广东统计年鉴

GUANGDONG STATISTICAL YEARBOOK

2023

（总第39期　No.39）

广　东　省　统　计　局
国家统计局广东调查总队　编

Compiled by

Statistics Bureau of Guangdong Province

Survey Office Of National Bureau of Statistics In Guangdong

图书在版编目（CIP）数据

广东统计年鉴. 2023 = Guangdong Statistical Yearbook 2023：汉英对照 / 广东省统计局，国家统计局广东调查总队编. -- 北京：中国统计出版社，2023.10
ISBN 978-7-5230-0271-1

Ⅰ. ①广… Ⅱ. ①广… ②国… Ⅲ. ①统计资料－广东－2023－年鉴－汉、英 Ⅳ. ①C832.65-54

中国国家版本馆 CIP 数据核字(2023)第 192362 号

广东统计年鉴 2023

作　　者/ 广东省统计局　国家统计局广东调查总队
责任编辑/ 高媛媛
装帧设计/ 广州九禾教育信息咨询有限公司
出版发行/ 中国统计出版社有限公司
地　　址/ 北京市丰台区西三环南路甲 6 号
邮政编码/ 100073
电　　话/ 邮购（010）63376909　书店（010）68783171
网　　址/ http://www.zgtjcbs.com
印　　刷/ 广州星河印刷有限公司
经　　销/ 新华书店
开　　本/ 890mm×1240mm　1/16
字　　数/ 1450 千字
印　　张/ 45
版　　别/ 2023 年 10 月第 1 版
版　　次/ 2023 年 10 月第 1 次印刷
定　　价/ 460.00 元　Price：460.00yuan(RMB)

本书附同版本 CD-ROM 一张，光盘内容以书面文字为准。
如有印装差错，由本社发行部调换。

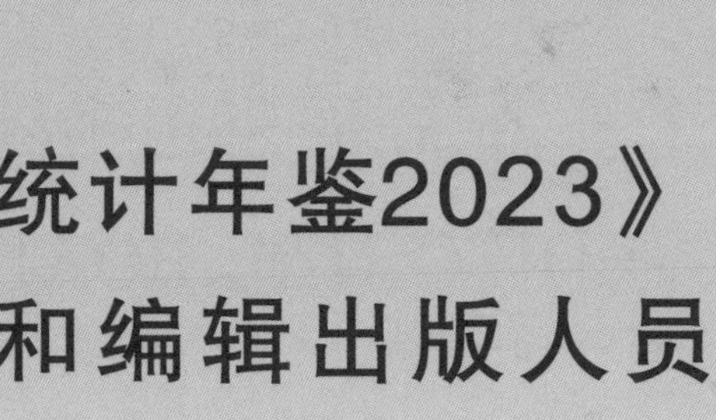

《广东统计年鉴2023》编委会和编辑出版人员

Guangdong Statistical Yearbook 2023
EDITORIAL BOARD AND STAFF

2023

编者说明

一、《广东统计年鉴2023》系统收录了全省及各市、县（区）2022年经济、社会各方面的统计数据，以及1978年以来各个主要时期全省主要统计数据，是一部全面反映广东国民经济和社会发展情况的资料性年刊。

二、本年鉴正文内容分为23个篇章，即：1.综合；2.国民经济核算；3.人口；4.就业和工资；5.固定资产投资；6.对外经济；7.能源、资源和环境；8.财政、银行和保险；9.价格；10.人民生活；11.农业；12.工业；13.建筑业；14.规模以上服务业；15.运输和邮电；16.批发零售业；17.住宿餐饮业和旅游；18.房地产业；19.教育和科技；20.文化和体育；21.卫生、社会福利、社会保障和其他；22.区域经济主要指标；23.县（市、区）主要经济指标。同时，附录有4个篇章：1.全国31个省（市）主要统计指标；2.中国香港特别行政区和中国澳门特别行政区主要统计资料；3.中国台湾省主要统计指标；4.部分国家和地区主要统计资料。

为方便读者使用，各篇章前设有《简要说明》，对本篇章的主要内容、资料来源、统计范围、统计方法以及历史变动情况予以简要概述，篇末附有《主要统计指标解释》。

三、本年鉴资料主要来自政府各级统计局、国家统计局调查总队的各种统计报表和抽样调查资料；部分资料来自中央部属单位和省直有关部门。附录资料根据国家统计局有关资料整理。

四、本年鉴涉及珠三角、东翼、西翼和山区的具体划分为：

珠三角包括：广州、深圳、珠海、佛山、惠州、东莞、中山、江门和肇庆。

东翼指汕头、汕尾、潮州和揭阳。

西翼指阳江、湛江和茂名。

山区指韶关、河源、梅州、清远和云浮。

五、资料中所使用的度量衡单位，除灌溉、播种面积照顾我国使用习惯继续用“亩”为单位外，其余均采用国际统一标准计量单位。

六、本年鉴中涉及到的历史数据，均以最新出版的本年鉴数据为准；年鉴中部分数据合计数或相对数由于单位取舍不同而产生的计算误差，均未做机械调整。

七、本年鉴统计表中的符号使用说明：

“…”表示数据不足本表最小单位数；

“#”表示其中主要项；

“空格”表示该项统计指标数据不详或无该项数据；

“①”表示本表下有注解。

八、与《广东统计年鉴2022》相比较，本年鉴在篇章结构和内容上主要做了如下修订：“人口”部分取消广东第七次全国人口普查各市按性别、年龄、民族、户口登记状况受教育层年度分的人口表以及各市按家庭户规模分的户数表；“就业与工资”部分取消各市城镇非私营单位就业人员和在岗职工人数表、各市城镇非私营单位就业人员、各市城镇非私营单位在岗职工工资总额和年平均工资表、各市城镇新增就业人数表；“固定资产投资”部分取消按投资主体、建设性质和产业划分固定资产投资情况表、国有经济固定资产投资主要指标表、新增主要生产能力或效益表，增加各市按控股类型分固定资产投资增长速度表、各市按领域分固定资产投资比上年增长情况表；“人民生活”部分取消干鲜瓜果类、糖果糕点类指标；“工业”部分取消按总产值及营业收入排名的企业名单；“农业”部分取消农业中间消耗率、淡水养殖水面、生猪出栏率指标。

本年鉴在整理编辑过程中，得到省直有关部门和单位的大力支持，在此表示感谢!

EDITOR'S NOTES

Ⅰ. *Guangdong Statistical Yearbook 2023* is an annual statistical publication, which reflects comprehensively the economic and social development of Guangdong Province. It covers data for 2022 and key statistical data in some historically important years since 1978 at the provincial level and the local levels of city, county and district.

Ⅱ. The yearbook contains twenty-three chapters: 1. General Survey; 2. National Accounts; 3. Population; 4. Employment and Wages; 5. Investment in Fixed Assets; 6. Foreign Trade and Economic Cooperation ; 7. Energy, Resources and Environment ; 8. Government Finance, Banking and Insurance; 9. Prices; 10. People's Living Conditions; 11. Agriculture; 12. Industry; 13. Service Enterprises Above Designated Size;14.Construction; 15. Transport, Postal and Telecommunication Services; 16. Wholesale , Retail Trades and Tourism; 17. Hotels, Catering Services and Tourism; 18. Real Estate 19. Education, Science and Technology; 20. Culture and Sports. 21.Public Health, Social Welfare, Social Insurance and Others; 22. Main Economic Indicators of Economic Regions; 23. Main Economic Indicators of Counties (County-level Cities) and Districts. Meanwhile, four chapters are listed as appendices: 1. Main Statistical Indicators of 31 Provinces and Municipalities; 2. Main Statistics of Hong Kong and Macao Special Administrative Regions; 3. Main Statistical Indicators of Taiwan Province; 4. Main Statistics of Some Countries and Territories. To facilitate readers, the Brief Introduction at the beginning of each chapter provides a summary of the main contents of the chapter, data sources, statistical scope, statistical methods and historical changes. At the end of each chapter, Explanatory Notes on Main Statistical Indicators are included.

Ⅲ. The data in this yearbook are mainly obtained from regular statistical reports and sample surveys conducted by the Statistical Bureaus at all levels of government and Survey Office of the National Bureau of Statistics. Some data are collected from the departments of the central government and the provincial government. Data in the appendices are compiled from statistical publications published by the National Bureau of Statistics and other sources.

Ⅳ. The pearl river delta, east wing, west wing and mountainous areas in the yearbook are divided as following:

The pearl river delta include Guangzhou, Shenzhen, Zhuhai, Foshan, Jiangmen, Dongguan, Zhongshan, Huizhou and Zhaoqing.

The east wing includes Shantou, Shanwei, Chaozhou and Jieyang.

The west wing includes Zhanjiang, Maoming and Yangjiang.

The mountainous areas include Shaoguan, Heyuan, Meizhou, Qingyuan and Yunfu.

Ⅴ. The units of measurement used in the yearbook are internationally standard measurement units, except that the unit of cultivated land and sown areas uses"mu" with regard to the Chinese tradition.

Ⅵ. Please refer to the newly published version of the yearbook for updated historical data. Statistical discrepancies on totals and relative figures due to rounding are not adjusted in the yearbook.

Ⅶ. Notations used in the yearbook:

" … " indicates that the figure is not large enough to be measured with the smallest unit in the table;

" # " indicates a major breakdown of the total;

" blank space " indicates that the data are unknown or are not available;

" ① " indicates footnotes at the end of the table.

Ⅷ. In comparison with Guangdong Statistical Yearbook 2022,following revisions have been made in this new version in terms of the statistical contents and in editing: Of the chapter "Population", the annual population table by gender, age, ethnic group, household registration status and education level of each city and the household number table by household size of each city of the Guangdong 7th National Census have been deleted; Of the chapter "Employment and Wages", table of the Number of Employed Persons and of Fully Employed Staff and Workers in Urban Non-Private Units by City、table of total wages and annual average wages of employed persons and staff in urban non-private units、table of Number of New Employment in Urban Area by City have been deleted. Of the chapter "Investment in Fixed Assets", the table of Investment in Fixed Assets by Investment Entity, Construction Nature, and Industries、Main Indicators of Investment in Fixed Assets of Sector and by City、Newly Increased Production Capacity or Efficiency have been deleted, the growth rate of fixed asset investment by holding type by city and the year-on-year growth of fixed asset investment by field by city have been added; Of the chapter "Industry", the list of enterprises ranked by total output value and operating revenue has been deleted; Of the chapter "Agricultural", the indicators of agricultural intermediate consumption rate、freshwater aquatic cultivation area and slaughtered fattened hog rate have been deleted.

Acknowledgements: our gratitude goes to relevant departments and units under the provincial government, from which we have received tremendous support when compiling the yearbook.

目　　录
CONTENTS

一、综合
General Survey

简要说明 …… 2
Brief Introduction

1-1 行政区划（2022 年）…… 3
Divisions of Administrative Areas （2022）

1-2 国民经济和社会发展总量与速度指标 …… 4
Principal Aggregate Indicators on National Economic and Social Development and Growth Rates

1-3 国民经济和社会发展结构指标 …… 12
Composition Indicators of National Economic and Social Development

1-4 国民经济和社会发展比例和效益指标 …… 16
Indicators on National Economic and Social Development

1-5 国民经济和社会发展主要指标占全国比重 …… 18
Percentage of National Total of Main Indicators of Economic and Social Development of Guangdong

1-6 各部门机构数 …… 20
Grassroots Units in Various Sectors

1-7 法人和产业活动单位数 …… 21
Number of Legal Entities and Industrial Establishments

1-8 各市法人和产业活动单位数 …… 22
Number of Corporate Units and Industrial Establishments by City

1-9 按行业和登记注册类型分组的法人单位数（2022 年）…… 23
Number of Corporate Units by Sector and by Status of Registration（2022）

1-10 各市按机构类型分法人单位数（2022 年）…… 27
Number of Corporate Units by Type by City（2022）

1-11 各市按行业分法人单位数（2022 年）…… 28
Number of Corporate Units by Sector by City（2022）

1-12 各市按登记注册类型分法人单位数（2022 年）…… 32
Number of Corporate Units by Status of Registration by City（2022）

1-13 全省商品、服务类电子商务交易情况 …… 36
E-commerce Transactions in Commodities and Services of Guangdong

1-14 粤港澳大湾区主要经济指标（2022 年）…… 37
Main Indicators of Guangdong-Hong Kong-Macao Greater Bay Area（2022）
主要统计指标解释 …… 38
Explanatory Notes on Main Statistical Indicators

二、国民经济核算
National Economic Accounts

简要说明 …… 44
Brief Introduction
2-1 国民经济核算主要指标 …… 45
Main Indicators of Gross Domestic Product
2-2 地区生产总值 …… 46
Gross Domestic Product
2-3 地区生产总值指数（上年=100）…… 47
Indices of Gross Domestic Product（preceding year=100）
2-4 地区生产总值指数（1978 年=100）…… 48
Indices of Gross Domestic Product（year of 1978=100）
2-5 地区生产总值产业构成 …… 49
Composition of Gross Domestic Product
2-6 三次产业贡献率 …… 50
Contribution Rate of Three Industries
2-7 三次产业对地区生产总值增长的拉动 …… 51
Contribution of the Three Strata of Industry to GDP Growth
2-8 支出法地区生产总值 …… 52
Gross Domestic Product by Expenditure Approach
2-9 资本形成总额及构成 …… 53
Gross Capital Formation and Composition
2-10 最终消费及构成 …… 54
Final Consumption Expenditure and Composition
2-11 三大需求对地区生产总值增长的贡献率和拉动 …… 55
Contribution Share and Contribution of the Three Major Demands to GDP Growth
2-12 人均地区生产总值及人均消费水平指数（上年=100）…… 56
Indices of Per Capita Gross Domestic Product and Consumption（preceding year=100）
2-13 人均地区生产总值及人均消费水平指数（1978 年=100）…… 57
Indices of Per Capita Gross Domestic Product and Consumption（year of 1978=100）
2-14 各市地区生产总值 …… 58
Gross Domestic Product by City
2-15 各市地区生产总值指数（上年=100）…… 60
Indices of Gross Domestic Product by City（preceding year=100）

2-16 各市地区生产总值指数（2000年=100） …… 62
Indices of Gross Domestic Product by City（year of 2000=100）
2-17 各市第一产业增加值 …… 64
Value-added of the Primary Industry by City
2-18 各市第二产业增加值 …… 65
Value-added of the Secondary Industry by City
2-19 各市第三产业增加值 …… 66
Value-added of the Tertiary Industry by City
2-20 各市第一产业增加值指数 …… 67
Indices of Value-added of the Primary Industry by City
2-21 各市第二产业增加值指数 …… 68
Indices of Value-added of the Secondary Industry by City
2-22 各市第三产业增加值指数 …… 69
Indices of Value-added of the Tertiary Industry by City
2-23 各市地区生产总值（2022年） …… 70
Gross Domestic Product by City（2022）
2-24 各市地区生产总值指数（2022年） …… 72
Growth Indices of Gross Domestic Product by City（2022）
2-25 各市地区生产总值产业构成（2022年） …… 74
Composition of Gross Domestic Product by Industry by City（2022）
2-26 各市人均地区生产总值 …… 75
Per Capita Gross Domestic Product by City
2-27 各市人均地区生产总值指数（上年=100） …… 77
Indices of Per Capita Gross Domestic Product by City（preceding year=100）
2-28 各市人均地区生产总值指数（2000年=100） …… 79
Indices of Per Capita Gross Domestic Product by City（year of 2000=100）
2-29 文化及相关产业增加值 …… 81
Value-added of Culture and related Industry
主要统计指标解释 …… 82
Explanatory Notes on Main Statistical Indicators

三、人口
Population
简要说明 …… 88
Brief Introduction
3-1 人口主要指标 …… 89
Main Population Indicators
3-2 人口自然变动情况 …… 90
Status of Natural Population Changes

3-3 常住人口构成 …… 91
Composition of Permanent Population
3-4 常住人口年龄结构和抚养比 …… 92
Age Composition and Dependency Ratio of Permanent Population
3-5 年末户籍总人口 …… 93
Total Population with Residence Registration at Year-end
3-6 户籍人口迁移变动情况 …… 94
Status of Migrant Changes
3-7 各市年末常住人口数 …… 95
Permanent Population at Year-end by City
3-8 各市城镇人口占常住人口的比例 …… 96
Proportion of Urban Population to Permanent Population by City
3-9 各市年末户籍人口数（2022 年）…… 97
Total Population with Residence Registration at Year-end by City（2022）
3-10 各市年末户籍迁移人口数（2022 年）…… 98
Number of Migrant Population at the Year-end by City（2022）
主要统计指标解释 …… 99
Explanatory Notes on Main Statistical Indicators

四、就业和工资

Employment and Wages

简要说明 …… 102
Brief Introduction
4-1 就业基本情况 …… 103
Employment
4-2 就业人员年末人数 …… 104
Number of Employed Persons at the Year-end
4-3 按三次产业分就业人员年末人数 …… 105
Number of Employed Persons at Year-end by Three strata of Industry
4-4 各市就业人员年末人数 …… 106
Number of Employed Persons at the Year-end by City
4-5 各市按三次产业分就业人员年末人数 …… 107
Number of Employed Persons at the Year-end by Strata of Industry by City
4-6 各市按城乡分就业人员年末人数 …… 108
Number of Employed Persons at the Year-end by Strata of Industry by City
4-7 城镇非私营单位就业人员和在岗职工年末人数（2022 年）…… 109
Number of Employed Persons and Fully Employed Staff and Workers in Urban Non Private Units at the Year-end（2022）

4-8 各市城镇非私营单位各行业在岗职工年末人数 (2022 年) …… 111
Number of Fully Employed Staff and Workers in Urban Non Private Units at the Year-end by Sector and by City (2022)
4-9 城镇非私营单位女性就业人员年末人数（2022 年）…… 114
Number of Females Employed in Urban Non Private Units at the Year-end (2022)
4-10 城镇非私营单位职工工资总额与年平均工资 …… 115
Total Wages Bill and Average Wage of Staff and Workers in Urban Non Private Units
4-11 城镇非私营单位就业人员工资总额（2022 年）…… 116
Total Wages of Employed Persons in Urban Non Private Units (2022)
4-12 城镇非私营单位在岗职工工资总额（2022 年）…… 117
Total Wages of Fully Employed Staff and Workers in Urban Non Private Units (2022)
4-13 城镇非私营单位就业人员年平均工资（2022 年）…… 118
Average Annual Wages of Employed Persons in Urban Non Private Units (2022)
4-14 城镇非私营单位在岗职工年平均工资（2022 年）…… 119
Average Annual Wages of Fully Employed Staff and Workers in Urban Non Private Units (2022)
主要统计指标解释 …… 120
Explanatory Notes on Main Statistical Indicators

五、固定资产投资

Investment in Fixed Assets

简要说明 …… 124
Brief Introduction
5-1 固定资产投资主要指标增长速度 …… 125
Main Indicators of Investment in Fixed Assets
5-2 固定资产投资增长速度 …… 126
Growth Rate of Investment in Fixed Assets
5-3 按资金来源和构成分固定资产投资增速及比重 …… 127
Growth Rate and Percentage Investment in Fixed Assets by Source of Funds and Structure of Investment
5-4 按构成分固定资产投资增长速度 …… 129
Growth Rate of Investment in Fixed Assets by Structure
5-5 按行业分固定资产投资主要指标增长速度 (2022 年) …… 130
Growth Rate of Main Indicators of Investment by Sector (2022)
5-6 各行业财务拨贷款资金来源主要指标增长速度 (2022 年) …… 133
Growth Rate of Main Indicators on Sources of Funds and Loans for Investment by Sector (2022)
5-7 各市按项目和房地产开发分固定资产投资增长速度 …… 136
Growth Rate of Investment in Fixed Assets By Project and Real Estate Development and by City

5-8 各市按登记注册类型分固定资产投资增长速度 (2022 年) …… 137
Growth Rate of Investment in Fixed Assets by Status of Registration and City (2022)
5-9 各市按控股类型分固定资产投资增长速度 (2022 年) …… 138
Growth Rate of Investment in Fixed Assets Divided by Holding Type and by City
5-10 各市按行业分固定资产投资增长速度 (2022 年) …… 139
Growth Rate of Investment in Fixed Assets by Sector and by City (2022)
5-11 各市按领域分固定资产投资比上年增长情况 …… 142
Growth Rate of Investment in Fixed Assets by Sector and City
5-12 各市财务拨贷款资金来源主要指标增长速度 (2022 年) …… 143
Growth Rate of Main Indicators on Sources of Funds and Loans for Investment by City (2022)
5-13 各市按构成和建设性质分固定资产投资增长速度 (2022 年) …… 144
Growth Rate of Investment in Fixed Assets in Urban Area by Composition of Funds, Type of Construction and City (2022)
5-14 各市农业、能源、原材料、运输邮电业投资比重 …… 145
Proportion of Investment in Capital Construction of Agriculture, Energy,Raw Materials, Transport, Post and Telecommunications
5-15 各市工业投资比重 …… 146
Proportion of Industrial Investment by City
主要统计指标解释 …… 147
Explanatory Notes on Main Statistical Indicators

六、对外经济

Foreign Economy

简要说明 …… 150
Brief Introduction
6-1 对外经济主要指标 …… 151
Main Indicators of Foreign Trade and Economic Cooperation
6-2 人民币对主要外币中间价汇率（年平均价）…… 152
Middle Exchange Rate of RMB Against Major Foreign Currencies (Period Average)
6-3 进出口总额 …… 153
Total Value of Imports and Exports
6-4 按贸易方式和经济类型分的进出口额（人民币）…… 154
Total Value of Imports and Exports by Customs Regime and Ownership Type (RMB)
6-5 按贸易方式和经济类型分的进出口额（美元）…… 154
Total Value of Imports and Exports by Customs Regime and Ownership Type (USD)
6-6 按产品类型分的进出口额 …… 155
Total Value of Imports and Exports by Product Type
6-7 广东同主要国家（地区）进出口额（2022 年）…… 157
Total Value of Imports and Exports with Main Countries and Regions (2022)

6-8 进出口商品分类金额（2022 年）…… 157
Total Value of Imports and Exports by Category of Commodities（2022）
6-9 出口主要商品数量和金额（2022 年）…… 160
Volume and Value of Main Export Commodities（2022）
6-10 进口主要商品数量和金额（2022 年）…… 162
Volume and Value of Main Import Commodities（2022）
6-11 各市出口总额 …… 164
Total Value of Exports by City
6-12 各市进口总额 …… 165
Total Value of Imports by City
6-13 各市外商投资企业出口总额 …… 166
Total Value of Exports of Enterprises with Foreign Investment by City
6-14 各市外商投资企业进口总额 …… 167
Total Value of Imports of Enterprises with Foreign Investment by City
6-15 外商投资企业进出口主要指标（2022 年）…… 168
Main Indicators on Imports and Exports of Enterprises with Foreign Investment（2022）
6-16 外商投资企业出口主要商品数量和金额（2022 年）…… 169
Volume and Value of Main Export Commodities of Enterprises with Foreign Investment（2022）
6-17 外商投资企业进口主要商品数量和金额（2022 年）…… 171
Volume and Value of Main Import Commodities by Enterprises with Foreign Investment（2022）
6-18 私营企业进出口主要指标（2022 年）…… 173
Main Indicators on Imports and Exports of Private Enterprises（2022）
6-19 利用外资情况 …… 174
Utilization of Foreign Capital
6-20 分行业外商直接投资（2022 年）…… 175
Foreign Direct Investment by Sector（2022）
6-21 分国家（地区）实际使用外资金额 …… 176
Actual Value of Foreign Capital Used in Countries and Regions
6-22 各市外商直接投资 …… 177
Foreign Direct Investment by City
6-23 分行业外商投资企业工商注册登记情况（2022 年末）…… 178
Registration Status of Enterprises with Foreign Investment by Sector（Year-end of 2022）
6-24 各市外商投资企业工商注册登记情况（2022 年末）…… 179
Registration Status of Enterprises with Foreign Investment by City（Year-end of 2022）
6-25 一类口岸开放使用情况（2022 年末）…… 180
Opening and Operating Status of Category-1 Ports（Year-end of 2022）
6-26 对外经济技术合作情况 …… 181
Economic and Technical Cooperation with Foreign Countries and Regions

6-27 分国别（地区）对外直接投资 …… 182
Foreign Direct Investment by Country（Region）
6-28 分行业对外直接投资（2022 年）…… 183
Foreign Direct Investment by Sector（2022）
主要统计指标解释 …… 184
Explanatory Notes on Main Statistical Indicators

七、能源、资源和环境

Energy，Resources and Environment

简要说明 …… 188
Brief Introduction
7-1 能源主要指标 …… 190
Main Indicators of Energy
7-2 能源生产总量及构成 …… 190
Total Production of Energy and its Composition
7-3 能源消费总量及构成 …… 191
Total Consumption of Energy and Its Composition
7-4 综合能源平衡表 …… 192
Overall Energy Balance Sheet
7-5 分行业能源消费总量和原煤、电力消费量（2022 年）…… 193
Consumption of Total Energy，Coal and Electricity by Sector（2022）
7-6 各市电力消费量 …… 194
Electricity Consumption by City
7-7 各市单位 GDP 能耗增长速度 …… 195
Growth Rate of Energy Consumption Per Unit GDP by City
7-8 各市单位 GDP 电耗增长速度 …… 195
Growth Rate of Electricity Consumption per Unit of GDP by City
7-9 各市单位工业增加值能耗增长速度 …… 196
Growth Rate of Energy Consumption per Unit of Industrial Value-added by City
7-10 平均每天各种能源消费量 …… 196
Average Daily Energy Consumption by Variety
7-11 平均每人年生活用能源 …… 197
Annual per Capita Energy Consumption of Households
7-12 分品种生活能源年消费总量 …… 197
Annual Total Energy Consumption of Households by Variety
7-13 能源加工转换效率 …… 198
Efficiency of Energy Conversion

7-14 能源生产弹性系数 …… 199
Elasticity Ratio of Energy Production
7-15 能源消费弹性系数 …… 200
Elasticity Ratio of Energy Consumption
7-16 自然资源（2022 年）…… 201
Natural Resources（2022）
7-17 各地区年平均气温 …… 202
Average Temperature by Region
7-18 各地区年降雨量 …… 203
Annual Precipitation by Region
7-19 各地区年日照时数 …… 204
Annual Sunshine Hours by Region
7-20 各市土地面积和人口密度 …… 205
Land Area and Population Density by City
7-21 水资源及供水用水基本情况 …… 206
Water Resouces, Water Supply and Water use
7-22 环境保护基本情况 …… 207
Basic Conditions of Environmental Protection
7-23 各市水环境质量情况（2022 年）…… 209
Statistics on Water Environment Quality by City（2022）
7-24 各市大气环境质量情况（2022 年）…… 210
Statistics on Atmospheric Environmental Quality by City（2022）
7-25 各市城市建设基本情况 …… 211
Basic Statistics on Urban Sanitation by City
主要统计指标解释 …… 213
Explanatory Notes on Main Statistical Indicators

八、财政、银行和保险

Government Finance，Banking and Insurance

简要说明 …… 218
Brief Introduction
8-1 地方一般公共预算收支和增长速度 …… 219
Local Government General Public Budget Revenue and Expenditure and Their Growth Rates
8-2 地方一般公共预算收支基本情况 …… 220
Basic Items of General Public Budget Revenue and Expenditure
8-3 各市地方一般公共预算收支 …… 221
Local Government General Budgetary Revenue and Expenditure by City

8-4 各市人均地方一般公共预算收入 …… 223
Per Capita Local Government General Public Budget Revenue by City
8-5 各市财政收支（2022 年）…… 224
Basic Conditions of Local Government General Public Budget Revenue and Expenditure by City (2022)
8-6 历年金融机构存贷款 …… 228
Deposits and Loans in All Financial Institutions
8-7 金融机构本外币存贷款余额 …… 229
Deposits and Loans in Renminbi and Foreign Currencies in All Financial Institutions
8-8 金融机构人民币存贷款余额 …… 230
Deposits and Loans in Renminbi in All Financial Institutions
8-9 各市中资金融机构基本情况 …… 231
Basic Conditions of Chinese-funded Financial Institutions by City
8-10 各市金融机构本外币存贷款 …… 233
Deposits and Loans in Renminbi and Foreign Currencies in All Financial Institutions by City
8-11 各市金融机构住户存款 …… 235
Savings Deposit by Household in All Financial Institutions by City
8-12 财产保险公司主要指标 …… 237
Main Indicators of Property Insurance Companies
8-13 人身保险公司主要指标 …… 238
Main Indicators of Life Insurance Companies
8-14 保险业务主要指标 …… 239
Main Indicators of Insurance Business
8-15 分市原保险保费收入和赔付支出情况（2022 年）…… 240
Premium of Primary Insurance and Payment by City (2022)
主要统计指标解释 …… 241
Explanatory Notes on Main Statistical Indicators

九、价格

Price

简要说明 …… 244
Brief Introduction
9-1 各种价格指数 …… 245
Price Indices
9-2 各种价格定基指数 …… 246
Fixed-base Price Indices
9-3 居民消费价格分类指数（2022 年）…… 247
Consumer Price Indices by Category (2022)

9-4 商品零售价格分类指数（2022 年） …… 249
Retail Price Indices by Category（2022）
9-5 各市居民消费价格分类指数（2022 年） …… 251
Consumer Price Indices by Category and by City（2022）
9-6 各市服务项目价格分类指数（2022 年） …… 253
Service Price Indices by Category and by City（2022）
9-7 工业生产者出厂价格指数 …… 254
Producer Price Indices for Industrial Products
9-8 工业生产者购进价格指数 …… 255
Producer Price Indices for Industrial Products
9-9 各市工业生产者出厂价格指数 …… 256
Producer Price Indices for Industrial Products by City
9-10 分行业工业生产者出厂价格指数 …… 257
Producer Price Indices for Industrial Products by Sector
9-11 农产品生产者价格指数 …… 258
Producer Price Indices for Farm Products
主要统计指标解释 …… 259
Explanatory Notes on Main Statistical Indicators

十、人民生活

People's Living Conditions

简要说明 …… 262
Brief Introduction
10-1 全省居民家庭基本情况 …… 263
Basic Conditions of Households Province Wide
10-2 按收入五等份分组的全省居民人均可支配收入 …… 264
Per Capita Disposable Income of Households Province Wide by Income Quintile
10-3 全省居民人均主要食品消费量 …… 264
Per Capita Consumption of Major Foods Province Wide
10-4 全省居民平均每百户年末主要耐用消费品拥有量 …… 265
Main Durable Consumer Goods Owned per 100 Households Province Wide
10-5 各市全体居民人均可支配收入 …… 266
Per Capita Disposable Income of Households by City
10-6 各市全体居民人均可支配收入来源（2022 年） …… 267
Per Capita Disposable Income of Households by Sources and City（2022）
10-7 各市全体居民人均消费支出 …… 268
Per Capita Consumption Expenditure of Households by City

10-8 城镇居民家庭基本情况 …… 269
Basic Situation of Urban Households
10-9 历年城镇居民人均可支配收入及生活消费支出（1978-2012 年）…… 270
Per Capita Disposable Income and Consumption Expenditure of Urban Households（1978-2012）
10-10 全省城镇居民人均主要食品消费量 …… 271
Per Capita Consumption of Major Foods of Urban Households
10-11 全省城镇居民平均每百户年末主要耐用消费品拥有量 …… 271
Main Durable Consumer Goods Owned per 100 Urban Households at the Year-end
10-12 各市城镇居民人均可支配收入 …… 272
Per Capita Disposable Income of Urban Households by City
10-13 各市城镇居民人均可支配收入来源（2022 年）…… 273
Per Capita Disposable Income of Urban Households by Sources and City（2022）
10-14 各市城镇居民人均消费支出 …… 274
Per Capita Consumption Expenditure of Urban Households by City
10-15 农村居民家庭基本情况 …… 275
Basic Conditions of Rural Households
10-16 历年农村居民人均纯收入及生活消费支出（1978-2012 年）…… 276
Per Capita Income and Consumption Expenditure of Rural Households（1978-2012）
10-17 全省农村居民人均主要食品消费量 …… 277
Per Capita Consumption of Major Foods of Rural Households
10-18 全省农村居民平均每百户年末主要耐用品拥有量 …… 277
Main Durable Consumer Goods Owned per 100 Rural Households at the Year-end
10-19 各市农村居民人均可支配收入 …… 278
Per Capita Disposal Income of Rural Households by City
10-20 各市农村居民人均可支配收入来源（2022 年）…… 279
Per Capita Disposable Income of Rural Households by Sources and City（2022）
10-21 全省各市农村居民人均消费支出 …… 280
Per Capita Consumption Expenditure of Rural Households by City
10-22 全省、城镇、农村居民人均可支配收入及生活消费支出（2013-2022 年）…… 281
Per Capita Disposable Income and Consumption Expenditure of Households（2013-2022）
主要统计指标解释 …… 282
Explanatory Notes on Main Statistical Indicators

十一、农业

Agriculture

简要说明 …… 288
Brief Introduction
11-1 农业主要指标 …… 289
Main Indicators of Agriculture

11-2 各市农村基层组织情况（2022 年）…… 290
Basic Conditions of Rural Grassroots Units by City（2022）
11-3 农业生产条件 …… 291
Agricultural Production Basic Conditions
11-4 农业自然灾害情况 …… 291
Statistics on Agriculture Covered and Affected by Natural Disasters
11-5 农林牧渔业总产值 …… 292
Gross Output Value of Agriculture, Forestry, Animal Husbandry and Fishery
11-6 农林牧渔业总产值指数（1978 年=100）…… 293
Indices of Gross Output Value of Agriculture, Forestry, Animal Husbandry and Fishery（1978=100）
11-7 农林牧渔业总产值指数（上年=100）…… 294
Indices of Gross Output Value of Agriculture, Forestry, Animal Husbandry and Fishery（preceding year=100）
11-8 各市农林牧渔业总产值（2022 年）…… 295
Gross Output Value of Farming, Forestry, Animal Husbandry and Fishery by City（2022）
11-9 各市农林牧渔业总产值指数（2022 年）…… 296
Indices of Gross Output Value of Agriculture, Forestry, Animal Husbandry and Fishery by City（2022）
11-10 农作物播种面积 …… 297
Total Sown Area of Farm Crops
11-11 主要农产品产量 …… 299
Output of Major Farm Products
11-12 主要畜产品和水产品产量 …… 300
Output of Major Farm Products
11-13 主要农作物播种面积、亩产及总产量 …… 301
Sown Area, Yield per Mu and Total Output of Major Farm Crops
11-14 各市主要农作物播种面积、亩产及总产量（2022 年）…… 302
Sown Area, Yield per Mu and Total Output of Major Farm Crops by City（2022）
11-15 造林面积及主要林产品产量 …… 306
Area of Afforestation and Output of Major Forest Products
11-16 水产养殖面积和水产品产量 …… 306
Area of Cultivation and Output of Aquatic Products
11-17 牲畜头数及肉类产量 …… 307
Number of Livestock and Output of Meat
11-18 各市造林面积、水产品产量、牲畜头数及猪肉产量（2022 年）…… 308
Area of Afforestation, Output of Aquatic Products, Number of Livestock and Output of Pork by City（2022）

11-19 茶叶、桑、水果面积及产量 …… 309
Planted Area and Output of Tea, Mulberry and Fruits
11-20 各市水果面积及产量（2022 年）…… 310
Planted Area and Output of Fruits by City（2022）
11-21 主要农产品产量与最高年份比较（2022 年）…… 312
Output of Major Farm Products in Comparison with Peak Year（2022）
11-22 农林牧渔业分项产值 …… 313
Agricultural Production Basic Conditions
主要统计指标解释 …… 314
Explanatory Notes on Main Statistical Indicators

十二、工业

Industry

简要说明 …… 316
Brief Introduction
12-1 工业主要指标 …… 317
Main Indicators of Industry
12-2 规模以上工业企业增加值和指数 …… 318
Value-added of Industrial Enterprises above Designated Size and Their Indices
12-3 历年规模以上工业增加值增长速度 …… 319
Growth Rates of Industrial Enterprises above Designated Size
12-4 规模以上分行业工业增加值和增长速度 …… 320
Value-added and Growth Rates of Industry above Designated Size by Sector
12-5 规模以上工业企业单位数和产值 …… 321
Number of Industrial Enterprises above Designated Size and Their Gross Output Values
12-6 全部工业总产值和指数 …… 322
Gross Industrial Output Value of All Industrial Enterprises and Theirs Indices
12-7 规模以上工业总产值和指数 …… 323
Gross Output Value of Industrial Enterprises above Designated Size and Their Indices
12-8 规模以上工业产品产量 …… 324
Output of Industrial Products of Enterprises above Designated Size
12-9 各市规模以上工业企业单位数和工业总产值 …… 326
Number and Gross Output Value of Industrial Enterprises above Designated Size by City
12-10 各市规模以上工业增加值和指数 …… 328
Value-added and Indices of Industry above Designated Size by City
12-11 各市规模以上工业企业单位数（2022 年）…… 330
Number of Industrial Enterprises above Designated Size by City（2022）

12-12 各市规模以上工业总产值（2022 年）…… 334
Gross Output Value of Industry above Designated Size by City（2022）
12-13 各市规模以上工业增加值（2022 年）…… 338
Value-added of Industry above Designated Size by City（2022）
12-14 规模以上工业企业主要经济指标 …… 342
Main Indicators of Industrial Enterprises above Designated Size
12-15 规模以上国有控股工业企业主要经济指标 …… 343
Main Indicators of State-owned and State-holding Industrial Enterprises above Designated Size
12-16 规模以上工业企业主要经济指标（2022 年）…… 344
Main Economic Indicators of Industrial Enterprises above Designated Size（2022）
12-17 规模以上国有控股工业企业主要经济指标（2022 年）…… 346
Main Economic Indicators of State-holding Industrial Enterprises above Designated Size（2022）
12-18 规模以上集体工业企业主要经济指标（2022 年）…… 348
Main Economic Indicators of Collective-owned Industrial Enterprises above Designated Size（2022）
12-19 规模以上股份合作工业企业主要经济指标（2022 年）…… 350
Main Economic Indicators of Share-holding Cooperative Industrial Enterprises above Designated Size（2022）
12-20 规模以上股份制工业企业主要经济指标（2022 年）…… 352
Main Economic Indicators of Share-holding Industrial Enterprises above Designated Size（2022）
12-21 规模以上“三资”工业企业主要经济指标（2022 年）…… 354
Main Economic Indicators of Foreign-funded Industrial Enterprises above Designated Size（2022）
12-22 规模以上私营工业企业主要经济指标（2022 年）…… 356
Main Economic Indicators of Private Industrial Enterprises above Designated Size（2022）
12-23 规模以上大中型工业企业主要经济指标（2022 年）…… 358
Main Economic Indicators of Large and Medium-sized Industrial Enterprises above Designated Size（2022）
12-24 规模以上高技术制造业主要经济指标（2022 年）…… 360
Main Indicators on High-tech Manufacturing Enterprises above Designated Size（2022）
12-25 规模以上先进制造业主要经济指标（2022 年）…… 362
Main Indicators on Advanced Manufacturing Enterprises above Designated Size（2022）
12-26 规模以上工业企业主要经济效益指标（2022 年）…… 364
Main Indicators on Economic Benefit of Industrial Enterprises above Designated Size（2022）
12-27 规模以上制造业工业企业主要经济指标 …… 366
Main Economic Indicators of Manufacturing Enterprises above Designated Size
12-28 各市规模以上工业企业主要经济指标（2022 年）…… 367
Main Economic Indicators of Industrial Enterprises above Designated Size by City（2022）
12-29 各市规模以上私营工业企业主要经济指标（2022 年）…… 368
Main Economic Indicators of Private Industrial Enterprises above Designated Size by City（2022）

12-30 各市规模以上工业企业主要经济效益指标（2022 年）…… 369
Main Indicators on Economic Benefit of Industrial Enterprises above Designated Size by City（2022）
12-31 各市规模以上国有控股工业企业主要经济效益指标（2022 年）…… 371
Main Indicators on Economic Benefit of State-holding Industrial Enterprises above Designated Size by City（2022）
12-32 各市规模以上按经济类型分的工业企业资产（2022 年）…… 372
Total Assets of Industrial Enterprises above Designated Size by Ownership and by City（2022）
12-33 各市规模以上大中型工业企业产值资产（2022 年）…… 373
Gross Output Value and Total Assets of Large and Medium-sized Industrial Enterprises above Designated Size by City（2022）
12-34 各市现代产业增加值及比重（2022 年）…… 374
Value Added and Ratio of Modern Industries by City（2022）
12-35 规模以上工业主要产品生产能力 …… 375
Main Industrial Products above Designated Size
主要统计指标解释 …… 376
Explanatory Notes on Main Statistical Indicators

十三、建筑业

Construction

简要说明 …… 386
Brief Introduction
13-1 建筑业企业生产情况 …… 387
Production Conditions of Construction Enterprises
13-2 建筑业企业主要指标 …… 388
Main Indicators on Construction Enterprises
13-3 按登记注册类型分建筑业企业主要经济指标 (2022 年) …… 389
Main Economic Indicators of Construction Enterprises by Registration Type (2022)
13-4 按登记注册类型分建筑业企业财务状况 (2022 年) …… 391
Financial Situation of Construction Enterprises by Registration Type (2022)
13-5 按行业分建筑业企业主要经济指标和财务状况 (2022 年) …… 393
Main Economic Indicators and Financial Situation of Construction Enterprises by Sector (2022)
13-6 各市建筑业企业个数 …… 395
Number of Construction Enterprises by City
13-7 各市建筑业企业总产值 …… 396
Gross Output Value of Construction Enterprises by City
13-8 各市建筑业企业营业收入 (2022 年)
Operating Revenue of Construction Enterprises by City
13-9 各市建筑业企业利税总额 …… 398
Total Pre-tax Profits of Construction Enterprises by City

13-10 各市建筑业企业利润总额 …… 399
Total Profits of Construction Enterprises by City
13-11 各市建筑业企业房屋建筑施工面积 …… 400
Floor Space of Buildings under Construction by Construction Enterprises by City
13-12 各市建筑业企业房屋建筑施工新开工面积 …… 401
Floor Space of Buildings Started This Year by Construction Enterprises by City
13-13 各市建筑业企业期末就业人员 …… 402
Number of Employed Persons of Construction Enterprises at the Year-end by City
13-14 各市建筑业企业劳动生产率 …… 403
Labor Productivity of Construction Enterprises by City
主要统计指标解释 …… 404
Explanatory Notes on Main Statistical Indicators

十四、规模以上服务业
Service Enterprises Above Designated Size
简要说明 …… 408
Brief Introduction
14-1 规模以上服务业企业财务指标 …… 409
Main Financial Indicators of Service Enterprises above Designated Size
14-2 规模以上服务业企业分行业主要指标（2022 年） …… 410
Main Indicators of Service Enterprises above Designated Size by Sector（2022）
14-3 规模以上服务业企业分行业营业收入 …… 418
Business Revenue of Service Enterprises above Designated Size by Sector
14-4 规模以上服务业企业分行业营业利润 …… 419
Business Profits of Service Enterprises above Designated Size by Sector
14-5 规模以上服务业企业分行业应付职工薪酬 …… 420
Total Wages Payable of Service Enterprises above Designated Size by Sector
14-6 规模以上服务业企业分行业就业人员平均人数 …… 421
Average number of Employed Persons of Service Enterprises above Designated Size by Sector
14-7 各市规模以上服务业企业主要指标（2022 年） …… 422
Main Indicators of Service Enterprises above Designated Size by City（2022）
主要统计指标解释 …… 426
Explanatory Notes on Main Statistical Indicators

十五、运输和邮电
Transportation，Postal and Telecommunication Services
简要说明 …… 428
Brief Introduction

15-1 运输邮电主要指标 …… 430
Main Indicators on Transport, Postal and Telecommunication Services
15-2 全社会旅客运输量 …… 431
Total Passenger Traffic
15-3 旅客运输量指数 …… 432
Indices of Passenger Traffic
15-4 各市客运量 …… 433
Passenger Traffic by City
15-5 各市旅客周转量 …… 434
Passenger-kilometers by City
15-6 全社会货物运输量 …… 435
Total Freight Traffic
15-7 货物运输量指数 …… 436
Indices of Freight Traffic
15-8 各市货运量 …… 437
Freight Traffic by City
15-9 各市货物周转量 …… 438
Freight Ton-kilometers by City
15-10 运输工具和线路拥有量 …… 439
Number of Means of Transport and Length of Transport Routes
15-11 各市民用汽车拥有量（2022 年） …… 440
Possession of Civil Vehicles by City (2022)
15-12 各市私人汽车拥有量（2022 年） …… 442
Possession of Private Vehicles by City (2022)
15-13 各市公路基本情况（2022 年） …… 443
Basic Conditions of Highways by City (2022)
15-14 公路通车里程和桥梁数 …… 444
Length of Highways and Number of Bridges
15-15 输油（气）管道长度和运输量 …… 444
Length and Traffic of Petroleum and Gas Pipelines
15-16 民航航站吞吐量 …… 445
Throughput of Civil Aviation Airports
15-17 港口泊位及吞吐量 …… 446
Berth and Throughput of Coastal Ports
15-18 各市港口货物吞吐量 …… 447
Freight Throughput of Ports by City
15-19 各市城市公共交通情况（2022 年） …… 448
Basic Statistics on Public Transportation in Cities by City (2022)

15–20 邮电业务总量和指数 …… 450
Business Volume of Postal and Telecommunication Services and Their Indices
15–21 各市邮电业务总量 …… 451
Business Volume of Postal and Telecommunication Services by City
15–22 各市邮电业务情况（2022 年）…… 452
Conditions of Postal and Telecommunication Services by City（2022）
15–23 邮政通信业基本情况 …… 453
Basic Conditions of Postal and Telecommunication Services
主要统计指标解释 …… 454
Explanatory Notes on Main Statistical Indicators

十六、批发零售业
Wholesale and Retail Trades
简要说明 …… 460
Brief Introduction
16–1 批发零售业主要指标 …… 461
Main Indicators on Domestic Trade
16–2 按城乡分社会消费品零售总额 …… 462
Total Retail Sales of Consumer Goods by Urban and Rural Area
16–3 各市社会消费品零售总额（2022 年）…… 463
Total Retail Sales of Consumer Goods by City（2022）
16–4 各市社会消费品零售总额 …… 464
Total Retail Sales of Consumer Goods by City
16–5 批发零售业商品销售总额 …… 465
Total Sales of Commodities in Wholesale and Retail Trades
16–6 限额以上批发零售业商品批发额 …… 466
Total Wholesale Value of Commodities in Wholesale and Retail Trades
16–7 限额以上批发零售业商品零售额 …… 467
Total Retail Value of Commodities in Wholesale and Retail Trades
16–8 限额以上批发企业商品购、销、存总额（2022 年）…… 468
Total Purchases，Sales and Inventory of Enterprises above Designated Size in Wholesale Trade（2022）
16–9 限额以上零售企业商品购、销、存总额（2022 年）…… 470
Total Purchases，Sales and Inventory of Enterprises above Designated Size in Retail Trade（2022）
16–10 各市限额以上批发零售企业商品购、销、存总额（2022 年）…… 472
Total Purchases，Sales and Inventory of Enterprises above Designated Size in Wholesale and Retail Trades by City（2022）

16-11 限额以上连锁批发零售业经营情况（2022 年） …… 473
Business of Chain Stores above Designated Size in Wholesale and Retail Trade（2022）
16-12 亿元以上商品交易市场成交额 …… 475
Turnover of Commodity Exchange Markets with Transaction Value over 100 Million Yuan
16-13 限额以上批发零售企业财务状况（2022 年） …… 477
Financial Indicators of Enterprises above Designated Size in Wholesale and Retail Trades Services（2022）
16-14 限额以上批发企业财务状况（2022 年） …… 478
Financial Indicators of Enterprises above Designated Size in Wholesale Trade（2022）
16-15 限额以上零售企业财务状况（2022 年） …… 482
Financial Indicators of Enterprises above Designated Size in Retail Trade（2022）
16-16 各市限额以上批发零售企业财务状况（2022 年） …… 486
Financial Indicators of Enterprises above Designated Size in Wholesale and Retail Trades by City（2022）
主要统计指标解释 …… 490
Explanatory Notes on Main Statistical Indicators

十七、住宿餐饮业和旅游
Hotels, Catering Services and Tourism
简要说明 …… 494
Brief Introduction
17-1 住宿、餐饮业、旅游主要指标 …… 495
Main Indicators on Hotels, Catering Services and Tourism
17-2 限额以上住宿业经营情况（2022 年） …… 496
Business of Hotels above Designated Size（2022）
17-3 限额以上餐饮业经营情况（2022 年） …… 497
Business of Catering Services Enterprises above Designated Size（2022）
17-4 各市限额以上住宿餐饮业经营情况（2022 年） …… 498
Business of Enterprises above Designated Size of Hotels and Catering Services by City（2022）
17-5 限额以上连锁住宿餐饮业经营情况（2022 年） …… 499
Business of Chain Stores above Designated Size in Hotels and Catering Services（2022）
17-6 限额以上住宿餐饮企业财务状况（2022 年） …… 501
Financial Indicators of Enterprises above Designated Size in Hotels and Catering Services（2022）
17-7 限额以上住宿企业财务状况（2022 年） …… 502
Financial Indicators of Hotels above Designated Size（2022）
17-8 限额以上餐饮企业财务状况（2022 年） …… 506
Financial Indicators of Catering Services Enterprises above Designated Size（2022）

17-9 各市限额以上住宿和餐饮企业财务状况（2022 年）…… 510
Financial Indicators of Enterprises above Designated Size of Hotels and Catering Services by City（2022）
17-10 各市住宿餐饮业营业额 …… 514
Business of Enterprises above Designated Size of Hotels and Catering Services by City
17-11 旅游部门基本情况 …… 515
Basic Statistics on Tourism-related Agencies
17-12 城市接待外国游客人数 …… 515
Number of Foreign Visitors Received by Cities
17-13 各市旅游宾馆（酒店）住宿设施（2022 年）…… 516
Lodging Facilities of Tourist Hotels by City（2022）
17-14 各市接待过夜旅游者人数 …… 517
Number of Overnight Tourists by City
17-15 各市旅游业收入 …… 518
Tourism Earnings by City
17-16 各市国际旅游外汇收入 …… 519
Foreign Exchange Earnings from International Tourism by City
主要统计指标解释 …… 520
Explanatory Notes on Main Statistical Indicators

十八、房地产业

Real Estate

简要说明 …… 522
Brief Introduction
18-1 房地产开发主要指标 …… 523
Main Indicators on Real Estate Development
18-2 按用途分房地产开发企业房屋建筑及销售情况 …… 524
Situation of Real Estate Development, Corporate Building Construction and Sales by Purpose
18-3 按登记注册类型分组房地产开发投资情况 …… 525
Investment in Real Estate Development
18-4 按登记注册类型分组房地产开发房屋建筑面积及价值（2022 年）…… 525
Floor Space and Value of Buildings in Real Estate Development（2022）
18-5 各市房地产开发企业投资总规模及完成情况 (2022 年) …… 526
The Total Investment Scale and Completion Status of Real Estate Development Enterprises By City (2022)
18-6 各市房地产开发投资情况（2022 年）…… 527
Investment in Real Estate Development by City（2022）
18-7 各市房地产开发房屋建筑面积及价值（2022 年）…… 528
Floor Space and Value of Buildings in Real Estate Development by City（2022）

18-8 按用途分商品房销售面积（2022 年） …… 529
Floor Space of Commercial Buildings Sold by Use（2022）
18-9 按用途分商品房销售额（2022 年） …… 529
Sales of Commercial Buildings by Use（2022）
18-10 各市商品房屋销售情况（2022 年） …… 530
Sales of Commercial Buildings by City（2022）
主要统计指标解释 …… 531
Explanatory Notes on Main Statistical Indicators

十九、教育和科技

Education and Technology

简要说明 …… 534
Brief Introduction
19-1 教育、科技主要指标 …… 535
Main Indicators on Education，Science and Technology
19-2 各级各类学校在校学生数 …… 536
Number of Total Enrollment by Level and Type of School
19-3 各级各类学校情况 …… 537
Statistics on Various Levels and Types of Schools
19-4 研究生教育情况 …… 539
Statistics on Postgraduate Education
19-5 各级各类继续教育在校学生数 …… 539
Number of Total Enrollment by Level and Type of Continuing Education
19-6 高等学校情况（2022 年） …… 540
Statistics on Institutions of Higher Education（2022）
19-7 中等学校情况（2022 年） …… 540
Statistics on Secondary Schools（2022）
19-8 各市普通中学情况（2022 年） …… 541
Statistics on Regular Secondary Schools by City（2022）
19-9 各市中等职业教育基本情况（2022 年） …… 543
Basic Statistics on Vocational Secondary Education by City（2022）
19-10 各市小学情况（2022 年） …… 544
Statistics on Primary Schools by City（2022）
19-11 各市学龄儿童入学情况 …… 545
Statistics on School-age Children Enrolled in Schools by City
19-12 研究与试验发展（R&D）基本情况 …… 546
Basic Statistics on Research and Development（R&D）

19-13 公有经济企业、事业单位专业技术人员年末人数 …… 547
Number of Professional and Technical Personnel in State-owned Enterprises and Institutions at the Year-end
19-14 高层次人才情况 …… 548
Statistics on High-level Talents
19-15 各类技术合同签订情况 …… 548
Statistics on Technical Contracts Signed by Type
19-16 科技成果项数 …… 549
Number of Achievements for Scientific and Technological Research
19-17 县级政府部门属研究与开发机构基本情况 …… 549
Basic Statistics on Research and Development Institutions under Government Departments at County Level
19-18 县级以上政府部门属研究与开发机构基本情况 …… 550
Basic Statistics on Research and Development Institutions under Government Departments at and above County Level
19-19 各市县级及以上政府部门属研究与开发机构基本情况 …… 551
Basic Statistics on Research and Development Institutions under Government Departments at and above County Level by City
19-20 三种专利申请量与授权量 …… 553
Three Types of Patent Application and Granted
19-21 分市全社会研究与试验发展人员与经费（2021 年） …… 554
Research and Intramural Expenditure on R&D by City（2021）
19-22 规模以上工业企业的科技活动基本情况 …… 555
Basic Statistics on Science and Technology Activities of Industrial Enterprises above Designated size
19-23 规模以上工业企业研究与发展经费内部支出 …… 556
Internal Expenditures of Industrial Enterprises Above Designated Size
19-24 分市规模以上工业企业 R&D 活动人员和经费 …… 558
R&D Personnel and Expenditure of Industrial Enterprises by City
19-25 分市规模以上工业企业新产品开发与销售情况（2022 年） …… 559
New Products Development and Sale by Industrial Enterprises by City（2022）
19-26 科协机构及活动情况 …… 560
Statistics on Associations for Science and Technology and Their Activities
主要统计指标解释 …… 561
Explanatory Notes on Main Statistical Indicators

二十、文化与体育

Culture and Sports

简要说明 …… 566
Brief Introduction

20-1 文化、体育主要指标 …… 567
Main Indicators on Culture and Education
20-2 文化艺术、文物事业机构数 …… 568
Number of Institutions of Culture, Arts and Cultural Relics
20-3 文化部门艺术表演团体演出基本情况（2022 年） …… 569
Basic Statistics on Performances of Art Troupes under (of) Cultural Departments (2022)
20-4 文化、文物机构及人员数（2022 年） …… 570
Number of Institutions and Personnel in Culture and Cultural Relics (2022)
20-5 公共图书馆、群众文化事业机构及人员数（2022 年） …… 570
Number of Institutions and Personnel in Public Libraries and Mass Culture (2022)
20-6 各市文化、文物事业机构数（2022 年） …… 571
Number of Institutions in Culture and Cultural Relics by City (2022)
20-7 各市文化、文物事业机构的人员数（2022 年） …… 572
Number of Personnel in Culture and Cultural Relics by City (2022)
20-8 图书、杂志、报纸出版数量 …… 573
Number of Books, Magazines and Newspapers Published
20-9 图书出版情况（2022 年） …… 573
Statistics on Books Published (2022)
20-10 杂志出版情况（2022 年） …… 574
Statistics on Magazines Published (2022)
20-11 报纸出版情况（2022 年） …… 574
Statistics on Newspapers Published (2022)
20-12 广播、电视事业发展情况 …… 575
Statistics on Radio and Television Stations
20-13 广播电台宣传基本情况（2022 年） …… 575
Basic Statistics on Radio Stations (2022)
20-14 电视台宣传基本情况（2022 年） …… 576
Basic Statistics on Television Stations (2022)
20-15 各市广播、电视事业机构数（2022 年） …… 576
Number of Institutions of Radio and Television by City (2022)
20-16 体育事业情况 …… 577
Statistics on Sports
主要统计指标解释 …… 578
Explanatory Notes on Main Statistical Indicators

二十一、卫生、社会福利、社会保障和其他
Public Health, Social Welfare, Social Insurance and Others
简要说明 …… 580
Brief Introduction

21-1 卫生、社会福利和其他主要指标 …… 581
Main Indicators of Sports, Public Health, Social Welfare, Environmental Protection and Others
21-2 医疗卫生机构、床位及人员数 …… 582
Number of Health Care Institutions, Beds and Personnel
21-3 医疗卫生机构、床位和人员数（2022 年） …… 583
Number of Health Care Institutions, Beds and Personnel (2022)
21-4 各市医疗卫生机构、床位和人员数（2022 年） …… 584
Number of Health Care Institutions, Beds and Personnel by City (2022)
21-5 各类医疗卫生机构、床位和人员数 …… 585
Number of Health Institutions, Beds and Personnel by Type
21-6 各市社会保险基金征缴收入（2022 年） …… 586
Amount Collected of Security Insurance (2022)
21-7 各市社会保险参保人数（2022 年） …… 587
Number of Persons Participating in Social Insurance by City (2022)
21-8 优抚、社会救济和福利事业情况 …… 588
Statistics on Preferential Treatment and Resettlement, Social Relief and Welfare
21-9 婚姻登记情况 …… 590
Statistics on Marriage Registration
21-10 律师、公证、基层司法基本情况 …… 591
Basic Statistics on Lawyers, Notarization, Grassroots Judicial Work
21-11 交通事故发生情况（2022 年） …… 592
Statistics on Traffic Accidents (2022)
21-12 火灾事故发生情况（2022 年） …… 592
Statistics on Fire Accidents (2022)
21-13 各市亿元生产总值生产安全事故死亡率 …… 593
Rate of Death from Work Safety Accidents per 100 Million Yuan of Gross Domestic Product by City
主要统计指标解释 …… 594
Explanatory Notes on Main Statistical Indicators

二十二、区域主要经济指标

Major Economic Regions

简要说明 …… 596
Brief Introduction
22-1 区域主要经济指标 …… 597
Main Indicators on Regional Economies
22-2 区域主要经济指标占全省比重 …… 599
Percentage of Main Regional Economic Indicators to the Provincial Total

22-3 珠三角主要经济指标 …… 601
Main Economic Indicators of the Pearl River Delta Economic Zone
22-4 珠三角工业企业主要指标（2022年） …… 604
Main Indicators of Industrial Enterprises of the Pearl River Delta（2022）
22-5 广州、深圳主要经济指标（2022年） …… 608
Main Economic Indicators of Guangzhou and Shenzhen（2022）
22-6 粤东西北主要经济指标 …… 609
Main Economic Indicators of the East and West and Mountainous Area
22-7 东翼主要经济指标 …… 612
Main Economic Indicators of the East Wing
22-8 西翼主要经济指标 …… 613
Main Economic Indicators of the West Wing
22-9 山区主要经济指标 …… 614
Main Economic Indicators of Mountainous Areas
22-10 山区县（市、区）主要经济指标 …… 615
Main Economic Indicators of Counties（County-level Cities and Districts）in Mountainous Areas
22-11 少数民族县主要经济指标（2022年） …… 616
Main Economic Indicators of Minority Counties（2022）

二十三、县（市、区）主要经济指标
Counties and Districts Under City Administration

简要说明 …… 618
Brief Introduction
23-1 各县（市、区）地区生产总值 …… 619
Gross Domestic Product by County（County-level City and District）
23-2 各县（市、区）三次产业地区生产总值 …… 622
Gross Domestic Product of the Three Strata of Industry by County（County-level City and District）
23-3 各县（市、区）三次产业地区生产总值指数 …… 625
Gross Domestic Product of the Three Industries by County（County-level City and District）
23-4 各县（市、区）人均地区生产总值及指数 …… 628
Per Capita Gross Domestic Product and Growth Rates by County（County-level City and District）
23-5 各县（市、区）工、农林牧渔业总产值 …… 631
Gross Output Value of Industry Enterprises above Designated Size and Agriculture by County (County-level City and District)
23-6 各县（市、区）粮食产量 …… 634
Output of Grain by County（County-level City and District）
23-7 各县（市、区）糖蔗、水果和蔬菜产量 …… 637
Output of Sugarcane，Fruits and Vegetable by County（County-level City and District）

23-8 各县（市、区）猪肉产量、禽肉产量 …… 640
Output of Pork and Output of Meat of Poultry by County（County-level City and District）
23-9 各县（市、区）规模以上工业企业单位数及利润总额 …… 643
Number of Industrial Enterprises And Total Profits by County（County-level City and District）
23-10 各县（市、区）房地产开发投资 …… 646
Investment in Fixed Assets by County（County-level City and District）
23-11 各县（市、区）社会消费品零售总额 …… 649
Total Retail Sales of Consumer Goods by County（County-level City and District）
23-12 各县（市、区）财政收支 …… 652
Local Government Budgetary Revenue and Expenditure by County（County-level City and District）
23-13 各县（市、区）城镇居民人均可支配收入 …… 655
Per Capita Disposable Income of Urban Households by County（County-level City and District）
23-14 各县（市、区）农村居民人均可支配收入 …… 658
Per Capita Disposable Income of Rural Households by County（County-level City and District）

附录

Appendix

简要说明 …… 662
Brief Introduction
附录 A-1 人口及地区生产总值（2022 年）…… 664
Population and Gross Domestic Product（2022）
附录 A-2 固定资产投资完成情况（2022 年）…… 665
Investment in Fixed Assets（2022 年）
附录 A-3 居民人均收入与支出（2022 年）…… 666
Per Capita Income and Expenditure（2022）
附录 A-4 居民消费价格指数（2022 年）…… 667
Consumer Price Indices（2022）
附录 A-5 农林牧渔业总产值和增速（2022 年）…… 668
Gross Output Value of Farming，Forestry，Animal Husbandry and Fishery and Growth Rate（2022）
附录 A-6 主要农产品产量（2022 年）…… 669
Output of Major Agricultural Products（2022）
附录 A-7 规模以上工业企业主要经济指标（2022 年）…… 670
Main Economic Indicators of Industrial Enterprises above Designated Size（2022）
附录 A-8 主要工业产品产量（2022 年）…… 671
Output of Major Industrial Products（2022）
附录 A-9 建筑业主要指标（2022 年）…… 672
Indicators of Construction Industry（2022）

附录 A-10 客运量和旅客周转量（2022 年）…… 673
Passenger Traffic and Passenger-kilometers（2022）
附录 A-11 货运量和货物周转量（2022 年）…… 674
Freight Traffic and Freight Ton_Kilometers（2022）
附录 A-12 国内外贸易（2022 年）…… 675
Retail Trades and Foreign Trades（2022）
附录 B-1 中国香港特别行政区主要社会经济指标 …… 676
Main Statistical Indicators of Hong Kong Special Administrative Region
附录 B-2 中国澳门特别行政区主要社会经济指标 …… 677
Main Statistical Indicators of Macao Special Administrative Region
附录 C 中国台湾省主要社会经济指标 …… 678
Main Statistical Indicators of Taiwan Province
附录 D-1 部分国家和地区主要经济指标（2021 年）…… 679
Main Economic Indicators of Some Countries and Territories（2021）
附录 D-2 部分国家和地区国内生产总值 …… 681
Gross Domestic Product of Some Countries and Territories
附录 D-3 部分国家和地区国内生产总值增长率 …… 682
Growth Rates of GDP of Some Countries and Territories
附录 D-4 部分国家和地区人均国民总收入 …… 683
Per Capita Gross National Income of Some Countries and Territories
附录 D-5 部分国家和地区人均国内生产总值增长率 …… 684
Growth Rates of Per Capita GDP of Some Countries and Territories
主要统计指标解释 …… 685
Explanatory Notes on Main Statistical Indicators

一、综合

GENERAL SURVEY

一 综合

简要说明

一、本篇资料反映广东行政区划、国民经济和社会发展综合资料，并收录了基本单位统计情况。

二、本篇资料分别由广东省民政厅，广东省统计局各专业处、综合统计处、普查中心和国家统计局广东调查总队整理提供。

三、综合统计资料是根据广东省统计局各专业统计年报资料以及国家统计局、广东省有关部门提供的统计资料加工整理而成。

四、基本单位资料中的产业活动单位按“在地”原则，国民经济行业分类标准（GB/T 4754-2017)汇总。

1 General Survey

Brief Introduction

Ⅰ.The summary data in this chapter reflect the divisions of administrative areas, summary data on the national economy and social development, and related indications on.

Ⅱ.The data are prepared and provided by the Civil Affairs Department of Guangdong Province., the Division of Professional Statistics, the Division of Comprehensive Statistics, the Census Center of Statistics Bureau of Guangdong Province, and the Survey Office in Guangdong of National Bureau of Statistics respectively.

Ⅲ.The summary data are processed and prepared on the basis of the annual reports of various specialized fields provided by Statistics Bureau of Guangdong Province and the statistics provided by the National Bureau of Statistics and some related departments of Guangdong Province.

Ⅳ. The data on “Units of Industrial Establishments” of the basic industrial units are prepared on the principle of location and the standard of Industrial Classification of the National Economy(GB/T 4754-2017).

1-1 行政区划（2022年）

Divisions of Administrative Areas (2022)

单位：个 (unit)

市别	City	地级市 Number of Cities at Prefecture Level	县级市 Number of Cities at County Level	县 Number of Counties	自治县 Number of Autonomous Counties	市辖区 Number of Districts under the Jurisdiction of Cities	市辖镇 Number of Towns under the Jurisdiction of Cities	乡 Number of Townships	民族乡 Ethnic Townships	街道 Number of Street Communities
全　省	**Provincial Total**	**21**	**20**	**34**	**3**	**65**	**1112**	**4**	**7**	**489**
广　州	Guangzhou	1				11	34			142
深　圳	Shenzhen	1				9				74
珠　海	Zhuhai	1				3	15			10
汕　头	Shantou	1		1		6	30			37
佛　山	Foshan	1				5	21			11
韶　关	Shaoguan	1	2	4	1	3	94		1	10
河　源	Heyuan	1		5		1	94		1	6
梅　州	Meizhou	1	1	5		2	104			6
惠　州	Huizhou	1		3		2	48		1	22
汕　尾	Shanwei	1	1	2		1	40			14
东　莞	Dongguan	1					28			4
中　山	Zhongshan	1					15			8
江　门	Jiangmen	1	4			3	61			12
阳　江	Yangjiang	1	1	1		2	38			10
湛　江	Zhanjiang	1	3	2		4	82	2		38
茂　名	Maoming	1	3			2	86			26
肇　庆	Zhaoqing	1	1	4		3	87		1	17
清　远	Qingyuan	1	2	2	2	2	77		3	5
潮　州	Chaozhou	1		1		2	41			5
揭　阳	Jieyang	1	1	2		2	62	2		24
云　浮	Yunfu	1	1	2		2	55			8

注：本行政区划截至2022年底。

Note: The divisions of administrative areas reflect the status at the end of 2022.

1-2 国民经济和社会发展总量与速度指标

指　　标		Item		1978	1990	2000
人口与就业		**Population and Employment**				
人口	**(万人)**	**Population**	**(10000 persons)**			
年末户籍总人口		Population with Residence Registration at the Year-end		5064.15	6246.32	7498.54
年末常住人口		Permanent Population at the Year-end		5064.15	6347.19	8650.03
男性人口		Male		2586.68	3249.76	4402.87
女性人口		Female		2477.47	3097.43	4247.16
城镇人口		Urban Population			2335.77	4757.52
乡村人口		Rural Population			4011.42	3892.51
就业	**(万人)**	**Employment**	**(10000 persons)**			
年末就业人员人数		Employed Persons at the Year-end		2275.95	3118.10	3989.32
宏观经济		**Macro Economy**				
国民经济核算	**(亿元)**	**National Accounting**	**(100 million yuan)**			
地区生产总值		Gross Domestic Product		185.85	1559.03	10810.21
第一产业		Primary Industry		55.31	384.59	986.32
第二产业		Secondary Industry		86.62	615.86	5042.75
第三产业		Tertiary Industry		43.92	558.58	4781.15
人均地区生产总值	(元)	Per Capita Gross Domestic Product	(yuan)	370	2484	12817
支出法地区生产总值	(亿元)	Gross Domestic Product by Expenditure Approach	(100 million yuan)	194.14	1541.99	10810.21
最终消费支出		Final Consumption Expenditures		130.02	938.48	5717.11
居民消费		Household Consumption Expenditures		111.46	807.84	4474.11
政府消费		Government Consumption Expenditures		18.56	130.64	1243.00
资本形成总额		Gross Capital Formation		54.79	502.90	3917.11
固定资本形成总额		Gross Fixed Capital Formation		37.93	336.61	3160.12
存货增加		Changes in Inventories		16.86	166.29	756.99
货物和服务净流出		Net Exports of Goods and Services		9.33	100.61	1175.99
固定资产投资	**(亿元)**	**Investment in Fixed Assets**	**(100 million yuan)**			
房地产开发投资额		Real Estate Development			32.70	858.61
消费	**(亿元)**	**Domestic Trade**	**(100 million yuan)**			
社会消费品零售总额		Total Retail Sales of Consumer Goods		79.86	667.36	4320.73
对外贸易	**(亿美元)**	**Foreign Trade**	**(USD 100 million)**			
货物进出口总额		Total Exports and Imports			418.98	1701.06
出口额		Exports			222.21	919.19
进口额		Imports			196.77	781.87
利用外资		**Foreign Capital Utilized**				
实际利用外商直接投资	(亿美元)	Foreign Direct Investment Actually Utilized	(USD 100 million)		14.60	122.37
实际利用外商直接投资	(亿元)	Foreign Direct Investment Actually Utilized	(RMB 100 million)			
财政	**(亿元)**	**Government Finance**	**(100 million yuan)**			
地方一般公共预算收入		Local Public Budgetary Revenue		41.82	131.02	910.56
地方一般公共预算支出		Local Public Budgetary Expenditure		28.70	150.69	1069.86
价格指数	**(上年=100)**	**Price Indices**	**(preceding year=100)**			
商品零售价格指数		Retail Price Index		100.4	95.6	99.9
居民消费价格指数		Consumer Price Index			97.5	101.4
工业生产者出厂价格指数		Producer Price Index for Manufactured Goods				103.4
工业生产者购进价格指数		Producer Price Index for Purchased Goods				110.9
能源生产与消费	**(万吨标准煤)**	**Production and Consumption of Energy**	**(10000 tons of SCE)**			
能源生产总量		Total Energy Production			1006.24	3711.69
能源消费总量		Total Energy Consumption			4044.28	9447.70

Principal Aggregate Indicators on National Economic and Social Development and Growth Rates

2010	2021	2022	速度指标(%) Indices and Growth Rates (%)								
			指数(2022为以下各年) Index (2022 as percentage of the following years)					平均增长速度 Average Annual Growth Rate			
			1978	1990	2000	2010	2021	1979–2022	1991–2022	2001–2022	2011–2022
8521.55	9946.95	10049.72	198.4	160.9	134.0	117.9	101.0	1.6	1.5	1.3	1.4
10440.94	12684.00	12656.80	249.9	199.4	146.3	121.2	99.8	2.1	2.2	1.7	1.6
5444.95	6693.00	6673.80	258.0	205.4	151.6	122.6	99.7	2.2	2.3	1.9	1.7
4995.99	5991.00	5983.00	241.5	193.2	140.9	119.8	99.9	2.0	2.1	1.6	1.5
6909.85	9466.07	9465.40		405.2	199.0	137.0	100.0		4.5	3.2	2.7
3531.09	3217.93	3191.40		79.6	82.0	90.4	99.2		-0.7	-0.9	-0.8
6051.00	7072.00	6904.00	303.3	221.4	173.1	114.1	97.6	2.6	2.5	2.5	1.1
45944.62	124719.53	129118.58	12912.5	3062.8	739.8	222.6	101.9	11.7	11.3	9.5	6.9
2199.60	4984.70	5340.36	840.6	352.1	233.7	161.3	105.2	5.0	4.0	3.9	4.1
22917.43	50555.79	52843.51	24232.2	4931.2	819.7	210.0	102.5	13.3	13.0	10.0	6.4
20827.59	69179.04	70934.71	16725.2	2937.9	755.6	242.5	101.2	12.3	11.1	9.6	7.7
44669	98561	101905	5123.0	1517.1	492.4	180.7	101.7	9.4	8.9	7.5	5.1
45944.62	124719.53										
22501.78	62237.05										
17702.35	46666.46										
4799.43	15570.60										
18226.60	56914.11										
17035.10	50735.78										
1191.50	6178.33										
5216.24	5568.37										
3659.69	17465.85	14962.97		45758.3	1742.7	408.9	85.7		21.1	13.9	12.5
16991.39	44187.71	44882.92	56202.0	6725.4	1038.8	264.2	101.6	15.4	14.0	11.1	8.3
7848.96	12795.67	12469.69		2976.2	733.1	158.9	97.5		11.2	9.5	3.9
4531.91	7818.60	7999.02		3599.8	870.2	176.5	102.3		11.8	10.3	4.8
3317.05	4977.07	4470.67		2272.0	571.8	134.8	89.8		10.3	8.2	2.5
202.61											
	1840.02	1819.02					98.9				
4517.04	14105.04	13260.88	31709.4	10121.3	1456.3	293.6	94.0	14.0	15.5	12.9	9.4
5421.54	18247.01	18533.08	64575.2	12298.8	1732.3	341.8	101.6	15.8	16.2	13.8	10.8
103.3	101.4	102.5									
103.1	100.8	102.2									
103.2	103.4	103.0									
107.3	108.0	104.1									
4858.07	8892.72	9647.31		958.7	259.9	198.6	108.5		7.3	4.4	5.9
25445.22	36821.42	36519.05		903.0	386.5	143.5	99.2		7.1	6.3	3.1

1-2 续表 1

指　　标	Item	1978	1990	2000
产业	**Industry**			
农业	**Agriculture**			
农林牧渔业总产值　(亿元)	Gross Output Value of Farming, Forestry, Animal Husbandry and Fishery (100 million yuan)	85.94	600.71	1701.18
主要农产品产量　(万吨)	Output of Major Farm Products (10000 tons)			
粮食	Grain	1509.51	1896.29	1822.33
油料	Oil-bearing Crops	36.04	58.93	78.78
糖蔗	Sugarcane	835.42	2093.46	1137.59
茶叶	Tea	0.92	2.59	4.21
水果	Fruits	29.40	328.58	643.52
肉类	Meat	48.45	202.45	324.48
水产品	Aquatic Products	65.50	207.66	593.19
工业	**Industry**			
主要工业产品产量	Output of Major Industrial Products			
布　(亿米)	Cloth (100 million m)	2.27	4.59	16.99
机制纸及纸板　(万吨)	Machine-made Paper and Paperboard (10000 tons)	27.47	104.13	260.30
成品糖　(万吨)	Sugar (10000 tons)	96.15	184.50	91.30
家用电冰箱　(万台)	Household Refrigerators (10000 sets)		105.75	320.70
家用洗衣机　(万台)	Household Washing Machines (10000 sets)		143.01	244.18
彩色电视机　(万台)	Color Television Sets (10000 sets)		262.37	1531.53
照相机　(万架)	Cameras (10000 sets)		99.30	3545.88
原油　(万吨)	Crude Oil (10000 tons)	10.22	49.05	1393.17
发电量　(亿千瓦时)	Electricity (100 million kwh)	92.32	343.98	1292.69
粗钢　(万吨)	Raw Steel (10000 tons)	35.84	116.96	286.99
钢材　(万吨)	Steel Products (10000 tons)	43.67	133.74	406.28
水泥　(万吨)	Cement (10000 tons)	369.08	2070.91	5872.00
汽车　(万辆)	Motor Vehicles (10000 units)			3.94
规模以上工业企业主要指标	Main Indicators of Industrial Enterprises above Designated Size			
工业增加值　(亿元)	Value-added of Industry (101 million yuan)	55.59	391.19	3422.60
资产总计　(亿元)	Total Assets (100 million yuan)	104.06	546.72	14370.57
营业收入　(亿元)	Business Revenue (100 million yuan)	168.91	689.83	12480.93
利税总额　(亿元)	Pre-tax Profits (100 million yuan)	32.91	121.50	1042.77
建筑业	**Construction**			
建筑业企业年末就业人员(万人)	Number of Employed Persons in Construction Enterprises at the Year-end (10000 persons)	14.78	67.22	141.46
建筑业总产值(当年价)　(亿元)	Gross Output Value (at current prices) (100 million yuan)	5.47	113.40	944.61
交通运输业	**Transportation**			
客运量　(万人)	Passenger Traffic (10000 persons)	15906	78046	164791
铁路	Railways	2410	4467	12165
公路	Highways	10897	70681	148945
水运	Waterways	2546	2428	2363
民航	Civil Aviation	53	470	1318
货运量　(万吨)	Freight Traffic (10000 tons)	15204	85809	119216
铁路	Railways	3206	4803	15172
公路	Highways	3967	63709	75365
水运	Waterways	7887	16198	25696
民航	Civil Aviation	1	8	31
管道	Pipelines	143	1091	2952
港口货物吞吐量　(万吨)	Volume of Freight Handled at Ports (10000 tons)	7133	11904	31649

1-2 1 continued

2010	2021	2022	速度指标(%) Indices and Growth Rates (%)								
			指数(2022为以下各年) Index (2022 as percentage of the following years)					平均增长速度 Average Annual Growth Rate			
			1978	1990	2000	2010	2021	1979–2022	1991–2022	2001–2022	2011–2022
3697.18	8305.84	8892.29	919.5	401.7	236.2	156.7	104.8	5.2	4.4	4.0	3.8
1249.15	1279.87	1291.54	85.6	68.1	70.9	103.4	100.9	-0.4	-1.2	-1.6	0.3
83.34	117.30	117.43	325.8	199.3	149.1	140.9	100.1	2.7	2.2	1.8	2.9
1064.09	1118.20	1107.76	132.6	52.9	97.4	104.1	99.1	0.6	-2.0	-0.1	0.3
5.38	13.95	16.08	1748.2	621.0	382.0	298.7	115.3	6.7	5.9	6.3	9.5
1049.21	1826.73	1895.18	6446.2	576.8	294.5	180.6	103.7	9.9	5.6	5.0	5.1
454.86	457.42	481.01	992.8	237.6	148.2	105.7	105.2	5.4	2.7	1.8	0.5
729.03	884.52	894.03	1364.9	430.5	150.7	122.6	101.1	6.1	4.7	1.9	1.7
28.27	25.75	20.17	888.7	439.5	118.7	71.4	81.3	5.1	4.7	0.8	-2.8
1434.68	2410.29	2374.14	8642.7	2280.0	912.1	165.5	97.7	10.7	10.3	10.6	4.3
91.66	131.42	119.16	123.9	64.6	130.5	130.0	92.2	0.5	-1.4	1.2	2.2
1457.76	2091.56	1773.35		1676.9	553.0	121.6	82.8		9.2	8.1	1.6
467.83	757.57	686.72		480.2	281.2	146.8	90.6		5.0	4.8	3.3
4494.78	9810.91	10792.02		4113.3	704.7	240.1	111.5		12.3	9.3	7.6
3798.93	529.65	444.43		447.6	12.5	11.7	73.3		4.8	-9.0	-16.4
1287.15	1744.68	1884.62	18440.5	3842.2	135.3	146.4	108.0	12.6	12.1	1.4	3.2
3101.28	6306.23	6093.81	6600.8	1771.6	471.4	196.5	96.6	10.0	9.4	7.3	5.8
1239.34	3178.33	3571.77	9965.9	3053.8	1244.6	288.2	112.4	11.0	11.3	12.1	9.2
2918.89	5111.18	5627.44	12886.3	4207.7	1385.1	192.8	108.6	11.7	12.4	12.7	5.6
11536.67	17005.20	15131.17	4099.7	730.7	257.7	131.2	88.6	8.8	6.4	4.4	2.3
156.29	338.46	415.37			10542.3	265.8	122.0			23.6	8.5
20338.34	37306.53	37260.57			1306.8	220.6	101.6			12.3	6.8
62626.90	175746.01	196419.19			1317.9	302.4	111.7			12.5	9.7
85824.64	173649.71	183027.35			1416.5	206.0	103.8			12.8	6.2
9418.42	16325.16	15857.14			1415.2	156.7	91.6			12.7	3.7
196.32	355.40	345.04	2334.5	513.3	243.9	175.8	97.1	7.4	5.2	4.1	4.8
4742.09	21346.12	22956.50	419680.1	20243.8	2430.3	484.1	107.5	20.9	18.1	15.6	14.0
467049	62126	47632	297.7	221.6	107.4	57.2	76.7	2.5	2.5	0.3	-4.5
14956	23977	17526	779.5	432.0	228.4	133.6	73.1	4.8	4.7	3.8	2.4
442224	27567	23730	254.0	155.1	73.6	38.8	86.1	2.1	1.4	-1.4	-7.6
2241	1580	884	10.0	45.4	46.6	40.7	56.0	-5.1	-2.4	-3.4	-7.2
7628	9002	5492	10125.6	1138.1	405.9	70.1	61.0	11.1	7.9	6.6	-2.9
205034	398420	364199	1556.1	665.4	506.7	210.1	91.4	6.4	6.1	7.7	6.4
12170	9919	9374	391.6	229.7	127.8	109.1	95.5	3.2	2.6	1.1	0.7
142389	267489	242474	1446.1	779.1	658.6	225.4	90.6	6.3	6.6	8.9	7.0
43092	107206	97628	870.5	595.4	375.3	205.7	91.1	5.0	5.7	6.2	6.2
116	240	221	17782.0	2158.0	556.9	149.2	91.8	12.5	10.1	8.1	3.4
7267	13564	14503	7174.6	940.4	347.5	147.1	106.9	10.2	7.3	5.8	3.3
122258	209600	204802	3517.5	2107.7	792.8	205.2	97.7	8.4	10.0	9.9	6.2

1-2 续表 2

指　标	Item	1978	1990	2000
邮政、电信	**Postal，Telecommunication**			
邮政业务总量 (亿元)	Business Volume of Postal Services (100 million yuan)		3.91	50.40
电信业务总量 (亿元)	Business Volume of Telecommunications Services (100 million pieces)		22.39	706.82
固定电话用户 (万户)	Number of Subscribers of Local Telephones (10000 accounts)		113.00	1414.94
移动电话用户 (万户)	Number of Subscribers of Mobile Telephones (10000 accounts)		1.11	1357.26
固定互联网宽带接入用户 (万户)	Broadband Subscribers of Internet (10000 accounts)			216.41
国际旅游	**International Tourism**			
国际旅游外汇收入（亿美元）	Foreign Exchange Earnings from International Tourism (USD 100 million)		7.17	41.12
金融保险	**Banking and Insurance**			
金融机构存款余额 (亿元)	Deposits of Financial Institutions (100 million yuan)			19083.64
金融机构贷款余额 (亿元)	Loans in in Financial Institutions (100 million yuan)			13227.62
保费收入 (亿元)	Premium Income (100 million yuan)		18.05	191.88
教育、科技、文化	**Education, Science and Technology and Culture**			
教育	**Education**			
专任教师数 (万人)	Full-time Teachers (10000 persons)			
普通高等学校	Institutions of Higher Education	0.90	1.57	2.04
中等学校	Secondary Schools	15.93	16.33	27.24
小学	Primary Schools	26.09	27.73	36.41
在校学生数 (万人)	Students Enrollment (10000 persons)			
普通高等学校	Institutions of Higher Education	3.07	9.59	29.95
中等学校	Secondary Schools	316.96	284.52	541.72
小学	Primary Schools	743.02	747.29	929.93
财政教育支出 (亿元)	Government Expenditures on Education (100 million yuan)		21.34	144.39
科技	**Science and Technology**			
研究与试验发展(R&D)活动人员 (万人)	Number of R&D Personnel (10000 persons)			
研究与试验发展(R&D)经费内部支出 (亿元)	Internal Expenditure on R&D (100 million yuan)			
研究与试验发展(R&D)活动课题(项目)数 (个)	Number of R&D Programs/Projects (item)			
文化	**Culture**			
出版数量	Number of Publications			
图书 (亿册)	Number of Books Published (100 million copies)	1.72	2.81	2.70
杂志 (万册)	Number of Magazines Issued (10000 copies)	1519	11325	26299
报纸 (亿份)	Number of Newspapers Issued (100 million copies)	3.19	13.81	34.63

1-2 2 continued

2010	2021	2022	速度指标(%) Indices and Growth Rates (%)								
			指数(2022为以下各年) Index (2022 as percentage of the following years)					平均增长速度 Average Annual Growth Rate			
			1978	1990	2000	2010	2021	1979–2022	1991–2022	2001–2022	2011–2022
118.57	3021.10	3112.87		136852.8	10616.8	3359.5	103.0		25.3	23.6	34.0
4714.37	1933.49	1950.26		918199.5	29085.9	3473.7	118.6		33.0	29.4	34.4
3169.14	2072.20	1944.08		1720.4	137.4	61.3	93.8		9.3	1.5	-4.0
9710.09	16267.80	16650.76		1500068.5	1226.8	171.5	102.4		35.1	12.1	4.6
1523.22	4277.71	4628.72			2138.9	303.9	108.2			14.9	9.7
124.32	22.40	17.37		242.3	42.2	14.0	77.5		2.8	-3.8	-15.1
82019.40	293169.22	322357.66			1689.2	393.0	110.0			13.7	12.1
51799.30	222234.29	245722.94			1857.7	474.4	110.6			14.2	13.9
1421.68	5578.96	5894.16		32654.6	3071.8	414.6	105.6		19.8	16.8	12.6
7.86	12.88	13.59	1510.0	865.6	666.2	172.9	105.5	6.4	7.0	9.0	4.7
45.48	54.23	56.48	354.6	345.9	207.3	124.2	104.1	2.9	4.0	3.4	1.8
43.07	59.22	60.20	230.7	217.1	165.3	139.8	101.7	1.9	2.5	2.3	2.8
142.66	253.98	267.09	8700.0	2785.1	891.8	187.2	105.2	10.7	11.0	10.5	5.4
939.39	783.17	824.62	260.2	289.8	152.2	87.8	105.3	2.2	3.4	1.9	-1.1
848.55	1079.01	1084.05	145.9	145.1	116.6	127.8	100.5	0.9	1.2	0.7	2.1
921.48	3796.69	3871.14		18140.3	2681.0	420.1	102.0		17.6	16.1	12.7
44.66	124.85										
808.75	4002.18										
72747	284693										
2.31	5.06	5.06	294.1	180.0	187.4	219.0	100.0	2.5	1.9	2.9	6.8
21201	9539	9113	599.9	80.5	34.7	43.0	95.5	4.2	-0.7	-4.7	-6.8
45.59	14.48	13.19	413.5	95.5	38.1	28.9	91.1	3.3	-0.1	-4.3	-9.8

1-2 续表 3

指　　标	Item	1978	1990	2000
家庭、生活、环境	**Family, People's Livelihood and Environment**			
家庭	**Family**			
城镇居民平均每户家庭人口（人）	Average Permanent Household Size in Urban Areas (person)	4.84	3.85	3.57
农村居民平均每户家庭人口（人）	Average Permanent Household Size in Rural Areas (person)	5.99	5.65	5.15
婚姻	**Marriages and Divorces**			
结婚登记总数（万对）	Registered Number of Marriages (10000 couples)		50.66	56.21
离婚数（万对）	Number of Divorces (10000 couples)		2.58	4.75
居住	**Residence**			
全体居民人均住户建筑面积(平方米)	Per Capita housing construction are (sq.m)			
城镇居民人均住房建筑面积(平方米)	Per Capita Floor Space of Urban Residents (sq.m)	5.47	15.77	24.60
农村居民人均住房建筑面积(平方米)	Per Capita Floor Space of Rural Residents (sq.m)	8.73	17.39	22.42
生活	**People's Livelihood**			
全体居民人均可支配收入（元）	Per Capita Disposable Income of Residents (yuan)			
城镇居民人均可支配收入（元）	Per Capita Disposable Income of Urban Residents (yuan)	412	2303	9762
农村居民人均可支配收入（元）	Per Capita Disposable Income of Rural Residents (yuan)	193	1043	3654
人民币住户存款（亿元）	Savings Deposits by Households in Renminbi (100 million yuan)	17.56	752.16	8667.29
工资	**Wages**			
城镇单位就业人员工资总额（亿元）	Earnings of Employed Persons in Urban Areas (100 million yuan)	30.59	223.29	1057.57
城镇单位就业人员平均工资（元）	Average Earnings of Employed Persons in Urban Areas (yuan)	615	2929	13859
卫生	**Health Care**			
医院、卫生院（个）	Number of Hospitals (unit)	1968	1885	2426
执业(助理)医师（万人）	Number of Doctors (10000 persons)	4.79	8.11	11.12
医院、卫生院床位数（万张）	Number of Hospital Beds (10000 units)	8.41	11.41	15.72
环境、灾害	**Environment and Disaster**			
火灾发生数（起）	Number of Fire Disasters (time)		1725	8622
火灾损失（万元）	Fire Loss (10000 yuan)		9102	10065
交通事故发生数（起）	Number of Traffic Accidents (time)		25909	66072
交通事故损失（万元）	Loss of Traffic Accidents (10000 yuan)		5044	27526

注：1.2011—2020年年末常住人口根据2020年第七次全国人口普查数据进行平滑修正。
2.2003年起，职工改为单位从业人员，2000年数据作了相应调整。2006—2009年就业人员人数,根据第六次全国人口普查资料作了相应调整。从2020年起，国家统计局对各省、自治区、直辖市就业人数及其产业构成以常住人口口径统一测算，同时对2010—2019年就业人数及其产业结构进行平滑修正。
3.农业总产值、工业增加值绝对数按当年价格计算，增长速度按可比价计算。
4.工业指标统计范围为规模以上工业企业(即年主营业务收入2000万元以上的法人工业企业，2000—2006年为全部国有工业企业及年主营业务收入500万元以上的非国有工业企业，2011年起，调整为年主营业务收入2000万元及以上的法人工业企业)。
5.2000年起，粮食产量为抽样调查数据。
6.邮电业务总量2000年以前按1990年不变价计算，2000—2010年按2000年不变价计算,2011年起按2010年不变价计算,2017年起电信业务总量按2015年不变价格计算，邮政业务总量仍按2010年不变价计算，2021年起均按2020年不变价计算。2022年，电信业务总量按上年不变价计算。
7.1986年以前中等学校不含成人中专数据。
8.城镇居民人均住房建筑面积1995、2000年为使用面积， 2005年以后为建筑面积。
9.2011年起，固定资产投资项目统计起点由50万元提高至500万元，且不包含农村农户投资；2010年以前为全社会固定资产投资。
10.2015年起，地方公共财政预算收入和地方公共财政预算支出统一更名为地方一般公共预算收入和地方一般公共预算支出。
11.2013年起，居民人均可支配收入为城乡一体化住户收支与生活状况调查数据，与此前分城镇和农村住户调查的统计口径不可比，2013年以前农村居民收入为纯收入。
12.2018年起，外商直接投资使用商务部反馈人民币数据。

1-2 3 continued

2010	2021	2022	速度指标(%) Indices and Growth Rates (%)								
			指数(2022为以下各年) Index (2022 as percentage of the following years)					平均增长速度 Average Annual Growth Rate			
			1978	1990	2000	2010	2021	1979–2022	1991–2022	2001–2022	2011–2022
3.21	3.35	3.37	69.6	87.5	94.4	105.0	100.6	-0.8	-0.4	-0.3	0.4
4.95	3.74	3.72	62.1	65.8	72.2	75.2	99.5	-1.1	-1.3	-1.5	-2.4
85.71	59.11	57.31		113.1	101.9	66.9	96.9		0.4	0.1	-3.3
12.70	16.72	18.45		715.2	388.4	145.2	110.3		6.3	6.4	3.2
	42.23	42.62					100.9				
34.13	38.79	39.20	716.6	248.6	159.3	114.9	101.1	4.6	2.9	2.1	1.2
29.23	50.14	50.75	581.3	291.8	226.4	173.6	101.2	4.1	3.4	3.8	4.7
	44993	47065					104.6				
23898	54854	56905					103.7				
7890	22306	23598					105.8				
36318.66	96634.05	112555.17	640974.8	14964.3	1298.6	309.9	116.5	22.0	16.9	12.4	9.9
4484.29	24978.70	26200.89	85651.8	11734.0	2477.5	584.3	104.9	16.6	16.1	15.7	15.8
40432	118133	124916	20311.5	4264.8	901.3	309.0	105.7	12.8	12.4	10.5	9.9
2444	2935	2981	151.5	158.1	122.9	122.0	101.6	0.9	1.4	0.9	1.7
17.51	32.09	33.52	699.8	413.3	301.4	191.4	104.4	4.5	4.5	5.1	5.6
27.71	54.66	56.41	670.6	494.6	358.9	203.6	103.2	4.4	5.1	6.0	6.1
6065	64134	55629		3224.9	645.2	917.2	86.7		11.5	8.8	20.3
17500	79931	70995		780.0	705.4	405.7	88.8		6.6	9.3	12.4
30480	48206	38782		149.7	58.7	127.2	80.5		1.3	-2.4	2.0
8051	10534	8649		171.5	31.4	107.4	82.1		1.7	-5.1	0.6

Notes: a)Figures of permanent population at the year-end from 2011 to 2020 have been adjusted in accordance with the flash sums of the 7th National Population Census in 2020.

b)The number of staff and workers has been recoded as employed persons in units since 2003.The data of 2000 have been adjusted accordingly. The number of employed persons from 2006 to 2009 have been adjusted in accordance with the data of the 6th National Census. Since 2020, the NBS is uniformly calculated the number of employed persons and industrial composition by permanent resident method in all Provinces, Autonomous Regions and Municipalities, the number of employed persons and industrial compositon from 2010 to 2019 have been adjusted at the same time.

c)Figures in value terms on gross output value of agriculture and industry are calculated at current prices , whereas their growth rates are calculated at constant prices.

d)The statistical coverage of the industrial indicators refers to the industrial enterprises above designated size, i.e.legal person industrial enterprises with annual main business revenue over 5 million yuan.The industrial indicators from 2000 to 2006 covered all state-owned industrial enterprises and non-state-owned industrial enterprises with annual main business revenue over 5 million yuan. Since 2011, it refers to legal person industrial enterprises with annual principal business revenue of over 20 million yuan.

e) Figures of output of grain have been obtained from sample surveys since 2000.

f)The total business volume of postal and telecommunication services are at 1990 constant prices before 2000 and at 2000 constant prices from 2000 to 2010,and at 2010 constant price since 2011. The total bussiness volume of telecommunication services are at 2015 constant price since 2017, and the total bussiness volume of postal services are still at 2010 constant price, and since 2021 both at 2020 constant price. In 2022, the total business volume of postal and telecommunication services are at last year's constant prices.

g) Before 1986, the figures of secondary schools excluded those of specialized secondary schools for adults.

h) The per capital floor space of urban residents of 1995 and 2000 are useable area, and that since 2005 are building area.

i) Since 2011, the cut-off point of investment statistics is changed from a minimum of 500,000 yuan to a minimum of 5,000,000 yuan, and the data do not include the investment made by rural households. Data before 2010 refer to total investment in fixed assets.

j) From 2015, the name of local government budgetary revenue and local government budgetary expenditure have been changed to local public budgetary revenue and local public budgetary expenditure.

k) Since 2013, Per Capita Disposable Income of Residents are the data of investigation on income and expenditure and living conditions of urban and rural integrated households, it is not comparable with the statistical caliber of previous urban and rural househlods survey. Before 2013, the income of rural residents is net income.

l) Data of foreign direct investment in RMB that approved by Ministry of Commerce have been adopted since 2018.

1−3 国民经济和社会发展结构指标

Composition Indicators of National Economic and Social Development

单位：% (%)

指　标	Item	2000	2010	2015	2021	2022
人口与就业	**Population and Employment**					
人口	**Population**					
城乡结构(常住人口)	Urban and Rural Composition(by permanent population)					
城镇	Urban	55.0	66.2	69.5	74.6	74.8
乡村	Rural	45.0	33.8	30.5	25.4	25.2
性别结构(户籍人口)	Sexual Composition(by residential population)					
男	Male	51.6	51.5	51.5	51.2	51.1
女	Female	48.4	48.5	48.5	48.8	48.9
就业	**Employment**					
产业结构	Industrial Structure					
第一产业	Primary Industry	40.0	24.4	15.9	10.6	10.5
第二产业	Secondary Industry	27.9	42.4	40.0	36.3	36.6
第三产业	Tertiary Industry	32.1	33.2	44.1	53.1	53.0
宏观经济	**Macro Economy**					
国民经济核算	**National Accounts**					
地区生产总值产业结构	Industrial Structure of Gross Domestic Product					
第一产业	Primary Industry	9.1	4.8	4.3	4.0	4.1
第二产业	Secondary Industry	46.7	49.9	45.4	40.5	40.9
第三产业	Tertiary Industry	44.2	45.3	50.3	55.5	55.0
支出法地区生产总值结构	Domestic Expenditure Structure					
最终消费	Final Consumption	52.9	48.9	51.5	49.9	
居民消费	Household Consumption	41.4	38.5	39.8	37.4	
城镇居民	Urban Households	28.9	33.9	33.5	31.5	
农村居民	Rural Households	12.5	4.6	6.3	5.9	
政府消费	Government Consumption	11.5	10.4	11.7	12.5	
资本形成总额	Gross Capital Formation	36.2	39.3	40.6	45.6	
固定资本形成总额	Gross Fixed Capital Formation	29.2	36.6	39.1	40.7	
存货增加	Changes in Inventories	7.0	2.7	1.5	5.0	
净流出	Net Exports	10.9	11.9	7.8	4.5	
固定资产投资	**Investment**					
按登记注册类型分	Grouped by Status of Registration					
内资	Domestic-funded	82.8	85.4	88.4	91.3	91.0
国有	State-owned	37.7	32.0	21.2	27.6	29.7
集体	Collective-owned	12.2	4.6	4.3	1.5	1.5
股份合作	Cooperative	0.6	0.3	0.4	0.2	0.1
联营	Joint ownership	1.5	0.1	…	…	…
其他有限责任公司	Limited Liability	11.3	21.1	30.7	32.9	31.7
股份有限公司	Share-holding	4.7	5.4	4.2	3.8	3.4
私营	Private	6.4	13.7	22.6	24.2	23.4
个体	Individual	7.7	5.6	1.1	0.1	0.1
其他	Others	0.7	2.6	3.9	1.0	1.0
港澳台商投资	Investment from Hong Kong, Macao & Taiwan	12.9	9.2	6.9	4.7	5.0
外商投资	Foreign investment	4.3	5.4	4.7	4.0	4.0

注：2006−2009年就业人员人数，根据第六次全国人口普查资料作了调整。从2020年起，国家统计局对各省、自治区、直辖市就业人数及其产业构成以常住人口口径统一测算，同时对2010−2019年对就业人数及其产业结构进行平滑修正。

Note: Number of Employed Persons from 2006 to 2009 have been adjusted in accordance with the result of the 6th National Census. Since 2020, the National Bureau of Statistics calculates the number of Employed Persons and Industrial Composition of all Province, Autonomous Region and Municipality directly under the Central Government according to the caliber of permanent population， also adjusted the number of Employed Persons and Industrial Structure from 2010 to 2019.

1-3 续表 1 continued

单位：% (%)

指　　标	Item	2000	2010	2015	2021	2022
资金来源结构	Structure of Sources of Funds					
国家预算资金	State Budgetary Appropriation	1.7	2.2	4.9	9.8	14.2
国内贷款	Domestic Loans	17.2	16.8	12.5	16.2	15.9
利用外资	Foreign Investment	10.5	3.3	0.6	0.3	0.4
自筹投资	Fundraising	42.9	56.6	57.9	43.2	46.6
其他投资	Others	27.7	21.1	24.2	30.6	22.9
对外贸易(美元)	**Foreign Trade (USD)**					
出口按贸易方式分	Exports by Customs Regime					
一般贸易	Ordinary Trade	19.0	32.9	42.9	53.6	57.6
加工贸易	Processing Trade	78.1	60.8	43.7	28.8	26.4
其他	Others	2.9	6.3	13.4	17.6	16.0
进口按贸易方式分	Imports by Customs Regime					
一般贸易	Ordinary Trade	26.7	36.0	40.9	50.2	49.3
加工贸易	Processing Trade	63.1	51.4	41.9	25.0	25.0
其他	Others	10.2	12.6	17.2	24.8	25.7
国内贸易	**Domestic Trade**					
社会消费品零售总额结构	Structure of Total Retail Sales of Consumer Goods					
城镇	Urban Areas	76.2	86.9	89.3	88.1	87.5
乡村	Rural Areas	23.8	13.1	10.7	11.9	12.5
能源生产与消费	**Production and Consumption of Energy**					
能源生产总量结构	Structure of Total Energy Production					
原煤	Coal	8.0				
原油	Crude Oil	53.6	37.8	32.8	28.0	27.9
电力	Electricity	27.1	40.7	48.5	53.9	56.4
天然气	Natural Gas	11.3	21.5	18.7	18.1	15.6
一次能源消费总量结构	Structure of Total Primary Energy Consumption					
原煤	Coal	52.2	45.2	40.2	35.0	32.6
原油	Crude Oil	35.0	29.0	25.9	26.8	25.5
电力	Electricity	12.6	20.1	26.8	26.8	30.9
天然气	Natural Gas	0.2	5.7	7.1	11.4	11.0
其他	Others					
农业	**Agriculture**					
农林牧渔业产值结构	Structure of Gross Output Value of Farming, Forestry, Animal Husbandry and Fishery					
农业	Farming	47.5	45.1	47.0	47.6	48.4
林业	Forestry	3.5	4.9	5.8	6.0	6.2
牧业	Animal Husbandry	26.5	26.5	22.6	20.6	18.9
渔业	Fishery	22.5	19.9	20.8	21.0	21.3
农林牧渔专业及辅助性活动	Services for Farming, Forestry, Animal Husbandry and Fishery		3.6	3.9	4.9	5.1
工业(规模以上)	**Industry(above designated size)**					
按轻重工业分	Grouped by Light and Heavy Industry					
轻工业	Light Industry	52.9	38.3	38.2	33.4	33.5
重工业	Heavy Industry	47.1	61.7	61.8	66.6	66.5
按经济类型分	Grouped by Ownership					
#国有工业	State-owned Industry	11.6	5.4	0.5	0.4	0.6
集体工业	Collective-owned Industry	9.6	0.9	0.4	0.1	...
股份合作工业	Share-holding Cooperative Industry	0.9	0.2	0.1	...	...
股份制工业	Share-holding Industry	14.3	35.7	53.8	64.1	62.9
外商投资工业	Industry with Foreign Investment	20.2	25.4	20.8	15.8	15.7
港澳台商投资工业	Industry with Investment from Hong Kong, Macao and Taiwan	38.0	27.6	22.3	18.6	20.0
按企业规模分	Grouped by Size of Enterprise					
大型企业	Large	36.2	33.0	44.4	49.3	50.4
中型企业	Medium-sized	11.4	33.3	26.6	22.3	23.4
小微型企业	Small and Micro	52.3	33.7	29.0	28.4	26.2

注：2018年起资金来源中不含5000万元以下项目。
Note: Source of funds exclude projects below 50 million yuan since 2018.

1-3 续表 2 continued

单位：% (%)

指 标	Item	2000	2010	2015	2021	2022
建筑业	**Construction**					
按登记注册类型分	Grouped by Status of Registration					
内资	Domestic-funded	97.6	96.5	97.4	97.8	98.3
国有	State-owned	38.8	20.3	9.8	8.9	9.0
集体	Collective-owned	33.2	6.2	4.5	1.9	1.5
股份合作	Cooperative	0.8	0.3	0.1	0.1	0.1
联营	Joint ownership	1.2	0.4	0.1	0.1	0.1
有限责任公司	Limited Liability	13.9	42.0	53.7	48.5	52.2
股份有限公司	Share-holding	5.2	7.3	9.7	4.7	3.4
私营	Private	4.4	18.6	19.6	33.6	32.1
其他	Others	...	1.0	...	...	...
港澳台商投资	Investment from Hong Kong, Macao & Taiwan	1.6	1.5	0.8	0.9	0.9
外商投资	Foreign investment	0.8	2.0	1.7	1.2	0.8
交通运输和旅游	**Transportation and Tourism**					
客运量结构	Structure of Passenger Traffic					
铁路	Railways	7.4	3.2	12.8	38.6	36.8
公路	Highways	90.4	94.6	81.0	44.4	49.8
水运	Waterways	1.4	0.5	1.3	2.5	1.9
民用航空	Civil Aviation	0.8	1.6	4.8	14.5	11.5
货运量结构	Structure of Freight Traffic					
铁路	Railways	12.7	5.9	2.7	2.5	2.6
公路	Highways	63.2	69.4	74.4	67.1	66.6
水运	Waterways	21.6	21.0	20.7	26.9	26.8
民用航空	Civil Aviation	...	0.1	...	0.1	0.1
管道输油(气)	Pipelines	2.5	3.5	2.2	3.4	4.0
接待过夜旅游者人数	Composition of Tourists Staying Overnight					
入境旅游者	Overseas Visitor Arrivals Inbound Tourists	15.6	14.8	9.5	1.2	0.9
国内旅游者	Domestic Tourists	84.4	85.2	90.5	98.8	99.1
教育与科技	**Education and Technology**					
教育	**Education**					
在校学生结构	Structure of Enrolled Students					
大学生	Colleges and Universities	2.1	8.4	11.5	12.0	12.3
中学生	Regular Secondary Schools	32.4	41.7	34.7	37.0	37.9
小学生	Primary Schools	65.5	49.9	53.8	51.0	49.8
专任教师结构	Structure of Full-time Teachers					
大学	Colleges and Universities	3.3	8.7	10.0	10.2	10.4
中学	Secondary Schools	37.3	43.5	42.9	42.9	43.4
小学	Primary Schools	59.4	47.8	47.1	46.9	46.2
科技	**Science and Technology**					
研究与试验发展(R&D)经费内部支出	R&D Expenditure Internal Expenditure					
科学研究与技术开发机构	Scientific Research and Technological Development Institutions		2.6	3.6	4.9	
全日制普通高等学校	Full-time Regular Institutions of Higher Education		3.5	3.5	5.6	
工业企业	Industrial Enterprises		87.0	84.6	72.5	
其他	Others		6.8	8.4	17.0	
研究与试验发展(R&D)经费内部支出	R&D Expenditure Internal Expenditure					
#基础研究	Basic Research		2.1	3.0	6.9	
应用研究	Applied Research		4.6	9.2	8.9	
试验发展	Experimental Development		93.3	87.8	84.2	

1-3 续表 3 continued

单位：% (%)

指 标	Item	2000	2010	2015	2021	2022
生活、卫生、环境	**People's Livelihood，Health Care and Environment**					
生活	**People's Livelihood**					
全体居民消费结构	Composition of Consumption Expenditure Province Wide					
食品烟酒	Food,Tobacco and Liquor			34.5	33.2	34.3
衣着	Clothing			5.3	4.0	3.7
居住	Living			22.3	25.9	26.1
生活用品及服务	Daily Necessities and Services			5.9	5.1	5.1
交通通信	Transportation and Telecommunication			14.4	13.2	13.0
教育文化娱乐	Education,Culture and Entertainment			10.1	10.3	9.9
医疗保健	Health Service			4.7	6.0	5.5
其他用品和服务	Other Necessities and Services			2.8	2.3	2.4
城镇居民消费结构	Composition of Consumption Expenditure of Urban Households					
食品烟酒	Food,Tobacco and Liquor	38.6	36.5	33.2	31.7	32.8
衣着	Clothing	4.6	6.7	5.7	4.1	3.7
居住	Living	13.7	10.4	22.3	26.5	26.9
生活用品及服务	Daily Necessities and Services	7.5	6.5	5.9	5.1	5.2
交通通信	Transportation and Telecommunication	13.4	18.5	15.2	13.7	13.2
教育文化娱乐	Education,Culture and Entertainment	11.5	12.9	10.4	10.6	10.2
医疗保健	Health Service	4.3	5.0	4.3	5.9	5.5
其他用品和服务	Other Necessities and Services	6.4	3.5	3.0	2.4	2.5
农村居民消费结构	Composition of Consumption Expenditure of Rural Households					
食品烟酒	Food,Tobacco and Liquor	49.8	47.7	40.6	39.3	40.3
衣着	Clothing	3.9	3.9	3.3	3.6	3.3
居住	Living	14.3	17.9	22.5	23.6	23.0
生活用品及服务	Daily Necessities and Services	4.7	4.3	5.9	5.1	4.8
交通通信	Transportation and Telecommunication	7.8	11.6	10.5	11.1	11.9
教育文化娱乐	Education,Culture and Entertainment	11.8	5.9	8.6	8.9	9.0
医疗保健	Health Service	3.9	5.6	6.5	6.7	5.9
其他用品和服务	Other Necessities and Services	3.8	3.1	2.2	1.7	1.8
卫生	**Health Care**					
卫生技术人员结构	Structure of Medical Technical Personnel					
#执业(助理)医生	Doctors	42.0	37.7	36.4	36.6	36.5
注册护士	Nurses	31.4	37.1	41.3	45.9	45.8
床位结构	Structure of Hospital Beds					
#医院	Hospitals	71.4	74.7	79.2	81.5	81.7
事故、灾害	**Cash and Disaster**					
火灾事故损失额结构	Structure of Fire Losses Converted into Cash					
特大或重大	Extraordinarily Serious Fires					
较大	Serious Fires		0.2	0.8	0.1	0.6
一般	Ordinary Fires		99.8	99.2	99.9	99.4
交通事故损失额结构	Structure of Losses from Traffic Accidents Converted into Cash					
机动车道	Roads for Motored Vehicles		81.5	83.9	76.8	81.5
非机动车道	Roads for Nonmotored Vehicles		1.4	1.4	2.5	2.4
混合道	Mixed Roads		12.8	11.8	15.9	12.0
其他道	Others		4.3	3.0	4.8	4.1

注：1.由于数据计算进位的原因，部分结构总和不等于100。
2.按照国家统计局统一部署，广东省从2013年开始正式对外发布全省居民调查数据。

Note: a) Owing to the rounding-off of figures, some totals in this table are not equal to 100.
b) Under the unified deployment by NBS, Since 2013, Guangdong Province has officially released the provincial residents survey data.

1-4 国民经济和社会发展比例和效益指标

Indicators on National Economic and Social Development

指标	Item	2000	2015	2021	2022
人口	**Population and Employment**				
总抚养比 (%)	Gross Dependency Ratio (%)	43.31	34.86	38.61	39.01
少儿抚养比 (%)	Children Dependency Ratio (%)	34.64	23.43	25.97	25.67
老年抚养比 (%)	Old Dependency Ratio (%)	8.67	11.44	12.64	13.34
国民经济核算	**National Accounts**				
第一产业增加值占地区生产总值比重 (%)	Percentage of Value-added of Primary Industry in Gross Domestic Product (%)	9.1	4.3	4.0	4.1
第二产业增加值占地区生产总值比重 (%)	Percentage of Value-added of Secondary Industry in Gross Domestic Product (%)	46.7	45.4	40.5	40.9
第三产业增加值占地区生产总值比重 (%)	Percentage of Value-added of Tertiary Industry in Gross Domestic Product (%)	44.2	50.3	55.5	55.0
文化产业增加值占地区生产总值比重 (%)	Percentage of Value-added of Cultural Industry in Gross Domestic Product (%)		5.6	5.5	
新经济增加值占地区生产总值比重 (%)	Percentage of Value-added of New Economy in Gross Domestic Product (%)			25.6	25.8
全社会劳动生产率 (万元/人)	Gross labour productivity (million yuan/person)	2.78	11.50	17.68	18.48
人民生活	**People's Living Conditions**				
全省居民恩格尔系数 (%)	Engel coefficient for all permanent residents (%)		34.5	33.2	34.3
城镇居民恩格尔系数 (%)	Engel coefficient of permanent urban residents (%)	38.6	33.2	31.7	32.8
农村居民恩格尔系数 (%)	Engel coefficient of permanent rural residents (%)	49.8	40.6	39.3	40.3
城乡收入比 (农村居民收入为1)	Urban and Rural Income ratio (Rural Income as 1)	2.67	2.60	2.46	2.41
财政	**Government Finance**				
一般公共预算收入与地区生产总值之比(%)	Proportion of Government Revenue to GDP (%)	8.4	12.5	11.3	10.3
一般公共预算支出与地区生产总值之比(%)	Proportion of Government Expenditure to GDP (%)	9.9	17.2	14.6	14.4
能源	**Energy**				
能源生产弹性系数	Elasticity Ratio of Energy Production	0.50	2.84	0.48	4.47
电力生产弹性系数	Elasticity Ratio of Electricity Production	1.63	0.06	2.58	0.50
能源消费弹性系数	Elasticity Ratio of Energy Consumption	0.71	0.24	0.84	0.00
电力消费弹性系数	Elasticity Ratio of Electricity Consumption	1.99	0.18	1.70	0.02
能源加工转换总效率 (%)	Total Efficiency of Energy Conversion (%)	66.63	69.07	70.25	69.99
资源环境	**Resources and Environment**				
万元地区生产总值用水量 (立方米)	Water Use Per 10000 Yuan GDP (cu.m)		61	33	31
万元工业增加值用水量 (立方米)	Water Use Per 10000 Yuan of Industrial Added Value (cu.m)		37	17	15
固定资产投资	**Investment in Fixed Assets**				
项目建成投产率 (%)	Rate of Projects Completed and Put into Use (%)	49.3	70.8	37.4	33.8
对外贸易	**Foreign Trade**				
进出口总额相当于地区生产总值比重 (%)	Proportion of Total Value of Imports & Exports to GDP (%)	130.3	85.0	66.5	64.4
高新技术产品出口额占出口总额的比重(%)	Proportion of High and New-tech Products to Total Exports (%)	18.5	35.6	33.9	31.4
一般贸易进出口总额占进出口总额的比重 (%)	Proportion of Ordinary Trade to Total Value of Imports and Exports (%)	22.5	42.2	52.3	54.6
加工贸易进出口总额占进出口总额的比重 (%)	Proportion of Processing Trade to Total Value of Imports and Exports (%)	71.2	43.1	27.3	25.9

1-4 续表 continued

指 标	Item	2000	2015	2021	2022
农业	**Agriculture**				
每公顷播种面积农产品产量 (公斤)	Output of Farm Crops per Hectare of Sown Area (kg)				
粮食	Grain	5879	5524	5783	5791
糖料	Sugar Crops	70380	77619	87045	87778
油料	Oil-bearing Crops	2295	2963	3282	3306
工业	**Industry**				
高技术制造业增加值占规模以上工业比重 (%)	Ratio of Value Added of Advanced Manufacturing Industry to the Industry above designated sized (%)		25.6	31.3	31.6
先进制造业增加值占规模以上工业比重 (%)	Ratio of Value Added of High-tech Industry to the Industry above designated sized (%)		47.9	55.9	55.0
总资产贡献率 (%)	Ratio of Total Assets to Industrial Output Value (%)	8.86	13.58	9.71	8.47
资产负债率 (%)	Assets-Liability Ratio (%)	57.56	57.38	57.26	58.39
成本费用利润率 (%)	Ratio of Profits to Industrial Costs (%)	4.82	6.85	6.93	5.98
产品销售率 (%)	Proportion of Products Sold (%)	97.40	97.11	97.08	96.40
每百元营业收入的成本 (元)	Cost per Every 100 Yuan Revenue in Businesses (yuan)		84.40	82.90	83.72
建筑业	**Construction**				
建筑业劳动生产率 (元/人) (按增加值计算)	Overall Labor Productivity (yuan/person) (in terms of value-added per employee)	39831	103972	131242	131746
交通运输业	**Transport**				
铁路网密度 (公里/万平方公里)	Railway Density (km/10000sq.km)	108	215	284	287
公路网密度 (公里/万平方公里)	Highway Density (km/10000sq.km)	5710	12021	12404	12414
邮电通信业	**Postal and Telecommunication Services**				
电话普及率(含移动电话) (部/百人)	Popularization Rate of Telephone (set/100 persons)	39.5	164.2	144.6	146.9
移动电话普及率 (部/百人)	Popularization Rate of Mobile Telephone (set/100 persons)	15.7	138.4	128.3	131.6
金融业	**Financial Intermediation**				
金融机构存款与地区生产总值之比 (%)	Proportion of Deposits of Financial Institutions to GDP (%)	176.5	217.1	235.7	249.7
金融机构贷款与地区生产总值之比 (%)	Proportion of Loans of Financial Institutions to GDP (%)	122.4	129.5	178.7	190.3
金融机构年末人民币贷、存款余额比例 (%)	Proportion of Loans to Deposits of Financial Institutions in RMB at the year-end (%)	69.7	58.1	76.4	76.7
科技	**Science and Technology**				
研究与试验发展经费内部支出占地区生产总值比重 (%)	Porportion of R&D Expenditure to GDP (%)	0.99	2.43	3.21	
每万人口发明专利拥有量 (件/万人)	Number of patents per 10 000 persons (patents/10 000 persons)		12.80	34.89	42.51
教育	**Education**				
学龄儿童入学率 (%)	Percentage of School-age Children Enrolled (%)	99.70	99.98	100.00	99.93
高中毛入学率 (%)	Gross Enrollment Rate of Senior Secondary Schools (%)	38.70	95.70	97.71	97.58
高等教育毛入学率 (%)	Gross Enrollment Rate of High Education (%)	11.35	33.00	57.65	60.07
卫生	**Public Health**				
每千人口执业(助理)医师数 (人)	Number of Licensed(Assistant) Doctors per 10000 Population (person)	1.29	1.96	2.53	2.65
每千人口医疗卫生机构床位数 (张)	Number of Beds of Hospitals and Health Centers per 1000 Population (bed)	1.94	3.73	4.64	4.81
医院病床使用率 (%)	Beds Utilization Rate of Medical Organizations (%)	68.1	83.5	74.2	72.2
城市市政建设	**Municipal Works**				
人均公园绿地面积 (平方米)	Per Capita Public Green Area (Sq.m)		17.40	17.49	17.68

1-5 国民经济和社会发展主要指标占全国比重

Percentage of National Total of Main Indicators of Economic and Social Development of Guangdong

指标	Item	2021 广东 Guang-dong	2021 全国 National Total	2021 广东占全国(%) As Percentage of National Total	2022 广东 Guang-dong	2022 全国 National Total	2022 广东占全国(%) As Percentage of National Total
人口	**Population**						
年末常住人口数 (万人)	Permanent Population at the Year-end (10000 persons)	12684.0	141260.0	9.0	12656.8	141175.0	9.0
土地面积 (万平方公里)	**Land Area (10000 sp.km)**	**17.98**	**960**	**1.9**	**17.98**	**960**	**1.9**
国内(地区)生产总值(亿元)	**Gross Domestic Product (100 million yuan)**	**124719.5**	**1149237.0**	**10.9**	**129118.6**	**1210207.2**	**10.7**
第一产业	Primary Industry	4984.7	83216.5	6.0	5340.4	88345.1	6.0
第二产业	Secondary Industry	50555.8	451544.1	11.2	52843.5	483164.5	10.9
第三产业	Tertiary Industry	69179.0	614476.4	11.3	70934.7	638697.6	11.1
人均国内(地区)生产总值 (元)	**Per Capita Gross Domestic Product (yuan)**	**98561**	**81370**		**101905**	**85698**	
主要工农业产品产量	**Output of Major Farm Products and Industrial Products**						
粮食 (万吨)	Grain (10000 tons)	1279.9	68284.7	1.9	1291.5	68652.8	1.9
油料 (万吨)	Oil-bearing Crops (10000 tons)	117.3	3613.2	3.2	117.4	3654.2	3.2
肉类 (万吨)	Meat (10000 tons)	457.4	8990.0	5.1	481.0	9328.4	5.2
水产品 (万吨)	Aquatic Products (10000 tons)	884.5	6690.3	13.2	894.0	6868.8	13.0
甘蔗 (万吨)	sugarcane (10000 tons)	1306.6	10666.4	12.2	1292.1	10338.1	12.5
水果 (万吨)	Fruits (10000 tons)	1957.8	29970.2	6.5	2028.4	31296.2	6.5
茶叶 (万吨)	Tea (10000 tons)	14.0	316.4	4.4	16.1	334.2	4.8
农用化肥 (万吨)	Chemical Fertilizer (10000 tons)	6.4	5543.6	0.1	5.5	5573.3	0.1
发电量 (亿千瓦时)	Electricity (100 million kwh)	6306.2	85342.5	7.4	6093.8	88487.1	6.9
水泥 (亿吨)	Cement (100 million tons)	1.7	23.8	7.2	1.5	21.3	7.1
布 (亿米)	Cloth (100 million m)	25.8	502.0	5.1	20.2	467.5	4.3
机制纸及纸板 (万吨)	Machine-made Paper and Paperboard (10000 tons)	2410.3	13583.9	17.7	2374.1	13691.4	17.3
钢材 (万吨)	Steel (10000 tons)	5111.2	133666.8	3.8	5627.4	134033.5	4.2
成品糖 (万吨)	Sugar (10000 tons)	131.4	1449.7	9.1	119.2	1486.8	8.1
平板玻璃 (万重量箱)	Flat Glass (10000 wt.cases)	11083.8	101727.4	10.9	10336.0	101620.8	10.2
家用电冰箱 (万台)	Household Refrigerators (10000 units)	2091.6	8992.1	23.3	1773.3	8664.4	20.5
家用洗衣机 (万台)	Household Washing Machines (10000 units)	757.6	8618.5	8.8	686.7	9106.3	7.5
彩色电视机 (万台)	Color Television Sets (10000 sets)	9810.9	18496.5	53.0	10792.0	19578.3	55.1
房间空气调节器 (万台)	Air Conditioners (10000 sets)	6736.3	21835.7	30.8	6637.7	22247.3	29.8
汽车 (万辆)	Vehicles	338.5	2652.8	12.8	415.4	2718.0	15.1
微型计算机设备 (万台)	Microcomputers (10000 units)	5935.4	46692.0	12.7	6948.8	43418.2	16.0
房地产开发投资(亿元)	**Real Estate Development (100 million yuan)**	**17465.8**	**147602.1**	**11.8**	**14963.0**	**132895.4**	**11.3**

1−5 续表 continued

指 标	Item	2021 广东 Guang-dong	2021 全国 National Total	2021 广东占全国(%) As Percentage of National Total	2022 广东 Guang-dong	2022 全国 National Total	2022 广东占全国(%) As Percentage of National Total
运输、邮电	**Transport, Postal and Telecommunication Services**						
货物周转量 (亿吨公里)	Freight Traffic (100 million ton-kilometers)	28388.1	223600.4	12.7	28438.6	231782.7	12.3
旅客周转量 (亿人公里)	Passenger Traffic (100 million person-kilometers)	2352.2	19758.2	11.9	1621.4	12921.4	12.5
港口货物吞吐量 (万吨)	Volume of Freight Handled at Major Coastal Ports (10000 tons)	209599.7	1554534.3	13.5	204801.6	1568452.7	13.1
邮电业务总量 (亿元)	Total Business Volume of Postal and Telecommunication Services (100 million yuan)	4928.7	30895.8	16.0	5063.1	31814.3	15.9
财政金融	**Government Finance and Banking**						
地方一般公共预算收入 (亿元)	Local Public Budgetary Revenue (100 million yuan)	14105.0	111084.2	12.7	13260.9	108818.5	12.2
地方一般公共预算支出 (亿元)	Local Public Budgetary Expenditure (100 million yuan)	18247.0	210623.0	8.7	18533.1	225039.3	8.2
人民币住户存款 (亿元)	Savings Deposits by Residents in Renminbi (100 million yuan)	96634.1	1025011.6	9.4	112555.2	1203386.8	9.4
外经	**Foreign Trade**						
出口总额 (亿元)	Total Exports (RMB 100 million)	50525.5	217287.4	23.3	53319.5	239654.0	22.2
进口总额 (亿元)	Total Imports (RMB 100 million)	32156.1	173634.3	18.5	29778.7	181024.2	16.5
实际外商直接投资 (亿元)	Foreign Direct Investment(RMB 100 million)	1840.0	11493.6	16.0	1819.0	12326.8	14.8
国内贸易和物价	**Domestic Trade and Prices**						
社会消费品零售总额 (亿元)	Total Amount of Retail Sales of Consumer Goods (100 million yuan)	44187.7	440823.2	10.0	44882.9	439732.5	10.2
居民消费价格指数	General Consumer Price Index	100.8	100.9		102.2	102.0	
商品零售价格指数	General Retail Price Index	101.4	101.6		102.5	102.7	
人民生活	**People's Livelihood**						
城镇单位就业人员工资总额 (亿元)	Earnings of Urban Employed Persons (100 million yuan)	24978.7	180817.5	13.8	26200.9	190820.2	13.7
全体居民人均可支配收入 (元)	Per Capita Disposable Income of Residents (yuan)	44993.3	35128.1		47064.6	36883.3	
城镇居民人均可支配收入 (元)	Per Capita Disposable Income of Urban Residents (yuan)	54853.6	47411.8		56905.3	49282.9	
农村居民人均可支配收入 (元)	Per Capita Disposable Income of Rural Residents (yuan)	22306.0	18931.1		23597.8	20132.8	
教育、科技、卫生	**Education, Science and Technology and Health Care**						
普通本专科学校在校学生数 (万人)	Students Enrolled in Colleges and Universities (10000 persons)	254.0	3496.1	7.3	267.1	3659.4	7.3
研究与试验发展(R&D)经费内部支出 (亿元)	Internal Expenditure on R&D (100 million yuan)	4002.2	27956.3	15.7			
医疗卫生机构床位数(万张)	Number of Hospital Beds (10000 units)	58.9	945.0	6.2	60.8	975.0	6.2
专业卫生技术人员 (万人)	Number of Medical Technical Personnel (10000 persons)	87.6	1124.4	7.8	91.8	1165.8	7.9

注：1.本表水果产量含瓜果产量。
2.全国2022年数为快报数并来自中国统计摘要。
3.2019年起，广东实际外商直接投资使用商务部反馈人民币数据。

Note: a) Data of output of fruits in this table include melons.
b) The 2022data of the whole nation are based on flash reports and from China Statistical Abstract.
c)Data of foreign direct investment of Guangdong in RMB that are approved by Ministry of Commerce are adopted since 2019.

1-6 各部门机构数

Grassroots Units in Various Sectors

部　门	Sector	2010	2015	2021	2022
农村基层组织　（个）	**Rural Grassroots Units (unit)**				
村民委员会	Villagers' Committees	22140	19632	19430	19431
工业企业　（个）	**Industrial Enterprises (unit)**	**250853**	**379804**	**674522**	**732757**
规模以上工业	Industrial Enterprises above Designated Size	53418	42134	66329	70725
#国有工业	State-owned	567	200	215	258
集体工业	Collective-owned	872	212	88	73
建筑业企业　（个）	**Construction Enterprises (unit)**	**20195**	**36124**	**155020**	**186025**
#国有企业	State-owned	648	482	402	760
批发零售和住宿餐饮企业法人单位数　（万个）	**Number of Corporate Units in Wholesale and Retail Trades, Accommodations and Catering Services (10000 units)**	**22.18**	**41.58**	**119.92**	**126.74**
医疗卫生机构数　（个）	**Health Care (unit)**	**16541**	**21189**	**57955**	**59531**
#医院、卫生院	Hospitals and Health Centers	2444	2539	2935	2981
提供住宿的社会服务机构	Social Welfare Institutions	2514	1588	2109	2058
教育事业	**Education**				
普通高等学校　（所）	Regular Institutions of Higher Education (unit)	131	143	160	161
中等学校　（所）	Secondary Schools (unit)	5146	5078	5438	5541
#普通中学	Regular Secondary Schools	4334	4434	4908	5024
小学　（万所）	Primary Schools (10000 units)	1.68	1.01	1.06	1.06
幼儿园　（所）	Kindergartens (unit)	11161	16368	21101	21566
艺术表演团体　（个）	Art Performance Troupes (unit)	133	72	76	76
文化事业　（个）	Cultural Institutions (unit)	2384	2275	2305	2308
文物事业　（个）	Cultural Relic Establishments (unit)	208	260	236	227
广播电视　（座）	**Radio and Television (unit)**				
广播电台	Radio Stations	22	22	2	2
电视台	Television Stations	24	24	3	3
县、市广播电视台	Radio and Television Stations in Counties and County-level Cities	79	79	94	94
研究机构数　（个）	**Number of R&D Institutions (units)**	**4452**	**8164**	**37172**	
科学研究与技术开发机构	Scientific Research and Technological Development Institutions	186	189	201	
全日制普通高等学校	Full-time Regular Institutions of Higher Education	450	850	2085	
工业企业	Industrial Enterprises	3309	6553	32938	
其他	Others	507	572	1948	

1-7 法人和产业活动单位数

Number of Legal Entities and Industrial Establishments

单位：个 (unit)

项 目	Item	2021 法人单位数 Corporate Units	2021 产业单位数 Industrial Establishments	2022 法人单位数 Corporate Units	2022 产业单位数 Industrial Establishments
全 省	**Provincial Total**	**3634403**	**3894498**	**3838318**	**4085262**
按行业分	By Sector				
农、林、牧、渔业	Farming,Forestry,Animal Husbandry and Fishery	49050	49823	53402	54131
采矿业	Mining	2757	2944	2832	3029
制造业	Manufacture	661042	669491	708572	716790
电力、燃气及水的生产和供应业	Production and Supply of Electric Power, Gas and Water	10723	13015	11300	13385
建筑业	Construction	155020	165561	175128	186025
批发和零售业	Wholesale and Retail Trades	1135371	1217915	1201165	1280584
交通运输、仓储和邮政业	Transport, Storage and Postal Services	87925	102669	96391	110297
住宿和餐饮业	Hotels and Catering Services	63852	77765	70299	83847
信息传输、软件和信息技术服务业	Information Transmission, Computer Services and Software	185523	195172	192060	201347
金融业	Finance	31248	55016	32283	55552
房地产业	Real Estate	139385	160615	147384	167771
租赁和商务服务业	Leasing and Business Services	560720	587115	572160	596173
科学研究和技术服务业	Scientific Research, Technical Services	218335	229418	236298	247680
水利、环境和公共设施管理业	Management of Water Conservancy, Environment and Public Facilities	14912	16206	16521	17780
居民服务、修理和其他服务业	Services to Households,Repair and Other Services	70170	75253	74396	79181
教育	Education	78297	86210	77691	84698
卫生和社会工作	Health and Social Service	19346	24173	19072	22218
文化、体育和娱乐业	Culture, Sports and Entertainment	68047	71407	71134	74169
公共管理、社会保障和社会组织	Public Administration,Social Security and Social Organizations	82280	94730	80230	90605
按登记注册类型分	By Status of Registration				
内资	Domestic-funded	3548646	3790872	3750591	3979474
国有	State-owned	65282	94121	65876	90991
集体	Collective-owned	135573	143793	133542	140750
股份合作企业	Share-holding Cooperative Enterprises	5250	7430	5795	7740
联营企业	Joint-operation Enterprises	2177	2788	2358	2938
有限责任公司	Limited Liability Corporations	356709	407066	408707	457730
股份有限公司	Share-holding Corporations Ltd.	19418	42574	23635	46464
私营企业	Private Enterprises	2834689	2958964	2983063	3102555
其他	Other	129548	134136	127615	130306
港、澳、台商投资企业	Enterprises with Investment from Hong Kong,Macao and Taiwan	64722	72001	66052	73186
合资经营企业(港或澳、台资)	Joint Ventures	6430	7848	7414	8821
合作经营企业(港或澳、台资)	Cooperative Enterprises	1483	1657	1477	1652
港、澳、台商独资经营企业	Sole Investment Enterprises	54839	59795	54792	59610
港、澳、台商投资股份有限公司	Share-holding Corporations Ltd.	870	1169	1008	1303
其他港、澳、台商投资	Other Enterprises	1100	1532	1361	1800
外商投资企业	Enterprises with Foreign Investment	20635	31625	21675	32602
中外合资经营企业	Sino-foreign Joint Ventures	3862	5833	3865	5784
中外合作经营企业	Sino-foreign Cooperative Enterprises	347	453	345	444
外资企业	Foreign-funded Enterprises	14516	22075	15366	22964
外商投资股份有限公司	Share-holding Corporations Ltd.	738	1334	816	1393
其他外商投资	Other Enterprises	1172	1930	1283	2017

注：产业单位数包含法人单位数。

Note: The number of the industrial establishments include the number of the corporate units.

1-8 各市法人和产业活动单位数

Number of Corporate Units and Industrial Establishments by City

单位：个 (unit)

市别	City	2021 法人单位数 Corporate Units	2021 产业单位数 Industrial Establishments	2022 法人单位数 Corporate Units	2022 产业单位数 Industrial Establishments
全 省	**Provincial Total**	**3634003**	**3894498**	**3838318**	**4085262**
广 州	Guangzhou	837112	886204	876356	925731
深 圳	Shenzhen	939274	993874	942370	989981
珠 海	Zhuhai	128544	137029	136027	143651
汕 头	Shantou	66828	74016	84484	91973
佛 山	Foshan	277608	297191	297263	316834
韶 关	Shaoguan	49366	55014	53629	59155
河 源	Heyuan	35086	40733	40038	45778
梅 州	Meizhou	39986	46849	41108	46671
惠 州	Huizhou	185855	199090	208055	221079
汕 尾	Shanwei	19013	22254	20192	23537
东 莞	Dongguan	441075	463145	456383	477379
中 山	Zhongshan	136885	146284	184345	194391
江 门	Jiangmen	83222	90653	87954	95421
阳 江	Yangjiang	38812	42770	55031	59015
湛 江	Zhanjiang	80191	92215	73003	83598
茂 名	Maoming	80149	88061	77817	83943
肇 庆	Zhaoqing	42712	48537	45076	50994
清 远	Qingyuan	59523	66483	62428	68734
潮 州	Chaozhou	26211	28868	28887	31510
揭 阳	Jieyang	44705	49247	43820	47545
云 浮	Yunfu	21846	25981	24052	28342
按经济区域分	By Region				
珠 三 角	Pearl River Delta	3072287	3262007	3233829	3415461
东 翼	Eastern Region	156757	174385	177383	194565
西 翼	Western Region	199152	223046	205851	226556
山 区	Mountainous Region	205807	235060	221255	248680

1-9 按行业和登记注册类型分组的法人单位数（2022年）

Number of Corporate Units by Sector and by Status of Registration (2022)

单位：个 (unit)

项 目	Item	总 计 Total	内资 Domestic-funded	国有 State-owned	集体 Collective-owned	股份合作企业 Share-holding Cooperative Enterprises
全 省	**Provincial Total**	**3838318**	**3750591**	**65876**	**133542**	**5795**
农、林、牧、渔业	Farming,Forestry,Animal Husbandry and Fishery	53402	52703	447	957	68
采矿业	Mining	2832	2793	27	31	3
制造业	Manufacture	708572	679470	958	1523	1237
电力、燃气及水的生产和供应业	Production and Supply of Electric Power, Gas and Water	11300	10923	459	935	40
建筑业	Construction	175128	174045	427	539	228
批发和零售业	Wholesale and Retail Trades	1201165	1178585	2052	3329	1498
交通运输、仓储和邮政业	Transport, Storage and Postal Services	96391	94310	926	377	124
住宿和餐饮业	Hotels and Catering Services	70299	68871	253	203	238
信息传输、软件和信息技术服务业	Information Transmission, Computer Services and Software	192060	185725	459	83	95
金融业	Finance	32283	30853	390	40	101
房地产业	Real Estate	147384	143271	1356	3062	671
租赁和商务服务业	Leasing and Business Services	572160	560921	3360	116934	765
科学研究和技术服务业	Scientific Research, Technical Services	236298	230850	3617	497	222
水利、环境和公共设施管理业	Management of Water Conservancy, Environment and Public Facilities	16521	16341	2016	198	20
居民服务、修理和其他服务业	Services to Households,Repair and Other Services	74396	73825	451	349	200
教育	Education	77691	77450	16790	1777	139
卫生和社会工作	Health and Social Service	19072	18977	4301	709	40
文化、体育和娱乐业	Culture, Sports and Entertainment	71134	70455	1897	197	90
公共管理、社会保障和社会组织	Public Administration,Social Security and Social Organizations	80230	80223	25690	1802	16

1-9 续表 1 continued

单位：个 (unit)

项目	Item	联营企业 Joint-operation Enterprises	有限责任公司 Limited Liability Corporations	股份有限公司 Shareholding Corporations Ltd.	私营企业 Private Enterprises	其他 Other
全　省	**Provincial Total**	**2358**	**408707**	**23635**	**2983063**	**127615**
农、林、牧、渔业	Farming,Forestry,Animal Husbandry and Fishery	37	2989	319	21278	26608
采矿业	Mining	4	447	42	2215	24
制造业	Manufacture	256	89538	5092	576605	4261
电力、燃气及水的生产和供应业	Production and Supply of Electric Power, Gas and Water	83	2081	186	7062	77
建筑业	Construction	56	23249	1105	147456	985
批发和零售业	Wholesale and Retail Trades	431	116480	5820	1039533	9442
交通运输、仓储和邮政业	Transport, Storage and Postal Services	41	10917	646	80842	437
住宿和餐饮业	Hotels and Catering Services	37	8627	490	58466	557
信息传输、软件和信息技术服务业	Information Transmission, Computer Services and Software	24	20595	1401	162369	699
金融业	Finance	15	5601	1341	23177	188
房地产业	Real Estate	122	25439	1296	110713	612
租赁和商务服务业	Leasing and Business Services	448	52829	2749	373642	10194
科学研究和技术服务业	Scientific Research, Technical Services	75	26943	1666	194709	3121
水利、环境和公共设施管理业	Management of Water Conservancy, Environment and Public Facilities	17	2714	164	11025	187
居民服务、修理和其他服务业	Services to Households,Repair and Other Services	38	6875	438	63946	1528
教育	Education	171	4132	273	41267	12901
卫生和社会工作	Health and Social Service	63	1699	103	9472	2590
文化、体育和娱乐业	Culture, Sports and Entertainment	41	7415	486	58080	2249
公共管理、社会保障和社会组织	Public Administration,Social Security and Social Organizations	399	137	18	1206	50955

1-9 续表 2 continued

单位：个 (unit)

项 目	Item	港、澳、台商投资企业 Enterprises with Investment from Hong Kong, Macao and Taiwan	合资经营企业(港或澳、台资) Joint Ventures	合作经营企业(港或澳、台资) Cooperative Enterprises	港、澳、台商独资经营企业 Sole Investment Enterprises	港、澳、台商投资股份有限公司 Shareholding Corporations Ltd.	其他港、澳、台商投资 Other Enterprises
全 省	**Provincial Total**	**66052**	**7414**	**1477**	**54792**	**1008**	**1361**
农、林、牧、渔业	Farming,Forestry,Animal Husbandry and Fishery	624	60	12	535	4	13
采矿业	Mining	30	9	2	19		
制造业	Manufacture	21630	2377	445	18054	437	317
电力、燃气及水的生产和供应业	Production and Supply of Electric Power,Gas and Water	243	104	13	116	7	3
建筑业	Construction	973	121	19	791	20	22
批发和零售业	Wholesale and Retail Trades	16002	1246	101	14175	184	296
交通运输、仓储和邮政业	Transport, Storage and Postal Services	1587	212	408	916	27	24
住宿和餐饮业	Hotels and Catering Services	991	251	53	623	25	39
信息传输、软件和信息技术服务业	Information Transmission, Computer Services and Software	5358	389	34	4768	71	96
金融业	Finance	1001	372	10	565	13	41
房地产业	Real Estate	3178	597	242	2205	55	79
租赁和商务服务业	Leasing and Business Services	8816	896	49	7526	91	254
科学研究和技术服务业	Scientific Research, Technical Services	4272	487	30	3587	42	126
水利、环境和公共设施管理业	Management of Water Conservancy, Environment and Public Facilities	140	32	7	96	4	1
居民服务、修理和其他服务业	Services to Households,Repair and Other Services	425	72	10	315	11	17
教育	Education	167	35	6	119	4	3
卫生和社会工作	Health and Social Service	72	22	4	40		6
文化、体育和娱乐业	Culture, Sports and Entertainment	541	131	32	341	13	24
公共管理、社会保障和社会组织	Public Administration,Social Security and Social Organizations	2	1		1		

1-9 续表 3 continued

单位：个 (unit)

项　目	Item	外商投资企业 Enterprises with Foreign Investment	中外合资经营企业 Sino-foreign Joint Ventures	中外合作经营企业 Sino-foreign Cooperative Enterprises	外资企业 Foreign-funded Enterprises	外商投资股份有限公司 Share-holding Corporations Ltd.	其他外商投资 Other Enter-prises
全　省	**Provincial Total**	**21675**	**3865**	**345**	**15366**	**816**	**1283**
农、林、牧、渔业	Farming,Forestry,Animal Husbandry and Fishery	75	15	6	46	3	5
采矿业	Mining	9	5	1	3		
制造业	Manufacture	7472	1385	118	5515	221	233
电力、燃气及水的生产和供应业	Production and Supply of Electric Power,Gas and Water	134	52	9	59	8	6
建筑业	Construction	110	30	3	58	4	15
批发和零售业	Wholesale and Retail Trades	6578	705	28	5215	275	355
交通运输、仓储和邮政业	Transport, Storage and Postal Services	494	130	56	261	22	25
住宿和餐饮业	Hotels and Catering Services	437	92	11	256	44	34
信息传输、软件和信息技术服务业	Information Transmission, Computer Services and Software	977	222	6	652	22	75
金融业	Finance	429	184	3	167	40	35
房地产业	Real Estate	935	267	46	503	55	64
租赁和商务服务业	Leasing and Business Services	2423	330	24	1716	77	276
科学研究和技术服务业	Scientific Research, Technical Services	1176	346	17	687	32	94
水利、环境和公共设施管理业	Management of Water Conservancy, Environment and Public Facilities	40	8		22	2	8
居民服务、修理和其他服务业	Services to Households,Repair and Other Services	146	25	6	88	6	21
教育	Education	74	18	4	34	1	17
卫生和社会工作	Health and Social Service	23	12	1	7		3
文化、体育和娱乐业	Culture, Sports and Entertainment	138	39	6	75	4	14
公共管理、社会保障和社会组织	Public Administration,Social Security and Social Organizations	5			2		3

1-10 各市按机构类型分法人单位数（2022年）

Number of Corporate Units by Type by City (2022)

单位：个 (unit)

市别	city	法人单位 Corporate Units	企业 Enterprises	事业单位 Institutions	机关 Government Agencies	社会团体 Social Organizations	民办非企业 Non-enterprise Units Run by l NGO	其他组织机构 Other Organizations
全　省	**Provincial Total**	**3838318**	**3531854**	**43856**	**12467**	**27571**	**35321**	**187249**
广　州	Guangzhou	876356	844211	5515	1172	4752	4655	16051
深　圳	Shenzhen	942370	929977	2316	876	3369	4042	1790
珠　海	Zhuhai	136027	131053	956	514	1239	1359	906
汕　头	Shantou	84484	75527	2101	511	1170	1629	3546
佛　山	Foshan	297263	283370	1913	830	2485	2517	6148
韶　关	Shaoguan	53629	35807	2024	686	1166	710	13236
河　源	Heyuan	40038	30175	1260	492	625	934	6552
梅　州	Meizhou	41108	30567	1957	630	1080	1014	5860
惠　州	Huizhou	208055	189577	2202	585	1270	1853	12568
汕　尾	Shanwei	20192	13167	1230	424	623	688	4060
东　莞	Dongguan	456383	446132	1671	745	1211	3460	3164
中　山	Zhongshan	184345	178561	1137	196	713	1533	2205
江　门	Jiangmen	87954	72974	1944	547	1625	1026	9838
阳　江	Yangjiang	55031	40215	1025	422	737	927	11705
湛　江	Zhanjiang	73003	50084	3868	758	892	2227	15174
茂　名	Maoming	77817	38283	3352	491	843	1383	33465
肇　庆	Zhaoqing	45076	32639	1984	766	1019	1297	7371
清　远	Qingyuan	62428	33831	1672	532	853	1364	24176
潮　州	Chaozhou	28887	23464	1565	315	621	883	2039
揭　阳	Jieyang	43820	34625	2254	471	672	1366	4432
云　浮	Yunfu	24052	17615	1910	504	606	454	2963
按经济区域分	By Region							
珠三角	Pearl River Delta	3233829	3108494	19638	6231	17683	21742	60041
东　翼	Eastern Region	177383	146783	7150	1721	3086	4566	14077
西　翼	Western Region	205851	128582	8245	1671	2472	4537	60344
山　区	Mountainous Region	221255	147995	8823	2844	4330	4476	52787

1－11 各市按行业分法人单位数（2022年）

Number of Corporate Units by Sector by City (2021)

单位：个 (unit)

市别	city	总计 Total	农、林、牧、渔业 Farming, Forestry, Animal Husbandry and Fishery	采矿业 Mining	制造业 Manufacture	电力、燃气及水的生产和供应业 Production and Supply of Electric Power, Gas and Water
全　省	**Provincial Total**	**3838318**	**53402**	**2832**	**708572**	**11300**
广　州	Guangzhou	876356	3290	73	89455	823
深　圳	Shenzhen	942370	453	58	128604	472
珠　海	Zhuhai	136027	709	54	11615	214
汕　头	Shantou	84484	1555	26	19562	204
佛　山	Foshan	297263	1367	27	81341	351
韶　关	Shaoguan	53629	5002	232	3559	1290
河　源	Heyuan	40038	6748	321	3734	646
梅　州	Meizhou	41108	4526	287	3641	830
惠　州	Huizhou	208055	3421	234	35816	699
汕　尾	Shanwei	20192	1787	22	2103	227
东　莞	Dongguan	456383	642	29	176567	389
中　山	Zhongshan	184345	1087	10	72730	203
江　门	Jiangmen	87954	2022	107	25998	360
阳　江	Yangjiang	55031	2991	138	8149	572
湛　江	Zhanjiang	73003	4077	156	5617	289
茂　名	Maoming	77817	2689	236	4496	780
肇　庆	Zhaoqing	45076	2330	231	7172	706
清　远	Qingyuan	62428	4286	423	4799	1251
潮　州	Chaozhou	28887	1188	23	10458	253
揭　阳	Jieyang	43820	1905	35	8736	320
云　浮	Yunfu	24052	1327	110	4420	421
按经济区域分	By Region					
珠三角	Pearl River Delta	3233829	15321	823	629298	4217
东　翼	Eastern Region	177383	6435	106	40859	1004
西　翼	Western Region	205851	9757	530	18262	1641
山　区	Mountainous Region	221255	21889	1373	20153	4438

1-11 续表 1 continued

单位：个 (unit)

市 别	city	建筑业 Construction	批发和零售业 Wholesale and Retail Trades	交通运输、仓储和邮政业 Transport, Storage and Postal Services	住宿和餐饮业 Hotels and Catering Services	信息传输、软件和信息技术服务业 Information Transmission, Computer Services and Software
全 省	**Provincial Total**	**175128**	**1201165**	**96391**	**70299**	**192060**
广 州	Guangzhou	36041	305254	25262	20456	66635
深 圳	Shenzhen	26726	375832	29896	13902	67402
珠 海	Zhuhai	12140	32859	3229	3123	9370
汕 头	Shantou	2982	25104	2059	2230	2718
佛 山	Foshan	10435	99463	7069	6535	8976
韶 关	Shaoguan	3677	9883	1072	842	1512
河 源	Heyuan	3891	7766	783	703	1108
梅 州	Meizhou	3912	8500	815	495	1686
惠 州	Huizhou	21049	53445	3694	4558	6457
汕 尾	Shanwei	889	3489	340	611	424
东 莞	Dongguan	19804	130454	8379	6637	10235
中 山	Zhongshan	10544	42239	3822	3233	4735
江 门	Jiangmen	4993	17673	1940	1630	1814
阳 江	Yangjiang	2761	13652	1069	757	1319
湛 江	Zhanjiang	3742	18239	1771	1345	1810
茂 名	Maoming	2753	16403	1014	646	1393
肇 庆	Zhaoqing	2203	8454	1003	583	1328
清 远	Qingyuan	2709	7954	1340	679	1052
潮 州	Chaozhou	893	6096	464	414	455
揭 阳	Jieyang	1644	13116	823	643	1192
云 浮	Yunfu	1340	5290	547	277	439
按经济区域分	By Region					
珠 三 角	Pearl River Delta	143935	1065673	84294	60657	176952
东 翼	Eastern Region	6408	47805	3686	3898	4789
西 翼	Western Region	9256	48294	3854	2748	4522
山 区	Mountainous Region	15529	39393	4557	2996	5797

1-11 续表 2 continued

单位：个 (unit)

市别	city	金融业 Finance	房地产业 Real Estate	租赁和商务服务业 Leasing and Business Services	科学研究和技术服务业 Scientific Research, Technical Services and Geological Prospecting	水利、环境和公共设施管理业 Management of Water Conservancy, Environment and Public Facilities
全　省	**Provincial Total**	**32283**	**147384**	**572160**	**236298**	**16521**
广　州	Guangzhou	6999	36773	139586	74352	3136
深　圳	Shenzhen	13920	27282	136808	60048	2538
珠　海	Zhuhai	6207	7813	23760	11499	703
汕　头	Shantou	294	2732	7957	4959	480
佛　山	Foshan	985	11544	28434	16709	1105
韶　关	Shaoguan	183	1998	13131	2743	535
河　源	Heyuan	136	1965	3689	1767	407
梅　州	Meizhou	160	1338	4522	1660	571
惠　州	Huizhou	430	16195	30294	13766	1530
汕　尾	Shanwei	53	1149	3630	609	143
东　莞	Dongguan	1150	11467	46522	19313	1296
中　山	Zhongshan	353	7446	16443	9155	771
江　门	Jiangmen	246	4022	14614	2979	514
阳　江	Yangjiang	90	2157	13207	2401	391
湛　江	Zhanjiang	193	3331	16167	3044	400
茂　名	Maoming	134	2083	32810	2423	378
肇　庆	Zhaoqing	226	2345	7756	2546	382
清　远	Qingyuan	139	3215	24403	2552	486
潮　州	Chaozhou	97	494	1437	1227	186
揭　阳	Jieyang	155	1003	4573	1327	321
云　浮	Yunfu	133	1032	2417	1219	248
按经济区域分	By Region					
珠三角	Pearl River Delta	30516	124887	444217	210367	11975
东　翼	Eastern Region	599	5378	17597	8122	1130
西　翼	Western Region	417	7571	62184	7868	1169
山　区	Mountainous Region	751	9548	48162	9941	2247

1−11 续表 3 continued

单位：个 (unit)

市 别	city	居民服务、修理和其他服务业 Services to Households and Other Services	教育 Education	卫生和社会工作 Health Care, Social Security and Social Welfare	文化、体育和娱乐业 Culture, Sports and Recreation	公共管理、社会保障和社会组织 Public Administration and Social Organizations
全 省	**Provincial Total**	**74396**	**77691**	**19072**	**71134**	**80230**
广 州	Guangzhou	18982	14091	4124	20549	10475
深 圳	Shenzhen	18445	15098	3475	15229	6182
珠 海	Zhuhai	3329	2368	811	3643	2581
汕 头	Shantou	1954	2837	885	2400	3546
佛 山	Foshan	6352	4455	1241	6062	4812
韶 关	Shaoguan	905	1528	484	923	4130
河 源	Heyuan	804	1499	442	633	2996
梅 州	Meizhou	620	1626	498	671	4750
惠 州	Huizhou	4036	3607	984	3967	3873
汕 尾	Shanwei	432	1373	214	408	2289
东 莞	Dongguan	7520	5356	1094	6422	3107
中 山	Zhongshan	3816	2972	804	2521	1461
江 门	Jiangmen	1483	1772	563	1118	4106
阳 江	Yangjiang	692	1354	339	751	2241
湛 江	Zhanjiang	1341	4950	785	1282	4464
茂 名	Maoming	745	3768	513	949	3604
肇 庆	Zhaoqing	718	1850	457	829	3957
清 远	Qingyuan	901	1740	485	892	3122
潮 州	Chaozhou	352	1578	195	627	2450
揭 阳	Jieyang	661	2794	348	830	3394
云 浮	Yunfu	308	1075	331	428	2690
按经济区域分	By Region					
珠 三 角	Pearl River Delta	64681	51569	13553	60340	40554
东 翼	Eastern Region	3399	8582	1642	4265	11679
西 翼	Western Region	2778	10072	1637	2982	10309
山 区	Mountainous Region	3538	7468	2240	3547	17688

1-12　各市按登记注册类型分法人单位数（2022年）

Number of Corporate Units by Status of Registration by City (2022)

单位：个　　(unit)

市　别	city	总 计 Total	内资 Domestic-funded	国有 State-owned	集体 Collective-owned	股份合作企业 Share-holding Cooperative Enterprises
全　省	**Provincial Total**	**3838318**	**3750591**	**65876**	**133542**	**5795**
广　州	Guangzhou	876356	858467	8788	14486	1891
深　圳	Shenzhen	942370	918070	4254	586	902
珠　海	Zhuhai	136027	126387	1947	649	112
汕　头	Shantou	84484	83726	3434	2314	268
佛　山	Foshan	297263	293234	2886	5717	365
韶　关	Shaoguan	53629	52991	3177	8886	217
河　源	Heyuan	40038	38940	2118	387	106
梅　州	Meizhou	41108	38797	2897	939	87
惠　州	Huizhou	208055	203531	3299	9508	181
汕　尾	Shanwei	20192	19785	1984	2281	19
东　莞	Dongguan	456383	444222	2518	3836	827
中　山	Zhongshan	184345	180871	1155	2524	107
江　门	Jiangmen	87954	85325	2861	8145	157
阳　江	Yangjiang	55031	54653	1673	6951	19
湛　江	Zhanjiang	73003	72722	5182	9921	125
茂　名	Maoming	77817	77213	4357	29018	70
肇　庆	Zhaoqing	45076	44312	3142	4160	33
清　远	Qingyuan	62428	61471	2451	19498	85
潮　州	Chaozhou	28887	28594	2089	498	97
揭　阳	Jieyang	43820	43489	3039	1962	82
云　浮	Yunfu	24052	23791	2625	1276	45
按经济区域分	By Region					
珠三角	Pearl River Delta	3233829	3154419	30850	49611	4575
东　翼	Eastern Region	177383	175594	10546	7055	466
西　翼	Western Region	205851	204588	11212	45890	214
山　区	Mountainous Region	221255	215990	13268	30986	540

1-12 续表 1 continued

单位：个 (unit)

市 别	city	联营企业 Joint-operation Enterprises	有限责任公司 Limited Liability Corporations	股份有限公司 Share-holding Corporations Ltd.	私营企业 Private Enterprises	其他 Other
全 省	**Provincial Total**	**2358**	**408707**	**23635**	**2983063**	**127615**
广 州	Guangzhou	318	61977	4502	753106	13399
深 圳	Shenzhen	207	51300	4136	848029	8656
珠 海	Zhuhai	46	37396	615	82355	3267
汕 头	Shantou	85	12791	2681	56990	5163
佛 山	Foshan	115	15929	1091	261227	5904
韶 关	Shaoguan	56	4161	390	29766	6338
河 源	Heyuan	83	5215	401	22892	7738
梅 州	Meizhou	75	2940	391	24739	6729
惠 州	Huizhou	135	36615	1636	143916	8241
汕 尾	Shanwei	34	1222	127	11165	2953
东 莞	Dongguan	280	109143	3660	314184	9774
中 山	Zhongshan	83	24866	516	149185	2435
江 门	Jiangmen	205	13247	712	54653	5345
阳 江	Yangjiang	18	2650	223	36770	6349
湛 江	Zhanjiang	112	3125	480	45945	7832
茂 名	Maoming	207	9280	601	28065	5615
肇 庆	Zhaoqing	66	3581	305	27918	5107
清 远	Qingyuan	58	3157	296	29483	6443
潮 州	Chaozhou	46	2513	226	19987	3138
揭 阳	Jieyang	97	4924	461	28457	4467
云 浮	Yunfu	32	2675	185	14231	2722
按经济区域分	By Region					
珠 三 角	Pearl River Delta	1455	354054	17173	2634573	62128
东 翼	Eastern Region	262	21450	3495	116599	15721
西 翼	Western Region	337	15055	1304	110780	19796
山 区	Mountainous Region	304	18148	1663	121111	29970

1-12 续表 2 continued

单位：个 (unit)

市别	city	港、澳、台商投资企业 Enterprises with Investment from Hong Kong, Macao and Taiwan	合资经营企业(港或澳、台资) Joint Ventures	合作经营企业(港或澳、台资) Cooperative Enterprises	港、澳、台商独资经营企业 Sole Investment Enterprises	港、澳、台商投资股份有限公司 Share-holding Corporations Ltd.	其他港、澳、台商投资 Other Enterprises
全 省	**Provincial Total**	**66052**	**7414**	**1477**	**54792**	**1008**	**1361**
广 州	Guangzhou	10175	1567	391	7764	176	277
深 圳	Shenzhen	19995	1465	183	17805	207	335
珠 海	Zhuhai	8405	1574	105	6409	91	226
汕 头	Shantou	558	103	59	362	16	18
佛 山	Foshan	2477	640	55	1684	49	49
韶 关	Shaoguan	550	58	34	437	13	8
河 源	Heyuan	1022	49	27	907	23	16
梅 州	Meizhou	2253	91	29	2103	12	18
惠 州	Huizhou	3822	298	80	3286	91	67
汕 尾	Shanwei	378	26	16	324	5	7
东 莞	Dongguan	8706	509	131	7704	157	205
中 山	Zhongshan	2489	309	36	2027	68	49
江 门	Jiangmen	2105	341	68	1606	53	37
阳 江	Yangjiang	315	43	27	239	2	4
湛 江	Zhanjiang	174	51	28	85	4	6
茂 名	Maoming	558	50	14	478	9	7
肇 庆	Zhaoqing	591	83	23	457	16	12
清 远	Qingyuan	767	75	65	615	4	8
潮 州	Chaozhou	240	33	55	145	4	3
揭 阳	Jieyang	267	21	37	203	4	2
云 浮	Yunfu	205	28	14	152	4	7
按经济区域分	By Region						
珠 三 角	Pearl River Delta	58765	6786	1072	48742	908	1257
东 翼	Eastern Region	1443	183	167	1034	29	30
西 翼	Western Region	1047	144	69	802	15	17
山 区	Mountainous Region	4797	301	169	4214	56	57

1-12 续表 3 continued

单位：个 (unit)

市别	city	外商投资企业 Enterprises with Foreign Investment	中外合资经营企业 Sino-foreign Joint Ventures	中外合作经营企业 Sino-foreign Cooperative Enterprises	外资企业 Foreign-funded Enterprises	外商投资股份有限公司 Share-holding Corporations Ltd.	其他外商投资 Other Enterprises
全 省	**Provincial Total**	**21675**	**3865**	**345**	**15366**	**816**	**1283**
广 州	Guangzhou	7714	1242	89	5758	204	421
深 圳	Shenzhen	4305	970	47	2911	106	271
珠 海	Zhuhai	1235	272	33	766	39	125
汕 头	Shantou	200	38	11	125	12	14
佛 山	Foshan	1552	342	28	1056	66	60
韶 关	Shaoguan	88	26	1	54	3	4
河 源	Heyuan	76	12	3	53	5	3
梅 州	Meizhou	58	14	6	28	5	5
惠 州	Huizhou	702	114	15	499	31	43
汕 尾	Shanwei	29	6	2	17	2	2
东 莞	Dongguan	3455	355	34	2655	231	180
中 山	Zhongshan	985	152	6	701	66	60
江 门	Jiangmen	524	140	7	327	14	36
阳 江	Yangjiang	63	7	4	48	1	3
湛 江	Zhanjiang	107	43	3	52	3	6
茂 名	Maoming	46	12	2	25	4	3
肇 庆	Zhaoqing	173	49	11	102	3	8
清 远	Qingyuan	190	37	14	108	6	25
潮 州	Chaozhou	53	10	19	22	1	1
揭 阳	Jieyang	64	15	5	27	8	9
云 浮	Yunfu	56	9	5	32	6	4
按经济区域分	By Region						
珠三角	Pearl River Delta	20645	3636	270	14775	760	1204
东 翼	Eastern Region	346	69	37	191	23	26
西 翼	Western Region	216	62	9	125	8	12
山 区	Mountainous Region	468	98	29	275	25	41

1-13 全省商品、服务类电子商务交易情况

E-commerce Transactions in Commodities and Services of Guangdong

单位：亿元 (100 million yuan)

指　　标	Item	2022	2022比2021年增长(%) Growth Rate in 2022 over 2021(%)
广东商品、服务类电子商务交易额	E-commerce transactions in commodities and services of Guangdong	67833.59	3.4
按交易平台分	According to the Transaction Platform		
广东在本地平台实现的电子商务交易额	E-commerce Transaction Volume of Guangdong on the Local Platform	29540.94	0.0
广东在省外平台实现的电子商务交易额	E-commerce Transaction Volume of Guangdong not on the Local Platform	38292.65	6.2
按交易对象分	According to the Transaction Object		
B2B+B2G	B2B+B2G	32080.35	5.6
B2C+C2C	B2C+C2C	35753.23	1.6
按交易内容分	According to the Transaction Content		
商品	Commodity	55785.16	4.4
服务	Service	12048.42	-0.7

注：1.统计范围：辖区内规模以上工业、有资质的建筑业、限额以上批发和零售业、限额以上住宿和餐饮业、房地产开发经营业、规模以上服务业法人单位拥有的商品、服务类电子商务交易平台，辖区内规模以下法人单位拥有的且电子商务年交易额1000万元以上的商品、服务类电子商务交易平台。
2.电子商务交易额=在本地平台实现的电子商务交易额+在省外平台实现的电子商务交易额。
3.2016年起国家统计局仅反馈商品、服务类电子商务交易分地区数据，合约类电子商务交易数据不分地区反馈，增速按可比口径计算。

Note: a)Statistical scope: within the jurisdiction of the industrial enterprises above Designated Size, qualified construction enterprises, the enterprises above designated size in wholesale and retail industry, enterprises above designated size of hotels and catering services,real estate enterprises, the services enterprises above designated size have e-commerce trading platform,within the jurisdiction of the enterprises below the designated size have e-commerce trading platform with e-commerce transaction volume of more than 10 million yuan.
b)E-commerce transaction volume=E-commerce transaction volume of Guangdong on the local platform+E-commerce transaction volume not on the local platform.
c)since 2016, the National Bureau of statistics only feedback the data of commodity and service e-commerce transactions regard of region, but the data of contract e-commerce transaction data regardless of region.And the growth rates are calculated at constant prices.

1-14 粤港澳大湾区主要经济指标（2022年）

Main Indicators of Guangdong-Hong Kong-Macao Greater Bay Area (2022)

地 区	Region	土地面积（平方公里）Land Area (sq.m)	地区生产总值 Gross Domestic Product 绝对值（亿元）Absolute (100 million yuan)	指数（上年=100）Index (preceding year =100)	绝对值（亿美元）Absolute (USD 100 million)	人均地区生产总值 Per Capita GDP 绝对值（元）Absolute (yuan)	指数（上年=100）Index (preceding year =100)	绝对值（美元）Absolute (USD)
广 州	Guangzhou	7238.46	28839.00	101.0	4287.63	153625	101.0	22840
深 圳	Shenzhen	1987.00	32387.68	103.3	4815.22	183274	103.2	27248
珠 海	Zhuhai	1725.02	4045.45	102.3	601.46	163654	101.8	24331
佛 山	Foshan	3797.79	12698.39	102.1	1887.93	132517	101.9	19702
惠 州	Huizhou	11350.36	5401.24	104.2	803.03	89157	104.3	13255
东 莞	Dongguan	2460.38	11200.32	100.6	1665.20	106803	100.8	15879
中 山	Zhongshan	1780.99	3631.28	100.5	539.88	81620	100.5	12135
江 门	Jiangmen	9535.19	3773.41	103.3	561.01	78146	103.1	11618
肇 庆	Zhaoqing	14891.43	2705.05	101.1	402.17	65513	100.9	9740
香港特别行政区	Hong Kong Special Administrative Region	1114.40	24281.10	96.5	3609.98	330531	97.4	49142
澳门特别行政区	Macao Special Administrative Region	33.30	1478.60	73.2	219.83	218083	73.8	32423

1-14 续表 continued

地 区	Region	年末人口（万人）Population at the Year-end (10000 persons)	港口集装箱吞吐量（万标准集装箱）Container Throughput (10000 TEUs)	进出口总额（亿美元）Total Exports and Imports (USD 100 million)	出口总额（亿美元）Total Exports (USD 100 million)	进口总额（亿美元）Total Imports (USD 100 million)
广 州	Guangzhou	1873.41	2485.76	1639.43	926.85	712.58
深 圳	Shenzhen	1766.18	3003.62	5498.32	3279.04	2219.28
珠 海	Zhuhai	247.72	109.75	458.91	289.89	169.02
佛 山	Foshan	955.23	322.25	1001.94	840.49	161.45
惠 州	Huizhou	605.02	42.15	464.34	307.50	156.84
东 莞	Dongguan	1043.70	361.48	2095.67	1390.11	705.56
中 山	Zhongshan	443.11	136.24	422.22	351.37	70.85
江 门	Jiangmen	482.22	154.31	267.07	217.82	49.25
肇 庆	Zhaoqing	412.84	49.20	57.91	41.02	16.89
香港特别行政区	Hong Kong Special Administrative Region	734.60	1669.00	10466.42	5014.68	5451.74
澳门特别行政区	Macao Special Administrative Region	67.70	9.37	190.09	16.76	173.33

注：1.本表香港、澳门统计数据来自《中国统计摘要》、香港特别行政区政府统计处以及澳门特别行政区统计暨普查局。
2.香港特别行政区和澳门特别行政区地区生产总值为“本地生产总值 ”，年末人口为“年中人口 ”。澳门特别行政区集装箱吞吐量为载货集装箱吞吐量，其余为集装箱总吞吐量。
3.本表汇率按照100港币=85.89人民币元，100澳门元=83.41人民币元，100美元=672.61人民币元计算。
4.本表中，广州、深圳、珠海、佛山、惠州、东莞、中山、江门、肇庆九市土地面积为2021年数据。

Note:a)Data in this chart regarding Hong Kong and Macao come from the Hong Kong Special Administrative Region Census and Statistics Department and the Macao Special Administrative Region Statistics and Census Service.
b)The regional GDP of the Hong Kong Special Administrative Region and the Macao Special Administrative Region are labeled as “Regional GDP.”The container throughput of the Macao Special Adminis-trative Region is the cargo containing container throughput;the other container throughput data is total container throughput.
c)This chart is calculated using currency conversion rates of 100 HKD=85.89RMB,100MOP=83.41RMB, and 100USD=672.61RMB.
d) In this table, the land area data of Guangzhou, Shenzhen, Zhuhai, Foshan, Huizhou, Dongguan, Zhongshan, Jiangmen and Zhaoqing are the data of 2021.

主要统计指标解释

行政区划 指国家对行政区域的划分。根据有关法规规定，我国的行政区域划分如下：(1)全国分为省、自治区、直辖市；(2)省、自治区分为自治州、县、自治县、市；(3)自治州分为县、自治县、市；(4)县、自治县分为乡、民族乡、镇；(5)直辖市和较大的市分为区、县；(6)国家在必要时设立的特别行政区。

发展速度 用以反映社会经济发展程度的相对指标，根据两个不同时期发展水平的对比而得。由于比较的标准时期不同，发展速度可分为定期发展速度和环比发展速度两种。

增长速度 发展速度－1（或100%）就是增长速度。即增长速度＝发展速度－1（或100%）。

平均每年增长速度 我国计算平均增长速度有两种方法，一种是习惯上经常使用的"水平法"，又称几何平均法，是以间隔最后一年的水平同基期水平对比来计算平均每年增长（或下降）的速度；另一种是"累计法"又称代数平均法或方程法，是以间隔年内各年水平的总和同基期水平对比来计算平均每年增长（或下降）的速度。具体计算方法，可参照中国财经出版社出版的《平均增长速度查对表》。

在一般正常情况下，两种方法计算的平均每年增长速度比较接近，但在经济发展不平衡出现大起大落时，两种方法计算的结果差别较大。

本《年鉴》内所列的平均每年增长速度都是用水平法计算的。从某年到某年平均增长速度的年份，均不包基期年在内。如1981－2010年平均每年增长速度，是以1980年为基期，2010年为报告期，年份从1981年算起，共30年。

当年价格 是报告期的实际价格，如工厂的出厂价格、农产品的收购价格、商品的零售价格等。按当年价格计算，是指一些以货币表现的物量指标，如工业总产值、国内生产总值等，按照当年的实际价格来计算总量。按当年价格计算的价值指标，在不同年份之间进行对比时，因为包含有各年间价格变动的因素，不能确切地反映实物量的增减变动。因此，在计算增长速度时都使用按可比价格计算的数字。

国民经济行业分类 自2017年统计年报和2018年定期统计报表开始使用新的《国民经济行业分类》（GB/T 4754-2017）。该分类是由国家统计局组织修订，国家质量监督检验检疫总局和中国国家标准化管理委员会于2017年6月30日发布。这次修订是在2011年分类标准的基础上，参照联合国《所有经济活动的国际标准产业分类》（2006年，修订第四版，简称ISIC/Rev.4）进行的。修订后的《国民经济行业分类》（GB/T 4754-2017）共有门类20个，大类97个，中类473个，小类1382个。

企业（单位）登记注册类型 是以在工商行政管理机关登记注册的各类企业为划分对象，以工商行政管理部门对企业登记注册的类型为依据，将企业登记注册类型分为内资企业、港澳台商投资企业和外商投资企业三大类。内资企业包括国有企业、集体企业、股份合作企业、联营企业、有限责任公司、股份有限公司、私营企业和其他企业；港澳台商投资企业和外商投资企业分别包括合资经营企业、合作经营企业、独资经营企业和股份有限公司等。对不在工商行政管理部门进行登记注册的行政机关、事业单位和社会团体，主要按其经费来源和管理方式进行划分。

国有企业 指企业全部资产归国家所有，并按《中华人民共和国企业法人登记管理条例》规定登记注册的非公司制的经济组织。不包括有限责任公司中的国有独资公司。

集体企业 指企业资产归集体所有，并按《中华人民共和国企业法人登记管理条例》规定登记注册的经济组织。

股份合作企业 指以合作制为基础，由企业职工共同出资入股，吸收一定比例的社会资产投资组建，实行自主经营，自负盈亏，共同劳动，民主管理，按劳分配与按股分红相结合的一种集体经济组织。

联营企业 指两个及两个以上相同或不同所有制性质的企业法人或事业单位法人，按自愿、平等、互利的原则，共同投资组成的经济组织。联营企业包括国有联营企业、集体联营企业、国有与集体联营企业和其他联营企业。

有限责任公司 指根据《中华人民共和国公司登记管理条例》规定登记注册，由两个以上、五十个以下的股东共同出资，每个股东以其所认缴的出资额对公司承担有限责任，公司以其全部资产对其债务承担责任的经济组织。有限责任公司包括国有独资公司以及其他有限责任公司。

股份有限公司 指根据《中华人民共和国公司登记管理条例》规定登记注册，其全部注册资本由等额股份构成并通过发行股票筹集资本，股东以其认购的股份对公司承担有限责任，公司以其全部资产对其债务承担责任的经济组织。

私营企业 指由自然人投资设立或由自然人控股，以雇佣劳动为基础的营利性经济组织。包括按照《公司法》《合伙企业法》《私营企业暂行条例》规定登记注册的私营有限责任公司、私营股份有限公司、私营合伙企业和私营独资企业。

其他企业 指上述企业之外的其他内资经济组织。

合资经营企业（港或澳、台资） 指港澳台地区投资者与内地企业依照《中华人民共和国中外合资经营企业法》及有关法律的规定，按合同规定的比例投资设立、分享利润和分担风险的企业。

合作经营企业（港或澳、台资） 指港澳台地区投资者与内地企业依照《中华人民共和国中外合作经营企业法》及有关法律的规定，依照合作合同的约定进行投资或提供条件设立、分配利润和分担风险的企业。

港澳台商独资经营企业 指依照《中华人民共和国外资企业法》及有关法律的规定，在内地由港澳台地区投资者全额投资设立的企业。

港澳台商投资股份有限公司 指根据国家有关规定，经原外经贸部依法批准设立，其中港、澳、台商的股本占公司注册资本的比例达 25%以上的股份有限公司。凡其中港、澳、台商的股本占公司注册资本的比例小于 25%的，属于内资企业中的股份有限公司。

其他港澳台商投资企业 指在中国境内参照《外国企业或个人在中国境内设立合伙企业管理办法》和《外商投资合伙企业登记管理规定》，依法设立的港、澳、台商投资合伙企业等。

中外合资经营企业 指外国企业或外国人与中国内地企业依照《中华人民共和国中外合资经营企业法》及有关法律的规定，按合同规定的比例投资设立、分享利润和分担风险的企业。

中外合作经营企业 指外国企业或外国人与中国内地企业依照《中华人民共和国中外合作经营企业法》及有关法律的规定，依照合作合同的约定进行投资或提供条件设立、分配利润和分担风险的企业。

外资企业 指依照《中华人民共和国外资企业法》及有关法律的规定，在中国内地由外国投资者全额投资设立的企业。

外商投资股份有限公司 指根据国家有关规定，经原外经贸部依法批准设立，其中外资的股本占公司注册资本的比例达 25% 以上的股份有限公司。凡其中外资股本占公司注册资本的比例小于 25%的，属于内资企业中的股份有限公司。

其他外商投资企业 指在中国境内依照《外国企业或个人在中国境内设立合伙企业管理办法》和《外商投资合伙企业登记管理规定》，依法设立的外商投资合伙企业等。

行政机关、事业单位和社会团体 参照企业登记注册类型，主要按其经费来源和管理方式划分。具体规定如下：

⑴行政机关：包括国家机关和政党机关，原则上均列为“国有”。但有特殊规定的，如供销社等，则列为“集体”。

⑵事业单位：包括经国家机构编制部门和有关业务主管部门批准成立的各类事业单位，不包括实行企业化管理的事业单位。事业单位的划分办法如下：

①由国家财政预算拨款或列入财政预算外资金管理以及经费主要来源于国有主管部门或国有上级单位的事业单位，列为“国有”。

②经费主要来源于集体单位的事业单位，列为“集体”。

③公民个人(或个人合伙)开办的事业单位，列为“私营”。

④上述以外的其他事业单位，如果其经费来源不明确，按管理方式进行归类。

⑶社会团体：包括经民政部门批准成立以及未纳入社会团体管理条例范围的工会、妇联等各类社会团体。社会团体的划分办法如下：

①未纳入民政部社会团体管理条例范围的工会、妇联、共青团、青联、工商联、科协、侨联等社会团体，国家拨款设立的基金会或基金管理组织以及经费主要来源于国有业务主管部门或国有上级单位的社会团体，列为“国有”。

②经费主要来源于集体单位的社会团体，列为“集体”。

③公民个人(或个人合伙)开办的社会团体，划为“私营”。

④上述以外的其他社会团体，如果其经费来源不明确，改按管理方式进行归类。

电子商务交易平台 指在电子商务活动中为交易双方或多方提供交易撮合及相关服务的信息网络系统总合。

Explanatory Notes on Main Statistical Indicators

Divisions of Administrative Areas refer to the divisions of administrative areas by the state. Relevant laws of the People' s Republic of China stipulate the following principles for the divisions of administrative areas: 1)The whole country is divided into provinces, autonomous regions and municipalities directly under the central government; 2) Provinces and autonomous regions are divided into autonomous prefectures, counties, autonomous counties and cities; 3) Autonomous prefectures are divided into counties, autonomous counties and cities; 4) Counties and autonomous counties are divided into townships, ethnic townships and towns, 5) Municipalities under the central government and large cities are divided into districts and counties; 6) The state will, when necessary, establish special administrative regions.

Development Rate is a relative indicator of the degree of social and economic development calculated through the comparison of two different periods in the degree of development. Development rate can take the form of either fixed-base development rate or chain base development rate.

Growth Rate is equal to development rate minus one (or 100%), i.e. growth rate = development rate −1 (or 100%)

Average Annual Growth Rate Two methods for calculating average annual growth rate are applied in China, one is the more commonly-used “level approach” or the method of calculating geometric average, which is derived by comparing the level of the last year of the interval to that of the base year; the other is called “accumulative approach” or algebraic average or equation method, which is derived by comparing the summation of the actual figure of each year in the interval to the figure in the base year. The detailed calculating methods can be found by reference to the Check Table of Average Growth Rate published by China Financial Publishing House.

Under normal conditions the results calculated by the two methods are fairly close, but they differed sharply when uneven economic development occurred with striking fluctuations in growth.

The average annual growth rates listed in this statistical yearbook are calculated by level approach. The base years are not included when the years are listed for average annual growth rates. For instance, the average annual growth rate of 30 years since 1981 is listed as average annual growth rate of 1981-2010, among which 1980 is the base year and 2010 is the reference year.

Current Price refers to the actual price in the reference period, such as ex-factory price, purchasing price of agricultural products, retail price of commodities, etc. Total values of some quantum indicators in value terms at current prices, such as gross industrial output value and gross domestic product, are calculated in accordance with actual prices of the current year. When comparing indicators of value over time at current prices, they cannot accurately reflect the changes in real term due to price fluctuations of each year. That is why growth rates are calculated at constant prices.

Industrial Classification of the National Economy The new Industrial Classification of the National Economy (GB/T 4754-2017) is introduced starting from the compilation of 2017 annual statistics and 2018 regular statistics. The revision, based on the 2011 classification, was organized by the National Bureau of Statistics taking into consideration of the International Standards of the Industrial Classification of All Economic Activities (2006, Revised Fourth Edition, ISIC/Rev.4) of the United Nations. The new Classification was promulgated by the National Administration of Quality Supervision, Inspection and Quarantine and the Standardization Administration of the People's Republic of China on June 30, 2017. The revised version of the Industrial Classification of the National Economy (GB/T 4754-2017) is composed of 20 sections, 97divisions, 473 groups and 1382 classes.

Registration Status of Enterprises (Units) Enterprises are classified into 3 categories, namely domestic-funded enterprises, enterprises with investment from Hong Kong, Macao and Taiwan, and enterprises with foreign investment, according to the registration status of an enterprise in industrial and commercial administration agencies. Domestic-funded enterprises include State-owned enterprises, collective-owned enterprises, cooperative enterprises, joint ownership enterprises, limited liability corporations, share-holding corporations Ltd., private enterprises and other enterprises. Included in the enterprises with investment from Hong Kong, Macao and Taiwan and enterprises with foreign investment are joint-venture enterprises, cooperative enterprises, sole investment enterprises and share-holding corporations Ltd. For government agencies, institutions and social organizations which are not registered in industrial and commercial administration agencies, they are classified mainly by their sources of funding and manner of management.

State-owned Enterprises refer to non-corporation economic units where the entire assets are owned by the State and which have been registered in accordance with the Regulation of the People's Republic of China on the Management of Registration of Corporate Enterprises. Not included from this category are solely State-funded corporations in the limited liability corporations.

Collective-owned Enterprises refer to economic units where the assets are owned collectively and which have been registered in accordance with the Regulation of the People's Republic of China on the Management of Registration of Corporate Enterprises.

Cooperative Enterprises refer to a form of collective economic units (enterprises) where capitals come mainly from employees as their shares, with certain proportion of capital from the outside, where production is organized on the basis of independent operation, independent accounting for profits and losses, joint work, democratic management, and a distribution system that integrates remuneration according to work with dividend according to capital share.

Joint Ownership Enterprises refer to economic units established by two or more corporate enterprises or corporate institutions of the same or different ownership, through joint investment on the basis of voluntary participation, equality, and mutual benefits. They include State joint ownership enterprises; collective joint ownership enterprises; joint State-collective enterprises; and other joint ownership enterprises.

Limited Liability Corporations refer to economic units established with investment from 2-50 investors and registered in accordance with the Regulation of the People's Republic of China on the Management of Registration of Corporations, each investor bearing limited liability to the corporation depending on its share of investment, and the corporation bearing liability to its debt to the maximum of its total assets. Limited liability corporations include solely State-funded limited liability corporations and other limited liability corporations.

Share-holding Corporations Ltd. refer to economic units registered in accordance with the Regulation of the People's Republic of China on the Management of Registration of Corporations, with total registered capital divided into equal shares and raised through issuing stocks. Each investor bears limited liability to the corporation depending on the holding of shares, and the corporation bears liability to its debt to the maximum of its total assets.

Private Enterprises refer to profit-making economic units invested and established by natural persons, or controlled by natural persons using employed labour. Included in this category are private limited liability corporations, private share-holding corporations Ltd., private partnership enterprises and private-funded enterprises registered in accordance with the Company Law, the Law on Partnership Business and Interim Regulations on Private Enterprises.

Other Domestic-funded Enterprises refer to domestic-funded economic units other than those mentioned above.

Joint Venture Enterprises(Funds are from Hong Kong, Macao or Taiwan.) are enterprises established by investors from Hong Kong, Macao and Taiwan with enterprises in the mainland of China in accordance with the Law of the People's Republic of China on Sino-foreign Equity Joint Ventures and other relevant laws, where the establishment of the investment and the sharing of profits and risks are stipulated under joint venture contracts.

Cooperative Enterprises(Funds are from Hong Kong, Macao or Taiwan.) established by investors from Hong Kong, Macao and Taiwan with enterprises in the mainland of China in accordance with the Law of the People's Republic of China on Sino-foreign Contractual Joint Venture and other relevant laws, where the investment or provision of facilities and the sharing of profits and risks are stipulated under cooperative contracts.

Enterprises with Sole (exclusive) Investment from Hong Kong, Macao and Taiwan refer to enterprises established in the mainland of China with exclusive investment from investors from Hong Kong, Macao and Taiwan in accordance with the Law of the People's Republic of China on Wholly Foreign-owned Enterprises and other relevant laws.

Share-holding Corporations Ltd. with Investment from Hong Kong, Macao and Taiwan refer to share-holding corporations Ltd. established with the approval from the former Ministry of Foreign Trade and Economic Relations in line with relevant State regulations, where the share of investment from Hong Kong, Macao or Taiwan businessmen exceeds 25% of the total registered capital of the corporation. In case the share of investment from Hong Kong, Macao or Taiwan is less than 25% of the total registered capital, the enterprise is to be classified as domestic-funded share-holding corporation Ltd.

Other Enterprises with Funds From Hong Kong, Macao and Taiwan refer to partnership enterprises with investments from Hong Kong, Macao and Taiwan established within the territory of China in accordance

With Administrative Measures on the Establishment of Partnership Enterprises in China by Foreign Enterprises or Foreign Individuals and Regulations for the Administration of the Registration of Foreign-invested Partnership Enterprises.

Joint Venture Enterprises with Foreign Investment refer to enterprises jointly established by foreign enterprises or foreigners with enterprises in the mainland of China in accordance with the Law of the People's Republic of China on Sino-foreign Equity Joint Ventures and other relevant laws, where the sharing of investment, profits and risks is stipulated under contract.

Cooperative Enterprises with Foreign Investment refer to enterprises jointly established by foreign enterprises or foreigners with enterprises in the mainland of China in accordance with the Law of the People's Republic of China on Sino-foreign Contractual Joint Venture and other relevant laws, where the investment or provision of facilities and the sharing of profits and risks are stipulated under cooperative contracts.

Enterprises with Sole (exclusive) Foreign Investment refer to enterprises established in the mainland of China with exclusive investment from foreign investors in accordance with the Law of the People's Republic of China on Wholly Foreign-owned Enterprises and other relevant laws.

Share-holding Corporations Ltd. with Foreign Investment refer to share-holding corporations Ltd. established with the approval from the former Ministry of Foreign Trade and Economic Relations in line with relevant State regulations, where the share of investment from foreign investors exceeds 25% of the total registered capital of the corporation. In case the share of foreign investment is less than 25% of the total registered capital, the enterprise is to be classified as domestic-funded share-holding corporation Ltd.

Other Enterprises with Foreign Funds refer to partnership enterprises established within the territory of China in accordance with Administrative Measures on the Establishment of Partnership Enterprises in China by Foreign Enterprises or Foreign Individuals and Regulations for the Administration of the Registration of Foreign-invested Partnership Enterprises.

Government Agencies, Institutions and Social Organizations are classified into the following categories by source of funds and manner of management taking reference of the registration status of enterprises:

(1) Government agencies: include State and party agencies, classified in principle as State-owned. There are exceptions, such as supply and marketing cooperatives which are classified as collective-owned.

(2) Institutions: include institutions of various types established with the approval by organization and staffing departments of the government, but exclude institutions where enterprise management system is introduced. Institutions are further classified as follows:

(a) Institutions for which their main budgets are from government budget appropriations or extra-budget funds, or allocated from the budget of their competent government agencies. Such institutions are classified as state-owned.

(b) Institutions for which their budget mainly come from collective units. Such institutions are classified as collective-owned.

(c) Social institutions established by individual or a group of citizens, which are classified as private.

(d) Institutions other than those mentioned above for which their sources of budget are not clear. Such institutions are classified by the manner of management.

(3) Social organizations: include social organizations established with the approval from the Ministry of Civil Affairs, and organizations that are not covered by social organization management regulations such as trade unions, women's federations etc.. Social organizations are further classified as follows:

(a) Social organizations that are not covered by social organization management regulations of the Ministry of Civil Affairs such as trade unions, women federations, communist youth leagues, youth associations, industrial and commerce associations, scientist associations, overseas Chinese associations, etc., foundations and fund management organizations established with funds from the state, and social organizations whose funds mainly come from the budget of their competent government agencies. Such institutions are classified as State-owned.

(b) Social organizations for which their budget mainly come from collective units. Such institutions are classified as collective-owned.

(c) Social organizations established by individual or a group of citizens, which are classified as private.

(d) Social organizations other than those mentioned above for which their sources of budget are not clear. Such organizations are classified by the manner of management.

E-commerce Trading Platform refers to the total information network system which provide the deal making and related service for the transaction parties in e-commerce activities.

二、国民经济核算

NATIONAL ECONOMIC ACCOUNTS

二　国民经济核算

简要说明

一、本篇资料反映广东国民经济核算情况。

二、国民经济核算资料主要包括地区生产总值及其有关资料。地区生产总值是根据不同产业部门、不同支出构成的特点和资料来源情况而采用不同方法计算的。

三、本年鉴公布的地区生产总值以及与之有关的指标数据，最后一年数据不是最终数，还会在获得更多的财务和行政记录等资料后发生变动。如果遇到普查或者重大核算方法改革，在能够获得更详细的基础资料的情况下，地区生产总值的历史数据还会发生变动。2018 年，根据全国第四次经济普查结果和国家统计局地区生产总值统一核算要求，对历史年份全省生产总值进行了修订。2020 年，根据全国第七次人口普查结果，对 2010 年后的人均生产总值及支出法地区生产总值有关数据进行了修订。本年鉴中的数据是修订后的数据。

四、国民经济核算数据绝对数按当年价格计算，速度和指数按不变价格计算。

五、分市的国民经济核算历史数据在 2018 年以前采取分级核算，2018 年及以后采取统一核算方式核算。

六、本篇资料由广东省统计局国民经济核算处整理提供。

2　National Economic Accounts

Brief Introduction

Ⅰ.The data in this chapter reflect the national accounts of Guangdong Province.

Ⅱ. The data on national accounts mainly include gross domestic product (GDP) and related data. Data on GDP are calculated with various approaches in accordance with the features of various industrial sectors, various expenditure structures and the data resources.

Ⅲ. The data on gross domestic product (GDP) and related measures publicized in this statistical yearbook for the latest year is not final and may be altered when more financial and administrative information is available. Major changes to census and accounting policies will lead to changes to GDP and historical data, if more detailed basic information is obtainable. In 2018, provincial GDP data in previous statistical yearbooks was edited according to the results of the 4th National Economic Census and requirements for the unified calculation of national GDP. In 2020, according to the results of the 7th National census, the relevant data of GDP per capita and GDP by expenditure method after 2010 have been revised. Data in this statistical yearbook contains the edited data.

Ⅳ. The data on national accounts are calculated at current prices, and the growth rates and the index are calculated at constant prices.

Ⅴ. Historical data on the economies of sub-cities was calculated with separate hierarchies prior to 2018. Starting in 2018, data was calculated in a unified manner.

Ⅵ. The data in this chapter are prepared and provided by the Division of National Accounts of Statistics Bureau of Guangdong Province.

2-1 国民经济核算主要指标

Main Indicators of Gross Domestic Product

指　　标	Item	2000	2020	2021	2022
地区生产总值 (亿元)	Gross Domestic Product (100 million yuan)	10810.21	111151.63	124719.53	129118.58
第一产业	Primary Industry	986.32	4732.74	4984.70	5340.36
第二产业	Secondary Industry	5042.75	43868.05	50555.79	52843.51
第三产业	Tertiary Industry	4781.15	62550.84	69179.04	70934.71
地区生产总值指数（上年=100)	Indices of Gross Domestic Product (preceding year=100)	111.7	102.3	108.1	101.9
第一产业	Primary Industry	102.3	103.7	107.8	105.2
第二产业	Secondary Industry	112.3	101.9	109.2	102.5
第三产业	Tertiary Industry	113.5	102.5	107.4	101.2
地区生产总值构成 (%)	Composition of Gross Domestic Product (%)				
第一产业	Primary Industry	9.1	4.2	4.0	4.1
第二产业	Secondary Industry	46.7	39.5	40.5	40.9
第三产业	Tertiary Industry	44.2	56.3	55.5	55.0
地区生产总值贡献率 (%)	Share of the Contribution of the Three Strata of Industry (%)				
第一产业	Primary Industry	1.9	6.1	4.1	11.8
第二产业	Secondary Industry	59.7	36.1	44.8	52.9
第三产业	Tertiary Industry	38.4	57.8	51.1	35.3
地区生产总值拉动率 (%)	Contribution of the Three Strata of Industry to Gross Domestic Product Growth (%)	11.7	2.3	8.1	1.9
第一产业	Primary Industry	0.2	0.1	0.3	0.2
第二产业	Secondary Industry	7.0	0.8	3.7	1.0
第三产业	Tertiary Industry	4.5	1.3	4.2	0.7
人均地区生产总值 (元)	Per Capita Gross Gross Domestic Product Product (yuan)	12817	88521	98561	101905
人均地区生产总值指数 (上年=100)	Indices of Per Capita Gross Domestic Product (preceding year=100)	107.3	101.1	107.3	101.7
支出法地区生产总值 (亿元)	Gross Domestic Product by Expenditure Approach (100 million yuan)	10810.21	111151.63	124719.53	
最终消费支出	Final Consumption Expenditures	5717.11	56585.06	62237.05	
资本形成总额	Gross Capital Formation	3917.11	49319.71	56914.11	
货物和服务净流出	Net Exports of Goods and Services	1175.99	5246.86	5568.37	
支出法地区生产总值构成 (%)	Composition of Gross Domestic Product by Expenditure Approach (%)				
最终消费支出	Final Consumption Expenditures	52.9	50.9	49.9	
资本形成总额	Gross Capital Formation	36.2	44.4	45.6	
货物和服务净流出	Net Exports of Goods and Services	10.9	4.7	4.5	
支出法地区生产总值贡献率(%)	Share of the Contribution of Gross Domestic Product by Expenditure Approach (%)				
最终消费支出	Final Consumption Expenditures	32.9	-17.5	56.4	
资本形成总额	Gross Capital Formation	27.2	61.6	41.7	
货物和服务净流出	Net Exports of Goods and Services	39.9	55.9	1.9	
文化及相关产业增加值（亿元)	Value-added of Culture and Related Industries (100 million yuan)		6210.60	6910.06	
新经济增加值 (亿元)	Value-added of New Economy (100 million yuan)		28199.82	31958.60	33358.93
占地区生产总值比重 (%)	Percentage of Value-added of New Economy in Gross (%)		25.4	25.6	25.8

2-2 地区生产总值
Gross Domestic Product

单位：亿元 (100 million yuan)

年份 Year	地区生产总值 Gross Domestic Product	第一产业 Primary Industry	第二产业 Secondary Industry	第三产业 Tertiary Industry	#工业 Industry	#建筑业 Construction	#批发和零售业 Wholesale and Retail Trades	#交通运输、仓储和邮政业 Transport, Storage, and Post	#金融业 Financial Interme-diation	#房地产业 Real Estate
1978	185.85	55.31	86.62	43.92	76.12	10.49	19.39	10.05	4.53	1.42
1979	209.34	66.62	91.65	51.06	82.36	9.29	23.52	11.26	4.74	1.62
1980	249.65	82.97	102.53	64.14	89.87	12.66	29.53	13.72	6.10	2.13
1981	290.36	94.30	120.34	75.71	103.60	16.74	33.57	16.71	6.76	2.79
1982	339.92	118.17	135.37	86.39	113.13	22.24	38.07	18.34	7.98	3.39
1983	368.75	121.24	152.27	95.24	125.82	26.45	41.42	19.47	8.94	4.09
1984	458.74	145.25	187.55	125.93	154.33	33.22	54.41	25.68	11.76	5.09
1985	577.38	171.87	229.82	175.69	185.81	44.01	79.86	35.91	12.74	6.16
1986	667.53	188.37	255.88	223.28	208.46	47.42	89.78	40.18	20.84	11.69
1987	846.69	232.14	330.35	284.20	273.77	56.58	104.17	53.20	34.25	16.44
1988	1155.37	306.50	460.17	388.70	386.35	73.82	145.89	65.22	46.80	22.84
1989	1381.39	351.73	554.13	475.53	464.06	90.07	136.65	79.02	72.70	41.36
1990	1559.03	384.59	615.86	558.58	523.42	92.45	152.90	101.61	82.46	42.87
1991	1893.30	416.00	782.67	694.63	675.55	107.12	185.77	138.54	94.83	54.09
1992	2447.54	465.83	1098.75	882.96	899.28	201.04	202.75	96.40	122.79	81.74
1993	3469.28	558.70	1702.46	1208.12	1386.83	318.05	291.79	127.20	149.29	126.09
1994	4619.02	692.25	2249.99	1676.77	1865.44	387.80	416.88	183.19	199.84	170.68
1995	5940.34	864.49	2901.99	2173.86	2454.87	451.40	555.12	238.66	229.27	229.89
1996	6848.22	935.23	3313.55	2599.44	2853.85	464.66	684.33	277.41	264.86	282.32
1997	7792.97	978.32	3713.92	3100.73	3250.72	468.97	809.50	354.11	302.87	339.57
1998	8555.33	994.55	4080.96	3479.82	3584.54	502.87	919.83	388.75	306.39	415.38
1999	9289.64	1009.01	4384.22	3896.41	3864.77	526.56	1006.73	427.02	331.10	500.21
2000	10810.21	986.32	5042.75	4781.15	4518.65	537.06	1175.32	536.54	443.69	616.25
2001	12126.59	988.84	5564.66	5573.09	5012.16	565.75	1323.01	657.08	450.81	682.89
2002	13601.89	1015.08	6209.06	6377.76	5628.70	596.03	1509.35	725.85	454.65	788.40
2003	15979.77	1072.92	7684.41	7222.44	6991.52	710.77	1729.08	747.89	539.41	930.80
2004	18658.34	1219.83	9191.71	8246.80	8433.23	780.81	1950.55	840.80	614.36	1039.13
2005	21962.99	1395.23	11049.21	9518.55	10231.13	847.44	2175.03	1000.38	681.73	1274.31
2006	25961.24	1494.69	13158.01	11308.54	12259.42	934.97	2529.92	1164.22	923.73	1564.13
2007	31742.61	1663.49	16022.56	14056.56	14990.77	1073.17	2957.99	1351.81	1716.57	1969.26
2008	36704.16	1920.80	18519.40	16263.96	17356.70	1208.40	3524.94	1541.26	2019.35	1999.67
2009	39464.69	1945.95	19439.71	18079.03	18128.48	1350.61	4024.32	1486.63	2372.87	2374.45
2010	45944.62	2199.60	22917.43	20827.59	21387.71	1574.96	4825.08	1670.49	2890.11	2672.34
2011	53072.79	2553.17	26161.08	24358.54	24460.73	1755.04	5935.31	1889.87	3326.82	3084.98
2012	57007.74	2711.32	27346.12	26950.30	25526.22	1876.07	6670.82	2100.81	3757.12	3378.45
2013	62503.41	2876.42	29342.97	30284.02	27142.10	2260.48	7404.60	2237.30	4498.84	3956.04
2014	68173.03	3038.71	31930.37	33203.95	29497.80	2496.15	7946.25	2490.13	4872.81	4309.34
2015	74732.44	3189.76	33913.76	37628.92	31315.46	2684.40	8030.87	2662.73	6119.66	5280.52
2016	82163.22	3500.49	35499.24	43163.49	32677.94	2909.50	8924.66	2877.45	6570.01	6615.72
2017	91648.73	3611.44	38536.61	49500.68	35343.97	3289.32	9642.05	3166.69	7311.19	8178.60
2018	99945.22	3836.40	41398.45	54710.37	37651.05	3849.75	10476.03	3363.48	7962.26	8533.74
2019	107986.92	4350.61	43368.21	60268.10	39141.79	4333.96	11000.23	3657.96	8764.09	9543.22
2020	111151.63	4732.74	43868.05	62550.84	39353.92	4616.38	10728.95	3370.13	10016.11	10377.02
2021	124719.53	4984.70	50555.79	69179.04	45510.34	5167.75	12102.12	4054.91	10937.34	11042.82
2022	129118.58	5340.36	52843.51	70934.71	47723.04	5247.57	12319.74	4040.91	11825.76	10450.56

注：1.1991年以前第一产业不包括农林牧渔服务业，交通运输仓储和邮政业包括电信业，但不包括城市公共交通业，批发与零售业包括餐饮业（以下相关表同）。

2.2013年起，三次产业分类依据国家统计局2012年制定的《三次产业划分规定》执行(以下相关表同)。

Notes: a)In 1991 and prior to it, the primary industry did not include service activities for farming, forestry, animal husbandry and fishery; transport, storage,and postal services included telecommunication services,but excluded urban public transport;and wholesale and retail trades included catering services. The same applies to the following tables.

b)Since 2013, the Three Industries.' classification are divided according to "the Deputy of the three Industries Classification" which was developed by NBS in 2012(the same applies to the following table).

2-3 地区生产总值指数

Indices of Gross Domestic Product

上年=100 (preceding year=100)

年份 Year	地区生产总值 Gross Domestic Product	第一产业 Primary Industry	第二产业 Secondary Industry	第三产业 Tertiary Industry	#工业 Industry	#建筑业 Construction	#批发和零售业 Wholesale and Retail Trades	#交通运输、仓储和邮政业 Transport, Storage, and Post	#金融业 Financial Interme-diation	#房地产业 Real Estate
1978	101.0	105.2	98.0	102.1	102.8	70.8	107.4	104.8	93.1	97.5
1979	108.5	106.6	104.7	118.1	106.7	88.7	123.8	113.2	103.7	115.4
1980	116.6	112.4	116.6	121.7	114.4	138.0	119.5	119.4	126.1	136.3
1981	109.0	104.6	112.3	109.4	110.9	122.2	106.4	107.2	106.1	129.1
1982	112.0	112.0	111.5	112.6	109.2	126.3	108.0	117.5	110.0	121.1
1983	107.3	103.2	109.6	108.5	109.3	111.3	106.7	104.8	109.7	117.4
1984	115.6	112.0	118.3	115.2	119.5	112.0	116.6	105.7	116.8	109.5
1985	118.0	105.7	120.2	128.1	120.3	119.5	127.1	122.6	129.5	147.7
1986	112.7	106.2	108.6	125.4	109.1	105.7	118.6	121.6	130.9	161.9
1987	119.6	108.6	126.2	119.4	128.9	109.8	115.0	120.7	138.6	130.7
1988	115.8	105.3	123.4	112.4	125.4	109.1	106.7	120.0	113.3	125.7
1989	107.2	107.0	108.3	105.5	109.8	96.2	79.6	117.4	132.2	140.5
1990	111.6	107.1	112.5	113.2	113.6	102.0	112.7	107.3	117.8	98.1
1991	117.7	105.5	123.7	119.4	123.1	127.5	119.6	128.3	107.2	114.3
1992	122.1	105.6	133.6	119.0	130.6	149.6	119.4	119.6	121.2	146.2
1993	123.0	102.6	136.4	116.8	140.4	117.5	122.0	122.6	102.5	128.8
1994	119.7	103.2	125.8	118.5	127.4	116.5	119.4	127.4	107.4	127.3
1995	115.7	105.4	119.0	114.7	119.9	112.9	115.9	118.0	101.8	122.0
1996	111.3	104.9	112.7	111.5	114.2	102.8	114.2	109.2	107.5	115.6
1997	111.2	104.7	113.0	110.7	114.7	100.2	113.6	108.5	109.6	111.2
1998	110.9	103.8	112.5	110.4	113.1	107.7	115.0	105.6	103.1	110.4
1999	110.3	103.9	110.8	111.3	111.2	107.5	110.4	105.6	110.8	119.3
2000	111.7	102.3	112.3	113.5	113.8	99.4	109.4	118.4	122.7	114.8
2001	110.5	102.2	110.8	112.0	111.3	106.1	111.6	117.7	101.7	108.3
2002	112.4	104.3	113.7	112.5	114.8	103.5	113.3	108.0	100.6	111.3
2003	114.8	102.2	120.2	111.3	120.9	113.2	111.6	105.6	110.7	115.0
2004	113.2	103.8	116.8	110.5	118.4	101.1	108.0	113.0	107.6	105.3
2005	114.2	104.8	115.3	114.3	116.0	106.6	111.1	118.8	107.7	122.1
2006	114.9	103.9	117.2	113.8	117.8	109.0	113.1	116.1	124.1	113.6
2007	115.0	103.1	117.3	113.9	118.0	107.6	108.0	111.1	140.6	114.0
2008	110.5	103.8	111.6	110.0	112.3	100.6	112.6	108.1	109.5	94.2
2009	109.9	105.1	109.1	111.4	108.6	116.0	117.2	104.9	117.7	120.5
2010	112.5	104.5	114.5	110.9	114.7	112.0	114.8	111.3	114.2	104.2
2011	110.2	104.3	110.4	110.7	110.7	105.3	113.9	111.9	107.6	105.7
2012	108.3	103.9	107.3	109.8	107.5	103.5	110.1	112.5	110.7	108.6
2013	108.5	102.4	108.0	109.7	107.9	109.1	110.6	107.5	114.7	111.4
2014	107.8	103.3	108.0	108.0	108.1	106.3	107.3	110.8	108.1	103.0
2015	108.0	103.4	107.0	109.6	107.1	105.6	106.7	106.1	117.6	109.2
2016	107.5	103.1	106.1	109.2	106.3	104.3	107.1	108.2	106.4	110.9
2017	107.5	103.6	106.5	108.6	106.8	103.0	105.4	108.8	107.4	107.4
2018	106.8	104.4	105.9	107.8	105.9	105.5	104.7	106.3	107.9	103.1
2019	106.2	103.8	104.2	107.9	104.0	107.9	103.9	106.7	109.1	108.1
2020	102.3	103.7	101.9	102.5	101.4	107.3	95.7	96.6	109.0	104.2
2021	108.1	107.8	109.2	107.4	109.9	104.1	110.8	114.7	104.8	103.7
2022	101.9	105.2	102.5	101.2	102.6	101.5	100.6	94.4	107.8	94.1

2-4 地区生产总值指数

Indices of Gross Domestic Product

1978年=100 (year of 1978=100)

年份 Year	地区生产总值 Gross Domestic Product	第一产业 Primary Industry	第二产业 Secondary Industry	第三产业 Tertiary Industry	#工业 Industry	#建筑业 Construction	#批发和零售业 Wholesale and Retail Trades	#交通运输、仓储和邮政业 Transport, Storage, and Post	#金融业 Financial Intermediation	#房地产业 Real Estate
1978	100.0	100.0	100.0	100.0	100.0	100.0	100.0	100.0	100.0	100.0
1979	108.5	106.6	104.7	118.1	106.7	88.7	123.8	113.2	103.7	115.4
1980	126.5	119.8	122.1	143.7	122.0	122.4	147.9	135.2	130.8	157.3
1981	137.9	125.3	137.1	157.2	135.4	149.6	157.4	144.9	138.7	203.1
1982	154.4	140.4	152.9	177.0	147.9	188.9	169.9	170.2	152.7	245.9
1983	165.6	144.9	167.7	192.0	161.7	210.3	181.4	178.4	167.5	288.7
1984	191.4	162.3	198.4	221.2	193.2	235.5	211.5	188.6	195.6	316.1
1985	225.7	171.5	238.4	283.5	232.3	281.6	268.8	231.3	253.2	466.7
1986	254.5	182.2	259.0	355.4	253.6	297.6	318.6	281.1	331.5	755.4
1987	304.5	197.8	326.9	424.5	326.9	326.9	366.6	339.4	459.3	987.3
1988	352.5	208.2	403.3	477.0	409.9	356.8	391.0	407.1	520.4	1240.6
1989	377.9	222.9	437.0	503.1	450.1	343.3	311.3	478.2	687.9	1743.5
1990	421.6	238.7	491.4	569.3	511.3	350.0	351.0	512.9	810.3	1709.5
1991	496.1	251.8	608.0	679.7	629.2	446.4	419.8	658.1	868.6	1953.5
1992	605.8	266.0	812.3	809.2	822.1	667.9	501.3	787.0	1053.0	2856.3
1993	745.1	272.9	1108.1	945.0	1154.2	784.8	611.5	965.2	1079.1	3678.7
1994	891.9	281.5	1393.9	1119.5	1470.7	914.1	730.2	1229.7	1158.6	4682.6
1995	1031.9	296.8	1658.4	1284.3	1764.1	1032.0	846.3	1451.5	1178.9	5713.4
1996	1148.9	311.3	1869.5	1432.3	2015.2	1060.5	966.8	1585.5	1267.3	6605.0
1997	1278.1	325.9	2111.8	1585.8	2311.5	1062.7	1098.0	1720.9	1388.4	7345.6
1998	1416.9	338.3	2376.1	1751.2	2613.9	1144.7	1262.6	1818.2	1431.8	8111.2
1999	1562.4	351.5	2633.4	1949.3	2906.9	1230.9	1394.4	1920.5	1587.0	9674.1
2000	1745.4	359.7	2956.2	2213.4	3307.7	1223.3	1526.1	2273.9	1946.4	11110.7
2001	1929.2	367.7	3274.5	2478.9	3681.4	1297.8	1703.4	2676.0	1980.2	12036.3
2002	2167.8	383.5	3722.3	2789.5	4227.9	1343.4	1930.1	2891.0	1992.8	13396.0
2003	2488.6	392.1	4474.4	3104.6	5111.6	1520.2	2154.9	3052.3	2206.2	15408.0
2004	2816.2	407.1	5227.8	3429.6	6049.8	1537.2	2326.4	3449.8	2374.2	16219.1
2005	3215.4	426.5	6026.3	3919.2	7017.0	1638.6	2584.7	4098.3	2557.0	19811.1
2006	3693.6	443.2	7060.6	4460.8	8268.1	1786.6	2923.8	4760.0	3173.2	22502.1
2007	4247.7	456.9	8280.0	5080.1	9756.0	1922.4	3158.1	5289.0	4462.7	25655.5
2008	4693.4	474.2	9238.0	5587.0	10958.6	1933.7	3554.7	5719.9	4885.9	24165.1
2009	5156.0	498.6	10077.6	6221.5	11902.6	2242.5	4166.4	5998.2	5748.8	29112.8
2010	5800.4	521.2	11541.2	6898.3	13651.0	2511.1	4783.8	6676.1	6563.5	30332.9
2011	6392.9	543.8	12736.5	7635.2	15117.7	2644.1	5447.7	7471.7	7061.2	32051.5
2012	6920.7	564.8	13661.5	8382.1	16253.0	2737.2	5997.5	8407.9	7817.8	34808.3
2013	7511.9	578.5	14750.3	9197.8	17537.7	2985.0	6635.9	9035.2	8964.4	38783.5
2014	8098.3	597.6	15924.1	9937.5	18953.0	3172.3	7121.9	10009.3	9686.2	39940.8
2015	8749.5	617.8	17033.6	10888.2	20296.3	3349.7	7601.3	10621.5	11390.8	43622.1
2016	9407.4	637.2	18073.6	11885.9	21566.3	3493.0	8140.2	11489.8	12118.9	48381.0
2017	10112.3	660.0	19254.1	12914.0	23039.1	3599.4	8581.1	12505.1	13015.9	51984.1
2018	10801.1	688.9	20383.9	13922.2	24397.5	3797.4	8981.1	13288.9	14040.4	53616.6
2019	11465.5	715.4	21249.5	15025.9	25361.3	4098.7	9331.0	14184.0	15316.1	57968.9
2020	11723.4	741.6	21648.6	15394.4	25715.3	4399.3	8927.8	13698.7	16699.1	60396.3
2021	12677.6	799.3	23650.8	16531.7	28249.8	4580.9	9893.7	15717.8	17495.0	62604.8
2022	12912.5	840.6	24232.2	16725.2	28983.0	4648.2	9951.3	14833.1	18859.9	58922.4

2-5 地区生产总值产业构成

Composition of Gross Domestic Product

单位：%　　　　(%)

年份 Year	地区生产总值 Gross Domestic Product	第一产业 Primary Industry	第二产业 Secondary Industry	第三产业 Tertiary Industry	#工业 Industry
1978	100.0	29.8	46.6	23.6	41.0
1979	100.0	31.8	43.8	24.4	39.3
1980	100.0	33.2	41.1	25.7	36.0
1981	100.0	32.5	41.4	26.1	35.7
1982	100.0	34.8	39.8	25.4	33.3
1983	100.0	32.9	41.3	25.8	34.1
1984	100.0	31.7	40.9	27.4	33.6
1985	100.0	29.8	39.8	30.4	32.2
1986	100.0	28.2	38.3	33.5	31.2
1987	100.0	27.4	39.0	33.6	32.3
1988	100.0	26.5	39.8	33.7	33.4
1989	100.0	25.5	40.1	34.4	33.6
1990	100.0	24.7	39.5	35.8	33.6
1991	100.0	22.0	41.3	36.7	35.7
1992	100.0	19.0	44.9	36.1	36.7
1993	100.0	16.1	49.1	34.8	40.0
1994	100.0	15.0	48.7	36.3	40.4
1995	100.0	14.6	48.8	36.6	41.3
1996	100.0	13.6	48.4	38.0	41.7
1997	100.0	12.5	47.7	39.8	41.7
1998	100.0	11.6	47.7	40.7	41.9
1999	100.0	10.9	47.2	41.9	41.6
2000	100.0	9.1	46.7	44.2	41.8
2001	100.0	8.1	45.9	46.0	41.3
2002	100.0	7.5	45.6	46.9	41.4
2003	100.0	6.7	48.1	45.2	43.8
2004	100.0	6.5	49.3	44.2	45.2
2005	100.0	6.4	50.3	43.3	46.6
2006	100.0	5.7	50.7	43.6	47.2
2007	100.0	5.2	50.5	44.3	47.2
2008	100.0	5.2	50.5	44.3	47.3
2009	100.0	4.9	49.3	45.8	45.9
2010	100.0	4.8	49.9	45.3	46.6
2011	100.0	4.8	49.3	45.9	46.1
2012	100.0	4.7	48.0	47.3	44.8
2013	100.0	4.6	46.9	48.5	43.4
2014	100.0	4.5	46.8	48.7	43.3
2015	100.0	4.3	45.4	50.3	41.9
2016	100.0	4.3	43.2	52.5	39.8
2017	100.0	3.9	42.1	54.0	38.6
2018	100.0	3.8	41.4	54.8	37.7
2019	100.0	4.0	40.2	55.8	36.2
2020	100.0	4.2	39.5	56.3	35.4
2021	100.0	4.0	40.5	55.5	36.5
2022	100.0	4.1	40.9	55.0	37.0

2-6 三次产业贡献率
Contribution Rate of Three Industries

单位：% (%)

年份 Year	地区生产总值 Gross Domestic Product	第一产业 Primary Industry	第二产业 Secondary Industry	第三产业 Tertiary Industry	#工业 Industry
1979	100.0	23.9	25.7	50.4	32.4
1980	100.0	22.4	44.2	33.5	34.8
1981	100.0	17.0	56.2	26.8	43.7
1982	100.0	32.1	40.8	27.1	28.3
1983	100.0	14.1	55.7	30.2	45.8
1984	100.0	23.7	50.7	25.6	45.6
1985	100.0	9.5	49.6	41.0	42.6
1986	100.0	13.0	30.4	56.6	27.5
1987	100.0	11.0	57.8	31.2	54.7
1988	100.0	7.6	67.7	24.7	64.4
1989	100.0	20.3	56.5	23.3	59.3
1990	100.0	12.7	53.0	34.3	52.2
1991	100.0	7.6	53.0	39.3	43.8
1992	100.0	5.6	63.0	31.4	48.7
1993	100.0	2.2	71.9	25.9	66.0
1994	100.0	2.6	65.9	31.6	59.7
1995	100.0	4.8	63.9	31.3	58.0
1996	100.0	5.4	61.0	33.6	59.4
1997	100.0	4.9	63.5	31.6	63.5
1998	100.0	3.9	64.4	31.7	60.3
1999	100.0	4.0	59.8	36.2	55.7
2000	100.0	1.9	59.7	38.4	60.6
2001	100.0	1.9	47.7	50.4	44.9
2002	100.0	2.9	51.7	45.4	50.5
2003	100.0	1.2	64.6	34.3	60.8
2004	100.0	2.0	63.4	34.6	63.2
2005	100.0	2.1	55.1	42.8	53.4
2006	100.0	1.7	58.1	40.3	55.9
2007	100.0	1.2	59.1	39.7	57.3
2008	100.0	1.9	57.7	40.4	57.6
2009	100.0	2.5	48.7	48.8	43.6
2010	100.0	1.7	61.0	37.3	57.9
2011	100.0	2.0	50.6	47.4	49.0
2012	100.0	2.1	43.9	53.9	42.5
2013	100.0	1.2	46.2	52.6	43.0
2014	100.0	1.7	50.2	48.1	47.7
2015	100.0	1.7	42.7	55.6	40.8
2016	100.0	1.8	36.8	61.4	34.9
2017	100.0	2.0	39.0	59.0	37.7
2018	100.0	2.5	38.2	59.2	35.6
2019	100.0	2.4	30.4	67.2	26.2
2020	100.0	6.1	36.1	57.8	24.8
2021	100.0	4.1	44.8	51.1	42.9
2022	100.0	11.8	52.9	35.3	50.4

注：三次产业贡献率指各产业增加值增量与GDP增量之比。

Notes: The contribution rate of three industries refers to the ratio of the value-added increment of each industry to the GDP increment.

2-7 三次产业对地区生产总值增长的拉动

Contribution of the Three Strata of Industry to GDP Growth

单位：百分点 (percentage points)

年份 Year	地区生产总值 Gross Domestic Product	第一产业 Primary Industry	第二产业 Secondary Industry	第三产业 Tertiary Industry	#工 业 Industry
1979	8.5	2.0	2.2	4.3	2.7
1980	16.6	3.7	7.3	5.6	5.8
1981	9.0	1.5	5.1	2.4	3.9
1982	12.0	3.8	4.9	3.2	3.4
1983	7.3	1.0	4.1	2.2	3.3
1984	15.6	3.7	7.9	4.0	7.1
1985	18.0	1.7	8.9	7.4	7.6
1986	12.7	1.7	3.9	7.2	3.5
1987	19.6	2.2	11.4	6.1	10.7
1988	15.8	1.2	10.7	3.9	10.2
1989	7.2	1.5	4.1	1.7	4.3
1990	11.6	1.5	6.1	4.0	6.0
1991	17.7	1.4	9.4	7.0	7.7
1992	22.1	1.2	13.9	6.9	10.8
1993	23.0	0.5	16.5	6.0	15.2
1994	19.7	0.5	13.0	6.2	11.8
1995	15.7	0.7	10.0	4.9	9.1
1996	11.3	0.6	6.9	3.8	6.7
1997	11.2	0.6	7.1	3.5	7.1
1998	10.9	0.4	7.0	3.4	6.6
1999	10.3	0.4	6.1	3.7	5.7
2000	11.7	0.2	7.0	4.5	7.1
2001	10.5	0.2	5.0	5.3	4.7
2002	12.4	0.4	6.4	5.6	6.2
2003	14.8	0.2	9.6	5.1	9.0
2004	13.2	0.3	8.3	4.6	8.3
2005	14.2	0.3	7.8	6.1	7.6
2006	14.9	0.2	8.6	6.0	8.3
2007	15.0	0.2	8.9	6.0	8.6
2008	10.5	0.2	6.1	4.2	6.0
2009	9.9	0.2	4.8	4.8	4.3
2010	12.5	0.2	7.6	4.7	7.2
2011	10.2	0.2	5.2	4.8	5.0
2012	8.3	0.2	3.6	4.5	3.5
2013	8.5	0.1	3.9	4.5	3.7
2014	7.8	0.1	3.9	3.8	3.7
2015	8.0	0.1	3.4	4.5	3.3
2016	7.5	0.1	2.8	4.6	2.6
2017	7.5	0.1	2.9	4.4	2.8
2018	6.8	0.2	2.6	4.0	2.4
2019	6.2	0.1	1.9	4.1	1.6
2020	2.3	0.2	0.8	1.3	0.6
2021	8.1	0.3	3.7	4.2	3.5
2022	1.9	0.2	1.0	0.7	0.9

注：三次产业拉动指GDP增长速度与各产业贡献率之乘积。

Notes: The Three Industries pulling rate is the growth rate of GDP multiplying industrial contribution rate.

2-8 支出法地区生产总值

Gross Domestic Product by Expenditure Approach

年份 Year	支出法地区生产总值(亿元) Gross Domestic Product by Expenditure Approach (100 million yuan)	最终消费支出 Final Consumption Expenditure	资本形成总额 Gross Capital Formation	货物和服务净流出 Net Exports of Goods and Services	最终消费率(消费率)(%) Final Consumption Rate (Consumption Rate)(%)	资本形成率(投资率)(%) Capital Formation Rate (Investment Rate)(%)
1978	194.14	130.02	54.79	9.33	67.0	28.2
1979	215.43	147.11	55.86	12.46	68.3	25.9
1980	259.32	180.93	71.37	7.02	69.8	27.5
1981	305.22	201.43	96.74	7.05	66.0	31.7
1982	349.13	233.21	112.35	3.57	66.8	32.2
1983	367.36	252.07	113.49	1.80	68.6	30.9
1984	446.06	288.26	150.07	7.72	64.6	33.6
1985	568.98	347.18	238.58	-16.78	61.0	41.9
1986	650.99	415.91	256.75	-21.67	63.9	39.4
1987	815.05	516.02	312.33	-13.29	63.3	38.3
1988	1129.64	667.03	462.07	0.54	59.0	40.9
1989	1348.54	857.33	472.75	18.46	63.6	35.1
1990	1541.99	938.48	502.90	100.61	60.9	32.6
1991	1847.99	1081.39	610.18	156.42	58.5	33.0
1992	2440.58	1359.08	987.96	93.54	55.7	40.5
1993	3465.31	1852.06	1554.46	58.79	53.4	44.9
1994	4618.25	2598.57	1930.86	88.82	56.3	41.8
1995	5940.34	3363.65	2401.80	174.89	56.6	40.4
1996	6848.22	3859.84	2795.64	192.74	56.4	40.8
1997	7792.97	4245.89	2992.18	554.90	54.5	38.4
1998	8555.33	4583.10	3354.63	617.60	53.6	39.2
1999	9289.64	5085.11	3548.75	655.78	54.7	38.2
2000	10810.21	5717.11	3917.11	1175.99	52.9	36.2
2001	12126.59	6259.29	4476.48	1390.82	51.6	36.9
2002	13601.89	7290.47	4858.53	1452.89	53.6	35.7
2003	15979.77	8647.86	6022.16	1309.75	54.1	37.7
2004	18658.34	10167.48	7350.24	1140.62	54.5	39.4
2005	21962.99	11457.36	8399.25	2106.38	52.2	38.2
2006	25961.24	12643.78	9512.26	3805.20	48.7	36.6
2007	31742.61	14853.52	10967.58	5921.51	46.8	34.6
2008	36704.16	17215.48	12590.33	6898.35	46.9	34.3
2009	39464.69	19196.56	15378.86	4889.27	48.6	39.0
2010	45944.62	22501.78	18226.60	5216.24	49.0	39.7
2011	53072.79	26235.01	21689.40	5148.38	49.4	40.9
2012	57007.74	29581.98	23699.14	3726.62	51.9	41.6
2013	62503.41	30900.24	27020.20	4582.97	49.4	43.2
2014	68173.03	34595.53	29850.24	3727.26	50.7	43.8
2015	74732.44	38116.43	31602.04	5013.97	51.0	42.3
2016	82163.22	42095.22	34647.12	5420.89	51.2	42.2
2017	91648.73	46682.78	39657.57	5308.39	50.9	43.3
2018	99945.22	51531.96	44379.92	4033.34	51.6	44.4
2019	107986.92	55827.36	48076.62	4082.94	51.7	44.5
2020	111151.63	56585.06	49319.71	5246.86	50.9	44.4
2021	124719.53	62237.05	56914.11	5568.37	49.9	45.6

注：2013年起，国家统计局推行城乡住户调查一体化改革，支出法地区生产总值数据与以前年份不可比(以下相关表同)。

Notes: The data of gross domestic product by expenditure approach are not comparable to the previous years due to the integrated household reform conducted by the NBS(the same applied to the related table) since 2013.

2-9 资本形成总额及构成

Gross Capital Formation and Composition

年份 Year	资本形成总额（亿元） Gross Capital Formation (100 million yuan)	固定资本形成总额 Gross Fixed Capital Formation	存货变动 Change in Inventories	比重(资本形成总额＝100) Proportion (gross capital formation=100) 固定资本形成总额 Gross Fixed Capital Formation	存货变动 Change in Inventories
1978	54.79	37.93	16.86	69.2	30.8
1979	55.86	41.81	14.05	74.8	25.2
1980	71.37	57.15	14.23	80.1	19.9
1981	96.74	73.39	23.34	75.9	24.1
1982	112.35	94.64	17.71	84.2	15.8
1983	113.49	96.80	16.69	85.3	14.7
1984	150.07	133.04	17.03	88.7	11.3
1985	238.58	163.84	74.74	68.7	31.3
1986	256.75	182.15	74.59	70.9	29.1
1987	312.33	197.01	115.32	63.1	36.9
1988	462.07	286.00	176.07	61.9	38.1
1989	472.75	266.68	206.07	56.4	43.6
1990	502.90	336.61	166.29	66.9	33.1
1991	610.18	396.49	213.70	65.0	35.0
1992	987.96	683.66	304.30	69.2	30.8
1993	1554.46	1110.69	443.77	71.5	28.5
1994	1930.86	1375.09	555.76	71.2	28.8
1995	2401.80	1826.18	575.62	76.0	24.0
1996	2795.64	1932.16	863.48	69.1	30.9
1997	2992.18	2096.88	895.30	70.1	29.9
1998	3354.63	2497.33	857.30	74.4	25.6
1999	3548.75	2907.86	640.89	81.9	18.1
2000	3917.11	3160.12	756.99	80.7	19.3
2001	4476.48	3531.49	944.99	78.9	21.1
2002	4858.53	4119.36	739.17	84.8	15.2
2003	6022.16	5096.72	925.44	84.6	15.4
2004	7350.24	6093.41	1256.83	82.9	17.1
2005	8399.25	7577.75	821.50	90.2	9.8
2006	9512.26	8694.07	818.19	91.4	8.6
2007	10967.58	10230.11	737.47	93.3	6.7
2008	12590.33	11803.75	786.58	93.8	6.2
2009	15378.86	14452.53	926.33	94.0	6.0
2010	18226.60	17035.10	1191.50	93.5	6.5
2011	21689.40	20118.29	1571.11	92.8	7.2
2012	23699.14	22860.84	838.30	96.5	3.5
2013	27020.20	25966.92	1053.28	96.1	3.9
2014	29850.24	29021.09	829.15	97.2	2.8
2015	31602.04	30478.30	1123.74	96.4	3.6
2016	34647.12	33279.65	1367.47	96.1	3.9
2017	39657.57	38390.85	1266.72	96.8	3.2
2018	44379.92	42319.88	2060.04	95.4	4.6
2019	48076.62	45950.04	2126.58	95.6	4.4
2020	49319.71	46332.16	2987.55	93.9	6.1
2021	56914.11	50735.78	6178.33	89.1	10.9

2-10 最终消费及构成

Final Consumption Expenditure and Composition

年份 Year	最终消费支出(亿元) Final Consumption Expenditure (100 million yuan)	居民消费支出 Household Consumption	城镇居民 Urban Households	农村居民 Rural Households	政府消费支出 Government Consumption	比重 Proportion: 最终消费支出=100 Final Consumption Expenditure=100: 居民消费支出 Household Consumption	政府消费支出 Government Consumption	居民消费支出=100 Household Consumption=100: 城镇居民 Urban Households	农村居民 Rural Households
1978	130.02	111.46	40.12	71.34	18.56	85.7	14.3	36.0	64.0
1979	147.11	128.48	46.57	81.91	18.63	87.3	12.7	36.2	63.8
1980	180.93	156.51	60.55	95.95	24.42	86.5	13.5	38.7	61.3
1981	201.43	175.12	64.50	110.62	26.31	86.9	13.1	36.8	63.2
1982	233.21	202.70	74.76	127.93	30.51	86.9	13.1	36.9	63.1
1983	252.07	220.14	85.69	134.45	31.93	87.3	12.7	38.9	61.1
1984	288.26	250.92	105.87	145.05	37.34	87.0	13.0	42.2	57.8
1985	347.18	298.00	137.84	160.16	49.17	85.8	14.2	46.3	53.7
1986	415.91	349.52	164.49	185.03	66.39	84.0	16.0	47.1	52.9
1987	516.02	442.20	223.51	218.69	73.82	85.7	14.3	50.5	49.5
1988	667.03	566.25	283.39	282.86	100.77	84.9	15.1	50.0	50.0
1989	857.33	743.90	377.08	366.82	113.42	86.8	13.2	50.7	49.3
1990	938.48	807.84	406.22	401.62	130.64	86.1	13.9	50.3	49.7
1991	1081.39	923.37	511.00	412.36	158.02	85.4	14.6	55.3	44.7
1992	1359.08	1118.52	648.51	470.01	240.55	82.3	17.7	58.0	42.0
1993	1852.06	1574.61	957.16	617.45	277.45	85.0	15.0	60.8	39.2
1994	2598.57	2287.69	1442.66	845.03	310.88	88.0	12.0	63.1	36.9
1995	3363.65	2912.58	1890.75	1021.83	451.07	86.6	13.4	64.9	35.1
1996	3859.84	3343.00	2154.56	1188.44	516.84	86.6	13.4	64.4	35.6
1997	4245.89	3539.63	2317.15	1222.48	706.26	83.4	16.6	65.5	34.5
1998	4583.10	3781.21	2499.29	1281.92	801.89	82.5	17.5	66.1	33.9
1999	5085.11	4072.05	2774.14	1297.91	1013.06	80.1	19.9	68.1	31.9
2000	5717.11	4474.11	3125.44	1348.67	1243.00	78.3	21.7	69.9	30.1
2001	6259.29	4733.53	3318.28	1415.25	1525.76	75.6	24.4	70.1	29.9
2002	7290.47	5449.58	4025.54	1424.04	1840.89	74.7	25.3	73.9	26.1
2003	8647.86	6537.53	5273.69	1263.84	2110.33	75.6	24.4	80.7	19.3
2004	10167.48	7953.60	6729.38	1224.22	2213.88	78.2	21.8	84.6	15.4
2005	11457.36	8968.54	7560.24	1408.30	2488.82	78.3	21.7	84.3	15.7
2006	12643.78	9895.13	8470.02	1425.11	2748.65	78.3	21.7	85.6	14.4
2007	14853.52	11781.66	10229.41	1552.25	3071.86	79.3	20.7	86.8	13.2
2008	17215.48	13599.73	11812.60	1787.13	3615.75	79.0	21.0	86.9	13.1
2009	19196.56	15261.29	13233.01	2028.28	3935.27	79.5	20.5	86.7	13.3
2010	22501.78	17702.35	15438.42	2263.93	4799.43	78.7	21.3	87.2	12.8
2011	26235.01	20636.84	17860.12	2776.72	5598.17	78.7	21.3	86.5	13.5
2012	29581.98	23321.42	20179.53	3141.89	6260.56	78.8	21.2	86.5	13.5
2013	30900.24	23901.02	20109.64	3791.38	6999.22	77.3	22.7	84.1	15.9
2014	34595.53	26936.81	22536.12	4400.69	7658.72	77.9	22.1	83.7	16.3
2015	38116.43	29356.72	24734.89	4621.84	8759.71	77.0	23.0	84.3	15.7
2016	42095.22	32336.89	27234.11	5102.78	9758.33	76.8	23.2	84.2	15.8
2017	46682.78	35650.88	30154.13	5496.75	11031.90	76.4	23.6	84.6	15.4
2018	51531.96	39312.83	32963.41	6349.42	12219.13	76.3	23.7	83.8	16.2
2019	55827.36	42318.90	35556.70	6762.19	13508.47	75.8	24.2	84.0	16.0
2020	56585.06	42098.56	35482.91	6615.65	14486.50	74.4	25.6	84.3	15.7
2021	62237.05	46666.46	39322.44	7344.02	15570.60	75.0	25.0	84.3	15.7

2-11　三大需求对地区生产总值增长的贡献率和拉动

Contribution Share and Contribution of the Three Major Demands to GDP Growth

年份 Year	最终消费支出 Final Consumption Expenditure		资本形成总额 Gross Capital Formation		货物和服务净流出 Net Exports of Goods and Services	
	贡献率(%) Contribution Share (%)	拉动(百分点) Contribution (percentage points)	贡献率(%) Contribution Rate (%)	拉动(百分点) Contribution (percentage points)	贡献率(%) Contribution Rate (%)	拉动(百分点) Contribution (percentage points)
1979	95.7	5.3	-13.8	-0.8	18.2	1.0
1980	71.3	13.0	33.5	6.1	-4.8	-0.9
1981	50.5	6.3	56.4	7.1	-6.9	-0.9
1982	72.7	8.3	40.6	4.6	-13.2	-1.5
1983	124.4	5.6	-12.9	-0.6	-11.5	-0.5
1984	56.5	8.5	42.2	6.3	1.3	0.2
1985	32.0	6.9	80.6	17.4	-12.6	-2.7
1986	83.6	8.8	15.5	1.6	0.8	0.1
1987	38.6	4.9	34.9	4.4	26.4	3.3
1988	-2.8	-0.3	60.1	7.4	42.8	5.2
1989	110.8	9.4	-35.6	-3.0	24.8	2.1
1990	60.9	7.2	9.5	1.1	29.6	3.5
1991	39.9	7.1	35.1	6.3	25.0	4.5
1992	56.0	12.4	65.2	14.5	-21.1	-4.7
1993	50.2	11.6	60.1	13.9	-10.3	-2.4
1994	53.8	10.4	36.1	7.0	10.1	1.9
1995	48.5	8.0	39.6	6.5	11.9	2.0
1996	44.8	5.1	52.1	5.9	3.1	0.3
1997	21.6	2.4	7.5	0.8	71.0	8.0
1998	39.4	4.3	43.9	4.8	16.7	1.8
1999	54.5	5.6	22.5	2.3	23.1	2.4
2000	32.9	3.9	27.2	3.2	39.9	4.7
2001	45.8	4.8	49.0	5.2	5.3	0.6
2002	68.0	8.4	23.3	2.9	8.7	1.1
2003	63.4	9.4	50.4	7.5	-13.8	-2.0
2004	56.4	7.4	41.8	5.5	1.8	0.2
2005	43.3	6.1	31.2	4.4	25.6	3.6
2006	32.3	4.8	30.3	4.5	37.4	5.6
2007	46.3	7.0	24.7	3.7	28.9	4.3
2008	46.9	4.9	36.3	3.8	16.8	1.8
2009	65.2	6.4	83.4	8.2	-48.5	-4.8
2010	54.6	6.8	48.7	6.1	-3.3	-0.4
2011	51.0	5.2	50.5	5.2	-1.5	-0.1
2012	57.1	4.7	45.8	3.8	-2.9	-0.2
2013	46.1	0.3	43.5	6.2	10.3	2.0
2014	53.7	4.2	50.7	4.0	-4.4	-0.3
2015	51.9	4.2	49.1	3.9	-1.0	-0.1
2016	53.7	4.0	48.2	3.6	-1.9	-0.1
2017	53.3	4.0	44.7	3.3	2.0	0.2
2018	56.4	3.8	54.8	3.7	-11.1	-0.8
2019	55.1	3.4	49.5	3.0	-4.6	-0.3
2020	-17.5	-0.4	61.6	1.4	55.9	1.3
2021	56.4	4.6	41.7	3.4	1.9	0.2

注：1.三大需求指支出法地区生产总值的三大构成项目，即最终消费支出、资本形成总额、货物和服务净流出。
2.贡献率指三大需求增量与地区支出法生产总值增量之比。
3.拉动指地区生产总值增长速度与三大需求贡献率的乘积。

Notes: a) Three major demands refer to three major components of gross domestic product by expenditure approach,i.e.final consumption expenditure, gross capital formation, and net exports of goods and services.
b) Contribution rate refers to the proportion of the increment of three major demands to the increment of gross domestic product by expenditure approach.
c) Pulling rate refers to the growth rate of gross regional product multiplying the contribution rates of three major demands.

2-12 人均地区生产总值及人均消费水平指数

Indices of Per Capita Gross Domestic Product and Consumption

年份 Year	人均地区生产总值 Per Capita Gross Domestic Product		人均消费水平 Per Capita Consumption					
			全体居民 Households		城镇居民 Urban Households		农村居民 Rural Households	
	绝对数(元) Absolute Figure (yuan)	指数(上年=100) Index (preceding year=100)	绝对数(元) Absolute Figure (yuan)	指数(上年=100) Index (preceding year=100)	绝对数(元) Absolute Figure (yuan)	指数(上年=100) Index (preceding year=100)	绝对数(元) Absolute Figure (yuan)	指数(上年=100) Index (preceding year=100)
1978	370		222		466		171	
1979	410	106.9	252	108.3	507	102.6	196	109.8
1980	481	114.8	302	114.9	620	112.7	228	114.1
1981	550	107.1	332	107.9	627	98.1	260	113.3
1982	633	110.0	377	110.3	696	108.3	298	110.4
1983	675	105.6	403	107.2	764	108.5	310	105.1
1984	827	113.8	453	110.3	878	109.7	334	107.8
1985	1026	116.2	529	105.7	1038	110.2	372	97.4
1986	1164	110.6	609	109.5	1146	108.4	430	106.3
1987	1443	117.0	754	106.4	1382	101.1	515	104.9
1988	1926	113.2	944	96.5	1716	93.2	651	100.5
1989	2251	104.8	1212	119.7	2188	115.0	831	123.1
1990	2484	109.1	1287	109.3	2263	104.7	896	112.9
1991	2941	114.7	1434	108.3	2712	114.8	906	100.2
1992	3699	118.8	1690	114.7	3210	115.7	1023	109.7
1993	5085	119.3	2308	120.5	4280	117.0	1347	117.6
1994	6530	115.5	3234	117.8	5870	115.7	1831	114.3
1995	8139	112.1	3991	110.1	7091	107.6	2206	108.4
1996	9157	108.7	4470	106.9	7660	102.3	2547	111.6
1997	10154	108.4	4612	97.9	7807	95.2	2597	99.6
1998	10850	107.9	4796	104.2	8054	102.2	2681	105.8
1999	11463	107.3	5025	104.5	8598	105.9	2661	100.8
2000	12817	107.3	5305	100.2	9189	100.2	2680	98.7
2001	13952	107.3	5445	101.9	9312	100.3	2759	103.0
2002	15478	111.1	6199	113.2	10358	110.2	2904	105.7
2003	17950	113.3	7342	117.0	11136	106.4	3032	103.4
2004	20647	111.5	8800	115.9	12409	107.9	3386	108.2
2005	23997	112.7	9799	110.0	13609	108.6	3915	113.2
2006	27861	112.8	10619	107.4	14695	106.9	4010	102.2
2007	33236	112.2	12336	112.9	16982	112.6	4401	105.0
2008	37543	107.9	13911	107.1	19101	107.1	4975	105.6
2009	39418	107.3	15243	110.9	20852	111.3	5533	106.9
2010	44669	109.5	17211	109.3	23159	107.5	6255	109.4
2011	50076	107.0	19186	105.8	24943	102.9	7722	112.2
2012	52308	105.3	21123	106.9	27218	106.3	8663	106.7
2013	56029	106.0	21208	110.0	26206	109.6	10543	110.9
2014	59909	105.7	23446	107.6	28586	106.3	12206	112.3
2015	64516	106.1	25138	106.8	30472	105.6	12980	108.5
2016	69671	105.6	27156	105.6	32602	104.8	14356	106.8
2017	76218	105.4	29364	105.4	35110	104.5	15473	107.6
2018	81625	104.9	31837	105.7	37175	103.1	18241	115.2
2019	86956	104.7	33885	105.6	39188	105.1	19797	104.7
2020	88521	101.1	33348	96.1	37906	94.7	20273	98.4
2021	98561	107.3	36879	109.1	41773	107.5	22662	113.8
2022	101905	101.7						

注：2006—2009年人均地区生产总值根据2010年第六次全国人口普查结果进行修订，2011—2019年人均地区生产总值根据2020年第七次全国人口普查结果进行修订。

Note: The per capita GDP in 2006-2009 is revised according to the results of the sixth national census in 2010, and the per capita GDP in 2011-2019 is revised according to the results of the seventh national census in 2020.

2-13 人均地区生产总值及人均消费水平指数

Indices of Per Capita Gross Domestic Product and Consumption

年份 Year	人均地区生产总值 Per Capita Gross Domestic Product		人均消费水平 Per Capita Consumption					
			全体居民 Households		城镇居民 Urban Households		农村居民 Rural Households	
	绝对数（元） Value (yuan)	指数（1978年=100） Index (year of 1978=100)	绝对数（元） Value (yuan)	指数（1978年=100） Index (year of 1978=100)	绝对数（元） Value (yuan)	指数（1978年=100） Index (year of 1978=100)	绝对数（元） Value (yuan)	指数（1978年=100） Index (year of 1978=100)
1978	370	100.0	222	100.0	466	100.0	171	100.0
1979	410	106.9	252	108.3	507	102.6	196	109.8
1980	481	122.6	302	124.4	620	115.6	228	125.2
1981	550	131.3	332	134.2	627	113.4	260	141.9
1982	633	144.4	377	148.1	696	122.8	298	156.7
1983	675	152.4	403	158.7	764	133.3	310	164.8
1984	827	173.5	453	175.0	878	146.3	334	177.6
1985	1026	201.6	529	184.9	1038	161.2	372	172.9
1986	1164	223.1	609	202.5	1146	174.7	430	183.7
1987	1443	260.9	754	215.6	1382	176.6	515	192.6
1988	1926	295.4	944	208.1	1716	164.6	651	193.6
1989	2251	309.6	1212	249.0	2188	189.3	831	238.2
1990	2484	337.7	1287	272.1	2263	198.2	896	269.0
1991	2941	387.4	1434	294.7	2712	227.5	906	269.5
1992	3699	460.3	1690	338.1	3210	263.2	1023	295.7
1993	5085	549.0	2308	407.5	4280	308.1	1347	347.8
1994	6530	633.9	3234	480.2	5870	356.5	1831	397.6
1995	8139	710.7	3991	528.9	7091	383.5	2206	430.8
1996	9157	772.3	4470	565.4	7660	392.3	2547	480.6
1997	10154	837.2	4612	553.4	7807	373.4	2597	478.6
1998	10850	903.3	4796	576.9	8054	381.6	2681	506.5
1999	11463	969.2	5025	602.6	8598	404.2	2661	510.6
2000	12817	1040.3	5305	603.5	9189	405.0	2680	503.8
2001	13952	1115.8	5445	615.2	9312	406.3	2759	519.0
2002	15478	1240.1	6199	696.1	10358	447.6	2904	548.8
2003	17950	1405.3	7342	814.5	11136	476.2	3032	567.2
2004	20647	1566.6	8800	944.4	12409	513.8	3386	613.6
2005	23997	1766.1	9799	1039.2	13609	557.8	3915	694.5
2006	27861	1992.7	10619	1116.5	14695	596.5	4010	709.8
2007	33236	2235.7	12336	1260.3	16982	671.5	4401	745.1
2008	37543	2413.3	13911	1350.1	19101	719.3	4975	787.1
2009	39418	2588.9	15243	1496.8	20852	800.5	5533	841.2
2010	44669	2834.9	17211	1636.4	23159	860.4	6255	920.5
2011	50076	3032.2	19186	1730.9	24943	885.0	7722	1033.1
2012	52308	3192.2	21123	1850.9	27218	940.9	8663	1101.9
2013	56029	3385.1	21208	2035.2	26206	1031.1	10543	1222.5
2014	59909	3577.5	23446	2190.0	28586	1095.8	12206	1372.6
2015	64516	3797.1	25138	2338.3	30472	1157.7	12980	1489.9
2016	69671	4010.1	27156	2469.4	32602	1213.6	14356	1591.5
2017	76218	4227.6	29364	2602.2	35110	1268.1	15473	1711.8
2018	81625	4434.4	31837	2750.1	37175	1307.9	18241	1971.7
2019	86956	4641.2	33885	2903.7	39188	1375.3	19797	2063.7
2020	88521	4693.5	33348	2790.0	37906	1302.6	20273	2029.6
2021	98561	5036.4	36879	3043.1	41773	1400.7	22662	2310.2
2022	101905	5123.0						

2-14 各市地区生产总值

Gross Domestic Product by City

单位：亿元 (100 million yuan)

市 别	City	2000	2005	2010	2012	2013	2014	2015
广 州	Guangzhou	2505.58	5187.85	10640.67	13194.69	15050.40	16135.95	17347.37
深 圳	Shenzhen	2219.20	5035.77	10069.06	13496.27	15234.24	16795.35	18436.84
珠 海	Zhuhai	335.92	640.53	1241.74	1583.66	1780.87	2008.86	2216.54
汕 头	Shantou	450.16	637.68	1125.75	1422.98	1569.58	1710.57	1869.53
佛 山	Foshan	1050.38	2450.67	5665.45	6642.95	7064.30	7509.96	8107.60
韶 关	Shaoguan	192.72	337.03	624.77	818.55	898.41	961.90	987.86
河 源	Heyuan	87.22	204.81	444.03	591.42	668.92	734.84	768.68
梅 州	Meizhou	180.64	315.17	602.79	737.60	790.82	870.73	943.58
惠 州	Huizhou	439.19	805.11	1723.56	2352.46	2674.50	2959.11	3090.22
汕 尾	Shanwei	128.49	205.75	455.02	613.73	678.22	729.36	766.86
东 莞	Dongguan	821.14	2189.46	4339.85	5190.20	5740.44	6174.83	6665.34
中 山	Zhongshan	345.44	894.59	1808.48	2306.52	2470.06	2580.59	2711.36
江 门	Jiangmen	504.66	801.70	1574.73	1892.98	2020.97	2099.29	2274.26
阳 江	Yangjiang	160.20	294.55	614.99	831.81	971.17	1066.82	1108.12
湛 江	Zhanjiang	373.81	682.67	1390.02	1845.70	2031.80	2201.88	2319.49
茂 名	Maoming	417.36	739.13	1482.26	1931.69	2186.93	2375.38	2439.73
肇 庆	Zhaoqing	249.78	420.95	965.12	1279.64	1437.04	1580.50	1691.85
清 远	Qingyuan	157.92	323.60	867.13	1025.12	1099.54	1194.42	1266.26
潮 州	Chaozhou	177.87	283.44	556.51	699.44	772.28	833.19	891.11
揭 阳	Jieyang	311.09	414.00	969.82	1306.17	1465.36	1604.73	1664.39
云 浮	Yunfu	137.70	202.46	396.21	524.28	596.67	645.74	696.60
按经济区域分	By Region							
珠 三 角	Pearl River Delta	8471.28	18426.64	38028.65	47939.37	53472.83	57844.44	62541.37
东 翼	Eastern Region	1067.61	1540.87	3107.09	4042.32	4485.43	4877.85	5191.89
西 翼	Western Region	951.37	1716.35	3487.27	4609.20	5189.91	5644.08	5867.34
山 区	Mountainous Region	756.20	1383.07	2934.93	3696.98	4054.36	4407.64	4662.99

2-14 续表 continued

单位：亿元 (100 million yuan)

市 别	City	2016	2017	2018	2019	2020	2021	2022
广 州	Guangzhou	18559.73	19871.67	21002.44	23844.69	25068.75	28225.21	28839.00
深 圳	Shenzhen	20685.74	23280.27	25266.08	26992.33	27759.02	30820.10	32387.68
珠 海	Zhuhai	2452.61	2943.83	3216.78	3444.23	3518.26	3896.04	4045.45
汕 头	Shantou	2097.48	2368.16	2503.08	2687.28	2704.74	2949.58	3017.44
佛 山	Foshan	8756.31	9382.16	9976.72	10739.76	10758.50	12185.75	12698.39
韶 关	Shaoguan	1040.69	1133.62	1217.48	1316.35	1375.16	1550.06	1563.93
河 源	Heyuan	847.80	968.10	1006.98	1079.75	1114.31	1273.91	1294.57
梅 州	Meizhou	1029.74	1086.59	1127.24	1187.08	1227.27	1309.39	1318.21
惠 州	Huizhou	3359.52	3745.75	4003.33	4192.93	4283.72	5033.06	5401.24
汕 尾	Shanwei	843.92	904.57	1004.00	1076.27	1112.63	1285.41	1322.02
东 莞	Dongguan	7260.92	8079.20	8818.11	9474.43	9756.77	10931.69	11200.32
中 山	Zhongshan	2830.43	2939.52	3053.73	3123.79	3189.15	3578.88	3631.28
江 门	Jiangmen	2480.94	2745.89	3001.24	3150.22	3202.97	3598.04	3773.41
阳 江	Yangjiang	1117.03	1142.24	1167.73	1291.67	1349.53	1511.19	1535.02
湛 江	Zhanjiang	2487.25	2744.98	2944.48	3055.90	3103.32	3565.46	3712.56
茂 名	Maoming	2618.91	2881.07	3095.11	3248.11	3285.44	3695.90	3904.63
肇 庆	Zhaoqing	1810.67	1964.97	2102.29	2250.67	2313.24	2645.81	2705.05
清 远	Qingyuan	1404.30	1474.54	1575.32	1704.47	1804.36	2000.69	2032.02
潮 州	Chaozhou	948.16	960.68	1005.30	1082.94	1102.88	1244.52	1312.98
揭 阳	Jieyang	1804.26	1842.67	2002.09	2099.91	2088.00	2280.97	2260.98
云 浮	Yunfu	758.68	804.63	855.67	944.14	1033.62	1137.87	1162.43
按经济区域分	By Region							
珠 三 角	Pearl River Delta	68196.86	74953.26	80440.72	87213.05	89850.38	100914.59	104681.81
东 翼	Eastern Region	5693.82	6076.09	6514.48	6946.39	7008.25	7760.48	7913.42
西 翼	Western Region	6223.19	6768.29	7207.33	7595.68	7738.29	8772.55	9152.20
山 区	Mountainous Region	5081.21	5467.48	5782.69	6231.80	6554.71	7271.92	7371.15

注：2017年起，深圳市地区生产总值数据包含深汕合作区。
Notes: Since 2017, GDP of Shenshan Special Cooperation Zone is included in that of Shenzhen city.

2-15 各市地区生产总值指数

Indices of Gross Domestic Product by City

上年=100 (preceding year=100)

市 别	City	2000	2005	2010	2012	2013	2014	2015
广 州	Guangzhou	113.4	113.0	113.0	110.4	111.5	108.5	108.3
深 圳	Shenzhen	116.3	115.3	112.3	110.2	110.6	108.9	109.0
珠 海	Zhuhai	112.0	113.2	113.3	107.8	110.9	110.4	110.0
汕 头	Shantou	107.0	111.3	110.4	109.5	110.1	108.9	108.4
佛 山	Foshan	112.5	119.3	114.3	108.1	109.8	108.2	108.2
韶 关	Shaoguan	111.3	110.1	112.5	111.7	110.7	107.6	105.9
河 源	Heyuan	110.7	122.9	112.5	111.5	112.1	108.6	106.3
梅 州	Meizhou	108.1	107.9	114.1	109.9	111.0	108.6	108.6
惠 州	Huizhou	111.3	116.1	118.2	112.6	113.7	110.0	109.3
汕 尾	Shanwei	111.5	116.0	117.0	113.4	112.3	109.0	108.1
东 莞	Dongguan	119.7	119.5	110.4	106.3	110.0	108.0	108.4
中 山	Zhongshan	112.4	121.1	113.8	111.1	109.7	107.5	108.2
江 门	Jiangmen	110.2	112.6	114.5	108.2	109.6	107.5	108.4
阳 江	Yangjiang	109.6	113.9	116.3	112.5	115.0	110.2	107.9
湛 江	Zhanjiang	107.1	113.6	114.2	109.5	111.8	109.8	108.7
茂 名	Maoming	111.2	114.1	114.0	110.6	113.6	110.1	107.6
肇 庆	Zhaoqing	110.6	115.8	115.5	109.8	109.7	109.7	107.9
清 远	Qingyuan	108.3	127.7	112.8	104.8	108.1	107.7	108.0
潮 州	Chaozhou	105.6	111.5	114.0	110.5	110.8	108.1	108.2
揭 阳	Jieyang	105.4	111.3	119.3	110.7	114.1	110.3	107.8
云 浮	Yunfu	105.3	113.3	113.9	113.0	113.5	110.3	108.6
按经济区域分	By Region							
珠 三 角	Pearl River Delta	113.9	115.7	113.1	109.5	110.7	108.6	108.6
东 翼	Eastern Region	106.7	112.0	114.6	110.7	111.8	109.2	108.1
西 翼	Western Region	109.4	113.8	114.5	110.5	113.2	110.0	108.1
山 区	Mountainous Region	108.7	115.7	113.1	109.5	110.7	108.4	107.5

2−15 续表 continued

上年=100 (preceding year=100)

市别	City	2016	2017	2018	2019	2020	2021	2022
广州	Guangzhou	107.6	106.7	106.0	106.9	102.7	108.1	101.0
深圳	Shenzhen	109.3	108.8	107.7	106.7	103.1	107.0	103.3
珠海	Zhuhai	108.1	111.1	107.9	106.8	103.0	107.2	102.3
汕头	Shantou	108.6	109.1	106.9	106.1	102.0	106.4	101.0
佛山	Foshan	107.9	108.0	106.4	106.8	101.5	108.5	102.1
韶关	Shaoguan	106.1	106.4	104.0	106.0	103.0	108.6	100.2
河源	Heyuan	106.6	106.7	105.8	105.5	101.3	108.0	101.0
梅州	Meizhou	107.8	106.9	102.3	103.4	101.5	105.6	100.5
惠州	Huizhou	108.1	107.9	105.9	104.2	101.5	110.4	104.2
汕尾	Shanwei	107.0	108.1	108.0	106.7	104.6	112.7	101.5
东莞	Dongguan	108.0	108.8	107.5	107.4	101.1	108.5	100.6
中山	Zhongshan	104.3	103.8	103.1	102.0	101.5	108.4	100.5
江门	Jiangmen	107.3	108.1	107.8	104.3	102.2	108.4	103.3
阳江	Yangjiang	106.4	105.8	103.8	108.2	104.4	108.3	100.8
湛江	Zhanjiang	106.8	106.9	105.7	104.0	101.9	108.7	101.2
茂名	Maoming	107.4	107.6	105.8	104.3	101.5	107.6	100.5
肇庆	Zhaoqing	105.0	105.1	106.5	106.3	103.0	110.5	101.1
清远	Qingyuan	109.3	104.1	104.0	106.3	103.8	108.1	101.0
潮州	Chaozhou	107.0	106.1	104.9	105.0	101.3	109.3	102.3
揭阳	Jieyang	107.5	105.2	105.2	103.0	100.2	106.4	98.7
云浮	Yunfu	108.0	105.3	104.0	106.4	104.1	108.1	102.1
按经济区域分	By Region							
珠三角	Pearl River Delta	108.0	107.8	106.8	106.4	102.4	108.0	102.1
东翼	Eastern Region	107.8	107.2	106.2	105.0	101.7	107.9	100.6
西翼	Western Region	107.0	107.0	105.4	104.9	102.2	108.2	100.8
山区	Mountainous Region	107.7	105.8	103.9	105.5	102.8	107.7	100.9

2-16 各市地区生产总值指数

Indices of Gross Domestic Product by City

2000年=100 (year of 2000=100)

市别	City	2001	2005	2010	2012	2013	2014	2015
广州	Guangzhou	112.8	191.3	361.2	444.0	495.3	537.3	581.8
深圳	Shenzhen	114.5	213.8	402.8	488.6	540.5	588.7	641.5
珠海	Zhuhai	111.9	190.6	342.3	412.3	457.4	505.0	555.4
汕头	Shantou	98.1	139.9	234.4	282.7	311.1	338.7	367.1
佛山	Foshan	113.2	214.8	454.5	548.0	601.5	650.9	704.3
韶关	Shaoguan	110.2	165.0	301.8	371.8	411.7	443.0	469.1
河源	Heyuan	111.7	215.4	460.6	581.5	651.6	707.4	752.2
梅州	Meizhou	108.6	159.1	270.8	337.9	375.0	407.1	442.0
惠州	Huizhou	109.5	181.9	373.6	483.8	550.2	605.1	661.2
汕尾	Shanwei	108.9	179.3	383.3	496.0	557.1	607.2	656.3
东莞	Dongguan	120.0	252.1	473.2	545.2	599.9	648.0	702.3
中山	Zhongshan	117.0	245.0	467.3	586.9	643.9	692.1	748.7
江门	Jiangmen	105.3	160.2	295.2	360.9	395.6	425.2	460.8
阳江	Yangjiang	109.7	174.4	335.0	432.1	497.1	548.0	591.2
湛江	Zhanjiang	108.3	169.6	307.6	380.0	425.0	466.6	507.0
茂名	Maoming	110.3	176.6	314.5	385.5	437.9	482.1	518.8
肇庆	Zhaoqing	108.2	174.6	339.4	423.6	464.8	510.0	550.5
清远	Qingyuan	106.5	204.6	462.3	525.1	567.9	611.4	660.0
潮州	Chaozhou	106.9	160.4	296.2	370.5	410.5	443.7	480.1
揭阳	Jieyang	103.5	133.0	289.2	366.5	418.3	461.3	497.4
云浮	Yunfu	104.6	151.3	279.1	360.9	409.8	452.0	490.7
按经济区域分	By Region							
珠三角	Pearl River Delta	113.4	205.3	394.4	479.7	531.2	576.8	626.2
东翼	Eastern Region	102.4	146.0	277.8	346.2	387.1	422.7	457.1
西翼	Western Region	109.4	173.4	315.3	391.3	442.8	487.1	526.4
山区	Mountainous Region	108.2	175.2	341.5	416.5	461.0	499.6	536.9

2-16 续表 continued

2000年=100 (year of 2000=100)

市 别	City	2016	2017	2018	2019	2020	2021	2022
广 州	Guangzhou	626.1	668.2	708.6	757.6	778.1	841.4	850.0
深 圳	Shenzhen	701.5	763.3	822.4	877.1	903.9	967.1	999.1
珠 海	Zhuhai	600.6	667.2	720.1	769.0	792.0	849.3	869.0
汕 头	Shantou	398.7	434.9	464.8	493.2	503.0	535.3	540.7
佛 山	Foshan	760.0	820.6	872.8	932.0	945.7	1026.0	1047.1
韶 关	Shaoguan	497.8	529.9	551.0	584.1	601.8	653.4	654.9
河 源	Heyuan	801.7	855.2	904.8	954.6	967.3	1045.1	1055.5
梅 州	Meizhou	476.4	509.3	521.0	538.8	547.1	577.8	580.4
惠 州	Huizhou	714.5	771.2	816.4	850.8	863.6	953.8	994.0
汕 尾	Shanwei	702.4	759.6	820.7	875.7	916.0	1032.5	1047.6
东 莞	Dongguan	758.1	824.7	886.2	951.4	961.8	1043.5	1050.0
中 山	Zhongshan	781.0	811.1	836.3	853.3	866.4	938.9	943.5
江 门	Jiangmen	494.7	534.7	576.4	601.2	614.3	665.6	687.4
阳 江	Yangjiang	628.9	665.4	690.6	747.3	779.8	844.6	851.7
湛 江	Zhanjiang	541.5	578.9	612.1	636.5	648.6	705.2	713.4
茂 名	Maoming	557.1	599.4	633.9	661.2	670.9	722.2	725.8
肇 庆	Zhaoqing	578.1	607.7	647.2	687.7	708.1	782.5	790.8
清 远	Qingyuan	721.2	751.1	781.0	830.2	861.7	931.5	940.7
潮 州	Chaozhou	513.9	545.4	572.2	600.7	608.2	664.8	680.4
揭 阳	Jieyang	534.8	562.7	591.8	609.4	610.4	649.7	641.5
云 浮	Yunfu	530.2	558.2	580.7	618.2	643.2	695.5	710.3
按经济区域分	By Region							
珠 三 角	Pearl River Delta	676.4	729.4	778.7	828.8	848.4	916.5	935.5
东 翼	Eastern Region	492.5	528.0	560.5	588.7	598.7	645.8	649.9
西 翼	Western Region	563.0	602.3	634.8	665.8	680.4	736.1	742.2
山 区	Mountainous Region	578.1	611.5	635.6	670.8	689.7	743.0	749.8

2-17 各市第一产业增加值
Value-added of the Primary Industry by City

单位：亿元 (100 million yuan)

市 别	City	2000	2005	2010	2015	2018	2019	2020	2021	2022
广 州	Guangzhou	94.37	130.22	168.62	206.52	229.18	247.13	286.27	299.75	318.31
深 圳	Shenzhen	15.57	9.74	6.11	7.21	22.61	25.58	25.59	23.75	25.64
珠 海	Zhuhai	15.27	22.69	30.00	48.30	54.10	58.09	51.00	54.20	60.52
汕 头	Shantou	39.38	44.52	62.45	91.39	110.57	120.40	122.51	126.42	136.96
佛 山	Foshan	61.74	75.76	98.74	127.29	144.55	160.40	190.05	202.68	221.13
韶 关	Shaoguan	44.01	55.47	87.97	131.73	156.31	176.67	199.87	215.03	224.56
河 源	Heyuan	30.36	42.42	58.69	93.34	107.84	121.07	133.52	153.21	162.41
梅 州	Meizhou	56.02	72.73	118.40	172.97	196.14	223.63	238.66	241.07	257.91
惠 州	Huizhou	62.23	75.10	99.89	146.13	176.13	206.73	216.98	248.39	277.45
汕 尾	Shanwei	46.71	46.12	73.23	112.97	133.24	149.64	157.16	166.48	187.40
东 莞	Dongguan	25.91	21.82	15.56	19.92	25.83	28.85	30.40	34.83	36.50
中 山	Zhongshan	23.51	30.71	48.32	59.56	63.05	62.69	71.01	84.71	89.20
江 门	Jiangmen	69.83	72.47	115.91	170.46	201.85	254.35	272.91	294.89	324.61
阳 江	Yangjiang	62.95	80.38	129.98	190.04	219.98	244.42	254.74	245.58	251.44
湛 江	Zhanjiang	105.06	160.50	279.81	429.39	528.68	584.25	608.53	644.41	682.78
茂 名	Maoming	125.91	167.04	272.89	398.05	490.57	580.66	648.67	648.85	699.01
肇 庆	Zhaoqing	91.75	120.72	189.81	288.50	348.24	386.58	431.99	462.18	486.46
清 远	Qingyuan	61.43	71.54	118.22	192.30	231.33	262.16	288.85	303.81	330.61
潮 州	Chaozhou	28.76	32.64	38.76	62.64	76.81	98.90	108.93	115.98	124.88
揭 阳	Jieyang	71.06	65.20	100.86	141.33	164.75	186.69	203.41	208.29	223.68
云 浮	Yunfu	54.81	63.42	92.46	129.44	154.79	171.74	191.70	210.20	218.91
按经济区域分	By Region									
珠 三 角	Pearl River Delta	460.17	559.23	772.96	1073.87	1265.53	1430.38	1576.19	1705.36	1839.82
东 翼	Eastern Region	185.92	188.48	275.30	408.34	485.37	555.64	592.01	617.17	672.91
西 翼	Western Region	293.92	407.92	682.67	1017.49	1239.23	1409.33	1511.94	1538.85	1633.23
山 区	Mountainous Region	246.64	305.58	475.73	719.77	846.39	955.27	1052.60	1123.32	1194.40

2–18 各市第二产业增加值

Value-added of the Secondary Industry by City

单位：亿元 (100 million yuan)

市 别	City	2000	2005	2010	2015	2018	2019	2020	2021	2022
广 州	Guangzhou	1029.94	2067.00	4053.30	5777.17	6109.95	6509.40	6716.16	7736.13	7909.29
深 圳	Shenzhen	1108.76	2709.69	4727.94	7687.41	9995.87	10402.00	10380.65	11607.80	12405.88
珠 海	Zhuhai	176.30	344.14	670.63	1043.69	1450.82	1519.85	1463.16	1651.11	1808.08
汕 头	Shantou	217.39	328.07	594.67	937.58	1221.45	1282.67	1322.53	1422.03	1446.43
佛 山	Foshan	553.61	1494.20	3581.59	5003.35	5663.51	6088.54	5887.79	6780.94	7129.80
韶 关	Shaoguan	75.71	143.51	244.52	353.14	422.29	448.85	474.36	559.34	556.69
河 源	Heyuan	20.99	80.46	208.19	310.43	348.49	372.32	388.34	464.44	469.15
梅 州	Meizhou	63.30	129.80	248.19	347.19	352.04	369.04	396.35	422.62	407.69
惠 州	Huizhou	255.26	456.79	1022.99	1744.62	2122.20	2158.14	2137.61	2718.75	3019.87
汕 尾	Shanwei	37.31	83.10	199.88	321.40	371.29	390.94	411.63	491.47	490.90
东 莞	Dongguan	451.47	1232.14	2313.00	3479.05	4960.40	5298.93	5534.57	6359.21	6513.64
中 山	Zhongshan	180.83	548.21	1069.62	1516.61	1539.37	1556.02	1525.97	1777.09	1795.25
江 门	Jiangmen	235.11	425.57	868.35	1061.67	1328.64	1326.60	1400.69	1623.27	1723.64
阳 江	Yangjiang	47.03	110.83	258.10	503.26	389.33	443.23	473.81	590.12	596.35
湛 江	Zhanjiang	135.52	298.80	565.19	892.89	1058.79	1045.62	1098.46	1382.26	1457.77
茂 名	Maoming	147.72	260.23	560.77	920.24	1084.64	1078.28	1060.92	1278.32	1421.12
肇 庆	Zhaoqing	53.10	99.87	348.13	783.60	867.26	889.50	895.70	1106.37	1126.94
清 远	Qingyuan	40.72	127.21	397.65	483.73	537.95	558.19	669.69	774.20	767.59
潮 州	Chaozhou	86.52	151.68	309.50	476.77	500.20	517.69	516.15	581.94	625.52
揭 阳	Jieyang	141.91	202.13	537.79	865.09	804.38	809.87	775.62	859.99	793.61
云 浮	Yunfu	39.98	73.69	158.18	274.79	270.44	302.54	337.90	368.41	378.32
按经济区域分	By Region									
珠 三 角	Pearl River Delta	4044.38	9377.60	18655.55	28097.17	34038.02	35748.98	35942.30	41360.66	43432.38
东 翼	Eastern Region	483.13	764.98	1641.84	2600.84	2897.32	3001.16	3025.92	3355.43	3356.46
西 翼	Western Region	330.27	669.87	1384.06	2316.39	2532.76	2567.13	2633.18	3250.70	3475.24
山 区	Mountainous Region	240.70	554.68	1256.73	1769.29	1931.21	2050.94	2266.64	2589.00	2579.43

2-19 各市第三产业增加值

Value-added of the Tertiary Industry by City

单位：亿元 (100 million yuan)

市别	City	2000	2005	2010	2015	2018	2019	2020	2021	2022
广州	Guangzhou	1381.27	2990.63	6418.75	11363.68	14663.32	17088.17	18066.32	20189.34	20611.40
深圳	Shenzhen	1094.87	2316.34	5335.01	10742.22	15247.60	16564.75	17352.77	19188.56	19956.16
珠海	Zhuhai	144.35	273.71	541.10	1124.55	1711.86	1866.29	2004.10	2190.73	2176.86
汕头	Shantou	193.39	265.10	468.63	840.56	1171.05	1284.21	1259.71	1401.12	1434.05
佛山	Foshan	435.03	880.70	1985.13	2976.96	4168.66	4490.82	4680.66	5202.13	5347.46
韶关	Shaoguan	73.00	138.05	292.28	502.99	638.88	690.83	700.92	775.70	782.67
河源	Heyuan	35.87	81.93	177.15	364.91	550.66	586.36	592.44	656.26	663.01
梅州	Meizhou	61.32	112.64	236.20	423.42	579.07	594.41	592.26	645.70	652.60
惠州	Huizhou	121.70	273.22	600.68	1199.48	1705.00	1828.06	1929.14	2065.92	2103.91
汕尾	Shanwei	44.48	76.53	181.92	332.49	499.47	535.69	543.84	627.45	643.72
东莞	Dongguan	343.76	935.50	2011.28	3166.37	3831.87	4146.65	4191.80	4537.66	4650.18
中山	Zhongshan	141.09	315.67	690.54	1135.19	1451.32	1505.07	1592.17	1717.08	1746.83
江门	Jiangmen	199.72	303.66	590.47	1042.13	1470.76	1569.27	1529.37	1679.88	1725.16
阳江	Yangjiang	50.21	103.33	226.92	414.81	558.42	604.03	620.98	675.49	687.23
湛江	Zhanjiang	133.24	223.37	545.02	997.21	1357.01	1426.03	1396.33	1538.79	1572.00
茂名	Maoming	143.73	311.87	648.60	1121.44	1519.91	1589.17	1575.86	1768.73	1784.51
肇庆	Zhaoqing	104.93	200.37	427.18	619.76	886.79	974.60	985.55	1077.26	1091.65
清远	Qingyuan	55.77	124.85	351.27	590.24	806.04	884.12	845.82	922.68	933.83
潮州	Chaozhou	62.59	99.12	208.25	351.69	428.30	466.35	477.80	546.60	562.59
揭阳	Jieyang	98.11	146.66	331.16	657.97	1032.97	1103.35	1108.97	1212.69	1243.70
云浮	Yunfu	42.90	65.34	145.58	292.37	430.44	469.86	504.02	559.26	565.20
按经济区域分	By Region									
珠三角	Pearl River Delta	3966.73	8489.80	18600.14	33370.33	45137.18	50033.69	52331.89	57848.57	59409.60
东翼	Eastern Region	398.57	587.41	1189.95	2182.71	3131.79	3389.59	3390.31	3787.87	3884.06
西翼	Western Region	327.18	638.56	1420.54	2533.46	3435.34	3619.23	3593.17	3983.01	4043.73
山区	Mountainous Region	268.86	522.80	1202.47	2173.92	3005.09	3225.59	3235.47	3559.60	3597.31

2-20 各市第一产业增加值指数

Indices of Value-added of the Primary Industry by City

上年=100 (preceding year=100)

市别	City	2000	2005	2010	2015	2018	2019	2020	2021	2022
广州	Guangzhou	101.7	105.6	103.1	102.4	106.0	104.2	109.8	106.3	103.2
深圳	Shenzhen	103.1	79.6	88.8	104.2	107.3	105.9	96.1	101.0	100.8
珠海	Zhuhai	108.5	105.2	105.5	100.3	103.5	104.2	101.6	106.7	107.2
汕头	Shantou	105.2	104.6	105.1	103.0	103.8	102.2	100.0	102.5	104.4
佛山	Foshan	107.2	102.0	104.4	101.5	105.4	104.2	99.4	109.5	106.3
韶关	Shaoguan	103.6	102.6	105.7	103.8	105.3	104.6	104.4	113.1	104.9
河源	Heyuan	106.5	102.6	103.3	103.8	104.5	106.2	105.9	107.8	104.7
梅州	Meizhou	102.8	103.0	106.4	103.4	104.5	103.6	100.7	105.3	104.7
惠州	Huizhou	106.1	105.6	103.8	104.3	103.3	102.2	104.4	116.8	106.9
汕尾	Shanwei	106.1	102.5	106.1	104.5	104.4	104.8	103.9	109.0	107.2
东莞	Dongguan	99.8	102.3	101.5	102.6	108.8	108.3	105.9	112.3	100.3
中山	Zhongshan	101.9	101.9	103.2	99.6	104.1	96.0	117.5	113.1	105.9
江门	Jiangmen	104.9	100.9	104.9	103.2	104.2	106.6	103.3	109.8	107.0
阳江	Yangjiang	106.4	95.5	105.9	103.9	103.1	100.7	101.5	101.5	102.1
湛江	Zhanjiang	104.0	108.4	104.2	102.9	103.8	103.4	100.2	106.6	104.5
茂名	Maoming	108.5	104.0	104.1	104.0	105.2	103.8	105.4	106.8	105.6
肇庆	Zhaoqing	105.0	105.8	105.4	103.8	104.8	104.7	105.3	107.6	103.9
清远	Qingyuan	102.7	104.0	106.8	104.4	104.7	104.2	104.7	109.2	107.2
潮州	Chaozhou	101.0	102.1	104.5	102.9	105.0	103.3	104.4	109.8	105.4
揭阳	Jieyang	104.0	102.9	104.9	103.6	104.3	103.7	103.1	104.6	105.5
云浮	Yunfu	106.0	106.2	104.6	103.0	105.3	102.7	108.0	109.7	104.4
按经济区域分	By Region									
珠三角	Pearl River Delta	104.4	103.6	104.1	102.8	104.8	104.1	105.3	109.4	105.1
东翼	Eastern Region	104.3	103.0	105.2	103.6	104.3	103.6	102.8	106.3	105.7
西翼	Western Region	106.6	103.7	104.5	103.5	104.2	103.1	102.6	105.8	104.6
山区	Mountainous Region	104.1	103.9	105.6	103.7	104.8	104.1	104.4	109.0	105.4

2-21 各市第二产业增加值指数

Indices of Value-added of the Secondary Industry by City

上年=100 (preceding year=100)

市别	City	2000	2005	2010	2015	2018	2019	2020	2021	2022
广州	Guangzhou	111.9	113.0	113.0	106.8	105.4	105.4	103.3	108.7	101.1
深圳	Shenzhen	118.5	117.9	113.8	107.4	109.2	104.4	101.8	107.2	104.8
珠海	Zhuhai	114.7	116.9	118.2	110.2	112.6	104.1	101.9	108.5	107.1
汕头	Shantou	107.2	113.5	110.1	107.2	109.0	102.9	103.6	104.6	100.1
佛山	Foshan	112.4	125.2	115.2	107.3	106.0	106.8	101.2	108.9	102.8
韶关	Shaoguan	115.6	109.7	113.4	102.8	101.5	105.9	104.7	105.9	97.5
河源	Heyuan	113.1	145.6	113.9	104.3	106.0	105.9	101.9	110.5	100.5
梅州	Meizhou	109.2	108.0	118.3	108.5	101.4	103.1	101.7	102.7	96.5
惠州	Huizhou	113.1	117.4	124.2	109.8	105.9	101.5	101.6	117.1	107.2
汕尾	Shanwei	115.7	123.8	122.5	106.8	110.5	106.2	104.0	115.1	99.3
东莞	Dongguan	120.7	120.0	117.5	106.3	108.7	106.5	99.2	110.9	100.8
中山	Zhongshan	115.3	119.6	115.8	107.2	100.6	100.9	101.4	111.3	100.0
江门	Jiangmen	111.1	122.3	116.9	108.4	107.9	100.4	102.9	110.1	104.6
阳江	Yangjiang	111.7	125.2	121.3	110.1	102.8	113.5	109.5	113.7	99.5
湛江	Zhanjiang	106.2	111.4	116.9	109.9	104.6	100.8	104.9	112.7	99.1
茂名	Maoming	110.8	114.3	113.8	108.3	103.0	102.3	100.7	103.8	98.6
肇庆	Zhaoqing	114.2	120.6	130.8	109.6	108.1	101.4	102.7	116.1	101.1
清远	Qingyuan	104.6	162.1	111.1	106.2	106.4	104.4	106.3	108.7	99.1
潮州	Chaozhou	105.5	115.1	115.5	106.5	103.7	101.9	101.5	107.1	102.4
揭阳	Jieyang	104.9	114.3	125.6	106.5	103.8	100.1	97.4	106.3	91.3
云浮	Yunfu	105.2	128.3	120.2	106.3	99.5	108.8	104.8	105.0	102.7
按经济区域分	By Region									
珠三角	Pearl River Delta	114.6	118.3	115.5	107.5	107.2	104.7	101.7	109.5	103.1
东翼	Eastern Region	106.8	115.1	117.4	106.8	106.6	102.3	101.5	106.9	98.1
西翼	Western Region	109.2	114.8	116.6	109.3	103.6	104.0	104.3	109.3	99.0
山区	Mountainous Region	109.5	125.9	114.6	105.8	103.3	105.4	104.0	106.8	99.1

2-22 各市第三产业增加值指数

Indices of Value-added of the Tertiary Industry by City

上年=100 (preceding year=100)

市别	City	2000	2005	2010	2015	2018	2019	2020	2021	2022
广州	Guangzhou	116.4	113.3	113.2	109.3	106.4	107.7	102.3	108.0	101.0
深圳	Shenzhen	113.8	112.3	110.7	110.3	106.7	108.3	103.9	106.9	102.4
珠海	Zhuhai	108.9	109.2	107.5	110.1	103.8	109.5	104.1	106.3	98.6
汕头	Shantou	106.9	109.9	111.3	110.6	104.9	110.1	100.5	108.7	101.6
佛山	Foshan	113.6	112.2	113.0	110.2	107.0	106.8	102.0	108.0	101.0
韶关	Shaoguan	110.8	114.0	113.3	108.9	105.2	106.4	101.7	109.1	100.7
河源	Heyuan	112.4	117.1	113.5	109.7	105.9	105.1	99.9	106.5	100.5
梅州	Meizhou	112.6	110.9	113.2	110.6	102.2	103.5	101.7	107.7	101.3
惠州	Huizhou	108.6	117.3	110.3	108.9	106.0	107.8	101.1	102.4	100.0
汕尾	Shanwei	112.0	119.7	114.5	111.3	107.0	107.7	105.3	112.0	101.5
东莞	Dongguan	120.0	119.4	103.3	110.9	106.0	108.4	103.4	105.3	100.3
中山	Zhongshan	110.0	126.0	111.4	110.3	105.9	103.5	101.1	105.3	100.8
江门	Jiangmen	110.2	104.0	111.9	109.1	108.3	107.9	101.3	106.5	101.3
阳江	Yangjiang	111.1	120.5	116.6	106.2	105.1	105.4	99.5	107.0	101.4
湛江	Zhanjiang	110.4	119.4	115.8	109.6	107.5	107.0	100.1	106.5	101.4
茂名	Maoming	114.4	120.5	117.5	108.0	108.1	105.9	100.8	110.6	99.7
肇庆	Zhaoqing	112.2	120.2	110.2	107.6	105.5	112.2	102.4	106.7	99.7
清远	Qingyuan	120.0	118.2	117.3	111.0	102.1	108.3	101.8	107.3	100.4
潮州	Chaozhou	107.8	109.6	113.9	111.7	106.5	109.1	100.5	111.6	101.6
揭阳	Jieyang	107.2	112.0	113.1	111.5	106.7	105.8	102.3	106.8	102.7
云浮	Yunfu	104.7	107.8	112.4	114.2	107.0	106.1	102.1	109.6	100.9
按经济区域分	By Region									
珠三角	Pearl River Delta	114.1	113.7	110.9	109.8	106.4	107.9	102.9	107.0	101.3
东翼	Eastern Region	107.7	111.6	112.7	111.1	106.0	108.2	101.8	109.0	102.0
西翼	Western Region	112.3	120.1	116.8	108.4	107.3	106.3	100.3	108.4	100.6
山区	Mountainous Region	111.9	113.9	114.3	110.6	104.1	106.1	101.5	108.0	100.7

2-23 各市地区生产总值（2022年）
Gross Domestic Product by City (2022)

单位：亿元 (100 million yuan)

市别	City	地区生产总值 Gross Domestic Product	第一产业 Primary Industry	第二产业 Secondary Industry	第三产业 Tertiary Industry	#农、林、牧、渔业 Farming, Forestry, Animal Husbandry and Fishery	#工业 Industry
广州	Guangzhou	28839.00	318.31	7909.29	20611.40	354.65	6946.67
深圳	Shenzhen	32387.68	25.64	12405.88	19956.16	26.63	11357.09
珠海	Zhuhai	4045.45	60.52	1808.08	2176.86	65.08	1579.11
汕头	Shantou	3017.44	136.96	1446.43	1434.05	144.94	1229.45
佛山	Foshan	12698.39	221.13	7129.80	5347.46	235.20	6741.89
韶关	Shaoguan	1563.93	224.56	556.69	782.67	226.50	467.77
河源	Heyuan	1294.57	162.41	469.15	663.01	164.20	388.20
梅州	Meizhou	1318.21	257.91	407.69	652.60	262.54	297.58
惠州	Huizhou	5401.24	277.45	3019.87	2103.91	280.24	2717.80
汕尾	Shanwei	1322.02	187.40	490.90	643.72	194.37	415.49
东莞	Dongguan	11200.32	36.50	6513.64	4650.18	37.21	6251.51
中山	Zhongshan	3631.28	89.20	1795.25	1746.83	90.56	1677.81
江门	Jiangmen	3773.41	324.61	1723.64	1725.16	334.60	1483.99
阳江	Yangjiang	1535.02	251.44	596.35	687.23	257.85	541.02
湛江	Zhanjiang	3712.56	682.78	1457.77	1572.00	703.37	1222.54
茂名	Maoming	3904.63	699.01	1421.12	1784.51	713.71	1104.04
肇庆	Zhaoqing	2705.05	486.46	1126.94	1091.65	502.71	991.58
清远	Qingyuan	2032.02	330.61	767.59	933.83	346.55	690.68
潮州	Chaozhou	1312.98	124.88	625.52	562.59	129.90	578.31
揭阳	Jieyang	2260.98	223.68	793.61	1243.70	233.86	724.91
云浮	Yunfu	1162.43	218.91	378.32	565.20	226.87	315.62
按经济区域分	By Region						
珠三角	Pearl River Delta	104681.81	1839.82	43432.38	59409.60	1926.90	39747.44
东翼	Eastern Region	7913.42	672.91	3356.46	3884.06	703.07	2948.15
西翼	Western Region	9152.20	1633.23	3475.24	4043.73	1674.94	2867.60
山区	Mountainous Region	7371.15	1194.40	2579.43	3597.31	1226.66	2159.85

2-23 续表 continued

单位：亿元 (100 million yuan)

市 别	City	#建筑业 Construction	#批发和零售业 Wholesale and Retail Trades	#交通运输、仓储和邮政业 Transport, Storage and Post	#住宿和餐饮业 Hotels and Catering Services	#金融业 Financial Interme-diation	#房地产业 Real Estate
广 州	Guangzhou	1012.93	3801.59	1590.69	431.22	2596.15	3038.93
深 圳	Shenzhen	1079.38	2757.07	833.37	397.82	5137.98	2593.40
珠 海	Zhuhai	242.76	296.08	68.57	43.07	490.86	331.29
汕 头	Shantou	218.36	332.22	78.53	41.79	130.14	237.01
佛 山	Foshan	392.06	942.99	212.64	144.02	709.29	792.24
韶 关	Shaoguan	89.22	112.46	53.30	18.22	81.12	113.37
河 源	Heyuan	81.07	130.32	22.67	21.82	76.80	120.86
梅 州	Meizhou	110.33	92.61	33.42	20.15	93.73	104.90
惠 州	Huizhou	304.30	355.24	104.33	67.79	304.25	520.06
汕 尾	Shanwei	75.91	133.75	28.47	18.36	62.62	104.32
东 莞	Dongguan	269.07	804.10	234.27	182.45	749.81	773.94
中 山	Zhongshan	118.91	378.99	61.01	49.02	284.19	314.86
江 门	Jiangmen	241.11	205.62	102.40	59.80	281.06	229.90
阳 江	Yangjiang	55.72	157.58	58.58	21.15	75.92	88.99
湛 江	Zhanjiang	245.56	290.52	143.50	50.67	191.41	240.52
茂 名	Maoming	318.02	432.36	149.46	58.71	122.77	208.27
肇 庆	Zhaoqing	136.17	267.92	82.94	45.36	127.89	129.18
清 远	Qingyuan	77.31	125.38	41.76	27.75	130.74	165.24
潮 州	Chaozhou	47.50	136.14	32.85	16.82	62.82	73.55
揭 阳	Jieyang	68.99	453.31	62.38	30.67	73.00	178.45
云 浮	Yunfu	62.90	113.48	45.76	18.51	43.22	91.30
按经济区域分	By Region						
珠 三 角	Pearl River Delta	3796.69	9809.60	3290.22	1420.56	10681.47	8723.78
东 翼	Eastern Region	410.75	1055.42	202.24	107.65	328.58	593.33
西 翼	Western Region	619.31	880.47	351.54	130.52	390.09	537.78
山 区	Mountainous Region	420.82	574.25	196.91	106.46	425.62	595.67

2-24 各市地区生产总值指数（2022年）

Growth Indices of Gross Domestic Product by City (2022)

单位：%　　　　(%)

市别	City	地区生产总值 Gross Domestic Product	第一产业 Primary Industry	第二产业 Secondary Industry	第三产业 Tertiary Industry	#农、林、牧、渔业 Farming, Forestry, Animal Husbandry and Fishery	#工业 Industry
广州	Guangzhou	101.0	103.2	101.1	101.0	103.4	101.0
深圳	Shenzhen	103.3	100.8	104.8	102.4	101.0	104.7
珠海	Zhuhai	102.3	107.2	107.1	98.6	107.0	106.4
汕头	Shantou	101.0	104.4	100.1	101.6	104.5	101.9
佛山	Foshan	102.1	106.3	102.8	101.0	106.6	102.7
韶关	Shaoguan	100.2	104.9	97.5	100.7	104.9	99.7
河源	Heyuan	101.0	104.7	100.5	100.5	104.7	102.6
梅州	Meizhou	100.5	104.7	96.5	101.3	104.7	99.5
惠州	Huizhou	104.2	106.9	107.2	100.0	107.0	106.3
汕尾	Shanwei	101.5	107.2	99.3	101.5	107.2	101.1
东莞	Dongguan	100.6	100.3	100.8	100.3	100.2	100.6
中山	Zhongshan	100.5	105.9	100.0	100.8	105.9	99.4
江门	Jiangmen	103.3	107.0	104.6	101.3	107.1	104.0
阳江	Yangjiang	100.8	102.1	99.5	101.4	102.6	101.3
湛江	Zhanjiang	101.2	104.5	99.1	101.4	104.6	100.8
茂名	Maoming	100.5	105.6	98.6	99.7	105.7	98.1
肇庆	Zhaoqing	101.1	103.9	101.1	99.7	104.1	102.8
清远	Qingyuan	101.0	107.2	99.1	100.4	107.3	100.9
潮州	Chaozhou	102.3	105.4	102.4	101.6	105.4	102.1
揭阳	Jieyang	98.7	105.5	91.3	102.7	105.7	92.2
云浮	Yunfu	102.1	104.4	102.7	100.9	104.4	103.6
按经济区域分	By Region						
珠三角	Pearl River Delta	102.1	105.1	103.1	101.3	105.3	102.9
东翼	Eastern Region	100.6	105.7	98.1	102.0	105.8	99.2
西翼	Western Region	100.8	104.6	99.0	100.6	104.8	99.9
山区	Mountainous Region	100.9	105.4	99.1	100.7	105.4	101.1

2-24 续表 continued

单位：% (%)

市别	City	#建筑业 Construction	#批发和零售业 Wholesale and Retail Trades	#交通运输、仓储和邮政业 Transport, Storage and Post	#住宿和餐饮业 Hotels and Catering Services	#金融业 Financial Interme-diation	#房地产业 Real Estate
广州	Guangzhou	102.0	101.1	94.5	92.8	107.2	94.7
深圳	Shenzhen	105.9	102.7	93.3	89.2	108.2	95.6
珠海	Zhuhai	111.9	90.2	87.7	92.0	106.9	85.9
汕头	Shantou	90.9	98.1	98.7	96.4	107.5	98.9
佛山	Foshan	103.9	100.8	98.3	94.9	108.9	90.6
韶关	Shaoguan	87.7	98.8	96.6	98.1	105.3	97.9
河源	Heyuan	91.7	100.7	94.2	93.6	101.4	93.8
梅州	Meizhou	88.7	97.6	96.1	96.5	106.0	94.1
惠州	Huizhou	116.0	103.3	95.4	93.8	105.2	90.5
汕尾	Shanwei	90.5	101.7	94.3	95.9	106.3	94.3
东莞	Dongguan	106.9	97.5	90.3	96.3	109.0	91.7
中山	Zhongshan	109.7	101.8	99.0	96.3	106.9	92.0
江门	Jiangmen	108.1	98.4	96.3	95.6	107.4	95.7
阳江	Yangjiang	85.9	104.1	96.9	93.6	108.4	93.5
湛江	Zhanjiang	93.1	100.2	95.1	94.4	106.9	98.8
茂名	Maoming	100.1	96.0	92.6	95.2	105.8	99.4
肇庆	Zhaoqing	90.3	100.3	94.2	90.4	107.4	92.8
清远	Qingyuan	85.4	100.0	91.2	92.5	105.5	93.8
潮州	Chaozhou	105.7	99.0	99.4	95.5	106.6	101.8
揭阳	Jieyang	82.6	100.5	107.3	91.3	105.6	102.7
云浮	Yunfu	98.3	100.4	92.8	95.0	105.3	96.6
按经济区域分	By Region						
珠三角	Pearl River Delta	105.4	100.9	94.1	92.6	107.8	93.6
东翼	Eastern Region	90.8	99.7	100.7	94.7	106.7	99.6
西翼	Western Region	95.8	98.8	94.3	94.6	106.9	98.1
山区	Mountainous Region	89.7	99.6	94.2	94.9	104.8	95.0

2-25 各市地区生产总值产业构成（2022年）

Composition of Gross Domestic Product by Industry by City (2022)

单位：% (%)

市别	City	地区生产总值 Gross Domestic Product	第一产业 Primary Industry	第二产业 Secondary Industry	第三产业 Tertiary Industry	#工业 Industry
广州	Guangzhou	100.0	1.1	27.4	71.5	24.1
深圳	Shenzhen	100.0	0.1	38.3	61.6	35.1
珠海	Zhuhai	100.0	1.5	44.7	53.8	39.0
汕头	Shantou	100.0	4.5	47.9	47.5	40.7
佛山	Foshan	100.0	1.7	56.1	42.1	53.1
韶关	Shaoguan	100.0	14.4	35.6	50.0	29.9
河源	Heyuan	100.0	12.5	36.2	51.2	30.0
梅州	Meizhou	100.0	19.6	30.9	49.5	22.6
惠州	Huizhou	100.0	5.1	55.9	39.0	50.3
汕尾	Shanwei	100.0	14.2	37.1	48.7	31.4
东莞	Dongguan	100.0	0.3	58.2	41.5	55.8
中山	Zhongshan	100.0	2.5	49.4	48.1	46.2
江门	Jiangmen	100.0	8.6	45.7	45.7	39.3
阳江	Yangjiang	100.0	16.4	38.8	44.8	35.2
湛江	Zhanjiang	100.0	18.4	39.3	42.3	32.9
茂名	Maoming	100.0	17.9	36.4	45.7	28.3
肇庆	Zhaoqing	100.0	18.0	41.7	40.4	36.7
清远	Qingyuan	100.0	16.3	37.8	46.0	34.0
潮州	Chaozhou	100.0	9.5	47.6	42.8	44.0
揭阳	Jieyang	100.0	9.9	35.1	55.0	32.1
云浮	Yunfu	100.0	18.8	32.5	48.6	27.2
按经济区域分	By Region					
珠三角	Pearl River Delta	100.0	1.8	41.5	56.8	38.0
东翼	Eastern Region	100.0	8.5	42.4	49.1	37.3
西翼	Western Region	100.0	17.8	38.0	44.2	31.3
山区	Mountainous Region	100.0	16.2	35.0	48.8	29.3

2-26 各市人均地区生产总值

Per Capita Gross Domestic Product by City

单位：元 (yuan)

市 别	City	2000	2005	2010	2013	2014	2015	2016
广 州	Guangzhou	25758	54160	86582	104235	107528	111060	113400
深 圳	Shenzhen	33276	61843	99095	124208	130448	135271	142494
珠 海	Zhuhai	28068	45682	80024	100939	109846	117879	127167
汕 头	Shantou	9741	12919	21208	28985	31480	34294	38413
佛 山	Foshan	20231	42434	80511	87194	89742	94608	100699
韶 关	Shaoguan	7028	11608	21996	31726	33954	34854	36682
河 源	Heyuan	3826	7483	15234	22746	25034	26304	29216
梅 州	Meizhou	4731	7684	14315	18997	21115	23083	25402
惠 州	Huizhou	13877	21942	38507	52211	55900	56802	60361
汕 尾	Shanwei	5262	7419	15503	23527	25469	26968	29912
东 莞	Dongguan	13563	33383	53959	60843	63065	66810	72028
中 山	Zhongshan	15077	36800	59411	67973	67955	69129	70352
江 门	Jiangmen	12844	19546	35719	44718	46177	49767	53941
阳 江	Yangjiang	7377	12724	25640	39105	42717	44085	44144
湛 江	Zhanjiang	6231	10269	19945	29047	31487	33184	35602
茂 名	Maoming	7981	12743	25328	36984	40105	41171	44151
肇 庆	Zhaoqing	7422	11505	24875	36171	39625	42333	45151
清 远	Qingyuan	5003	9088	23497	29013	31247	32878	36258
潮 州	Chaozhou	7398	11256	21004	28774	31029	33738	36522
揭 阳	Jieyang	6001	7417	16585	25099	27558	28692	31239
云 浮	Yunfu	6399	8690	16871	25234	27300	29415	31943
按经济区域分	By Region							
珠 三 角	Pearl River Delta	20369	40661	69281	84537	88318	92510	97721
东 翼	Eastern Region	7287	9747	18561	26667	29025	31020	34190
西 翼	Western Region	7099	11626	22912	33719	36618	38027	40284
山 区	Mountainous Region	5345	8847	18338	25198	27411	29028	31676

2-26 续表 continued

单位：元 (yuan)

市 别	City	2017	2018	2019	2020	2021	2022
广 州	Guangzhou	116051	118511	131400	135315	150330	153625
深 圳	Shenzhen	150739	155320	159883	159820	174542	183274
珠 海	Zhuhai	146096	150345	151702	147164	158495	163654
汕 头	Shantou	43295	45672	48953	49191	53463	54504
佛 山	Foshan	105729	109272	114914	113545	127390	132517
韶 关	Shaoguan	39887	42775	46200	48200	54242	54665
河 源	Heyuan	33585	35131	37838	39209	44884	45563
梅 州	Meizhou	27037	28339	30149	31506	33800	34085
惠 州	Huizhou	66007	69206	70949	71220	83032	89157
汕 尾	Shanwei	33049	36976	39910	41532	47996	49242
东 莞	Dongguan	78637	84708	90696	93194	104010	106803
中 山	Zhongshan	71198	72119	72014	72329	80442	81620
江 门	Jiangmen	59244	64163	66622	67027	74654	78146
阳 江	Yangjiang	44816	45526	50031	51937	57827	58556
湛 江	Zhanjiang	39304	42169	43769	44453	50893	52787
茂 名	Maoming	48330	51394	53326	53411	59613	62685
肇 庆	Zhaoqing	48781	51879	55176	56357	64167	65513
清 远	Qingyuan	37858	40198	43228	45514	50289	51001
潮 州	Chaozhou	37053	38822	41885	42834	48414	50988
揭 阳	Jieyang	32124	35235	37192	37243	40748	40192
云 浮	Yunfu	33805	35941	39635	43365	47639	48538
按经济区域分	By Region						
珠 三 角	Pearl River Delta	103863	108094	114120	115880	128684	133437
东 翼	Eastern Region	36677	39560	42375	42842	47425	48190
西 翼	Western Region	43684	46290	48607	49192	55456	57621
山 区	Mountainous Region	34132	36165	38870	41126	45630	46217

2-27 各市人均地区生产总值指数

Indices of Per Capita Gross Domestic Product by City

上年=100 (preceding year=100)

市 别	City	2000	2005	2010	2013	2014	2015	2016
广 州	Guangzhou	108.4	114.3	105.8	106.7	104.4	104.0	102.7
深 圳	Shenzhen	105.8	111.8	107.8	104.6	103.8	102.9	102.7
珠 海	Zhuhai	104.9	110.5	111.4	106.4	106.5	107.0	105.4
汕 头	Shantou	104.5	110.4	107.8	109.8	108.5	108.1	108.4
佛 山	Foshan	106.3	117.7	109.2	105.5	104.8	105.7	106.3
韶 关	Shaoguan	111.8	108.7	113.2	110.7	107.6	105.8	106.0
河 源	Heyuan	111.9	118.3	110.5	112.2	108.8	106.8	107.3
梅 州	Meizhou	108.9	106.5	113.0	111.9	109.6	109.5	108.7
惠 州	Huizhou	107.7	113.2	112.7	109.4	106.4	106.3	105.6
汕 尾	Shanwei	110.2	113.3	116.6	113.2	109.7	108.8	107.9
东 莞	Dongguan	105.1	119.5	105.5	105.0	104.1	106.4	106.8
中 山	Zhongshan	105.4	120.7	108.2	104.2	102.9	104.7	101.7
江 门	Jiangmen	108.7	112.1	112.3	108.9	106.8	107.8	106.7
阳 江	Yangjiang	109.6	112.7	114.8	114.0	109.6	107.2	105.7
湛 江	Zhanjiang	106.0	111.6	113.5	111.9	109.8	108.7	106.9
茂 名	Maoming	110.5	111.9	115.1	113.0	109.9	107.6	107.3
肇 庆	Zhaoqing	109.9	114.1	113.8	109.1	109.3	107.7	104.7
清 远	Qingyuan	108.8	124.7	112.3	107.2	106.7	107.1	108.7
潮 州	Chaozhou	104.3	110.8	112.4	110.6	108.0	110.0	108.9
揭 阳	Jieyang	103.0	110.2	118.3	114.4	110.6	108.2	108.0
云 浮	Yunfu	105.1	111.8	113.3	113.5	110.3	108.4	107.7
按经济区域分	By Region							
珠 三 角	Pearl River Delta	106.5	114.6	108.2	106.3	104.9	105.2	104.6
东 翼	Eastern Region	105.0	111.1	113.1	112.0	109.3	108.6	108.3
西 翼	Western Region	109.0	112.1	114.3	112.8	109.9	108.0	106.8
山 区	Mountainous Region	109.0	113.5	112.3	110.7	108.4	107.6	107.8

2-27 续表 continued

上年=100 (preceding year=100)

市 别	City	2017	2018	2019	2020	2021	2022
广 州	Guangzhou	102.0	102.5	104.4	100.6	106.7	101.0
深 圳	Shenzhen	102.7	102.3	102.8	100.2	105.2	103.2
珠 海	Zhuhai	106.3	101.7	100.6	97.8	104.3	101.8
汕 头	Shantou	108.9	106.7	105.9	101.8	106.0	100.7
佛 山	Foshan	105.8	103.4	104.3	100.1	107.5	101.9
韶 关	Shaoguan	106.3	103.8	105.9	102.9	108.4	100.1
河 源	Heyuan	107.4	106.4	106.0	101.8	108.2	100.9
梅 州	Meizhou	107.8	103.4	104.5	102.6	106.2	100.6
惠 州	Huizhou	105.9	103.9	102.0	99.7	109.6	104.3
汕 尾	Shanwei	109.0	108.9	107.4	105.3	112.7	101.2
东 莞	Dongguan	106.7	106.1	107.0	100.9	108.1	100.8
中 山	Zhongshan	101.2	100.5	99.6	99.9	107.4	100.5
江 门	Jiangmen	107.3	106.8	103.2	101.1	107.4	103.1
阳 江	Yangjiang	105.0	103.1	107.5	103.7	107.7	100.5
湛 江	Zhanjiang	106.9	105.8	104.0	101.9	108.3	100.8
茂 名	Maoming	107.1	104.7	103.1	100.5	106.8	100.0
肇 庆	Zhaoqing	104.6	105.9	105.6	102.3	110.0	100.9
清 远	Qingyuan	103.6	103.3	105.7	103.2	107.7	100.8
潮 州	Chaozhou	106.3	105.0	105.1	101.7	109.5	102.2
揭 阳	Jieyang	105.9	106.2	103.6	100.9	106.6	98.3
云 浮	Yunfu	105.1	104.0	106.4	104.0	107.9	101.9
按经济区域分	By Region						
珠 三 角	Pearl River Delta	104.3	103.6	104.0	100.5	106.8	102.0
东 翼	Eastern Region	107.8	106.6	105.3	102.1	107.8	100.3
西 翼	Western Region	106.7	104.9	104.3	101.7	107.6	100.4
山 区	Mountainous Region	105.9	104.1	105.7	103.0	107.7	100.8

2-28 各市人均地区生产总值指数

Indices of Per Capita Gross Domestic Product by City

2000年=100 (year of 2000=100)

市 别	City	2001	2005	2010	2013	2014	2015	2016
广 州	Guangzhou	110.2	194.3	285.9	333.7	348.3	362.3	372.1
深 圳	Shenzhen	107.2	175.1	264.6	294.1	305.2	314.2	322.5
珠 海	Zhuhai	106.3	162.6	263.9	310.2	330.4	353.4	372.6
汕 头	Shantou	95.8	130.9	203.9	265.2	287.7	310.9	337.0
佛 山	Foshan	108.6	193.1	335.3	385.5	403.9	426.7	453.8
韶 关	Shaoguan	109.7	155.9	291.4	398.7	428.9	453.9	481.2
河 源	Heyuan	109.3	179.3	360.2	505.1	549.4	586.8	629.8
梅 州	Meizhou	107.5	148.1	245.7	344.2	377.2	413.1	449.0
惠 州	Huizhou	105.6	156.9	264.3	340.1	362.0	384.9	406.5
汕 尾	Shanwei	106.2	157.9	318.9	471.8	517.7	563.5	608.0
东 莞	Dongguan	111.8	232.7	356.2	384.9	400.6	426.2	455.3
中 山	Zhongshan	112.9	230.9	351.9	406.2	417.8	437.5	445.0
江 门	Jiangmen	123.6	183.1	311.1	406.8	434.6	468.6	499.8
阳 江	Yangjiang	108.4	163.6	303.7	435.2	477.1	511.4	540.4
湛 江	Zhanjiang	106.0	153.1	264.8	364.5	400.3	435.2	465.0
茂 名	Maoming	108.2	159.2	281.0	387.2	425.6	457.8	491.0
肇 庆	Zhaoqing	106.4	160.6	294.4	393.7	430.3	463.5	485.2
清 远	Qingyuan	104.7	181.4	395.5	473.1	505.0	541.1	587.9
潮 州	Chaozhou	105.8	153.1	268.7	367.6	397.2	436.9	475.8
揭 阳	Jieyang	101.1	123.6	256.5	371.7	411.0	444.8	480.3
云 浮	Yunfu	103.0	139.7	255.8	373.0	411.3	446.0	480.5
按经济区域分	By Region							
珠 三 角	Pearl River Delta	109.4	186.2	294.6	344.4	361.1	379.8	397.4
东 翼	Eastern Region	101.5	140.1	252.3	349.9	382.5	415.2	449.7
西 翼	Western Region	107.6	158.9	283.0	392.9	431.6	466.0	497.8
山 区	Mountainous Region	106.8	158.7	303.2	407.1	441.5	475.0	512.2

2-28 续表 continued

2000年=100 (year of 2000=100)

市 别	City	2017	2018	2019	2020	2021	2022
广 州	Guangzhou	379.6	388.9	406.1	408.6	435.9	440.5
深 圳	Shenzhen	331.3	338.9	348.3	348.8	367.1	379.0
珠 海	Zhuhai	396.1	402.7	405.2	396.4	413.4	420.6
汕 头	Shantou	367.0	391.5	414.7	422.3	447.9	450.9
佛 山	Foshan	480.1	496.3	517.8	518.2	556.8	567.3
韶 关	Shaoguan	511.3	530.9	562.2	578.4	627.0	627.8
河 源	Heyuan	676.3	719.6	762.6	776.0	839.4	846.9
梅 州	Meizhou	484.2	500.5	522.8	536.5	569.8	573.4
惠 州	Huizhou	430.4	446.9	455.9	454.7	498.3	519.6
汕 尾	Shanwei	662.8	721.9	775.6	816.7	920.8	932.0
东 莞	Dongguan	485.9	515.4	551.4	556.2	601.1	606.1
中 山	Zhongshan	450.3	452.7	450.9	450.4	483.7	486.1
江 门	Jiangmen	536.1	572.6	590.8	597.3	641.8	661.5
阳 江	Yangjiang	567.6	585.4	629.3	652.5	702.7	706.4
湛 江	Zhanjiang	497.3	525.9	547.0	557.4	603.9	608.5
茂 名	Maoming	525.7	550.4	567.6	570.3	609.1	609.3
肇 庆	Zhaoqing	507.7	537.5	567.4	580.6	638.7	644.6
清 远	Qingyuan	608.9	629.2	664.8	686.2	739.2	745.5
潮 州	Chaozhou	505.6	531.1	558.4	567.8	621.6	635.0
揭 阳	Jieyang	508.9	540.2	559.9	564.8	602.0	591.6
云 浮	Yunfu	504.8	525.0	558.6	580.9	626.7	638.4
按经济区域分	By Region						
珠 三 角	Pearl River Delta	414.4	429.3	446.5	448.9	479.4	489.2
东 翼	Eastern Region	484.6	516.6	544.2	555.4	599.0	600.6
西 翼	Western Region	531.0	556.9	580.9	590.7	635.6	638.2
山 区	Mountainous Region	542.5	564.9	597.1	614.9	662.5	668.1

2-29 文化及相关产业增加值

Value-added of Culture and related Industry

单位：亿元 (100 million yuan)

指　标	Item	2015	2018	2019	2020	2021
文化及相关产业增加值	**Value-added of Culture and related Industry**	**3879.99**	**5787.81**	**6227.18**	**6210.60**	**6910.06**
分行业大类	Grouped by Sector					
文化制造业	Cultural Manufacturing	2101.45	2327.75	2419.32	2265.07	2575.56
文化批发和零售业	Cultural Wholesale and Retail Sale	282.13	532.89	509.38	506.48	599.55
文化服务业	Cultural Services	1496.41	2927.17	3298.48	3439.05	3734.95
分活动性质	Grouped by Nature of Activities					
文化核心领域	Core Areas of Culture	2003.64	3370.22	3718.36	3855.85	4224.20
新闻信息服务	New Information Services	341.74	835.95	1016.98	1185.11	1153.57
内容创作生产	Content Creation and Production	815.92	1136.88	1241.31	1341.66	1533.50
创意设计服务	Creative Design Services	472.34	835.13	848.30	850.02	954.49
文化传播渠道	Cultural Transmission Channel	231.11	385.48	403.53	333.03	410.80
文化投资运营	Cultural Investment and Operation	21.08	32.05	3.94	31.30	29.87
文化娱乐休闲服务	Culture and Recreation Services	121.45	144.73	204.30	114.73	141.96
文化相关领域	Culture Related Areas	1876.35	2417.58	2508.83	2354.75	2685.85
文化辅助生产和中介服务	Cultural Auxiliary Production and Intermediary Services	644.69	920.49	982.26	935.27	1038.30
文化装备生产	Cultural Equipment Production	449.94	504.19	576.37	496.93	543.79
文化消费终端生产	Cultural Consumer Terminal Production	781.72	992.90	950.20	922.55	1103.76

注：若数据分项合计与总计不等，是由于数值修约误差所致。
Note: If the itemized total data is different from the total，caused by Numerical rounding error.

主要统计指标解释

国内（地区）生产总值 指一个国家（或地区）所有常住单位在一定时期内生产活动的最终成果。国内（地区）生产总值有三种表现形态，即价值形态、收入形态和产品形态。从价值形态看，它是所有常住单位在一定时期内生产的全部货物和服务价值与同期投入的全部非固定资产货物和服务价值的差额，即所有常住单位的增加值之和；从收入形态看，它是所有常住单位在一定时期内创造的各项收入之和，包括劳动者报酬、生产税净额、固定资产折旧和营业盈余；从产品形态看，它是所有常住单位在一定时期内最终使用的货物和服务价值与货物和服务净出口价值之和。在实际核算中，国内（地区）生产总值有三种计算方法，即生产法、收入法和支出法。三种方法分别从不同的方面反映国内（地区）生产总值及其构成。

三次产业 三次产业的划分是世界上较为常用的产业结构分类，但各国的划分不尽一致。根据《国民经济行业分类》（GB/T 4754—2017）和国家统计局 2018 年修订的《三次产业划分规定》，我国的三产产业划分是：

第一产业是指农、林、牧、渔业（不含农、林、牧、渔服务业）。

第二产业是指采矿业（不含开采专业及辅助性活动），制造业（不含金属制品、机械和设备修理业），电力、热力、燃气及水生产和供应业，建筑业。

第三产业即服务业，是指除第一产业、第二产业以外的其他行业。

劳动者报酬 指劳动者从事生产活动应获得的全部报酬，既包括货币形式的报酬，也包括实物形式的报酬。主要包括工资、奖金、津贴和补贴，单位为其员工交纳的社会保险费、补充社会保险费和住房公积金、行政事业单位职工的离退休金、单位为其员工提供的其他各种形式的福利和报酬等。

生产税净额 指生产税减生产补贴后的差额。其中，生产税指政府对生产单位从事生产、销售和经营活动，以及因从事生产活动使用某些生产要素（如固定资产和土地等）所征收的各种税收、附加费和其他规费。生产税分为产品税和其他生产税，产品税主要有：增值税、消费税、进口关税、出口税等；其他生产税主要有：房产税、车船使用税、城镇土地使用税等。生产补贴则相反，它是政府为影响生产单位的生产、销售及定价等生产活动而对其提供的无偿支付，包括农业生产补贴、政策亏损补贴、进口补贴等。生产补贴作为负生产税处理。

固定资产折旧 指由于自然退化、正常淘汰或损耗而导致的固定资产价值下降，用以代表固定资产通过生产过程被转移到其产出中的价值。原则上，固定资产折旧应按照固定资产的重置价值计算。

营业盈余 指常住单位创造的增加值扣除劳动者报酬、生产税净额和固定资产折旧后的余额。

支出法国内生产总值 是从最终使用的角度反映一个国家(或地区)一定时期内生产活动最终成果的一种方法，包括最终消费支出、资本形成总额及货物和服务净出口三部分。计算公式为：

支出法国内生产总值=最终消费支出+资本形成总额+货物和服务净出口

最终消费支出 指常住单位为满足物质、文化和精神生活的需要，从本国经济领土和国外购买的货物和服务的支出。它不包括非常住单位在本国经济领土内的消费支出。最终消费支出分为居民消费支出和政府消费支出。

居民消费支出 指常住住户在一定时期内对于货物和服务的全部最终消费支出。居民消费支出除了直接以货币形式购买的货物和服务的消费支出外，还包括以其他方式获得的货物和服务的消费支出，后者称为虚拟消费支出。居民虚拟消费支出主要包括：单位以实物报酬及实物转移的形式提供给劳动者的货物和服务；住户生产用于自身消费的货物（如自产自用的农产品），以及纳入生产核算范围并用于自身消费的服务（如住户的自有住房服务）；银行和保险机构提供的间接计算的金融服务。

政府消费支出 指政府部门为全社会提供的公共服务的消费支出和免费或以较低的价格向居民住户提供的货物和服务的净支出，前者等于政府服务的产出价值减去政府单位所获得的经营收入的价值，后者等于政府部门免费或以较低价格向居民住户提供的货物和服务的市场价值减去向住户收取的价值。

资本形成总额 指常住单位在一定时期内获得减去处置的固定资产和存货的净额，包括固定资本形成总额和存货变动两部分。

固定资本形成总额 指常住单位在一定时期内获得的固定资产减处置的固定资产的价值总额。固定资产是通过生产活动生产出来的，且其使用年限在一年以上、单位价值在规定标准以上的资产，不包括自然资产、耐用消费品、小型工器具。固定资本形成总额包括住宅、其他建筑和构筑物、机器和设备、培育性生物资源、知识产权产品（研发支出、矿藏的勘探、计算机软件）的价值获得减处置。

存货变动 指常住单位在一定时期内存货实物量变动的市场价值，即期末价值减期初价值的差额，再扣除当期由于价格变动而产生的持有收益。存货变动可以是正值，也可以是负值，正值表示存货上升，负值表示存货下降。存货包括生产单位购进的原材料、燃料和储备物资等存货，以及生产单位生产的产成品、在制品和半成品等存货。

货物和服务净出口 指货物和服务出口减货物和服务进口的差额。出口包括常住单位向非常住单位出售或无偿转让的各种货物和服务的价值；进口包括常住单位从非常住单位购买或无偿得到的各种货物和服务的价值。货物的出口和进口都按离岸价格计算。

新经济增加值占地区生产总值比重 是指新经济增加值占地区生产总值之比。新经济增加值是指一个国家（或地区）所有常住单位在一定时期内从事新产业、新业态、新商业模式经济生产活动的最终成果，是常住单位进行新产业、新业态、新商业模式经济生产活动的增加值之和。

Explanatory Notes on Main Statistical Indicators

Gross Domestic (Regional) Product refers to the final products produced by all resident units in a country during a certain period of time. Gross domestic (regional) product is expressed in three different perspectives, namely value, income, and products respectively. GDP in its value perspective refers to the balance of total value of all goods and services produced by all resident units during a certain period of time, minus the total value of input of goods and services of the nature of non-fixed assets; in other words, it is the sum of the value-added of all resident units. GDP from the perspective of income refers to the sum of all kinds of revenue, including Compensation of Employees, Net Taxes on Production, Depreciation of Fixed Assets, and Operating Surplus. GDP from the perspective of products refers to the value of all goods and services for final demand by all resident units plus the net exports of goods and services during a given period of time. In the practice of national accounting, gross domestic (regional) product is calculated from three approaches, namely production approach, income approach and expenditure approach, which reflect gross domestic (regional) product and its composition from different angles.

Three Strata of Industry Classification of economic activities into three strata of industry is a common practice in the world, although the grouping varies to some extent from country to country. In China, according to Industrial classification for National Economic Activities (GB/T 4754—2017) and Dividing Basis of Three Industries revised by National Bureau of Statistics in 2018, economic activities are categorized into the following three strata of industry:

Primary industry refers to agriculture, forestry, animal husbandry and fishery industries (not including services in support of agriculture, forestry, animal husbandry and fishery industries).

Secondary industry refers to mining and quarrying(not including support activities for mining), manufacturing(not including repair service of metal products, machinery and equipment), production and supply of electricity, heat, gas and water, and construction.

Tertiary industry refers to all other economic activities not included in the primary or secondary industries.

Compensation of Employees refers to the total payment of various forms to employees for the productive activities they are engaged in. It includes the employees earn in cash or in kind. It mainly include: wages, bonuses and allowances, subsidies, social insurance paid by company or unit for its staff, supplementary social insurance, housing fund, the pension for the employees of the administrative institution, other forms of welfare and remuneration provide by the units for its employees.

Net Taxes on Production refers to taxes on production less subsidies on production. The taxes on production refers to the various taxes, extra charges and fees levied on the production units on their production, sale and business activities as well as on the use of some factors of production, such as fixed assets, land etc. in the production activities they are engaged in. Taxes on production are divided into product tax and other kinds of taxes on production, product tax mainly includes: value-added tax, consumption tax, import duty, export duty; other taxes on production mainly include: House Property Tax, Tax on Vehicles and Boat Operation, Urban Land Use Tax, etc. In contrast to taxes on production, subsidies on production refer to the payment by the government for free to the production units to influence production activities of production units such as production, sales and pricing, which include agricultural production subsidies, subsidies for policy losses, import subsidies, etc. Subsidies on production are therefore regarded as negative taxes on production.

Depreciation of Fixed Assets refers to the decline of the value of fixed assets due to natural deterioration, normal elimination or loss, it reflects the value of transfer of the fixed assets in the production of the current period. In principle, the depreciation of fixed assets should be calculated on the basis of the re-purchased value of the fixed assets.

Operating Surplus refers to the balance of the value added created by the resident units after deducting the labourers remuneration, net taxes on production and the depreciation of fixed assets.

Gross Domestic (Regional) Product Calculated by Expenditure Approach refers to the method of measuring the final results of production activities of a country (region) during a given period from the perspective of final uses. It includes final consumption expenditure, gross capital formation and net export of goods and services. The formula for computation is:

GDP by expenditure approach = final consumption expenditure + gross capital formation + net export of goods and services

Final Consumption Expenditure refers to the total expenditure of resident units for purchases of goods and services from both the domestic economic territory and abroad to meet the needs of material, cultural and spiritual life. It does not include the expenditure of non-resident units on consumption in the economic territory of the country. The final consumption expenditure is broken down into household consumption expenditure and government consumption expenditure.

Household Consumption Expenditure refers to the total expenditure of resident households on the final consumption of goods and services. In addition to the consumption of goods and services bought by the households directly with money, the household consumption expenditure also includes expenditure on goods and services obtained by the households in other ways, i.e. the latter so-called imputed consumption expenditure, which mainly includes: (a) the goods and services provided to households by employers in the form of payment in kind and transfer in kind; (b) goods and services produced and consumed by the households themselves (such as self produced agricultural products); (c) financial intermediate services provided by banking and insurance institutions.

Government Consumption Expenditure refers to the consumption expenditure spent for the provision of public services provided by the government to the whole country and the net expenditure on the goods and services provided by the government to households free of charge or at reduced prices. The former equals to the output value of the government services minus the value of operating income obtained by the government departments. The latter equals to the market value of the goods and services provided by the government free of charge or at reduced prices to the households minus the value received by the government from the households.

Gross Capital Formation refers to the fixed assets acquired less disposals and the net value of inventory, thus including gross fixed capital formation and changes in inventories.

Gross Fixed Capital Formation refers to the value of acquisitions less those disposals of fixed assets during a given period. Fixed assets are the assets produced through production activities with unit value above a specified amount and which could be used for over one year. Natural assets, consumer durables, small instruments are not included. Gross Fixed Capital Formation includes the value of housing, other buildings and structure, equipment and machinery, breeding biological resources, intellectual property right product (expenditure for R&D, the prospecting of minerals and the acquisition of computer software) minus the disposal of them.

Changes in Inventories refers to the market value of the change in the physical volume of inventory of resident units during a given period, i.e. the difference between the values at the beginning and at the end of the period minus the gains due to the change in prices. The changes in inventories can have a positive or a negative value. A positive value indicates an increase in inventory while a negative value indicates a decrease in inventory. The inventory includes raw materials, fuels and reserve materials purchased by the production units as well as the inventory of finished products, semi-finished products and work-in-progress.

Net Export of Goods and Services refers to the exports of goods and services subtracting the imports of goods and services. Exports include the value of various goods and services sold or gratuitously transferred by resident units to non-resident units. Imports include the value of various goods and services purchased or gratuitously acquired resident units from non-resident units. Because the provision of services and the use of them happen simultaneously, the acquisition of services by resident units from abroad is usually treated as import while the acquisition of services by non-resident units in this country is usually treated as export. The exports and imports of goods are calculated at FOB.

Percentage of Value-added of New Economy in Gross Domestic Product refers to the percentage of value-added of new economy in GDP. The value -added of new economy refers to the final result of all resident units in a country (or a region) engaging in economic production activities of new industries, new forms of business and new business models during a certain period of time. It is the sum of the value-added of economy production activities of permanent units in new industries, new forms of business and new business models.

三、人口

POPULATION

三 人口

简要说明

一、本篇资料反映广东人口发展变化基本情况，主要内容包括：

1. 年末常住人口、年龄性别比例、城镇人口比例以及人口自然增长。数据由广东省统计局根据人口普查、1%人口抽样调查或年度人口变动情况抽样调查评估测算。

2. 1990-2019年年末常住人口数、出生率、死亡率以及自然增长率，除人口普查和1%人口抽样调查年份直接计算外，其余年份数据均已按人口普查和1%人口抽样调查结果作平滑调整。

3. 年末户籍人口、分性别以及迁移变动等，数据来源于广东省公安厅人口统计年报。

二、本资料由广东省统计局人口和就业统计处整理提供。

3 Population

Brief Introduction

Ⅰ. The data in this chapter show the basic conditions of development and changes of population in Guangdong, including mainly:

（1）Permanent population at the end of the year, age and sex ratio, urban population ratio and natural population growth. The data are evaluated and calculated by Guangdong Provincial Bureau of statistics according to the population census, national one-percent sample survey or annual population change sampling survey.

（2）Permanent population at the year-end, birth rate, death rate and natural growth rate of population from 1990 to 2019 result from smooth adjustment on population census and national one-percent sample survey on population with the exceptions of 1990 and 2020 data, which are direct calculated from the result of population censuses.

（3）Registered residence population at the end of the year by gender and migration change etc, the data are obtained from the annual reports of population of Guangdong Provincial Department of Public Security.

Ⅱ. The date in this chapter are prepared and provided by the Division of Population and Employment Statistics of Statistics Bureau of Guangdong Province.

3-1 人口主要指标
Main Population Indicators

项 目	Item	2000	2010	2015	2020	2021	2022
年末常住人口 （万人）	**Permanent Population at the Year-end (10000 persons)**	**8650.03**	**10440.94**	**11678.00**	**12624.00**	**12684.00**	**12656.80**
男性比例 (%)	Proportion of Male Population (%)	50.90	52.15	52.29	53.07	52.77	52.73
女性比例 (%)	Proportion of Female Population (%)	49.10	47.85	47.71	46.93	47.23	47.27
0-14岁人口比例 (%)	Proportion of Population Aged 0-14 (%)	24.17	16.88	17.37	18.85	18.73	18.47
15-64岁人口比例 (%)	Proportion of Population Aged 15-64 (%)	69.78	76.33	74.15	72.57	72.15	71.94
65岁及以上人口比例(%)	Proportion of Population Aged 65 And Over (%)	6.05	6.79	8.48	8.58	9.12	9.59
城镇人口比例 (%)	Proportion of Urban Population (%)	55.00	66.18	69.51	74.15	74.63	74.79
人口密度（人/平方公里）	Population Density (person/sq.km.)	486	581	650	702	705	704
户籍人口	**Population with Residence Registration**						
年末总户数 （万户）	Total Households at the Year-end (10000 households)	1901.91	2296.61	2415.90	2622.10	2681.91	2734.83
年末总人口 （万人）	Total Population at the Year-end(10000 persons)	7498.54	8521.55	9008.38	9808.66	9946.95	10049.72
性别比 (女=100)	Sex Ratio (female=100)	106.70	106.20	106.08	104.97	104.75	104.57
人口变动情况 （‰）	**Status of Population Changes (‰)**						
出生率	Birth Rate	12.91	11.18	11.12	10.28	9.35	8.30
死亡率	Death Rate	4.77	4.21	4.32	4.70	4.83	4.97
自然增长率	Natural Growth Rate	8.14	6.97	6.80	5.58	4.52	3.33
迁入率	Immigration Rate	16.59	12.07	8.34	14.65	14.65	12.13
迁出率	Emigration Rate	12.94	8.35	7.45	8.71	8.43	7.27
总迁移率	Total Migration Rate	29.53	20.42	15.79	23.37	23.08	19.40
净迁移率	Net Migration Rate	3.65	3.72	0.89	5.94	6.23	4.86
跨省净迁移率	Net Cross-Provincial Migration Rate	1.01	2.52	0.80	5.51	5.87	4.68

3-2 人口自然变动情况

Status of Natural Population Changes

单位：万人、‰ (10000 persons, ‰)

年 份 Year	常住人口 Permanent Population	出生 Birth		死亡 Death		自然增长 Natural Growth		人口密度（人/平方公里） Population Density (person/sq.km.)
		出生人数 Number of Birth	出生率 Birth Rate	死亡人数 Number of Death	死亡率 Death Rate	自然增长人数 Number of Natural Growth	自然增长率 Rate of Natural Growth	
1978	5064.15	111.23	22.14	27.35	5.44	83.88	16.70	285
1980	5230.00	118.31	22.82	28.40	5.48	89.91	17.34	294
1982	5419.35	123.98	23.09	31.79	5.92	92.19	17.17	304
1983	5501.85	114.55	21.00	34.47	6.32	80.08	14.68	309
1984	5585.61	114.86	20.75	34.37	6.21	80.49	14.54	313
1985	5670.65	115.70	20.60	35.53	6.33	80.17	14.27	318
1986	5799.75	126.23	22.15	32.48	5.70	93.75	16.45	323
1987	5931.79	128.00	22.12	32.98	5.70	95.02	16.42	328
1988	6066.84	122.90	20.90	29.81	5.07	93.09	15.83	333
1989	6204.96	121.15	20.27	34.25	5.73	86.90	14.54	338
1990	6347.19	140.11	22.26	36.25	5.76	103.86	16.50	353
1991	6527.01	131.31	20.40	38.04	5.91	93.27	14.49	363
1992	6706.45	125.17	18.92	40.00	6.05	85.17	12.87	373
1993	6936.69	120.00	17.59	38.00	5.57	82.00	12.02	386
1994	7209.58	121.00	17.11	38.00	5.37	83.00	11.74	401
1995	7387.49	123.54	16.93	38.91	5.33	84.63	11.60	411
1996	7569.78	124.80	16.69	42.11	5.63	82.69	11.06	421
1997	7779.69	118.40	15.43	37.83	4.93	80.57	10.50	433
1998	7990.03	117.00	14.84	40.00	5.07	77.00	9.77	444
1999	8217.91	110.00	13.57	39.00	4.81	71.00	8.76	457
2000	8650.03	108.85	12.91	40.21	4.77	68.64	8.14	486
2001	8733.18	107.99	12.42	39.63	4.56	68.36	7.86	486
2002	8842.08	103.94	11.82	39.73	4.52	64.21	7.30	492
2003	8962.69	108.00	12.13	41.98	4.71	66.02	7.42	499
2004	9110.66	106.73	11.81	41.62	4.60	65.11	7.21	507
2005	9194.00	107.11	11.70	42.24	4.68	64.87	7.02	511
2006	9442.07	108.96	11.69	41.53	4.46	67.43	7.24	525
2007	9659.52	112.00	11.73	44.00	4.61	68.00	7.12	537
2008	9893.48	112.00	11.46	43.00	4.40	69.00	7.06	550
2009	10130.19	113.00	11.29	43.00	4.29	70.00	6.99	563
2010	10440.94	115.00	11.18	43.27	4.21	71.73	6.97	581
2011	10756.00	109.44	10.45	45.56	4.35	63.88	6.10	598
2012	11041.00	122.37	11.60	49.06	4.65	73.31	6.95	614
2013	11270.00	113.73	10.71	49.80	4.69	63.93	6.02	627
2014	11489.00	115.39	10.80	50.21	4.70	65.18	6.10	639
2015	11678.00	119.95	11.12	46.60	4.32	73.35	6.80	650
2016	11908.00	129.45	11.85	48.17	4.41	81.28	7.44	663
2017	12141.00	151.63	13.68	50.10	4.52	101.53	9.16	676
2018	12348.00	143.98	12.79	51.22	4.55	92.76	8.24	687
2019	12489.00	143.38	12.54	50.99	4.46	92.38	8.08	695
2020	12624.00	129.08	10.28	59.02	4.70	70.06	5.58	702
2021	12684.00	118.31	9.35	61.12	4.83	57.19	4.52	705
2022	12656.80	105.20	8.30	63.00	4.97	42.20	3.33	704

注：2011—2019年年末常住人口根据2020年第七次全国人口普查结果平滑调整。

Note: Figures of permanent population at the year-end from 2011 to 2019 have been adjusted in accordance with the flash sums of the 7th National Population Census in 2020.

3-3 常住人口构成
Composition of Permanent Population

单位：万人、% (10000 persons, %)

年份 Year	按性别分 By Sex				按城乡分 By Residence			
	男 Male		女 Female		城镇 Urban		农村 Rural	
	人口数 Population	比重 Proportion	人口数 Population	比重 Proportion	人口数 Population	比重 Proportion	人口数 Population	比重 Proportion
1982	2774.17	51.19	2645.18	48.81	972.23	17.94	4447.12	82.06
1990	3249.76	51.20	3097.43	48.80	2335.77	36.80	4011.42	63.20
2000	4402.87	50.90	4247.16	49.10	4757.52	55.00	3892.51	45.00
2005	4655.84	50.64	4538.16	49.36	5578.92	60.68	3615.08	39.32
2006	4787.13	50.70	4654.94	49.30	5948.50	63.00	3493.57	37.00
2007	4926.36	51.00	4733.16	49.00	6099.02	63.14	3560.50	36.86
2008	5065.46	51.20	4828.02	48.80	6269.50	63.37	3623.98	36.63
2009	5166.40	51.00	4963.79	49.00	6422.54	63.40	3707.65	36.60
2010	5444.95	52.15	4995.99	47.85	6909.85	66.18	3531.09	33.82
2011	5689.92	52.90	5066.08	47.10	7160.27	66.57	3595.73	33.43
2012	5807.57	52.60	5233.43	47.40	7414.03	67.15	3626.97	32.85
2013	5871.67	52.10	5398.33	47.90	7673.74	68.09	3596.26	31.91
2014	6081.13	52.93	5407.87	47.07	7883.75	68.62	3605.25	31.38
2015	6106.43	52.29	5571.57	47.71	8117.38	69.51	3560.62	30.49
2016	6239.79	52.40	5668.21	47.60	8353.46	70.15	3554.54	29.85
2017	6372.81	52.49	5768.19	47.51	8588.54	70.74	3552.46	29.26
2018	6443.19	52.18	5904.81	47.82	8867.10	71.81	3480.90	28.19
2019	6528.00	52.27	5961.00	47.73	9073.26	72.65	3415.74	27.35
2020	6699.56	53.07	5924.44	46.93	9360.70	74.15	3263.30	25.85
2021	6693.00	52.77	5991.00	47.23	9466.07	74.63	3217.93	25.37
2022	6673.80	52.73	5983.00	47.27	9465.40	74.79	3191.40	25.21

注：2011—2019年年末常住人口根据2020年第七次全国人口普查结果平滑调整。

Note: Figures of permanent population at the year-end from 2011 to 2019 have been adjusted in accordance with the flash sums of the 7th National Population Census in 2020.

3-4 常住人口年龄结构和抚养比

Age Composition and Dependency Ratio of Permanent Population

单位：万人、% (10000 persons, %)

年份 Year	0—14岁 Aged 0-14		15—64岁 Aged 15-64		65岁及以上 Aged 65 and Over		少年儿童抚养比 Children Dependency Ratio	老年人口抚养比 Old Dependency Ratio	总抚养比 Gross Dependency Ratio
	人数 Population	比重 Proportion	人数 Population	比重 Proportion	人数 Population	比重 Proportion			
1982	1802.68	33.61	3267.68	60.93	292.83	5.46	55.16	8.96	64.12
1990	1879.73	29.92	4030.66	64.15	372.58	5.93	46.64	9.24	55.88
2000	2088.56	24.17	6029.96	69.78	523.65	6.05	34.64	8.67	43.31
2005	1960.16	21.32	6552.56	71.27	681.28	7.41	29.91	10.40	40.31
2006	1935.62	20.50	6807.73	72.10	698.71	7.40	28.43	10.26	38.70
2007	1941.56	20.10	6983.83	72.30	734.12	7.60	27.80	10.51	38.31
2008	1949.02	19.70	7162.88	72.40	781.58	7.90	27.21	10.91	38.12
2009	1955.13	19.30	7364.65	72.70	810.42	8.00	26.55	11.00	37.55
2010	1760.40	16.88	7963.03	76.33	708.62	6.79	22.11	8.90	31.01
2011	1817.76	16.90	8206.83	76.30	731.41	6.80	22.15	8.91	31.06
2012	1766.56	16.00	8501.57	77.00	772.87	7.00	20.78	9.09	29.87
2013	1649.93	14.64	8699.31	77.19	920.76	8.17	18.97	10.58	29.55
2014	1767.01	15.38	8771.85	76.35	950.14	8.27	20.14	10.83	30.98
2015	2028.47	17.37	8659.24	74.15	990.29	8.48	23.43	11.44	34.86
2016	2051.75	17.23	8838.12	74.22	1018.13	8.55	23.21	11.52	34.73
2017	2089.47	17.21	9004.98	74.17	1046.55	8.62	23.20	11.62	34.83
2018	2121.39	17.18	9162.21	74.20	1064.40	8.62	23.15	11.62	34.77
2019	2033.21	16.28	9331.78	74.72	1124.01	9.00	21.79	12.04	33.83
2020	2374.99	18.85	9144.96	72.57	1081.30	8.58	25.97	11.82	37.79
2021	2376.00	18.73	9151.00	72.15	1157.00	9.12	25.97	12.64	38.61
2022	2337.30	18.47	9105.10	71.94	1214.40	9.59	25.67	13.34	39.01

注：1982、1990、2000、2010、2020年常住人口年龄结构使用普查数据，其合计数据与表3-2不一致。

Note: Age composition of permanent population for the years 1982, 1990, 2000, 2010 and 2020 are census year estimates. Therefore, the total data is inconsistent with table 3-2.

3-5 年末户籍总人口

Total Population with Residence Registration at Year-end

单位：万人、% (10000 persons,%)

年份 Year	总人口 Total Population	按性别分 By Sex			
		男 Male		女 Female	
		人口数 Total Population	比例 Proportion	人口数 Total Population	比例 Proportion
1978	5064.15	2586.68	51.08	2477.47	48.92
1980	5227.67	2671.28	51.10	2556.39	48.90
1982	5415.35	2771.86	51.19	2643.49	48.81
1983	5494.12	2818.92	51.31	2675.20	48.69
1984	5576.62	2865.90	51.39	2710.72	48.61
1985	5655.60	2909.52	51.44	2746.08	48.56
1986	5740.70	2955.68	51.49	2785.02	48.51
1987	5832.15	3003.09	51.49	2829.06	48.51
1988	5928.31	3053.50	51.51	2874.81	48.49
1989	6024.98	3106.37	51.56	2918.61	48.44
1990	6246.32	3213.20	51.44	3033.12	48.56
1991	6348.95	3266.26	51.45	3082.69	48.55
1992	6463.17	3327.67	51.49	3135.50	48.51
1993	6581.60	3390.37	51.51	3191.23	48.49
1994	6691.46	3450.68	51.57	3240.78	48.43
1995	6788.74	3501.19	51.57	3287.55	48.43
1996	6896.77	3559.54	51.61	3337.23	48.39
1997	7013.73	3620.32	51.62	3393.41	48.38
1998	7115.65	3676.95	51.67	3438.70	48.33
1999	7298.88	3769.70	51.65	3529.18	48.35
2000	7498.54	3871.13	51.63	3627.41	48.37
2001	7565.33	3905.28	51.62	3660.05	48.38
2002	7649.29	3948.25	51.62	3701.04	48.38
2003	7723.42	3989.24	51.65	3734.18	48.35
2004	7804.75	4025.87	51.58	3778.88	48.42
2005	7899.64	4080.74	51.66	3818.90	48.34
2006	8048.71	4154.03	51.61	3894.68	48.39
2007	8156.05	4204.47	51.55	3951.58	48.45
2008	8267.09	4263.24	51.57	4003.85	48.43
2009	8365.98	4309.11	51.51	4056.87	48.49
2010	8521.55	4388.61	51.50	4132.94	48.50
2011	8637.19	4445.48	51.47	4191.71	48.53
2012	8635.89	4448.45	51.51	4187.44	48.49
2013	8759.46	4513.51	51.53	4245.95	48.47
2014	8886.88	4577.10	51.50	4309.78	48.50
2015	9008.38	4637.13	51.48	4371.25	48.52
2016	9164.90	4717.29	51.47	4447.61	48.53
2017	9316.91	4788.55	51.40	4528.36	48.60
2018	9502.12	4877.64	51.33	4624.48	48.67
2019	9663.41	4955.32	51.28	4708.09	48.72
2020	9808.66	5023.14	51.21	4785.52	48.79
2021	9946.95	5088.93	51.16	4858.02	48.84
2022	10049.72	5137.03	51.12	4912.69	48.88

3-6 户籍人口迁移变动情况

Status of Migrant Changes

单位：万人、‰ (10000 persons, ‰)

年份 Year	迁入 Immigration		迁出 Emigration		总迁移 Total Migration		净迁移 Net Migration	
	迁入人数 Number of Immigration	迁入率 Immigration Rate	迁出人数 Number of Emigration	迁出率 Emigration Rate	总迁人数 Total Number of Migration	总迁移率 Total Migration Rate	净迁移人数 Net Number of Migration	净迁移率 Net Migration Rate
1978	81.83	16.29	75.58	15.04	157.41	31.33	6.25	1.25
1980	91.45	17.64	82.09	15.83	173.54	33.47	9.36	1.81
1982	71.63	13.34	65.06	12.11	136.69	25.45	6.57	1.23
1983	66.26	12.14	59.35	10.88	125.61	23.02	6.91	1.26
1984	92.30	16.67	83.31	15.05	175.61	31.72	8.99	1.62
1985	100.10	17.82	84.90	15.12	185.00	32.94	15.20	2.70
1986	85.61	15.02	70.83	12.43	156.44	27.45	14.78	2.59
1987	92.89	16.05	73.26	12.66	166.15	28.71	19.63	3.39
1988	93.82	15.96	73.46	12.49	167.28	28.45	20.36	3.47
1989	95.26	15.94	73.87	12.36	169.13	28.30	21.39	3.58
1990	94.39	15.38	77.07	12.56	171.46	27.94	17.32	2.82
1991	97.23	15.44	83.74	13.30	180.97	28.74	13.49	2.14
1992	135.89	21.21	108.39	16.92	244.28	38.13	27.50	4.29
1993	158.20	24.25	128.06	19.63	286.26	43.88	30.14	4.62
1994	140.93	21.24	115.72	17.44	256.65	38.68	25.21	3.80
1995	108.09	16.04	89.74	13.31	197.83	29.35	18.35	2.73
1996	113.47	16.58	88.88	12.99	202.35	29.57	24.59	3.59
1997	130.94	18.83	98.90	14.22	229.84	33.05	32.04	4.61
1998	117.93	16.69	94.18	13.33	212.11	30.02	23.75	3.36
1999	107.68	14.94	89.13	12.37	196.81	27.31	18.55	2.57
2000	122.72	16.59	95.76	12.94	218.48	29.53	26.96	3.65
2001	109.88	14.59	92.34	12.26	202.22	26.85	17.54	2.33
2002	102.26	13.44	81.95	10.77	184.21	24.21	20.31	2.67
2003	105.27	13.70	83.22	10.83	188.49	24.53	22.05	2.87
2004	133.91	17.25	104.26	13.43	238.17	30.68	29.65	3.82
2005	107.21	13.65	70.45	8.97	177.66	22.62	36.76	4.68
2006	145.49	18.25	80.56	10.10	226.05	28.35	64.93	8.14
2007	119.95	14.80	71.67	8.85	191.62	23.65	48.28	5.96
2008	110.56	13.46	79.47	9.68	190.03	23.14	31.09	3.79
2009	96.80	11.64	64.93	7.81	161.73	19.45	31.87	3.83
2010	101.90	12.07	70.48	8.35	172.38	20.42	31.43	3.72
2011	94.47	11.01	65.37	7.62	159.84	18.63	29.10	3.39
2012	97.91	11.34	112.62	13.04	210.53	24.38	-14.70	-1.70
2013	97.86	11.25	77.72	8.94	175.58	20.19	20.14	2.32
2014	93.48	10.60	68.29	7.74	161.78	18.34	25.19	2.85
2015	74.65	8.34	66.67	7.45	141.32	15.79	7.98	0.89
2016	88.31	9.72	73.84	8.13	162.15	17.84	14.47	1.59
2017	133.09	14.40	85.91	9.30	219.00	23.70	47.18	5.11
2018	160.20	17.02	95.20	10.12	255.40	27.14	64.99	6.91
2019	148.35	15.48	84.90	8.86	233.25	24.34	63.45	6.62
2020	142.67	14.65	84.82	8.71	227.50	23.37	57.85	5.94
2021	144.74	14.65	83.24	8.43	227.98	23.08	61.50	6.23
2022	121.27	12.13	72.68	7.27	193.94	19.40	48.59	4.86

3-7 各市年末常住人口数

Permanent Population at Year-end by City

单位：万人 (10000 persons)

市 别	City	2000	2005	2010	2016	2017	2018	2019	2020	2021	2022
全 省	**Provincial Total**	**8650.03**	**9194.00**	**10440.94**	**11908.00**	**12141.00**	**12348.00**	**12489.00**	**12624.00**	**12684.00**	**12656.80**
广 州	Guangzhou	994.80	949.68	1270.96	1678.38	1746.27	1798.13	1831.21	1874.03	1881.06	1873.41
深 圳	Shenzhen	701.24	827.75	1043.76	1501.51	1587.31	1666.12	1710.40	1763.38	1768.16	1766.18
珠 海	Zhuhai	123.65	141.57	156.16	195.98	207.02	220.90	233.18	244.96	246.67	247.72
汕 头	Shantou	467.78	494.45	539.62	546.46	547.51	548.59	549.31	550.37	553.04	554.19
佛 山	Foshan	534.05	580.03	719.91	874.77	899.99	926.04	943.14	951.88	961.26	955.23
韶 关	Shaoguan	273.65	292.26	283.02	283.95	284.47	284.78	285.07	285.53	286.01	286.18
河 源	Heyuan	226.78	278.24	295.82	289.13	287.38	285.89	284.83	283.56	284.09	284.17
梅 州	Meizhou	380.52	411.84	424.46	403.76	400.02	395.51	391.96	387.10	387.69	385.80
惠 州	Huizhou	321.80	370.69	460.11	562.73	572.22	584.72	597.23	605.72	606.60	605.02
汕 尾	Shanwei	245.71	279.87	287.34	274.87	272.55	270.50	268.85	266.94	268.69	268.26
东 莞	Dongguan	644.84	656.07	822.48	1016.58	1038.22	1043.77	1045.50	1048.36	1053.68	1043.70
中 山	Zhongshan	236.47	243.46	312.27	407.69	418.04	428.82	438.73	443.11	446.69	443.11
江 门	Jiangmen	395.24	410.29	445.08	461.85	465.12	470.38	475.32	480.41	483.51	482.22
阳 江	Yangjiang	217.20	232.14	242.53	254.02	255.73	257.26	259.09	260.59	262.07	262.22
湛 江	Zhanjiang	603.43	668.95	700.38	698.49	698.30	698.23	698.16	698.07	703.09	703.54
茂 名	Maoming	524.82	584.04	582.64	593.72	598.52	605.95	612.26	618.00	621.97	623.82
肇 庆	Zhaoqing	337.69	367.60	392.22	401.75	403.88	406.58	409.24	411.69	412.97	412.84
清 远	Qingyuan	314.98	359.37	370.38	388.32	390.66	393.12	395.48	397.40	398.28	398.57
潮 州	Chaozhou	240.44	252.01	267.21	259.46	259.09	258.81	258.29	256.66	257.46	257.56
揭 阳	Jieyang	524.61	559.69	588.30	576.60	570.62	565.81	563.42	557.87	561.68	563.41
云 浮	Yunfu	215.49	233.99	236.29	237.98	238.07	238.09	238.33	238.37	239.33	239.65
按经济区域分	By Region										
珠 三 角	Pearl River Delta	4289.78	4547.14	5622.95	7101.24	7338.07	7545.46	7683.95	7823.54	7860.60	7829.43
东 翼	Eastern Region	1478.54	1586.02	1682.47	1657.39	1649.77	1643.71	1639.87	1631.84	1640.87	1643.42
西 翼	Western Region	1345.45	1485.13	1525.55	1546.23	1552.55	1561.44	1569.51	1576.66	1587.13	1589.58
山 区	Mountainous Region	1411.42	1575.70	1609.97	1603.14	1600.60	1597.39	1595.67	1591.96	1595.40	1594.37

注：1.2000年全省数据含根据普查误差率推算的漏登人口。
2.2006—2009年年末常住人口根据2010年第六次全国人口普查结果平滑调整。
3.2010年开始，深圳市包含深汕合作区人口。
4.2011—2019年年末常住人口根据2020年第七次全国人口普查结果平滑调整。

Note: a)Data for the permanent population of 2000 has been adjusted to account for the unregistered population,per the Population Census Error Rate.
b)Data for the permanent population from 2006 to 2009 have been adjusted with flash sums from the 6th National Population Census in 2010.
c)Data for the 2010 permanent population of Shenzhen includes the permanent population of the Shenshan Special Cooperation Zone.
d)Figures of permanent population at the year-end from 2011 to 2019 have been adjusted in accordance with the flash sums of the 7th National Population Census in 2020.

3-8 各市城镇人口占常住人口的比例

Proportion of Urban Population to Permanent Population by City

单位：% (%)

市别	City	2000	2005	2010	2016	2017	2018	2019	2020	2021	2022
全省	**Provincial Total**	**55.00**	**60.68**	**66.18**	**70.15**	**70.74**	**71.81**	**72.65**	**74.15**	**74.63**	**74.79**
广州	Guangzhou	83.79	91.51	83.79	84.35	84.41	84.75	85.13	86.19	86.46	86.48
深圳	Shenzhen	92.46	100.00	99.76	99.85	99.80	99.82	99.52	99.54	99.81	99.79
珠海	Zhuhai	85.48	87.90	87.66	88.25	88.34	88.79	89.21	90.47	90.75	90.76
汕头	Shantou	67.00	72.34	68.47	69.11	69.22	69.58	69.96	70.70	70.74	70.75
佛山	Foshan	75.06	78.39	94.10	94.33	94.36	94.50	94.67	95.20	95.21	95.22
韶关	Shaoguan	51.13	49.76	52.54	53.87	54.10	55.11	55.96	57.33	58.13	58.54
河源	Heyuan	26.53	32.47	40.06	42.38	42.81	44.59	46.13	48.50	49.75	50.25
梅州	Meizhou	37.21	41.63	43.03	45.44	45.91	47.59	49.10	51.58	52.38	52.68
惠州	Huizhou	51.66	55.01	61.85	65.08	65.67	67.61	69.61	72.80	72.90	72.91
汕尾	Shanwei	52.58	51.88	54.03	54.80	54.82	55.32	56.29	57.12	57.56	57.86
东莞	Dongguan	60.04	73.02	88.47	89.34	89.44	89.93	90.31	92.15	92.24	92.25
中山	Zhongshan	60.67	74.29	87.84	87.32	87.24	87.15	87.06	86.96	87.00	87.02
江门	Jiangmen	47.08	56.78	62.31	63.85	64.13	65.12	66.04	67.63	67.84	67.85
阳江	Yangjiang	41.92	44.09	46.82	48.82	49.18	50.77	52.08	54.16	54.96	55.26
湛江	Zhanjiang	38.47	39.71	36.69	39.22	39.72	41.33	42.88	45.46	46.46	47.31
茂名	Maoming	37.45	39.30	35.08	37.51	37.99	39.58	41.09	43.56	45.06	45.84
肇庆	Zhaoqing	32.52	38.99	42.40	44.83	45.30	46.99	48.52	51.02	51.91	52.14
清远	Qingyuan	32.60	38.46	47.56	49.53	49.89	51.26	52.47	54.50	55.40	56.30
潮州	Chaozhou	43.41	53.62	62.78	63.18	63.24	63.55	63.82	64.19	64.80	64.81
揭阳	Jieyang	37.91	41.15	47.33	48.29	48.47	49.09	49.68	50.65	51.52	51.93
云浮	Yunfu	35.86	37.26	36.97	38.80	39.14	40.65	41.90	43.77	44.55	45.04
按经济区域分	By Region										
珠三角	Pearl River Delta	71.59	77.32	82.71	84.75	85.04	85.66	86.10	87.24	87.47	87.48
东翼	Eastern Region	50.45	54.75	57.71	58.56	58.73	59.23	59.78	60.60	61.07	61.26
西翼	Western Region	38.64	40.23	37.69	40.14	40.61	42.21	43.70	46.15	47.31	48.04
山区	Mountainous Region	36.96	40.16	44.31	46.39	46.77	48.26	49.56	51.62	52.52	53.06

注：1.本表2000年、2005年数据按国家统计局1999年发布的《关于统计上划分城乡的规定（试行）》计算；2006年起数据按国家统计局2006年颁布的《关于统计上划分城乡的暂行规定》计算。
2.2006—2009年年末常住人口根据2010年第六次全国人口普查结果平滑调整，城镇人口比例也作相应调整。
3.2011—2019年年末常住人口根据2020年第七次全国人口普查结果平滑调整，城镇人口比例也作相应调整。

Note: a) The 2000 and 2005 data in this table are calculated according to Interim Regulations on Statistical Classification of Urban and Rural Populationissued by National Bureau of Statistics in 1999. The 2006 data are calculated according to Provisional Regulations on Statistical Classification of Urban and Rural Population issued by National Bureau of Statistics in 2006.
b) Figures of permanent population at the year-end from 2006 to 2009 have been adjusted in accordance with the flash sums of the 6th National Population Census in 2010 and the proportion of urban population to permanent population is also adjusted.
c) Figures of permanent population at the year-end from 2011 to 2019 have been adjusted in accordance with the flash sums of the 7th National Population Census in 2020. and the proportion of urban population to permanent population is also adjusted.

3-9 各市年末户籍人口数（2022年）

Total Population with Residence Registration at Year-end by City (2022)

单位：万人、% (10000 persons,%)

市别	City	总人口 Total Population	按性别分 By Sex			
			男 Male		女 Female	
			人口数 Total Population	比例 Proportion	人口数 Total Population	比例 Proportion
全　省	**Provincial Total**	**10049.72**	**5137.03**	**51.12**	**4912.69**	**48.88**
广　州	Guangzhou	1034.91	511.55	49.43	523.36	50.57
深　圳	Shenzhen	654.74	322.89	49.32	331.85	50.68
珠　海	Zhuhai	154.99	75.48	48.70	79.51	51.30
汕　头	Shantou	578.84	291.57	50.37	287.27	49.63
佛　山	Foshan	495.40	238.80	48.20	256.60	51.80
韶　关	Shaoguan	336.71	173.91	51.65	162.80	48.35
河　源	Heyuan	371.27	191.64	51.62	179.62	48.38
梅　州	Meizhou	539.35	279.76	51.87	259.59	48.13
惠　州	Huizhou	415.77	206.82	49.74	208.95	50.26
汕　尾	Shanwei	364.53	190.72	52.32	173.82	47.68
东　莞	Dongguan	292.45	142.16	48.61	150.29	51.39
中　山	Zhongshan	208.13	99.01	47.57	109.12	52.43
江　门	Jiangmen	403.41	201.72	50.00	201.69	50.00
阳　江	Yangjiang	303.23	160.89	53.06	142.34	46.94
湛　江	Zhanjiang	869.28	464.26	53.41	405.02	46.59
茂　名	Maoming	825.97	443.54	53.70	382.43	46.30
肇　庆	Zhaoqing	458.35	238.74	52.09	219.61	47.91
清　远	Qingyuan	453.50	235.56	51.94	217.94	48.06
潮　州	Chaozhou	274.75	139.71	50.85	135.05	49.15
揭　阳	Jieyang	712.71	368.80	51.75	343.91	48.25
云　浮	Yunfu	301.43	159.52	52.92	141.91	47.08
按经济区域分	By Region					
珠三角	Pearl River Delta	4118.15	2037.16	49.47	2081.00	50.53
东　翼	Eastern Region	1930.83	990.79	51.31	940.04	48.69
西　翼	Western Region	1998.48	1068.69	53.48	929.79	46.52
山　区	Mountainous Region	2002.26	1040.40	51.96	961.86	48.04

3-10 各市年末户籍迁移人口数（2022年）
Number of Migrant Population at the Year-end by City (2022)

单位：人 (person)

市别	City	迁入 Immigration		迁出 Emigration		净迁移 Net Migration	
		省内迁入 Within Guangdong	省外迁入 Outside Guangdong	迁往省内 Within Guangdong	迁往省外 Outside Guangdong	省内 Within Guangdong	省外 Outside Guangdong
全　省	**Provincial Total**	**618169**	**594484**	**600175**	**126582**	**17994**	**467902**
广　州	Guangzhou	114402	103296	17760	18725	96642	84571
深　圳	Shenzhen	77113	142501	14042	24515	63071	117986
珠　海	Zhuhai	28602	39644	4100	4398	24502	35246
汕　头	Shantou	7896	5022	29621	4138	-21725	884
佛　山	Foshan	52553	48765	10738	3985	41815	44780
韶　关	Shaoguan	7374	5728	25552	3112	-18178	2616
河　源	Heyuan	6084	3971	29903	3995	-23819	-24
梅　州	Meizhou	5816	4250	49157	3907	-43341	343
惠　州	Huizhou	68963	51065	47556	5971	21407	45094
汕　尾	Shanwei	16385	4150	37494	6957	-21109	-2807
东　莞	Dongguan	43572	80726	5019	2547	38553	78179
中　山	Zhongshan	35802	51355	3511	1726	32291	49629
江　门	Jiangmen	27049	13882	29705	5296	-2656	8586
阳　江	Yangjiang	2501	2134	14651	1561	-12150	573
湛　江	Zhanjiang	21863	5032	56503	6861	-34640	-1829
茂　名	Maoming	34293	5706	62687	9865	-28394	-4159
肇　庆	Zhaoqing	19241	7535	29880	2875	-10639	4660
清　远	Qingyuan	12047	7875	21087	2896	-9040	4979
潮　州	Chaozhou	2381	1646	14376	1686	-11995	-40
揭　阳	Jieyang	27803	7743	74087	9001	-46284	-1258
云　浮	Yunfu	6429	2458	22746	2565	-16317	-107
按经济区域分	By Region						
珠三角	Pearl River Delta	467297	538769	162311	70038	304986	468731
东　翼	Eastern Region	54465	18561	155578	21782	-101113	-3221
西　翼	Western Region	58657	12872	133841	18287	-75184	-5415
山　区	Mountainous Region	37750	24282	148445	16475	-110695	7807

主要统计指标解释

总人口 指一定时点、一定地区范围内有生命的个人的总和。按不同的统计范围可分为常住人口和户籍人口；统计时点通常为每年 12 月 31 日 24 时。

0-14 岁人口比例 （少年儿童人口系数或少年儿童人口比例） 指 0-14 岁的少年儿童人口与同期总人口之比，反映人口的年龄结构特征。通常以百分比表示。

15-64 岁人口比例 （成年人口系数或成年人口比例） 指 15-64 岁的成年人口与同期总人口之比，反映人口的年龄结构特征。通常以百分比表示。

65 岁及以上人口比例 （老年人口系数或老年人口比例） 指 65 岁及以上的老年人口与同期总人口之比，反映人口的老龄化程度。通常以百分比表示。

城镇人口比例 指城镇人口与同期总人口之比，反映该区域人口的城镇化水平。通常以百分比表示。

人口密度 指某一时点单位土地面积上居住的人口数。通常以每平方公里常住的人口数表示。

性别比 总人口（或分年龄人口）中男性人数与女性人数之比。通常以每 100 个女性人口相应有多少男性人口表示。

其计算公式为：性别比=男性人口数/女性人口数×100

出生率 也称粗出生率。指某一人口在一定时期（通常为一年）内活产婴儿数与同期总人口的生存人口数（或同期平均总人口、年中人口数）之比。通常以千分比表示。

死亡率 也称粗死亡率。指一定时期（通常为一年）内全部死亡人数与同期平均总人口之比，反映该时期人口的死亡强度。通常以千分比表示。

自然增长率 指一定时期（通常为一年）内人口自然增加数（出生人口减死亡人口）与同期平均总人口之比。通常以千分比表示。

迁入率（迁出率） 指一定时期（通常为一年）内迁入（迁出）人数与同期平均总人口之比。通常以千分比表示。

总迁移率 指一定时期（通常为一年）内人口迁移总量（迁入人口加迁出人口）与同期平均总人口之比。通常以千分比表示。

净迁移率 指一定时期（通常为一年）内人口迁入迁出相抵后（迁入人口减迁出人口）与同期平均总人口之比。通常以千分比表示。

跨省净迁移率 指一定时期（通常为一年）内省外迁入人口和迁往省外（含出国）人口之差与同期平均总人口之比。通常以千分比表示。

总抚养比 总抚养比也称总负担系数，是指人口总体中非劳动年龄人口数（0-14 岁人口+65 岁及以上人口）与劳动年龄人口数（15-64 岁人口）之比，通常用百分比表示。

少年儿童抚养比 少年儿童抚养比也称少年儿童抚养系数，是指某一人口中少年儿童人口数（0-14 岁人口）与劳动年龄人口数（15-64 岁人口）之比，通常用百分比表示。

老年人口抚养比 老年人口抚养比也称老年人口抚养系数，是指某一人口中老年人口数（65 岁及以上人口）与劳动年龄人口数（15-64 岁人口）之比，通常用百分比表示。

Explanatory Notes on Main Statistical Indicators

Total Population refers to the total number of people alive within a given area at a certain point of time. It can be divided into the permanent population and the population with residence registration according to different statistical coverage. The reference time of the statistics on total population is usually taken at midnight of December 31.

Proportion of Population Aged 0-14 (coefficient of child population or proportion of child population) refers to the proportion of population aged 0-14 in the total population during the same period of time. It is an indicator of age structure, usually expressed in percentage.

Proportion of Population Aged 15-64 (coefficient of adult population or proportion of adult population) refers to the proportion of population aged 15-64 in the total population during the same period of time. It is an indicator of age structure, usually expressed in percentage.

Proportion of Population Aged 65 and Over (coefficient of aged population or proportion of aged population) refers to the proportion of population aged 65 and over in the total population during the same period of time. It is an indicator of population ageing, usually expressed in percentage.

Proportion of Urban Population refers to the proportion of urban population in the total population during the same period of time. It is an indicator of population urbanization in a certain region, usually expressed in percentage.

Population Density refers to the number of people located in a given land area at a certain point of time, usually expressed in the number of permanent population per square kilometer.

Sex Ratio refers to the ratio of the male population to the female population among the total population (or population grouped by age), usually expressed in the number of males per 100 females.

The following formula is used:

Sex Ration = Number of Male Population / Number of Female Population ×100

Birth Rate (or Crude Birth Rate) refers to the ratio of live births to the total number of population alive (or average population, mid-year population) during a certain period of time (usually one year), expressed in ‰.

Death Rate (or Crude Death Rate) refers to the ratio of deaths to the average population during a certain period of time (usually one year), expressed in ‰. Death rate reflects the death intensity of the population during the same period of time.

Natural Growth Rate refers to the ratio of natural increase in population (number of births minus number of deaths) during a certain period of time (usually one year) to the average population of the same period, expressed in ‰.

Immigration Rate (Emigration Rate) refers to the ratio of the number of immigration (emigration) to the average population during a certain period of time (usually one year), expressed in ‰.

Total Migration Rate refers to the ratio of the total number of migration (number of immigration plus number of emigration) to the average population during a certain period of time (usually one year),expressed in ‰.

Net Migration Rate refers to the ratio of the net number of migration (number of immigration minus number of emigration) to the average population during a certain period of time (usually one year), expressed in ‰

Net Migration Rate across Province refers to the ratio of the number of immigration from outside the province minus the number of emigration to outside the province (including those going abroad) to the average population during a certain period of time (usually one year), expressed in ‰.

Total Dependency Ratio Total dependency ratio is also called total burden coefficient,refers to the ratio of the number of people of non working age (0-14 years old+65 years old and above) to the number of people of working age (15-64 years old) in the population, usually expressed as a percentage.

Child Dependency ratio Child dependency ratio is also called child dependency coefficient,refers to the ratio of the population of children (0-14 years old) to the population of working age (15-64 years old) in a certain population, usually expressed as a percentage.

Old Age Dependency Ratio The dependency ratio of the elderly population is also called the dependency coefficient of the elderly population,refers to the ratio of the number of middle-aged and elderly people (65 years old and above) to the number of working age people (15-64 years old), usually expressed as a percentage.

四、就业和工资

EMPLOYMENT AND WAGES

四　就业和工资

简要说明

一、本篇资料反映广东劳动就业与工资的基本情况。主要内容包括全社会就业人员数，城镇非私营单位就业人员、在岗职工人数，城镇非私营单位就业人员、在岗职工工资总额、平均工资。

二、本篇资料由广东省统计局人口和就业统计处整理提供。

三、本篇资料主要根据国家统计调查制度搜集汇总。

四、本篇资料中的城镇单位就业人员、在岗职工及其工资统计范围只包括城镇国有、集体及其他经济类型单位，不包括私营企业和个体劳动者。根据国家劳动统计报表制度的统一规定，从2013年年报起，将原属于乡镇企业且符合城镇非私营单位条件的“四上”企业（即规模以上工业企业、有资质的建筑业及全部房地产开发经营企业、限额以上批发和零售业、限额以上住宿和餐饮业、部分规模以上服务业企业）纳入城镇单位就业人员及工资统计的范围。

五、1998 年，劳动统计年报中对全部调查单位改按企业登记注册类型分组。即国有单位中不再包括国有联营和有限责任公司中的国有独资公司；城镇集体单位中不再包括集体联营和股份合作企业；其他单位则包括国有联营和有限责任公司中的国有独资公司，集体联营和股份合作企业。

4 Employment and Wages

Brief Introduction

Ⅰ. The data in this chapter reflects the basic situation of labor employment and wages in Guangdong Province. The main content includes the number of employees in the whole society, the number of Urban Non private employees and on-the-job employees, the total wages and average wages of Urban Non private employees and on-the-job employees etc.

Ⅱ. The data in this chapter are prepared and provided by the Division of Population and Employment Statistics of Statistics Bureau of Guangdong Province.

Ⅲ. The data in this chapter are collected and tabulated mainly in accordance with the statistical survey scheme of the National Bureau of Statistics.

Ⅳ. The statistical coverage of urban unit employed persons, fully employed staff and workers, staff and workers and wages in this chapter only includes state-owned units, collective-owned units and other types of ownership in urban areas, but excludes private enterprises and self-employed individuals. According to the The National Reporting Form System on Labour Wage Statistics, from the 2013 annual report.,the four enterprises original part of township enterprise and urban corporate unit excluding private units those are industrial enterprises above designated size,quality of the construction industry and real estate development enterprises,wholesale and retail trade enterprises above designated size, hotels and catering service enterprises above designated size and part of the service industry above designated size, are brought into the scope of statistics on employed person in urban areas and total wage bills.

Ⅴ. In annual labor reports since 1998, survey units are categorized by registration status. As a result, exclusively state-invested companies in state-owned joint ownership units and limited liability companies are no longer entered as state-owned units, and collective-owned joint ownership units and cooperative units are no longer entered as urban collective-owned units. These units excluded from the categories of state-owned joint ownership units and urban collective-owned units are now categorized as units of other types of ownership.

4-1 就业基本情况
Employment

指　标	Item	2000	2010	2015	2020	2021	2022
就业人员（万人）	**Number of Employed Persons (10000 persons)**	**3989.32**	**6051.00**	**6566.00**	**7039.00**	**7072.00**	**6904.00**
第一产业	Primary Industry	1593.68	1476.00	1046.00	767.00	753.00	722.00
第二产业	Secondary Industry	1114.86	2566.00	2627.00	2526.00	2565.00	2524.00
第三产业	Tertiary Industry	1280.78	2009.00	2893.00	3746.00	3754.00	3658.00
按城乡分就业人员（万人）	**Number of Employed Persons by Urban and Rural Areas (10 000 persons)**						
城镇就业人员	Urban Employed Persons		4004.55	4822.00	5418.00	5473.00	5389.00
乡村就业人员	Rural Employed Persons		2046.45	1744.00	1621.00	1599.00	1515.00
#城镇非私营单位就业人员（万人）	Urban Employed Persons (10000 persons)	759.21	1118.52	1948.04	2085.27	2110.88	2066.65
国有单位	State-owned Units	425.52	400.65	388.81	423.26	431.54	438.30
城镇集体单位	Urban Collective-owned Units	105.97	57.66	50.34	36.85	36.32	33.06
其他各种单位	Units of Other Types of Ownership	227.73	660.21	1508.89	1625.16	1643.02	1595.29
城镇非私营单位就业人员工资总额（亿元）	**Earnings of Urban Employed Persons (100 million yuan)**	**1057.57**	**4484.29**	**12918.81**	**22421.98**	**24978.70**	**26200.89**
国有单位	State-owned Units	612.17	1951.16	2975.96	6287.53	6855.32	7272.19
城镇集体单位	Urban Collective-owned Units	93.04	129.01	227.71	261.87	273.36	256.00
其他各种单位	Units of Other Types of Ownership	352.37	2404.12	9715.14	15872.58	17850.02	18672.70
城镇非私营单位就业人员年平均工资（元）	**Average Labor Remuneration of Urban Employed Persons (yuan)**	**13859**	**40432**	**65788**	**108045**	**118133**	**124916**
国有单位	State-owned Units	14296	49027	76870	149783	160329	167521
城镇集体单位	Urban Collective-owned Units	8605	22453	45027	72174	76875	78973
其他各种单位	Units of Other Types of Ownership	15538	36779	63664	98028	108095	114489

注：2006—2009年就业人员人数，根据第六次全国人口普查资料作了相应调整。从2020年起，国家统计局对各省、自治区、直辖市就业人数及其产业构成以常住人口口径统一测算，同时对2010—2019年就业人数及其产业、城乡结构进行平滑修正。

Note: The number of Employed Persons from 2006 to 2009 have been adjusted in accordance with the data of the 6th National Census. Since 2020, the National Bureau of Statistics calculates the number of Employed Persons and Industrial Composition of all Province、Autonomous Region and Municipality directly under the Central Government according to the caliber of permanent population, also adjusted the number of Employed Persons and Industrial Structure from 2010 to 2019.

4-2 就业人员年末人数
Number of Employed Persons at the Year-end

单位：万人 (10000 persons)

年份 Year	就业人员年末人数 Number of Employed Persons at the Year-end	#城镇非私营单位就业人员 Urban Employed Persons	国有单位 State-owned Units	城镇集体单位 Urban Collective-owned Units	其他单位 Units of Other Types of Ownership	城镇就业人员 Urban Employed Persons	乡村就业人员 Rural Employed Persons
1978	2275.95	515.85	369.04	146.81			
1979	2304.95	535.37	378.57	156.80			
1980	2367.78	563.62	400.19	163.43			
1981	2423.79	587.34	422.03	165.31			
1982	2521.38	608.12	443.43	164.69			
1983	2569.70	612.65	446.51	166.14			
1984	2637.49	631.77	429.65	197.89	4.23		
1985	2731.11	660.82	449.40	203.32	8.10		
1986	2811.92	686.20	465.59	208.85	11.76		
1987	2910.99	720.34	485.59	216.16	18.59		
1988	2994.72	747.67	503.20	216.96	27.51		
1989	3041.27	762.61	511.88	212.50	38.23		
1990	3118.10	785.49	528.13	207.62	49.74		
1991	3259.20	827.58	544.55	216.86	66.17		
1992	3367.21	858.12	559.71	216.57	81.84		
1993	3433.91	877.16	563.63	199.99	113.54		
1994	3493.15	901.57	568.80	202.86	129.91		
1995	3551.20	931.58	565.48	204.12	161.98		
1996	3641.30	920.55	565.68	193.24	161.63		
1997	3701.90	912.74	556.56	181.44	174.74		
1998	3783.87	897.98	521.34	161.50	215.13		
1999	3796.32	793.54	449.87	122.70	220.97		
2000	3989.32	759.21	425.52	105.97	227.73		
2001	4058.63	737.12	400.12	91.33	245.67		
2002	4134.37	751.23	382.91	82.81	285.51		
2003	4395.93	781.14	376.56	78.47	326.11		
2004	4681.89	830.72	374.34	72.28	384.10		
2005	5022.97	904.27	380.19	68.70	455.38		
2006	5177.02	954.44	384.78	67.25	502.41		
2007	5341.50	1001.46	381.00	65.49	554.97		
2008	5471.72	1007.87	385.14	60.64	562.09		
2009	5688.62	1055.03	389.17	58.33	607.53		
2010	6051.00	1118.52	400.65	57.66	660.21	4004.55	2046.45
2011	6087.00	1238.22	423.88	62.83	751.51	4150.51	1936.49
2012	6171.00	1303.98	430.33	55.28	818.38	4305.70	1865.30
2013	6273.00	1966.98	402.75	58.52	1505.71	4454.56	1818.44
2014	6428.00	1973.28	396.20	56.69	1520.39	4642.00	1786.00
2015	6566.00	1948.04	388.81	50.34	1508.89	4822.00	1744.00
2016	6703.00	1957.57	387.75	47.83	1521.99	4998.00	1705.00
2017	6858.00	1963.10	384.09	45.46	1533.56	5187.00	1671.00
2018	6960.00	1994.14	375.11	42.62	1576.41	5314.00	1646.00
2019	6995.00	2064.59	385.06	37.94	1641.59	5364.00	1631.00
2020	7039.00	2085.27	423.26	36.85	1625.16	5418.00	1621.00
2021	7072.00	2110.88	431.54	36.32	1643.02	5473.00	1599.00
2022	6904.00	2066.65	438.30	33.06	1595.29	5389.00	1515.00

注：2006—2009年就业人员人数，根据第六次全国人口普查资料作了相应调整。从2020年起，国家统计局对各省、自治区、直辖市就业人数及其产业构成以常住人口口径统一测算，同时对2010—2019年就业人数及其产业、城乡结构进行平滑修正。1993年及以前城镇单位就业人员为城镇单位职工人数。

Note: Figures of “Number of Employed Persons" from 2006 to 2009 have been adjusted in accordance with the results of the 6th population census. Since 2020, the National Bureau of Statistics calculates the number of Employed Persons and Industrial Composition of all Province、Autonomous Region and Municipality directly under the Central Government according to the caliber of permanent population,also adjusted the number of Employed Persons and Industrial Structure from 2010 to 2019. Employed persons of urban units are the number of staff and workers of urban units in 1993 and before.

4-3 按三次产业分就业人员年末人数

Number of Employed Persons at Year-end by Three strata of Industry

年 份 Year	就业人数（万人） Total Employed Persons (10000 persons)	第一产业 Primary Industry	第二产业 Secondary Industry	第三产业 Tertiary Industry	构成（%） Composition in Percentage(%) 第一产业 Primary Industry	第二产业 Secondary Industry	第三产业 Tertiary Industry
1978	2275.95	1677.01	312.94	286.00	73.7	13.7	12.6
1979	2304.95	1659.01	381.11	264.83	72.0	16.5	11.5
1980	2367.78	1673.57	404.80	289.41	70.7	17.1	12.2
1981	2423.79	1699.85	409.93	314.01	70.1	16.9	13.0
1982	2521.38	1723.46	447.18	350.74	68.4	17.7	13.9
1983	2569.70	1729.47	458.80	381.43	67.3	17.9	14.8
1984	2637.49	1679.46	498.09	459.94	63.7	18.9	17.4
1985	2731.11	1646.82	614.52	469.77	60.3	22.5	17.2
1986	2811.92	1624.15	637.76	550.01	57.8	22.6	19.6
1987	2910.99	1605.10	704.24	601.65	55.1	24.2	20.7
1988	2994.72	1607.11	743.91	643.70	53.7	24.8	21.5
1989	3041.27	1632.36	747.78	661.13	53.7	24.6	21.7
1990	3118.10	1651.71	848.37	618.02	53.0	27.2	19.8
1991	3259.20	1645.25	932.76	681.19	50.5	28.6	20.9
1992	3367.21	1594.32	1024.98	747.91	47.3	30.5	22.2
1993	3433.91	1512.88	1115.42	805.61	44.1	32.4	23.5
1994	3493.15	1478.37	1172.84	841.94	42.3	33.6	24.1
1995	3551.20	1473.60	1199.00	878.60	41.5	33.8	24.7
1996	3641.30	1481.40	1218.00	941.90	40.7	33.4	25.9
1997	3701.90	1511.38	1217.25	973.27	40.8	32.9	26.3
1998	3783.87	1554.33	1214.96	1014.58	41.1	32.1	26.8
1999	3796.32	1574.25	1181.58	1040.49	41.5	31.1	27.4
2000	3989.32	1593.68	1114.86	1280.78	40.0	27.9	32.1
2001	4058.63	1587.48	1131.96	1339.19	39.1	27.9	33.0
2002	4134.37	1572.92	1202.92	1358.53	38.0	29.1	32.9
2003	4395.93	1617.69	1557.19	1221.05	36.8	35.4	27.8
2004	4681.89	1622.50	1727.86	1331.53	34.7	36.9	28.4
2005	5022.97	1609.89	1916.16	1496.92	32.1	38.1	29.8
2006	5177.02	1562.17	2015.88	1598.97	30.2	38.9	30.9
2007	5341.50	1562.19	2102.28	1677.04	29.2	39.4	31.4
2008	5471.72	1526.66	2172.93	1772.13	27.9	39.7	32.4
2009	5688.62	1514.04	2292.05	1882.53	26.6	40.3	33.1
2010	6051.00	1476.00	2566.00	2009.00	24.4	42.4	33.2
2011	6087.00	1340.00	2611.00	2136.00	22.0	42.9	35.1
2012	6171.00	1243.00	2628.00	2300.00	20.1	42.6	37.3
2013	6273.00	1172.00	2620.00	2481.00	18.7	41.8	39.6
2014	6428.00	1112.00	2606.00	2710.00	17.3	40.5	42.2
2015	6566.00	1046.00	2627.00	2893.00	15.9	40.0	44.1
2016	6703.00	987.00	2611.00	3105.00	14.7	39.0	46.3
2017	6858.00	933.00	2592.00	3333.00	13.6	37.8	48.6
2018	6960.00	864.00	2506.00	3590.00	12.4	36.0	51.6
2019	6995.00	823.00	2522.00	3650.00	11.8	36.1	52.2
2020	7039.00	767.00	2526.00	3746.00	10.9	35.9	53.2
2021	7072.00	753.00	2565.00	3754.00	10.6	36.3	53.1
2022	6904.00	722.00	2524.00	3658.00	10.5	36.6	53.0

注：2006—2009年就业人员人数，根据第六次全国人口普查资料作了相应调整。从2020年起，国家统计局对各省、自治区、直辖市就业人数及其产业构成以常住人口口径统一测算，同时对2010—2019年就业人数及其产业、城乡结构进行平滑修正。

Note: Data for the employed population from 2006 to 2009 have been adjusted from the 6th National Census.Since 2020, the National Bureau of Statistics calculates the number of Employed Persons and Industrial Composition of all Province、Autonomous Region and Municipality directly under the Central Government according to the caliber of permanent population, also adjusted the number of Employed Persons and Industrial Structure from 2010 to 2019.

4-4 各市就业人员年末人数

Number of Employed Persons at the Year-end by City

单位：万人 (10000 persons)

市 别	City	2005	2010	2015	2020	2021	2022
全 省	**Provincial Total**	**5022.97**	**6051.00**	**6566.00**	**7039.00**	**7072.00**	**6904.00**
广 州	Guangzhou	574.46	732.93	927.91	1158.01	1163.44	1119.82
深 圳	Shenzhen	576.26	781.45	1083.35	1239.61	1245.42	1193.41
珠 海	Zhuhai	94.01	106.19	124.11	147.79	148.48	135.13
汕 头	Shantou	179.81	245.22	243.92	246.81	247.97	252.30
佛 山	Foshan	348.69	457.09	523.37	598.10	600.90	575.57
韶 关	Shaoguan	138.44	146.89	137.53	124.99	125.58	120.06
河 源	Heyuan	118.20	137.25	131.40	134.50	135.13	139.01
梅 州	Meizhou	211.98	214.47	183.28	169.43	170.22	175.45
惠 州	Huizhou	222.62	268.14	299.29	320.88	337.58	330.51
汕 尾	Shanwei	117.78	122.81	122.34	124.96	125.55	128.33
东 莞	Dongguan	388.13	645.51	680.09	714.59	717.94	679.31
中 山	Zhongshan	188.85	213.71	241.21	274.62	275.91	262.71
江 门	Jiangmen	214.53	257.22	254.36	256.81	258.01	263.04
阳 江	Yangjiang	146.63	135.38	117.13	113.16	113.69	107.34
湛 江	Zhanjiang	305.00	329.61	343.98	321.14	322.65	324.77
茂 名	Maoming	287.36	281.58	282.89	270.72	271.99	269.70
肇 庆	Zhaoqing	215.05	219.61	209.87	200.74	201.68	204.19
清 远	Qingyuan	195.95	202.10	196.50	182.75	183.61	181.81
潮 州	Chaozhou	129.18	142.74	116.98	108.49	109.00	112.49
揭 阳	Jieyang	253.70	278.57	232.25	231.65	217.54	226.33
云 浮	Yunfu	114.30	132.53	114.24	99.25	99.71	102.72
按经济区域分	By Region						
珠 三 角	Pearl River Delta	2822.60	3681.85	4343.56	4911.15	4949.36	4763.69
东 翼	Eastern Region	680.47	789.34	715.49	711.91	700.06	719.45
西 翼	Western Region	738.99	746.57	744.00	705.02	708.33	701.81
山 区	Mountainous Region	778.87	833.24	762.95	710.92	714.25	719.05

注：从2020年起，国家统计局对各省、自治区、直辖市就业人数及其产业构成以常住人口口径统一测算，同时对2010—2019年就业人数及其产业、城乡结构进行平滑修正。

Note: Since 2020, the National Bureau of Statistics calculates the number of Employed Persons and Industrial Composition of all Province、Autonomous Region and Municipality directly under the Central Government according to the caliber of permanent population, also adjusted the number of Employed Persons and Industrial、City-countryside Structure from 2010 to 2019.

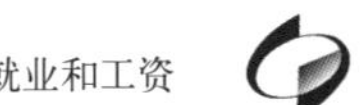

4-5 各市按三次产业分就业人员年末人数

Number of Employed Persons at the Year-end by Strata of Industry by City

单位：万人 (10000 persons)

市别	City	2021 合计 Total	2021 第一产业 Primary Industry	2021 第二产业 Secondary Industry	2021 第三产业 Tertiary Industry	2022 合计 Total	2022 第一产业 Primary Industry	2022 第二产业 Secondary Industry	2022 第三产业 Tertiary Industry
全　省	**Provincial Total**	**7072.00**	**753.00**	**2565.00**	**3754.00**	**6904.00**	**722.00**	**2524.00**	**3658.00**
广　州	Guangzhou	1163.44	58.22	263.78	841.44	1119.82	46.84	255.66	817.31
深　圳	Shenzhen	1245.42	1.21	486.40	757.81	1193.41	0.65	467.95	724.81
珠　海	Zhuhai	148.48	4.62	61.41	82.45	135.13	2.19	58.21	74.73
汕　头	Shantou	247.97	36.60	98.99	112.38	252.30	36.72	100.76	114.82
佛　山	Foshan	600.90	22.44	301.19	277.27	575.57	14.56	295.68	265.33
韶　关	Shaoguan	125.58	32.69	25.86	67.03	120.06	30.35	25.23	64.48
河　源	Heyuan	135.13	33.06	29.41	72.66	139.01	33.17	30.57	75.27
梅　州	Meizhou	170.22	42.18	38.81	89.23	175.45	43.03	40.43	91.98
惠　州	Huizhou	337.58	36.41	152.08	149.09	330.51	33.89	151.54	145.08
汕　尾	Shanwei	125.55	31.16	30.33	64.06	128.33	31.52	31.32	65.48
东　莞	Dongguan	717.94	5.41	454.00	258.53	679.31	3.96	435.87	239.48
中　山	Zhongshan	275.91	9.85	157.64	108.42	262.71	6.76	151.34	104.62
江　门	Jiangmen	258.01	31.38	85.48	141.15	263.04	32.31	88.80	141.93
阳　江	Yangjiang	113.69	27.34	26.62	59.73	107.34	25.05	25.90	56.39
湛　江	Zhanjiang	322.65	95.62	75.93	151.10	324.77	95.33	79.16	150.28
茂　名	Maoming	271.99	77.19	61.81	132.99	269.70	75.64	62.36	131.70
肇　庆	Zhaoqing	201.68	49.94	46.43	105.31	204.19	50.48	48.03	105.68
清　远	Qingyuan	183.61	43.43	40.64	99.54	181.81	42.58	40.67	98.56
潮　州	Chaozhou	109.00	26.78	39.15	43.07	112.49	27.33	40.78	44.38
揭　阳	Jieyang	217.54	58.83	64.65	94.06	226.33	60.41	68.32	97.60
云　浮	Yunfu	99.71	28.64	24.39	46.68	102.72	29.22	25.40	48.10
按经济区域分	By Region								
珠三角	Pearl River Delta	4949.36	219.48	2008.41	2721.47	4763.69	191.64	1953.09	2618.96
东　翼	Eastern Region	700.06	153.37	233.12	313.57	719.45	155.98	241.19	322.28
西　翼	Western Region	708.33	200.15	164.36	343.82	701.81	196.03	167.41	338.37
山　区	Mountainous Region	714.25	180.00	159.11	375.14	719.05	178.35	162.31	378.39

注：从2020年起，国家统计局对各省、自治区、直辖市就业人数及其产业构成以常住人口口径统一测算，同时对2010—2019年就业人数及其产业、城乡结构进行平滑修正。

Note: Since 2020, the National Bureau of Statistics calculates the number of Employed Persons and Industrial Composition of all Province、Autonomous Region and Municipality directly under the Central Government according to the caliber of permanent population, also adjusted the number of Employed Persons and Industrial、City-countryside Structure from 2010 to 2019.

4-6 各市按城乡分就业人员年末人数

Number of Employed Persons at the Year-end by Strata of Industry by City

单位：万人 (10000 persons)

市别	City	2010 合计 Total	2010 城镇 Urban	2010 乡村 Rural	2021 合计 Total	2021 城镇 Urban	2021 乡村 Rural	2022 合计 Total	2022 城镇 Urban	2022 乡村 Rural
全 省	**Provincial Total**	**6051.00**	**4004.55**	**2046.45**	**7072.00**	**5473.00**	**1599.00**	**6904.00**	**5389.00**	**1515.00**
广 州	Guangzhou	732.93	614.14	118.79	1163.44	1015.68	147.76	1119.82	975.42	144.40
深 圳	Shenzhen	781.45	781.04	0.41	1245.42	1240.20	5.22	1193.41	1190.90	2.51
珠 海	Zhuhai	106.19	93.09	13.10	148.48	135.45	13.03	135.13	125.64	9.49
汕 头	Shantou	245.22	123.76	121.46	247.97	134.21	113.76	252.30	143.00	109.30
佛 山	Foshan	457.09	378.33	78.76	600.90	573.48	27.42	575.57	563.06	12.51
韶 关	Shaoguan	146.89	72.77	74.12	125.58	66.79	58.79	120.06	70.28	49.78
河 源	Heyuan	137.25	54.98	82.27	135.13	67.45	67.68	139.01	69.85	69.16
梅 州	Meizhou	214.47	92.29	122.18	170.22	88.63	81.59	175.45	92.43	83.02
惠 州	Huizhou	268.14	165.84	102.30	337.58	243.83	93.75	330.51	249.93	80.58
汕 尾	Shanwei	122.81	61.44	61.37	125.55	67.34	58.21	128.33	74.25	54.08
东 莞	Dongguan	645.51	534.04	111.47	717.94	661.57	56.37	679.31	631.00	48.31
中 山	Zhongshan	213.71	164.32	49.39	275.91	240.61	35.30	262.71	236.61	26.10
江 门	Jiangmen	257.22	160.27	96.95	258.01	180.69	77.32	263.04	185.47	77.57
阳 江	Yangjiang	135.38	63.38	72.00	113.69	61.75	51.94	107.34	59.32	48.02
湛 江	Zhanjiang	329.61	120.93	208.68	322.65	152.78	169.87	324.77	153.65	171.12
茂 名	Maoming	281.58	98.78	182.80	271.99	122.25	149.74	269.70	123.63	146.07
肇 庆	Zhaoqing	219.61	93.11	126.50	201.68	109.46	92.22	204.19	106.46	97.73
清 远	Qingyuan	202.10	81.56	120.54	183.61	99.98	83.63	181.81	102.36	79.45
潮 州	Chaozhou	142.74	69.63	73.11	109.00	55.70	53.30	112.49	62.90	49.59
揭 阳	Jieyang	278.57	131.85	146.72	217.54	110.46	107.08	226.33	126.53	99.80
云 浮	Yunfu	132.53	49.00	83.53	99.71	44.69	55.02	102.72	46.27	56.45
按经济区域分	By Region									
珠 三 角	Pearl River Delta	3681.85	2984.18	697.67	4949.36	4400.97	548.39	4763.69	4264.50	499.19
东 翼	Eastern Region	789.34	386.68	402.66	700.06	367.71	332.35	719.45	406.69	312.76
西 翼	Western Region	746.57	283.09	463.48	708.33	336.78	371.55	701.81	336.60	365.21
山 区	Mountainous Region	833.24	350.60	482.64	714.25	367.54	346.71	719.05	381.19	337.86

注：从2020年起，国家统计局对各省、自治区、直辖市就业人数及其产业构成以常住人口口径统一测算，同时对2010—2019年就业人数及其产业、城乡结构进行平滑修正。

Note: Since 2020, the National Bureau of Statistics calculates the number of Employed Persons and Industrial Composition of all Province、Autonomous Region and Municipality directly under the Central Government according to the caliber of permanent population, also adjusted the number of Employed Persons and Industrial、City-countryside Structure from 2010 to 2019.

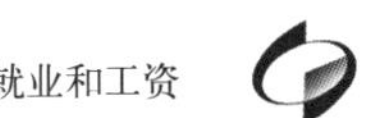

4-7 城镇非私营单位就业人员和在岗职工年末人数（2022年）
Number of Employed Persons and Fully Employed Staff and Workers in Urban Non Private Units at the Year-end (2022)

单位：万人 (10000 persons)

行业	Item	就业人员 Employed Persons	国有单位 State-owned Units	城镇集体单位 Urban Collective-owned Units	其他单位 Other Types of Ownership
全省	**Provincial Total**	**2066.65**	**438.30**	**33.06**	**1595.29**
农、林、牧、渔业	Farming, Forestry, Animal Husbandry and Fishery	1.91	1.08	0.04	0.79
采矿业	Mining and Quarrying	1.46	0.16		1.30
制造业	Manufacture	782.16	2.89	1.50	777.77
电力、热力、燃气及水生产和供应业	Production and Supply of Electric Power, Gas and Water	26.77	3.75	0.55	22.46
建筑业	Construction	119.58	12.30	12.18	95.09
批发和零售业	Wholesale and Retail Trade	109.09	2.76	0.67	105.65
交通运输、仓储和邮政业	Transport, Storage and Postal Services	80.00	9.45	0.34	70.21
住宿和餐饮业	Hotels and Catering Services	40.53	1.45	0.16	38.93
信息传输、软件和信息技术服务业	Information Transmission, Computer Services and Software	83.90	2.36	0.05	81.50
金融业	Finance	79.00	8.28	0.06	70.66
房地产业	Real Estate	90.76	7.12	1.96	81.67
租赁和商务服务业	Leasing and Business Services	130.60	14.66	5.76	110.18
科学研究和技术服务业	Scientific Research and Technical Services	52.37	11.40	0.27	40.70
水利、环境和公共设施管理业	Water Conservancy, Environment and Public Facilities Management	22.43	8.80	0.43	13.20
居民服务、修理和其他服务业	Household's Services,Repair and Other Services	12.96	1.33	0.19	11.44
教育	Education	169.67	113.55	5.41	50.71
卫生和社会工作	Health Care and Social Work	96.92	79.80	2.85	14.27
文化、体育和娱乐业	Culture, Sports and Recreation	12.49	5.28	0.09	7.12
公共管理、社会保障和社会组织	Public Administration and Social Security and Social Organizations	154.04	151.87	0.55	1.63

4-7 续表 continued

单位：万人 (10000 persons)

行 业	Item	在岗职工 Fully Employed Staff and Workers	国有单位 State-owned Units	城镇集体单位 Urban Collecti-ve-owned Units	其他单位 Other Types of Ownership
全 省	**Provincial Total**	**1993.65**	**426.04**	**30.92**	**1536.69**
农、林、牧、渔业	Farming, Forestry, Animal Husbandry and Fishery	1.84	1.05	0.04	0.74
采矿业	Mining and Quarrying	1.42	0.16		1.25
制造业	Manufacture	777.09	2.81	1.49	772.79
电力、热力、燃气及水生产和供应业	Production and Supply of Electric Power, Gas and Water	26.65	3.73	0.53	22.39
建筑业	Construction	107.53	11.02	11.27	85.23
批发和零售业	Wholesale and Retail Trade	106.66	2.64	0.65	103.37
交通运输、仓储和邮政业	Transport, Storage and Postal Services	78.92	9.27	0.30	69.35
住宿和餐饮业	Hotels and Catering Services	34.70	1.42	0.15	33.12
信息传输、软件和信息技术服务业	Information Transmission, Computer Services and Software	82.63	2.31	0.04	80.27
金融业	Finance	55.48	8.15	0.04	47.29
房地产业	Real Estate	89.07	7.07	1.71	80.29
租赁和商务服务业	Leasing and Business Services	125.43	14.15	5.13	106.15
科学研究和技术服务业	Scientific Research and Technical Services	50.89	10.97	0.26	39.66
水利、环境和公共设施管理业	Water Conservancy, Environment and Public Facilities Management	21.36	8.04	0.36	12.96
居民服务、修理和其他服务业	Household's Services,Repair and Other Services	12.37	1.30	0.19	10.88
教育	Education	164.40	110.05	5.32	49.03
卫生和社会工作	Health Care and Social Work	94.70	78.34	2.81	13.55
文化、体育和娱乐业	Culture, Sports and Recreation	11.89	5.03	0.08	6.79
公共管理、社会保障和社会组织	Public Administration and Social Security and Social Organizations	150.64	148.54	0.54	1.56

4-8 各市城镇非私营单位各行业在岗职工年末人数（2022年）

Number of Fully Employed Staff and Workers in Urban Non Private Units at the Year-end by Sector and by City (2022)

单位：万人 (10000 persons)

市别	City	合计 Total	农、林、牧、渔业 Farming, Forestry, Animal Husbandry and Fishery	采矿业 Mining and Quarrying	制造业 Manuf-acture	电力、热力、燃气及水生产和供应业 Production and Supply of Electric Power,Gas and Water	建筑业 Const-ruction	批发和零售业 Wholesale and Retail Trade
全　省	**Provincial Total**	**1993.65**	**1.84**	**1.42**	**777.09**	**26.65**	**107.53**	**106.66**
广　州	Guangzhou	403.47	0.17	0.01	71.16	5.03	16.70	30.00
深　圳	Shenzhen	497.33	0.02	0.46	200.97	3.93	25.64	29.50
珠　海	Zhuhai	78.06	0.08	0.03	32.99	0.74	4.57	3.50
汕　头	Shantou	47.13	0.02		9.63	0.77	11.19	1.99
佛　山	Foshan	145.58	0.04	0.01	77.10	2.04	3.38	7.40
韶　关	Shaoguan	25.73	0.07	0.11	5.23	0.79	3.25	1.04
河　源	Heyuan	28.38	0.04	0.02	9.84	0.62	0.92	0.81
梅　州	Meizhou	25.73	0.06	0.08	4.72	0.96	2.00	0.87
惠　州	Huizhou	100.81	0.07	0.04	58.54	1.61	3.73	4.06
汕　尾	Shanwei	18.48	0.05		4.75	0.38	0.47	0.42
东　莞	Dongguan	266.15	0.08	0.01	183.00	2.08	6.14	12.22
中　山	Zhongshan	73.03	0.06		44.41	0.70	1.42	3.18
江　门	Jiangmen	60.49	0.06	0.01	27.41	0.90	3.52	3.12
阳　江	Yangjiang	16.06	0.03	0.01	2.12	0.53	1.56	0.61
湛　江	Zhanjiang	41.15	0.59	0.25	4.31	0.85	3.85	1.81
茂　名	Maoming	44.32	0.04	0.07	3.75	1.57	11.55	1.93
肇　庆	Zhaoqing	34.97	0.06	0.12	13.49	0.74	1.48	0.95
清　远	Qingyuan	30.86	0.02	0.02	10.42	0.65	2.00	1.01
潮　州	Chaozhou	14.74	0.02	0.01	4.27	0.55	1.05	0.42
揭　阳	Jieyang	24.42	0.03		4.98	0.84	2.01	0.94
云　浮	Yunfu	16.74	0.22	0.18	4.00	0.35	1.09	0.90
按经济区域分	By Region							
珠三角	Pearl River Delta	1659.89	0.64	0.68	709.08	17.79	66.59	93.92
东　翼	Eastern Region	104.78	0.12	0.01	23.63	2.54	14.71	3.77
西　翼	Western Region	101.53	0.66	0.33	10.18	2.95	16.96	4.35
山　区	Mountainous Region	127.45	0.42	0.40	34.20	3.37	9.26	4.63

4-8 续表 1 continued 1

单位：万人 (10000 persons)

市 别	City	交通运输、仓储和邮政业 Transport, Storage and Postal Services	住宿和餐饮业 Hotels and Catering Services	信息传输、软件和信息技术服务业 Information Transmission, Computer Services and Software	金融业 Finance	房地产业 Real Estate	租赁和商务服务业 Leasing and Business Services	科学研究和技术服务业 Scientific Research and Technical Services
全 省	**Provincial Total**	**78.92**	**34.70**	**82.63**	**55.48**	**89.07**	**125.43**	**50.89**
广 州	Guangzhou	30.31	12.17	28.16	10.81	30.04	54.92	21.20
深 圳	Shenzhen	21.83	9.47	39.76	20.21	31.48	32.67	14.66
珠 海	Zhuhai	2.85	1.84	3.24	1.80	3.90	8.33	1.75
汕 头	Shantou	1.15	0.65	1.21	1.45	1.22	1.05	0.54
佛 山	Foshan	4.71	1.74	1.97	2.87	4.44	4.78	2.76
韶 关	Shaoguan	0.69	0.30	0.27	1.10	0.36	0.40	0.29
河 源	Heyuan	0.45	0.18	0.30	0.97	0.58	1.23	0.33
梅 州	Meizhou	0.65	0.12	0.34	0.80	0.31	0.36	0.27
惠 州	Huizhou	2.40	1.12	0.77	1.14	2.91	2.45	0.98
汕 尾	Shanwei	0.40	0.23	0.31	0.70	0.49	0.32	0.15
东 莞	Dongguan	4.35	3.02	2.11	3.76	3.59	10.15	3.69
中 山	Zhongshan	1.31	0.90	0.87	1.42	2.97	2.32	1.05
江 门	Jiangmen	1.53	0.69	0.53	1.39	1.27	1.23	0.78
阳 江	Yangjiang	0.42	0.16	0.21	0.65	0.50	0.57	0.21
湛 江	Zhanjiang	1.94	0.49	0.42	1.30	1.39	0.84	0.58
茂 名	Maoming	1.32	0.35	0.74	0.99	1.49	1.72	0.44
肇 庆	Zhaoqing	0.67	0.25	0.28	1.09	0.60	0.31	0.28
清 远	Qingyuan	0.71	0.48	0.29	0.71	0.71	0.63	0.46
潮 州	Chaozhou	0.21	0.13	0.25	0.96	0.17	0.18	0.16
揭 阳	Jieyang	0.63	0.26	0.41	0.76	0.42	0.68	0.14
云 浮	Yunfu	0.40	0.14	0.22	0.58	0.22	0.30	0.17
按经济区域分	By Region							
珠 三 角	Pearl River Delta	69.96	31.20	77.68	44.51	81.21	117.16	47.15
东 翼	Eastern Region	2.38	1.27	2.17	3.88	2.29	2.22	0.99
西 翼	Western Region	3.68	1.00	1.36	2.94	3.39	3.13	1.24
山 区	Mountainous Region	2.90	1.22	1.41	4.16	2.18	2.91	1.52

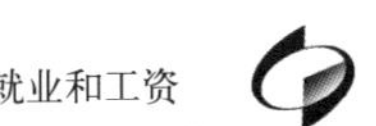

4-8 续表 2 continued 2

单位：万人 (10000 persons)

市别	City	水利、环境和公共设施管理业 Management of Water Conservancy, Environment and Public Facilities	居民服务、修理和其他服务业 Household's Services, Repair and Other Services	教育 Education	卫生和社会工作 Health and Social Service	文化、体育和娱乐业 Culture, Sports and Entertainment	公共管理、社会保障和社会组织 Public Management, Social Security and Social Organizations
全　省	**Provincial Total**	**21.36**	**12.37**	**164.40**	**94.70**	**11.89**	**150.64**
广　州	Guangzhou	5.64	3.00	29.93	23.86	3.78	26.57
深　圳	Shenzhen	4.07	3.86	19.11	13.46	2.45	23.77
珠　海	Zhuhai	1.22	0.55	3.81	2.78	0.86	3.22
汕　头	Shantou	0.39	0.28	7.07	3.36	0.28	4.91
佛　山	Foshan	2.24	0.98	12.16	6.46	0.86	9.65
韶　关	Shaoguan	0.67	0.14	4.44	2.53	0.18	3.90
河　源	Heyuan	0.26	0.11	4.60	2.12	0.13	4.88
梅　州	Meizhou	0.30	0.04	5.15	2.42	0.17	6.11
惠　州	Huizhou	0.51	0.31	7.57	4.10	0.41	8.08
汕　尾	Shanwei	0.18	0.06	4.12	1.11	0.07	4.28
东　莞	Dongguan	1.96	1.50	11.03	6.59	0.92	9.95
中　山	Zhongshan	0.77	0.32	5.00	2.88	0.32	3.11
江　门	Jiangmen	0.63	0.30	6.25	3.77	0.27	6.83
阳　江	Yangjiang	0.48	0.04	3.52	1.44	0.12	2.90
湛　江	Zhanjiang	0.49	0.19	9.28	4.85	0.22	7.51
茂　名	Maoming	0.38	0.15	8.99	3.69	0.27	4.88
肇　庆	Zhaoqing	0.45	0.16	5.58	2.97	0.21	5.28
清　远	Qingyuan	0.18	0.14	5.22	1.99	0.16	5.06
潮　州	Chaozhou	0.20	0.04	2.80	1.01	0.08	2.23
揭　阳	Jieyang	0.25	0.14	5.62	1.97	0.09	4.27
云　浮	Yunfu	0.10	0.05	3.16	1.36	0.06	3.25
按经济区域分	By Region						
珠三角	Pearl River Delta	17.49	10.99	100.44	66.86	10.08	96.47
东　翼	Eastern Region	1.01	0.52	19.61	7.45	0.51	15.70
西　翼	Western Region	1.35	0.37	21.78	9.97	0.60	15.28
山　区	Mountainous Region	1.51	0.48	22.57	10.41	0.70	23.19

4-9 城镇非私营单位女性就业人员年末人数（2022年）

Number of Females Employed in Urban Non Private Units at the Year-end (2022)

单位：万人 (10000 persons)

行业	Sector	合计 Total	国有单位 State-owned Units	城镇集体单位 Urban Collective-owned Units	其他单位 Other Types of Ownership
全省	**Provincial Total**	**870.36**	**207.08**	**12.68**	**650.60**
农、林、牧、渔业	Farming, Forestry, Animal Husbandry and Fishery	0.58	0.29	0.01	0.28
采矿业	Mining and Quarrying	0.25	0.03		0.23
制造业	Manufacture	313.55	0.78	0.91	311.86
电力、热力、燃气及水生产和供应业	Production and Supply of Electric Power, Gas and Water	6.05	1.00	0.15	4.90
建筑业	Construction	18.50	1.54	2.17	14.79
批发和零售业	Wholesale and Retail Trade	54.52	1.11	0.30	53.11
交通运输、仓储和邮政业	Transport, Storage and Postal Services	21.45	2.97	0.11	18.37
住宿和餐饮业	Hotels and Catering Services	22.24	0.67	0.08	21.48
信息传输、软件和信息技术服务业	Information Transmission, Computer Services and Software	31.50	0.80	0.02	30.69
金融业	Finance	43.35	3.85	0.04	39.46
房地产业	Real Estate	35.52	2.46	0.60	32.46
租赁和商务服务业	Leasing and Business Services	49.47	3.83	1.69	43.95
科学研究和技术服务业	Scientific Research and Technical Services	18.37	4.07	0.08	14.22
水利、环境和公共设施管理业	Management of Water Conservancy, Environment and Public Facilities	9.00	2.94	0.15	5.91
居民服务、修理和其他服务业	Household's Services,Repair and Other Services	7.07	0.47	0.09	6.51
教育	Education	113.98	71.88	4.12	37.97
卫生和社会工作	Health Care and Social Service	67.10	55.08	1.91	10.11
文化、体育和娱乐业	Culture, Sports and Entertainment	6.09	2.50	0.04	3.56
公共管理、社会保障和社会组织	Public Administration and Social Security and Social Organizations	51.76	50.81	0.19	0.76

4-10 城镇非私营单位职工工资总额与年平均工资

Total Wages Bill and Average Wage of Staff and Workers in Urban Non Private Units

年份 Year	工资总额（亿元） Total Wages Bill (100 million yuan)				平均工资（元） Average Wage (yuan)			
	合计 Total	国有单位 State-owned Units	城镇集体单位 Urban Collective-owned Units	其他单位 Other Types of Ownership	合计 Total	国有单位 State-owned Units	城镇集体单位 Urban Collective-owned Units	其他单位 Other Types of Ownership
1978	30.59	22.67	7.92		615	638	558	
1979	35.56	26.37	9.19		685	718	605	
1980	42.83	32.00	10.83		789	828	691	
1981	49.40	37.01	12.39		873	912	774	
1982	56.69	43.03	13.66		961	1000	856	
1983	60.85	46.25	14.60		1021	1061	907	
1984	72.82	52.66	19.59	0.57	1187	1261	1017	1697
1985	88.91	63.42	23.85	1.64	1393	1458	1216	2209
1986	102.13	73.10	26.69	2.34	1541	1619	1330	2198
1987	121.10	84.99	31.99	4.12	1743	1805	1544	2469
1988	162.76	113.60	41.23	7.93	2250	2320	1979	3134
1989	200.39	139.38	47.74	13.27	2678	2763	2302	3641
1990	223.29	154.96	50.06	18.27	2929	3000	2508	3972
1991	268.19	179.81	60.15	28.23	3358	3383	2931	4558
1992	334.61	222.27	72.06	40.28	4027	4059	3510	5157
1993	455.33	300.91	83.79	70.63	5327	5431	4388	6435
1994	612.73	401.80	107.03	103.90	7117	7410	5565	8216
1995	734.14	458.86	124.32	150.96	8250	8540	6395	9546
1996	803.50	512.22	124.35	166.93	9127	9494	6799	10569
1997	858.35	539.95	120.36	198.04	9698	10032	6814	11635
1998	899.68	530.11	105.59	263.98	10233	10432	6671	12410
1999	970.70	567.54	101.72	301.44	11309	11579	7025	13492
2000	1038.38	604.59	91.81	341.98	13823	14387	8615	15240
2001	1146.11	663.85	82.67	399.59	15682	16779	9040	16392
2002	1306.32	737.63	80.26	488.43	17814	19696	9881	17597
2003	1515.58	841.02	83.52	591.05	19986	22944	10836	18782
2004	1771.05	942.39	84.73	743.94	22116	25979	11937	20267
2005	2085.64	1058.97	88.63	938.04	23959	28835	13240	21500
2006	2413.63	1165.88	94.91	1152.84	26186	31352	14520	23794
2007	2854.99	1343.92	104.01	1407.06	29443	36396	16328	26215
2008	3294.17	1520.88	110.28	1663.02	33110	40775	18461	29580
2009	3698.34	1687.96	114.71	1895.66	36355	44964	20347	32377
2010	4363.82	1913.19	125.99	2324.64	40358	49610	22470	36347
2011	5444.34	2235.58	149.68	3059.08	45152	54739	25679	41390
2012	6397.01	2508.29	165.71	3723.02	50577	60116	31219	46860
2013	10213.35	2434.53	196.96	7581.85	53611	63390	35812	51717
2014	11471.24	2667.14	221.64	8582.47	59827	69694	40850	57972
2015	12596.61	2927.11	220.22	9449.28	66296	78058	45436	63994
2016	13790.07	3255.53	223.74	10310.80	72848	87482	50159	69844
2017	15110.67	3684.67	238.28	11187.73	80020	99809	55813	75772
2018	17232.72	4096.16	234.67	12901.89	89826	113316	59896	85005
2019	19945.83	5041.31	221.06	14683.47	100689	137123	62239	93065
2020	21804.42	6195.82	251.59	15357.01	110324	152860	73806	99916
2021	24346.28	6749.41	262.95	17333.93	120299	163492	78446	109884
2022	25639.81	7179.19	245.75	18214.86	126925	170091	80913	116194

注：从2000年起统计口径为在岗职工。
Note: Since 2000, statistical coverage refers to the fully employed staff and workers.

4-11 城镇非私营单位就业人员工资总额（2022年）

Total Wages of Employed Persons in Urban Non Private Units (2022)

单位：亿元 (100 million yuan)

行业	Item	合计 Total	国有单位 State-owned Units	城镇集体单位 Urban Collective Owned Units	其他单位 Other Types of Ownership
全省	**Provincial Total**	**26200.89**	**7272.19**	**256.00**	**18672.70**
农、林、牧、渔业	Farming, Forestry, Animal Husbandry and Fishery	14.54	7.80	0.21	6.53
采矿业	Mining and Quarrying	33.00	2.84	0.01	30.15
制造业	Manufacture	7949.57	27.63	10.09	7911.85
电力、热力、燃气及水生产和供应业	Production and Supply of Electric Power, Gas and Water	467.65	53.35	2.80	411.50
建筑业	Construction	1024.29	105.04	59.24	860.01
批发和零售业	Wholesale and Retail Trade	1232.23	38.10	4.00	1190.12
交通运输、仓储和邮政业	Transport, Storage and Postal Services	1043.16	125.85	2.09	915.22
住宿和餐饮业	Hotels and Catering Services	232.34	12.88	0.92	218.53
信息传输、软件和信息技术服务业	Information Transmission, Computer Services and Software	1951.08	38.79	0.54	1911.75
金融业	Finance	1889.12	243.92	0.99	1644.20
房地产业	Real Estate	906.48	78.94	13.43	814.12
租赁和商务服务业	Leasing and Business Services	1330.50	134.51	37.29	1158.71
科学研究和技术服务业	Scientific Research and Technical Services	927.46	236.84	2.72	687.90
水利、环境和公共设施管理业	Management of Water Conservancy, Environment and Public Facilities	189.25	91.94	2.88	94.43
居民服务、修理和其他服务业	Household's Services,Repair and Other Services	90.80	15.27	1.06	74.47
教育	Education	2429.92	1881.97	65.03	482.91
卫生和社会工作	Health Care and Social Service	1817.76	1606.55	45.58	165.63
文化、体育和娱乐业	Culture, Sports and Entertainment	164.27	89.03	0.78	74.46
公共管理、社会保障和社会组织	Public Administration and Social Security and Social Organizations	2507.47	2480.93	6.34	20.20

4-12 城镇非私营单位在岗职工工资总额（2022年）

Total Wages of Fully Employed Staff and Workers in Urban Non Private Units (2022)

单位：亿元 (100 million yuan)

行　业	Item	合计 Total	国有单位 State-owned Units	城镇集体单位 Urban Collective Owned Units	其他单位 Other Types of Ownership
全　省	**Provincial Total**	**25639.81**	**7179.19**	**245.75**	**18214.86**
农、林、牧、渔业	Farming, Forestry, Animal Husbandry and Fishery	14.28	7.68	0.21	6.39
采矿业	Mining and Quarrying	32.70	2.84	0.01	29.85
制造业	Manufacture	7890.44	27.32	10.06	7853.06
电力、热力、燃气及水生产和供应业	Production and Supply of Electric Power, Gas and Water	466.88	53.24	2.74	410.91
建筑业	Construction	944.91	93.71	54.81	796.39
批发和零售业	Wholesale and Retail Trade	1215.75	37.46	3.90	1174.39
交通运输、仓储和邮政业	Transport, Storage and Postal Services	1034.46	124.40	1.86	908.20
住宿和餐饮业	Hotels and Catering Services	222.95	12.73	0.91	209.30
信息传输、软件和信息技术服务业	Information Transmission, Computer Services and Software	1944.38	38.47	0.54	1905.37
金融业	Finance	1669.88	242.96	0.72	1426.20
房地产业	Real Estate	896.35	78.59	12.4	805.35
租赁和商务服务业	Leasing and Business Services	1290.86	131.55	34.63	1124.69
科学研究和技术服务业	Scientific Research and Technical Services	913.09	231.54	2.63	678.91
水利、环境和公共设施管理业	Management of Water Conservancy, Environment and Public Facilities	185.20	89.28	2.55	93.38
居民服务、修理和其他服务业	Household's Services,Repair and Other Services	88.00	15.16	1.04	71.80
教育	Education	2385.37	1854.86	64.46	466.05
卫生和社会工作	Health Care and Social Service	1793.22	1586.02	45.24	161.96
文化、体育和娱乐业	Culture, Sports and Entertainment	161.26	87.68	0.72	72.85
公共管理、社会保障和社会组织	Public Administration and Social Security and Social Organizations	2489.83	2463.72	6.31	19.80

4-13 城镇非私营单位就业人员年平均工资（2022年）

Average Annual Wages of Employed Persons in Urban Non Private Units (2022)

单位：元 (yuan)

行 业	Item	合计 Total	国有单位 State-owned Units	城镇集体单位 Urban Collective Owned Units	其他单位 Other Types of Ownership
全 省	**Provincial Total**	**124916**	**167521**	**78973**	**114489**
农、林、牧、渔业	Farming, Forestry, Animal Husbandry and Fishery	76074	72514	49222	82370
采矿业	Mining and Quarrying	228763	174715	57059	235861
制造业	Manufacture	98026	94608	63627	98106
电力、热力、燃气及水生产和供应业	Production and Supply of Electric Power, Gas and Water	174716	140131	51233	183601
建筑业	Construction	87892	94899	51112	91607
批发和零售业	Wholesale and Retail Trade	110346	136088	59229	109999
交通运输、仓储和邮政业	Transport, Storage and Postal Services	128931	132465	59888	128797
住宿和餐饮业	Hotels and Catering Services	55727	88818	57650	54522
信息传输、软件和信息技术服务业	Information Transmission, Computer Services and Software	228692	165243	124480	230543
金融业	Finance	233820	295134	157300	226893
房地产业	Real Estate	98507	105796	66214	98641
租赁和商务服务业	Leasing and Business Services	102877	91534	66380	106287
科学研究和技术服务业	Scientific Research and Technical Services	175554	208873	101150	166875
水利、环境和公共设施管理业	Management of Water Conservancy, Environment and Public Facilities	84782	104058	68046	72288
居民服务、修理和其他服务业	Household's Services,Repair and Other Services	68835	115816	56148	63738
教育	Education	144300	167364	120892	95501
卫生和社会工作	Health Care and Social Service	189974	204362	161576	116226
文化、体育和娱乐业	Culture, Sports and Entertainment	127404	165990	91071	100022
公共管理、社会保障和社会组织	Public Administration and Social Security and Social Organizations	164092	164697	116143	124123

4-14 城镇非私营单位在岗职工年平均工资（2022年）

Average Annual Wages of Fully Employed Staff and Workers in Urban Non Private Units (2022)

单位：元 (yuan)

行　业	Item	合计 Total	国有单位 State-owned Units	城镇集体单位 Urban Collective Owned Units	其他单位 Other Types of Ownership
全　省	**Provincial Total**	**126925**	**170091**	**80913**	**116194**
农、林、牧、渔业	Farming, Forestry, Animal Husbandry and Fishery	77711	73513	50639	85052
采矿业	Mining and Quarrying	234479	174852	57059	242590
制造业	Manufacture	98008	96404	63770	98082
电力、热力、燃气及水生产和供应业	Production and Supply of Electric Power, Gas and Water	175235	140912	51869	183954
建筑业	Construction	90179	95916	50662	94591
批发和零售业	Wholesale and Retail Trade	111529	139792	59812	111132
交通运输、仓储和邮政业	Transport, Storage and Postal Services	129651	133633	61793	129414
住宿和餐饮业	Hotels and Catering Services	62638	89795	57849	61528
信息传输、软件和信息技术服务业	Information Transmission, Computer Services and Software	233147	167219	124630	235077
金融业	Finance	301949	298682	173349	302626
房地产业	Real Estate	99410	106233	72970	99342
租赁和商务服务业	Leasing and Business Services	104449	92881	68739	107741
科学研究和技术服务业	Scientific Research and Technical Services	177697	212958	102304	168654
水利、环境和公共设施管理业	Water Conservancy, Environment and Public Facilities Management	87251	111005	71698	72790
居民服务、修理和其他服务业	Household's Services,Repair and Other Services	70292	117447	56714	65007
教育	Education	146071	169845	122010	95482
卫生和社会工作	Health Care and Social Work	192036	205555	162991	120452
文化、体育和娱乐业	Culture, Sports and Recreation	132958	173323	95296	104172
公共管理、社会保障和社会组织	Public Administration and Social Security and Social Organizations	166475	167081	116728	126574

主要统计指标解释

就业人员 指在一定年龄以上，有劳动能力，为取得劳动报酬或经营收入而从事一定社会劳动的人员。具体指年满16周岁，为取得报酬或经营利润，在调查周内从事了1小时（含1小时）以上劳动的人员；或由于学习、休假等原因在调查周内暂时处于未工作状态，但有工作单位或场所的人员；或由于临时停工放假、单位不景气放假等原因在调查周内暂时处于未工作状态，但不满三个月的人员。

单位就业人员 指报告期末最后一日24时在本单位中工作，并取得工资或其他形式劳动报酬的人员数。该指标为时点指标，不包括最后一日当天及以前已经与单位解除劳动合同关系的人员，是在岗职工、劳务派遣人员及其他就业人员之和。就业人员不包括：

(1)离开本单位仍保留劳动关系，并定期领取生活费的人员；

(2)在本单位实习的各类在校学生；

(3)本单位因劳务外包而使用的人员。

在岗职工 指在本单位工作且与本单位签订劳动合同，并由单位支付各项工资和社会保险、住房公积金的人员，以及上述人员中由于学习、病伤、产假等原因暂未工作仍由单位支付工资的人员。在岗职工还包括：

(1)应订立劳动合同而未订立劳动合同人员(如使用的农村户籍人员)；

(2)处于试用期人员；

(3)编制外招用的人员；

(4)派往外单位工作，但工资仍由本单位发放的人员(如挂职锻炼、外派工作等情况)。

工资总额 指根据《关于工资总额组成的规定》(1990年1月1日国家统计局发布的一号令)进行修订，在报告期内(季度或年度)直接支付给本单位全部就业人员的劳动报酬总额。包括计时工资、计件工资、奖金、津贴和补贴、加班加点工资、特殊情况下支付的工资，是在岗职工工资总额、劳务派遣人员工资总额和其他就业人员工资总额之和。

工资总额是税前工资，包括单位从个人工资中直接为其代扣或代缴的房费、水费、电费、住房公积金、职工年金和社会保险基金个人缴纳部分等。

工资总额不论是计入成本的还是不计入成本的，不论是以货币形式支付的还是以实物形式支付的，均应列入工资总额的计算范围。

平均工资 是指在报告期内单位发放工资的人均水平。计算公式为：

$$\text{平均工资} = \frac{\text{报告期工资总额}}{\text{报告期平均人数}}$$

平均工资通常是以年平均工资的形式表现，月平均工资就是用年平均工资除以12求得。

Explanatory Notes on Main Statistical Indicators

Employed Persons refer to persons, aged 16 and over, who performed some work for compensation or business gains for one hour or more during the reference period; or persons who do not work for the reasons of study or on holiday, but had work units or sites during the reference period; or persons temporary absence from a job for disorganization or suspension of work, recession, etc, but not exceeding three months during the reference period.

Persons Employed in Various Units refer to the total number of employees who work at his unit and obtain wages or other forms of payment at the end of the reporting period. This indicator is a kind of time point index and it equals to the sum of the number of employed staff and workers, labor dispatch personnel and other employed persons. Employed persons do not include:

1)persons who have left their working units while keeping their labour contract (employment relation) unchanged and receiving regular alimony;

2)students who do part-time jobs in spare time and all kinds of enrolled students who do internship in various units;

3)persons employed due to labor outsourcing;

Employed Staff and Workers refer to persons who signed labor contracts with working units and working units would pay wages, social insurance and housing funds for them. Persons who have their work posts but are temporarily absent from work for reasons of study or on sick, injury or maternal leave and still receive wages from their working units are also included. Employed staff and workers also include:

1)Persons who should have signed the labor contracts but not (like people with rural household registration);

2)Employees on probation;

3)Employees beyond the staffing quota;

4)Employees who are sent to other working units but still obtain wages from their original units (situations like on-the-job placement, expatriated assignment, etc.)

Total Wage Bill It is revised according to the "Provision of Composition of Total Wages" (Order No.1 by National Bureau of Statistics on January, 1st, ,1990), total wage bill refers to the total remuneration payment to all employed persons in various units during the reporting period (by quarter or by year), including hourly-paid wages, piece-rate wages, bonuses, allowance and subsidies, overtime wages and wages paid under special circumstances. It equals to the sum of total wages of employed staff and workers, dispatch labors and other employed persons.

Total wage bill is pre-tax wages, including the room charges, utility bills, housing funds and social insurance paid or withheld by employee's units.

Total wage bill, whether or not included in cost, whether or not paid in money or in kind, shall be included in the calculation of total wage.

Average Wage refers to the average per capita wage in money terms during a certain period of time for employed persons. It shows the general level of wage income of staff and worker during a certain period of time, one major indicator to reflect the wage level. It is calculated as follows:

$$\text{Average Wage} = \frac{\text{Total Wage Bill of Employed Persons at Reference Time}}{\text{Average Number of Persons Employed at Reference Time}}$$

Average Wage in this yearbook is the annual average wage.The average monthly wage is calculated by dividing the annual average wage by 12.

五、固定资产投资

INVESTMENT IN FIXED ASSETS

五　固定资产投资

简要说明

一、本篇资料反映广东省固定资产投资的基本情况，主要包括：固定资产投资以及各市固定资产投资的主要指标数据。

二、本篇资料由广东省统计局固定资产投资统计处整理提供。

三、固定资产投资统计的资料来源主要为全面统计报表。按照现行的固定资产投资统计报表制度，固定资产投资按登记注册类型可分为：国有、集体、股份合作、联营、其他有限责任公司、股份有限公司、私营、个体、其他、港澳台投资、外商投资。

四、2011 年起，固定资产投资项目统计起点由 50 万元提高到 500 万元，且不包含农户投资；2010 年以前为全社会固定资产投资。

五、2011 年定报起，原国家预算内资金改为国家预算资金。

六、2014 年定报起，固定资产投资取消城乡分组。

5　Investment in Fixed Assets

Brief Introduction

Ⅰ.The data in this chapter reflect the basic conditions of investment in fixed assets of Guangdong Province, mainly including investment in fixed assets in the whole province, and main indicators on investment in fixed assets by city.

Ⅱ.The data in this chapter are prepared and provided by the Division of Investment and Construction Statistics of Statistics Bureau of Guangdong Province.

Ⅲ.The data sources for the statistics of investment in fixed assets mainly come from complete statistical report forms. According to the present regulations on the statistics of investment in fixed assets, the investment in fixed assets is classified by the following status of registration: state-owned units, collective-owned units, Cooperative Units joint ownership units, other Limited liability units, share-holding corporations, units with funds from Hong Kong, Macao and Taiwan, foreign-funded units, private, self-employed individuals and others.

Ⅳ.Since 2011, the cut-off point of investment statistics is changed from a minimum of 500,000 yuan to a minimum of 5,000,000 yuan, and the data do not include the investment made by rural households. Data before 2010 refer to total investment in fixed assets.

Ⅴ.Since 2011, state budget is changed to state and local budget.

VI.Since 2014, fixed asset investment grouped by urban and rural areas is canceled.

5-1 固定资产投资主要指标增长速度

Main Indicators of Investment in Fixed Assets

单位：% (%)

项　　目	Item	2018	2019	2020	2021	2022
投资完成额	**Investment**	**10.7**	**11.1**	**7.2**	**6.3**	**-2.6**
#房地产开发	Real Estate Development	19.3	10.0	9.2	0.9	-14.3
#民间投资		8.9	6.4	1.1	7.8	-9.4
按登记注册类型分	Grouped by Status of Registration					
内资	Domestic	12.0	12.6	8.8	5.3	-3.1
国有	State-owned	13.9	26.8	20.4	6.1	4.5
集体	Collective-owned	5.7	4.5	-20.0	19.0	-3.1
股份合作	Cooperative	147.7	-48.7	-30.7	120.7	-38.4
联营	Joint	112.0	-69.1	-62.1	-42.6	-69.0
其他有限责任公司	Other Limited Liability	12.2	2.7	7.7	-0.4	-6.3
股份有限公司	Share-holding	23.9	28.9	-3.0	8.2	-12.9
私营	Private	7.6	17.6	8.9	13.7	-5.8
个体	Self-employed Individual	17.7	-11.7	-76.3	10.6	27.4
其他	Others	8.1	0.0	-35.3	-27.3	-2.6
港澳台商投资	Funds from Hong Kong, Macao and Taiwan	-15.1	-0.3	-3.6	12.6	4.3
外商投资	Foreign Funded	29.5	-0.9	-14.3	18.3	-3.4
按构成分	Grouped by Use of Funds					
建筑安装工程	Construction and Installation	3.4	12.0	7.3	7.9	-3.5
设备工具器具购置	Purchase of Equipments and Instruments	3.0	2.0	-11.7	6.8	-3.1
其他费用	Others	38.8	14.4	15.6	2.1	-1.1
按三次产业分	Grouped by Three Strata of Industry					
第一产业	Primary Industry	-20.9	-18.0	81.0	31.8	-21.2
第二产业	Secondary Industry	0.6	6.3	-1.1	19.4	10.4
第三产业	Tertiary Industry	14.9	13.0	9.3	2.2	-6.9
按财务拨贷款合计	**Grouped by Source of Funds**	**10.3**	**10.5**	**14.7**	**9.4**	**-11.5**
国家预算资金	State and Local Budget	26.3	19.5	53.5	3.4	28.1
国内贷款	Domestic Loans	8.3	1.9	9.6	4.4	-13.0
利用外资	Foreign Investment	-28.9	-6.6	-14.6	37.7	26.6
自筹资金	Self-raising Funds	4.7	12.3	18.8	13.3	-4.5
其他资金	Others	16.3	11.9	5.0	8.9	-33.7

注：1. 2011年起固定资产投资项目统计起点由50万元提高至500万元，且不包含农村农户投资；2010年以前为全社会固定资产投资，下表同。
2. 2011年报起，原国家预算内资金改为国家预算资金，下表同。
3. 2018年—2020年，资金来源指标不包含5000万元以下项目数据，增速为可比口径，下表同。

Note:a) Since 2011,the cut-off point of investment statistics is changed from a minimum of 500,000 yuan to a minimum of 5,000,000 yuan, and the data do not include the investment made by rural households. Data before 2010 refer to total investment in fixed assets. The same applies to all tables following.
b) Since 2011, state budget is changed to state and local budget.The same applies to all tables following.
c) From 2018 to 2020, sources of funds for investment do not include projects under 50 million yuan. The growth rate is caculated by comparable coverage, and the same applies to the following table.

5-2 固定资产投资增长速度

Growth Rate of Investment in Fixed Assets

单位：% (%)

年份 Year	全部投资 Total Investment	#房地产开发 Real Estate Development	按产业分 Grouped by Three Strata of Industry 第一产业 Primary Industry	第二产业 Secondary Industry	第三产业 Tertiary Industry
1978					
1979	3.9		-40.4	74.9	-33.2
1980	35.3		…	33.3	54.1
1981	57.7		11.2	21.3	136.9
1982	40.3		10.7	33.9	50.0
1983	4.7		-13.1	1.3	9.2
1984	47.0		4.5	34.8	59.5
1985	41.6		33.2	91.4	9.4
1986	17.3		-8.4	48.0	-16.5
1987	15.9	62.9	-6.7	18.4	12.3
1988	40.9	34.8	12.6	42.8	38.2
1989	-1.8	119.3	5.7	-46.8	97.6
1990	9.8	-32.1	13.4	25.1	0.6
1991	25.4	52.1	61.0	9.1	36.5
1992	92.8	152.4	-17.8	56.8	117.5
1993	76.8	152.1	25.9	91.7	71.1
1994	31.4	27.7	12.7	36.3	29.2
1995	8.7	39.5	34.2	-4.6	15.2
1996	…	-6.2	36.0	-2.5	0.7
1997	-1.3	-0.1	-15.2	-9.3	2.1
1998	16.1	14.1	18.3	9.4	18.5
1999	13.5	17.8	8.2	11.1	14.3
2000	6.8	20.9	11.2	4.7	7.4
2001	9.4	13.2	-0.1	16.0	7.4
2002	12.3	14.7	3.0	36.5	4.1
2003	26.7	10.6	-39.6	12.2	33.7
2004	19.8	9.9	68.2	57.7	5.4
2005	18.9	17.4	17.3	33.2	10.9
2006	13.5	15.8	71.3	13.2	13.3
2007	18.0	36.6	42.1	8.2	24.4
2008	16.3	16.4	56.7	12.1	18.4
2009	19.6	1.0	18.9	13.2	23.1
2010	20.7	23.6	39.6	17.6	22.0
2011	17.6	31.4	53.9	17.8	17.0
2012	14.6	11.3	28.4	17.7	12.8
2013	18.2	21.2	29.1	13.4	20.5
2014	15.9	17.7	-1.2	16.8	15.9
2015	15.8	11.8	52.5	20.8	12.8
2016	10.0	20.7	5.9	8.9	10.5
2017	13.5	17.2	-11.2	9.4	16.2
2018	10.7	19.3	-20.9	0.6	14.9
2019	11.1	10.0	-18.0	6.3	13.0
2020	7.2	9.2	81.0	-1.1	9.3
2021	6.3	0.9	31.8	19.4	2.2
2022	-2.6	-14.3	-21.2	10.4	-6.9

注：1993年以前房地产开发投资主要是商品房建设投资。
Notes: Prior to 1993, investment in real estate development focused mainly on the construction of commercial buildings.

5-3 按资金来源和构成分固定资产投资增速及比重

Growth Rate and Percentage Investment in Fixed Assets by Source of Funds and Structure of Investment

单位：% (%)

年份 Year	按财务拨贷款资金来源分 By Source of Funds				按构成分 By Structure of Investment		
	国家预算资金 State Budget Funds	国内贷款 Domestic Loans	利用外资 Foreign Investment	自筹和其他资金 Fundraising and Others	建筑安装工程 Construction and Installation	设备工具器具购置 Purchase of Equipment and Instruments	其他费用 Others
增长速度 Growth Rate							
1985	1.8	45.7	73.2	43.1			
1990	7.8	32.5	15.5	-1.7			
1995	30.3	12.1	-3.0	27.1	11.1	-6.9	24.5
1996	-16.5	-7.5	6.4	-4.1	-0.1	7.3	-9.2
1997	-3.4	-14.7	-3.4	2.0	0.3	-6.9	0.1
1998	113.9	39.8	-17.4	22.8	11.7	17.5	34.8
1999	31.0	32.7	-18.0	9.9	16.1	7.7	10.4
2000	-6.8	6.2	10.3	10.7	7.3	1.5	11.2
2001	2.3	1.4	1.1	11.7	9.0	16.9	2.1
2002	26.6	26.4	21.7	13.4	11.1	12.2	17.3
2003	22.6	26.9	29.5	31.5	25.6	24.8	33.5
2004	-19.8	19.0	15.3	21.7	18.2	27.6	16.7
2005	-4.5	20.7	19.9	17.7	19.5	27.7	5.6
2006	52.7	21.5	10.1	16.3	15.5	12.7	6.2
2007	70.0	5.8	13.7	27.5	16.6	10.2	37.3
2008	41.1	7.0	-20.8	9.4	17.3	14.4	15.1
2009	50.0	43.5	-12.5	30.5	23.3	9.0	18.4
2010	8.3	17.7	-7.6	20.8	18.1	20.2	32.0
2011	3.2	-10.0	-0.8	21.9	20.2	16.1	10.2
2012	142.9	15.1	4.4	12.7	16.1	11.4	12.3
2013	17.1	27.4	14.0	21.1	19.3	18.3	13.9
2014	28.9	8.5	-37.1	11.1	16.8	14.0	20.6
2015	24.4	4.5	-49.6	24.5	14.9	25.1	10.4
2016	8.4	9.8	29.2	8.4	6.9	8.8	24.5
2017	27.3	37.3	-1.5	1.7	11.6	11.0	23.6
2018	26.3	8.3	-28.9	9.9	3.4	3.0	38.8
2019	19.5	1.9	-6.6	12.1	12.0	2.0	14.4
2020	53.5	9.6	-14.6	12.4	7.3	-11.7	15.6
2021	3.4	4.4	37.7	11.3	7.9	6.8	2.1
2022	28.1	-13.0	26.6	-16.6	-3.5	-3.1	-1.1

5-3 续表 continued

单位：%　　(%)

年份 Year	按财务拨贷款资金来源分 By Source of Funds				按构成分 By Structure of Investment		
	国家预算资金 State Budget Funds	国内贷款 Domestic Loans	利用外资 Foreign Investment	自筹和其他资金 Fundraising and Others	建筑安装工程 Construction and Installation	设备工具器具购置 Purchase of Equipment and Instruments	其他费用 Others
比重 Percentage							
1985	8.1	24.8	10.3	56.8	74.9	17.7	7.4
1990	3.2	18.1	14.9	63.9	64.6	27.3	8.1
1995	1.1	15.0	18.5	65.4	64.8	20.0	15.2
1996	0.9	14.3	20.3	64.5	64.7	21.4	13.8
1997	0.9	12.3	19.9	66.9	65.8	20.2	14.0
1998	1.6	14.7	14.0	69.7	63.3	20.5	16.3
1999	2.0	17.7	10.4	69.9	64.7	19.4	15.8
2000	1.7	17.2	10.5	70.6	65.1	18.5	16.5
2001	1.6	16.1	9.8	72.6	64.9	19.8	15.4
2002	1.7	17.4	10.2	70.7	64.2	19.7	16.1
2003	1.6	17.0	10.1	71.3	63.6	19.4	16.9
2004	1.1	16.8	9.8	72.3	62.8	20.7	16.5
2005	0.9	17.2	9.9	72.1	63.1	22.2	14.7
2006	1.1	17.9	9.3	71.7	64.2	22.1	13.7
2007	1.6	15.4	8.6	74.4	63.4	20.6	15.9
2008	2.1	15.4	6.4	76.1	64.0	20.3	15.7
2009	2.4	16.9	4.3	76.4	65.9	18.5	15.6
2010	2.2	16.8	3.3	77.7	64.5	18.4	17.1
2011	2.1	14.4	2.9	80.6	65.4	17.9	16.6
2012	4.4	14.4	2.6	78.6	66.3	17.4	16.3
2013	4.3	15.0	2.5	78.2	66.9	17.4	15.7
2014	4.7	14.4	1.3	79.5	67.4	16.5	16.1
2015	4.9	12.5	0.6	82.1	66.9	17.8	15.4
2016	4.8	12.6	0.7	81.9	65.0	17.6	17.4
2017	5.7	16.1	0.6	77.5	63.9	17.2	18.9
2018	6.8	20.2	0.4	72.6	59.7	14.0	26.3
2019	7.4	18.6	0.3	73.7	60.1	12.8	27.0
2020	9.9	17.8	0.2	72.1	60.3	10.6	29.2
2021	9.8	16.2	0.3	73.7	61.3	10.7	28.1
2022	14.2	15.9	0.4	69.5	60.9	10.6	28.5

注：1986年及以后的资金来源为财务拨贷款数，各项相加不等于投资总额；从2012年定报开始，资金来源中的“国家预算内资金”改为“国家预算资金”，包括中央预算资金和地方预算资金，口径有所扩大；2018年—2020年，资金来源不含计划总投资5000万元以下项目。

Note: Source of funds for investment since 1986 refers to financial appropriations, which do not add up to total investment.Since 2012,state budget is changed to state and local budget including central budget funds and local budget funds,the caliber has been expanded.From 2018 to 2020, sources of funds for Investment do not include projects with total planed investment under 50 million yuan.

 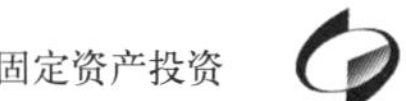

5-4 按构成分固定资产投资增长速度

Growth Rate of Investment in Fixed Assets by Structure

单位：% (%)

项 目	Item	2021年 全部投资 Total	项目投资 Project	房地产开发 Real Estate Devel-opment	2022年 全部投资 Total	项目投资 Project	房地产开发 Real Estate Devel-opment
建设项目个数	**Number of Projects**	**9.4**	**9.4**		**0.8**	**0.8**	
其中：本年新开工	Newly-commenced Projects	-15.2	-15.2		-7.3	-7.3	
全部建成投产项目	Projects Completed and Put into Use	6.7	6.7		-8.9	-8.9	
计划总投资	**Total Planned Investment**	**15.6**	**18.2**	**12.8**	**11.0**	**18.9**	**2.3**
本年投资总额	**Total Investment in this year**	**6.3**	**9.8**	**0.9**	**-2.6**	**4.7**	**-14.3**
#住宅	Residential Buildings	3.4	-24.7	4.4	-14.3	-24.1	-14.0
按隶属关系分	Investment by Jurisdiction of Management						
中央	Central Investment	1.5	3.1	-3.9	0.4	5.3	-17.2
地方	Local Investment	6.4	10.3	1.1	-2.9	4.8	-14.2
按构成分	Grouped by Structure						
建筑安装工程	Construction and Installation	7.9	9.0	6.1	-3.5	3.9	-17.3
设备工具器具购置	Purchase of Equipment and Instruments	6.8	7.8	-17.5	-3.1	-2.4	-27.8
其他费用	Others	2.1	15.2	-4.4	-1.1	14.5	-10.5
财务拨贷款合计	**Total Financial Appropriations**	**9.4**	**12.9**	**6.9**	**-11.5**	**14.4**	**-33.2**
国家预算资金	State and Local Budget	3.4	3.4		28.1	28.1	
国内贷款	Domestic Loans	4.4	24.3	-8.8	-13.0	12.7	-36.5
利用外资	Foreign Investment	37.7	40.6	16.4	26.6	31.0	-13.9
自筹资金	Self-raising Funds	13.3	16.3	9.7	-4.5	8.3	-22.8
其他资金	Others	8.9	-13.2	10.8	-33.7	26.5	-38.9
新增固定资产	**Newly Increased Fixed Assets**	**12.0**	**9.9**	**14.7**	**2.0**	**1.3**	**3.3**
房屋建筑面积	**Floor Space of Buildings**						
施工面积	Floor Space under Construction			2.8			-5.9
竣工面积	Floor Space Completed			3.6			1.5
#住宅	Residential Buildings			0.3			1.0

注：建设项目个数不含房地产开发。
Note: The total number of projects under construction excludes the projects of real estate development.

5-5 按行业分固定资产投资主要指标增长速度(2022年)

Growth Rate of Main Indicators of Investment by Sector (2022)

单位：% (%)

行业	Sector	投资额 Investment	施工项目个数 Number of Projects under Construction	全部建成投产项目个数 Number of Projects Completed and Put into Use	新增固定资产 Newly Increased Fixed Assets
全省	**Provincial Total**	**-2.6**	**0.8**	**-8.9**	**2.0**
农、林、牧、渔业	**Farming, Forestry, Animal Husbandry and Fishery**	**-15.3**	**-8.9**	**-32.9**	**-16.4**
农业	Farming	-4.3	-11.1	-38.3	-21.1
林业	Forestry	-28.8	-22.7	-66.7	-77.1
畜牧业	Animal Husbandry	-36.6	-18.8	-28.6	-17.3
渔业	Fishery	20.7	4.3	3.0	2.0
农、林、牧、渔专业及辅助性活动	Service Activities for Farming, Forestry, Animal Husbandry and Fishery	27.8	11.8	-24.0	4.0
采矿业	**Mining**	**33.6**	**-17.2**	**-34.0**	**17.0**
煤炭开采和洗选业	Mining and Washing of Coal				
石油和天然气开采业	Extraction of Petroleum and Natural Gas	48.9	-27.3		68.1
黑色金属矿采选业	Mining and Dressing of Ferrous Metal Ores	116.9			
有色金属矿采选业	Mining and Dressing of Non-Ferrous Metal Ores	-12.7		-28.6	-16.5
非金属矿采选业	Mining and Dressing of Nonmetal Ores	14.0	-17.6	-37.8	-76.4
开采专业及辅助性活动	Auxiliary Mining Operations	2.4	-50.0	100.0	1332.6
其他采矿业	Mining of Other Ores	4297.3			-23.4
制造业	**Manufacture**	**12.2**	**0.8**	**-4.0**	**4.1**
农副食品加工业	Processing of Farm and Sideline Food	19.8	7.4	-8.3	4.3
食品制造业	Manufacture of Food	3.0	-6.3	-17.1	-19.1
酒、饮料和精制茶制造业	Manufacture of Wine, Beverage and Refined Tea	24.6	2.4	-9.9	15.0
烟草制品业	Tobacco Products	-32.9	100.0	40.0	171.3
纺织业	Textile Industry	-16.5	-18.6	-28.4	-10.3
纺织服装、服饰业	Manufacture of Textile Garments, Apparel	26.8	-7.3	-10.8	11.7
皮革、毛皮、羽毛及其制品和制鞋业	Leather, Fur, Feather and Related Products, and Footwear	22.5	-13.3	-30.6	30.3
木材加工及木、竹、藤、棕、草制品业	Timber Processing, Bamboo, Cane, Palm Fiber & Straw Products	-30.8	-16.7	-1.8	-16.9
家具制造业	Manufacture of Furniture	9.2	-0.2	9.0	-14.9
造纸和纸制品业	Papermaking and Paper Products	3.0	-7.6	-9.6	-17.5
印刷业和记录媒介复制业	Printing and Record Medium Reproduction	-4.8	-9.9	-14.7	-12.3
文教、工美、体育和娱乐用品制造业	Manufacture of Culture, Arts, Sports and Entertainment Articles	6.9	-11.8	-7.2	39.6
石油加工、炼焦和核燃料加工业	Petroleum Refining, Coking and Nuclear Fuel Processing	-37.8	27.5	-17.8	244.0
化学原料和化学制品制造业	Manufacture of Raw Chemical Materials and Chemical Products	44.6	-0.4	-4.3	23.1
医药制造业	Manufacture of Medicines	8.8	-0.5	-24.5	-6.1
化学纤维制造业	Manufacture of Chemical Fibers	33.1	9.7	22.2	-33.6
橡胶和塑料制品业	Manufacture of Rubber and Plastic Products	-6.5	-4.7	-8.8	-16.7
非金属矿物制品业	Nonmetal Mineral Products	-8.1	-13.7	-5.2	-19.8
黑色金属冶炼及压延加工业	Smelting and Pressing of Ferrous Metals	-21.9	1.6	-5.6	125.3
有色金属冶炼及压延加工业	Smelting and Pressing of Nonferrous Metals	-11.4	2.0	18.4	-19.0
金属制品业	Metal Products	4.9	1.1	0.4	14.4
通用设备制造业	Manufacture of General-purpose Machinery	9.0	3.3	3.9	1.7
专用设备制造业	Manufacture of Special-purpose Machinery	24.5	4.3	2.0	8.8
汽车制造业	Manufacture of Automobile	16.4	11.0	-2.6	3.6

注：建设项目个数不含房地产开发；2018年—2020年，本年新增固定资产不含计划总投资5000万元以下项目。

Note: Projects under construction do not include real estate investment and newly increased fixed assets do not include project under 50 million from 2018 to 2020.

5-5 续表 1 continued 1

单位：% (%)

行 业	Sector	投资额 Investment	施工项目个数 Number of Projects under Construction	全部建成投产项目个数 Number of Projects Completed and Put into Use	新增固定资产 Newly Increased Fixed Assets
铁路、船舶、航空航天和其他运输设备制造业	Manufacture of Railway, Slip, Aeronautics and Other Transport Equipment	2.5	8.1	15.1	6.2
电气机械及器材制造业	Manufacture of Electrical Machinery and Equipment	24.5	7.5	5.0	-9.9
计算机、通信和其他电子设备制造业	Manufacture of Computers, Communication Equipment and Other Electronic Equipment	25.6	7.1	1.4	-2.5
仪器仪表制造业	Manufacture of Instruments and Meters	33.7	10.3	9.1	59.8
其他制造业	Other Manufactures	18.9	39.8	50.0	53.5
废弃资源综合利用业	Comprehensive Utilization of Waste	-17.6	-3.0	-15.9	10.4
金属制品、机械和设备修理业	Manufacture of Metal Products, Machinery and Equipment Maintenance	-34.8		44.4	43.3
电力、热力、燃气及水生产和供应业	**Production and Supply of Electric Power, Heat Power, Gas and Water**	**2.0**	**21.5**	**11.6**	**25.8**
电力、热力生产和供应业	Production and Supply of Electric Power and Heat Power	1.6	32.5	22.7	37.1
燃气生产和供应业	Production and Supply of Gas	19.6	38.7	-36.8	-37.3
水的生产和供应业	Production and Supply of Water	-0.7	4.8	10.1	7.0
建筑业	**Construction**	**86.2**		**33.3**	**-2.1**
房屋建筑业	Housing Construction	83.7		100.0	489.8
土木工程建筑业	Civil Engineering Construction	93.6			-51.9
建筑安装业	Construction and Installation				
建筑装饰和其他建筑业	Architectural Decoration and Other Construction	-23.4			-23.4
批发和零售业	**Wholesale and Retail Trades**	**6.4**	**-16.1**	**-24.5**	**-36.4**
批发业	Wholesale	-11.0	1.9	-4.3	-33.7
零售业	Retail Trade	22.9	-24.5	-32.1	-38.3
交通运输、仓储和邮政业	**Transport, Storage and Postal Services**	**-0.6**	**-0.8**	**-11.4**	**6.8**
铁路运输业	Railway Transport	23.5	6.7	75.0	153.4
道路运输业	Road Transport	-5.4	-10.3	-26.2	-11.7
水上运输业	Waterway Transport	-18.0	21.0	18.2	-65.6
航空运输业	Air Transport	-9.5	58.0	200.0	15.7
管道运输业	Pipeline Transport	-28.0	-3.8	-75.0	-99.5
多式联运和运输代理业	Multimodal Transportation and Transport Agency Industry	22.2	-3.3	87.5	578.8
装卸搬运和仓储业	Handling, handling and storage	11.6	14.9	42.3	136.5
邮政业	Postal Services	422.0	41.7	20.0	819.6
住宿和餐饮业	**Hotels and Catering Services**	**-21.3**	**8.9**	**2.4**	**23.4**
住宿业	Hotels	-23.3	10.4	4.3	27.1
餐饮业	Catering Services	21.3		-3.1	-6.9
信息传输、软件和信息技术服务业	**Information Transmission, Software and Information Technology Services**	**3.3**	**-12.3**	**-15.8**	**-7.7**
电信、广播电视和卫星传输服务	Telecommunications, Broadcasting Television and Satellite Transmission Services	-10.5	-29.5	-32.4	-8.1
互联网和相关服务	Internet and Related Services	-28.7	13.8	50.0	122.6
软件和信息技术服务业	Software and Information Technology Services	77.6	3.1	7.1	-32.5
金融业	**Finance**	**2.7**	**16.1**	**-15.4**	**60.5**
货币金融服务	Monetary and Financial Services	48.3	20.0	-22.2	1053.9

5-5 续表 2 continued 2

单位：% (%)

行 业	Sector	投资额 Investment	施工项目个数 Number of Projects under Construction	全部建成投产项目个数 Number of Projects Completed and Put into Use	新增固定资产 Newly Increased Fixed Assets
资本市场服务	Capital Market Services	-9.6	50.0	200.0	-98.1
保险业	Insurance	-51.1	-10.0		-60.3
其他金融活动	Other Financial Activities	-38.6	-25.0	-50.0	-96.1
房地产业	**Real Estate**	**-13.4**	**1.1**	**-4.3**	**-23.4**
房地产业	Real Estate	-13.4	1.1	-4.3	-23.4
租赁和商务服务业	**Leasing and Business Services**	**-5.5**	**16.9**	**5.8**	**-6.1**
租赁业	Leasing	9.3		-8.3	4.6
商务服务业	Business Services	-5.7	17.1	6.7	-6.4
科学研究、技术服务业	**Scientific Research, Technological Services**	**11.3**	**7.5**	**19.4**	**58.0**
研究与试验发展	Research and Experimental Development	13.6	4.7	26.5	61.6
专业技术服务业	Professional Technical Services	40.0	11.1	11.5	42.4
科技推广和应用服务业	Science and Technology Popularization and Application Services	-24.7	6.5	29.4	83.9
水利、环境和公共设施管理业	**Management of Water Conservancy, Environment and Public Facilities**	**7.5**	**-3.2**	**-18.6**	**-14.7**
水利管理业	Management of Water Conservancy	9.6	4.8	-4.7	-0.6
生态保护和环境治理业	Ecological Protection and Environmental Treatment	-11.3	-20.1	-34.1	13.0
公共设施管理业	Management of Public Facilities	8.8	-3.0	-19.2	-16.8
土地管理业	Land Management	-0.8	20.0	122.2	192.6
居民服务、修理和其他服务业	**Households' service, Repair and Other Services**	**19.9**	**8.7**	**2.2**	**88.1**
居民服务业	Services to Households	21.7	3.0	-3.2	89.3
机动车、电子产品和日用产品修理业	Motor Vehicle, Electronic Products and Consumer Products Repair	95.9		16.7	153.7
其他服务业	Other Services	-2.7	40.0	11.1	57.4
教育	**Education**	**-14.0**	**-2.9**	**-3.9**	**15.4**
教育	Education	-14.0	-2.9	-3.9	15.4
卫生和社会工作	**Health and Social Work**	**29.4**	**15.6**	**-2.4**	**20.0**
卫生	Health	31.0	16.9	-3.3	21.9
社会工作	Social Work	4.4	4.6	8.0	-10.0
文化、体育和娱乐业	**Culture, Sports and Recreation**	**-10.4**	**-11.8**	**-23.7**	**-37.0**
新闻出版业	Publication	-63.5	33.3		
广播、电视、电影和影视录音制作业	Production of Radio, Television, Film and Video Recording	-34.3	-18.5	-38.5	-64.9
文化艺术业	Culture and Arts	3.1	-11.8	-31.1	-20.9
体育	Sports	-17.3	-17.2	-28.8	-64.3
娱乐业	Recreation	-19.3	-8.9	-9.4	-18.3
公共管理、社会保障和社会组织	**Public Administration, Social Security and Social Organizations**	**23.9**	**3.6**	**-14.3**	**3.9**
中国共产党机关	Organs of Communist Party of China	-74.1	-50.0	-66.7	-74.3
国家机构	Government Agencies	28.6	7.7	-5.4	11.9
人民政协、民主党派	Chinese Peoples Political Consultative Conference, Democratic Parties				
社会保障	Social Security				
群众社团、社会团体和其他成员组织	Mass Organizations, Social Organizations and Other Member Organizations	-33.9	-28.1	-82.4	-78.4
基层群众自治组织	Self-governing Mass Organizations at the Grass-roots Level	-9.4	-29.0	-31.6	-6.8

5-6 各行业财务拨贷款资金来源主要指标增长速度(2022年)
Growth Rate of Main Indicators on Sources of Funds and Loans for Investment by Sector (2022)

单位：% (%)

项　目	Item	本年资金来源合计 Sources of Funds	国家预算资金 State and Local Budget	国内贷款 Domestic Loans	利用外资 Foreign Investment	自筹资金 Self-raising Fund	其他资金 Others
全　省	**Provincial Total**	**-11.5**	**28.1**	**-13.0**	**26.6**	**-4.5**	**-33.7**
农、林、牧、渔业	**Farming, Forestry, Animal Husbandry and Fishery**	**-4.9**	**45.0**	**22.4**	**-1.4**	**-16.0**	**-14.8**
农业	Farming	7.7	4.9	113.4		19.1	-32.3
林业	Forestry	2.3	52.6			-22.1	-59.3
畜牧业	Animal Husbandry	-30.2	-32.3	9.4	-100.0	-34.3	31.7
渔业	Fishery	73.1	278.8	58.4		55.2	-56.1
农、林、牧、渔服务业	Service Activities for Farming, Forestry, Animal Husbandry and Fishery	42.8	112.7	40.0		-7.8	23.0
采矿业	**Mining**	**62.6**	**-100.0**	**64.4**		**62.0**	**95.1**
煤炭开采和洗选业	Mining and Washing of Coal						
石油和天然气开采业	Extraction of Petroleum and Natural Gas	48.9				48.9	
黑色金属矿采选业	Mining and Dressing of Ferrous Metal Ores	109.9				109.9	
有色金属矿采选业	Mining and Dressing of Non-Ferrous Metal Ores	-14.7				-14.9	
非金属矿采选业	Mining and Dressing of Nonmetal Ores	82.0	-100.0	64.4		122.0	56.8
开采辅助活动	Auxiliary Mining Operations	1.9				1.9	
其他采矿业	Mining of Other Ores	4297.3				-32.1	
制造业	**Manufacture**	**17.8**	**152.3**	**39.9**	**49.7**	**13.3**	**42.2**
农副食品加工业	Processing of Farm and Sideline Food	26.4	123.9	61.6	-72.4	18.2	44.0
食品制造业	Manufacture of Food	7.0	-77.3	95.5	-43.3	7.9	-46.5
酒、饮料和精制茶制造业	Manufacture of Wine,Beverage and refined tea	37.4	-54.1	13.6	-60.5	40.2	63.8
烟草制品业	Tobacco Products	-32.3				-33.6	
纺织业	Textile Industry	-10.6	-100.0	-59.2	-75.5	-9.4	101.5
纺织服装、服饰业	Manufacture of Textile Garments, Apparel	37.8	280.0	153.1		25.5	83.8
皮革、毛皮、羽毛及其制品和制鞋业	Leather, Fur, Feather and Related Products, and Footwear	35.3	-24.5	34.5	-100.0	32.6	588.2
木材加工及木、竹、藤、棕、草制品业	Timber Processing, Bamboo, Cane, Palm Fiber & Straw Products	-25.5	-100.0	-64.7	-100.0	-21.7	23.4
家具制造业	Manufacture of Furniture	17.5		79.8	-62.3	13.3	-8.7
造纸和纸制品业	Papermaking and Paper Products	6.1	3054.6	100.7	-1.6	-7.5	22.7
印刷业和记录媒介复制业	Printing and Record Medium Reproduction	0.0		-21.0		0.8	-3.3
文教、工美、体育和娱乐用品制造业	Manufacture of Culture, Arts, Sports and Entertainment Articles	14.2		68.7	-84.8	14.6	-12.0
石油加工、炼焦及核燃料加工业	Petroleum Refining, Coking and Nuclear Fuel Processing	-24.3		-97.3	-100.0	-17.8	-100.0
化学原料及化学制品制造业	Manufacture of Raw Chemical Materials and Chemical Products	43.8	274.7	41.9	62.3	39.1	63.0
医药制造业	Manufacture of Medicines	8.5	1192.0	6.7	500.0	-1.7	184.7
化学纤维制造业	Manufacture of Chemical Fibers	-39.7				-48.6	
橡胶和塑料制品业	Manufacture of Rubber and Plastic Products	0.4	-21.3	1.3	-18.2	-3.6	174.2
非金属矿物制品业	Nonmetal Mineral Products	-4.4	-76.2	-41.6	441.4	0.2	-12.6
黑色金属冶炼及压延加工业	Smelting and Pressing of Ferrous Metals	-21.4		0.7		-22.5	165.4
有色金属冶炼及压延加工业	Smelting and Pressing of Nonferrous Metals	1.8	-100.0	59.7		-1.8	25.3
金属制品业	Metal Products	10.5	31.3	44.6	-74.7	7.8	55.0
通用设备制造业	Manufacture of General-purpose Machinery	22.2	-51.3	7.4	237.4	22.7	29.3
专用设备制造业	Manufacture of Special-purpose Machinery	34.4	180.6	82.2	-33.3	28.7	75.2
汽车制造业	Manufacture of Automobile	12.3	-44.9	-23.9	-58.2	18.3	-60.6

5-6 续表 1 continued 1

单位：% (%)

项 目	Item	本年资金来源合计 Sources of Funds	国家预算内资金 State Budget	国内货款 Domestic Loans	利用外资 Foreign Inves-tment	自筹资金 Self-raising Fund	其他资金 Others
铁路、船舶、航空航天和其他运输设备制造业	Manufacture of Railway, Slip, Aeronautics and Other Transport Equipment	20.1	385.9	494.1	-100.0	10.4	59.5
电气机械及器材制造业	Manufacture of Electrical Machinery and Equipment	23.3	830.0	57.0	71.0	21.0	-21.6
计算机、通信和其他电子设备制造业	Manufacture of Computers, Communication Equipment and Other Electronic Equipment	30.9	232.5	74.0	152.5	21.0	104.8
仪器仪表制造业	Manufacture of Instruments and Meters	40.8		-33.8	-24.3	52.4	1.8
其他制造业	Other Manufactures	38.9	-25.0	453.4		29.1	-65.4
废弃资源综合利用业	Comprehensive Utilization of Waste	-19.1	-100.0	-33.7		-16.7	6.8
金属制品、机械和设备修理业	Manufacture of Metal Products, Machinery and Equipment Maintenance	-33.8	-100.0	-41.5	-63.2	-27.3	-86.4
电力、热力、燃气及水生产和供应业	**Production and Supply of Electric Power, Heat Power, Gas and Water**	**17.1**	**59.3**	**-11.5**	**-72.7**	**35.6**	**9.8**
电力、热力生产和供应业	Production and Supply of Electric Power and Heat Power	16.3	40.5	-13.0	-92.7	44.8	55.4
燃气生产和供应业	Production and Supply of Gas	32.5	18.4	63.4	556.6	40.4	-45.1
水的生产和供应业	Production and Supply of Water	15.7	70.2	-25.3	-100.0	-5.7	4.7
建筑业	**Construction**	**73.8**	**-100.0**	**-36.9**		**337.6**	
房屋建筑业	Housing Construction	76.9				-31.1	
土木工程建筑业	Civil Engineering Construction	79.5	-100.0	-41.5		540.3	
建筑安装业	Construction and Installation						
建筑装饰和其他建筑业	Architectural Decoration and Other Construction	-23.1		-100.0		-17.3	
批发和零售业	**Wholesale and Retail Trades**	**10.7**	**-19.3**	**6.3**	**243.1**	**14.5**	**-16.1**
批发业	Wholesale	-0.4	532.2	121.9		-7.6	-63.9
零售业	Retail Trade	20.4	-95.3	-28.7	241.5	37.0	57.4
交通运输、仓储和邮政业	**Transport, Storage and Postal Services**	**6.2**	**16.2**	**5.9**	**125.0**	**1.0**	**-26.9**
铁路运输业	Railway Transport	21.1	45.8	43.9		-0.2	-80.2
道路运输业	Road Transport	6.9	7.9	5.0	-100.0	12.0	0.7
水上运输业	Waterway Transport	-13.3	-11.5	-39.2		-12.2	103.9
航空运输业	Air Transport	-18.7	11.8	-37.3		-19.3	-35.3
管道运输业	Pipeline Transport	-46.4		-59.3		-43.0	-97.1
多式联运和运输代理业	Multimodal Transportation and Transport Agency Industry	25.9	1448.8	-58.6		49.2	1301.9
装卸搬运和仓储业	Handling, handling and storage	11.9	44.9	34.5	34.0	-1.1	29.3
邮政业	Postal Services	18.8		-100.0		15.4	104.2
住宿和餐饮业	**Hotels and Catering Services**	**-5.2**	**-62.9**	**39.7**	**420.0**	**6.4**	**60.0**
住宿业	Hotels	-5.7	-62.9	43.3		6.7	60.3
餐饮业	Catering Services	2.7	-100.0	-29.8	-100.0	2.0	54.8
信息传输、软件和信息技术服务业	**Information Transmission, Software and Information Technology Services**	**2.1**	**-28.7**	**-40.4**	**350.7**	**3.9**	**282.9**
电信、广播电视和卫星传输服务	Telecommunications, Broadcasting Television and Satellite Transmission Services	-9.9	110.0	-81.5		-9.0	330.5
互联网和相关服务	Internet and Related Services	-30.8	-65.7	19.0		-26.4	181.7
软件和信息技术服务业	Software and Information Technology Services	71.9	82.0	5.5	-100.0	68.5	325.2
金融业	**Finance**	**6.9**	**-22.2**	**-75.9**		**12.2**	**-80.3**
货币金融服务	Monetary and Financial Services	56.0		-100.0		67.7	-42.9

5-6 续表 2 continued 2

单位：% (%)

项　　目	Item	本年资金来源合计 Sources of Funds	国家预算内资金 State Budget	国内货款 Domestic loans	利用外资 Foreign Inives-tment	自筹资金 Self-raising Fund	其他资金 Others
资本市场服务	Capital Market Services	-1.4				-2.4	
保险业	Insurance	-50.8				-50.8	
其他金融活动	Other Financial Activities	-39.1	-22.2			-83.4	-100.0
房地产业	**Real Estate**	**-31.2**	**-33.3**	**-30.7**	**-14.6**	**-20.6**	**-38.6**
房地产业	Real Estate	-31.2	-33.3	-30.7	-14.6	-20.6	-38.6
租赁和商务服务业	**Leasing and Business Services**	**6.2**	**37.8**	**50.0**	**-43.5**	**-1.2**	**22.0**
租赁业	Leasing	18.9		-37.0		4.4	523.2
商务服务业	Business Services	6.0	37.8	50.3	-49.5	-1.3	19.0
科学研究、技术服务业	**Scientific Research, Technological Services**	**6.9**	**-2.9**	**37.5**	**14507.4**	**-19.5**	**317.2**
研究与试验发展	Research and Experimental Development	2.9	-5.2	50.7		-12.6	132.9
专业技术服务业	Professional Technical Services	69.6	28.1	142.6	3603.7	4.7	1327.9
科技推广和应用服务业	Science and Technology Popularization and Application Services	-39.8	-33.9	-83.9		-46.2	250.3
水利、环境和公共设施管理业	**Management of Water Conservancy, Environment and Public Facilities**	**23.4**	**41.2**	**-15.0**	**-46.8**	**-13.6**	**41.5**
水利管理业	Management of Water Conservancy	21.0	32.2	-52.3		-9.7	107.5
生态保护和环境治理业	Ecological Protection and Environmental Treatment	-8.9	-22.4	-27.3	-32.4	4.7	93.2
公共设施管理业	Management of Public Facilities	26.3	47.8	-7.5	-56.1	-14.7	30.9
土地管理业	Land Management	29.0	502.2			-31.2	-74.3
居民服务、修理和其他服务业	**Households'service,Repair and Other Services**	**23.4**	**-22.2**	**143.9**	**40.0**	**22.0**	**42.8**
居民服务业	Services to Households	28.8	-21.2	143.9	40.0	27.6	38.3
机动车、电子产品和日用产品修理业	Motor Vehicle, Electronic Products and Consumer Products repair	120.5				120.5	
其他服务业	Other Services	-14.0	-28.3			-13.0	
教育	**Education**	**-6.3**	**6.1**	**-12.4**	**-100.0**	**-31.3**	**87.1**
教育	Education	-6.3	6.1	-12.4	-100.0	-31.3	87.1
卫生和社会工作	**Health and Social Work**	**41.8**	**70.9**	**-26.3**	**-74.7**	**3.2**	**12.1**
卫生	Health	43.7	71.8	-17.1	-74.7	2.3	5.2
社会工作	Social Work	13.0	42.2	-59.8		10.3	161.2
文化、体育和娱乐业	**Culture, Sports and Recreation**	**2.4**	**47.2**	**14.3**	**277.5**	**-32.6**	**27.7**
新闻出版业	Publication	-70.0		-83.9		-66.7	
广播、电视、电影和影视录音制作业	Production of Radio, Television, Film and Video Recording	-33.3	352.1	62.4	-100.0	-60.7	-12.1
文化艺术业	Culture and Arts	24.7	73.4	899.2		-39.8	-16.5
体育	Sports	5.7	6.0	866.4		-28.0	60.3
娱乐业	Recreation	-14.2	32.3	-14.4	1279.1	-26.3	50.1
公共管理、社会保障和社会组织	**Public Administration, Social Security and Social Organizations**	**45.4**	**40.6**	**-59.4**		**48.8**	**85.6**
中国共产党机关	Organs of Communist Party of China	-67.5	-75.3				-100.0
国家机构	Government Agencies	51.3	41.4	-59.4		87.2	85.7
人民政协、民主党派	Chinese Peoples Political Consultative Conference, Democratic Parties						
社会保障	Social Security						
群众社团、社会团体和其他成员组织	Mass Organizations, Social Organizations and Other Member Organizations	-22.7	1034.4			-61.2	76.8
基层群众自治组织	Self-governing Mass Organizations at the Grass-roots Level	20.4	-66.7			32.4	599.6

5-7 各市按项目和房地产开发分固定资产投资增长速度

Growth Rate of Investment in Fixed Assets By Project and Real Estate Development and by City

单位：% (%)

市别	City	2021 全部投资 Total	2021 项目投资 Project	2021 房地产开发 Real Estate Development	2022 全部投资 Total	2022 项目投资 Project	2022 房地产开发 Real Estate Development
全　省	**Provincial Total**	**6.3**	**9.8**	**0.9**	**-2.6**	**4.7**	**-14.3**
广　州	Guangzhou	11.7	13.0	10.1	-2.1	0.3	-5.4
深　圳	Shenzhen	3.7	19.2	-15.4	8.4	5.5	13.3
珠　海	Zhuhai	-3.1	-13.4	8.0	-8.8	21.5	-34.8
汕　头	Shantou	-25.3	-33.6	6.5	-14.5	-11.3	-22.0
佛　山	Foshan	7.6	14.8	2.3	-3.6	11.8	-16.5
韶　关	Shaoguan	2.2	-2.4	14.5	-19.7	-7.1	-48.5
河　源	Heyuan	8.9	11.0	4.2	-29.3	-20.8	-49.1
梅　州	Meizhou	-14.8	-19.7	-6.3	-11.0	15.4	-49.8
惠　州	Huizhou	21.8	39.0	5.6	8.8	30.2	-17.9
汕　尾	Shanwei	16.9	21.0	6.2	-6.2	8.1	-49.4
东　莞	Dongguan	8.2	6.3	11.7	0.8	6.0	-7.9
中　山	Zhongshan	15.3	15.7	14.7	-0.7	14.7	-23.4
江　门	Jiangmen	1.4	9.0	-10.3	-0.8	11.4	-23.4
阳　江	Yangjiang	37.8	58.0	-20.3	-32.8	-33.9	-26.2
湛　江	Zhanjiang	19.1	15.1	27.2	-9.6	2.0	-31.1
茂　名	Maoming	0.4	1.1	-0.5	6.3	24.5	-19.7
肇　庆	Zhaoqing	11.6	15.5	3.2	-14.9	-3.9	-41.7
清　远	Qingyuan	9.5	33.6	-17.0	-6.9	2.5	-23.6
潮　州	Chaozhou	1.6	4.4	-6.6	0.4	4.1	-11.6
揭　阳	Jieyang	-6.4	-6.2	-7.0	-23.5	-16.1	-44.3
云　浮	Yunfu	4.5	0.7	12.8	5.3	24.7	-32.3
按经济区域分	By Region						
珠三角	Pearl River Delta	8.1	14.1	0.7	0.4	7.9	-9.9
东　翼	Eastern Region	-10.5	-14.2	1.3	-13.4	-6.2	-32.8
西　翼	Western Region	16.7	20.9	8.8	-10.6	-3.2	-26.4
山　区	Mountainous Region	2.9	6.0	-2.6	-14.4	-1.6	-39.6

5-8 各市按登记注册类型分固定资产投资增长速度（2022年）
Growth Rate of Investment in Fixed Assets by Status of Registration and City (2022)

单位：% (%)

市 别	City	全部投资 Total	内资 Domestic	港、澳、台商 Funds from Hong Kong Macao and Taiwan	外商 Foreign Funded
全 省	**Provincial Total**	**-2.6**	**-3.1**	**4.3**	**-3.4**
广 州	Guangzhou	-2.1	-5.3	11.9	51.5
深 圳	Shenzhen	8.4	9.1	22.8	-23.0
珠 海	Zhuhai	-8.8	2.6	-33.9	-73.3
汕 头	Shantou	-14.5	-13.7	-42.5	-21.4
佛 山	Foshan	-3.6	-2.3	3.9	-33.9
韶 关	Shaoguan	-19.7	-19.8	-31.9	0.2
河 源	Heyuan	-29.3	-28.9	-33.8	-38.9
梅 州	Meizhou	-11.0	-10.9	10.1	-54.6
惠 州	Huizhou	8.8	6.2	5.0	80.3
汕 尾	Shanwei	-6.2	-5.0	-48.3	12.7
东 莞	Dongguan	0.8	1.3	-5.3	-3.0
中 山	Zhongshan	-0.7	-1.5	14.9	-3.2
江 门	Jiangmen	-0.8	-0.6	4.8	-12.6
阳 江	Yangjiang	-32.8	-33.0	-27.7	28.3
湛 江	Zhanjiang	-9.6	-11.5	12.2	-0.3
茂 名	Maoming	6.3	3.8	47.5	96.4
肇 庆	Zhaoqing	-14.9	-16.1	63.3	-46.5
清 远	Qingyuan	-6.9	-6.0	-21.5	-8.6
潮 州	Chaozhou	0.4	0.1	27.0	37.0
揭 阳	Jieyang	-23.5	-24.7	122.5	502.0
云 浮	Yunfu	5.3	2.7	84.1	-15.8
按经济区域分	By Region				
珠 三 角	Pearl River Delta	0.4	0.3	7.1	-4.7
东 翼	Eastern Region	-13.4	-13.2	-28.2	2.8
西 翼	Western Region	-10.6	-12.4	3.9	16.7
山 区	Mountainous Region	-14.4	-14.4	-14.0	-16.7

注：内资含个体经济，下表同。
Note: Domestic investment include individuals and the same applies to the following table.

5-9 各市按控股类型分固定资产投资增长速度（2022年）

Growth Rate of Investment in Fixed Assets Divided by Holding Type and by City

单位：% (%)

市别	City	全部投资 Total	#国有控股 State Holding	集体控股 Collective Holding	私人控股 Private Holding
全省	**Provincial Total**	**-2.6**	**4.7**	**-6.5**	**-8.6**
广州	Guangzhou	-2.1	-1.2	1.7	-9.7
深圳	Shenzhen	8.4	11.8	1.3	-2.3
珠海	Zhuhai	-8.8	36.6	-4.8	-10.3
汕头	Shantou	-14.5	-15.3	-16.3	-11.3
佛山	Foshan	-3.6	2.0	-26.3	4.0
韶关	Shaoguan	-19.7	-11.6	123.8	-26.7
河源	Heyuan	-29.3	-19.0	-5.6	-37.7
梅州	Meizhou	-11.0	20.4	291.5	-34.5
惠州	Huizhou	8.8	11.3	57.7	6.5
汕尾	Shanwei	-6.2	4.7	57.4	-10.5
东莞	Dongguan	0.8	9.4	19.4	0.8
中山	Zhongshan	-0.7	27.1	-1.7	-19.3
江门	Jiangmen	-0.8	22.6	-24.5	-9.8
阳江	Yangjiang	-32.8	-37.9	90.0	-22.6
湛江	Zhanjiang	-9.6	-5.6	-36.1	-24.0
茂名	Maoming	6.3	17.3	-48.2	-10.4
肇庆	Zhaoqing	-14.9	-13.9	-9.3	-17.5
清远	Qingyuan	-6.9	51.2	32.0	-30.0
潮州	Chaozhou	0.4	13.0	-64.3	-6.6
揭阳	Jieyang	-23.5	-16.8	43.7	-32.2
云浮	Yunfu	5.3	32.1	97.9	-14.6
按经济区域分	By Region				
珠三角	Pearl River Delta	0.4	7.9	-5.2	-4.0
东翼	Eastern Region	-13.4	-8.3	-10.6	-14.7
西翼	Western Region	-10.6	-10.1	-40.1	-18.6
山区	Mountainous Region	-14.4	8.7	41.2	-30.2

5-10 各市按行业分固定资产投资增长速度（2022年）

Growth Rate of Investment in Fixed Assets by Sector and by City (2022)

单位：% (%)

市别	City	全部投资 Total	农、林、牧、渔业 Agriculture, Forestry, Animal Husbandry and Fishery	采矿业 Mining	制造业 Manufacturing	电力、热力、燃气及水的生产和供应业 Production and Supply of Electricity, Gas and Water	建筑业 Construction	批发和零售业 Wholesale and Retail Trades
全　省	**Provincial Total**	**-2.6**	**-15.3**	**33.6**	**12.2**	**2.0**	**86.2**	**6.4**
广　州	Guangzhou	-2.1	-24.6	-48.3	21.5	-12.1	77.4	-34.5
深　圳	Shenzhen	8.4	-97.4	73.0	15.4	16.6		164.0
珠　海	Zhuhai	-8.8	-37.5	-78.7	81.6	1.3		-37.8
汕　头	Shantou	-14.5	58.1		-12.4	28.1	20.5	-7.3
佛　山	Foshan	-3.6	1.5	-79.0	9.8	-9.1		58.0
韶　关	Shaoguan	-19.7	-23.2	42.2	-2.8	-27.3		14.2
河　源	Heyuan	-29.3	-24.1	-26.4	-8.4	-41.7		-91.3
梅　州	Meizhou	-11.0	91.0	-51.4	11.1	12.2		-38.3
惠　州	Huizhou	8.8	6.8	13.3	50.2	19.2		-13.3
汕　尾	Shanwei	-6.2	59.1		1.5	-10.9	-66.7	-86.6
东　莞	Dongguan	0.8	-96.2		3.2	21.4		-43.5
中　山	Zhongshan	-0.7	-28.3		20.2	21.9		
江　门	Jiangmen	-0.8	-31.4	62.5	18.9	16.8		-18.4
阳　江	Yangjiang	-32.8	126.5	-88.6	-21.1	-54.3		894.1
湛　江	Zhanjiang	-9.6	-46.0	23.6	-23.2	-1.8		-31.4
茂　名	Maoming	6.3	1.0	-63.7	7.2	13.9		102.2
肇　庆	Zhaoqing	-14.9	-35.9	-70.6	-5.0	277.9		-57.3
清　远	Qingyuan	-6.9	32.6		-2.0	29.0		-42.7
潮　州	Chaozhou	0.4	-47.5	-47.6	0.6	16.4		-6.4
揭　阳	Jieyang	-23.5	-35.6	1444.8	-29.1	18.8		-44.2
云　浮	Yunfu	5.3	2.3	555.5	6.0	80.9		-35.3
按经济区域分	By Region							
珠三角	Pearl River Delta	0.4	-28.5	17.6	19.6	16.6	86.2	15.3
东　翼	Eastern Region	-13.4	18.6	413.2	-15.7	7.1	-34.8	-24.9
西　翼	Western Region	-10.6	-26.7	20.7	-14.2	-29.1	314.4	70.7
山　区	Mountainous Region	-14.4	-6.7	405.9	-1.7	3.7		-47.4

5−10 续表 1 continued 1

单位：% (%)

市别	City	交通运输、仓储和邮政业 Transport, Storage and Post	住宿和餐饮业 Hotels and Catering Services	信息传输、软件和信息技术服务业 Information Transmission, Software and Information Technology Services	金融业 Financial Intermediation	房地产业 Real Estate	租赁和商务服务业 Leasing and Business Services	科学研究和技术服务业 Scientific Research, Technical Service
全　省	**Provincial Total**	**-0.6**	**-21.3**	**3.3**	**2.7**	**-13.4**	**-5.5**	**11.3**
广　州	Guangzhou	3.5	-0.7	-15.4	-21.7	-3.7	-10.0	15.3
深　圳	Shenzhen	8.3	-54.8	43.8	17.1	7.4	-17.8	-15.0
珠　海	Zhuhai	-3.9	-22.6	5.7		-34.5	0.9	47.2
汕　头	Shantou	0.3	-15.4	46.2	40.3	-18.3	99.5	59.0
佛　山	Foshan	6.7	2.2	39.2	73.3	-15.4	0.3	-6.7
韶　关	Shaoguan	-31.7	-1.7	-15.4	1019.9	-44.3	21.9	6.4
河　源	Heyuan	-38.1	28.1	-53.5		-48.8	-17.8	53.9
梅　州	Meizhou	16.5		6.6	145.6	-46.6	-0.8	-79.0
惠　州	Huizhou	18.1	-6.9	26.0		-17.7	-39.8	3.8
汕　尾	Shanwei	5.4	56.3	28.6		-47.5	-18.4	23.4
东　莞	Dongguan	9.4	-8.2	-32.4	-24.8	-6.1	-11.7	-8.7
中　山	Zhongshan	-11.3	-44.6	-8.0	-44.2	-22.6	7.8	44.6
江　门	Jiangmen	8.4	-9.4	-41.8	-52.7	-23.4	-40.1	-43.8
阳　江	Yangjiang	-9.8	-4.3	24.4		-22.2	404.4	128.7
湛　江	Zhanjiang	-5.9	-57.3	7.6	-21.5	-31.6	-6.0	-1.4
茂　名	Maoming	12.5	4.1	-32.8		-19.4	77.7	57.4
肇　庆	Zhaoqing	-4.4	-34.6	-21.9	79.9	-36.5	-23.2	-32.3
清　远	Qingyuan	-71.1	-41.2	-0.1		-22.4	127.3	1460.4
潮　州	Chaozhou	-17.0	26.3	-25.3		-18.0	-8.4	-21.0
揭　阳	Jieyang	-10.4	16.1	-29.5		-41.2	21.8	3.6
云　浮	Yunfu	-1.8	-47.6	22.6		-29.5	-13.5	140.0
按经济区域分	By Region							
珠 三 角	Pearl River Delta	5.0	-29.7	9.7	2.2	-9.4	-12.1	1.8
东　翼	Eastern Region	-3.4	26.1	13.8	40.3	-30.0	42.8	39.9
西　翼	Western Region	-0.6	-20.6	-7.7	14.9	-26.2	56.8	16.9
山　区	Mountainous Region	-38.7	-18.7	-20.4	357.7	-37.7	31.8	273.9

5-10 续表 2 continued 2

单位：% (%)

市　别	City	水利、环境和公共设施管理业 Management of Water Conservancy, Environment and Public Facilities	居民、修理服务和其他服务业 Household's Services, Repair and Other Services	教育 Education	卫生和社会工作 Health and Social Service	文化、体育和娱乐业 Culture, Sports and Entert-ainment	公共管理、社会保障和社会组织 Public Management, Social Security and Social Organization
全　省	**Provincial Total**	**7.5**	**19.9**	**-14.0**	**29.4**	**-10.4**	**23.9**
广　州	Guangzhou	-4.9	88.4	-19.5	-17.4	-6.8	-30.7
深　圳	Shenzhen	-9.9	-16.5	-13.0	64.1	22.9	6.4
珠　海	Zhuhai	17.1	124.8	5.3	-8.9	-45.8	102.5
汕　头	Shantou	-40.0	23.4	-55.0	-2.3	-49.2	145.3
佛　山	Foshan	20.7	-18.6	13.1	110.0	-19.4	51.4
韶　关	Shaoguan	17.7	-4.9	16.4	-21.7	-7.8	22.2
河　源	Heyuan	16.0	-61.4	-25.2	-40.7	-20.9	-29.6
梅　州	Meizhou	10.1	-96.6	-6.7	77.1	-59.7	150.1
惠　州	Huizhou	23.6	2.5	-33.0	63.3	-37.3	18.2
汕　尾	Shanwei	56.3	-74.5	-34.5	-6.8	54.1	-16.4
东　莞	Dongguan	2.0	-65.8	30.3	75.4	57.0	18.9
中　山	Zhongshan	93.8		-15.9	337.8	-45.1	34.2
江　门	Jiangmen	15.1	-60.8	-13.7	66.9	-65.0	63.0
阳　江	Yangjiang	22.9		7.3	79.3	-23.5	-3.7
湛　江	Zhanjiang	33.5	247.4	68.7	71.7	174.8	172.5
茂　名	Maoming	79.7	73.5	-6.0	93.6	-17.2	20.9
肇　庆	Zhaoqing	-6.8	2193.3	-33.8	-34.6	-66.3	6.4
清　远	Qingyuan	117.1		-73.3	117.1	-13.8	219.2
潮　州	Chaozhou	47.6	82.5	-11.8	-24.3	-84.7	397.2
揭　阳	Jieyang	-12.2	-27.9	-37.0	-7.0	64.1	92.6
云　浮	Yunfu	9.9		-5.7	83.7	-62.5	-59.4
按经济区域分	By Region						
珠三角	Pearl River Delta	4.9	35.9	-11.7	29.9	-8.3	14.6
东　翼	Eastern Region	-9.4	16.4	-37.7	-7.3	-23.1	77.8
西　翼	Western Region	49.5	205.7	27.8	78.4	55.1	99.4
山　区	Mountainous Region	34.0	-57.9	-33.8	28.7	-26.4	22.3

5-11 各市按领域分固定资产投资比上年增长情况

Growth Rate of Investment in Fixed Assets by Sector and City

单位：%　　　　(%)

市别	City	全部投资 Total	#基础设施 Infrastructure	制造业 Manufacture	房地产开发 Real Estate Development
全　省	**Provincial Total**	**-2.6**	**2.0**	**12.2**	**-14.3**
广　州	Guangzhou	-2.1	-1.5	21.5	-5.4
深　圳	Shenzhen	8.4	1.7	15.4	13.3
珠　海	Zhuhai	-8.8	6.4	81.6	-34.8
汕　头	Shantou	-14.5	-16.7	-12.4	-22.0
佛　山	Foshan	-3.6	10.6	9.8	-16.5
韶　关	Shaoguan	-19.7	-12.9	-2.8	-48.5
河　源	Heyuan	-29.3	-26.3	-8.4	-49.1
梅　州	Meizhou	-11.0	12.7	11.1	-49.8
惠　州	Huizhou	8.8	18.5	50.2	-17.9
汕　尾	Shanwei	-6.2	6.5	1.5	-49.4
东　莞	Dongguan	0.8	8.1	3.2	-7.9
中　山	Zhongshan	-0.7	11.5	20.2	-23.4
江　门	Jiangmen	-0.8	10.4	18.9	-23.4
阳　江	Yangjiang	-32.8	-40.0	-21.1	-26.2
湛　江	Zhanjiang	-9.6	4.9	-23.2	-31.1
茂　名	Maoming	6.3	35.3	7.2	-19.7
肇　庆	Zhaoqing	-14.9	21.9	-5.0	-41.7
清　远	Qingyuan	-6.9	-7.0	-2.0	-23.6
潮　州	Chaozhou	0.4	18.4	0.6	-11.6
揭　阳	Jieyang	-23.5	1.2	-29.1	-44.3
云　浮	Yunfu	5.3	27.9	6.0	-32.3
按经济区域分	By Region				
珠三角	Pearl River Delta	0.4	5.6	19.6	-9.9
东　翼	Eastern Region	-13.4	-2.7	-15.7	-32.8
西　翼	Western Region	-10.6	-6.3	-14.2	-26.4
山　区	Mountainous Region	-14.4	-6.8	-1.7	-39.6

5-12 各市财务拨贷款资金来源主要指标增长速度（2022年）

Growth Rate of Main Indicators on Sources of Funds and Loans for Investment by City (2022)

单位：% (%)

市 别	City	本年资金来源合计 Sources of Funds	国家预算资金 State and Local Budget	国内贷款 Domestic Loans	利用外资 Foreign Investment	自筹资金 Self-raising Fund	其他资金 Others
全 省	**Provincial Total**	**-11.5**	**28.1**	**-13.0**	**26.6**	**-4.5**	**-33.7**
广 州	Guangzhou	-14.6	-8.4	8.9	62.6	-13.8	-32.0
深 圳	Shenzhen	-6.2	6.9	-17.7	452.1	19.8	-33.5
珠 海	Zhuhai	-23.6	69.1	-24.4	15.7	-16.5	-50.6
汕 头	Shantou	-5.0	60.0	-22.3	-100.0	-14.9	24.0
佛 山	Foshan	-17.8	86.4	-24.6	-65.5	-9.2	-38.4
韶 关	Shaoguan	-14.7	52.0	-24.3	-95.9	-19.0	-31.3
河 源	Heyuan	-18.6	55.4	-62.0	-100.0	-13.2	-34.4
梅 州	Meizhou	2.3	46.1	9.9	32.3	13.9	-33.1
惠 州	Huizhou	-11.8	47.6	-16.7	33.9	12.6	-45.7
汕 尾	Shanwei	1.9	78.2	-25.8	-89.8	18.3	-27.7
东 莞	Dongguan	-8.8	25.1	-13.2	-87.5	6.9	-31.2
中 山	Zhongshan	-20.2	151.7	-10.9	67.2	-21.1	-42.5
江 门	Jiangmen	-4.8	184.1	-40.9	-0.3	1.1	-22.7
阳 江	Yangjiang	-13.0	17.6	0.4	-78.9	-13.3	-31.4
湛 江	Zhanjiang	-8.7	93.5	-23.2	109.2	-25.2	-22.0
茂 名	Maoming	4.3	70.0	-28.7	-66.3	-0.1	-6.2
肇 庆	Zhaoqing	-12.6	21.2	-11.2	71.3	-9.5	-35.9
清 远	Qingyuan	-20.4	63.2	-31.2	55.3	-19.3	-31.0
潮 州	Chaozhou	4.2	41.8	-52.7	681.3	-0.4	-2.7
揭 阳	Jieyang	-14.9	46.3	50.8	485.0	-28.6	-11.6
云 浮	Yunfu	26.7	46.9	115.0	151081.5	11.7	8.2
按经济区域分	By Region						
珠 三 角	Pearl River Delta	-12.6	18.9	-11.7	18.7	-2.2	-36.2
东 翼	Eastern Region	-4.9	57.7	-15.3	-67.5	-12.2	-10.6
西 翼	Western Region	-5.7	68.2	-18.3	59.4	-16.5	-18.2
山 区	Mountainous Region	-10.5	53.2	-22.6	99.1	-9.6	-27.8

5-13 各市按构成和建设性质分固定资产投资增长速度（2022年）

Growth Rate of Investment in Fixed Assets in Urban Area by Composition of Funds, Type of Construction and City (2022)

单位：% (%)

市别	City	全部投资 Total	按构成分 By Composition of Funds			按建设性质分 By Type of Construction		
			建筑安装工程 Construction and Installation	设备、工具器具购置 Purchase of Equipment and Instruments	其他费用 Others	新建 New Construction	扩建 Expansion	改建和技术改造 Reconstruction and Technological Transformation
全　省	**Provincial Total**	**-2.6**	**-3.5**	**-3.1**	**-1.1**	**-2.0**	**0.6**	**-7.2**
广　州	Guangzhou	-2.1	-6.2	8.0	0.2	-0.2	-14.0	-12.0
深　圳	Shenzhen	8.4	2.2	-3.6	24.0	11.4	-7.2	-5.7
珠　海	Zhuhai	-8.8	16.8	-5.6	-42.7	-10.5	36.6	-0.3
汕　头	Shantou	-14.5	-10.3	-8.9	-34.0	-8.2	-40.0	-38.2
佛　山	Foshan	-3.6	-2.7	6.4	-7.6	-6.8	19.3	15.4
韶　关	Shaoguan	-19.7	-14.2	-13.2	-47.1	-22.0	-27.3	-2.5
河　源	Heyuan	-29.3	-24.1	-32.9	-53.6	-29.9	-4.9	-37.2
梅　州	Meizhou	-11.0	-9.8	20.8	-30.7	-18.6	266.9	-5.1
惠　州	Huizhou	8.8	12.7	15.6	-5.7	10.2	7.6	-9.9
汕　尾	Shanwei	-6.2	-6.5	2.8	-13.4	-7.0	15.6	-10.1
东　莞	Dongguan	0.8	1.9	-19.0	9.6	2.0	45.5	-10.9
中　山	Zhongshan	-0.7	-1.5	-1.8	1.5	-0.1	23.3	-17.4
江　门	Jiangmen	-0.8	2.1	13.6	-22.4	-1.2	3.0	2.6
阳　江	Yangjiang	-32.8	-20.3	-71.4	-0.3	-32.9	-66.5	44.8
湛　江	Zhanjiang	-9.6	-11.3	-2.1	-9.1	-11.5	14.3	7.7
茂　名	Maoming	6.3	0.9	-8.7	33.8	12.4	-21.9	-30.8
肇　庆	Zhaoqing	-14.9	-17.1	6.6	-23.4	-14.1	-27.0	-13.9
清　远	Qingyuan	-6.9	-21.2	15.8	41.9	-8.4	6.5	32.0
潮　州	Chaozhou	0.4	6.7	-14.4	-23.8	10.0	8.1	-35.1
揭　阳	Jieyang	-23.5	-24.4	-7.1	-31.2	-23.7	-24.5	-24.6
云　浮	Yunfu	5.3	-6.9	18.9	82.1	-0.5	145.4	-1.2
按经济区域分	By Region							
珠三角	Pearl River Delta	0.4	0.2	1.3	0.6	1.4	3.8	-4.7
东　翼	Eastern Region	-13.4	-11.4	-5.5	-28.2	-10.7	-20.0	-30.3
西　翼	Western Region	-10.6	-9.3	-34.7	5.0	-10.1	-31.4	-3.3
山　区	Mountainous Region	-14.4	-17.2	-3.2	-10.9	-17.2	40.5	-6.5

5-14 各市农业、能源、原材料、运输邮电业投资比重

Proportion of Investment in Capital Construction of Agriculture, Energy, Raw Materials, Transport, Post and Telecommunications

单位：% (%)

市别	City	2021（以投资总额为100） Proportion (total investment=100)				2022（以投资总额为100） Proportion (total investment=100)			
		农、林、牧、渔业 Farming, Forestry, Animal Husbandry and Fishery	能源 Energy	原材料 Raw Materials	交通运输、仓储和邮政业 Transport, Storage and Postal Services	农、林、牧、渔业 Farming, Forestry, Animal Husbandry and Fishery	能源 Energy	原材料 Raw Materials	交通运输、仓储和邮政业 Transport, Storage and Postal Services
全 省	**Provincial Total**	**0.8**	**5.9**	**2.6**	**10.4**	**0.7**	**5.9**	**3.0**	**10.7**
广 州	Guangzhou	0.3	2.8	0.9	12.9	0.2	2.5	1.0	13.7
深 圳	Shenzhen	…	2.9	0.5	12.9	0.0	3.9	0.3	12.9
珠 海	Zhuhai	0.1	2.6	2.4	5.1	0.1	2.4	1.5	5.3
汕 头	Shantou	0.6	5.2	2.0	8.9	1.0	8.2	1.9	10.5
佛 山	Foshan	0.1	1.4	2.2	4.3	0.1	1.4	2.1	4.8
韶 关	Shaoguan	5.2	7.9	6.4	10.3	5.0	7.0	8.1	8.8
河 源	Heyuan	3.6	5.5	3.9	12.0	3.8	3.7	2.5	10.5
梅 州	Meizhou	1.3	7.6	2.0	13.8	2.7	9.5	2.0	18.0
惠 州	Huizhou	0.5	6.4	5.7	7.8	0.5	7.1	9.2	8.5
汕 尾	Shanwei	2.5	19.0	0.9	10.9	4.3	19.0	2.8	12.3
东 莞	Dongguan	…	4.8	1.7	5.7	0.0	5.0	1.7	6.2
中 山	Zhongshan	…	2.1	1.0	22.9	0.0	1.9	1.5	20.5
江 门	Jiangmen	1.2	3.6	5.8	8.8	0.8	4.4	7.2	9.6
阳 江	Yangjiang	0.1	51.4	2.5	15.1	0.3	34.8	3.4	20.3
湛 江	Zhanjiang	3.1	19.8	8.1	10.0	1.9	19.4	8.1	10.4
茂 名	Maoming	3.1	7.3	5.0	15.6	3.0	6.9	6.0	16.5
肇 庆	Zhaoqing	4.2	1.2	6.8	4.9	3.2	8.2	6.7	5.5
清 远	Qingyuan	1.1	6.6	4.4	17.6	1.5	9.8	7.0	5.4
潮 州	Chaozhou	2.8	5.9	1.1	12.0	1.5	8.0	1.2	9.9
揭 阳	Jieyang	0.9	31.0	3.4	10.2	0.8	33.1	4.5	12.0
云 浮	Yunfu	2.7	6.4	10.6	6.2	2.6	10.5	16.3	5.8
按经济区域分	By Region								
珠 三 角	Pearl River Delta	0.4	3.1	2.1	10.0	0.3	3.7	2.4	10.5
东 翼	Eastern Region	1.4	15.4	2.0	10.1	1.9	16.8	2.6	11.2
西 翼	Western Region	2.4	23.8	5.9	12.8	2.0	17.9	6.6	14.3
山 区	Mountainous Region	2.8	6.7	5.0	12.8	3.0	8.0	6.8	9.2

5-15 各市工业投资比重

Proportion of Industrial Investment by City

单位：%　　　　(%)

市别	City	2021（以投资总额为100） Proportion (total investment=100)				2022（以投资总额为100） Proportion (total investment=100)			
		合计 Total	采矿业 Mining	制造业 Manufa-cturing	电力、燃气及水的生产和供应业 Production and Supply of Electri-city,Gas and Water	合计 Total	采矿业 Mining	制造业 Manufa-cturing	电力、燃气及水的生产和供应业 Production and Supply of Electri-city,Gas and Water
全　省	**Provincial Total**	**24.6**	**0.6**	**18.2**	**5.9**	**27.9**	**0.8**	**21.0**	**6.2**
广　州	Guangzhou	12.9	…	9.5	3.4	14.9	0.0	11.8	3.1
深　圳	Shenzhen	16.6	1.0	12.4	3.2	18.3	1.7	13.2	3.4
珠　海	Zhuhai	17.6	1.3	13.3	3.0	30.1	0.3	26.5	3.4
汕　头	Shantou	25.7		19.0	6.7	29.6	0.0	19.5	10.1
佛　山	Foshan	24.7	…	22.3	2.3	27.6	0.0	25.4	2.2
韶　关	Shaoguan	29.6	0.4	19.2	10.0	32.9	0.7	23.2	9.0
河　源	Heyuan	28.1	0.3	20.8	7.0	33.0	0.3	27.0	5.8
梅　州	Meizhou	21.9	0.1	11.4	10.4	27.4	0.0	14.3	13.0
惠　州	Huizhou	33.1	1.5	24.7	6.8	43.2	1.6	34.1	7.4
汕　尾	Shanwei	39.4	…	18.3	21.0	39.8		19.8	19.9
东　莞	Dongguan	39.2		34.2	5.0	41.0		35.0	6.1
中　山	Zhongshan	22.4		20.1	2.3	27.2		24.4	2.8
江　门	Jiangmen	36.8	0.5	31.3	5.0	44.2	0.8	37.5	5.9
阳　江	Yangjiang	62.1	0.1	9.9	52.1	47.1	0.0	11.6	35.5
湛　江	Zhanjiang	35.1	4.0	14.0	17.1	35.9	5.5	11.9	18.6
茂　名	Maoming	20.4	0.2	12.6	7.6	20.9	0.1	12.7	8.2
肇　庆	Zhaoqing	33.3	1.4	29.7	2.2	43.3	0.5	33.2	9.7
清　远	Qingyuan	22.0		13.9	8.1	27.7	1.9	14.6	11.2
潮　州	Chaozhou	26.1	0.1	17.0	9.0	27.6	0.0	17.1	10.5
揭　阳	Jieyang	43.8	…	36.2	7.6	45.8	0.5	33.5	11.8
云　浮	Yunfu	30.9	0.9	21.6	8.4	41.7	5.5	21.7	14.4
按经济区域分	By Region								
珠三角	Pearl River Delta	22.3	0.6	18.1	3.6	26.4	0.7	21.6	4.2
东　翼	Eastern Region	33.8	…	23.2	10.5	35.7	0.1	22.6	13.0
西　翼	Western Region	37.4	2.0	12.6	22.8	32.8	2.6	12.1	18.1
山　区	Mountainous Region	26.1	0.3	17.3	8.6	31.8	1.5	19.8	10.4

主要统计指标解释

固定资产投资额　是以货币形式表现的在一定时期内建造和购置固定资产的工作量以及与此有关的费用的总称。它是反映固定资产投资规模、结构和发展速度的综合性指标，又是观察工程进度和考核投资效果的重要依据。

固定资产投资的资金来源　根据固定资产投资的资金来源不同，分为国家预算资金、国内贷款、利用外资、自筹资金和其他资金来源。

(1)国家预算资金　自 2011 年起，按照全国人大和国务院的要求，各级财政的所有资金，包括税收和非税收入，均必须纳入预算管理，我国已不存在预算外资金的概念，因此各级政府用于固定资产投资的财政资金均为预算资金。由于已经没有预算外资金，因此名称改为国家预算资金，包括中央预算资金和地方预算资金，旧的国家预算内资金的内容和现中央预算资金的内容基本一致。

国家预算包括一般预算、政府性基金预算、国有资本经营预算和社保基金预算。各类预算中用于固定资产投资的资金全部作为国家预算资金填报，其中一般预算中用于固定资产投资的部分包括基建投资、车购税、灾后恢复重建基金和其他财政投资。各级政府债券也应归入国家预算资金。

(2)国内贷款　指报告期固定资产投资单位向银行及非银行金融机构借入的用于固定资产投资的各种国内借款，包括银行利用自有资金及吸收存款发放的贷款、上级主管部门拨入的国内贷款、国家专项贷款（包括煤代油贷款、劳改煤矿专项贷款等)，地方财政专项资金安排的贷款、国内储备贷款、周转贷款等。

(3)利用外资　指报告期内收到的用于固定资产建造和购置的国外资金（包括设备、材料、技术)。包括对外借款、外商直接投资、外商其他投资。不包括我国自有外汇资金。

(5)自筹资金　指固定资产投资单位报告期内收到的，由各地区、各部门及企事业单位筹集用于固定资产投资的预算外资金，包括中央各部门、各级地方和企事业单位的自筹资金。

(6)其他资金来源　指报告期收到的除以上各种资金之外其他用于固定资产投资的资金。包括集资、个人资金、无偿捐赠的资金及其他单位拨入的资金。

新增固定资产　指已经完成建造和购置过程，并已交付生产或使用单位的固定资产的价值。它是表示固定资产投资成果的价值指标，也是反映建设进度，计算固定资产投资效果的重要依据。

基础设施　基础设施投资指在电力、热力的生产和供应业，燃气生产和供应业，水的生产和供应业，铁路运输业，道路运输业，水上运输业，航空运输业，管道运输业，装卸搬运和运输代理业，邮政业，电信、广播电视和卫星传输服务，互联网和相关服务，水利管理业，生态保护和环境治理业和公共设施管理业等行业方面的固定资产投资。

Explanatory Notes on Main Statistical Indicators

Amount of Investment in Fixed Assets　refers to the sum in monetary terms of the volume of activities in the construction and purchase of fixed assets as well as related expenses. It is not only a comprehensive indicator of the size, proportional relations and developmental pace of investment in fixed assets, but also an important basis to follow the progress of projects and check the result of investment on.

Sources of Funds for Investment in Fixed Assets　are categorized as funds from the State budget, domestic loans, foreign investment, self-raised funds, and others, depending on the sources of investment.

(1)State Budgetary Funds Since 2011, in accordance with the requirements of the National People's Congress and the State Council, budgetary funds at all levels, including tax and non-tax revenues, must be included into budgetary management. As a result, the concept of "extra-budgetary funds" no longer exist. Therefore, all the fiscal funds used in fixed asset investment by governments at all levels are state budgetary funds. Without extra-budgetary funds, the name is changed into State Budgetary Funds. It includes central budgetary funds and local budgetary funds. The contents of the previously named "Fund from the State budget" is basically the same as the content of the central budgetary funds.

State budget includes general budget, government fund budget, state-owned capital operation budget and social insurance fund budget. Of all the budgets, the funds used in fixed asset investment are recorded as state budgetary funds. In general budget, the funds used in fixed asset investment include investment in infrastructure, vehicle purchase tax, post-disaster reconstruction fund and other fiscal investments. Government bonds at all levels shall also be included in state budgetary funds.

(2) Domestic loans refer to loans of various forms borrowed by investing units from banks and non-bank financial institutions during the reference period for the purpose of investment in fixed assets, including loans issued by banks from their self-owned funds and deposit, loans appropriated by higher authorities, special loans by government, loans arranged by local government from special funds, domestic reserve loan, and working loan.

(3) Foreign investment refers to foreign funds received during the reference period for the purpose of construction and purchase of fixed assets (including equipment, materials and technologies). It includes foreign loans, foreign direct investment and other foreign investment, but excludes self-owned foreign exchanges of China.

(4) Fundraising refers to extra-budgetary funds received and raised by enterprises and institutions at all levels during the reference period for the purpose of investment in fixed assets, including funds raised by various departments under the central government, government departments of various levels, enterprises and institutions.

(5) Other funds refer to funds received during the reference period for the purpose of investment in fixed assets which are not included in the above-mentioned sources, including mass financing, individual funds, donations and funds from other units.

Newly Increased Fixed Assets refer to the value of fixed assets which have been completed and transferred to production units or users. It is a value indicator of the achievements of investment in fixed assets as well as an important basis to evaluate the result of investment in fixed assets on.

Infrastructure Investment Infrastructure investment refers to the fixed assets investments in the industry of electric power, hot water production and supply industry, gas production and supply industry, water production and supply industry, railway transport, road transport, water transport, air transport industry, pipeline transportation, handling and transportation agent industry, postal services, telecommunications, radio, television and satellite transmission service, Internet and related services, water management industry, ecological protection and environmental governance industry and public facilities management.

六、对外经济

FOREIGN ECONOMY

六　对外经济

简要说明

一、本篇资料综合反映广东对外贸易、利用外资、对外承包工程和劳务合作以及外商投资企业工商登记等历年概况和近年发展的详细情况。

二、本篇资料由广东省统计局贸易外经统计处负责整理、编辑。

三、资料来源和统计范围：

1.人民币对美元、日元、港元的年平均汇价资料来源于外汇管理部门，是根据当年国家外汇管理局提供的每日汇价进行加权平均计算而得出的。

2.进出口贸易规模、结构情况资料，来源于海关总署广东分署，统计范围为在广东境内经海关报关注册登记的经营单位（包括有进出口经营权和无进出口经营权的经营单位）。进出口商品价值，出口按离岸价（FOB）、进口按到岸价（CIF）统计；进出口商品分类按海关合作理事会制定的《商品名称及编码协调制度》（HS）目录进行分类统计。

3.利用外资规模、结构、对外直接投资和广东对外承包工程和劳务合作状况资料来源于广东省商务厅。

4.外商投资企业注册登记情况资料来源于广东省市场监督管理局。

5.对外开放使用口岸分布状况资料来源于广东省商务厅。

6　Foreign Economy

Brief Introduction

Ⅰ. This data in this chapter comprehensively reflects the situation of Guangdong's foreign trade, utilization of foreign capital, foreign contracted projects and labor cooperation and the industrial and commercial registration of foreign-funded enterprises over the years and the detailed development in recent years.

Ⅱ. The data in this chapter are prepared and edited by the Division of Trade and External Economic Relations Statistics of Statistics Bureau of Guangdong Province.

Ⅲ. Data sources and statistical coverage:

(1) The data on the average exchange rates of RMB yuan to US dollar, Japanese yen and Hong Kong dollar over the years come from the State Administration of Foreign Exchange. The annual average exchange rate is calculated as the weighted mean of the daily exchange rates provided by the State Administration of Foreign Exchange in current year.

(2) The data on the size and composition of Guangdong's imports and exports come from Guangdong Customs Office. The statistics cover the operating units (with or without the right to handle imports and exports) which have a declaration and register at customs within the boundary of Guangdong. The values of export commodities are calculated on an FOB basis, while the values of import commodities are calculated on a CIF basis. The Harmonized Commodity Description and Coding System (HS) stipulated by the Customs Cooperation Council is used in the classification of import and export commodities.

(3) The data on the scale and composition of the utilization of foreign capital,overseas direct invest ment and the conditions of contracted projects and labor cooperation with foreign countries or territories in Guangdong come from the Department of Commerce of Guangdong Province.

(4) The data on registration status of enterprises with foreign investment come from Guangdong Administration for Market Regulation.

(5) The data on the distribution of ports opening to the outside world come from the Department of Commerce of Guangdong Province.

6-1 对外经济主要指标
Main Indicators of Foreign Trade and Economic Cooperation

指　标	Item	2018	2019	2020	2021	2022
进出口总额 (亿元)	Total Value of Imports and Exports (RMB 100 million)	71645.73	71484.39	70862.64	82681.56	83098.11
出口总额	Total Exports	42744.06	43416.04	43493.07	50525.46	53319.46
进口总额	Total Imports	28901.67	28068.35	27369.58	32156.10	29778.65
进出口总额 (亿美元)	Total Value of Imports and Exports (USD 100 million)	10851.03	10365.78	10239.02	12795.67	12469.69
出口总额	Total Exports	6470.46	6294.64	6282.99	7818.60	7999.02
#农产品	Farm Produce	102.70	98.69	93.13	105.98	172.98
机电产品	Machanical and Electrical Products	4470.83	4280.73	4300.84	5407.11	5320.92
高新技术产品	High and New-tech Products	2337.57	2192.95	2174.99	2655.31	2510.13
进口总额	Total Imports	4380.57	4071.14	3956.03	4977.07	4470.67
#农产品	Farm Produce	199.64	214.80	244.05	292.61	321.71
机电产品	Machanical and Electrical Products	3025.71	2774.47	2733.19	3315.71	2893.43
高新技术产品	High and New-tech Products	2410.23	2219.25	2213.40	2750.61	2333.80
签订外商直接投资协议(合同)项目 (个)	Number of Projects with Contracted Foreign Direct Investment (unit)	35774	14350	12864	16155	13365
签订外商直接投资协议(合同)金额 (亿元)	Amount of Contracted Foreign Direct Investment (RMB 100 million)	5900.98	5523.84	5032.99	4894.14	4051.57
实际利用外商直接投资额 (亿元)	Amount of Foreign Capital Actually Utilized (RMB 100 million)	1450.88	1522.00	1620.29	1840.02	1819.02
外商投资企业年底工商登记数 (户)	Number of Registered Enterprises with Foreign Investment at the Year-end (unit)	170968	179268	175378	185553	189439
投资总额 (亿美元)	Total Investment (USD 100 million)	19234.65	19532.52	21670.90	23284.71	24141.48
注册资本 (亿美元)	Registered Capital (USD 100 million)	7964.06	8542.58	9853.35	10723.77	11363.18
对外承包工程合同数 (份)	Number of Contracted Projects with Foreign Countries and Territories (unit)	1136	1030	878	787	859
合同金额 (亿美元)	Contracted Value (USD 100 million)	191.47	255.61	187.31	183.52	197.94
完成营业额 (亿美元)	Value of Turnover Fulfilled (USD 100 million)	175.67	167.06	156.65	156.23	162.02
对外劳务人员合同工资总额 (亿美元)	Contracted Value (USD 100 million)	6.75	7.36	5.59	6.37	4.40
对外劳务人员实际工资总额 (亿美元)	Value of Turnover Fulfilled (USD 100 million)	8.56	9.29	7.92	8.74	8.82
对外直接投资合同数 (个)	Number of Agreement(Contract)Signed of Overseas Direct Investment (unit)	1012	932	865	1075	1230
对外直接投资额 (亿美元)	Amount of Overseas Direct Investment (USD 100 million)	138.00	102.77	158.16	169.67	220.72

注：1.2018年起，外商直接投资使用商务部反馈人民币数据，计量单位为亿元。
2.2018年起，省商务厅未对外公布利用外资签订项目、合同外资额和实际利用外资数据。

Note: a)Data of foreign direct investment in RMB that are approved by Ministry of Commerce are adopted since 2018. The unit of measurement is 100 million yuan.
b)Data of signed projects, contracted foreign capital and foreign capital actually utilized are not published by Department of Commerce of Guangdong Province since 2018.

6-2 人民币对主要外币中间价汇率（年平均价）

Middle Exchange Rate of RMB Against Major Foreign Currencies (Period Average)

单位：人民币，元 (RMB/yuan)

年份 Year	100美元 100 US Dollars	100日元 100 Japanese Yen	100港元 100 Hong Kong Dollars	100欧元 100 Euros
1987	372.21	2.5799	47.74	
1988	372.21	2.9082	47.70	
1989	376.51	2.7360	48.28	
1990	478.32	3.3233	61.39	
1991	532.33	3.9602	68.45	
1992	551.46	4.3608	71.24	
1993	576.20	5.2020	74.41	
1994	861.87	8.4370	111.53	
1995	835.10	8.9225	107.96	
1996	831.42	7.6352	107.51	
1997	828.98	6.8600	107.09	
1998	827.91	6.3488	106.88	
1999	827.83	7.2932	106.66	
2000	827.84	7.6864	106.18	
2001	827.70	6.8075	106.08	
2002	827.70	6.6237	106.07	800.58
2003	827.70	7.1466	106.24	936.13
2004	827.68	7.6552	106.23	1029.00
2005	819.17	7.4484	105.30	1019.53
2006	797.18	6.8570	102.62	1001.90
2007	760.40	6.4632	97.46	1041.75
2008	694.51	6.7427	89.19	1022.27
2009	683.10	7.2986	88.12	952.70
2010	676.95	7.7279	87.13	897.25
2011	645.88	8.1050	82.97	900.11
2012	631.25	7.9037	81.38	810.78
2013	619.36	6.3323	79.85	822.19
2014	614.28	5.8196	79.22	816.51
2015	622.84	5.1543	80.34	691.41
2016	664.23	6.1243	85.58	734.26
2017	675.18	6.0244	86.64	763.03
2018	661.74	5.9890	84.43	780.16
2019	689.85	6.3389	88.05	772.55
2020	689.76	6.4626	88.93	787.55
2021	645.15	5.8735	83.00	762.93
2022	672.61	5.1261	85.89	707.21

6–3 进出口总额

Total Value of Imports and Exports

年份 Year	亿元人民币 RMB 100 million				亿美元 USD 100 million			
	进出口总额 Total Imports and Exports	出口 Exports	进口 Imports	差额 Balance	进出口总额 Total Imports and Exports	出口 Exports	进口 Imports	差额 Balance
1987	782.91	377.37	405.54	-28.17	210.37	101.40	108.97	-7.57
1988	1154.40	551.43	602.97	-51.54	310.19	148.17	162.02	-13.85
1989	1324.07	674.09	649.98	24.11	355.78	181.13	174.65	6.48
1990	1994.18	1057.63	936.55	121.08	418.98	222.21	196.77	25.44
1991	2774.47	1430.16	1344.31	85.85	525.21	270.73	254.48	16.25
1992	3584.97	1824.33	1760.64	63.69	657.48	334.58	322.90	11.68
1993	4507.68	2151.54	2356.14	-204.60	783.44	373.94	409.50	-35.56
1994	8354.58	4339.74	4014.84	324.90	966.63	502.11	464.52	37.59
1995	8700.58	4735.73	3964.85	770.88	1039.72	565.92	473.80	92.12
1996	9144.27	4935.21	4209.06	726.15	1099.60	593.46	506.14	87.32
1997	10789.42	6182.77	4606.65	1576.12	1301.20	745.64	555.56	190.08
1998	10745.98	6260.41	4485.56	1774.85	1297.98	756.18	541.80	214.38
1999	11620.08	6432.65	5187.43	1245.22	1403.68	777.05	626.63	150.42
2000	14082.06	7609.42	6472.63	1136.79	1701.06	919.19	781.87	137.32
2001	14608.01	7898.09	6709.91	1188.18	1764.87	954.21	810.66	143.55
2002	18299.78	9804.77	8495.02	1309.75	2210.92	1184.58	1026.34	158.24
2003	23467.12	12651.23	10815.89	1835.34	2835.22	1528.48	1306.74	221.74
2004	29559.57	15856.17	13703.40	2152.76	3571.29	1915.69	1655.60	260.09
2005	35121.80	19542.06	15579.74	3962.32	4280.02	2381.71	1898.31	483.40
2006	42114.53	24119.13	17995.40	6123.73	5272.07	3019.48	2252.59	766.89
2007	48445.43	28210.96	20234.46	7976.50	6340.35	3692.39	2647.96	1044.43
2008	47869.07	28342.66	19526.41	8816.25	6834.92	4041.88	2793.04	1248.83
2009	41736.14	24517.40	17218.74	7298.66	6111.18	3589.56	2521.62	1067.93
2010	53203.22	30718.98	22484.24	8234.74	7848.96	4531.91	3317.05	1214.86
2011	59276.15	34519.93	24756.22	9763.71	9133.34	5317.93	3815.41	1502.52
2012	62123.46	36242.50	25880.96	10361.54	9839.47	5740.59	4098.88	1641.71
2013	67806.10	39513.95	28292.14	11221.81	10918.22	6363.64	4554.58	1809.06
2014	66137.28	39693.38	26443.90	13249.48	10765.84	6460.87	4304.97	2155.90
2015	63559.70	39983.10	23576.60	16406.50	10227.96	6434.68	3793.28	2641.41
2016	63099.68	39520.54	23579.14	15941.40	9552.86	5985.64	3567.21	2418.43
2017	68168.86	42192.86	25976.00	16216.86	10066.80	6228.73	3838.06	2390.67
2018	71645.73	42744.06	28901.67	13842.39	10851.03	6470.46	4380.57	2089.89
2019	71484.39	43416.04	28068.35	15347.69	10365.78	6294.64	4071.14	2223.49
2020	70862.64	43493.07	27369.58	16123.49	10239.02	6282.99	3956.03	2326.96
2021	82681.56	50525.46	32156.10	18369.37	12795.67	7818.60	4977.07	2841.52
2022	83098.11	53319.46	29778.65	23540.81	12469.69	7999.02	4470.67	3528.35

注：进出口差额负数为入超。

Note: A negative balance indicates trade deficit. That is, imports surpassing exports.

6-4 按贸易方式和经济类型分的进出口额(人民币)

Total Value of Imports and Exports by Customs Regime and Ownership Type (RMB)

单位：亿元人民币 (RMB 100 million)

项目	Item	2020		2021		2022	
		出口 Exports	进口 Imports	出口 Exports	进口 Imports	出口 Exports	进口 Imports
全　省	**Provincial Total**	**43493.07**	**27369.58**	**50525.46**	**32156.10**	**53319.46**	**29778.65**
按贸易方式分	By Customs Regime						
一般贸易	Ordinary Trade	22893.16	13401.73	27099.60	16135.87	30717.26	14656.01
来料加工	Processing and Assembling with Customer's Materials	974.81	690.77	1136.83	900.18	1092.90	824.91
补偿贸易	Compensation Trade						
进料加工	Processing and Assembling with Import Materials	11948.55	6362.33	13422.88	7147.74	12985.96	6634.05
加工设备	Processing Equipments		20.76		14.18		11.57
外资设备	Foreign-funded Equipments		75.74		29.46		26.55
保税仓库	Bonded Warehouse	4385.31	6599.57	5356.47	7733.07	6276.15	7463.06
捐赠	Donation	5.53	2.45	0.14	0.01	0.83	0.19
其他	Others	3285.70	216.23	3509.54	195.61	2246.36	162.31
按经济类型分	By Type of Ownership						
国有经济	State-owned Economy	2263.86	1492.07	2544.77	1708.17	2751.31	2062.31
集体经济	Collective-owned Economy	1072.73	257.67	1061.14	77.97	1117.18	83.28
私营经济	Private Economy	23150.36	14529.75	27965.10	17522.95	31020.37	15558.60
外商投资经济	Foreign-funded Economy	16896.57	10985.77	18854.71	12728.75	18352.18	11990.75
其他经济	Others	109.53	104.32	99.75	118.25	78.42	83.71

6-5 按贸易方式和经济类型分的进出口额(美元)

Total Value of Imports and Exports by Customs Regime and Ownership Type(USD)

单位：亿美元 (USD 100 million)

项目	Item	2020		2021		2022	
		出口 Exports	进口 Imports	出口 Exports	进口 Imports	出口 Exports	进口 Imports
全　省	**Provincial Total**	**6282.99**	**3956.03**	**7818.60**	**4977.07**	**7999.02**	**4470.67**
按贸易方式分	By Customs Regime						
一般贸易	Ordinary Trade	3306.09	1934.04	4193.24	2496.13	4606.20	2206.03
来料加工	Processing and Assembling with Customer's Materials	141.00	100.12	176.02	139.42	163.70	123.80
补偿贸易	Compensation Trade						
进料加工	Processing and Assembling with Import Materials	1728.18	922.52	2078.04	1106.87	1947.99	993.62
加工设备	Processing Equipments		2.98		2.20		1.76
外资设备	Foreign-funded Equipments		10.88		4.55		4.05
保税仓库	Bonded Warehouse	633.99	953.93	829.32	1197.75	939.06	1117.02
捐赠	Donation	0.79	0.35	0.02	…	0.13	0.03
其他	Others	472.95	31.20	541.95	30.17	341.94	24.36
按经济类型分	By Type of Ownership						
国有经济	State-owned Economy	326.99	215.23	393.75	264.38	413.24	310.06
集体经济	Collective-owned Economy	155.11	36.98	164.19	12.05	167.75	12.51
私营经济	Private Economy	3344.20	2099.50	4326.86	2711.92	4649.92	2335.08
外商投资经济	Foreign-funded Economy	2441.08	1589.25	2918.51	1970.52	2756.34	1800.38
其他经济	Others	15.61	15.07	15.29	18.20	11.77	12.64

6-6 按产品类型分的进出口额

Total Value of Imports and Exports by Product Type

项 目	Item	亿元人民币 RMB 100 million			亿美元 USD 100 million		
		2020	2021	2022	2020	2021	2022
出口总额	**Total Exports**	**43493.07**	**50525.46**	**53319.46**	**6282.99**	**7818.60**	**7999.02**
#农产品	Farm Produce	644.68	684.63	1157.91	93.13	105.98	172.98
机电产品	Machanical and Electrical Products	29756.14	34936.80	35460.42	4300.84	5407.11	5320.92
自动数据处理设备及其零部件	Automated Data Processing Equipment and their Parts	2827.57	3356.13	3563.06	409.02	519.75	534.69
电工器材	Electrical Equipment	2565.79	3114.09	3705.11	370.72	482.02	555.00
电子元件	Electrical Components	3772.46	4457.55	4489.21	545.88	690.15	671.69
汽车零配件	Automobile Parts	450.87	553.48	574.58	65.20	85.59	86.14
液晶显示板	LCD Display Panels	547.10	722.41		79.08	111.78	
液晶平板显示模组	Liquid Crystal Display Modules			755.20			113.72
计量检测分析自控仪器及器具	Automated Measurement, Detection, Analysis Equipment and their Parts	473.96	461.89	482.17	68.40	71.49	72.20
高新技术产品	High and New-tech Products	15035.76	17150.36	16741.88	2174.99	2655.31	2510.13
生物技术	Biotechnology	1.90	13.29	2.31	0.28	2.07	0.35
生命科学技术	Life Sciences Technology	298.04	382.12	452.49	42.99	59.14	68.38
光电技术	Photoelectric Technology	695.54	897.30	934.38	100.53	138.85	140.55
计算机与通信技术	Computer and Communication Technology	10620.01	11832.41	11031.19	1536.49	1831.96	1654.48
电子技术	Electronic Technology	2978.56	3506.25	3641.25	430.84	542.98	544.42
计算机集成制造技术	Computer Integrated Manufacturing Technology	282.48	326.33	333.07	40.79	50.49	49.96
材料技术	Material Technology	82.75	102.94	113.50	11.96	15.93	17.04
航空航大技术	Aerospace Technology	64.99	66.98	213.69	9.45	10.37	31.94
其他	Others	11.50	22.75	20.01	1.67	3.52	3.02
进口总额	**Total Imports**	**27369.58**	**32156.10**	**29778.65**	**3956.03**	**4977.07**	**4470.67**
#农产品	Farm Produce	1690.53	1892.15	2143.83	244.05	292.61	321.71
机电产品	Machinery and Electrical Products	18912.22	21420.52	19258.07	2733.19	3315.71	2893.43
自动数据处理设备及其零部件	Automatic Data Processing Equipment and their Parts	1270.26	1388.24	1254.78	183.13	214.96	188.97
电工器材	Electrical Equipment	958.88	989.96	828.18	138.57	153.24	124.49
电子元件	Electrical Components	10598.19	12842.47	12169.86	1530.66	1988.21	1829.30
汽车零配件	Automobile Parts	300.90	278.76	210.15	43.39	43.05	31.73
液晶显示板	LCD Display Panels	494.53	511.57		71.46	79.19	
液晶平板显示模组	Liquid Crystal Display Modules			384.03			58.03
计量检测分析自控仪器及器具	Automated Measurement, Detection, Analysis Equipment and their Parts	441.82	377.98	374.75	63.81	58.49	56.13
高新技术产品	High and New-tech Products	15314.65	17767.27	15530.54	2213.40	2750.61	2333.80
生物技术	Biotechnology	20.42	23.73	16.70	2.95	3.66	2.49
生命科学技术	Life Sciences Technology	293.05	316.29	332.22	42.34	48.95	49.81
光电技术	Photoelectric Technology	657.66	663.60	532.16	95.01	102.71	80.20
计算机与通信技术	Computer and Communication Technology	3272.16	3606.88	2069.81	473.80	558.35	310.73
电子技术	Electronic Technology	10132.47	12286.34	11770.73	1463.27	1902.20	1769.12
计算机集成制造技术	Computer Integrated Manufacturing Technology	567.85	527.55	492.90	81.85	81.60	74.06
材料技术	Material Technology	85.35	95.52	90.51	12.33	14.79	13.62
航空航天技术	Aerospace Technology	269.23	237.38	216.25	39.45	36.77	32.33
其他	Others	16.46	9.98	9.26	2.39	1.56	1.44

注：自2022年1月起，海关删除编码“液晶显示板”，新增编码“液晶平板显示模组”。

Note: Since January 2022, the customs has deleted the item "LCD Display Panel" and added the item "Liquid Crystal Display Modules".

6-7 广东同主要国家(地区)进出口额 (2022年)
Total Value of Imports and Exports with Main Countries and Regions (2022)

国别（地区）	Country (Region)	亿元人民币 RMB 100 million			亿美元 USD 100 million		
		进出口 Total	出口 Exports	进口 Imports	进出口 Total	出口 Exports	进口 Imports
合计	**Total**	**83098.11**	**53319.46**	**29778.65**	**12469.69**	**7999.02**	**4470.67**
亚洲	**Asia**	**49866.34**	**26915.30**	**22951.04**	**7479.37**	**4031.93**	**3447.44**
#香港	Hong Kong, China	10522.26	10340.07	182.19	1571.65	1544.50	27.15
韩国	Republic of Korea	4075.91	1202.98	2872.93	613.53	180.90	432.62
台湾省	Taiwan, China	6452.45	878.25	5574.20	969.89	132.00	837.89
日本	Japan	4643.25	2042.17	2601.08	696.80	306.08	390.71
越南	Vietnam	3157.98	1720.35	1437.62	473.46	258.85	214.61
马来西亚	Malaysia	3095.27	1422.12	1673.15	463.36	212.41	250.95
泰国	Thailand	2202.64	1032.82	1169.82	331.20	155.28	175.92
印度	India	1837.30	1694.19	143.12	275.81	254.32	21.49
新加坡	Singapore	1548.48	1082.91	465.56	231.01	160.93	70.08
菲律宾	Philippines	1317.12	748.10	569.01	197.75	112.24	85.51
印度尼西亚	Indonesia	1554.40	938.56	615.84	233.61	141.22	92.39
阿联酋	United Arab Emirates	895.84	731.10	164.73	134.60	109.80	24.80
沙特阿拉伯	Saudi Arabia	805.69	587.93	217.76	121.00	88.40	32.59
东盟	Association of Southeast Asian Nations	13546.59	7289.46	6257.12	2029.93	1092.83	937.09
非洲	**Africa**	**2651.82**	**1969.07**	**682.74**	**397.71**	**295.09**	**102.62**
#南非	South Africa	671.38	301.81	369.57	100.50	45.23	55.28
尼日利亚	Nigeria	300.15	277.47	22.68	44.97	41.52	3.44
欧洲	**Europe**	**12893.57**	**10106.85**	**2786.72**	**1936.17**	**1518.67**	**417.51**
#德国	Germany	2166.34	1501.06	665.29	325.39	225.62	99.77
英国	United Kingdom	1470.09	1317.77	152.31	220.72	197.88	22.84
荷兰	Netherlands	1776.49	1650.79	125.71	266.69	247.91	18.78
法国	France	1028.78	730.56	298.22	154.62	110.02	44.60
意大利	Italy	963.75	767.78	195.96	145.28	115.92	29.36
俄罗斯	Russia	1071.25	827.36	243.89	159.51	123.22	36.29
西班牙	Spain	657.30	571.92	85.38	98.98	86.18	12.80
波兰	Poland	575.34	546.36	28.98	86.58	82.22	4.36
比利时	Belgium	515.42	325.23	190.19	77.43	48.89	28.55
瑞士	Switzerland	428.67	102.68	325.99	64.40	15.46	48.93
匈牙利	Hungary	288.73	249.67	39.06	43.37	37.53	5.84
瑞典	Sweden	196.45	155.50	40.95	29.54	23.39	6.15
捷克	Czech	262.06	224.06	38.00	39.30	33.59	5.71
欧盟	European Union	9657.50	7657.34	2000.16	1451.53	1151.83	299.70
拉丁美洲	**Latin America**	**4367.55**	**3102.84**	**1264.70**	**655.12**	**465.71**	**189.41**
#墨西哥	Mexico	1380.93	1229.60	151.33	207.32	184.61	22.70
巴西	Brazil	1048.38	586.12	462.26	156.79	87.76	69.03
智利	Chile	506.15	204.88	301.27	76.37	30.89	45.47
阿根廷	Argentina	235.64	152.43	83.21	35.34	22.95	12.40
北美洲	**North America**	**11252.87**	**9910.98**	**1341.89**	**1692.44**	**1491.21**	**201.22**
#美国	United States of America	10245.37	9112.56	1132.82	1541.09	1371.09	170.00
加拿大	Canada	1003.88	797.81	206.07	150.81	120.03	30.78
大洋洲及其他	**Oceania and others**	**2065.97**	**1314.41**	**751.56**	**308.87**	**196.41**	**112.47**
#澳大利亚	Australia	1704.46	1130.75	573.72	254.75	168.93	85.82
新西兰	New Zealand	255.31	136.51	118.80	38.33	20.45	17.88

注：本表数字按产销国别原则统计。
Note: The data in the table are calculated on the basis of production and consumption countries.

6-8 进出口商品分类金额（2022年）

Total Value of Imports and Exports by Category of Commodities (2022)

商品类别	Category of Commodities	万元人民币 RMB10 000		万美元 USD 10 000	
		出口 Exports	进口 Imports	出口 Exports	进口 Imports
全　省	**Provincial Total**	**533194609**	**297786534**	**79990201**	**44706684**
第一类 活动物；动物产品	**Live Animals and Animal Products**	**1468433**	**6674216**	**219454**	**1000782**
活动物	Live Animals	170254	15132	25232	2335
肉及食用杂碎	Meat and Edible Haslets	384522	3836485	57636	574116
水产品	Aquatic Products	812897	1967670	121434	295012
乳品、蛋品、天然蜂蜜、其他食用动物产品	Dairy Products, Eggs, Natural Honey and Other Edible Animal Products	66587	717658	9965	108674
其他动物产品	Other Animal Products	34172	137271	5186	20646
第二类 植物产品	**Plant Products**	**1446170**	**8293009**	**215197**	**1252591**
树苗及花草	Saplings, Flowers and Herbs	82012	24740	12271	3664
蔬菜	Edible Vegetables	436656	193682	65237	29472
水果及坚果	Fruits and Nuts	401233	4023036	59157	612098
咖啡、茶叶及调味香料	Coffee, Tea and Spices	134890	177225	20329	26399
谷物	Cereals	71	1750912	11	264990
制粉工业产品	Flour, Starch and Related Products	139886	129736	20758	19492
植物油籽及果实、种子、药材及饲料	Oil Seeds and Kernels, Seeds, Medical Materials and Forage	157736	1932381	23466	287257
虫胶、树胶、树脂	Shellac, Gum, Resin	59798	36645	8857	5504
编结植物材料、其他植物产品	Stuff of Knitting Plant, Other Plants and Related Products	33889	24651	5111	3715
第三类 动、植物油脂及蜡	**Animal Fat, Vegetable Oil and Wax**	**221580**	**1027062**	**33361**	**152878**
第四类 食品、烟草及制品	**Food, Tobacco and Related Products**	**8345776**	**5236839**	**1247145**	**779782**
动物产品制品	Animal Products	1292281	53309	194184	7968
糖及糖食	Sugar and Sugar Products	572606	464651	85709	68815
可可及可可制品	Cocoa and Cocoa Products	90800	109216	13432	16129
粮食及乳制品、糕饼点心	Foodstuff, Dairy Products and Pastry Products	556935	1601203	83295	238644
蔬菜、水果等植物制品	Products of Vegetables and Fruits	203205	349155	30369	51685
杂项制品	Miscellaneous Edible Products	550440	1068981	82508	159091
饮料、酒及醋	Beverages, Liquor and Vinegar	700806	907218	104599	134965
食品的残渣、动物饲料	Dreg of Food, Animal Forage	182311	562897	27172	84372
烟草及烟草制品	Tobacco and Related Products	4196392	120207	625878	18112
第五类 矿产品	**Minerals**	**4564601**	**18888928**	**682304**	**2834739**
盐、硫磺、建筑材料	Salt, Sulphur, Building Materials	622377	358586	93341	54217
矿砂、矿渣及矿灰	Ore, Slag and Mortar	84176	4764526	12501	718707
矿物燃料、矿物油及产品	Mineral Fuels, Mineral Oils and Related Products	3858049	13765816	576463	2061816
第六类 化工产品	**Chemicals**	**11081844**	**13579439**	**1668921**	**2034530**
无机化学品	Inorganic Chemicals	1194501	1503850	179834	221547
有机化学品	Organic Chemicals	2009668	2986267	302953	449762
药品	Medicinal and Pharmaceutical Products	1107823	2751592	166966	411669
肥料	Fertilizer	41093	120489	6146	18369
鞣料、染料浸膏、染料、颜料、油漆、油墨	Tanning Materials, Dyeing Extracts, Dyestuff, Colourant, Paint and Printing Ink	760904	631204	114206	94938

6-8 续表 1 continued 1

商品类别	Category of Commodities	万元人民币 RMB10 000		万美元 USD 10 000	
		出口 Exports	进口 Imports	出口 Exports	进口 Imports
化妆品及其原料、芳香料制品	Cosmetics and Cosmetic Raw Materials, Perfume Products	1424294	1772740	212926	265651
洗涤用品	Detergents	837888	672512	125717	100820
蛋白类物质、改性淀粉、胶、酶	Protein Materials, Modified Starch, Gum and Enzyme	581973	561392	87434	84394
炸药、烟火制品、易燃材料制品	Explosive, Pyrotechnic Products, Inflammable Material Products	10937	57	1637	9
照相及电影用品	Photographic and Film Products	104559	433855	15655	65257
杂项化学产品	Miscellaneous Chemical Products	3008204	2145482	455448	322114
第七类 塑料、橡胶及其制品	**Plastics, Rubber and Related Products**	**21653537**	**13042709**	**3251952**	**1964316**
塑料及其制品	Plastics and Related Products	20217843	11993552	3036240	1806776
橡胶及其制品	Rubber and Related Products	1435694	1049158	215712	157541
第八类 皮革、毛皮及其制品、旅行用品、手提包	**Leather, Furs and Related Products, Travel Articles, Handbags**	**7666388**	**802605**	**1147809**	**120593**
生皮及皮革	Raw Hides and Leather	215183	552734	32523	83428
皮革制品、旅行用品及手提包	Leather Products, Travel Articles and Handbags	7433180	229953	1112604	34225
毛皮、人造毛皮及制品	Furs, Artificial Furs and Related Products	18024	19918	2682	2940
第九类 木及木制品、草柳编结品	**Wood and Wooden Products, Straw and Wicker Knitting Products**	**1260762**	**1432094**	**189474**	**215751**
木及木制品、木炭	Wood and Wooden Products, Charcoal	1136866	1428559	170756	215215
软木及软木制品	Cork and Related Products	1510	1759	228	267
草柳编结品	Straw and Wicker Knitting Products	122386	1776	18490	269
第十类 木浆、纸、纸板及制品	**Wood Pulp, Paper, Paperboard and Related Products**	**6178124**	**3190371**	**926069**	**477364**
木浆及其他纤维素浆、废碎纸板	Wood Pulp and Cellulose Pulp, Waste Paper and Paperboard	7382	1902946	1107	284150
纸及纸板、纸浆、纸制品	Paper, Paperboard, Paper Pulp, Paper Products	4579659	976140	685948	146493
书籍、印刷品、设计图纸	Books, Printed Matter, Design Blueprint	1591083	311284	239015	46720
第十一类 纺织原料及纺织制品	**Textile Materials and Products**	**28252969**	**2272526**	**4246494**	**341987**
蚕丝	Natural Silk	57391	3988	8626	596
羊毛、动物毛、毛纱线及制品	Wool, Animal Hair, Woolen Yarn and Woven Fabrics	24385	50657	3711	7703
棉花	Cotton	940799	466330	141785	70332
其他纺织纤维、纸纱线及机织物	Other Textile Fibers, Yarn and Related Woven Fabrics	140930	48147	20923	7245
化学纤维长丝	Chemical Fiber, Continuous Filament	610295	386154	92174	58141
化学纤维短丝	Chemical Fiber, Staple Fiber	214076	114514	32170	17200
絮胎、毡尼及无纺物、特种纱线、线绳索缆	Wadding, Felt and Adhesive-bond Fabrics, Special Yarn, Threads, Ropes, Cables	796162	183257	119610	27555
地毯及纺织铺地制品	Carpets and Related Woven Products	161792	4516	24223	675
特种机织物、纺织装饰品、刺绣品	Special Woven Fabrics, Woven Ornaments, Embroidery	826708	63664	124209	9551
浸渍、涂布、包覆或层压的纺织物	Impregnated, Coated, Covered or Laminated Textile Products	928716	211379	139722	31754
针织物及钩编织物	Knit Wear and Crocheted Fabrics	2289515	202043	346177	30426
针织或钩编的服装及衣着附件	Knitted or Crocheted Garments and Clothing Accessories	9269828	240341	1391246	36122
非针织或非钩编的服装及衣着附件	Garments Not Knitted or Not Crocheted and Clothing Accessories	9528591	246840	1431223	37051
其他纺织制成品、成套物品	Other Textile Products	2463779	50697	370695	7635
第十二类 鞋帽伞杖、加工羽毛、人造花、人发制品	**Footwear, Headgear, Umbrellas, Canes, Processed Feather, Artificial Flowers, Wigs**	**11958965**	**569006**	**1543249**	**47058**
鞋类及零件	Footwear and Accessories	9349385	286802	1403977	42776
帽类及零件	Headgear and Accessories	851216	17255	127923	2579

6-8 续表 2 continued 2

商品类别	Category of Commodities	万元人民币 RMB10 000		万美元 USD 10 000	
		出口 Exports	进口 Imports	出口 Exports	进口 Imports
伞、杖、鞭及零件	Umbrellas, Canes, Whips and Accessories	224138	1710	33657	252
加工羽毛、羽绒及制品、人造花、人发制品	Processed Feathers, Down and Related Products, Artificial Flowers, Wigs	1534225	9639	231292	1452
第十三类 石材制品、陶瓷产品、玻璃及其制品	**Stone Products, Ceramics, Glass and Glassware**	**11253137**	**1808699**	**1689003**	**272059**
矿物材料的制品	Stone and Related Products	1889691	273546	283881	41058
陶瓷产品	Ceramics	6197977	103110	929650	15485
玻璃及其制品	Glass and Glassware	3165468	1432043	475472	215517
第十四类 珠宝首饰、硬币	**Jewellery, Coins**	**10937704**	**13506201**	**1619000**	**2007060**
第十五类 贱金属及其制品	**Base Metals and Related Products**	**30322997**	**14101790**	**4561312**	**2120606**
钢铁	Iron and Steel	2403334	2858140	364090	431500
钢铁制品	Iron and Steel Products	11734639	740727	1763920	111420
铜及其制品	Copper and Related Products	909892	6054363	137012	909968
镍及其制品	Nickel and Related Products	103420	674086	15462	101325
铝及其制品	Aluminum and Related Products	5181986	2460356	779649	368100
铅及其制品	Lead and Related Products	4063	12085	614	1803
锌及其制品	Zinc and Related Products	34207	117437	5139	17815
锡及其制品	Tin and Related Products	19079	160270	2931	24138
其他贱金属金属陶瓷及其制品	Other Base Metals, Metallic Ceramics and Related Products	575147	528636	86467	79943
贱金属工具器具利口器餐具及零件	Base Metal Tools, Utensils, Sharp Tools, Dinner-sets and Accessories	3393056	285633	509838	42993
贱金属杂项制品	Miscellaneous Base Metal Products	5964175	210058	896190	31600
第十六类 机械、电气设备、电视机及音响设备	**Machinery, Electric Equipment, TV Sets, Sound Appliances**	**280488584**	**178294623**	**42083745**	**26791650**
核反应堆、锅炉、机械设备及零件	Nuclear Reactor, Boilers, Mechanic Equipment and Accessories	77273523	24067251	11612378	3621974
机电、电气设备、电视机及音响设备	Machinery, Electric Equipment, TV Sets and Sound Appliances	203215061	154227372	30471367	23169675
第十七类 车辆、航空器、船舶及有关运输设备	**Vehicles, Aircraft, Ships and Related Transport Equipment**	**16115394**	**3808069**	**2414009**	**571149**
铁道及电车机车、车辆及零件	Rail Locomotives, Tramcars and Accessories	1885267	18991	285753	2816
车辆及零附件	Vehicles and Related Parts and Accessories	11114311	2768013	1662869	416369
航空器、航天器及零件	Aircraft, Spacecraft and Related Parts and Accessories	1569588	968269	234693	143962
船舶及浮动结构体	Ships and Related Products	1546228	52795	230694	8003
第十八类 仪器、医疗器械、钟表及乐器	**Instruments, Medical Instruments and Equipm-ent,Clocks and Watches, Musical Instruments**	**15061302**	**8515359**	**2257877**	**1276566**
光学、照相电影、计量检验、医疗仪器设备	Optical, Photographic, Film, Measuring and Checking, Medical Instruments and Equipment	12757359	7968809	1912831	1194684
钟表及零件	Clocks, Watches and Parts	1839977	509364	275487	76320
乐器及零附件	Musical Instruments and Parts	463966	37186	69559	5562
第十九类杂项制品	**Miscellaneous Manufactured Articles**	**50520248**	**1432656**	**7587167**	**214317**
家具、床上用品、照明装置、发光标志	Furniture, Bed Articles, Lighting Apparatus, Radiate Marks	27009126	260596	4059426	39144
玩具、游戏、运动用品及零附件	Toys, Game Goods, Sports Articles and Related Parts and Accessories	20619414	770516	3094474	115046
杂项制品	Miscellaneous Manufactured Articles	2891707	401543	433267	60127
第二十类 艺术品、收藏品及古物	**Works of Art, Collection Pieces and Antiques**	**30999**	**539692**	**4613**	**76639**

6-9 出口主要商品数量和金额（2022年）

Volume and Value of Main Export Commodities (2022)

商品名称		Item		数量 Volume	金额 Value 万元人民币 RMB 10 000	万美元 USD 10 000
肉类(包含杂碎)	(吨)	Meat Products (Including Minced Products)	(tonnes)	136763	385722	57815
水产品	(吨)	Aquatic Products	(tonnes)	512262	1915574	287234
蔬菜及食用菌	(吨)	Vegetables and Edible Fungi	(tonnes)	618356	463441	69278
干鲜瓜果及坚果	(吨)	Dried and Fresh Fruits and Nuts	(tonnes)	375752	399551	58907
茶叶	(吨)	Tea Leaves	(tonnes)	4250	46542	6954
粮食	(吨)	Grain	(tonnes)	106742	43731	6518
罐头	(吨)	Canned Products	(tonnes)	37927	49619	7406
酒类及饮料	(吨)	Liquor and Drinks	(tonnes)	1327406	701608	104703
烟草及其制品	(吨)	Tobacco and Tobacco Products	(tonnes)	6783	29390	4472
制盐	(吨)	Salt	(tonnes)	8019	3557	538
水泥及水泥熟料	(吨)	Cement and Cement Clinker	(tonnes)	846849	39064	5824
钨品	(吨)	Tungsten Products	(tonnes)	2000	52967	7994
煤及褐煤	(吨)	Coal and Lignite	(tonnes)	268432	59298	9006
焦炭及半焦炭	(吨)	Coke and Semi-coke	(tonnes)	331806	86151	12946
成品油	(吨)	Refined Oil	(tonnes)	1999810	1230298	184856
氧化铝	(吨)	Aluminum Oxide	(tonnes)	1035	1694	254
稀土及其制品	(吨)	Rare Earths and Rare Earth Products	(tonnes)	4417	155616	23343
基本有机化学品		Basic Organic Chemical Products			1490981	224983
医药材及药品	(吨)	Medicinal Materials and Drugs	(tonnes)	105359	1617184	243302
肥料	(吨)	Fertilizer	(tonnes)	152076	41083	6144
合成有机染料	(吨)	Synthetic Organic Dyes	(tonnes)	8076	25674	3840
美容化妆品及洗护用品	(吨)	Cosmetics and Skincare Products	(tonnes)	387762	1263791	188800
烟花、爆竹	(吨)	Fireworks and Firecrackers	(tonnes)	1773	4739	711
橡胶轮胎	(吨)	Rubber Tires	(tonnes)	260041	472113	70960
皮革、毛皮及其制品		Leather, Furs, and their Products			1125113	168707
箱包及类似容器	(吨)	Luggage Bags and Similar Containers	(tonnes)	667960	6882386	1030243
木及其制品	(吨)	Wood and Wood Products	(tonnes)	818652	1134792	170451
植物材料编结品	(吨)	Knitted Plant Material Products	(tonnes)	41026	122386	18490
纸浆、纸及其制品	(吨)	Paper Pulp, Paper, and their Products	(tonnes)	2143252	4586936	687040
纺织原料	(吨)	Textile Raw Materials	(tonnes)	28206	54298	8197
纺织纱线、织物及其制品		Textile Yarn, Fabric, and their Products			9400184	1415819
服装及衣着附件		Clothing and Clothing Accessories			19317815	2900453
鞋靴	(吨)	Footwear	(tonnes)	800733	8258660	1239693
帽类	(万个)	Hats	(ten thousand)	640578	810120	121732
伞	(吨)	Umbrellas	(tonnes)	26574	146468	21945
花岗岩石材及其制品	(吨)	Granite Materials and Products	(tonnes)	105334	73052	10990
陶瓷产品	(吨)	Pottery Products	(tonnes)	8089954	6197977	929650
玻璃及其制品		Glass and Glassware			3289056	494027

6-9 续表 continued

商品名称	Item	数量 Volume	金额 Value 万元人民币 RMB 10 000	万美元 USD 10 000
珍珠、宝石及半宝石	Pearls, Precious Stones, and Semi-Precious Stones		903333	134656
贵金属或包贵金属的首饰(吨)	Precious Metals or Jewelry with Precious Metals(tonnes)	521	8711506	1287138
铁合金 (吨)	Ferroalloy (tonnes)	459494	566522	86015
钢材 (吨)	Steel (tonnes)	2194916	2152542	325569
未锻轧铜及铜材 (吨)	Unwrought Copper and Copper Materials (tonnes)	102529	698782	105259
未锻轧铝及铝材 (吨)	Unwrought Aluminum and Aluminum Materials (tonnes)	1013425	2545976	384382
家具及其零件	Furniture and Furniture Parts		12637372	1898534
玩具	Toys		12803768	1921168
体育用品及设备	Sports Equipment and Devices		3188137	480696
笔及其零件	Pens and Pen Parts		206728	30868
机械基础件	Basic Mechanical Parts		2548392	381781
手用或机用工具 (吨)	Hand or Machine Tools (tonnes)	230642	1624206	243652
农业机械	Agricultural Machinery		329139	49809
食品加工机械 (万台)	Food Processing Machinery (10000 units)	326	402620	60309
包装机械 (万台)	Packaging Machinery (10000 units)	707	555575	83302
印刷、装订机械及其零件	Printing and Binding Machinery and their Parts		5946187	891185
通用机械设备	General Machinery		8192970	1235442
纺织机械及其零件	Textile Machinery and their Parts		340608	51112
缝制机械及其零件	Sewing Machinery and their Parts		134585	20189
机床 (万台)	Machine Tools (10000 units)	164	1080088	161573
自动数据处理设备及其零部件	Automatic Data Processing Equipment and their Parts		35630640	5346939
电工器材	Electrical Equipment		37051114	5550042
手机 (万台)	Mobile Phones (10000 units)	248881	26360856	3940242
家用电器	Household Appliances		28478367	4293633
音视频设备及其零件	Audiovisual Equipment and their Parts		11782672	1767545
电子元件	Electrical Components		44892110	6716868
集装箱 (万个)	Containers (10000 units)	45	1852121	280802
摩托车 (万辆)	Motorcycles (10000 units)	743	2104360	316458
自行车 (万辆)	Bicycles (10000 units)	319	280868	42506
摩托车及自行车的零配件	Motorcycle and Bicycle Parts		2511061	376395
汽车 (包含底盘)	Automobiles (Including Chassis)		1424214	208400
汽车零配件	Automobile Parts		5745803	861396
婴孩车及其零件 (吨)	Baby Carriages and their Parts (tonnes)	84089	447082	67137
船舶	Ships		1482072	221092
眼镜及其零件	Eyeglasses and their Parts		1727835	258927
液晶平板显示模组	Liquid Crystal Display Modules	83095	7552027	1137217
计量检测分析自控仪器及器具	Automated Measurement, Detection, Analysis Devices		4821724	722034
医疗仪器及器械	Medical Equipment and Devices		3897316	585559
钟表及其零件	Clocks and their Parts		1839977	275487
灯具、照明装置及其零件	Lamps, Lighting Devices, and their Parts		12531229	1883682
游戏机及其零附件	Gaming Consoles and their Parts		1416639	211857

注：自2022年起，海关删除编码“液晶显示板”，新增编码“液晶平板显示模组”。
Note: Since 2022, the customs has deleted the item "LCD Display Panel" and added the item "Liquid Crystal Display Modules".

6-10 进口主要商品数量和金额（2022年）

Volume and Value of Main Import Commodities (2022)

商品名称		Item		数量 Volume	金额 Value 万元人民币 RMB 10 000	万美元 USD 10 000
肉类(包含杂碎)	(吨)	Meat Products (Including Minced Products)	(tonnes)	1553378	3936596	589197
#猪肉及猪杂碎	(吨)	Pork and Minced Pork Products	(tonnes)	555874	919391	137977
水产品	(吨)	Aquatic Products	(tonnes)	468556	2046655	306804
乳品	(吨)	Dairy Products	(tonnes)	376229	1621238	243158
#奶粉	(吨)	Milk Powder	(tonnes)	197952	1370745	205405
干鲜瓜果及坚果	(吨)	Dried and Fresh Fruit and Nuts	(tonnes)	1953949	3837177	584502
粮食	(吨)	Grain	(tonnes)	10222447	3412323	512863
#稻谷及大米	(吨)	Unmilled and Milled Rice	(tonnes)	2378129	695399	105077
大豆	(吨)	Soybeans	(tonnes)	3395135	1550865	231359
食用植物油	(吨)	Edible Vegetable Oils	(tonnes)	505134	455594	67174
#棕榈油	(吨)	Palm Oil	(tonnes)	352452	268203	39278
食糖	(吨)	Sugar	(tonnes)	1005817	326281	48109
酒类及饮料		Liquor and Drinks			967678	143954
#葡萄酒	(升)	Wine	(liters)	56938	204900	30708
制盐	(吨)	Salt	(tonnes)	10477	3572	532
金属矿及矿砂	(吨)	Metal Ores and Other Ores	(tonnes)	53161747	4768428	719295
#铁矿砂及其精矿	(吨)	Iron Ore and Iron Ore Concentrate	(tonnes)	42445243	3377753	509575
煤及褐煤	(吨)	Coal and Lignite	(tonnes)	39869492	3256595	488462
原油	(吨)	Crude Oil	(tonnes)	6756220	3201534	482539
成品油	(吨)	Refined Oil	(tonnes)	1236562	713207	108447
#航空煤油	(吨)	Aviation Kerosene	(tonnes)	171428	104057	16130
天然气	(吨)	Natural Gas	(tonnes)			
#液化天然气	(吨)	Liquid Natural Gas	(tonnes)			
多晶硅	(吨)	Polysilicon	(tonnes)	49	592	91
基本有机化学品		Basic Organic Chemicals			3084580	464508
医药材及药品	(吨)	Medicinal Materials and Drugs	(tonnes)	56640	2855606	427140
肥料	(吨)	Fertilizer	(tonnes)	310924	120492	18369
美容化妆品及洗护用品	(吨)	Cosmetics and Skincare Products	(tonnes)	61025	1747010	261701
初级形状的塑料	(吨)	Plastics in their Initial Form	(tonnes)	7135518	9203917	1387369
塑料制品		Plastic Products			2967891	446136
天然及合成橡胶(包括胶乳)	(吨)	Natural and Synthetic Rubber (Including Latex)	(tonnes)	295049	413795	62109
皮革、毛皮及其制品		Leather, Furs, and their Products		157397	633257	95367
木及其制品	(吨)	Wood and Wood Products	(tonnes)	4930881	1238448	186662
#锯材	(吨)	Saws	(tonnes)	2943255	832876	125577
纸浆、纸及其制品	(吨)	Paper Pulp, Paper, and their Products	(tonnes)	6055003	2788296	417017
#纸浆	(吨)	Paper Pulp	(tonnes)	4123002	1812155	270524
纺织原料	(吨)	Textile Raw Materials	(tonnes)	186367	89948	13567
纺织纱线、织物及其制品		Textile Yarn, Fabric, and their Products			1695234	255223
#纺织纱线	(吨)	Textile Yarn	(tonnes)	244777	621457	93872

注：自2022年1月起，海关总署未公布天然气进出口数据。
Note: Since January 2022, the General Administration of Customs has not released the import and export data of natural gas.

6-10 续表 continued

商品名称	Item	数量 Volume	金额 Value 万元人民币 RMB 10 000	万美元 USD 10 000
服装及衣着附件	Clothing and Clothing Accessories		603333	90602
玻璃及其制品	Glass and Glassware		1440986	216848
珍珠、宝石及半宝石	Pearls, Precious Stones, Semi-Precious Stones		6713774	992604
#钻石 (克拉)	Diamonds (carats)	6902	3719193	556884
钢材 (吨)	Steel (tonnes)	2606760	2328791	351694
未锻轧铜及铜材 (吨)	Unwrought Copper and Copper Materials (tonnes)	668108	4265685	641892
未锻轧铝及铝材 (吨)	Unwrought Aluminum and Aluminum Materials (tonnes)	398790	834691	125232
机械基础件	Basic Mechanical Parts		934297	140742
农业机械	Agricultural Machinery		21334	3217
食品加工机械 (台)	Food Processing Machinery (units)	31952	60167	8965
包装机械 (台)	Packaging Machinery (units)	14778	143484	21731
印刷、装订机械及其零件	Printing and Binding Machinery, and their Parts		1246379	187341
#打印机、复印机及一体机 (万台)	Printers, Copiers, and All-in-one Machines (10000 units)	116	266498	40084
通用机械设备	General Mechanical Equipment		1271381	191209
机床 (台)	Machine Tools (units)	11322	604527	90393
自动数据处理设备及其零部件	Automatic Data Processing Equipment and their Parts		12547751	1889711
#存储部件 (万台)	Storage Components (10000 units)	8388	4286476	645793
自动数据处理设备的零件、附件 (吨)	Parts and Accessories of Automatic Data Processing Equipment (tonnes)	19853	5573584	839131
半导体制造设备 (台)	Semiconductor Manufacturing Equipment (units)	10127	2199006	330292
#制造平板显示器用的机器及装置(台)	Flat Panel Display Manufacturing Machinery and Equipment (units)	2074	957860	143902
电工器材	Electrical Equipment		8281764	1244855
#电气控制装置	Electrical Control Devices		4020958	604723
电线及电缆 (吨)	Electrical Wires and Cables (tonnes)	43532	921393	138487
音视频设备及其零件	Audiovisual Equipment and their Parts		2172458	320686
#音视频设备的零件	Audiovisual Equipment Parts		1880996	277098
电子元件	Electrical Components		121698590	18293040
#集成电路 (万个)	Integrated Circuits (10000 units)	188270602	105019662	15785401
汽车 (包含底盘)	Automobiles (Including Chassis)		715262	106481
#乘用车 (辆)	Passenger Automobiles (units)	11734	683088	101694
汽车零配件	Automobile Parts		2101485	317349
飞机及其他航空器 (架)	Aircraft and other Aviation Vehicles (units)	37633	677927	100384
航空器零部件	Aircraft Parts		1189522	178504
船舶	Ships		49881	7570
液晶平板显示模组 (万个)	Liquid Crystal Display Modules (10000 units)	76880	3840324	580345
计量检测分析自控仪器及器具	Automated Measurement, Detection, Analysis Equipment and Appliances		3747542	561348
医疗仪器及器械	Medical Devices and Equipment		724405	108773
钟表及其零件	Clocks and their Parts		509364	76320
#手表 (万只)	Wristwatches (10000 units)	807	194376	29167

注：自2022年起，海关删除编码“液晶显示板”，新增编码“液晶平板显示模组”。
Note: Since 2022, the customs has deleted the item "LCD Display Panel" and added the item "Liquid Crystal Display Modules".

6-11 各市出口总额
Total Value of Exports by City

市别	City	亿元 RMB100 million					亿美元 USD100 million				
		2018	2019	2020	2021	2022	2018	2019	2020	2021	2022
全省	**Provincial Total**	**42744.06**	**43416.04**	**43493.07**	**50525.46**	**53319.46**	**6470.46**	**6294.64**	**6282.99**	**7818.60**	**7999.02**
广州	Guangzhou	5607.50	5258.47	5423.35	6311.24	6195.42	848.50	762.24	782.18	976.18	926.85
深圳	Shenzhen	16295.17	16715.50	16973.87	19262.61	21943.77	2463.36	2422.16	2453.29	2982.12	3279.04
珠海	Zhuhai	1886.97	1654.56	1608.52	1885.62	1927.48	286.51	239.89	232.44	291.76	289.89
汕头	Shantou	408.67	464.00	542.47	601.15	634.88	61.95	67.33	78.03	92.91	95.89
佛山	Foshan	3527.26	3727.67	4131.13	5007.31	5561.65	535.60	540.88	597.85	773.59	840.49
韶关	Shaoguan	72.47	75.24	71.06	92.49	90.90	10.95	10.91	10.30	14.32	13.68
河源	Heyuan	215.30	251.20	242.05	246.64	193.95	32.44	36.27	35.05	38.17	29.16
梅州	Meizhou	117.90	100.74	86.79	97.83	91.51	17.92	14.64	12.52	15.14	13.73
惠州	Huizhou	2208.83	1821.63	1687.77	2132.23	2044.93	334.62	264.61	243.88	330.06	307.50
汕尾	Shanwei	87.73	87.56	88.88	112.17	98.46	13.23	12.70	12.80	17.37	14.77
东莞	Dongguan	7955.59	8658.71	8280.87	9559.22	9239.61	1204.42	1255.11	1195.20	1479.61	1390.11
中山	Zhongshan	1801.70	1929.14	1815.00	2231.46	2327.81	273.22	280.24	262.05	345.33	351.37
江门	Jiangmen	1122.99	1136.08	1125.69	1465.60	1446.10	170.35	164.89	162.58	226.82	217.82
阳江	Yangjiang	107.20	117.12	142.59	186.84	179.02	16.22	16.98	20.59	28.92	27.06
湛江	Zhanjiang	206.68	209.38	193.03	212.70	212.21	31.29	30.37	27.94	32.92	31.85
茂名	Maoming	127.32	170.55	169.24	170.84	179.98	18.98	24.69	24.62	26.41	26.78
肇庆	Zhaoqing	237.61	271.67	299.87	271.96	273.41	35.99	39.33	43.48	42.09	41.02
清远	Qingyuan	200.25	214.54	210.06	238.62	257.09	30.28	31.10	30.32	36.93	38.65
潮州	Chaozhou	173.95	180.75	152.52	193.02	206.91	26.35	26.23	22.05	29.87	31.13
揭阳	Jieyang	320.26	308.36	181.08	163.46	125.49	48.75	44.89	26.10	25.29	18.90
云浮	Yunfu	62.70	63.15	67.25	82.47	88.88	9.51	9.15	9.72	12.76	13.32
按经济区域分	By Region										
珠三角	Pearl River Delta	40643.62	41173.44	41346.06	48127.25	50960.18	6152.58	5969.36	5972.95	7447.57	7644.09
东翼	Eastern Region	990.61	1040.68	964.94	1069.80	1065.73	150.28	151.16	138.97	165.44	160.69
西翼	Western Region	441.21	497.05	504.86	570.38	571.22	66.49	72.04	73.15	88.25	85.69
山区	Mountainous Region	668.62	704.87	677.20	758.04	722.33	101.10	102.07	97.91	117.33	108.55

6-12 各市进口总额

Total Value of Imports by City

市 别	City	亿元 RMB100 million					亿美元 USD100 million				
		2018	2019	2020	2021	2022	2018	2019	2020	2021	2022
全 省	**Provincial Total**	**28901.67**	**28068.35**	**27369.58**	**32156.10**	**29778.65**	**4380.57**	**4071.14**	**3956.03**	**4977.07**	**4470.67**
广 州	Guangzhou	4204.09	4745.04	4108.57	4513.85	4752.76	636.55	688.29	593.94	698.35	712.58
深 圳	Shenzhen	13702.08	13065.11	13534.75	16174.13	14794.43	2075.86	1893.54	1955.72	2503.65	2219.28
珠 海	Zhuhai	1360.72	1253.98	1124.38	1433.95	1123.37	207.01	182.26	162.54	221.82	169.02
汕 头	Shantou	146.92	136.52	139.17	152.28	136.06	22.32	19.84	20.05	23.56	20.57
佛 山	Foshan	1071.78	1100.73	929.29	1153.93	1075.21	162.06	159.79	134.54	178.60	161.45
韶 关	Shaoguan	83.53	107.03	115.43	127.89	105.75	12.64	15.54	16.67	19.79	15.88
河 源	Heyuan	55.35	51.77	51.14	60.24	49.94	8.35	7.51	7.42	9.33	7.47
梅 州	Meizhou	17.32	19.88	12.20	23.94	18.52	2.63	2.90	1.76	3.71	2.78
惠 州	Huizhou	1125.84	888.02	800.61	922.82	1046.20	170.96	129.00	115.92	142.89	156.84
汕 尾	Shanwei	89.99	80.18	80.76	91.23	63.42	13.66	11.64	11.64	14.13	9.52
东 莞	Dongguan	5464.32	5175.60	5022.73	5687.35	4686.64	829.06	751.05	725.79	880.36	705.56
中 山	Zhongshan	539.90	458.01	393.91	463.34	470.72	81.87	66.51	56.94	71.71	70.85
江 门	Jiangmen	349.22	289.28	303.25	323.71	327.67	52.84	42.00	43.90	50.11	49.25
阳 江	Yangjiang	30.66	34.66	49.14	81.74	89.66	4.64	5.03	7.09	12.65	13.52
湛 江	Zhanjiang	172.34	204.51	251.61	331.80	411.42	26.13	29.67	36.55	51.38	62.11
茂 名	Maoming	24.42	25.82	30.03	58.52	77.16	3.71	3.75	4.36	9.06	11.52
肇 庆	Zhaoqing	152.22	132.71	113.28	133.49	112.16	23.05	19.33	16.38	20.67	16.89
清 远	Qingyuan	212.24	201.70	216.40	297.83	295.70	32.22	29.30	31.34	46.11	44.47
潮 州	Chaozhou	32.37	34.85	29.41	48.40	54.31	4.94	5.07	4.26	7.48	8.17
揭 阳	Jieyang	21.17	16.15	13.23	24.99	37.20	3.22	2.35	1.91	3.87	5.43
云 浮	Yunfu	45.19	46.82	50.30	50.67	50.37	6.84	6.78	7.30	7.83	7.51
按经济区域分	By Region										
珠 三 角	Pearl River Delta	27970.16	27108.47	26330.76	30806.57	28389.16	4239.27	3931.77	3805.68	4768.16	4261.73
东 翼	Eastern Region	290.45	267.70	262.57	316.90	290.98	44.14	38.89	37.86	49.04	43.69
西 翼	Western Region	227.42	264.99	330.78	472.05	578.24	34.48	38.45	48.00	73.10	87.14
山 区	Mountainous Region	413.63	427.19	445.47	560.58	520.27	62.68	62.03	64.48	86.78	78.11

6-13 各市外商投资企业出口总额

Total Value of Exports of Enterprises with Foreign Investment by City

市 别	City	亿元人民币 RMB100 million					亿美元 USD100 million				
		2018	2019	2020	2021	2022	2018	2019	2020	2021	2022
全 省	**Provincial Total**	**19382.28**	**18091.48**	**16896.57**	**18854.71**	**18352.18**	**2934.98**	**2624.40**	**2441.08**	**2918.51**	**2756.34**
广 州	Guangzhou	2040.15	1942.14	1622.74	1910.52	1874.14	309.42	282.03	234.42	295.63	282.11
深 圳	Shenzhen	6875.74	6296.21	6255.14	6677.36	6819.79	1039.29	912.28	904.63	1033.84	1020.16
珠 海	Zhuhai	829.52	748.36	702.53	747.33	824.16	125.85	108.53	101.57	115.69	123.52
汕 头	Shantou	77.93	70.04	54.17	55.23	53.47	11.82	10.17	7.82	8.55	8.03
佛 山	Foshan	1297.25	1279.29	1229.00	1442.58	1328.13	196.85	185.81	177.36	223.20	200.47
韶 关	Shaoguan	43.55	46.05	39.11	49.05	44.36	6.58	6.67	5.64	7.59	6.68
河 源	Heyuan	141.98	136.48	125.73	142.30	140.30	21.50	19.81	18.14	22.02	21.14
梅 州	Meizhou	34.76	28.09	24.43	26.60	25.27	5.27	4.08	3.53	4.12	3.82
惠 州	Huizhou	1922.73	1491.07	1305.07	1562.47	1383.42	291.39	216.68	188.57	241.86	208.25
汕 尾	Shanwei	75.93	79.21	65.52	88.07	73.46	11.43	11.49	9.47	13.64	11.01
东 莞	Dongguan	3990.31	3992.17	3727.36	4080.36	3662.84	604.24	578.98	537.93	631.56	551.29
中 山	Zhongshan	1012.20	977.99	882.02	1009.53	1075.14	153.53	142.04	127.25	156.25	162.17
江 门	Jiangmen	594.92	579.04	533.62	667.32	654.06	90.29	84.07	77.08	103.28	98.46
阳 江	Yangjiang	11.63	10.69	12.25	20.83	17.36	1.76	1.55	1.77	3.22	2.62
湛 江	Zhanjiang	51.19	44.32	26.24	27.25	27.12	7.77	6.43	3.78	4.22	4.06
茂 名	Maoming	11.10	10.46	7.95	7.89	8.89	1.68	1.52	1.15	1.22	1.34
肇 庆	Zhaoqing	126.17	121.36	86.91	105.83	111.48	19.13	17.63	12.56	16.38	16.78
清 远	Qingyuan	146.59	143.82	128.56	148.52	161.15	22.20	20.88	18.57	22.99	24.24
潮 州	Chaozhou	16.89	15.85	10.40	10.22	9.18	2.57	2.30	1.50	1.58	1.38
揭 阳	Jieyang	46.51	40.42	25.75	25.70	21.01	7.08	5.88	3.71	3.98	3.16
云 浮	Yunfu	35.24	38.41	32.08	49.74	37.45	5.32	5.57	4.65	7.70	5.66
按经济区域分	By Region										
珠 三 角	Pearl River Delta	18688.99	17427.64	16344.38	18203.30	17733.16	2829.99	2528.05	2361.36	2817.68	2663.21
东 翼	Eastern Region	217.27	205.52	155.84	179.23	157.13	32.90	29.84	22.50	27.75	23.58
西 翼	Western Region	73.91	65.47	46.44	55.96	53.37	11.21	9.50	6.70	8.66	8.02
山 区	Mountainous Region	402.11	392.85	349.92	416.21	408.52	60.88	57.01	50.52	64.42	61.53

6-14 各市外商投资企业进口总额

Total Value of Imports of Enterprises with Foreign Investment by City

市别	City	亿元人民币 RMB100 million					亿美元 USD100 million				
		2018	2019	2020	2021	2022	2018	2019	2020	2021	2022
全省	**Provincial Total**	**13020.99**	**11877.35**	**10985.77**	**12728.75**	**11990.75**	**1970.90**	**1723.27**	**1589.25**	**1970.52**	**1800.38**
广州	Guangzhou	2157.97	2277.76	1863.76	1950.82	1804.01	326.74	330.88	269.03	301.78	271.68
深圳	Shenzhen	5338.23	4497.07	4267.97	5081.87	4618.44	806.48	651.55	618.07	786.81	691.23
珠海	Zhuhai	707.40	696.59	633.48	755.26	661.38	107.43	101.03	91.55	116.92	99.53
汕头	Shantou	50.37	39.72	32.60	32.08	42.91	7.62	5.78	4.70	4.96	6.49
佛山	Foshan	560.52	527.14	481.82	569.39	479.89	84.71	76.52	69.71	88.13	72.43
韶关	Shaoguan	14.45	17.15	14.69	20.81	18.11	2.17	2.49	2.12	3.22	2.72
河源	Heyuan	46.37	38.48	34.93	45.55	36.68	7.01	5.57	5.06	7.06	5.52
梅州	Meizhou	9.99	8.54	8.63	9.84	8.77	1.52	1.24	1.24	1.52	1.32
惠州	Huizhou	960.37	687.88	550.25	623.30	601.72	146.10	100.08	79.67	96.50	90.55
汕尾	Shanwei	82.85	75.03	64.42	60.76	47.91	12.56	10.89	9.29	9.41	7.20
东莞	Dongguan	2170.83	2228.26	2305.80	2719.63	2796.13	328.89	323.43	333.55	421.15	420.14
中山	Zhongshan	431.92	357.51	303.26	351.13	342.66	65.45	51.92	43.79	54.35	51.60
江门	Jiangmen	234.51	171.50	181.18	188.18	197.54	35.53	24.91	26.21	29.13	29.66
阳江	Yangjiang	21.02	24.73	25.61	30.63	32.54	3.18	3.60	3.68	4.74	4.85
湛江	Zhanjiang	33.96	47.57	64.98	118.98	127.67	5.11	6.88	9.53	18.44	19.21
茂名	Maoming	4.55	4.62	9.61	19.70	24.52	0.69	0.67	1.40	3.04	3.64
肇庆	Zhaoqing	67.69	57.78	48.41	44.86	43.42	10.26	8.43	6.99	6.94	6.53
清远	Qingyuan	82.07	71.12	70.84	84.52	79.11	12.49	10.31	10.23	13.09	11.96
潮州	Chaozhou	15.80	19.65	6.93	10.48	16.12	2.40	2.86	1.00	1.62	2.42
揭阳	Jieyang	6.10	5.44	3.31	3.36	5.60	0.93	0.79	0.48	0.52	0.84
云浮	Yunfu	24.01	23.79	13.29	7.59	5.61	3.63	3.45	1.92	1.17	0.85
按经济区域分	By Region										
珠三角	Pearl River Delta	12629.45	11501.49	10635.93	12284.45	11545.19	1911.59	1668.74	1538.59	1901.71	1733.35
东翼	Eastern Region	155.12	139.85	107.26	106.69	112.54	23.51	20.33	15.47	16.51	16.96
西翼	Western Region	59.52	76.92	100.20	169.31	184.74	8.98	11.15	14.61	26.23	27.71
山区	Mountainous Region	176.90	159.08	142.38	168.30	148.28	26.82	23.06	20.57	26.07	22.36

6-15 外商投资企业进出口主要指标（2022年）

Main Indicators on Imports and Exports of Enterprises with Foreign Investment(2022)

项 目	Item	亿元人民币 RMB 100 million			亿美元 USD 100 million		
		进出口总额 Total	出口 Exports	进口 Imports	进出口总额 Total	出口 Exports	进口 Imports
全 省	**Provincial Total**	**30342.92**	**18352.18**	**11990.75**	**4556.72**	**2756.34**	**1800.38**
按贸易方式分	By Customs Regime						
一般贸易	Ordinary Trade	9654.33	5982.89	3671.44	1452.64	900.40	552.24
来料加工	Processing and Assembling with Customer's Materials	1293.72	751.45	542.27	194.07	112.63	81.44
进料加工	Processing and Assembling with Import Materials	15088.54	10244.06	4844.48	2264.39	1537.47	726.92
加工设备	Processing Equipments	11.00		11.00	1.67		1.67
外资设备	Foreign-funded Equipments	26.55		26.55	4.05		4.05
保税仓库	Bonded Warehouse	4233.76	1360.39	2873.37	634.67	203.87	430.81
其他	Others	35.02	13.38	21.64	5.22	1.97	3.25
按经济类型分	By Type of Ownership						
合作经营企业	Joint Ventures	184.06	152.18	31.88	27.68	22.88	4.80
合资经营企业	Cooperative Enterprises	8210.99	4679.05	3531.94	1234.22	703.57	530.65
外资(独资)企业	Enterprises with Sole Foreign Investment	21947.88	13520.95	8426.93	3294.82	2029.89	1264.93
按产品类型分	By Type of Product						
#机电产品	Machanical and Electrical Products	22358.38	14247.40	8110.97	3357.03	2139.29	1217.74
高新技术产品	High and New-tech Products	13344.03	7106.30	6237.73	2000.60	1064.71	935.89
#计算机与通信技术	Computer and Communication Technology	5569.43	4800.10	769.33	833.87	718.49	115.38
电子技术	Electronic Technology	6155.89	1463.43	4692.46	922.75	219.29	703.46
按主要国家(地区)分	By Main Country (Region)						
亚洲	**Asia**	**19745.32**	**10178.14**	**9567.18**	**2963.26**	**1525.92**	**1437.34**
中国香港	Hong Kong, China	5692.87	5624.53	68.34	850.82	840.63	10.19
中国澳门	Macao, China	50.32	47.04	3.28	7.61	7.11	0.49
中国台湾	Taiwan, China	2800.51	387.36	2413.15	420.47	58.38	362.09
日本	Japan	2613.63	1041.66	1571.98	392.39	156.25	236.15
韩国	Republic of Korea	1889.82	427.13	1462.69	284.46	64.47	219.99
东盟	Association of Southeast Asian Nations	3809.19	1811.07	1998.13	572.49	272.75	299.74
中东十七国	The Seventeen Countries of the Middle East	801.90	477.21	324.69	120.85	71.86	48.99
非洲	**Africa**	**496.11**	**248.19**	**247.92**	**74.68**	**37.47**	**37.21**
欧洲	**Europe**	**4208.66**	**3198.31**	**1010.35**	**632.38**	**480.84**	**151.55**
欧盟	European Union	3380.14	2551.70	828.43	507.93	383.77	124.16
#英国	United Kingdom	465.96	421.64	44.33	70.04	63.41	6.62
德国	Germany	893.15	610.70	282.45	134.15	91.77	42.38
法国	France	342.92	212.83	130.09	51.56	32.02	19.54
意大利	Italy	294.42	197.63	96.79	44.35	29.86	14.50
荷兰	Netherlands	699.13	629.11	70.02	104.96	94.50	10.46
芬兰	Finland	20.34	10.81	9.53	3.06	1.64	1.43
瑞士	Switzerland	131.55	43.64	87.91	19.73	6.56	13.16
俄罗斯	Russia	167.49	140.82	26.66	25.07	21.01	4.06
拉丁美洲	**Latin America**	**1373.52**	**931.16**	**442.35**	**205.86**	**139.98**	**65.88**
北美洲	**North America**	**3975.91**	**3455.39**	**520.52**	**599.03**	**520.97**	**78.06**
加拿大	Canada	314.87	257.89	56.98	47.37	38.82	8.55
美国	United States of America	3661.03	3197.49	463.54	551.66	482.15	69.51
大洋洲及其他	**Oceania and Others**	**543.41**	**340.98**	**202.43**	**81.51**	**51.16**	**30.35**
澳大利亚	Australia	436.76	296.62	140.14	65.55	44.53	21.01
新西兰	New Zealand	83.34	38.25	45.09	12.49	5.72	6.77

6-16 外商投资企业出口主要商品数量和金额（2022年）

Volume and Value of Main Export Commodities of Enterprises with Foreign Investment (2022)

商品名称		Item		数量 Volume	金额 Value 万元人民币 RMB10 000	万美元 USD 10 000
肉类(包含杂碎)	(吨)	Meat Products (Including Minced Meat)	(tonnes)	18467	52558	7872
水产品	(吨)	Aquatic Products	(tonnes)	60127	314589	47125
蔬菜及食用菌	(吨)	Vegetables and Edible Fungi	(tonnes)	72127	82395	12449
干鲜瓜果及坚果	(吨)	Dried and Fresh Fruits and Nuts	(tonnes)	9508	33117	4872
茶叶	(吨)	Tea Leaves	(tonnes)	970	6036	889
粮食	(吨)	Grain	(tonnes)	79500	31580	4721
罐头	(吨)	Canned Products	(tonnes)	13685	14154	2135
酒类及饮料		Liquor and Drinks			559510	83522
烟草及其制品	(吨)	Tobacco and Tobacco Products	(tonnes)	1	29	4
制盐	(吨)	Salt	(tonnes)	1435	1501	224
水泥及水泥熟料	(吨)	Cement and Cement Clinker	(tonnes)	812548	35379	5271
钨品	(吨)	Tungsten Products	(tonnes)	0	57	8
成品油	(吨)	Refined Oil	(tonnes)	779098	501046	75382
氧化铝	(吨)	Alumina	(tonnes)	141	446	67
稀土及其制品	(吨)	Rare Earths and their Products	(tonnes)	686	45006	6725
基本有机化学品		Basic Organic Chemical Products			432125	65398
医药材及药品	(吨)	Medicinal Materials and Drugs	(tonnes)	37773	249381	37481
肥料	(吨)	Fertilizer	(tonnes)	29484	10197	1533
合成有机染料	(吨)	Synthetic Organic Dyes	(tonnes)	719	5513	832
美容化妆品及洗护用品	(吨)	Cosmetics and Skincare Products	(tonnes)	208124	496708	74318
塑料制品	(吨)	Plastic Products		1500184	4280659	644945
橡胶轮胎	(吨)	Rubber Tires	(tonnes)	105669	179818	27204
皮革、毛皮及其制品		Leather, Furs, and their Products			424715	63971
箱包及类似容器	(吨)	Luggage Bags and Similar Containers	(tonnes)	115896	1253290	188176
木及其制品	(吨)	Wood and Wood Products	(tonnes)	144827	286737	43072
植物材料编结品	(吨)	Woven Plant Material Products	(tonnes)	2520	9605	1456
纸浆、纸及其制品	(吨)	Paper Pulp, Paper, and their Products	(tonnes)	751122	1142341	171402
纺织原料	(吨)	Textile Raw Materials	(tonnes)	312	1005	149
纺织纱线、织物及其制品		Textile Yarn, Fabric, and their Products			3229993	487993
服装及衣着附件		Clothing and Clothing Accessories			3322608	499426
鞋靴	(吨)	Footwear	(tonnes)	112096	1851677	278841
帽类	(个)	Hats	(units)	201191	324813	49023
伞	(吨)	Umbrellas	(tonnes)	5585	27885	4200
花岗岩石材及其制品	(吨)	Granite Materials and Products	(tonnes)	12296	10467	1594
陶瓷产品	(吨)	Pottery Products	(tonnes)	468831	282120	42320
玻璃及其制品		Glass and Glassware			975227	147082
珍珠、宝石及半宝石		Pearls, Precious Stones and Semi-precious Stones			755405	112713
贵金属或包贵金属的首饰	(克)	Precious Metals or Jeweler with Precious Metals	(carats)	117645	2904336	431896

6-16 续表 continued

商品名称		Item		数量 Volume	金额 Value 万元人民币 RMB10 000	万美元 USD 10 000
钢材	(吨)	Steel	(tonnes)	412064	482450	72437
未锻轧铜及铜材	(吨)	Unwrought Copper and Copper Materials	(tonnes)	51668	341502	51455
未锻轧铝及铝材	(吨)	Unwrought Aluminum and Aluminum Materials	(tonnes)	282127	671335	101625
家具及其零件		Furniture and their Parts			2625163	395638
玩具		Toys			3578505	538305
体育用品及设备		Sports Equipment and Devices			1515495	228820
笔及其零件		Pens and Pen Parts			59463	8974
机械基础件		Basic Mechanical Parts			698420	104748
手用或机用工具	(吨)	Hand or Machine Tools	(tonnes)	65950	436722	65914
农业机械	(万台)	Agricultural Machinery	(10000 units)	3304	233568	35519
食品加工机械	(万台)	Food Processing Machinery	(10000 units)	38	79303	11984
包装机械		Packaging Machinery			105821	15914
印刷、装订机械及其零件		Printing, Binding Machinery and their Parts			4018283	602245
通用机械设备		General Mechanical Equipment			3543282	535453
纺织机械及其零件		Textile Machinery and their Parts			125890	18813
缝制机械及其零件		Sewing Machinery and their Parts			16606	2497
机床	(万台)	Machine Tools	(10000 units)	77	144058	21614
自动数据处理设备及其零部件		Automatic Data Processing Equipment and their Parts			16788839	2517582
电工器材		Electrical Equipment			14861763	2229941
手机	(万台)	Mobile Phones	(10000 units)	6547	14746336	2190674
家用电器		Household Appliances			13207465	1995548
音视频设备及其零件		Audiovisual Equipment and their Parts			3602579	541219
电子元件		Electrical Components			17621368	2643263
集装箱	(万个)	Containers	(10000 units)	30	1176086	178154
摩托车	(万辆)	Motorcycles	(10000 units)	189	780747	117504
自行车	(万辆)	Bicycles	(10000 units)	71	77065	11636
摩托车及自行车的零配件		Motorcycle and Bicycle Parts			893160	
汽车	(包含底盘)	Automobiles	(Including Chassis)		873975	126924
汽车零配件		Automobile Parts			2105693	316099
婴孩车及其零件	(吨)	Baby Carriages and their Parts	(tonnes)	43609	246089	36847
船舶		Ships			78683	11850
眼镜及其零件		Eyeglasses and their Parts			635449	95271
液晶平板显示模组	(万个)	Liquid Crystal Display Modules	(10000 units)	46065	4543830	685476
计量检测分析自控仪器及器具		Automated Measurement, Detection, Analysis Devices and Appliances			2190195	328709
医疗仪器及器械		Medical Devices and Equipment			1561585	234824
钟表及其零件		Clocks and their Parts			1222242	183254
灯具、照明装置及其零件		Lamps, Lighting Devices, and their Parts			1600372	240937
游戏机及其零附件		Gaming Consoles and their Parts			929056	138941

注：自2022年起，海关删除编码“液晶显示板”，新增编码“液晶平板显示模组”。
Note: Since 2022, the customs has deleted the item "LCD Display Panel" and added the item "Liquid Crystal Display Modules".

 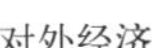 

6-17 外商投资企业进口主要商品数量和金额（2022年）

Volume and Value of Main Import Commodities by Enterprises with Foreign Investment (2022)

商品名称		Item		数量 Volume	金额 Value 万元人民币 RMB10 000	金额 Value 万美元 USD 10 000
肉类(包含杂碎)	(吨)	Meat Products (Including Minced Products)	(tonnes)	76495	380579	56977
#牛肉及牛杂碎	(吨)	Beef and Minced Beef Products	(tonnes)	68745	363554	54413
猪肉及猪杂碎	(吨)	Pork and Minced Pork Products	(tonnes)	4176	7697	1157
水产品	(吨)	Aquatic Products	(tonnes)	54115	178060	26718
#冻鱼	(吨)	Frozen Fish	(tonnes)	12866	21129	3218
乳品	(吨)	Dairy Products	(tonnes)	190817	936125	140007
#奶粉	(吨)	Milk Powder	(tonnes)	89909	830862	124106
干鲜瓜果及坚果	(吨)	Dried and Fresh Fruit and Nuts	(tonnes)	157894	378528	57941
粮食	(吨)	Grain	(tonnes)	1534313	683102	101026
#小麦	(吨)	Wheat	(tonnes)	136386	39301	5804
大麦	(吨)	Barley	(tonnes)	1095	260	36
大豆	(吨)	Soybeans	(tonnes)	1253792	589832	87135
食用植物油	(吨)	Edible Vegetable Oils	(tonnes)	413237	352830	51924
#棕榈油	(吨)	Palm Oil	(tonnes)	352240	268009	39249
食糖	(吨)	Sugar	(tonnes)	27465	10538	1573
酒类及饮料		Liquor and Drinks			150179	22422
#啤酒	(升)	Beer	(liters)	7392	7185	1072
制盐	(吨)	Salt	(tonnes)	1657	520	77
金属矿及矿砂	(吨)	Metal Ores and Other Ores	(tonnes)	17083454	1596233	239836
铁矿砂及其精矿	(吨)	Iron Ore and Iron Ore Concentrate	(tonnes)	13996384	1123759	168829
煤及褐煤	(吨)	Coal and Lignite	(tonnes)	6816292	521097	78579
原油	(吨)	Crude Oil	(tonnes)	3210508	1554140	233410
成品油	(吨)	Refined Oil	(tonnes)	277912	192556	29339
天然气	(吨)	Natural Gas	(tonnes)			
基本有机化学品		Basic Organic Chemicals			1928733	290700
#二甲苯	(吨)	Xylene	(tonnes)	1001692	732752	110444
医药材及药品	(吨)	Medicinal Materials and Drugs	(tonnes)	19795	995226	148880
肥料	(吨)	Fertilizer	(tonnes)	307397	118605	18098
#氯化钾	(吨)	Potassium Chloride	(tonnes)	306865	117629	17953
美容化妆品及洗护用品	(吨)	Cosmetics and Skincare Products	(tonnes)	14536	158770	23765
初级形状的塑料	(吨)	Plastics in their Initial Form	(tonnes)	2973947	4544454	686018
塑料制品	(吨)	Plastic Products		165740	1766801	265409
天然及合成橡胶(包括胶乳)	(吨)	Natural and Synthetic Rubber (Including Latex)	(tonnes)	90610	168800	25412
皮革、毛皮及其制品	(吨)	Leather, Furs, and their Products		73842	296866	44855
#牛皮革及马皮革	(吨)	Cow Leather and Horse Leather	(tonnes)	69932	260250	39330
木及其制品	(吨)	Wood and Wood Products	(tonnes)	242611	81197	12266
#锯材	(吨)	Saws	(tonnes)	78730	38440	5773
纸浆、纸及其制品	(吨)	Paper Pulp, Paper, and their Products	(tonnes)	3899347	1742469	261309
#纸浆	(吨)	Paper Pulp	(tonnes)	2945748	1212148	181510

注：自2022年1月起，海关总署未公布天然气进出口数据。

Note: Since January 2022, the General Administration of Customs has not released the import and export data of natural gas.

6-17 续表 continued

商品名称		Item		数量 Volume	金额 Value 万元人民币 RMB10 000	万美元 USD 10 000
纺织原料	(吨)	Textile Raw Materials	(tonnes)	23922	36659	5537
#棉花	(吨)	Cotton	(tonnes)	4515	8757	1329
纺织纱线、织物及其制品		Yarn, Fabric, and their Products			1221969	183947
#纺织纱线	(吨)	Textile Yarn	(tonnes)	127117	432320	65285
服装及衣着附件		Clothing and Clothing Accessories			188887	28374
玻璃及其制品		Glass and Glassware			1188976	178780
#玻璃纤维及其制品	(吨)	Glass Fibre and Glass Fibre Products	(tonnes)	34266	132560	20000
珍珠、宝石及半宝石		Pearls, Precious Stones, and Semi-precious Stones			2007898	301518
#钻石	(克拉)	Diamonds	(carats)	3678450	1945665	292222
钢材	(吨)	Steel	(tonnes)	2182091	1803627	272990
未锻轧铜及铜材	(吨)	Unwrought Copper and Copper Materials	(tonnes)	253409	1908039	288256
未锻轧铝及铝材	(吨)	Unwrought Aluminium and Aluminium Materials	(tonnes)	110658	297501	44481
机械基础件		Basic Mechanical Parts			682971	102840
农业机械	(万台)	Agricultural Machinery	(10000 units)	80	4570	694
食品加工机械	(台)	Food Processing Machinery	(units)	6208	29581	4370
包装机械	(台)	Packaging Machinery	(units)	1085	77025	11670
印刷、装订机械及其零件		Printing, Binding Machinery and their Parts			750298	112639
#打印机、复印机及一体机	(万台)	Printers, Copiers, and All-in-one Machines	(10000 units)	28	56960	8598
通用机械设备		General Mechanical Equipment			720752	108478
#阀门及类似装置	(万套)	Valves and Similar Devices	(10000 sets)	7335	289450	43511
机床	(台)	Machine Tools	(units)	3102	229551	34349
自动数据处理设备及其零部件		Automatic Data Processing Equipment and their Parts			3049059	460430
存储部件	(台)	Storage Components	(units)	12477108	712800	107724
#自动数据处理设备的零件、附件	(吨)	Accessories and Parts of Automatic Data Processing Equipment	(tonnes)	11039	1536521	232442
半导体制造设备	(台)	Semiconductor Manufacturing Equipment	(units)	2101	999633	151615
#制造平板显示器用的机器及装置	(台)	Flat Panel Display Manufacturing Equipment and Devices	(units)	663	433315	65755
电工器材		Electrical Equipment			4737915	712038
#电气控制装置		Electrical Control Devices			2179063	327612
音视频设备及其零件		Audiovisual Equipment and their Parts			1801715	265241
#电子元件		Electrical Components			48771612	7312910
二极管及类似半导体器件	(万个)	Diodes and Similar Semiconductor Devices	(10000 units)	9322966	3917828	587887
#集成电路	(万个)	Integrated Circuits	(10000 units)	7410155	40505129	6071451
汽车(包含底盘)	(辆)	Automobiles (Including Chassis)	(units)	242	15239	2377
汽车零配件		Automobile Parts			1652914	249745
船舶		Ships			14454	2116
液晶平板显示模组	(万个)	Liquid Crystal Display Modules	(10000 units)	23099	2372791	359223
计量检测分析自控仪器及器具		Automatic Measuring, Detection, Analysis Devices and Equipment			1380470	207245
医疗仪器及器械		Medical Devices and Equipment			143423	21445
钟表及其零件		Clocks and their Parts			344781	51788
手表	(万只)	Wristwatches	(10000 units)	568	78063	11849

注：自2022年起，海关删除编码“液晶显示板”，新增编码“液晶平板显示模组”。
Note: Since 2022, the customs has deleted the item "LCD Display Panel" and added the item "Liquid Crystal Display Modules".

6-18 私营企业进出口主要指标（2022年）

Main Indicators on Imports and Exports of Private Enterprises (2022)

项 目	Item	亿元人民币 RMB100 million			亿美元 USD 100 million		
		进出口总额 Total	出口 Exports	进口 Imports	进出口总额 Total	出口 Exports	进口 Imports
全 省	**Provincial Total**	**46578.97**	**31020.37**	**15558.60**	**6985.00**	**4649.92**	**2335.08**
按贸易方式分	By Customs Regime						
一般贸易	Ordinary Trade	31860.40	22484.70	9375.70	4779.88	3367.94	1411.94
来料加工	Processing and Assembling with Customer's Materials	568.45	303.74	264.71	85.08	45.41	39.68
进料加工	Processing and Assembling with Import Materials	4222.10	2500.80	1721.30	630.84	374.38	256.46
加工设备	Processing Equipments	0.57		0.57	0.09		0.09
保税仓库	Bonded Warehouse	7704.07	3568.45	4135.62	1150.59	532.73	617.86
其他	Others	2223.39	2162.68	60.71	338.52	329.46	9.06
按产品类型分	By Type of Product						
#机电产品	Machanical and Electrical Products	28548.25	18303.87	10244.39	4284.16	2744.82	1539.34
#自动数据处理设备及其零部件	Automatic Data Processing Machine and Components	2604.65	1712.59	892.05	391.29	257.15	134.15
高新技术产品	High and New-tech Products	16807.17	8253.61	8553.57	2523.80	1237.58	1286.21
#计算机与通信技术	Computer and Communication Technology	6338.42	5134.99	1203.43	951.72	771.06	180.66
电子技术	Electronic Technology	8609.00	2030.92	6578.07	1292.98	303.07	989.91
按主要国家(地区)分	By Main Country (Region)						
亚洲	**Asia**	**27076.28**	**14930.30**	**12145.98**	**4058.52**	**2235.07**	**1823.46**
中国香港	Hong Kong, China	4470.28	4372.87	97.41	667.09	652.60	14.49
中国澳门	Macao, China	68.73	68.20	0.53	10.34	10.27	0.08
中国台湾	Taiwan, China	3369.04	410.15	2958.89	506.77	61.57	445.20
日本	Japan	1743.12	872.54	870.58	261.28	130.63	130.65
韩国	Republic of Korea	1970.95	656.75	1314.19	296.59	98.54	198.05
东盟	Association of Southeast Asian Nations	8755.51	4922.35	3833.16	1309.77	736.50	573.27
中东十七国	The Seventeen Countries of the Middle East	2245.55	1998.14	247.41	337.61	300.35	37.26
非洲	**Africa**	**1802.75**	**1462.91**	**339.84**	**269.80**	**218.85**	**50.95**
欧洲	**Europe**	**7381.64**	**5963.52**	**1418.12**	**1108.22**	**895.77**	**212.45**
欧盟	European Union	6260.34	5138.63	1121.71	940.89	772.82	168.07
#英国	United Kingdom	923.94	826.79	97.16	138.63	124.03	14.59
德国	Germany	1124.53	798.97	325.56	168.88	120.10	48.79
法国	France	617.24	474.37	142.87	92.77	71.48	21.28
意大利	Italy	593.21	501.54	91.67	89.41	75.67	13.73
荷兰	Netherlands	862.01	811.93	50.08	129.55	122.08	7.48
俄罗斯	Russia	693.36	624.11	69.25	103.00	92.77	10.23
拉丁美洲	**Latin America**	**2492.56**	**1810.97**	**681.59**	**374.03**	**271.57**	**102.47**
北美洲	**North America**	**6651.47**	**5969.21**	**682.26**	**998.99**	**896.87**	**102.12**
加拿大	Canada	594.45	486.96	107.49	89.16	73.23	15.93
美国	United States of America	6053.47	5481.69	571.78	909.29	823.56	85.73
大洋洲及其他	**Oceania and others**	**1174.27**	**883.45**	**290.82**	**175.44**	**131.79**	**43.65**
澳大利亚	Australia	978.67	769.39	209.28	146.07	114.69	31.38
新西兰	New Zealand	154.36	85.75	68.62	23.19	12.85	10.34

6-19 利用外资情况
Utilization of Foreign Capital

年份 Year	签订项目 (个) Number of Signed Projects (unit)	#外商直接投资 Foreign Direct Investment	合同外资额 (万美元) Amount of Contracted Foreign Capital (USD 10000)	#外商直接投资 Foreign Direct Investment	实际使用外资 (万美元) Amount of Foreign Capital Actually Utilized (USD 10000)	#外商直接投资 Foreign Direct Investment
1979	1642	70	22889	14616	9143	3074
1980	5048	188	138920	120046	21419	12320
1981	6803	236	167507	156206	28837	17326
1982	8171	151	155916	147698	28103	17123
1983	11318	412	72660	61552	40685	24523
1984	17452	1105	144489	116958	64379	54163
1985	13621	1640	256521	200073	91910	51529
1986	9417	774	183480	85902	142829	64392
1987	6999	1186	201750	124647	121671	59396
1988	7662	2741	382748	224196	243965	91906
1989	6636	2438	362311	243813	239915	115644
1990	7196	3042	316751	268958	202347	145984
1991	8507	4554	580152	490530	258250	182286
1992	12916	9769	1986673	1885764	486147	355150
1993	19012	16768	3489660	3314887	965225	749805
1994	11956	10558	2638753	2382441	1144664	939708
1995	9345	8177	2610480	2483244	1210037	1018028
1996	5955	4608	1744639	1554584	1389943	1162362
1997	17737	3744	964527	769202	1420519	1171083
1998	15459	4349	1237802	916180	1509945	1202005
1999	14824	3013	871592	617451	1447383	1220300
2000	16879	4245	1108598	868393	1457466	1223720
2001	13198	5317	1580386	1343463	1575526	1297240
2002	11706	6613	1890108	1617119	1658946	1311071
2003	11472	7306	2446711	2178926	1894081	1557779
2004	10530	8322	2217800	1936046	1289900	1001158
2005	11786	8384	2675695	2374365	1517358	1236391
2006	11276	8452	2838923	2456820	1780780	1451065
2007	11705	9506	3646583	3393817	1961771	1712603
2008	8980	6999	3071447	2863991	2126657	1916703
2009	5693	4346	1824109	1755834	2028688	1953460
2010	6022	5641	2516987	2460075	2102646	2026098
2011	7289	7035	3485492	3469238	2232847	2179836
2012	6263	6043	3544579	3499424	2410578	2354911
2013	5740	5520	3666273	3631343	2532719	2495210
2014	6175	6016	4339446	4305905	2727751	2687144
2015	7033	7029	5614566	5611000	2702512	2687546
2016	8078	8078	8673350	8667477	2340689	2334921
2017	15599	15599	7309658	7308672	2294813	2290668
2018		35774		5900.98④		1450.88④
2019		14350		5523.84		1522.00
2020		12864		5032.99		1620.29
2021		16155		4894.14		1840.02
2022		13365		4051.57		1819.02

注：1.2002年起，外商直接投资统计口径调整，企业投资总额内的境外借款只包括外方股东贷款。
2.2004年实际利用外商直接投资统计口径作了调整，与2003年以前的年份不可比。
3.2004年起，签订项目数、合同外资额、实际利用外资不包含对外借款。
4.2018年起，外商直接投资使用商务部反馈人民币数据，单位为亿元。
5.2018年起，省商务厅未对外公布利用外资签订项目、合同外资额和实际利用外资数据。

Notes: a)Since 2002, the foreign direct investment statistic has been adjusted, of which the overseas borrowings in total investment of enterprises only include loans by foreign shareholders.
b)The foreign direct investment actually utilized of 2004 is adjusted, incomparable to values of preceding years.
c)Since2004,the number of signed projects,amount of contracted foreign capital and foreign capital actually utilized exclude foreign borrowings.
d)Data of foreign direct investment in RMB that are approved by Ministry of Commerce are adopted since 2018. The data unit in 2018 is RMB 100 million.
e)Data of signed projects, contracted foreign capital and foreign capital actually utilized are not published by Department of Commerce of Guangdong Province since 2018.

6-20 分行业外商直接投资（2022年）

Foreign Direct Investment by Sector (2022)

指标	Item	签订项目（个）Number of Signed Projects (unit)	合同利用金额（万元）Amount of Contracted Foreign Capital (RMB 10000)	实际使用金额（万元）Amount of Foreign Capital Actually Utilized (RMB 10000)
全 省	**Provincial Total**	**13365**	**40515729**	**18190177**
农、林、牧、渔业	Farming,Forestry,Anima Husbandry and Fishery	84	37155	174458
采矿业	Mining	3	1003500	2382
制造业	Manufacture	830	5864303	4406544
电力、热力、燃气及水生产和供应业	Production and Supply of Electric Power, Gas and Water	38	928213	250452
建筑业	Construction	252	1196741	46975
批发和零售业	Wholesale and Retail Trades	4440	3313422	1224132
交通运输、仓储和邮政业	Transport, Storage and Postal Services	232	1341802	597051
住宿和餐饮业	Hotels and Catering Services	416	101768	20082
信息传输、软件和信息技术服务业	Information Transmission, Computer Services and Software	1198	3843821	2511450
金融业	Finance	94	888870	231591
房地产业	Real Estate	307	3866996	1859456
租赁和商务服务业	Leasing and Business Services	2577	11078092	4579676
科学研究和技术服务业	Scientific Research, Technical Services	1950	6159997	2167968
水利、环境和公共设施管理业	Management of Water Conservancy,Environment and Public Facilities	27	158720	35897
居民服务、修理和其他服务业	Services to Households,Repair and Other Services	232	567180	1665
教育	Education	43	7305	39215
卫生和社会工作	Health and Social Service	31	39853	7552
文化、体育和娱乐业	Culture, Sports and Entertainment	610	117789	33631
公共管理、社会保障和社会组织	Public Administration,Social Security and Social Organizations	1	202	

6-21 分国家(地区)实际使用外资金额

Actual Value of Foreign Capital Used in Countries and Regions

单位：万美元 (USD 10000)

指　　标	Item	2000	2010	2015	2020	2021	2022
合　计	**Total**	**1223720**	**2026098**	**2687546**	**16202914**	**18400192**	**18190177**
亚洲	**Asia**	**927071**	**1486723**	**2268764**	**14759426**	**16972216**	**16705805**
#中国香港	Hong Kong, China	744826	1291738	2047856	11892901	14314569	15308147
中国台湾	Taiwan, China	49746	24543	10525	53266	43919	34491
中国澳门	Macao, China	26137	30189	73718	1352295	1200837	490977
日本	Japan	30852	51044	45514	399495	226567	202781
新加坡	Singapore	49115	46482	47343	826600	769122	644005
韩国	Republic of Korea	13671	20658	34770	191592	405758	13028
文莱	Brunei		8825	3133		3287	110
马来西亚	Malaysia	4993	5133	4541	3818	748	666
泰国	Thailand	2895	998	822	22109	2433	914
印度尼西亚	Indonesia	3352	877	36	18	29	1129
阿联酋	United Arab Emirates	100	5370	10		39	174
菲律宾	Philippines	191	91	5	134		441
印度	India	964	69	148	1678	2406	494
非洲	**Africa**	**4272**	**16972**	**12060**	**62619**	**29763**	**24720**
#毛里求斯	Mauritius	4576	14738	7327	39189	17554	10965
塞舌尔	Seychelles		1772	4635	23430	12072	13755
欧洲	**Europe**	**38643**	**78713**	**83864**	**322300**	**629418**	**642562**
#荷兰	Netherlands	7886	9646	7246	21553	36216	78847
英国	United Kingdom	8258	1859	13139	16183	70093	57821
法国	France	4551	52008	21078	13301	11318	172
德国	Germany	10057	3657	33898	95280	292691	401620
瑞士	Switzerland	3349	2839	1191	10764	51117	75254
意大利	Italy		1736	1344	752	2194	624
西班牙	Spain	44	2089	444	1656	4536	606
芬兰	Finland	2302	18		18345	31062	52
卢森堡	Luxembourg	90	660	860	57709	116900	376
爱尔兰	Ireland		2010	3762	101	3637	
瑞典	Sweden	360	500	647	1294	4799	1356
奥地利	Austria	101	1000		17335	3600	25262
比利时	Belgium	499	60	129			
丹麦	Denmark		201	11	1423	455	32
拉丁美洲	**Latin America**	**161983**	**303059**	**142932**	**959389**	**576009**	**633176**
#维尔京群岛	Virgin Islands	149200	270979	123429	810268	498419	571883
开曼群岛	Cayman Islands	6694	24644	16671	148307	74566	60009
巴哈马	Bahamas	3543	1649	1019			
巴巴多斯	Barbados		3254	701		346	
巴拿马	Panama	1544	1953	288			
北美洲	**North America**	**74453**	**40816**	**35221**	**29500**	**113355**	**66101**
#美国	United States of America	66972	25388	19049	23376	103948	47486
百慕大	Bermuda	2320	13341	15808	3117	800	13172
加拿大	Canada	5161	2087	364	3007	8607	5443
大洋洲	**Oceania**	**14510**	**53171**	**57284**	**64291**	**79429**	**117813**
#萨摩亚	Samoa	8942	49714	54362	56063	72567	116810
澳大利亚	Australia	4697	2869	2538	5672	800	631
马绍尔群岛	Marshall Islands	680	183	384	713		
新西兰	New Zealand	86	181		202		372
其它	**Others**	**2788**	**46644**	**87276**	**5389**	**2**	
#投资性公司投资	Investment Companies		35196	87119			
创业投资公司投资	Resuccess Investments Limited			157			

注：2018年起，外商直接投资使用商务部反馈人民币数据，单位为万元。

Note: Data of direct investment in RMB that are approved by Ministry of Commerce are adopted since 2018. The data unit in 2018 is RMB 10000.

6-22 各市外商直接投资
Foreign Direct Investment by City

市 别	City	2021			2022		
		签订项目(个) Number of Signed Projects (unit)	合同利用金额(万元) Amount of Contracted Foreign Capital (RMB 10000)	实际使用金额(万元) Amount of Foreign Capital Actually Utilized (RMB 10000)	签订项目(个) Number of Signed Projects (unit)	合同利用金额(万元) Amount of Contracted Foreign Capital (RMB 10000)	实际使用金额(万元) Amount of Foreign Capital Actually Utilized (RMB 10000)
广 州	Guangzhou	4048	14489159	5432585	3442	12921431	5741290
深 圳	Shenzhen	5788	16968456	7300994	4289	13903531	7143307
珠 海	Zhuhai	2578	8037428	2022408	1942	3949588	877322
汕 头	Shantou	47	142449	52437	58	156191	19247
佛 山	Foshan	668	1109147	335367	727	1485306	731415
韶 关	Shaoguan	25	40446	68327	43	235947	51832
河 源	Heyuan	28	220494	106059	36	352467	113835
梅 州	Meizhou	26	110103	16071	23	5214	11507
惠 州	Huizhou	410	1654722	743862	364	1548920	1039938
汕 尾	Shanwei	49	135050	31617	53	128589	28390
东 莞	Dongguan	1205	2260347	953237	1104	1057170	788673
中 山	Zhongshan	522	966339	377290	581	576393	416276
江 门	Jiangmen	432	622561	229831	395	1247381	352032
阳 江	Yangjiang	15	55779	60172	27	69637	60702
湛 江	Zhanjiang	44	1449675	296818	37	136741	408219
茂 名	Maoming	27	184692	45516	29	1020606	18886
肇 庆	Zhaoqing	121	190141	81279	90	732121	110570
清 远	Qingyuan	63	56045	100091	63	775631	111487
潮 州	Chaozhou	7	58679	57966	5	68873	70183
揭 阳	Jieyang	17	93667	27368	12	2953	43405
云 浮	Yunfu	35	96064	23476	45	141039	51661
按经济区域分	By Region						
珠三角	Pearl River Delta	15772	46298300	17476853	12934	37421841	17200823
东 翼	Eastern Region	120	429845	169388	128	356606	161225
西 翼	Western Region	86	1690146	402506	93	1226984	487807
山 区	Mountainous Region	177	523152	314024	210	1510298	340322

注：2018年起，外商直接投资使用商务部反馈人民币数据。
Note: Data of direct investment in RMB approved by Ministry of Commerce are adopted since 2018.

6–23 分行业外商投资企业工商注册登记情况（2022年末）

Registration Status of Enterprises with Foreign Investment by Sector (Year-end of 2022)

行业	Sector	企业数（户）Number of Registered Enterprises (unit)	投资总额（亿美元）Total Investment (USD 100 million)	注册资本（亿美元）Registered Capital (USD 100 million)	#外方 Capital Invested by Foreign Partners
全　省	**Provincial Total**	**189439**	**24141.48**	**11363.18**	**8521.27**
农、林、牧、渔业	Farming,Forestry,Anima Husbandry and Fishery	1843	8579.39	205.46	198.79
采矿业	Mining	66	24.40	21.14	18.48
制造业	Manufacture	35659	3782.70	2390.23	1761.03
电力、热力、燃气及水生产和供应业	Production and Supply of Electric Power, Gas and Water	754	674.60	291.44	119.09
建筑业	Construction	3006	265.79	191.63	127.22
批发和零售业	Wholesale and Retail Trades	62168	988.56	755.42	591.90
交通运输、仓储和邮政业	Transport, Storage and Postal Services	4217	323.99	219.61	148.50
住宿和餐饮业	Hotels and Catering Services	8579	68.92	50.32	40.84
信息传输、软件和信息技术服务业	Information Transmission, Computer Services and Software	13472	937.14	655.58	598.79
金融业	Finance	3804	1067.91	1121.99	680.62
房地产业	Real Estate	5906	1619.13	1190.50	946.06
租赁和商务服务业	Leasing and Business Services	26201	4223.80	3211.50	2456.51
科学研究和技术服务业	Scientific Research, Technical Services	15821	1277.77	835.14	652.19
水利、环境和公共设施管理业	Management of Water Conservancy,Environment and Public Facilities	344	73.01	44.72	35.26
居民服务、修理和其他服务业	Services to Households,Repair and Other Services	2961	80.36	66.12	55.07
教育	Education	331	2.75	2.54	1.73
卫生和社会工作	Health and Social Service	150	22.51	17.65	9.40
文化、体育和娱乐业	Culture, Sports and Entertainment	3105	92.87	66.75	58.98
其他	Others	1052	35.86	25.42	20.81

6-24 各市外商投资企业工商注册登记情况（2022年末）

Registration Status of Enterprises with Foreign Investment by City(Year-end of 2022)

市别	City	企业数(户) Number of Registered Enterprises(unit)	投资总额(亿美元) Total Investment (USD 100 million)	注册资本(亿美元) Registered Capital (USD 100 million)	#外方 Capital Invested by Foreign Partners
全省	**Provincial Total**	**189439**	**24141.48**	**11363.18**	**8521.27**
广州	Guangzhou	38392	12574.17	3296.57	2330.69
深圳	Shenzhen	71520	5286.32	4130.68	2989.49
珠海	Zhuhai	17464	1245.00	1085.64	854.65
汕头	Shantou	1381	102.11	76.64	55.69
佛山	Foshan	8818	1027.32	554.12	450.81
韶关	Shaoguan	1054	51.49	34.92	27.70
河源	Heyuan	1917	104.37	66.30	55.44
梅州	Meizhou	3469	48.91	35.21	31.29
惠州	Huizhou	8443	1016.62	373.38	306.77
汕尾	Shanwei	859	41.97	32.99	28.94
东莞	Dongguan	15559	882.42	631.09	580.12
中山	Zhongshan	5839	241.92	183.73	155.46
江门	Jiangmen	5013	514.81	260.66	195.97
阳江	Yangjiang	713	225.18	66.96	33.25
湛江	Zhanjiang	990	207.62	100.48	76.83
茂名	Maoming	1531	56.11	47.79	38.48
肇庆	Zhaoqing	2791	225.23	176.36	167.53
清远	Qingyuan	1639	143.88	91.20	71.24
潮州	Chaozhou	598	16.45	14.77	11.48
揭阳	Jieyang	727	25.21	17.99	14.79
云浮	Yunfu	644	34.35	22.52	17.42
局本部	Unclassified by Region	78	70.02	63.17	27.24

6-25　一类口岸开放使用情况（2022年末）
Opening and Operating Status of Category-1　Ports (Year-end of 2022)

市　别	City	个　数 Number	口岸类型 Name of Ports				
			水　运	Water Transport	陆　运	Land Transport	空　运 Air Transport
合　计	**Total**	**56**	**35**		**16**		**5**
广　州	Guangzhou	6	广州港口岸	Guangzhou Port	广州火车东站铁路口岸	Guangzhou East Railway Station for Passenger Service	白云国际机场 Baiyun International Airport
			广州南沙港口岸	Nansha Port			
			广州莲花山港口岸	Lianhuashan Port			
			增城新塘港客运口岸	Xintang Port			
深　圳	Shenzhen	16	蛇口工业区码头	Shekou Port	罗湖	Luohu	深圳宝安国际机场 Shenzhen International Airport
			赤湾码头	Chiwan Port	文锦渡	Wenjindu	
			大铲湾港区	Dachan Bay Port	沙头角	Shatoujiao	
			妈湾码头	Mawan Port	皇岗	Huanggang	
			盐田码头	Yantian Port	深圳湾	Shenzhen Bay	
			大亚湾核电站专用码头	Dayawan Port	福田	Futian	
					广深港高铁西九龙站	Guangzhou-Shenzhen-Hong Kong Express Rail Link West Kowloon Terminus	
					莲塘	Liantang	
					深圳(笋岗)铁路口岸	Shenzhen(Sungang) Railway Station	
珠　海	Zhuhai	10	九州港口岸	Jiuzhou Port	拱北	Gongbei	
			湾仔口岸	Wanzai Port	横琴	Hengqin	
			珠海港口岸	Zhuhai Port	珠澳跨境工业区专用口岸	The Industrial Zone Dedicated port cross-border between The Pearl River Delta and Macao	
			万山港口岸	Wanshan Port			
			斗门港口岸	Doumen Port			
					港珠澳大桥珠海公路口岸	Zhuhai Port of Hong Kong Zhuhai Macao Bridge	
					珠海青茂口岸	Qingmao Port	
汕　头	Shantou	2	汕头港口岸	Shantou Port			
			潮阳港口岸	Chaoyang Port			
梅　州	Meizhou	1					梅县机场 Meixian Airport
惠　州	Huizhou	1	惠州港口岸	Huizhou Port			
汕　尾	Shanwei	1	汕尾港口岸	Shanwei Port			
东　莞	Dongguan	2	虎门港口岸	Humen Port	东莞常平铁路客运	Dongguan Changping Railway Stations for Passenger Service	
中　山	Zhongshan	1	中山港口岸	Zhongshan Port			
江　门	Jiangmen	5	江门客运港口岸	Jiangmen Port			
			开平三埠港客运口岸	Sanfu Port			
			台山广海港口岸	Guanghai Port			
			鹤山港客运口岸	Heshan Port			
			新会港口岸	Xinhui Port			
佛　山	Foshan	3	顺德容奇港口岸	Shunde Port			
			南海港口岸	Nanhai Port			
			高明港客运口岸	Gaoming Port			
阳　江	Yangjiang	1	阳江港口岸	Yangjiang Port			
湛　江	Zhanjiang	2	湛江港口岸	Zhanjiang Port			湛江机场 Zhanjiang Airport
茂　名	Maoming	1	茂名港口岸	Maoming Port			
肇　庆	Zhaoqing	1	肇庆港客运口岸	Zhaoqing Port			
潮　州	Chaozhou	1	潮州港口岸	Chaozhou Port			
揭　阳	Jieyang	2	揭阳港口岸	Jieyang Port			揭阳潮汕国际机场 Jieyang International Airport

注：目前为止江门三埠港客运口岸、肇庆港客运口岸暂停运作。
Note: To date，Jiangmen Sanfu Port，Zhaoqing Port are temporarily out of operation.

6–26 对外经济技术合作情况
Economic and Technical Cooperation with Foreign Countries and Regions

年 份 Year	对外承包工程 Contracted Projects				对外劳务合作 Labor Services		
	签订合同数 (个) Number of Contracts Signed (unit)	合同金额 (万美元) Contracted Value (USD 10000)	营业金额 (万美元) Value of Turnover (USD 10000)	年末在外人数 (人) Number of Persons Abroad at the Year-end (person)	劳务人员合同工资总额 (万美元) Total Wages of Contract Workers (USD 10000)	劳务人员实际收入总额 (万美元) Actual Total Income of Contract Workers (USD 10000)	年末在外人数 (人) Number of Persons Abroad at the Year-end (person)
1985	28	1897	2491	305	424	433	1197
1990	23	5953	7586	688	6055	3189	8045
1995	29	19183	10924	850	20593	17775	33263
1996	37	14823	9474	1680	11784	19365	23319
1997	67	22435	10940	354	17356	14743	22857
1998	28	13331	17526	566	12925	14464	20816
1999	63	52961	21857	603	9327	13230	19128
2000	86	36555	34515	634	12941	10777	19564
2001	250	53924	26192	641	13271	11752	30695
2002	165	64827	58986	643	19114	17059	18922
2003	193	97055	86898	730	23132	21926	21738
2004	810	168338	161287	856	27392	28315	17043
2005	2061	326752	247189	606	32762	30878	20469
2006	1625	458442	344170	752	41898	37030	27024
2007	757	597733	546069	946	80824	62927	27880
2008	331	844352	686045	886	68209	58420	33691
2009	556	814859	758799	2105	45718	59469	33124
2010	605	986740	820815	4554	76575	58428	33901
2011	528	1343526	1134158	4017	46578	46445	38621
2012	517	1905053	1605342	3863	46643	38600	44301
2013	617	2366492	2286507	3243	53917	44689	54272
2014	1139	1524873	1241121	3405	138820	66218	72788
2015	1937	2072350	1987790	3633	139705	117787	81600
2016	1503	2198726	1816382	4350	65540	89185	80468
2017	1151	2218294	1809649	6293	72805	86660	79440
2018	1136	1914713	1756733	10507	67494	85623	82329
2019	1030	2556123	1670589	9025	73640	92860	84216
2020	878	1873148	1566539	10542	55850	79177	60035
2021	787	1835162	1562286	2303	63696	87394	10601
2022	859	1979411	1620215	8617	44027	88198	58453

注：1.2009年以后，“对外承包工程”包含“对外设计咨询”。
2.2011年对外劳务合作统计口径调整。

Note: a) After 2009, foreign design consultation is included in foreign contracted projects.
b) The statistics coverage of foreign labor service has been adjusted in 2011.

6-27 分国别(地区)对外直接投资

Foreign Direct Investment by Country (Region)

国家(地区)	Country of Region	企业个数(个) Number of Projects (unit)			对外直接投资额(万美元) Net Overseas Direct Investment (USD10000)		
		2020	2021	2022	2020	2021	2022
合计	**Total**	**865**	**1075**	**1230**	**1581557**	**1696707**	**2207193**
亚洲	**Asia**	**681**	**887**	**970**	**993956**	**1128470**	**1557865**
#中国香港	Hong Kong, China	449	712	743	945305	1067363	1511149
中国澳门	Macao, China	22	29	29	1579	6752	6912
印度尼西亚	Indonesia	9	5	14	2032	2799	947
泰国	Thailand	12	7	11	2450	3653	1467
新加坡	Singapore	37	32	48	10858	29299	17719
韩国	Republic of Korea	6	14	9	222	1453	1733
日本	Japan	19	15	33	882	1778	1207
中国台湾	Taiwan, China	8	5	1	10	184	18
马来西亚	Malaysia	11	11	6	8536	4143	2532
印度	India	16	7	7	1801	42	1809
越南	Vietnam	61	26	41	8538	6162	5337
柬埔寨	Cambodia	4	3	3	5023	3144	4978
以色列	Israel	4	3	1	400	473	945
老挝	Laos	3	1	2	303	306	55
非洲	**Africa**	**9**	**20**	**18**	**3610**	**1343**	**210**
#加纳	Ghana	1	2	0	704	222	0
肯尼亚	Kenya	1	2	1	20	30	6
塞舌尔	Seychelles		3	0	135	5	87
欧洲	**Europe**	**70**	**59**	**87**	**37443**	**38388**	**20941**
#法国	France	5	2	1	9	108	479
爱尔兰	Ireland				241	1308	
荷兰	Netherlands	10		9	670		2274
俄罗斯	Russia	5	4		11	1	
德国	Germany	19	15	35	26401	8056	3702
英国	United Kingdom	9	12	9	2498	179	121
卢森堡	Luxembourg				788	1270	242
意大利	Italy	3	5	4	2484	2084	1961
瑞士	Switzerland		2	4		1	142
瑞典	Sweden	2	2	3	1	2838	6411
挪威	Norway	1			91	47	
波兰	Poland	4	4	1	886	1464	3804
匈牙利	Hungary	1	1	3	829	1934	1236
拉丁美洲	**Latin America**	**17**	**43**	**45**	**167123**	**104955**	**103392**
#英属维尔京群岛	Virgin Islands	3	2	4	139095	64397	35384
开曼群岛	Cayman Islands	11	29	30	26934	38285	65666
巴西	Brazil	1	2	5	185	906	10
秘鲁	Peru		2	1		190	
墨西哥	Mexico		6	5		160	542
智利	Chile		1		50	50	
北美洲	**North America**	**74**	**64**	**104**	**15665**	**14287**	**27331**
#美国	United States of America	69	58	94	15213	12796	26352
加拿大	Canada	5	5	10	452	1490	979
大洋洲	**Oceania**	**14**	**2**	**6**	**4770**	**5105**	**7374**
#新西兰	New Zealand	5		1	3082	185	12
澳大利亚	Australia	9	1	5	507	1539	5161
巴布亚新几内亚	Papua New Guinea				1180	3380	2200
利润再投资分摊	**Reinvested profit sharing**				**358990**	**404160**	**490080**

6-28　分行业对外直接投资（2022年）
Foreign Direct Investment by Sector (2022)

单位：万美元　　(USD 10 000)

分组指标	Indexes by Group	新增企业个数 Number of New Companies	对外直接投资额 Direct Investment in Foreign Companies
全　省	**Provincial Total**	**1230**	**2207193**
农、林、牧、渔业	Agricultural, Forestry, Husbandry, and Fishing Industries	8	98
采矿业	Mining Industry	5	19730
制造业	Manufacturing Industry	156	159466
电力、热力、燃气及水的生产和供应业	Electricity, Heat, Gas, and Water Production and Supply Industries	3	20293
建筑业	Construction Industry	10	3438
批发和零售业	Wholesale and Retail Industries	581	520305
交通运输、仓储和邮政业	Transportation, Storage, and Postal Industries	52	11785
住宿和餐饮业	Accommodation and Catering Industries	1	12705
信息传输、软件和信息技术服务业	Information Transmission, Software, and Information Technology Industries	108	42091
金融业	Financial Industry	1	11481
房地产业	Real Estate Industry	1	40103
租赁和商务服务业	Leasing and Business Services Industries	69	856047
科学研究和技术服务业	Scientific Research and Technical Services Industries	75	13035
水利、环境和公共设施管理业	Water Conservation, Environment, and Public Facility Management Industries	3	
居民服务、修理和其他服务业	Resident Services, Repairs, and Other Service Industries	2	6151
教育	Education	1	70
卫生和社会工作	Health and Social Work		307
文化、体育和娱乐业	Culture, Sports and Entertainment Industries	1	6
公共管理、社会保障和社会组织	Public Management, Social Security, Social Organization		
其他	Others	153	
利润再投资分摊	Profit Reinvestment and Sharing		490080

主要统计指标解释

货物进出口总额 指实际进出我国国境的货物总金额。包括对外贸易实际进出口货物，来料加工装配进出口货物，国家间、联合国及国际组织无偿援助物资和赠送品，华侨、港澳台同胞和外籍华人捐赠品，租赁期满归承租人所有的租赁货物，进料加工进出口货物，边境地方贸易及边境地区小额贸易进出口货物，中外合资企业、中外合作经营企业、外商独资经营企业进出口货物和公用物品，到、离岸价格在规定限额以上的进出口货样和广告品(无商业价值、无使用价值和免费提供出口的除外)，从保税仓库提取在中国境内销售的进口货物，以及其他进出口货物。该指标可以观察一个国家在对外贸易方面的总规模。我国规定出口货物按离岸价格统计，进口货物按到岸价格统计。

商品目的地进口额和商品货源地出口额 目的地进口额指进口货物的消费、使用或最终抵运地的实际进口额；货源地出口额指出口货物的产地或原始发货地的实际出口额。

利用外资 指我国政府、部门、企业和其他经济组织通过对外借款、吸收客商直接投资以及向境外发行债券、股票等方式筹借的境外资金。

外资的形式可以是现汇、实物、工业产权或专有技术等有形资本和无形资本。

我国自有外汇和中国银行自有外汇资金发放的外汇贷款购置国外设备和材料，华侨、港澳同胞的捐赠，联合国或其他国际组织的无偿赠送资金、无偿援建的项目均不属于外资范围 。

利用外资的方式有：对外借款，外国（或港澳地区）企业和经济组织或个人在我国境内开办独资企业、与我国境内的企业或组织共同开办合资企业、合作经营(企业)项目或合作开发资源，以及补偿贸易、国际租赁等。

补偿贸易 是以商品或劳务偿还贷款的一种贸易方式。即由客商提供设备、原材料、生产技术，以这些设备、原材料、生产技术生产的产品或是用双方协商的其他产品价值去支付 （偿还）进口设备、原材料价款。

对外借款 指我国政府、部门、企业和中国银行等单位向国际金融组织 、外国政府、企业等借用的长期、短期资本，到期需还本付息。借款按不同渠道划分为：①外国政府贷款； ②国际金融组织贷款；③外国银行贷款；④出口信贷；⑤发行债券。

外商直接投资 指外国企业和经济组织或个人（包括华侨、港澳同胞以及我在境外注册的企业）按我国有关政策、法规，在我国境内开办外商独资企业，与我国境内的企业或经济组织共同举办中外合资企业、合作经营企业或合作开发资源的投资，以及外商从企业得到收益的再投资。2002 年起“外商直接投资”统计口径调整，“企业投资总额内的境外借款”只包括“企业投资总额内直接投资者对企业的贷款, 即外方股东贷款”。不包括“直接投资者提供担保的第三方对企业的贷款即外方股东担保贷款”和“其他方式的企业境外借款即其他境外借款。”

国际租赁 指出租者用自有资金，或向银行借款购买资本设备租给承租者在约定的期限内使用，承租者依约按期付给出租者一定租金，在租赁期内设备的使用属于承租者，设备的所有权属于出租者，租期满后，出租者对设备具有支配权：收回、作价出卖或赠送企业。

对外直接投资 指我国企业、团体等(简称境内投资主体) 在国外及港澳台地区以现金、实物、无形资产等方式投资，并以控制国(境)外企业的经营管理权为核心的经济活动。对外直接投资的内涵主要体现在一经济体通过投资于另一经济体而实现其持久利益的目标。

Explanatory Notes on Main Statistical Indicators

Total Import and Export of Goods refer to the real value of commodities imported and exported across the border of China. They include the actual imports and exports through foreign trade, imported and exported goods under the processing and assembling trades and materials, supplies and gifts as aid given gratis between governments and by the United Nations and other international organizations, and contributions donated by overseas Chinese, compatriots in Hong Kong and Macao and Chinese with foreign citizenship, leasing commodities owned by tenant at the expiration of leasing period, the imported and exported commodities processed with imported materials, commodities trading in border areas, the imported and exported commodities and articles for public use of the Sino-foreign joint ventures, cooperative enterprises and ventures with sole foreign investment. Also included is import or export of samples and advertising goods for which CIF or FOB value are beyond the permitted ceiling (excluding goods of no trading or use value and free commodities for export), imported goods sold in China from bonded warehouses and other imported or exported goods. The indicator of the total imports and exports at customs can be used to observe the total size of external trade in a country. In accordance with the stipulation of the Chinese government, imports are calculated at CIF, while exports are calculated at FOB.

Import or Export Value by Location of China's Foreign Trade Managing Units refers to actual value of imports and exports carried out by corporations which have been registered by the local Customs house and are vested with right to run import export business.

Utilization of Foreign Capital refers to funds financed from abroad by means of loans, foreign direct investment, and issuing bonds and shares undertaken by the Chinese governments at all levels, various departments, enterprises and other economic units.

The types of foreign capital include tangible capital and intangible capital, such as remittance, goods, industrial property rights and know-how.

Those excluded are the purchases of foreign equipment and materials with loans from state-owned foreign exchange and foreign exchange owned by the Bank of China, donations by overseas Chinese, compatriots in Hong Kong and Macao, and funds and projcets as aid given gratis by the United Nations and other international organizations.

Utilization of foreign capital takes the forms of loans from abroad, sole investment in enterprises in the boundary of China by foreign (or Hong Kong and Macao) enterprises, economic organizations or individuals, investment in Sino-foreign joint ventures, cooperative projects (enterprises), cooperative exploitation of natural resources with enterprises or organizations in China, compensation trade and international lease, etc.

Compensation Trade refers to a kind of trade returning loans with commodities or services, i.e. imported equipment, raw materials and production technology provided by foreign entrepreneurs are repaid (returned) by means of the products produced with such equipment, raw materials and production technology or by means of the value of other products negotiated by both sides.

Foreign Loans refer to long-term capital and short-term capital borrowed from international financial organizations, foreign governments and enterprises by the Chinese governments at all levels, by various departments, enterprises and the Bank of China, etc, and repaid with interest at maturity. Foreign loans can be divided according to channels into: ①loans from foreign governments; ②loans from international financial organizations; ③loans from foreign banks; ④export credit; ⑤bonds and shares issued abroad.

Foreign Direct Investment refers to investment inside China by foreign enterprises and economic organizations or individuals (including overseas Chinese, compatriots from Hong Kong and Macao, and Chinese enterprises registered abroad), following the relevant policies and laws of China, for the establishment of foreign sole investment enterprises, Sino-foreign joint ventures and cooperative enterprises or for cooperative exploitation of resources with enterprises or economic organizations in China, and re-investment of foreign entrepreneurs with the profits gained from such enterprises and corporations. Starting from 2002, the foreign direct investment statistic has been adjusted such that the overseas borrowings in total investment of enterprises only include loans to the enterprises by direct investors or, in other terms, loans by foreign shareholders, but exclude loans from the third party guaranteed by the direct investors or, in other terms, loans guaranteed by the foreign shareholders, and overseas borrowings by enterprises in other manners or, in other terms, other overseas borrowings.

International Lease refers to the lease of which tenants rent the equipment purchased by lessors with their own money or loans from banks during a fixed period and repay a sum of leasing expenses to lessors according to contracts. During the leasing period, tenants have the right to use the equipment while lessors maintain possession of the equipment. At the expiration of the leasing period, lessors have the right to dispose the equipment: take it back, sell it at a fixed price, or donate it to an enterprise.

Overseas Direct Investment refers to investment made by domestic enterprises and organizations (referred to as domestic investors) in foreign countries and Hong Kong SAR, Macao SAR and Taiwan province in forms of cash, physical investment and intangible assets, and the economic activities centring on operation and management of those enterprises are under the control of domestic investors. The content of overseas direct investment mainly reflects one economic entity by investing in another economic entity to achieve its goal of lasting interest.

七、能源、资源和环境

ENERGY, RESOURCES AND ENVIRONMENT

七　能源、资源和环境

简要说明

一、本篇资料反映广东自然资源状况、能源生产、能源消费、能耗水平和生态环境事业等情况。能源情况主要包括：能源生产、消费及品种构成，分行业能源消费总量，综合能源平衡，各市能源单耗，能源生产和消费弹性系数，能源加工转换效率，生活用能源消费等资料。自然资源包括土地 、气候、森林、水利、矿产资源情况。环保部分主要包括水环境、大气环境、生态环境、城市环境、农村环境、自然灾害等。

二、本篇资料由广东省统计局综合统计处、能源统计处根据有关资料和调查结果整理提供。

三、能源资料取自全省《地区能源平衡表》《工业企业能源购进、消费及库存表》等。地区能源平衡表编制范围为辖区内生产和消费能源的单位；规模以上工业企业的能源消费根据国家统计局制定的报表制度由统计系统搜集资料逐级汇总上报；加工转换消费来源于《工业企业能源购进、消费及库存附表》；其他数据来源于有关厅 (局)、公司或企业。矿产、土地资源、海洋资料由省自然资源厅提供；气象资料由省气象局提供；森林资源资料由省林业局提供；水利资料由省水利厅提供；环保事业情况由省生态环境厅提供；城市建设情况由省住房和城乡建设厅提供。

四、关于数据口径与计算的说明：

1．2015 年以后的数据已按第四次全国经济普查结果进行调整。

2．能源生产与消费弹性系数分别按能源生产、消费增长速度与地区生产总值增长速度计算。

3．在地区能源平衡表中，进口量和出口量采用海关统计数据，电力折算标准煤系数按平均发电煤耗计算。

4．能源加工转换效率表中的电力折算标准煤系数采用当量值计算，每千瓦小时折 0.1229 千克标准煤。

7 Energy ,Resources and Environment

Brief Introduction

Ⅰ. The data in this chapter reflect the natural resource, energy production, consumption, and efficiency and environmental protection of Guangdong Province. The data on energy mainly including the energy production and consumption and their composition, the energy consumption by sector, the overall balance of energy, energy consumption per unit by city, the elasticity ratios of energy production and consumption, the efficiency of energy conversion and the consumption of energy for non-production use, etc. The data on natural resource cover land, climate, forest, water conservancy and mineral resources. The data on environmental protection mainly include water environment, atmospheric environment, ecological environment, urban environment, rural environment, natural disasters, etc.

Ⅱ. The data in this chapter are prepared and provided by the Division of Comprehensive Statistics of Statistics Bureau of Guangdong Province and the Division of Energy Statistics of Statistics Bureau of Guangdong Province.

Ⅲ. The data in this chapter come from the Energy Balance Sheet of the whole province and the Sheets of Energy Purchase, Consumption and Storage of Key Energy Consumption Industrial Enterprises. The coverage of the regional energy balance includes the units that produce and consume energy. Among them, the data on the energy consumption of industrial enterprises above designated size are collected by the statistical agencies in accordance with the statistical reporting scheme stipulated by the National Bureau of Statistics and tabulated and reported to the higher authorities level by level; the data on the energy processing, transformation and consumption are derived from the Sheets of Energy Purchase, Consumption and Storage of Key Energy Consumption Industrial Enterprises; other data are provided by related government departments, companies and enterprises. The data on mineral and land resources an ocean are provided by Department of Natural Resources of Guangdong Province. The data on meteorological phenomena are provided by the Meteorological Bureau of Guangdong Province. The data on forest are provided by the Forestry Administration of Guangdong Province. The data on water conservancy are provided by the Water Resources Department of Guangdong Province. The data on environmental protection are provided by Department of Ecology and Environment of Guangdong Province. The data on urban construction are provided by Department of Housing and Urban Rural Development of Guangdong Province.

Ⅳ. Data coverage and calculation:

(1) Since 2015,data have been adjusted in accordance with the figures from the third china economics census.

(2) The elasticity ratio of energy production is calculated as the quotient of the growth rate of energy production divided by the growth rate of GDP; and the elasticity ratio of energy consumption is calculated as the quotient of the growth rate of energy consumption divided by the growth rate of GDP.

(3) In the energy balance sheet, the data on the imports and exports are data from the customs statistics.The ratio for converting electric power into the standard coal equivalent is calculated according to the average consumption of coal for generating electricity.

(4) In the table on the efficiency of energy conversion, the ratio for converting electric power into the standard coal equivalent is calculated on the basis of heat value equivalent.One kilowatt is equal to 0.1229 kg SCE.

7-1 能源主要指标

Main Indicators of Energy

项　　目	item	2020	2021	2022
一、能源生产	**Production of Energy**			
(一)一次能源生产量	Primary Energy Output			
原油 (万吨)	Crude Oil (10000tons)	1613.15	1744.68	1884.62
天然气 (亿立方米)	Natural Gas (100 million cu.m)	131.59	132.48	124.39
一次电 (亿千瓦时)	Primary Electricity (100 million kwh)	1622.79	1667.66	1896.53
(二)二次能源生产量	Secondary Energy Output			
原油加工量 (万吨)	Crude Oil Processing Capacity (10000tons)	6211.95	6740.95	6560.33
汽油 (万吨)	Gasoline (10000tons)	1206.19	1417.41	1371.76
煤油 (万吨)	Kerosene (10000tons)	668.74	633.73	532.74
柴油 (万吨)	Diesel Oil (10000tons)	1592.53	1649.54	1964.18
燃料油 (万吨)	Fuel Oil (10000tons)	576.73	644.22	568.29
液化石油气 (万吨)	Liquefied Petroleum Gas (10000tons)	464.49	503.72	468.50
发电量 (亿千瓦时)	Power Generation (100 million kwh)	3603.12	4638.57	4469.17
二、能源消费 (万吨标准煤)	**Consumption of Energy (10000 tons of SCE)**			
能源消费总量	Total Energy Consumption	34502.92	36821.42	36519.05
第一产业	Primary Industry	670.30	711.81	746.20
第二产业	Secondary Industry	20510.49	21881.43	21920.27
第三产业	Tertiary Industry	7634.13	8343.72	7867.70
居民消费量	Household Consumption	5688.01	5884.46	5984.88
三、节能减排 (%)	**Energy Conservation (%)**			
单位GDP能耗上升或下降(±)	Energy Consumption per Unit of GDP rises or decreases (±)	-1.16	-1.20	-2.60
规模以上工业单位工业增加值能耗上升或下降(±)	Energy Consumption per Unit of Industrial Value-added rises or decreases (±)	1.21	1.70	-3.00
单位GDP电耗上升或下降(±)	Electricity Consumption per Unit of GDP rises or decreases (±)	1.16	5.20	-1.90

7-2 能源生产总量及构成

Total Production of Energy and its Composition

项　目	Item	2000	2005	2010	2015	2020	2021	2022
能源生产总量 (万吨标准煤)	**Total Energy Production (10000 tons of SCE)**	**3711.69**	**4758.79**	**4858.07**	**6862.51**	**8563.01**	**8892.72**	**9647.31**
构　成 (%)	Composition (%)	100.0	100.0	100.0	100.0	100.0	100.0	100.0
原　煤	Coal	8.0	7.2					
原　油	Crude Oil	53.6	44.1	37.8	32.8	26.9	28.0	27.9
天然气	Natural Gas	11.3	12.5	21.5	18.7	17.7	18.1	15.6
一次电力及其他能源	Primary Electricity and Other Energy	27.1	36.2	40.7	48.5	55.4	53.9	56.5

7-3 能源消费总量及构成

Total Consumption of Energy and Its Composition

年份 Year	一次能源消费量(万吨标准煤) Primary Energy Consumption (10000 tons of SCE)	构成(%) Composition(%)				终端能源消费量(万吨标准煤) Final Energy Consumption (10000 tons of SCE)	构成(%) Composition(%)			
		原煤 Coal	原油 Crude Oil	天然气 Natural Gas	一次电力及其他能源 Primary Electricity and Other Energy		原煤 Coal	油品 Oil Products	电力 Elect-ricity	其他 Others
1990	3690.25	56.5	35.3		8.2	3936.44	33.6	22.4	33.0	11.0
1995	6147.61	56.4	28.5	0.2	14.9	7062.28	27.0	20.9	39.7	12.4
2000	7983.46	52.2	35.0	0.2	12.6	9080.20	17.1	22.6	45.4	14.9
2001	8169.60	52.5	34.0		13.5	9775.15	15.9	22.6	46.1	15.4
2002	9036.40	51.9	31.0		17.1	10861.68	14.5	21.6	49.2	14.7
2003	10462.09	53.5	28.6	0.2	17.7	12414.48	17.8	22.6	44.5	15.1
2004	12013.14	51.4	28.4	0.2	20.0	14487.74	11.7	20.7	52.6	15.0
2005	13086.58	52.8	26.1	0.3	20.8	17255.84	10.9	23.6	50.7	14.8
2006	15281.00	50.4	26.2	1.3	22.1	19254.03	12.5	23.7	48.7	15.1
2007	17344.10	52.0	24.2	3.5	20.3	21427.33	12.0	22.2	49.3	16.5
2008	17679.13	50.8	24.6	4.1	20.5	22671.76	13.8	21.2	48.5	16.5
2009	19235.86	46.5	27.5	5.4	20.6	23943.39	12.2	20.9	46.3	20.6
2010	21942.15	45.2	29.0	5.7	20.1	24594.92	9.7	18.8	50.4	21.1
2011	23318.44	50.2	27.0	6.4	16.4	26223.64	10.3	16.8	51.5	21.4
2012	23786.60	46.4	27.1	6.4	20.1	26763.90	9.7	16.7	52.2	21.4
2013	24930.93	46.4	27.1	6.5	20.0	27666.36	10.4	16.8	51.0	21.8
2014	25636.29	43.7	26.6	6.8	22.9	28669.57	10.2	16.6	53.5	19.7
2015	26999.64	40.2	25.9	7.1	26.8	29359.74	10.0	16.8	52.2	21.0
2016	28179.17	38.2	25.6	7.8	28.4	30700.98	9.8	18.1	52.6	19.5
2017	29253.74	38.7	25.4	8.2	27.7	31645.79	8.1	17.7	54.5	19.7
2018	30154.66	37.2	28.1	8.3	26.4	32760.73	7.2	17.2	54.6	21.0
2019	31122.99	34.2	25.9	8.7	31.2	33359.42	6.4	16.9	57.1	19.6
2020	32818.22	31.3	27.2	10.3	31.2	33774.90	6.3	15.6	58.0	20.1
2021	36221.32	35.0	26.8	11.4	26.8	35955.63	5.2	13.6	61.0	20.2
2022	36230.97	33.5	26.2	11.3	29.0	35700.97	4.8	11.3	61.3	22.6

7-4 综合能源平衡表

Overall Energy Balance Sheet

单位：万吨标准煤 (10000 tons of SCE)

项 目	Item	2000	2010	2015	2020	2021	2022
可供本地区消费的能源量	**Total Energy Available for Consumption by Locality**	**9447.70**	**25445.22**	**30117.44**	**34502.92**	**36821.42**	**36519.05**
年初库存量	Stock at the Year-beginning	675.20	1347.93	1635.41	2810.98	2389.88	2243.64
一次能源生产量	Primary Energy Output	3711.69	4858.07	7126.26	8563.01	8892.72	9647.31
外省调入量	Allocation from Other Provinces	5628.27	15570.94	20486.80	18114.15	19247.95	22186.34
进口量	Imports	2757.39	8112.34	6732.49	18952.08	20027.99	18737.66
境内轮船和飞机在境外加油量	Petroleum Consumed by Chinese Airplanes and Ships Abroad		183.44	220.81	117.84	175.81	305.26
本省调出量(−)	Allocation over Other Provinces(-)	-1599.39	-1294.98	-2392.60	-9703.98	-9369.68	-12205.82
出口量(−)	Exports(-)	-980.31	-1700.12	-1377.99	-1819.78	-2145.51	-1628.38
境外轮船和飞机在境内加油量(−)	Petroleum Consumed by Foreign Airplanes and Ships in China(-)	-62.51	-275.16	-336.16	-110.38	-158.04	-304.70
年末库存量(−)	Stock at the Year-end(-)	-779.26	-1357.25	-1977.58	-2421.02	-2239.69	-2462.26
加工转换投入(−)产出(+)量	**Input Output in Processing and Transformation**	**-35.74**	**-92.50**	**-0.11**	**-42.04**	**-72.39**	**-0.41**
火力发电	Thermal Power						
供热	Heating		-90.80	-128.38	-223.60	-216.53	-250.51
洗选煤	Coal Washing						
炼焦	Coking	-3.85	-2.25	-8.76	-54.66	-43.07	-25.41
炼油及煤制油	Petroleum Refining	-26.89	205.83	-185.30	-408.96	-463.28	-500.75
制气	Gas Production	-5.00	-1.08	-31.76	-35.07	-57.87	-78.43
回收能	Recovery of Energy	96.59	123.70	365.40	680.70	709.15	855.33
损失量	**Losses**	**331.76**	**757.80**	**757.59**	**685.97**	**793.40**	**817.67**
#运输和输配损失	Losses in Transmission	318.75	732.46	741.70	654.40	696.47	740.62
终端消费量	**End-use**	**9080.20**	**24594.92**	**29359.74**	**33774.90**	**35955.63**	**35700.97**
第一产业	Primary Industry	353.56	400.60	501.98	670.30	711.81	746.20
农、林、牧、渔业	Farming, Forestry, Animal Husbandry and Fishery	353.56	400.60	501.98	670.30	711.81	746.20
第二产业	Secondary Industry	5790.91	16452.13	18179.56	19791.89	21025.50	21123.25
工业	Industry	5693.02	15813.16	17445.74	19056.24	20304.99	20545.42
#用作原料材料	As Raw Materials and Fuel	86.44	990.06	586.76	1328.70	1193.32	1430.02
建筑业	Construction	97.90	638.97	733.82	735.65	720.51	577.83
第三产业	Tertiary Industry	1648.93	4749.44	6256.26	7624.71	8333.86	7846.63
交通运输仓储及邮电通信业	Transport, Storage, Postal and Telecommunication Services	957.92	2332.91	3137.15	3395.70	3307.71	2743.23
批发和零售贸易业、餐饮业	Wholesale and Retail Trade and Catering Services	403.21	1202.83	1479.01	1765.40	2096.29	2136.42
其他	Others	287.81	1213.70	1640.10	2463.61	2929.85	2966.98
生活消费	Residential Consumption	1286.80	2992.75	4421.95	5688.01	5884.46	5984.88
城镇	Urban Areas	818.33	1896.70	2796.08	3527.24	3650.28	3703.40
乡村	Rural Areas	468.45	1096.05	1625.86	2160.77	2234.18	2281.48
平衡差额	**Balance**						
消费量合计	**Total Energy Consumption**	**9447.70**	**25445.22**	**30117.44**	**34502.92**	**36821.42**	**36519.05**

7-5 分行业能源消费总量和原煤、电力消费量（2022年）
Consumption of Total Energy, Coal and Electricity by Sector (2022)

行业	Sector	能源消费总量(万吨标准煤) Total Energy Consumption (10000 tons of SCE)	原煤消费量(万吨) Coal Consumption (10000 tons)	电力消费量(亿千瓦小时) Electricity Consumption (100 million kwh)
消费总量	**Total**	**36519.05**	**18628.88**	**7870.34**
农、林、牧、渔业	**Farming,Forestry,Animal Husbandry and Fishery**	**746.20**	**39.74**	**164.62**
工业合计	**Industry**	**21350.59**	**18570.43**	**4565.47**
采矿业	**Mining and Quarrying**	**224.70**	**5.58**	**24.02**
煤炭开采和洗选业	Mining and Washing of Coal			
石油和天然气开采业	Extraction of Petroleum and Natural Gas	137.14		0.99
黑色金属矿采选业	Mining and Dressing of Ferrous Metal Ores	12.99		3.04
有色金属矿采选业	Mining and Dressing of Nonferrous Metal Ores	18.52	1.46	5.69
非金属矿采选业	Mining and Dressing of Nonmetal Ores	52.78	4.12	14.16
开采专业及辅助性活动	Auxiliary Minning Operations Mining	3.08		0.14
其他采矿业	Mining and Dressing of Other Ores	0.18		
制造业	**Manufacturing**	**18325.62**	**3646.17**	**3627.39**
农副食品加工业	Processing of Farm and Sideline Food	275.89	12.49	62.81
食品制造业	Manufacture of Food	185.75	19.89	42.01
酒、饮料和精制茶制造业	Manufacture of Wine, Beverage and Tea	99.69	6.68	23.72
烟草制品业	Tobacco Products	8.36		2.21
纺织业	Textile Industry	536.53	169.60	106.31
纺织服装、服饰业	Manufacture of Textile Garments, Footwear and	116.79	11.53	32.03
皮革、毛皮、羽毛(绒)及其制品业	Leather, Fur, Feather, Down and Related Products	99.47	1.15	29.91
木材加工及木、竹、藤、棕、草制品业	Timber Processing, Bamboo, Cane, Palm Fiber & Straw Products	81.19	0.80	23.74
家具制造业	Manufacture of Furniture	100.84	0.66	31.33
造纸及纸制品业	Papermaking and Paper Products	936.71	652.85	194.31
印刷业和记录媒介的复制	Printing and Record Medium Reproduction	122.79	0.37	36.73
文教、工美、体育和娱乐用品制造业	Manufacture of Cultural, Educational and Sports Articles	151.60	0.22	48.20
石油加工、炼焦及核燃料加工业	Petroleum Refining, Coking, and Nuclear Fuel Processing	2305.68	448.70	122.41
化学原料及化学制品制造业	Manufacture of Raw Chemical Materials and Chemical Products	1925.81	95.61	232.07
医药制造业	Manufacture of Medicines	133.66	4.13	34.51
化学纤维制造业	Manufacture of Chemical Fibers	55.83	2.08	14.24
橡胶和塑料制品业	Rubber Products	871.15	20.89	266.36
非金属矿物制品业	Nonmetal Mineral Products	2778.88	1507.78	364.59
黑色金属冶炼及压延加工业	Smelting and Pressing of Ferrous Metals	2256.15	575.18	314.00
有色金属冶炼及压延加工业	Smelting and Pressing of Nonferrous Metals	590.18	80.18	136.60
金属制品业	Metal Products	791.96	13.63	232.62
通用设备制造业	Manufacture of General-purpose Machinery	209.96	5.54	66.57
专用设备制造业	Manufacture of Special-purpose Machinery	245.28	2.69	80.49
汽车制造业	Manufacture of Automobile	330.28		104.57
铁路、船舶、航空航天和其他运输设备制造业	Manufacture of Railway ,Ship,Aeronautics and Other Transport Equipment	63.08	0.04	16.56
电气机械及器材制造业	Manufacture of Electrical Machinery and Equipment	787.29	0.51	255.50
通信设备、计算机及其他电子设备制造业	Manufacture of Communication Equipment, Computers and Other Electronic Equipment	2068.37	3.98	698.61
仪器仪表制造业	Manufacture of Instruments and Meters	58.59		18.89
其他制造业	Handicraft and Other Manufactures	37.94	1.20	10.90
废弃资源综合利用业	Recycling and Disposal of Waste	94.87	7.79	23.04
金属制品、机械和设备修理业	Manufacture of Metal Products,Machinery and Equipment Maintenance	5.07		1.55
电力、燃气及水的生产和供应业	**Production and Supply of Electric Power,Gas and Water**	**2800.27**	**14918.68**	**914.06**
电力、热力的生产和供应业	Production and Supply of Electric Power and Heat Power	2504.09	14905.37	816.73
燃气生产和供应业	Production and Supply of Gas	27.33	0.58	6.42
水的生产和供应业	Production and Supply of Water	268.86	12.73	90.91
建筑业	**Construction**	**577.83**	**2.85**	**104.26**
交通运输、仓储及邮政业	**Transport, Storage,Postal and Telecommunication Services**	**2756.15**		**178.41**
批发和零售贸易餐饮业	**Wholesale and Retail Trade and Catering Services**	**2136.42**	**3.24**	**520.30**
其他行业	**Others**	**2966.98**	**2.12**	**984.33**
生活消费	**Non-production Consumption**	**5984.88**	**10.50**	**1352.95**

7–6 各市电力消费量

Electricity Consumption by City

单位：亿千瓦小时 (100 million kwh)

市别	City	2000	2005	2010	2015	2018	2019	2020	2021	2022
全省	**Provincial Total**	**1334.58**	**2673.56**	**4060.13**	**5310.69**	**6323.35**	**6695.85**	**6926.12**	**7866.63**	**7870.34**
广州	Guangzhou	238.78	425.67	625.90	779.32	936.90	1005.58	996.72	1119.73	1118.76
深圳	Shenzhen	190.35	440.21	663.55	806.68	907.19	972.98	983.34	1103.40	1073.82
珠海	Zhuhai	30.82	61.58	102.26	145.37	175.99	189.91	193.20	218.22	224.64
汕头	Shantou	43.91	87.60	136.81	178.01	209.36	211.99	218.46	249.30	251.14
佛山	Foshan	168.84	316.29	463.08	587.84	690.85	702.65	710.30	780.79	758.91
韶关	Shaoguan	35.81	58.72	84.06	111.31	133.64	144.23	154.09	167.61	189.35
河源	Heyuan	9.27	23.90	51.52	78.06	89.84	97.40	99.38	115.75	117.57
梅州	Meizhou	22.70	40.40	60.88	77.98	99.11	104.67	112.07	123.41	118.98
惠州	Huizhou	43.53	105.22	192.46	290.62	408.38	425.88	447.84	510.36	516.62
汕尾	Shanwei	9.35	16.87	29.73	47.05	56.83	60.56	65.95	73.91	75.48
东莞	Dongguan	179.78	419.83	562.00	666.84	806.64	850.70	873.90	1001.18	967.71
中山	Zhongshan	54.54	123.63	186.65	245.51	293.01	310.04	316.58	357.17	344.71
江门	Jiangmen	64.65	113.63	165.21	237.13	281.78	294.71	309.07	350.84	342.41
阳江	Yangjiang	12.09	22.46	40.43	98.21	119.84	134.26	145.20	148.99	155.71
湛江	Zhanjiang	24.15	49.09	78.68	116.04	196.43	212.65	237.97	280.77	294.72
茂名	Maoming	29.98	40.11	65.80	98.40	115.18	123.63	133.38	152.87	153.93
肇庆	Zhaoqing	24.00	48.58	105.08	152.30	171.81	180.44	182.28	210.64	211.98
清远	Qingyuan	22.60	59.47	125.53	179.27	198.72	216.03	240.18	276.33	262.98
潮州	Chaozhou	13.95	33.17	59.16	75.59	91.10	95.59	101.11	115.34	114.67
揭阳	Jieyang	22.51	51.13	98.68	152.71	155.88	157.06	166.94	188.19	195.43
云浮	Yunfu	12.14	21.55	34.89	57.81	68.58	74.45	78.56	85.17	95.26
按经济区域分	By Region									
珠三角	Pearl River Delta	995.29	2054.64	3066.18	3911.61	4672.54	4932.88	5013.23	5652.34	5559.56
东翼	Eastern Region	89.72	188.77	324.38	453.34	513.18	525.21	552.46	626.74	636.72
西翼	Western Region	66.22	111.66	184.91	312.65	431.45	470.54	516.55	582.63	604.36
山区	Mountainous Region	102.52	204.04	356.88	504.43	589.89	636.79	684.29	768.27	784.14

注：由于各市电力消费量不包含不分区域线损，全省数不等于分市数合计。

Note: Because the electricity consumption by region doesn't include line losses , the sum of electricity consumption by cities is different from the provincial total.

7-7 各市单位GDP能耗增长速度

Growth Rate of Energy Consumption Per Unit GDP by City

单位：%　　　　(%)

市 别	City	2010	2013	2014	2015	2016	2017	2018	2019	2020	2021	2022
全 省	**Provincial Total**	**-2.94**	**-4.55**	**-3.56**	**-5.71**	**-3.62**	**-3.69**	**-3.42**	**-3.52**	**-1.16**	**-1.2**	**-2.6**
广 州	Guangzhou	-4.60	-5.14	-3.52	-4.52	-4.96	-4.81	-3.24	-3.86	-4.23	-1.8	-3.1
深 圳	Shenzhen	-2.94	-5.12	-4.35	-3.26	-4.21	-4.23	-4.20	-3.54	-5.54	1.0	-5.8
珠 海	Zhuhai	-3.67	-4.98	-4.12	-2.80	-3.94	-4.20	-1.26	-3.09	-0.44	-2.1	-0.2
汕 头	Shantou	-3.19	-3.99	-3.85	-6.81	-3.00	-5.04	-4.13	-2.75	-2.19	-0.3	2.8
佛 山	Foshan	-4.38	-4.54	-4.45	-5.64	-6.63	-5.13	-5.20	-4.90	-5.26	-1.7	-3.7
韶 关	Shaoguan	-1.57	-4.31	-5.01	-7.95	-3.81	3.20	1.76	-1.00	-1.46	-5.4	-1.1
河 源	Heyuan	-1.06	-3.67	-2.21	-4.08	-4.08	-4.15	0.14	-0.50	-8.32	5.6	-1.8
梅 州	Meizhou	-3.23	-4.51	-3.69	-5.91	-3.80	-4.80	12.80	-0.02	2.15	-2.2	-3.3
惠 州	Huizhou	-5.82	-4.35	-3.69	-7.10	-1.52	6.28	10.25	1.72	2.28	-5.3	-5.0
汕 尾	Shanwei	-2.02	-5.69	-1.12	2.03	-3.01	-0.94	-4.57	1.43	-0.69	-3.2	-0.7
东 莞	Dongguan	-2.02	-5.35	-5.88	-7.90	-4.65	-4.87	-5.55	-4.46	-2.91	-4.0	-1.9
中 山	Zhongshan	-1.50	-3.98	-3.81	-3.91	-3.89	-3.73	-3.78	-1.33	-6.22	-0.3	-4.0
江 门	Jiangmen	-2.30	-4.49	-3.02	-6.63	-4.52	-4.61	-4.89	-2.46	-2.51	-2.3	-3.3
阳 江	Yangjiang	-1.00	-3.97	-3.38	-4.12	7.16	5.46	5.65	4.01	-1.06	-12.7	2.8
湛 江	Zhanjiang	-0.30	-4.04	-4.03	-2.57	38.35	8.77	-3.81	-1.68	11.36	13.6	9.8
茂 名	Maoming	-4.25	-4.21	-2.38	-7.36	-2.82	-4.41	-0.75	-3.82	-7.09	-5.0	-7.9
肇 庆	Zhaoqing	-2.44	-4.03	-3.51	-4.51	-5.35	-1.97	-6.90	-3.49	-2.63	-8.0	-2.5
清 远	Qingyuan	-1.96	-2.81	-3.03	-7.73	-4.04	-3.93	3.60	-3.08	-3.12	-8.0	-9.7
潮 州	Chaozhou	-3.32	-4.82	-3.55	-6.67	-4.07	-3.82	-4.26	-3.45	-2.12	-2.2	-3.5
揭 阳	Jieyang	-2.21	-4.50	-2.00	-6.35	-4.43	2.79	-6.93	-3.50	-4.81	0.8	10.5
云 浮	Yunfu	-1.54	-3.90	-3.08	-2.86	-4.76	-4.17	-5.15	-4.09	-3.59	-6.2	2.8

注：本表为当年节能考核确认数。
Note: Data in this table is the confirmed figure of energy saving assessment in the current year.

7-8 各市单位GDP电耗增长速度

Growth Rate of Electricity Consumption per Unit of GDP by City

单位：%　　　　(%)

市 别	City	2010	2013	2014	2015	2016	2017	2018	2019	2020	2021	2022
全 省	**Provincial Total**	**0.03**	**-3.62**	**0.59**	**-6.10**	**-1.73**	**-1.19**	**-0.64**	**-0.24**	**1.16**	**5.2**	**-1.9**
广 州	Guangzhou	-2.53	-8.21	-0.77	-6.13	-2.36	-1.32	-2.27	0.50	-3.49	3.9	-1.1
深 圳	Shenzhen	1.00	-8.30	-0.65	-5.01	-4.17	-4.82	-3.62	-0.39	-1.93	5.2	-5.9
珠 海	Zhuhai	-1.21	-6.23	0.04	-1.61	-3.10	-2.54	0.18	1.04	-1.23	5.6	0.7
汕 头	Shantou	-0.62	-5.37	-0.79	-5.78	-1.33	-3.61	-2.19	-4.57	1.03	7.5	-0.3
佛 山	Foshan	-2.76	-5.07	-1.44	-3.95	-2.48	0.08	-3.52	-4.86	-0.45	1.5	-4.8
韶 关	Shaoguan	2.44	0.80	-0.04	-12.00	-5.49	0.96	7.25	2.03	3.73	0.1	1.6
河 源	Heyuan	3.54	0.30	2.97	-2.96	-1.69	-1.47	7.23	2.76	0.68	7.9	0.3
梅 州	Meizhou	-4.67	-5.32	1.06	-6.18	0.60	-0.52	8.14	2.14	5.37	3.8	-4.2
惠 州	Huizhou	-1.64	-3.82	1.15	-3.56	2.83	5.80	4.59	0.08	3.61	3.5	-2.7
汕 尾	Shanwei	-5.82	-4.46	6.59	-0.63	0.06	0.48	-1.12	-0.13	3.53	0.8	0.7
东 莞	Dongguan	2.84	-6.17	-1.50	-6.54	-2.62	0.23	-1.28	-1.82	1.62	5.9	-4.0
中 山	Zhongshan	1.38	-4.42	1.35	-4.73	-1.97	1.10	-0.98	4.56	0.57	4.3	-4.0
江 门	Jiangmen	1.60	-3.71	1.96	-4.00	-2.43	-0.56	-2.15	0.14	2.52	4.7	-5.5
阳 江	Yangjiang	5.66	4.50	6.41	-0.21	0.06	0.90	2.55	3.46	3.54	-5.3	3.6
湛 江	Zhanjiang	-0.12	-6.17	1.39	-2.28	22.37	10.83	2.13	4.10	9.83	8.6	3.8
茂 名	Maoming	-4.65	-6.32	4.75	-3.86	-1.38	-4.31	2.09	2.79	6.26	6.5	0.2
肇 庆	Zhaoqing	1.74	-2.46	-0.40	-9.92	-0.42	0.74	-4.53	-1.16	-1.89	4.6	-0.5
清 远	Qingyuan	-2.32	1.74	2.82	-4.91	-0.04	-12.64	7.85	2.21	2.07	6.6	-5.8
潮 州	Chaozhou	0.85	-7.05	1.12	-6.44	-1.35	0.33	0.95	-0.07	4.46	4.4	-2.8
揭 阳	Jieyang	-3.58	-1.80	3.66	-11.03	-0.87	-12.04	-0.47	-2.18	6.11	6.2	5.2
云 浮	Yunfu	0.24	1.74	1.64	-2.85	-1.09	0.22	2.89	2.32	1.42	0.3	9.5

7-9 各市单位工业增加值能耗增长速度

Growth Rate of Energy Consumption per Unit of Industrial Value-added by City

单位：% (%)

市别	City	2010	2013	2014	2015	2016	2017	2018	2019	2020	2021	2022
全省	**Provincial Total**	**-6.88**	**-4.97**	**-9.25**	**-10.47**	**-3.75**	**-0.01**	**-2.35**	**-5.21**	**1.21**	**1.7**	**-3.0**
广州	Guangzhou	-12.61	-10.89	-11.91	-13.03	-6.55	-4.85	-6.54	-7.50	-1.67	-3.7	-3.7
深圳	Shenzhen	-3.72	-9.49	-8.45	-11.07	-4.98	-0.75	-11.24	-3.89	-4.82	5.5	-5.2
珠海	Zhuhai	-10.52	-9.17	-8.49	-1.88	-7.12	-6.76	-8.79	-9.57	-1.21	6.6	-7.5
汕头	Shantou	18.74	5.35	-11.22	-16.00	-16.78	4.86	3.28	-11.19	-0.78	2.7	0.5
佛山	Foshan	-10.48	-11.45	-12.54	-13.77	-8.32	-6.36	-8.77	-8.92	-8.28	-3.9	-11.1
韶关	Shaoguan	-2.11	-10.61	-12.81	-8.66	-0.49	12.52	4.52	-2.18	2.82	2.2	-5.4
河源	Heyuan	-1.15	-15.94	-19.33	-13.26	-9.65	1.44	-2.77	-14.16	-12.56	35.9	27.0
梅州	Meizhou	-15.33	-3.25	-14.92	-15.48	1.49	-23.41	26.20	4.12	4.58	6.9	-6.7
惠州	Huizhou	-16.87	-18.18	-14.15	-12.31	-4.59	10.28	11.61	6.10	5.28	-9.4	-7.6
汕尾	Shanwei	-14.25	-30.74	-14.92	26.15	-2.24	14.78	-4.74	21.16	1.99	-0.3	3.9
东莞	Dongguan	-10.92	-8.45	-9.74	-10.88	-3.93	-7.95	-9.15	-11.94	-3.24	-1.6	2.2
中山	Zhongshan	-3.84	-12.34	-3.84	4.91	-1.58	-1.62	-6.02	-2.30	-2.02	-10.8	-10.3
江门	Jiangmen	-12.91	-0.53	-17.45	-14.93	-10.89	-4.84	0.02	-10.32	0.65	5.5	1.4
阳江	Yangjiang	58.95	-16.69	-1.16	-10.30	4.58	5.45	8.01	-11.08	-4.48	-12.5	1.9
湛江	Zhanjiang	-4.35	-7.40	-17.83	-11.45	43.40	13.09	-3.68	-1.26	17.93	16.4	13.4
茂名	Maoming	-9.91	-11.53	-5.04	-11.60	-6.55	-3.09	2.78	-2.17	5.26	5.9	-0.4
肇庆	Zhaoqing	-7.65	-9.31	-9.80	-12.94	-8.39	-0.51	-8.21	-7.19	0.25	-16.6	-6.5
清远	Qingyuan	-16.28	-0.74	-9.52	-9.16	-7.39	-0.73	-1.59	-5.51	-3.94	-10.2	-9.8
潮州	Chaozhou	17.93	-16.05	-21.13	-13.16	-11.45	11.53	-3.79	-3.90	-8.42	6.2	-6.8
揭阳	Jieyang	-15.49	24.31	-18.62	-15.54	-17.50	15.12	-5.74	-6.49	4.39	9.8	35.0
云浮	Yunfu	-9.70	-21.35	-14.19	-10.32	-7.55	-2.37	-8.81	-11.54	-3.43	-8.6	-2.1

7-10 平均每天各种能源消费量

Average Daily Energy Consumption by Variety

能源品种	Energy Variety	2000	2005	2010	2015	2020	2021	2022
合计(吨标准煤)	**Total (ton of SCE)**	**248773**	**472363**	**721776**	**804376**	**925340**	**985086**	**978109**
煤炭 (吨)	Coal (Ton)	59590	78227	143273	135415	100542	75952	70515
焦炭 (吨)	Coke (Ton)	3973	8058	13314	14875	27718	25546	29460
原油 (吨)	Crude Oil (Ton)	250	178	480	635	772	808	1555
燃料油 (吨)	Fuel Oil (Ton)	9248	18288	13141	8253	7812	10123	8603
汽油 (吨)	Gasoline (Ton)	8226	19330	29693	33601	41242	34725	28164
煤油 (吨)	Kerosene (Ton)	2444	4212	5532	7510	7655	9984	9140
柴油 (吨)	Diesel Oil (Ton)	18726	34920	45370	43303	42118	37197	29895
液化石油气 (吨)	Liquefied Petroleum Gas(Ton)	8720	16676	16023	18510	16956	16671	21535
电力(万千瓦时)	Electricity (10000 kwh)	33978	69671	105290	139035	183624	208886	208683

7-11 平均每人年生活用能源

Annual per Capita Energy Consumption of Households

能源品种	Energy Variety	2000	2005	2010	2015	2020	2021	2022
合　计(千克标准煤)	**Total (kg of SCE)**	**148.90**	**227.85**	**290.97**	**381.75**	**452.99**	**465.03**	**472.35**
煤　炭　(千克)	Coal (kg)	9.63	10.54	6.14	5.75	5.17	3.54	1.17
汽　油　(千克)	Gasoline (kg)	4.42	14.57	36.95	46.50	62.03	49.45	40.41
煤　油　(千克)	Kerosene (kg)	0.24	0.33	0.35	0.35	0.26	0.23	0.17
柴　油　(千克)	Diesel Oil (kg)	0.57	0.98	1.39	1.65	1.67	1.55	1.90
液化石油气　(千克)	Liquefied Petroleum Gas(kg)	31.47	43.66	27.42	40.19	33.54	33.78	39.16
电　力　(千瓦时)	Electricity (kwh)	239.09	359.06	536.60	730.31	939.33	1040.97	1067.80

7-12 分品种生活能源年消费总量

Annual Total Energy Consumption of Households by Variety

能源品种	Energy Variety	2000	2005	2010	2015	2020	2021	2022
合　计(万吨标准煤)	**Total (10000 tons of SCE)**	**1286.80**	**2100.39**	**2992.75**	**4421.95**	**5688.01**	**5884.46**	**5984.88**
煤　炭　(万吨)	Coal (10000 tons)	83.22	96.46	63.19	66.57	64.91	44.77	14.77
汽　油　(万吨)	Gasoline (10000 tons)	38.20	133.36	380.05	538.63	778.93	625.71	512.07
煤　油　(万吨)	Kerosene (10000 tons)	2.10	2.98	3.60	4.11	3.30	2.87	2.16
柴　油　(万吨)	Diesel Oil (10000 tons)	4.90	8.93	14.30	19.10	20.97	19.58	24.13
液化石油气　(万吨)	Liquefied Petroleum Gas(10000 tons)	271.96	399.55	282.01	465.57	421.12	427.45	496.19
电　力(亿千瓦小时)	Electricity (100 million kwh)	206.62	328.62	551.92	845.96	1179.47	1317.24	1352.95

7-13 能源加工转换效率
Efficiency of Energy Conversion

单位：%　　(%)

年 份 Year	火力发电 Thermal Power Generation	供 热 Heating	炼 焦 Coking	炼 油 Petroleum Refining	制 气 Gas Production
1990	31.13	79.21	93.48	99.44	
1995	31.85	80.07	90.93	99.89	86.17
2000	37.20	87.19	94.35	99.02	79.18
2001	37.21	85.09	95.23	99.12	77.90
2002	36.36	76.40	94.27	98.40	80.08
2003	40.69	71.43	82.36	98.57	78.67
2004	35.53	86.10	91.53	99.29	79.70
2005	36.22	95.99	96.66	99.53	79.18
2006	37.74	88.49	96.95	99.80	95.40
2007	38.80	70.66	99.02	99.79	97.22
2008	38.00	77.34	98.43	99.10	95.65
2009	38.69	82.15	98.31	99.58	93.47
2010	38.90	82.80	99.08	98.12	87.81
2011	38.22	79.19	98.69	98.54	89.87
2012	38.49	78.26	97.57	98.17	89.77
2013	39.66	79.57	96.01	98.48	91.00
2014	39.72	75.73	96.15	97.42	71.51
2015	40.62	84.02	97.15	97.69	57.39
2016	40.78	83.32	97.91	99.03	60.99
2017	40.79	84.41	96.56	95.78	62.77
2018	41.70	81.59	92.63	99.47	57.40
2019	41.58	79.64	93.56	97.10	62.80
2020	42.04	82.00	93.10	96.43	64.00
2021	42.75	85.02	94.79	97.07	65.00
2022	42.80	83.48	97.46	96.65	58.81

7-14 能源生产弹性系数

Elasticity Ratio of Energy Production

年份 Year	能源生产比上年增长(%) Growth Rate of Energy Production over Preceding Year(%)	电力生产比上年增长(%) Growth Rate of Electricity Production over Preceding Year(%)	本省生产总值比上年增长(%) Growth Rate of Gross Domestic Product(GDP) over Preceding Year(%)	能源生产弹性系数 Elasticity Ratio of Energy Production	电力生产弹性系数 Elasticity Ratio of Electricity Production
1986	1.0	8.0	12.7	0.08	0.63
1990	0.3	15.3	11.6	0.02	1.32
1995	14.7	6.6	15.6	0.94	0.42
1996	43.3	10.7	11.3	3.83	0.95
1997	8.5	8.0	11.2	0.76	0.71
1998	-4.1	5.6	10.8		0.52
1999	-10.3	9.8	10.1		0.97
2000	5.8	18.7	11.5	0.50	1.63
2001	-8.2	5.9	10.5		0.56
2002	6.5	12.4	12.4	0.52	1.00
2003	12.7	17.7	14.8	0.86	1.20
2004	18.6	11.9	14.8	1.26	0.80
2005	-6.7	7.4	13.8		0.54
2006	-8.1	8.5	14.6		0.58
2007	-5.7	8.9	14.7		0.61
2008	12.5	-0.4	10.1	1.24	
2009	-0.6	-0.6	9.7		
2010	10.6	20.1	12.4	0.85	1.62
2011	-0.2	15.6	10.0		1.56
2012	5.0	-1.8	8.2	0.61	
2013	5.4	6.7	8.5	0.64	0.79
2014	4.3	0.5	7.8	0.55	0.06
2015	22.7	0.5	8.0	2.84	0.06
2016	4.0	5.7	7.5	0.53	0.76
2017	-1.4	6.4	7.5		0.85
2018	0.6	3.5	6.8	0.09	0.51
2019	18.3	7.1	6.2	2.96	1.14
2020	2.2	7.1	2.3	0.96	1.51
2021	3.9	20.7	8.1	0.48	2.58
2022	8.5	0.9	1.9	4.47	0.50

7-15 能源消费弹性系数

Elasticity Ratio of Energy Consumption

年份 Year	能源消费比上年增长（%） Growth Rate of Energy Consumption over Preceding Year(%)	电力消费比上年增长(%) Growth Rate of Electricity Consumption over Preceding Year(%)	本省生产总值比上年增长(%) Growth Rate of Gross Domestic Product(GDP) over Preceding Year(%)	能源消费弹性系数 Elasticity Ratio of Energy Consumption	电力消费弹性系数 Elasticity Ratio of Electricity Consumption
1986	8.4	4.7	12.7	0.66	0.37
1990	4.1	14.3	11.6	0.35	1.24
1995	9.2	7.6	15.6	0.59	0.49
1996	5.5	8.9	11.3	0.48	0.79
1997	2.7	7.1	11.2	0.24	0.64
1998	5.3	7.5	10.8	0.49	0.70
1999	4.3	10.0	10.1	0.42	0.99
2000	8.2	22.9	11.5	0.71	1.99
2001	7.7	9.3	10.5	0.74	0.88
2002	11.6	15.7	12.4	0.93	1.27
2003	15.4	20.3	14.8	1.04	1.37
2004	16.1	17.5	14.8	1.09	1.18
2005	16.8	12.0	13.8	1.22	0.87
2006	11.2	12.4	14.6	0.77	0.85
2007	10.9	13.0	14.7	0.74	0.88
2008	5.3	3.3	10.1	0.52	0.32
2009	6.9	2.9	9.7	0.71	0.30
2010	8.9	12.5	12.4	0.72	1.00
2011	5.8	8.3	10.0	0.58	0.83
2012	2.3	5.0	8.2	0.28	0.61
2013	3.6	4.5	8.5	0.42	0.53
2014	3.9	8.4	7.8	0.50	1.08
2015	1.9	1.4	8.0	0.24	0.18
2016	3.6	5.6	7.5	0.48	0.75
2017	3.5	6.2	7.5	0.47	0.83
2018	3.2	6.1	6.8	0.47	0.90
2019	2.4	5.9	6.2	0.39	0.95
2020	1.1	3.4	2.3	0.46	1.50
2021	6.7	13.6	8.1	0.84	1.70
2022	-0.8	0.0	1.9	0.00	0.02

7-16 自然资源（2022年）
Natural Resources (2022)

项　　目		Item		2022
一、土地资源和海洋		**Land Resources and Sea**		
土地面积	(万平方公里)	Total Land Area	(10000 sq.km)	17.98
耕　地	(万公顷)	Cultivated Land	(10000 hectares)	189.97
林　地	(万公顷)	Afforested Land	(10000 hectares)	1074.23
园　地	(万公顷)	Plantation	(10000 hectares)	131.66
牧草地	(万公顷)	Grass Land	(10000 hectares)	0.04
海域总面积	(万平方公里)	Total Area of Sea	(10000 sq.km)	41.90
海洋滩涂面积	(万公顷)	Sea Beach Area	(10000 hectares)	18.02
海岛面积	(平方公里)	Area of Islands	(sq.km)	1513.17
大陆海岸线长度	(公里)	Length of Continental Coastline	(km)	4084.48
岛屿岸线长度	(公里)	Length of Island Coastline	(km)	2378.71
岛屿个数	(个)	Number of Islands	(unit)	1963
二、气候		**Climate**		
年平均降雨量	(毫米)	Annual Average Precipitation	(mm)	2057.6
年平均气温	(摄氏度)	Annual Average Temperature	(℃)	22.2
年日照时数	(小时)	Annual Sunshine Hours	(hour)	1856.3
三、森林		**Forest**		
森林蓄积量	(亿立方米)	Total Standing Stock Volume	(100 million cu.m)	
森林覆盖率	(%)	Forest Coverage Rate	(%)	
四、水力水产		**Hydropower and Aquatic Products**		
水能资源理论蕴藏量	(万千瓦)	Theoretical Hydropower Resources	(10000 kw)	1137.2
#技术可开发量		Developable Resources		864.6
五、矿产		**Mineral Resources**		
煤保有资源储量	(万吨)	Ensured Reserve of Coal	(10000 tons)	48383.59
铁矿石保有资源储量	(万吨)	Ensured Reserve of Iron Ore	(10000 tons)	58972.31
硫铁矿保有资源储量	(万吨)	Ensured Reserve of Pyrite Ore	(10000 tons)	31119.84

注：1.表中土地面积、耕地、林地、园地、牧草地数据为2021年数据。
2.海域总面积包括内水领海专属经济区面积。
3.大陆海岸长度来源于2008年省政府批复岸线；海岛面积、岛岸线长度、岛屿个数来源于2013年广东省海岛地名普查；海域总面积包括内水领海专属经济区面积。
4.2022年森林覆盖率、森林蓄积量数据暂缺。

Notes: a) The data of Total Land Area, Cultivated Land, Afforested Land, Plantation, Grass Land in the table is based on the data of 2021.
b) Total Area of Sea includes the area of exclusive economic zone of internal waters and territorial waters.
c) The length of continental coastline approved by the Guangdong Provincial Government in 2008; the area of islands, the length of the island coastline, and the number of islands are from the geographical name survey of Guangdong Province in 2013; the total area of sea includes the area of the exclusive economic zone of internal waters and territorial waters.
d) Data on forest coverage rate and total standing stock volume in 2022 are currently lacking.

7-17 各地区年平均气温

Average Temperature by Region

单位：摄氏度 (℃)

年份 Year	粤北 Northern Regions	粤东北 North Eastern Regions	粤西北 North Western Regions	粤东 Eastern Regions	粤中 Central Regions	粤西 Western Regions
1980	20.7	21.5	22.5	21.2	22.2	23.4
1985	20.2	20.9	22.0	21.1	21.6	22.6
1990	21.1	21.5	22.8	21.8	22.6	23.4
1995	20.0	20.0	22.2	21.6	22.3	23.0
1996	19.9	21.4	22.4	21.9	21.6	23.3
1997	20.4	21.3	22.7	22.1	22.0	23.7
1998	21.2	22.5	23.3	23.0	22.8	24.5
1999	20.8	21.9	22.7	22.6	22.5	24.0
2000	20.4	21.9	22.6	22.5	22.5	23.8
2001	20.5	22.0	22.5	22.7	22.6	23.8
2002	21.0	22.3	22.8	23.0	23.0	24.1
2003	20.9	21.9	22.9	22.6	23.0	24.4
2004	20.8	21.6	22.6	22.6	22.8	23.2
2005	20.5	21.6	22.5	22.3	22.8	23.0
2006	20.8	22.1	23.1	22.8	23.2	23.4
2007	21.2	22.0	23.0	22.9	23.2	23.2
2008	20.5	21.5	22.1	22.3	22.5	22.4
2009	20.6	22.3	22.9	22.6	23.0	23.3
2010	20.0	21.8	22.4	22.3	22.5	23.3
2011	19.6	21.7	22.3	22.1	21.4	22.4
2012	19.6	22.0	22.4	22.3	21.7	23.2
2013	20.0	21.2	22.7	22.6	21.5	23.0
2014	20.4	21.7	22.8	22.8	21.7	23.3
2015	20.8	22.0	23.4	23.5	22.3	24.3
2016	20.7	21.7	22.5	23.3	22.0	23.6
2017	20.8	22.0	22.6	23.5	22.1	23.7
2018	21.2	21.7	20.7	22.7	22.4	22.9
2019	21.4	22.0	20.9	23.1	22.9	23.7
2020	21.2	22.5	23.1	23.9	22.7	24.3
2021	21.4	23.0	23.3	24.2	22.9	24.2
2022	20.8	21.9	22.6	23.4	22.1	23.3

7-18 各地区年降雨量

Annual Precipitation by Region

单位：毫米 (mm)

年份 Year	粤北 Northern Regions	粤东北 North Eastern Regions	粤西北 North Western Regions	粤东 Eastern Regions	粤中 Central Regions	粤西 Western Regions
1980	1459.4	1461.7	1586.1	1369.1	1492.2	2274.0
1985	1360.2	1607.8	1726.9	1481.3	1706.0	2411.3
1990	1436.6	1709.0	1284.8	2236.9	1239.5	1510.2
1995	1506.9	1171.0	1766.4	1512.2	1752.4	2082.9
1996	1633.1	1361.5	1693.1	1409.0	1683.4	1222.6
1997	2045.3	1847.5	1815.3	2040.9	1997.3	2344.3
1998	1862.3	1458.2	1737.5	1593.6	1736.1	1266.4
1999	1314.3	1033.8	1318.7	1517.4	1620.4	1392.6
2000	1565.8	1850.9	1318.2	1486.7	1798.9	1762.7
2001	1689.8	1560.3	1889.2	1947.9	2678.9	2314.5
2002	1814.9	1110.3	1480.9	1409.7	1866.7	2263.3
2003	1388.2	1415.2	1251.8	1406.6	1338.7	1372.4
2004	1156.3	1251.8	1034.7	1379.7	1636.5	1068.5
2005	1772.2	1647.3	1905.2	1631.3	1986.2	1387.3
2006	1782.8	2040.2	1727.0	2507.7	2175.7	1149.8
2007	1502.3	1399.2	1252.4	1482.2	1370.3	1620.8
2008	1553.1	1300.2	2221.0	2123.6	2284.0	1865.2
2009	1275.5	1246.7	1440.4	927.9	1472.6	1849.9
2010	2104.4	1416.1	1419.6	1350.3	2353.6	1952.3
2011	1443.0	1233.1	1277.2	1027.0	1632.3	1408.5
2012	2056.3	1460.5	1919.2	1247.1	1813.9	2068.6
2013	1654.0	1930.2	1736.2	1887.2	2095.4	2084.2
2014	1517.0	1164.9	1788.2	1416.5	2234.0	1468.9
2015	2128.7	1696.3	1848.1	1446.6	2471.9	1328.9
2016	2428.9	2410.3	2132.5	2174.7	2939.7	1820.0
2017	1397.2	1396.3	1275.8	1419.0	2067.4	1760.7
2018	1547.0	1364.9	1691.3	1672.6	1795.1	1902.7
2019	1963.4	1872.2	1988.1	1721.9	1918.4	1716.0
2020	1719.5	1122.7	1057.4	1207.5	1916.2	1568.9
2021	1168.9	823.4	1064.3	923.5	1544.1	1123.8
2022	2423.9	1841.3	1666.1	2024.4	1959.7	1928.4

7–19 各地区年日照时数

Annual Sunshine Hours by Region

单位：小时　　(hour)

年份 Year	粤 北 Northern Regions	粤东北 North Eastern Regions	粤西北 North Western Regions	粤 东 Eastern Regions	粤 中 Central Regions	粤 西 Western Regions
1980	1754.1	1811.1	1945.8	1989.2	1921.8	2036.5
1985	1701.6	1926.7	1613.3	1900.6	1406.0	1868.4
1990	1613.9	1893.1	1542.8	1921.3	1648.7	1877.4
1995	1420.6	1868.7	1704.6	2038.3	1559.6	1828.3
1996	1626.5	1965.7	1796.9	2094.8	1564.7	2042.3
1997	1349.1	1490.2	1454.9	1985.8	1209.8	1895.1
1998	1578.3	1689.6	1546.1	1917.5	1469.4	1994.0
1999	1564.0	1819.7	1699.0	2237.0	1599.5	2050.7
2000	1497.2	1672.6	1714.1	2126.3	1609.2	1855.3
2001	1613.0	1884.0	1559.2	2199.8	1651.0	1794.6
2002	1506.4	1813.2	1521.7	2266.6	1566.5	1783.8
2003	1821.1	2030.1	1762.6	2341.5	1741.6	2144.5
2004	1818.5	2117.1	1640.2	2433.5	1767.4	2024.7
2005	1491.2	1736.4	1345.6	1849.5	1288.5	1784.4
2006	1487.7	1779.4	1454.8	1843.5	1328.7	1664.3
2007	1736.3	1750.6	1722.4	1961.2	1616.0	1778.7
2008	1545.0	1853.1	1638.8	1852.1	1482.2	1864.4
2009	1852.9	1962.9	1531.8	2059.8	1671.8	1981.8
2010	1631.0	1676.9	1356.5	1855.5	1484.0	1878.4
2011	1783.8	1901.1	1709.7	2077.9	1878.4	1822.3
2012	1501.0	1660.3	1361.1	1650.4	1471.2	1544.0
2013	1731.5	1827.8	1624.2	1865.8	1582.9	1811.2
2014	1886.2	1997.5	1744.5	1957.8	1613.6	1991.5
2015	1540.8	1740.4	1583.0	2010.7	1594.3	2008.1
2016	1629.2	1553.6	1466.2	1701.0	1451.8	1963.9
2017	1738.9	1831.4	1605.4	1994.6	1671.5	1891.9
2018	1609.7	1700.5	1541.2	2066.9	1556.8	1687.7
2019	1653.8	1757.2	1566.6	1971.3	1660.3	1771.2
2020	1581.8	1830.7	1724.0	2426.4	1661.4	1803.9
2021	1898.0	2142.3	1948.9	2567.0	1946.8	2080.8
2022	1684.6	1851.6	1779.5	2431.4	1774.6	1801.8

7-20 各市土地面积和人口密度

Land Area and Population Density by City

市 别	City	土地面积(平方公里) Land Area (sq.km)	人口密度（人/平方公里） Population Density (persons/sq.km)								
			2000	2005	2010	2015	2018	2019	2020	2021	2022
全 省	**Provincial Total**	**179800.00**	**486**	**511**	**581**	**650**	**687**	**695**	**702**	**705**	**704**
广 州	Guangzhou	7238.46	1337	1277	1744	2200	2480	2530	2589	2599	2588
深 圳	Shenzhen	1987.00	3596	4239	5311	7081	8341	8611	8877	8899	8889
珠 海	Zhuhai	1725.02	758	839	944	1095	1272	1352	1420	1430	1436
汕 头	Shantou	2204.52	2263	2395	2400	2481	2495	2492	2497	2509	2514
佛 山	Foshan	3797.79	1400	1507	1871	2276	2438	2483	2506	2531	2515
韶 关	Shaoguan	18412.66	149	159	154	154	155	155	155	155	155
河 源	Heyuan	15653.63	143	176	189	186	183	182	181	181	182
梅 州	Meizhou	15864.51	240	259	267	257	249	247	244	244	243
惠 州	Huizhou	11350.36	288	332	405	485	515	526	534	534	533
汕 尾	Shanwei	4865.56	465	531	600	569	556	553	549	552	551
东 莞	Dongguan	2460.38	2615	2662	3328	4063	4243	4249	4261	4283	4242
中 山	Zhongshan	1780.99	1313	1352	1735	2226	2404	2463	2488	2508	2488
江 门	Jiangmen	9535.19	414	430	467	482	495	498	504	507	506
阳 江	Yangjiang	7966.79	278	297	304	317	323	325	327	329	329
湛 江	Zhanjiang	13263.80	487	536	530	527	526	526	526	530	530
茂 名	Maoming	11451.80	457	510	510	519	530	535	540	543	545
肇 庆	Zhaoqing	14891.43	227	247	265	269	273	275	276	277	277
清 远	Qingyuan	19035.48	164	188	193	203	207	208	209	209	209
潮 州	Chaozhou	3159.89	780	810	862	826	823	817	812	815	815
揭 阳	Jieyang	5266.10	999	1068	1117	1099	1074	1070	1059	1067	1070
云 浮	Yunfu	7785.16	277	301	304	304	306	306	306	307	308

注：1. 2000、2010、2020年所使用人口数据为第五次、第六次、第七次全国人口普查结果，2005年使用人口数据为广东省2005年全国1%人口抽样调查结果。2015-2019年人口数据根据第七次全国人口普查结果修正后使用。

2. 表中土地面积数为2021年数据，2021、2022年计算人口密度所使用的土地面积均为2021年数据。

Note: a) The population data used in 2000、2010 and 2020 are the results of the 5th、6th and 7th Population Censuses, the population data used in 2005 is the result of 1% national population sample survey in Guangdong Province in 2005. The population data of 2015-2019 are used according to revised results of the 7th National Census.

b) The number of land area in table is based on the data of 2021, all land areas used in population density in 2021、2022 are the data of 2021.

7-21 水资源及供水用水基本情况

Water Resources, Water Supply and Water use

项　　目	Item	2010	2015	2020	2021	2022
年平均降水量 （毫米）	Precipitation per Year (mm)	1927.1	1875.7	1574.1	1420.9	2114.3
水资源总量 （亿立方米）	Total Amount of Water Resource (100 million cu.m)	1998.8	1933.4	1626.0	1221.1	2223.6
#地表水资源量	Surface Water Resources	1989.5	1923.4	1616.3	1211.3	2213.3
地下水资源量	Groundwater Resources	478.3	461.4	399.1	301.3	546.2
人均水资源量 （立方米/人）	Per Capita Amount of Water Resource (cu.m/person)	1915	1782	1296	966	1755
供水总量 （亿立方米）	Water Supply (100 million cu.m)	469.0	443.1	405.1	407.0	401.7
地表水	Surface Water	446.4	426.0	390.4	394.0	383.5
地下水	Groundwater	21.3	15.3	11.1	8.6	6.5
其他	Others	1.3	1.7	3.6	4.4	11.7
用水总量 （亿立方米）	Total Water Consumption (100 million cu.m)	469.0	443.1	405.1	407.0	401.7
#农业用水	Agriculture	231.3	227.0	210.8	204.2	198.7
工业用水	Industry	138.8	112.5	80.4	78.2	73.4
生活用水	Living	90.4	98.3	107.9	117.9	116.7
生态环境补水	Ecology	8.5	5.3	6.0	6.7	12.9
人均用水量 （立方米/人）	Per Capita Water Consumption (cu.m/person)	450	411	323	322	317
万元GDP用水量 （立方米/万元）	Water Consumption per 10000 Yuan of GDP (cu.m/10000 yuan)	103	61	37	33	31
万元工业增加值用水量 （立方米/万元）	Water Consumption per 10000 Yuan of Value-added of Industry (cu.m/10000 yuan)	65	37	21	17	15

7−22 环境保护基本情况

Basic Conditions of Environmental Protection

项　目	item	2010	2015	2020	2021	2022
水环境	**Water Environment**					
优良水体比例 (%)	Proportion of Excellent Water (%)					
地表水国考断面	National Examination Section of Surface water		77.5	87.3	90.5	92.6
地表水省考断面	Provincial Section of Surface Water		76.2	86.3	87.5	92.2
劣V类水体比例 (%)	Proportion of Inferior Class V water (%)					
地表水国考断面	National Examination Section of Surface water		8.5	0.0	1.4	0.0
地表水省考断面	Provincial Section of Surface Water		9.8	1.2	1.2	0.0
大气环境	**Atmospheric Environment**					
二氧化硫浓度 (微克/立方米)	Sulfur Dioxide Concentration (microgram / cubic meter)		12	8	8	8
二氧化氮浓度 (微克/立方米)	Nitrogen Dioxide Concentration (microgram / cubic meter)		24	21	22	19
颗粒物PM10浓度 (微克/立方米)	Respirable Suspended Particulates Concentration (microgram / cubic meter)		47	38	40	34
颗粒物PM2.5浓度(微克/立方米)	Fine Suspended Particulates Concentration (microgram / cubic meter)		31	22	22	20
一氧化碳浓度 (毫克/立方米)	Carbon Monoxide Concentration (milligram / cubic meter)		1.3	1.0	0.9	0.9
臭氧浓度 (微克/立方米)	Ozone Concentration (microgram / cubic meter)		126	138	144	157
空气质量达二级标准城市数 (个)	Number of Cities Meeting Grade Ⅱ Air Quality Standard (unit)	21	16	20	18	14
生态环境	**Ecological Environment**					
人均耕地面积 (亩)	Per Capita Area of Cultivated Land (mu)	0.37	0.36	0.23	0.23	0.22
新增水土流失治理面积 (千公顷)	Area of Soil Erosion under Control (1000 hectares)	44.56	72.61	95.63	80.83	86.85
森林面积 (万公顷)	Forest Area (10000 hectares)	1036.28	1086.11	1053.22	1054.70	
森林覆盖率 (%)	Forest Coverage Rate (%)	57.00	58.88	58.66	58.74	
人均森林面积 (公顷)	Per Capita Forest Area (hectare)	0.1	0.1	0.1	0.1	
活立木蓄积量 (万立方米)	Volume of Standing Forest Stock (10000 cu.m)	43936	56636	60422	62824	
森林蓄积量 (万立方米)	Stock Volume of Forest (10000 cu.m)	43190	56128	58400	62370	
当年造林面积 (万公顷)	Afforested Area in Current Year (10000 hectares)	30.77	107.34	78.07	17.56	17.72
自然保护区数 (个)	Number of Natural Reserves (unit)	357	377	377	377	377
自然保护区面积 (万公顷)	Area of Natural Reserves (10000 hectares)	164.44	168.89	169.50	169.50	169.50

7-22 续表 continued

项　　目	item	2010	2015	2020	2021	2022
城市环境	**Urban Environment**					
城市供水普及率 (%)	Popularization Rate of Tap Water in Urban Areas (%)	98.4	98.5		100.0	100.0
城市污水排放量 (万吨)	Volume of Municipal Sewage Discharge (10000 tons)	506546	671363	830750	961591	999541
城市污水处理量 (万吨)	Volume of Municipal Sewage Disposal (10000 tons)	436041	628706	811273	944597	983837
城市污水处理厂集中处理率(%)	Rate of Municipal Sewage Disposal (%)	73.1	93.3	97.6	97.6	98.0
城市生活垃圾无害化处理率(%)	Rate of Harmless Disposal of Urban Domestic Waste (%)	72.1	91.6	99.95	100.0	100.0
城市燃气普及率 (%)	Popularization Rate of Gas in Urban Areas (%)	95.8	97.6	98.8	98.2	98.6
城市人均公园绿地面积(平方米)	Per Capita Urban Public Green Area (sq.m)	13.29	17.40	17.87	17.49	17.68
建成区绿化覆盖率 (%)	Green Coverage Rate in Built-up Areas (%)	41.3	41.4	43.4	42.3	43.9
城市公共交通车辆运营数 (标台)	Number of Public Transportation Vehicles (Unit)	45850	62947	77687	76570	74032
农村环境	**Rural Environment**					
农村自来水普及率 (%)	Popularization Rate of Tap Water in Rural Areas (%)	59.5	83.4	92.7	99.1	99.3
无害化卫生厕所普及率 (%)	Popularization Rate of Harmless Sanitary Toilets (%)	77.7	87.2	99.0	99.4	95.9
农村沼气池产气总量 (万立方米)	Total Output of Biogas from Rural Biogas Pools (10000 cu.m)	18724	36617	21443	33661	44900
自然灾害	**Natural Disasters**					
地质灾害次数 (次)	Number of Geological Disasters (unit)	600	191	230	3	352
地质灾害直接经济损失 (万元)	Direct Economic Loss due to Geological Disasters (10000 yuan)	22732	3666	1956	21	16261
海洋灾害发生次数 (次)	Number of Marine Disasters (time)	14	9	24	35	38
海洋灾害直接经济损失 (亿元)	Direct Economic Loss due to Marine Disasters (100 million yuan)		28.77	0.49	0.28	7.65
森林火灾次数 (次)	Number of Forest Fires (time)	59	273	114	98	45

注：1.2022年森林面积、森林覆盖率、人均森林面积、活立木蓄积量、森林蓄积量数据暂缺。

2.2022年农村卫生厕所普及率的统计参照《农村三格式户厕建设技术规范》(GBT 38836-2020)开展。

Note: a)Data on forest area, forest coverage rate, per capita forest area, volume of standing forest stock and stock volume of forest in 2022 are temporarily lacking.

b)The statistics of the penetration rate of rural sanitary toilets in 2022 is carried out according to the Technical Code for the Construction of Rural Three-format Household Toilets(GBT 38836-2020).

7-23 各市水环境质量情况（2022年）

Statistics on Water Environment Quality by City(2022)

单位：% (%)

市 别	City	国控地表水断面 State Controlled Surface Water Sections		省考地表水断面 Provincial Surface Water Section	
		优良率 Excellent Rate	劣V类比例 Proportion of Inferior to Class V	优良率 Excellent Rate	劣V类比例 Proportion of Inferior to Class V
全 省	**Provincial Total**	**92.6**	**0.0**	**92.2**	**0.0**
广 州	Guangzhou	92.3	0.0	85.0	0.0
深 圳	Shenzhen	91.7	0.0	95.2	0.0
珠 海	Zhuhai	100.0	0.0	100.0	0.0
汕 头	Shantou	80.0	0.0	85.7	0.0
佛 山	Foshan	85.7	0.0	85.7	0.0
韶 关	Shaoguan	100.0	0.0	100.0	0.0
河 源	Heyuan	100.0	0.0	100.0	0.0
梅 州	Meizhou	100.0	0.0	100.0	0.0
惠 州	Huizhou	100.0	0.0	94.7	0.0
汕 尾	Shanwei	100.0	0.0	100.0	0.0
东 莞	Dongguan	85.7	0.0	88.9	0.0
中 山	Zhongshan	100.0	0.0	100.0	0.0
江 门	Jiangmen	83.3	0.0	93.3	0.0
阳 江	Yangjiang	100.0	0.0	100.0	0.0
湛 江	Zhanjiang	100.0	0.0	83.3	0.0
茂 名	Maoming	90.9	0.0	86.7	0.0
肇 庆	Zhaoqing	100.0	0.0	100.0	0.0
清 远	Qingyuan	100.0	0.0	90.9	0.0
潮 州	Chaozhou	75.0	0.0	85.7	0.0
揭 阳	Jieyang	40.0	0.0	63.6	0.0
云 浮	Yunfu	100.0	0.0	100.0	0.0

7-24 各市大气环境质量情况（2022年）

Statistics on Atmospheric Environmental Quality by City(2022)

市 别	City	SO2年平均浓度(μg/m3) Annual Average Concentration of Sulfur Dioxide (μg/m3)	NO2年平均浓度(μg/m3) Annual Average Concentration of Nitrogen Dioxide (μg/m3)	颗粒物PM10年平均浓度(μg/m3) Annual Average Concentration of Respirable Suspended Particulates (μg/m3)	颗粒物PM2.5年平均浓度(μg/m3) Annual Average Concentration of Fine Suspended Particulates (μg/m3)	O3-8h第90百分位数浓度(μg/m3) O3-8h 90th Percentile Concentration (μg/m3)	CO第95百分位数浓度(mg/m3) 95th Percentile Concentration of CO (mg/m3)	空气质量达到及好于二级的天数(天) Days with Air Quality Reaching or Better than Grade II (day)	AQI达标率(%) AQI Compliance Rate (%)
全 省	**Provincial Total**	**8**	**19**	**34**	**20**	**157**	**0.9**	**6999**	**91.3**
广 州	Guangzhou	6	29	39	22	179	1.0	306	83.8
深 圳	Shenzhen	5	20	31	16	147	0.8	336	92.1
珠 海	Zhuhai	8	19	30	17	160	0.8	328	89.9
汕 头	Shantou	9	14	33	17	142	0.8	350	95.9
佛 山	Foshan	6	29	38	21	184	1.0	307	84.1
韶 关	Shaoguan	11	15	35	22	155	0.9	336	92.1
河 源	Heyuan	4	16	31	18	142	1.0	351	96.2
梅 州	Meizhou	6	18	28	18	135	0.8	362	99.2
惠 州	Huizhou	5	16	33	17	151	0.8	342	93.7
汕 尾	Shanwei	7	8	27	15	134	0.8	354	97.0
东 莞	Dongguan	8	26	36	20	189	1.0	292	80.0
中 山	Zhongshan	5	22	34	19	184	0.8	305	83.6
江 门	Jiangmen	7	27	40	20	194	1.0	299	81.9
阳 江	Yangjiang	7	16	34	21	146	0.8	347	95.1
湛 江	Zhanjiang	9	12	32	21	138	0.8	352	96.4
茂 名	Maoming	11	12	35	19	138	0.9	355	97.3
肇 庆	Zhaoqing	9	23	35	22	175	0.9	314	86.0
清 远	Qingyuan	6	18	33	21	161	1.0	328	89.9
潮 州	Chaozhou	10	14	33	20	143	0.9	351	96.2
揭 阳	Jieyang	8	16	41	23	146	0.9	351	96.2
云 浮	Yunfu	12	20	40	21	153	0.9	333	91.7

7-25 各市城市建设基本情况

Basic Statistics on Urban Sanitation by City

市别	City	城市污水处理率 (%) Rate of Sewage Treatment				城市生活垃圾无害化处理率 (%) Rate of Consumption Waste Treatment			
		2010	2015	2021	2022	2010	2015	2021	2022
全省	**Province Total**	**73.1**	**93.7**	**98.2**	**98.4**	**72.1**	**91.6**	**100.0**	**100.0**
广州	Guangzhou	88.1	93.2	97.7	99.4	92.0	95.2	100.0	100.0
深圳	Shenzhen	88.9	96.6	98.3	96.1	94.6	100.0	100.0	100.0
珠海	Zhuhai	84.7	95.7	99.6	99.2	92.3	100.0	100.0	100.0
汕头	Shantou	57.9	90.2	98.7	99.1	64.4	92.6	100.0	100.0
佛山	Foshan	79.7	94.4	101.3	104.1	95.6	100.0	100.0	100.0
韶关	Shaoguan	53.6	86.2	101.9	100.0	100.0	100.0	100.0	100.0
河源	Heyuan	43.0	92.9	97.7	96.9	96.5	100.0	100.0	100.0
梅州	Meizhou	33.7	88.6	99.0	100.0	100.0	100.0	100.0	100.0
惠州	Huizhou	71.5	97.6	98.0	90.7	100.0	100.0	100.0	100.0
汕尾	Shanwei	18.6	89.1	96.5	98.7		100.0	100.0	100.0
东莞	Dongguan	91.1	96.5	97.2	98.0	100.0	100.0	100.0	100.0
中山	Zhongshan	85.1	96.0	89.6	99.1	100.0	100.0	100.0	100.0
江门	Jiangmen	63.5	91.6	97.5	98.1	100.0	100.0	100.0	100.0
阳江	Yangjiang	54.6	85.5	119.4	100.0	100.0	100.0	100.0	100.0
湛江	Zhanjiang	39.6	88.5	96.7	99.6	97.4	100.0	100.0	100.0
茂名	Maoming	34.4	88.4	103.3	123.2		100.0	100.0	100.0
肇庆	Zhaoqing	70.5	85.1	96.7	99.0	83.8	100.0	100.0	100.0
清远	Qingyuan	70.4	87.6	93.8	97.9	100.0	100.0	100.0	100.0
潮州	Chaozhou	33.5	79.7	106.7	120.2	100.0	79.3	100.0	100.0
揭阳	Jieyang	20.8	89.8	97.0	96.9	90.0	95.0	100.0	100.0
云浮	Yunfu	63.7	93.1	96.9	99.1	100.0	100.0	100.0	100.0

7-25 续表 continued

市 别	City	城市公共交通车辆标准运营数（标台）Number of Public Transportation Vehicles (unit)				城市人均公园绿地面积（平方米）Per Capital Area of Parks and Green Land in City (sq.m)			
		2010	2015	2021	2022	2010	2015	2021	2022
全 省	**Province Total**	**45850**	**62947**	**76570**	**74032**	**13.29**	**17.40**	**17.49**	**17.68**
广 州	Guangzhou	10232	16179	18842	18138	11.87	21.82	24.51	23.66
深 圳	Shenzhen	14677	17943	19820	18564	16.40	16.91	12.44	12.58
珠 海	Zhuhai	1557	2349	3117	3205	13.70	19.50	22.18	22.25
汕 头	Shantou	1111	1253	2279	2225	12.20	15.01	11.97	15.25
佛 山	Foshan	3715	6783	7164	6984	10.20	14.69	19.25	19.58
韶 关	Shaoguan	460	635	776	749	11.80	12.50	15.59	16.75
河 源	Heyuan	294	330	520	520	12.10	12.55	14.62	13.88
梅 州	Meizhou	238	925	1816	1758	11.80	16.70	16.76	16.95
惠 州	Huizhou	1124	2446	3144	3045	11.10	17.75	16.15	16.14
汕 尾	Shanwei	199	344	1311	1102	10.70	13.48	10.79	11.66
东 莞	Dongguan	6129	5346	6650	6650	15.30	19.36	21.61	19.56
中 山	Zhongshan	2151	2436	2657	2902	11.90	18.39	11.80	15.05
江 门	Jiangmen	924	1524	1872	1872	11.00	17.75	20.17	20.39
阳 江	Yangjiang	143	242	412	399	10.60	11.17	21.92	20.99
湛 江	Zhanjiang	735	1167	1246	1095	12.70	13.94	13.71	17.19
茂 名	Maoming	392	511	1134	1032	10.00	13.74	17.68	17.71
肇 庆	Zhaoqing	443	814	1145	1187	22.70	20.73	17.57	19.24
清 远	Qingyuan	633	778	1147	1064	11.30	13.03	15.04	14.81
潮 州	Chaozhou	140	192	388	380	10.30	10.57	13.71	13.92
揭 阳	Jieyang	377	387	651	718	12.90	8.65	13.84	15.15
云 浮	Yunfu	176	362	480	444	12.10	12.70	17.49	19.55

注：标台营运数为不含轨道交通数。
Note: Data of track transport is not included in the number of vehicles.

主要统计指标解释

能源生产总量　指一定时期内全国（地区）一次能源生产量的总和，是观察全国（地区）能源生产水平、规模、构成和发展速度的总量指标。一次能源生产量包括原煤、原油、天然气、水电、核能及其他动力能（如风能、地热能等）发电量。不包括低热值燃料生产量、生物质能、太阳能等的利用和由一次能源加工转换而成的二次能源产量。

能源消费总量　指一定时期内全国（地区）生产和生活消费的各种能源的总和，是观察能源消费水平、构成和增长速度的总量指标，能源消费总量包括原煤和原油及其制品、天然气、电力。不包括低热值燃料、生物质能和太阳能等的利用 。能源消费总量分为三部分，即终端能源消费量、能源加工转换损失量和损失量。

(1)终端能源消费量　指一定时期内全国（地区）生产和生活消费的各种能源在扣除了用于加工转换二次能源消费量和损失量以后的数量。

(2)能源加工转换损失量　指一定时期内全国（地区）投入加工转换的各种能源数量之和与产出各种能源产品之和的差额。它是观察能源在加工转换过程中损失量变化的指标。

(3)能源损失量　指一定时期内能源在输送、分配、储存过程中发生的损失和由客观原因造成的各种损失量。不包括各种气体能源放空、放散量。

能源生产弹性系数　是研究能源生产增长速度与国民经济增长速度之间关系的指标。计算公式：

$$能源生产弹性系数=\frac{能源生产总量增长速度}{国民经济增长速度}$$

国民经济增长速度，可根据不同的目的或需要，用国民生产总值，国内生产总值等指标来计算，本资料是采用国内生产总值指标计算的。

电力生产弹性系数　是研究电力生产增长速度与国民经济增长速度之间关系的指标。一般来说，电力的发展应当快于国民经济的发展，也就是说电力应超前发展。计算公式：

$$电力生产弹性系数=\frac{电力生产量增长速度}{国民经济增长速度}$$

能源消费弹性系数　是反映能源消费增长速度与国民经济增长速度之间比例关系的指标。计算公式：

$$能源消费弹性系数=\frac{能源消费量增长速度}{国民经济增长速度}$$

电力消费弹性系数　是反映电力消费增长速度与国民经济增长速度之间比例关系的指标。计算公式：

$$电力消费弹性系数=\frac{电力消费量增长速度}{国民经济增长速度}$$

能源加工转换效率　指一定时期内能源经过加工、转换后，产出的各种能源产品的数量与同期内投入加工转换的各种能源数量的比率。它是观察能源加工转换装置和生产工艺先进与落后、管理水平高低等的重要指标。计算公式：

$$能源加工转换效率=\frac{能源加工、转换产出量}{能源加工、转换投入量}\times 100\%$$

土地资源　土地指陆地的表层部分，它主要由岩石、岩石的风化物和土壤构成。土地资源按利用类型可以分为农用地、建筑用地和未利用地。农用地包括耕地、园地、林地、牧草地和水面。建筑用地包括居民点及工矿用地、交通用地和水利设施用地。未利用地指农用地和建筑用地以外的土地，包括滩涂、荒漠、戈壁、冰川和石山等。

耕地面积 指经过开垦用以种植农作物并经常进行耕耘的土地面积。包括种有作物的土地面积、休闲地、新开荒地和抛荒未满三年的土地面积。

林业用地面积 指生长乔木、竹类、灌木、沿海红树林等林木的土地面积，包括有林地、灌木林、疏林地、未成林造林地、迹地、苗圃等。

草地面积 指牧区和农区用于放牧牲畜或割草，植被盖度在 5% 以上的草原、草坡、草山等面积。包括天然的和人工种植或改良的草地面积。

森林资源 指森林、林木、林地以及依托森林、林木、林地生存的野生动物、植物和微生物。林木指树木和竹子。森林指以乔木为主体的植物群落，是集生的乔木及与共同作用的植物、动物、微生物和土壤、气候等的总体。

活立木总蓄积量 指一定范围内土地上全部树木蓄积的总量，包括森林蓄积、疏林蓄积、散生木蓄积和四旁树蓄积。

森林覆盖率 指一个国家或地区森林面积占土地总面积的百分比。森林覆盖率是反映森林资源的丰富程度和生态平衡状况的重要指标。在计算森林覆盖率时，森林面积包括郁闭度 0.2 以上的乔木林地面积和竹林地面积，国家特别规定的灌木林地面积、农田林网以及四旁(村旁、路旁、水旁、宅旁)林木的覆盖面积。计算公式为:

$$\text{森林覆盖率(\%)}=\frac{\text{森林面积}}{\text{土地总面积}}\times 100\%$$

森林面积 指由乔木树种构成，郁闭度 0.2 以上(含 0.2)的林地或冠幅宽度 10 米以上的林带的面积，即有林地面积。森林面积包括天然起源和人工起源的针叶林面积、阔叶林面积、针阔混交林面积和竹林面积，不包括灌木林地面积和疏林地面积。

森林蓄积量 指一定森林面积上存在着的林木树干部分的总材积。它是反映一个国家或地区森林资源总规模和水平的基本指标之一，也是反映森林资源的丰富程度、衡量森林生态环境优劣的重要依据。

水资源 水在自然界中以固体、液体和气态三种聚集状态存在，分布于海洋、陆地(包括土壤)以及大气之中，通过水循环形成水资源。水资源包括经人类控制并直接可供灌溉、发电、给水、航运、养殖等用途的地表水和地下水，以及江河、湖泊、井、泉、潮汐、港湾和养殖水域等。水资源是发展国民经济不可缺少的重要自然资源。

矿产资源 矿产资源指由地质作用形成的，具有利用价值的，呈固态、液态、气态的自然资源，是社会发展的重要物质基础。

矿产基础储量 基础储量是查明矿产资源的一部分。它能满足现行采矿和生产所需的指标要求，是控制的、探明的并通过可行性或预可行性研究认为属于经济的、边界经济的部分，用未扣除设计、采矿损失的数量表表示。

矿产保有资源储量 指查明的矿产资源储量（资源储量=基础储量+资源量）扣除已开采部分损失量和加减应勘查，重算或其它原因增减量而得出的年底实有资源储量。

Explanatory Notes on Main Statistical Indicators

Total Energy Production refers to the total production of primary energy by all energy producing enterprises in the country (region) in a given period of time. It is a comprehensive indicator of the capacity, scale, composition and development speed of energy production of the country (region). The production of primary energy includes that of coal, crude oil, natural gas, hydropower and electricity generated by nuclear energy and other means such as wind power and geothermal power. However, it excludes the production of fuel of low calorific value, bioenergy, solar energy and secondary energy converted from primary energy.

Total Domestic Energy Consumption refers to the total consumption of energy of various kinds by production sectors and households in the country (region) in a given period of time. It is a comprehensive indicator of the scale, composition and development speed of energy consumption. The total energy consumption includes that of coal, crude oil and their products, natural gas and electricity, but excludes the consumption of fuel of low calorific value, bioenergy and solar energy. Total domestic energy consumption can be divided into three parts:

(1) Final Energy Consumption: This refers to the total energy consumption by production sectors and households in the country (region) in a given period of time, excluding primary energy consumption and loss in the process of conversion into secondary energy.

(2)Loss During the Process of Energy Conversion: This refers to the total input of various kinds of energy for conversion minus the total output of various kinds of energy in the country (region) in a given period of time. It is an indicator of the loss that occurs during the process of energy conversion.

(3)Loss: This refers to the total loss of energy during the course of energy transmission, distribution and storage and the loss caused by any objective reason in a given period of time, excluding the loss of various kinds of gas due to gas discharges and stocktaking.

Elasticity Ratio of Energy Production is an indicator of the relationship between the growth rate of energy production and the growth rate of the national economy. The formula is:

$$\text{Elasticity Ratio of Energy Production} = \frac{\text{Growth Rate of Energy Production}}{\text{Growth Rate of National Economy}}$$

The average annual growth rate of the national economy can be shown by the gross national product, gross domestic product and other indicators, depending on the purposes or needs. The gross domestic product is used in the calculation of the ratio in this chapter.

Elasticity Ratio of Electricity Production is an indicator of the relationship between the growth rate of electricity production and the growth rate of the national economy. Generally speaking, the growth rate of electricity production should be higher than that of the national economy; in other words, electricity production should develop in advance of the national economy. Its formula is:

$$\text{Elasticity Ratio of Electricity Production} = \frac{\text{Growth Rate of Electricity Production}}{\text{Growth Rate of National Economy}}$$

Elasticity Ratio of Energy Consumption is an indicator of the relationship between the growth rate of energy consumption and the growth rate of the national economy. The formula is:

$$\text{Elasticity Ratio of Energy Consumption} = \frac{\text{Growth Rate of Energy Consumption}}{\text{Growth Rate of National Economy}}$$

Elasticity Ratio of Electricity Consumption is an indicator of the relationship between the growth rate of electricity consumption and the growth rate of the national economy. The formula is:

$$\text{Elasticity Ratio of Electricity Consumption} = \frac{\text{Growth Rate of Electricity Consumption}}{\text{Growth Rate of National Economy}}$$

Efficiency of Energy Processing and Conversion refers to the ratio of the total output of energy products of various kinds after processing and conversion to the total input of energy of various kinds for processing and conversion in the same reference period. It is an important indicator of the current conditions of energy processing and conversion equipment, production technique and management. The formula is:

$$\text{Efficiency of Energy Processing \& Conversion} = \frac{\text{Output of Energy after Processing \& Conversion}}{\text{Input of Energy for Processing \& Conversion}} \times 100\%$$

Land Resource Land refers to the surface of the earth，consisting of mainly rocks and its weathering and earth. Land resource can be classified，by its utilization，as land for agriculture，land for construction and unused land. Land for agriculture includes cultivated land，plantation，forestland，grassland and waters. Land for construction includes land for residential purpose, for manufacturing and mining, for transportation and for water conservancy projects. Unused land refers to land other than land for agriculture and construction, including beaches, deserts, Gobi, glaciers and rock mountains.

Area of Cultivated Land refers to area of land reclaimed for the regular cultivation of various farm crops, including crop-cover land, fallow, newly reclaimed land and land laid idle for less than 3 years.

Area of Afforested Land refers to land for trees, bamboos, bushes and mangrove including forest-cover land, bush-covered land, sparse forest land, land planned for forestation, slash and nurseries of young trees.

Area of Grassland refers to areas of grassland, grass-slopes and grass-covered hills with a vegetation-covering rate of over 5% that are used for animal husbandry or harvesting of grass. It includes natural, cultivated and improved grassland areas.

Forest Resource refers to forests, trees, forestland and wild animals, plants and microorganism that live on forests and trees. Trees include trees and bamboos. Forest refers to the population of clusters of trees and other plants, animals and microorganism as well as the earth and climate that have interactions with the trees.

Total Standing Stock Volume refers to the total stock volume of trees growing in land, including trees in forests, tress in sparse forests, scattered trees and trees planted by the side of villages, farm houses and along roads and rivers.

Forest Coverage Rate refers to the ratio of area of afforested land to total land area. It is a very important indicator that reflects the status of abundance of forest resource and ecosystem balance. Forest area includes the area of trees and bamboo growing with a canopy density above 0.2, the area of shrubby trees according to regulations of the government, the area of forest land inside farm land and the area of trees planted by the side of villages, farm houses and along roads and rivers. The formula for calculating forest coverage rate is as follows:

$$\text{Forest Coverage Rate (\%)} = \frac{\text{Area of Afforested Land}}{\text{Area of Total Land}} \times 100\%$$

Forest Area refers to wooded area, i.e. the area of forest where trees and bamboo grow with a canopy density above 0.2 (inclusive) or a crown width above 10 meters, including natural and planted coniferous forest, broad-leaved forest, mixed forest, and bamboo groves, but excluding shrubbery and open forest.

Stock Volume of Forest refers to total stock volume of wood growing in forest area, which shows the total size and level of forest resources of a country or a region. It is also an important indicator of the richness of forest resource and the status of forest ecological environment.

Water Resource Water exists in the nature in solid, liquid and gaseous states, is distributed in the ocean, land (including earth) and air, and constitutes water resource through circulation. Water resource includes surface water and underground water that is controlled by human beings for irrigation, power-generation, water supply, navigation and cultivation. It also includes rivers, lakes, wells, springs, tides, gulfs and water area for cultivation. Water resource as an indispensable natural resource for the development of national economy.

Mineral Resources refer to useful natural resources enriched due to geological processes, in the form of solid, liquid or gas. Minerals are important material basis for social development.

Basic Reserves of Mineral Resources Basic reserves are part of total identified mineral resources that meet present mining and production standards, which is the part of reserve controlled, proven, and found to be of economic or marginal value through feasibility assessment or pre-feasibility study. Basic reserves are indicated as a figure including designing and mining loss.

Ensured Reserves of Mineral Resources refer to the actual reserves of mineral resources at the year-end, calculated as the proven reserves of mineral resources (Reserves of Mineral Resources = Basic Reserves + Resource) minus losses in previous extraction processes, plus or minus increases or losses due to exploration, recalculation or other reasons.

八、财政、银行和保险

GOVERNMENT FINANCE, BANKING AND INSURANCE

八 财政、银行和保险

简要说明

一、本篇资料反映广东地方公共财政预算收支、银行、保险等方面的基本情况。

二、本篇资料由广东省统计局综合统计处负责整理、编辑。

三、资料来源：

财政资料根据广东省财政厅提供的历年《广东省财政总决算报表》有关项目加工整理。

银行资料由中国人民银行广州分行提供。

保险业务资料由国家金融监督管理总局广东监管局提供

8 Government Finance，Banking and Insurance

Brief Introduction

Ⅰ. The data in this chapter show the basic situation of local government general budgetary revenue and expenditure, banking and insurance of Guangdong Province.

Ⅱ. The data in this chapter are prepared by the Division of Comprehensive Statistics of Statistics Bureau of Guangdong Province.

Ⅲ. Data sources:

The data on local government finance are prepared in accordance with the related tables of the Total Final Accounts of Government Finance of Guangdong provided by Guangdong Provincial Department of Finance.

The data on banking are provided by Guangzhou Branch of the People's Bank of China.

The data on insurance are provided by Guangdong Financial Supervisory Authority.

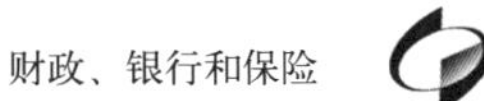

8-1 地方一般公共预算收支和增长速度

Local Government General Public Budget Revenue and Expenditure and Their Growth Rates

单位：亿元 (100 million yuan)

年份 Year	地方一般公共预算收入 Local Government General Public Budget Revenue	#税收收入 Taxes	地方一般公共预算支出 Local Government General Public Budget Expenditure	收支差额 Balance	增长速度(%) Growth Rate (%) 地方一般公共预算收入 Local General Government Public Budget Revenue	地方一般公共预算支出 Local General Government Public Budget Expenditure	地方一般公共预算收入占地区生产总值的比重(%) Percentage of Budgetary Revenue to GDP (%)
1978	41.82	25.78	28.70	13.12	17.9	42.6	22.5
1979	36.25	25.98	29.88	6.37	-13.3	4.1	17.3
1980	37.79	27.72	27.04	10.75	4.2	-9.5	15.1
1981	41.01	30.84	29.60	11.41	8.5	9.5	14.1
1982	42.23	34.72	33.34	8.89	3.0	12.6	12.4
1983	44.29	38.52	37.45	6.84	4.9	12.3	12.0
1984	49.28	43.59	47.18	2.10	11.3	26.0	10.7
1985	69.27	65.25	66.74	2.53	40.6	41.5	12.0
1986	82.41	73.29	89.55	-7.14	19.0	34.2	12.3
1987	95.88	88.65	96.59	-0.71	16.3	7.9	11.3
1988	107.57	119.17	115.20	-7.63	12.2	19.3	9.3
1989	136.87	145.02	141.16	-4.29	27.2	22.5	9.9
1990	131.02	135.62	150.69	-19.67	-4.3	6.8	8.4
1991	177.35	158.31	182.48	-5.13	35.4	21.1	9.4
1992	222.64	195.98	219.61	3.03	25.5	20.3	9.1
1993	346.56	310.78	331.27	15.29	55.7	50.8	10.0
1994	298.70	275.06	416.83	-118.13	-13.8	25.8	6.5
1995	382.34	353.64	525.63	-143.29	28.0	26.1	6.4
1996	479.45	438.25	601.23	-121.78	25.4	14.4	7.0
1997	543.95	494.76	682.66	-138.71	13.5	13.5	7.0
1998	640.75	545.62	825.61	-184.86	17.8	20.9	7.5
1999	766.19	645.28	1034.44	-268.25	19.6	25.3	8.3
2000	910.56	798.61	1069.86	-159.30	18.8	3.4	8.4
2001	1160.51	1014.72	1321.33	-160.82	27.5	23.5	9.6
2002	1201.61	1032.33	1521.08	-319.47	3.5	15.1	8.8
2003	1315.52	1109.50	1695.63	-380.11	9.5	11.5	8.2
2004	1418.51	1191.55	1852.95	-434.44	7.8	9.3	7.6
2005	1807.20	1526.97	2289.07	-481.87	27.4	23.5	8.2
2006	2179.46	1850.44	2553.34	-373.88	20.6	11.5	8.4
2007	2785.80	2415.47	3159.57	-373.77	27.8	23.7	8.8
2008	3310.32	2864.79	3778.57	-468.25	18.8	19.6	9.0
2009	3649.81	3130.61	4334.37	-684.56	10.3	14.7	9.2
2010	4517.04	3803.47	5421.54	-904.50	23.8	25.1	9.8
2011	5514.84	4548.66	6712.40	-1197.56	22.1	23.8	10.4
2012	6229.18	5073.88	7387.86	-1158.68	13.0	10.1	10.9
2013	7081.47	5767.94	8411.00	-1329.53	13.7	13.8	11.3
2014	8065.08	6510.47	9152.64	-1087.56	13.9	8.8	11.8
2015	9366.78	7377.07	12827.80	-3461.01	11.9	40.1	12.5
2016	10390.35	8098.63	13446.09	-3055.74	10.3	4.8	12.6
2017	11320.35	8871.89	15037.48	-3717.13	10.9	11.8	12.4
2018	12105.26	9737.51	15729.26	-3624.00	7.9	4.6	12.1
2019	12654.53	10063.95	17297.85	-4643.32	4.5	10.0	11.8
2020	12923.85	9881.95	17430.79	-4506.94	2.1	0.8	11.7
2021	14105.04	10785.23	18247.01	-4141.97	9.1	4.7	11.3
2022	13260.88	9286.11	18533.08	-5272.20	-6.0	1.6	10.3

注：2015年起，地方公共财政预算收入和地方公共财政预算支出统一更名为地方一般公共预算收入和地方一般公共预算支出，财政收入按可比口径计算。

Note: From 2015, the name of local government budgetary revenue and local government budgetary expenditure have been changed to local public budgetary revenue and local public budgetary expenditure.Growth rates of revenue are caculated by comparable caliber.

8-2 地方一般公共预算收支基本情况

Basic Items of General Public Budget Revenue and Expenditure

单位：亿元 (100 million yuan)

指　　标	Item	2010	2015	2018	2019	2020	2021	2022
一、地方一般公共预算收入	**General Public Budget Revenue**	**4517.04**	**9366.78**	**12105.26**	**12654.53**	**12923.85**	**14105.04**	**13260.88**
税收收入	Tax Revenue	3803.47	7377.07	9737.51	10063.95	9881.95	10785.23	9286.11
#增值税	Value-added Tax	657.82	1339.16	3922.94	3977.07	3693.94	4091.37	3114.09
企业所得税	Corporate Income Tax	678.75	1303.11	1876.46	2001.21	1946.60	2111.31	1880.53
个人所得税	Individual Income Tax	287.26	510.14	868.08	656.19	760.88	916.19	985.30
城市维护建设税	City Maintenance and Construction Tax	135.97	457.05	592.94	598.98	581.28	630.05	558.98
房产税	House Property Tax	122.44	241.00	361.21	356.76	315.94	374.14	430.69
印花税	Stamp Tax	69.93	141.41	152.27	152.10	166.46	196.79	201.21
土地增值税	Land Appreciation Tax	189.79	576.75	1056.11	1402.89	1375.09	1392.05	1243.62
耕地占用税	Farm Land Occupation Tax	56.03	95.38	53.78	58.34	58.71	50.96	59.92
契税	Deed Tax	235.51	427.24	601.70	640.89	783.82	809.80	597.03
非税收入	Non-tax Revenue	713.57	1989.71	2367.74	2590.58	3041.90	3319.80	3974.77
专项收入	Special Program Receipts	97.35	598.77	956.92	892.51	974.77	1199.34	1217.41
行政事业性收费收入	Charge of Administrative and Units	293.43	408.19	230.79	292.06	226.87	292.42	284.35
罚没收入	Penalty Receipts	95.62	155.77	236.07	231.11	238.46	263.19	418.65
国有资本经营收入	Operation Income from State-owned Assets	90.00	62.70	40.74	90.03	93.26	101.15	204.73
国有资源(资产)有偿使用收入	Income from Use of State-owned Resources Assets	81.88	355.19	562.62	731.60	1190.99	1110.55	1472.94
其他收入	Other Non-tax Revenue	55.29	409.09	340.59	353.28	317.54	353.14	376.69
二、地方一般公共预算支出	**General Public Budget Expenditure**	**5421.54**	**12827.80**	**15729.26**	**17297.85**	**17430.79**	**18247.01**	**18533.08**
#一般公共服务	Expenditure for General Public Services	685.39	1018.91	1556.29	1855.32	1889.53	1828.89	1773.74
教育	Expenditure for Education	921.48	2040.65	2792.90	3210.51	3510.56	3796.69	3871.14
科学技术	Expenditure for Science and Technology	214.44	569.55	1034.71	1168.79	955.73	982.76	983.78
文化旅游体育与传媒	Expenditure for Culture, Tourism, Sports and Media	166.16	194.58	321.84	350.33	417.22	395.59	350.19
社会保障和就业	Expenditure for Social Safety Net and Employment Effort	469.58	1064.91	1508.02	1703.48	1807.20	2131.89	2153.96
卫生健康	Expenditure for Health Care	304.04	918.36	1407.51	1579.60	1772.99	1857.10	2081.25
节能环保	Expenditure for Energy Conservation and Environment Protection	239.16	322.33	567.41	747.44	517.76	493.55	464.89
城乡社区	Expenditure for Urban and Rural Community Affairs	407.64	1174.16	2083.14	2413.84	1574.89	1556.64	1429.03
农林水	Expenditure for Agriculture, Forestry and Water Conservancy	325.02	811.90	909.78	957.68	1125.81	1109.47	1067.57
交通运输	Expenditure for Transportation	318.17	1982.63	617.33	525.23	652.43	728.22	759.61
其他支出	Other Expenditure	331.54	428.10	100.62	39.55	30.47	43.99	46.77

8-3 各市地方一般公共预算收支

Local Government General Budgetary Revenue and Expenditure by City

单位：亿元

市别	City	地方一般公共预算收入 Local Government General Budgetary Revenue								
		2000	2005	2010	2015	2018	2019	2020	2021	2022
全　省	**Provincial Total**	**910.56**	**1807.20**	**4517.04**	**9366.78**	**12105.26**	**12654.53**	**12923.85**	**14105.04**	**13260.88**
广　州	Guangzhou	200.55	371.26	872.65	1349.47	1634.22	1699.04	1722.79	1884.26	1855.10
深　圳	Shenzhen	221.92	412.38	1106.82	2726.85	3538.44	3773.38	3857.46	4257.70	4012.44
珠　海	Zhuhai	24.23	48.97	124.53	269.96	331.47	344.49	379.13	448.19	437.41
汕　头	Shantou	18.94	29.44	72.65	131.26	131.52	138.25	143.47	146.35	127.98
佛　山	Foshan	59.53	130.85	306.05	557.55	703.14	731.62	753.56	808.26	796.76
韶　关	Shaoguan	8.63	19.93	47.81	85.23	94.70	101.05	105.12	109.08	89.40
河　源	Heyuan	2.55	8.52	25.09	67.48	76.95	77.48	79.81	84.30	69.32
梅　州	Meizhou	7.18	15.18	38.95	103.59	97.09	91.59	88.19	95.01	82.22
惠　州	Huizhou	12.94	34.72	131.23	340.02	393.01	400.86	412.25	455.39	441.73
汕　尾	Shanwei	4.16	7.09	26.23	28.83	41.83	42.45	46.01	52.77	61.30
东　莞	Dongguan	30.22	103.97	277.84	517.97	649.91	673.27	694.75	769.57	766.13
中　山	Zhongshan	17.46	54.26	139.38	287.51	315.23	283.42	287.57	316.47	316.04
江　门	Jiangmen	21.24	41.63	104.29	199.01	244.05	256.83	264.00	279.87	263.03
阳　江	Yangjiang	3.89	8.70	26.77	67.93	62.62	64.30	65.70	77.67	76.35
湛　江	Zhanjiang	12.44	24.01	66.23	121.86	121.84	131.27	137.78	160.40	136.94
茂　名	Maoming	9.08	21.26	51.95	113.92	136.14	139.89	142.66	148.42	140.69
肇　庆	Zhaoqing	10.97	20.44	76.80	143.36	106.04	114.21	124.51	146.46	160.84
清　远	Qingyuan	4.53	13.25	72.79	108.38	111.90	118.54	123.62	137.42	141.01
潮　州	Chaozhou	4.60	8.64	23.25	47.20	47.37	48.01	48.63	51.77	49.22
揭　阳	Jieyang	9.24	11.19	38.65	77.40	79.34	73.02	73.97	79.31	71.39
云　浮	Yunfu	3.65	9.33	23.54	58.70	57.64	60.48	65.89	75.24	99.83
按经济区域分	By Region									
珠三角	Pearl River Delta	599.06	1218.48	3139.58	6391.70	7915.51	8277.11	8496.03	9366.17	9049.47
东　翼	Eastern Region	36.94	56.38	160.78	284.69	300.07	301.73	312.09	330.21	309.90
西　翼	Western Region	25.41	53.96	144.95	303.71	320.59	335.46	346.15	386.49	353.99
山　区	Mountainous Region	26.54	66.21	208.18	423.38	438.28	449.14	462.62	501.05	481.78

8-3 续表 continued

单位：亿元

市 别	City	地方一般公共预算支出 Local Government General Budgetary Expenditure								
		2000	2005	2010	2015	2018	2019	2020	2021	2022
全　省	**Provincial Total**	**1069.86**	**2289.07**	**5421.54**	**12827.80**	**15729.26**	**17297.85**	**17430.79**	**18247.01**	**18533.08**
广　州	Guangzhou	240.72	438.41	977.32	1727.72	2506.18	2865.33	2952.65	3021.18	3022.45
深　圳	Shenzhen	225.04	599.16	1266.07	3521.67	4282.56	4552.73	4178.42	4570.22	4997.38
珠　海	Zhuhai	31.14	57.77	166.41	388.77	572.52	615.74	677.62	786.66	754.13
汕　头	Shantou	27.90	50.14	121.71	280.98	327.10	386.54	427.26	412.92	379.75
佛　山	Foshan	72.48	150.85	363.35	799.93	806.54	941.32	1003.04	1072.01	1022.33
韶　关	Shaoguan	19.94	44.55	100.24	287.07	338.73	377.59	370.14	370.19	356.47
河　源	Heyuan	16.78	37.00	94.55	268.38	331.15	370.22	361.76	347.08	335.92
梅　州	Meizhou	23.84	46.25	117.98	376.37	445.14	443.84	474.35	443.07	449.51
惠　州	Huizhou	20.14	52.41	185.44	486.07	544.22	614.86	637.37	663.31	693.03
汕　尾	Shanwei	9.99	20.05	56.51	212.95	251.92	278.92	266.51	279.62	296.72
东　莞	Dongguan	33.61	117.04	289.83	581.24	765.41	863.01	840.33	882.53	861.60
中　山	Zhongshan	19.24	56.71	145.85	355.37	437.92	411.74	375.63	472.48	463.10
江　门	Jiangmen	28.18	54.24	132.98	292.90	377.88	421.24	442.38	460.25	450.67
阳　江	Yangjiang	11.00	23.17	64.92	170.91	226.21	242.34	249.84	242.62	271.39
湛　江	Zhanjiang	27.82	57.95	153.65	412.36	481.37	503.10	538.59	547.39	535.56
茂　名	Maoming	20.67	45.28	122.49	346.78	425.12	458.12	479.75	489.54	510.14
肇　庆	Zhaoqing	20.09	40.64	127.66	267.71	315.72	351.65	430.58	396.80	397.56
清　远	Qingyuan	16.35	38.15	132.81	292.59	342.01	395.28	411.84	406.78	423.79
潮　州	Chaozhou	11.31	21.36	55.99	147.67	184.89	197.16	217.17	209.97	214.93
揭　阳	Jieyang	19.50	30.99	94.68	276.88	313.74	349.69	374.48	365.75	374.84
云　浮	Yunfu	11.18	23.87	69.28	157.42	215.61	242.99	263.10	255.68	273.54
按经济区域分	By Region									
珠 三 角	Pearl River Delta	690.64	1567.23	3654.91	8421.36	10608.94	11637.61	11538.02	12325.44	12662.25
东　翼	Eastern Region	68.70	122.50	328.89	918.47	1077.65	1212.31	1285.41	1268.25	1266.24
西　翼	Western Region	59.49	126.40	341.06	930.04	1132.70	1203.57	1268.18	1279.55	1317.09
山　区	Mountainous Region	88.09	189.83	514.86	1381.84	1672.63	1829.92	1881.20	1822.80	1839.23

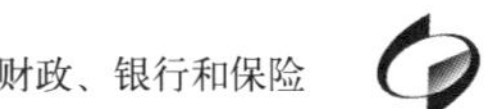

8-4 各市人均地方一般公共预算收入

Per Capita Local Government General Public Budget Revenue by City

单位：元 (yuan)

市 别	City	2000	2005	2010	2015	2018	2019	2020	2021	2022
全 省	**Provincial Total**	**1087.68**	**1974.59**	**4390.34**	**8683.80**	**10753.06**	**11067.94**	**10292.55**	**11146.70**	**10466.03**
广 州	Guangzhou	2061.72	3875.93	7100.70	10153.45	11116.11	11248.07	9299.20	10035.75	9882.06
深 圳	Shenzhen	3327.64	5064.37	10892.78	24613.26	27692.86	28515.59	22209.02	24112.41	22705.45
珠 海	Zhuhai	2024.57	3492.54	8025.47	16621.83	18130.46	17599.19	15858.65	18232.99	17694.79
汕 头	Shantou	409.83	596.51	1368.64	2370.24	2338.90	2446.25	2609.28	2652.74	2311.78
佛 山	Foshan	1146.57	2265.69	4349.20	7544.00	9036.42	9108.59	7953.07	8449.55	8314.83
韶 关	Shaoguan	314.70	686.57	1683.27	2918.61	3168.95	3352.84	3684.42	3816.95	3124.79
河 源	Heyuan	111.86	311.21	860.81	2199.23	2488.34	2499.49	2808.12	2970.08	2439.81
梅 州	Meizhou	188.06	370.01	924.97	2391.27	2218.36	2090.60	2264.01	2452.61	2125.89
惠 州	Huizhou	408.85	946.27	2931.87	7171.79	8181.66	8256.63	6853.94	7512.70	7291.51
汕 尾	Shanwei	170.37	255.84	893.66	956.42	1297.17	1413.00	1717.59	1970.40	2283.23
东 莞	Dongguan	503.97	1585.20	3454.53	6241.63	7767.23	7988.12	6636.08	7322.12	7305.60
中 山	Zhongshan	762.08	2231.98	4578.83	8981.32	9595.95	8472.91	6522.11	7113.32	7103.52
江 门	Jiangmen	540.87	1014.97	2365.62	4407.32	5328.61	5566.01	5524.66	5807.00	5447.34
阳 江	Yangjiang	179.12	375.62	1116.06	2711.43	2456.27	2508.51	2528.64	2972.00	2912.67
湛 江	Zhanjiang	207.35	361.18	950.34	1686.16	1664.81	1786.90	1973.61	2289.50	1947.05
茂 名	Maoming	173.63	366.48	887.70	1878.43	2175.17	2198.76	2319.25	2393.93	2258.69
肇 庆	Zhaoqing	325.95	558.68	1979.41	3541.77	2565.42	2739.21	3033.31	3552.04	3895.28
清 远	Qingyuan	143.50	372.24	1972.39	2832.14	2893.65	3055.15	3118.16	3454.22	3539.13
潮 州	Chaozhou	192.52	343.30	877.50	1760.93	1785.08	1806.18	1888.80	2014.12	1911.50
揭 阳	Jieyang	178.24	200.52	660.97	1280.02	1303.27	1197.53	1319.44	1416.77	1269.08
云 浮	Yunfu	169.61	400.53	1002.33	2393.45	2290.94	2384.84	2764.31	3149.97	4168.42
按经济区域分	By Region									
珠三角	Pearl River Delta	1442.48	2688.72	5717.85	10984.52	12714.12	12985.86	10957.32	11943.50	11535.31
东 翼	Eastern Region	252.38	356.63	960.44	1647.57	1729.46	1732.96	1907.79	2017.93	1887.15
西 翼	Western Region	189.61	365.50	952.37	1922.57	1987.99	2061.61	2200.44	2443.18	2228.63
山 区	Mountainous Region	187.58	423.54	1300.73	2550.51	2602.53	2655.95	2902.57	3143.97	3020.76

注：本表按年中常住人口数计算。

Note: The data in this table are calculated by permanent population of the year.

8-5 各市财政收支（2022年）

单位：亿元

项　　目	Item	全　省 Provincial Total	广　州 Guangzhou
一、地方一般公共预算收入	**General Public Budget Revenue of Local Governments**	**13260.88**	**1855.10**
税收收入	Tax Revenue	9286.11	1256.90
#增值税	Value-added Tax	3114.09	297.96
企业所得税	Corporate Income Tax	1880.53	217.76
个人所得税	Individual Income Tax	985.30	102.80
城市维护建设税	City Maintenance and Construction Tax	558.98	137.45
房产税	House Property Tax	430.69	123.93
土地增值税	Land Appreciation Tax	1243.62	119.56
耕地占用税	Farm Land Occupation Tax	59.92	14.52
契税	Deed Tax	597.03	154.18
非税收入	Non-tax Revenue	3974.77	598.20
专项收入	Special Program Receipts	1217.41	217.40
行政性收费收入	Charge of Administrative and Units	284.35	37.28
罚没收入	Penalty Receipts	418.65	182.60
国有资本经营收入	Operation Income from State-owned Assets	204.73	2.51
国有资源(资产)有偿使用收入	Income from Use of State-owned Resources Assets	1472.94	60.26
其他收入	Other Non-tax Revenue	376.69	98.15
二、地方一般公共预算支出	**General Public Budget Expenditure of Local Governments**	**18533.08**	**3022.45**
#一般公共服务	Expenditure for General Public Services	1773.74	301.01
教育	Expenditure for Education	3871.14	626.94
科学技术	Expenditure for Science and Technology	983.78	198.21
文化旅游体育与传媒	Expenditure for Culture, Tourism, Sports and Media	350.19	54.36
社会保障和就业	Expenditure for Social Safety Net and Employment Effort	2153.96	380.49
卫生健康	Expenditure for Health Care	2081.25	357.75
节能环保	Expenditure for Energy Conservation and Environment Protection	464.89	70.09
城乡社区	Expenditure for Urban and Rural Community Affairs	1429.03	247.97
农林水	Expenditure for Agriculture, Forestry and Water Conservancy	1067.57	83.81
交通运输	Expenditure for Transportation	759.61	78.22

Basic Conditions of Local Government General Public Budget Revenue and Expenditure by City(2022)

(100 million yuan)

深 圳 Shenzhen	珠 海 Zhuhai	汕 头 Shantou	佛 山 Foshan	韶 关 Shaoguan	河 源 Heyuan	梅 州 Meizhou	惠 州 Huizhou	汕 尾 Shanwei
4012.44	**437.41**	**127.98**	**796.76**	**89.40**	**69.32**	**82.22**	**441.73**	**61.30**
3114.45	290.63	75.63	448.74	43.64	34.00	42.02	268.88	25.43
1028.21	62.30	18.95	127.47	8.52	6.22	5.46	69.65	4.74
721.87	64.63	9.82	51.86	3.46	3.37	4.22	28.69	2.39
514.14	30.78	3.59	23.80	2.41	1.08	1.65	9.24	0.58
176.93	24.70	7.65	41.91	6.95	3.08	7.66	25.66	2.03
87.53	15.45	7.70	50.61	4.93	3.07	3.53	20.10	2.30
362.20	37.36	9.92	53.96	2.53	3.32	5.33	47.96	4.87
1.88	1.61	0.40	2.86	1.92	3.94	2.40	4.98	1.22
141.86	38.14	8.84	54.35	4.87	4.31	5.46	36.78	4.04
897.99	146.78	52.35	348.03	45.76	35.33	40.20	172.84	35.87
433.48	104.38	12.65	47.40	5.73	3.14	6.49	59.85	2.00
48.86	5.22	5.48	15.19	2.77	3.46	4.26	12.22	2.34
28.24	8.41	4.73	14.52	4.85	4.81	2.55	17.62	4.06
108.32	1.15	0.56	36.16	2.62	0.26	0.08	7.48	0.61
189.32	24.93	23.33	193.02	22.30	18.00	24.91	45.94	19.54
89.78	2.69	5.61	41.74	7.49	5.65	1.90	29.73	7.32
4997.38	**754.13**	**379.75**	**1022.33**	**356.47**	**335.92**	**449.51**	**693.03**	**296.72**
408.15	71.58	42.06	124.75	42.87	37.13	50.75	75.76	25.48
948.94	116.74	94.65	205.99	61.93	72.04	91.08	144.44	65.78
458.74	41.84	3.34	83.60	2.90	1.86	1.83	27.29	3.73
89.15	22.88	5.77	17.54	5.47	3.93	6.51	17.54	7.04
287.50	75.19	66.94	103.00	62.93	59.62	87.05	89.28	50.16
675.35	56.54	48.33	108.73	38.06	38.64	54.25	71.58	35.90
201.68	15.41	5.85	13.31	8.79	5.01	3.85	13.28	3.24
646.54	77.78	19.01	71.02	16.15	15.42	16.94	75.22	23.77
119.37	19.16	23.98	36.07	54.53	44.34	52.69	50.61	37.60
211.89	26.50	12.20	53.49	14.51	13.47	25.32	17.44	11.60

8-5 续表

单位：亿元

项　目	Item	东 莞 Dongguan	中 山 Zhongshan
一、地方一般公共预算收入	**General Public Budget Revenue of Local Governments**	**766.13**	**316.04**
税收收入	Tax Revenue	558.16	188.71
#增值税	Value-added Tax	223.07	61.64
企业所得税	Corporate Income Tax	61.27	21.21
个人所得税	Individual Income Tax	31.63	7.88
城市维护建设税	City Maintenance and Construction Tax	44.80	16.49
房产税	House Property Tax	38.96	20.88
土地增值税	Land Appriciation Tax	69.78	22.70
耕地占用税	Farm Land Occupation Tax	2.48	1.06
契税	Deed Tax	47.35	21.70
非税收入	Non-tax Revenue	207.97	127.33
专项收入	Special Program Receipts	58.11	28.49
行政性收费收入	Charge of Administrative and Units	21.58	11.71
罚没收入	Penalty Receipts	22.10	9.53
国有资本经营收入	Operation Income from State-owned Assets	16.30	
国有资源(资产)有偿使用收入	Income from Use of State-owned Resources Assets	75.66	61.85
其他收入	Other Non-tax Revenue	14.22	15.74
二、地方一般公共预算支出	**General Public Budget Expenditure of Local Governments**	**861.60**	**463.10**
#一般公共服务	Expenditure for General Public Services	86.68	49.64
教育	Expenditure for Education	215.19	102.17
科学技术	Expenditure for Science and Technology	32.90	28.79
文化旅游体育与传媒	Expenditure for Culture, Tourism, Sports and Media	23.21	9.01
社会保障和就业	Expenditure for Social Safety Net and Employment Effort	57.12	51.12
卫生健康	Expenditure for Health Care	78.26	40.38
节能环保	Expenditure for Energy Conservation and Environment Protection	45.69	15.03
城乡社区	Expenditure for Urban and Rural Community Affairs	42.88	46.31
农林水	Expenditure for Agriculture, Forestry and Water Conservancy	36.59	23.81
交通运输	Expenditure for Transportation	37.89	19.14

continued

(100 million yuan)

江门 Jiangmen	阳江 Yangjiang	湛江 Zhanjiang	茂名 Maoming	肇庆 Zhaoqing	清远 Qingyuan	潮州 Chaozhou	揭阳 Jieyang	云浮 Yunfu
263.03	**76.35**	**136.94**	**140.69**	**160.84**	**141.01**	**49.22**	**71.39**	**99.83**
139.88	47.55	83.25	63.77	74.23	75.26	28.61	29.09	28.51
32.72	12.08	25.53	16.63	15.91	21.44	7.79	-1.47	5.26
14.86	7.56	8.18	6.32	7.31	9.58	2.23	3.42	2.87
5.11	1.31	2.56	1.69	3.01	2.54	1.13	1.08	1.64
12.43	4.56	15.04	9.54	6.20	7.03	2.51	3.76	2.47
16.45	3.64	4.93	3.01	8.05	5.88	2.84	4.18	2.73
17.05	3.81	8.50	8.22	6.31	8.62	2.43	4.97	3.40
3.01	2.38	1.42	2.86	3.59	1.86	1.66	2.24	1.63
20.13	5.71	8.14	8.34	11.83	10.03	3.49	4.59	2.91
123.16	28.80	53.69	76.92	86.61	65.74	20.61	42.31	71.32
23.91	4.00	11.49	7.42	4.96	6.01	3.30	3.40	2.23
6.62	2.86	4.29	8.43	4.83	2.89	1.06	5.06	1.22
7.61	2.73	8.29	6.28	5.67	6.51	5.44	6.36	2.66
14.10	0.01	0.43	2.01	0.09	0.19	0.02	0.79	0.41
67.34	14.78	23.99	49.20	68.92	41.71	8.97	23.80	62.29
3.58	4.41	5.19	3.58	2.15	8.42	1.84	2.89	2.51
450.67	**271.39**	**535.56**	**510.14**	**397.56**	**423.79**	**214.93**	**374.84**	**273.54**
44.68	26.80	48.64	45.80	45.02	43.09	22.91	33.96	37.92
90.05	48.65	127.69	140.42	86.20	92.48	48.13	92.79	57.58
15.93	1.31	1.17	2.47	7.52	2.53	1.17	1.98	0.65
8.36	4.63	6.45	8.43	5.38	6.87	2.88	4.01	2.97
84.10	44.10	117.18	84.67	67.15	69.94	37.62	72.54	43.52
52.39	32.25	73.69	64.59	46.47	46.32	27.01	61.46	30.75
3.35	2.82	6.25	16.43	3.73	5.11	2.24	7.68	2.97
13.87	9.83	15.73	14.99	24.19	18.67	12.30	7.11	11.61
41.08	35.87	49.18	50.21	45.74	59.95	22.39	33.73	30.43
16.54	18.22	18.97	23.45	8.87	12.65	9.96	14.84	13.68

8-6 历年金融机构存贷款

Deposits and Loans in All Financial Institutions

单位：亿元　　(100million yuan)

年 份 Year	金融机构本外币存款余额 Deposits in Renminbi and Foreign Currencies in All Financial Institutions	#住户存款 Savings Deposit by Household	金融机构本外币贷款余额 Loans and Loans in Renminbi and Foreign Currencies in Financial Institutions	金融机构人民币存款余额 Deposits in Renminbi Currencies in Financial Institutions	#人民币住户存款 Savings Deposit by Household in Renminbi	金融机构人民币贷款余额 Loans in Renminbi Currencies in Financial Institutions
2000	19083.64	10031.68	13227.62	16919.98	8667.29	11787.14
2001	21714.85	11386.03	14472.08	19449.34	9930.12	13192.74
2002	25409.90	13372.85	16840.39	22975.88	11819.09	15314.56
2003	29640.83	15590.68	20126.24	27240.23	14061.77	18287.58
2004	33252.01	17631.07	21955.28	30869.62	16193.41	19671.52
2005	38119.91	20267.76	23261.21	35958.71	19051.35	20965.55
2006	43262.20	22677.19	25935.19	41146.58	21584.60	23617.49
2007	48955.03	23013.34	30617.27	47016.48	22242.70	27497.88
2008	56119.28	28181.18	33755.62	54309.57	27481.56	30964.62
2009	69691.46	32136.32	44510.22	67742.59	31411.40	39683.65
2010	82019.40	36965.75	51799.30	79957.97	36318.66	47191.56
2011	91590.15	41061.56	58615.27	89168.60	40405.07	53411.83
2012	105099.55	46265.58	67077.08	99934.60	45533.78	59967.26
2013	119685.15	50638.64	75664.16	114855.02	49891.35	68491.93
2014	127881.47	53215.87	84921.79	121964.85	52410.55	77889.50
2015	160388.22	55008.70	95661.12	153551.79	54238.30	89289.27
2016	179829.19	59768.75	110928.41	171024.47	58618.89	103649.79
2017	194535.75	62942.27	126031.95	184779.60	61890.08	118978.62
2018	208051.16	70293.46	145169.39	199576.08	69231.95	139100.04
2019	232458.64	78959.14	167994.58	222962.37	77943.89	162378.43
2020	267638.26	88976.65	195680.62	257851.63	87969.94	189802.41
2021	293169.22	97598.57	222234.29	282489.30	96634.05	215784.19
2022	322357.66	113554.76	245722.94	312286.48	112555.17	239605.98

注：2015年前，住户存款主要为居民储蓄存款。

Note: Before 2015, the savings by households are mainly savings by residents.

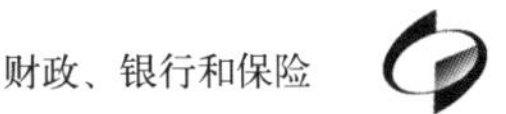

8-7 金融机构本外币存贷款余额

Deposits and Loans in Renminbi and Foreign Currencies in All Financial Institutions

单位：亿元 (100million yuan)

指　　标	Item	2019	2020	2021	2022
一、各项存款	**Total Deposits**	**232458.64**	**267638.26**	**293169.22**	**322357.66**
境内存款	Domestic Deposits	223582.69	257410.78	282596.96	311848.67
住户存款	Deposits of Households	78959.14	88976.65	97598.57	113554.76
活期存款	Demand Deposits	42187.05	46576.09	49607.97	54921.52
定期及其他存款	Time & Other Deposits	36772.10	42400.57	47990.60	58633.24
非金融企业存款	Deposits of Non-financial Enterprises	87267.57	102596.79	110133.55	120746.78
活期存款	Demand Deposits	26923.32	28669.72	29772.63	29956.91
定期及其他存款	Time & Other Deposits	60344.25	73927.07	80360.92	90789.87
广义政府存款	Deposits of Government	37231.19	38421.43	41917.79	44130.53
财政性存款	Fiscal Deposits	3560.84	4304.07	5140.81	4389.18
机关团体存款	Deposits of Government Departments &	33670.35	34117.36	36776.99	39741.35
非银行业金融机构存款	Deposits of Non-banking Financial Institutions	20124.78	27415.91	32947.06	33416.60
境外存款	Overseas Deposits	8875.95	10227.49	10572.25	10509.00
二、各项贷款	**Total Loans**	**167994.58**	**195680.62**	**222234.29**	**245722.94**
境内贷款	Domestic Loans	164261.54	192014.72	218200.07	241522.58
住户贷款	Loans to Households	72312.44	82517.46	93239.77	98214.21
#短期贷款	Short-term Loans	14687.59	13205.25	14771.61	14459.37
中长期贷款	Mid & Long-term Loans	57624.85	69312.21	78468.16	83754.84
非金融企业及机关团体贷款	Loans to Non-financial Enterprises and	91669.98	109221.81	124834.12	143029.86
#短期贷款	Short-term Loans	27252.97	31123.74	32697.21	34246.93
中长期贷款	Mid & Long-term Loans	55386.69	68304.93	79496.95	92867.50
非银行业金融机构贷款	Loans to Non-banking Financial Institutions	279.12	275.45	126.18	278.51
境外贷款	Overseas Loans	3733.05	3665.90	4034.22	4200.36

注：2015年起银行资金来源项目使用新的分类。
Note: Since 2015, new categorization is applied to items of bank fund sources.

8-8 金融机构人民币存贷款余额

Deposits and Loans in Renminbi in All Financial Institutions

单位：亿元 (100 million yuan)

指　　标	Item	2019	2020	2021	2022
一、各项存款	**Total Deposits**	**222962.37**	**257851.63**	**282489.30**	**312286.48**
境内存款	Domestic Deposits	217840.14	251502.64	275598.99	304470.53
住户存款	Deposits of Households	77943.89	87969.94	96634.05	112555.17
活期存款	Demand Deposits	41594.95	45943.18	48985.03	54318.44
定期及其他存款	Time & Other Deposits	36348.94	42026.76	47649.03	58236.72
非金融企业存款	Deposits of Non-financial Enterprises	82738.79	97912.35	104492.67	114585.73
活期存款	Demand Deposits	25199.33	26713.28	27374.28	27633.52
定期及其他存款	Time & Other Deposits	57539.47	71199.07	77118.39	86952.21
广义政府存款	Deposits of Government	37215.83	38409.77	41908.58	44120.07
财政性存款	Fiscal Deposits	3560.84	4304.07	5140.81	4389.18
机关团体存款	Deposits of Government Departments & Organizations	33654.99	34105.70	36767.77	39730.88
非银行业金融机构存款	Deposits of Non-banking Financial Institutions	19941.63	27210.58	32563.69	33209.56
境外存款	Overseas Deposits	5122.23	6349.00	6890.31	7815.95
二、各项贷款	**Total Loans**	**162378.43**	**189802.41**	**215784.19**	**239605.98**
境内贷款	Domestic Loans	161326.61	188651.84	214464.29	237918.53
住户贷款	Loans to Households	72302.73	82512.79	93234.78	98207.90
#短期贷款	Short-term Loans	14679.39	13201.52	14767.38	14453.98
中长期贷款	Mid & Long-term Loans	57623.34	69311.27	78467.40	83753.91
非金融企业及机关团体贷款	Loans to Non-financial Enterprises and Government Departments & Organizations	88744.77	105863.59	121103.34	139434.22
#短期贷款	Short-term Loans	25140.19	28699.38	29969.33	31554.60
中长期贷款	Mid & Long-term Loans	54724.22	67510.75	78625.19	92093.74
非银行业金融机构贷款	Loans to Non-banking Financial Institutions	279.12	275.45	126.18	276.42
境外贷款	Overseas Loans	1051.82	1150.58	1319.90	1687.45

注：2015年起银行资金来源项目使用新的分类。
Note: Since 2015, new categorization is applied to items of bank fund sources.

8-9 各市中资金融机构基本情况

Basic Conditions of Chinese-funded Financial Institutions by City

市别	City	2005				2010			
		机构数(个) Number of Financial Institutions	年末从业人员(人) Number of Employed Persons at the Year-end	人民币存款(亿元) Total Deposits (100 million yuan)	人民币贷款(亿元) Total Loans (100 million yuan)	机构数(个) Number of Financial Institutions	年末从业人员(人) Number of Employed Persons at the Year-end	人民币存款(亿元) Total Deposits (100 million yuan)	人民币贷款(亿元) Total Loans (100 million yuan)
全省合计	**Provincial Total**	**15433**	**222738**	**35783.57**	**20745.27**	**14983**	**258254**	**78285.89**	**46099.26**
广　州	Guangzhou	2053	45800	11065.22	6873.34	2395	58412	22775.49	14597.74
深　圳	Shenzhen	1119	28354	8478.18	6168.03	1286	41483	20210.75	13708.16
珠　海	Zhuhai	417	6798	925.47	424.33	406	7664	2542.56	1203.85
汕　头	Shantou	655	9196	955.34	391.08	632	9476	1849.14	627.91
佛　山	Foshan	1913	21732	3770.74	2056.29	1775	25815	8293.02	4729.61
韶　关	Shaoguan	406	5153	461.78	166.55	401	5317	903.67	346.28
河　源	Heyuan	349	3759	204.20	107.99	325	3828	496.83	335.32
梅　州	Meizhou	635	7373	429.79	206.37	529	6371	835.07	330.25
惠　州	Huizhou	664	8012	781.79	367.23	650	9065	2038.58	1096.21
汕　尾	Shanwei	246	2937	140.77	57.21	217	2965	326.96	130.20
东　莞	Dongguan	1262	14985	2933.40	1500.52	1221	19395	5915.54	3302.49
中　山	Zhongshan	586	7837	1131.19	479.02	568	9017	2596.88	1324.65
江　门	Jiangmen	906	11627	1163.76	534.17	819	11194	2214.97	973.75
阳　江	Yangjiang	289	3986	245.37	99.66	268	3806	564.19	283.93
湛　江	Zhanjiang	931	10663	705.32	285.97	780	10321	1556.00	714.40
茂　名	Maoming	717	7915	521.02	225.46	612	7670	1025.39	361.30
肇　庆	Zhaoqing	551	7120	478.15	229.43	494	6874	1057.35	642.04
清　远	Qingyuan	471	5510	386.23	175.08	447	5620	986.45	510.26
潮　州	Chaozhou	304	4087	324.04	132.34	275	4187	649.81	205.91
揭　阳	Jieyang	613	6120	468.15	169.19	586	6178	963.79	400.68
云　浮	Yunfu	346	3774	213.66	96.02	297	3596	483.45	274.32
按经济区域分	By Region								
珠三角	Pearl River Delta	9471	152265	30727.90	18632.36	9614	188919	67645.13	41578.51
东　翼	Eastern Region	1818	22340	1888.30	749.81	1710	22806	3789.69	1364.70
西　翼	Western Region	1937	22564	1471.71	611.09	1660	21797	3145.59	1359.62
山　区	Mountainous Region	2207	25569	1695.66	752.01	1999	24732	3705.47	1796.43

8-9 续表 continued

市 别	City	2021 机构数(个) Number of Financial Institutions	2021 年末从业人员(人) Number of Employed Persons at the Year-end	2021 人民币存款(亿元) Total Deposits (100 million yuan)	2021 人民币贷款(亿元) Total Loans (100 million yuan)	2022 机构数(个) Number of Financial Institutions	2022 年末从业人员(人) Number of Employed Persons at the Year-end	2022 人民币存款(亿元) Total Deposits (100 million yuan)	2022 人民币贷款(亿元) Total Loans (100 million yuan)
全省合计	**Provincial Total**	**16349**	**347556**	**278763.89**	**212409.63**	**16296**	**348922**	**308385.92**	**236227.69**
广 州	Guangzhou	2699	95669	71463.08	58991.30	2678	93659	77119.84	66682.86
深 圳	Shenzhen	1869	63828	105322.09	72218.17	1896	66555	116577.32	78704.75
珠 海	Zhuhai	490	11106	10121.57	8649.11	496	11408	11408.41	10030.38
汕 头	Shantou	639	10930	4444.39	2460.97	634	10892	4948.44	2765.58
佛 山	Foshan	1722	30932	20035.34	16140.67	1704	31305	23200.95	17968.20
韶 关	Shaoguan	409	5456	2217.74	1494.19	407	5407	2413.05	1640.09
河 源	Heyuan	350	4646	1550.99	1664.13	348	4652	1630.84	1743.69
梅 州	Meizhou	574	6943	2573.49	1754.08	569	6870	2799.87	1967.44
惠 州	Huizhou	740	12317	7201.05	8058.49	746	12440	7774.16	9055.26
汕 尾	Shanwei	209	2937	1051.41	811.78	207	2956	1059.78	982.59
东 莞	Dongguan	1374	25247	19114.29	14003.50	1393	25802	22339.83	15655.23
中 山	Zhongshan	614	11407	6803.61	6251.09	612	11557	7712.98	6784.89
江 门	Jiangmen	865	12598	5730.05	4904.58	862	12551	6412.91	5458.29
阳 江	Yangjiang	277	4420	1737.13	1518.08	275	4195	1964.66	1720.02
湛 江	Zhanjiang	741	11003	4175.58	3139.17	736	10743	4358.81	3649.89
茂 名	Maoming	602	8108	3424.27	2121.35	588	7991	3678.62	2409.42
肇 庆	Zhaoqing	512	8068	3011.24	2623.83	511	8063	3382.11	2926.97
清 远	Qingyuan	460	6672	2797.95	2468.47	458	6702	3032.78	2715.37
潮 州	Chaozhou	294	4450	1725.68	654.53	274	4386	1883.90	734.61
揭 阳	Jieyang	602	7037	2763.62	1354.72	597	7004	3042.14	1410.73
云 浮	Yunfu	307	3782	1499.33	1127.41	305	3784	1644.54	1221.45
按经济区域分	By Region								
珠 三 角	Pearl River Delta	10885	271172	248802.31	191840.75	10898	273340	275928.50	213266.83
东 翼	Eastern Region	1744	25345	9985.10	5282.00	1712	25238	10934.26	5893.52
西 翼	Western Region	1620	23531	9336.99	6778.60	1599	22929	10002.08	7779.32
山 区	Mountainous Region	2100	27499	10639.49	8508.28	2087	27415	11521.07	9288.03

注：1．本表存贷款统计口径为中资金融机构人民币存贷款。
2．机构数和年末从业人员统计范围为银行业及相关金融机构(不含人民银行、外资银行及资产管理公司)。

Notes: a) Deposits and loans in this table refer to the deposits and loans in Renminbi in domestic-funded financial institutions.
b) The number of financial institutions and the number of employed persons at the year-end refer to those in banking and related financial institutions (excluding the People's Bank of China, foreign-funded banks and assets management companies).

8-10 各市金融机构本外币存贷款

Deposits and Loans in Renminbi and Foreign Currencies in All Financial Institutions by City

单位：亿元 (100 million yuan)

市 别	City	各项存款 Total Deposits								
		2000	2005	2010	2015	2018	2019	2020	2021	2022
全省合计	**Provincial Total**	**19083.64**	**38119.91**	**82019.40**	**160388.22**	**208051.16**	**232458.64**	**267638.26**	**293169.22**	**322357.66**
广 州	Guangzhou	6200.47	11734.10	23953.96	42843.67	54788.09	59131.20	67798.81	74988.86	80495.07
深 圳	Shenzhen	3942.00	9486.76	21937.89	57778.90	72550.36	83942.45	101897.31	112545.17	123400.52
珠 海	Zhuhai	521.71	1014.08	2748.70	5383.73	7542.91	9047.24	9604.51	10496.05	11794.30
汕 头	Shantou	600.21	995.64	1873.03	2857.20	3579.40	3861.01	4130.81	4516.63	5045.42
佛 山	Foshan	2119.08	3906.93	8462.33	11867.67	15372.81	16948.10	19161.40	20606.98	23787.77
韶 关	Shaoguan	263.73	468.35	907.75	1532.91	1849.76	1944.17	2089.98	2231.08	2423.78
河 源	Heyuan	91.12	205.94	500.02	988.90	1376.19	1448.09	1544.34	1567.98	1647.28
梅 州	Meizhou	219.47	438.71	839.63	1565.28	2132.87	2251.36	2438.24	2579.03	2807.60
惠 州	Huizhou	394.44	823.96	2090.14	3836.10	6171.35	6558.61	7235.61	7809.67	8396.63
汕 尾	Shanwei	78.19	144.45	332.70	631.03	940.46	1002.60	1073.29	1057.07	1062.96
东 莞	Dongguan	1327.79	3036.77	6077.87	9968.80	14157.22	16426.44	18232.83	20315.59	23514.02
中 山	Zhongshan	619.44	1186.76	2665.35	4378.36	5930.49	6345.05	6921.69	7332.85	8267.18
江 门	Jiangmen	805.18	1279.67	2285.75	3766.81	4528.88	4946.81	5475.45	5864.34	6570.65
阳 江	Yangjiang	142.73	248.75	575.32	1014.74	1386.49	1486.24	1639.46	1744.28	1973.00
湛 江	Zhanjiang	408.90	716.97	1565.19	2684.61	3343.59	3651.54	3938.27	4191.05	4377.76
茂 名	Maoming	332.55	524.90	1028.67	1974.75	2725.29	3012.91	3246.33	3432.91	3686.02
肇 庆	Zhaoqing	281.64	493.23	1072.54	1785.01	2495.80	2642.47	2893.08	3052.70	3429.96
清 远	Qingyuan	213.85	393.96	995.36	1699.82	2336.34	2564.42	2710.50	2827.48	3085.55
潮 州	Chaozhou	162.70	328.97	653.27	1076.19	1369.72	1489.43	1621.68	1735.33	1895.52
揭 阳	Jieyang	240.07	473.60	967.03	1837.87	2273.64	2429.00	2599.43	2770.96	3048.35
云 浮	Yunfu	118.37	217.40	486.93	915.88	1199.50	1329.49	1385.24	1503.20	1648.32
按经济区域分	By Region									
珠 三 角	Pearl River Delta	16211.75	32962.25	71294.51	141609.04	183537.91	205988.39	239220.69	263012.21	289656.10
东 翼	Eastern Region	1081.18	1942.66	3826.04	6402.29	8163.22	8782.04	9425.22	10080.00	11052.26
西 翼	Western Region	884.18	1490.63	3169.17	5674.10	7455.37	8150.69	8824.06	9368.24	10036.79
山 区	Mountainous Region	906.54	1724.37	3729.68	6702.78	8894.66	9537.52	10168.30	10708.77	11612.52

8−10 续表 continued

单位：亿元 (100 million yuan)

市别	City	各项贷款 Total Loans								
		2000	2005	2010	2015	2018	2019	2020	2021	2022
全省合计	**Provincial Total**	**13227.62**	**23261.21**	**51799.30**	**95661.12**	**145169.39**	**167994.58**	**195680.62**	**222234.29**	**245722.94**
广　州	Guangzhou	4241.87	7622.20	16284.31	27296.16	40749.32	47103.31	54387.64	61399.61	68918.60
深　圳	Shenzhen	3032.13	7596.72	16808.12	32449.04	52539.79	59461.39	68020.54	77240.78	83422.99
珠　海	Zhuhai	349.20	486.72	1472.54	2969.70	5238.24	6358.61	7626.26	8909.80	10312.70
汕　头	Shantou	476.66	421.36	661.52	1199.00	1955.95	2168.92	2220.33	2516.74	2812.05
佛　山	Foshan	1581.90	2122.74	4868.99	7950.53	10457.65	12175.18	14507.62	16474.11	18234.52
韶　关	Shaoguan	149.23	169.68	376.06	731.84	956.33	1110.56	1316.85	1504.19	1651.32
河　源	Heyuan	62.19	108.13	338.69	801.08	1154.17	1346.12	1572.17	1671.36	1756.15
梅　州	Meizhou	147.02	206.44	331.10	736.41	1171.70	1352.38	1588.81	1758.09	1969.06
惠　州	Huizhou	221.42	409.44	1225.71	2701.60	4886.82	5848.89	7183.93	8478.86	9479.08
汕　尾	Shanwei	68.74	57.21	131.12	306.14	425.40	521.64	680.92	819.04	984.03
东　莞	Dongguan	642.33	1540.48	3441.99	5980.90	8209.70	10132.14	12777.12	14931.21	16780.23
中　山	Zhongshan	382.09	498.05	1373.62	2894.32	4036.39	4912.91	5711.18	6486.49	7055.21
江　门	Jiangmen	574.26	565.45	1032.46	2218.01	3140.85	3667.71	4390.98	4970.31	5497.83
阳　江	Yangjiang	89.71	100.66	292.24	757.74	1006.16	1173.23	1353.97	1522.11	1722.80
湛　江	Zhanjiang	294.70	310.03	721.00	1568.76	2164.16	2508.25	2932.33	3153.76	3660.83
茂　名	Maoming	211.96	230.93	362.40	858.33	1326.32	1582.35	1871.39	2126.26	2412.27
肇　庆	Zhaoqing	217.44	232.13	652.01	1281.52	1825.47	2156.79	2485.60	2639.61	2939.68
清　远	Qingyuan	150.82	179.13	520.62	1061.23	1559.72	1886.24	2218.01	2487.61	2739.91
潮　州	Chaozhou	118.57	137.20	219.41	369.04	417.44	467.17	549.47	657.41	738.59
揭　阳	Jieyang	131.25	169.40	407.06	931.72	1154.75	1182.07	1236.62	1358.28	1412.24
云　浮	Yunfu	84.12	97.10	278.34	598.05	793.07	878.74	1048.88	1128.67	1222.87
按经济区域分	By Region									
珠三角	Pearl River Delta	11242.64	21073.93	47159.74	85741.78	131084.22	151816.93	177090.87	201530.79	222640.84
东　翼	Eastern Region	795.23	785.17	1419.10	2805.90	3953.54	4339.79	4687.33	5351.47	5946.91
西　翼	Western Region	596.37	641.62	1375.65	3184.82	4496.65	5263.82	6157.70	6802.13	7795.89
山　区	Mountainous Region	593.39	760.49	1844.81	3928.63	5634.99	6574.04	7744.72	8549.91	9339.30

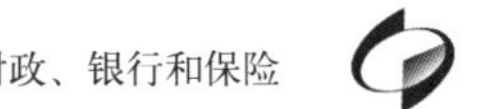

8-11 各市金融机构住户存款

Savings Deposit by Household in All Financial Institutions by City

单位：亿元 (100 million yuan)

市别	City	中外资金融机构本外币住户存款 Savings Deposit by Household in Renminbi and Foreign Currencies in All Financial Institutions								
		2000	2005	2010	2015	2018	2019	2020	2021	2022
全省合计	**Provincial Total**	**10031.68**	**20267.76**	**36965.75**	**55008.70**	**70293.46**	**78959.14**	**88976.65**	**97598.57**	**113554.76**
广州	Guangzhou	2683.38	5475.77	9302.33	13602.38	16456.56	18383.44	21177.97	23151.08	26878.13
深圳	Shenzhen	1391.78	3525.70	6918.19	9680.24	13810.06	16327.05	19031.88	20834.08	24928.72
珠海	Zhuhai	262.41	513.72	982.54	1322.97	1772.01	1985.20	2243.02	2498.01	2949.27
汕头	Shantou	401.88	765.26	1305.62	1918.05	2345.66	2614.33	2825.22	3066.23	3504.56
佛山	Foshan	1359.52	2465.51	4460.82	6232.20	7577.50	8383.03	9259.24	10124.60	11843.25
韶关	Shaoguan	172.46	320.00	562.11	925.18	1195.08	1315.94	1459.06	1607.29	1820.97
河源	Heyuan	71.32	146.36	314.33	591.09	786.26	864.07	950.91	1045.01	1163.96
梅州	Meizhou	166.95	326.86	582.20	1061.20	1347.89	1517.82	1679.03	1864.83	2088.83
惠州	Huizhou	276.61	548.27	1044.17	1729.01	2376.43	2614.95	2910.72	3244.63	3753.98
汕尾	Shanwei	58.89	111.83	231.32	388.93	501.36	534.84	582.34	628.54	711.20
东莞	Dongguan	753.78	1796.69	3425.89	4630.69	5656.01	6365.70	6998.52	7655.09	9071.89
中山	Zhongshan	409.23	764.69	1462.96	2108.53	2642.90	2896.31	3246.66	3560.37	4155.30
江门	Jiangmen	607.54	951.96	1516.72	2270.52	2783.43	3059.53	3394.16	3757.84	4266.61
阳江	Yangjiang	107.92	192.35	386.82	665.27	870.85	976.68	1102.18	1217.15	1382.16
湛江	Zhanjiang	310.23	514.85	945.28	1684.28	2127.66	2339.16	2525.38	2771.94	3104.97
茂名	Maoming	251.70	413.71	752.61	1413.64	1813.69	1996.80	2192.91	2426.31	2725.01
肇庆	Zhaoqing	197.68	347.39	657.31	1160.94	1532.75	1645.21	1787.68	1992.83	2248.07
清远	Qingyuan	152.70	279.69	593.11	1013.87	1380.66	1517.73	1676.20	1848.61	2081.13
潮州	Chaozhou	111.07	246.32	461.35	748.54	919.27	1016.19	1116.17	1222.22	1402.82
揭阳	Jieyang	190.83	392.24	716.17	1251.86	1607.27	1734.69	1870.86	2048.80	2320.41
云浮	Yunfu	93.82	168.58	343.92	609.30	790.18	870.46	946.56	1033.09	1153.53
按经济区域分	By Region									
珠三角	Pearl River Delta	7941.93	16389.71	29770.92	42737.49	54607.65	61660.42	70049.84	76818.54	90095.22
东翼	Eastern Region	762.66	1515.65	2714.46	4307.37	5373.55	5900.06	6394.59	6965.80	7938.99
西翼	Western Region	669.84	1120.91	2084.70	3763.19	4812.19	5312.63	5820.47	6415.40	7212.14
山区	Mountainous Region	657.25	1241.49	2395.67	4200.64	5500.07	6086.03	6711.76	7398.83	8308.40

8-11 续表 continued

单位：亿元 (100 million yuan)

市别	City	中资金融机构人民币住户存款 Savings Deposit by Household in Renminbi in Chinese-funded Financial Institutions 2000	2005	2010	2015	2018	2019	2020	2021	2022
全省合计	**Provincial Total**	**8667.29**	**19051.35**	**36219.15**	**54114.45**	**69083.50**	**77790.28**	**87826.30**	**96486.15**	**112381.27**
广　州	Guangzhou	2239.64	5024.69	9013.15	13236.26	15965.46	17903.24	20703.72	22696.13	26401.54
深　圳	Shenzhen	1082.43	3229.38	6717.05	9429.42	13441.61	15971.13	18674.43	20484.90	24544.92
珠　海	Zhuhai	216.08	480.87	957.58	1296.96	1736.03	1950.23	2209.72	2465.54	2914.90
汕　头	Shantou	351.40	733.50	1291.11	1897.90	2323.45	2592.37	2802.94	3045.15	3482.50
佛　山	Foshan	1216.98	2358.78	4406.34	6170.92	7496.55	8306.48	9185.36	10053.82	11770.37
韶　关	Shaoguan	165.47	313.97	559.16	921.64	1190.82	1311.80	1455.19	1603.75	1817.44
河　源	Heyuan	69.96	145.12	313.64	590.09	785.18	863.11	949.95	1044.09	1163.02
梅　州	Meizhou	155.14	318.77	578.33	1057.84	1343.90	1514.10	1675.55	1861.56	2085.53
惠　州	Huizhou	249.31	522.21	1031.63	1717.05	2359.43	2599.07	2895.98	3230.42	3739.44
汕　尾	Shanwei	54.18	108.39	229.73	385.72	498.56	532.67	580.30	625.57	709.41
东　莞	Dongguan	672.07	1728.28	3384.45	4587.86	5595.25	6308.80	6944.74	7603.58	9019.34
中　山	Zhongshan	354.65	725.06	1442.18	2082.30	2611.80	2866.87	3217.59	3532.27	4126.79
江　门	Jiangmen	483.75	851.93	1461.98	2228.65	2732.50	3011.77	3348.82	3713.01	4221.58
阳　江	Yangjiang	104.99	189.91	385.69	663.22	868.71	974.68	1100.25	1215.29	1380.36
湛　江	Zhanjiang	298.14	505.70	940.08	1675.56	2117.25	2329.34	2516.73	2763.52	3096.37
茂　名	Maoming	247.45	410.02	750.67	1410.49	1810.33	1993.71	2189.85	2423.38	2722.04
肇　庆	Zhaoqing	184.21	335.91	650.23	1151.53	1523.58	1636.17	1779.19	1984.74	2239.84
清　远	Qingyuan	146.27	273.86	590.26	1010.55	1376.56	1513.83	1672.42	1844.92	2077.44
潮　州	Chaozhou	104.19	242.65	459.60	744.83	914.90	1011.24	1111.19	1217.59	1399.16
揭　阳	Jieyang	180.82	387.29	714.16	1247.84	1603.18	1730.83	1867.38	2045.39	2317.29
云　浮	Yunfu	90.13	165.09	342.13	607.82	788.45	868.86	944.99	1031.56	1151.99
按经济区域分	By Region									
珠三角	Pearl River Delta	6699.12	15257.09	29064.60	41900.94	53462.21	60553.76	68959.55	75764.409	88978.71
东　翼	Eastern Region	690.59	1471.82	2694.60	4276.29	5340.09	5867.1	6361.81	6933.6899	7908.35
西　翼	Western Region	650.58	1105.62	2076.44	3749.27	4796.3	5297.73	5806.83	6402.1891	7198.77
山　区	Mountainous Region	626.97	1216.81	2383.51	4187.95	5484.91	6071.69	6698.11	7385.8629	8295.43

8-12 财产保险公司主要指标

Main Indicators of Property Insurance Companies

单位：万元 (10000 yuan)

项目	Item	2019		2020	
		保费收入 Premium Income	赔款支出 Indemnity Expenditure	保费收入 Premium Income	赔款支出 Indemnity Expenditure
合计	**Total**	**15868667.50**	**8397135.54**	**15540749.10**	**9300861.80**
企业财产保险	Enterprise Property Insurance	726256.25	387038.64	795692.90	337640.99
家庭财产保险	Household Property Insurance	100856.05	39296.98	123852.11	51618.44
#投资型家财险	Of Which: Investment-Linked Household Property Insurance	221.39	72.21	209.94	100.90
机动车辆保险	Motor Vehicle Insurance	9326355.14	4968514.02	9289970.36	5268930.42
工程保险	Project Insurance	233185.71	147642.64	222866.03	123111.41
责任保险	Liability Insurance	1090525.02	387151.55	1350390.88	481196.97
信用保险	Credit Insurance	413078.26	303198.34	393167.30	273109.91
保证保险	Guarantee Insurance	1736033.55	1011352.95	692276.82	1439051.39
#机动车辆消费贷款保证保险	Of Which: Motor Vehicle Consumption Loan Guarantee Insurance	620.60	5109.25	468.51	9104.92
个人贷款抵押房屋保证保险	Personal Loan Home Mortgage Guarantee Insurance	25.48	69.39	233.49	29.40
船舶保险	Ship Insurance	54546.38	34094.35	66021.87	33693.26
货物运输保险	Freight Transport Insurance	142316.35	83312.90	144588.33	66686.97
特殊风险保险	Peculiar Risk Insurance	208530.16	93605.45	231570.91	104803.11
农业保险	Agriculture Insurance	188238.06	132954.33	267447.12	141322.47
健康险	Health Insurance	699523.49	569635.07	1085692.57	684118.60
意外伤害保险	Accident Injury Insurance	837302.90	171666.96	722298.68	197367.52
其他险	Other Property Insurance	111920.19	67671.36	154913.21	98210.35

8-12 续表 continued

单位：万元 (10000 yuan)

项目	Item	2021		2022	
		保费收入 Premium Income	赔款支出 Indemnity Expenditure	保费收入 Premium Income	赔款支出 Indemnity Expenditure
合计	**Total**	**16162145.15**	**9269796.23**	**17807307.13**	**10049442.80**
企业财产保险	Enterprise Property Insurance	871085.52	367995.38	932947.97	407063.66
家庭财产保险	Household Property Insurance	139119.85	59634.32	228049.37	47285.92
#投资型家财险	Of Which: Investment-Linked Household Property Insurance	332.23	48.50	246.64	3.28
机动车辆保险	Motor Vehicle Insurance	9067603.25	5665520.84	9664915.76	5844835.69
工程保险	Project Insurance	246614.23	121676.47	268807.52	92822.72
责任保险	Liability Insurance	1578364.74	645465.10	1827164.53	732709.51
信用保险	Credit Insurance	409657.71	116910.98	503318.20	138071.10
保证保险	Guarantee Insurance	471839.57	493981.50	491917.88	635329.83
#机动车辆消费贷款保证保险	Of Which: Motor Vehicle Consumption Loan Guarantee Insurance	373.31	-1327.18	403.83	-606.73
个人贷款抵押房屋保证保险	Personal Loan Home Mortgage Guarantee Insurance	27.16	9.63	142.29	-815.49
船舶保险	Ship Insurance	62585.61	44302.37	81930.19	28432.77
货物运输保险	Freight Transport Insurance	205967.37	90788.05	269613.24	126173.86
特殊风险保险	Peculiar Risk Insurance	189015.06	66699.20	210781.90	56664.73
农业保险	Agriculture Insurance	483778.60	247499.63	819655.59	497839.18
健康险	Health Insurance	1342157.14	918064.21	1410894.10	926997.96
意外伤害保险	Accident Injury Insurance	860881.05	251506.67	741969.44	290242.01
其他险	Other Property Insurance	233475.44	179751.52	355341.41	224973.89

注：因部分机构正在风险处置，表中2021年保险统计数据均不包括该部分机构数据。
Note: As some institutions are under risk disposal, the insurance statistics of 2021 in the table do not include the data of these institutions.

8-13 人身保险公司主要指标
Main Indicators of Life Insurance Companies

单位：亿元　　　　(100 million yuan)

项　目	Item	2019	2020	2021	2022
保费收入	**Premium Income**	**3909.83**	**4098.78**	**3963.50**	**4113.43**
按险种分	Premium by Line of Business:				
寿险	Life Insurance	3011.38	3062.64	2921.43	3022.68
个人业务	Personal Business	3000.94	3052.12	2912.23	3014.20
新单保费	New Business Premium	1313.48	1189.49	1129.28	1106.56
续期保费	Renewal Premium	1687.46	1862.63	1782.95	1907.63
团体业务	Group Business	10.44	10.53	9.21	8.48
新单保费	New Business Premium	8.78	8.43	6.57	5.84
续期保费	Renewal Premium	1.66	2.10	2.64	2.64
意外伤害险	Accident Injury Insurance	111.26	103.39	97.38	85.95
一年期以内业务	Within One-year	16.64	15.74	13.47	10.79
一年期业务	One Year	47.75	45.27	44.25	39.24
一年以上业务	Over One-year Period Business	46.87	42.37	39.65	35.93
健康险	Health Insurance	787.19	932.75	944.69	1004.79
一年期以内及一年期业务	Within One Year and One-year Period Business	152.02	171.37	165.95	206.96
个人业务	Personal Business	72.18	81.81	74.62	90.41
团体业务	Group Business	79.83	89.56	91.33	116.56
一年期以上业务	Over One-year Period Business	635.17	761.38	778.74	797.83
个人业务	Personal Business	618.08	728.70	759.35	779.24
团体业务	Group Business	17.09	32.69	19.39	18.59
按新型产品分：	Premium by New Product:				
寿险保费收入合计	Total Life Insurance Premium Income	3011.38	3062.64	2921.43	3022.68
普通寿险	Ordinary Insurance	1476.98	1725.99	1816.49	2104.84
新单保费	New Business Premium	600.56	582.89	635.45	726.46
续期保费	Renewal Premium	876.42	1143.09	1181.04	1378.38
分红寿险	Dividend Insurance	1522.57	1324.96	1093.88	906.28
新单保费	New Business Premium	720.60	613.49	498.78	383.45
续期保费	Renewal Premium	801.96	711.47	595.10	522.83
投资连结保险	Investment Link Insurance	1.36	1.37	1.37	1.39
万能寿险	Universal Life Insurance	10.48	10.32	9.70	10.17
赔付支出	**Total Payment Expenditure**	**585.79**	**659.43**	**954.09**	**740.14**
赔款支出	Total Indemnity Expenditure	102.17	112.56	131.51	140.57
意外伤害险	Accident Injury Insurance	14.21	14.80	15.79	17.48
一年期以内业务	Within One-year Period Business	3.07	3.96	3.97	4.42
一年期业务	One-year Period Business	11.14	10.84	11.81	13.06
一年期以内及一年期健康险	Within One Year and One-year Period Health Insurance Business	87.96	97.76	115.72	123.09
个人业务	Personal Business	25.57	27.24	32.66	38.78
团体业务	Group Business	62.39	70.52	83.06	84.31
死伤医疗给付合计	Total Payment for Death, Injury and Medical Treatment	104.99	129.56	175.01	191.09
寿险	Life Insurance	28.10	30.26	34.25	36.28
个人业务	Personal Business	25.08	26.98	31.05	32.92
团体业务	Group Business	3.02	3.28	3.20	3.36
一年期以上健康险	Over One-year Period Health Insurance	76.90	99.30	140.77	154.82
个人业务	Personal Business	74.89	97.76	137.91	150.90
团体业务	Group Business	2.01	1.53	2.86	3.92
满期给付合计	Total Mature Payment	253.36	306.68	538.22	285.96
寿险	Life Insurance	252.88	248.17	260.92	250.63
个人业务	Personal Business	250.24	245.48	257.52	246.10
团体业务	Group Business	2.64	2.69	3.40	4.53
一年期以上健康险	Over One-year Period Health Insurance	0.48	58.51	277.31	35.33
个人业务	Personal Business	0.48	58.51	277.31	35.32
团体业务	Group Business	…			0.00
年金给付合计	Total Annuity Payment	125.01	110.59	109.32	122.52
个人业务	Personal Business	121.81	107.09	104.72	118.96
团体业务	Group Business	3.20	3.49	4.60	3.57
退保金	**Withdrawal Amount Insured**	**633.82**	**372.69**	**388.14**	**604.60**
寿险	Life Insurance	596.32	351.68	360.06	575.10
个人业务	Personal Business	594.90	351.03	357.26	574.77
团体业务	Group Business	1.42	0.65	2.80	0.33
一年期以上健康险	Over One-year Period Health Insurance	37.50	21.01	28.09	29.50

注：因部分机构正在风险处置，表中2021年保险统计数据均不包括该部分机构数据。
Note: As some institutions are under risk disposal, the insurance statistics of 2021 in the table do not include the data of these institutions.

8-14 保险业务主要指标
Main Indicators of Insurance Business

指　标	Indicators	2015	2016	2017	2018	2019	2020	2021	2022
保费收入　　（亿元）	**Premium of Insurance (100 million yuan)**	**2814.37**	**3820.51**	**4304.60**	**4663.89**	**5496.70**	**5652.86**	**5578.96**	**5894.16**
财产险	Property Insurance	879.87	945.52	1105.34	1271.17	1433.18	1373.28	1395.91	1565.44
人寿险	Life Insurance	1537.11	2038.11	2533.14	2571.73	3011.38	3062.64	2920.67	3022.68
健康险	Health Insurance	310.52	723.85	527.79	648.14	857.14	1041.32	1078.91	1145.88
人身意外伤害险	Personal Accident Insurance	86.88	113.02	138.34	172.85	194.99	175.62	183.46	160.15
各项赔款和给付（亿元）	**Payment (100 million yuan)**	**882.32**	**1035.42**	**1142.38**	**1403.46**	**1425.25**	**1589.47**	**1881.04**	**1745.09**
财产险	Property Insurance	435.38	469.07	549.07	744.73	765.58	841.94	810.02	883.22
人寿险	Life Insurance	355.92	449.50	450.70	477.64	405.98	389.01	404.48	409.43
健康险	Health Insurance	76.95	97.16	118.98	152.29	222.30	323.98	625.60	405.94
人身意外伤害险	Personal Accident Insurance	14.07	19.70	23.63	28.80	31.38	34.54	40.94	46.50
保险公司数　（家）	**Number of Insurance Companies (unit)**	**90**	**103**	**109**	**111**	**113**	**114**	**118**	**118**
#财产保险公司	Property Insurance Companies	40	47	51	52	53	54	55	55
人身保险公司	Life Insurance Companies	50	56	58	59	60	60	63	63
#中资保险公司	Domestic Funded Insurance Companies	60	68	74	76	78	79	82	82
外资保险公司	Foreign-funded Insurance Companies	30	35	35	35	35	35	36	36
保险公司总资产（亿元）	**Total Assets of Insurance Companies(100 million yuan)**	**9959.67**	**10811.14**	**12101.88**	**13037.68**	**14884.76**	**16916.68**	**18619.97**	**20662.10**
#财产险公司	Property Insurance Companies	776.08	1017.09	1058.64	1110.77	1196.67	1345.15	1404.12	1596.39
寿险公司	Life Insurance Companies	8190.30	9472.37	10583.70	11529.09	13179.93	14892.66	16411.30	18105.24
保险公司分支机构（家）	**Number of Institutions of Insurance Companies (Unit)**	**5578**	**5815**	**6005**	**6098**	**6167**	**6306**	**6256**	**5959**
从业人员数　　（万人）	**Employed Persons (person)**	**51.98**	**69.64**	**76.56**	**81.40**	**82.16**	**79.15**	**54.37**	**44.72**

注：“保险公司分支机构(家)”统计指标从2014年起进行了调整，包括省级分公司、地市级分公司和中心支公司、支公司、营业部、营销服务部及电销专属机构。

Note: The number of institutions of insurance companies were adjusted from 2014, including the provincial branch, municipal branch,central branch, sales department, marketing department and telemarketing exclusive agency.

8-15 分市原保险保费收入和赔付支出情况（2022年）

Premium of Primary Insurance and Payment by City (2022)

单位：亿元　　(100 million yuan)

地　区	Region	原保险保费收入 Premium of Primary Insurance			赔付支出 Payment		
		小计 Sub-total	财产险业务 Property Insurance	人身险业务 Life Insurance	小计 Sub-total	财产险业务 Property Insurance	人身险业务 Life Insurance
全　省	**Provincial Total**	**5894.16**	**1565.44**	**4328.71**	**1745.09**	**883.22**	**861.87**
广　州	Guangzhou	1544.89	374.21	1170.68	468.19	217.86	250.33
深　圳	Shenzhen	1527.65	417.92	1109.73	440.61	220.95	219.66
珠　海	Zhuhai	172.24	37.62	134.62	45.07	21.54	23.54
汕　头	Shantou	127.84	28.98	98.85	34.94	16.90	18.04
佛　山	Foshan	600.40	140.35	460.04	155.32	79.88	75.44
韶　关	Shaoguan	63.96	18.66	45.31	22.06	12.17	9.89
河　源	Heyuan	38.56	16.25	22.31	16.83	9.81	7.01
梅　州	Meizhou	62.09	21.59	40.50	24.73	12.16	12.56
惠　州	Huizhou	176.86	54.33	122.54	53.16	30.32	22.85
汕　尾	Shanwei	25.24	10.43	14.81	10.78	5.63	5.16
东　莞	Dongguan	556.02	157.73	398.29	161.34	88.54	72.80
中　山	Zhongshan	227.54	56.93	170.60	59.65	31.24	28.41
江　门	Jiangmen	180.33	42.86	137.48	45.66	22.82	22.84
阳　江	Yangjiang	51.65	15.40	36.25	16.77	10.19	6.58
湛　江	Zhanjiang	121.42	35.15	86.28	41.71	21.24	20.47
茂　名	Maoming	97.45	33.84	63.61	38.91	21.01	17.91
肇　庆	Zhaoqing	82.04	26.22	55.82	26.20	14.29	11.91
清　远	Qingyuan	74.00	25.36	48.64	28.74	16.45	12.29
潮　州	Chaozhou	53.02	14.48	38.54	14.82	7.95	6.87
揭　阳	Jieyang	73.73	23.54	50.18	26.20	14.40	11.80
云　浮	Yunfu	37.23	13.59	23.63	13.39	7.88	5.52

注：赔付支出不包括直保公司的分保赔付支出。
Note: The payment does not include the reinsurance payment of the direct insurance company.

主要统计指标解释

一般公共预算收入 指国家财政参与社会产品分配所取得的收入，是实现国家职能的财力保证。主要包括：

（1）各项税收：包括国内增值税、国内消费税、进口货物增值税和消费税、出口货物退增值税和消费税、营业税、企业所得税、个人所得税、资源税、城市维护建设税、房产税、印花税、城镇土地使用税、土地增值税、车船税、船舶吨税、车辆购置税、关税、耕地占用税、契税、烟叶税等。财政收入按现行分税制财政体制划分为中央本级收入和地方本级收入。

（2）非税收入：包括专项收入、行政事业性收费、罚没收入和其他收入。

一般公共预算支出 指国家财政将筹集起来的资金进行分配使用，以满足经济建设和各项事业的需要。主要包括：一般公共服务、外交、国防、公共安全、教育、科学技术、文化体育与传媒、社会保障和就业、医疗卫生与计划生育、节能环保、城乡社区、农林水、交通运输、资源勘探信息等、商业服务业等、金融、援助其他地区、国土海洋气象等、住房保障、粮油物资储备、政府债务付息等方面的支出。财政支出根据政府在经济和社会活动中的不同职权，划分为中央财政支出和地方财政支出。

信贷资金 指金融机构以信用方式集聚和分配的货币资金。金融机构信贷资金的来源有各项存款、金融债券、对国家金融机构负债、流通中现金、其他项目等；信贷自己的运用有各项贷款、有价证券及投资、黄金占款、外汇买卖、财政借款及在国家金融机构中的资产等。

存款 指企业、机关、团体或居民根据资金必须收回的原则，把货币资金存入银行或其他信用机构保管并取得一定利息的一种信用活动形式。根据存款对象或性质的不同可划分为住户存款、非金融企业存款、政府存款、非银行业金融存款等科目。它是银行信贷资金的主要来源。

贷款 指银行或其他信贷机构根据资金必须归还的原则，按一定利率，为企业、个人等提供资金的一种信用活动形式。我国银行贷款分为短期贷款、中长期贷款、融资租赁、票据融资、各项垫款、境外贷款等。

住户存款 个人客户在其他存款性公司开立账户并存入资金或货币，由其他存款性公司出具存款凭证，个人客户凭存款凭证可以支取本金或利息的存款。

保险金额 指保险人承担赔偿或者给付保险金责任的最高限额。

保费 指投保人为取得保险人在约定范围内所承担赔偿责任而支付给保险人的费用。

赔款 指保险人根据保险合同的规定，向被保险人支付的赔偿保险责任损失的金额。

给付 包括死伤医疗给付和满期给付。死伤医疗给付是指保险人根据人寿保险及长期健康保险合同的规定，因被保险人在保险期内发生保险责任范围内的保险事故支付给被保险人（或受益人）的金额。满期给付是指被保险人生存期满，保险人按人寿保险合同规定支付给被保险人的满期保险金额。

Explanatory Notes on Main Statistical Indicators

General Public Budgetary Revenue refers to income for the government finance through participating in the distribution of social products. It is the financial guarantee to ensure government functioning. The contents of government revenue include the following main items:

(1) Various tax revenues, including domestic value added tax (VAT), domestic consumption tax, VAT and consumption tax from imports, VAT and consumption tax rebate for exports, business tax, corporate income tax, individual income tax, resource tax, city maintenance and construct tax, house property tax, stamp tax, urban land use tax, land appreciation tax, tax on vehicles and boat operation, ship tonnage tax, vehicle purchase tax, tariffs, farm land occupation tax, deed tax, and tobacco leaf tax, etc.

(2) Non-tax revenue, including special program receipts, charge of administrative and institutional units, penalty receipts and others non-tax receipts.

General Public Budgetary Expenditure refers to the distribution and use of the funds which the government finance has raised, so as to meet the needs of economic construction and various undertakings. It includes the following main items: expenditure for general public services, expenditure for foreign affairs, expenditure for national defence expenditure for public security, expenditure for education, expenditure for science and technology, expenditure for culture, sport and media, expenditure for social safety net and employment effort, expenditure for medical and health care and family planning, expenditure for energy conservation and environment protection, expenditure for urban and rural community affairs, expenditure for agriculture, forestry and water conservancy, expenditure for transportation, expenditure for resource exploration and information, expenditure for affairs of commerce and services, expenditure for finance, aid to other regions, expenditure for land, ocean and weather, expenditure for housing security, expenditure for grain & oil reserves, interest payment for public debts. General public budget expenditure is divided into general public budget expenditure of central government and general public budget expenditure of local government according to the different functions of the governments played in economic and social activities.

Credit Funds refer to the monetary funds accumulated and distributed in the means of credit by the financial institutions. The sources of credit funds include various deposits, financial bonds, liabilities to international financial institutions, currency in circulation, other items. The uses of credit funds include loans, securities and investment, position for bullion purchase, foreign exchange trading, advances to treasury, and assets with international financial institutions.

Deposit is a form of credit by which enterprises, institutions, organizations or households can put money into banks and other credit institutions for safekeeping and interest earning under the principle of free withdrawal. According to different depositors, deposits are divided into household deposits, non financial enterprise deposits, government deposits, non banking financial institutions deposits. Deposits are major sources of the credit funds of banks.

Loan is a form of credit by which banks and other credit institutions provide funds at certain interest rate to enterprises and individuals in the light of the principle of unconditional repayment. Loans from Chinese banks include short-term loan, medium-term and long-term loans, financial lease, bill financing, various money advanced, foreign loans.

Savings Deposits refer to the capital which is deposited in the account opened in the reserve corporation by the individual with a deposit certificate as the proof, the principal and interest of which can be withdrew with the deposit certificate.

Amount Insured refers to the maximum that the insurant will get for the claim of the case insured.

Premium is the fee paid by the insurant to the insurer to obtain the obligation of compensation from the insurance within the agreed terms. is the compensation paid by the insurer to the insurant in accordance with the insurance contract.

Settled Claim is the compensation paid by the insurer to the insurant in accordance with the insurance contract.

Payment includes payment for death, injury or medical treatment and payment at maturity. Payment for death, injury or medical treatment refers to the money paid to the insurant (or the beneficiary) in accordance with the life or health insurance contract when the insurant encounters accidents within the insured period covered in the contract. Payment at maturity refers to the payment to the insurant in accordance with the life insurance contract at the end of the insured period.

九、价格

PRICE

九 价格

简要说明

一、本篇资料反映生产、流通、消费与投资等环节的价格变动情况。主要包括居民消费价格指数、商品零售价格指数、工业生产者出厂价格指数、工业生产者购进价格指数、农产品生产者价格指数。

二、本篇资料由国家统计局广东调查总队消费价格调查处和生产投资价格调查处整理提供。

三、居民消费价格指数、商品零售价格指数采用分层随机抽样调查方法编制，即在全省选择不同经济区域的市、县以及有代表性的商品和服务项目作为样本，对市场价格进行经常性调查，以样本推断总体。

四、工业生产者出厂价格指数和工业生产者购进价格指数均采用重点调查与典型调查相结合的方法统计。

五、农产品生产者价格指数采用抽样调查和重点调查相结合的调查方法进行统计。

9 Price

Brief Introduction

Ⅰ. The data in this chapter reflect price changes in production, circulation，consumption and investment, including mainly consumer price indices, retail price indices, price indices of means of agricultural production, producer price indices for manufactured goods, producer price indices for purchased goods, producers' price indices for farm products.

Ⅱ. The data are prepared and provided by the Division of Consumers Price Survey and the Division of Production Price Survey under Guangdong Survey Office of the National Bureau of Statistics.

Ⅲ. The data for the calculation of consumer price indices and retail price indices in the province are collected through stratified random sampling. Cities and counties distributed in different economic regions of the province are selected as sample areas, and representative commodities and services are selected as sample commodities and services. Regular surveys are conducted to collect data on market prices. The data on the population are estimated on the basis of the sample.

Ⅳ. The data for the calculation of producer price indices for manufactured goods and producer price indices for purchased goods are all collected through key-point survey combined with typical survey.

Ⅴ. The data for the calculation of producers' price indices of farm products are collected through sampling survey combined with key-point survey.

9-1 各种价格指数

Price Indices

上年=100 (preceding year=100)

年份 Year	商品零售价格指数 Retail Price Indices	居民消费价格指数 Consumer Price Indices	城市居民消费价格指数 Urban	农村居民消费价格指数 Rural	工业生产者出厂价格指数 Producer Price Index for Industrial Products	工业生产者购进价格指数 Purchasing Price Index for Industrial Products
1978	100.4		100.3			
1979	103.0		104.6			
1980	108.5		109.5			
1981	109.3		106.3			
1982	102.3		102.6			
1983	100.7		102.8			
1984	101.2	101.3	101.9	100.4		
1985	113.6	114.8	117.1	111.2		
1986	104.8	104.9	104.7	105.3		
1987	111.7	111.2	112.8	109.7		
1988	130.2	129.4	129.5	129.3		
1989	121.0	122.1	121.9	122.4		
1990	95.6	97.5	97.4	97.6		
1991	100.6	101.2	102.3	99.9		
1992	105.8	107.3	108.4	105.9		
1993	118.2	121.6	122.0	120.6		
1994	118.9	121.7	121.0	122.5		
1995	111.6	114.0	113.1	115.3		
1996	104.4	107.0	107.2	106.5		
1997	100.1	101.9	102.1	101.5	100.1	97.3
1998	97.0	98.2	98.3	98.1	94.8	91.4
1999	96.7	98.2	98.4	97.7	97.7	97.8
2000	99.9	101.4	102.2	100.0	103.4	110.9
2001	98.7	99.3	99.2	99.6	98.5	99.1
2002	98.5	98.6	98.6	98.6	96.5	96.3
2003	100.0	100.6	100.7	100.4	99.3	104.1
2004	102.9	103.0	102.6	103.7	101.7	110.6
2005	101.8	102.3	102.0	102.7	101.5	105.0
2006	101.5	101.8	101.8	101.6	101.4	103.6
2007	103.4	103.7	103.7	103.5	101.3	103.3
2008	106.0	105.6	105.5	105.8	103.1	107.9
2009	96.8	97.7	97.6	97.8	95.8	93.8
2010	103.3	103.1	103.1	103.2	103.2	107.3
2011	105.1	105.3	105.3	105.6	103.7	107.3
2012	102.2	102.8	102.8	102.9	99.5	99.5
2013	101.0	102.5	102.4	102.7	98.8	98.2
2014	101.4	102.3	102.3	102.1	98.9	98.8
2015	99.6	101.5	101.6	101.3	96.8	95.3
2016	100.8	102.3	102.4	102.0	99.4	98.0
2017	101.6	101.5	101.7	100.8	103.3	105.3
2018	102.1	102.2	102.2	101.9	101.8	102.5
2019	101.4	103.4	103.1	104.6	100.2	99.2
2020	100.8	102.6	102.6	103.0	99.0	97.4
2021	101.4	100.8	101.0	100.1	103.4	108.0
2022	102.5	102.2	102.2	102.3	103.0	104.1

9-2 各种价格定基指数

Fixed-base Price Indices

年份 Year	商品零售价格指数(1978年为100) Retail Price Indices (1978=100)	居民消费价格指数(1983年为100) Consumer Price Indices (1983=100)	城市居民消费价格指数(1983年为100) Urban (1983=100)	农村居民消费价格指数(1983年为100) Rural (1983=100)	工业生产者出厂价格指数(1996年为100) Producer Price Index for Industrial Products (1996=100)	工业生产者购进价格指数(1996年为100) Purchasing Price Index for Industrial Products (1996=100)
1978	100.0					
1979	103.0					
1980	111.8					
1981	122.0					
1982	124.9					
1983	125.7	100.0	100.0	100.0		
1984	127.2	101.3	101.9	100.4		
1985	144.5	116.3	119.3	111.6		
1986	151.5	122.0	124.9	117.6		
1987	169.2	135.7	140.9	129.0		
1988	220.3	175.5	182.5	166.8		
1989	266.6	214.3	222.5	204.1		
1990	254.8	209.0	216.7	199.2		
1991	256.4	211.5	221.7	199.0		
1992	271.3	226.9	240.3	210.7		
1993	320.6	275.9	293.1	254.2		
1994	381.3	335.8	354.7	311.3		
1995	425.6	382.8	401.2	359.0		
1996	444.3	409.6	430.1	382.3	100.0	100.0
1997	444.7	417.4	439.1	388.1	100.1	97.3
1998	431.4	409.9	431.6	380.7	94.9	88.9
1999	417.1	402.5	424.7	371.9	92.7	86.9
2000	416.7	408.1	434.1	371.9	95.9	96.4
2001	411.3	405.3	430.6	370.4	94.5	95.5
2002	405.1	399.6	424.6	365.3	91.2	92.0
2003	405.1	402.0	427.5	366.7	90.6	95.8
2004	416.9	414.1	438.6	380.3	92.1	106.0
2005	424.4	423.6	447.4	390.5	93.5	111.3
2006	430.8	431.2	455.5	396.8	94.8	115.3
2007	445.4	447.2	472.3	410.7	96.0	119.1
2008	472.2	472.2	498.3	434.5	99.0	128.4
2009	457.1	461.3	486.3	424.9	94.9	120.4
2010	472.2	475.6	501.4	438.5	97.9	129.2
2011	496.3	500.8	528.0	463.1	101.4	138.6
2012	507.2	514.8	542.8	476.5	100.9	137.9
2013	512.3	527.7	555.8	489.4	99.7	135.4
2014	519.5	539.8	568.6	499.7	98.6	134.0
2015	517.4	547.9	577.7	506.2	95.4	127.7
2016	521.5	560.5	591.6	516.3	94.8	125.1
2017	529.8	568.9	601.7	520.4	97.9	131.8
2018	540.9	581.4	614.9	530.3	99.7	135.1
2019	548.5	601.2	634.0	554.7	99.9	134.0
2020	553.1	616.9	650.4	571.4	98.9	130.5
2021	560.8	621.8	656.9	572.0	102.3	140.9
2022	574.8	635.5	671.4	585.2	105.3	146.7

9-3 居民消费价格分类指数（2022年）

Consumer Price Indices by Category (2022)

上年=100 (preceding year=100)

项 目	Item	全省 Provincial Indices	城市 Urban Indices	农村 Rural Indices
居民消费价格总指数	**Consumer Price Index**	**102.2**	**102.2**	**102.3**
非食品烟酒价格指数	**Non food,tobacco and alcohol price index**	**101.9**	**101.9**	**102.0**
服务价格指数	**Service Price Index**	**100.8**	**100.9**	**100.3**
消费品价格指数	**Consumer Goods Price Index**	**103.2**	**103.1**	**103.5**
扣除鲜菜鲜果价格指数	**Price Index Deducting Fresh Vegetables and Fruits**	**102.0**	**102.0**	**101.8**
食品烟酒	**Foods,tobacco and alcohol**	**102.9**	**102.9**	**103.0**
食品	Foods	102.9	102.7	103.8
粮食	Grain	101.6	102.0	100.4
#大米	Rice	100.9	101.5	99.2
粮食制品	Grain Products	103.1	103.3	102.5
薯类	Tubers	105.6	104.3	112.9
豆类	beans	104.3	104.1	104.7
食用油	edible oil	106.3	106.5	105.8
菜及食用菌	Vegetables and Edible Fungi	105.9	104.0	114.3
#鲜菜	Fresh Vegetables	106.2	104.1	115.4
畜肉类	Neat of animal	93.5	93.0	95.0
#猪肉	Pork	89.9	89.1	92.4
禽肉类	Meat of poultries	103.5	102.9	105.3
水产品	Aquatic Products	105.8	106.0	105.2
蛋类	Eggs	106.4	106.0	107.7
奶类	Milk	100.4	101.1	96.7
干鲜瓜果类	Dried and Fresh Melons and Fruits	110.9	110.9	110.7
#鲜果	Fresh Fruits	112.7	112.8	112.3
糖果糕点类	Candy and pastry	102.7	102.7	103.0
调味品	Condiment	104.3	104.7	103.0
其他食品类	Other Foods	102.5	102.6	102.2
茶及饮料	Tea and Beverages	103.1	103.4	101.4
烟酒	Tobacco and Alcohol	102.7	102.9	102.2
卷烟	Cigarettes	102.9	103.1	102.4
酒类	Alcohol	102.0	102.2	101.4
在外餐饮	Outside catering	102.8	103.1	100.3
衣着	**Clothing**	**100.6**	**100.8**	**99.2**
服装	Garments	101.0	101.4	99.1
衣着材料及配件	Clothing Materials and Accessories	101.1	100.8	102.9
衣着服务费	Clothing Services Fee	101.9	101.9	101.5
鞋类	Footwear	98.6	98.4	99.6
鞋类服务	Footwear Services	102.3	102.2	102.8
居住	**Residence**	**100.6**	**100.5**	**101.2**
租赁房房租	Rental housing	99.6	99.5	100.1
住房保养维修及管理	Housing maintenance and management	102.3	102.3	102.3
水电燃料	Hydropower fuel	103.4	103.0	105.9
自有住房	Own housing	99.3	99.3	98.9

9-3 续表 continued

上年=100 (preceding year=100)

项 目	Item	全省 Provincial Indices	城市 Urban Indices	农村 Rural Indices
生活用品及服务	**Daily Necessities and Services**	**101.2**	**101.1**	**101.8**
家具及室内装饰品	Furniture and Interior Decorations	101.7	101.9	101.0
家具	Furniture	101.9	102.1	101.0
室内装饰品	Interior Decorations	99.6	99.7	98.8
家用器具	Home Appliances	101.5	101.4	102.2
家用纺织品	Home Textiles	97.9	97.4	100.6
家庭日用杂品	Household Groceries	100.1	99.9	100.5
个人护理用品	Personal-care Supply	101.1	100.8	103.0
家庭服务	Domestic Service	103.2	103.0	105.1
交通通信	**Transportation and Communication**	**105.8**	**105.8**	**105.6**
交通	Transportation	108.0	107.9	108.6
交通工具	The Traffic Tools	98.6	99.0	96.7
交通工具用燃料	The Vehicles Fuel	120.4	120.3	121.1
交通工具使用和维修	Vehicle usage and Maintenance	102.0	102.1	101.0
交通费	Transportation	105.4	105.6	102.4
通信	Communication	99.3	99.5	98.3
通信工具	Communication Tools	98.9	99.1	97.5
通信服务	Communication Service	99.4	99.6	98.5
邮递服务	Postal Service	99.8	99.9	99.5
教育文化娱乐	**Education Culture and Entertainment**	**102.2**	**102.2**	**102.2**
教育	Education	102.5	102.4	102.9
教育用品	Education Supplies	102.6	102.8	101.4
教育服务	Education Services	102.5	102.4	102.9
文化娱乐	Cultural Entertainment	101.7	101.8	100.7
文娱耐用消费品	Recreational Consumer Goods	100.1	100.0	100.4
其他文娱用品	Other Entertainment Items	100.6	100.5	100.8
文化娱乐服务	Cultural Entertainment Service	100.2	100.2	100.7
旅游	Tourism	104.4	104.7	100.9
医疗保健	**Health care**	**100.4**	**100.6**	**99.7**
药品及医疗器具	Medicines and Medical Instruments	100.8	100.8	100.5
中药	Traditional Chinese Medicine	102.9	103.8	100.4
西药	Western Medicines	100.7	100.8	100.5
滋补保健品	Nourishing Health Products	100.6	100.5	101.9
医疗卫生器具	Medical Appliance	98.1	98.2	97.0
保健器具	Health Care Appliances	101.2	101.6	100.0
医疗服务	Medical Services	100.3	100.5	99.6
其他用品及服务	**Other Goods and Services**	**101.6**	**101.5**	**102.3**
其他用品	Other Products	101.5	101.3	102.7
其他服务	Other Service Class	101.7	101.6	101.9

9-4 商品零售价格分类指数（2022年）
Retail Price Indices by Category (2022)

上年=100 (preceding year=100)

项 目	Item	全省 Provincial Indices	城市 Urban Indices	农村 Rural Indices
商品零售价格指数	**Retail Price Index**	**102.5**	**102.5**	**102.8**
食品	**Foods**	**102.9**	**102.9**	**102.9**
粮食	Grain	101.8	102.0	100.5
#大米	Rice	101.1	101.5	99.5
粮食制品	Grain Products	103.1	103.2	102.2
薯类	Tubers	104.6	104.0	109.8
豆类	Beans	104.2	104.3	103.8
食用油	Edible Oil	106.1	106.3	105.1
菜及食用菌	Vegetables and Edible Fungi	104.9	103.9	111.9
#鲜菜	Fresh Vegetables	105.1	104.0	112.9
畜肉类	Neat of Animal	93.4	93.0	95.3
#猪肉	Pork	89.7	89.0	92.9
禽肉类	Meat of Poultry	103.1	102.7	105.0
水产品	Aquatic Products	106.0	106.0	105.6
蛋类	Eggs	106.3	106.1	107.6
奶类	Milk	100.6	101.0	97.2
干鲜瓜果类	Dried and Fresh Melons and Fruits	111.0	111.1	110.2
#鲜果	Fresh Fruits	112.8	113.0	111.7
糖果糕点类	Candy and Pastry	102.8	102.7	103.3
调味品	Condiment	104.5	105.0	102.1
其他食品类	Other Foods	102.7	102.7	102.4
餐饮业零售	Catering Retail	103.1	103.3	100.2
饮料、烟酒	**Beverages, Tobacco and Alcohol**	**102.8**	**102.9**	**102.2**
茶及饮料	Tea and Beverages	103.3	103.5	101.5
卷烟	Cigarettes	102.8	102.9	102.3
酒类	Alcohol	102.2	102.1	103.1
服装、鞋帽	**Garments, Shoes and Hats**	**100.8**	**100.9**	**99.4**
服装	Garments	101.3	101.5	99.2
鞋帽袜	Shoes, Hats and Socks	98.9	98.7	100.4
其他衣着配件	Other Clothing Accessories	99.3	99.3	98.9
纺织品	**Textiles**	**100.3**	**100.2**	**101.9**
服装材料	Clothing Material	102.3	102.2	103.4
床上用品	Bed Articles	98.1	97.7	101.0

9-4 续表 continued

上年=100 (preceding year=100)

项 目	Item	全 省 Provincial Indices	城 市 Urban Indices	农 村 Rural Indices
家用电器及音像器材	**Household Appliances, Audio and Video Equipment**	**100.6**	**100.4**	**102.3**
家庭设备	Household Facilities	101.4	101.2	102.5
文娱用耐用消费品	Durable Consumer Goods for Cultural and Recreational Use	98.8	98.6	100.5
专业音像器材	Audio and Video Equipment	102.5	101.9	107.5
文化办公用品	**Cultural and Office Appliances**	**100.8**	**100.7**	**101.6**
日用品	**Articles for Daily Use**	**101.2**	**101.1**	**101.4**
日用百货	General Merchandise for Daily Use	102.3	102.3	101.9
厨具餐具茶具	Kitchenware, Tableware and Tea Set	101.7	101.5	102.8
清洗用品	Cleaning Supplies	97.4	97.7	96.4
其他日用品	Other Articles for Daily Use	101.3	101.1	102.3
体育娱乐用品	**Sports and Recreation Articles**	**100.0**	**99.9**	**100.9**
体育户外用品	Sports Outdoor Products	103.9	103.8	106.9
娱乐用品	Recreation Articles	99.5	99.4	100.5
交通、通信用品	**Transportation and Communication Appliances**	**98.7**	**98.7**	**98.7**
交通运输机械	Transportation Machinery	98.6	98.6	98.8
通信器材	Communication Equipment	99.4	99.5	96.6
家具	**Furniture**	**102.1**	**102.1**	**102.1**
化妆品	**Cosmetics**	**100.9**	**100.7**	**103.2**
金银饰品	**Gold and Silver Jewelry**	**100.8**	**100.8**	**101.4**
中西药品及医疗保健用品	**Traditional Chinese & Western Medicines and Health Care Articles**	**100.8**	**100.8**	**100.7**
医疗卫生器具	Medical Appliance	98.2	98.3	96.4
中药	Traditional Chinese Medicine	103.0	103.5	100.4
西药	Western Medicines	100.6	100.6	100.7
保健器具及用品	Health Equipment and Supplies	100.9	100.8	102.6
书报杂志及电子出版物	**Books, Newspapers, Magazines and Electronic Publications**	**102.8**	**103.0**	**100.6**
教材及参考书	Teaching Materials and Reference Books	102.6	102.7	101.5
书报杂志及音像制品	Books, Newspapers, Magazines and Audio-Visual Products	103.5	103.8	99.5
计算机办公软件	Computer Office Software	102.5	102.6	99.9
燃料	**Fuels**	**115.5**	**115.2**	**117.5**
煤炭及制品	Coal and Its Products	113.9	115.5	98.6
石油及制品	Petroleum and Its Products	115.5	115.2	117.5
建筑材料及五金电料	**Building Materials and Hardware**	**101.0**	**101.0**	**101.0**
建筑装璜材料	Building Decoration Materials	102.2	102.3	101.4
五金水暖	Plumbing Hardware	99.6	99.5	100.4

9-5 各市居民消费价格分类指数（2022年）

Consumer Price Indices by Category and by City (2022)

上年=100 (preceding year=100)

市 别	City	总指数 General Indices	服务价格 Service Price	食品烟酒 Foods Tobacco and Alcohol	食品 Foods	#粮食 Grain	食用油 Edible Oil	鲜菜 Vegetables	畜肉类 Meat of Livestock	禽肉类 Meat of Poultry	水产品 Aquatic Products	蛋类 Eggs
广 州	Guangzhou	102.4	101.2	103.3	103.2	105.4	106.4	103.1	91.7	100.9	105.1	101.7
深 圳	Shenzhen	102.3	101.0	103.4	102.4	99.1	105.3	104.0	95.0	101.7	106.2	108.3
珠 海	Zhuhai	101.2	99.5	101.3	101.4	103.4	103.2	98.2	92.9	103.9	109.0	104.8
汕 头	Shantou	101.6	99.2	102.9	103.6	102.5	107.7	106.4	96.4	103.0	107.4	103.4
佛 山	Foshan	102.2	101.0	102.0	102.5	101.5	105.8	106.3	92.3	105.8	106.8	109.7
韶 关	Shaoguan	101.9	99.9	102.0	102.9	101.6	112.9	105.6	90.1	104.0	102.5	108.1
河 源	Heyuan	101.8	100.8	102.6	102.7	99.3	112.3	107.5	89.7	107.7	104.6	110.3
梅 州	Meizhou	101.8	99.6	101.6	102.0	98.4	107.7	102.7	93.8	104.0	102.7	109.0
惠 州	Huizhou	102.7	100.8	103.4	103.7	101.7	107.4	105.4	92.6	102.7	110.1	108.0
汕 尾	Shanwei	102.0	101.0	103.1	103.0	98.6	105.9	103.9	92.7	103.0	108.2	106.4
东 莞	Dongguan	102.7	100.9	102.9	102.8	103.0	107.6	104.9	92.4	106.4	104.1	107.8
中 山	Zhongshan	101.9	101.0	101.4	101.7	100.0	111.8	103.2	91.5	102.5	103.0	107.2
江 门	Jiangmen	102.2	100.8	101.2	101.6	101.7	110.6	101.5	92.1	105.7	99.7	108.6
阳 江	Yangjiang	102.1	101.1	102.3	102.6	94.4	113.1	107.1	89.9	109.2	103.0	105.5
湛 江	Zhanjiang	101.8	100.1	102.4	102.7	97.1	110.5	103.4	90.2	107.2	108.3	103.5
茂 名	Maoming	101.6	100.4	101.4	101.6	95.7	101.6	105.3	95.6	100.5	105.6	109.4
肇 庆	Zhaoqing	102.3	100.7	102.4	101.2	99.6	107.0	98.8	90.4	105.6	105.7	107.9
清 远	Qingyuan	101.6	100.0	100.9	99.6	99.6	110.3	90.7	90.6	98.1	103.6	107.8
潮 州	Chaozhou	102.0	100.4	102.2	103.4	100.8	107.9	112.1	92.5	102.5	105.6	103.4
揭 阳	Jieyang	101.6	99.4	102.7	102.2	95.9	105.6	103.9	96.4	105.6	102.8	107.1
云 浮	Yunfu	101.7	100.0	101.7	102.1	103.8	105.4	99.4	91.3	99.8	105.9	105.3

9-5 续表 continued

上年=100 (preceding year=100)

市别	City	干鲜瓜果类 Fruits and Nuts	茶及饮料 Tea and Beverages	烟酒 Tobacco and Alcohol	在外餐饮 Dining Out	衣着 Clothing	居住 Housing	生活用品及服务 Articles for Daily Use and Services	交通通信 Transport and Communi-cations	教育文化娱乐 Education Culture and Recreation	医疗保健 Health Care	其他用品及服务 Other Articles and Services
广 州	Guangzhou	117.8	100.5	102.7	103.9	101.6	100.8	100.5	105.7	102.8	100.4	100.7
深 圳	Shenzhen	107.5	107.6	103.5	104.5	100.9	100.3	101.3	105.5	102.6	100.0	102.3
珠 海	Zhuhai	104.0	101.0	101.5	100.9	99.6	100.0	100.6	105.9	99.7	100.4	100.2
汕 头	Shantou	110.9	99.8	106.4	100.2	102.0	98.9	101.6	104.5	101.5	99.9	100.8
佛 山	Foshan	106.2	105.0	99.2	101.2	99.9	100.4	101.6	106.2	101.7	102.2	101.5
韶 关	Shaoguan	109.6	102.8	99.9	100.3	101.2	100.1	100.5	106.1	101.6	100.2	100.3
河 源	Heyuan	105.5	100.4	104.0	102.0	97.9	100.0	99.8	104.0	102.2	103.9	100.3
梅 州	Meizhou	111.9	103.1	102.6	99.8	102.5	101.9	100.8	104.8	100.4	99.7	101.2
惠 州	Huizhou	113.7	103.2	101.9	103.3	100.2	100.5	101.9	107.4	102.1	99.7	101.8
汕 尾	Shanwei	110.4	99.4	101.6	104.1	94.8	101.2	100.0	104.4	101.1	102.2	102.2
东 莞	Dongguan	107.1	108.9	105.1	102.4	98.5	100.9	102.0	107.3	101.5	99.9	103.5
中 山	Zhongshan	105.6	102.3	102.1	100.7	101.7	101.1	103.0	105.0	101.8	100.4	101.0
江 门	Jiangmen	108.2	102.8	105.0	99.6	102.0	101.4	101.8	106.0	101.5	101.8	102.0
阳 江	Yangjiang	109.9	98.4	99.9	102.3	99.5	100.6	101.4	106.0	103.0	99.5	99.5
湛 江	Zhanjiang	113.4	101.0	103.2	101.9	102.4	100.9	99.6	104.8	101.5	99.3	100.0
茂 名	Maoming	106.2	101.2	102.0	100.8	98.0	101.4	100.3	105.5	101.1	100.6	101.1
肇 庆	Zhaoqing	108.1	98.0	99.9	105.3	99.1	100.5	101.3	106.5	102.6	101.1	101.0
清 远	Qingyuan	111.2	105.5	104.1	103.1	100.4	99.6	103.2	105.1	101.9	101.5	102.3
潮 州	Chaozhou	109.6	100.1	100.7	99.9	100.8	101.5	101.8	104.6	100.7	100.6	103.1
揭 阳	Jieyang	109.3	102.8	102.9	103.7	98.6	99.3	100.5	104.1	100.9	103.0	101.8
云 浮	Yunfu	115.4	100.8	101.7	100.7	100.2	100.8	100.7	105.6	99.7	100.5	103.0

9-6 各市服务项目价格分类指数（2022年）

Service Price Indices by Category and by City (2022)

上年=100 (preceding year=100)

市 别	City	服务价格 Service Price	#租赁房房租 Rent of Rental Housing	家庭服务 Household Services	交通费 Traffic Fee	通信服务 Communication Services	邮递服务 Postal Service	教育服务 Education Service	文化娱乐服务 Cultural and Recreational Services	旅游 Tourism	医疗服务 Medical Service	其他服务 Other Service
广 州	Guangzhou	101.2	100.0	103.4	106.1	99.3	100.0	102.9	100.9	107.0	100.0	100.5
深 圳	Shenzhen	101.0	99.6	101.4	106.0	100.0	99.9	102.8	100.3	104.9	100.0	103.1
珠 海	Zhuhai	99.5	98.5	99.4	103.0	100.0	99.8	100.9	97.8	93.1	100.0	99.8
汕 头	Shantou	99.2	94.4	106.0	103.1	100.0	99.3	101.2	99.5	106.4	100.0	101.0
佛 山	Foshan	101.0	99.1	105.0	105.6	98.8	99.9	102.3	98.7	103.2	102.8	101.2
韶 关	Shaoguan	99.9	98.0	100.0	105.9	100.0	99.8	102.2	97.0	102.5	100.0	100.1
河 源	Heyuan	100.8	97.9	100.3	105.1	100.0	100.5	102.3	101.0	107.1	103.6	99.3
梅 州	Meizhou	99.6	98.6	99.6	102.2	100.0	99.8	100.8	100.9	99.3	99.2	100.6
惠 州	Huizhou	100.8	98.6	106.0	103.8	100.5	98.8	102.3	101.0	102.9	100.4	100.8
汕 尾	Shanwei	101.0	99.2	99.5	108.6	100.0	100.9	101.9	100.3	101.8	102.0	99.8
东 莞	Dongguan	100.9	98.8	103.2	105.4	98.9	100.0	102.0	100.3	101.0	100.0	102.7
中 山	Zhongshan	101.0	99.0	108.6	103.8	100.0	100.0	102.2	100.9	101.6	100.4	100.8
江 门	Jiangmen	100.8	99.9	101.9	105.2	100.0	100.0	101.0	101.3	101.2	101.6	101.7
阳 江	Yangjiang	101.1	99.6	106.7	106.2	100.2	99.8	102.9	100.8	107.2	100.0	100.0
湛 江	Zhanjiang	100.1	99.3	100.8	103.9	100.0	100.0	100.9	99.6	106.8	98.5	100.5
茂 名	Maoming	100.4	98.2	102.6	103.0	100.0	102.8	102.5	96.8	93.4	100.0	100.9
肇 庆	Zhaoqing	100.7	99.4	105.3	106.6	100.0	100.0	103.3	100.6	102.7	100.0	102.4
清 远	Qingyuan	100.0	97.1	106.3	104.9	100.0	98.5	102.5	100.9	99.9	101.5	100.4
潮 州	Chaozhou	100.4	98.6	105.8	103.7	99.7	99.0	101.0	101.6	98.2	100.0	101.3
揭 阳	Jieyang	99.4	95.5	105.0	102.6	100.0	98.0	101.4	100.2	99.2	104.7	100.5
云 浮	Yunfu	100.0	96.4	101.2	105.9	99.4	100.0	99.3	100.4	101.0	100.0	103.4

9-7 工业生产者出厂价格指数
Producer Price Indices for Industrial Products

上年=100 (preceding year=100)

项　目	Item	2017	2018	2019	2020	2021	2022
工业生产者出厂价格指数	**Producer Price Index for Industrial Products**	**103.3**	**101.8**	**100.2**	**99.0**	**103.4**	**103.0**
按轻重工业分	**Grouped by Light and Heavy Industries**						
轻工业	Light Industry	101.9	100.7	100.7	99.7	101.7	102.3
以农产品为原料	Using Farm Products as Raw Materials	102.2	101.2	101.4	100.3	101.8	103.2
以非农产品为原料	Using Non-farm Products as Raw Materials	101.7	100.3	100.2	99.3	101.7	101.8
重工业	Heavy Industry	104.1	102.4	99.9	98.6	104.2	103.3
采　掘	Mining and Quarrying	116.8	108.8	100.2	92.9	118.5	121.5
原　料	Raw Materials	107.5	104.6	98.1	94.5	110.9	112.0
加　工	Processing	102.9	101.6	100.4	99.9	102.6	101.1
按生产生活资料分	**Grouped by Production and Living Materials**						
生产资料	Means of Production	104.5	102.6	100.0	98.6	105.0	104.2
采　掘	Mining and Quarrying	116.8	108.8	100.2	92.9	118.5	121.5
原　料	Raw Materials	107.5	104.6	98.0	94.2	110.9	112.0
加　工	Processing	103.5	101.8	100.5	99.9	103.5	102.2
生活资料	Living Materials	101.3	100.5	100.5	99.7	100.4	100.6
食　品	Food	101.9	101.0	102.3	102.7	101.5	102.4
衣　着	Clothing	101.3	99.8	102.2	99.0	98.4	102.6
一般日用品	Articles for Daily Use	101.2	100.4	101.3	100.8	100.6	102.0
耐用消费品	Durable Consumer Goods	101.0	100.5	99.0	98.4	100.3	99.1
按工业部门分	**Grouped by Industrial Sectors**						
冶金工业	Metallurgical Industry	114.6	106.6	100.6	100.2	115.7	104.9
电力工业	Power Industry	98.7	96.0	98.8	97.5	98.8	105.2
石油工业	Petroleum Industry	118.1	115.0	95.9	83.8	124.5	131.0
化学工业	Chemical Industry	104.2	103.0	99.1	98.1	106.2	102.3
机械工业	Machine Manufacturing Industry	100.6	100.0	100.2	99.4	100.6	101.0
建筑材料工业	Building Materials Industry	104.8	106.4	100.2	100.1	104.0	96.8
森林工业	Timber Industry	101.2	100.8	101.2	99.9	100.4	102.5
食品工业	Food Industry	101.4	101.1	102.0	102.9	103.5	103.8
纺织工业	Textile Industry	102.1	101.7	101.7	99.1	99.9	104.7
缝纫工业	Tailoring Industry	102.6	100.4	102.3	98.9	98.8	103.2
皮革工业	Leather Industry	99.1	98.7	102.3	99.2	96.2	101.3
造纸工业	Paper Making Industry	107.2	105.7	96.0	96.5	106.0	101.2
文教艺术用品工业	Industry for Cultural, Educational & Art Articles	101.3	100.0	102.7	101.0	100.6	101.9
其它工业	Others	101.4	98.0	103.0	104.4	101.1	101.6

9-8 工业生产者购进价格指数

Purchasing Price Indices for Industrial Producers

上年=100 (preceding year=100)

项 目	Item	2017	2018	2019
工业生产者购进价格指数	**Producer Price Index for Purchased Goods**	**105.3**	**102.5**	**99.2**
按材料类别分	**Grouped by Type of Material**			
燃料、动力类	Fuels and Power	106.2	103.7	99.7
黑色金属材料类	Ferrous Materials	115.8	104.8	101.1
#钢材	Steel	115.8	105.0	98.2
其它	Others	115.9	104.4	106.0
有色金属材料和电线类	Nonferrous Materials and Wires	115.0	104.2	96.9
化工原料类	Chemical Materials	107.1	103.4	97.3
木材及纸浆类	Timber and Paper Pulp	108.6	106.2	96.2
建筑材料及非金属矿类	Building Materials and Nonmetal Minerals	108.2	115.2	103.4
其它工业原材料及半成品类	Other Raw Materials and Semi-finished Products	102.4	100.3	99.2
农副产品类	Agricultural Products	103.6	99.0	100.6
纺织原料类	Textile Raw Materials	103.5	103.0	100.2

9-8 续表 continued

上年=100 (preceding year=100)

项 目	Item	2020	2021	2022
工业生产者购进价格指数	**Producer Price Index for Purchased Goods**	**97.4**	**108.0**	**104.1**
按材料类别分	**Grouped by Type of Material**			
燃料、动力类	Fuels and Power	91.4	118.4	117.9
黑色金属材料类	Ferrous Materials	98.8	119.5	98.8
#钢材	Steel	98.1	119.5	99.2
其它	Others	100.1	120.6	93.1
有色金属材料和电线类	Nonferrous Materials and Wires	99.9	126.4	102.5
化工原料类	Chemical Materials	94.6	109.8	104.5
木材及纸浆类	Timber and Paper Pulp	96.2	104.7	108.6
建筑材料及非金属矿类	Building Materials and Nonmetal Minerals	102.4	102.1	99.6
其它工业原材料及半成品类	Other Raw Materials and Semi-finished Products	99.3	102.8	102.3
农副产品类	Agricultural Products	103.6	99.5	104.1
纺织原料类	Textile Raw Materials	96.4	100.0	101.9

9-9 各市工业生产者出厂价格指数
Producer Price Indices for Industrial Products by City

上年=100 (preceding year=100)

市 别	City	2015	2016	2017	2018	2019	2020	2021	2022
全 省	**Provincial Total**	**96.8**	**99.4**	**103.3**	**101.8**	**100.2**	**99.0**	**103.4**	**103.0**
广 州	Guangzhou	96.8	98.8	102.3	101.0	99.1	99.4	104.1	102.6
深 圳	Shenzhen	97.6	99.3	101.8	100.2	100.0	99.0	101.9	101.7
珠 海	Zhuhai	96.9	99.4	103.2	101.9	100.1	97.9	103.5	103.4
汕 头	Shantou	98.6	100.3	102.0	100.8	100.9	99.5	101.6	102.8
佛 山	Foshan	97.2	99.2	104.5	101.9	100.2	99.0	104.1	103.3
韶 关	Shaoguan	92.1	99.0	110.2	104.8	99.8	99.3	111.6	104.7
河 源	Heyuan	93.6	100.2	107.9	102.1	100.4	99.7	103.9	101.4
梅 州	Meizhou	95.8	99.5	103.2	103.1	101.6	100.3	103.2	100.5
惠 州	Huizhou	92.5	98.3	104.2	102.8	99.3	97.5	107.1	104.6
汕 尾	Shanwei	98.6	100.9	102.0	99.6	101.1	100.6	101.2	101.9
东 莞	Dongguan	98.2	99.9	101.7	100.6	100.4	99.4	101.8	101.4
中 山	Zhongshan	98.0	99.7	102.5	101.1	100.3	99.1	102.1	102.2
江 门	Jiangmen	97.8	99.3	103.5	102.0	99.8	98.7	103.7	102.8
阳 江	Yangjiang	95.2	99.9	106.9	103.4	100.0	99.9	110.5	104.1
湛 江	Zhanjiang	91.7	99.2	105.6	103.4	99.7	97.4	111.3	109.9
茂 名	Maoming	81.8	95.5	110.7	109.0	97.6	91.4	119.0	121.1
肇 庆	Zhaoqing	96.3	98.9	105.2	102.4	99.8	99.4	105.8	102.0
清 远	Qingyuan	94.6	97.8	107.9	104.6	99.6	98.8	108.0	102.3
潮 州	Chaozhou	97.2	99.4	101.7	101.6	101.2	99.3	104.7	106.1
揭 阳	Jieyang	97.6	100.4	104.4	102.3	101.1	98.9	103.0	103.0
云 浮	Yunfu	96.8	98.9	102.6	103.4	98.1	97.3	102.5	100.5

9-10 分行业工业生产者出厂价格指数

Producer Price Indices for Industrial Products by Sector

上年=100 (preceding year=100)

项　目	Item	2019	2020	2021	2022
工业生产者出厂价格指数	**Producer Price Index for Manufactured Goods**	**100.2**	**99.0**	**103.4**	**103.0**
按工业行业分	**Grouped by Industrial Sector**				
#石油和天然气开采业	Extraction of Petroleum and Natural Gas	96.7	82.6	123.5	131.1
黑色金属矿采选业	Mining and Processing of Ferrous Metal Ores	112.1	115.9	155.9	82.9
有色金属矿采选业	Mining and Processing of Non-ferrous Metal Ores	95.6	106.3	110.5	104.0
非金属矿采选业	Mining and Processing of Nonmetal Ores	104.0	102.5	99.2	98.8
农副食品加工业	Processing of Foods from Agricultural Products	101.8	104.7	107.3	106.5
食品制造业	Processing of Foodstuff	100.3	99.9	100.1	102.8
酒、饮料和精制茶制造业	Manufacture of Liquor, Beverages and Refined Tea	103.7	102.4	99.4	100.5
烟草制品业	Manufacture of Tobacco	104.5	103.1	102.1	100.3
纺织业	Textile Industry	102.8	99.2	99.5	106.2
纺织服装、服饰业	Manufacture of Textile, Wearing Apparel and Accessories	101.4	98.8	98.6	101.9
皮革、毛皮、羽毛及其制品和制鞋业	Manufacture of Leather,Fur, Feather and Related Products and Footware	102.4	99.3	98.4	101.6
木材加工及木、竹、藤、棕、草制品业	Processing of Timber, Manufacture of Wood, Bamboo, Rattan, Palm and Straw Products	97.7	99.4	103.6	102.6
家具制造业	Manufacture of Furniture	102.2	98.7	98.7	100.6
造纸和纸制品业	Manufacture of Paper and Paper Products	96.0	96.5	106.0	101.2
印刷和记录媒介复制业	Printing, Reproduction of Recording Media	102.6	99.8	99.5	101.3
文教、工美、体育和娱乐用品制造业	Manufacture of Articles for Culture, Education, Arts and Crafts, Sport and Entertainment Activities	103.8	104.9	102.8	102.5
石油加工、炼焦和核燃料加工业	Processing of Petroleum, Coking, Processing of Nuclear Fuel	95.6	82.2	130.0	135.6
化学原料和化学制品制造业	Manufacture of Raw Chemical Materials and Chemical Products	97.0	97.1	112.1	103.3
医药制造业	Manufacture of Medicines	103.4	101.4	97.6	99.4
化学纤维制造业	Manufacture of Chemical Fibers	96.9	89.4	114.3	99.7
橡胶和塑料制品业	Manufacture of Rubber and Plastic Products	100.4	98.1	102.3	101.9
非金属矿物制品业	Manufacture of Non-metallic Mineral Products	100.1	99.9	103.9	97.3
黑色金属冶炼和压延加工业	Smelting and Pressing of Ferrous Metals	99.1	98.3	123.3	109.4
有色金属冶炼和压延加工业	Smelting and Pressing of Nonferrous Metals	99.3	101.2	123.5	105.6
金属制品业	Manufacture of Metal Products	101.2	100.1	107.6	101.9
通用设备制造业	Manufacture of General-purpose Machinery	101.4	101.2	101.3	101.2
专用设备制造业	Manufacture of Special-purpose Machinery	100.5	100.3	100.3	100.6
汽车制造业	Manufacture of Automobiles	100.3	101.4	99.5	100.6
铁路、船舶、航空航天和其他运输设备制造业	Manufacture of Railway, Ship, Aerospace and Other Electronic Equipment	101.1	100.3	101.0	101.8
电气机械和器材制造业	Manufacture of Electrical Machinery and Equipment	98.9	97.7	101.4	105.3
计算机、通信和其他电子设备制造业	Manufacture of Communication Equipment, Computers and Other Electronic Equipment	100.4	99.6	100.2	99.5
仪器仪表制造业	Manufacture of Measuring Instruments and Machinery	102.3	98.0	98.7	101.1
其他制造业	Other Manufacturing	100.3	98.8	99.4	102.8
废弃资源综合利用业	Utilization of Waste Resources	102.7	98.9	113.9	103.5
金属制品、机械和设备修理业	Repair Service of Metal Products,Machinery and Equipment	98.8	120.3	99.0	103.2
电力、热力生产和供应业	Production and Supply of Electric Power and Heat Power	99.1	97.6	98.8	105.2
燃气生产和供应业	Production and Supply of Gas	96.5	93.7	110.3	118.5
水的生产和供应业	Production and Supply of Water	98.3	100.0	100.8	100.7

注:2016年起，由于使用新的国民经济行业分类GB/4754—2011，之前年份个别行业数据缺失或数据涵盖范围存在差异。

Note: Since 2016 indices are by the industrial classification standard of 2011's version. Dates are lost in some sub-industries and there are differences in the scope of dates calculated.

9-11 农产品生产者价格指数

Producer Price Indices for Farm Products

上年=100 (preceding year=100)

项 目	Item	2017	2018	2019	2020	2021	2022
农产品生产者价格指数	**Producer Price Indices for Farm Products**	**99.4**	**101.3**	**107.3**	**104.7**	**98.8**	**100.1**
农业产品	**Farm Products**	**100.9**	**100.1**	**103.5**	**99.8**	**100.8**	**102.8**
谷物	Cereal	100.5	101.0	98.3	100.5	104.1	101.8
#稻谷	Rice	100.5	101.0	98.3	100.5	104.1	101.6
薯类	Potato	107.6	106.3	103.1	99.4	95.5	98.8
油料	Oil-Bearing Crops	98.8	102.2	103.8	106.2	100.9	101.0
豆类	Beans	96.4	102.2	99.4	102.3	106.6	102.2
糖料	Sugar Crops	114.4	91.4	93.6	105.0	101.0	104.0
未加工烟草	Raw Tobacco	99.4	97.5	102.8	101.8	104.9	102.1
蔬菜及食用菌	Vegetables & Edible Fungi	95.6	101.1	102.3	100.4	103.3	101.6
#叶菜类蔬菜	Leaf Vegetable	90.9	103.1	103.2	99.0	102.8	103.6
白菜类蔬菜	Chinese Cabbage Vegetable	90.3	100.6	102.3	101.0	102.6	101.3
芥菜类蔬菜	Mustard Vegetable	95.1	99.2	100.7	101.3	106.5	100.8
甘蓝类蔬菜	Brassica Vegetable	85.9	100.7	98.6	102.8	103.6	97.4
根茎类蔬菜	Root Vegetable	93.9	104.9	92.8	98.5	102.7	101.0
瓜菜类蔬菜	Cucurbita Vegetable	104.8	98.6	104.8	101.5	100.4	101.9
豆类蔬菜	Bean Vegetable	102.8	99.2	105.6	97.7	108.8	102.1
茄果类蔬菜	Solanaceous Vegetable	101.7	103.0	113.1	94.3	102.7	102.6
莴苣及菊苣类蔬菜	Lettuce Vegetable	94.5	102.9	101.3	108.7	100.0	102.5
葱蒜类蔬菜	Bulb Vegetable	98.9	102.1	97.1	101.7	106.9	100.1
花卉	Flowers	104.4	101.6	94.5	102.3	96.0	99.5
盆景及园艺产品	Potted Landscape and Gardening Products	94.7	99.2	94.1	93.2	98.8	100.8
水果及坚果	Fruit and Nuts	106.1	95.0	124.0	96.7	93.7	105.2
茶及饮料原料	Tea and Beverage Raw Meterials	103.7	104.6	102.2	99.8	101.6	102.6
林业产品	**Forestry Products**	**102.0**	**99.4**	**98.0**	**99.5**	**109.3**	**99.8**
育种和育苗	Seed Breeding and Seedling	93.5	100.1	98.2	103.9	102.0	99.9
木材采伐产品	Wood Logging	100.5	101.2	99.9	98.4	108.0	97.8
竹材采伐产品	Bamboo Logging	99.8	100.5	100.1	96.1	102.5	100.5
林产品	Forestry Products	117.1	93.2	91.2	99.4	127.1	100.1
饲养动物及其产品	**Farm Animal and Products**	**92.0**	**101.6**	**121.0**	**119.5**	**88.2**	**92.0**
活牲畜	Live Animals	89.1	89.7	140.5	157.9	69.1	83.5
#猪	Pig	89.1	89.7	140.5	157.9	69.1	83.5
活家禽	Live Birds	96.7	107.5	109.3	89.0	103.1	102.0
#鸡	Chicken	98.6	103.9	108.8	92.0	103.2	102.1
鸭	Duck	99.7	111.9	107.5	89.3	107.0	101.5
畜禽产品	Animal and Bird Products	87.6	120.3	95.7	88.7	104.3	103.5
#鸡蛋	Chicken Eggs	81.2	112.9	99.7	94.7	100.4	103.1
鸭蛋	Duck Eggs	103.1	138.4	85.9	74.0	113.9	110.7
渔业产品	**Fishery Products**	**103.9**	**103.6**	**102.1**	**99.2**	**105.0**	**101.6**
海水养殖产品	Marine Farm Products	104.9	103.2	103.5	97.3	102.4	101.3
#海水养殖鱼	Marine Farm Fish	104.8	104.6	105.1	99.3	101.3	98.1
海水养殖虾	Marine Farm Shrimp	103.1	100.3	99.1	99.6	101.5	103.5
海水捕捞产品	Marine Catching Products	104.7	105.6	105.2	101.2	106.0	101.6
#海水捕捞鲜鱼	Marine Catching Fish	104.3	106.3	105.7	100.5	101.4	100.9
海水捕捞虾	Marine Catching Shrimp	107.4	103.4	105.0	105.8	105.8	119.4
淡水养殖产品	Freshwater Farm Products	103.0	101.9	100.4	98.5	104.3	101.9
#养殖淡水鱼	Freshwater Fram Fish	103.2	102.0	99.4	101.5	105.2	101.3
淡水养殖虾	Freshwater Fram Shrimp	102.0	101.3	104.0	87.1	100.6	103.6
淡水捕捞产品	Freshwater Catching Products	102.8	109.9	100.2	106.2	110.1	
#捕捞淡水鱼	Freshwater Catching Fish	101.7	112.4	100.0	107.0	102.3	
淡水捕捞鲜虾	Freshwater Catching Shrimp	105.9	106.7	100.1	102.5	110.1	

主要统计指标解释

居民消费价格指数 是度量生活消费品及服务项目价格水平随着时间而变动的相对数，反映居民家庭购买的消费品及服务项目价格水平的变动情况。该指数是宏观经济分析、决策、调控和价格总水平监测以及国民经济核算的重要指标，其按年度计算的变动率通常被用来作为反映通货膨胀(或紧缩)程度的指标。

城市居民消费价格指数 是反映城市居民家庭所购买的生活消费品和服务项目价格变动趋势和变动程度的相对数。编制该指数，可以观察和分析消费品的零售价格和服务项目价格变动对城市居民生活消费支出的影响，作为研究城市居民生活和制定工资政策的依据。

农村居民消费价格指数 是反映农村居民家庭所购买的生活消费品和服务项目价格变动趋势和变动程度的相对数。编制该指数，可以观察农村消费品的零售价格和服务项目价格变动对农村居民生活消费支出的影响，反映农村居民生活水平的实际变化情况，为分析和研究农村居民生活问题提供依据。

商品零售价格指数 是度量市场商品零售价格水平变动趋势和变动程度的相对数，反映商品在流通过程中最后一个环节的价格即工业、商业、餐饮业和其他零售企业向城乡居民、机关团体出售生活消费品和办公用品价格水平的变动趋势和变动程度。其目的在于掌握商品价格的变动趋势，为国家宏观调控和国民经济核算提供参考依据。

工业生产者出厂价格指数 是反映工业企业产品第一次出售时的出厂价格变化趋势和变动幅度的相对数（2010年前称工业品出厂价格指数），是综合了工业企业出售给本企业以外所有单位和个人的各种产品价格指数计算取得。是反映某一时期工业生产领域价格变动情况的重要经济指标，也是制定有关经济政策和国民经济核算的重要依据。

工业生产者购进价格指数 是反映工业企业作为中间投入产品购进价格的变化趋势和变动幅度的相对数（2010年前称原材料、燃料、动力购进价格指数）。反映工业企业作为生产投入而从物资交易市场和能源、原材料生产企业购买原材料，燃料和动力产品时，所支付的价格水平变动趋势和程度的重要指标，是扣除工业企业物质消耗成本中的价格变动影响的重要依据。

农产品生产者价格指数 是反映农产品生产者第一手(直接)出售其产品时实际获得的单位产品价格。开展农产品生产者价格调查是为了全面收集农产品生产者价格资料，客观反映农产品生产者价格水平和结构变动情况，满足农业与国民经济核算需要，为各级政府制定农业保护与农产品流通政策提供决策依据，向社会各界提供优质的农产品价格信息服务。

Explanatory Notes on Main Statistical Indicators

Consumer Price Indices measure the relative change with time in prices of consumer goods and services, reflecting the rates of change in consumer goods and services purchased by households. It is an important indicator for macroeconomic analysis, decision-making, regularization and control, supervision of general price level and national economic accounting. The annualized rates of change are generally considered as an indicator of inflation or deflation.

Consumer Price Indices of Urban Households reflect the trend and degree of changes in prices of consumer goods and services purchased by urban households and can be used to observe and analyze the impact of price changes in consumer goods and services on urban household living expenditures, thus providing the basis for policy making concerning the living cost and the wages of urban staff and workers.

Consumer Price Indices of Rural Households reflect the trend and degree of changes in prices of consumer goods and services purchased by rural households and can be used to observe and analyze the impact of change in prices of consumer goods and services on living expenditure and actual changes in the living standards of rural residents, thus providing the basis for analysis and research on the conditions of life in rural areas.

Retail Price Indices measure the relative trend and degree of changes in retail prices of commodities, reflecting the trend of changes in prices in the last link of circulation, i.e. prices of consumer goods and office appliances sold to households or organizations by enterprises of industry, commerce, catering services and other retail trades. It reflects the trend of price changes and provides a reference for macroeconomic adjustment and control as well as national economic accounting.

Producer Price Indices for Manufactured Goods reflect the trend and degree of changes in general ex-factory prices of all manufactured goods on first sale (it was referred to as Ex-factory Price Indices for Industrial Goods). It is calculated on the basis of sales of manufactured goods by an industrial enterprise to all units outside the enterprise, as well as sales of consumer goods to residents.It is an import index reflecting the price changes on the course of industrial production, and provides important data for economic policy making and national economic accounting

Producer Price Indices for Purchased Goods reflect the trend and degree of changes in prices paid by industrial enterprises when they purchase production input (it was referred to as Purchasing Price Indices of Raw Materials, Fuels and Power). They reflect changes in the level and degree of prices paid by industrial enterprises when they purchase production input such as raw materials, fuels and power from the market or from other energy or raw materials producing enterprises. These indices provide an important basis for measuring the material consumption of industrial enterprises after removing the influence of price changes.

Producer Price Indices of Agricultural Products refer to the actual prices per unit of agricultural products at which the producers of the agricultural products directly sell them. The purpose of conducting the survey of producer prices of agricultural products is to comprehensively collect the data on the producer prices of agricultural products, objectively reflect the situations of the level and structural changes of the producer prices of agricultural products, meet the needs of conducting the agricultural accounts and national accounts, provide the government at different levels with the base data for making the policies of protecting agriculture and circulation of agricultural products and provide the various social circles with the high quality information on the prices of agricultural products.

十、人民生活

PEOPLE'S LIVING CONDITIONS

十 人民生活

简要说明

一、本篇资料反映广东居民生活状况，主要内容包括广东全体居民及分城乡居民家庭人口、收入与消费支出结构、住房面积和主要耐用消费品拥有量等。

二、本篇资料由国家统计局广东调查总队居民收支调查处整理提供。

三、居民调查资料采用二相抽样和多阶段抽样相结合的调查方法统计。

四、2013 年国家统计局实行城乡住户一体化调查改革，将过去城镇与农村分别开展的调查体系，按照统一指标、统一方法、统一标准、统一调查、统一程序的原则，整合为城乡一体化住户调查新体系。由于新旧调查体系在调查范围和对象、城乡划分标准、样本抽选方法、计算和汇总方式、指标名称和口径等都发生了变化，新旧口径指标数据衔接困难。

五、旧调查体系的农村居民纯收入指标在新的调查体系中统一为城乡可比的可支配收入，旧调查体系中的城乡经营性收入、财产性收入与转移性收入在新的调查体系中统一为经营净收入、财产净收入与转移净收入。

六、2013 年起为新口径数据， 2013 年以前的为旧调查体系的数据。

七、珠三角地区 9 市指广州、深圳、珠海、佛山、惠州、东莞、中山、江门、肇庆。粤东西北 12 市指汕头、韶关、河源、梅州、汕尾、阳江、湛江、茂名、清远、潮州、揭阳和云浮市。东翼 4 市指汕头、汕尾、潮州、揭阳市。西翼 3 市指阳江、湛江、茂名市。山区 5 市指韶关、河源、梅州、清远、云浮。

10 People's Living Conditions

Brief Introduction

Ⅰ. The data in this chapter show the basic conditions of the people' s livelihood in the urban and rural areas of Guangdong Province. The main contents include urban and rural households population, per capita income and consumption expenditure structure, housing area and possession of the major consumer goods.

Ⅱ.The data in this chapter are prepared and provided by Division of Income and Expenditure Survey and under Guangdong Survey Office of the National Bureau of Statistics.

Ⅲ.The survey data of urban and rural residents are collected through two-phase sampling scheme combined with multi-stage sampling scheme.

Ⅳ.The National Bureau of Statistics of China started an integrated reform of household survey in 2013, including both rural and urban households. According to the principle of unified index, unified standard, unified survey, unified software, unified release, the separate urban and rural household surveys are changed to the integrated household income and expenditure survey. Because there are great difference of survey scope and object, survey methodology, sample selection, data collection methodology between the integrated and the separate household survey, the data produced by the integrated system of household survey are not comparable to those produced by the separate urban and rural household surveys prior to 2013.

V.The net income of rural households of the old household survey are integrated to the disposal income of rural households in the new household survey since 2013. Income from properties, transfers and business of the old household survey are unified to net income from properties, transfers and business in the new household survey.

Ⅵ.Data before 2013 are produced by the old survey system , data since 2013 are new scope.

VII. The 9 Cities of the Pearl River Delta refer to Guangzhou, Shenzhen, Zhuhai, Foshan, Huizhou, Dongguan, Zhongshan, Jiangmen, and Zhaoqing. The 12 Cities of the Eastern-Western-Northern Region refer to Shantou, Shaoguan, Heyuan Meizhou, Shanwei, Yangjiang, Zhanjiang, Maoming, Qingyuan, Chaozhou, Jieyang, and Yunfu. The 4 Cities of the Eastern Region refer to Shantou, Shanwei, Chaozhou, and Jieyang. The 3 Cities of the Western Region refer to Yangjiang, Zhanjiang, and Maoming. The 5 Cities of the Mountainous Region refer to Shaoguan, Heyuan, Meizhou, Qingyuan, and Yunfu.

10-1 全省居民家庭基本情况

Basic Conditions of Households Province Wide

指　　标	Item	2017	2018	2019	2020	2021	2022
调查户数　　　（户）	**Survey of households　　(households)**	**8082**	**7900**	**7900**	**7900**	**7900**	**7900**
平均每户常住人口（人）	Average Number of per Permanent Household (person)	3.08	3.26	3.28	3.29	3.46	3.47
平均每户就业人口（人）	Average Number of Employed Persons per Household (person)	1.77	1.75	1.74	1.70	1.80	1.78
人均住房建筑面积（平方米）	**Per Capita housing construction area (square meter)**	**36.94**	**38.46**	**39.75**	**40.89**	**42.23**	**42.62**
人均可支配收入（元）	**Per Capita Disposable Income　　(yuan)**	**33003.3**	**35809.9**	**39014.3**	**41028.6**	**44993.3**	**47064.6**
1.工资性收入	Income of Wages and Salaries	23052.9	24749.0	26554.3	27824.4	30777.3	32200.8
2.经营净收入	Net Business Income	4420.9	4734.5	5154.7	5037.4	5729.1	5977.5
3.财产净收入	Net Income from Properties	3602.0	4131.4	4776.9	5339.1	5831.3	6107.7
4.转移净收入	Net Income from Transfers	1927.5	2194.9	2528.4	2827.7	2655.6	2778.6
可支配收入构成（%）	**Composition of Disposable Income　　(%)**	**100.0**	**100.0**	**100.0**	**100.0**	**100.0**	**100.0**
1.工资性收入	Income of Wages and Salaries	69.9	69.1	68.1	67.8	68.4	68.4
2.经营净收入	Net Business Income	13.5	13.2	13.2	12.3	12.7	12.7
3.财产净收入	Net Income from Properties	10.8	11.5	12.2	13.0	13.0	13.0
4.转移净收入	Net Income from Transfers	5.8	6.1	6.5	6.9	5.9	5.9
人均消费支出　（元）	**Per Capita Consumption Expenditure　(yuan)**	**24819.6**	**26054.0**	**28994.7**	**28491.9**	**31589.3**	**32168.7**
1.食品烟酒	Food,Tobacco and Liquor	8317.0	8480.8	9369.2	9629.3	10484.6	11025.8
2.衣着	Clothing	1230.3	1135.3	1192.2	1044.5	1278.0	1178.3
3.居住	Living	5790.9	6643.3	7329.1	7733.0	8189.6	8406.2
4.生活用品及服务	Daily Necessities and Services	1447.4	1440.8	1560.2	1560.6	1614.1	1636.0
5.交通通信	Transportation and Telecommunication	3380.0	3423.9	3833.6	3808.7	4164.6	4174.3
6.教育文化娱乐	Education,Culture and Entertainment	2620.4	2750.9	3244.4	2442.9	3241.6	3196.3
7.医疗保健	Health Service	1319.5	1520.8	1770.4	1677.9	1900.9	1783.0
8.其他用品和服务	Other Necessities and Services	714.1	658.2	695.5	595.1	715.9	768.8
消费支出构成　（%）	**Composition of Consumption Expenditure (%)**	**100.0**	**100.0**	**100.0**	**100.0**	**100.0**	**100.0**
1.食品烟酒	Food,Tobacco and Liquor	33.5	32.6	32.3	33.8	33.2	34.3
2.衣着	Clothing	5.0	4.4	4.1	3.7	4.0	3.7
3.居住	Living	23.3	25.5	25.3	27.1	25.9	26.1
4.生活用品及服务	Daily Necessities and Services	5.8	5.5	5.4	5.4	5.1	5.1
5.交通通信	Transportation and Telecommunication	13.6	13.1	13.2	13.4	13.2	13.0
6.教育文化娱乐	Education,Culture and Entertainment	10.6	10.6	11.2	8.6	10.3	9.9
7.医疗保健	Health Service	5.3	5.8	6.1	5.9	6.0	5.5
8.其他用品和服务	Other Necessities and Services	2.9	2.5	2.4	2.1	2.3	2.4

10-2 按收入五等份分组的全省居民人均可支配收入

Per Capita Disposable Income of Households Province Wide by Income Quintile

单位：元 (yuan)

年份 Year	低收入户 (20%) Low Income Households (20%)	中等偏下户 (20%) Lower Middle Income Households (20%)	中等收入户 (20%) Middle Income Households (20%)	中等偏上户 (20%) Upper Middle Income Households (20%)	高收入户 (20%) High Income Households (20%)
2016	9544.65	19574.65	30598.48	41989.63	68599.33
2017	10534.31	20963.27	32339.36	45235.77	75774.57
2018	11241.71	21673.77	33984.26	49984.23	82444.32
2019	11824.33	23226.18	36697.84	54261.18	89717.48
2020	12665.68	23627.34	37656.83	55938.37	93242.94
2021	14229.00	26527.86	40839.11	60156.03	98481.33
2022	14617.01	27922.28	42696.36	63101.77	104311.94

10-3 全省居民人均主要食品消费量

Per Capita Consumption of Major Foods Province Wide

单位:千克 (Kg)

指 标	Item	2017	2018	2019	2020	2021	2022
粮食	Grain	116.80	108.67	115.90	128.21	111.59	106.47
谷物	Cereal	108.86	101.08	106.67	118.36	103.75	98.98
薯类	Tuber	1.64	1.54	1.65	1.62	1.29	1.26
豆类	Beans and the Products	6.30	6.05	7.59	8.22	6.54	6.22
油脂类	Oil and Fats	9.23	9.16	9.03	9.94	10.35	10.05
#植物油	Vegetable Oil	8.83	8.58	8.47	9.50	9.78	9.57
蔬菜及菜制品	Vegetable and Mushroom	100.76	100.57	109.45	113.01	97.86	101.15
#鲜菜	Fresh Vegetables	96.66	97.19	105.74	109.33	95.02	98.53
肉类	Products of Meat	36.51	40.99	38.73	33.61	37.58	42.76
#猪肉	Pork	29.07	34.02	30.71	25.96	29.61	34.20
禽类	Poultry	20.62	21.08	25.92	31.12	24.56	24.34
#鸡	Chick	13.40	13.74	16.62	19.54	15.71	15.68
水产品	Aquatic Products	22.85	22.03	28.61	30.01	27.55	24.43
#鱼类	Fresh	16.86	16.35	21.05	22.28	20.19	16.68
蛋类及蛋制品	Eggs and Egg Products	7.32	7.39	8.37	9.87	8.40	8.77
#鲜蛋	Fresh Eggs	6.89	7.06	8.01	9.50	8.09	8.50
奶及奶制品	Milk and Dairy Products	7.71	8.63	8.83	9.59	12.85	9.28
#鲜奶	Fresh Milk	4.21	4.65	5.36	6.40	9.18	6.71
鲜瓜果	Fresh Melons and Fruits	36.39	35.66	43.04	43.55	41.35	40.82
食糖	Sugar	1.54	1.56	1.55	1.58	1.15	1.04

10-4 全省居民平均每百户年末主要耐用消费品拥有量
Main Durable Consumer Goods Owned per 100 Households Province wide

指　标		Item		2017	2018	2019	2020	2021	2022
家用汽车	(辆)	Car	(set)	31.58	36.94	41.27	42.68	47.63	53.04
摩托车	(辆)	Motorcycle	(set)	64.24	67.25	66.44	65.54	63.55	61.95
助力车	(台)	Electric Bicycle	(set)	30.88	34.60	39.65	41.77	54.64	57.70
洗衣机	(台)	Washing Machine	(set)	78.18	89.73	92.65	93.16	98.08	98.27
电冰箱(柜)	(台)	Refrigerator	(set)	84.44	94.41	97.64	98.23	103.16	103.57
微波炉	(台)	Microwave Oven	(set)	38.13	39.16	41.12	41.82	42.84	43.02
彩色电视机	(台)	Color Television	(set)	106.91	109.07	110.19	110.48	108.36	108.84
空调	(台)	Air Conditioner	(set)	145.24	176.07	187.85	190.13	224.33	229.07
热水器	(台)	Water Heater	(unit)	88.72	99.43	101.52	104.22	104.65	105.59
排油烟机	(台)	Fume hood	(set)	55.35	65.54	68.33	69.39	72.29	73.14
移动电话	(部)	Mobile Phone	(set)	248.76	268.23	270.56	268.44	280.13	281.85
计算机	(台)	Computer	(set)	75.83	69.34	72.59	74.33	67.81	68.07
照相机	(台)	Camera	(set)	24.61	15.88	16.26	16.21	11.41	11.76

10-5 各市全体居民人均可支配收入

Per Capita Disposable Income of Households by City

单位：元 (yuan)

市别	City	2017	2018	2019	2020	2021	2022
全省	**Provincial Total**	**33003.3**	**35809.9**	**39014.3**	**41028.6**	**44993.3**	**47064.6**
广州	Guangzhou	50782.2	55276.1	60073.8	63289.2	68908.3	71357.9
深圳	Shenzhen	52938.0	57543.6	62522.4	64877.7	70847.3	72718.2
珠海	Zhuhai	44043.1	48107.1	52495.1	55936.1	61390.0	62976.1
汕头	Shantou	22521.0	24428.0	26612.8	28220.5	30969.7	32653.8
佛山	Foshan	45813.3	49629.5	54042.7	56244.8	61700.2	64150.2
韶关	Shaoguan	21865.9	23676.0	25805.5	27546.2	30211.5	31411.1
河源	Heyuan	17717.7	19397.1	21052.3	22291.1	24626.5	25825.1
梅州	Meizhou	19635.0	21217.0	22903.9	23872.6	26209.8	27431.1
惠州	Huizhou	31090.6	33929.9	37159.6	39745.4	43350.5	44890.4
汕尾	Shanwei	19325.8	21001.1	22782.9	24427.0	27422.8	29020.1
东莞	Dongguan	45450.6	49331.0	53657.2	56533.1	62126.5	63832.9
中山	Zhongshan	43553.7	46865.0	50477.6	52753.6	57900.8	59764.0
江门	Jiangmen	26850.6	29546.9	32323.3	33666.5	37068.4	38756.2
阳江	Yangjiang	21443.9	23281.8	25131.1	26591.4	29167.9	30514.4
湛江	Zhanjiang	19631.6	21426.9	23320.4	24986.3	27646.3	28861.4
茂名	Maoming	19885.2	21349.9	23179.0	24600.4	26728.6	27787.9
肇庆	Zhaoqing	22360.0	24070.9	26121.5	27496.2	30394.1	31469.8
清远	Qingyuan	20692.0	22369.4	24362.0	26055.0	28741.3	29911.6
潮州	Chaozhou	19429.0	20895.1	22542.4	23302.5	25083.7	26420.0
揭阳	Jieyang	18750.1	20042.3	21341.1	21821.5	23780.5	24788.2
云浮	Yunfu	17874.5	19239.1	20938.1	22306.2	24610.9	25951.9
按经济区域分	By Region						
珠三角	Pearl River Delta	43840.1	47911.0	52213.7	54809.6	60729.7	62700.0
东翼	Eastern Region	20166.7	21754.2	23483.6	24575.6	27006.0	28388.3
西翼	Western Region	20016.4	21691.0	23550.9	25087.4	27538.1	28713.6
山区	Mountainous Region	19657.1	21288.0	23120.3	24504.7	27038.0	28256.0

注：按照国家统计局的统一部署，广东省分市县城乡一体化住户调查工作从2013年底正式启动，从2014年开始正式对外发布分市全体居民人均可支配收入数据。

Note: Under the unified deployment by NBS, Guangdong province started an integrated household survey by city and county since 2013,including both urban and rural households. Since 2014 the data of per capita disposal income and expenditures of all households in the province by city is released officially after the transitional period.

10-6 各市全体居民人均可支配收入来源（2022年）

Per Capita Disposable Income of Households by Sources and City (2022)

单位：元 (yuan)

地　区	City	可支配收入 Disposable Income	工资性收入 Income of Wages and Salaries	经营净收入 Net Business Income	财产净收入 Net Income from Property	转移净收入 Net Income from Transfer
全　省	**Provincial Total**	**47064.6**	**32200.8**	**5977.5**	**6107.7**	**2778.6**
广　州	Guangzhou	71357.9	47247.4	4412.4	13534.2	6163.9
深　圳	Shenzhen	72718.2	61156.8	6989.5	6761.4	-2189.5
珠　海	Zhuhai	62976.1	46621.9	4419.2	8220.7	3714.3
汕　头	Shantou	32653.8	22831.5	4018.0	1908.2	3896.1
佛　山	Foshan	64150.2	39082.9	7681.5	12705.1	4680.7
韶　关	Shaoguan	31411.1	19382.6	5985.9	1648.4	4394.1
河　源	Heyuan	25825.1	16236.2	4508.0	868.5	4212.3
梅　州	Meizhou	27431.1	15672.5	4788.8	1220.3	5749.4
惠　州	Huizhou	44890.4	29758.4	8192.1	4803.0	2136.9
汕　尾	Shanwei	29020.1	16788.8	6239.5	1313.6	4678.2
东　莞	Dongguan	63832.9	44182.9	6512.2	13406.2	-268.3
中　山	Zhongshan	59764.0	40482.9	7191.5	7091.6	4998.0
江　门	Jiangmen	38756.2	27583.6	3626.6	3409.1	4136.9
阳　江	Yangjiang	30514.4	17796.4	7122.1	1725.6	3870.2
湛　江	Zhanjiang	28861.4	15598.7	5549.4	1747.7	5965.5
茂　名	Maoming	27787.9	16311.6	4499.6	1351.0	5625.6
肇　庆	Zhaoqing	31469.8	19743.8	5321.0	1784.8	4620.3
清　远	Qingyuan	29911.6	18704.0	5787.4	1355.5	4064.7
潮　州	Chaozhou	26420.0	15802.1	4602.6	1485.4	4529.8
揭　阳	Jieyang	24788.2	14042.4	5382.1	1236.9	4126.8
云　浮	Yunfu	25951.9	17365.7	4053.5	1237.8	3294.9

10-7 各市全体居民人均消费支出

Per Capita Consumption Expenditure of Households by City

单位：元 (yuan)

市别	City	2017	2018	2019	2020	2021	2022
全省	**Provincial Total**	**24819.6**	**26054.0**	**28994.7**	**28491.9**	**31589.3**	**32168.7**
广州	Guangzhou	37496.1	39467.1	42308.7	41400.3	44253.1	44036.6
深圳	Shenzhen	38320.1	40535.0	43112.7	40581.1	46285.7	44792.9
珠海	Zhuhai	32981.4	35081.4	38211.8	36359.7	42333.7	41333.3
汕头	Shantou	18789.2	19186.8	20944.5	21256.8	22493.0	22824.0
佛山	Foshan	32648.0	34052.6	37160.3	36936.0	40545.2	41129.2
韶关	Shaoguan	16055.7	17207.8	18727.2	18800.2	21335.8	21486.7
河源	Heyuan	13580.7	14593.5	15604.9	16003.5	18030.4	18426.3
梅州	Meizhou	15298.6	15912.5	16822.5	17071.0	18931.3	19624.1
惠州	Huizhou	22968.8	24461.9	26610.7	26232.4	29175.7	29408.0
汕尾	Shanwei	15180.9	16414.2	17834.1	18773.8	20497.6	21635.4
东莞	Dongguan	31849.5	33208.9	35729.7	34259.8	39078.9	39432.5
中山	Zhongshan	29034.2	31057.9	33959.0	32735.5	37852.7	38648.1
江门	Jiangmen	19302.4	19751.6	21647.4	21898.7	24192.8	24538.9
阳江	Yangjiang	17217.9	17850.1	18918.8	19181.0	21018.8	21371.9
湛江	Zhanjiang	14513.9	15302.6	16312.4	16559.7	18858.3	19141.6
茂名	Maoming	14494.5	15440.7	16517.1	17014.9	18276.5	18740.1
肇庆	Zhaoqing	14867.7	15505.6	17021.7	16777.3	19094.7	19592.8
清远	Qingyuan	15580.2	16709.5	17981.4	18247.9	20404.0	20710.6
潮州	Chaozhou	14561.9	15616.1	16840.8	17472.2	18887.9	19568.3
揭阳	Jieyang	14036.1	14574.3	15140.1	15565.8	17824.2	18662.0
云浮	Yunfu	13383.4	13672.1	14882.9	14833.8	16428.5	16840.2

注：按照国家统计局的统一部署，广东省分市县城乡一体化住户调查工作从2013年底正式启动，从2014年开始正式对外发布分市全体居民人均消费支出数据。

Note: Under the unified deployment by NBS, Guangdong province started an integrated household survey by city and county since 2013, including both urban and rural households. Since 2014 the data of per capita disposal income and expenditures of all households in the province by city is released officially after the transitional period.

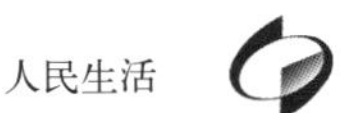

10-8 城镇居民家庭基本情况

Basic Situation of Urban Households

指　　标	Item	2017	2018	2019	2020	2021	2022
调查户数　　（户）	**Survey of households　　(household)**	**5477**	**5550**	**5550**	**5550**	**5550**	**5550**
平均每户常住人口　（人）	Average number of residents per Permanent Household　(person)	2.87	3.18	3.21	3.23	3.35	3.37
平均每户就业人口　（人）	Average Number of Employed Persons per Permanent Household　(person)	1.67	1.73	1.73	1.69	1.77	1.75
人均住房建筑面积（平方米）	**Per Capita housing construction area (sq.m)**	**33.09**	**34.49**	**35.73**	**37.35**	**38.79**	**39.20**
人均可支配收入　　（元）	**Per Capita Disposable Income　　(yuan)**	**40975.1**	**44341.0**	**48117.6**	**50257.0**	**54853.6**	**56905.3**
1.工资性收入	Income of Wages and Salaries	30087.3	32180.1	34151.9	35429.3	38605.8	40017.6
2.经营净收入	Net Business Income	4560.8	4872.6	5473.8	5237.3	5855.2	6069.1
3.财产净收入	Income from Properties	5077.2	5816.6	6686.2	7425.9	8020.1	8304.6
4.转移净收入	Income from Transfers	1249.8	1471.7	1805.7	2164.4	2372.5	2514.0
人均消费支出　　（元）	**Per Capita Consumption Expenditure(yuan)**	**30197.9**	**30924.3**	**34424.1**	**33511.3**	**36621.1**	**36936.2**
1.食品烟酒	Food,Tobacco and Liquor	9711.7	9780.2	10757.5	10794.7	11622.0	12129.8
2.衣着	Clothing	1587.1	1415.3	1480.8	1282.1	1519.9	1381.4
3.居住	Living	7127.8	8147.8	8961.6	9457.9	9696.4	9925.7
4.生活用品及服务	Daily Necessities and Services	1782.8	1726.2	1894.8	1895.3	1874.8	1905.8
5.交通通信	Transportation and Telecommunication	4285.5	4107.3	4597.1	4626.3	5008.5	4888.5
6.教育文化娱乐	Education,Culture and Entertainment	3284.3	3335.7	3984.5	2958.7	3872.8	3747.8
7.医疗保健	Health Service	1503.6	1591.3	1883.0	1748.6	2143.7	2019.2
8.其他用品和服务	Other Necessities and Services	915.1	820.5	864.9	747.7	882.9	937.8
消费支出构成　　（%）	**Composition of Consumption Expenditure**	**100.0**	**100.0**	**100.0**	**100.0**	**100.0**	**100.0**
1.食品烟酒	Food,Tobacco and Liquor	32.2	31.6	31.2	32.2	31.7	32.8
2.衣着	Clothing	5.3	4.6	4.3	3.8	4.1	3.7
3.居住	Living	23.5	26.3	26.0	28.2	26.5	26.9
4.生活用品及服务	Daily Necessities and Services	5.9	5.6	5.5	5.7	5.1	5.2
5.交通通信	Transportation and Telecommunication	14.2	13.3	13.4	13.8	13.7	13.2
6.教育文化娱乐	Education,Culture and Entertainment	10.9	10.8	11.6	8.8	10.6	10.2
7.医疗保健	Health Service	5.0	5.1	5.5	5.2	5.9	5.5
8.其他用品和服务	Other Necessities and Services	3.0	2.7	2.5	2.3	2.4	2.5

10-9 历年城镇居民人均可支配收入及生活消费支出(1978-2012年)

Per Capita Disposable Income and Consumption Expenditure of Urban Households (1978-2012)

年份 Year	人均可支配收入(元) Per Capita Disposable Income (yuan)	指数 Index			人均消费支出(元) Per Capita Consumption Expenditure (yuan)	指数 Index		恩格尔系数(%) Engle Coefficient (%)
		名义增长(上年为100) Nominal Growth (preceding year=100)	实际增长(上年为100) Real Growth (preceding year=100)	实际增长(1978年为100) Real Growth (1978=100)		名义增长(上年为100) Nominal Growth (preceding year=100)	实际增长(上年为100) Real Growth (preceding year=100)	
1978	412.13	101.0	96.6	100.0	399.96	106.3	101.5	66.6
1979	416.33	101.0	96.6	96.6	424.96	106.3	101.5	67.0
1980	472.57	113.5	103.7	100.1	485.76	114.3	104.5	65.5
1981	560.69	118.6	111.6	111.7	517.44	106.5	100.2	65.8
1982	631.45	112.6	109.8	122.7	592.08	114.4	111.5	64.2
1983	714.20	113.1	110.0	135.0	660.12	111.5	108.5	64.5
1984	818.37	114.6	112.4	151.8	744.36	112.8	110.7	63.6
1985	954.12	116.6	99.6	151.1	889.56	119.5	102.1	58.3
1986	1102.09	115.5	110.3	166.7	998.88	112.3	107.2	58.6
1987	1320.89	119.9	106.3	177.1	1215.84	121.7	107.9	56.7
1988	1583.13	119.9	92.6	163.9	1506.99	123.9	95.7	56.7
1989	2086.21	131.8	108.1	177.2	1921.05	127.5	104.6	56.5
1990	2303.15	110.4	113.3	200.8	1983.86	103.3	106.0	57.2
1991	2752.18	119.5	116.8	234.6	2388.77	120.4	117.7	53.1
1992	3476.70	126.3	116.5	273.4	2830.62	118.5	110.4	51.5
1993	4632.38	133.2	109.2	298.6	3777.43	133.4	110.3	48.9
1994	6367.08	137.4	113.6	339.2	5181.30	137.2	113.4	46.4
1995	7438.68	116.8	103.3	350.4	6253.68	120.7	106.7	48.0
1996	8157.81	109.7	102.3	358.4	6736.09	107.7	100.5	47.3
1997	8561.71	105.0	102.8	368.4	6853.48	101.7	99.7	46.0
1998	8839.68	103.2	105.0	387.0	7054.09	102.9	104.7	44.1
1999	9125.92	103.2	104.9	406.0	7517.81	106.6	108.3	40.6
2000	9761.57	107.0	104.7	424.9	8016.91	106.6	104.3	38.6
2001	10415.19	106.7	107.6	457.0	8099.63	101.0	101.8	38.1
2002	11137.20	109.1	110.6	495.7	8988.48	111.0	112.6	38.5
2003	12380.40	111.2	110.4	547.2	9636.24	107.2	106.5	37.2
2004	13627.65	110.1	107.3	587.0	10694.79	111.0	108.2	37.0
2005	14769.94	108.4	106.3	623.8	11809.87	110.4	108.2	36.1
2006	16015.58	108.4	106.5	664.3	12432.22	105.3	103.4	36.2
2007	17699.30	110.5	106.6	707.9	14336.87	115.3	111.2	35.3
2008	19732.86	111.5	105.7	748.3	15527.97	108.3	102.7	37.8
2009	21574.72	109.3	112.0	838.1	16857.51	108.6	111.3	36.9
2010	23897.80	110.8	107.5	901.0	18489.53	109.7	106.4	36.5
2011	26897.48	112.6	106.9	963.2	20251.82	109.5	104.0	36.9
2012	30226.71	112.4	109.3	1052.8	22396.35	110.6	107.6	36.9

10-10 全省城镇居民人均主要食品消费量

Per Capita Consumption of Major Foods of Urban Households

单位：千克 (Kg)

指 标	Item	2017	2018	2019	2020	2021	2022
粮食	Grain	93.75	93.89	100.79	108.86	94.50	90.41
谷物	Cereal	85.89	86.28	91.70	99.56	86.98	83.30
薯类	Tuber	1.59	1.54	1.71	1.75	1.40	1.36
豆类	Beans and the Products	6.26	6.07	7.38	7.55	6.13	5.75
油脂类	Oil and Fats	8.98	8.16	8.42	9.14	9.30	9.26
#植物油	Vegetable Oil	8.70	7.77	7.97	8.81	8.91	8.91
蔬菜及菜制品	Vegetable and Mushroom	100.76	98.52	110.64	113.70	94.22	96.60
#鲜菜	Fresh Vegetables	96.08	94.86	106.65	109.81	91.22	93.82
肉类	Products of Meat	36.59	40.71	39.44	34.35	36.56	40.86
#猪肉	Pork	28.17	33.07	30.56	25.81	27.97	31.75
禽类	Poultry	19.28	19.80	23.86	28.06	21.93	22.31
#鸡	Chick	12.46	13.06	15.69	18.06	14.19	14.55
水产品	Aquatic Products	24.51	23.06	29.49	30.07	28.74	24.33
#鱼类	Fresh	17.75	16.76	21.19	21.71	20.84	16.15
蛋类及制品	Eggs and Egg Products	7.57	7.58	8.66	10.19	8.52	8.83
#鲜蛋	Fresh Eggs	7.04	7.19	8.24	9.76	8.17	8.52
奶及奶制品	Milk and Dairy Products	9.74	10.76	10.80	11.75	14.97	10.91
#鲜奶	Fresh Milk	5.55	5.79	6.55	7.84	10.61	7.90
鲜瓜果	Fresh Melons and Fruits	41.35	41.07	49.30	49.18	44.89	43.51
食糖	Sugar	1.26	1.41	1.40	1.45	1.07	0.94

10-11 全省城镇居民平均每百户年末主要耐用消费品拥有量

Main Durable Consumer Goods Owned per 100 Urban Households at the Year-end

项 目		Item		2017	2018	2019	2020	2021	2022
家用汽车	(辆)	Car	(set)	36.69	42.92	47.63	48.88	53.77	59.15
摩托车	(辆)	Motorcycle	(set)	42.62	46.42	45.55	44.90	45.13	43.93
助力车	(台)	Electric Bicycle	(set)	28.10	34.08	39.31	41.50	53.95	56.74
洗衣机	(台)	Washing Machine	(set)	78.08	91.84	93.75	94.33	98.65	98.68
电冰箱	(台)	Refrigerator	(set)	83.18	95.04	97.91	98.55	103.27	103.68
微波炉	(台)	Microwave Oven	(set)	43.69	44.28	46.14	46.91	46.15	46.14
彩色电视机	(台)	Color Television	(set)	101.97	105.94	107.57	108.23	106.94	107.40
空调	(台)	Air Conditioner	(set)	164.88	202.39	212.11	213.87	244.28	248.54
热水器	(台)	Water Heater	(unit)	88.81	101.71	102.99	105.27	105.84	106.49
排油烟机	(台)	Fume Hood	(set)	61.90	72.47	75.09	75.91	77.53	78.26
移动电话	(部)	Mobile Telephone	(set)	234.79	258.88	263.99	264.56	274.77	276.37
计算机	(台)	Computer	(set)	88.29	83.66	86.82	88.63	80.19	80.19
照相机	(台)	Camera	(set)	32.00	20.50	21.21	21.42	14.82	15.05

10−12 各市城镇居民人均可支配收入

Per Capita Disposable Income of Urban Households by City

单位：元 (yuan)

市别	City	2017	2018	2019	2020	2021	2022
全省	**Provincial Total**	**40975.1**	**44341.0**	**48117.6**	**50257.0**	**54853.6**	**56905.3**
广州	Guangzhou	55400.5	59982.1	65052.1	68304.1	74416.2	76849.4
深圳	Shenzhen	52938.0	57543.6	62522.4	64877.7	70847.3	72718.2
珠海	Zhuhai	46826.4	50713.0	55219.3	58474.7	64233.7	65743.2
汕头	Shantou	27175.1	29077.3	31415.8	32921.9	35600.7	37036.9
佛山	Foshan	46848.5	50736.9	55232.8	57444.9	62942.3	65416.8
韶关	Shaoguan	28305.9	30287.3	32633.9	34418.2	37623.5	38742.0
河源	Heyuan	23779.6	25491.8	27128.5	28018.2	30445.7	31517.6
梅州	Meizhou	25694.6	27385.3	29235.3	29942.2	32751.5	33923.6
惠州	Huizhou	36608.3	39573.6	42999.4	45474.5	49243.0	50811.1
汕尾	Shanwei	24085.5	26012.3	28051.3	29860.3	33081.8	34766.3
东莞	Dongguan	46739.1	50721.3	55155.9	58051.9	63739.8	65405.9
中山	Zhongshan	45295.3	48803.6	52502.4	54737.3	60322.7	62195.7
江门	Jiangmen	32477.8	35465.8	38595.2	39922.9	43621.8	45399.8
阳江	Yangjiang	27568.1	29360.1	31255.7	32310.8	35069.1	36319.1
湛江	Zhanjiang	27119.3	29046.3	31240.7	32925.6	35988.8	37098.6
茂名	Maoming	25315.4	27163.4	29404.9	30733.0	33423.9	34303.5
肇庆	Zhaoqing	28276.1	30679.6	33259.8	34752.0	37791.4	38711.1
清远	Qingyuan	27610.0	29377.0	31597.1	33159.2	36171.6	37244.0
潮州	Chaozhou	22695.0	24170.2	25827.7	26440.2	28403.1	29758.2
揭阳	Jieyang	24099.7	25425.2	26745.5	27066.4	29397.1	30273.1
云浮	Yunfu	23446.0	24946.5	26806.5	28329.8	30951.9	32380.5
按经济区域分	By Region						
珠三角	Pearl River Delta	47926.9	52129.1	56638.7	59225.1	65118.6	67092.6
东翼	Eastern Region	25029.1	26694.2	28569.8	29622.2	32240.7	33521.5
西翼	Western Region	26542.6	28404.7	30552.5	31971.0	34861.6	35906.0
山区	Mountainous Region	26084.4	27826.9	29828.0	31095.7	34008.9	35151.8

注：按照国家统计局的统一部署，广东省分市县城乡一体化住户调查工作从2013年底正式启动，从2014年开始正式对外发布分市城镇居民人均可支配收入数据。

Note: Under the unified deployment by NBS, Guangdong province started an integrated household survey by city and county since 2013,including both urban and rural households . Since 2014 the data of per capita disposal income of all households in the province by city is released officially after the transitional period.

10-13 各市城镇居民人均可支配收入来源（2022年）

Per Capita Disposable Income of Urban Households by Sources and City (2022)

单位：元 (yuan)

地区	City	可支配收入 Disposable Income	工资性收入 Income of Wages and Salaries	经营净收入 Net Business Income	财产净收入 Net Income from Property	转移净收入 Net Income from Transfer
全　省	**Provincial Total**	**56905.3**	**40017.6**	**6069.1**	**8304.6**	**2514.0**
广　州	Guangzhou	76849.4	50474.7	4457.3	15093.2	6824.2
深　圳	Shenzhen	72718.2	61156.8	6989.5	6761.4	-2189.5
珠　海	Zhuhai	65743.2	48869.2	4349.3	8684.3	3840.4
汕　头	Shantou	37036.9	25051.0	5016.7	2744.2	4225.0
佛　山	Foshan	65416.8	39768.0	7767.8	13070.0	4811.0
韶　关	Shaoguan	38742.0	26187.9	4798.6	2175.1	5580.3
河　源	Heyuan	31517.6	20791.1	4619.7	1528.7	4578.1
梅　州	Meizhou	33923.6	20533.2	4789.1	2279.6	6321.7
惠　州	Huizhou	50811.1	34535.9	8233.4	5979.4	2062.4
汕　尾	Shanwei	34766.3	19984.1	7204.5	2121.4	5456.3
东　莞	Dongguan	65405.9	44834.1	6739.9	14078.9	-247.0
中　山	Zhongshan	62195.7	42031.9	7463.5	7413.7	5286.6
江　门	Jiangmen	45399.8	31996.5	3822.1	4519.4	5061.8
阳　江	Yangjiang	36319.1	22537.3	6193.2	3033.6	4555.1
湛　江	Zhanjiang	37098.6	22050.2	5065.7	3482.3	6500.5
茂　名	Maoming	34303.5	22861.9	5510.1	2184.3	3747.1
肇　庆	Zhaoqing	38711.1	25835.8	4680.2	2868.5	5326.6
清　远	Qingyuan	37244.0	24680.4	5533.9	2202.1	4827.6
潮　州	Chaozhou	29758.2	18151.8	3747.9	2245.5	5612.9
揭　阳	Jieyang	30273.1	16730.2	6703.8	2320.8	4518.3
云　浮	Yunfu	32380.5	22265.5	3547.9	2742.6	3824.5

10-14 各市城镇居民人均消费支出

Per Capita Consumption Expenditure of Urban Households by City

单位：元 (yuan)

市别	City	2017	2018	2019	2020	2021	2022
全省	**Provincial Total**	**30197.9**	**30924.3**	**34424.1**	**33511.3**	**36621.1**	**36936.2**
广州	Guangzhou	40636.8	42181.0	45049.3	44283.4	47161.9	46825.2
深圳	Shenzhen	38320.1	40535.0	43112.7	40581.1	46285.7	44792.9
珠海	Zhuhai	34734.7	36818.8	40030.5	37777.6	43956.5	42856.5
汕头	Shantou	21777.6	21998.3	23853.7	24049.9	25268.0	25094.0
佛山	Foshan	33451.0	34803.5	37970.2	37664.0	41327.2	41897.2
韶关	Shaoguan	19630.2	20808.0	22472.7	22162.1	25079.0	25168.5
河源	Heyuan	16458.2	17343.1	18227.6	18320.0	20165.0	20214.2
梅州	Meizhou	18474.0	18659.0	19447.4	19479.0	21415.2	22063.9
惠州	Huizhou	26423.8	27772.5	30008.8	29369.0	32431.0	32578.6
汕尾	Shanwei	18497.3	19800.8	21421.5	22492.5	24292.0	25379.2
东莞	Dongguan	32498.3	33675.1	36198.4	34706.3	39802.6	40131.4
中山	Zhongshan	30131.5	32180.4	35173.2	33773.6	39143.7	39887.3
江门	Jiangmen	22905.9	23237.4	25679.4	25477.6	27912.1	28182.6
阳江	Yangjiang	21514.3	21782.2	22838.0	22895.4	23892.6	23908.9
湛江	Zhanjiang	20014.0	20214.0	21058.9	21006.8	23270.4	23422.2
茂名	Maoming	17511.8	18022.0	19256.0	19440.4	20638.6	20789.8
肇庆	Zhaoqing	18945.0	19984.4	21685.4	20990.2	23028.1	23385.0
清远	Qingyuan	19232.3	20270.2	21620.2	21774.1	23987.5	24146.0
潮州	Chaozhou	16257.3	17386.4	18569.1	19109.3	20533.8	21147.1
揭阳	Jieyang	16746.7	16907.5	17183.7	17416.5	19781.6	20393.5
云浮	Yunfu	15920.8	16398.4	17638.7	17536.5	19057.1	19149.6

注：按照国家统计局的统一部署，广东省分市县城乡一体化住户调查工作从2013年底正式启动，从2014年开始正式对外发布分市城镇居民人均消费支出数据。

Note: Under the unified deployment by NBS, Guangdong province started an integrated household survey by city and county since 2013, including both urban and rural households. Since 2014 the data of per capita expenditures of all households in the province by city is released officially after the transitional period.

10-15 农村居民家庭基本情况
Basic Conditions of Rural Households

指　　标	Item	2017	2018	2019	2020	2021	2022
调查户数　（户）	**Survey of households　(household)**	**2605**	**2350**	**2350**	**2350**	**2350**	**2350**
平均每户常住人口（人）	Average number of residents per Permanent Household　(person)	3.65	3.45	3.47	3.45	3.74	3.72
平均每户就业人口（人）	Average Number of Employed Persons per Permanent Household　(person)	2.03	1.81	1.76	1.72	1.88	1.86
人均住房建筑面积(平方米)	**Per Capita housing construction area (sq.m)**	**45.27**	**47.13**	**48.68**	**48.92**	**50.14**	**50.75**
人均可支配收入　（元）	**Per Capita Disposable Income (yuan)**	**15779.7**	**17167.7**	**18818.4**	**20143.4**	**22306.0**	**23597.8**
1.工资性收入	Income of Wages and Salaries	7854.6	8510.7	9698.7	10613.5	12765.0	13560.2
2.经营净收入	Net Business Income	4118.6	4432.7	4446.9	4584.9	5438.8	5759.3
3.财产净收入	Income from Properties	414.8	448.9	541.0	616.1	795.3	868.8
4.转移净收入	Income from Transfers	3391.7	3775.5	4131.7	4328.9	3306.8	3409.5
人均消费支出　（元）	**Per Capita Consumption Expenditure (yuan)**	**13199.6**	**15411.3**	**16949.4**	**17132.3**	**20011.8**	**20800.0**
1.食品烟酒	Food,Tobacco and Liquor	5303.9	5641.2	6289.3	6991.8	7867.4	8393.1
2.衣着	Clothing	459.5	523.6	552.0	506.9	721.4	694.0
3.居住	Living	2902.4	3355.8	3707.4	3829.2	4722.4	4782.7
4.生活用品及服务	Daily Necessities and Services	722.8	817.0	817.9	803.2	1014.2	992.5
5.交通通信	Transportation and Telecommunication	1423.6	1930.4	2139.8	1958.1	2222.9	2471.2
6.教育文化娱乐	Education,Culture and Entertainment	1186.0	1473.0	1602.7	1275.5	1789.4	1881.0
7.医疗保健	Health Service	921.7	1366.7	1520.7	1517.9	1342.2	1219.6
8.其他用品和服务	Other Necessities and Services	279.7	303.6	319.8	249.8	331.8	365.9
消费支出构成　（%）	**Composition of Consumption Expenditure**	**100.0**	**100.0**	**100.0**	**100.0**	**100.0**	**100.0**
1.食品烟酒	Food,Tobacco and Liquor	40.2	36.6	37.1	40.8	39.3	40.3
2.衣着	Clothing	3.5	3.4	3.3	3.0	3.6	3.3
3.居住	Living	22.0	21.8	21.9	22.3	23.6	23.0
4.生活用品及服务	Daily Necessities and Services	5.5	5.3	4.8	4.7	5.1	4.8
5.交通通信	Transportation and Telecommunication	10.8	12.5	12.6	11.4	11.1	11.9
6.教育文化娱乐	Education,Culture and Entertainment	9.0	9.6	9.5	7.4	8.9	9.0
7.医疗保健	Health Service	6.9	8.9	9.0	8.9	6.7	5.9
8.其他用品和服务	Other Necessities and Services	2.1	2.0	1.9	1.5	1.7	1.8

注：2013年起为新口径数据。
Note: Since 2013, the relative data of rural households have been calculated according to the new standard.

10-16 历年农村居民人均纯收入及生活消费支出（1978-2012年）

Per Capita Income and Consumption Expenditure of Rural Households (1978-2012)

年份 Year	人均纯收入（元） Per Capita Net Income (yuan)	指数 Index			人均消费支出（元） Per Capita Living Expenditure (yuan)	指数 Index		恩格尔系数（%） Engle Coefficient (%)
		名义增长（上年为100） Nominal Growth (Preceding year=100)	实际增长（上年为100） Real Growth (Preceding year=100)	实际增长（1978年为100） Real Growth (1978=100)		名义增长（上年为100） Nominal Growth (Preceding year=100)	实际增长（上年为100） Real Growth (Preceding year=100)	
1978	193.25	107.9		100.0	184.89	97.4		61.7
1979	222.72	115.2	113.6	113.6	205.18	111.0	110.1	59.9
1980	274.37	123.2	119.4	135.6	222.22	108.3	103.9	60.4
1981	325.37	118.6	111.4	151.1	266.05	119.7	112.1	59.3
1982	381.79	117.3	112.7	170.3	312.44	117.4	116.2	58.4
1983	395.92	103.7	107.0	182.2	328.76	105.2	106.3	60.3
1984	425.34	107.4	107.2	195.3	346.19	105.3	105.0	59.3
1985	495.31	116.5	109.8	214.5	388.00	112.1	105.7	60.4
1986	546.43	110.3	107.6	230.8	454.06	117.0	111.1	58.8
1987	662.24	121.2	111.1	256.4	545.25	120.1	109.5	57.3
1988	808.70	122.1	102.7	263.3	684.67	125.6	103.2	55.2
1989	955.02	118.1	102.0	268.6	870.59	127.2	107.3	53.7
1990	1043.03	109.2	101.6	272.9	932.63	107.1	99.7	57.7
1991	1143.06	109.6	109.4	298.5	942.40	101.1	101.2	57.4
1992	1307.65	114.4	110.4	329.6	1060.29	112.5	108.8	54.0
1993	1674.78	128.1	106.1	349.7	1391.01	131.2	106.8	52.8
1994	2181.52	130.3	103.8	363.0	1882.00	135.3	103.6	55.6
1995	2699.24	123.7	106.5	386.6	2255.01	119.8	105.3	54.5
1996	3183.46	117.9	107.6	415.9	2584.16	114.6	106.9	51.6
1997	3467.69	108.9	104.2	433.4	2617.65	101.3	100.3	52.3
1998	3527.14	101.7	103.4	448.2	2683.18	102.5	103.8	51.1
1999	3628.93	102.9	106.2	475.9	2645.94	98.6	101.7	50.7
2000	3654.48	100.7	100.9	480.2	2646.02	100.0	100.0	49.8
2001	3769.79	103.2	103.5	497.0	2703.36	102.2	102.5	49.9
2002	3911.91	103.8	105.1	522.4	2825.01	104.5	106.0	47.6
2003	4054.58	103.6	103.4	540.1	2927.35	103.6	103.4	47.9
2004	4365.87	107.7	104.0	561.8	3240.78	110.7	106.7	48.8
2005	4690.49	107.4	104.5	587.0	3707.73	114.4	111.4	48.3
2006	5079.78	108.3	106.4	624.6	3885.97	104.8	103.2	48.6
2007	5624.04	110.7	106.5	665.5	4202.32	108.1	104.5	49.7
2008	6399.77	113.8	107.6	715.8	4872.96	115.9	109.6	49.0
2009	6906.93	107.9	110.7	792.4	5019.81	103.0	105.3	48.3
2010	7890.25	114.2	110.3	874.0	5515.58	109.9	106.5	47.7
2011	9371.73	118.8	111.9	978.0	6725.55	121.9	115.5	49.1
2012	10542.84	112.5	109.3	1069.0	7458.56	110.9	107.8	49.1

注：本表数据来源于2013年之前分别开展的城镇住户调查和农村住户调查。
Note: The data shown in the table are compiled on the basis of the urban and rural household surveys before year 2013.

10−17 全省农村居民人均主要食品消费量

Per Capita Consumption of Major Foods of Rural Households

单位:千克 (Kg)

指 标	Item	2017	2018	2019	2020	2021	2022
粮食	Grain	166.58	140.98	149.44	171.99	150.91	144.76
谷物	Cereal	158.47	133.41	139.86	160.93	142.35	136.38
薯类	Tuber	1.74	1.56	1.52	1.32	1.05	1.05
豆类	Beans and the Products	6.37	6.02	8.05	9.74	7.50	7.33
油脂类	Oil and Fats	9.78	11.34	10.40	11.76	12.75	11.94
#植物油	Vegetable Oil	9.12	10.37	9.56	11.06	11.78	11.15
蔬菜及菜制品	Vegetable and Mushroom	100.75	105.04	106.80	111.45	106.24	112.01
#鲜菜	Fresh Vegetables	97.90	102.29	103.70	108.25	103.75	109.76
肉类	Products of Meat	36.35	41.62	37.14	31.92	39.93	47.28
#猪肉	Pork	31.02	36.12	31.06	26.32	33.39	40.06
禽类	Poultry	23.50	23.87	30.49	38.04	30.62	29.17
#鸡	Chick	15.42	15.25	18.68	22.88	19.23	18.37
水产品	Aquatic Products	19.24	19.79	26.64	29.86	24.81	24.67
#鱼类	Fresh	14.95	15.47	20.73	23.56	18.70	17.94
蛋类及蛋制品	Eggs ang Egg Products	6.77	6.96	7.73	9.14	8.13	8.62
#鲜蛋	Fresh Eggs	6.55	6.78	7.50	8.92	7.92	8.45
奶及奶制品	Milk and Dairy Products	3.32	3.99	4.48	4.72	7.97	5.39
#鲜奶	Fresh Milk	1.33	2.16	2.72	3.14	5.88	3.87
鲜瓜果	Fresh Melons and Fruits	25.69	23.83	29.16	30.81	33.18	34.41
食糖	Sugar	2.12	1.90	1.88	1.87	1.33	1.26

10−18 全省农村居民平均每百户年末主要耐用品拥有量

Main Durable Consumer Goods Owned per 100 Rural Households at the Year-end

项 目		Item		2017	2018	2019	2020	2021	2022
家用汽车	(辆)	Car	(set)	17.57	22.73	26.01	27.69	31.84	36.93
摩托车	(辆)	Motorcycle	(set)	123.63	116.73	116.58	115.45	110.87	109.43
助力车	(台)	Electric Bicycle	(set)	38.50	35.84	40.49	42.42	56.40	60.22
洗衣机	(台)	Washing Machine	(set)	78.46	84.71	89.98	90.32	96.62	97.18
电冰箱(柜)	(台)	Refrigerator	(set)	87.93	92.94	97.00	97.48	102.86	103.27
微波炉	(台)	Microwave Oven	(set)	22.90	27.01	29.09	29.52	34.33	34.81
彩色电视机	(台)	Color Television	(set)	120.47	116.51	116.47	115.93	112.01	112.65
空调	(台)	Air Conditioner	(set)	91.33	113.53	129.63	132.71	173.09	177.77
热水器	(台)	Water Heater	(unit)	88.49	94.02	97.99	101.70	101.59	103.20
排油烟机	(台)	Fume hood	(set)	37.30	49.07	52.12	53.62	58.82	59.68
移动电话	(部)	Mobile Phone	(set)	287.12	290.44	286.34	277.85	293.90	296.27
计算机	(台)	Computer	(set)	41.61	35.29	38.45	39.75	36.02	36.14
照相机	(台)	Camera	(set)	4.20	4.88	4.38	3.60	2.65	3.11

10-19 各市农村居民人均可支配收入

Per Capita Disposal Income of Rural Households by City

单位：元 (yuan)

市别	City	2017	2018	2019	2020	2021	2022
全　省	**Provincial Total**	**15779.7**	**17167.7**	**18818.4**	**20143.4**	**22306.0**	**23597.8**
广　州	Guangzhou	23483.9	26020.1	28867.9	31266.3	34533.3	36292.3
深　圳	Shenzhen						
珠　海	Zhuhai	23496.4	26198.4	29069.3	31118.6	34394.0	35828.6
汕　头	Shantou	14904.7	16246.1	17735.3	18962.5	20819.2	22056.8
佛　山	Foshan	26389.6	28764.7	31503.4	33440.2	37067.0	38971.3
韶　关	Shaoguan	14107.6	15433.7	16940.1	18288.7	20252.9	21234.3
河　源	Heyuan	13300.8	14620.3	16030.3	17313.4	19146.3	20189.6
梅　州	Meizhou	14088.5	15173.3	16447.2	17430.1	19241.2	20289.6
惠　州	Huizhou	19284.3	21039.1	23027.4	24925.1	27580.0	28963.7
汕　尾	Shanwei	13501.3	14851.5	16304.7	17732.3	19884.5	21226.8
东　莞	Dongguan	29078.3	32276.9	35904.5	38827.2	43187.8	45135.8
中　山	Zhongshan	30012.4	32263.3	35121.6	37632.8	41749.9	43490.2
江　门	Jiangmen	16473.3	18153.6	19873.3	21129.4	23376.4	24742.2
阳　江	Yangjiang	15341.7	16799.1	18331.9	19981.8	22195.6	23431.1
湛　江	Zhanjiang	14484.0	15888.9	17343.0	18758.2	20692.7	21713.2
茂　名	Maoming	15695.2	16950.8	18482.2	19621.2	21561.2	22444.0
肇　庆	Zhaoqing	16430.5	17695.7	19217.0	20627.5	22688.7	23653.4
清　远	Qingyuan	14026.8	15162.9	16523.8	17881.3	19841.2	20803.4
潮　州	Chaozhou	13672.9	14944.5	16359.6	17265.7	19133.6	20274.8
揭　阳	Jieyang	13206.7	14421.7	15675.4	16311.9	18015.8	18959.3
云　浮	Yunfu	14124.4	15240.3	16646.2	17776.9	19675.1	20786.9
按经济区域分	By Region						
珠三角	Pearl River Delta	20813.5	22805.6	25025.8	26856.5	30464.7	31956.7
东　翼	Eastern Region	13732.9	15013.2	16386.8	17357.1	19211.4	20335.4
西　翼	Western Region	15081.6	16434.7	17932.4	19267.8	21261.0	22254.3
山　区	Mountainous Region	13924.7	15111.5	16490.8	17698.0	19599.6	20627.7

注：1.按照国家统计局的统一部署广东省分市县城乡一体化住户调查工作从2013年底正式启动，从2014年开始正式对外发布分市农村居民人均可支配收入数据，不再发布分市农村居民人均纯收入数据，这两项收入指标数据在调查范围、调查方法和统计口径上均有一定变化，不完全可比。

2.深圳因完全城市化，无相关数据。

Note: a)Under the unified deployment by NBS, Guangdong province started an integrated household survey by city and county since the end of the 2013, including both urban and rural households. Since 2014 the data of per capita disposal income and expenditures of all households in the province by city is released officially after the transitional period. The coverage, methodology and definitions used in the integrated rural survey are different from the survey prior to 2013, therefore the disposable income of rural household of 2014 are different from the net income of rural household prior to 2013.

b)There is no data of Shenzhen city due to its totally urbanization.

10–20 各市农村居民人均可支配收入来源（2022年）

Per Capita Disposable Income of Rural Households by Sources and City(2022)

单位：元 (yuan)

地区	City	可支配收入 Disposable Income	工资性收入 Income of Wages and Salaries	经营净收入 Net Business Income	财产净收入 Net Income from Property	转移净收入 Net Income from Transfer
全省	**Provincial Total**	**23597.8**	**13560.2**	**5759.3**	**868.8**	**3409.5**
广州	Guangzhou	36292.3	26639.5	4125.7	3579.3	1947.8
深圳	Shenzhen					
珠海	Zhuhai	35828.6	24574.5	5105.0	3672.4	2476.8
汕头	Shantou	22056.8	16240.0	2568.6	616.1	2632.1
佛山	Foshan	38971.3	25463.2	5966.0	5452.1	2090.0
韶关	Shaoguan	21234.3	9935.5	7634.2	917.3	2747.3
河源	Heyuan	20189.6	11726.9	4397.5	215.0	3850.2
梅州	Meizhou	20289.6	10325.9	4788.4	55.2	5120.0
惠州	Huizhou	28963.7	16907.6	8080.5	1638.5	2337.1
汕尾	Shanwei	21226.8	12455.1	4930.8	218.1	3622.8
东莞	Dongguan	45135.8	36442.5	3805.8	5409.6	-522.1
中山	Zhongshan	43490.2	30117.0	5371.0	4936.1	3066.1
江门	Jiangmen	24742.2	18275.2	3214.2	1067.0	2185.8
阳江	Yangjiang	23431.1	12011.5	8255.6	129.5	3034.5
湛江	Zhanjiang	21713.2	10000.2	5969.1	242.6	5501.2
茂名	Maoming	22444.0	10939.2	3670.8	667.6	7166.4
肇庆	Zhaoqing	23653.4	13167.8	6012.7	615.0	3857.9
清远	Qingyuan	20803.4	11280.3	6102.3	303.9	3117.0
潮州	Chaozhou	20274.8	11476.1	6176.4	86.3	2536.0
揭阳	Jieyang	18959.3	11186.2	3977.5	85.0	3710.7
云浮	Yunfu	20786.9	13429.0	4459.8	28.7	2869.4

10–21 全省各市农村居民人均消费支出

Per Capita Consumption Expenditure of Rural Households by City

单位：元 (yuan)

市　别	City	2017	2018	2019	2020	2021	2022
全　省	**Provincial Total**	**13199.6**	**15411.3**	**16949.4**	**17132.3**	**20011.8**	**20800.0**
广　州	Guangzhou	18932.3	20633.9	22521.9	22990.1	26099.2	26229.7
深　圳	Shenzhen						
珠　海	Zhuhai	20038.1	20474.7	22573.0	22498.4	26928.2	26389.0
汕　头	Shantou	13345.6	14054.2	15373.1	15743.2	16914.0	17267.0
佛　山	Foshan	18262.0	19905.6	21822.5	22258.9	25035.2	25861.4
韶　关	Shaoguan	11810.1	12719.5	13864.3	14271.2	16306.6	16375.7
河　源	Heyuan	11484.1	12438.4	13437.2	13990.0	16020.0	16656.2
梅　州	Meizhou	12392.0	13221.5	14145.7	14515.1	16285.3	16940.3
惠　州	Huizhou	15576.2	16900.2	18387.4	18118.6	20462.9	20879.3
汕　尾	Shanwei	11122.6	12258.2	13422.8	14191.6	15443.0	16557.8
东　莞	Dongguan	23090.2	25354.5	27720.6	26890.2	30583.7	31124.8
中　山	Zhongshan	20832.6	22603.3	24750.6	24824.9	29243.7	30355.0
江　门	Jiangmen	12655.9	13041.6	13643.5	14727.1	16422.2	16853.1
阳　江	Yangjiang	12931.4	13656.4	14603.2	14888.4	17623.3	18276.2
湛　江	Zhanjiang	10732.6	11732.8	12730.1	13071.1	15180.8	15426.9
茂　名	Maoming	12481.2	13487.4	14450.9	15045.5	16453.4	17059.1
肇　庆	Zhaoqing	10925.6	11358.5	12510.3	12789.0	14997.4	15499.4
清　远	Qingyuan	12168.2	13047.7	14039.3	14190.8	16111.6	16443.2
潮　州	Chaozhou	11573.9	12399.6	13588.0	14322.4	15937.7	16662.8
揭　阳	Jieyang	11227.2	12138.1	12997.6	13621.7	15815.3	16821.9
云　浮	Yunfu	11169.9	11761.9	12867.5	12801.6	14382.1	14984.8

注：按照国家统计局的统一部署，广东省分市县城乡一体化住户调查工作从2013年底正式启动，从2014年开始正式对外发布分市农村居民人均消费支出数据。

Note: Under the unified deployment by NBS, Guangdong province started an integrated household survey by city and county since the end of the 2013, including both urban and rural households. Since 2014 the data of per capita disposal income and expenditures of all households in the province by city is released officially after the transitional period.

10-22 全省、城镇、农村居民人均可支配收入及生活消费支出(2013-2022年)

Per Capita Disposable Income and Consumption Expenditure of Households (2013-2022)

年份 Year	人均可支配收入(元) Per Capita Disposable Income (yuan)	指数 Index 名义增长(上年为100) Nominal Growth (Preceding year=100)	指数 Index 实际增长(上年为100) Real Growth (Preceding year=100)	人均消费支出(元) Per Capita Consumption Expenditure (yuan)	指数 Index 名义增长(上年为100) Nominal Growth (Preceding year=100)	指数 Index 实际增长(上年为100) Real Growth (Preceding year=100)	恩格尔系数(%) Engle Coefficient (%)
全省居民 Provincial Household							
2013	23420.7	110.1	107.4	17421.0	108.9	106.2	35.0
2014	25685.0	109.7	107.2	19205.5	110.2	107.7	34.3
2015	27858.9	108.5	106.9	20975.7	109.2	107.6	34.5
2016	30295.8	108.7	106.3	23448.4	111.8	109.3	34.2
2017	33003.3	108.9	107.3	24819.6	105.8	104.2	33.5
2018	35809.9	108.5	106.2	26054.0	105.0	102.7	32.6
2019	39014.3	108.9	105.3	28994.7	111.3	107.6	32.3
2020	41028.6	105.2	102.5	28491.9	98.3	95.8	33.8
2021	44993.3	109.7	108.8	31589.3	110.9	110.0	33.2
2022	47064.6	104.6	102.4	32168.7	101.8	99.6	34.3
城镇居民 Urban Household							
2013	29537.3	109.5	106.9	21621.5	107.8	105.3	33.6
2014	32148.1	108.8	106.4	23611.7	109.2	106.7	33.2
2015	34757.2	108.1	106.4	25673.1	108.7	107.0	33.2
2016	37684.3	108.4	105.9	28613.3	111.5	108.8	32.9
2017	40975.1	108.7	106.9	30197.9	105.5	103.7	32.2
2018	44341.0	108.2	105.9	30924.3	102.4	100.2	31.6
2019	48117.6	108.5	105.2	34424.1	111.3	108.0	31.2
2020	50257.0	104.4	101.8	33511.3	97.3	94.9	32.2
2021	54853.6	109.1	108.1	36621.1	109.3	108.2	31.7
2022	56905.3	103.7	101.5	36936.2	100.9	98.7	32.8
农村居民 Rural Household							
2013	11067.8	110.7	107.8	8937.8	111.9	109.0	42.1
2014	12245.6	110.6	108.3	10043.2	112.4	110.1	39.5
2015	13360.4	109.1	107.7	11103.0	110.6	109.2	40.6
2016	14512.2	108.6	106.5	12414.8	111.8	109.6	40.4
2017	15779.7	108.7	107.8	13199.6	106.3	105.5	40.2
2018	17167.7	108.8	106.8	15411.3	116.8	114.6	36.6
2019	18818.4	109.6	104.8	16949.4	110.0	105.2	37.1
2020	20143.4	107.0	103.9	17132.3	101.1	98.1	40.8
2021	22306.0	110.7	110.6	20011.8	116.8	116.7	39.3
2022	23597.8	105.8	103.4	20800.0	103.9	101.6	40.3

注：本表数据来源于自2013年起开展的城乡一体化住户收支和生活状况调查。

Notes: The data shown in the table are compiled on the basis of the integrated household income and expenditure survey carried out since 2013, including both urban and rural households.

主要统计指标解释

一、城乡一体化住户收支与生活状况调查指标解释

从2012年四季度起，国家统计局对分别进行的城乡住户调查实施了一体化改革，规范了城乡划分范围，统一了城乡居民收入指标名称、分类和统计标准，建立了城乡统一的一体化住户调查，并据此采集全国居民有关数据。

（一）居民可支配收入

居民可支配收入指居民可用于最终消费支出和储蓄的总和，即居民可用于自由支配的收入。既包括现金收入，也包括实物收入。按照收入的来源，可支配收入包含四项，分别为：工资性收入、经营净收入、财产净收入和转移净收入。

工资性收入　指就业人员通过各种途径得到的全部劳动报酬和各种福利，包括受雇于单位或个人、从事各种自由职业、兼职和零星劳动得到的全部劳动报酬和福利。

经营净收入　指住户或住户成员从事生产经营活动所获得的净收入，是全部经营收入中扣除经营费用、生产性固定资产折旧和生产税之后得到的净收入。计算公式为：

经营净收入=经营收入-经营费用-生产性固定资产折旧-生产税

财产净收入　指住户或住户成员将其所拥有的金融资产、住房等非金融资产和自然资源交由其他机构单位、住户或个人支配而获得的回报并扣除相关的费用之后得到的净收入。财产净收入包括利息净收入、红利收入、储蓄性保险净收益、转让承包土地经营权租金净收入、出租房屋净收入、出租其他资产净收入和自有住房折算净租金等。财产净收入不包括转让资产所有权的溢价所得。

转移净收入　计算公式为：转移净收入=转移性收入-转移性支出

转移性收入　指国家、单位、社会团体对住户的各种经常性转移支付和住户之间的经常性收入转移。包括养老金或退休金、社会救济和补助、政策性生产补贴、政策性生活补贴、救灾款、经常性捐赠和赔偿、报销医疗费、住户之间的赡养收入，本住户非常住成员寄回带回的收入等。转移性收入不包括住户之间的实物馈赠。

转移性支出　指调查户对国家、单位、住户或个人的经常性或义务性转移支付。包括缴纳的税款、各项社会保障支出、赡养支出、经常性捐赠和赔偿支出以及其他经常转移支出等。

（二）居民消费支出

居民消费支出是指居民用于满足家庭日常生活消费需要的全部支出，既包括现金消费支出，也包括实物消费支出。消费支出可划分为食品烟酒、衣着、居住、生活用品及服务、交通通信、教育文化娱乐、医疗保健以及其他用品及服务八大类。

食品烟酒　指用于各种食品和烟草、酒类的支出。

衣着　指与居民穿着有关的支出，包括服装、服装材料、鞋类、其他衣类及配件、衣着相关加工服务的支出。

居住　指与居住有关的支出，包括房租、水、电、燃料、物业管理等方面的支出，也包括自有住房折算租金。

生活用品及服务　指家庭及个人的各类生活品及家庭服务。包括家具及室内装饰品、家用器具、家用纺织品、家庭日用杂品、个人用品和家庭服务。

交通通信　指用于交通和通信工具及相关的各种服务费、维修费和车辆保险等支出。

教育文化娱乐　指用于教育和文化娱乐方面的支出。

医疗保健　指用于医疗和保健的药品、用品和服务的总费用。包括医疗器具及药品，以及医疗服务。

其他用品及服务　指无法直接归入上述各类支出的其他用品与服务支出。

二、2012 年及以前的分城镇和农村住户调查指标解释

2012 年及以前年份，中国的住户调查一直分城乡分别开展。由于分别调查，农村与城镇居民收入、支出等指标的统计口径有所不同，数据也不完全可比，城镇调查城镇居民可支配收入，农村调查农村居民纯收入。城镇居民收入与支出数据，指现金收入或现金支出，不包括实物收支；其中，计算城镇居民人均可支配收入和消费支出时，不包括自有住房折算租金，也不包括购建房支出。农村居民收入与支出数据，分为总收支和现金收支，即农村居民的总收支部分包括了自产自用的实物收支；其中，计算农村居民人均纯收入和消费支出时，也不包括自有住房折算租金，但农村居民居住消费支出中，包括了购建房支出。为了保持历史数据的可比，本年鉴中 2012 年及以前年份的数据和指标解释仍保持了原城镇住户调查和农村住户调查方案的原貌。

（一）城镇住户调查

城镇家庭人口　指居住在一起，经济上合在一起共同生活的家庭成员。凡计算为家庭人口的成员其全部收支都包括在本家庭中。

城镇居民家庭可支配收入　指家庭成员得到可用于最终消费支出和其他非义务性支出以及储蓄的总和，即居民家庭可以用来自由支配的收入。它是家庭总收入扣除交纳的个人所得税、个人交纳的社会保障支出以及记账补贴后的收入。计算公式为：

城镇居民家庭可支配收入=家庭总收入-交纳个人所得税-个人交纳的社会保障支出-记账补贴

（二）农村住户调查

农村住户　指农村常住户。农村常住户指长期(一年以上)居住在乡镇(不包括城关镇)行政管理区域内的住户，以及长期居住在城关镇所辖行政村范围内的农村住户。户口不在本地而在本地居住一年及以上的住户也包括在本地农村常住户范围内；有本地户口，但举家外出谋生一年以上的住户，无论是否保留承包耕地都不包括在本地农村住户范围内。

农村居民家庭纯收入　指农村住户当年从各个来源得到的总收入相应地扣除所发生的费用后的收入总和。计算公式为：

农村居民家庭纯收入=总收入-家庭经营费用支出-税费支出-生产性固定资产折旧-赠送农村内部亲友

纯收入主要用于再生产投入和当年生活消费支出，也可用于储蓄和各种非义务性支出。“农民人均纯收入”是按人口平均的纯收入水平，反映的是一个地区农村居民的平均收入水平。

Explanatory Notes on Main Statistical Indicators

Ⅰ. Integrated Urban and Rural Households Survey on Income and Expenditures and Living Conditions

Since the fourth quarter of 2012, the NBS has launched its reform on the household survey programme, to form an integrated survey, instead of the two separate urban and rural household surveys. The reform regulates the division of urban and rural areas, integrates the concepts, classifications and standards, conducts the integrated household survey, and collects household data in the whole country thereafter.

1. Disposable Income of Households

Disposable Income of Households refers to the income of households for purpose of final expenditure and savings. It includes income both in cash and in kind. By sources of income, disposable income includes four categories: income from wages and salaries, net business income, net income from properties and net income from transfer.

Income from Wages and Salaries　refers to remuneration of labour and salaries from all kinds of sources, including those employed by other units or individuals, freelance work, part-time jobs, and sporadic labour.

Net Business Income refers to net income earned by households and their members engaged in production and business activities. It refers to the net income of operating revenue minus operating costs, depreciation of productive fixed assets, and production tax. The formula is:

Net Business Income=Operating Revenue-Operating Costs-Depreciation of Productive Fixed Assets-Production Tax

Net Income from Properties refers to the net income received as returns by households or members of financial assets, non-financial assets such as housing, to other institutions, households or individuals, and minus relevant costs. Net income from properties includes net income of interest, bonus income, net income of saving insurance, net income of rents of transferring management right of contract land, income of renting housing, income of renting other assets, net converted rents of self-owned housing. Net income from properties do not include premium of transferring ownership of assets.

Net Income from Transfer The formula is:

Net Income from Transfer=Income from Transfers-Expenditure from Transfer

Income from Transfer refers to the regular transfer from country, institutions, social communities to households and between households. It includes old-age and retirement pension, disaster relief funds, regular donation and compensation, applying for medical fees, supporting income between households, income from non-usual-residing members of households, etc. Income from transfer do not include presents in kinds between households.

Expenditure from Transfer refers to regular or deontic transfer from households to country, institutions, households or individuals. It includes taxes paid, expenditure of all kinds of social security, supporting expenditure, regular donation and compensation and other regular transfer expenditure, etc.

2. Consumption Expenditure of Households

Consumption Expenditure of Households refers to all expenditure of households for living expenditure to satisfy family daily living. It includes expenditure in cash and in kind. It includes eight categories: food, tobacco and liquor, clothing, residence, household facilities, articles and services, transport and communications, education, cultural and recreational activities, health care and medical services, and miscellaneous goods and services.

Food, Tobacco and Liquor refers to expenditure for food, tobacco and liquor of all kinds.

Clothing refers to expenditure related to clothing, including clothes, clothing materials, footwear, other clothing and accessories, processing services related to clothing.

Residence refers to expenditure related to residence, including housing rents, water, electricity, fuel, property management, and including converted self-owned housing rents.

Household Facilities, Articles and Services refers to expenditure for family and individual articles for living purpose and family services. It includes furniture and interior decoration, home appliances, home textiles, household miscellaneous daily articles, personal articles, and family services.

Transport and Communications refers to expenditure for transport and communication and related services, maintenance and repairs, and vehicle insurance.

Education, Cultural and Recreational Activities refers to expenditure on education, cultural and recreational activities.

Health Care and Medical Services refers to expenditure on drugs, supplies and services of medical and health care. It includes medical appliances and drugs, and medical services.

Miscellaneous Goods and Services refers to expenditure of all kinds of expenditure of other articles and services that can not divided into the category above.

II. Explanatory on Indicators before 2012

Prior to 2012, household surveys in China were conducted separately in urban and rural areas. Statistical coverage of indicators of household income and expenditure of urban and rural households were different, data were not comparable completely. Disposable income was surveyed in urban households, and net income was surveyed in rural households. Income and expenditure of urban households refer to that in cash, not including physical payments. Among which, when calculating per capita disposable income and consumption, self-owned housing conversion rental is not included, and expenditure of purchasing housing is not included either. Income and expenditure of rural households are divided into that of total and in cash, that is, total income and expenditure include self occupied physical payments. Among which, when computing per capita net income and expenditure of rural households, self-owned housing conversion rental is not included, but purchasing of housing is included in consumption expenditure of rural households.

For comparable reason, data prior to 2012 in this yearbook were still original urban households and rural households survey.

1. Urban Household Survey

Population of Urban Households refer to members of households living and sharing economically together in the urban areas. All the income and expenditure of all the members of such households are included in the income and expenditure of the household.

Disposable Income of Urban Households refers to the actual income at the disposal of members of the households which can be used for final consumption, other non-compulsory expenditure and savings. This equals to total income minus income tax, personal contribution to social security and subsidy for keeping diaries in being a sample household. The following formula is used:

Disposable Income of Urban Households= total household income - income tax - personal contribution to social security - subsidy for keeping diaries for a sampled household

2. Rural Household Survey

Rural Households refer to usual resident households in rural areas. Usual resident households in rural areas are households residing on a long term basis(for more than one year) in the areas under the administration of township governments (not including county towns), and in the areas under the administration of villages in county towns. Households residing in the current addresses for over one year with their household registration in other places are still considered as resident households of the locality. For households with their household registration in one place but all members of the households having moved away to make a living in another place for over one year, they will not be included in the rural households of the area where they are registered, irrespective of whether they still keep their contracted land.

Net Income of Rural Households refers to the total income of rural households from all sources minus all corresponding expenses. The formula for calculation is as follows:

Net income of rural households = total income - household operation expenses - taxes and fees-depreciation of fixed assets for production - gifts to rural relatives.

Net income is mainly used as input for reinvestment in production and as consumption expenditure of the year, and also used for savings and non-compulsory expenses of various forms. "Per capita net income of farmers" is the level of net income averaged by population, reflecting the average income level of rural population in a given area.

十一、农业

AGRICULTURE

十一　农业

简要说明

一、本篇资料反映广东省农业生产和农村经济的基本情况。内容主要包括农业产值、主要产品产量、农业自然灾害等方面的统计资料。

二、本篇资料主要由广东省统计局农村社会经济统计处，国家统计局广东调查总队农业调查处、农村调查处整理提供。

三、本篇资料根据国家统计局农业统计报表制度填报，统计范围包括各市县区各种经济类型的全部农林牧渔业生产活动。

四、根据《全国农业普查条例》，本篇资料的 1996 年部分数据以第一次全国农业普查结果为基础做了调整，2006 年部分数据以第二次全国农业普查结果为基础做了调整，2007-2017 年部分数据以第三次全国农业普查结果为基础做了调整。

11 Agriculture

Brief Introduction

Ⅰ.The data in this chapter show the basic conditions of agricultural production and rural economy in Guangdong Province, including mainly rural labor force, output value of agriculture, output of major products, as well as statistics on natural disasters in agriculture enterprises.

Ⅱ.The data in this chapter are mainly prepared and provided by the rural social and Economic Statistics Department of the Guangdong Provincial Bureau of statistics, the agricultural investigation department and the rural investigation department of the Guangdong Survey Corps of the National Bureau of Statistics.

Ⅲ.This data is filled according to the agricultural statistical reporting system of the National Bureau of Statistics, and the statistical scope includes all agricultural, forestry, animal husbandry and fishery production activities of various economic types in cities, counties and districts.

Ⅳ. Some data of 1996 in this chapter are adjusted in accordance with the regulations of the first national agricultural census，some data of 2006 in this chapter are adjusted in accordance with the regulations of the second national agricultural census，some data from 2007-2017 in this chapter are adjusted in accordance with the regulations of the third national agricultural census.

11-1 农业主要指标
Main Indicators of Agriculture

指　标	Item	2000	2010	2015	2020	2021	2022
化肥施用量(折纯)（万吨）	Consumption of Chemical Fertilizers (100 percent equivalent,10000 tons)	176.20	233.42	238.17	219.80	212.87	208.74
#氮肥	Nitrogenous Fertilizer	95.89	94.93	90.78	84.11	80.06	78.26
磷肥	Phosphate Fertilizer	18.36	24.75	29.03	25.80	25.98	25.19
钾肥	Potash Fertilizer	35.84	46.74	47.00	41.68	40.80	40.21
农药使用量（万吨）	Consumption of Pesticides (10000 tons)	8.47	9.10	9.23	8.32	7.74	7.60
农林牧渔业总产值(亿元)	Gross Output Value of Agriculture (100 million yuan)	1701.18	3697.18	5303.63	7901.92	8305.84	8892.29
农林牧渔业增加值(亿元)	Value-added of Agriculture (100 million yuan)	1005.14	2254.49	3275.05	4880.83	5151.27	5531.56
农作物总播种面积(万亩)	Total Sown Area (10000 mu)	7735.35	6394.16	6291.83	6677.71	6747.53	6830.20
粮食作物	Grain Corps	4649.83	3579.49	3289.94	3307.03	3319.55	3345.43
经济作物	Economics Corps	2940.05	2814.67	3001.88	3370.68	3427.98	3484.77
人工造林面积（万亩）	Afforested Area in Barren Mountains(10000 mu)	25.76	142.72	177.69	30.03	29.61	15.48
主要产品产量（万吨）	Output of Major Products (10000 tons)						
粮食	Grain	1822.33	1249.15	1211.66	1267.56	1279.87	1291.54
糖蔗	Sugarcane	1137.59	1064.09	1093.58	1176.25	1118.20	1107.76
花生	Peanuts	77.68	81.59	94.48	112.05	115.87	115.93
烟叶	Tobacco	6.21	5.00	4.52	4.12	3.88	3.71
蔬菜	Vegetables	2214.80	2550.50	2994.65	3706.85	3855.73	3999.11
水果	Fruits	643.52	1049.21	1298.52	1756.16	1826.73	1895.18
水产品	Aquatic Products	593.19	729.03	803.71	875.81	884.52	894.03
猪肉	Pork	206.85	285.14	296.31	192.42	263.23	279.81

注：1.2004年起粮食播种面积含大豆，下表同。
2.经济作物包括甘蔗、油料作物、麻类、烟叶、药材、蔬菜、瓜果类、其他农作物，下表同。
3.2022年农林牧渔业增加值为快报数。

Notes: a) Since 2004, the sown area of grain has included that of soybeans. The same applies to the following tables.
b) Economics crops include sugarcane, oil crops, hemp, tobacco leaves, medicinal materials, vegetables, melons and fruits, and other crops, the same below.
c) In 2022, the Value-added of Agriculture is the result of express report.

11-2 各市农村基层组织情况（2022年）

Basic Conditions of Rural Grassroots Units by City (2022)

市别	City	乡镇个数 (个) Number of Townships (unit)	村民委员会个数 (个) Number of Villagers' Committees (unit)
全省	**Provincial Total**	**1123**	**19431**
广州	Guangzhou	34	1145
深圳	Shenzhen		
珠海	Zhuhai	15	122
汕头	Shantou	30	558
佛山	Foshan	21	329
韶关	Shaoguan	95	1207
河源	Heyuan	95	1251
梅州	Meizhou	104	2048
惠州	Huizhou	49	1043
汕尾	Shanwei	40	723
东莞	Dongguan	28	350
中山	Zhongshan	15	150
江门	Jiangmen	61	1056
阳江	Yangjiang	38	710
湛江	Zhanjiang	84	1638
茂名	Maoming	86	1628
肇庆	Zhaoqing	88	1255
清远	Qingyuan	80	1031
潮州	Chaozhou	41	894
揭阳	Jieyang	64	1446
云浮	Yunfu	55	847
按经济区域分	By Region		
珠三角	Pearl River Delta	311	5450
东翼	Eastern Region	175	3621
西翼	Western Region	208	3976
山区	Mountainous Region	429	6384

11-3 农业生产条件

Agricultural Production Basic Conditions

指标	Item	2019	2020	2021	2022
农业机械化情况	**Mechanization of Agriculture**				
农业机械总动力 (万千瓦)	Total Agricultural Machinery Power (10 000 kw)	2455.79	2495.43	2524.48	2556.34
机耕面积 (千公顷)	Total Area Cultivated Using Machinery (10 000 hectares)	3724.21	3825.98	3877.57	3980.79
机播面积 (千公顷)	Total Area Sown Using Machinery (1 000 hectares)	404.32	504.99	616.27	721.93
农用物资使用情况	**Use of Agricultural Materials**				
化肥施用量(折纯量) (万吨)	Consumption of Chemical Fertilizers(pure) (10 000 tons)	225.79	219.80	212.87	208.74
农用塑料薄膜使用量 (万吨)	Plastic Agricultural Film Used (10 000 tons)	4.38	4.26	4.30	4.53
农用柴油使用量 (万吨)	Diesel Used in Agriculture (10 000 tons)	85.55	85.81	85.42	85.99
农药使用量 (万吨)	Consumption of Pesticides (10 000 tons)	8.75	8.32	7.74	7.60
农田水利情况	**Agricultural Water Conservation**				
耕地灌溉面积 (千公顷)	Irrigated Area of Cultivated Land (10 000 hectares)	1773.40	1776.46	1776.46	1529.21
高效节水灌溉建设任务 (千公顷)	Construction task of efficient and water-saving irrigation (10 000 hectares)	6.10	5.34	7.39	3.61
除涝面积 (千公顷)	Areas with Flood Prevention Measures (10 000 hectares)	541.89	543.82	552.74	535.06
新增水土流失治理面积 (千公顷)	Areas Newly Treated for Water and Soil Erosion (10 000 hectares)	110.93	95.63	80.83	86.85
堤防长度 (公里)	Total Length of Dikes (10 000 km)	32135.54	31929.09	31910.76	30304.25
堤防保护耕地面积 (千公顷)	Dike protection Area of Cultivated Land(10 000 hectares)	1132.66	1135.29	1136.61	1101.76

11-4 农业自然灾害情况

Statistics on Agriculture Covered and Affected by Natural Disasters

项目	Item	2000	2010	2020	2021	2022
农作物受灾面积 (万亩)	Area of Farm Crops Covered by Natural Disasters(10000 mu)	948.43	916.21	126.15	119.56	383.16
#绝收面积	Area without Output	84.14	106.45	12.30	22.61	67.79
受灾人口 (万人)	Number of Persons Covered by Natural Disasters (10000 persons)	1801.00	1197.00	120.08	96.05	442.17
紧急转移安置人口(万人)	Number of Persons Receiving Evacuation and Re-settlement (10000 persons)	27.73	71.61	12.42	0.89	25.47
因灾死亡人口 (人)	Death Toll in Natural Disasters (person)	102	177	17	2	19
因灾伤病人口 (人)	Number of Wounded Persons in Natural Disasters (person)	14454	1121	11	2	4
倒塌房屋 (间)	Number of Broken Buildings (room)	27743	73666	1894	267	6551
损坏房屋 (间)	Number of Damaged Buildings (room)	74052	137066	3820	1778	3090
因灾死亡大牲畜(头、只)	Number of Large Livestock Killed in Natural Disasters (head)	62417	74002	256	2388	3412
直接经济损失 (亿元)	Volume of Direct Economic Loss (100 million yuan)	38.20	180.01	54.33	25.59	191.77

11-5 农林牧渔业总产值

Gross Output Value of Agriculture, Forestry, Animal Husbandry and Fishery

单位：亿元 (100 million yuan)

年份 Year	农林牧渔业总产值 Total	农业产值 Farming	林业产值 Forestry	牧业产值 Animal Husbandry	渔业产值 Fishery	农林牧渔专业及辅助性活动产值 Professional and Support Activities for Agriculture, Forestry, Animal Husbandry, Fishery
1978	85.94	59.56	4.98	15.98	5.42	
1979	91.53	67.19	7.67	13.58	3.09	
1980	126.25	97.15	6.83	17.75	4.52	
1981	133.85	99.33	7.81	21.62	5.09	
1982	135.52	98.33	8.33	21.73	7.13	
1983	169.96	120.06	10.72	28.57	10.61	
1984	200.07	141.22	12.13	33.81	12.91	
1985	245.21	149.09	21.09	54.68	20.35	
1986	279.15	168.68	24.38	60.74	25.35	
1987	348.61	214.47	16.74	78.26	39.14	
1988	473.78	277.38	27.66	114.28	54.46	
1989	548.60	323.15	28.00	134.60	62.85	
1990	600.71	359.39	28.46	143.68	69.18	
1991	654.82	388.90	29.64	156.08	80.20	
1992	737.11	428.99	32.86	175.36	99.90	
1993	899.03	486.46	35.51	223.16	153.90	
1994	1151.38	628.17	41.07	279.98	202.16	
1995	1445.48	777.72	46.12	349.11	272.53	
1996	1577.89	825.60	49.64	398.12	304.53	
1997	1656.46	851.35	52.10	425.67	327.34	
1998	1705.44	861.97	54.65	441.61	347.21	
1999	1745.02	859.66	58.77	457.51	369.08	
2000	1701.18	807.94	59.64	450.18	383.42	
2001	1722.35	817.95	56.78	457.56	390.06	
2002	1781.06	841.77	57.09	465.91	416.29	
2003	1908.66	851.72	55.72	482.83	432.74	85.65
2004	2154.79	959.97	61.72	571.09	466.45	95.56
2005	2447.57	1109.18	66.25	638.61	523.79	109.74
2006	2536.27	1235.40	67.60	623.34	519.03	90.90
2007	2810.45	1268.70	116.96	781.97	540.58	102.24
2008	3276.02	1398.82	125.23	983.84	650.23	117.89
2009	3301.86	1442.40	139.95	939.67	657.65	122.18
2010	3697.18	1668.66	180.20	978.33	737.01	132.97
2011	4301.86	1910.21	213.71	1193.73	835.41	148.80
2012	4550.29	2060.91	228.75	1189.80	908.12	162.71
2013	4802.01	2229.64	256.99	1168.73	968.42	178.23
2014	5053.72	2357.16	289.66	1145.87	1068.00	193.03
2015	5303.63	2490.20	308.72	1195.97	1102.12	206.62
2016	5817.55	2763.79	330.04	1318.89	1179.15	225.68
2017	5969.87	2889.97	356.14	1202.30	1276.11	245.34
2018	6318.12	3089.57	390.62	1184.72	1383.81	269.39
2019	7175.89	3530.21	408.48	1404.13	1524.78	308.30
2020	7901.92	3769.26	414.29	1778.18	1581.54	358.64
2021	8305.84	3951.14	495.44	1707.82	1747.34	404.10
2022	8892.29	4308.23	549.15	1680.24	1898.24	456.43

11-6 农林牧渔业总产值指数（1978年＝100）

Indices of Gross Output Value of Agriculture, Forestry, Animal Husbandry and Fishery (1978=100)

1978年＝100 (year of 1978=100)

年份 Year	农林牧渔业总产值 Total	农业产值 Farming	林业产值 Forestry	牧业产值 Animal Husbandry	渔业产值 Fishery	农林牧渔专业及辅助性活动产值 Professional and Support Activities for Agriculture, Forestry, Animal Husbandry, Fishery
1978	100.0	100.0	100.0	100.0	100.0	
1979	99.2	99.4	85.1	104.6	93.7	
1980	110.2	111.8	108.3	104.4	102.8	
1981	112.8	110.3	119.6	122.9	111.9	
1982	131.2	127.4	133.4	148.6	135.0	
1983	134.6	127.2	140.4	159.8	164.3	
1984	147.1	138.9	147.6	175.5	185.5	
1985	157.8	145.5	154.8	202.2	216.2	
1986	167.5	151.0	173.4	219.6	257.0	
1987	183.6	165.8	166.9	237.7	313.2	
1988	197.7	173.4	223.2	259.2	350.3	
1989	213.2	186.9	232.3	279.4	389.9	
1990	228.9	201.5	215.7	306.2	429.3	
1991	243.0	211.9	213.8	332.6	470.1	
1992	257.7	220.3	218.9	357.8	536.5	
1993	267.6	213.7	222.6	398.9	644.5	
1994	279.5	219.5	227.5	415.1	716.3	
1995	302.7	237.1	239.6	443.5	800.1	
1996	320.9	245.0	246.5	485.9	882.9	
1997	342.7	263.7	249.2	509.5	953.5	
1998	359.3	272.7	258.1	535.8	1033.7	
1999	379.1	286.8	271.8	563.9	1101.9	
2000	389.3	288.6	281.3	579.6	1184.5	
2001	400.1	295.6	294.0	592.7	1230.1	
2002	426.1	323.4	285.8	601.4	1310.6	
2003	438.2	331.6	277.8	614.8	1367.5	100.0
2004	457.9	350.5	287.2	625.9	1433.1	107.8
2005	479.9	362.3	295.5	660.4	1514.2	120.5
2006	499.1	375.2	280.8	680.7	1605.1	132.3
2007	515.5	385.5	289.1	701.2	1670.8	143.1
2008	536.1	392.4	289.9	750.8	1749.5	155.0
2009	562.9	414.3	310.6	779.3	1839.0	163.2
2010	586.9	434.2	324.5	803.9	1921.4	171.4
2011	609.9	458.6	351.1	795.6	2023.4	180.8
2012	632.7	476.3	373.0	811.3	2123.6	191.1
2013	647.0	490.9	393.7	796.8	2211.8	203.2
2014	666.4	512.8	413.2	788.5	2292.0	213.5
2015	687.0	534.0	437.6	785.6	2369.7	224.7
2016	707.1	554.6	467.1	777.7	2451.0	238.3
2017	730.8	580.3	490.1	771.7	2542.1	255.3
2018	761.2	609.8	521.8	780.5	2634.9	274.3
2019	787.7	645.5	548.4	739.9	2734.3	303.6
2020	819.3	681.8	555.1	716.3	2891.0	344.8
2021	877.7	713.7	559.4	824.6	3023.8	385.5
2022	919.5	743.7	603.3	856.7	3162.4	427.1

注：本表按可比价格计算。
Note: The indices are calculated at comparable prices.

11-7 农林牧渔业总产值指数（上年=100）

Indices of Gross Output Value of Agriculture, Forestry, Animal Husbandry and Fishery (preceding year=100)

上年=100 (preceding year=100)

年份 Year	农林牧渔业总产值 Total	农业产值 Farming	林业产值 Forestry	牧业产值 Animal Husbandry	渔业产值 Fishery	农林牧渔专业及辅助性活动产值 Professional and Support Activities for Agriculture, Forestry, Animal Husbandry, Fishery
1979	99.2	99.4	85.1	104.6	93.7	
1980	111.1	112.5	127.3	99.8	109.7	
1981	102.4	98.7	110.4	117.6	108.9	
1982	116.3	115.5	111.5	120.9	120.6	
1983	102.6	99.9	105.2	107.6	121.7	
1984	109.3	109.2	105.1	109.8	112.9	
1985	107.3	104.8	104.9	115.2	116.5	
1986	106.1	103.8	112.0	108.6	118.9	
1987	109.6	109.8	96.3	108.2	121.9	
1988	107.7	104.6	133.7	109.0	111.8	
1989	107.8	107.8	104.1	107.8	111.3	
1990	107.4	107.8	92.9	109.6	110.1	
1991	106.2	105.1	99.1	108.6	109.5	
1992	106.0	103.9	102.4	107.6	114.1	
1993	103.8	97.0	101.7	111.5	120.1	
1994	104.4	102.7	102.2	104.1	111.1	
1995	108.3	108.0	105.3	106.8	111.7	
1996	106.0	103.3	102.9	109.6	110.3	
1997	106.8	107.6	101.1	104.8	108.0	
1998	104.8	103.4	103.6	105.2	108.4	
1999	105.5	105.2	105.3	105.2	106.6	
2000	102.7	100.6	103.5	102.8	107.5	
2001	102.8	102.4	104.5	102.2	103.8	
2002	106.5	109.4	97.2	101.5	106.5	
2003	102.8	102.5	97.2	102.2	104.3	
2004	104.5	105.7	103.4	101.8	104.8	107.8
2005	104.8	103.4	102.9	105.5	105.7	111.8
2006	104.0	103.6	95.0	103.1	106.0	109.8
2007	103.3	102.7	103.0	103.0	104.1	108.2
2008	104.0	101.8	100.3	107.1	104.7	108.3
2009	105.0	105.6	107.1	103.8	105.1	105.3
2010	104.3	104.8	104.5	103.2	104.5	105.0
2011	103.9	105.6	108.2	99.0	105.3	105.5
2012	103.7	103.9	106.3	102.0	105.0	105.7
2013	102.3	103.1	105.5	98.2	104.2	106.3
2014	103.0	104.5	105.0	99.0	103.6	105.1
2015	103.1	104.1	105.9	99.6	103.4	105.2
2016	102.9	103.9	106.8	99.0	103.4	106.1
2017	103.3	104.6	104.9	99.2	103.7	107.1
2018	104.2	105.1	106.5	101.1	103.7	107.4
2019	103.5	105.8	105.1	94.8	103.8	110.7
2020	104.0	105.6	101.2	96.8	105.7	113.6
2021	107.1	104.7	100.8	115.1	104.6	111.8
2022	104.8	104.2	107.8	103.9	104.6	110.8

注：本表按可比价格计算。
Note: The indices are calculated at comparable prices.

11-8 各市农林牧渔业总产值（2022年）

Gross Output Value of Farming, Forestry, Animal Husbandry and Fishery by City (2022)

单位：亿元　　　　(100 million yuan)

市别	City	农林牧渔业总产值 Total	农业产值 Farming	林业产值 Forestry	牧业产值 Animal Husbandry	渔业产值 Fishery	农林牧渔专业及辅助性活动产值 Professional and Support Activities for Agriculture, Forestry, Animal Husbandry, Fishery
全　省	**Provincial Total**	**8892.29**	**4308.23**	**549.15**	**1680.24**	**1898.24**	**456.43**
广　州	Guangzhou	568.77	312.13	4.61	36.32	129.54	86.17
深　圳	Shenzhen	48.26	15.67	0.36	3.15	26.86	2.23
珠　海	Zhuhai	121.41	15.02	0.03	3.78	91.76	10.82
汕　头	Shantou	254.95	124.89	0.41	32.73	79.79	17.13
佛　山	Foshan	429.40	146.72	1.42	62.36	185.41	33.50
韶　关	Shaoguan	375.39	211.61	35.64	109.29	14.23	4.62
河　源	Heyuan	253.75	144.76	43.73	53.89	7.10	4.27
梅　州	Meizhou	410.94	274.11	20.64	91.76	13.43	10.99
惠　州	Huizhou	434.25	288.28	15.69	65.66	57.94	6.68
汕　尾	Shanwei	309.24	121.64	7.56	34.59	129.12	16.34
东　莞	Dongguan	55.08	40.71	0.27	1.18	11.24	1.68
中　山	Zhongshan	146.79	50.89	0.10	3.22	89.35	3.24
江　门	Jiangmen	595.20	178.47	13.41	127.62	251.71	23.99
阳　江	Yangjiang	420.33	116.74	13.20	80.82	194.14	15.44
湛　江	Zhanjiang	1104.08	597.79	21.37	161.54	274.44	48.95
茂　名	Maoming	1130.02	594.59	97.01	266.31	133.52	38.59
肇　庆	Zhaoqing	759.42	344.61	116.59	164.79	94.81	38.60
清　远	Qingyuan	552.45	271.98	55.93	164.13	22.41	38.01
潮　州	Chaozhou	209.99	126.56	2.17	23.17	46.16	11.92
揭　阳	Jieyang	354.38	206.92	40.22	52.39	30.66	24.18
云　浮	Yunfu	358.19	124.15	58.79	141.55	14.63	19.08
按经济区域分	By Region						
珠三角	Pearl River Delta	3158.58	1392.50	152.48	468.07	938.62	206.92
东　翼	Eastern Region	1128.56	580.01	50.37	142.88	285.73	69.58
西　翼	Western Region	2654.43	1309.12	131.57	508.67	602.09	102.98
山　区	Mountainous Region	1950.71	1026.61	214.73	560.62	71.79	76.96

注：本表按当年价格计算。
Note: Data in this table are calculated at current prices.

11-9 各市农林牧渔业总产值指数(2022年)

Indices of Gross Output Value of Agriculture,Forestry, Animal Husbandry and Fishery by City (2022)

上年=100 (preceding year=100)

市别	City	农林牧渔业总产值 Total	农业产值 Farming	林业产值 Forestry	牧业产值 Animal Husbandry	渔业产值 Fishery	农林牧渔专业及辅助性活动产值 Professional and Support Activities for Agriculture, Forestry, Animal Husbandry, Fishery
全　省	**Provincial Total**	**104.8**	**104.2**	**107.8**	**103.9**	**104.6**	**110.8**
广　州	Guangzhou	102.7	101.6	83.2	100.5	103.8	107.6
深　圳	Shenzhen	101.2	100.0	62.4	102.6	102.3	109.0
珠　海	Zhuhai	106.5	92.0	146.6	148.6	108.4	106.1
汕　头	Shantou	105.5	102.8	72.3	104.8	109.8	108.6
佛　山	Foshan	106.5	102.7	82.5	110.5	107.4	113.0
韶　关	Shaoguan	104.3	103.4	109.1	104.8	101.2	108.5
河　源	Heyuan	104.7	103.2	106.9	106.4	107.5	107.5
梅　州	Meizhou	104.1	104.4	101.7	103.4	101.9	109.2
惠　州	Huizhou	107.7	106.3	130.3	107.5	109.4	114.2
汕　尾	Shanwei	106.2	104.9	110.8	103.5	107.5	109.3
东　莞	Dongguan	97.5	97.3	428.9	108.2	95.4	99.3
中　山	Zhongshan	105.4	110.0	51.2	94.9	103.6	103.6
江　门	Jiangmen	104.9	105.5	108.2	106.2	103.0	111.1
阳　江	Yangjiang	101.7	102.0	102.6	101.0	100.3	125.1
湛　江	Zhanjiang	104.1	104.0	106.3	105.0	102.6	109.5
茂　名	Maoming	105.1	103.5	116.5	101.6	109.5	116.2
肇　庆	Zhaoqing	103.4	103.1	103.5	101.1	104.2	114.9
清　远	Qingyuan	106.6	105.2	123.5	103.8	101.6	111.4
潮　州	Chaozhou	105.5	108.1	77.7	101.4	102.7	106.4
揭　阳	Jieyang	105.0	105.2	107.1	100.8	104.8	110.9
云　浮	Yunfu	104.3	103.5	107.6	104.2	95.5	107.2
按经济区域分	By Region						
珠三角	Pearl River Delta	104.6	103.6	103.8	104.7	104.9	110.1
东　翼	Eastern Region	105.4	105.2	103.0	102.4	107.0	109.2
西　翼	Western Region	104.0	103.6	111.4	102.6	103.3	114.1
山　区	Mountainous Region	104.8	104.1	109.8	104.3	100.8	109.6

注：本表按可比价格计算。
Note: The indices are calculated at comparable prices.

11-10 农作物播种面积

Total Sown Area of Farm Crops

单位：万亩 (10000 mu)

年份 Year	农作物总播种面积 Total Sown Area	一、粮食作物 Grain Crops	#稻谷 Rice	#薯类 Tubers	#大豆 Soybean
1978	9962.46	7603.47	5790.39	873.02	163.71
1979	9492.62	7300.54	5691.88	845.65	185.91
1980	8954.84	6908.02	5596.10	800.67	198.18
1981	8567.83	6548.40	5450.29	767.07	199.33
1982	8539.77	6475.65	5373.51	778.51	218.52
1983	8364.03	6485.66	5406.97	780.98	197.43
1984	8313.00	6269.47	5272.01	765.51	193.21
1985	8036.82	5750.76	4815.81	730.83	175.22
1986	8037.18	5731.76	4804.77	745.48	177.59
1987	8064.78	5679.94	4750.06	743.22	174.25
1988	8063.89	5598.29	4678.26	726.61	172.60
1989	8322.71	5777.18	4768.32	743.93	173.64
1990	8507.35	5822.06	4763.67	751.70	172.44
1991	8489.09	5643.92	4596.92	746.74	163.30
1992	8231.36	5303.82	4313.79	710.56	157.48
1993	7718.41	4840.76	3944.83	681.66	160.54
1994	7807.99	4959.10	4005.47	747.93	157.12
1995	7957.19	5052.24	4052.13	775.96	155.84
1996	8156.22	5120.09	4066.33	778.70	155.04
1997	8267.25	5144.06	4055.92	772.52	149.14
1998	8310.73	5147.65	4029.10	768.09	146.06
1999	7894.24	4912.04	3836.30	697.22	144.52
2000	7735.35	4649.83	3619.05	640.15	145.46
2001	7868.21	4634.79	3638.28	661.15	132.19
2002	7207.37	4021.44	3151.22	582.81	102.14
2003	7294.58	4012.81	3144.56	578.14	114.54
2004	7211.96	4184.55	3208.50	581.55	120.60
2005	7223.06	4179.75	3206.40	579.75	125.70
2006	6573.85	3700.00	2912.90	468.40	96.90
2007	6444.51	3662.24	2895.53	448.58	85.95
2008	6410.77	3638.75	2896.11	425.09	81.17
2009	6416.17	3638.09	2900.39	404.84	73.18
2010	6394.16	3579.49	2877.21	392.65	72.66
2011	6367.10	3524.67	2847.03	372.05	63.76
2012	6372.63	3497.08	2847.31	355.91	61.87
2013	6363.36	3399.78	2774.98	339.63	58.22
2014	6337.79	3346.61	2740.15	333.84	54.53
2015	6291.83	3289.94	2707.15	319.78	51.71
2016	6271.95	3266.67	2709.05	304.07	48.47
2017	6341.26	3254.59	2708.13	300.04	46.74
2018	6419.04	3226.56	2681.09	299.72	47.68
2019	6536.07	3240.96	2690.51	303.74	48.86
2020	6677.71	3307.03	2751.65	304.33	48.92
2021	6747.53	3319.55	2741.13	317.08	48.95
2022	6830.20	3345.43	2753.84	324.51	52.05

11-10 续表 continued

单位：万亩 (10000 mu)

年份 Year	二、经济作物 Economic Crops	#糖蔗 Sugarcane	#花生 Peanuts	#烟叶 Tobacco	#蔬菜 Vegetables
1978	2195.28	258.96	486.62	69.19	
1979	2006.17	227.15	519.73	59.44	
1980	1848.64	218.57	553.24	38.62	
1981	1820.10	272.52	595.41	45.06	
1982	1845.60	331.53	588.01	48.73	
1983	1680.94	312.86	489.74	43.25	
1984	1850.32	341.02	523.56	39.06	
1985	2110.84	442.83	545.78	55.25	
1986	2127.83	405.07	560.80	41.87	
1987	2210.59	344.72	533.13	41.42	
1988	2293.00	354.90	497.82	61.39	
1989	2371.89	338.02	486.05	72.25	
1990	2512.85	419.73	485.96	68.55	776.00
1991	2681.87	453.90	472.15	81.93	867.95
1992	2770.06	461.14	471.88	79.08	946.88
1993	2717.11	353.65	499.78	73.92	1057.02
1994	2691.77	325.62	505.35	53.15	1147.53
1995	2749.11	320.18	499.60	44.33	1244.96
1996	2881.09	329.28	497.42	45.10	1348.64
1997	2974.06	334.02	499.70	55.45	1416.62
1998	3017.02	325.59	510.83	50.30	1484.82
1999	2837.68	261.47	468.50	42.72	1441.85
2000	2940.05	239.60	496.61	46.64	1515.15
2001	3101.23	215.25	511.57	53.48	1685.69
2002	3083.79	222.66	472.49	46.27	1692.00
2003	3167.23	198.29	488.66	44.86	1792.29
2004	3027.41	193.45	462.20	47.42	1720.01
2005	3043.31	188.08	464.11	47.47	1744.08
2006	2873.85	195.13	462.28	30.23	1627.80
2007	2782.27	206.37	446.50	28.62	1570.07
2008	2772.02	203.87	455.75	33.57	1612.13
2009	2778.08	203.79	459.64	34.44	1621.20
2010	2814.67	205.08	461.08	32.54	1651.25
2011	2842.42	211.58	461.80	32.31	1662.82
2012	2875.55	219.42	466.41	31.22	1669.40
2013	2963.58	231.18	469.80	29.99	1736.59
2014	2991.19	225.68	470.91	28.23	1772.00
2015	3001.88	215.36	474.87	27.42	1782.70
2016	3005.28	214.36	471.77	26.71	1784.79
2017	3086.67	219.36	478.65	26.11	1840.83
2018	3192.48	223.17	498.73	26.21	1908.37
2019	3295.11	220.60	510.77	25.10	1980.78
2020	3370.68	205.18	521.36	24.73	2045.32
2021	3427.98	192.60	524.52	23.77	2088.37
2022	3484.77	189.14	520.19	22.98	2142.56

11-11 主要农产品产量

Output of Major Farm Products

单位：万吨 (10000 tons)

年份 Year	粮食作物 Grain Crops	#稻谷 Rice	#薯类 Tubers	#大豆 Soybean	糖蔗 Sugarcane	花生 Peanuts	烟叶 Tobacco	蔬菜 Vegetables	茶叶 Tea	水果 Fruits
1978	1509.51	1328.56	121.04	7.99	835.42	35.17	4.73		0.92	29.40
1979	1605.36	1435.22	125.15	9.56	742.90	40.70	4.00		0.89	26.20
1980	1681.91	1523.92	123.68	11.47	834.73	50.00	2.72		1.00	29.10
1981	1521.00	1372.22	122.53	12.01	1235.50	57.39	3.68		1.13	39.20
1982	1795.72	1627.37	138.98	14.44	1496.10	61.90	4.67		1.31	46.30
1983	1817.48	1673.12	138.98	10.80	1159.83	48.08	3.41		1.45	53.00
1984	1819.33	1666.08	130.21	11.90	1454.15	53.40	3.50		1.61	73.90
1985	1604.37	1454.29	131.88	11.32	1831.40	57.07	4.89		1.75	116.28
1986	1567.00	1421.55	128.01	12.27	1622.13	60.40	3.50		2.03	185.50
1987	1701.81	1536.46	146.48	12.43	1338.60	53.50	4.05		2.28	264.10
1988	1636.70	1472.95	143.42	12.32	1538.68	51.80	5.80		2.39	277.98
1989	1817.21	1630.29	153.47	13.25	1681.34	55.38	7.15	916.88	2.35	275.83
1990	1896.29	1687.00	167.05	13.87	2093.46	57.95	7.08	976.83	2.59	328.58
1991	1873.50	1651.65	176.59	12.60	2286.38	56.11	8.46	1106.19	2.67	394.19
1992	1810.40	1602.27	170.28	13.94	2271.06	60.30	8.62	1203.54	2.87	453.62
1993	1629.11	1425.81	169.20	15.28	1603.11	66.02	7.70	1367.22	3.07	402.44
1994	1662.66	1434.04	194.68	15.44	1397.22	63.71	5.30	1509.93	3.32	401.55
1995	1803.33	1553.90	209.40	16.50	1472.21	69.98	5.04	1703.86	3.96	414.51
1996	1891.43	1626.29	210.28	17.32	1392.00	73.05	5.29	1865.10	3.62	381.17
1997	1966.75	1669.33	228.35	17.61	1629.27	74.10	7.33	1995.99	3.66	414.48
1998	1884.13	1688.53	238.28	17.32	1616.94	69.38	6.61	2011.13	3.89	453.12
1999	1935.82	1630.13	214.38	17.91	1218.30	73.31	5.80	2109.68	4.06	622.68
2000	1822.33	1528.53	199.05	18.73	1137.59	77.68	6.21	2214.80	4.21	643.52
2001	1721.55	1441.35	198.15	17.36	1073.38	79.73	6.79	2377.60	4.15	590.74
2002	1484.16	1243.46	171.02	12.67	1136.45	75.19	6.08	2442.53	4.24	698.91
2003	1488.00	1250.38	166.77	14.92	952.87	80.73	6.00	2584.20	4.14	718.59
2004	1390.00	1123.13	180.28	18.10	940.77	76.47	6.27	2557.65	4.04	787.85
2005	1394.97	1116.99	185.48	18.87	946.02	75.86	6.30	2596.02	4.45	831.69
2006	1242.42	1015.90	150.48	14.92	1025.66	76.54	4.23	2380.56	4.74	893.47
2007	1267.03	1041.38	148.04	12.64	1078.06	75.45	4.07	2316.01	4.91	934.12
2008	1210.02	994.97	136.91	12.10	1043.21	77.93	4.71	2355.51	4.88	948.32
2009	1261.99	1044.00	133.43	11.08	1062.73	79.58	4.98	2446.67	5.20	1004.99
2010	1249.15	1041.80	129.01	11.20	1064.09	81.59	5.00	2550.50	5.38	1049.21
2011	1275.73	1072.65	122.86	9.60	1111.28	83.72	5.00	2633.02	6.04	1100.20
2012	1295.69	1097.00	120.06	10.15	1164.49	86.66	5.06	2722.03	6.39	1147.12
2013	1202.48	1012.80	112.48	9.88	1218.46	89.17	4.83	2808.09	7.09	1206.39
2014	1229.97	1053.29	106.12	9.45	1159.89	91.77	4.61	2898.53	7.51	1248.18
2015	1211.66	1040.82	102.34	9.03	1093.58	94.48	4.52	2994.65	8.07	1298.52
2016	1204.22	1039.53	96.53	8.63	1096.56	95.48	4.40	3036.45	8.92	1331.99
2017	1208.56	1046.34	95.43	8.48	1144.14	98.42	4.26	3177.49	9.29	1421.23
2018	1193.49	1032.07	94.67	8.71	1207.97	104.40	4.33	3330.24	9.99	1547.81
2019	1240.80	1075.05	97.41	9.04	1241.64	108.69	4.17	3527.96	11.08	1644.38
2020	1267.56	1099.58	97.29	9.10	1176.25	112.05	4.12	3706.85	12.82	1756.16
2021	1279.87	1104.41	102.72	8.64	1118.20	115.87	3.88	3855.73	13.95	1826.73
2022	1291.54	1108.63	107.01	9.27	1107.76	115.93	3.71	3999.11	16.08	1895.18

11-12 主要畜产品和水产品产量
Output of Major Farm Products

单位：万吨 Units: (10000 tons)

年份 Year	肉类 Meat	#猪肉 Pork	牛奶 Cow Milk	水产品 Aquatic Products	海水产品 Seawater Aquatic Products	淡水产品 Freshwater Aquatic Products
1978	48.45	48.09	1.66	65.50	46.47	19.03
1979	58.96	58.30	1.90	57.44	36.71	20.73
1980	63.20	62.62	2.18	63.34	41.54	21.80
1981	69.61	69.10	2.56	64.17	39.63	24.54
1982	76.85	76.20	2.88	76.32	47.12	29.20
1983	85.24	84.50	3.16	85.61	51.58	34.03
1984	90.00	89.00	3.89	95.63	54.33	41.30
1985	128.12	97.59	4.09	109.44	58.74	50.70
1986	154.16	106.60	4.39	136.54	78.18	58.36
1987	154.15	114.12	4.55	155.36	90.17	65.19
1988	172.45	124.64	4.99	174.66	102.02	72.64
1989	181.66	132.40	5.08	189.75	113.47	76.28
1990	202.45	145.35	5.51	207.66	124.53	83.13
1991	225.08	158.01	6.03	225.31	135.11	90.20
1992	245.69	166.22	5.72	251.06	147.42	103.64
1993	271.46	173.89	5.71	280.75	158.46	122.29
1994	278.50	176.89	5.71	314.10	174.80	139.30
1995	305.06	188.75	5.49	354.34	197.21	157.13
1996	252.03	162.03	5.81	395.08	218.39	176.69
1997	275.62	176.59	6.03	520.96	330.66	190.30
1998	305.45	197.53	6.97	554.28	346.20	208.07
1999	315.86	204.40	7.77	575.95	355.37	220.58
2000	324.48	206.85	9.19	593.19	360.45	232.73
2001	333.25	213.65	10.18	609.67	367.07	242.60
2002	343.63	220.17	10.82	628.06	374.36	253.70
2003	358.50	232.77	10.55	648.55	379.21	269.34
2004	365.32	242.14	10.94	664.56	381.79	282.78
2005	384.31	256.28	11.64	695.23	397.95	297.28
2006	382.08	251.46	12.00	658.84	373.59	285.25
2007	388.60	237.41	12.17	664.34	373.12	291.22
2008	418.32	258.39	13.62	680.41	376.81	303.60
2009	436.92	268.98	14.75	702.60	387.15	315.45
2010	454.86	285.14	14.95	729.03	401.50	327.53
2011	451.65	282.93	14.95	762.53	418.23	344.31
2012	464.13	291.09	14.33	739.35	408.92	330.43
2013	459.22	295.09	14.46	764.29	418.58	345.71
2014	456.69	302.86	14.20	783.22	426.44	356.78
2015	454.71	296.31	13.61	803.71	434.71	369.00
2016	448.70	288.24	13.61	818.29	441.54	376.75
2017	444.08	277.96	13.88	833.54	451.81	381.73
2018	449.90	281.52	13.89	842.44	449.17	393.28
2019	412.12	221.93	13.92	866.40	455.49	410.91
2020	400.99	192.42	15.10	875.81	450.53	425.28
2021	457.42	263.23	17.23	884.52	455.04	429.47
2022	481.01	279.81	19.81	894.03	458.29	435.74

注：2012—2017年水产品数据以第三次全国农业普查数据为基础做了调整。下表同。

Note: From 2012 to 2017, data of aquatic products are adjusted in accordance with the Third National Agricultural Census. The same applies to the following tables.

11-13 主要农作物播种面积、亩产及总产量

Sown Area, Yield per Mu and Total Output of Major Farm Crops

单位：万亩、公斤、万吨 (10000 mu, kg, 10000 tons)

作物名称	Farm Crop	2010			2021			2022		
		播种面积 Sown Area	亩产 Yield per Mu	总产量 Total Output	播种面积 Sown Area	亩产 Yield per Mu	总产量 Total Output	播种面积 Sown Area	亩产 Yield per Mu	总产量 Total Output
农作物播种面积	**Total Sown Area**	**6394.16**			**6747.53**			**6830.20**		
粮食作物	**Grain Crops**	**3579.49**	**349**	**1249.15**	**3319.55**	**386**	**1279.87**	**3345.43**	**386**	**1291.54**
稻谷	Rice	2877.21	362	1041.80	2741.13	403	1104.41	2753.84	403	1108.63
早稻	Early Rice	1386.98	362	502.04	1287.84	407	524.15	1296.34	401	520.09
晚稻	Late Rice	1490.23	362	539.76	1453.29	399	580.26	1457.50	404	588.54
小麦	Wheat	1.30	191	0.25	0.37	243	0.09	0.63	235	0.15
玉米	Corn	209.12	296	61.94	194.68	312	60.80	197.86	320	63.41
薯类(折粮)	Tubers	392.65	329	129.01	317.08	324	102.72	324.51	330	107.01
大豆	Soybean	72.66	154	11.20	48.95	177	8.64	52.05	178	9.27
经济作物	**Economic Crops**	**2814.67**			**3427.98**			**3484.77**		
甘蔗	Sugarcane and Fruit Cane	233.16	5253	1224.73	225.16	5803	1306.60	220.79	5852	1292.05
#糖蔗	Sugarcane	205.08	5189	1064.09	192.60	5806	1118.20	189.14	5857	1107.76
油料作物	Oil-bearing Crops	477.28	175	83.34	536.16	219	117.30	532.82	220	117.43
#花生	Peanuts	461.08	177	81.59	524.52	221	115.87	520.19	223	115.93
麻类	Fiber Crops	0.29	164	0.05	0.09	212	0.02	0.06	245	0.01
烟叶	Tobacco	32.54	154	5.00	23.77	163	3.88	22.98	162	3.71
中草药材	Chinese Herbal Medicine	16.92			84.57			102.74		
蔬菜	Vegetables	1651.25	1544	2550.50	2088.37	1846	3855.73	2142.56	1867	3999.11
瓜果类	Melons and Fruits	57.67	1724	99.43	64.70	2026	131.06	64.91	2052	133.20
其他农作物	Other Crops	345.56			405.16			397.91		
#木薯	Cassava	114.94	1223	140.61	95.41	1429	136.33	91.47	1450	132.67

11−14 各市主要农作物播种面积、亩产及总产量（2022年）

Sown Area, Yield per Mu and Total Output of Major Farm Crops by City (2022)

单位：亩、公斤、吨 (mu, kg, ton)

市别	City	粮食作物 Grain Crops			#稻谷 Rice		
		播种面积 Sown Area	亩产 Yield per Mu	总产量 Total Output	播种面积 Sown Area	亩产 Yield per Mu	总产量 Total Output
全　省	**Provincial Total**	**33454285**	**386**	**12915441**	**27538401**	**403**	**11086285**
广　州	Guangzhou	448213	343	153841	357214	352	125878
深　圳	Shenzhen	28070	340	9552	11496	323	3711
珠　海	Zhuhai	82256	364	29948	67772	390	26402
汕　头	Shantou	1032088	448	462245	692009	468	323649
佛　山	Foshan	140140	353	49508	104566	374	39083
韶　关	Shaoguan	1833950	414	759026	1554023	436	676732
河　源	Heyuan	2011380	405	815442	1844429	420	774792
梅　州	Meizhou	2763267	412	1137704	2437896	434	1057183
惠　州	Huizhou	1707772	363	619501	1277028	374	476905
汕　尾	Shanwei	1245611	357	444580	1042472	369	384239
东　莞	Dongguan	29985	336	10067	21766	367	7997
中　山	Zhongshan	43904	347	15240	35780	355	12693
江　门	Jiangmen	2807108	353	990323	2546832	362	921591
阳　江	Yangjiang	1822835	349	635310	1612937	362	583130
湛　江	Zhanjiang	4258005	363	1546427	3381474	376	1270376
茂　名	Maoming	3767458	407	1531722	3158323	424	1337728
肇　庆	Zhaoqing	3005524	411	1233610	2529988	430	1087835
清　远	Qingyuan	2264948	325	736291	1826851	348	636528
潮　州	Chaozhou	639374	435	278446	481754	470	226274
揭　阳	Jieyang	1978966	411	814174	1230664	427	526036
云　浮	Yunfu	1543431	416	642486	1323126	444	587523
按经济区域分	By Region						
珠三角	Pearl River Delta	8292972	375	3111589	6952442	389	2702095
东　翼	Eastern Region	4896039	408	1999445	3446899	424	1460198
西　翼	Western Region	9848298	377	3713459	8152734	391	3191234
山　区	Mountainous Region	10416976	393	4090949	8986325	415	3732758

11-14 续表 1 continued

单位：亩、公斤、吨 (mu, kg, ton)

市别	City	#大豆 Soybean 播种面积 Sown Area	亩产 Yield per Mu	总产量 Total Output	经济作物 Economic Crops 播种面积 Sown Area	#糖蔗 Sugarcane 播种面积 Sown Area	亩产 Yield per Mu	总产量 Total Output
全　省	**Provincial Total**	**520500**	**178**	**92661**	**34847713**	**1891425**	**5857**	**11077591**
广　州	Guangzhou	5749	185	1062	2736460			
深　圳	Shenzhen	398	161	64	145081	116	3112	361
珠　海	Zhuhai	1992	166	330	149367			
汕　头	Shantou	6429	184	1180	750079			
佛　山	Foshan	1181	180	213	816248			
韶　关	Shaoguan	47308	178	8417	2017124	4491	5674	25481
河　源	Heyuan	39785	182	7223	1094336	5101	5008	25546
梅　州	Meizhou	61213	172	10499	1939689	1105	2050	2265
惠　州	Huizhou	19820	169	3346	2265071	7250	7380	53502
汕　尾	Shanwei	20091	186	3741	1135930	1042	4821	5023
东　莞	Dongguan	1084	147	160	335733			
中　山	Zhongshan	616	178	110	373550	10	4600	46
江　门	Jiangmen	33125	185	6117	1946778	11822	6423	75938
阳　江	Yangjiang	49709	174	8634	1354742	2689	4636	12466
湛　江	Zhanjiang	27722	188	5205	5802852	1729799	5857	10131424
茂　名	Maoming	43601	166	7241	3246282	102842	5160	530687
肇　庆	Zhaoqing	35302	178	6292	2656675	2258	5102	11521
清　远	Qingyuan	51642	183	9436	3565767	22900	8879	203331
潮　州	Chaozhou	10610	187	1989	323702			
揭　阳	Jieyang	41149	182	7485	1094383			
云　浮	Yunfu	21974	178	3917	1097865			
按经济区域分	By Region							
珠三角	Pearl River Delta	99267	178	17694	11424962	21456	6589	141368
东　翼	Eastern Region	78279	184	14395	3304094	1042	4821	5023
西　翼	Western Region	121032	174	21080	10403876	1835330	5816	10674577
山　区	Mountainous Region	221922	178	39492	9714781	33597	7638	256623

11-14 续表 2 continued

单位：亩、公斤、吨 (mu, kg, ton)

市别	City	#花生 Peanuts			#烟叶 Tobacco		
		播种面积 Sown Area	亩产 Yield per Mu	总产量 Total Output	播种面积 Sown Area	亩产 Yield per Mu	总产量 Total Output
全　省	**Provincial Total**	**5201912**	**223**	**1159262**	**229802**	**162**	**37137**
广　州	Guangzhou	48171	194	9349			
深　圳	Shenzhen	2348	128	300			
珠　海	Zhuhai	2539	261	663			
汕　头	Shantou	18053	168	3037			
佛　山	Foshan	10026	204	2050	27	593	16
韶　关	Shaoguan	550226	244	134448	125906	154	19438
河　源	Heyuan	365651	217	79265			
梅　州	Meizhou	190127	195	37169	65153	160	10414
惠　州	Huizhou	255967	205	52433			
汕　尾	Shanwei	196165	176	34454			
东　莞	Dongguan	416	214	89			
中　山	Zhongshan	215	316	68			
江　门	Jiangmen	185841	183	33959	5	200	1
阳　江	Yangjiang	310038	159	49310	55	200	11
湛　江	Zhanjiang	967754	259	250763	1772	202	358
茂　名	Maoming	683217	233	158873	11706	209	2445
肇　庆	Zhaoqing	426026	217	92574	15968	183	2929
清　远	Qingyuan	573528	223	127662	9140	165	1505
潮　州	Chaozhou	28443	180	5113			
揭　阳	Jieyang	123120	280	34497	70	286	20
云　浮	Yunfu	264041	201	53186			
按经济区域分	By Region						
珠三角	Pearl River Delta	931549	206	191485	16000	184	2946
东　翼	Eastern Region	365781	211	77101	70	286	20
西　翼	Western Region	1961009	234	458946	13533	208	2814
山　区	Mountainous Region	1943573	222	431730	200199	157	31357

11-14 续表 3 continued

单位：亩、公斤、吨 (mu, kg, ton)

市别	City	#木薯 Cassava			#蔬菜 Vegetables		
		播种面积 Sown Area	亩产 Yield per Mu	总产量 Total Output	播种面积 Sown Area	亩产 Yield per Mu	总产量 Total Output
全　省	**Provincial Total**	**914684**	**1450**	**1326724**	**21425627**	**1867**	**39991095**
广　州	Guangzhou	1610	1125	1811	2240526	1837	4115685
深　圳	Shenzhen	152	2263	344	133278	1290	171964
珠　海	Zhuhai	52	846	44	107188	1306	140024
汕　头	Shantou	300	3433	1030	698448	2586	1806333
佛　山	Foshan	143	1748	250	502204	1696	851627
韶　关	Shaoguan	8685	1692	14693	936368	1601	1499562
河　源	Heyuan	30850	999	30824	611847	1358	831102
梅　州	Meizhou	100654	1129	113647	1120548	2313	2592263
惠　州	Huizhou	830	1675	1390	1907374	1857	3542043
汕　尾	Shanwei	25062	2325	58272	840567	1778	1494858
东　莞	Dongguan				300663	1367	410887
中　山	Zhongshan	100	1470	147	226992	1643	372920
江　门	Jiangmen	32781	1572	51530	1155533	1709	1974455
阳　江	Yangjiang	50239	1071	53797	851019	1156	983673
湛　江	Zhanjiang	144087	1921	276839	2445862	1856	4539338
茂　名	Maoming	77056	1377	106123	1915715	2021	3871504
肇　庆	Zhaoqing	229059	1355	310436	1441287	2233	3218728
清　远	Qingyuan	68406	1329	90938	2456491	1648	4047773
潮　州	Chaozhou	2528	1205	3047	245419	2322	569957
揭　阳	Jieyang	8293	1651	13688	872072	2630	2293892
云　浮	Yunfu	133797	1479	197874	416225	1592	662506
按经济区域分	By Region						
珠三角	Pearl River Delta	264727	1382	365952	8015045	1846	14798334
东　翼	Eastern Region	36183	2101	76037	2656506	2321	6165040
西　翼	Western Region	271382	1609	436759	5212596	1802	9394515
山　区	Mountainous Region	342392	1308	447976	5541479	1738	9633206

11-15 造林面积及主要林产品产量

Area of Afforestation and Output of Major Forest Products

项　目	Item	2000	2010	2015	2020	2021	2022
人工造林面积（万亩）	Artificial Afforestation Area (10000 mu)	25.76	142.72	177.69	30.03	29.61	15.48
年末实有育苗面积（万亩）	Actual Area of Seedlings Raising at the Year-end (10000 mu)	3.12	4.54	12.17	3.57	3.63	2.70
主要林产品产量	Output of Major Forest Products						
油茶籽（吨）	Tea-oil Seeds (ton)	26268	82417	149374	162656	177622	179745
竹笋干（吨）	Dried Bamboo Shoots (ton)	14132	30291	39805	55591	66153	
板栗（吨）	Chinese Chestnuts (ton)	5440	10616	21229	46006	55592	55092
松香类产品（万吨）	Rosin Products (10000 tons)	9.61	12.91	15.62	18.90	18.64	14.61
木材竹材产量	Output of Wood and Bamboo						
木材（万立方米）	Wood (10000 cubic meters)	275	655	791	1011	1264	1254
大径竹（万根）	Large Diameter Bamboo (10000 sticks)	6809	13252	12754	25737	30907	

11-16 水产养殖面积和水产品产量

Area of Cultivation and Output of Aquatic Products

指　标	Item	2000	2010	2015	2020	2021	2022
水产品产量(万吨)	**Output of Aquatic Products(10000 tons)**	**593.19**	**729.03**	**803.71**	**875.81**	**884.52**	**894.03**
海水产品	Seawater Aquatic Products	360.45	401.50	434.71	450.53	455.04	458.29
捕捞	Catches	191.48	152.43	154.00	119.29	118.80	118.61
养殖	Artificially Cultured	168.97	249.07	280.71	331.24	336.24	339.68
淡水产品	Freshwater Aquatic Products	232.73	327.53	369.00	425.28	429.47	435.74
捕捞	Catches	13.52	12.86	12.26	9.87	8.91	7.68
养殖	Artificially Cultured	219.21	314.67	356.74	415.41	420.57	428.06
养殖面积（万亩）	**Area of Cultivation (10000 mu)**	**846.76**	**845.12**	**734.88**	**711.15**	**713.43**	**710.49**
海水养殖	Seawater	292.33	298.89	247.76	247.05	248.58	249.90
淡水养殖	Freshwater	554.43	546.24	487.12	464.10	464.85	460.59

11-17 牲畜头数及肉类产量

Number of Livestock and Output of Meat

项 目	Item	2000	2010	2015	2020	2021	2022
牛年末存栏头数（万头）	**Number of Cattle and Buffaloes (at the year-end) (10000 heads)**	**420.64**	**175.49**	**132.92**	**122.41**	**112.99**	**108.55**
役用牛	Farming Cattle	295.20	89.62	54.61	29.69	25.24	21.36
肉用牛	Beef Cattle	121.72	80.29	72.52	85.87	81.55	80.99
奶牛	Milch Cows	3.72	5.57	5.79	6.84	6.20	6.20
牛奶产量（万吨）	**Output of Milk (10000 tons)**	**9.19**	**14.95**	**13.61**	**15.10**	**17.23**	**19.81**
山羊年末存栏只数（万只）	**Number of Goats on Hand at the Year-end (10000 heads)**	**29.33**	**50.52**	**83.55**	**94.31**	**88.64**	**85.12**
生猪年末存栏头数（万头）	**Number of Hogs at the Year-end (10000 heads)**	**2034.79**	**2332.51**	**2308.54**	**1767.27**	**2075.48**	**2195.86**
#能繁殖母猪	Number of Female Hogs with Fertility	143.75	262.65	242.52	184.72	191.18	204.38
肉猪出栏头数（万头）	**Number of Slaughtered Fattened Hogs (10000 heads)**	**2954.98**	**3863.23**	**3959.62**	**2537.36**	**3336.63**	**3496.79**
家禽年末存栏（亿只）	**Poultry at year-end (100 million heads)**	**3.89**	**4.09**	**3.74**	**4.03**	**3.94**	**3.88**
出售和自宰的家禽（亿只）	**Poultry sold or slaughtered (100 million heads)**	**9.29**	**11.75**	**10.48**	**13.74**	**12.80**	**13.37**
禽蛋产量（万吨）	**Poultry Eggs (10 000 tons)**	**33.08**	**35.54**	**36.40**	**44.63**	**43.66**	**47.2**
肉类产量（万吨）	**Output of Meat (10000 tons)**	**324.48**	**454.86**	**454.71**	**400.99**	**457.42**	**481.01**
#猪肉	Pork	206.85	285.14	296.31	192.42	263.23	279.81
牛肉	Beef	5.17	4.97	4.14	4.22	4.37	4.53
羊肉	Mutton	0.43	1.24	1.83	1.92	1.96	2.00
禽肉	Meat of Poultry	111.50	158.04	145.01	195.27	182.19	189.48
兔肉	Rabbit Meat	0.53	0.65	0.90	0.79	0.68	0.57

11−18 各市造林面积、水产品产量、牲畜头数及猪肉产量（2022年）
Area of Afforestation, Output of Aquatic Products, Number of Livestock and Output of Pork by City (2022)

市别	City	人工造林面积（万亩）Artificial Afforestation Area (10000 mu)	水产品产量（万吨）Output of Aquatic Products (10000 tons)	#淡水养殖 Freshwater	牛年末存栏头数（万头）Number of Cattles and Buffalos at the Year-end (10000 heads)	生猪年末存栏头数（万头）Number of Hogs at the Year-end (10000 heads)	肉猪出栏头数（万头）Number of Slaughtered Fattened Hogs (10000 heads)	猪肉产量（万吨）Output of Pork (10000 tons)
全　省	**Provincial Total**	**15.48**	**894.03**	**428.06**	**108.55**	**2195.86**	**3496.79**	**279.81**
广　州	Guangzhou		49.83	33.53	1.22	35.93	63.84	5.06
深　圳	Shenzhen	0.02	8.16	0.72	0.14	3.94	7.89	0.57
珠　海	Zhuhai	0.03	33.96	21.63	...	6.67	10.16	0.81
汕　头	Shantou	0.06	47.44	9.39	0.38	28.24	55.84	4.54
佛　山	Foshan	0.21	77.28	76.71	0.41	55.76	100.21	7.92
韶　关	Shaoguan	5.22	8.29	8.06	3.44	193.59	281.39	22.84
河　源	Heyuan	2.86	4.90	4.71	6.13	94.66	136.40	10.78
梅　州	Meizhou	2.67	10.68	9.63	9.13	127.65	201.25	15.90
惠　州	Huizhou	0.67	21.01	13.96	4.33	92.85	143.51	11.35
汕　尾	Shanwei	1.06	59.88	5.03	7.04	58.02	92.29	7.46
东　莞	Dongguan		5.01	4.29	...	1.13	1.65	0.13
中　山	Zhongshan	0.03	37.10	36.96	0.02	0.96	1.66	0.14
江　门	Jiangmen		84.79	52.99	1.87	145.53	222.07	17.59
阳　江	Yangjiang	0.10	119.10	10.08	6.72	174.98	264.66	21.31
湛　江	Zhanjiang	0.27	122.20	17.80	21.46	281.45	400.01	32.13
茂　名	Maoming	0.57	92.64	34.66	14.70	309.54	587.25	47.21
肇　庆	Zhaoqing		52.23	51.90	16.28	168.16	311.53	25.12
清　远	Qingyuan	0.93	13.80	13.62	7.51	199.50	292.37	23.28
潮　州	Chaozhou	0.18	20.90	4.77	0.62	25.34	41.32	3.40
揭　阳	Jieyang	0.53	14.91	7.81	4.42	78.26	119.04	9.40
云　浮	Yunfu	0.08	9.92	9.81	2.71	113.70	162.46	12.87
按经济区域分	By Region							
珠三角	Pearl River Delta	0.96	369.37	292.70	24.28	510.93	862.51	68.69
东　翼	Eastern Region	1.83	143.13	26.99	12.46	189.85	308.49	24.81
西　翼	Western Region	0.94	333.95	62.54	42.88	765.97	1251.92	100.65
山　区	Mountainous Region	11.75	47.59	45.84	28.92	729.11	1073.87	85.67

注：分市人工造林数据未包括当地国家级自然保护区和省属林场完成量。
Note: The artificial afforestation data by city do not include the completed amount of local national nature reserves and provincial forest farms.

11−19 茶叶、桑、水果面积及产量

Planted Area and Output of Tea, Mulberry and Fruits

指　标	Item	2000	2010	2015	2020	2021	2022
茶叶年末实有面积（万亩）	Planted Area of Tea at the Year-end(10000 mu)	64.80	62.76	78.07	117.29	133.90	149.19
茶叶总产量（万吨）	Output of Tea (10000 tons)	4.21	5.38	8.07	12.82	13.95	16.08
桑地年末实有面积（万亩）	Planted Area of Mulberries at the Year-end (10000 mu)	26.89	47.73	51.25	39.62	31.00	31.18
桑叶产量（万吨）	Output of mulberry leaves (10000 tons)	51.25	94.35	113.54	105.62	87.77	90.05
水果年末实有面积（万亩）	Planted Area of Fruits at the Year-end (10000 mu)	1502.35	1510.61	1452.71	1546.97	1576.14	1603.68
水果总产量（万吨）	Gross Output of Fruits (10000 tons)	643.52	1049.21	1298.52	1756.16	1826.73	1895.18
#柑橘橙年末实有面积（万亩）	Planted Area of Citruses at the Year-end (10000 mu)	123.34	326.83	296.62	292.47	287.95	287.33
柑橘橙总产量（万吨）	Output of Citruses (10000 tons)	81.06	259.34	317.53	388.20	399.72	420.18
香(大)蕉年末实有面积（万亩）	Planted Area of Bananas at the Year-end (10000 mu)	151.51	171.85	162.22	166.89	167.13	165.95
香(大)蕉总产量（万吨）	Output of Bananas (10000 tons)	235.30	334.13	357.83	478.73	483.30	488.55
菠萝年末实有面积(万亩)	Planted Area of Pineapples at the Year-end (10000 mu)	44.58	38.81	44.58	58.44	58.87	58.73
菠萝总产量（万吨）	Output of Pineapples (10000 tons)	47.53	63.21	83.76	121.02	125.98	129.47
荔枝年末实有面积(万亩)	Planted Area of Lychees at the Year-end (10000 mu)	474.83	390.99	371.82	381.21	393.98	406.84
荔枝总产量（万吨）	Output of Lychees (10000 tons)	64.75	96.53	116.18	135.09	151.62	146.74
龙眼年末实有面积(万亩)	Planted Area of Longans at the Year-end (10000 mu)	236.31	182.45	170.54	171.37	172.39	172.64
龙眼总产量（万吨）	Output of Longans (10000 tons)	34.68	58.22	76.04	93.10	104.23	96.05

11−20 各市水果面积及产量（2022年）

Planted Area and Output of Fruits by City (2022)

单位：万亩、万吨 (10000 mu，10000 tons)

市别	City	水果合计 Fruits		#柑橘橙 Citrus		#香(大)蕉 Banana	
		年末面积 Year-end Area	总产量 Total Output	年末面积 Year-end Area	总产量 Total Output	年末面积 Year-end Area	总产量 Total Output
全省	**Provincial Total**	**1603.68**	**1895.18**	**287.33**	**420.18**	**165.95**	**488.55**
广州	Guangzhou	105.68	81.86	5.96	8.82	7.50	28.04
深圳	Shenzhen	6.10	3.27	0.43	0.49	0.18	0.28
珠海	Zhuhai	8.32	10.01	0.07	0.08	1.14	3.24
汕头	Shantou	21.20	31.26	1.30	3.02	3.16	6.41
佛山	Foshan	2.62	4.13	0.17	0.27	0.85	2.60
韶关	Shaoguan	72.22	71.44	34.85	37.67	0.67	0.63
河源	Heyuan	56.87	47.23	13.70	13.36	1.34	1.24
梅州	Meizhou	127.04	160.90	11.45	17.26	5.58	8.13
惠州	Huizhou	102.14	102.41	28.09	30.16	14.90	39.61
汕尾	Shanwei	56.06	36.73	1.55	4.21	3.54	4.35
东莞	Dongguan	20.40	6.55	0.03	0.02	2.42	3.78
中山	Zhongshan	5.30	11.66	0.25	0.34	1.48	4.97
江门	Jiangmen	37.60	40.30	13.21	18.64	4.75	8.80
阳江	Yangjiang	74.82	41.94	6.94	9.56	7.52	10.96
湛江	Zhanjiang	172.76	328.96	9.30	11.30	41.95	129.72
茂名	Maoming	367.14	457.53	14.62	16.70	43.80	191.60
肇庆	Zhaoqing	121.02	217.70	83.69	171.16	10.10	18.01
清远	Qingyuan	72.89	85.78	34.48	42.15	2.92	4.97
潮州	Chaozhou	24.78	29.22	2.17	3.56	0.88	3.14
揭阳	Jieyang	86.68	73.48	6.71	9.05	6.21	11.64
云浮	Yunfu	62.05	52.84	18.38	22.34	5.06	6.43
按经济区域分	By Region						
珠三角	Pearl River Delta	409.19	477.87	131.89	229.99	43.33	109.33
东翼	Eastern Region	188.72	170.69	11.72	19.84	13.79	25.53
西翼	Western Region	614.71	828.43	30.86	37.56	93.27	332.28
山区	Mountainous Region	391.07	418.18	112.86	132.79	15.56	21.40

11-20 续表 continued

单位：万亩、万吨 (10000 mu，10000 tons)

市 别	City	#菠萝 Pineapple		#荔枝 Lychee		#龙眼 Longan	
		年末面积 Year-end Area	总产量 Total Output	年末面积 Year-end Area	总产量 Total Output	年末面积 Year-end Area	总产量 Total Output
全 省	**Provincial Total**	**58.73**	**129.47**	**406.84**	**146.74**	**172.64**	**96.05**
广 州	Guangzhou	0.04	0.14	56.44	11.29	12.14	4.30
深 圳	Shenzhen	0.17	0.13	3.85	0.80	0.56	0.26
珠 海	Zhuhai	0.04	0.13	4.21	0.50	0.77	0.23
汕 头	Shantou	0.01	…	4.94	1.13	0.60	0.57
佛 山	Foshan	0.01	0.02	0.20	0.12	0.73	0.17
韶 关	Shaoguan	…	…	…	0.01	0.22	0.13
河 源	Heyuan			5.31	0.94	1.71	0.74
梅 州	Meizhou	0.23	0.13	4.49	2.01	5.18	3.11
惠 州	Huizhou	0.38	0.53	32.88	10.03	11.98	6.25
汕 尾	Shanwei	2.11	1.24	24.74	11.85	3.66	2.68
东 莞	Dongguan	…	…	15.58	1.77	1.61	0.32
中 山	Zhongshan	0.38	0.59	1.04	0.54	0.65	0.58
江 门	Jiangmen	0.05	0.16	8.07	2.66	5.37	1.88
阳 江	Yangjiang	0.05	0.05	32.31	8.17	14.96	5.36
湛 江	Zhanjiang	48.27	116.20	36.43	22.19	6.74	4.32
茂 名	Maoming	0.05	0.06	139.22	55.06	80.96	49.18
肇 庆	Zhaoqing	0.74	0.61	2.77	2.91	3.33	2.55
清 远	Qingyuan	0.01	0.01	2.40	1.17	1.48	0.93
潮 州	Chaozhou	0.61	0.76	2.88	2.58	5.43	5.79
揭 阳	Jieyang	5.45	8.45	18.07	7.58	8.53	3.49
云 浮	Yunfu	0.14	0.25	11.02	3.45	6.03	3.21
按经济区域分	By Region						
珠 三 角	Pearl River Delta	1.80	2.31	125.03	30.61	37.14	16.55
东 翼	Eastern Region	8.18	10.46	50.62	23.14	18.21	12.53
西 翼	Western Region	48.37	116.30	207.96	85.43	102.67	58.86
山 区	Mountainous Region	0.39	0.39	23.23	7.57	14.62	8.12

11-21 主要农产品产量与最高年份比较（2022年）
Output of Major Farm Products in Comparison with Peak Year (2022)

指　标	Item	2022	新中国成立以来最高年份 Peak Year since 1949		
			年份 Year	产量 Output	2022年为新中国成立以来最高年份% Percentage of 2022 to Peak Year%
粮食总产量　（万吨）	**Total Output of Grain　(10000 tons)**	**1291.54**	**1997**	**1966.75**	**65.7**
#稻谷	Output of Rice	1108.63	1998	1688.53	65.7
#早稻	Early Rice	520.09	1983	862.25	60.3
晚稻	Late Rice	588.54	1998	866.51	67.9
薯类	Tubers	107.01	1998	238.28	44.9
经济作物　（万吨）	**Economic Crops　(10000 tons)**				
甘蔗	Sugarcane and Fruit Canes	1292.05	1992	2376.62	54.4
#糖蔗	Sugarcane	1107.76	1992	2271.06	48.8
油料作物	Oil-bearing Crops	117.43	2021	117.30	100.1
#花生	Peanuts	115.93	2021	115.87	100.0
烟叶	Tobacco	3.71	1992	8.62	43.1
蔬菜　（万吨）	Vegetables　(10000 tons)	3999.11	2021	3855.73	103.7
水果　（万吨）	**Fruits　(10000 tons)**	**1895.18**	**2021**	**1826.73**	**103.7**
水产品　（万吨）	**Aquatic Products　(10000 tons)**	**894.03**	**2021**	**884.52**	**101.1**
生猪年末存栏量　（万头）	**Number of Hogs at the Year-end　(10000 heads)**	**2195.86**	**2009**	**2455.11**	**89.4**
生猪出栏头数　（万头）	**Number of Slaughtered Fattened Hogs　(10000 heads)**	**3496.79**	**2014**	**4062.02**	**86.1**
猪肉产量　（万吨）	**Output of Pork　(10000 tons)**	**279.81**	**2014**	**302.86**	**92.4**
家禽年末存栏　（亿只）	**Poultry at year-end　(100 million heads)**	**3.88**	**2010**	**4.09**	**94.8**
出售和自宰的家禽（亿只）	**Poultry sold or slaughtered(100 million heads)**	**13.37**	**2020**	**13.74**	**97.3**
禽肉产量　（万吨）	**Output of Poultry Meat　(10 000 tons)**	**189.48**	**2020**	**195.27**	**97.0**

11−22 农林牧渔业分项产值

Agricultural Production Basic Conditions

单位：亿元 (100 million yuan)

指 标	Item	2019	2020	2021	2022
农林牧渔业总产值	**Gross Output Value of Agriculture**	**7175.89**	**7901.92**	**8305.84**	**8892.29**
农业产值	**Farming**	**3530.21**	**3769.26**	**3951.14**	**4308.23**
谷物及其他作物	Cereal and other Crops	742.91	768.96	783.80	812.49
#谷物	Cereal	361.50	375.02	390.66	401.97
薯类	Tubers	97.11	98.20	98.32	106.71
豆类	Beans	8.88	9.13	9.33	9.93
糖料	Sugar Crops	82.72	84.14	82.02	82.72
油料	Oil Bearing Crops	97.83	105.44	110.10	111.67
蔬菜园艺作物	Horticulture Vegetables	1564.92	1682.44	1834.07	1972.57
#蔬菜(含菜用瓜、食用菌)	Vegetables	1387.68	1464.81	1574.19	1680.55
水果、坚果、饮料和香料作物	Fruits, Nuts, Drink, and Spice Crops	1114.38	1194.48	1208.42	1372.15
#水果(含果用瓜)、坚果	Fruits (Including Fruit Melons), Nuts	1017.53	1084.18	1057.52	1187.11
中草药材	Chinese Medicinal Herbs	108.00	123.38	124.85	151.03
林业产值	**Forestry**	**408.48**	**414.29**	**495.44**	**549.15**
林木的培育和种植	Planting and Nurturing of Trees	34.20	35.14	32.49	35.75
竹木采运	Lumbering and Transport of Bamboo	132.30	134.76	165.29	174.51
林产品	Forestry Production	241.98	244.38	297.67	338.89
牧业产值	**Animal Husbandry**	**1404.13**	**1778.18**	**1707.82**	**1680.24**
牲畜饲养	Breeding and Raising of Domestic Animals	42.61	54.97	56.49	63.03
猪的饲养	Raising of Swine	677.45	1000.35	940.13	874.34
家禽饲养	Raising of Poultry	572.63	632.64	633.00	670.02
其他畜牧业	Raising of Other Animals	111.43	90.22	78.19	72.85
渔业产值	**Fishery**	**1524.78**	**1581.54**	**1747.34**	**1898.24**
海水产品	Seawater Aquatic Production	789.84	793.73	909.96	997.50
淡水产品	Freshwater Aquatic Production	734.94	787.81	837.38	900.73
农林牧渔专业及辅助性活动产值	**Professional and Auxiliary Activities of Agriculture, Forestry,Animal Husbandry, and Fishery Industries**	**308.30**	**358.64**	**404.10**	**456.43**

主要统计指标解释

农林牧渔业总产值 是以货币表现的农林牧渔业的全部产品总量和对农林牧渔业生产活动进行的各种支持性服务活动的价值。它反映一定时期内农林牧渔业生产总规模和总成果，是观察农林牧渔业生产水平和发展速度，研究农林牧渔业内部比例关系、农林牧渔业与工业、农林牧渔业与国家建设、人民生活比例关系的重要指标，同时也是计算农林牧渔业劳动生产率和农林牧渔业增加值的基础资料。

农林牧渔业总产值的计算，一般采用“产品法”，即凡有产品产量的，都按单位产品价格乘产量的办法求得每种产品产量的产值，然后相加求得各业的产值，最后各业相加求出农林牧渔业总产值。

农作物播种面积 指农业生产经营者在日历年度内收获的农作物在全部土地（耕地或非耕地）上的播种或移植面积。凡是本年内收获的作物，无论是本年还是上年播种，都算为当年播种面积，但不包括本年播种，下年收获的作物面积。

农作物产量 指农业生产经营者日历年度内生产的农作物数量。

Explanatory Notes on Main Statistical Indicators

Gross Output Value of Agriculture Forestry, Animal Husbandry and Fishery refers to the total volume of products of farming, forestry, animal husbandry, and fishery and the value of various services supporting the production of farming, forestry, animal husbandry and fishery in monetary terms, which reflects the total scale and total results of farming, forestry, animal husbandry and fishery production during a given period of time. It is an important indicator to observe the production level and development speed of farming, forestry, animal husbandry and fishery, to study the internal structure of farming, forestry, animal husbandry and fishery, and to review the proportionate relationship of farming, forestry, animal husbandry and fishery to industry, to national construction and to people’s life. It is also the foundation for calculating the labor productivity and value-added of farming, forestry, animal husbandry and fishery.

Generally, the gross output value of farming, forestry, animal husbandry and fishery is calculated with the production approach. Where applicable, the gross output value of each single product is obtained by multiplying the output of each product by its price. These values are then summed up to obtain the output value of each sector. The sum of output values of all sectors is the gross output value of farming, forestry, animal husbandry and fishery.

Sown Area of Crops refers to area of all land (cultivated or non-cultivated area) sown or transplanted with crops that are harvested within the calendar year by agricultural producers. All crops harvested within the year are counted as sown area, regardless of being sown in this year or the previous year. Crops sown this year but will be harvested in the coming year are excluded.

Crops Output refers to total output of crops produced by agricultural producers within a calendar year.

十二、工业

INDUSTRY

十二　工业

简要说明

一、本篇主要包括如下资料：1. 全省及各地市全部工业和规模以上工业生产主要指标总量及速度。2. 规模以上工业主要产品产量。3. 全省及各地市规模以上工业主要经济效益指标。4. 规模以上工业企业按主要经济类型和企业规模分组的主要财务指标。5. 规模以上工业中高技术制造业、先进制造业主要经济指标。

二、本篇资料由广东省统计局工业交通统计处整理提供。

三、本篇工业资料是根据国家统计局工业统计报表制度填报。2011 年定报及以前数据经各市、县统计局布置、收集、汇总整理，2011 年起通过网上直报系统收集、汇总整理。其中 1995 年度资料通过第三次全国工业普查取得，2004 年数据根据第一次全国经济普查取得，2008 年数据根据第二次全国经济普查取得。2013 年数据根据第三次全国经济普查取得。2018 年数据根据 2018 年广东省第四次全国经济普查取得。

四、规模以上工业法人单位的统计范围。1998 年至 2006 年为全部国有和年主营业务收入 500 万元及以上的非国有工业企业；2007 至 2010 年为年主营业务收入 500 万元及以上的工业企业(即规模以上工业企业)；从 2011 年开始，为年主营业务收入 2000 万元及以上的工业企业（即规模以上工业企业）；2021 年起，为年主营业务收入 2000 万元及以上的工业企业和个体经营户（即规模以上工业法人单位）。

五、从 2017 年年报起，工业行业分类按 2017 年《国民经济行业分类标准》划分；企业规模划分按 2017 年《统计上大中小微型企业划分办法》标准执行，增加了微型企业分组。

六、本篇规模以上工业增加值从 2011 年起按收入法公布。

12 Industry

Brief Introduction

Ⅰ. This chapter covers the following data:（1）Principal aggregate indicators and growth rates of industrial production of total industry and industry above designated size of the province and cities;（2）Output of major products of industry above designated size;（3）Main indicators on economic benefits of industry above designated size of the province and cities;（4）Main financial indicators on industry above designated size grouped by sector and scale;（5）Main economic indicators on advanced manufacturing industries and hi-tech manufacturing industries above designated size;

Ⅱ. The data in this chapter are prepared and provided by the Division of Industry and Transport Statistics of Statistics Bureau of Guangdong Province.

Ⅲ. The data in this chapter are compiled mainly in accordance with the industrial statistical reporting scheme stipulated by the National Bureau of Statistics. The annual data of 2011 and before 2011 are collected, tabulated and prepared by the municipal and county statistical bureaus. Since 2011, the annual data are collected, tabulated and prepared by the network reporting system. Of which the annual data of 1995 were collected in the Third National Industrial Census and the data of 2004 were collected in the First National Economic Census of Guangdong, the data of 2008 were collected in the Second National Economic Census of Guangdong, the data of 2013 were collected in the Third National Economic Census of Guangdong, the data of 2018 were collected in the Third Fourth Economic Census of Guangdong..

Ⅳ. Industrial legal entities above designated size refers to all State-owned industrial enterprises and non-State-owned industrial enterprises with revenue from principal business over 5 million yuan from 1998 to 2006. For 2007 to 2010, the scopes of industrial statistics were all industrial enterprises with revenue from principal business over 5 million yuan, (or the industrial enterprises above designated size). Since 2011, the scope is adjusted to all industrial enterprises with revenue from principal business above 20 million yuan (i.e. industrial enterprises above designated size). From 2021, the scope is industrial enterprise and self-employed household with an annual main business income of 20 million yuan or more(i.e. industrial legal entities above designated size).

Ⅴ. Industrial sectors since 2017 in this chapter has been categorized in accordance with the 2017 Industrial Classification of the National Economy and the size of industrial enterprises have been categorized in accordance with the 2017 Interim Regulations on Statistical Categorization of Large, Medium , Small and Micro Industrial Enterprises. Micro industrial enterprises are added.

Ⅵ. The value-added of industrial enterprises above designated size in this chapter is calculated by income approach since 2011.

12-1 工业主要指标

Main Indicators of Industry

指 标	Item	2000	2010	2015	2020	2021	2022
全部工业	**All Industrial Enterprises**						
企业单位数 (个)	Number of Enterprises (unit)	380231	481022	582813	660897	674522	732757
工业总产值 (亿元)	Gross Industrial Output Value (100 million yuan)	16904.47	93462.97	135308.14	155210.54	182919.33	193108.50
工业增加值 (亿元)	Value-added of Industry (100 million yuan)	4518.65	21387.71	31315.46	38903.90	45510.34	47723.04
规模以上工业	**Industrial Enterprises above Designated Size**						
企业单位数 (个)	Number of Enterprises (unit)	19695	53418	42134	58504	66329	70725
亏损企业数 (个)	Number of Loss-making Enterprises (unit)	4805	6385	5850	9524	10759	14953
工业总产值 (亿元)	Gross Industrial Output Value (100 million yuan)	12480.93	85824.64	124649.16	148469.69	171979.82	180933.44
工业增加值 (亿元)	Value-added of Industry (100 million yuan)	3422.60	20338.34	29446.21	32500.17	37306.53	37260.57
工业销售产值 (亿元)	Sales Output Value of Industry (100 million yuan)	12156.19	83646.51	121049.68	143226.67	164660.77	173713.57
出口交货值 (亿元)	Export Delivery Value (100 million yuan)	4634.44	25919.08	32035.16	33551.22	37553.99	38598.36
营业收入 (亿元)	Business Revenue (100 million yuan)	12480.93	85824.64	124649.16	149930.12	173649.71	183027.35
资产总计 (亿元)	Total Assets (100 million yuan)	14370.57	62626.90	95411.22	150717.82	175746.01	196419.19
流动资产合计 (亿元)	Average Balance of Circulating Funds (100 million yuan)	6891.49	34339.97	54715.38	90365.50	105030.92	117937.22
固定资产合计 (亿元)	Average Balance of Net Value of Fixed Assets (100 million yuan)	5884.78	22407.53	26943.69	30415.82	32626.99	36649.71
负债总计 (亿元)	Total Liabilities (100 million yuan)	8272.36	35073.74	54747.90	84861.65	100629.77	114686.14
所有者权益合计(亿元)	Total Creditors' Equity (100 million yuan)	6098.21	27461.84	40239.01	65856.33	75120.93	81498.85
利润总额 (亿元)	Total Profits (100 million yuan)	564.75	6239.64	7723.16	9572.09	11278.35	10329.25
亏损企业亏损额(亿元)	Loss Value of Loss-making Enterprises (100 million yuan)	156.03	227.26	510.18	1016.48	1219.85	1801.76
利税总额 (亿元)	Total Pre-tax Profits (100 million yuan)	1042.77	9418.42	12375.00	14119.76	16325.16	15857.14
应交增值税 (亿元)	Value-added Tax Payable (100 million yuan)	360.83	2280.56	3284.50	3008.71	3259.11	3598.56
所得税费用 (亿元)	Fee of Income Tax Payable (100 million yuan)	62.79	820.89	1179.43	1357.92	1511.50	1303.74
本年应付工资总额 (亿元)	Total Salary Payable in Current Year (100 million yuan)	676.06	5747.72	9888.11	13380.36	15585.50	16983.35
就业人员平均人数 (万人)	Average Employed Persons (10000 persons)	572.89	1568.00	1439.33	1277.06	1343.58	1332.56

注：1.2011年起，规模以上工业统计口径从年主营业务收入500万元及以上调整为2000万元及以上工业企业,2021年调整为主业务收入2000万元及以上工业企业和工业个体经营户，为反映可比口径速度，本表规模以上工业主要指标使用快报增速，全部工业数据含个体数据。

2.表中全部工业增加值及增长速度是核算的年度数据，2010年及以后规模以上工业增加值按照收入法计算，与全社会工业增加值不可直接比对。2010年全部工业增加值按照第三次全国经济普查数据修正。

3.2011年起，本年应付工资总额指标数据为本年应付职工薪酬；所得税费用数据2014年以前为应交所得税。

4.本表中营业收入数据2017年及以前为主营业务收入数据，2018年后为营业收入数据。

Notes: a) Since 2011, the annual principal business revenue of industrial enterprises above designated size is changed from industrial enterprises of 5 million yuan or above to 20 million yuan or above. It is adjusted to industrial enterprises and industrial self-employed households with main business income of 20 million yuan and above in 2021. Growth rates in this table are calculated at current price with flash statistics report in order to compare the rate. Data on all industrial enterprises include self-employed individuals.

b) The value-added and growth rates of all industries in this table are calculated figures of the year. The value-added of industry above designated size is calculated by income approach since 2010, and hence is not directly comparable with the value-added of all industries. All value-added of industry from 2010 have been adjusted with the third economic census.

c) Total salary payable in current year from 2011 are total employee pay payable and income tax payable are tax expenses.Data of fee of income tax payable before 2014 are income tax payable.

d) The indicator was Revenue from Principal Business in 2017 and before,and are Business Revenue since 2018.

12-2 规模以上工业企业增加值和指数

Value-added of Industrial Enterprises above Designated Size and Their Indices

项　　目	Item	2000	2010	2015	2020	2021	2022
工业增加值　　（亿元）	**Value-added of Industry (100 million yuan)**	**3422.60**	**20338.34**	**29446.21**	**32500.17**	**37306.53**	**37260.57**
按工业门类分	Grouped by Industries						
采矿业	Mining	267.07	673.52	577.51	562.38	819.09	1205.69
制造业	Manufacturing	2769.10	18317.70	26568.90	29737.47	34319.83	33636.96
电力、热力、燃气及水生产和供应业	Production and Supply of Electricity Gas and Water	386.43	1347.08	2299.80	2200.32	2167.63	2417.91
按经济类型分	Grouped by Ownership						
#国有控股工业	Of the Total: State-holding Industry	1035.41	3729.48	5051.87	4806.95	6210.72	6407.02
国有工业	State-owned Industry	574.73	1172.21	173.46	169.27	150.33	229.35
集体工业	Collective-owned Industry	301.48	199.38	116.59	30.04	30.99	13.74
股份合作工业	Share-holding Cooperative Industry	29.15	42.23	23.10	16.46	14.72	13.03
股份制工业	Share-holding Industry	158.86	7351.85	16289.21	20688.83	23915.12	23426.65
外商投资工业	Foreign-funded Industry	575.31	5200.37	5689.44	5291.74	5912.13	5860.16
港澳台投资工业	Industry with Funds from Hong Kong, Macao and Taiwan	1290.47	5393.8	6545.58	6008.66	6952.86	7441.79
按轻重工业分	Grouped by Light and Heavy Industries						
轻工业	Light Industry	1628.13	8038.97	11387.50	10872.65	12472.98	12475.18
重工业	Heavy Industry	1794.47	12299.37	18058.71	21627.52	24833.56	24785.39
按企业规模分	Grouped by Size of Enterprises						
大型企业	Large Enterprises	610.13	6579.38	13698.60	15916.19	18384.41	18776.54
中型企业	Medium Enterprises	1513.26	7107.28	7864.85	7610.08	8318.96	8720.97
小微型企业	Small and Micro Enterprises	1298.55	6651.68	7882.76	8973.89	10603.16	9763.06
工业增加值指数 (2000年=100)	**Indices of Value-added of Industry (2000=100)**	**100.0**	**592.4**	**913.2**	**1180.0**	**1286.2**	**1306.8**
按经济类型分	Grouped by Ownership						
#国有控股工业	Of the Total: State-holding Industry	100.0	354.9	502.2	635.7	718.3	752.0
国有工业	State-owned Industry	100.0	226.2	304.3	404.6	488.4	520.7
集体工业	Collective-owned Industry	100.0	81.0	110.3	77.1	80.8	47.0
股份合作工业	Share-holding Cooperative Industry	100.0	188.0	345.9	425.7	402.3	388.3
股份制工业	Share-holding Industry	100.0	4296.3	7734.8	11171.2	12187.8	12460.8
外商投资工业	Foreign-funded Industry	100.0	844.5	1126.3	1290.0	1377.7	1359.7
港澳台投资工业	Industry with Funds from Hong Kong, Macao and Taiwan	100.0	468.8	640.9	676.1	754.5	776.3
按轻重工业分	Grouped by Light and Heavy Industries						
轻工业	Light Industry	100.0	532.0	790.1	932.2	1020.7	1019.8
重工业	Heavy Industry	100.0	653.6	1032.2	1399.2	1522.3	1559.7
按企业规模分	Grouped by Size of Enterprises						
大型企业	Large Enterprises	100.0	978.4	1481.0	1988.7	2086.1	2181.8
中型企业	Medium Enterprises	100.0	412.9	578.4	734.5	831.5	844.8
小微型企业	Small and Micro Enterprises	100.0	637.7	1095.9	1341.9	1507.0	1473.1

注：1.2011年起，规模以上工业统计口径从年主营业务收入500万元及以上调整为2000万元及以上工业企业，2021年调整为主业务收入2000万元及以上工业企业和工业个体经营户。

2.本表工业增加值2010年以前采用生产法计算，2011年起采用收入法计算，按当年价格计算，速度为可比口径计算。

3.企业规模划分：2003年以前为一个标准，2003-2010年为一个标准，2011年起采用新的标准，并增加微型企业。

Note: a) Since 2011, the annual principal business revenue of industrial enterprises above designated size is changed from industrial enterprises of 5 million yuan or above to 20 million yuan or above. It is adjusted to industrial enterprises and industrial self-employed households with main business income of 20 million yuan and above in 2021.

b)Data of value-added in this table prior to 2010 are calculated with production approach and since 2011 calculated with income approach.Data of value-added of industry are calculated at current prices and the growth rates are calculated at comparable coverage.

c) Size of Industrial enterprise categorization: The standard prior to 2003 is not the same as the period from 2003 to 2010.Since 2011, New standard is adopted and micro-enterprises is added.

12-3 历年规模以上工业增加值增长速度

Growth Rates of Industrial Enterprises above Designated Size

单位：% (%)

年份 Year	工业增加值 Gross Industrial Output Value	按轻重工分 Grouped by Light & Heavy Industry		按规模分 Grouped by Size			按经济类型分 Grouped by Ownership	
		轻工业 Light Industry	重工业 Heavy Industry	大型企业 Large Enterprises	中型企业 Medium Enterprises	小微型企业 Small and Micro Enterprises	国有控股工业 Of the Total: State-holding Industry	外商及港澳台商投资工业 Industry with Investment from Foreign Country , Hong Kong, Macao and Taiwan
2001	15.1	12.4	18.4				4.0	14.2
2002	20.0	20.4	19.7				14.7	15.9
2003	28.4	23.4	38.5				20.8	22.2
2004	28.0	26.0	31.1	30.8	26.8	27.4	20.8	23.9
2005	24.7	20.6	25.0	23.2	21.5	28.0	6.1	16.2
2006	23.4	18.2	24.2	15.5	19.3	32.4	19.4	14.8
2007	18.2	24.2	13.2	19.2	14.2	22.1	12.6	16.9
2008	12.8	14.2	12.2	14.2	9.1	16.3	7.8	10.9
2009	8.9	7.4	10.0	11.4	-0.1	17.5	7.0	4.1
2010	16.8	16.4	17.1	15.0	13.4	22.2	12.8	14.5
2011	12.6	12.4	12.8	12.1	8.8	17.7	12.5	8.4
2012	8.4	9.2	7.9	8.1	6.0	8.8	7.3	5.7
2013	8.7	7.7	9.3	8.5	6.9	10.9	8.0	7.1
2014	8.4	7.4	9.1	8.3	7.4	9.7	6.3	5.0
2015	7.2	4.6	8.8	6.3	5.8	10.3	2.1	4.1
2016	6.7	3.3	8.7	7.0	4.8	7.9	5.0	2.3
2017	7.2	6.1	7.8	7.6	6.7	6.8	2.0	5.6
2018	6.3	4.6	7.2	8.5	5.0	3.4	7.2	2.0
2019	4.7	2.4	5.9	5.7	4.1	3.6	4.6	-0.1
2020	1.5	0.5	1.9	1.7	3.9	-0.8	5.4	-0.4
2021	9.0	9.5	8.8	4.9	13.2	12.3	13.0	9.2
2022	1.6	-0.1	2.5	4.6	1.6	-2.3	4.7	0.9

注：本表按可比口径计算。
Note: Data in this table are calculated in comparable coverage.

12-4 规模以上分行业工业增加值和增长速度

Value-added and Growth Rates of Industry above Designated Size by Sector

行业	Sector	工业增加值(亿元) Value-added of Industry (100 million yuan)		2022比2021增长(%) Growth Rate in 2022 over 2021 (%)
		2021	2022	
总计	**Total**	**37306.53**	**37260.57**	**1.6**
煤炭开采和洗选业	Mining and Washing of Coal			
石油和天然气开采业	Extraction of Petroleum and Natural Gas	639.26	1032.98	4.6
黑色金属矿采选业	Mining and Dressing of Ferrous Metal Ores	27.62	21.25	50.9
有色金属矿采选业	Mining and Dressing of Nonferrous Metal Ores	38.73	45.99	9.9
非金属矿采选业	Mining and Dressing of Nonmetal Ores	100.67	83.14	-13.6
开采专业及辅助性活动	Mining Specialized and Auxiliary Operations	12.81	22.33	65.8
其他采矿业	Mining and Dressing of Other Ores			
农副食品加工业	Processing of Farm and Sideline Food	405.51	407.73	-0.7
食品制造业	Manufacture of Food	705.28	668.26	-0.7
酒、饮料和精制茶制造业	Manufacture of Wine, Beverage and Refined Tea	340.82	322.48	0.7
烟草制品业	Tobacco Products	453.41	471.22	44.2
纺织业	Textile Industry	521.78	481.85	-6.9
纺织服装、服饰业	Manufacture of Textile Garments, Footwear and Headgear	759.88	647.38	-11.4
皮革、毛皮、羽毛及其制品和制鞋业	Leather, Fur, Feather, Down and Related Products	371.45	380.25	2.1
木材加工和木、竹、藤、棕、草制品业	Timber Processing, Bamboo, Cane, Palm Fiber & Straw Products	109.95	74.81	-23.1
家具制造业	Manufacture of Furniture	556.16	502.04	-5.3
造纸和纸制品业	Papermaking and Paper Products	539.94	450.08	-4.8
印刷和记录媒介复制业	Printing and Record Medium Reproduction	360.85	361.00	-2.4
文教、工美、体育和娱乐用品制造业	Manufacture of Cultural, Educational,Sports and Entertainment Articles	669.24	667.83	-1.6
石油、煤炭及其他燃料加工业	Petroleum, Coal and other Fuel Processing	1084.33	898.80	-18.5
化学原料和化学制品制造业	Manufacture of Raw Chemical Materials and Chemical Products	1416.87	1213.73	8.3
医药制造业	Manufacture of Medicines	702.36	808.74	15.1
化学纤维制造业	Manufacture of Chemical Fibers	67.54	42.08	-13.0
橡胶和塑料制品业	Rubber and Plastic Products	1499.68	1396.03	-6.5
非金属矿物制品业	Nonmetal Mineral Products	1607.23	1295.59	-5.0
黑色金属冶炼和压延加工业	Smelting and Pressing of Ferrous Metals	469.24	362.56	-5.2
有色金属冶炼和压延加工业	Smelting and Pressing of Nonferrous Metals	543.53	407.57	-2.8
金属制品业	Metal Products	1850.14	1796.81	-4.1
通用设备制造业	Manufacture of General-purpose Machinery	1204.59	1272.78	-0.1
专用设备制造业	Manufacture of Special-purpose Machinery	1454.63	1558.47	4.1
汽车制造业	Manufacture of Automobile	2007.74	2280.35	20.8
铁路、船舶、航空航天和其他运输设备制造业	Manufacture of Railway ,Ship,Aeronautics and Other Transport equipment	235.07	302.19	-5.3
电气机械和器材制造业	Manufacture of Electrical Machinery and Equipment	4134.74	4430.59	2.8
计算机、通信和其他电子设备制造业	Manufacture of Communication Equipment, Computers and Other Electronic Equipment	9555.10	9367.69	1.1
仪器仪表制造业	Manufacture of Instruments and Meters	417.04	451.18	3.7
其他制造业	Other Manufactures	109.58	175.23	4.9
废弃资源综合利用业	Comprehensive Utilization of Waste	99.36	72.81	-0.6
金属制品、机械和设备修理业	Manufacture of Metal Products,Machinery and Equipment Maintenance	66.80	68.83	11.3
电力、热力生产和供应业	Production and Supply of Electric Power and Heat Power	1603.18	1893.49	5.4
燃气生产和供应业	Production and Supply of Gas	255.62	193.06	3.3
水的生产和供应业	Production and Supply of Water	308.83	331.36	7.5

注：本表工业增加值按当年价格计算，增长速度按快报可比价格计算。

Note: Data of value-added of industry in this table are calculated at current prices whereas their growth rates are calculated at constant prices in accordance with flash reports.

12-5 规模以上工业企业单位数和产值

Number of Industrial Enterprises above Designated Size and Their Gross Output Values

项 目	Item	2000	2010	2020	2021	2022
工业企业单位数（个）	**Total Number of Industrial Enterprises (unit)**	**19695**	**53418**	**58504**	**66329**	**70725**
按经济类型分	Grouped by Ownership					
#国有控股工业	Of the Total: State-holding Industry	3320	1279	1250	1439	1573
国有工业	State-owned Industry	2383	567	244	215	258
集体工业	Collective-owned Industry	4158	872	105	88	73
股份合作工业	Share-holding Cooperative Industry	299	223	45	39	46
股份制工业	Share-holding Industry	1875	25490	44574	52183	56499
外商投资工业	Foreign-funded Industry	1682	5790	3864	3880	3794
港澳台投资工业	Industry with Funds from Hong Kong, Macao and Taiwan	6731	13151	7953	7994	7942
按轻重工业分	Grouped by Light and Heavy Industries					
轻工业	Light Industry	12255	29678	26962	29844	31685
重工业	Heavy Industry	7440	23740	31542	36485	39040
按企业规模分	Grouped by Size of Enterprises					
大型企业	Large Enterprises	823	524	1448	1564	1438
中型企业	Medium Enterprises	1228	6968	6769	6812	6449
小微型企业	Small and Micro Enterprises	17644	45926	50287	57953	62838
工业总产值 （亿元）	**Gross Industrial Output Value (100 million yuan)**	**12480.93**	**85824.64**	**148469.69**	**171979.82**	**180933.44**
按经济类型分	Grouped by Ownership					
#国有控股工业	Of the Total: State-holding Industry	3126.12	13166.37	21191.00	28733.57	32513.46
国有工业	State-owned Industry	1450.86	4595.82	633.27	801.98	941.32
集体工业	Collective-owned Industry	1202.49	767.03	102.77	102.59	48.66
股份合作工业	Share-holding Cooperative Industry	106.87	175.69	86.73	77.96	67.62
股份制工业	Share-holding Industry	1780.64	30626.84	96637.42	111887.28	118899.83
外商投资工业	Foreign-funded Industry	2527.06	23705.89	24877.60	27596.08	27898.05
港澳台投资工业	Industry with Funds from Hong Kong, Macao and Taiwan	4747.30	21813.34	24624.51	29834.65	31506.28
按轻重工业分	Grouped by Light and Heavy Industries					
轻工业	Light Industry	6607.84	32867.30	45387.73	53378.95	54766.14
重工业	Heavy Industry	5873.09	52957.34	103081.95	118600.86	126167.29
按企业规模分	Grouped by Size of Enterprises					
大型企业	Large Enterprises	4523.92	28306.79	69073.57	77076.51	82354.91
中型企业	Medium Enterprises	1427.65	28566.98	32689.04	38215.85	40038.23
小微型企业	Small and Micro Enterprises	6529.37	28950.88	46707.07	56687.45	58540.30

注：1.2011年起，规模以上工业统计口径从年主营业务收入500万元及以上调整为2000万元及以上工业企业,2021年调整为主业务收入2000万元及以上工业企业和工业个体经营户。

2.企业规模划分：2003年以前为一个标准，2003—2010年为一个标准，2011年起采用新的标准，并增加微型企业.

Note: a) Since 2011,the annual principal business revenue of industrial enterprises above designated size is changed from industrial enterprises of 5 million yuan or above to 20 million yuan or above. It is adjusted to industrial enterprises and industrial self-employed households with main business income of 20 million yuan and above in 2021.

b) Size of Industrial enterprise categorization: The standard prior to 2003 is not the same as the period from 2003 to 2010. Since 2011, New standard is adopted and micro-enterprises is added.

12-6 全部工业总产值和指数

Gross Industrial Output Value of All Industrial Enterprises and Theirs Indices

年份 Year	绝对数（亿元） Absolute Figures (100 million yuan)			指数（1978年＝100） Indices(1978=100)	
	全部工业总产值 Gross Industrial Output Value	#国有控股工业 State-holding Industry	#国有工业 State-owned Industry	全部工业总产值 Gross Industrial Output Value	#国有工业 State-owned Industry
1978	206.56		131.83	100.0	100.0
1979	221.46		142.64	107.5	106.1
1980	248.68		146.95	117.4	109.2
1981	282.95		165.53	134.5	120.3
1982	313.76		178.78	145.7	129.5
1983	356.91		204.68	163.4	144.1
1984	433.40		240.19	196.4	164.0
1985	534.72		298.42	249.6	194.0
1986	632.89		334.59	288.3	209.7
1987	878.29		427.10	384.6	255.4
1988	1318.90		594.98	519.3	316.7
1989	1647.24		714.93	603.9	335.8
1990	1902.25		765.43	707.1	366.9
1991	2524.12		973.59	909.6	442.1
1992	3479.39		1202.46	1243.0	532.5
1993	5237.37		1445.38	1731.0	552.4
1994	7273.95		1562.24	2305.9	536.8
1995	9720.54		1709.89	2880.8	539.8
1995(新规定) (New Stipulations)	8849.90		1465.82		
1996	10530.93		1544.58	3404.9	549.8
1997	12372.69		1574.39	4040.7	590.0
1998	13799.16		1453.79	4708.5	526.3
1999	15303.33	3025.68	1427.42	5385.9	487.2
2000	16904.47	3126.12	1536.50	6376.7	472.1
2001	18909.91	3309.51	1186.24	7428.9	374.8
2002	21788.71	3369.50	1217.66	8847.8	392.4
2003	27375.56	4017.54	979.19	11281.8	379.3
2004	34443.48	6039.24	1862.55	13958.7	709.5
2005	41661.74	6375.54	2068.75	16634.5	776.4
2006	51131.94	7253.17	2923.76	20137.8	1082.3
2007	62759.92	8603.94	2791.73	24399.0	1267.4
2008	74414.31	11144.50	2877.31	27636.7	1267.0
2009	75886.62	10790.11	3654.86	29405.4	1280.4
2010	93462.97	13166.37	4595.82	35110.0	1554.0
2011	103493.35	13927.70	5102.02	39358.3	1765.3
2012	105049.54	15529.16	5938.25	43490.9	1899.5
2013	119139.72	17525.16	1242.18	48796.8	2076.2
2014	130081.02	18225.94	635.82	52944.5	2153.0
2015	135308.14	17032.30	605.34	54956.4	2200.4
2016	144926.09	17172.18	665.85	58418.7	2347.8
2017	148173.99	19525.92	802.95	65078.4	2014.4
2018	148876.81	20855.98	153.00	70610.1	2433.4
2019	157662.91	21270.03	240.20	73858.2	2762.0
2020	155210.54	21191.00	633.27	73569.1	3134.1
2021	182919.33	28733.57	801.98	81220.3	3773.5
2022	193108.50	32513.46	941.32	82194.9	4079.1

注：1.工业总产值按当年价计算，2008年根据经济普查结果进行调整，指数按可比价计算。
2.2000年起全部工业总产值中规模以下部分为抽样调查数。

Notes: a) Gross industrial output values are calculated at current prices, whereas their indices have been adjusted in accordance with the national economic census in 2008 and are calculated at constant prices.

b) Since 2000, data of the industrial enterprises below designated size in the gross industrial output value have been obtained from sample surveys.

12-7 规模以上工业总产值和指数

Gross Output Value of Industrial Enterprises above Designated Size and Their Indices

单位:亿元 (100 million yuan)

年份 Year	工业总产值 Gross Industrial Output Value	轻工业 Light Industry	重工业 Heavy Industry	#大中型工业 Large and Medium-sized Industry	指数(1978年=100) Indices (1978=100)	轻工业 Light Industry	重工业 Heavy Industry	#大中型工业 Large and Medium-sized Industry
1978	180.73	102.32	78.41	49.34	100.0	100.0	100.0	100.0
1979	194.64	110.28	84.36	54.91	105.8	105.3	106.4	109.5
1980	212.69	128.17	84.52	56.33	115.8	127.7	100.7	103.1
1981	241.93	152.97	88.96	66.89	128.7	151.3	102.1	133.0
1982	263.02	164.17	98.85	75.37	139.9	164.2	111.2	148.5
1983	293.70	180.60	113.10	92.78	157.1	184.5	124.7	181.5
1984	359.87	223.29	136.58	110.63	188.1	226.1	142.8	209.9
1985	471.83	289.68	182.15	166.11	236.0	279.6	179.8	302.0
1986	550.49	344.70	205.79	210.27	269.5	327.7	194.7	379.7
1987	747.47	472.45	275.02	299.19	350.1	426.5	252.2	522.3
1988	1118.00	718.03	399.97	459.74	472.5	582.1	332.2	720.2
1989	1399.45	893.20	506.25	622.42	543.2	594.3	389.2	863.6
1990	1605.80	1057.02	548.78	734.35	637.6	795.5	435.8	1042.2
1991	2144.93	1371.46	773.47	1057.02	820.0	1009.7	622.1	1476.1
1992	2884.93	1796.12	1088.23	1408.48	1096.0	1331.0	854.4	1980.5
1993	4252.70	2515.77	1736.93	1891.29	1470.7	1751.6	1188.8	2412.8
1994	5565.48	3224.69	2340.79	2563.27	1819.1	2135.9	1507.6	2863.3
1995(原规定) (Original Stipulations)	7189.24	4148.78	3040.46	3227.59	2274.1	2581.8	1993.2	3519.7
1995(新规定) (New Stipulations)	6502.97	3776.94	2726.03	2824.61				
1996	7490.49	4344.25	3146.24	3470.81	2625.4	2989.5	2290.2	4253.6
1997	8442.32	4914.09	3528.23	3950.86	3045.3	3470.5	2652.8	5176.4
1998	9738.56	5765.51	3973.05	4169.16	3508.2	3866.1	3228.5	5927.0
1999	10538.17	6011.06	4527.11	4711.94	4016.9	4299.1	3861.3	7070.9
2000	12480.93	6607.84	5873.09	5951.56	4757.4	4737.6	5027.4	8590.8
2001	14035.35	7165.90	6869.44	7534.70	5637.5	5400.9	6234.0	12181.8
2002	16378.60	8161.63	8216.97	8755.02	6787.6	6313.7	7742.6	14472.0
2003	21513.46	9959.51	11553.95	14353.53	9051.9	7845.4	11063.4	19955.4
2004	29554.92	12146.01	17408.91	19799.88	12228.7	9549.6	15380.9	27054.8
2005	35942.74	14506.76	21435.97	24403.13	14652.0	11434.3	17914.1	32852.0
2006	44674.75	17148.09	27526.65	30828.93	17963.7	13549.8	21927.5	40937.6
2007	55252.86	21221.12	34031.74	37718.60	21931.9	16667.6	26370.0	49436.3
2008	65424.61	25035.86	40388.76	43866.65	25188.6	19373.2	29468.8	55765.6
2009	68275.77	26685.86	41589.91	44755.10	27430.4	20806.8	32415.7	57494.3
2010	85824.64	32867.30	52957.34	56873.77	33437.7	25200.5	39064.6	70824.4
2011	94871.68	36005.33	58866.35	67492.96	38954.9	29333.4	45549.3	79606.6
2012	95602.09	35817.39	59784.70	70178.27	43162.0	32032.1	49147.7	86134.3
2013	109673.07	41669.48	68003.59	76417.82	48686.7	36420.5	55192.9	95695.2
2014	119713.04	45756.65	73956.39	85194.40	53019.8	39953.3	59829.1	103446.5
2015	124649.16	47604.61	77044.55	88503.28	54981.5	41471.5	62042.8	106239.6
2016	133768.04	50237.52	83530.51	94758.85	58555.4	43379.2	66758.0	112826.4
2017	135722.42	47827.76	87894.65	95951.23	65582.0	47587.0	75703.6	126252.8
2018	140398.93	44520.43	95878.50	99544.89	71156.5	50394.6	83046.9	133954.2
2019	146121.72	46185.68	99936.04	101521.68	74429.7	51956.9	87531.4	144335.9
2020	148469.69	45387.73	103081.95	101762.61	75546.1	52216.6	89194.5	147800.0
2021	171979.82	53378.95	118600.86	115292.36	83176.3	58743.7	97222.0	160658.6
2022	180933.44	54766.14	126167.29	122393.14	83924.8	57745.1	99263.7	165317.7

注：1.工业总产值按当年价格计算，指数按可比价计算。
2.1997年以前为乡及乡以上工业，2011年起规模以上工业统计口径从年主营业务收入500万元及以上调整为2000万元及以上，2021年调整为主业务收入2000万元及以上工业企业和工业个体经营户。

Notes: a) Gross industrial output values are calculated at current prices, whereas their indices are calculated at constant prices.
b) Data prior to 1997 refer to the industrial enterprises at or above the township level.Since 2011,the annual principal business revenue of 20 industrial enterprises above designated size is changed from industrial enterprises of 5 million yuan or above to million yuan or above. It is adjusted to industrial enterprises and industrial self-employed households with main business income of 20 million yuan and above in 2021.

12-8 规模以上工业产品产量

Output of Industrial Products of Enterprises above Designated Size

产品名称		Item		2000	2010	2020	2021	2022
化学纤维	(万吨)	Chemical Fiber	(10000 tons)	45.00	44.54	83.05	84.71	75.51
#合成纤维	(万吨)	Synthetic Fiber	(10000 tons)	45.00	42.45	44.28	55.27	51.93
纱	(万吨)	Yarn	(10000 tons)	16.99	45.16	25.36	25.27	25.42
布	(亿米)	Cloth	(100 million m)	16.99	28.27	19.50	25.75	20.17
#棉布	(亿米)	Pure Cotton Cloth	(100 million m)	7.49	19.54	10.51	11.37	8.85
蚕丝	(万吨)	Silk	(10000 tons)	0.05	0.17	0.04	0.04	0.03
呢绒	(万米)	Woolen Piece Goods	(10000 m)	676.00	13.00	580.00	694.50	631.50
服装	(亿件)	Clothing	(100 million pieces)	21.99	70.26	37.29	39.16	35.20
皮革鞋靴	(亿双)	Leather Shoes and Boots	(100 million pair)	9.05	12.18	3.06	3.36	3.64
机制纸及纸板	(万吨)	Machine-made Paper and Paperboard	(10000 tons)	260.30	1434.68	2435.96	2410.29	2374.14
家用电冰箱	(万台)	Household Refrigerators	(10000 sets)	320.70	1457.76	2305.76	2091.56	1773.35
家用冷柜	(万台)	Freezers	(10000 sets)		180.14	512.12	554.31	464.34
家用洗衣机	(万台)	Household Washing Machines	(10000 sets)	244.18	467.83	741.57	757.57	686.72
家用吸尘器	(万台)	Vacuum Cleaners	(10000 sets)	251.80	2626.67	3216.94	2551.32	2321.83
家用电风扇	(万台)	Electric Fans	(10000 sets)	6759.02	14813.38	20552.78	21170.92	16057.12
房间空气调节器	(万台)	House Air Conditioners	(10000 sets)	697.91	5477.85	6714.61	6736.25	6637.70
家用吸排油烟机	(万台)	Smoke Absorbers	(10000 sets)	43.39	1324.67	1979.95	2427.27	2328.77
电饭锅	(万个)	Electric Rice Cookers	(10000 sets)		15207.47	10728.50	10357.51	9445.49
微波炉	(万台)	Microwave Ovens	(10000 sets)	906.51	5341.00	8471.34	9140.69	9108.53
程控交换机	(万线)	Program Controlled Switchboards	(10000 lines)	3554.88	1602.61	596.26	591.11	829.71
电话单机	(万部)	Telephone Sets	(10000 sets)	7700.05	14766.80	4413.19	4758.81	3730.57
移动通信手持机(手机)	(万台)	Mobile Telephone	(10000 units)	1001.30	48626.59	61979.77	66965.36	62690.03
#智能手机	(万台)	Smart Telephone	(10000 units)			51592.27	52476.53	50603.90
微型计算机设备	(万台)	Micro-computers Equipment	(10000 units)	169.74	3581.11	4621.58	5935.41	6948.85
服务器	(万台)	Servers	(10000 units)		2.98	135.97	148.36	85.22
集成电路	(亿块)	Semiconductor Integrated Circuit	(100 million pieces)	11.76	161.01	373.57	539.39	516.87
彩色电视机	(万部)	Color TV Sets	(10000 sets)	1531.53	4494.78	11233.36	9810.91	10792.02
#智能电视	(万台)	Smart TV	(10000 sets)			6701.71	7418.27	7957.95
数字激光音、视盘机	(万台)	Laser Digital Audio,Video Disc Machine	(10000sets)	637.69	7589.01	1113.54	572.78	351.82
组合音响	(万部)	Hi-fi Stereo Component System	(10000 sets)	2344.58	9713.01	12352.10	17252.45	15545.19
照相机	(万架)	Cameras	(10000 sets)	3545.88	3798.93	487.45	529.65	444.43
#数码照相机	(万台)	Digital Cameras	(10000 sets)		3687.89	336.95	466.00	360.02
表	(万只)	Watches	(10000 units)	19123.23	11892.26	7284.44	8032.13	8238.43
日用玻璃制品	(万吨)	Daily Use Glassware	(10000 tons)	51.46	150.93	125.98	112.86	103.57
合成洗涤剂	(万吨)	Synthetic Detergents	(10000 tons)	26.31	224.61	345.78	324.62	325.08
精制食用植物油	(万吨)	Refined Edible Vegetable oil	(100000tons)	7.87	244.21	799.53	756.40	711.04
成品糖	(万吨)	Refined Sugar	(10000 tons)	91.30	91.66	119.54	131.42	119.16
食用盐	(万吨)	Edible Salt	(10000 tons)			0.41	0.18	0.47
卷烟	(万箱)	Cigarettes	(10000 units)	177.30	260.69	255.67	258.30	259.30
罐头	(万吨)	Canned Food	(10000 tons)	7.11	30.18	25.16	22.87	17.12
饮料酒	(万千升)	Alcoholic Beverages (mixed weight)	(10000 kiloliter)	178.66	415.80	374.42	428.86	414.88
#白酒	(万千升)	Spirits	(10000 kiloliter)	17.88	10.27	10.10	10.74	10.48
啤酒	(万千升)	Beer	(10000 kiloliter)	158.89	401.40	357.46	408.25	394.11
乳制品	(万吨)	Dairy Products	(10000 tons)	1.29	58.12	96.37	82.74	77.86
中成药	(万吨)	Traditional Chinese Patent Medicine	(10000 tons)	6.05	19.01	20.08	24.41	22.37
化学药品原药	(万吨)	Chemical Active Pharmaceutical Ingredient	(10000 tons)	1.94	4.78	10.28	11.73	9.61

12-8 续表 continued

产品名称		Item		2000	2010	2020	2021	2022
农用氮、磷、钾化学肥料(折纯)	(万吨)	Chemical Fertilizer	(10000 tons)	34.65	62.15	10.49	6.44	5.52
#磷肥(折五氧化二磷100%)	(万吨)	Phosphate Fertilizer	(10000 tons)	18.67	50.66	5.69	2.45	3.77
化学农药原药(折有效成分100%)	(万吨)	Chemical Pesticide	(10000 tons)	0.84	0.86	1.98	2.28	3.10
乙烯	(万吨)	Ethylene	(10000 tons)	54.85	203.96	365.68	417.75	391.15
合成橡胶	(万吨)	Synthetic Rubber	(10000 tons)	5.45	38.36	74.82	72.78	70.33
橡胶轮胎外胎	(万条)	Tires	(10000 pieces)	359.13	6907.25	2215.67	3277.46	3404.11
交流电动机	(万千瓦)	Alternating Current Motors	(10000 kw)	236.21	753.39	1634.06	5185.75	8191.64
汽车	(万辆)	Motor Vehicles	(10000 units)	3.94	156.29	313.31	338.46	415.37
#载货汽车	(万辆)	Trucks	(10000 units)	0.53	0.34	0.62	0.82	0.63
客车	(万辆)	Buses	(10000 units)	0.18	0.20	0.64	0.45	0.75
轿车	(万辆)	Cars	(10000 units)	3.22	132.67	172.70	183.34	235.02
#新能源汽车	(万辆)	New Energy Vehicle	(10000 units)			20.87	53.54	129.73
城市轨道车辆	(辆)	Urban Rail Vehicle	(unit)			184	246	172
民用钢质船舶	(万载重吨)	Civil Steel ship	(10000ton)		177.18	89.87	71.73	82.56
摩托车整车	(万辆)	Motorcycles	(10000 units)	146.31	917.60	659.37	732.23	628.72
两轮脚踏自行车	(万辆)	Bicycles	(10000 units)	1038.00	788.75	570.89	884.83	901.50
生铁	(万吨)	Pig Iron	(10000 tons)	201.57	806.68	2158.74	2053.64	2420.90
粗钢	(万吨)	Crude Steel	(10000 tons)	286.99	1239.34	3382.34	3178.33	3571.77
钢材	(万吨)	Rolled Steel Products	(10000 tons)	406.28	2918.89	4866.19	5111.18	5627.44
十种有色金属	(万吨)	Ten Kinds of Nonferrous Metals	(10000 tons)		45.31	46.13	49.99	53.29
铝材	(万吨)	Aluminum	(10000 tons)		496.85	528.32	510.11	553.07
汽车用发动机	(万千瓦)	Automotive engines	(10000 kw)		8727.56	28164.86	24047.87	26369.58
工业机器人	(万套)	Industrial Robots	(10000 sets)			7.04	12.44	16.57
光纤	(万千米)	Optical fiber	(10000km)			730.26	672.97	1261.15
光缆	(万芯千米)	Optical Cable	(10000km)		835.99	2542.34	2975.71	3356.84
太阳能电池(光伏电池)	(万千瓦)	Solar cells (photovoltaic cells)	(10000kw)			269.91	216.46	320.56
水泥	(万吨)	Cement	(10000 tons)	5872.00	11536.67	17075.63	17005.20	15131.17
平板玻璃	(万重量箱)	Plate Glass	(10000 wt.cases)	632.59	7821.07	9963.69	11083.79	10336.04
硫酸(折100%)	(万吨)	Sulphuric Acid	(10000 tons)	138.75	236.74	229.43	251.57	237.38
纯碱（碳酸钠)	(万吨)	Soda Ash	(10000 tons)	24.28	40.01	54.39	57.28	55.66
烧碱(折100%)	(万吨)	Caustic Soda	(10000 tons)	16.43	27.62	33.16	34.56	33.98

注：1.纱包括纯棉纱、棉混纺纱、化学纤维纱，不包括棉线、代用纤维纱和手工纺纱。
2.布包括纯棉布、棉混纺布、化学纤维布，不包括代用纤维布、手工织布。
3.农用化肥按有效成分100%计算。

Notes: a) Yarn includes pure and blended cotton yarn, chemical fiber yarn, but excludes cotton thread, substitute fiber yarn and handmade yarn.
b) Cloth includes pure and blended cotton cloth,chemical fiber cloth and canvas,but excludes substitute fiber cloth,hand-woven cloth and cord fabric.
c) Output of chemical fertilizers is calculated on the basis of 100 percent effective content equivalent.

12-9 各市规模以上工业企业单位数和工业总产值

Number and Gross Output Value of Industrial Enterprises above Designated Size by City

市别	City	工业企业单位数（个） Number of Industrial Enterprises (unit)								
		2000	2005	2010	2015	2018	2019	2020	2021	2022
广　州	Guangzhou	4531	5240	6969	4644	4809	5802	6208	6757	6878
深　圳	Shenzhen	1834	5214	8249	6539	9006	10337	11255	13027	13790
珠　海	Zhuhai	771	992	1347	1023	1236	1388	1492	1655	1792
汕　头	Shantou	794	1490	2580	1771	1983	1972	1928	2061	2181
佛　山	Foshan	2180	5148	7684	5787	6631	7902	8020	9370	9851
韶　关	Shaoguan	406	392	559	628	439	475	504	603	641
河　源	Heyuan	148	226	440	575	611	567	581	623	627
梅　州	Meizhou	371	392	521	440	467	474	505	536	547
惠　州	Huizhou	689	1243	1853	1893	2546	2764	3055	3873	4365
汕　尾	Shanwei	94	179	452	238	248	244	258	289	316
东　莞	Dongguan	1663	4504	5899	5688	10054	10658	11525	12778	13844
中　山	Zhongshan	1074	3291	5063	3045	3376	3635	3868	4626	4959
江　门	Jiangmen	1599	2365	3246	2036	2300	2458	2535	2903	3264
阳　江	Yangjiang	250	498	596	571	309	334	386	461	512
湛　江	Zhanjiang	458	578	850	828	893	870	780	788	815
茂　名	Maoming	447	590	792	957	949	810	751	652	674
肇　庆	Zhaoqing	981	684	1131	1110	1189	1269	1321	1446	1562
清　远	Qingyuan	304	426	813	611	733	772	834	949	1034
潮　州	Chaozhou	326	727	1245	890	889	936	939	1035	1075
揭　阳	Jieyang	455	714	2525	2030	1581	1393	1376	1464	1572
云　浮	Yunfu	320	264	604	830	342	355	383	433	426
按经济区域分	By Region									
珠三角	Pearl River Delta	15322	28681	41441	31765	41147	46213	49279	56435	60305
东　翼	Eastern Region	1669	3110	6802	4929	4701	4545	4501	4849	5144
西　翼	Western Region	1155	1666	2238	2356	2151	2014	1917	1901	2001
山　区	Mountainous Region	1549	1700	2937	3084	2592	2643	2807	3144	3275

注：2011年起，规模以上工业统计口径从年主营业务收入500万元及以上调整为2000万元及以上工业企业,2021年为主业务收入2000万元及以上工业企业和工业个体经营户。

Note: Since 2011, the annual principal business revenue of industrial enterprises above designated size is changed from industrial enterprises of 5 million yuan or above to 20 million yuan or above. It is adjusted to industrial enterprises and industrial self-employed households with main business income of 20 million yuan and above in 2021.

12-9 续表 continued

市别	City	工业总产值（亿元） Gross Industrial Output Value（100 million yuan）								
		2000	2005	2010	2015	2018	2019	2020	2021	2022
广　州	Guangzhou	2568.57	6032.05	13831.25	18424.73	18595.11	19407.64	20310.16	23121.00	23928.58
深　圳	Shenzhen	2566.93	9867.55	18526.82	25542.44	35439.02	37326.16	38460.79	42453.96	46259.43
珠　海	Zhuhai	630.17	1569.56	2976.18	3966.02	4481.34	4646.99	4565.80	5272.44	5916.09
汕　头	Shantou	344.34	761.37	1897.57	2968.80	3405.47	3060.82	2985.44	3378.20	3404.18
佛　山	Foshan	1560.55	4780.88	14527.47	19544.95	21595.71	23222.05	23037.41	26312.48	27965.42
韶　关	Shaoguan	151.01	393.36	773.37	1221.78	1128.83	1210.17	1256.83	1645.23	1617.80
河　源	Heyuan	35.81	182.10	832.73	1443.02	1333.76	1352.91	1244.61	1459.68	1459.82
梅　州	Meizhou	81.81	206.98	455.97	704.76	639.19	713.19	725.80	865.46	858.68
惠　州	Huizhou	657.83	1428.66	3905.17	7044.73	7700.39	7431.43	7714.43	9949.28	11099.46
汕　尾	Shanwei	30.08	113.45	432.42	1166.08	1165.46	1236.29	1180.04	1462.56	1251.04
东　莞	Dongguan	914.64	3940.11	7739.09	12744.42	20392.92	21561.78	21862.96	24513.14	24772.97
中　山	Zhongshan	532.95	2221.45	5023.63	6345.28	5115.30	5162.50	5375.84	6619.31	6772.54
江　门	Jiangmen	871.15	1453.25	3828.91	3998.76	4409.29	4246.64	4382.58	5451.19	5631.70
阳　江	Yangjiang	66.17	213.82	693.46	1990.04	949.29	1237.44	1526.51	2124.62	2320.70
湛　江	Zhanjiang	269.10	644.27	1404.95	2272.40	2399.65	2231.12	2102.93	2951.80	3371.13
茂　名	Maoming	373.22	702.04	1360.15	2328.05	2125.61	1988.87	1771.25	2231.07	2477.57
肇　庆	Zhaoqing	392.04	321.20	1744.19	4034.37	2881.44	3123.28	3272.42	4272.96	4385.41
清　远	Qingyuan	77.51	364.34	2887.04	1680.13	1846.42	2003.40	2173.68	2864.73	2833.26
潮　州	Chaozhou	73.88	293.72	723.12	1325.80	1358.37	1543.11	1196.57	1458.80	1387.93
揭　阳	Jieyang	136.46	298.82	1794.82	4803.12	2941.07	2873.24	2745.02	2900.65	2502.81
云　浮	Yunfu	146.71	153.77	466.34	1099.49	495.32	542.68	578.59	671.27	716.92
按经济区域分	By Region									
珠三角	Pearl River Delta	10694.83	31614.71	72102.70	101645.70	120610.50	126128.47	128982.41	147965.76	156731.60
东　翼	Eastern Region	584.76	1467.36	4847.93	10263.80	8870.36	8713.46	8107.07	9200.20	8545.96
西　翼	Western Region	708.49	1560.13	3458.56	6590.49	5474.55	5457.43	5400.69	7307.49	8169.40
山　区	Mountainous Region	492.85	1300.55	5415.45	6149.17	5443.52	5822.36	5979.52	7506.36	7486.48

注：本表产值按当年价格计算。
Note: Data of gross industrial output value in this table are calculated at current prices.

12-10 各市规模以上工业增加值和指数

Value-added and Indices of Industry above Designated Size by City

市别	City	工业增加值(亿元) Value-add of Industry (100 million yuan)								
		2000	2005	2010	2015	2018	2019	2020	2021	2022
广　州	Guangzhou	708.40	1654.03	4073.35	4535.25	4209.48	4324.08	4544.60	4963.72	4912.19
深　圳	Shenzhen	706.85	2571.95	5015.33	6426.39	8290.54	8893.21	8565.79	9578.00	10106.69
珠　海	Zhuhai	156.16	328.74	683.98	916.94	1190.46	1206.38	1190.66	1329.49	1450.09
汕　头	Shantou	88.56	190.30	483.20	694.62	799.46	676.71	676.32	739.85	721.67
佛　山	Foshan	401.78	1303.31	3915.12	4364.33	4569.02	4874.23	4650.46	5432.94	5603.21
韶　关	Shaoguan	50.72	108.63	219.25	309.71	325.51	313.85	321.22	361.23	321.82
河　源	Heyuan	10.66	57.78	312.36	327.57	277.27	279.92	284.91	345.77	343.68
梅　州	Meizhou	29.46	72.49	166.00	214.34	208.46	229.76	242.47	264.09	240.18
惠　州	Huizhou	129.08	315.32	881.16	1617.38	1630.40	1654.17	1689.86	2215.85	2185.30
汕　尾	Shanwei	8.74	29.17	112.34	245.10	208.14	184.14	178.24	191.95	174.34
东　莞	Dongguan	259.44	1060.49	1760.02	2611.96	3914.38	4192.78	4477.91	5187.03	4959.60
中　山	Zhongshan	136.16	551.20	1263.08	1281.05	1127.44	1140.09	1172.11	1361.97	1363.20
江　门	Jiangmen	189.49	355.10	1053.39	965.74	1060.78	1008.60	1027.95	1201.92	1136.07
阳　江	Yangjiang	21.55	66.26	184.14	452.02	269.94	298.09	299.11	359.84	372.83
湛　江	Zhanjiang	99.80	229.87	528.83	721.26	772.53	636.54	653.64	855.33	836.44
茂　名	Maoming	78.44	165.28	362.29	757.29	608.75	502.47	463.25	537.14	385.04
肇　庆	Zhaoqing	36.36	76.86	434.51	961.07	656.83	668.90	653.82	765.69	728.56
清　远	Qingyuan	21.22	90.83	686.02	396.65	453.19	482.07	546.58	678.83	570.34
潮　州	Chaozhou	20.19	69.46	194.91	352.08	276.26	269.93	251.75	273.11	240.10
揭　阳	Jieyang	39.09	77.62	512.46	1054.89	587.20	525.30	462.04	511.51	484.50
云　浮	Yunfu	22.37	41.70	146.58	240.58	121.05	132.77	147.47	151.27	124.73
按经济区域分	By Region									
珠三角	Pearl River Delta	2723.72	8217.00	19079.95	23680.10	26649.33	27962.44	27973.15	32036.61	32444.89
东　翼	Eastern Region	156.58	366.55	1302.91	2346.69	1871.05	1656.07	1568.36	1716.42	1620.60
西　翼	Western Region	199.79	461.41	1075.26	1930.57	1651.22	1437.10	1416.01	1752.31	1594.31
山　区	Mountainous Region	134.43	371.44	1530.20	1488.84	1385.48	1438.37	1542.65	1801.19	1600.76

注：1.本表统计口径从2011年起从年主营业务收入500万元及以上调整为2000万元及以上。
2.本表增加值2010年及以前用生产法计算，2011年起用收入法计算。

Note:a) Since 2011, the annual principal business revenue of industrial enterprises above designated size is changed from 5 million yuan or above to 20 million yuan or above.
b) The value-added in this table in 2010 and prior to are calculated with production approach and since 2011 calculated with income approach.

12-10 续表 continued

市 别	City	指数(2000年=100) Indices (2000=100)								
		2000	2005	2010	2015	2018	2019	2020	2021	2022
广 州	Guangzhou	100.0	223.8	455.8	723.0	840.8	883.7	905.8	976.4	984.2
深 圳	Shenzhen	100.0	391.6	723.3	1118.2	1432.0	1499.3	1529.3	1601.2	1678.0
珠 海	Zhuhai	100.0	229.9	426.1	709.1	947.6	985.5	999.3	1087.2	1162.3
汕 头	Shantou	100.0	183.0	407.9	749.7	989.7	1013.5	1031.7	1120.4	1094.7
佛 山	Foshan	100.0	312.0	851.3	1461.5	1820.5	1947.9	1990.8	2175.9	2210.7
韶 关	Shaoguan	100.0	159.8	332.4	587.4	638.6	668.6	688.7	776.1	762.2
河 源	Heyuan	100.0	460.0	1844.7	3922.0	4803.8	5096.8	5209.0	5860.1	6000.7
梅 州	Meizhou	100.0	210.7	422.1	808.0	868.1	882.9	884.6	980.2	952.7
惠 州	Huizhou	100.0	215.2	582.5	1215.0	1526.1	1553.6	1570.7	1792.1	1905.0
汕 尾	Shanwei	100.0	367.4	1541.3	3972.2	5283.6	5738.0	5887.2	7152.9	6702.3
东 莞	Dongguan	100.0	327.6	512.0	741.1	928.1	1007.0	995.9	1097.5	1083.2
中 山	Zhongshan	100.0	494.0	1026.2	1779.4	2053.4	2012.3	2056.6	2303.4	2271.1
江 门	Jiangmen	100.0	207.7	525.1	959.0	1234.8	1253.3	1282.1	1470.6	1516.2
阳 江	Yangjiang	100.0	266.8	705.0	2038.0	2389.6	2795.8	3271.1	3954.8	3998.3
湛 江	Zhanjiang	100.0	183.7	340.2	618.1	785.1	782.7	825.0	947.1	931.0
茂 名	Maoming	100.0	163.6	276.9	577.5	679.5	682.9	667.2	697.9	642.1
肇 庆	Zhaoqing	100.0	211.8	952.6	2127.1	2496.7	2669.0	2738.4	3242.2	3290.9
清 远	Qingyuan	100.0	353.0	2310.0	3850.6	4685.9	4971.7	5304.8	6058.1	6009.7
潮 州	Chaozhou	100.0	321.1	796.0	1576.1	1853.8	1916.8	1868.9	2022.2	1923.1
揭 阳	Jieyang	100.0	188.3	879.7	2142.6	2435.3	2423.1	2357.7	2407.2	1985.9
云 浮	Yunfu	100.0	174.7	517.4	1428.8	1627.6	1726.9	1790.8	1917.9	1917.9
按经济区域分	By Region									
珠 三 角	Pearl River Delta	100.0	205.0	399.6	606.8	746.1	783.4	795.9	864.4	885.1
东 翼	Eastern Region	100.0	208.4	532.7	1060.8	1279.0	1308.4	1286.2	1390.4	1284.7
西 翼	Western Region	100.0	199.8	373.3	726.2	868.2	893.4	939.8	1062.0	1030.2
山 区	Mountainous Region	100.0	207.5	638.6	1142.6	1316.9	1384.1	1432.5	1610.1	1600.5

注：本表工业增加值按当年价格计算，指数按可比价格计算。

Note: Data of value-added of industry in this table are calculated at current prices, whereas their indices are calculated at constant prices.

12-11 各市规模以上工业企业单位数（2022年）

单位：个

项 目	Item	全 省 Provincial Total	广 州 Guangzhou
总 计	**Total**	**70725**	**6878**
按经济类型分	Grouped by Ownership		
在总计中：国有控股工业	Of the Total:State-holding Industry	1573	335
国有工业	State-owned Industry	258	28
集体工业	Collective-owned Industry	73	12
股份合作工业	Share-holding Cooperative Industry	46	14
股份制工业	Share-holding Industry	56499	5415
外商投资工业	Foreign-funded Industry	3794	647
港澳台投资工业	Industry with Funds from Hong Kong, Macao and Taiwan	7942	639
按轻重工业分	Grouped by Light and Heavy Industries		
轻工业	Light Industry	31685	3327
重工业	Heavy Industry	39040	3551
按企业规模分	Grouped by Size of Enterprises		
大型企业	Large Enterprises	1438	162
中型企业	Medium Enterprises	6449	596
小微型企业	Small and Micro Enterprises	62838	6120
按行业分	Grouped by Sector		
煤炭开采和洗选业	Mining and Washing of Coal		
石油和天然气开采业	Extraction of Petroleum and Natural Gas	3	
黑色金属矿采选业	Mining and Dressing of Ferrous Metal Ores	12	
有色金属矿采选业	Mining and Dressing of Nonferrous Metal Ores	28	
非金属矿采选业	Mining and Dressing of Nonmetal Ores	226	4
开采专业及辅助性活动	Mining Specialized and Auxiliary Operations	8	
其他采矿业	Mining and Dressing of Other Ores		
农副食品加工业	Processing of Farm and Sideline Food	1285	145
食品制造业	Manufacture of Food	930	181
酒、饮料和精制茶制造业	Manufacture of Wine, Beverage and Refined Tea	237	39
烟草制品业	Tobacco Products	46	1
纺织业	Textile Industry	1685	147
纺织服装、服饰业	Manufacture of Textile Garments, Footwear and Headgear	2671	430
皮革、毛皮、羽毛及其制品和制鞋业	Leather, Fur, Feather, Down and Related Products	1757	323
木材加工和木、竹、藤、棕、草制品业	Timber Processing, Bamboo, Cane, Palm Fiber & Straw Products	570	57
家具制造业	Manufacture of Furniture	1956	158
造纸和纸制品业	Papermaking and Paper Products	1598	163
印刷和记录媒介复制业	Printing and Record Medium Reproduction	1213	125
文教、工美、体育和娱乐用品制造业	Manufacture of Cultural, Educational,Sports and Entertainment Articles	2081	151
石油、煤炭及其他燃料加工业	Petroleum, Coal and other Fuel Processing	122	16
化学原料和化学制品制造业	Manufacture of Raw Chemical Materials and Chemical Products	3321	682
医药制造业	Manufacture of Medicines	628	147
化学纤维制造业	Manufacture of Chemical Fibers	93	12
橡胶和塑料制品业	Rubber and Plastic Products	6241	461
非金属矿物制品业	Nonmetal Mineral Products	3890	299
黑色金属冶炼和压延加工业	Smelting and Pressing of Ferrous Metals	531	28
有色金属冶炼和压延加工业	Smelting and Pressing of Nonferrous Metals	1149	63
金属制品业	Metal Products	7175	383
通用设备制造业	Manufacture of General-purpose Machinery	4095	479
专用设备制造业	Manufacture of Special-purpose Machinery	4234	452
汽车制造业	Manufacture of Automobile	1140	343
铁路、船舶、航空航天和其他运输设备制造业	Manufacture of Railway ,Ship,Aeronautics and Other Transport equipment	541	92
电气机械和器材制造业	Manufacture of Electrical Machinery and Equipment	8246	520
计算机、通信和其他电子设备制造业	Manufacture of Communication Equipment, Computers and Other Electronic Equipment	9672	646
仪器仪表制造业	Manufacture of Instruments and Meters	1186	112
其他制造业	Other Manufactures	535	37
废弃资源综合利用业	Comprehensive Utilization of Waste	271	19
金属制品、机械和设备修理业	Manufacture of Metal Products,Machinery and Equipment Maintenance	89	25
电力、热力生产和供应业	Production and Supply of Electric Power and Heat Power	567	62
燃气生产和供应业	Production and Supply of Gas	291	39
水的生产和供应业	Production and Supply of Water	402	37

Number of Industrial Enterprises above Designated Size by City (2022)

(unit)

深 圳 Shenzhen	珠 海 Zhuhai	汕 头 Shantou	佛 山 Foshan	韶 关 Shaoguan	河 源 Heyuan	梅 州 Meizhou	惠 州 Huizhou	汕 尾 Shanwei
13790	**1792**	**2181**	**9851**	**641**	**627**	**547**	**4365**	**316**
236	71	45	125	81	21	35	75	28
33	9	12	21	8	13	2	7	7
	1	6	5	1		1	3	9
	1	7	7			1	1	
11449	1278	1903	8347	551	464	488	3328	233
572	201	54	378	21	23	12	224	7
1587	294	109	624	55	109	30	670	42
4105	601	1746	4573	155	219	175	1990	175
9685	1191	435	5278	486	408	372	2375	141
326	71	13	161	14	20	7	123	21
1250	237	147	807	59	91	54	429	25
12214	1484	2021	8883	568	516	486	3813	270
1	1							
	1			1	5	1		
				7	2	3		
		1	2	6	13	8	30	4
3	1							
58	30	51	133	16	17	25	59	21
48	35	71	100	9	12	13	26	12
17	10	7	29	4	7	10	13	5
34		2		3		1	2	1
70	14	198	474	9	9	9	64	13
169	33	584	274	3	18	7	65	25
76	1	13	154	3	7	5	192	6
21	5	2	73	17	21	5	63	6
120	8	7	636		9	8	322	1
233	29	70	194	11	8	4	84	5
232	38	75	129	1	10	5	50	3
407	21	263	95	19	33	24	192	24
6	8	1	20			1	8	
270	141	94	445	121	11	13	214	7
112	37	26	58	7	9	13	21	
1	5	3	14		2	1	4	
951	134	278	784	27	40	16	521	28
214	72	52	559	85	111	118	246	43
32	5	1	213	6	16	6	15	
137	17	3	353	17	8	4	47	
818	106	43	1629	70	30	15	398	28
947	124	49	751	30	30	11	148	3
1322	122	65	613	21	33	17	139	4
104	32	12	248	6	2	17	64	
105	27	2	69	1	2	1	41	2
1988	227	71	1254	29	36	21	451	14
4415	373	43	317	31	74	111	713	25
553	68	5	62	3	10	3	55	
185	1	10	32	3	9	1	29	1
19	14	27	30	16	1	8	20	1
20	5	2	2	1			4	2
35	23	19	31	44	19	24	29	14
20	13	6	22	7	10	9	10	4
47	11	25	52	7	3	9	26	14

12-11 续表

单位：个

项　目	Item	东 莞 Dongguan	中 山 Zhongshan
总　计	**Total**	**13844**	**4959**
按经济类型分	Grouped by Ownership		
在总计中：国有控股工业	Of the Total:State-holding Industry	67	41
国有工业	State-owned Industry	4	
集体工业	Collective-owned Industry	17	5
股份合作工业	Share-holding Cooperative Industry	4	
股份制工业	Share-holding Industry	10388	3904
外商投资工业	Foreign-funded Industry	987	301
港澳台投资工业	Industry with Funds from Hong Kong, Macao and Taiwan	2176	547
按轻重工业分	Grouped by Light and Heavy Industries		
轻工业	Light Industry	5868	3140
重工业	Heavy Industry	7976	1819
按企业规模分	Grouped by Size of Enterprises		
大型企业	Large Enterprises	269	87
中型企业	Medium Enterprises	1394	433
小微型企业	Small and Micro Enterprises	12181	4439
按行业分	Grouped by Sector		
煤炭开采和洗选业	Mining and Washing of Coal		
石油和天然气开采业	Extraction of Petroleum and Natural Gas		
黑色金属矿采选业	Mining and Dressing of Ferrous Metal Ores		
有色金属矿采选业	Mining and Dressing of Nonferrous Metal Ores		
非金属矿采选业	Mining and Dressing of Nonmetal Ores	2	
开采专业及辅助性活动	Mining Specialized and Auxiliary Operations		
其他采矿业	Mining and Dressing of Other Ores		
农副食品加工业	Processing of Farm and Sideline Food	91	35
食品制造业	Manufacture of Food	97	47
酒、饮料和精制茶制造业	Manufacture of Wine, Beverage and Refined Tea	17	12
烟草制品业	Tobacco Products		1
纺织业	Textile Industry	214	136
纺织服装、服饰业	Manufacture of Textile Garments, Footwear and Headgear	479	271
皮革、毛皮、羽毛及其制品和制鞋业	Leather, Fur, Feather, Down and Related Products	472	80
木材加工和木、竹、藤、棕、草制品业	Timber Processing, Bamboo, Cane, Palm Fiber & Straw Products	70	27
家具制造业	Manufacture of Furniture	375	153
造纸和纸制品业	Papermaking and Paper Products	418	129
印刷和记录媒介复制业	Printing and Record Medium Reproduction	280	84
文教、工美、体育和娱乐用品制造业	Manufacture of Cultural, Educational,Sports and Entertainment Articles	557	137
石油、煤炭及其他燃料加工业	Petroleum, Coal and other Fuel Processing	12	6
化学原料和化学制品制造业	Manufacture of Raw Chemical Materials and Chemical Products	482	180
医药制造业	Manufacture of Medicines	27	35
化学纤维制造业	Manufacture of Chemical Fibers	27	5
橡胶和塑料制品业	Rubber and Plastic Products	1776	467
非金属矿物制品业	Nonmetal Mineral Products	318	160
黑色金属冶炼和压延加工业	Smelting and Pressing of Ferrous Metals	58	19
有色金属冶炼和压延加工业	Smelting and Pressing of Nonferrous Metals	182	61
金属制品业	Metal Products	1538	543
通用设备制造业	Manufacture of General-purpose Machinery	913	289
专用设备制造业	Manufacture of Special-purpose Machinery	1026	186
汽车制造业	Manufacture of Automobile	125	59
铁路、船舶、航空航天和其他运输设备制造业	Manufacture of Railway ,Ship,Aeronautics and Other Transport equipment	46	15
电气机械和器材制造业	Manufacture of Electrical Machinery and Equipment	1525	1332
计算机、通信和其他电子设备制造业	Manufacture of Communication Equipment, Computers and Other Electronic Equipment	2222	318
仪器仪表制造业	Manufacture of Instruments and Meters	225	64
其他制造业	Other Manufactures	144	51
废弃资源综合利用业	Comprehensive Utilization of Waste	7	2
金属制品、机械和设备修理业	Manufacture of Metal Products,Machinery and Equipment Maintenance	12	4
电力、热力生产和供应业	Production and Supply of Electric Power and Heat Power	28	16
燃气生产和供应业	Production and Supply of Gas	37	9
水的生产和供应业	Production and Supply of Water	42	26

12-11 continued

(unit)

江 门 Jiangmen	阳 江 Yangjiang	湛 江 Zhanjiang	茂 名 Maoming	肇 庆 Zhaoqing	清 远 Qingyuan	潮 州 Chaozhou	揭 阳 Jieyang	云 浮 Yunfu
3264	**512**	**815**	**674**	**1562**	**1034**	**1075**	**1572**	**426**
41	40	106	63	42	44	19	33	25
4	5	36	34	5	7	6	14	3
1			3	1	1	3	4	
3						7	1	
2451	425	674	557	1280	808	836	1389	331
165	16	36	9	64	43	7	12	15
522	38	39	26	138	138	43	61	55
1747	290	429	328	550	363	741	1043	120
1517	222	386	346	1012	671	334	529	306
59	8	9	5	30	30	5	7	11
283	57	69	33	174	134	43	88	46
2922	447	737	636	1358	870	1027	1477	369
		1						
				1	1	1		1
		8	4	2	1			1
27	10	18	36	26	19	8	4	8
2		1		1				
104	43	148	152	32	32	41	41	11
52	10	19	18	32	10	63	68	7
9	3	11	2	15	10	9	7	1
		1						
113	1	10	9	39	38	6	103	9
75	9	3	9	18	8	37	147	7
50	4	46	29	28	35	49	183	1
43	9	47	23	29	12	11	21	8
92	1	13	2	26	18	2	4	1
101	11	22	5	41	11	33	21	5
44	4	12	4	8	7	70	31	1
38	3	3	13	28	29	10	30	4
6	1	4	25	1	1	2	4	
180	14	30	69	153	133	20	17	45
19	2	12	28	10	10	9	29	17
5				3	4		5	2
268	38	23	26	76	107	68	143	9
192	39	122	117	200	190	422	176	155
24	13	2	3	8	12	9	59	2
60	4	3	1	100	51	14	12	12
668	174	32	20	285	55	102	210	28
147	25	7	6	69	33	11	13	10
75	3	14	7	65	21	4	30	15
39	3	6		38	31		3	8
116	1	1	1	1	12		6	
402	25	103	4	62	25	15	125	17
206	5	2	16	75	33	8	26	13
12			1	6	2	1	2	2
20	1	2	1	4	2	1	1	
13	7	13	4	26	22	3	14	5
3		6		3				
26	31	46	23	25	37	9	17	9
11	7	10	7	15	13	30	6	6
22	11	14	9	11	9	7	14	6

12-12 各市规模以上工业总产值（2022年）

单位：亿元

项 目	Item	全 省 Provincial Total	广 州 Guangzhou
总 计	**Total**	**180933.44**	**23928.58**
按经济类型分	Grouped by Ownership		
在总计中：国有控股工业	Of the Total:State-holding Industry	32513.46	11249.21
国有工业	State-owned Industry	941.32	119.74
集体工业	Collective-owned Industry	48.66	13.68
股份合作工业	Share-holding Cooperative Industry	67.62	8.8
股份制工业	Share-holding Industry	118899.83	12348.9
外商投资工业	Foreign-funded Industry	27898.05	9162.86
港澳台投资工业	Industry with Funds from Hong Kong, Macao and Taiwan	31506.28	2213.71
按轻重工业分	Grouped by Light and Heavy Industries		
轻工业	Light Industry	54766.14	5745.73
重工业	Heavy Industry	126167.29	18182.85
按企业规模分	Grouped by Size of Enterprises		
大型企业	Large Enterprises	82354.91	12847.12
中型企业	Medium Enterprises	40038.23	3740.78
小微型企业	Small and Micro Enterprises	58540.3	7340.68
按行业分	Grouped by Sector		
煤炭开采和洗选业	Mining and Washing of Coal		
石油和天然气开采业	Extraction of Petroleum and Natural Gas	1159.37	
黑色金属矿采选业	Mining and Dressing of Ferrous Metal Ores	53.95	
有色金属矿采选业	Mining and Dressing of Nonferrous Metal Ores	114.99	
非金属矿采选业	Mining and Dressing of Nonmetal Ores	237.24	31.84
开采专业及辅助性活动	Mining Specialized and Auxiliary Operations	56.27	
其他采矿业	Mining and Dressing of Other Ores		
农副食品加工业	Processing of Farm and Sideline Food	4272.63	433.96
食品制造业	Manufacture of Food	2232.95	575.09
酒、饮料和精制茶制造业	Manufacture of Wine, Beverage and Refined Tea	1173.87	360.24
烟草制品业	Tobacco Products	601.72	245.45
纺织业	Textile Industry	2261.45	136.28
纺织服装、服饰业	Manufacture of Textile Garments, Footwear and Headgear	2798.78	261.66
皮革、毛皮、羽毛及其制品和制鞋业	Leather, Fur, Feather, Down and Related Products	1599.61	153.51
木材加工和木、竹、藤、棕、草制品业	Timber Processing, Bamboo, Cane, Palm Fiber & Straw Products	426.31	24.18
家具制造业	Manufacture of Furniture	2207.71	374.93
造纸和纸制品业	Papermaking and Paper Products	2767.12	170.5
印刷和记录媒介复制业	Printing and Record Medium Reproduction	1438.37	125.42
文教、工美、体育和娱乐用品制造业	Manufacture of Cultural, Educational,Sports and Entertainment Articles	4145.36	152.27
石油、煤炭及其他燃料加工业	Petroleum, Coal and other Fuel Processing	4945.41	759.73
化学原料和化学制品制造业	Manufacture of Raw Chemical Materials and Chemical Products	7233.54	1327.49
医药制造业	Manufacture of Medicines	2264.35	601.35
化学纤维制造业	Manufacture of Chemical Fibers	196.54	8.99
橡胶和塑料制品业	Rubber and Plastic Products	6283.5	573.79
非金属矿物制品业	Nonmetal Mineral Products	6789.28	608.61
黑色金属冶炼和压延加工业	Smelting and Pressing of Ferrous Metals	3845.87	269.22
有色金属冶炼和压延加工业	Smelting and Pressing of Nonferrous Metals	5066.77	663.54
金属制品业	Metal Products	8816.38	405.16
通用设备制造业	Manufacture of General-purpose Machinery	5793.28	801.59
专用设备制造业	Manufacture of Special-purpose Machinery	5673.58	531.9
汽车制造业	Manufacture of Automobile	11593.39	6470.48
铁路、船舶、航空航天和其他运输设备制造业	Manufacture of Railway ,Ship,Aeronautics and Other Transport equipment	1583.18	556.65
电气机械和器材制造业	Manufacture of Electrical Machinery and Equipment	20991.1	1310.11
计算机、通信和其他电子设备制造业	Manufacture of Communication Equipment, Computers and Other Electronic Equipment	46693.22	2573.07
仪器仪表制造业	Manufacture of Instruments and Meters	1614.87	198.06
其他制造业	Other Manufactures	632.72	21.36
废弃资源综合利用业	Comprehensive Utilization of Waste	649.08	38.28
金属制品、机械和设备修理业	Manufacture of Metal Products,Machinery and Equipment Maintenance	236.63	96.65
电力、热力生产和供应业	Production and Supply of Electric Power and Heat Power	9184.45	1920.13
燃气生产和供应业	Production and Supply of Gas	2466.14	1019.57
水的生产和供应业	Production and Supply of Water	832.44	127.57

注：本表产值按当年价格计算。

Gross Output Value of Industry above Designated Size by City (2022)

(100 million yuan)

深 圳 Shenzhen	珠 海 Zhuhai	汕 头 Shantou	佛 山 Foshan	韶 关 Shaoguan	河 源 Heyuan	梅 州 Meizhou	惠 州 Huizhou	汕 尾 Shanwei
46259.43	**5916.09**	**3404.18**	**27965.42**	**1617.8**	**1459.82**	**858.68**	**11099.46**	**1251.04**
5497.03	850.61	383.03	1713.02	768.35	164.15	250.06	2399.25	173.11
171.08	98.09	102.77	105.67	6.95	71.23	1.48	3.82	16.08
	0.18	5.05	7.79	0.92		0.56	1.52	1.87
	0.23	7.58	40.15			0.96	0.41	
30653.4	3492.14	2779.35	20099.44	1377.58	942.84	759.17	6635.87	898.24
5090.37	1541.63	177.98	3110.94	114.48	143	30.84	1931.55	91.23
10232.9	778.58	236.81	4112.61	116.23	292.65	54.29	2468.55	217.81
7938.68	1851.58	2397.73	14039.53	264.06	313.44	238.89	2441.28	461.27
38320.76	4064.51	1006.44	13925.89	1353.74	1146.38	619.79	8658.18	789.77
26062.54	2494.29	339.68	10605.82	662.12	623.51	167.49	6343.06	666.03
7934.25	1321.55	1000.84	8947.85	418.68	353.94	354.91	1838.3	277.12
12262.64	2100.25	2063.66	8411.74	537.01	482.38	336.28	2918.09	307.89
714.04	170.43							
	14.83			0.6	35.74			
				44.64	4.92	7.46		
		1.58	1.47	2.97	7.29	5.09	25.54	1.14
40.77	2.8							
265.88	121.69	112.15	637.7	27.54	24.96	44.76	101.56	42.7
77.72	71.71	86.33	365.63	8.41	22.76	12.83	16.21	13.12
173.63	19.45	8.42	244.72	3.1	32.49	11.84	62.99	3.29
148.47		2.4		76.89		90.3	5.42	0.51
110.26	14.66	272.47	906.49	13.97	5.71	5.6	37.28	26.27
256.82	25.58	798.74	414.12	1.64	25.35	1.69	65.02	91.29
83.42	0.37	24.27	226.77	1.19	23.39	11.47	113.54	1.99
16.82	5.21	0.91	84.96	21.25	8.8	1	38.72	3.72
90.46	19.35	3.84	729.23		8.33	2.17	196.56	0.21
137.64	79.55	97.96	318.33	13.14	9.6	5.69	76.5	7.05
265.55	19.2	103.19	250.59	2.7	6.64	1.9	38.11	4.58
1764.11	21.31	337.11	601.62	31.8	73.88	10.21	132.95	68.84
33.24	97.55	0.28	120.42			0.24	1342.28	
396.97	499.31	235.47	1235.45	168.21	11.78	7.65	1147.88	7.5
499.22	237.13	78.78	291.45	11.14	12.52	8.91	39	
0.24	81.17	8.6	26.04		0.55	0.38	2.35	
816	145.8	327.58	1371.25	23.77	34.97	13.96	426.3	87.78
606.16	173.56	98.41	1687.72	78.77	87.97	103.86	383.99	70.34
33.63	114.53	0.15	647.64	409.27	168.96	19.27	17.7	
737.07	90.48	3.74	1402.57	139.47	11.16	15.96	82.51	
787.98	143.77	57.86	3046.07	84.62	28.92	8.44	290.05	28.48
1322.1	209.09	28.44	1308.09	41.2	24.79	7.4	138.77	95.29
2241.92	150.89	59.87	977.43	17.4	37.66	10.47	259.42	1.1
2090.58	70.13	41.44	1524.93	2.52	8.01	22.82	197.86	
207.89	69.33	0.74	107.48	0.42	1.99	0.31	66.54	16.27
3782.58	1416.62	109.9	7128.82	58.1	37	29.32	1310.69	141.47
25575.79	1092.75	107.35	706.01	78.45	524.33	206.05	3822.49	320.22
694.62	93.07	1.65	155.92	9.28	9.02	1.49	67.39	
342.56	0.35	11.31	28.96	1.2	6.44	0.23	17.29	0.45
118.37	16.26	45.77	139.95	30.19	0.51	5.59	35.37	1.34
24.81	93.54	1.97	0.22	0.53			3.33	0.68
1256.77	322.64	304.44	671.28	202.87	154.94	173.22	479.88	206.77
391.91	190.87	8.84	303.51	6.52	7.05	5.54	26.92	2.8
153.43	21.1	22.21	302.57	4.03	1.41	5.55	31.03	5.83

Note: Data in this table are calculated at current prices.

12-12 续表

单位：亿元

项 目	Item	东 莞 Dongguan	中 山 Zhongshan
总 计	**Total**	**24772.97**	**6772.54**
按经济类型分	Grouped by Ownership		
在总计中：国有控股工业	Of the Total:State-holding Industry	1289.31	496.64
国有工业	State-owned Industry	17.18	
集体工业	Collective-owned Industry	5.49	1.46
股份合作工业	Share-holding Cooperative Industry	2.51	
股份制工业	Share-holding Industry	16209.53	3815.87
外商投资工业	Foreign-funded Industry	3122.93	1669.34
港澳台投资工业	Industry with Funds from Hong Kong, Macao and Taiwan	5292.39	1219.97
按轻重工业分	Grouped by Light and Heavy Industries		
轻工业	Light Industry	7559.71	3259.82
重工业	Heavy Industry	17213.26	3512.72
按企业规模分	Grouped by Size of Enterprises		
大型企业	Large Enterprises	10363.74	2626.44
中型企业	Medium Enterprises	5556.18	1483.53
小微型企业	Small and Micro Enterprises	8853.05	2662.58
按行业分	Grouped by Sector		
煤炭开采和洗选业	Mining and Washing of Coal		
石油和天然气开采业	Extraction of Petroleum and Natural Gas		
黑色金属矿采选业	Mining and Dressing of Ferrous Metal Ores		
有色金属矿采选业	Mining and Dressing of Nonferrous Metal Ores		
非金属矿采选业	Mining and Dressing of Nonmetal Ores	1.23	
开采专业及辅助性活动	Mining Specialized and Auxiliary Operations		
其他采矿业	Mining and Dressing of Other Ores		
农副食品加工业	Processing of Farm and Sideline Food	850.61	55.06
食品制造业	Manufacture of Food	203.73	67.44
酒、饮料和精制茶制造业	Manufacture of Wine, Beverage and Refined Tea	89.8	41.27
烟草制品业	Tobacco Products		3.81
纺织业	Textile Industry	220.7	103.43
纺织服装、服饰业	Manufacture of Textile Garments, Footwear and Headgear	418.73	176.52
皮革、毛皮、羽毛及其制品和制鞋业	Leather, Fur, Feather, Down and Related Products	370.64	63.39
木材加工和木、竹、藤、棕、草制品业	Timber Processing, Bamboo, Cane, Palm Fiber & Straw Products	46.94	21.58
家具制造业	Manufacture of Furniture	378.13	154.79
造纸和纸制品业	Papermaking and Paper Products	998.7	122.5
印刷和记录媒介复制业	Printing and Record Medium Reproduction	342.34	53.06
文教、工美、体育和娱乐用品制造业	Manufacture of Cultural, Educational,Sports and Entertainment Articles	570.37	165.91
石油、煤炭及其他燃料加工业	Petroleum, Coal and other Fuel Processing	13.21	4.58
化学原料和化学制品制造业	Manufacture of Raw Chemical Materials and Chemical Products	649.05	289.83
医药制造业	Manufacture of Medicines	69.01	97.88
化学纤维制造业	Manufacture of Chemical Fibers	23.52	1.46
橡胶和塑料制品业	Rubber and Plastic Products	1334.4	369.97
非金属矿物制品业	Nonmetal Mineral Products	546.41	221.92
黑色金属冶炼和压延加工业	Smelting and Pressing of Ferrous Metals	68.93	112.05
有色金属冶炼和压延加工业	Smelting and Pressing of Nonferrous Metals	293.18	70.29
金属制品业	Metal Products	1428.29	412.72
通用设备制造业	Manufacture of General-purpose Machinery	1075.78	357.17
专用设备制造业	Manufacture of Special-purpose Machinery	1001.96	144.74
汽车制造业	Manufacture of Automobile	321.29	168.86
铁路、船舶、航空航天和其他运输设备制造业	Manufacture of Railway ,Ship,Aeronautics and Other Transport equipment	104.99	12.81
电气机械和器材制造业	Manufacture of Electrical Machinery and Equipment	2360.2	1981.78
计算机、通信和其他电子设备制造业	Manufacture of Communication Equipment, Computers and Other Electronic Equipment	9502.5	949.01
仪器仪表制造业	Manufacture of Instruments and Meters	276.58	74.37
其他制造业	Other Manufactures	127.93	49.93
废弃资源综合利用业	Comprehensive Utilization of Waste	3.33	4.48
金属制品、机械和设备修理业	Manufacture of Metal Products,Machinery and Equipment Maintenance	6.05	2.1
电力、热力生产和供应业	Production and Supply of Electric Power and Heat Power	888.54	339.32
燃气生产和供应业	Production and Supply of Gas	125.76	56.79
水的生产和供应业	Production and Supply of Water	60.12	21.72

12-12 continued

(100 million yuan)

江 门 Jiangmen	阳 江 Yangjiang	湛 江 Zhanjiang	茂 名 Maoming	肇 庆 Zhaoqing	清 远 Qingyuan	潮 州 Chaozhou	揭 阳 Jieyang	云 浮 Yunfu
5631.7	**2320.7**	**3371.13**	**2477.57**	**4385.41**	**2833.26**	**1387.93**	**2502.81**	**716.92**
655.79	1366.87	2140.47	1689.92	456.67	375.65	185.66	263.86	144.78
129.55	11.13	23.99	22.05	5.29	8.83	4.36	10.45	11.59
0.22			0.81	0.64	0.42	3.09	4.96	
1.04						5.43	0.51	
3320.6	1935.96	1855.87	2367.83	3442.11	2029.95	1157.31	2239.49	538.39
633.83	98.85	373.3	39.06	281.83	179.06	52.74	10.92	41.33
1484.37	260.56	1106.48	29.05	528.98	588.53	60.82	106.71	104.27
2326.36	358.34	837.26	346.13	1312.36	761.45	658.11	1468.13	186.28
3305.35	1962.36	2533.87	2131.44	3073.05	2071.81	729.82	1034.68	530.64
1500.39	862.36	2254.33	1551.88	1038.18	676.01	171.88	277.78	220.26
1694.81	985.69	388.42	348.55	1298.6	1115.94	185.35	576.51	216.45
2436.51	472.65	728.38	577.15	2048.64	1041.31	1030.7	1648.52	280.21
		274.9						
				2.32	0.16	0.2		0.09
		23.54	11.67	19.67	0.74			2.34
46.18	6.39	14.38	15.8	35.76	19.76	2.04	2.29	16.5
4.69		7.78		0.23				
294.79	157.71	463.76	247.35	100.61	105.66	70.38	81.81	31.98
310.61	52.46	17.69	8.26	73.41	6.5	64.67	174.23	4.14
18.96	1.9	18.92	0.13	32.24	34.53	11.93	3.39	0.64
		28.48						
127.3	1.19	5.36	3.36	89.86	43.6	3.12	131.02	3.51
39.9	5.78	3.43	15.08	19.48	2.33	11.95	154.69	9
32.39	3.18	16.02	6.89	63.38	117.06	37.03	249.32	0.38
32.95	5.91	19.21	9.73	48.5	11.25	3.37	14.25	7.04
88.29	8.64	17.45	0.36	74.29	53.6	0.72	6.05	0.31
316.73	12.14	160.06	4.17	99.17	24.79	35.23	50.25	27.43
61.9	2.05	9.93	1.11	26.83	11.01	52.97	58.47	0.82
28.3	1.05	0.63	8.58	59.4	59.71	10.79	37.66	8.86
5.12	0.06	1021.19	1477.73	0.21	0.59	50.28	18.71	
270.26	10.14	79.17	315.17	242.24	236.69	23.58	26.55	53.13
28.3	2.05	33.55	22.08	35.7	60.26	24.69	85.53	25.78
20.61				2.23	1.07		18.56	0.78
228.99	13.91	16.02	20.21	136.73	114.19	40.2	171.01	16.67
302.39	79.45	107.64	63.29	531.19	376.16	319.3	211.34	130.82
20.13	794.59	643.99	11.23	10.94	211.67	7.28	230.9	53.77
180.04	428.09	0.95	0.32	291.61	372.63	204.08	14.38	64.68
654.69	139.53	11.32	7.64	765.86	159.75	87.62	217.68	49.92
187.39	30.52	4.51	4.18	64.84	55	19.35	10.06	7.72
73.03	1.12	5.46	12.23	67.18	10.87	4.73	54.57	9.63
100.08	1.24	11.9		440.62	64.68		17.53	38.41
352.77	1.7	0.12	0.41	0.5	61.22		21.05	
604.89	85.35	46.3	2.47	349.52	71.14	12.58	133.33	18.92
620.21	3.26	2.69	6.14	262.22	215.17	60.41	34.05	31.06
6.48			0.21	7.93	1.16	3.2	11.96	2.5
14.93	0.25	0.44	0.22	3.4	2.49	0.27	2.7	
18.64	4.46	26.63	2.65	95.84	42.87	2.49	13.34	2.73
2.61		2.94		1.21				
460.63	441.65	255.15	186.38	223.07	232.7	161.48	213.83	88.74
56.74	19.69	9	7.85	97.77	44.05	57.75	21	6.21
19.81	5.22	10.59	4.67	9.43	8.2	4.24	11.3	2.41

12-13 各市规模以上工业增加值（2022年）

单位：亿元

项　　目	Item	全　省 Provincial Total	广　州 Guangzhou
总　计	**Total**	**37260.57**	**4912.19**
按经济类型分	Grouped by Ownership		
在总计中：国有控股工业	Of the Total:State-holding Industry	6407.02	2106.10
国有工业	State-owned Industry	229.35	44.80
集体工业	Collective-owned Industry	13.74	7.53
股份合作工业	Share-holding Cooperative Industry	13.03	2.49
股份制工业	Share-holding Industry	23426.65	2290.23
外商投资工业	Foreign-funded Industry	5860.16	2006.52
港澳台投资工业	Industry with Funds from Hong Kong, Macao and Taiwan	7441.79	551.22
按轻重工业分	Grouped by Light and Heavy Industries		
轻工业	Light Industry	12475.18	1623.83
重工业	Heavy Industry	24785.39	3288.36
按企业规模分	Grouped by Size of Enterprises		
大型企业	Large Enterprises	18776.54	2977.27
中型企业	Medium Enterprises	8720.97	877.57
小微型企业	Small and Micro Enterprises	9763.06	1057.35
按行业分	Grouped by Sector		
煤炭开采和洗选业	Mining and Washing of Coal		
石油和天然气开采业	Extraction of Petroleum and Natural Gas	1032.98	
黑色金属矿采选业	Mining and Dressing of Ferrous Metal Ores	21.25	
有色金属矿采选业	Mining and Dressing of Nonferrous Metal Ores	45.99	
非金属矿采选业	Mining and Dressing of Nonmetal Ores	83.14	-4.21
开采专业及辅助性活动	Mining Specialized and Auxiliary Operations	22.33	
其他采矿业	Mining and Dressing of Other Ores		
农副食品加工业	Processing of Farm and Sideline Food	407.73	43.44
食品制造业	Manufacture of Food	668.26	209.85
酒、饮料和精制茶制造业	Manufacture of Wine, Beverage and Refined Tea	322.48	104.40
烟草制品业	Tobacco Products	471.22	214.46
纺织业	Textile Industry	481.85	29.02
纺织服装、服饰业	Manufacture of Textile Garments, Footwear and Headgear	647.38	68.82
皮革、毛皮、羽毛及其制品和制鞋业	Leather, Fur, Feather, Down and Related Products	380.25	33.09
木材加工和木、竹、藤、棕、草制品业	Timber Processing, Bamboo, Cane, Palm Fiber & Straw	74.81	3.68
家具制造业	Manufacture of Furniture	502.04	73.27
造纸和纸制品业	Papermaking and Paper Products	450.08	27.48
印刷和记录媒介复制业	Printing and Record Medium Reproduction	361.00	39.85
文教、工美、体育和娱乐用品制造业	Manufacture of Cultural, Educational and Sports Articles	667.83	47.61
石油、煤炭及其他燃料加工业	Petroleum, Coal and other Fuel Processing	898.80	157.49
化学原料和化学制品制造业	Manufacture of Raw Chemical Materials and Chemical Products	1213.73	333.68
医药制造业	Manufacture of Medicines	808.74	222.31
化学纤维制造业	Manufacture of Chemical Fibers	42.08	1.80
橡胶和塑料制品业	Rubber and Plastic Products	1396.03	117.97
非金属矿物制品业	Nonmetal Mineral Products	1295.59	94.92
黑色金属冶炼和压延加工业	Smelting and Pressing of Ferrous Metals	362.56	19.44
有色金属冶炼和压延加工业	Smelting and Pressing of Nonferrous Metals	407.45	13.12
金属制品业	Metal Products	1796.81	89.46
通用设备制造业	Manufacture of General-purpose Equipment	1272.90	195.87
专用设备制造业	Manufacture of Special-purpose Equipment	1558.47	141.01
汽车制造业	Manufacture of Transport Equipment	2280.35	1298.82
铁路、船舶、航空航天和其他运输设备制造业	Manufacture of Railway ,Ship,Aeronautics and Other Transport equipment	302.19	77.83
电气机械和器材制造业	Manufacture of Electrical Machinery and Equipment	4430.59	216.26
计算机、通信和其他电子设备制造业	Manufacture of Communication Equipment, Computers and Other Electronic Equipment	9367.69	562.56
仪器仪表制造业	Manufacture of Instruments and Meters	451.18	52.84
其他制造业	Other Manufactures	175.23	5.36
废弃资源综合利用业	Comprehensive Utilization of Waste	72.81	2.68
金属制品、机械和设备修理业	Manufacture of Metal Products,Machinery and Equipment Maintenance	68.83	39.29
电力、热力生产和供应业	Production and Supply of Electric Power and Heat Power	1893.49	282.10
燃气生产和供应业	Production and Supply of Gas	193.06	28.44
水的生产和供应业	Production and Supply of Water	331.36	68.19

注：本表工业增加值按收入法、当年价格计算。

Value-added of Industry above Designated Size by City (2022)

(100 million yuan)

深 圳 Shenzhen	珠 海 Zhuhai	汕 头 Shantou	佛 山 Foshan	韶 关 Shaoguan	河 源 Heyuan	梅 州 Meizhou	惠 州 Huizhou	汕 尾 Shanwei
10106.69	**1450.09**	**721.67**	**5603.21**	**321.82**	**343.68**	**240.18**	**2185.30**	**174.34**
1281.95	153.92	71.41	302.49	170.71	34.66	111.77	425.22	57.78
51.26	12.44	18.77	20.43	4.36	14.38	1.19	1.53	1.81
	0.05	1.09	1.77	0.39		0.03	0.90	0.38
	0.03	1.36	7.18			0.41	0.07	
6725.93	887.82	571.53	3969.11	270.77	226.18	214.00	1305.68	115.40
916.21	344.01	49.68	656.44	15.20	29.90	9.54	299.51	21.46
2391.41	204.36	59.23	864.37	30.87	70.03	13.77	563.90	32.80
1676.55	629.66	530.78	3097.12	109.68	81.11	108.87	566.49	52.56
8430.14	820.42	190.88	2506.08	212.15	262.58	131.31	1618.80	121.77
6364.22	757.97	78.79	2472.78	96.77	135.43	43.40	1187.21	83.18
1812.80	282.07	230.36	1854.77	120.21	100.97	137.32	443.96	25.38
1929.66	410.04	412.52	1275.66	104.84	107.28	59.46	554.13	65.77
698.42	76.06							
	4.20			0.11	15.83	-0.01		
				33.81	1.47	3.71		
		0.39	0.18	1.42	2.17	1.33	5.81	26.47
16.77	1.22							
22.99	7.25	10.93	71.64	1.45	1.78	4.21	10.81	4.44
22.86	32.96	21.56	106.45	2.27	4.22	2.88	3.30	1.53
48.56	5.42	1.31	62.29	1.06	14.34	2.73	18.06	0.41
83.12		0.84		67.13		78.90	0.95	-0.16
27.50	3.80	54.50	187.71	2.54	1.26	1.05	9.55	4.72
66.39	6.30	174.13	97.20	0.58	7.11	0.69	19.31	9.84
18.96	0.09	5.38	47.29	0.35	5.88	5.56	37.44	0.28
1.88	1.91	0.20	14.85	3.73	1.48	0.17	6.38	0.48
17.05	5.89	1.00	149.68		2.34	0.39	48.80	0.01
24.33	10.56	16.65	58.06	1.91	1.68	0.21	12.55	0.88
72.62	4.85	25.00	49.86	1.03	1.98	0.32	11.91	0.55
130.32	6.32	78.53	75.35	12.67	19.55	2.18	34.25	3.61
0.63	15.33	0.07	21.26			0.03	228.50	
80.02	56.51	44.61	213.80	36.16	2.24	1.69	88.71	0.96
181.09	100.11	32.23	88.06	5.00	3.28	2.17	10.70	
0.07	16.72	1.81	7.71		0.17	0.28	0.89	
182.31	44.72	70.77	289.85	4.60	8.51	3.33	111.90	11.12
81.07	28.16	18.48	336.79	17.65	21.81	25.45	67.22	8.89
2.66	12.74		82.13	9.09	34.19	1.21	2.42	
16.50	4.25	0.82	170.21	15.50	2.26	2.04	6.06	
174.67	35.88	10.25	563.09	9.63	6.19	2.40	69.34	2.02
325.66	42.46	6.99	242.58	8.90	5.61	1.80	32.46	2.27
664.02	47.57	13.36	212.98	4.17	9.57	2.81	68.07	0.22
348.49	16.35	9.79	332.99	0.79	1.61	5.22	52.35	
60.74	21.85	0.05	23.16	0.03	0.92	0.05	13.55	0.94
713.01	436.46	17.10	1663.36	13.18	9.13	4.51	266.51	15.59
5261.85	271.26	25.65	144.81	16.76	116.01	45.83	794.42	37.29
188.32	31.81	0.64	37.13	1.45	2.78	0.43	20.14	
105.94	0.10	3.21	6.08	0.30	1.87	0.05	4.62	0.10
5.08	2.82	6.93	11.72	6.21	0.28	0.43	4.72	0.08
11.39	14.51	0.48	0.15	0.15			0.79	0.08
317.52	56.68	57.53	122.55	39.82	34.75	33.12	102.70	38.83
72.58	15.45	1.76	22.29	0.74	0.67	0.62	4.14	0.60
61.32	11.52	8.72	89.97	1.64	0.73	2.40	15.98	2.29

Note: Data of value-added of industry in this table are calculated with income approach and at current prices.

12-13 续表

单位：亿元

项 目	Item	东 莞 Dongguan	中 山 Zhongshan
总 计	**Total**	**4959.60**	**1363.20**
按经济类型分	Grouped by Ownership		
在总计中：国有控股工业	Of the Total:State-holding Industry	227.05	94.07
国有工业	State-owned Industry	5.27	
集体工业	Collective-owned Industry	-0.85	0.44
股份合作工业	Share-holding Cooperative Industry	0.60	
股份制工业	Share-holding Industry	3024.11	742.00
外商投资工业	Foreign-funded Industry	632.87	312.56
港澳台投资工业	Industry with Funds from Hong Kong, Macao and Taiwan	1275.09	294.58
按轻重工业分	Grouped by Light and Heavy Industries		
轻工业	Light Industry	1647.48	745.19
重工业	Heavy Industry	3312.12	618.01
按企业规模分	Grouped by Size of Enterprises		
大型企业	Large Enterprises	2102.76	510.88
中型企业	Medium Enterprises	1286.17	357.31
小微型企业	Small and Micro Enterprises	1570.66	495.00
按行业分	Grouped by Sector		
煤炭开采和洗选业	Mining and Washing of Coal		
石油和天然气开采业	Extraction of Petroleum and Natural Gas		
黑色金属矿采选业	Mining and Dressing of Ferrous Metal Ores		
有色金属矿采选业	Mining and Dressing of Nonferrous Metal Ores		
非金属矿采选业	Mining and Dressing of Nonmetal Ores	0.12	
开采专业及辅助性活动	Mining Specialized and Auxiliary Operations		
其他采矿业	Mining and Dressing of Other Ores		
农副食品加工业	Processing of Farm and Sideline Food	70.94	6.23
食品制造业	Manufacture of Food	45.80	20.46
酒、饮料和精制茶制造业	Manufacture of Wine, Beverage and Refined Tea	23.39	11.63
烟草制品业	Tobacco Products		1.11
纺织业	Textile Industry	60.05	22.09
纺织服装、服饰业	Manufacture of Textile Garments, Footwear and Headgear	95.78	44.02
皮革、毛皮、羽毛及其制品和制鞋业	Leather, Fur, Feather, Down and Related Products	89.03	18.44
木材加工和木、竹、藤、棕、草制品业	Timber Processing, Bamboo, Cane, Palm Fiber & Straw	9.72	3.95
家具制造业	Manufacture of Furniture	105.51	40.70
造纸和纸制品业	Papermaking and Paper Products	149.34	19.29
印刷和记录媒介复制业	Printing and Record Medium Reproduction	85.29	14.51
文教、工美、体育和娱乐用品制造业	Manufacture of Cultural, Educational and Sports Articles	160.62	45.25
石油、煤炭及其他燃料加工业	Petroleum, Coal and other Fuel Processing	0.96	0.46
化学原料和化学制品制造业	Manufacture of Raw Chemical Materials and Chemical Products	97.77	59.39
医药制造业	Manufacture of Medicines	31.06	31.75
化学纤维制造业	Manufacture of Chemical Fibers	4.59	0.25
橡胶和塑料制品业	Rubber and Plastic Products	316.66	82.15
非金属矿物制品业	Nonmetal Mineral Products	105.34	35.46
黑色金属冶炼和压延加工业	Smelting and Pressing of Ferrous Metals	6.15	6.42
有色金属冶炼和压延加工业	Smelting and Pressing of Nonferrous Metals	26.17	6.05
金属制品业	Metal Products	373.42	93.36
通用设备制造业	Manufacture of General-purpose Equipment	233.09	88.16
专用设备制造业	Manufacture of Special-purpose Equipment	296.76	37.75
汽车制造业	Manufacture of Transport Equipment	70.85	42.91
铁路、船舶、航空航天和其他运输设备制造业	Manufacture of Railway ,Ship,Aeronautics and Other Transport equipment	22.42	0.90
电气机械和器材制造业	Manufacture of Electrical Machinery and Equipment	492.96	371.67
计算机、通信和其他电子设备制造业	Manufacture of Communication Equipment, Computers and Other Electronic Equipment	1677.23	145.70
仪器仪表制造业	Manufacture of Instruments and Meters	86.66	21.98
其他制造业	Other Manufactures	28.23	13.25
废弃资源综合利用业	Comprehensive Utilization of Waste	0.32	0.60
金属制品、机械和设备修理业	Manufacture of Metal Products,Machinery and Equipment Maintenance	2.57	0.36
电力、热力生产和供应业	Production and Supply of Electric Power and Heat Power	161.86	59.76
燃气生产和供应业	Production and Supply of Gas	9.45	6.85
水的生产和供应业	Production and Supply of Water	19.50	10.33

12-13 continued

(100 million yuan)

江门 Jiangmen	阳江 Yangjiang	湛江 Zhanjiang	茂名 Maoming	肇庆 Zhaoqing	清远 Qingyuan	潮州 Chaozhou	揭阳 Jieyang	云浮 Yunfu
1136.07	**372.83**	**836.44**	**385.04**	**728.56**	**570.34**	**240.10**	**484.50**	**124.73**
120.00	245.82	445.40	266.80	75.56	71.33	38.94	76.90	29.16
27.64	4.32	3.53	3.74	1.82	5.88	2.50	2.89	0.77
0.24			0.24	0.24	-0.01	0.42	0.88	
0.13						0.73	0.02	
589.89	212.61	316.68	359.21	527.41	352.48	201.56	434.69	89.34
151.78	12.58	272.68	8.17	56.09	45.35	8.09	1.15	10.37
357.62	140.97	241.98	9.22	120.77	163.89	11.95	21.40	22.37
497.16	71.72	129.12	53.30	232.88	177.20	126.28	277.27	40.93
638.91	301.12	707.32	331.74	495.69	393.14	113.82	207.23	83.80
363.71	197.63	652.57	246.23	199.23	165.68	51.75	50.78	38.28
364.52	68.71	74.70	39.17	216.05	231.60	41.80	112.13	43.40
407.84	106.50	109.17	99.64	313.28	173.07	146.55	321.59	43.05
		258.50						
				1.02	0.02	0.05		0.02
		2.03	1.77	1.68	0.07			1.46
13.85	2.71	2.46	6.07	7.85	5.20	0.49	0.52	10.31
0.32		3.92		0.10				
26.73	10.86	28.98	27.57	12.51	15.95	13.33	12.44	3.27
110.43	16.39	2.87	2.21	13.47	1.34	12.08	34.54	0.80
3.87	0.92	3.91		7.17	10.11	1.78	1.05	0.05
		24.88						
26.28	0.07	0.95	1.08	16.29	8.02	0.57	23.85	0.95
10.21	1.44	0.96	4.26	3.89	0.82	3.42	28.22	4.01
8.52	2.07	2.70	2.02	14.94	35.44	6.12	46.43	0.23
5.53	1.03	2.48	2.25	9.15	1.75	0.69	2.68	0.82
19.54	2.72	1.64	0.22	13.99	18.23	0.16	0.82	0.07
51.86	3.03	32.37	1.13	15.26	2.79	4.17	8.99	7.54
19.28	0.48	3.83	0.25	6.05	3.04	7.41	12.76	0.13
6.85	0.26	0.15	2.72	11.71	17.74	1.86	8.01	2.27
1.02		229.00	215.92	0.04	0.10	7.16	20.83	
48.59	1.64	3.28	30.03	36.51	62.90	3.73	4.23	7.28
11.27	0.46	12.12	5.06	11.41	20.74	14.63	17.68	7.61
4.60				0.72	0.12		2.29	0.06
50.25	3.59	3.63	4.94	27.33	23.16	4.55	33.43	1.26
56.44	15.67	18.31	13.81	120.12	104.38	68.50	36.13	20.98
2.02	31.17	103.35	2.37	1.74	16.31	0.25	31.96	-3.05
26.41	30.76	0.18	0.06	48.77	21.98	9.50	2.73	4.09
131.48	32.57	2.31	2.31	107.94	23.90	8.47	45.18	12.94
41.21	8.99	1.30	1.17	15.54	11.26	3.91	2.01	1.65
21.49	0.24	2.03	2.95	15.85	2.98	1.93	10.56	2.14
21.63	0.38	3.51		40.72	20.16		3.61	10.19
67.70	0.52	0.01	0.12	0.15	8.24		3.01	
121.79	9.51	7.89	0.53	32.67	12.23	2.39	21.78	2.05
121.85	0.61	0.44	2.05	68.30	39.97	20.23	6.93	7.93
1.69			0.08	2.20	0.75	0.60	1.35	0.36
3.86	0.08	0.07	0.04	0.80	0.68	0.05	0.53	
3.09	0.78	5.46	1.15	13.47	3.48	0.25	2.66	0.59
1.25		1.36		-3.55				
83.20	188.07	63.86	46.72	42.75	69.81	35.51	42.00	14.37
0.30	2.55	0.46	0.73	5.64	4.08	3.08	11.71	0.93
11.67	3.26	5.24	3.46	4.35	2.56	3.22	3.59	1.43

12-14 规模以上工业企业主要经济指标
Main Indicators of Industrial Enterprises above Designated Size

年份 Year	全部就业人员平均人数(万人) Annual Average Number of Employed Persons (10000 persons)	总产值(亿元) Gross Output Value of Industry (100 million yuan)	固定资产原价(亿元) Original Value of Fixed Assets (100 million yuan)	营业收入(亿元) Business Revenue (100 million yuan)	利润总额(亿元) Total Profits (100 million yuan)	利税总额(亿元) Total Pre-tax Profits (100 million yuan)	百元固定资产实现利税(元) Pre-tax Profits per 100 yuan of Original Value of Fixed Assets (yuan)	总资产贡献率(%) Ratio of Total Assets to Industrial Output Value (%)	产值利税率(%) Ratio of Pre-tax Profits to Gross Output Value (%)	百元营业收入实现利税(元) Pre-tax Profits per 100 yuan of Business Revenue (yuan)	全员劳动生产率(元/人) Overall Labor Productivity (yuan/person)
1978	170.51	168.91	111.42		16.78	32.91	29.54		19.48		9906
1979	171.76	181.96	129.09	170.09	15.21	34.48	26.71		18.45	20.27	10594
1980	182.39	198.83	136.59	189.97	19.41	38.51	28.19		19.37	20.27	10902
1981	189.08	226.26	152.58	215.09	21.18	42.12	27.60		18.61	19.58	11966
1982	194.33	245.54	172.00	231.20	22.44	44.62	25.94		18.17	19.30	12635
1983	197.50	275.25	226.58	226.91	26.17	48.59	21.45		17.65	21.42	13937
1984	241.42	336.45	221.46	313.33	30.44	56.83	25.66		16.89	18.14	13937
1985	298.66	438.91	269.13	412.77	39.09	75.99	29.23		17.31	18.41	14696
1986	323.16	522.35	335.19	498.80	37.74	80.90	24.14		15.49	16.22	16164
1987	353.95	711.04	433.95	692.47	51.35	102.24	23.56		14.38	14.76	20089
1988	382.19	1056.47	540.37	1016.20	68.67	140.65	26.03		13.31	13.84	27643
1989	387.90	1321.33	700.66	1222.20	60.42	138.71	19.80		10.50	11.35	34064
1990	390.28	1379.98	843.88	1287.91	37.04	121.50	14.40		8.80	9.43	35359
1991	433.18	2018.62	1339.04	1875.02	71.83	188.08	14.05		9.32	10.03	46600
1992	450.99	2696.47	1485.36	2537.84	115.34	248.78	22.32		9.23	9.80	59790
1993	478.39	4085.35	2099.09	3920.98	211.80	397.40	18.93		9.73	10.14	85379
1994	537.57	5325.35	3309.63	4826.68	210.36	478.41	14.46		8.89	9.91	99063
1995	537.83	6325.19	4298.15	6195.84	171.87	445.53	10.37		7.04	7.19	117606
1996	529.13	7308.51	5066.23	6808.08	178.75	489.26	9.66		6.69	7.19	36094
1997	522.94	8201.71	5904.95	7767.79	270.90	617.90	10.46	7.54	7.53	7.95	40040
1998	548.59	9738.56	6968.36	9243.42	224.89	622.82	8.94	7.37	6.40	6.74	44553
1999	537.77	10538.17	7399.10	10208.99	356.79	778.94	10.53	7.62	7.39	7.63	50307
2000	572.89	12480.93	8005.77	12380.65	564.75	1042.77	13.03	8.86	8.35	8.42	58836
2001	578.94	14035.35	8655.82	13891.46	595.60	1139.98	13.17	8.70	8.12	8.21	67012
2002	644.39	16378.60	9550.47	16247.73	769.09	1380.24	14.45	9.17	8.43	8.50	58940
2003	741.17	21513.46	10768.77	21566.93	1075.41	1850.90	17.19	10.42	8.60	8.56	77150
2004	996.44	29554.92	12713.34	28998.45	1449.96	2329.79	18.33	10.52	7.90	8.03	74661
2005	1085.65	35942.74	14453.16	34781.58	1693.99	2877.81	19.91	11.29	8.01	8.27	86735
2006	1203.58	44674.75	17824.33	43550.87	2217.73	3907.10	21.92	12.24	8.75	8.97	97882
2007	1307.40	55252.86	19763.42	53927.94	3061.60	5105.93	25.83	13.59	9.24	9.46	107880
2008	1493.38	65424.61	24529.17	63371.65	3272.60	6136.69	25.02	14.32	9.38	9.68	117940
2009	1436.02	68275.77	26293.23	66117.81	4204.40	6793.59	25.84	14.18	9.95	10.27	126984
2010	1568.00	85824.64	33489.49	84114.85	6239.64	9418.42	28.12	15.63	10.97	11.20	129709
2011	1463.86	94871.68	33244.26	92996.88	5874.03	9608.33	28.9	14.98	10.13	10.33	147987
2012	1452.16	95602.09	35983.70	93821.74	5464.90	9383.63	26.08	13.94	9.82	10.00	156463
2013	1455.81	109673.07	39339.68	106361.21	6496.42	11008.36	27.98	14.53	10.04	10.35	182303
2014	1455.78	119713.04	43635.95	115451.13	7014.99	11663.66	26.73	13.97	9.74	10.10	193633
2015	1439.33	124649.16	48104.10	119157.86	7723.16	12375.00	25.73	13.58	9.93	10.39	204582
2016	1417.84	133768.04	52729.34	129151.31	8383.04	13150.85	24.94	12.98	9.83	10.18	220972
2017	1403.19	135722.42	52619.74	133924.37	8864.36	13769.27	26.17	12.45	10.15	10.28	223415
2018	1341.31	140398.93	53725.45	142597.86	8748.68	13706.38	25.51	11.56	9.31	9.61	235271
2019	1315.80	146121.72	58026.73	146726.43	9140.48	13766.51	23.72	10.49	9.42	9.38	246953
2020	1277.06	148469.69	62452.78	149930.12	9572.09	14119.76	22.61	9.82	9.51	9.42	254491
2021	1343.58	171979.82	68125.54	173649.71	11278.35	16325.16	23.96	9.71	9.49	9.40	277665
2022	1332.56	180933.44	74967.63	183027.35	10329.25	15857.14	21.15	8.47	8.76	8.66	279615

注：1.利税总额包括增值税。
2.全员劳动生产率1996年后按工业增加值计算。
3.1997年以前为独立核算工业企业，1998年起统计口径改为年主营业务收入500万元及以上的规模以上工业，2011年调整为年主营业务收入2000万元及以上工业企业，2021年调整为主业务收入2000万元及以上工业企业和工业个体经营户。
4.本表中营业收入数据2017年及以前为主营业务收入数据，2018年后为营业收入数据。

Note:a) Total pre-tax profits include value-added tax.
b) Since 1996, figures of overall labor productivity have been calculated by value-added of industry.
c) From 1998 to 2010, data are statistics of industrial enterprises above designated size with annual principal business revenue of over 5 million yuan, while data prior to 1997 are statistics of industrial enterprises with independent accounting systems. Since 2011, data are statistics of legal person industrial enterprises with annual principal business revenue of over 20 million yuan. It is adjusted to industrial enterprises and industrial self-employed households with main business income of 20 million yuan and above in 2021.
d) The indicator was Revenue from Principal Business in 2017 and before,and are Business Revenue since 2018.

12-15 规模以上国有控股工业企业主要经济指标
Main Indicators of State-owned and State-holding Industrial Enterprises above Designated Size

年份 Year	全部就业人员平均人数（万人） Annual Average Number of Employed Persons (10000 persons)	总产值（亿元） Gross Output Value of Industry (100 million yuan)	固定资产原价（亿元） Original Value of Fixed Assets (100 million yuan)	营业收入（亿元） Business Revenue (100 million yuan)	利润总额（亿元） Total Profits (100 million yuan)	利税总额（亿元） Total Pre-tax Profits (100 million yuan)	百元固定资产实现利税（元） Pre-tax Profits per 100 yuan of Original Value of Fixed Assets (yuan)	总资产贡献率（%） Ratio of Total Assets to Industrial Output Value (%)	产值利税率（%） Ratio of Pre-tax Profits to Gross Output Value (%)	百元主营业务收入实现利税（元） Pre-tax Profits per 100 yuan of Principal Business Revenue (yuan)	全员劳动生产率（元/人） Overall Labor Productivity (yuan/person)
1978	120.35	122.28	96.06			26.09	27.16		21.34		10159
1979	121.97	132.30	103.51	126.87		26.89	25.96		20.31	21.18	10847
1980	126.09	136.30	107.27	127.97		28.33	25.90		20.57	22.19	10829
1981	132.60	153.54	118.82	147.85		31.18	26.24		20.31	21.09	11579
1982	139.90	165.82	131.82	158.43		33.29	25.26		20.08	21.01	11853
1983	142.18	188.09	147.53	178.04		38.18	25.88		20.30	21.45	13228
1984	143.08	222.35	162.13	205.73		44.02	27.15		19.80	21.39	15540
1985	144.14	277.87	203.80	265.05		56.34	27.64		20.28	21.26	19278
1986	150.14	312.74	235.47	305.42		59.70	25.36		19.09	19.55	20829
1987	156.48	400.55	294.46	402.63		72.44	24.60		18.09	17.99	25598
1988	162.43	555.41	328.58	545.00		91.05	27.71		16.39	16.71	34194
1989	162.85	670.95	404.50	631.61		94.11	23.26		14.93	14.90	41200
1990	163.80	713.88	488.36	689.83		84.35	17.27		11.82	12.23	43582
1991	173.85	906.72	612.24	853.62		116.26	18.99		12.82	13.62	52155
1992	171.60	1118.86	751.42	1073.94		131.24	17.47		11.73	12.22	65202
1993	153.26	1371.58	856.85	1372.66		169.40	19.77		12.35	12.34	89494
1994	152.25	1498.80	1076.47	1400.87		176.81	16.42		11.80	12.62	98443
1995	142.83	1396.35	1315.16	1499.25		160.57	12.21		11.50	10.71	97763
1996	137.50	1476.12	1599.77	1555.28		139.01	8.69		9.42	8.94	34057
1997	124.71	1505.06	1794.89	1657.79		160.92	8.97		10.69	9.71	36596
1998	102.67	1453.79	1790.91	1616.64		163.10	9.11		11.22	10.09	47019
1999	128.16	3025.68	3520.17	3153.04		376.11	10.68	8.63	12.34	11.93	72606
2000	104.39	3126.12	3513.50	3583.55	226.08	433.35	12.33	9.09	13.86	12.09	91413
2001	91.77	3236.65	3982.54	3757.95	241.30	486.46	12.21	9.53	15.03	12.94	112515
2002	83.25	3264.46	3942.57	3800.38	224.39	483.25	12.26	9.34	14.80	12.72	132894
2003	75.20	3949.03	4603.66	4717.48	623.49	623.49	13.54	10.88	15.79	13.22	191590
2004	72.53	6039.24	4913.92	6031.47	423.55	779.41	15.86	12.39	12.91	12.92	213941
2005	69.42	6375.54	5153.83	6261.70	387.31	800.26	15.53	13.03	12.55	12.78	243447
2006	60.80	7253.17	6557.86	6887.69	672.39	1213.73	18.50	14.89	16.73	17.62	391250
2007	60.86	8603.94	6702.65	8258.85	926.24	1603.72	23.92	17.68	18.63	19.41	464322
2008	77.84	11144.50	8327.10	11045.88	782.48	1676.74	20.14	15.49	15.05	15.18	430063
2009	75.33	10790.11	9249.22	10637.39	861.47	1747.60	18.89	14.73	16.20	16.43	457743
2010	78.89	13166.37	10456.03	13418.41	1235.97	2398.44	22.94	17.21	18.22	17.87	518203
2011	82.98	13927.70	10891.43	13871.28	723.19	1963.69	18.03	13.54	14.10	14.16	441471
2012	82.87	15529.16	12395.46	15602.52	700.33	2172.26	17.52	14.03	13.99	13.92	515822
2013	81.67	17525.16	13124.26	17095.26	1105.5	2800.64	21.34	16.57	15.98	16.38	625429
2014	79.95	18225.94	14561.95	17804.39	1081.26	2810.73	19.30	15.61	15.42	15.79	615329
2015	83.23	17032.30	15949.18	16453.02	1196.46	2660.82	16.68	13.53	15.62	16.17	606956
2016	82.67	17172.18	17041.31	16266.66	1437.99	2889.08	16.95	13.36	16.82	17.76	626612
2017	78.17	19525.92	17858.14	19783.07	1597.99	3144.43	17.61	13.04	16.10	15.89	699173
2018	74.93	20855.98	19117.62	22071.06	1559.97	3150.36	16.48	12.93	14.93	14.27	742900
2019	71.17	21270.03	20440.64	21286.03	1343.26	2636.84	12.90	10.21	12.40	12.39	725147
2020	68.68	21191.00	21222.22	21279.76	1250.19	2512.04	11.84	9.16	11.85	11.80	699905
2021	74.91	28733.57	24230.32	28816.61	1676.42	3387.13	13.98	9.40	11.79	11.75	829085
2022	76.62	32513.46	27246.31	32626.42	1436.88	3311.11	12.15	8.16	10.18	10.15	836185

注：1998年以前为国有工业，1999年起为国有及国有控股工业，2007年起改为国有控股工业。

Note: Data prior to 1998 are statistics of state-owned industrial enterprises,data since 1999 are statistics of state-owned and state-holding industrial enterprises, and data since 2007 are statistics of state-holding industrial enterprises.

12-16 规模以上工业企业主要经济指标（2022年）

单位：亿元

项　　目	Item	企业单位数（个） Number of Enterprises (unit)	工业总产值（当年价） Gross Industrial Output Value (at current prices)
全　省	**Provincial Total**	**70725**	**180933.44**
按经济类型分	Grouped by Ownership		
在总计中：国有控股工业	Of the Total: State-holding Industry	1573	32513.46
国有工业	State-owned Industry	258	941.32
集体工业	Collective-owned Industry	73	48.66
股份合作工业	Share-holding Cooperative Industry	46	67.62
股份制工业	Share-holding Industry	56499	118899.83
外商投资工业	Foreign-funded Industry	3794	27898.05
港澳台投资工业	Industry with Funds from Hong Kong, Macao and Taiwan	7942	31506.28
按轻重工业分	Grouped by Light and Heavy Industries		
轻工业	Light Industry	31685	54766.14
重工业	Heavy Industry	39040	126167.29
按企业规模分	Grouped by Size of Enterprises		
大型企业	Large Enterprises	1438	82354.91
中型企业	Medium Enterprises	6449	40038.23
小微型企业	Small and Micro Enterprises	62838	58540.30
按行业分	Grouped by Sector		
煤炭开采和洗选业	Mining and Washing of Coal		
石油和天然气开采业	Extraction of Petroleum and Natural Gas	3	1159.37
黑色金属矿采选业	Mining and Dressing of Ferrous Metal Ores	12	53.95
有色金属矿采选业	Mining and Dressing of Nonferrous Metal Ores	28	114.99
非金属矿采选业	Mining and Dressing of Nonmetal Ores	226	237.24
开采专业及辅助性活动	Mining Specialized and Auxiliary Operations	8	56.27
其他采矿业	Mining and Dressing of Other Ores		
农副食品加工业	Processing of Farm and Sideline Food	1285	4272.63
食品制造业	Manufacture of Food	930	2232.95
酒、饮料和精制茶制造业	Manufacture of Wine, Beverage and Refined Tea	237	1173.87
烟草制品业	Tobacco Products	46	601.72
纺织业	Textile Industry	1685	2261.45
纺织服装、服饰业	Manufacture of Textile Garments, Footwear and Headgear	2671	2798.78
皮革、毛皮、羽毛及其制品和制鞋业	Leather, Fur, Feather, Down and Related Products	1757	1599.61
木材加工和木、竹、藤、棕、草制品业	Timber Processing, Bamboo, Cane, Palm Fiber & Straw Products	570	426.31
家具制造业	Manufacture of Furniture	1956	2207.71
造纸和纸制品业	Papermaking and Paper Products	1598	2767.12
印刷和记录媒介复制业	Printing and Record Medium Reproduction	1213	1438.37
文教、工美、体育和娱乐用品制造业	Manufacture of Cultural, Educational,Sports and Entertainment Articles	2081	4145.36
石油、煤炭及其他燃料加工业	Petroleum, Coal and other Fuel Processing	122	4945.41
化学原料和化学制品制造业	Manufacture of Raw Chemical Materials and Chemical Products	3321	7233.54
医药制造业	Manufacture of Medicines	628	2264.35
化学纤维制造业	Manufacture of Chemical Fibers	93	196.54
橡胶和塑料制品业	Rubber and Plastic Products	6241	6283.50
非金属矿物制品业	Nonmetal Mineral Products	3890	6789.28
黑色金属冶炼和压延加工业	Smelting and Pressing of Ferrous Metals	531	3845.87
有色金属冶炼和压延加工业	Smelting and Pressing of Nonferrous Metals	1149	5066.77
金属制品业	Metal Products	7175	8816.38
通用设备制造业	Manufacture of General-purpose Machinery	4095	5793.28
专用设备制造业	Manufacture of Special-purpose Machinery	4234	5673.58
汽车制造业	Manufacture of Automobile	1140	11593.39
铁路、船舶、航空航天和其他运输设备制造业	Manufacture of Railway ,Ship,Aeronautics and Other Transport equipment	541	1583.18
电气机械和器材制造业	Manufacture of Electrical Machinery and Equipment	8246	20991.10
计算机、通信和其他电子设备制造业	Manufacture of Communication Equipment, Computers and Other Electronic Equipment	9672	46693.22
仪器仪表制造业	Manufacture of Instruments and Meters	1186	1614.87
其他制造业	Other Manufactures	535	632.72
废弃资源综合利用业	Comprehensive Utilization of Waste	271	649.08
金属制品、机械和设备修理业	Manufacture of Metal Products,Machinery and Equipment Maintenance	89	236.63
电力、热力生产和供应业	Production and Supply of Electric Power and Heat Power	567	9184.45
燃气生产和供应业	Production and Supply of Gas	291	2466.14
水的生产和供应业	Production and Supply of Water	402	832.44

Main Economic Indicators of Industrial Enterprises above Designated Size (2022)

(100 million yuan)

工业增加值 Value-added of Industry	年末资产总计 Total Assets at the Year-end	流动资产合计 Total Working Capital	营业收入 Business Revenue	营业成本 Cost of Business	税金及附加 Tax and Extra Charges on Main Business	利润总额 Total Profits	利税总额 Total Pre-tax Profits	本年应交增值税 Value-added Tax Payable in Current Year	全部就业人员年平均人数(万人) Annual Average Number of Employed Persons (10000 persons)
37260.57	**196419.19**	**117937.22**	**183027.35**	**153237.94**	**1929.33**	**10329.25**	**15857.14**	**3598.56**	**1332.56**
6407.02	43476.12	15372.26	32626.42	28152.26	1248.27	1436.88	3311.11	625.97	76.62
229.35	1890.76	576.14	988.58	867.49	4.08	49.39	79.58	26.10	4.33
13.74	62.45	31.38	45.67	37.42	0.23	0.35	1.59	1.01	1.23
13.03	27.44	17.03	66.71	59.25	0.29	4.08	5.86	1.48	0.42
23426.65	133856.70	79280.08	119887.97	99822.91	1229.98	6250.96	9945.07	2464.13	821.13
5860.16	26288.61	15941.26	29033.85	24824.57	328.70	1776.10	2623.43	518.63	173.51
7441.79	33516.08	21566.98	31482.25	26290.10	359.05	2184.49	3099.01	555.47	317.63
12475.18	52562.72	34605.73	54997.64	44490.78	556.97	3706.98	5619.25	1355.30	562.21
24785.39	143856.47	83331.49	128029.71	108747.16	1372.36	6622.27	10237.89	2243.26	770.35
18776.54	99583.63	57966.57	83677.58	68574.75	1355.46	5870.69	8854.21	1628.06	444.80
8720.97	40782.44	24241.09	40737.67	34153.47	358.17	2361.14	3554.73	835.41	355.71
9763.06	56053.12	35729.56	58612.10	50509.72	215.71	2097.42	3448.20	1135.08	532.06
1032.98	1462.82	317.76	1067.11	398.51	59.54	582.96	737.33	94.82	0.51
21.25	53.26	25.63	47.84	32.25	0.87	11.59	14.46	2.00	0.14
45.99	112.83	40.16	113.90	79.28	2.86	22.37	31.76	6.53	0.63
83.14	395.41	152.39	223.60	165.54	6.70	10.52	25.63	8.42	1.38
22.33	102.99	56.92	55.80	42.33	0.12	9.88	10.79	0.79	0.18
407.73	2771.08	1904.04	4789.05	4452.69	8.03	145.71	197.65	43.90	15.17
668.26	2147.44	1229.58	2413.12	1628.15	15.32	247.03	353.90	91.55	19.20
322.48	1238.32	748.81	1250.66	935.77	22.40	100.64	164.89	41.84	7.38
471.22	523.89	387.73	600.30	193.74	302.04	51.93	407.65	53.69	1.81
481.85	1695.35	1011.98	2198.00	1881.95	9.72	126.54	183.36	47.10	22.79
647.38	1827.71	1248.55	2550.54	2076.88	13.87	109.19	182.29	59.22	46.35
380.25	809.56	606.99	1575.22	1359.02	6.95	56.20	88.53	25.38	31.95
74.81	470.11	326.05	409.91	357.60	2.24	10.07	23.40	11.10	5.15
502.04	2216.69	1472.17	2146.62	1762.37	10.46	135.17	197.22	51.59	31.50
450.08	2635.91	1491.20	2683.29	2379.38	12.02	55.45	140.51	73.04	19.77
361.00	1591.42	909.99	1421.63	1185.14	6.67	100.31	138.25	31.27	20.07
667.83	2686.31	2098.16	4037.96	3577.10	13.18	131.31	185.64	41.15	53.73
898.80	2744.19	904.13	5065.54	4350.42	637.47	-23.95	701.39	87.87	2.39
1213.73	6881.79	4015.60	7648.41	6407.21	35.57	379.95	579.19	163.66	33.67
808.74	4490.77	2602.48	2194.06	1155.60	15.79	385.26	497.13	96.07	17.04
42.08	180.61	90.09	184.61	152.99	0.96	17.46	22.46	4.04	1.22
1396.03	5785.84	3736.64	6315.41	5307.34	25.57	379.65	530.89	125.67	79.92
1295.59	7152.01	4378.26	6625.61	5711.39	32.74	270.66	473.27	169.87	51.94
362.56	2174.22	925.98	3932.88	3701.29	9.76	53.15	119.38	56.48	7.14
407.45	2415.13	1768.61	5441.13	5108.51	11.19	116.51	180.65	52.96	15.08
1796.81	6180.66	4252.62	8704.00	7483.58	34.48	435.84	654.21	183.89	92.42
1272.90	6154.11	4529.86	5773.69	4705.99	22.49	372.21	513.38	118.68	59.06
1558.47	7637.27	5572.48	5391.75	4071.46	26.94	509.29	669.44	133.21	66.67
2280.35	10008.90	7058.99	12143.00	10152.40	273.64	705.32	1209.62	230.67	16.57
302.19	2070.00	1440.69	1564.95	1370.22	7.45	80.39	109.01	21.17	11.71
4430.59	23313.48	16381.96	21135.24	17380.20	82.81	1521.64	2130.58	526.13	176.42
9367.69	55846.49	37992.83	47447.99	39227.08	158.26	2401.82	3178.13	618.05	332.06
451.18	2179.35	1580.61	1638.34	1243.50	7.45	137.75	185.32	40.12	21.33
175.23	680.53	521.99	632.07	491.88	3.30	59.72	72.57	9.55	9.45
72.81	526.87	323.53	661.94	598.59	2.41	22.30	37.30	12.60	2.16
68.83	303.95	213.95	239.57	203.75	1.19	12.31	19.45	5.95	2.50
1893.49	21978.12	4178.85	9335.73	8628.98	37.94	380.07	636.08	218.07	17.30
193.06	1547.07	545.61	2507.46	2343.46	3.20	117.07	139.19	18.92	2.39
331.36	3426.73	893.38	859.42	634.38	5.74	87.95	115.22	21.54	6.44

12-17 规模以上国有控股工业企业主要经济指标（2022年）

单位：亿元

项 目	Item	企业单位数（个）Number of Enterprises (unit)	工业总产值（当年价）Gross Industrial Output Value (at current prices)
全 省	**Provincial Total**	**1573**	**32513.46**
按轻重工业分	Grouped by Light and Heavy Industries		
轻工业	Light Industry	345	2458.83
重工业	Heavy Industry	1228	30054.62
按企业规模分	Grouped by Size of Enterprises		
大型企业	Large Enterprises	135	23100.86
中型企业	Medium Enterprises	268	4214.89
小微型企业	Small and Micro Enterprises	1170	5197.70
按行业分	Grouped by Sector		
煤炭开采和洗选业	Mining and Washing of Coal		
石油和天然气开采业	Extraction of Petroleum and Natural Gas		
黑色金属矿采选业	Mining and Dressing of Ferrous Metal Ores	1	0.90
有色金属矿采选业	Mining and Dressing of Nonferrous Metal Ores	8	63.45
非金属矿采选业	Mining and Dressing of Nonmetal Ores	17	45.72
开采专业及辅助性活动	Mining Specialized and Auxiliary Operations	3	43.51
其他采矿业	Mining and Dressing of Other Ores		
农副食品加工业	Processing of Farm and Sideline Food	123	399.31
食品制造业	Manufacture of Food	25	99.96
酒、饮料和精制茶制造业	Manufacture of Wine, Beverage and Refined Tea	23	181.63
烟草制品业	Tobacco Products	6	521.58
纺织业	Textile Industry	1	46.16
纺织服装、服饰业	Manufacture of Textile Garments, Footwear and Headgear	4	3.22
皮革、毛皮、羽毛及其制品和制鞋业	Leather, Fur, Feather, Down and Related Products	1	0.25
木材加工和木、竹、藤、棕、草制品业	Timber Processing, Bamboo, Cane, Palm Fiber & Straw Products	6	6.83
家具制造业	Manufacture of Furniture	1	0.84
造纸和纸制品业	Papermaking and Paper Products	9	111.53
印刷和记录媒介复制业	Printing and Record Medium Reproduction	26	38.63
文教、工美、体育和娱乐用品制造业	Manufacture of Cultural, Educational,Sports and Entertainment Articles	6	23.10
石油、煤炭及其他燃料加工业	Petroleum, Coal and other Fuel Processing	8	4543.18
化学原料和化学制品制造业	Manufacture of Raw Chemical Materials and Chemical Products	56	469.69
医药制造业	Manufacture of Medicines	47	545.68
化学纤维制造业	Manufacture of Chemical Fibers	1	29.86
橡胶和塑料制品业	Rubber and Plastic Products	34	124.13
非金属矿物制品业	Nonmetal Mineral Products	73	204.52
黑色金属冶炼和压延加工业	Smelting and Pressing of Ferrous Metals	14	1842.47
有色金属冶炼和压延加工业	Smelting and Pressing of Nonferrous Metals	28	1372.99
金属制品业	Metal Products	62	416.49
通用设备制造业	Manufacture of General-purpose Machinery	38	171.59
专用设备制造业	Manufacture of Special-purpose Machinery	28	80.79
汽车制造业	Manufacture of Automobile	41	4984.39
铁路、船舶、航空航天和其他运输设备制造业	Manufacture of Railway ,Ship,Aeronautics and Other Transport equipment	29	586.41
电气机械和器材制造业	Manufacture of Electrical Machinery and Equipment	69	496.12
计算机、通信和其他电子设备制造业	Manufacture of Communication Equipment, Computers and Other Electronic Equipment	133	4374.89
仪器仪表制造业	Manufacture of Instruments and Meters	11	42.91
其他制造业	Other Manufactures	4	5.50
废弃资源综合利用业	Comprehensive Utilization of Waste	15	42.75
金属制品、机械和设备修理业	Manufacture of Metal Products,Machinery and Equipment Maintenance	20	93.25
电力、热力生产和供应业	Production and Supply of Electric Power and Heat Power	322	8216.31
燃气生产和供应业	Production and Supply of Gas	76	1741.39
水的生产和供应业	Production and Supply of Water	204	541.51

Main Economic Indicators of State-holding Industrial Enterprises above Designated Size (2022)

(100 million yuan)

工业增加值 Value-added of Industry	年末资产总计 Total Assets at the Year-end	流动资产合计 Total Working Capital	营业收入 Business Revenue	营业成本 Cost of Business	税金及附加 Tax and Other Charges on Principal Business	利润总额 Total Profits	利税总额 Total Pre-tax Profits	本年应交增值税 Value-added Tax Payable in Current Year	全部就业人员年平均人数(万人) Annual Average Number of Employed Persons (10000 persons)
6407.02	**43476.12**	**15372.26**	**32626.42**	**28152.26**	**1248.27**	**1436.88**	**3311.11**	**625.97**	**76.62**
940.33	3291.40	1912.83	2583.11	1714.05	315.95	274.61	693.04	102.47	12.05
5466.69	40184.71	13459.42	30043.31	26438.21	932.31	1162.26	2618.07	523.49	64.57
4607.04	27708.23	9904.46	22509.27	19258.10	1042.70	1085.87	2509.81	381.24	50.71
1009.66	6981.19	2730.81	4423.74	3707.57	184.59	147.49	459.02	126.94	14.93
790.32	8786.70	2736.99	5693.41	5186.58	20.98	203.51	342.28	117.78	10.98
0.21	0.86	0.16	0.80	0.74		-0.12	-0.06	0.06	0.01
38.16	83.53	20.33	64.43	35.93	2.48	20.03	26.99	4.48	0.48
29.33	147.99	37.61	44.70	44.80	1.27	-5.73	-2.46	2.00	0.26
16.17	79.65	40.18	43.51	33.17	0.10	7.07	7.71	0.54	0.11
36.07	155.04	99.02	453.81	425.62	1.12	11.81	14.99	2.07	1.05
27.47	191.33	62.41	103.33	84.55	0.73	0.94	5.07	3.40	1.50
47.08	270.42	201.48	160.55	114.15	5.31	21.69	33.05	6.05	0.62
453.28	471.34	350.54	519.85	126.61	301.72	47.58	402.53	53.22	0.55
9.62	12.96	4.00	48.09	39.57	0.15	6.81	8.65	1.69	0.10
1.09	4.88	3.64	2.92	2.54	0.01	-0.08	0.08	0.14	0.09
0.05	0.14	0.13	0.25	0.21			0.01	0.01	0.01
1.61	45.98	31.26	7.45	6.29	0.10	-0.09	0.22	0.20	0.48
0.65	1.39	0.65	0.83	0.72		0.06	0.08	0.02	0.04
14.95	226.57	115.28	126.24	115.47	0.52	4.10	6.52	1.90	0.45
17.17	223.42	80.75	44.29	34.16	0.29	4.63	6.60	1.69	0.61
9.31	43.01	32.22	23.90	17.05	0.26	2.75	4.26	1.25	0.33
845.78	2394.19	682.45	4556.24	3884.32	627.87	-32.71	674.60	79.44	1.68
50.49	328.24	136.86	481.04	449.66	2.26	7.45	20.39	10.68	0.88
245.30	1258.72	680.81	570.58	284.69	3.95	152.60	182.11	25.57	3.27
10.65	18.67	7.35	29.07	20.38	0.20	7.28	8.72	1.24	0.04
33.20	211.83	107.92	133.63	109.49	0.81	5.94	9.17	2.42	1.52
41.77	306.51	148.07	216.89	188.64	1.53	6.30	14.28	6.45	0.93
153.51	1212.78	358.86	1909.68	1819.50	5.29	11.30	45.76	29.17	1.64
52.32	507.27	361.89	1693.89	1652.75	2.97	18.58	29.66	8.12	1.10
65.63	392.94	260.04	471.10	423.14	1.36	19.74	29.10	8.00	1.63
30.69	370.79	241.94	185.73	158.60	0.80	2.75	7.43	3.88	1.25
21.58	141.67	97.96	85.89	68.92	0.58	4.39	7.83	2.87	0.66
916.92	2768.63	1777.70	4990.75	4283.17	221.88	338.54	642.52	82.10	6.87
100.41	1016.83	679.87	584.50	535.64	2.71	28.33	36.19	5.15	2.09
67.01	480.55	355.18	522.61	470.32	1.55	17.58	23.72	4.59	2.72
892.39	6025.47	3748.50	3716.36	2780.78	18.21	239.47	307.32	49.65	20.36
11.56	168.38	87.22	59.24	44.43	0.31	-2.59	-0.61	1.67	0.36
0.83	6.92	5.00	4.20	3.42	0.01	-0.21	-0.11	0.09	0.06
10.45	65.56	19.93	43.37	37.20	0.25	2.36	4.26	1.65	0.20
35.65	156.32	92.30	93.82	82.29	0.81	-0.47	3.66	3.31	1.42
1735.14	19920.05	3447.17	8320.53	7708.35	34.06	348.23	574.60	192.31	15.30
149.86	1111.62	340.28	1754.46	1638.22	2.40	100.82	118.20	14.99	1.28
233.68	2653.66	655.31	557.90	426.76	4.39	39.75	58.07	13.94	4.69

12-18 规模以上集体工业企业主要经济指标（2022年）

单位：亿元

项　　目	Item	企业单位数（个）Number of Enterprises (unit)	工业总产值（当年价）Gross Industrial Output Value (at current prices)
全　省	**Provincial Total**	**73**	**48.66**
按轻重工业分	Grouped by Light and Heavy Industries		
轻工业	Light Industry	21	16.83
重工业	Heavy Industry	52	31.83
按企业规模分	Grouped by Size of Enterprises		
大型企业	Large Enterprises		
中型企业	Medium Enterprises	7	10.69
小微型企业	Small and Micro Enterprises	66	37.96
按行业分	Grouped by Sector		
煤炭开采和洗选业	Mining and Washing of Coal		
石油和天然气开采业	Extraction of Petroleum and Natural Gas		
黑色金属矿采选业	Mining and Dressing of Ferrous Metal Ores		
有色金属矿采选业	Mining and Dressing of Nonferrous Metal Ores		
非金属矿采选业	Mining and Dressing of Nonmetal Ores	1	0.46
开采专业及辅助性活动	Mining Specialized and Auxiliary Operations		
其他采矿业	Mining and Dressing of Other Ores		
农副食品加工业	Processing of Farm and Sideline Food	2	1.72
食品制造业	Manufacture of Food	1	1.51
酒、饮料和精制茶制造业	Manufacture of Wine, Beverage and Refined Tea		
烟草制品业	Tobacco Products		
纺织业	Textile Industry		
纺织服装、服饰业	Manufacture of Textile Garments, Footwear and Headgear	1	0.31
皮革、毛皮、羽毛及其制品和制鞋业	Leather, Fur, Feather, Down and Related Products	4	0.68
木材加工和木、竹、藤、棕、草制品业	Timber Processing, Bamboo, Cane, Palm Fiber & Straw Products		
家具制造业	Manufacture of Furniture	2	0.49
造纸和纸制品业	Papermaking and Paper Products	2	3.54
印刷和记录媒介复制业	Printing and Record Medium Reproduction		
文教、工美、体育和娱乐用品制造业	Manufacture of Cultural, Educational,Sports and Entertainment Articles	3	0.59
石油、煤炭及其他燃料加工业	Petroleum, Coal and other Fuel Processing	1	0.13
化学原料和化学制品制造业	Manufacture of Raw Chemical Materials and Chemical Products		
医药制造业	Manufacture of Medicines		
化学纤维制造业	Manufacture of Chemical Fibers		
橡胶和塑料制品业	Rubber and Plastic Products	2	0.41
非金属矿物制品业	Nonmetal Mineral Products	7	4.07
黑色金属冶炼和压延加工业	Smelting and Pressing of Ferrous Metals		
有色金属冶炼和压延加工业	Smelting and Pressing of Nonferrous Metals	1	0.42
金属制品业	Metal Products	1	0.52
通用设备制造业	Manufacture of General-purpose Machinery	1	1.43
专用设备制造业	Manufacture of Special-purpose Machinery	3	7.02
汽车制造业	Manufacture of Automobile		
铁路、船舶、航空航天和其他运输设备制造业	Manufacture of Railway ,Ship,Aeronautics and Other Transport equipment	1	0.31
电气机械和器材制造业	Manufacture of Electrical Machinery and Equipment	2	2.29
计算机、通信和其他电子设备制造业	Manufacture of Communication Equipment, Computers and Other Electronic Equipment	5	8.27
仪器仪表制造业	Manufacture of Instruments and Meters		
其他制造业	Other Manufactures		
废弃资源综合利用业	Comprehensive Utilization of Waste		
金属制品、机械和设备修理业	Manufacture of Metal Products,Machinery and Equipment Maintenance		
电力、热力生产和供应业	Production and Supply of Electric Power and Heat Power	2	0.85
燃气生产和供应业	Production and Supply of Gas	2	2.89
水的生产和供应业	Production and Supply of Water	29	10.73

Main Economic Indicators of Collective-owned Industrial Enterprises above Designated Size (2022)

(100 million yuan)

工业增加值 Value-added of Industry	年末资产总计 Total Assets at the Year-end	流动资产合计 Total Working Capital	营业收入 Business Revenue	营业成本 Cost of Business	税金及附加 Tax and Other Charges on Principal Business	利润总额 Total Profits	利税总额 Total Pre-tax Profits	本年应交增值税 Value-added Tax Payable in Current Year	全部就业人员年平均人数(万人) Annual Average Number of Employed Persons (10000 persons)
13.74	**62.45**	**31.38**	**45.67**	**37.42**	**0.23**	**0.35**	**1.59**	**1.01**	**1.23**
3.83	10.29	5.89	16.11	13.58	0.07	0.99	1.55	0.49	0.34
9.91	52.16	25.50	29.57	23.84	0.16	-0.64	0.04	0.52	0.88
7.26	3.65	2.73	10.71	7.13	0.03	0.10	0.14	0.01	0.77
6.48	58.80	28.65	34.96	30.29	0.20	0.25	1.45	1.00	0.46
0.12	0.23	0.05	0.46	0.35	0.01	0.05	0.08	0.01	
0.29	0.23	0.12	1.72	1.40		0.15	0.19	0.04	0.01
0.22	0.11	0.03	1.48	1.23	0.01	0.08	0.14	0.05	0.01
0.05	2.18	2.00	0.28	0.25			0.01	0.01	
0.31	0.71	0.48	0.81	0.86		-0.23	-0.19	0.04	0.04
0.11	0.45	0.10	0.46	0.39		0.05	0.06	0.01	0.01
0.67	1.38	1.03	3.12	2.62	0.01	0.19	0.28	0.08	0.04
0.49	2.54	0.24	0.59	0.30	0.02	0.15	0.23	0.07	0.04
0.01	0.28	0.28	0.17	0.16					
0.22	0.10	0.08	0.42	0.35		-0.02	-0.02		0.04
0.75	4.06	3.39	4.06	3.35	0.02	0.12	0.26	0.12	0.08
0.05	0.10	0.10	0.41	0.39			0.01	0.01	0.01
	0.53	0.53	0.42	0.42					
1.01	0.38	0.33	1.43	0.89		0.03	0.03		0.09
1.47	2.28	1.48	6.84	5.76	0.02	0.63	0.84	0.18	0.11
0.05	0.20	0.19	0.31	0.25		-0.01		0.01	0.01
0.36	0.25	0.20	1.49	1.42		0.04	0.05	0.01	0.01
5.78	2.97	2.34	8.37	5.49	0.02	0.10	0.15	0.02	0.56
0.48	2.24	0.26	0.68	0.43	0.01	0.04	0.07	0.02	0.03
0.37	1.36	0.46	2.81	2.52	0.01	0.20	0.27	0.07	0.01
0.93	39.86	17.67	9.34	8.59	0.09	-1.19	-0.87	0.24	0.12

12-19 规模以上股份合作工业企业主要经济指标（2022年）

单位：亿元

项　　目	Item	企业单位数（个） Number of Enterprises (unit)	工业总产值（当年价） Gross Industrial Output Value (at current prices)
全　省	**Provincial Total**	**46**	**67.62**
按轻重工业分	Grouped by Light & Heavy Industries		
轻工业	Light Industry	32	55.34
重工业	Heavy Industry	14	12.28
按企业规模分	Grouped by Size of Enterprises		
大型企业	Large Enterprises		
中型企业	Medium Enterprises	4	36.38
小微型企业	Small and Micro Enterprises	42	31.24
按行业分	Grouped by Sector		
煤炭开采和洗选业	Mining and Washing of Coal		
石油和天然气开采业	Extraction of Petroleum and Natural Gas		
黑色金属矿采选业	Mining and Dressing of Ferrous Metal Ores		
有色金属矿采选业	Mining and Dressing of Nonferrous Metal Ores		
非金属矿采选业	Mining and Dressing of Nonmetal Ores		
开采专业及辅助性活动	Mining Specialized and Auxiliary Operations		
其他采矿业	Mining and Dressing of Other Ores		
农副食品加工业	Processing of Farm and Sideline Food	1	0.51
食品制造业	Manufacture of Food		
酒、饮料和精制茶制造业	Manufacture of Wine, Beverage and Refined Tea		
烟草制品业	Tobacco Products		
纺织业	Textile Industry	4	11.26
纺织服装、服饰业	Manufacture of Textile Garments, Footwear and Headgear	3	0.67
皮革、毛皮、羽毛及其制品和制鞋业	Leather, Fur, Feather, Down and Related Products	2	0.86
木材加工和木、竹、藤、棕、草制品业	Timber Processing, Bamboo, Cane, Palm Fiber & Straw Products		
家具制造业	Manufacture of Furniture	1	0.71
造纸和纸制品业	Papermaking and Paper Products	1	1.20
印刷和记录媒介复制业	Printing and Record Medium Reproduction	5	2.73
文教、工美、体育和娱乐用品制造业	Manufacture of Cultural, Educational,Sports and Entertainment Articles	1	1.49
石油、煤炭及其他燃料加工业	Petroleum, Coal and other Fuel Processing		
化学原料和化学制品制造业	Manufacture of Raw Chemical Materials and Chemical Products	4	4.03
医药制造业	Manufacture of Medicines		
化学纤维制造业	Manufacture of Chemical Fibers		
橡胶和塑料制品业	Rubber and Plastic Products	3	0.82
非金属矿物制品业	Nonmetal Mineral Products	3	4.04
黑色金属冶炼和压延加工业	Smelting and Pressing of Ferrous Metals		
有色金属冶炼和压延加工业	Smelting and Pressing of Nonferrous Metals		
金属制品业	Metal Products	4	29.11
通用设备制造业	Manufacture of General-purpose Machinery	1	0.25
专用设备制造业	Manufacture of Special-purpose Machinery	2	1.10
汽车制造业	Manufacture of Automobile		
铁路、船舶、航空航天和其他运输设备制造业	Manufacture of Railway ,Ship,Aeronautics and Other Transport equipment		
电气机械和器材制造业	Manufacture of Electrical Machinery and Equipment	5	1.77
计算机、通信和其他电子设备制造业	Manufacture of Communication Equipment, Computers and Other Electronic Equipment	4	6.13
仪器仪表制造业	Manufacture of Instruments and Meters	1	0.22
其他制造业	Other Manufactures	1	0.72
废弃资源综合利用业	Comprehensive Utilization of Waste		
金属制品、机械和设备修理业	Manufacture of Metal Products,Machinery and Equipment Maintenance		
电力、热力生产和供应业	Production and Supply of Electric Power and Heat Power		
燃气生产和供应业	Production and Supply of Gas		
水的生产和供应业	Production and Supply of Water		

Main Economic Indicators of Share-holding Cooperative Industrial Enterprises above Designated Size (2022)

(100 million yuan)

工业增加值 Value-added of Industry	年末资产总计 Total Assets at the Year-end	流动资产合计 Total Working Capital	营业收入 Business Revenue	营业成本 Cost of Business	税金及附加 Tax and Other Charges on Principal Business	利润总额 Total Profits	利税总额 Total Pre-tax Profits	本年应交增值税 Value-added Tax Payable in Current Year	全部就业人员年平均人数(万人) Annual Average Number of Employed Persons (10000 persons)
13.03	**27.44**	**17.03**	**66.71**	**59.25**	**0.29**	**4.08**	**5.86**	**1.48**	**0.42**
9.37	15.43	7.77	54.63	50.42	0.26	2.44	3.87	1.18	0.26
3.65	12.00	9.26	12.08	8.83	0.04	1.65	1.99	0.30	0.15
7.37	9.98	6.45	37.36	33.12	0.19	2.90	3.99	0.90	0.13
5.66	17.45	10.59	29.34	26.13	0.10	1.18	1.87	0.58	0.29
0.02	0.47	0.10	0.41	0.34		0.02	0.02		0.01
1.91	4.35	0.96	10.79	10.06	0.05	0.52	0.73	0.16	0.03
0.12	0.47	0.33	0.60	0.54		0.02	0.02		0.01
0.18	0.35	0.33	0.69	0.62		0.01	0.06	0.05	0.02
0.26	0.29	0.26	0.63	0.51		0.01	0.04	0.03	0.02
0.12	0.22	0.06	0.52	0.46	0.01	0.02	0.04	0.01	0.02
0.17	1.69	0.89	2.20	2.06		0.05	0.06	0.01	0.01
0.07	0.04	0.02	1.49	1.39		0.01	0.01		0.02
0.67	3.59	3.22	4.24	3.49	0.02	0.22	0.35	0.11	0.02
0.61	1.19	1.02	0.93	0.83		0.03	0.04	0.01	0.02
1.79	6.71	5.03	4.33	3.28	0.02	0.73	0.95	0.19	0.06
5.00	2.61	0.90	30.27	28.27	0.17	1.54	2.47	0.76	0.05
0.04	0.08	0.07	0.25	0.22		0.01	0.02	0.01	
0.33	0.87	0.69	1.18	0.99		0.04	0.09	0.05	0.02
0.23	0.88	0.76	1.71	1.50		0.08	0.09	0.01	0.02
1.35	3.04	2.00	5.63	3.99		0.78	0.83	0.04	0.07
0.06	0.35	0.34	0.22	0.17			0.01	0.01	0.01
0.09	0.24	0.06	0.62	0.54		0.01	0.02	0.02	0.01

12-20 规模以上股份制工业企业主要经济指标（2022年）

单位：亿元

项目	Item	企业单位数（个） Number of Enterprises (unit)	工业总产值（当年价） Gross Industrial Output Value (at current prices)
全 省	**Provincial Total**	**56499**	**118899.83**
按轻重工业分	Grouped by Light and Heavy Industries		
轻工业	Light Industry	24749	36402.45
重工业	Heavy Industry	31750	82497.38
按企业规模分	Grouped by Size of Enterprises		
大型企业	Large Enterprises	685	47099.63
中型企业	Medium Enterprises	3902	26053.03
小微型企业	Small and Micro Enterprises	51912	45747.17
按行业分	Grouped by Sector		
煤炭开采和洗选业	Mining and Washing of Coal		
石油和天然气开采业	Extraction of Petroleum and Natural Gas		
黑色金属矿采选业	Mining and Dressing of Ferrous Metal Ores	8	35.73
有色金属矿采选业	Mining and Dressing of Nonferrous Metal Ores	26	111.37
非金属矿采选业	Mining and Dressing of Nonmetal Ores	199	217.30
开采专业及辅助性活动	Mining Specialized and Auxiliary Operations	5	15.50
其他采矿业	Mining and Dressing of Other Ores		
农副食品加工业	Processing of Farm and Sideline Food	1006	2979.15
食品制造业	Manufacture of Food	720	1139.68
酒、饮料和精制茶制造业	Manufacture of Wine, Beverage and Refined Tea	166	475.18
烟草制品业	Tobacco Products	42	593.66
纺织业	Textile Industry	1282	1478.68
纺织服装、服饰业	Manufacture of Textile Garments, Footwear and Headgear	2126	1964.63
皮革、毛皮、羽毛及其制品和制鞋业	Leather, Fur, Feather, Down and Related Products	1313	922.55
木材加工和木、竹、藤、棕、草制品业	Timber Processing, Bamboo, Cane, Palm Fiber & Straw Products	463	346.32
家具制造业	Manufacture of Furniture	1646	1613.34
造纸和纸制品业	Papermaking and Paper Products	1236	1577.13
印刷和记录媒介复制业	Printing and Record Medium Reproduction	938	930.18
文教、工美、体育和娱乐用品制造业	Manufacture of Cultural, Educational,Sports and Entertainment Articles	1394	2055.98
石油、煤炭及其他燃料加工业	Petroleum, Coal and other Fuel Processing	96	3757.04
化学原料和化学制品制造业	Manufacture of Raw Chemical Materials and Chemical Products	2655	4202.22
医药制造业	Manufacture of Medicines	496	1536.62
化学纤维制造业	Manufacture of Chemical Fibers	65	95.15
橡胶和塑料制品业	Rubber and Plastic Products	4845	4172.24
非金属矿物制品业	Nonmetal Mineral Products	3306	5434.48
黑色金属冶炼和压延加工业	Smelting and Pressing of Ferrous Metals	437	3130.60
有色金属冶炼和压延加工业	Smelting and Pressing of Nonferrous Metals	958	3944.73
金属制品业	Metal Products	5882	6536.40
通用设备制造业	Manufacture of General-purpose Machinery	3407	3625.82
专用设备制造业	Manufacture of Special-purpose Machinery	3517	3938.26
汽车制造业	Manufacture of Automobile	703	2465.44
铁路、船舶、航空航天和其他运输设备制造业	Manufacture of Railway ,Ship,Aeronautics and Other Transport equipment	403	1122.04
电气机械和器材制造业	Manufacture of Electrical Machinery and Equipment	6829	15714.01
计算机、通信和其他电子设备制造业	Manufacture of Communication Equipment, Computers and Other Electronic Equipment	7763	30269.12
仪器仪表制造业	Manufacture of Instruments and Meters	938	1064.29
其他制造业	Other Manufactures	402	379.15
废弃资源综合利用业	Comprehensive Utilization of Waste	247	599.87
金属制品、机械和设备修理业	Manufacture of Metal Products,Machinery and Equipment Maintenance	65	69.19
电力、热力生产和供应业	Production and Supply of Electric Power and Heat Power	413	7926.52
燃气生产和供应业	Production and Supply of Gas	204	1855.21
水的生产和供应业	Production and Supply of Water	298	605.04

Main Economic Indicators of Share-holding Industrial Enterprises above Designated Size (2022)

(100 million yuan)

工业增加值 Value-added of Industry	年末资产总计 Total Assets at the Year-end	流动资产合计 Total Working Capital	营业收入 Business Revenue	营业成本 Cost of Business	税金及附加 Tax and Other Charges on Principal Business	利润总额 Total Profits	利税总额 Total Pre-tax Profits	本年应交增值税 Value-added Tax Payable in Current Year	全部就业人员年平均人数(万人) Annual Average Number of Employed Persons (10000 persons)
23426.65	**133856.70**	**79280.08**	**119887.97**	**99822.91**	**1229.98**	**6250.96**	**9945.07**	**2464.13**	**821.13**
8035.64	34365.71	22534.97	36180.17	29262.51	456.37	2459.13	3853.44	937.94	336.78
15391.01	99490.99	56745.10	83707.80	70560.39	773.61	3791.83	6091.62	1526.19	484.35
10655.33	65033.05	36173.32	47987.59	38471.12	795.41	3281.80	5073.90	996.68	203.97
5405.39	26022.84	15696.19	26242.39	21973.46	282.19	1498.41	2337.34	556.74	204.67
7365.94	42800.81	27410.57	45657.99	39378.33	152.38	1470.75	2533.83	910.71	412.48
15.81	41.22	21.76	27.08	15.03	0.78	8.52	10.68	1.38	0.07
43.44	101.79	37.09	109.94	76.80	2.70	22.01	30.90	6.19	0.54
77.78	367.16	142.02	206.54	151.78	6.18	9.72	23.79	7.88	1.27
5.56	10.07	6.45	15.03	11.56	0.09	2.63	3.20	0.48	0.05
297.29	2036.30	1379.31	3337.62	3094.27	5.71	95.97	137.89	36.22	11.60
263.56	1144.81	601.64	1132.85	901.49	5.98	109.33	147.55	32.24	10.99
123.19	556.72	333.47	458.75	354.38	10.61	46.77	72.93	15.54	2.67
470.02	519.42	383.86	592.66	186.82	302.02	51.86	407.49	53.62	1.68
296.58	966.47	553.78	1446.96	1240.71	5.68	82.32	121.59	33.59	13.11
413.86	1233.96	801.76	1762.47	1422.35	9.48	76.00	127.53	42.06	27.91
187.78	403.81	312.11	897.65	788.76	3.46	25.07	43.34	14.81	15.31
61.36	358.54	239.29	331.64	289.72	1.54	9.64	20.69	9.51	4.11
361.29	1599.14	1038.41	1570.21	1284.59	7.38	81.95	130.16	40.83	22.76
246.10	1383.46	769.25	1514.39	1326.66	5.95	40.47	79.92	33.49	12.54
205.08	933.82	518.32	907.74	764.75	4.00	46.25	70.40	20.15	11.06
314.37	1248.28	943.74	2052.15	1812.87	6.10	73.16	104.39	25.13	21.81
645.32	2044.43	641.48	3878.16	3371.03	462.28	-27.75	501.47	66.95	1.90
711.14	3946.60	2346.31	4380.79	3674.60	21.91	226.19	351.51	103.41	23.36
576.55	3065.98	1654.58	1483.09	805.34	9.92	305.77	374.05	58.36	11.30
16.46	87.21	44.21	82.21	70.14	0.40	6.36	8.40	1.64	0.65
848.56	3554.10	2196.78	4118.68	3477.11	15.27	214.15	318.92	89.51	47.48
946.86	5419.72	3419.34	5284.33	4581.81	25.17	169.44	331.12	136.51	40.98
292.96	1716.70	678.28	3138.92	2948.53	8.12	47.20	106.53	51.21	5.79
275.92	1787.47	1302.35	4249.91	4021.65	8.07	77.02	123.59	38.50	10.48
1244.87	4331.99	2969.05	6393.50	5505.98	24.80	302.38	468.54	141.37	64.57
787.04	4238.93	3033.66	3536.41	2837.79	13.96	207.94	305.24	83.35	38.92
1020.93	5350.62	3982.99	3670.11	2760.44	16.58	278.47	392.02	96.97	45.94
343.82	3136.30	1895.36	2576.50	2318.30	23.18	22.22	81.22	35.82	15.11
175.13	1522.41	1065.89	1073.07	948.57	4.04	52.86	71.93	15.04	7.07
3267.74	17305.84	12370.58	15747.89	12740.62	61.01	1204.52	1689.79	424.26	115.65
6504.51	39110.39	27414.27	31258.64	24578.75	111.63	1838.19	2436.06	486.24	190.23
307.53	1613.74	1161.77	1077.23	781.38	5.16	85.39	123.83	33.28	13.29
93.74	329.10	227.05	375.98	308.78	1.62	20.66	29.77	7.49	6.44
66.67	474.53	293.64	611.89	554.19	2.16	19.47	33.23	11.60	1.98
18.35	89.05	63.05	73.90	64.45	0.40	-0.50	2.84	2.94	1.10
1518.26	18237.41	3401.43	8013.09	7512.83	30.10	280.29	487.10	176.71	15.17
139.68	1077.95	339.09	1874.85	1763.27	2.23	82.06	98.14	13.85	1.72
241.54	2511.24	696.68	625.17	474.79	4.30	56.99	77.31	16.01	4.53

12-21　规模以上“三资”工业企业主要经济指标（2022年）

单位：亿元

项　目	Item	企业单位数（个） Number of Enterprises (unit)	工业总产值（当年价） Gross Industrial Output Value (at current prices)
全　省	**Provincial Total**	**11736**	**59404.33**
按经济类型分	Grouped by Ownership		
外商投资工业	Foreign-funded Industry	3794	27898.05
港澳台投资工业	Industry with Funds from Hong Kong, Macao and Taiwan	7942	31506.28
按轻重工业分	Grouped by Light and Heavy Industries		
轻工业	Light Industry	5623	17309.67
重工业	Heavy Industry	6113	42094.66
按企业规模分	Grouped by Size of Enterprises		
大型企业	Large Enterprises	747	35179.86
中型企业	Medium Enterprises	2456	13101.97
小微型企业	Small and Micro Enterprises	8533	11122.50
按行业分	Grouped by Sector		
煤炭开采和洗选业	Mining and Washing of Coal		
石油和天然气开采业	Extraction of Petroleum and Natural Gas	3	1159.37
黑色金属矿采选业	Mining and Dressing of Ferrous Metal Ores	2	17.16
有色金属矿采选业	Mining and Dressing of Nonferrous Metal Ores	1	2.34
非金属矿采选业	Mining and Dressing of Nonmetal Ores	8	8.18
开采专业及辅助性活动	Mining Specialized and Auxiliary Operations	2	7.84
其他采矿业	Mining and Dressing of Other Ores		
农副食品加工业	Processing of Farm and Sideline Food	142	1129.05
食品制造业	Manufacture of Food	190	1078.95
酒、饮料和精制茶制造业	Manufacture of Wine, Beverage and Refined Tea	64	694.44
烟草制品业	Tobacco Products	1	3.77
纺织业	Textile Industry	311	635.25
纺织服装、服饰业	Manufacture of Textile Garments, Footwear and Headgear	466	796.95
皮革、毛皮、羽毛及其制品和制鞋业	Leather, Fur, Feather, Down and Related Products	325	630.36
木材加工和木、竹、藤、棕、草制品业	Timber Processing, Bamboo, Cane, Palm Fiber & Straw Products	57	54.50
家具制造业	Manufacture of Furniture	255	575.57
造纸和纸制品业	Papermaking and Paper Products	272	1086.23
印刷和记录媒介复制业	Printing and Record Medium Reproduction	202	441.51
文教、工美、体育和娱乐用品制造业	Manufacture of Cultural, Educational,Sports and Entertainment Articles	640	2060.31
石油、煤炭及其他燃料加工业	Petroleum, Coal and other Fuel Processing	24	1187.74
化学原料和化学制品制造业	Manufacture of Raw Chemical Materials and Chemical Products	582	2952.99
医药制造业	Manufacture of Medicines	116	703.11
化学纤维制造业	Manufacture of Chemical Fibers	21	99.98
橡胶和塑料制品业	Rubber and Plastic Products	1165	1959.43
非金属矿物制品业	Nonmetal Mineral Products	361	1181.47
黑色金属冶炼和压延加工业	Smelting and Pressing of Ferrous Metals	59	668.52
有色金属冶炼和压延加工业	Smelting and Pressing of Nonferrous Metals	135	1006.78
金属制品业	Metal Products	949	1979.26
通用设备制造业	Manufacture of General-purpose Machinery	593	2109.90
专用设备制造业	Manufacture of Special-purpose Machinery	637	1669.36
汽车制造业	Manufacture of Automobile	421	9093.50
铁路、船舶、航空航天和其他运输设备制造业	Manufacture of Railway ,Ship,Aeronautics and Other Transport equipment	106	404.66
电气机械和器材制造业	Manufacture of Electrical Machinery and Equipment	1247	5176.81
计算机、通信和其他电子设备制造业	Manufacture of Communication Equipment, Computers and Other Electronic Equipment	1771	16266.52
仪器仪表制造业	Manufacture of Instruments and Meters	235	537.53
其他制造业	Other Manufactures	119	248.50
废弃资源综合利用业	Comprehensive Utilization of Waste	18	34.82
金属制品、机械和设备修理业	Manufacture of Metal Products,Machinery and Equipment Maintenance	19	143.63
电力、热力生产和供应业	Production and Supply of Electric Power and Heat Power	104	895.36
燃气生产和供应业	Production and Supply of Gas	75	564.25
水的生产和供应业	Production and Supply of Water	38	138.41

Main Economic Indicators of Foreign-funded Industrial Enterprises above Designated Size (2022)

(100 million yuan)

工业增加值 Value-added of Industry	年末资产总计 Total Assets at the Year-end	流动资产合计 Total Working Capital	营业收入 Business Revenue	营业成本 Cost of Business	税金及附加 Tax and Other Charges on Principal Business	利润总额 Total Profits	利税总额 Total Pre-tax Profits	本年应交增值税 Value-added Tax Payable in Current Year	全部就业人员年平均人数(万人) Annual Average Number of Employed Persons (10000 persons)
13301.96	**59804.69**	**37508.24**	**60516.10**	**51114.67**	**687.75**	**3960.59**	**5722.44**	**1074.10**	**491.14**
5860.16	26288.61	15941.26	29033.85	24824.57	328.70	1776.10	2623.43	518.63	173.51
7441.79	33516.08	21566.98	31482.25	26290.10	359.05	2184.49	3099.01	555.47	317.63
4247.10	17728.04	11782.78	17788.93	14325.11	95.87	1197.24	1688.34	395.23	215.54
9054.86	42076.65	25725.46	42727.16	36789.56	591.87	2763.35	4034.10	678.87	275.59
8095.39	34256.76	21736.35	35616.69	30039.62	559.49	2589.77	3779.37	630.11	239.69
3127.15	13974.55	8235.69	13582.51	11364.41	71.93	821.84	1150.76	256.98	146.11
2079.42	11573.38	7536.20	11316.90	9710.64	56.32	548.98	792.31	187.01	105.34
1032.98	1462.82	317.76	1067.11	398.51	59.54	582.96	737.33	94.82	0.51
5.22	11.06	3.59	19.75	16.28	0.09	3.18	3.83	0.56	0.05
1.46	4.94	1.77	2.42	1.72	0.10	0.24	0.52	0.18	0.03
2.19	9.85	5.36	7.62	5.92	0.27	0.30	0.83	0.26	0.04
5.75	21.53	15.26	7.84	4.93	0.01	2.66	2.79	0.13	0.06
96.43	686.65	494.44	1289.98	1208.71	2.17	45.45	54.30	6.69	2.74
401.85	996.13	623.90	1266.02	714.74	9.24	137.20	205.41	58.97	8.01
198.98	671.53	411.51	787.93	577.97	11.78	53.79	91.86	26.29	4.69
0.68	3.15	2.70	3.66	3.27	0.01	0.02	0.06	0.03	0.07
157.28	672.76	436.71	606.32	514.47	3.54	32.27	46.23	10.42	8.97
224.55	571.31	429.68	751.85	623.46	4.09	31.34	51.79	16.36	17.78
180.63	388.22	280.83	632.04	529.57	3.24	30.21	43.20	9.75	15.67
9.66	97.04	76.84	52.75	44.63	0.60	0.10	1.79	1.09	0.76
136.83	604.90	427.37	557.94	461.84	2.99	52.61	65.96	10.37	8.48
184.02	1226.55	706.08	1068.99	966.92	5.38	8.37	50.39	36.64	6.63
138.54	591.57	352.92	449.16	367.56	2.23	50.76	62.08	9.09	8.47
345.78	1420.56	1145.38	1957.56	1739.77	6.98	56.73	78.99	15.28	31.29
253.42	699.24	262.14	1186.74	978.85	175.19	3.79	199.89	20.91	0.48
490.90	2886.32	1638.39	3191.26	2666.46	13.46	149.54	222.02	59.01	9.87
227.48	1412.00	938.46	686.47	330.53	5.67	77.78	120.29	36.84	5.57
25.40	92.82	45.43	101.01	81.63	0.56	11.08	14.01	2.37	0.55
520.80	2161.16	1494.09	2047.86	1698.10	9.68	159.81	202.60	33.11	30.81
314.22	1610.31	895.40	1174.98	984.19	6.67	94.33	130.40	29.39	9.35
62.80	443.74	239.14	754.63	716.55	1.48	4.82	11.13	4.83	1.20
125.52	595.62	445.51	1074.48	974.49	2.96	37.85	54.47	13.66	4.33
503.21	1681.93	1170.20	2016.69	1717.44	8.15	120.97	165.19	36.07	25.39
475.52	1877.62	1470.15	2189.21	1828.83	8.39	162.00	204.68	34.29	19.50
521.74	2224.75	1546.30	1649.36	1249.29	10.03	227.65	271.51	33.83	20.02
1928.08	6846.30	5145.39	9531.20	8103.70	250.30	681.88	1126.01	193.83	31.16
113.09	484.00	331.86	434.79	372.47	2.86	24.83	32.59	4.89	4.31
1143.94	5945.46	3960.88	5289.30	4555.13	21.44	313.05	434.37	99.88	59.55
2812.50	16575.33	10465.92	16034.78	14528.44	46.18	547.97	720.49	126.34	140.04
141.72	560.90	414.52	548.14	451.38	2.26	51.76	60.49	6.46	7.96
80.62	349.20	293.28	251.12	178.76	1.67	38.89	42.53	1.97	2.94
5.22	46.04	27.00	35.98	30.96	0.21	2.88	4.01	0.91	0.14
43.67	157.60	115.02	143.45	120.07	0.68	12.79	16.25	2.78	1.10
288.12	2965.27	610.28	913.04	742.10	6.15	86.59	120.89	28.15	1.51
50.34	373.72	165.23	584.20	534.67	0.87	28.70	34.04	4.47	0.62
50.86	374.79	101.57	148.45	90.33	0.62	33.43	37.21	3.17	0.46

12-22 规模以上私营工业企业主要经济指标（2022年）

单位：亿元

项　　目	Item	企业单位数（个） Number of Enterprises (unit)	工业总产值（当年价） Gross Industrial Output Value (at current prices)
全　省	**Provincial Total**	**47503**	**63718.10**
按轻重工业分	Grouped by Light & Heavy Industries		
轻工业	Light Industry	21855	27060.15
重工业	Heavy Industry	25648	36657.95
按企业规模分	Grouped by Size of Enterprises		
大型企业	Large Enterprises	321	14208.99
中型企业	Medium Enterprises	2735	16053.30
小微型企业	Small and Micro Enterprises	44447	33455.81
按行业分	Grouped by Sector		
煤炭开采和洗选业	Mining and Washing of Coal		
石油和天然气开采业	Extraction of Petroleum and Natural Gas		
黑色金属矿采选业	Mining and Dressing of Ferrous Metal Ores	6	10.15
有色金属矿采选业	Mining and Dressing of Nonferrous Metal Ores	17	38.95
非金属矿采选业	Mining and Dressing of Nonmetal Ores	153	113.88
开采专业及辅助性活动	Mining Specialized and Auxiliary Operations	2	1.95
其他采矿业	Mining and Dressing of Other Ores		
农副食品加工业	Processing of Farm and Sideline Food	720	1490.48
食品制造业	Manufacture of Food	570	790.91
酒、饮料和精制茶制造业	Manufacture of Wine, Beverage and Refined Tea	105	161.89
烟草制品业	Tobacco Products	30	63.91
纺织业	Textile Industry	1208	1340.84
纺织服装、服饰业	Manufacture of Textile Garments, Footwear and Headgear	1944	1796.04
皮革、毛皮、羽毛及其制品和制鞋业	Leather, Fur, Feather, Down and Related Products	1241	869.89
木材加工和木、竹、藤、棕、草制品业	Timber Processing, Bamboo, Cane, Palm Fiber & Straw Products	431	296.52
家具制造业	Manufacture of Furniture	1504	1388.32
造纸和纸制品业	Papermaking and Paper Products	1159	1178.46
印刷和记录媒介复制业	Printing and Record Medium Reproduction	861	785.61
文教、工美、体育和娱乐用品制造业	Manufacture of Cultural, Educational,Sports and Entertainment Articles	1201	1480.44
石油、煤炭及其他燃料加工业	Petroleum, Coal and other Fuel Processing	64	136.40
化学原料和化学制品制造业	Manufacture of Raw Chemical Materials and Chemical Products	2162	2592.68
医药制造业	Manufacture of Medicines	322	502.29
化学纤维制造业	Manufacture of Chemical Fibers	59	62.34
橡胶和塑料制品业	Rubber and Plastic Products	4277	3530.48
非金属矿物制品业	Nonmetal Mineral Products	2844	4115.58
黑色金属冶炼和压延加工业	Smelting and Pressing of Ferrous Metals	407	1179.96
有色金属冶炼和压延加工业	Smelting and Pressing of Nonferrous Metals	836	1997.36
金属制品业	Metal Products	5266	5294.76
通用设备制造业	Manufacture of General-purpose Machinery	2896	2529.89
专用设备制造业	Manufacture of Special-purpose Machinery	2858	2776.37
汽车制造业	Manufacture of Automobile	509	779.82
铁路、船舶、航空航天和其他运输设备制造业	Manufacture of Railway ,Ship,Aeronautics and Other Transport equipment	339	455.32
电气机械和器材制造业	Manufacture of Electrical Machinery and Equipment	5822	11618.17
计算机、通信和其他电子设备制造业	Manufacture of Communication Equipment, Computers and Other Electronic Equipment	6135	12467.98
仪器仪表制造业	Manufacture of Instruments and Meters	755	665.70
其他制造业	Other Manufactures	338	272.79
废弃资源综合利用业	Comprehensive Utilization of Waste	197	503.18
金属制品、机械和设备修理业	Manufacture of Metal Products,Machinery and Equipment Maintenance	39	24.90
电力、热力生产和供应业	Production and Supply of Electric Power and Heat Power	83	202.41
燃气生产和供应业	Production and Supply of Gas	76	163.95
水的生产和供应业	Production and Supply of Water	67	37.54

Main Economic Indicators of Private Industrial Enterprises above Designated Size (2022)

(100 million yuan)

工业增加值 Value-added of Industry	年末资产总计 Total Assets at the Year-end	流动资产合计 Total working Capital	营业收入 Business Revenue	营业成本 Cost of Business	税金及附加 Tax and Other Charges on Principal Business	利润总额 Total Profits	利税总额 Total Pre-tax Profits	本年应交增值税 Value-added Tax Payable in Current Year	全部就业人员年平均人数(万人) Annual Average Number of Employed Persons (10000 persons)
11867.72	**53847.96**	**38551.42**	**63239.38**	**53227.71**	**240.75**	**3208.86**	**4847.49**	**1397.89**	**564.39**
5552.44	20411.72	13747.82	26040.11	21537.04	112.46	1581.46	2366.05	672.12	265.97
6315.28	33436.24	24803.60	37199.26	31690.67	128.29	1627.40	2481.45	725.76	298.42
3069.97	16058.53	11501.81	14746.74	11911.57	56.26	1183.40	1631.14	391.48	81.86
3312.77	12192.08	8141.30	15806.69	13290.12	74.95	979.03	1393.25	339.27	140.03
5484.97	25597.34	18908.31	32685.94	28026.01	109.54	1046.43	1823.10	667.14	342.49
7.56	11.12	7.74	10.32	3.56	0.28	5.53	6.72	0.90	0.04
4.53	15.06	10.99	37.31	33.30	0.23	1.64	2.83	0.96	0.09
30.00	137.43	63.98	106.80	75.55	2.93	6.69	13.66	4.04	0.78
0.22	1.19	0.96	1.48	1.35		0.07	0.12	0.05	0.01
165.02	1259.06	827.02	1661.70	1524.54	2.97	55.70	79.77	21.09	7.39
181.20	693.51	384.23	783.57	623.62	4.07	83.05	110.02	22.90	7.42
33.99	160.37	79.26	159.02	131.98	4.96	7.68	16.38	3.74	1.35
14.84	41.75	28.24	61.40	50.44	0.27	3.80	4.60	0.54	1.00
264.45	805.93	458.04	1308.33	1140.06	5.02	72.85	107.26	29.39	11.28
384.94	982.54	691.61	1622.65	1328.62	8.94	73.48	120.58	38.17	25.17
178.17	351.32	269.65	847.10	746.05	3.06	23.87	40.76	13.83	14.31
52.66	237.13	161.80	284.74	248.09	1.28	8.99	18.51	8.24	3.18
301.44	1235.66	838.61	1342.54	1100.96	6.29	73.97	113.35	33.09	18.90
179.41	741.89	482.26	1109.50	979.89	4.07	27.57	57.30	25.66	10.10
166.72	505.29	313.89	766.35	651.58	3.58	35.99	57.50	17.94	9.06
224.90	935.73	712.05	1471.14	1311.13	4.43	38.34	61.24	18.48	17.42
15.71	112.09	58.15	151.89	139.56	0.41	5.74	8.28	2.13	0.30
459.11	2013.86	1358.62	2519.41	2063.95	10.85	144.13	214.66	59.69	17.29
146.80	759.40	492.32	463.35	287.58	2.78	69.68	87.84	15.38	4.20
12.24	54.79	32.68	56.16	46.77	0.31	5.48	7.05	1.26	0.51
692.66	2595.63	1635.44	3464.58	2938.24	12.62	187.03	274.64	74.99	38.43
704.57	3605.94	2344.02	3958.45	3437.94	18.45	127.78	248.74	102.52	31.45
139.22	563.71	337.65	1136.18	1046.42	3.15	29.25	55.30	22.90	4.04
192.26	939.59	709.56	1951.99	1793.45	4.22	52.75	83.74	26.77	7.90
1005.31	3180.93	2172.03	5153.46	4439.93	21.14	239.58	377.44	116.72	53.80
548.50	2459.26	1809.98	2467.90	1989.84	9.24	142.89	211.34	59.21	28.99
702.44	3264.27	2490.81	2611.25	1993.22	11.27	185.89	266.07	68.91	33.15
151.99	889.27	580.00	800.32	675.59	4.47	30.42	52.78	17.90	8.18
86.02	436.03	315.46	451.50	383.77	2.53	19.53	30.05	8.00	4.37
2419.83	10022.40	7160.38	11061.48	8911.01	44.09	805.56	1184.83	335.19	88.19
2034.94	12900.09	10469.39	13608.10	11640.37	35.96	541.76	782.37	204.64	99.11
194.31	842.46	652.92	660.29	476.49	3.07	58.81	82.87	20.99	8.71
71.84	237.17	162.46	271.80	224.69	1.29	13.50	21.10	6.31	5.25
46.00	347.73	237.87	516.15	472.26	1.56	15.17	24.87	8.14	1.40
7.81	27.80	20.57	25.30	20.50	0.12	1.24	2.33	0.96	0.52
23.70	298.80	105.85	130.86	111.92	0.49	6.43	11.42	4.50	0.42
7.15	61.77	38.84	164.38	155.24	0.15	2.28	3.17	0.73	0.23
15.29	119.98	36.07	40.65	28.26	0.21	4.75	6.02	1.06	0.43

12-23 规模以上大中型工业企业主要经济指标（2022年）

单位：亿元

项　　目	Item	企业单位数（个） Number of Enterprises (unit)	工业总产值（当年价） Gross Industrial Output Value (at current prices)
全　省	**Provincial Total**	**7887**	**122393.14**
按轻重工业分	Grouped by Light & Heavy Industry		
轻工业	Light Industry	3582	33623.10
重工业	Heavy Industry	4305	88770.04
按企业规模分	Grouped by Size of Enterprises		
大型企业	Large	1438	82354.91
中型企业	Medium	6449	40038.23
按行业分	Grouped by Sector		
煤炭开采和洗选业	Mining and Washing of Coal		
石油和天然气开采业	Extraction of Petroleum and Natural Gas	2	988.93
黑色金属矿采选业	Mining and Dressing of Ferrous Metal Ores	1	2.32
有色金属矿采选业	Mining and Dressing of Nonferrous Metal Ores	4	56.63
非金属矿采选业	Mining and Dressing of Nonmetal Ores	3	45.45
开采专业及辅助性活动	Mining Specialized and Auxiliary Operations	3	45.60
其他采矿业	Mining and Dressing of Other Ores		
农副食品加工业	Processing of Farm and Sideline Food	117	1690.57
食品制造业	Manufacture of Food	135	1530.38
酒、饮料和精制茶制造业	Manufacture of Wine, Beverage and Refined Tea	52	906.15
烟草制品业	Tobacco Products	18	573.28
纺织业	Textile Industry	142	1155.93
纺织服装、服饰业	Manufacture of Textile Garments, Footwear and Headgear	314	1431.25
皮革、毛皮、羽毛及其制品和制鞋业	Leather, Fur, Feather, Down and Related Products	192	701.36
木材加工和木、竹、藤、棕、草制品业	Timber Processing, Bamboo, Cane, Palm Fiber & Straw Products	14	71.96
家具制造业	Manufacture of Furniture	210	1328.53
造纸和纸制品业	Papermaking and Paper Products	116	1451.33
印刷和记录媒介复制业	Printing and Record Medium Reproduction	136	782.71
文教、工美、体育和娱乐用品制造业	Manufacture of Cultural, Educational,Sports and Entertainment Articles	372	2671.15
石油、煤炭及其他燃料加工业	Petroleum, Coal and other Fuel Processing	8	4605.30
化学原料和化学制品制造业	Manufacture of Raw Chemical Materials and Chemical Products	201	3225.53
医药制造业	Manufacture of Medicines	141	1697.34
化学纤维制造业	Manufacture of Chemical Fibers	11	109.31
橡胶和塑料制品业	Rubber and Plastic Products	461	2529.61
非金属矿物制品业	Nonmetal Mineral Products	315	2986.37
黑色金属冶炼和压延加工业	Smelting and Pressing of Ferrous Metals	41	2936.73
有色金属冶炼和压延加工业	Smelting and Pressing of Nonferrous Metals	86	2100.25
金属制品业	Metal Products	542	4091.21
通用设备制造业	Manufacture of General-purpose Machinery	352	3418.94
专用设备制造业	Manufacture of Special-purpose Machinery	408	3135.80
汽车制造业	Manufacture of Automobile	315	10491.88
铁路、船舶、航空航天和其他运输设备制造业	Manufacture of Railway ,Ship,Aeronautics and Other Transport equipment	84	1165.34
电气机械和器材制造业	Manufacture of Electrical Machinery and Equipment	1039	15652.92
计算机、通信和其他电子设备制造业	Manufacture of Communication Equipment, Computers and Other Electronic Equipment	1669	38856.10
仪器仪表制造业	Manufacture of Instruments and Meters	171	832.06
其他制造业	Other Manufactures	57	332.82
废弃资源综合利用业	Comprehensive Utilization of Waste	12	161.21
金属制品、机械和设备修理业	Manufacture of Metal Products,Machinery and Equipment Maintenance	19	193.35
电力、热力生产和供应业	Production and Supply of Electric Power and Heat Power	67	7528.26
燃气生产和供应业	Production and Supply of Gas	8	343.92
水的生产和供应业	Production and Supply of Water	49	565.32

Main Economic Indicators of Large and Medium-sized Industrial Enterprises above Designated Size (2022)

(100 million yuan)

工业增加值 Value-added of Industry	年末资产总计 Total Assets at the Year-end	流动资产合计 Total Working Capital	营业收入 Business Revenue	营业成本 Cost of Business	税金及附加 Tax and Other Charges	利润总额 Total Profits	利税总额 Total Pre-tax Profits	本年应交增值税 Value-added Tax Payable in Current Year	全部就业人员年平均人数(万人) Annual Average Number of Employed Persons (10000 persons)
27497.51	**140366.07**	**82207.66**	**124415.25**	**102728.22**	**1713.62**	**8231.83**	**12408.93**	**2463.48**	**800.51**
8713.51	36213.92	23393.64	34130.13	26626.05	478.14	2972.14	4415.26	964.98	312.69
18784.00	104152.15	58814.02	90285.12	76102.17	1235.48	5259.69	7993.67	1498.50	487.82
18776.54	99583.63	57966.57	83677.58	68574.75	1355.46	5870.69	8854.21	1628.06	444.80
8720.97	40782.44	24241.09	40737.67	34153.47	358.17	2361.14	3554.73	835.41	355.71
956.92	1098.84	108.99	975.96	355.57	54.73	536.49	684.31	93.09	0.49
1.02	3.69	0.99	2.03	1.71	0.02	0.11	0.26	0.13	0.04
34.96	76.63	16.18	58.09	32.44	1.65	18.82	24.57	4.10	0.45
21.07	49.74	29.50	44.20	23.08	1.53	10.44	13.94	1.97	0.28
18.66	84.68	44.68	45.60	34.37	0.07	7.82	8.31	0.42	0.15
191.68	1270.34	839.93	1904.67	1753.93	3.73	86.10	107.39	17.56	6.12
522.48	1477.62	858.22	1716.32	1060.39	11.69	208.28	292.43	72.47	11.43
253.72	814.85	534.13	966.29	708.90	15.78	84.91	133.57	32.87	5.39
464.39	490.48	370.01	567.25	165.58	301.85	51.47	406.77	53.44	1.39
263.99	815.24	499.26	1154.72	973.54	5.17	89.23	121.60	27.19	10.45
379.49	970.02	667.13	1322.11	1032.08	8.49	62.24	106.89	36.17	24.78
200.62	394.38	279.58	696.62	585.29	4.02	34.57	49.34	10.74	16.91
19.83	83.59	48.50	70.15	56.94	0.57	5.39	9.19	3.23	1.08
343.86	1577.60	983.13	1303.96	1045.24	7.06	119.32	160.31	33.93	17.21
260.11	1722.42	850.36	1403.73	1242.31	7.87	31.24	87.18	48.07	7.87
218.03	960.85	511.85	777.42	639.74	3.81	66.64	87.23	16.79	10.79
442.80	1725.86	1384.29	2565.20	2259.45	9.28	100.30	132.99	23.41	34.27
838.76	1721.71	663.98	4624.16	3925.26	631.18	7.89	686.84	47.78	1.57
606.92	3405.73	1779.01	3595.45	2985.00	19.42	192.73	296.44	84.30	12.01
640.55	3662.86	2083.75	1667.99	857.70	12.46	308.64	398.26	77.16	11.99
26.39	103.38	44.70	108.24	87.53	0.59	11.56	14.67	2.52	0.50
669.38	2840.92	1718.73	2671.99	2218.69	13.11	241.74	307.20	52.36	33.96
681.62	3538.88	1811.59	2943.59	2537.21	15.48	158.91	245.09	70.70	23.25
280.82	1761.50	613.05	3015.60	2841.14	7.81	35.27	88.84	45.76	4.30
259.93	1156.67	773.93	2227.59	2030.39	6.36	79.73	119.45	33.36	8.41
988.54	2900.54	1858.10	4041.07	3404.91	18.82	304.37	411.50	88.31	38.89
773.79	3744.49	2674.26	3445.84	2829.58	14.26	274.38	349.54	60.90	29.98
955.36	4414.43	3192.04	2931.48	2152.65	16.78	368.91	454.15	68.46	33.90
2083.33	8988.03	6399.52	11026.65	9485.96	269.36	662.47	1137.39	205.56	37.98
233.80	1618.68	1113.15	1157.81	1019.53	5.39	69.98	88.34	12.97	7.51
3533.59	18358.14	12614.62	15895.59	12932.60	66.06	1341.95	1837.95	429.93	112.78
8144.65	47495.36	31857.35	39306.86	32226.66	137.36	2198.04	2829.52	494.12	256.81
243.86	1224.89	825.37	857.22	672.66	4.04	57.95	81.23	19.25	11.94
114.09	427.09	337.85	336.08	246.79	2.22	49.61	55.98	4.15	4.75
23.93	149.84	83.02	155.93	136.86	0.53	8.37	12.39	3.50	0.61
57.11	248.53	170.07	191.98	165.72	0.94	10.27	14.98	3.77	1.87
1465.10	16357.10	2991.48	7698.92	7263.48	29.20	247.46	440.39	163.73	13.84
56.32	476.68	102.87	357.12	304.85	0.96	27.85	33.71	4.89	0.81
226.02	2153.78	472.49	583.77	432.47	3.96	60.38	78.76	14.42	3.71

12-24 规模以上高技术制造业主要经济指标（2022年）

单位：亿元

项　　目	Item	企业单位数（个） Number of Enterprises (unit)	工业总产值（当年价） Gross Industrial Output Value (at current prices)
高技术制造业合计	**Total**	**13271**	**55632.52**
信息化学品制造	**Manufacture of Information Chemical Products**	**13**	**25.07**
医药制造业	**Manufacture of Medicines**	**628**	**2264.35**
#化学药品制造	Manufacture of Chemical Medicines	139	710.93
中成药生产	Manufacture of Traditional Chinese Patent Medicines	102	528.96
生物药品制造	Manufacture of Biological and Biochemical Products	109	466.37
航空航天器及设备制造	**Manufacture of Aircraft and Spacecraft**	**30**	**173.36**
飞机制造	Manufacture of Aircraft	7	17.49
航天器制造	Manufacture of Spacecraft	2	0.80
航空、航天相关设备制造	Manufacture of Aircraft and Spacecraft related products	5	4.11
其他飞行器制造	Manufacture of Air Vehicle	8	17.09
航空航天器修理	Repair of Aircraft and Spacecraft	8	133.86
电子及通信设备制造业	**Manufacture of Electronic and Communication Equipment**	**9488**	**44977.32**
电子工业专用设备制造	Equipment for Electronic Industry	669	1074.15
光纤、光缆及锂离子电池制造	Optical Fiber,Cable Manufacturing	574	2426.28
通信设备、雷达及配套设备制造	Manufacture of Communication Equipment	813	20454.90
通信系统设备制造	Manufacture of Communication Transmission Equipment	330	3539.40
通信终端设备制造	Manufacture of Communication Exchange Equipment	474	16895.92
雷达及配套设备制造	Manufacture of Radar Equipment	9	19.58
广播电视设备制造	Manufacture of Broadcasting and Television Equipment	227	545.32
非专业视听设备制造	Manufacture of Audio-visual Equipment	715	2501.57
电子器件制造	Manufacture of Electronic Parts	2086	6720.76
电子元件及电子专用材料制造	Manufacture of Electronic component and Electronic Specialized Materials	3104	7760.99
智能消费设备制造	Manufacturing of Intelligent Consumption Equipment	464	1604.56
其他电子设备制造	Manufacture of Electronic Devices	836	1888.78
电子计算机及办公设备制造业	**Manufacture of Computers and Office Equipment**	**1510**	**5567.94**
计算机整机制造	Manufacture of Complete Computers	220	1957.23
计算机零部件制造	Manufacture of Computer part Equipment	450	1028.72
计算机外围设备制造	Manufacture of Computer Peripheral Equipment	461	1348.76
工业控制计算机及系统制造	Manufacture of Industrial Control Computer and System	55	44.83
信息安全设备制造	Manufacture of Information Security Equipment	29	27.48
其他计算机制造	Other computer equipment	168	729.85
办公设备制造	Manufacture of Office Equipment	127	431.07
医疗设备及仪器仪表制造业	**Manufacture of Medical Equipment, Instruments and Meters**	**1602**	**2624.48**
#医疗设备及器械制造	Manufacture of Medical Equipment and Appliances	624	1227.06
通用仪器仪表制造	Manufacture of General Measuring Instruments and Machinery	584	749.99
专用仪器仪表制造	Manufacture of Special Measuring Instruments and Machinery	216	223.52

Main Indicators on High-tech Manufacturing Enterprises above Designated Size (2022)

(100 million yuan)

工业增加值 Value-added of Industry	年末资产总计 Total Assets at the Year-end	流动资产合计 Total Working Capital	营业收入 Business Revenue	营业成本 Cost of Business	税金及附加 Tax and Other Charges	利润总额 Total Profits	利税总额 Total Pre-tax Profits	本年应交增值税 Value-added Tax Payable in Current Year	全部就业人员年平均人数(万人) Annual Average Number of Employed Persons (10000 persons)
11783.82	**69523.37**	**47225.52**	**56285.06**	**45649.10**	**3315.54**	**200.62**	**4353.43**	**837.28**	**412.65**
5.87	**20.09**	**12.78**	**20.36**	**17.65**	**0.69**	**0.06**	**1.07**	**0.32**	**0.16**
808.74	**4490.77**	**2602.48**	**2194.06**	**1155.60**	**385.26**	**15.79**	**497.13**	**96.07**	**17.04**
247.17	1565.98	933.62	669.70	339.15	138.31	5.36	176.57	32.91	4.50
166.94	945.05	486.84	526.53	320.15	72.81	4.07	99.90	23.01	4.62
181.55	1020.95	548.05	457.27	172.40	63.64	2.88	87.40	20.87	2.70
51.16	**252.98**	**169.00**	**171.81**	**140.61**	**15.43**	**0.83**	**19.50**	**3.25**	**1.32**
6.62	66.20	39.45	17.10	11.81	2.09	0.06	2.83	0.68	0.19
0.08	0.94	0.88	0.80	0.68	-0.05	0.00	-0.02	0.03	0.00
1.70	20.37	10.91	4.57	3.57	0.52	0.07	0.63	0.04	0.06
4.01	15.15	9.08	15.62	12.12	2.00	0.07	2.32	0.25	0.13
38.74	150.31	108.68	133.72	112.43	10.87	0.62	13.75	2.25	0.93
9263.58	**55746.85**	**38149.23**	**45678.81**	**37545.26**	**2301.40**	**155.78**	**3076.20**	**619.01**	**324.54**
275.14	1567.68	1326.27	963.67	737.83	74.72	4.25	102.46	23.48	12.85
378.44	3270.03	2322.62	2580.39	2291.52	60.62	5.81	95.53	29.11	16.79
4352.48	24489.62	18371.46	21213.19	16448.50	1309.29	72.00	1676.67	295.38	84.18
769.47	3401.46	2579.45	2946.36	2267.50	146.39	14.76	189.96	28.81	20.53
3580.38	21050.77	15761.24	18249.35	14167.36	1165.94	57.18	1489.36	266.23	63.46
2.63	37.39	30.77	17.48	13.64	-3.04	0.06	-2.64	0.34	0.19
134.60	739.72	417.66	537.93	415.85	45.43	2.63	56.04	7.99	5.84
298.66	2738.13	2086.19	2509.89	2258.14	51.06	7.16	74.75	16.54	20.97
1325.17	10617.81	5454.88	6288.06	5543.88	121.77	24.17	234.61	88.66	58.84
1843.19	9250.72	5673.41	8031.15	6861.43	455.87	29.28	587.03	101.88	93.91
258.64	1395.07	1108.10	1629.71	1368.77	74.86	4.70	96.85	17.28	11.18
397.25	1678.06	1388.65	1924.82	1619.33	107.78	5.77	152.26	38.71	19.99
840.29	**5258.94**	**3695.89**	**5667.43**	**5023.51**	**282.51**	**14.12**	**351.31**	**54.68**	**40.38**
179.37	1369.20	1071.78	2028.66	1877.26	72.96	2.97	82.86	6.93	6.13
167.59	997.30	564.49	981.49	870.54	47.86	2.48	60.98	10.64	11.80
243.82	1554.25	1076.63	1412.16	1238.49	74.30	4.22	94.13	15.61	12.44
10.52	49.38	40.31	46.91	35.81	3.91	0.15	4.90	0.84	0.50
4.43	47.76	37.62	26.69	20.47	0.19	0.06	0.58	0.33	0.24
141.85	743.83	585.55	733.12	606.32	54.09	2.42	71.43	14.92	4.98
92.71	497.22	319.51	438.41	374.61	29.21	1.81	36.42	5.39	4.29
814.17	**3753.73**	**2596.15**	**2552.59**	**1766.47**	**330.25**	**14.03**	**408.23**	**63.95**	**29.21**
432.23	1813.06	1177.94	1129.29	693.16	201.63	7.62	237.18	27.93	13.64
210.09	1120.91	829.16	751.36	548.02	73.50	3.89	101.21	23.82	7.97
71.52	339.21	261.96	225.37	155.02	20.34	0.99	27.22	5.89	3.06

12-25 规模以上先进制造业主要经济指标（2022年）

单位：亿元

项　　目	Item	企业单位数（个）Number of Enterprises (unit)	工业总产值（当年价）Gross Industrial Output Value (at current prices)	工业增加值 Value-added of Industry
合　计	**Total**	**41624**	**98170.91**	**20507.83**
高端电子信息制造业	**Manufacture of Advanced Electronic Equipment and Communication Equipment**	**6832**	**37940.67**	**7985.05**
集成电路及关键元器件	Integrated Circuits and Key Components	5850	15924.98	3463.97
信息通信设备	Communication Equipment	804	20435.32	4349.85
新型显示	New-Type Displays	178	1580.36	171.23
先进装备制造业	**Manufacture of Advanced Equipment**	**11304**	**30485.21**	**6677.80**
智能制造装备	Intelligent Manufacturing Equipment	3372	5209.25	1425.25
船舶与海洋工程装备	Equipment for Ships and Marine Engineering	94	596.65	102.04
节能环保装备	Equipment for Energy Conservation and Environmental Protection	1401	2537.52	519.19
轨道交通设备	Equipment for Rail Transportation	38	98.12	21.89
航空装备	Equipment for Aviation	57	393.91	48.80
新能源装备	Equipment for New Energy	1960	3673.25	791.58
汽车制造	Automobiles	1140	11593.39	2280.35
卫星及应用	Satellites and Applications	595	3901.83	852.11
重要基础件	Critical Basic Components	2647	2481.30	636.59
石油化工产业	**Petrochemical Manufacturing**	**3218**	**11515.68**	**1966.23**
先进轻纺制造业	**Manufacture of Advanced Light Textiles**	**12501**	**11513.94**	**2651.58**
绿色食品饮料	Green Foods and Drinks	2541	2360.05	433.04
高附加值纺织服装	High Added-value Textile Clothing	6226	2163.40	489.09
环保多功能家具	Environmental Friendly and Multi-purpose Furniture	1956	662.31	150.61
智能节能型家电	Intelligent Energy Saving Household Appliances	1778	6328.18	1578.84
新材料制造业	**Manufacture of New Materials**	**8221**	**9994.41**	**1672.22**
高端精品钢材	High-end Fine Steel	495	2986.88	273.83
高性能复合材料及特种功能材料	High Performance Composite Materials and Special Purpose Materials	7720	6990.23	1395.64
战略前沿材料	Strategic Materials	6	17.30	2.75
生物医药及高性能医疗器械	**Manufacture of Biological Medicines and Advanced Medical Equipment**	**1345**	**2904.15**	**1034.95**
生物制药	Biological Medicine	628	1811.48	646.99
高性能医疗器械	Advanced Medical Equipment	717	1092.67	387.95

Main Indicators on Advanced Manufacturing Enterprises above Designated Size (2022)

(100 million yuan)

年末资产总计 Total Assets at the Year-end	流动资产合计 Total Working Capital	营业收入 Business Revenue	营业成本 Cost of Business	税金及附加 Tax and Other Charges on Principal Business	利润总额 Total Profits	利税总额 Total Pre-tax Profits	本年应交增值税 Value-added Tax Payable in Current Year	全部就业人员年平均人数(万人) Annual Average Number of Employed Persons (10000 persons)
106467.96	**70223.98**	**99568.85**	**81981.82**	**1241.30**	**5763.40**	**8878.84**	**1874.13**	**843.71**
48065.44	**32081.90**	**38546.25**	**31458.02**	**134.66**	**2061.88**	**2709.85**	**513.31**	**258.34**
21360.33	12156.67	15737.47	13591.44	58.19	695.02	961.75	208.54	165.86
24452.23	18340.69	21195.71	16434.87	71.94	1312.33	1679.31	295.04	83.99
2252.88	1584.54	1613.07	1431.71	4.53	54.54	68.79	9.73	8.50
32035.00	**22920.32**	**29961.31**	**24619.99**	**352.85**	**2003.91**	**2929.91**	**573.15**	**228.41**
7106.19	5152.93	4940.10	3654.72	25.14	499.66	646.77	121.98	55.29
1183.53	769.61	574.63	533.10	2.00	21.50	27.29	3.80	2.62
3004.68	2155.26	2488.43	2086.29	9.87	145.39	207.39	52.13	25.83
168.27	120.07	102.24	86.22	0.58	4.96	8.63	3.08	0.62
353.32	286.34	400.90	337.09	1.49	15.84	20.90	3.57	2.06
4069.93	2873.38	3573.17	2910.69	13.52	290.54	364.73	60.66	35.18
10008.90	7058.99	12143.00	10452.40	273.64	705.32	1209.62	230.67	46.57
3764.15	2860.75	3295.01	2543.80	16.11	159.32	210.74	35.31	25.58
2376.05	1642.99	2443.83	2015.68	10.50	161.39	233.85	61.95	34.66
9004.28	**4521.13**	**11996.84**	**10239.81**	**669.85**	**297.40**	**1193.98**	**226.73**	**33.01**
10757.78	**7579.54**	**11724.84**	**9410.73**	**56.13**	**951.05**	**1368.04**	**360.86**	**235.57**
1903.09	1203.96	2589.54	2147.93	13.91	150.30	218.66	54.45	42.67
1460.78	986.80	2069.10	1734.27	9.87	102.71	156.31	43.73	102.39
665.01	441.65	643.99	528.71	3.14	40.55	59.17	15.48	31.50
6728.91	4947.13	6422.21	4999.82	29.21	657.49	933.91	247.21	59.01
8032.16	**4745.63**	**10058.34**	**8867.09**	**35.22**	**416.10**	**624.35**	**173.02**	**106.01**
1711.64	721.56	3058.69	2884.21	7.58	35.71	86.67	43.39	6.85
6304.29	4011.91	6979.69	5965.11	27.60	379.10	536.27	129.56	99.08
16.23	12.16	19.96	17.77	0.04	1.30	1.40	0.07	0.08
5141.66	**3081.00**	**2769.44**	**1575.59**	**19.41**	**473.24**	**592.41**	**99.76**	**34.68**
3592.62	2081.98	1755.25	924.48	12.64	308.21	397.70	76.86	17.04
1549.04	999.02	1014.19	651.10	6.77	165.03	194.71	22.91	17.64

12-26 规模以上工业企业主要经济效益指标（2022年）

项　　目	Item
全　省	**Provincial Total**
按经济类型分	Grouped by Ownership
在总计中：国有控股工业	Of the Total: State-holding Industry
国有工业	State-owned Industry
集体工业	Collective-owned Industry
股份合作工业	Share-holding Cooperative Industry
股份制工业	Share-holding Industry
外商投资工业	Foreign-funded Industry
港澳台投资工业	Industry with Funds from Hong Kong, Macao and Taiwan
按轻重工业分	Grouped by Light and Heavy Industries
轻工业	Light Industry
重工业	Heavy Industry
按企业规模分	Grouped by Size of Enterprises
大型企业	Large Enterprises
中型企业	Medium Enterprises
小微型企业	Small and Micro Enterprises
按行业分	Grouped by Sector
煤炭开采和洗选业	Mining and Washing of Coal
石油和天然气开采业	Extraction of Petroleum and Natural Gas
黑色金属矿采选业	Mining and Dressing of Ferrous Metal Ores
有色金属矿采选业	Mining and Dressing of Nonferrous Metal Ores
非金属矿采选业	Mining and Dressing of Nonmetal Ores
开采专业及辅助性活动	Mining Specialized and Auxiliary Operations
其他采矿业	Mining and Dressing of Other Ores
农副食品加工业	Processing of Farm and Sideline Food
食品制造业	Manufacture of Food
酒、饮料和精制茶制造业	Manufacture of Wine, Beverage and Refined Tea
烟草制品业	Tobacco Products
纺织业	Textile Industry
纺织服装、服饰业	Manufacture of Textile Garments, Footwear and Headgear
皮革、毛皮、羽毛及其制品和制鞋业	Leather, Fur, Feather, Down and Related Products
木材加工和木、竹、藤、棕、草制品业	Timber Processing, Bamboo, Cane, Palm Fiber & Straw Products
家具制造业	Manufacture of Furniture
造纸和纸制品业	Papermaking and Paper Products
印刷和记录媒介复制业	Printing and Record Medium Reproduction
文教、工美、体育和娱乐用品制造业	Manufacture of Cultural, Educational,Sports and Entertainment Articles
石油、煤炭及其他燃料加工业	Petroleum, Coal and other Fuel Processing
化学原料和化学制品制造业	Manufacture of Raw Chemical Materials and Chemical Products
医药制造业	Manufacture of Medicines
化学纤维制造业	Manufacture of Chemical Fibers
橡胶和塑料制品业	Rubber and Plastic Products
非金属矿物制品业	Nonmetal Mineral Products
黑色金属冶炼和压延加工业	Smelting and Pressing of Ferrous Metals
有色金属冶炼和压延加工业	Smelting and Pressing of Nonferrous Metals
金属制品业	Metal Products
通用设备制造业	Manufacture of General-purpose Machinery
专用设备制造业	Manufacture of Special-purpose Machinery
汽车制造业	Manufacture of Automobile
铁路、船舶、航空航天和其他运输设备制造业	Manufacture of Railway ,Ship,Aeronautics and Other Transport equipment
电气机械和器材制造业	Manufacture of Electrical Machinery and Equipment
计算机、通信和其他电子设备制造业	Manufacture of Communication Equipment, Computers and Other Electronic Equipment
仪器仪表制造业	Manufacture of Instruments and Meters
其他制造业	Other Manufactures
废弃资源综合利用业	Comprehensive Utilization of Waste
金属制品、机械和设备修理业	Manufacture of Metal Products,Machinery and Equipment Maintenance
电力、热力生产和供应业	Production and Supply of Electric Power and Heat Power
燃气生产和供应业	Production and Supply of Gas
水的生产和供应业	Production and Supply of Water

Main Indicators on Economic Benefit of Industrial Enterprises above Designated Size (2022)

总资产贡献率 (%) Ratio of Total Assets to Industrial Output Value (%)	资产负债率 (%) Assets-Liability Ratio (%)	成本费用利润率 (%) Ratio of Profits to Industrial Costs (%)	全员劳动生产率 (元/人) Overall Labor Productivity (yuan/person)	产品销售率 (%) Proportion of Products Sold (%)
8.47	**58.39**	**5.98**	**279615**	**96.40**
8.16	58.39	4.75	836185	97.94
5.13	56.67	5.20	529675	98.47
2.77	68.04	0.78	111999	97.22
21.54	51.08	6.55	312881	95.76
7.85	60.20	5.49	285297	96.03
10.38	54.10	6.55	337749	98.50
9.49	54.44	7.49	234291	95.87
10.94	55.41	7.24	221894	94.97
7.56	59.48	5.45	321741	97.03
9.13	58.65	7.54	422135	96.25
9.25	53.81	6.18	245172	96.39
6.72	61.25	3.71	183496	96.62
50.23	78.69	136.75	20183276	98.75
28.00	73.40	32.76	1565655	97.44
28.69	61.07	25.25	732978	97.06
7.13	69.74	5.18	601750	90.11
10.54	29.51	21.47	1267406	99.96
7.69	66.89	3.12	268804	100.11
16.61	46.00	11.30	348117	94.83
13.33	49.60	8.86	436935	97.41
77.00	18.47	21.57	2610216	99.38
11.23	54.88	6.10	211473	94.67
10.33	49.13	4.50	139684	90.85
11.20	61.24	3.71	119015	98.00
5.62	58.94	2.53	145289	96.89
9.32	61.01	6.61	159382	96.76
5.97	54.21	2.11	227672	95.82
9.01	44.13	7.44	179895	97.45
7.23	64.03	3.36	124301	92.30
25.93	61.53	-0.54	3763042	98.98
8.98	51.48	5.23	360466	98.42
11.34	42.97	21.05	474552	91.41
12.47	36.69	10.28	344771	93.25
9.65	54.83	6.34	174679	98.12
7.19	62.67	4.28	249463	96.25
6.00	60.06	1.38	507603	97.22
8.04	74.43	2.19	270203	98.56
11.13	60.18	5.29	194409	96.65
8.60	56.58	6.85	215539	95.53
9.02	51.53	10.25	233767	93.48
12.09	64.02	6.29	489702	99.65
5.37	65.71	5.36	258068	98.23
9.26	60.31	7.73	251139	93.27
5.96	58.04	5.24	282110	96.02
8.86	48.46	9.05	211479	96.65
11.49	47.28	10.45	185345	95.24
7.81	64.94	3.48	336636	96.15
6.99	60.05	5.46	275102	99.82
3.89	61.91	4.19	1094446	99.81
9.53	53.96	4.83	806221	99.88
4.71	60.01	11.28	514629	96.99

12-27 规模以上制造业工业企业主要经济指标
Main Economic Indicators of Manufacturing Enterprises above Designated Size

项　目	Item	2000	2010	2015	2020	2021	2022
企业单位数 （个）	Number of Enterprises (unit)	18571	52102	42134	57230	64919	69188
工业总产值 （亿元）	Gross Industrial Output Value (100 million yuan)	11352.62	79504.12	124649.16	138707.96	159796.90	166828.59
工业增加值 （亿元）	Value-added of Industry (100 million yuan)	2768.88	18317.74	29446.21	29737.46	34319.83	33636.96
营业收入 （亿元）	Business Revenue (100 million yuan)	10865.66	77730.85	120886.73	140163.33	161397.04	168816.49
资产总计 （亿元）	Total Assets (100 million yuan)	11653.11	52734.31	95411.22	129502.06	148971.08	167339.96
流动资产合计 （亿元）	Total Liquid Assets (100 million yuan)		32414.52	54715.38	86415.14	99693.71	111726.52
固定资产净额 （亿元）	Total Fixed Assets (100 million yuan)		16420.14	26943.69	19812.10	21734.04	24030.33
负债总计 （亿元）	Total Liabilities (100 million yuan)	6950.47	29407.47	54747.90	73749.37	84636.43	96623.44
所有者权益合计（亿元）	Total Creditors' Equity (100 million yuan)	4576.24	23243.24	40239.01	55752.84	64335.99	70483.21
利润总额 （亿元）	Total Profits (100 million yuan)	348.92	5313.74	7723.16	8597.54	10371.61	9106.84
亏损企业亏损额（亿元）	Loss Value of Loss-making Enterprises (100 million yuan)	131.89	195.53	510.18	975.92	1035.17	1553.64
利税总额 （亿元）	Total Pre-tax Profits (100 million yuan)	729.92	8150.46	12375.00	12845.43	15076.96	14146.68
应交增值税 （亿元）	Value-added Tax Payable(100 million yuan)	277.66	2003.07	3284.50	2780.71	3011.58	3227.47
从业人员平均人数 （万人）	Average Employed Persons (10000 persons)	546.03	1533.72	1439.33	1248.52	1314.70	1303.60

注：1.本表总产值和增加值绝对数按当年价格计算，增加值2009年及以前用生产法计算，2010年起用收入法计算，2011年统计口径从年业务收入500万元及以上调整为2000万元及以上工业企业,2021年为主业务收入2000万元及以上工业企业和工业个体经营户。

2.本表中营业收入指标数据2017年及以前为主营业务收入数据，2018年后为营业收入数据。

Note: a) Gross industrial output values and value-added are calculated at current prices.Value-added is calculated by production approach in 2009 and prior to and since 2010 by income approach. Since 2011,the annual principal business revenue of industrial enterprises above designated size is changed from industrial enterprises of 5 million yuan or above to 20 million yuan or above. It is adjusted to industrial enterprises and industrial self-employed households with main business income of 20 million yuan and above in 2021.

b) The indicator was Revenue from Principal Business in 2017 and before,and are Business Revenue since 2018.

12-28 各市规模以上工业企业主要经济指标（2022年）

Main Economic Indicators of Industrial Enterprises above Designated Size by City (2022)

单位：亿元 (100 million yuan)

市 别	City	营业收入 Business Revenue	营业成本 Cost of Principal Business	资产合计 Total Assets	负债合计 Total Liabilities	利润总额 Total Profits	利税总额 Total Pre-tax Profits	全部就业人员年平均人数(万人) Annual Average Number of Employed Persons (10000 persons)
广 州	Guangzhou	25181.62	20941.77	31134.74	17245.93	1528.23	2591.82	127.58
深 圳	Shenzhen	46591.23	36965.90	60367.01	34525.85	3315.56	4305.22	303.52
珠 海	Zhuhai	6642.99	5403.31	10239.31	6271.92	596.53	757.38	44.58
汕 头	Shantou	3157.51	2638.12	3155.13	1575.64	201.43	285.56	27.63
佛 山	Foshan	27764.31	23381.98	19978.06	11400.90	2005.51	2874.82	156.23
韶 关	Shaoguan	1718.17	1512.46	2053.05	1351.49	20.94	110.95	11.86
河 源	Heyuan	1431.96	1271.52	1260.46	790.82	52.63	94.98	16.70
梅 州	Meizhou	899.87	731.68	1367.94	730.38	27.27	111.31	8.84
惠 州	Huizhou	10862.73	9603.11	9849.38	6095.50	304.40	669.06	102.03
汕 尾	Shanwei	1118.93	1040.40	1240.95	836.18	13.31	31.21	8.10
东 莞	Dongguan	25355.88	21821.21	23060.30	14207.43	925.67	1463.05	273.75
中 山	Zhongshan	6635.09	5630.23	6571.91	3839.67	302.19	480.49	84.29
江 门	Jiangmen	5460.25	4682.89	6166.34	3708.96	193.64	364.39	52.57
阳 江	Yangjiang	2324.23	2023.31	2945.40	1959.34	147.06	182.36	8.77
湛 江	Zhanjiang	3541.31	2970.10	4087.01	2701.08	189.26	497.56	10.61
茂 名	Maoming	2661.16	2399.58	1459.62	809.81	4.79	214.32	7.15
肇 庆	Zhaoqing	4247.70	3724.95	3680.59	2190.78	174.03	277.72	28.01
清 远	Qingyuan	3147.18	2733.75	3412.80	2092.18	154.97	230.95	23.77
潮 州	Chaozhou	1297.53	1135.55	1122.36	493.95	82.54	119.49	12.41
揭 阳	Jieyang	2262.92	1982.50	2463.75	1404.90	80.00	166.44	16.43
云 浮	Yunfu	724.80	643.61	803.09	453.43	9.30	28.06	7.75
按经济区域分	By Region							
珠 三 角	Pearl River Delta	158741.80	132155.35	171047.63	99486.93	9345.75	13783.96	1172.55
东 翼	Eastern Region	7836.87	6796.57	7982.18	4310.67	377.28	602.70	64.57
西 翼	Western Region	8526.70	7393.00	8492.03	5470.23	341.11	894.24	26.53
山 区	Mountainous Region	7921.97	6893.02	8897.35	5418.30	265.11	576.24	68.92

12-29　各市规模以上私营工业企业主要经济指标（2022年）

Main Economic Indicators of Private Industrial Enterprises above Designated Size by City (2022)

单位：亿元　　(100 million yuan)

市　别	City	营业收入 Business Revenue	营业成本 Cost of Business	资产合计 Total Assets	负债合计 Total Liabilities	利润总额 Total Profits	利税总额 Total Pre-tax Profits	全部就业人员年平均人数(万人) Annual Average Number of Employed Persons (10000 persons)
广　州	Guangzhou	4182.23	3389.00	4313.10	2505.77	230.46	329.95	43.93
深　圳	Shenzhen	12685.49	10596.53	12917.14	7810.55	555.89	792.25	114.81
珠　海	Zhuhai	1395.30	1137.27	2039.77	1145.42	95.42	128.14	14.72
汕　头	Shantou	1993.26	1652.01	1288.25	670.36	123.07	174.50	18.40
佛　山	Foshan	16055.31	13330.57	10599.87	6369.92	1194.43	1753.85	90.25
韶　关	Shaoguan	397.09	357.05	413.11	297.14	3.03	13.33	3.53
河　源	Heyuan	505.47	422.24	393.00	225.18	35.16	54.69	5.65
梅　州	Meizhou	342.30	301.12	449.03	307.65	2.64	12.17	4.88
惠　州	Huizhou	2514.11	2173.54	2193.48	1472.93	90.70	154.54	32.13
汕　尾	Shanwei	269.52	246.78	133.31	81.52	4.57	8.99	3.00
东　莞	Dongguan	11413.83	9684.76	10398.77	7268.28	428.11	672.84	107.62
中　山	Zhongshan	2733.58	2317.45	2358.58	1549.72	91.06	163.14	42.78
江　门	Jiangmen	1983.40	1708.14	1699.53	1126.77	64.37	125.68	23.58
阳　江	Yangjiang	272.86	237.20	228.21	140.56	9.24	16.16	4.92
湛　江	Zhanjiang	460.46	413.58	513.56	406.61	4.54	14.91	5.07
茂　名	Maoming	358.44	318.24	299.11	176.93	12.55	22.35	3.53
肇　庆	Zhaoqing	2021.54	1738.15	1168.64	712.43	105.53	164.24	13.66
清　远	Qingyuan	1008.15	893.81	868.18	628.07	21.23	46.13	8.21
潮　州	Chaozhou	852.12	751.10	605.50	236.47	48.97	70.57	9.57
揭　阳	Jieyang	1485.41	1275.62	653.94	325.35	90.12	124.51	10.87
云　浮	Yunfu	309.51	283.55	313.90	184.89	-2.23	4.55	3.28
按经济区域分	By Region							
珠三角	Pearl River Delta	54984.79	46075.41	47688.89	29961.79	2855.97	4284.64	483.48
东　翼	Eastern Region	4600.31	3925.51	2680.98	1313.69	266.73	378.57	41.84
西　翼	Western Region	1091.76	969.02	1040.88	724.09	26.33	53.42	13.52
山　区	Mountainous Region	2562.52	2257.77	2437.21	1642.93	59.83	130.87	25.54

12-30 各市规模以上工业企业主要经济效益指标（2022年）

Main Indicators on Economic Benefit of Industrial Enterprises above Designated Size by City (2022)

市 别	City	总资产贡献率 (%) Ratio of Total Assets to Industrial Output Value (%)	资产负债率 (%) Assets-Liability Ratio (%)	成本费用利润率 (%) Ratio of Profits to Industrial Costs (%)	全员劳动生产率 (元/人) Overall Labor Productivity (yuan/person)	产品销售率 (%) Proportion of Products Sold (%)
全 省	**Provincial Total**	**8.47**	**58.39**	**5.98**	**279615**	**96.40**
广 州	Guangzhou	8.56	55.39	6.50	385042	99.03
深 圳	Shenzhen	7.47	57.19	7.55	332985	96.41
珠 海	Zhuhai	7.38	61.25	9.80	325314	94.61
汕 头	Shantou	9.56	49.94	6.82	261201	92.50
佛 山	Foshan	14.83	57.07	7.80	358641	96.12
韶 关	Shaoguan	6.32	65.83	1.27	271437	98.39
河 源	Heyuan	8.28	62.74	3.84	205791	95.30
梅 州	Meizhou	8.84	53.39	3.34	271574	98.29
惠 州	Huizhou	7.20	61.89	2.94	214174	94.32
汕 尾	Shanwei	3.28	67.38	1.21	215168	94.38
东 莞	Dongguan	6.62	61.61	3.76	181176	95.90
中 山	Zhongshan	7.82	58.43	4.77	161731	95.68
江 门	Jiangmen	6.80	60.15	3.69	216111	95.15
阳 江	Yangjiang	7.50	66.52	6.76	425164	98.58
湛 江	Zhanjiang	13.06	66.09	6.00	788310	100.60
茂 名	Maoming	15.29	55.48	0.19	538695	99.01
肇 庆	Zhaoqing	8.18	59.52	4.29	260097	96.38
清 远	Qingyuan	7.54	61.30	5.22	239907	97.49
潮 州	Chaozhou	11.06	44.01	6.78	193441	95.29
揭 阳	Jieyang	7.22	57.02	3.72	294972	91.14
云 浮	Yunfu	4.11	56.46	1.31	161030	99.86

12-30 续表 continued

市别	City	总资产贡献率比去年增减(百分点) Percentage Gain in Ratio of Total Assets to Industrial Output Value over Preceding Year	资产负债率比去年增减(百分点) Percentage Gain in Assets-Liability Ratio over Preceding Year	成本费用利润率比去年增减(百分点) Percentage Gain in Ratio of Profits to Industrial Costs over Preceding Year	全员劳动生产率比去年增长(%) Growth in Overall Labor Productivity over Preceding Year (%)	产品销售率比去年增减(百分点) Percentage Gain in Proportion of Products Sold over Preceding Year
全　省	**Provincial Total**	**-1.24**	**1.13**	**-0.95**	**0.70**	**-0.68**
广　州	Guangzhou	-0.63	-1.23	-0.35	-3.02	0.40
深　圳	Shenzhen	-1.22	2.11	-1.15	6.34	-0.33
珠　海	Zhuhai	0.21	3.02	0.03	9.54	-1.56
汕　头	Shantou	-0.19	4.19	-0.06	5.80	-4.21
佛　山	Foshan	0.67	-0.23	-0.13	4.22	0.23
韶　关	Shaoguan	-3.71	3.41	-3.76	-12.43	-0.87
河　源	Heyuan	-0.22	3.08	-0.78	-1.04	0.22
梅　州	Meizhou	-3.06	0.20	-2.78	-5.81	0.10
惠　州	Huizhou	-2.31	1.33	-1.79	-3.91	-2.23
汕　尾	Shanwei	-0.34	7.75	0.36	58.11	3.17
东　莞	Dongguan	-2.00	1.90	-1.16	-3.45	-1.29
中　山	Zhongshan	-0.19	-2.04	-0.07	1.47	-2.83
江　门	Jiangmen	-0.96	1.02	-0.94	-7.80	-2.23
阳　江	Yangjiang	-1.57	0.95	-1.14	3.14	-1.86
湛　江	Zhanjiang	-1.84	-1.27	-2.84	-2.95	0.02
茂　名	Maoming	-11.50	5.83	-7.02	-27.46	-0.61
肇　庆	Zhaoqing	-2.30	0.09	-1.25	-7.99	0.54
清　远	Qingyuan	-0.89	-2.23	-1.28	-19.08	-0.90
潮　州	Chaozhou	-0.01	2.43	0.49	-4.41	-1.38
揭　阳	Jieyang	-10.60	11.41	-4.22	5.69	-3.66
云　浮	Yunfu	-3.64	-1.97	-4.63	-18.21	-0.43

12-31 各市规模以上国有控股工业企业主要经济效益指标（2022年）

Main Indicators on Economic Benefit of State-holding Industrial Enterprises above Designated Size by City (2022)

市 别	City	总资产贡献率 (%) Ratio of Total Assets to Industrial Output Value (%)	资产负债率 (%) Assets-Liability Ratio (%)	成本费用利润率 (%) Ratio of Profits to Industrial Costs (%)	全员劳动生产率 (元/人) Overall Labor Productivity (yuan/person)	产品销售率 (%) Proportion of Products Sold (%)
全 省	**Provincial Total**	**8.16**	**58.39**	**4.75**	**836185**	**97.94**
广 州	Guangzhou	8.54	57.98	6.27	919572	99.65
深 圳	Shenzhen	7.53	55.21	9.45	761002	91.99
珠 海	Zhuhai	5.38	51.83	3.81	670768	98.71
汕 头	Shantou	3.52	55.16	0.84	521311	97.36
佛 山	Foshan	7.51	58.49	5.04	612342	97.60
韶 关	Shaoguan	7.89	65.83	-0.18	669892	99.70
河 源	Heyuan	3.56	70.36	-2.86	880459	98.27
梅 州	Meizhou	20.04	50.39	5.55	1415161	98.51
惠 州	Huizhou	16.66	60.30	1.94	979410	99.24
汕 尾	Shanwei	3.02	66.09	3.18	1405610	95.22
东 莞	Dongguan	3.19	64.17	-0.16	411648	96.97
中 山	Zhongshan	4.77	55.12	2.92	461617	98.14
江 门	Jiangmen	3.06	66.44	0.39	848528	98.94
阳 江	Yangjiang	8.40	66.87	10.10	1721662	99.66
湛 江	Zhanjiang	13.26	58.95	1.23	1830669	99.31
茂 名	Maoming	23.67	49.78	-0.34	1969718	100.00
肇 庆	Zhaoqing	3.55	47.58	2.95	330017	99.93
清 远	Qingyuan	6.16	63.25	3.82	727226	99.95
潮 州	Chaozhou	7.35	62.28	5.51	925922	99.98
揭 阳	Jieyang	1.22	60.68	-10.70	629896	93.30
云 浮	Yunfu	4.18	51.13	1.05	422529	101.10

12−32 各市规模以上按经济类型分的工业企业资产（2022年）

Total Assets of Industrial Enterprises by Ownership and above Designated Size by Ownership and by City (2022)

单位：亿元　　(100 million yuan)

市 别	City	资产合计 Total Assets	#国有控股工业 State-holding Industry	集体工业 Collective-owned Industry	股份合作制工业 Share-holding Cooperative Industry	股份制工业 Share-holding Industry	外商投资工业 Foreign-funded Industry	港澳台投资工业 Industry with Funds from Hong Kong,Macao and Taiwan
广 州	Guangzhou	31134.74	16288.55	9.53	10.30	20634.14	7220.96	2774.15
深 圳	Shenzhen	60367.01	8325.93			41342.11	5961.65	12693.03
珠 海	Zhuhai	10239.31	1054.29	0.39	0.07	7456.13	1601.27	1064.88
汕 头	Shantou	3155.13	646.63	4.84	5.71	2398.60	164.23	325.39
佛 山	Foshan	19978.06	1834.41	4.93	4.28	14288.49	2021.89	3307.75
韶 关	Shaoguan	2053.05	965.71	0.40		1769.93	88.86	161.34
河 源	Heyuan	1260.46	233.07			815.12	73.31	238.04
梅 州	Meizhou	1367.94	402.69	0.22	1.40	1220.45	35.96	97.77
惠 州	Huizhou	9849.38	1600.03	4.22	0.39	5577.63	1837.56	2353.65
汕 尾	Shanwei	1240.95	431.37	1.80		842.22	205.15	169.51
东 莞	Dongguan	23060.30	1421.65	29.85	1.26	16225.84	2406.77	4293.78
中 山	Zhongshan	6571.91	577.10	0.98		3492.54	1694.98	1342.20
江 门	Jiangmen	6166.34	1628.27	0.18	0.55	2888.74	1514.98	1592.99
阳 江	Yangjiang	2945.40	2061.87			1942.55	59.69	845.05
湛 江	Zhanjiang	4087.01	2197.44			2651.44	647.16	723.87
茂 名	Maoming	1459.62	784.63	0.92		1337.88	43.33	43.95
肇 庆	Zhaoqing	3680.59	730.19	2.06		2929.05	278.19	393.76
清 远	Qingyuan	3412.80	455.87	0.06		2248.22	355.56	752.78
潮 州	Chaozhou	1122.36	236.12	1.52	3.01	934.68	10.23	100.62
揭 阳	Jieyang	2463.75	1429.66	0.55	0.47	2254.66	33.52	94.04
云 浮	Yunfu	803.09	170.64			606.30	33.37	147.51
按经济区域分	By Region							
珠 三 角	Pearl River Delta	171047.63	33460.41	52.14	16.85	114834.66	24538.24	29816.20
东 翼	Eastern Region	7982.18	2743.78	8.71	9.19	6430.16	413.13	689.56
西 翼	Western Region	8492.03	5043.94	0.92		5931.87	750.18	1612.88
山 区	Mountainous Region	8897.35	2227.99	0.68	1.40	6660.01	587.06	1397.44

12-33 各市规模以上大中型工业企业产值资产（2022年）
Gross Output Value and Total Assets of Large and Medium-sized Industrial Enterprises above Designated Size by City (2022)

单位：亿元 (100 million yuan)

市 别	City	企业个数(个) Number of Enterprises (unit)	#大型 Large sized	工业总产值(当年价) Gross Industrial Output Value (at current prices)	#大型 Large sized	资产总计 Total Assets	#大型 Large sized
全 省	**Provincial Total**	**7887**	**1438**	**122393.14**	**82354.91**	**140366.07**	**99583.63**
广 州	Guangzhou	758	162	16587.90	12847.12	24404.71	19363.86
深 圳	Shenzhen	1576	326	33996.79	26062.54	47012.63	35649.89
珠 海	Zhuhai	308	71	3815.84	2494.29	7487.49	5709.37
汕 头	Shantou	160	13	1340.52	339.68	1318.38	373.08
佛 山	Foshan	968	161	19553.67	10605.82	14081.17	9021.67
韶 关	Shaoguan	73	14	1080.80	662.12	1110.67	546.35
河 源	Heyuan	111	20	977.45	623.51	665.83	405.24
梅 州	Meizhou	61	7	522.40	167.49	744.44	275.90
惠 州	Huizhou	552	123	8181.37	6343.06	7003.27	5344.20
汕 尾	Shanwei	46	21	943.15	666.03	728.41	508.90
东 莞	Dongguan	1663	269	15919.92	10363.74	16222.95	11443.40
中 山	Zhongshan	520	87	4109.97	2626.44	4157.93	2719.76
江 门	Jiangmen	342	59	3195.20	1500.39	3929.78	1451.61
阳 江	Yangjiang	65	8	1848.05	862.36	1704.99	1103.23
湛 江	Zhanjiang	78	9	2642.75	2254.33	2923.78	2189.63
茂 名	Maoming	38	5	1900.43	1551.88	894.41	571.43
肇 庆	Zhaoqing	204	30	2336.77	1038.18	2191.56	1235.81
清 远	Qingyuan	164	30	1791.95	676.01	2145.44	726.81
潮 州	Chaozhou	48	5	357.23	171.88	486.54	277.33
揭 阳	Jieyang	95	7	854.29	277.78	674.19	409.39
云 浮	Yunfu	57	11	436.71	220.26	477.48	256.76
按经济区域分	By Region						
珠 三 角	Pearl River Delta	6891	1288	107697.42	73881.58	126491.50	91939.57
东 翼	Eastern Region	349	46	3495.19	1455.37	3207.53	1568.70
西 翼	Western Region	181	22	6391.22	4668.57	5523.17	3864.29
山 区	Mountainous Region	466	82	4809.31	2349.39	5143.87	2211.06

12–34 各市现代产业增加值及比重（2022年）

Value Added and Ratio of Modern Industries by City (2022)

市别	City	先进制造业增加值（亿元）Value-added of Advanced Manufacturing Industry (100 Million yuan)	先进制造业增加值占规模以上工业比重（%）Ratio of Value-added to that of Industry (%)	高技术制造业增加值（亿元）Value-added of High-tech Industry (100 Million yuan)	高技术制造业增加值占规模以上工业比重（%）Ratio of Value-added to that of Industry (%)
全　省	**Provincial Total**	**20507.83**	**55.0**	**11783.82**	**31.6**
广　州	Guangzhou	2973.45	60.5	934.28	19.0
深　圳	Shenzhen	6726.97	66.6	6190.80	61.3
珠　海	Zhuhai	867.64	59.8	476.44	32.9
汕　头	Shantou	272.68	37.8	69.16	9.6
佛　山	Foshan	2804.49	50.1	313.30	5.6
韶　关	Shaoguan	85.37	26.5	22.70	7.1
河　源	Heyuan	169.93	49.4	123.37	35.9
梅　州	Meizhou	73.42	30.6	50.62	21.1
惠　州	Huizhou	1349.89	61.8	946.95	43.3
汕　尾	Shanwei	60.74	34.8	51.42	29.5
东　莞	Dongguan	2559.29	51.6	1993.41	40.2
中　山	Zhongshan	669.71	49.1	207.03	15.2
江　门	Jiangmen	451.27	39.7	140.70	12.4
阳　江	Yangjiang	76.74	20.6	1.21	0.3
湛　江	Zhanjiang	354.34	42.4	13.77	1.6
茂　名	Maoming	269.56	70.0	8.45	2.2
肇　庆	Zhaoqing	249.52	34.2	99.09	13.6
清　远	Qingyuan	221.20	38.8	61.89	10.9
潮　州	Chaozhou	60.90	25.4	37.29	15.5
揭　阳	Jieyang	174.39	36.0	26.00	5.4
云　浮	Yunfu	36.32	29.1	15.94	12.8
按经济区域分	By Region				
珠三角	Pearl River Delta	18652.23	57.5	11302.00	34.8
东　翼	Eastern Region	568.72	35.1	183.87	11.3
西　翼	Western Region	700.64	43.9	23.43	1.5
山　区	Mountainous Region	586.24	36.6	274.51	17.1

注：本表现代产业增加值按年报收入法计算；高技术制造业增加值采用新的国家统计局高技术产业(制造业)分类(2017)。

Note: Value-added of modern industries in this table is calculated in accordance with the income method of the annual report. Date of high-tech industry are based on National Classification of High-tech Industry(2017).

12-35 规模以上工业主要产品生产能力
Main Industrial Products above Designated Size

名　　称	Item	2019	2020	2021	2022
天然原油 (万吨)	Crude Oil (10 000 tons)	1498.29	1696.60	1857.88	1927.48
卷烟 (亿支)	Cigarettes (100 million pieces)	2905.98	1616.40	1611.76	1640.93
棉纺锭 (万锭)	Cotton Hasp (10 000 ingots)	61.59	50.32	44.42	47.21
气流纺锭 (万头)	Rotor Hasp (10 000 ingots)	2.41	1.94	2.78	2.97
棉布织机 (万台)	Printing and Dyeing Cotton Cloth (10 000 sets)	2.32	1.86	2.88	2.04
原油加工能力 (万吨)	Crude Oil Processing Capacity (10 000 tons)	6159.41	7160.54	7138.12	9205.59
焦炭 (万吨)	Coke (10 000 tons)	629.00	626.00	786.00	786.00
烧碱(折100%) (万吨)	Caustic Soda (10 000 tons)	37.40	37.40	37.40	33.40
农用氮、磷、钾化肥 (万吨)	Chemical Fertilizers (10 000 tons)	85.49	60.50	30.71	34.27
初级形态塑料 (万吨)	Primary Plastic (10 000 tons)	863.81	906.68	932.91	971.43
化学纤维 (万吨)	Chemical Fibre (10 000 tons)	77.37	77.54	84.60	122.76
硅酸盐水泥熟料 (万吨)	Clinker (10 000 tons)	10796.50	11302.28	11257.50	11376.29
水泥 (万吨)	Cement (10 000 tons)	22034.98	22161.03	22612.75	23480.72
平板玻璃 (万重量箱)	Plate Glass (10 000 weight cases)	11294.03	10746.76	14493.47	11629.01
生铁 (万吨)	Pig Iron (10 000 tons)	1951.50	2000.00	1950.80	2352.00
粗钢 (万吨)	Crude Steel (10 000 tons)	3550.20	4644.66	4909.36	4668.36
钢材 (万吨)	Rolled Steel (10 000 tons)	5738.23	6270.86	6750.80	6796.90
金属切削机床 (万台)	Metal- cutting Machine Tools (10 000 tons)	5.78	5.82	6.83	10.48
汽车 (万辆)	Motor Vehicles (10 000 sets)	416.16	363.00	379.60	455.96
#乘用车 (万辆)	Passenger Vehicle (10 000 sets)	406.70	358.70	367.00	443.15
新能源乘用车 (万辆)	New energy Passenger Vehicle (10 000 sets)	31.30	36.30	41.00	107.00
商用车 (万辆)	Commercial vehicle (10 000 sets)	9.46	3.80	12.10	12.81
新能源商用车 (万辆)	New energy Commercial Vehicle (10 000 sets)	2.87	2.22	2.52	2.96
民用钢质船舶 (万载重吨)	Civil Steel Ship (10 000 tons)	178.44	188.38	193.96	179.86
太阳能电池 (万千瓦)	Solar Cells (10 000kw)	413.38	388.06	827.07	625.40
家用电冰箱 (万台)	Household Refrigerators (10 000 sets)	2049.55	2518.88	2490.10	2547.74
房间空气调节器 (万台)	Air Conditioners (10 000 sets)	10515.18	11084.01	10319.57	10710.08
微型计算机设备 (万台)	Micro Computer Equipment (10 000 sets)	8833.13	8006.55	8298.74	10112.46
移动通信手持机(手机)(万台)	Mobile Telephones (10 000 sets)	47811.34	66804.00	67565.07	61498.03
彩色电视机 (万台)	Color TV Set (10 000 sets)	12614.83	13687.49	13113.82	13771.02
发电设备容量总计 (万千瓦)	Installed Capacity of Power Generation(10 000 Kw)	11675.13	12866.83	13970.00	14798.19
#火电设备容量 (万千瓦)	Thermal Power (10 000 Kw)	8523.74	9580.73	10183.91	10665.34
水电设备容量 (万千瓦)	Hydropower (10 000 Kw)	942.38	959.24	941.49	961.15
核电设备容量 (万千瓦)	Nuclear Power (10 000 Kw)	1613.81	1613.81	1613.81	1613.81
风电设备容量 (万千瓦)	Wind Power (10 000 Kw)	388.55	424.56	883.20	1224.25

注：农用氮、磷、钾化肥指农用氮、磷、钾化学肥料总计(折纯)。
Note: Output of chemical fertilizers is calculated on the basis of 100 percent effective content equivalent.

主要统计指标解释

工业 指从事自然资源的开采，对采掘品和农产品进行加工和再加工的物质生产部门。具体包括：(1)对自然资源的开采，如采矿、晒盐、森林采伐等（但不包括禽兽捕猎和水产捕捞）；(2)对农副产品的加工、再加工，如粮油加工、食品加工、轧花、缫丝、纺织、制革等；(3)对采掘品的加工、再加工，如炼铁、炼钢、化工生产、石油加工、机器制造、木材加工等，以及电力、自来水、煤气的生产和供应等；(4)对工业品的修理、翻新，如机器设备的修理、交通运输工具（包括小卧车）的修理等。

1984 年以前农村的村及村以下办工业归属农业，1984 年以后划归工业。

工业统计调查单位 工业统计调查单位分为两类：独立核算法人工业企业和工业生产活动单位。

(1)独立核算法人工业企业 是指从事工业生产经营活动的单位。独立核算法人工业企业应同时具备以下条件：①依法成立，有自己的名称、组织机构和场所，能够承担民事责任；②独立拥有和使用资产，承担负债，有权与其他单位签订合同；③独立核算盈亏，并能够编制资产负债表。

(2)工业生产活动单位 是指在一个场所从事一种或主要从事一种工业生产活动的经济单位。它包括独立核算工业企业按主营业务活动(即工业生产活动)划分的主营业务活动单位和非工业企业所属的工业生产活动单位（即原非独立核算工业生产单位）。工业生产活动单位，一般应同时具备以下三个条件：①具有一个场所，从事一种或主要从事一种工业活动；②单独组织工业生产、经营或业务活动；③单独核算收入和支出。

轻工业 指主要提供生活消费品和制作手工工具的工业。按其所使用的原料不同，可分为两大类：(1)以农产品为原料的轻工业，是指直接或间接以农产品为基本原料的轻工业。主要包括食品制造、饮料制造、烟草加工、纺织、缝纫、皮革和毛皮制作、造纸以及印刷等工业；(2)以非农产品为原料的轻工业，是指以工业品为原料的轻工业。主要包括文教体育用品、化学药品制造、合成纤维制造、日用化学制品、日用玻璃制品、日用金属制品、手工工具制造、医疗器械制造、文化和办公用机械制造等工业。

重工业 是指为国民经济各部门提供物质技术基础的主要生产资料的工业。按其生产性质和产品用途，可分为下列三类：(1)采掘（伐）工业，是指对自然资源的开采，包括石油开采、煤炭开采、金属矿开采、非金属矿开采和木材采伐等工业；(2)原材料工业，指向国民经济各部门提供基本材料、动力和燃料的工业。包括金属冶炼及加工、炼焦及焦炭化学、化工原料、水泥、人造板以及电力、石油和煤炭加工等工业；(3)加工工业，是指对工业原材料进行再加工制造的工业。包括装备国民经济各部门的机械设备制造工业、金属结构、水泥制品等工业，以及为农业提供的生产资料如化肥、农药等工业。

根据上述划分原则，修理业中以重工业产品为修理作业对象的划为重工业，反之划为轻工业。

工业总产值 是以货币表现的工业企业在一定时期内生产的已出售或可供出售工业产品总量，它反映一定时间内工业生产的总规模和总水平。它包括：在本企业内不再进行加工，经检验、包装入库（规定不需包装的产品除外）的成品价值，对外加工费收入，自制半成品、在产品期末期初差额价值。工业总产值采用“工厂法”计算，即以工业企业作为一个整体，按企业工业生产活动的最终成果来计算，企业内部不允许重复计算，不能把企业内部各个车间（分厂）生产的成果相加。但在企业之间、行业之间、地区之间存在着重复计算。

轻重工业总产值的划分也是按“工厂法”计算的，即一个工业企业在正常情况下生产的主要产品的性质属于轻工业，则该企业的全部总产值作为轻工业总产值；一个工业企业生产的主要产品的性质属于重工业，则该企业的全部总产值作为重工业总产值。

工业销售产值（当年价格） 是以货币形式表现的，工业企业在本年内销售的本企业生产的工业产品或提供工业性劳务价值的总价值量。工业销售产值包括的内容为：

（1）销售成品价值：指企业在报告期内实际销售（包括本期生产和非本期生产）的全部成品、半成品的总价值，即按报告期产品的实际销售数量乘以不含增值税（销项税额）的产品实际销售平均单价计算。销售成品价值中包括企业生产的自制设备及提供给本企业在建工程、其他非工业部门和生活福利部门等单位使用的成品价值，但不包括用订货者来料加工，并且只收取加工费的成品（半成品）价值。

（2）对外加工费收入：指企业在报告期内完成的对外承接的工业品加工（包括用定货者来料加工的产品）的加工费收入；对外工业品修理作业可收取的加工费收入和对内非工业部门提供的加工修理、设备安装等收入。对外加工费收入按不含增值税（销项税额）的价格计算。

对于以对外加工生产为主，对外加工费收入所占比重较大的企业，如果对外加工费收入出现跨年度支付的情况，为保证总产值生产口径计算的准确性，则应将对外加工费收入按实际情况调整，记录本年应实际收取的对外加工费收入。

出口交货值 指工业企业交给外贸部门或自营（委托）出口（包括销往香港、澳门、台湾），用外汇价格结算的产品价值，以及外商来样、来料加工、来件装配和补偿贸易等生产的产品价值。在计算出口交货值时，要把外汇价格按交易时的汇率折成人民币计算。

工业增加值 是指工业行业在报告期内以货币表现的工业生产活动的最终成果，是企业全部生产活动的总成果扣除了在生产过程中消耗或转移的物质产品和劳务价值后的余额，是企业生产过程中新增加的价值。

计算工业增加值通常采用两种方法。

一是“生产法”，即从工业生产过程中产品和劳务价值形成的角度入手，剔除生产环节中间投入的价值，从而得到新增价值的方法。公式为：

工业增加值＝工业总产值－工业中间投入＋本期应交增值税

二是“收入法”，即从工业生产过程中创造的原始收入初次分配的角度，对工业生产活动最终成果进行核算的一种方法，其计算公式为：

工业增加值＝固定资产折旧＋劳动者报酬＋生产税净额＋营业盈余

流动资产合计 资产满足以下条件之一应归为流动资产：（1）预计在一个正常营业周期中变现、出售或耗用，主要包括存货、应收账款等；（2）主要为交易目的而持有；（3）预计在资产负债表日起一年内（含一年）变现；（4）自资产负债日起一年内，交换其他资产或清偿负债的能力不受限制的现金或现金等价物。包括货币资金、应收票据、应收账款、存货等项目。来源于“资产负债表”中“流动资产合计”项目的期末余额数。

应收账款 指企业因销售商品、提供劳务等经营活动所形成的债权，包括应向客户收取的货款、增值税款和为客户代垫的运杂费等。来源于会计“资产负债表”中“应收账款”项目的期末余额数。

存货 指企业在日常活动中持有以备出售的产成品或商品、处在生产过程中的在产品、在生产过程或提供劳务过程中耗用的材料或物料等，通常包括原材料、在产品、半成品、产成品、商品以及周转材料等。来源于会计“资产负债表”中“存货”项目的期末余额数。

产成品 指企业已经完成全部生产过程并验收入库，可以按照合同规定的条件送交订货单位，或者可以作为商品对外销售的产品。来源于会计“产成品”科目的借方余额。

固定资产合计 指企业为生产商品、提供劳务、出租或经营管理而持有的，使用寿命超过一个会计年度的有形资产。包括使用期限超过一年的房屋、建筑物、机器、机械、运输工具以及其他与生产、经营有关的设备、器具、工具等。固定资产合计是时点指标，表示固定资产经过扣减折旧、减值准备等后的期末余额。执行《企业会计准则》或《小企业会计准则》的企业，来源于会计“资产负债表”中“固定资产”项目的期末余额数。

资产总计 指企业过去的交易或者事项形成的、由企业拥有或者控制的、预期会给企业带来经济利益的资源。资产一般按流动性（资产的变现或耗用时间长短）分为流动资产和非流动资产。其中流动资产可分为货币资金、交易性金融资产、应收票据、应收账款、预付款项、其他应收款、存货等；非流动资产可分为长期股权投资、固定资产、无形资产及其他非流动资产等。来源于会计“资产负债表”中“资产总计”项目的期末余额数。

负债合计 指企业过去的交易或者事项形成的，预期会导致经济利益流出企业的现时义务。负债一般按偿还期长短分为流动负债和非流动负债。来源于会计“资产负债表”中“负债合计”项目的期末余额数。

流动负债合计 负债满足下列条件之一的应归为流动负债：（1）预计在一个正常营业周期中清偿；（2）主要为交易目的而持有；（3）自资产负债表日起一年内到期应予清偿；（4）企业无权自主地将清偿推迟至资产负债表日后一年以上。包括短期借款、应付票据、应付账款、应付职工薪酬、应交税费等项目。来源于会计“资产负债表”中“流动负债合计”项目的期末余额数。

所有者权益合计　指企业资产扣除负债后由所有者享有的剩余权益。公司的所有者权益又称股东权益。包括实收资本、资本公积、盈余公积、未分配利润等。来源于会计“资产负债表”中“所有者权益合计”项目的期末余额数。

实收资本　指企业各投资者实际投入的资本（或股本）总额，包括货币、实物、无形资产等各种形式的投入。实收资本按投资主体可分为国家资本、集体资本、法人资本、个人资本、港澳台资本和外商资本。来源于会计“资产负债表”中“所有者权益”项下“实收资本”的期末余额数。

国家资本　指有权代表国家投资的政府部门或机构、直属事业单位对企业形成的资本金。来源于会计“实收资本”科目。

集体资本　指由本企业职工等自然人集体投资或各种机构对企业进行扶持形成的集体性质的资本金。来源于会计“实收资本”科目。

法人资本　指法人以其依法可支配的资产投入企业形成的资本金。来源于会计“实收资本”科目。

个人资本　指自然人实际投入企业的资本金。来源于会计“实收资本”科目。

港澳台资本　指我国香港、澳门和台湾地区投资者实际投入企业的资本金。来源于会计“实收资本”科目。

外商资本　指外国投资者实际投入企业的资本金。来源于会计“实收资本”科目。

营业收入　指企业经营主要业务和其他业务所确认的收入总额。营业收入合计包括“主营业务收入”和“其他业务收入”。来源于会计“利润表”中“营业收入”项目的本期金额数。

营业成本　指企业从事销售商品、提供劳务和让渡资产使用权等生产经营活动发生的实际成本。“营业成本”应当与“营业收入”进行配比。包括“主营业务成本”和“其他业务成本”。根据会计“利润表”中“营业成本”项目的本年累计数填报。

销售费用　指企业在销售商品和材料、提供劳务的过程中发生的各种费用，包括保险费、包装费、展览费和广告费、商品维修费、预计产品质量保证损失、运输费、装卸费等以及为销售本企业商品而专设的销售机构（含销售网点、售后服务网点等）的职工薪酬、业务费、折旧费等经营费用。

管理费用　指企业为组织和管理企业生产经营所发生的费用，包括企业在筹建期间内发生的开办费、董事会和行政管理部门在企业经营管理中发生的，或者应当由企业统一负担的公司经费等。根据会计“利润表”中“管理费用”项目的本期金额数填报。

研发费用　指企业在新知识、新技术、新产品、新工艺等的研究与开发过程中发生的费用化支出，以及计入“管理费用”会计科目的企业自行开发无形资产的摊销。费用化支出主要包括研发活动的人工费用、直接投入费用、用于研发活动的仪器、设备的折旧费、用于研发活动的软件、专利权、非专利技术的摊销费用、新产品设计费、新工艺规程制定费以及其他研发活动相关费用。执行企业会计准则的企业,根据会计“利润表”中“研发费用”项目的本年累计数填报。执行《小企业会计准则》的企业,根据会计“利润表”中“研究费用”项目的本年累计数填报。执行其他企业会计制度的企业以及会计“利润表”未列示“研发费用”或“研究费用”的企业，根据会计“管理费用”科目下“研究费用”明细科目的本期发生额，以及“管理费用”科目下“无形资产摊销”明细科目的本期发生额分析填报。

财务费用　指企业为筹集生产经营所需资金等而发生的筹资费用，包括企业生产经营期间发生的利息支出（减利息收入）、汇兑损失（减汇兑收益）以及相关的手续费等。根据会计“利润表”中“财务费用”项目的本期金额数填报。

利润总额　指企业在一定会计期间的经营成果，是生产经营过程中各种收入扣除各种耗费后的盈余，反映企业在报告期内实现的盈亏总额。来源于会计“利润表”中“利润总额”项目的本期金额数。

本年应交增值税　指企业按税法规定，从事货物销售或提供加工、修理修配劳务等增加货物价值的活动本期应交纳的税金。计算公式为：

本年应交增值税=销项税额－（进项税额－进项税额转出）－出口抵减内销产品应纳税额
－减免税款+出口退税

本年进项税额：指工业企业在报告期内购入货物或接受应税劳务而支付的、准予从销项税额中抵扣的增值税额。

本年销项税额：指工业企业在报告期内销售货物或提供应税劳务应收取的增值税额。

利税总额　指企业利润总额、产品销售税金及附加和应交增值税之和。

工业经济效益综合指数　是指现行综合评价工业经济效益总体水平及工业经济运行质量的指数。它是用工业产品销售率、总资产贡献率、资本保值增值率、资产负债率、流动资金周转率、成本费用利润率、全员劳动生产率等七项代表性经济效益指标，分别除以各项指标的标准值，再乘以各自的权数，加总后除以总权数求得。其计算公式为：

$$工业经济效益综合指数=\sum(\frac{某项经济效益指标报告期数值}{该项指标标准值}\times 权数)\div 总权数$$

上式总权数为100。

总资产贡献率 是指企业一定时期内全部资产获利能力，是企业经营业绩和管理水平的集中体现，是评价和考核企业盈利能力的核心指标。计算公式为：

$$总资产贡献率（\%）=\frac{利润总额+税金总额+利息支出}{平均资产总额}\times 100\%$$

税金总额为产品销售税金及附加与应交增值税之和，平均资产总额为期初、期末资产总计的算术平均值 。

资产负债率 是指反映企业经营风险的大小，反映企业利用债权人提供的资金从事经营活动的能力。计算公式为：

$$资产负债率（\%）=\frac{负债总计}{资产总计}\times 100\%$$

资产及负债均为报告期末数。

成本费用利润率 是指工业企业投入生产成本及费用的经济效益，同时也反映企业降低成本所取得的经济效益。计算公式为：

$$成本费用利润率（\%）=\frac{利润总额}{成本费用总额}\times 100\%$$

成本费用总额为主营业务成本和营业费用、管理费用、财务费用三项期间费用。

全员劳动生产率 是指反映企业的生产效率和劳动投入的经济效益。一般用平均每人一年创造的工业增加值表示。计算公式为：

$$全员劳动生产率（元/人）=\frac{工业增加值}{全部职工平均人数}\times 100\%$$

全部职工平均人数为企业在报告期内全部从业人员的平均人数，计算公式为：

$$全部从业人员年平均人数=\frac{1至12月各月全部从业人员平均人数之和}{12}$$

或：

$$全部从业人员年平均人数=\frac{1至12月各月月初、月末全部从业人员之和}{24}$$

工业产品销售率 是指反映工业产品已实现销售的程度，是分析工业产销衔接情况、研究工业产品满足社会需求的指标。计算公式为：

$$产品销售率（\%）=\frac{现价工业销售产值}{现价工业总产值}\times 100\%$$

Explanatory Notes on Main Statistical Indicators

Industry refers to the material production sector which is engaged in extraction of natural resources and processing and reprocessing of minerals and agricultural products. It includes: (1) Extraction of natural resources, such as mining, salt production, and logging (but excluding hunting and fishing); (2) Processing and reprocessing of farm and sideline produces, such as rice husking, flour milling, wine making, oil pressing, cotton ginning, silk reeling, spinning and weaving, and leather making; (3) Manufacture of industrial products, such as steel making, iron smelting, chemicals manufacturing, petroleum processing, machine building, timber processing; and production and supply of electricity, water and gas; (4) Repair and renovation of industrial products, such as the repair of machinery and means of transport (including cars).

Prior to 1984, industrial enterprises run by villages and cooperative organizations under village were classified into agriculture. Since 1984, these enterprises have been grouped into industry.

Units of Industrial Statistics Survey These are classified into two categories: corporate industrial enterprises with independent accounting system and industrial establishments.

(1) Corporate industrial enterprises with independent accounting system refer to enterprises engaging in industrial production activities which simultaneously meet the following requirements: ①They are established legally, having their own names, organizations, location, able to take civil liability; ②They possess and use their assets independently, assume liabilities, and are entitled to sign contracts with other units; ③They are financially independent and compile their own balance sheets.

(2) Industrial establishments refer to economic units located in one single place and engaged entirely or primarily in one kind of industrial production activity, including units engaged in main business activities (industrial production activities) under industrial enterprises with independent accounting system and units engaged in industrial production activities under non-industrial enterprises (formerly industrial establishments with dependent accounting system). Industrial establishments generally meet the following requirements simultaneously: ① They have each one location and are engaged entirely or primarily in one kind of industrial activity each; ② They operate and manage their industrial production activities separately; ③ They have accounts of income and expenditure separately.

Light Industry refers to the industry that produces consumer goods and hand tools. It consists of two categories, depending on the materials used:

(1) Industries using farm products as raw materials. These are branches of light industry which directly or indirectly use farm products as basic raw materials, including the manufacture of food and beverages, tobacco processing, textile, clothing, fur and leather manufacturing, paper making, printing, etc.

(2) Industries using non-farm products as raw materials. These are branches of light industry which use manufactured goods as raw materials, including the manufacture of cultural, educational and sports articles, chemicals, synthetic fiber, chemical products for daily use, glass products for daily use, metal products for daily use, hand tools, medical apparatus and instruments, and the manufacture of cultural and clerical machinery.

Heavy Industry refers to the industry which produces capital goods and provides various sectors of the national economy with necessary material and technical basis. It consists of the following three branches according to the purpose of production or the use of products:

(1) Mining, quarrying and logging industry refers to the industry that extracts natural resources, including extraction of petroleum, coal, metal and non-metal ores, and logging.

(2) Raw materials industry refers to the industry that provides various sectors of the national economy with raw materials, fuels and power. It includes smelting and processing of metals, coking and coke chemistry, chemical materials and building materials such as cement, plywood, and power, petroleum refining and coal dressing.

(3) Manufacturing industry refers to the industry that processes raw materials. It includes machine-building industry which equips sectors of the national economy, industries of metal structure and cement products, industries producing means of agricultural production, such as chemical fertilizers and pesticides.

According to the above principle of classification, repairing trades engaged primarily in repairing products of heavy industry are classified into heavy industry, while those engaged in repairing products of light industry are classified into light industry.

Gross Industrial Output Value refers to the total volume of industrial products sold or available for sale in monetary terms during a given period, which reflects the total achievements and overall scale of industrial production during a given period. It includes the value of the finished products in the enterprises, which are not to be further processed and have been inspected, packed and put in storage (where applicable), the income from external processing and the value gain of semi-finished products at the end of the reference period over the beginning. The gross industrial output value is calculated by the factory approach, i.e. the whole industrial enterprise is regarded as the basic accounting unit in calculating the gross industrial output value. No double calculations are to be made within the same enterprise and the output value of different workshops (branch factories) should not be added. However, this approach does not exclude the possibility of double calculations between enterprises, sectors and regions.

Output value of light and heavy industries is also classified by the factory approach. Under normal conditions, if the major products of an industrial enterprise belong to light industry products, the gross output value of that enterprise is classified wholly into light industry; the same principle applies to heavy industry.

Sales Value of Industry (Current Price) refers to refers to the total value of industrial products sold or industrial services provided in monetary terms within the current year. It includes:

(1) Sales Value of Finished Products. Sale value of finished products refers to the total value of finished and semi-finished products sold within the reporting period (including those produced within and outside the period). It equals the actual sales volume of products sold within the reporting period timing the actual average sales price (excluding value added or sales tax). It includes the equipment made by the enterprise itself, as well as the finished products provided to the projects under construction, non-industrial departments and welfare department, and excludes the value of finished or semi-finished products of external processing with supplied materials that produces only processing charges.

(2) Income from External Processing: refers to income from contracted external processing of industrial products (including processing of industrial products using materials from the clients), and the income from industrial repairing work provided to other units. Income from external processing is calculated using information from the item "products sales income" in the enterprise accounting at the prices excluding value-added tax.

For an enterprise whose main business is external processing and the charges of external processing constitute a large proportion of its income, in case of cross-year payment, the income of external processing charges shall be adjusted and the actual income of external processing charges of the current year shall be recorded to ensure the accuracy of the coverage of gross industrial output.

Export Delivery Value refers to the value of the products that an industrial enterprises have delivered to export units or have exported on its own or per procuration (including those sold to Hong Kong, Macaw and Taiwan), and the value of the products from processing and compensation trades(processing with given materials or samples, assembling supplied components). In calculating the export delivery value, the foreign exchanges shall be converted into yuan at current exchange rates.

Value-added of Industry refers to the final results of industrial production of industrial enterprises in monetary terms during the reference period. It equals to the total achievements of all industrial production minus the goods and services consumed or transferred during the industrial production of enterprises, in other terms the newly added value during the industrial production of enterprises. It is calculated by the following two approaches:

a) The production approach. The value added is calculated by taking the value of industrial intermediate input out of the final value of products and labor services that comes from industrial production. The formula used is:

Value-added of industry = gross industrial output—industrial intermediate input + value-added tax

b) The income approach. It is calculation of the final value of industrial activities by approaching the primary distribution of the primary income of industrial production. The formula used is:

Value-added of industry = depreciation of fixed assets + remuneration of laborers + net production tax+ operating surplus

Total Current Assets refer to the assets that meet one of the following requirements: (1) expected to be cashed, sold or used in a normal operation cycle, mainly including inventory and accounts receivable; (2) be owned for trading purpose mainly; (3) expected to be cashed in one year (including one year) from the day of the Balance

Sheet; (4) unlimited cash or cash equivalents that can be exchanged with other assets or being capable of settling debts during one year since the day of the Balance Sheet. Included are monetary capital, notes receivable, accounts receivable and inventories. Data on this indicator can be obtained from the year-end figures of Total Current Assets in the Balance Sheet of accounting records.

Accounts Receivable refers to creditor's rights formed by business activities such as selling goods, providing labor, which include payment for goods that should be charged to the customer, value-added tax and advance freight for the clients. It comes from the ending balance of Accounts Receivable in Balance Sheet of accounting records.

Inventories refers to finished goods or commodities held in preparation for sale in enterprises' daily activities, goods in the production process, material or the physical materials consumed in the production process or in the process of providing labor, usually include raw materials, goods in the production process, semi-finished products, finished products, goods and materials in flow. It comes from the ending balance of Inventory in Balance Sheet of accounting records.

Finished Goods refers to the products that the enterprises have completed all of the production process and accepted and put in storage, and can be sent to the ordering units in accordance with the contract stipulations, or can be on sale. It comes from the debit balance of Finished Products of accounting.

Fixed Assets refers to houses, buildings machines, vehicles and other equipment, appliances and tools related to production and operation that have been used for more than one year. It also includes articles that are not major equipment of production or operation, but the value of which exceeds 2000 yuan and the service period of which exceeds 2 years. Data can be obtained from the year-end figures of Fixed Assets in the Balance Sheet of accounting records.

Total Assets refer to all resources that are owned or controlled by enterprises through previous trades or transactions with expectation of making economic profits. Classified by the degree of liquidity, total assets include current assets and non-current assets. Current assets can be classified into monetary capital, trading financial assets, notes receivable, accounts receivable, advanced payments, other receivables and inventories. Non-current assets can be divided into long-term equity investment, fixed assets, intangible assets and other non-current assets. Data on this indicator can be obtained from the year-end figures of total assets in the Balance Sheet of accounting records.

Total Liabilities refer to payable liabilities of enterprises that accumulated from previous trades or transactions with expectation of economic profits leaking out. In terms of payment, it can be divided into liquid liabilities and long-term liabilities. Data on this indicator can be obtained from the year-end figures of total liabilities in the Balance Sheet of accounting records. It comes from the debit balance of Total Liabilities in the Balance Sheet of accounting records.

Total Liquid Liabilities refer to total debt payable by enterprises within an operating cycle of one year or over one year, including short-term loans, payables and advance payments, wages payable, taxes payable and profits payable, etc. Data can be obtained from the year-end figures of Total Liquid Liabilities in the Balance Sheet of accounting records.

Creditors' Equity refers to investors' ownership of net assets of the enterprise. It is equal to the total assets of the enterprise minus its total liabilities, including the primary input from investors, capital accumulation fund, surplus accumulation fund and undistributed profit. Data can be obtained from the year-end figures of Creditors' Equity in the Balance Sheet of accounting records.

Paid-in Capital refers to the capital (or share) actually invested by the investors of an enterprise, including currency, goods, intangible assets, etc. Classified by the investing bodies, paid-in capital includes state capital, collective capital, corporate capital, individual capital, Hong Kong, Macaw and Taiwan capital and foreign capital. Data on this indicator can be obtained from the accounting subject of Paid-in Capital in the accounting record of enterprise.

State Capital refers to the investment in an enterprises made by government departments or agencies under government's jurisdiction on behalf of state. Data on this indicator can be obtained from the accounting subject of Paid-in Capital in the accounting record of enterprise.

Collective Capital refers to the collective capital contributed by work staff or other institutions to support an enterprise. Data on this indicator can be obtained from the accounting subject of Paid-in Capital in the accounting record of enterprise.

Corporate Capital refers to the investment in an enterprise made by a corporate body out of its legal disposable assets. Data on this indicator can be obtained from the accounting subject of Paid-in Capital in the accounting record of enterprise.

Individual Capital refers to the capital actually invested in an enterprise by an individual. Data on this indicator can be obtained from the accounting subject of Paid-in Capital in the accounting record of enterprise.

Hong Kong, Macaw and Taiwan Capital refers to the capital actually invested in an enterprises by investors from Hong Kong, Macaw and Taiwan. Data on this indicator can be obtained from the accounting subject of Paid-in Capital in the accounting record of enterprise.

Foreign Capital refers to the capital actually invested in an enterprise by a foreign investor. Data on this indicator can be obtained from the accounting subject of Paid-in Capital in the accounting record of enterprise.

Business Revenue refers to the revenue from the sales of products (or commodities) and from rendering of industrial services by industrial enterprises. It is classified into two categories: principal business revenue (or basic business revenue) and other business revenue (or additional business revenue). It comes from current amount of Business Revenue in income statement.

Business Cost refers to the total cost incurred by an enterprise in its principal business and other business operations.It includes "Cost of principal business" and "Cost of other business".It come from this year's cumulative report of "operating cost" items from the "income statement".

Selling Expense refers to the cost during the sale of goods and materials, providing labour services, including insurance, packing, exhibition fees and advertising fees, merchandise maintenance costs, expected product quality guarantee loss, transportation fees, handling fees, and operating expenses for the sales of the company's products such as employee compensation, business expenses, depreciation costs for dedicated sales offices (including sales outlets, after-sales service outlets, etc.).

Administrative Expense refers to the expenses for the organization and management of enterprise operating, including the start-up costs during the construction of enterprises, funds occurred during enterprises operating by board of directors and executive management in the enterprise management, or burden by enterprises. It comes from current amount of management cost in income statement.

Financial Expenses refers to cost of raising fund for enterprises to raise funds for production and operation, including interest payments (a reduction in interest income), exchange loss (less exchange gains) and related fees during the period of production. It comes from current amount of financial expenses in income statement.

Total Profits refers to the operation results in a certain accounting period, and it is the balance of various incomes minus various spending in the course of operation, reflecting the total profits and losses of enterprises in reference period. Data are obtained from the amount of total profits in the profit statement of the accounting record of enterprise.

Value-added Tax Payable refers to the amount of the value-added tax which should be paid by the enterprises according to tax laws during the reference period of selling goods or providing such services as processing, repairing or assembling that add value to goods. The formula used is:

Value-added Tax Payable=Output Tax－(Input Tax－Input Tax Returns)－
Export Deduct Domestic Sales Goods Tax－Tax Deduction+ Export Tax Refund

Amount of Input Tax at Current Year refers to the VAT an industrial enterprise pays for purchasing goods or receiving taxable services within the reference period, which is allowed to be deducted from the amount of output tax.

Amount of Output Tax at Current Year refers to the VAT an industrial enterprise pays for selling goods or providing taxable services within the reference period.

Total Pre-Tax Profits refers to the sum of total profits, sales tax as well as additional and payable value-added taxes.

Comprehensive Index on Economic Benefit of Industry refers to the current comprehensive evaluation of the general level of economic benefit of industry and the performance of industrial economy. It is calculated by a selection of representative indicators on economic benefit divided by the standard value of each indicator respectively, multiplied by the weight of each indicator, summed and divided by total weight. The formula used is:

$$\text{Comprehensive Index on Economic Benefit of Industry} = \left(\frac{\text{Value of an Indicator on Economic Benefit in the Reference Period}}{\text{Standard Value of the Indicator}} \times \text{Weight}\right) \div \text{Total Weight where Total Weight} = 100$$

Ratio of Total Assets to Industrial Output Value refers to the profit-making capability of all assets of the enterprise. As a core indicator for the evaluation and assessment of the profit-making potential of the enterprise, it is a focused reflection of the performance and management efficiency of the enterprise. This ratio is calculated as follows:

$$\text{Ratio of Total Assets to Industrial Output Value (\%)} = \left(\frac{\text{Total Profits} + \text{Total Taxes} + \text{Interest Expenditure}}{\text{Average Assets}}\right) \times 100\% \times \left(\frac{12}{\text{cumulative number of months}}\right)$$

where Total Taxes are the sum of tax and extra charges on the sales of products and value-added tax payable; and Average Assets are the arithmetic mean of beginning assets and ending assets.

Ratio of Capital Maintenance and Appreciation is an important indicator of the changes of net assets of an enterprise and a focused reflection of the development capability of enterprises. It is the ratio of total creditors' equity at the end of the reference period to that of the same period of the previous year, calculated as follows:

$$\text{Ratio of Capital Maintenance and Appreciation (\%)} = \left(\frac{\text{Total Creditors' Equity at the End of the Reference Period}}{\text{Total Creditors' Equity of the Same Period of the Previous Year}}\right) \times 100\%$$

where Creditors' equity is equal to the total assets of the enterprise minus its total liabilities.

Assets-Liability Ratio reflects both the operation risk and the capability of the enterprise in making use of the capital from the creditors. It is calculated as follows:

$$\text{Assets-Liability Ratio(\%)} = \left(\frac{\text{Total Debts}}{\text{Total Assets}}\right) \times 100\%$$

where both assets and debts are figures at the end of the reference period.

Ratio of Profits to Industrial Costs refers to the ratio of profits realized in a given period to the total production costs of industrial enterprises in the same period, which also reflects the economic benefit attained by the enterprises from reduced costs. This ratio is calculated as follows:

$$\text{Ratio of Profits to Industrial Costs (\%)} = \left(\frac{\text{Total Profits}}{\text{Total Costs}}\right) \times 100\%$$

where Total costs are the sum of cost of products sold, marketing cost, management cost and financial cost.

Value-added Labor Productivity reflects the production efficiency of the enterprise and economic benefit of its labor input. It is usually expressed as the industrial value-added created by an average member of an industrial enterprise in a year. The formula used is:

$$\text{Value-added Labor Productivity (yuan/person)} = \left(\frac{\text{Value-added of Industry}}{\text{Average Number of Staff and Workers}}\right) \times \left(\frac{12}{\text{Cumulative Number of Months}}\right)$$

Average Number of Staff and Workers refers to the average number of all employed persons by an industrial enterprise within the reference period. The formula used is:

$$\text{Average Number of Staff and Workers} = \frac{\text{Sum of Average Monthly Numbers from January to December}}{12}$$

Or

$$\text{Average Number of Staff and Workers} = \frac{\text{Sum of Average Numbers at the Beginning and End of Each Month from January to December}}{24}$$

Proportion of Products Sold refers to the sales of industrial products to the gross industrial output value, and is used to analyze the linkage between production and sales and the extent to which the needs of the society are met by the supply of industrial products. It is calculated as follows:

$$\text{Proportion of Products Sold (\%)} = \left(\frac{\text{Value of Industrial Sales at Current Prices}}{\text{Gross Industrial Output Value at Current Prices}}\right) \times 100\%$$

十三、建筑业

CONSTRUCTION

十三　建筑业

简要说明

一、本篇资料反映广东省建筑业发展的基本情况。主要内容包括全省和各市建筑业企业生产经营的情况，主要指标有企业个数、就业人员数、建筑业总产值、房屋建筑面积、房屋建筑施工新开工面积、利润总额、利税总额和建筑业劳动生产率等。

二、本篇资料由广东省统计局固定资产投资统计处整理提供。

三、本篇资料是根据国家统计局制定的《建筑业统计报表制度》整理汇总的。统计范围包括：广东境内具有法人资格的独立核算建筑业企业和辖区内建筑业法人所属的产业活动单位。

四、从 2004 年开始到 2018 年止，统计范围为具有建筑业资质的独立核算建筑业企业（包括具有总承包和专业承包资质和劳务分包资质的独立核算建筑业企业）。从 2019 年开始，统计范围为具有总承包和专业承包资质的独立核算建筑业企业。

五、本篇资料中，2018 年的数据修正为第四次全国经济普查的数据。

13 Construction

Brief Introduction

Ⅰ. The data in this chapter show the development of the construction industry in Guangdong Province. They cover mainly the statistics of production and management of the enterprises of construction of the whole province and its cities, including the number of enterprises, the number of employed persons, gross output value of construction, floor space of buildings, value-added of construction, total profits and total pre-tax profits, construction enterprise labor productivity, etc.

Ⅱ. The data in this chapter are prepared and provided by the Division of Investment and Construction Statistics of Statistics Bureau of Guangdong Province.

Ⅲ. The data in this chapter are collected in accordance with the Reporting Scheme of Construction Statistics stipulated by the National Bureau of Statistics. The coverage of construction statistics includes construction enterprises with legal person qualifications and independent accounting system and industrial establishments affiliated with corporate construction enterprises under the jurisdiction of Guangdong Province.

Ⅳ. From 2004 to 2018, the scope of the construction statistics include all construction enterprises with construction qualifications and independent accounting system (including independent accounting construction enterprises with general contracting and professional contracting qualification and labor subcontracting qualification). Starting from 2019, the statistical scope is independent accounting construction enterprises with general contracting and professional contracting qualifications.

Ⅴ. In this chapter,the data in 2018 have been adjusted in accordance with the result of the fourth national economic census.

13-1 建筑业企业生产情况

Production Conditions of Construction Enterprises

项目	Item	2021 合计 Total of 2021	2021 #国有及国有控股企业 State-owned and State-holding	2022 合计 Total of 2022	2022 #国有及国有控股企业 State-owned and State-holding
企业个数 （个）	**Number of Construction Enterprises (unit)**	**9674**	**585**	**10960**	**725**
建筑业合同情况	**Contracts of Construction**				
签订的合同额 （亿元）	Value of Contracts Signed (100 million yuan)	60427.40	35675.22	68170.24	43248.45
上年结转合同额(亿元)	Value of Contracts Carried-over from the Previous Year (100 million yuan)	30637.32	18838.74	35748.13	21992.25
本年新签合同额(亿元)	Value of Newly-signed Contracts in Current Year (100 million yuan)	29790.08	16836.99	32422.11	21256.19
承包工程完成情况	**Contracted Projects Completed**				
直接从建设单位承揽工程完成产值 （亿元）	Completed Output Value of Contracted Projects Directly from Construction Units (100 million yuan)	21574.33	10394.07	22478.24	11628.19
自行完成施工产值 （亿元）	Output Value of Self-completed Projects (100 million yuan)	19467.23	8862.44	20253.66	9964.55
分包出去工程的产值 （亿元）	Output Value of Outsourcing Projects (100 million yuan)	2107.10	1531.63	2224.59	1663.64
从建设单位以外承揽工程完成产值 （亿元）	Completed Output Valuc of Contracted Projects outside Construction Units (100 million yuan)	1878.89	1153.73	2702.85	1903.64
建筑业总产值 （亿元）	**Gross Output Value of Construction (100 million yuan)**	**21346.12**	**10016.17**	**22956.50**	**11868.20**
#装配式建筑工程产值 （亿元）	Output value of prefabricated construction (100 million yuan)	475.68	339.34	476.15	363.92
#装饰装修产值 （亿元）	Output Value of Decoration Projects (100 million yuan)	1446.91	180.80	1549.76	258.30
#在外省完成的产值 （亿元）	Output Value Completed in Other Provinces (100 million yuan)	4974.99	2901.42	5262.14	3465.21
建筑工程产值 （亿元）	Output Value of Construction Projects (100 million yuan)	18940.78	9443.38	20398.87	11073.59
安装工程产值 （亿元）	Output Value of Installation Projects (100 million yuan)	1745.71	409.40	1965.54	654.37
其他产值 （亿元）	Other Output Values (100 million yuan)	659.63	163.39	592.10	140.24
竣工产值 （亿元）	**Output Value Completed (100 million yuan)**	**6788.49**	**2458.41**	**7261.45**	**2647.16**
房屋建筑施工面积 （万平方米）	**Floor Space of Buildings under Construction (10000 sq.m)**	**105978.61**	**52420.27**	**107372.69**	**53938.33**
#新开工面积 （万平方米）	Floor Space of Newly-started Buildings (10000 sq.m)	30525.21	13086.68	30605.05	17660.24
劳动人员情况	**Labor Force**				
从事建筑业活动的就业人员平均人数 （万人）	Average Number of Employed Persons in the Main Business Activities (10000 persons)	393.94	160.52	398.31	166.85
期末就业人数 （万人）	Number of Employed Persons at the Year-end (10000 persons)	355.40	138.12	345.04	145.21
#工程技术人员 （万人）	Number of Engineering Technical Personnel (10000 persons)	37.62	14.59	38.89	16.82

13−2 建筑业企业主要指标

Main Indicators on Construction Enterprises

年份 Year	建筑业企业单位数(个) Number of Construction Enterprises (unit)	建筑业企业总产值(亿元) Gross Output Value of Construction Enterprises (100 million yuan)	建筑业企业增加值(亿元) Value-added of Construction Enterprises (100 million yuan)	建筑业企业利税总额(亿元) Total Pre-tax Profits of Construction Enterprises (100 million yuan)	建筑业企业期末就业人员(万人) Number of Employed Persons of Construction Enterprises at the Year-end (10000 persons)
1978	178	5.47	10.49	0.20	14.78
1979	188	6.32	9.29	0.23	16.27
1980	204	8.88	12.66	0.32	19.45
1981	224	13.44	16.74	0.49	24.29
1982	246	19.66	22.24	0.72	29.94
1983	269	24.51	26.45	0.90	36.23
1984	357	36.83	33.22	1.31	47.12
1985	462	50.45	44.01	1.54	54.47
1986	448	57.14	47.42	1.28	58.24
1987	492	65.96	56.58	1.56	59.08
1988	596	86.74	73.82	2.74	66.56
1989	646	125.65	90.07	3.62	71.88
1990	686	113.40	92.45	3.12	67.22
1991	705	137.30	107.12	4.33	67.71
1992	910	216.56	201.04	9.65	84.80
1993	1766	459.95	318.05	23.03	144.12
1994	1587	535.75	387.80	31.29	150.05
1995	1618	635.83	451.40	39.47	135.56
1996	2031	632.16	464.66	35.74	146.56
1997	2399	732.97	468.97	38.26	143.89
1998	2961	800.00	502.87	43.11	142.82
1999	3283	954.44	526.56	53.06	144.78
2000	4593	944.61	537.06	58.24	141.46
2001	3699	1179.03	565.75	84.51	147.07
2002	4019	1418.41	596.03	88.95	150.12
2003	4488	1702.87	710.77	127.48	161.48
2004	4166	1901.86	780.81	143.75	152.10
2005	4182	2200.58	847.44	164.38	166.78
2006	4172	2594.04	934.97	191.62	169.33
2007	4326	3005.32	1073.17	256.59	179.13
2008	4470	3375.03	1208.40	205.07	173.77
2009	4508	3826.83	1350.61	329.00	179.34
2010	4551	4742.09	1574.96	393.87	196.32
2011	4589	5804.21	1755.04	470.75	190.28
2012	4637	6564.37	1876.07	517.82	198.31
2013	4977	7927.13	2260.48	653.70	204.79
2014	4982	8440.29	2496.15	675.99	211.07
2015	4926	8984.86	2684.40	724.74	185.50
2016	5054	9805.00	2909.50	736.98	246.17
2017	5606	11571.33	3289.32	851.86	289.97
2018	6509	14199.49	3849.75	1083.08	313.50
2019	7171	16633.41	4333.96	1041.77	329.51
2020	8334	18429.84	4651.50	1024.55	342.44
2021	9674	21346.12	5170.10	938.58	355.40
2022	10960	22956.50	5247.57	996.42	345.04

13-3 按登记注册类型分建筑业企业主要经济指标（2022年）

Main Economic Indicators of Construction Enterprises by Registration Type(2022)

项　　目	Item	合计 Total	内资企业 Domestic	国有 State-owned
企业个数 (个)	Number of Construction Enterprises (unit)	10960	10871	196
签订的合同额 (亿元)	Value of Contracts Signed (100 million yuan)	68170.24	66781.46	5076.33
#本年新签合同额 (亿元)	Value of Newly-signed Contracts in Current Year (100 million yuan)	32422.11	31884.75	2350.88
建筑业总产值 (亿元)	Gross Output Value of Construction (100 million yuan)	22956.50	22575.79	2068.71
#建筑工程	Construction Projects	20398.87	20058.27	1915.56
安装工程	Installation Projects	1965.54	1931.57	123.64
竣工产值 (亿元)	Output Value Completed (100 million yuan)	7261.45	7023.68	564.29
房屋建筑施工面积（万平方米）	Floor Space of Buildings under Construction (10000 sq.m)	107372.69	100211.88	9700.89
#本年新开工面积	Floor Space of Newly-started Buildings this year (10000 sq.m)	30605.05	29196.61	3276.34
房屋建筑竣工面积（万平方米）	Floor Space of Buildings Completed (10000 sq.m)	24943.47	23443.11	1196.69
从事建筑业活动的平均人数 (万人)	Average Number of Employed Persons in the Main Business Activities (10000 persons)	398.31	394.94	34.21
年末从业人员数 (万人)	Number of Employed Persons at the Year-end (10000 persons)	345.04	342.02	33.24

13-3 续表1 continued

项　　目	Item	集体 Collective-owned	股份合作 Cooperative	联营 Joint
企业个数 (个)	Number of Construction Enterprises (unit)	195	7	7
签订的合同额 (亿元)	Value of Contracts Signed (100 million yuan)	823.08	23.19	20.33
#本年新签合同额 (亿元)	Value of Newly-signed Contracts in Current Year (100 million yuan)	308.19	11.30	12.55
建筑业总产值 (亿元)	Gross Output Value of Construction (100 million yuan)	352.19	12.86	13.08
#建筑工程	Construction Projects	320.24	9.97	12.48
安装工程	Installation Projects	24.90	0.02	0.42
竣工产值 (亿元)	Output Value Completed (100 million yuan)	206.73	11.06	6.78
房屋建筑施工面积（万平方米）	Floor Space of Buildings under Construction (10000 sq.m)	2776.60	154.90	71.61
#本年新开工面积	Floor Space of Newly-started Buildings this year (10000 sq.m)	664.88	20.16	51.73
房屋建筑竣工面积（万平方米）	Floor Space of Buildings Completed (10000 sq.m)	847.68	89.06	45.74
从事建筑业活动的平均人数 (万人)	Average Number of Employed Persons in the Main Business Activities (10000 persons)	11.56	0.27	0.35
年末从业人员数 (万人)	Number of Employed Persons at the Year-end (10000 persons)	11.58	0.25	0.35

13-3 续表2 continued

项 目	Item	有限责任公司 Limited Liability	股份有限公司 Share-holding	私营 Private
企业个数 (个)	Number of Construction Enterprises (unit)	1943	132	8389
签订的合同额 (亿元)	Value of Contracts Signed (100 million yuan)	42226.67	2488.36	16123.38
#本年新签合同额 (亿元)	Value of Newly-signed Contracts in Current Year (100 million yuan)	20738.21	930.80	7532.72
建筑业总产值 (亿元)	Gross Output Value of Construction (100 million yuan)	11980.33	769.36	7379.14
#建筑工程	Construction Projects	11049.64	606.01	6144.24
安装工程	Installation Projects	735.29	114.61	932.68
竣工产值 (亿元)	Output Value Completed (100 million yuan)	3462.04	205.16	2567.50
房屋建筑施工面积 (万平方米)	Floor Space of Buildings under Construction (10000 sq.m)	53342.51	2170.41	31994.22
#本年新开工面积	Floor Space of Newly-started Buildings this year (10000 sq.m)	16286.12	554.73	8341.91
房屋建筑竣工面积 (万平方米)	Floor Space of Buildings Completed (10000 sq.m)	10754.14	591.86	9917.18
从事建筑业活动的平均人数 (万人)	Average Number of Employed Persons in the Main Business Activities (10000 persons)	168.26	16.51	163.79
年末从业人员数 (万人)	Number of Employed Persons at the Year-end (10000 persons)	145.83	10.36	140.41

13-3 续表3 continued

项 目	Item	其他 Others	港澳台商投资企业 Investment Enterprises from Hong Kong,Macao and Taiwan	外商投资企业 Foreign Funded Enterprises
企业个数 (个)	Number of Construction Enterprises (unit)	2	68	21
签订的合同额 (亿元)	Value of Contracts Signed (100 million yuan)	0.12	835.61	553.17
#本年新签合同额 (亿元)	Value of Newly-signed Contracts in Current Year (100 million yuan)	0.12	343.92	193.43
建筑业总产值 (亿元)	Gross Output Value of Construction (100 million yuan)	0.12	196.09	184.63
#建筑工程	Construction Projects	0.12	163.55	177.05
安装工程	Installation Projects		26.61	7.35
竣工产值 (亿元)	Output Value Completed (100 million yuan)	0.12	68.11	169.66
房屋建筑施工面积 (万平方米)	Floor Space of Buildings under Construction (10000 sq.m)	0.75	2298.41	4862.39
#本年新开工面积	Floor Space of Newly-started Buildings this year (10000 sq.m)	0.75	524.36	884.08
房屋建筑竣工面积 (万平方米)	Floor Space of Buildings Completed (10000 sq.m)	0.75	295.84	1204.52
从事建筑业活动的平均人数 (万人)	Average Number of Employed Persons in the Main Business Activities (10000 persons)	…	2.32	1.05
年末从业人员数 (万人)	Number of Employed Persons at the Year-end (10000 persons)	…	2.21	0.81

13-4 按登记注册类型分建筑业企业财务状况（2022年）
Financial Situation of Construction Enterprises by Registration Type (2022)

单位：亿元 (100 million yuan)

项　目	Item	合计 Total	内资企业 Domestic	国有 State-owned	集体 Collective-owned	股份合作 Cooperative	联营 Joint
年初存货	Inventory at the beginning of the year	2008.11	1804.91	62.23	61.94	0.25	0.78
流动资产合计	Total Current Assets	23600.66	21600.32	1188.63	210.17	5.98	5.72
#存货	Inventory	2064.41	1845.45	75.72	42.71	0.71	0.78
固定资产原价合计	Total Original Value of Fixed Assets	1271.53	1249.12	62.87	21.20	1.89	0.69
累计折旧	Accumulated Depreciation	631.28	619.17	34.61	10.29	0.59	0.28
#本年折旧	Depreciation for the Current Year	95.75	94.67	6.80	0.79	0.04	0.01
在建工程	Construction In Progress	202.43	189.29	8.84	14.42	0.02	0.15
资产总计	Total Assets	28578.15	26392.03	1364.54	238.12	7.84	6.92
流动负债合计	Total Current Liabilities	20048.32	18541.01	1107.27	157.36	5.24	4.38
非流动负债合计	Total Non-current Liabilities	1461.84	1286.62	41.61	0.71	0.07	0.09
负债合计	Total liabilities	21900.27	20217.24	1149.89	163.04	5.43	4.49
所有者权益合计	Total Owner's Equity	6678.10	6175.00	214.65	75.08	2.41	2.43
主营业务收入	Main Business Income	21884.66	21323.16	1637.68	353.89	9.96	13.47
主营业务成本	Main Business Cost	20219.71	19728.08	1558.67	332.13	9.31	12.47
主营业务税金及附加	Main Business Taxes and Surcharges	70.20	69.12	6.30	4.85	0.04	0.05
其他业务利润	Other Business Profits	16.19	15.58	0.26	0.06	0.06	
销售费用	Selling Expenses	42.14	41.05	0.40	0.57	0.01	…
管理费用	Administration Expenses	622.16	611.37	22.41	7.58	0.37	0.29
财务费用	Financial Expenses	129.17	117.79	1.52	-0.05	0.01	…
营业利润	Operating Profit	505.02	472.73	26.00	11.11	0.15	0.19
利润总额	Total Profit	504.07	471.77	26.62	10.94	0.16	0.19
所得税费用	Income Tax Expenses	95.16	89.81	6.63	3.85	0.01	0.09
应付职工薪酬	Payroll Payable	2511.76	2484.32	208.36	60.32	3.07	0.74
应交增值税	Value-Added Tax Payable	417.07	406.51	24.65	13.22	0.21	0.29

13-4 续表 continued

单位：亿元 (100 million yuan)

项　　目	Item	有限责任公司 Limited Liability	股份有限公司 Share-holding	私营 Private	其他 Others	港澳台商投资企业 Investment Enterprises from Hong Kong,Macao and Taiwan	外商投资企业 Foreign Funded Enterprises
年初存货	Inventory at the beginning of the year	629.34	42.32	1008.06		23.14	180.06
流动资产合计	Total Current Assets	10647.35	1387.73	8154.68	0.07	932.76	1067.58
#存货	Inventory	610.85	46.78	1067.90		22.40	196.55
固定资产原价合计	Total Original Value of Fixed Assets	620.63	52.14	489.70	0.01	18.12	4.28
累计折旧	Accumulated Depreciation	310.05	25.24	238.10	…	10.10	2.01
#本年折旧	Depreciation for the Current Year	46.66	3.16	37.20	…	0.83	0.25
在建工程	Construction In Progress	82.96	7.42	75.50		12.87	0.26
资产总计	Total Assets	14041.89	1737.45	8995.19	0.08	1096.74	1089.38
流动负债合计	Total Current Liabilities	10081.70	1202.35	5982.63	0.07	676.63	830.68
非流动负债合计	Total Non-current Liabilities	847.70	153.23	243.21		113.05	62.17
负债合计	Total liabilities	11059.49	1360.33	6474.49	0.07	790.18	892.85
所有者权益合计	Total Owner's Equity	2982.56	377.13	2520.74	…	306.56	196.53
主营业务收入	Main Business Income	11377.79	855.03	7075.19	0.14	337.91	223.59
主营业务成本	Main Business Cost	10576.77	804.42	6434.19	0.12	285.74	205.89
主营业务税金及附加	Main Business Taxes and Surcharges	27.42	2.28	28.17	…	0.52	0.56
其他业务利润	Other Business Profits	8.64	3.44	3.12		0.61	…
销售费用	Selling Expenses	10.06	2.81	27.19		0.70	0.40
管理费用	Administration Expenses	230.17	20.93	329.61	0.01	7.61	3.18
财务费用	Financial Expenses	49.88	10.86	55.58	…	7.97	3.40
营业利润	Operating Profit	272.04	4.48	158.76	0.01	28.22	4.07
利润总额	Total Profit	271.70	7.54	154.61	0.01	28.19	4.11
所得税费用	Income Tax Expenses	45.43	0.65	33.14	…	4.43	0.92
应付职工薪酬	Payroll Payable	1178.05	88.30	945.47	0.01	15.42	12.02
应交增值税	Value-Added Tax Payable	164.10	12.84	191.21	…	6.74	3.81

13-5 按行业分建筑业企业主要经济指标和财务状况（2022年）

Main Economic Indicators and Financial Situation of Construction Enterprises by Sector(2022)

单位：亿元 (100 million yuan)

项目	Item	合计 Total	房屋建筑业 housing industry	土木工程建筑业 Civil engineering and construction industry
企业个数 (个)	Number of Construction Enterprises (unit)	10960	4277	2616
签订的合同额 (亿元)	Value of Contracts Signed (100 million yuan)	68170.24	32224.38	29046.56
#本年新签合同额	Value of Newly-signed Contracts in Current Year (100 million yuan)	32422.11	15693.10	12747.01
建筑业总产值	Gross Output Value of Construction (100 million yuan)	22956.50	12105.01	7458.02
#建筑工程	Construction Projects	20398.87	11220.46	6883.99
安装工程	Installation Projects	1965.54	653.38	387.21
竣工产值	Output Value Completed (100 million yuan)	7261.45	5114.26	1268.61
房屋建筑施工面积（万平方米）	Floor Space of Buildings under Construction (10000 sq.m)	107372.69	89347.27	15384.54
#本年新开工面积	Floor Space of Newly-started Buildings this year (10000 sq.m)	30605.05	25512.22	4344.23
房屋建筑竣工面积（万平方米）	Floor Space of Buildings Completed (10000 sq.m)	24943.47	20435.92	2909.11
从事建筑业活动的平均人数 (万人)	Average Number of Employed Persons in the Main Business Activities (10000 persons)	398.31	221.48	106.11
年末从业人员数 (万人)	Number of Employed Persons at the Year-end (10000 persons)	345.04	194.91	93.96
年初存货	Inventory at the beginning of the year	2008.11	1242.72	433.29
流动资产合计	Total Current Assets	23600.66	12246.73	7523.21
#存货	Inventory	2064.41	1295.53	455.01
固定资产原价合计	Total Original Value of Fixed Assets	1271.53	418.04	631.59
累计折旧	Accumulated Depreciation	631.28	190.48	336.85
#本年折旧	Depreciation for the Current Year	95.75	29.16	50.36
在建工程	Construction In Progress	202.43	109.09	60.62
资产总计	Total Assets	28578.15	13886.85	10401.70
流动负债合计	Total Current Liabilities	20048.32	10132.45	6996.94
非流动负债合计	Total Non-current Liabilities	1461.84	594.65	744.34
负债合计	Total liabilities	21900.27	10921.45	7871.26
所有者权益合计	Total Owner's Equity	6678.10	2965.41	2530.44
主营业务收入	Main Business Income	21884.66	10767.79	7499.84
主营业务成本	Main Business Cost	20219.71	10051.12	6936.41
主营业务税金及附加	Main Business Taxes and Surcharges	70.20	40.80	18.51
其他业务利润	Other Business Profits	16.19	7.53	6.75
销售费用	Selling Expenses	42.14	10.84	9.60
管理费用	Administration Expenses	622.16	249.80	183.91
财务费用	Financial Expenses	129.17	70.19	33.28
营业利润	Operating Profit	505.02	221.96	193.96
利润总额	Total Profit	504.07	221.87	192.99
所得税费用	Income Tax Expenses	95.16	46.42	30.88
应付职工薪酬	Payroll Payable	2511.76	1236.53	845.69
应交增值税	Value-Added Tax Payable	417.07	230.09	109.87

13-5 续表 continued

单位：亿元 (100 million yuan)

项 目	Item	建筑安装业 Construction and installation industry	建筑装饰、装修和其他建筑业 Building decoration, decoration, and other construction industries
企业个数 (个)	Number of Construction Enterprises (unit)	1587	2480
签订的合同额 (亿元)	Value of Contracts Signed (100 million yuan)	2389.01	4510.28
#本年新签合同额	Value of Newly-signed Contracts in Current Year (100 million yuan)	1403.88	2578.13
建筑业总产值	Gross Output Value of Construction (100 million yuan)	1131.82	2261.66
#建筑工程	Construction Projects	443.05	1851.37
安装工程	Installation Projects	627.51	297.45
竣工产值	Output Value Completed (100 million yuan)	351.57	527.01
房屋建筑施工面积（万平方米）	Floor Space of Buildings under Construction (10000 sq.m)	1055.20	1585.68
#本年新开工面积	Floor Space of Newly-started Buildings this year (10000 sq.m)	395.87	352.72
房屋建筑竣工面积（万平方米）	Floor Space of Buildings Completed (10000 sq.m)	413.75	1184.70
从事建筑业活动的平均人数 (万人)	Average Number of Employed Persons in the Main Business Activities (10000 persons)	20.87	49.85
年末从业人员数 (万人)	Number of Employed Persons at the Year-end (10000 persons)	16.64	39.52
年初存货	Inventory at the beginning of the year	164.19	167.92
流动资产合计	Total Current Assets	1313.11	2517.61
#存货	Inventory	140.48	173.38
固定资产原价合计	Total Original Value of Fixed Assets	108.37	113.53
累计折旧	Accumulated Depreciation	54.53	49.42
#本年折旧	Depreciation for the Current Year	7.20	9.02
在建工程	Construction In Progress	13.11	19.61
资产总计	Total Assets	1487.63	2801.97
流动负债合计	Total Current Liabilities	993.21	1925.72
非流动负债合计	Total Non-current Liabilities	36.10	86.76
负债合计	Total liabilities	1052.58	2054.98
所有者权益合计	Total Owner's Equity	435.09	747.15
主营业务收入	Main Business Income	1305.05	2311.98
主营业务成本	Main Business Cost	1157.96	2074.22
主营业务税金及附加	Main Business Taxes and Surcharges	3.45	7.45
其他业务利润	Other Business Profits	1.38	0.52
销售费用	Selling Expenses	8.72	12.98
管理费用	Administration Expenses	85.43	103.02
财务费用	Financial Expenses	8.09	17.60
营业利润	Operating Profit	28.90	60.20
利润总额	Total Profit	29.13	60.08
所得税费用	Income Tax Expenses	6.45	11.41
应付职工薪酬	Payroll Payable	154.41	275.13
应交增值税	Value-Added Tax Payable	24.81	52.29

13-6 各市建筑业企业个数

Number of Construction Enterprises by City

单位：个 (unit)

市 别	City	2000	2005	2010	2015	2018	2019	2020	2021	2022
全 省	**Provincial Total**	**4593**	**4182**	**4551**	**4926**	**6509**	**7171**	**8334**	**9674**	**10960**
广 州	Guangzhou	757	764	779	877	1177	1330	1639	2011	2203
深 圳	Shenzhen	447	604	808	776	1117	1262	1389	1501	1788
珠 海	Zhuhai	143	165	144	393	349	407	510	517	584
汕 头	Shantou	271	199	212	175	173	174	175	187	198
佛 山	Foshan	248	502	497	427	524	612	719	802	858
韶 关	Shaoguan	110	66	76	94	146	187	257	335	352
河 源	Heyuan	117	82	85	104	126	135	160	168	186
梅 州	Meizhou	154	111	146	151	169	181	191	194	201
惠 州	Huizhou	241	124	111	103	284	259	328	663	902
汕 尾	Shanwei	100	43	38	36	39	41	58	87	128
东 莞	Dongguan	183	361	444	540	869	949	1017	1096	1181
中 山	Zhongshan	385	273	314	319	369	395	460	509	601
江 门	Jiangmen	342	156	165	164	235	235	269	286	328
阳 江	Yangjiang	122	91	95	113	115	108	142	172	194
湛 江	Zhanjiang	238	125	106	127	176	195	211	241	264
茂 名	Maoming	146	100	97	129	195	206	219	252	286
肇 庆	Zhaoqing	136	122	119	90	96	117	142	169	176
清 远	Qingyuan	136	74	80	88	114	123	153	174	204
潮 州	Chaozhou	139	90	83	66	55	61	61	63	67
揭 阳	Jieyang	121	84	107	111	128	142	166	175	178
云 浮	Yunfu	57	46	45	43	53	52	68	72	81
按经济区域分	By Region									
珠 三 角	Pearl River Delta	2882	3071	3381	3689	5020	5566	6473	7554	8621
东 翼	Eastern Region	631	416	440	388	395	418	460	512	571
西 翼	Western Region	506	316	298	369	486	509	572	665	744
山 区	Mountainous Region	574	379	432	480	608	678	829	943	1024

13-7 各市建筑业企业总产值

Gross Output Value of Construction Enterprises by City

单位：亿元 (100 million yuan)

市别	City	2000	2005	2010	2015	2018	2019	2020	2021	2022
全省	**Provincial Total**	**944.61**	**2200.58**	**4742.09**	**8984.86**	**14199.49**	**16633.41**	**18429.84**	**21346.12**	**22956.50**
广州	Guangzhou	256.13	633.99	1296.19	2546.94	4118.51	5304.90	5961.63	7069.68	7522.52
深圳	Shenzhen	153.02	545.62	1460.99	2275.20	3715.70	4361.44	4772.22	5412.91	6243.27
珠海	Zhuhai	33.11	52.48	100.81	477.45	795.05	986.91	1106.13	1235.98	1359.03
汕头	Shantou	80.67	127.78	219.12	405.52	609.74	713.30	787.63	827.85	752.91
佛山	Foshan	73.08	154.68	315.42	497.09	569.88	616.92	713.07	880.15	986.79
韶关	Shaoguan	24.14	29.25	102.76	214.35	211.89	213.35	239.64	271.26	235.34
河源	Heyuan	5.74	17.01	20.68	69.31	128.42	138.34	138.69	160.89	170.49
梅州	Meizhou	15.14	54.81	125.91	241.12	375.09	392.94	402.36	400.61	341.53
惠州	Huizhou	20.35	46.94	69.83	141.29	215.14	237.03	273.55	425.69	524.32
汕尾	Shanwei	5.49	6.95	15.44	14.41	42.49	43.77	55.64	62.15	54.29
东莞	Dongguan	40.45	84.35	122.06	224.59	479.76	562.68	664.48	842.63	960.57
中山	Zhongshan	26.20	73.41	133.70	153.67	263.99	256.81	313.35	404.56	495.18
江门	Jiangmen	47.18	56.06	119.18	225.24	314.85	316.38	334.60	367.51	428.76
阳江	Yangjiang	18.80	32.97	66.18	120.05	115.01	133.89	117.91	124.08	110.94
湛江	Zhanjiang	45.61	75.96	168.08	461.75	795.20	838.24	881.02	967.14	929.02
茂名	Maoming	39.05	92.14	134.67	481.04	860.01	938.44	1024.10	1227.18	1216.25
肇庆	Zhaoqing	15.40	39.99	99.40	125.49	157.70	169.03	183.33	210.89	202.01
清远	Qingyuan	11.49	20.19	52.78	101.72	166.10	142.50	198.03	207.30	183.53
潮州	Chaozhou	12.71	18.99	25.98	43.84	47.36	50.70	51.29	54.36	57.89
揭阳	Jieyang	12.24	21.78	75.06	133.02	164.82	152.24	139.38	103.36	88.96
云浮	Yunfu	8.61	15.20	17.85	31.75	52.79	63.60	71.79	89.95	92.88
按经济区域分	By Region									
珠三角	Pearl River Delta	664.92	1687.53	3717.58	6666.97	10630.57	12812.10	14322.35	16850.00	18722.46
东翼	Eastern Region	111.11	175.50	335.60	596.79	864.41	960.01	1033.94	1047.71	954.05
西翼	Western Region	103.46	201.08	368.93	1062.85	1770.22	1910.58	2023.03	2318.39	2256.22
山区	Mountainous Region	65.12	136.47	319.98	658.26	934.29	950.72	1050.52	1130.01	1023.77

13-8 各市建筑业企业营业收入(2022年)

Operating Revenue of Construction Enterprises by City

单位：亿元　　(100 million yuan)

市别	City	营业收入 Operating Revenue	#主营业务收入 Main Business Income	营业成本 Operating Costs	#主营业务成本 Main Business Costs	其他营业收入 Other Operating Income	#其他业务利润 Other Business Profits
全　省	**Provincial Total**	**22196.70**	**21884.66**	**20555.99**	**20219.71**	**312.04**	**16.19**
广　州	Guangzhou	7969.58	7900.81	7452.93	7382.69	68.77	7.13
深　圳	Shenzhen	5721.28	5590.93	5292.01	5140.08	130.35	2.99
珠　海	Zhuhai	1359.02	1346.63	1228.19	1210.71	12.39	0.62
汕　头	Shantou	536.31	535.70	505.56	503.97	0.61	0.11
佛　山	Foshan	1030.06	1012.24	934.45	917.71	17.82	1.59
韶　关	Shaoguan	212.55	207.58	194.24	188.48	4.97	0.09
河　源	Heyuan	132.93	128.04	117.48	114.31	4.88	0.01
梅　州	Meizhou	357.09	355.31	316.11	313.16	1.78	0.13
惠　州	Huizhou	458.15	453.92	421.47	417.17	4.23	0.39
汕　尾	Shanwei	39.08	38.49	34.81	34.26	0.60	0.01
东　莞	Dongguan	956.04	951.78	866.20	860.18	4.27	0.37
中　山	Zhongshan	487.73	485.12	443.21	441.26	2.62	0.44
江　门	Jiangmen	326.20	322.28	297.58	293.18	3.92	0.16
阳　江	Yangjiang	113.66	113.51	103.33	103.18	0.15	0.00
湛　江	Zhanjiang	779.26	767.03	741.75	729.88	12.23	0.43
茂　名	Maoming	1145.37	1115.31	1096.79	1071.70	30.06	0.66
肇　庆	Zhaoqing	149.69	144.95	139.49	135.61	4.74	0.54
清　远	Qingyuan	192.03	191.82	166.53	165.88	0.21	0.08
潮　州	Chaozhou	56.04	55.08	52.42	50.90	0.96	0.01
揭　阳	Jieyang	85.58	80.59	76.97	72.14	4.99	0.04
云　浮	Yunfu	89.05	87.55	74.48	73.25	1.50	0.38
按经济区域分	By Region						
珠三角	Pearl River Delta	18457.75	18208.65	17075.53	16798.59	249.10	14.24
东　翼	Eastern Region	717.02	709.85	669.76	661.28	7.16	0.17
西　翼	Western Region	2038.29	1995.86	1941.87	1904.76	42.43	1.09
山　区	Mountainous Region	983.64	970.29	868.83	855.08	13.35	0.69

13-9 各市建筑业企业利税总额

Total Pre-tax Profits of Construction Enterprises by City

单位：亿元 (100 million yuan)

市　别	City	2000	2005	2010	2015	2018	2019	2020	2021	2022
全　省	**Provincial Total**	**58.24**	**164.38**	**393.87**	**724.74**	**1083.08**	**1041.77**	**1024.55**	**938.58**	**996.42**
广　州	Guangzhou	15.17	45.42	118.16	171.85	265.62	224.60	264.28	247.84	223.58
深　圳	Shenzhen	13.79	39.76	105.09	212.92	245.38	259.51	211.86	144.15	270.58
珠　海	Zhuhai	1.43	4.16	7.44	34.12	65.02	60.08	64.95	72.06	87.76
汕　头	Shantou	4.14	9.86	17.64	32.64	70.77	91.92	80.07	56.42	33.04
佛　山	Foshan	4.70	14.31	30.47	38.40	39.29	42.93	34.07	44.83	46.34
韶　关	Shaoguan	2.00	1.57	6.66	14.55	16.75	10.06	12.58	10.38	12.15
河　源	Heyuan	0.53	1.23	2.08	10.72	16.55	16.94	12.70	12.02	13.00
梅　州	Meizhou	0.81	6.47	13.70	26.53	44.16	39.87	39.26	31.95	27.83
惠　州	Huizhou	1.02	3.63	4.96	5.44	14.58	12.69	16.16	17.92	21.70
汕　尾	Shanwei	0.58	0.58	1.43	1.29	5.99	4.28	3.42	4.08	3.40
东　莞	Dongguan	2.25	6.36	9.80	17.09	40.63	36.91	36.86	42.77	36.60
中　山	Zhongshan	1.53	6.09	13.71	11.87	19.08	20.90	20.82	21.99	20.75
江　门	Jiangmen	2.37	3.79	9.61	20.34	23.94	22.75	21.11	20.11	20.84
阳　江	Yangjiang	1.15	3.24	6.26	9.09	13.50	14.60	10.98	9.44	6.79
湛　江	Zhanjiang	1.69	3.80	10.69	23.94	54.28	42.30	49.68	52.60	43.49
茂　名	Maoming	1.82	5.97	10.01	52.94	96.42	88.22	81.99	82.86	75.33
肇　庆	Zhaoqing	0.77	2.55	6.32	7.79	11.28	7.96	9.48	10.25	8.95
清　远	Qingyuan	0.40	1.20	6.24	5.78	11.85	11.91	28.83	35.21	20.73
潮　州	Chaozhou	0.66	1.17	2.12	3.18	4.82	5.01	4.32	3.67	3.65
揭　阳	Jieyang	0.73	2.09	9.48	21.01	17.51	20.31	13.17	9.35	8.48
云　浮	Yunfu	0.70	1.13	1.98	3.26	5.68	8.01	7.96	8.71	11.41
按经济区域分	By Region									
珠 三 角	Pearl River Delta	43.03	126.06	305.57	519.81	724.81	688.33	679.59	621.90	737.11
东　翼	Eastern Region	6.11	13.70	30.68	58.12	99.09	121.52	100.98	73.53	48.58
西　翼	Western Region	4.66	13.01	26.96	85.97	164.20	145.13	142.66	144.89	125.61
山　区	Mountainous Region	4.44	11.61	30.66	60.84	94.98	86.79	101.33	98.26	85.12

13–10 各市建筑业企业利润总额

Total Profits of Construction Enterprises by City

单位：亿元 (100 million yuan)

市 别	City	2000	2005	2010	2015	2018	2019	2020	2021	2022
全 省	**Provincial Total**	**22.73**	**70.53**	**205.47**	**396.36**	**543.03**	**570.14**	**541.11**	**445.33**	**504.07**
广 州	Guangzhou	5.20	18.64	65.51	96.23	129.95	122.71	150.99	139.73	121.54
深 圳	Shenzhen	7.57	15.65	50.44	115.51	121.92	154.70	116.91	40.88	154.51
珠 海	Zhuhai	0.37	1.98	3.47	19.05	48.99	44.06	48.90	53.58	60.91
汕 头	Shantou	1.36	3.74	8.23	15.63	42.75	61.77	45.36	29.21	13.83
佛 山	Foshan	2.00	6.54	19.27	24.99	22.80	23.06	15.36	19.22	20.66
韶 关	Shaoguan	0.23	0.43	2.95	5.44	6.61	4.23	4.97	3.97	4.19
河 源	Heyuan	0.29	0.48	0.95	7.71	9.53	9.39	7.28	6.89	7.26
梅 州	Meizhou	0.21	4.56	8.44	17.08	30.59	26.08	27.66	20.12	17.97
惠 州	Huizhou	0.35	1.02	1.68	2.37	4.34	4.88	7.31	7.86	8.63
汕 尾	Shanwei	0.22	0.18	0.56	0.55	1.99	1.38	1.13	1.72	1.53
东 莞	Dongguan	1.14	3.81	5.78	9.67	18.23	20.81	17.34	18.46	10.99
中 山	Zhongshan	0.78	3.63	7.46	6.25	11.30	14.61	14.09	14.51	11.04
江 门	Jiangmen	0.34	1.55	4.88	11.33	10.54	11.10	10.47	9.73	9.73
阳 江	Yangjiang	0.61	1.38	3.59	4.71	5.35	5.58	4.47	4.81	3.15
湛 江	Zhanjiang	0.28	1.19	3.76	8.68	20.15	13.16	11.34	13.08	11.14
茂 名	Maoming	0.77	2.49	4.43	27.67	35.53	29.41	22.01	18.72	17.36
肇 庆	Zhaoqing	0.09	0.65	2.51	3.26	3.91	2.65	3.47	3.58	2.48
清 远	Qingyuan	0.01	0.46	3.44	3.24	4.64	3.75	19.50	27.21	13.98
潮 州	Chaozhou	0.28	0.49	1.12	1.77	1.71	1.61	2.25	1.71	1.78
揭 阳	Jieyang	0.26	1.22	5.90	13.46	10.23	11.29	5.51	4.42	3.42
云 浮	Yunfu	0.37	0.43	1.10	1.77	1.97	3.89	4.79	5.92	7.96
按经济区域分	By Region									
珠 三 角	Pearl River Delta	17.84	53.48	161.00	288.67	371.99	398.59	384.84	307.55	400.48
东 翼	Eastern Region	2.12	5.62	15.81	31.41	56.67	76.06	54.25	37.06	20.56
西 翼	Western Region	1.66	5.06	11.78	41.05	61.03	48.16	37.82	36.61	31.65
山 区	Mountainous Region	1.11	6.36	16.87	35.23	53.35	47.34	64.20	64.11	51.37

13-11 各市建筑业企业房屋建筑施工面积

Floor Space of Buildings under Construction by Construction Enterprises by City

单位：万平方米 (10000 sq.m)

市别	City	2000	2005	2010	2015	2018	2019	2020	2021	2022
全省	**Provincial Total**	**16333.82**	**26886.00**	**33140.39**	**50461.59**	**74183.34**	**84392.33**	**91890.63**	**105978.61**	**107372.69**
广州	Guangzhou	3161.25	5311.14	7135.48	15163.70	27932.75	32046.22	35123.20	39243.58	38614.01
深圳	Shenzhen	1999.65	4800.07	5980.34	7682.65	10792.06	15901.54	16948.79	20769.52	22419.28
珠海	Zhuhai	733.57	625.51	877.39	1969.64	1672.12	1826.83	2374.35	3972.99	2947.55
汕头	Shantou	1477.16	2176.29	2381.63	4218.81	5429.38	5976.68	5992.08	5896.33	5152.85
佛山	Foshan	1763.57	2782.45	3335.62	2731.91	3639.70	3240.81	5141.61	8638.64	9626.77
韶关	Shaoguan	362.44	424.57	781.78	1063.36	1254.89	1201.06	955.25	1149.05	1039.68
河源	Heyuan	79.80	294.41	218.83	453.06	648.15	647.47	567.99	639.97	529.74
梅州	Meizhou	273.56	776.23	1315.80	1632.23	2519.37	2242.01	2017.01	1749.27	1461.86
惠州	Huizhou	366.05	772.13	942.90	1162.39	1335.43	1522.36	2529.10	3538.18	3177.93
汕尾	Shanwei	127.42	114.77	175.11	118.61	302.60	284.54	250.63	217.73	211.80
东莞	Dongguan	1217.56	1234.98	733.44	1045.99	1316.67	1517.73	2269.60	2845.68	3954.25
中山	Zhongshan	400.99	945.60	601.02	470.87	559.48	654.55	919.87	1505.28	3138.46
江门	Jiangmen	1329.02	1585.95	1640.13	2457.27	2833.76	2401.03	2554.04	2173.77	2353.38
阳江	Yangjiang	270.81	525.95	825.31	920.64	817.25	732.08	760.53	673.78	542.04
湛江	Zhanjiang	857.19	1399.47	1943.66	3361.23	4624.23	5243.37	4840.73	4330.77	3951.85
茂名	Maoming	734.43	1395.55	1770.78	3264.79	5664.90	6021.54	5768.60	5792.18	5526.36
肇庆	Zhaoqing	386.93	531.11	728.47	640.44	516.21	586.08	514.49	498.22	508.22
清远	Qingyuan	249.02	466.45	632.87	562.07	763.72	728.31	754.23	915.57	942.90
潮州	Chaozhou	217.15	206.67	373.12	597.67	471.52	507.10	586.08	565.22	532.41
揭阳	Jieyang	193.91	277.75	559.41	638.29	607.42	599.14	539.17	370.64	304.68
云浮	Yunfu	132.34	238.96	187.29	305.99	481.73	511.88	483.28	492.23	436.68
按经济区域分	By Region									
珠三角	Pearl River Delta	11358.59	18588.94	21974.80	33324.85	50598.17	59697.16	68375.04	83185.86	86739.85
东翼	Eastern Region	2015.64	2775.47	3489.27	5573.38	6810.92	7367.46	7367.96	7049.92	6201.74
西翼	Western Region	1862.43	3320.97	4539.75	7546.67	11106.38	11996.99	11369.86	10796.73	10020.25
山区	Mountainous Region	1097.16	2200.62	3136.57	4016.70	5667.86	5330.73	4777.76	4946.10	4410.86

13−12 各市建筑业企业房屋建筑施工新开工面积

Floor Space of Buildings Started This Year by Construction Enterprises by City

单位：万平方米 (10000 sq.m)

市 别	City	2000	2005	2010	2015	2018	2019	2020	2021	2022
全 省	**Provincial Total**	**6423.16**	**11879.41**	**14529.68**	**15802.23**	**26316.94**	**26469.33**	**29175.62**	**30525.21**	**30605.05**
广 州	Guangzhou	1153.97	2313.48	2995.47	3473.80	8645.05	7929.47	9866.93	8959.73	9825.71
深 圳	Shenzhen	791.59	1933.19	2443.02	1833.43	4757.48	5229.78	5669.14	5361.42	8057.59
珠 海	Zhuhai	236.23	298.50	476.92	687.28	718.85	535.43	804.74	1363.85	923.15
汕 头	Shantou	576.48	942.72	1129.55	1421.14	1796.75	2051.94	1631.85	1606.44	826.09
佛 山	Foshan	943.98	1230.74	931.63	682.05	1225.51	971.21	1709.02	3721.59	2179.74
韶 关	Shaoguan	160.10	196.57	360.77	551.67	447.81	350.82	270.43	294.38	249.37
河 源	Heyuan	40.48	151.18	126.65	283.87	409.20	380.26	284.69	309.44	224.06
梅 州	Meizhou	124.38	323.52	655.48	541.14	1521.14	996.67	652.37	572.65	288.56
惠 州	Huizhou	185.75	380.49	444.14	325.94	394.37	437.96	1248.76	1021.09	982.89
汕 尾	Shanwei	84.60	50.11	122.07	55.53	89.93	65.10	86.18	84.32	94.52
东 莞	Dongguan		589.95	345.07	328.25	468.08	708.78	1120.94	1222.85	1396.47
中 山	Zhongshan	200.38	503.83	287.82	212.48	187.51	248.78	410.65	592.32	1138.25
江 门	Jiangmen	668.83	631.55	833.99	928.62	813.06	690.12	528.54	664.31	905.35
阳 江	Yangjiang	354.20	249.55	369.70	326.31	229.41	225.77	150.17	123.05	158.77
湛 江	Zhanjiang	290.52	639.64	922.67	1299.72	1604.86	2326.96	1726.68	1680.67	935.41
茂 名	Maoming	138.54	600.67	848.76	1614.28	1723.16	2212.01	1970.72	2080.79	1792.89
肇 庆	Zhaoqing	115.93	248.72	298.32	337.26	230.20	260.08	178.64	159.06	171.20
清 远	Qingyuan	97.89	235.35	318.47	269.03	316.72	229.65	281.33	330.25	199.11
潮 州	Chaozhou	99.95	96.79	134.94	98.21	41.09	56.54	148.70	85.38	51.76
揭 阳	Jieyang	108.93	147.23	388.76	408.95	513.71	405.94	337.88	184.71	99.95
云 浮	Yunfu	50.43	115.64	95.48	123.25	183.04	156.06	97.25	106.91	104.21
按经济区域分	By Region									
珠三角	Pearl River Delta	4296.66	8130.45	9056.38	8809.12	17440.12	17011.62	21537.36	23066.21	25580.37
东 翼	Eastern Region	869.96	1236.84	1775.32	1983.84	2441.49	2579.51	2204.62	1960.85	1072.32
西 翼	Western Region	783.26	1489.86	2141.14	3240.31	3557.43	4764.74	3847.57	3884.52	2887.06
山 区	Mountainous Region	473.28	1022.26	1556.84	1768.97	2877.90	2113.47	1586.07	1613.63	1065.30

13-13 各市建筑业企业期末就业人员

Number of Employed Persons of Construction Enterprises at the Year-end by City

单位：万人 (10000 persons)

市别	City	2000	2005	2010	2015	2018	2019	2020	2021	2022
全省	**Provincial Total**	**141.46**	**166.78**	**196.32**	**185.50**	**313.50**	**329.51**	**342.44**	**355.40**	**345.04**
广州	Guangzhou	26.40	30.80	39.65	40.03	77.50	84.73	87.41	88.27	81.59
深圳	Shenzhen	20.15	26.85	45.59	41.35	69.42	79.94	82.70	90.54	95.54
珠海	Zhuhai	3.55	3.24	4.36	6.37	21.22	21.24	25.87	22.25	26.29
汕头	Shantou	14.29	12.63	14.35	13.60	16.00	16.57	15.90	16.14	13.67
佛山	Foshan	8.62	13.71	11.02	10.49	8.85	9.44	9.72	10.99	10.92
韶关	Shaoguan	4.46	3.69	5.71	6.81	6.47	6.97	7.71	7.91	7.24
河源	Heyuan	1.74	2.09	1.72	1.92	4.56	3.80	3.68	4.13	4.36
梅州	Meizhou	3.58	7.27	9.13	6.55	10.66	10.39	10.59	8.38	7.07
惠州	Huizhou	3.33	3.94	3.24	1.57	4.97	4.53	4.70	7.21	8.08
汕尾	Shanwei	1.25	1.28	1.31	0.70	1.34	1.18	1.35	1.46	1.37
东莞	Dongguan	6.65	7.78	5.73	7.58	12.58	14.36	15.10	17.91	17.43
中山	Zhongshan	3.71	5.75	5.32	4.00	4.65	4.82	5.46	6.92	7.85
江门	Jiangmen	10.26	10.58	8.50	6.12	8.63	7.38	7.75	7.77	7.91
阳江	Yangjiang	3.54	4.54	5.49	4.85	4.91	4.86	4.68	3.76	3.54
湛江	Zhanjiang	8.03	7.87	10.29	10.71	24.65	24.25	23.53	23.29	17.66
茂名	Maoming	8.92	10.44	8.27	10.53	17.12	17.41	18.23	20.35	18.23
肇庆	Zhaoqing	3.61	3.70	4.12	2.53	6.11	4.01	3.47	3.77	3.54
清远	Qingyuan	2.74	2.46	3.43	2.87	4.93	4.00	4.89	5.59	4.53
潮州	Chaozhou	2.10	2.17	1.46	1.54	1.90	1.95	2.02	2.01	2.03
揭阳	Jieyang	2.88	3.86	5.75	3.85	4.89	5.48	5.07	3.94	3.59
云浮	Yunfu	1.65	2.13	1.85	1.51	2.13	2.18	2.59	2.82	2.59
按经济区域分	By Region									
珠三角	Pearl River Delta	86.28	106.35	127.54	120.03	213.93	230.46	242.19	255.63	259.15
东翼	Eastern Region	20.52	19.94	22.88	19.70	24.13	25.18	24.34	23.55	20.66
西翼	Western Region	20.49	22.86	24.06	26.09	46.68	46.53	46.44	47.39	39.43
山区	Mountainous Region	14.17	17.64	21.84	19.67	28.76	27.33	29.46	28.83	25.80

13-14 各市建筑业企业劳动生产率

Labor Productivity of Construction Enterprises by City

单位：元/人 (yuan/person)

市别	City	2000	2005	2010	2015	2018	2019	2020	2021	2022
全　省	**Provincial Total**	**70137**	**132056**	**239595**	**382570**	**435580**	**475704**	**493524**	**541866**	**576342**
广　州	Guangzhou	91086	204454	315033	552068	491331	574751	573454	623186	681875
深　圳	Shenzhen	107549	183515	300502	345823	496908	474309	484905	527352	575034
珠　海	Zhuhai	85936	162503	228342	385938	353682	448816	415380	534504	486602
汕　头	Shantou	56057	99266	159623	296273	400077	454946	498467	522338	544946
佛　山	Foshan	86795	115051	285616	586097	641907	641674	714819	757575	766971
韶　关	Shaoguan	57743	83704	189045	313316	307486	320481	315172	349030	360597
河　源	Heyuan	33395	82741	121383	280999	282586	354389	334064	335343	331741
梅　州	Meizhou	44258	78866	141903	327465	354976	405335	405034	480570	433026
惠　州	Huizhou	60374	119974	217933	406527	400993	490286	559940	595367	543417
汕　尾	Shanwei	46496	51367	116927	211873	343840	235210	329961	355300	351846
东　莞	Dongguan	64176	108136	218052	263489	371984	410150	457503	484333	488335
中　山	Zhongshan	73597	119772	249502	333178	545571	510957	534601	620575	576016
江　门	Jiangmen	49612	64418	147038	336038	367407	425974	425780	469581	525951
阳　江	Yangjiang	59689	78360	123368	241168	245808	293671	269880	315154	305884
湛　江	Zhanjiang	57160	98452	173336	315036	339105	355164	405312	419062	523488
茂　名	Maoming	46992	90457	170522	396918	493231	517968	572739	605481	640703
肇　庆	Zhaoqing	46380	107435	257334	385010	233086	431525	522676	527241	543245
清　远	Qingyuan	42073	90596	158598	266337	383481	310542	439627	384343	371505
潮　州	Chaozhou	57817	91838	146120	237822	219501	197879	241983	251802	282466
揭　阳	Jieyang	40672	57368	131884	242247	343561	275180	260243	257864	231980
云　浮	Yunfu	49773	74640	101721	204748	232881	299633	268503	313760	338307
按经济区域分	By Region									
珠三角	Pearl River Delta	82426	156714	283028	418380	465450	510891	519647	573671	604975
东　翼	Eastern Region	53458	87357	149042	274993	368911	374504	414196	440862	449102
西　翼	Western Region	55234	90945	160692	334707	388504	412842	459920	490318	559067
山　区	Mountainous Region	47252	81395	151686	298647	326671	352562	363911	387438	375857

主要统计指标解释

建筑业总产值　是以货币表现的建筑业企业在一定时期内生产的建筑业产品和服务的总和。建筑业总产值包括三部分内容：

⑴建筑工程产值：指列入建筑工程预算内的各种工程价值。

⑵安装工程产值：指设备安装工程价值以及将预制品部件安装成建筑工程产品的价值，但不包括被安装设备、被安装部品部件本身的价值。

⑶其他产值：建筑业总产值中除建筑工程、安装工程以外的产值。包括房屋构筑物修理产值、非标准设备制造产值、总包企业向分包企业收取的管理费以及不能明确划分的施工活动所完成的产值。

①房屋构筑物修理产值：指房屋和构筑物的修理所完成的价值，但不包括被修理房屋构筑物的本身价值和生产设备的修理价值。

②非标准设备制造产值：指加工制造没有定型的非标准生产设备的加工费和原材料价值以及附属加工厂为本企业承建工程制作的非标准设备的价值。

竣工产值　一般是以单位工程为对象，当该工程按照设计所规定的工程内容全部完成，达到了设计规定的交工条件，经有关部门检查验收鉴定合格的单位工程价值，即为竣工产值。

房屋施工面积　指在报告期内施工的全部房屋建筑面积，它包括本期新开工的房屋面积、上期跨入本期继续施工的房屋面积、上期停缓建在本期恢复施工的房屋面积、本期竣工的房屋面积以及本期施工后又停缓建的房屋面积。

房屋新开工面积　指报告期内本年新开工建设的房屋建筑面积，以单位工程为核算对象。不包括在上年开工跨入本年继续施工的房屋建筑面积和上年停缓建而在本年恢复施工的房屋建筑面积。房屋的开工应以房屋正式开始破土刨槽（地基处理或打永久桩）的日期为准。房屋新开工面积指整栋房屋的全部建筑面积，不能分割计算。

从事建筑业活动的就业人员平均人数　指建筑业企业(或单位)报告期实际拥有的、与建筑施工活动有关的人员的平均人数，包括参加本企业(或单位)建筑施工活动的非本企业(或单位)人员，但不包括企业内部社会服务性机构的人员以及由本企业支付工资但所从事的工作与本企业生产基本无关的人员。

年末就业人员中工程技术人员　指负担工程技术和工程技术管理工作，并具有工程技术工作能力的人员。

利润总额　指企业在生产经营过程中各种收入扣除各种耗费后的盈余，反映企业在报告期内实现的亏盈总额，包括营业利润、补贴收入、投资净收益和营业外收支净额。

工程结算税金及附加　指因从事建筑业生产活动，取得工程价款结算收入而按规定应该交纳的营业税、城市维护建设税等以及随同营业税金一并计算交纳的教育费附加等。

应交增值税　指按照税法规定，以销售货物、服务、无形资产、不动产或提供加工、修理修配劳务的增值额和货物进口金额为计税依据而课征的一种流转税。指按照税法规定，针对销售货物或提供加工、修理修配劳务以及进口货物实现的增值额，企业在报告期内应交纳的税金。填报本指标时，应按权责发生制核算企业本期应负担的增值税，按销项税额与进项税额之间的差额填写。如果一般纳税人企业进项税大于销项税，致使应交税金出现负数时，该项一律填零，不填负数。

应交增值税=销项税额-(进项税额-进项税额转出)-出口抵减内销产品应纳税额-减免税款+出口退税

利税总额=工程结算税金及附加+应交增值税+利润总额

建筑业全员劳动生产率=建筑业总产值÷计算建筑业劳动生产率的平均人数

Explanatory Notes on Main Statistical Indicators

Gross Output Value of Construction　refers to the sum in monetary terms of construction products and services completed by construction enterprises during a given period of time. It includes:

(1) Output value of construction projects, which is the value of various projects covered by the project budgets.

(2) Output value of equipment installation projects refers to the value of the installation of equipment and the value of installing prefabricated parts into construction engineering products. It does not include the value of the equipment and the part itself.

(3) Other output values, which are output values other than output value of construction projects and output value of installation projects, including output value of house and building repair, output value of non-standard equipment manufacture, management expenses received by overall contractor enterprises from subcontractor enterprises and output value completed in unclassified construction activities.

①Output value of house and building repair is the value created through the repairs of houses and buildings, excluding the value of houses or buildings being repaired and the value of the repair of production equipment.

②Output value of non-standard equipment manufacture is the value of non-standard production equipment with unique specifications (including raw materials and manufacturing costs), and equipment manufactured by subsidiary workshops for construction projects contracted by construction enterprises.

Output Value Completed refers to the value of unit project completed, which has come up to the designed standards for putting into use and has been checked and accepted as qualified project by related departments.

Floor Space of Buildings under Construction refers to the floor space of buildings under construction during the reference period, including newly started buildings, buildings started earlier and continued into the reference period, buildings suspended in preceding periods but resumed during the reference period, buildings completed during the reference period, and buildings started and then suspended during the reference period.

Floor Space of Buildings Started This Year refers to the total floor space area of the buildings started in the year by real estate development companies. It excludes the buildings started in previous years and continued in the year, and the buildings suspended in previous years but restarted in the year. The start of a construction is defined by the date of ground breaking or pile driving. The floor space of the building includes that of the entire building.

Average Number of Persons for Labor Productivity Calculation of the Construction Industry refers to the average number of persons actually employed in the construction enterprises (units) and engaged in related activities of construction in the reference period, including non-staff personnel engaged in the construction activities of the enterprises (units), but excluding personnel employed in social service institutions of the enterprises and those receiving remunerations therefrom but engaged in activities basically irrelevant to the production of the enterprises.

Number of Engineering Technical Personnel Employed at the Year-end refers to personnel capable of and engaged in engineering technical work and related management.

Total Profits refer to the surplus of various incomes in the production and operation of the enterprises after deducting all expenses. This reflects the total profits or losses realized by the enterprises in the reference period, including profits from operation, income from subsidies, net investment earnings and net income from activities other than operations.

Taxes and Extra Charges on Project Settlement Accounts refer to business tax, city maintenance and construction tax and extra charges for education calculated and paid with business tax, which should be borne by the enterprises obtaining project settlement incomes from the production activities of construction.

Value added tax payable According to the tax law refers to, in order to sell goods, services, intangible assets, real estate or providing processing, repairs and replacement services appreciation and the amount of goods imported for a turnover tax assessed on profits realized from tax basis.In accordance with the provisions of the tax law, the enterprise shall pay the tax in the report period according to the value added value of goods sold or provided for processing, repair and repair services and import goods.When filling in this index, the value added tax shall be calculated according to the accrual basis of accrual basis, and the difference between the output tax and the input tax shall be filled in.If the average taxpayer enterprise enters into a tax more than the sales tax, resulting in the negative tax payable, the item will be filled to zero, and no negative value will be filled.

Value added tax payable = sales tax - (input tax - input tax) - export offset shall be tax payable - tax deduction Export tax rebate

Total Pre-tax Profits = Taxes and Extra Charges on Project Settlement Accounts +Value added tax payable + Total Profits

Overall Labor Productivity of Construction = Gross Output Value of Construction ÷ Average Number of Persons for Labor Productivity Calculation

十四、规模以上服务业

SERVICE ENTERPRISES ABOVE DESIGNATED SIZE

十四　规模以上服务业

简要说明

一、本篇资料主要反映规模以上服务业的基本情况、财务状况、从业人员及劳动报酬情况等。

二、本篇资料由广东省统计局服务业统计处整理、编辑。

三、据国家统计报表制度，2012 年规模以上服务业年报首次纳入“一套表”联网直报系统。规模以上服务业统计范围：辖区内年营业收入 2000 万元及以上服务业法人单位。包括：交通运输、仓储和邮政业，信息传输、软件和信息技术服务业，水利、环境和公共设施管理业，卫生。辖区内年营业收入 1000 万元及以上服务业法人单位。包括：租赁和商务服务业，科学研究和技术服务业，教育，以及物业管理、房地产中介服务、房地产租赁经营和其他房地产业。辖区内年营业收入 500 万元及以上服务业法人单位。包括：居民服务、修理和其他服务业，文化、体育和娱乐业，社会工作。调查方法为符合上述条件企业的全面调查。

14 Service Enterprises Above Designated Size

Brief Introduction

Ⅰ. This data in this chapter reflect the basic information, financial condition, employed persons, labor remuneration and ecommerce transactions of some service enterprises above designated size.

Ⅱ. Data of some service enterprises above designated size are prepared and edited by the Division of Service Statistics of Statistics Bureau of Guangdong Province.

Ⅲ. According to the National Statistical Reporting System, some service enterprises above designated size have been integrated into the "network reporting" system since 2012. Statistics coverage of some service enterprises above designated size: All the service legal entity with annual business revenue of 20 million yuan or above within the jurisdiction, including transport, storage and postal services, information transmission, software and information technology services, management of water conservancy, environment and public facilities, hygiene. All the service legal entity with annual business revenue of 10 million yuan or above within the jurisdiction, including leasing and business services, scientific research and technical services, education, estate management, real estate agent services, real estate intermediary services, own real estate business activities and other real estate,etc.All the service legal entity with annual business revenue of 5 million yuan or above within the jurisdiction, including households service, repair and other services, culture, sports and entertainment services, social work. Survey method is a comprehensive survey.

14-1 规模以上服务业企业财务指标

Main Financial Indicators of Service Enterprises above Designated Size

单位：亿元 (100 million yuan)

项目	Item	2019	2020	2021	2022	2022年比2021年增长(%) Growth Rate in 2022 Over 2021(%)
年初存货	**Inventory at Year-beginning**	**2538.04**	**2747.27**	**3169.54**	**4200.69**	**23.0**
期末资产负债	**Closing Balance**					
固定资产原价	Original Value of Fixed Assets	34434.71	37402.65	39758.55	43348.30	6.0
本年折旧	Depreciation Drawn in Current Year	1919.26	1752.55	1872.23	1915.25	1.3
资产总计	Total Assets	137989.75	163089.18	182956.23	197977.09	8.2
负债合计	Total Liabilities	73587.25	90997.01	103752.20	114026.95	9.9
所有者权益合计	Total Creditors'Equity	64402.50	72092.17	79204.03	83949.85	5.9
损益及分配	**Profits and Loss**					
营业收入	Business Revenue	33516.56	35728.23	44419.85	46722.88	4.2
营业成本	Business Costs	23684.36	25677.66	32352.12	34881.30	7.0
税金及附加	Tax and Extra Charges	253.80	226.93	269.94	273.73	-1.1
销售费用	Sales Expenses	1827.46	1973.81	2439.96	2486.28	0.5
管理费用	Management Expenses	3585.28	3817.65	4641.61	4710.37	-0.2
财务费用	Financial Expenses	943.08	1029.83	1026.18	1105.68	5.3
其中：利息收入	Interest Revenue	480.48	607.03	730.38	746.82	3.4
利息支出	Interest Expense	1174.94	1408.93	1539.25	1613.21	4.2
投资收益(损失以“-”号记)	Investment Income(loss with “-”mark)	2509.06	3009.38	2982.87	2995.11	4.4
营业利润	Business Profits	5035.18	5068.14	5339.28	4720.94	-10.3
利润总额	Total Profits	5131.67	5180.83	5316.25	4802.85	-8.3
所得税费用	Income Taxes Payable	640.65	588.00	632.66	618.85	0.1
人工成本及增值税	**Labor Cost and Value-added Tax**					
应付职工薪酬(本年贷方累计发生额)	Total Wages Payable(Credit Accumulated Amount in this year)	6883.07	7522.62	8898.92	9802.91	8.0
应交增值税(本期累计发生额)	Value-added Tax Payable	746.21	766.86	960.12	1170.85	19.5

注：增速按可比口径计算。
Note: The growth rates are calculated on comparable coverage.

14-2 规模以上服务业企业分行业主要指标（2022年）

单位：亿元

项　　目	Item	企业单位数(个) Number of Enterprises (unit)	营业收入 Business Revenue 总量 Total	2022年比2021年增长(%) Growth Rate in 2022 Over 2021(%)
全　省	**Provincial Total**	**35692**	**46722.88**	**4.2**
按经济类型分	Grouped by Ownership			
内资企业	Domestic-funded Enterprises	32943	39030.67	3.8
#国有企业	State-owned Enterprises	809	1695.05	7.9
集体企业	Collective-owned Enterprises	651	253.10	5.4
有限责任公司	Limited Liability Corporations	8796	15008.50	9.0
私营企业	Private Enterprises	20988	17932.55	1.0
港澳台商投资企业	Enterprises with Investment from Hong Kong, Macao and Taiwan	1858	5755.65	3.7
外商投资企业	Enterprises with Foreign Investment	891	1936.56	13.7
按行业分	Grouped by Sector			
交通运输、仓储和邮政业	Transport, Storage and Postal Services	5803	11679.85	-0.1
铁路运输业	Railway Transport Service	21	894.32	-7.5
#铁路旅客运输	Railway Passenger Transport	8	852.19	-7.1
铁路货物运输	Railway Freight Transport	12	36.78	-19.2
道路运输业	Road Transport Services	1919	2287.20	-3.5
#城市公共交通运输	Urban Public Transport	163	353.74	-23.1
公路旅客运输	Highway Passenger Transport	120	55.70	-14.2
道路货物运输	Road Freight Transport	1480	1205.44	7.0
水上运输业	Waterway Transport Service	285	905.45	1.0
#水上旅客运输	Waterway Passenger Transport	22	6.51	-31.3
水上货物运输	Waterway Freight Transport	156	586.26	3.2
航空运输业	Air Transport Service	42	1128.17	-10.8
#航空客货运输	Air Passenger and Freight Transport	15	1012.62	-11.0
管道运输业	Pipeline Transport Service	5	38.26	33.5
多式联运和运输代理业	Multimodal Transport and Transport Agency Industry	2529	4523.13	2.4
#运输代理业	Transportation Agency	2486	4234.83	2.3
装卸搬运和仓储业	Handling and Storage	671	656.56	11.3
邮政业	Postal Service	331	1246.76	8.0
#快递服务	Express Service	288	1011.15	7.5
信息传输、软件和信息技术服务业	Information Transmission, Software and Information Technology Services	5614	16580.39	9.1
电信、广播电视和卫星传输服务	Telecommunications, Broadcasting Television and Satellite Transmission Services	322	2373.81	5.9
#电信	Telecommunications	297	2277.08	6.2
互联网和相关服务	Internet and Related Services	905	5509.18	5.0
#互联网信息服务	Internet Information Services	403	3607.85	2.3
软件和信息技术服务业	Software and Information Technology Services	4387	8697.41	12.9
#软件开发	Software Development	2629	5241.59	7.0
信息系统集成和物联网技术服务	Information System Integration and Internet of Things Technology Services	634	906.45	7.1
信息技术咨询服务	Information Technology Consulting Services	444	1313.11	71.7
房地产业(不含房地产开发经营)	Realty Industry	5802	3702.70	-0.6
#物业管理业	Property Management Industry	2369	1982.39	3.6
房地产中介服务业	Real Estate Agent Services	595	377.74	-23.3

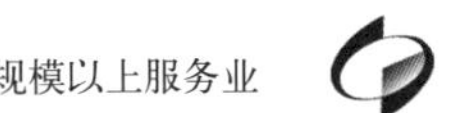

Main Indicators of Service Enterprises above Designated Size by Sector(2022)

(100 million yuan)

营业成本 Business Costs		税金及附加 Tax and Extra Charges		销售费用 Selling Expenses		管理费用 Management Expenses	
总量 Total	2022年比2021年增长(%) Growth Rate in 2022 Over 2021(%)	总量 Total	2022年比2021年增长(%) Growth Rate in 2022 Over 2021(%)	总量 Total	2022年比2021年增长(%) Growth Rate in 2022 Over 2021(%)	总量 Total	2022年比2021年增长(%) Growth Rate in 2022 Over 2021(%)
34881.30	**7.0**	**273.73**	**-1.1**	**2486.28**	**0.5**	**4710.37**	**-0.2**
30376.34	7.1	220.76	-2.1	1976.79	5.3	3851.77	-1.2
1375.57	11.5	12.14	5.4	34.96	-9.6	171.42	4.9
75.87	11.2	6.41	0.2	3.18	-21.8	49.33	-0.3
11864.17	13.9	104.66	-8.6	637.82	6.7	1270.30	-3.5
13748.79	2.4	71.01	11.3	1098.52	6.7	1845.76	-0.8
3268.76	2.7	36.99	6.3	412.59	-17.3	615.26	2.7
1236.20	17.0	15.98	-3.5	96.90	-0.8	243.34	10.3
11084.54	3.9	31.81	-43.6	182.69	2.1	639.69	4.8
977.35	-1.4	0.68	-59.7	0.03	-34.8	24.30	-5.8
932.17	-1.0	0.53	-66.0	0.00	-61.4	22.04	-7.3
40.08	-11.9	0.15	11.1	0.02	-23.7	2.09	8.1
2182.43	4.5	14.51	-60.1	36.66	-3.9	166.15	-1.3
644.68	3.1	7.90	-72.9	4.19	15.6	46.25	-1.7
63.14	-7.1	0.45	-25.0	0.62	-39.2	12.68	-10.9
1076.20	8.6	2.38	-16.3	30.10	-6.2	77.10	1.0
716.21	4.9	3.10	-2.1	4.31	-10.1	57.55	-2.3
13.70	-7.2	0.04	-32.0	0.41	-35.8	1.77	-10.0
503.65	7.5	1.13	-7.6	2.34	-15.6	29.07	-3.1
1365.90	5.5	3.22	-34.2	47.09	-5.5	47.66	2.1
1234.48	5.4	1.87	-33.4	45.18	-6.4	39.34	2.3
18.32	28.3	0.14	-1.1	0.05	-4.2	1.39	43.2
4172.10	2.3	2.56	-4.1	64.05	14.7	197.77	12.5
3901.76	2.3	2.28	-3.7	60.46	14.6	185.53	13.0
509.26	13.6	5.71	10.8	18.01	-1.2	61.65	8.1
1142.97	6.3	1.88	-15.4	12.49	4.4	83.22	8.1
931.44	6.2	0.63	-33.6	11.39	2.6	60.22	6.4
10405.43	12.0	65.93	34.7	1502.08	3.5	1448.14	0.7
1622.18	6.2	7.36	-3.3	185.53	-1.7	116.39	1.2
1551.17	6.4	7.20	-3.1	179.08	-1.9	101.98	2.4
3485.65	4.1	27.43	109.2	595.33	0.9	425.17	0.9
2392.37	5.9	23.80	136.9	175.91	-27.8	222.76	8.7
5297.60	20.1	31.15	10.3	721.22	7.3	906.58	0.6
2813.71	10.5	19.55	-0.3	529.42	1.4	556.51	0.1
667.88	6.9	2.93	8.2	36.35	8.5	81.85	12.0
1020.80	109.0	3.82	79.8	55.00	10.4	90.96	-14.7
2578.04	5.5	74.17	-5.5	118.59	-14.1	592.27	-5.7
1541.73	9.6	17.78	-1.2	40.95	-2.4	240.84	-7.2
286.59	-23.4	1.45	-37.2	37.85	-24.8	59.34	-15.7

14-2 续表 1

单位：亿元

项　　目	Item	财务费用 Financial Expenses 总量 Total	2022年比2021年增长(%) Growth Rate in 2022 Over 2021(%)
全　省	**Provincial Total**	**1105.68**	**5.3**
按经济类型分	Grouped by Ownership		
内资企业	Domestic-funded Enterprises	1019.95	6.2
#国有企业	State-owned Enterprises	52.60	23.9
集体企业	Collective-owned Enterprises	2.57	4.5
有限责任公司	Limited Liability Corporations	611.01	16.3
私营企业	Private Enterprises	170.48	-13.3
港澳台商投资企业	Enterprises with Investment from Hong Kong,Macao and Taiwan	50.93	1.2
外商投资企业	Enterprises with Foreign Investment	34.80	-12.2
按行业分	Grouped by Sector		
交通运输、仓储和邮政业	Transport, Storage and Postal Services	472.11	22.3
铁路运输业	Railway Transport Service	37.28	45.7
#铁路旅客运输	Railway Passenger Transport	30.16	45.0
铁路货物运输	Railway Freight Transport	7.11	49.6
道路运输业	Road Transport Services	268.50	15.3
#城市公共交通运输	Urban Public Transport	95.01	28.7
公路旅客运输	Highway Passenger Transport	2.93	-1.1
道路货物运输	Road Freight Transport	6.41	-13.7
水上运输业	Waterway Transport Service	10.13	-64.1
#水上旅客运输	Waterway Passenger Transport	1.38	14.9
水上货物运输	Waterway Freight Transport	2.53	-87.5
航空运输业	Air Transport Service	115.91	131.9
#航空客货运输	Air passenger and freight Transport	108.94	139.6
管道运输业	Pipeline Transport Service	3.76	131.6
多式联运和运输代理业	Multimodal Transport and Transport Agency Industry	1.95	-82.8
#运输代理业	Transportation Agency	0.32	-96.6
装卸搬运和仓储业	Handling and Storage	28.01	-6.2
邮政业	Postal Service	6.56	-0.7
#快递服务	Express Service	4.28	6.2
信息传输、软件和信息技术服务业	Information Transmission, Software and Information Technology Services	-67.91	-76.4
电信、广播电视和卫星传输服务	Telecommunications, Broadcasting Television and Satellite Transmission Services	-9.96	-52.0
#电信	Telecommunications	-11.20	-42.7
互联网和相关服务	Internet and Related Services	-41.15	-29.2
#互联网信息服务	Internet Information Services	-47.84	-15.6
软件和信息技术服务业	Software and Information Technology Services	-16.80	-17337.0
#软件开发	Software Development	-20.67	-215.1
信息系统集成和物联网技术服务	Information System Integration and Internet of Things Technology Services	0.84	-73.0
信息技术咨询服务	Information Technology Consulting services	0.48	-69.6
房地产业(不含房地产开发经营)	Realty Industry	299.34	-4.6
#物业管理业	Property Management Industry	40.83	33.7
房地产中介服务业	Real Estate Agent Services	0.27	77.0

14-2 1 continued

(100 million yuan)

利润总额 Total Profits		所得税费用 Income Taxes Payable		应付职工薪酬 Total Wages Payable		应交增值税 Value-added Taxes Payable		期末用工人数(万人) Total number of employed persons at the year-end (10000 persons)
总量 Total	2022年比2021年增长(%) Growth Rate in 2022 Over 2021(%)	总量 Total	2022年比2021年增长(%) Growth Rate in 2022 Over 2021(%)	总量 Total	2022年比2021年增长(%) Growth Rate in 2022 Over 2021(%)	总量 Total	2022年比2021年增长(%) Growth Rate in 2022 Over 2021(%)	
4802.85	**-8.3**	**648.85**	**0.4**	**9802.91**	**8.0**	**1170.85**	**19.5**	**639.52**
3186.00	-12.8	444.20	0.4	8048.97	7.7	954.57	19.3	571.74
252.34	-13.3	30.72	-27.0	460.69	6.9	41.41	15.4	29.34
118.71	5.3	3.47	-10.5	45.50	15.0	6.35	9.9	5.97
1291.45	-17.8	229.63	-9.6	3144.86	9.8	487.10	41.8	198.03
836.07	11.7	125.74	3.4	3250.03	6.9	330.15	-0.1	278.66
1219.37	-0.9	149.69	-1.2	1191.95	8.2	168.12	22.1	45.53
397.48	12.7	54.96	5.0	561.99	12.6	48.16	13.9	22.25
-88.82	-130.9	112.16	44.4	1776.47	6.3	266.72	73.9	107.55
-103.04	-46.7	-0.46	72.7	242.90	5.5	54.88	3.6	14.13
-96.20	-47.0	-3.16	-80.6	234.83	5.2	47.48	-9.0	13.58
-6.94	-44.8	2.69	5882.4	7.82	13.0	7.35	797.5	0.53
77.55	-60.1	44.69	-9.2	557.89	3.1	145.64	159.8	41.36
-86.60	-397.7	1.04	-41.4	316.57	2.8	76.79	527.9	19.47
-4.65	-18.9	1.79	423.5	31.23	-10.3	1.08	-42.0	3.73
14.29	-33.3	5.59	-2.9	121.86	6.4	17.48	9.5	11.97
132.14	-18.5	17.39	-40.9	132.02	4.7	12.93	53.5	4.57
-9.14	-11.3	-0.15	62.0	5.44	-13.8	0.22	26.5	0.31
44.53	-16.2	-1.06	-112.3	69.38	8.4	3.96	-1.2	1.70
-386.47	-170.1	8.27	121.7	314.64	4.0	7.71	-0.9	11.40
-358.68	-159.4	15.25	142.1	273.41	4.9	2.71	-46.1	9.70
17.03	47.3	4.41	55.3	3.08	13.0	6.60	2929.0	0.09
110.91	9.9	19.79	-4.6	277.07	15.7	18.23	57.6	18.16
109.98	10.4	19.26	-3.6	205.57	13.4	16.70	66.0	14.06
36.33	13.7	12.70	4.3	104.13	19.2	13.41	49.4	8.03
26.72	44487.3	5.37	68.9	144.73	2.3	7.31	-0.7	9.81
29.04	213.5	6.40	26.8	82.30	-1.0	4.78	-17.7	6.40
2105.77	3.7	294.70	14.1	3031.30	11.4	390.04	13.8	108.35
503.03	4.5	107.54	7.1	303.40	2.7	57.31	26.3	11.23
499.25	5.0	107.65	7.3	273.25	2.8	56.44	25.6	9.79
779.89	18.8	102.58	58.6	625.67	8.4	113.44	29.8	17.53
724.92	4.0	93.05	65.8	383.58	6.3	84.14	32.1	6.63
822.86	-7.9	84.58	-9.3	2102.23	13.7	219.29	4.5	79.59
631.17	-2.7	55.92	-11.2	1380.23	14.7	148.19	1.9	47.34
66.06	17.8	8.00	5.6	173.04	13.9	18.83	-14.8	7.80
62.68	3.5	9.39	33.0	223.41	9.1	20.70	39.8	9.45
306.13	-22.8	67.71	-40.7	982.71	2.2	145.76	1.6	100.04
128.92	-43.0	37.48	-24.5	714.99	7.5	67.39	-2.6	84.68
42.03	37.0	0.81	-55.4	115.15	-22.5	15.28	-13.2	5.81

14-2 续表 2

单位：亿元

项　　目	Item	企业单位数(个) Number of Enterprises (unit)	营业收入 Business Revenue 总量 Total	2022年比2021年增长(%) Growth Rate in 2022 Over 2021(%)
租赁和商务服务业	Leasing and Business Services	9383	8137.07	4.0
租赁业	Leasing	650	306.12	-2.5
#机械设备经营租赁	Machinery Equipment Operating Leasing	634	291.05	-2.9
商务服务业	Business Services	8733	7830.95	4.3
#组织管理服务	Organizational Management Services	1573	1357.48	1.5
咨询与调查	Consultation and Investigation	1196	788.52	1.7
广告业	Advertising	1164	1578.59	7.0
其他商务服务	Other Business Services	753	442.84	-4.2
科学研究和技术服务业	Scientific Research and Technical Services	4108	3755.05	2.8
研究和试验发展	Research and Experimental Development	407	356.31	18.9
#工程和技术研究和试验发展	Engineering and Technology Research and Experimental Development	255	258.42	15.8
专业技术服务业	Professional Technical Services	3127	2982.04	0.2
科技推广和应用服务业	Services of Science and Technology Exchanges and Promotion	574	416.69	10.3
水利环境和公共设施管理业	Management of Water Conservancy, Environment and Public Facilities	594	666.93	3.8
水利管理业	Management of Water Conservancy	19	21.93	1.2
生态保护和环境治理业	Ecological Protection and Environmental Treatment	168	131.04	-6.2
#生态保护	Ecological Protection	2	1.57	-31.9
环境治理业	Environmental Treatment	166	129.48	-5.8
公共设施管理业	Management of Public Facilities	393	371.19	-3.3
土地管理业	Management of Land	14	142.76	47.3
居民服务、修理和其他服务业	Households' service, Repair and Other Services	1425	472.21	6.9
居民服务业	Services to Households	352	118.46	0.2
机动车、电子产品和日用产品修理业	Motor Vehicle, Electronic Products and Consumer Products repair	428	137.45	15.4
#汽车、摩托车等修理与维护	Automobile, Motorcycle and Others Repair and Maintenance	291	70.02	20.7
其他服务业	Other Services	645	216.29	5.8
教育	Education	898	437.71	-6.6
#中等教育	Secondary Education	195	138.54	15.8
高等教育	Higher Education	19	39.50	8.6
卫生和社会工作	Health and Social Work	759	780.36	20.1
卫生	Health	643	754.14	20.2
#医院	Hospital	387	433.92	3.9
基层医疗卫生服务	Primary Health Care Services	117	56.60	2.8
社会工作	Social Work	116	26.22	15.6
文化、体育和娱乐业	Culture, Sports and Entertainment	1306	510.61	-10.0
新闻和出版业	News and Publication	98	102.81	-1.3
#出版业	Publication	91	97.05	-4.0
广播、电视、电影和影视录音制作业	Production of Radio, Television, Film and Video Recording	417	149.48	-17.0
文化艺术业	Culture and Arts	151	26.15	-23.4
体育	Sports	216	88.11	3.8
娱乐业	Entertainment	424	144.07	-12.0

14-2 2 continued

(100 million yuan)

营业成本 Business Costs		税金及附加 Tax and Extra Charges		销售费用 Selling Expenses		管理费用 Management Expenses	
总量 Total	2022年比2021年增长(%) Growth Rate in 2022 Over 2021(%)	总量 Total	2022年比2021年增长(%) Growth Rate in 2022 Over 2021(%)	总量 Total	2022年比2021年增长(%) Growth Rate in 2022 Over 2021(%)	总量 Total	2022年比2021年增长(%) Growth Rate in 2022 Over 2021(%)
6125.47	7.1	58.96	6.3	320.09	-3.9	1087.65	-0.8
225.39	-2.0	1.08	-8.2	22.88	-7.9	36.16	-5.4
216.82	-2.0	1.07	-6.8	18.06	-0.1	34.91	-4.7
5900.07	7.5	57.88	6.7	297.21	-3.5	1051.49	-0.6
663.24	6.3	26.31	-1.3	26.72	-3.0	377.60	2.1
438.24	6.8	3.09	-18.2	81.28	2.1	193.44	-9.4
1437.67	10.3	5.29	133.6	50.28	-2.3	66.86	5.0
345.24	-1.4	1.51	-1.3	27.75	-17.2	54.08	-10.5
2659.28	4.1	15.41	-7.4	152.71	7.8	475.84	-2.2
215.86	23.5	1.80	11.4	20.77	19.4	44.92	1.5
169.20	20.4	1.39	10.4	6.80	17.5	29.54	4.7
2172.01	1.3	11.69	-11.4	103.64	6.8	365.83	-2.6
271.41	15.7	1.92	4.8	28.31	4.0	65.10	-2.6
483.10	1.5	17.46	65.4	14.56	-5.1	62.04	2.0
14.93	5.9	0.13	-22.6	0.14	68.0	5.02	37.6
95.00	-6.9	0.58	-5.7	3.14	-7.5	15.62	3.7
1.37	-5.4	0.03	-1.8	0.09	43.0	0.31	4.8
93.63	-6.9	0.55	-5.9	3.04	-8.5	15.32	3.7
290.71	-1.8	1.41	14.4	7.19	-23.7	37.14	-3.5
82.47	29.5	15.35	79.6	4.09	67.4	4.26	17.6
347.44	11.1	1.83	-8.1	42.31	2.3	73.75	1.0
72.80	5.4	0.37	-7.6	22.32	3.1	23.93	-2.6
108.24	21.4	0.40	-22.0	12.46	-2.6	15.13	-0.1
54.04	29.5	0.18	-27.0	6.40	-7.8	9.52	-2.0
166.39	7.6	1.06	-1.5	7.52	8.7	34.69	4.1
275.95	-6.6	0.67	-27.8	30.17	-38.0	113.92	-1.4
101.43	12.3	0.06	9.8	0.65	2.6	36.00	13.4
24.93	17.0	0.07	-38.4	0.25	-30.4	6.96	10.6
539.77	25.3	0.86	9.3	78.43	8.2	107.33	9.2
519.40	25.6	0.85	9.6	77.29	8.4	101.10	9.5
316.61	7.3	0.66	3.8	37.71	-2.3	72.35	2.5
37.02	5.3	0.02	-32.7	10.42	-2.5	9.48	6.2
20.36	19.5	0.01	-5.9	1.14	-2.1	6.23	4.7
382.29	-8.6	6.62	0.1	44.64	-16.5	109.73	-2.2
73.25	2.7	1.27	49.5	5.05	-11.1	23.05	2.8
68.91	-1.0	1.00	20.5	5.03	-11.0	20.03	-6.8
120.01	-16.1	1.49	-24.9	10.49	-31.8	20.98	-7.5
19.98	-18.2	0.14	-17.5	1.99	-23.0	8.06	2.7
52.54	-14.9	3.03	22.8	12.68	2.6	21.61	-3.8
116.51	-1.2	0.69	-39.2	14.43	-17.2	36.03	-2.1

14-2 续表 3

单位：亿元

项　　目	item	财务费用 Financial Expenses 总量 Total	2022年比2021年增长(%) Growth Rate in 2022 Over 2021(%)
租赁和商务服务业	Leasing and Business Services	323.72	7.4
租赁业	Leasing	13.20	1.0
#机械设备经营租赁	Machinery Equipment Operating Leasing	13.12	1.8
商务服务业	Business Services	310.52	7.7
#组织管理服务	Organizational Management Services	230.61	3.0
咨询与调查	Consultation and Investigation	14.86	-9.7
广告业	Advertising	-1.82	-208.2
其他商务服务业	Other Business Services	0.14	-95.4
科学研究和技术服务业	Scientific Research and Technical Services	26.19	-25.1
研究和试验发展	Research and Experimental Development	-1.70	-275.1
#工程和技术研究和试验发展	Engineering and Technology Research and Experimental Development	-1.76	-2417.9
专业技术服务业	Professional Technical Services	9.19	-49.5
科技推广和应用服务业	Services of Science and Technology Exchanges and Promotion	18.70	18.1
水利环境和公共设施管理业	Management of Water Conservancy, Environment and Public Facilities	23.87	0.0
水利管理业	Management of Water Conservancy	2.89	79.2
生态保护和环境治理业	Ecological Protection and Environmental Treatment	2.38	100.4
#生态保护	Ecological Protection	0.09	-15.6
环境治理业	Environmental Treatment	2.28	112.1
公共设施管理业	Management of Public Facilities	14.84	-7.6
土地管理业	Management of Land	3.75	-25.2
居民服务、修理和其他服务业	Households' service, Repair and Other Services	3.35	14.9
居民服务业	Services to Households	1.41	3.6
机动车、电子产品和日用产品修理业	Motor Vehicle, Electronic Products and Consumer Products repair	0.65	55.5
#汽车、摩托车等修理与维护	Automobile, Motorcycle and Others Repair and Maintenance	0.39	100.5
其他服务业	Other Services	1.29	13.6
教育	Education	9.19	7.7
#中等教育	Secondary Education	2.90	-0.7
高等教育	Higher Education	1.89	24.2
卫生和社会工作	Health and Social Work	9.48	9.4
卫生	Health	9.01	8.6
#医院	Hospital	6.95	9.2
基层医疗卫生服务	Primary Health Care Services	0.45	34.3
社会工作	Social Work	0.47	28.4
文化、体育和娱乐业	Culture, Sports and Entertainment	6.33	-23.5
新闻和出版业	News and Publication	-1.54	-56.8
#出版业	Publication	-1.11	-17.0
广播、电视、电影和影视录音制作业	Production of Radio, Television, Film and Video Recording	4.93	-21.2
文化艺术业	Culture and Arts	0.05	-77.6
体育	Sports	4.31	7.1
娱乐业	Entertainment	-1.41	-14.5

14-2 3 continued

(100 million yuan)

利润总额 Total Profits		所得税费用 Income Taxes Payable		应付职工薪酬 Total Wages Payable		应交增值税 Value-added Tax Payable		期末用工人数（万人）Total number of employed persons at the year-end (10000 persons)
总量 Total	2022年比2021年增长(%) Growth Rate in 2022 Over 2021(%)	总量 Total	2022年比2021年增长(%) Growth Rate in 2022 Over 2021(%)	总量 Total	2022年比2021年增长(%) Growth Rate in 2022 Over 2021(%)	总量 Total	2022年比2021年增长(%) Growth Rate in 2022 Over 2021(%)	
2014.61	-4.9	100.20	-17.6	2023.07	10.0	208.73	12.0	179.81
11.81	597.9	5.09	86.5	40.54	-1.6	11.48	26.7	3.57
12.30	833.3	5.08	87.4	37.84	1.5	11.41	33.9	3.37
2002.80	-5.6	95.11	-20.0	1982.53	10.2	197.25	11.2	176.24
1604.67	-5.2	36.97	-19.3	347.11	4.2	54.19	2.8	17.94
103.35	-22.2	8.91	-51.6	283.81	1.1	23.47	-4.8	15.55
22.45	-40.0	7.59	-4.4	134.06	28.4	10.08	-11.8	5.11
17.37	-33.2	5.97	-18.0	65.54	-12.0	21.43	142.5	5.48
294.74	1.9	40.21	-3.5	1087.94	7.7	102.83	-1.9	53.46
50.14	11.4	7.56	-12.3	93.23	18.9	8.80	17.6	3.58
45.53	6.1	5.71	-11.0	61.22	15.9	6.63	13.2	2.13
234.68	2.2	27.48	-0.9	872.72	4.9	83.48	-4.2	44.85
9.91	-32.2	5.17	-3.2	121.99	22.7	10.56	3.4	5.03
75.22	11.0	14.15	27.8	144.36	6.7	20.80	20.9	19.09
0.61	-87.3	0.26	8.8	7.26	20.2	0.74	11.0	0.31
14.15	-8.7	2.02	-15.2	21.07	3.9	2.94	-17.9	1.39
1.01	-9.3	0.25	-8.8	0.77	-5.8	0.06	-75.2	0.08
13.14	-8.7	1.76	-16.0	20.31	4.3	2.88	-13.9	1.31
26.44	-13.3	5.42	4.3	112.99	6.7	11.61	47.4	17.30
34.02	100.5	6.46	97.8	3.04	0.1	5.52	8.4	0.09
3.71	-55.8	3.02	-13.7	186.86	7.1	14.69	11.0	29.67
-3.40	-533.4	1.07	-24.8	43.97	10.0	2.45	27.7	4.92
0.17	-79.7	0.77	14.9	24.74	5.2	3.87	-2.4	2.27
-0.39	36.8	0.34	24.0	12.26	0.5	1.79	-7.9	1.18
6.95	2.3	1.19	-16.1	118.14	6.4	8.37	13.9	22.49
6.38	326.3	3.36	17.7	193.83	-4.7	4.83	3.2	14.64
-0.85	81.6	0.49	31.1	67.95	17.5	0.21	12.0	4.75
5.99	-15.1	0.12	0.9	13.46	14.3	0.13	-8.2	0.94
26.59	-18.6	8.68	-7.4	233.13	16.8	1.55	12.0	17.16
27.51	-18.8	8.59	-7.9	218.19	16.5	1.43	10.4	14.21
-4.20	-167.8	3.27	-30.4	147.44	6.8	0.36	-13.3	10.11
-0.89	-1060.8	0.15	-49.5	15.05	7.3	0.17	5.1	1.12
-0.92	24.3	0.09	112.4	14.94	20.7	0.12	35.6	2.95
58.53	1018.0	4.66	-21.7	143.24	-9.7	14.89	15.8	9.75
17.68	-37.6	1.83	-20.6	34.02	-2.2	2.90	-1.1	1.16
17.23	-38.1	1.83	-20.7	29.52	-11.2	2.69	-3.9	1.01
-6.05	-1039.8	1.02	436.7	27.91	1.2	3.73	29.0	1.96
-0.83	-129.6	0.22	-48.9	9.70	-6.3	0.71	-26.8	0.63
-4.04	81.6	1.19	-11.8	31.88	-26.0	4.20	64.5	2.67
51.77	1217.1	0.40	-81.3	39.73	-7.2	3.34	-4.6	3.32

14-3 规模以上服务业企业分行业营业收入

Business Revenue of Service Enterprises above Designated Size by Sector

单位：亿元 (100 million yuan)

项　目	Item	营业收入 Business Revenue 2017	2018	2019
全　省	**Provincial Total**	**24325.20**	**28553.34**	**33516.56**
按行业分	Grouped by Sector			
交通运输、仓储和邮政业	Traffic, Transport, Storage and Post	7174.80	8264.88	8708.66
信息传输、软件和信息技术服务业	Information Transfer, Software and Information Technology Services	7589.40	8522.24	10665.72
房地产业(不含房地产开发经营)	Realty Industry	1547.30	2002.50	2598.26
租赁和商务服务业	Tenancy and Business Services	4195.30	5351.76	6195.57
科学研究和技术服务业	Scientific Research and Technical Service	2249.50	2579.68	3084.71
水利、环境和公共设施管理业	Management of Water Conservancy, Environment and Public Facilities	324.80	380.08	460.72
居民服务、修理和其他服务业	Resident Services, Repair and other Services	252.90	292.23	369.21
教育	Education	249.20	333.38	398.25
卫生和社会工作	Health and Social Work	264.20	324.20	406.93
文化、体育和娱乐业	Culture, Sports and Entertainment	477.90	502.38	628.51

14-3 续表 continued

单位：亿元 (100 million yuan)

项　目	Item	营业收入 Business Revenue 2020	2021	2022
全　省	**Provincial Total**	**35728.23**	**44419.85**	**46722.88**
按行业分	Grouped by Sector			
交通运输、仓储和邮政业	Traffic, Transport, Storage and Post	8704.79	11391.18	11679.85
信息传输、软件和信息技术服务业	Information Transfer, Software and Information Technology Services	12482.65	15107.78	16580.39
房地产业(不含房地产开发经营)	Realty Industry	3016.96	3577.55	3702.70
租赁和商务服务业	Tenancy and Business Services	6096.01	7819.10	8137.07
科学研究和技术服务业	Scientific Research and Technical Service	3293.50	3840.64	3755.05
水利、环境和公共设施管理业	Management of Water Conservancy, Environment and Public Facilities	516.40	643.37	666.93
居民服务、修理和其他服务业	Resident Services, Repair and other Services	372.62	445.97	472.21
教育	Education	405.97	471.35	437.71
卫生和社会工作	Health and Social Work	428.23	565.79	780.36
文化、体育和娱乐业	Culture, Sports and Entertainment	411.09	557.12	510.61

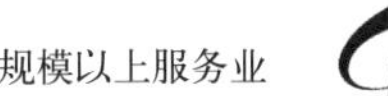

14−4 规模以上服务业企业分行业营业利润

Business Profits of Service Enterprises above Designated Size by Sector

单位：亿元 (100 million yuan)

项　　目	Item	营业利润 Business Profits 2017	2018	2019
全　省	**Provincial Total**	**4281.80**	**4450.17**	**5035.18**
按行业分	Grouped by Sector			
交通运输、仓储和邮政业	Traffic, Transport, Storage and Post	433.60	490.76	591.81
信息传输、软件和信息技术服务业	Information Transfer, Software and Information Technology Services	1742.70	1628.82	1985.38
房地产业(不含房地产开发经营)	Realty Industry	269.00	423.91	337.80
租赁和商务服务业	Tenancy and Business Services	1462.00	1543.85	1760.50
科学研究和技术服务业	Scientific Research and Technical Service	249.30	294.48	251.66
水利、环境和公共设施管理业	Management of Water Conservancy, Environment and Public Facilities	74.40	44.28	39.92
居民服务、修理和其他服务业	Resident Services, Repair and other Services	13.40	13.76	14.30
教育	Education	9.00	5.42	0.04
卫生和社会工作	Health and Social Work	11.70	10.26	8.83
文化、体育和娱乐业	Culture, Sports and Entertainment	16.60	-5.37	44.94

14−4 续表 continued

单位：亿元 (100 million yuan)

项　　目	Item	营业利润 Business Profits 2020	2021	2022
全　省	**Provincial Total**	**5068.14**	**5339.28**	**4720.94**
按行业分	Grouped by Sector			
交通运输、仓储和邮政业	Traffic, Transport, Storage and Post	209.63	282.52	-154.85
信息传输、软件和信息技术服务业	Information Transfer, Software and Information Technology Services	2109.54	2025.74	2150.01
房地产业(不含房地产开发经营)	Realty Industry	527.37	475.32	260.71
租赁和商务服务业	Tenancy and Business Services	1882.80	2146.27	2015.59
科学研究和技术服务业	Scientific Research and Technical Service	321.02	313.00	288.62
水利、环境和公共设施管理业	Management of Water Conservancy, Environment and Public Facilities	51.95	58.48	72.56
居民服务、修理和其他服务业	Resident Services, Repair and other Services	11.17	9.51	2.85
教育	Education	-10.18	-3.24	6.07
卫生和社会工作	Health and Social Work	8.32	20.67	29.00
文化、体育和娱乐业	Culture, Sports and Entertainment	-43.49	11.02	50.38

14-5 规模以上服务业企业分行业应付职工薪酬

Total Wages Payable of Service Enterprises above Designated Size by Sector

单位：亿元 (100 million yuan)

项　　目	Item	应付职工薪酬 Total Wages Payable 2017	2018	2019
全　省	**Provincial Total**	**4813.60**	**5919.15**	**6883.07**
按行业分	Grouped by Sector			
交通运输、仓储和邮政业	Traffic, Transport, Storage and Post	1398.60	1585.44	1507.99
信息传输、软件和信息技术服务业	Information Transfer, Software and Information Technology Services	1148.30	1439.38	1844.25
房地产业(不含房地产开发经营)	Realty Industry	484.60	645.54	737.74
租赁和商务服务业	Tenancy and Business Services	834.40	1066.75	1344.03
科学研究和技术服务业	Scientific Research and Technical Service	515.80	636.47	762.46
水利、环境和公共设施管理业	Management of Water Conservancy, Environment and Public Facilities	48.30	68.45	86.14
居民服务、修理和其他服务业	Resident Services, Repair and other Services	95.10	108.59	135.47
教育	Education	99.40	148.68	175.39
卫生和社会工作	Health and Social Work	75.00	95.77	122.33
文化、体育和娱乐业	Culture, Sports and Entertainment	114.20	124.09	167.27

14-5 续表 continued

单位：亿元 (100 million yuan)

项　　目	Item	应付职工薪酬 Total Wages Payable 2020	2021	2022
全　省	**Provincial Total**	**7522.62**	**8898.92**	**9802.91**
按行业分	Grouped by Sector			
交通运输、仓储和邮政业	Traffic, Transport, Storage and Post	1455.49	1622.86	1776.47
信息传输、软件和信息技术服务业	Information Transfer, Software and Information Technology Services	2151.83	2677.49	3031.30
房地产业(不含房地产开发经营)	Realty Industry	836.82	932.83	982.71
租赁和商务服务业	Tenancy and Business Services	1505.35	1792.73	2023.07
科学研究和技术服务业	Scientific Research and Technical Service	853.26	1021.38	1087.94
水利、环境和公共设施管理业	Management of Water Conservancy, Environment and Public Facilities	104.55	131.72	144.36
居民服务、修理和其他服务业	Resident Services, Repair and other Services	152.26	172.37	186.86
教育	Education	188.88	212.76	193.83
卫生和社会工作	Health and Social Work	134.60	179.31	233.13
文化、体育和娱乐业	Culture, Sports and Entertainment	139.58	155.47	143.24

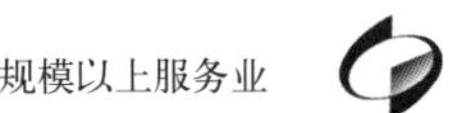

14-6 规模以上服务业企业分行业就业人员平均人数

Average number of Employed Persons of Service Enterprises above Designated Size by Sector

单位：万人 (10000 persons)

项　　目	Item	就业人员平均人数 Average Number of Employed Persons		
		2018	2019	2020
全　省	**Provincial Total**	**496.20**	**539.58**	**590.85**
按行业分	Grouped by Sector			
交通运输、仓储和邮政业	Traffic, Transport, Storage and Post	115.67	109.32	109.12
信息传输、软件和信息技术服务业	Information Transfer, Software and Information Technology Services	77.34	87.44	95.74
房地产业(不含房地产开发经营)	Realty Industry	83.39	88.93	96.13
租赁和商务服务业	Tenancy and Business Services	112.96	133.59	160.23
科学研究和技术服务业	Scientific Research and Technical Service	41.91	45.92	48.72
水利、环境和公共设施管理业	Management of Water Conservancy, Environment and Public Facilities	10.93	12.57	15.89
居民服务、修理和其他服务业	Resident Services, Repair and other Services	21.64	25.09	27.30
教育	Education	13.94	15.38	16.38
卫生和社会工作	Health and Social Work	9.03	10.43	11.66
文化、体育和娱乐业	Culture, Sports and Entertainment	9.39	10.92	9.69

注：本表中，2020年及以前为就业人员平均人数，2021年起改为期末用工人数，与历史数据不具可比性。

Notes: In this chart, the average number of employed persons in 2020 and before is changed to the number of employees at the year-end since 2021, which is not comparable with historical data.

14-6 续表 continued

单位：万人 (10000 persons)

项　　目	Item	期末用工人数 The number of Employed Persons at the Year-end	
		2021	2022
全　省	**Provincial Total**	**620.58**	**639.52**
按行业分	Grouped by Sector		
交通运输、仓储和邮政业	Traffic, Transport, Storage and Post	105.67	107.55
信息传输、软件和信息技术服务业	Information Transfer, Software and Information Technology Services	109.49	108.35
房地产业(不含房地产开发经营)	Realty Industry	98.98	100.04
租赁和商务服务业	Tenancy and Business Services	164.52	179.81
科学研究和技术服务业	Scientific Research and Technical Service	54.82	53.46
水利、环境和公共设施管理业	Management of Water Conservancy, Environment and Public Facilities	17.94	19.09
居民服务、修理和其他服务业	Resident Services, Repair and other Services	28.88	29.67
教育	Education	15.71	14.64
卫生和社会工作	Health and Social Work	14.14	17.16
文化、体育和娱乐业	Culture, Sports and Entertainment	10.43	9.75

14-7 各市规模以上服务业企业主要指标（2022年）

单位：亿元

市别	City	企业单位数（个）Number of Enterprises (unit)	营业收入 Business Revenue 总量 Total	营业收入 Business Revenue 2022年比2021年增长(%) Growth Rate in 2022 Over 2021(%)	营业成本 Business Costs 总量 Total	营业成本 Business Costs 2022年比2021年增长(%) Growth Rate in 2022 Over 2021(%)
广州	Guangzhou	13032	17315.24	2.7	13624.15	5.7
深圳	Shenzhen	11547	21372.67	4.6	15496.23	8.0
珠海	Zhuhai	1299	1334.52	2.9	886.01	3.0
汕头	Shantou	566	346.89	2.9	270.84	6.3
佛山	Foshan	2243	1416.96	5.2	1044.77	6.5
韶关	Shaoguan	192	106.71	0.8	84.80	3.1
河源	Heyuan	112	78.99	5.3	49.90	3.5
梅州	Meizhou	83	81.14	7.0	65.94	9.1
惠州	Huizhou	1215	623.42	2.7	461.52	3.2
汕尾	Shanwei	184	106.00	12.1	90.48	11.7
东莞	Dongguan	2488	2100.09	12.6	1420.69	13.8
中山	Zhongshan	927	502.53	1.9	378.38	4.5
江门	Jiangmen	397	248.92	0.8	182.91	0.4
阳江	Yangjiang	121	85.49	-1.4	66.58	-1.3
湛江	Zhanjiang	367	287.18	2.1	215.36	2.2
茂名	Maoming	247	152.60	-0.7	117.03	-0.5
肇庆	Zhaoqing	139	123.72	10.9	93.34	15.0
清远	Qingyuan	268	213.15	20.2	155.33	19.6
潮州	Chaozhou	58	57.65	13.0	46.71	16.8
揭阳	Jieyang	133	122.99	10.3	96.98	10.0
云浮	Yunfu	74	46.01	1.3	33.33	0.2
按经济区域分	By Region					
珠三角	Pearl River Delta	33287	45038.08	4.1	33588.01	7.0
东翼	Eastern Region	941	633.53	6.6	505.01	8.9
西翼	Western Region	735	525.27	0.7	398.97	0.8
山区	Mountainous Region	729	526.01	9.7	389.31	10.0

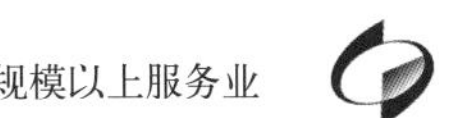

Main Indicators of Service Enterprises above Designated Size by City (2022)

(100 million yuan)

税金及附加 Tax and Extra Charges		销售费用 Selling Expenses		管理费用 Management Expenses	
总量 Total	2022年比2021年增长(%) Growth Rate in 2022 Over 2021(%)	总量 Total	2022年比2021年增长(%) Growth Rate in 2022 Over 2021(%)	总量 Total	2022年比2021年增长(%) Growth Rate in 2022 Over 2021(%)
94.80	-0.9	843.40	-3.2	1665.91	0.5
105.26	-8.3	1301.37	2.7	2131.80	-2.3
24.09	36.0	55.08	1.3	188.10	1.7
1.86	-17.8	20.47	7.6	33.41	-0.1
12.95	2.9	63.82	-1.5	171.24	6.9
0.46	-8.6	4.21	6.3	11.32	6.7
0.35	-6.1	2.93	-9.3	22.42	14.3
0.33	-11.1	3.05	-11.2	8.20	5.6
5.87	10.2	19.76	-0.7	69.87	-3.7
0.39	4.2	3.16	0.1	12.03	14.5
14.54	2.2	92.99	9.1	210.91	9.4
4.95	5.2	24.59	4.3	56.88	-1.1
2.41	3.3	9.17	-7.3	25.62	0.2
0.35	-3.3	3.88	-3.1	8.53	-1.8
1.66	-5.5	10.11	-2.5	30.46	-1.9
0.53	-20.8	7.23	-9.7	13.85	1.9
0.84	7.3	4.92	-11.8	12.24	7.6
1.19	8.7	5.92	-1.6	19.64	
0.22	-2.3	3.06	-7.6	3.41	-3.4
0.43	2.3	4.90	-12.3	9.38	6.5
0.27	-9.4	2.27	4.3	5.17	-1.0
265.70	-0.9	2415.09	0.6	4532.58	-0.3
2.89	-11.6	31.59	1.6	58.22	3.4
2.54	-8.8	21.22	-5.2	52.83	-0.9
2.60	-1.5	18.38	-2.3	66.74	6.2

14-7 续表

单位：亿元

市别	City	财务费用 Financial Expenses 总量 Total	财务费用 Financial Expenses 2022年比2021年增长(%) Growth Rate in 2022 Over 2021(%)	利润总额 Total Profits 总量 Total	利润总额 Total Profits 2022年比2021年增长(%) Growth Rate in 2022 Over 2021(%)
广　州	Guangzhou	471.95	21.2	1399.07	-16.6
深　圳	Shenzhen	345.87	-3.6	2342.76	-14.6
珠　海	Zhuhai	46.34	16.7	206.60	14.4
汕　头	Shantou	10.28	-77.4	4.41	115.5
佛　山	Foshan	48.31	6.5	96.67	-12.2
韶　关	Shaoguan	4.62	57.0	-0.16	-102.5
河　源	Heyuan	1.41	-20.4	3.94	71.7
梅　州	Meizhou	6.97	0.6	-3.80	-21.1
惠　州	Huizhou	46.21	-5.3	168.75	168.7
汕　尾	Shanwei	2.00	-11.1	0.55	-65.6
东　莞	Dongguan	61.72	1.9	422.38	34.2
中　山	Zhongshan	12.72	3.4	41.54	-34.7
江　门	Jiangmen	12.40	15.6	23.99	-0.9
阳　江	Yangjiang	0.92	-3.7	6.35	4.8
湛　江	Zhanjiang	8.55	0.1	29.28	1.2
茂　名	Maoming	2.66	12.8	12.72	-8.6
肇　庆	Zhaoqing	2.66	2.5	11.03	-3.9
清　远	Qingyuan	18.09	105.8	16.92	42.3
潮　州	Chaozhou	0.50	-7.6	3.98	45.0
揭　阳	Jieyang	0.71	46.6	11.37	26.3
云　浮	Yunfu	0.81	6.3	4.52	217.3
按经济区域分	By Region				
珠三角	Pearl River Delta	1048.16	8.3	4712.78	-9.2
东　翼	Eastern Region	13.49	-72.3	20.31	-234.3
西　翼	Western Region	12.13	2.3	48.35	-1.2
山　区	Mountainous Region	31.90	50.5	21.41	57.3

14-7 continued

(100 million yuan)

所得税费用 Income Taxes Payable		应付职工薪酬 Total Wages Payable		应交增值税 Value-added Tax Payable		期末用工人数(万人) Total number of employed persons at the year-end (10000 persons)
总量 Total	2022年比2021年增长(%) Growth Rate in 2022 Over 2021(%)	总量 Total	2022年比2021年增长(%) Growth Rate in 2022 Over 2021(%)	总量 Total	2022年比2021年增长(%) Growth Rate in 2022 Over 2021(%)	
230.68	0.3	3809.37	6.0	497.99	34.7	242.07
267.56	0.1	4257.97	9.0	460.59	7.0	241.94
34.72	6.9	361.07	6.3	55.69	46.8	24.73
5.15	12.6	74.07	6.5	6.52	9.4	6.57
23.31	4.3	318.76	9.2	33.73	-0.2	28.40
0.44	-48.2	21.75	7.0	8.07	224.9	2.55
1.29	44.0	14.83	8.0	1.23	-75.5	1.58
1.66	12.0	17.90	-0.2	1.99	4.5	1.62
12.83	3.5	135.48	7.5	14.92	2.9	14.79
1.02	-2.8	28.69	16.9	1.77	20.4	2.66
36.34	-7.6	380.77	17.4	43.90	18.0	35.11
7.63	-22.6	122.89	13.9	9.81	-12.1	12.39
5.21	0.4	51.40	11.0	5.55	11.0	4.87
1.24	18.9	23.47	6.9	2.40	-7.4	2.07
5.89	10.2	62.12	7.8	11.97	54.3	5.32
2.90	5.9	30.41	11.5	3.93	6.5	3.32
2.74	-1.8	22.88	9.2	2.56	-3.5	2.19
4.38	49.0	30.49	1.5	5.51	35.8	3.31
0.89	25.0	8.23	11.8	0.58	-15.0	0.90
2.15	5.1	19.61	6.6	1.07	-4.8	2.14
0.83	-3.3	10.76	1.4	1.08	8.0	0.99
621.00	-0.1	9460.58	8.0	1124.74	19.4	606.49
9.21	9.9	130.60	9.0	9.94	7.7	12.27
10.04	9.9	116.00	8.6	18.29	30.4	10.71
8.60	22.4	95.72	3.3	17.88	23.6	10.06

主要统计指标解释

期末用工人数 指报告期最后一日24时企业实际拥有的、参与本企业生产经营活动的人员数，无论是否从本企业领取劳动报酬均视为用工人数。该指标为时点指标，不包括最后一日当天及以前已经不再参与本企业生产经营活动的人员。包括企业的正式人员、劳务派遣人员和其他临时人员。

Explanatory Notes on Main Statistical Indicators

The number of Employed Persons at the Year-end refers to the number of personnel actually owned by the enterprise and participating in the production and business activities of the enterprise at 24 on the last day of the reporting period, whether or not they receive labor remuneration from the enterprise shall be regarded as the number of employees. This indicator is a time point indicator, excluding the personnel who have ceased to participate in the production and business activities of the enterprise on the last day and before. It includes the enterprise's regular personnel, labor dispatch personnel and other temporary personnel.

十五、运输和邮电

TRANSPORTATION, POSTAL AND TELECOMMUNICATION SERVICES

十五　运输和邮电

简要说明

一、本篇资料反映广东运输和邮电通信业发展的基本状况。

交通运输业资料主要包括：运输线路里程、运输设备拥有量、货物运输量和旅客运输量、港口设备和吞吐量、航站吞吐量等。

邮电通信业资料主要包括：邮电通信主要工具及设备情况，主要邮电业务完成情况，邮电通信发展水平等。

二、资料调查范围和统计单位

1. 铁路资料：包括国家铁路、地方铁路和合资铁路运营情况，不含军用铁路及由厂矿企事业单位自建的铁路专用线和专用铁道。

2. 公路、水路、港口资料：(1)公路和水路线路里程为年末通车和通航里程数。公路里程、桥梁、渡口统计从 2006 年起包括农村公路。(2)民用汽车拥有量，根据公安交通管理局所属车管部门登记注册的车辆资料整理；(3)民用运输船舶拥有量，不含渔船、水上施工作业船，根据水上航运管理部门登记注册的船舶资料整理；(4)公路、水路客货运输量资料，包括在广东公路水路运输管理部门注册登记或审批备案的、从事营业性公路、水路客、货运输的营业性运输工具(包括个体联户)所完成的运输量。此部分数据 2005 年之前由统计局收集整理，2005 年起改由省交通运输厅通过抽样调查方法负责收集整理。2009 年，交通运输部统一部署更换调查方法收集整理。2014-2015 年，按交通运输部要求，公路水路客货运输量采用经济调查结果进行推算。2016 年，公路水路客货运输量采用 2015 年专项调查结果进行推算。2020 年客货运输量中，公路货物运输量根据 2019 年道路货物运输量专项调查结果推算，海洋水路客货运输量统计方式改为企业一套表联网直报，管道运输纳统增加 6 家企业，增速按可比口径计算。2021 年，道路货物运输量统计方法调整为“规上企业全面调查+规下业户波动推算”。每次更换调查方法，均会导致公路水路客货运输量数据与以往不可比，使用时敬请注意。(5)港口设备及吞吐量，根据各地港务管理部门注册的港口企业和从事港口生产活动单位的资料整理。2019 年起，港口统计数据采集方式改为企业一套表联网直报，统计范围是辖区内各港口。

3. 管道运输资料：包括输原油、输成品油、输天然气、输其他气体的管线长度、输送能力及完成的运输量。数据主要来源于中国石油天然气集团公司和中国石油化工集团公司所属的本地各管道运输单位。

4. 民航运输资料：统计对象为在广东境内注册、从事民用航空运输飞行和通用飞行的航空运输企业和民用航空机场，不包括在境内运输飞行的国内其他航空公司及外国航空公司。统计范围为各航空公司从事国内运输、港澳台运输、国际运输的定期航班航线条数及里程、运输量及期末飞机在册架数、民用航空机场航班起降架次和客货吞吐量等。

5. 邮电通信资料：包括全省电信和邮政运营企业为社会公众提供的各类电信和邮政服务，不含专用网业务资料。资料主要来源于省通信管理局、邮政管理局以及邮政、电信、移动、联通等运营单位。

三、本篇资料由广东省统计局服务业统计处整理、编辑。资料主要来源于省内民航、铁路、公路、水运、港口、公安、邮政、通信等行业主管部门以及各有关单位。

15 Transportation,Postal and Telecommunication Services

Brief Introduction

Ⅰ. The data in this chapter cover mainly the basic conditions of the development of transport, postal and telecommunication services in Guangdong Province.

The data on transport cover mainly the route length of five means of transportation, the possession of transport equipment, the freight and passenger traffic the possession of port equipment and the volume of freight handled in ports, the passenger and freight throughput of airports, etc.

The data on postal and telecommunication services cover mainly major means and equipment of post and telecommunications, achievements of main businesses of postal and telecommunication services, and the level of development of postal and telecommunication services, etc.

Ⅱ. Coverage and Statistical Units

1. Data on railway transportation: including the operation and management of the national, local and joint-venture railways, but excluding the railways for military purpose, lines built by factories, mines, enterprises and institutions for exclusive use, and special railways.

2. Data on highways, waterways and ports: (1) The length of highways and waterways refer to the length open to traffic or navigation at the end of the year. The Statistical of length of highways,bridges,ferries from 2006 include rural highway. (2) The data on the possession of civil motor vehicles are compiled according to registration data of vehicles at the divisions of vehicle management under the traffic management departments of public security authorities. (3) The data on the possession of civil vessels exclusive of fishing boats and engineering ships over water are compiled according to registration data of vessels at the authorities of navigation and port management. (4) The data on the volume of transportation by highways and waterways, including all enterprises, institutions, and individuals (or individual partnerships) registered in Guangdong for passenger and freight transportation by highways and waterways, were collected and prepared by the Bureau of Statistics before 2005. Since 2005, the data were collected and prepared by the Department of Transport of Guangdong through sample survey. Since 2009, the data are collected and prepared in accordance with the new survey method stipulated by the Ministry of Transport. Since 2015, the data are prepared according to the third economic census of Guangdong Province.In the passenger and cargo traffic in 2020, cargo traffic by highway have been calculated according special survey of road cargo traffic in 2019,statistics of passenger and cargo traffic by waterway have been obtained by corporations reporting directly online,pipeline transportation enterprises increased by 6,the growth rate is calculated by comparable coverage.In 2021, the statistical method of road freight transport volume have adjusted to "comprehensive survey of Enterprises above Designated Size + fluctuating calculation of enterprises below Designated Size". Since the new survey method has new criteria for survey target and urban-rural division, the data are not comparable with those of the previous years. (5) The data on possession of port equipment and production capacity and handling capacity of ports are compiled according to registration data of port enterprises and production units at local port authorities. Starting in 2019, data related to ports have been compiled from direct online reporting by port enterprises, with the statistical scope being ports within each jurisdiction.

3. Data on pipeline transport: the data on pipeline transport cover the length, transport capacity and the volume transported of pipelines of petroleum (crude oil), petroleum products, natural gas and other gases. The data are mainly provided by enterprises engaged in the pipeline transport subordinate to the China National Petroleum Corporation and China Petrochemical Corporation.

4. Data on civil aviation transport: data on civil aviation transport include air transport enterprises and civil airports registered for civil aviation transport and general aviation, excluding other domestic aviation companies and foreign aviation companies engaged in air transport within Chinese territory. The statistics cover regular flights of domestic transport, transport between the mainland of China and Hong Kong, Macao and Taiwan, and international transport managed by various aviation companies, concerning the number of lines, length, transport volume, number of registered aircrafts at the end of the reference period, sorties at civil airports, and volumes of passenger and freight handled at civil airports.

5. Data on post and telecommunications: data in this category include telecommunications and postal services rendered to the public by telecommunications and postal enterprises of the whole province, but exclude services provided through dedicated networks. Statistics are mainly provided by Guangdong Communications Administration and corresponding enterprises, including China Post, China Telecom, China Mobile, China Unicom ,and China Netcom.

Ⅲ. The data in this chapter are prepared and compiled by the Division of Service Industry Statistics of Statistics Bureau of Guangdong Province. Raw data are mainly provided by authorities and related enterprises and institutions within the province of civil aviation, railways, highways, waterways, ports, public securities, and post and telecommunications.

15-1 运输邮电主要指标

Main Indicators on Transport, Postal and Telecommunication Services

指　标	Item	2000	2010	2021	2022	2022年比2021年增长% Growth Rate in 2022 over 2021 (%)
铁路营业里程 (公里)	Length of Railways in Operation (km)	1942	2297	5101	5158	1.1
公路通车里程 (公里)	Length of Highways (km)	102606	190144	222987	223081	0.0
内河通航里程 (公里)	Length of Navigable Inland Waterways (km)	13696	13596	12266	12266	0.0
民航航线里程 (万公里)	Length of Civil Aviation Routes (10000 km)	50.03	180.74	339.56	273.44	-19.5
管道输油(气)里程 (公里)	Length of Petroleum and Gas Pipelines (km)	1535.57	6033.62	9664.23	11769.84	21.8
港口码头泊位 (个)	Number of Berths in Coastal Ports (unit)	3191	3082	2295	2252	-1.9
#万吨级泊位	Berths at 10000 Ton Class	126	245	349	368	5.4
码头泊位长度 (米)	Length of Quay Line (m)	180238	252762	241392	244557	1.3
公路桥梁 (座)	Number of Highway Bridges (unit)	19668	42330	51302	62112	21.1
#永久式	Permanent	19656	42233	51243	62049	21.1
民用汽车 (万辆)	Number of Civil Motor Vehicles (10000 units)	172.91	783.50	2702.55	2898.36	7.2
机动船艘数 (艘)	Number of Motor Vessels (unit)	21733	8793	6646	6359	-4.3
吨位数 (万净载重吨)	Tonnage (10000 dead weight ton)	526.88	1140.71	2369.96	2305.98	-2.7
民用运输飞机 (架)	Number of Civil Aircrafts (unit)	106	441	901	909	0.9
移动电话交换机容量 (万户)	Capacity of Mobile Telephone Exchanges (10000 subscribers)	1825.40	14766.90	23803.81	24521.58	3.0
固定电话用户 (万户)	Subscribers of Local Fixed Telephones	1414.94	3169.14	2072.20	1944.08	-6.2
固定互联网宽带接入用户 (万户)	Subscribers of Fixed Internet Broadband (10000 subscribers)			4277.71	4628.72	8.2
移动互联网用户 (万户)	Subscribers of Mobile Internet (10000 subscribers)			15070.27	15097.28	0.2
移动电话用户 (万户)	Subscribers of Mobile Telephones (10000 subscribers)	1357.26	9710.09	16267.80	16650.76	2.4
客运量 (万人)	Passenger Traffic (10000 persons)	164791	467049	62126	47632	-23.3
旅客周转量 (亿人公里)	Passenger-kilometers (100 million passenger-km)	1218.59	3342.23	2352.19	1621.36	-31.1
货运量 (万吨)	Freight Traffic (10000 tons)	119216	205034	398420	364199	-8.6
货物周转量 (亿吨公里)	Freight Ton-kilometers (100 million ton-km)	3064.51	5933.88	28388.06	28438.62	0.2
港口货物吞吐量 (万吨)	Volume of Freight Handled in Ports (10000 tons)	31649	122258	209600	204802	-2.3
港口旅客吞吐量 (万人)	Volume of Passengers Handled in Ports (10000 persons)	1670.32	2483.21	1849.17	1464.19	-20.8
航站旅客吞吐量 (万人)	Volume of Passengers Handled at Airports (10000 persons)	2142.84	7188.64	9594.04	5824.95	-39.3
邮电业务总量 (亿元)	Business Volume of Postal and Telecommunication Services (100 million yuan)	757.22	4832.94	4954.59	5063.13	2.2
邮政 (亿元)	Postal Service (100 million yuan)	50.40	118.57	3021.10	3112.87	3.0
电信 (亿元)	Telecommunication Service (100 million yuan)	706.82	4714.37	1933.49	1950.26	18.6

注：1.邮电业务总量1988年及以前按1980年不变价格计算，1989—2000年按1990年不变价格计算，2001—2010年按2000年不变价格计算，2011—2016年按2010年不变价格计算，2017年起，电信业务总量按2015年不变价格计算，邮政业务总量仍按2010年不变价格计算。2021年起，按2020年不变价计算。2022年，电信业务总量按上年不变价计算。增速按可比价格计算。

2.2017年起，铁路客运量和货运量改为按发送量计算，客运量货运量数据与往年不可比。增长速度按可比口径计算。

3.从2019年起，港口统计数据采集方式改为企业一套表联网直报，统计范围是辖区内各港口，增长速度按可比口径计算。

Notes:a) The business volume of postal and telecommunication services in and before 1998 was calculated at 1980 constant prices, that from 1998 to 2000 was calculated at 1990 constant prices, that from 2001 to 2010 was calculated at 2000 constant prices and that from 2011 to 2016 was calculated at 2010 constant prices. Since 2017, the total amount of telecommunications was calculated at 2015 constant prices, while the total amount of postal business was calculated at 2010 constant prices. From 2021, that was calculated at 2020 constant prices. In 2022, the total amount of telecommunications was calculated at last year's constant prices.The growth rate was calculated at comparable prices.

b) Since 2017, passenger and cargo traffic by rail have been calculated according traffic sent, as such, data of cargo and passenger traffic by rail is incomparable with previous years. Growth rate is calculated with a comparable prices.

c) Since 2019, dockyard statistics have been obtained by corporations reporting directly online, the statistical scope of the data is organized by dockyards within each jurisdiction, growth rates are calculated with comparable data

15-2 全社会旅客运输量
Total Passenger Traffic

年份 Year	客运量(万人) Passenger Traffic (10000 persons)					旅客周转量（亿人公里） Passenger-kilometers (100 million passenger-km)				
	合计 Total	铁路 Railways	公路 Highways	水路 Waterways	民航 Civil Aviation	合计 Total	铁路 Railways	公路 Highways	水路 Waterways	民航 Civil Aviation
1985	49848	3357	41826	4427	238	270.23	50.41	178.27	20.46	21.09
1986	126890	3742	113561	9295	292	450.35	56.70	346.81	19.82	27.02
1987	158715	4129	144684	9557	345	796.86	66.98	678.04	21.20	30.64
1988	218915	4828	204278	9420	389	402.34	82.53	261.18	22.43	36.20
1989	66727	4882	58110	3377	358	447.62	84.38	309.25	20.50	33.49
1990	78046	4467	70681	2428	470	453.21	82.56	307.40	19.68	43.57
1991	83460	5004	75570	2317	569	526.66	102.11	348.85	20.89	54.81
1992	93678	6243	83128	3503	804	624.55	131.99	385.76	25.75	81.05
1993	95468	6835	84708	3078	847	696.92	161.04	422.88	25.60	87.40
1994	125036	6920	111447	5636	1033	929.48	164.11	619.52	33.21	112.64
1995	130998	6283	118406	5146	1163	936.29	163.11	613.07	31.13	128.98
1996	128831	5593	117815	4232	1191	938.65	153.86	626.60	20.65	137.54
1997	123649	6201	113259	3032	1157	957.20	177.61	616.48	17.21	145.90
1998	132462	6743	121795	2729	1195	994.84	194.16	630.65	13.87	156.16
1999	148636	7553	137324	2605	1154	1082.14	212.13	700.74	13.62	155.65
2000	164791	12165	148945	2363	1318	1218.59	241.51	780.74	11.65	184.69
2001	178676	12783	161967	2382	1544	1342.12	252.37	858.86	11.40	219.49
2002	188657	13310	171191	2347	1809	1490.34	273.19	945.16	11.31	260.68
2003	191202	12935	174288	2208	1771	1505.83	267.14	983.67	11.41	243.61
2004	202414	15142	183012	1827	2433	1738.21	308.38	1076.06	10.17	343.60
2005	212104	16106	189881	2062	4055	2122.14	327.74	1190.73	9.54	594.13
2005(调整) (adjusted)	161357	16106	139158	2038	4055	2043.23	327.74	1111.57	9.79	594.13
2006	197314	15109	175567	2073	4565	2245.37	347.60	1212.76	12.14	672.87
2007	211215	16762	186835	2071	5548	2626.71	387.61	1410.72	10.98	817.40
2007(调整) (adjusted)	206504	12050	186835	2071	5548	2626.71	387.61	1410.72	10.98	817.40
2008	238375	13739	216902	1902	5832	2844.79	420.12	1566.73	9.80	848.14
2008(调整) (adjusted)	484161	13739	462997	1593	5832	2551.92	420.12	1276.12	7.54	848.14
2009	428705	13394	406704	1873	6734	2853.30	407.72	1470.06	7.06	968.46
2010	467049	14956	442224	2241	7628	3342.23	456.46	1736.34	8.36	1141.07
2011	522095	17902	493618	2594	7981	3851.84	505.16	2082.68	9.63	1254.37
2012	586299	18528	556510	2725	8535	4372.06	514.88	2470.11	10.01	1377.06
2013	636816	20459	604934	2426	8997	4852.41	565.91	2776.08	10.23	1500.19
2013(调整) (adjusted)	175109	20459	143406	2247	8997	3538.10	565.91	1462.82	9.18	1500.19
2014	193363	23744	157234	2613	9771	3967.28	670.78	1629.79	10.67	1656.05
2015	207345	26536	168028	2728	10054	4335.79	747.05	1769.61	10.50	1808.63
2015(调整) (adjusted)	137368	26536	98050	2728	10054	3601.12	747.05	1034.94	10.50	1808.63
2016	144262	28954	102094	2648	10566	3842.58	793.44	1079.80	10.34	1959.00
2017	148549	28476	105919	2733	11420	4140.29	872.08	1129.53	10.85	2127.82
2018	154682	33745	105249	2775	12913	4501.97	953.75	1120.71	11.13	2416.38
2019	155770	38213	101012	2614	13931	4764.98	1023.05	1092.97	9.71	2639.26
2019(调整) (adjusted)	155892	38213	101012	2736	13931	4765.31	1023.05	1092.97	10.04	2639.26
2020	87777	22609	54946	1345	8878	2617.23	630.33	556.31	4.27	1426.32
2021	62126	23977	27567	1580	9002	2352.19	670.39	265.96	4.51	1411.33
2022	47632	17526	23730	884	5492	1621.36	526.81	193.83	2.31	898.40

15-3 旅客运输量指数

Indices of Passenger Traffic

上年=100 (preceding year=100)

年份 Year	客运量 Passenger Traffic					旅客周转量 Passenger-kilometers				
	合计 Total	铁路 Railways	公路 Highways	水路 Waterways	民航 Civil Aviation	合计 Total	铁路 Railways	公路 Highways	水路 Waterways	民航 Civil Aviation
1978	107.9	105.6	109.0	104.8	144.8	110.4	112.8	109.8	102.3	151.9
1979	114.9	115.5	116.0	109.2	144.2	123.5	129.1	119.8	117.1	165.2
1980	117.3	101.0	125.2	97.7	118.6	121.2	120.4	128.0	109.3	97.4
1981	107.4	100.0	110.0	99.1	125.1	110.9	109.0	112.2	106.0	121.0
1982	119.7	95.7	126.6	99.9	122.4	111.8	102.6	117.1	102.4	125.4
1983	107.2	107.2	108.6	96.4	89.6	111.9	117.8	114.0	99.7	94.6
1984	119.7	109.2	124.4	87.3	142.9	125.6	115.3	130.4	98.3	183.2
1985	109.2	112.6	109.1	103.6	131.6	118.1	121.3	116.1	101.0	148.7
1986	90.0	102.8	88.2	91.7	125.2	95.0	106.7	86.0	91.4	130.8
1987	125.1	110.3	127.4	102.8	118.2	176.9	118.1	195.5	107.0	113.4
1988	137.9	116.9	141.2	98.6	112.8	50.5	123.2	38.5	105.8	118.1
1989	30.5	101.1	28.4	35.8	92.0	111.3	102.2	118.4	91.4	92.5
1990	117.0	91.5	121.6	71.9	131.3	101.2	97.8	99.4	96.0	130.1
1991	106.9	112.0	106.9	95.4	121.1	116.2	123.7	113.5	106.1	125.8
1992	112.2	124.8	110.0	151.2	141.3	118.6	129.3	110.6	123.3	147.9
1993	101.9	109.5	101.9	87.9	105.3	111.6	122.0	109.6	99.4	107.8
1994	131.0	101.2	131.6	183.1	122.0	133.4	101.9	146.5	129.7	128.9
1995	104.8	90.8	106.2	91.3	112.6	100.7	99.4	99.0	93.7	114.5
1996	98.3	89.0	99.5	82.2	102.4	100.3	94.3	102.2	66.3	106.6
1997	96.0	110.9	96.1	71.6	97.1	102.0	115.4	98.4	83.3	106.1
1998	107.1	108.7	107.5	90.0	103.3	103.9	109.3	102.3	80.6	107.0
1999	112.2	112.0	112.8	95.5	96.6	108.8	109.3	111.1	98.2	99.7
2000	108.4	111.9	108.5	90.7	114.2	112.6	113.8	111.4	85.5	118.7
2001	108.4	105.1	108.7	100.8	117.1	110.1	104.5	110.0	97.9	118.8
2002	105.6	104.1	105.7	98.5	117.2	111.0	108.2	110.0	99.2	118.8
2003	101.3	97.2	101.8	94.1	97.9	101.0	97.8	104.1	100.9	93.5
2004	105.9	117.1	105.0	82.7	137.4	115.4	115.4	109.4	89.1	141.0
2005	104.8	106.4	103.8	112.9	166.7	122.1	106.3	110.7	93.8	172.9
2006	122.3	93.8	126.2	101.7	112.6	109.9	106.1	109.1	124.0	113.3
2007	107.0	110.9	106.4	99.9	121.5	117.0	111.5	116.3	90.4	121.5
2008	115.4	114.0	116.1	91.8	105.1	108.3	108.4	111.1	89.3	103.8
2009	88.5	97.5	87.8	117.6	115.4	111.8	97.0	115.2	93.6	114.2
2010	108.9	111.7	108.7	119.6	113.3	117.1	112.0	118.1	118.4	117.8
2011	111.8	119.7	111.6	115.8	104.6	115.2	110.7	119.9	115.2	109.9
2012	112.3	103.5	112.7	105.1	106.9	113.5	101.9	118.6	103.9	109.8
2013	108.6	110.4	108.7	89.0	105.4	111.0	109.9	112.4	102.2	108.9
2014	110.4	116.1	109.6	116.3	108.6	112.1	118.5	111.4	116.2	110.4
2015	107.2	111.8	106.9	104.4	102.9	109.3	111.4	108.6	98.4	109.2
2016	105.0	109.1	104.1	97.1	105.1	106.7	106.2	104.3	98.5	108.3
2017	105.6	112.1	103.7	103.2	108.1	107.6	109.4	104.6	104.9	108.6
2018	103.9	118.5	99.4	101.5	110.2	107.5	109.4	99.2	102.6	111.1
2019	100.7	113.2	96.0	94.2	107.9	105.8	107.3	97.5	87.2	109.2
2020	56.3	59.2	54.4	49.1	63.7	54.9	61.6	50.9	42.6	54.0
2021	70.8	106.1	50.2	117.5	101.4	89.9	106.4	47.8	105.5	98.9
2022	76.7	73.1	86.1	56.0	61.0	68.9	78.6	72.9	51.3	63.7

15-4 各市客运量

Passenger Traffic by City

单位：万人 (10000 persons)

市别	City	2005	2010	2015	2018	2019	2020	2021	2022
全　省	**Provincial Total**	**161357**	**467049**	**207345**	**154682**	**155770**	**87777**	**62126**	**47632**
广　州	Guangzhou	22583	47872	85170	25780	25658	18063	6731	6772
深　圳	Shenzhen	9500	151404	7040	6654	6907	5266	4636	4523
珠　海	Zhuhai	4874	19078	4017	3191	3121	1406	1003	695
汕　头	Shantou	1991	2539	1642	1635	1676	1133	305	263
佛　山	Foshan	11472	25166	5387	5057	4359	1448	2000	1780
韶　关	Shaoguan	2280	10200	5515	5558	5638	2934	1173	892
河　源	Heyuan	1969	3294	3257	3654	2980	783	992	855
梅　州	Meizhou	3550	4399	2859	3027	2598	863	340	272
惠　州	Huizhou	5049	12763	6799	6616	4686	926	889	563
汕　尾	Shanwei	3800	7250	1237	1348	1221	514	537	580
东　莞	Dongguan	30951	77446	5071	3383	3276	831	899	704
中　山	Zhongshan	9200	13258	1822	1401	1488	523	624	441
江　门	Jiangmen	8249	18096	10272	9417	8935	5127	1360	936
阳　江	Yangjiang	1585	4111	1586	1582	1594	532	266	165
湛　江	Zhanjiang	6413	12745	9026	9187	9439	3729	2674	1851
茂　名	Maoming	5079	6830	6367	6658	6753	5783	1419	960
肇　庆	Zhaoqing	4436	6388	3119	2893	2722	1245	813	555
清　远	Qingyuan	1959	9874	3088	3060	3251	2390	1182	829
潮　州	Chaozhou	733	2056	2255	2334	1953	797	156	146
揭　阳	Jieyang	3014	4789	2041	2363	2398	1381	658	507
云　浮	Yunfu	2509	4907	3188	3225	2972	619	489	326
不分地区	Unclassified	20161	22584	36589	46658	52144	31487	32979	23018
按经济区域分	By Region								
珠三角	Pearl River Delta	126475	394055	165285	111050	113296	66321	51934	39987
东　翼	Eastern Region	9538	16634	7175	7680	7248	3825	1656	1495
西　翼	Western Region	13077	23686	16979	17427	17787	10044	4359	2976
山　区	Mountainous Region	12267	32674	17907	18525	17440	7588	4177	3175

注：分市数据仅含公路和水路运输，铁路和民航运输在“不分地区”反映。下表同。

Note: Data by city only include the figures of highway and waterway transportation, whereas data of railway and civil aviation transportation are reflected in the category “Unclassified by Region”. The same applies to the following table.

15-5 各市旅客周转量

Passenger-kilometers by City

单位：亿人公里 (100 million passenger-km)

市 别	City	2005	2010	2015	2018	2019	2020	2021	2022
全 省	**Provincial Total**	**2043.23**	**3342.23**	**4335.79**	**4501.97**	**4764.98**	**2617.23**	**2352.19**	**1621.36**
广 州	Guangzhou	193.24	461.34	861.08	265.45	263.18	180.69	66.86	56.97
深 圳	Shenzhen	71.42	242.13	144.31	129.04	134.93	60.08	31.85	22.98
珠 海	Zhuhai	41.69	68.90	69.18	48.59	47.94	22.60	8.60	5.35
汕 头	Shantou	21.08	51.67	22.45	22.71	23.42	17.02	6.80	5.06
佛 山	Foshan	50.94	82.76	59.31	65.18	57.88	16.53	18.76	15.08
韶 关	Shaoguan	14.17	40.41	28.55	28.75	29.17	15.38	5.91	3.86
河 源	Heyuan	36.97	38.18	38.44	43.16	37.55	11.10	10.93	9.06
梅 州	Meizhou	41.73	51.79	39.52	41.74	35.70	12.17	5.53	3.98
惠 州	Huizhou	35.97	49.46	57.43	55.94	40.80	10.01	8.95	4.54
汕 尾	Shanwei	26.90	52.98	14.05	15.71	15.66	6.79	6.03	6.19
东 莞	Dongguan	158.53	129.07	81.55	45.63	42.29	11.46	9.49	6.44
中 山	Zhongshan	48.84	88.99	21.77	23.04	23.36	8.75	5.55	3.62
江 门	Jiangmen	60.30	58.99	64.71	61.34	58.54	33.12	9.88	6.37
阳 江	Yangjiang	26.29	21.80	11.01	10.74	10.96	4.13	3.37	2.12
湛 江	Zhanjiang	62.10	82.45	95.49	95.10	105.51	37.75	20.76	11.29
茂 名	Maoming	64.83	61.47	59.23	62.26	63.27	56.27	21.20	13.29
肇 庆	Zhaoqing	25.40	33.22	14.71	13.41	12.73	6.36	7.41	4.60
清 远	Qingyuan	35.45	38.68	24.08	24.59	26.23	20.26	10.95	6.54
潮 州	Chaozhou	19.37	23.93	27.53	29.93	24.93	11.13	3.21	2.61
揭 阳	Jieyang	67.53	37.28	22.22	25.45	25.84	12.33	4.03	3.47
云 浮	Yunfu	18.62	29.21	23.49	24.08	22.77	6.63	4.39	2.71
不分地区	Unclassified	921.87	1597.53	2555.68	3370.13	3662.31	2056.65	2081.72	1425.21
按经济区域分	By Region								
珠 三 角	Pearl River Delta	1608.20	2812.37	3929.73	4077.75	4343.96	2406.25	2249.09	1551.16
东 翼	Eastern Region	134.87	165.86	86.25	93.80	89.85	47.28	20.06	17.33
西 翼	Western Region	153.23	165.72	165.73	168.10	179.74	98.15	45.33	26.71
山 区	Mountainous Region	146.93	198.27	154.08	162.32	151.43	65.55	37.71	26.15

15-6 全社会货物运输量

Total Freight Traffic

年份 Year	货运量(万吨) Freight Traffic (10000 tons)						货物周转量(亿吨公里) Freight Ton-kilometers (100 million ton-km)					
	合计 Total	铁路 Railways	公路 Highways	水路 Waterways	民航 Civil Aviation	管道 Pipelines	合计 Total	铁路 Railways	公路 Highways	水路 Waterways	民航 Civil Aviation	管道 Pipelines
1985	58726	3000	42813	12045	4	864	1767.86	102.29	156.45	1503.47	0.38	5.27
1986	65078	4269	49030	10831	4	944	1845.33	130.02	127.28	1581.60	0.45	5.98
1987	74571	4493	57393	11664	5	1016	1982.59	142.56	179.41	1653.81	0.54	6.27
1988	79811	4504	57717	16583	6	1001	2209.11	151.55	216.22	1834.41	0.67	6.26
1989	85054	4888	63254	15820	6	1086	2419.57	168.39	301.16	1942.79	0.71	6.52
1990	85809	4803	63709	16198	8	1091	2598.88	179.54	346.27	2065.69	0.90	6.48
1991	94136	5347	69784	17718	10	1277	3181.83	206.18	386.49	2580.79	1.06	7.31
1992	113119	6089	84181	21346	12	1491	3560.59	239.34	583.36	2727.97	1.41	8.51
1993	125273	6595	87567	29660	14	1437	3797.09	261.91	428.17	3097.19	1.70	8.12
1994	119901	6971	81361	30165	20	1384	4326.09	280.31	443.54	3592.35	2.39	7.50
1995	111063	7634	68884	32952	21	1572	4642.91	290.78	352.45	3990.19	2.75	6.74
1996	95598	8138	60131	25699	24	1606	3761.09	294.12	327.81	3129.27	3.27	6.62
1997	99763	8430	62728	26873	25	1707	3837.78	294.45	341.08	3185.26	3.99	13.00
1998	101933	8288	65682	25669	28	2266	3453.92	290.65	371.08	2750.19	4.90	37.10
1999	106334	8150	70626	24857	31	2670	2980.69	282.68	426.70	2223.75	5.45	42.11
2000	119216	15172	75365	25696	31	2952	3064.51	295.97	472.49	2247.86	6.45	41.74
2001	131621	15435	86555	26434	35	3162	3221.47	296.79	522.89	2350.73	7.54	43.52
2002	137032	14790	92736	26263	42	3201	3229.39	277.87	576.35	2323.27	9.94	41.96
2003	143964	15375	97806	27412	42	3329	3666.83	285.02	614.01	2719.83	11.76	36.21
2004	156094	19495	102843	29783	49	3924	4148.54	341.26	657.49	3091.39	13.22	45.18
2005	158470	18647	105581	30179	73	3989	4359.97	319.68	781.41	3195.85	17.45	45.58
2005(调整) (adjusted)	133992	18647	84861	26422	73	3989	3917.43	319.68	646.55	2888.17	17.45	45.58
2006	145911	16170	97461	27503	79	4698	4162.77	333.12	742.67	2964.89	18.70	103.39
2007	165426	16480	112611	30893	87	5355	4430.93	337.31	906.84	3043.53	20.14	123.11
2007(调整) (adjusted)	160455	11285	112611	30893	87	5578	4489.69	337.31	906.84	3043.53	20.14	181.87
2008	176279	11545	126068	32318	85	6263	4520.12	344.96	1064.55	2878.85	18.38	213.38
2008(调整) (adjusted)	153256	11545	101428	33935	85	6263	4591.22	344.96	1225.30	2853.92	18.38	148.66
2009	179722	11254	125433	36623	90	6322	4942.83	309.55	1518.43	2937.94	18.83	158.08
2010	205034	12170	142389	43092	116	7267	5933.88	329.49	1753.40	3642.22	32.98	175.79
2011	234978	12034	166567	48856	118	7403	7113.29	322.25	2150.04	4427.64	37.00	176.36
2012	266359	12002	189034	57737	128	7458	9780.56	306.04	2434.95	6820.29	42.40	176.89
2013	305833	12042	217630	68378	131	7652	12495.93	301.55	2875.68	9104.57	44.20	169.94
2013(调整) (adjusted)	328138	12042	239462	68851	131	7652	12212.56	301.55	2668.03	9028.84	44.20	169.94
2014	353732	11143	257135	77220	144	8090	15020.92	274.81	3113.84	11407.80	51.05	173.42
2015	376434	10072	279983	78093	149	8137	15130.59	253.90	3454.99	11190.91	56.47	174.33
2015(调整) (adjusted)	349832	10072	255993	75481	149	8137	14667.43	253.90	3108.81	11073.92	56.47	174.33
2016	377645	10135	272826	85633	160	8891	22032.27	254.41	3381.92	18160.35	61.85	173.74
2017	400601	7254	288904	94871	166	9407	28192.23	261.97	3636.89	24011.92	68.73	212.71
2018	424996	7617	304743	102352	226	10058	28644.77	267.99	3890.32	24177.41	80.53	228.53
2019	446018	8185	319279	108371	238	9944	29230.88	297.35	4113.62	24508.26	82.98	228.67
2019(调整) (adjusted)	374823	8185	239744	113159	238	13496	27635.28	297.35	2563.96	24432.75	82.98	258.24
2020	356221	7845	231171	103759	238	13209	27575.18	278.44	2524.20	24404.83	85.93	281.78
2021	398420	9816	267489	107206	240	13564	28388.06	362.51	2980.46	24688.52	92.35	270.20
2022	364199	9374	242474	97628	221	14503	28438.62	362.74	2710.33	25005.04	89.09	271.42

15-7 货物运输量指数

Indices of Freight Traffic

上年=100 (preceding year=100)

年份 Year	货运量 Freight Traffic						货物周转量 Freight Ton-kilometers					
	合计 Total	铁路 Railways	公路 Highways	水路 Waterways	民航 Civil Aviation	管道 Pipelines	合计 Total	铁路 Railways	公路 Highways	水路 Waterways	民航 Civil Aviation	管道 Pipelines
1978	96.3	109.2	74.9	104.5	126.6		110.9	110.9	93.0	111.1	140.0	
1979	92.1	103.5	88.9	87.2	100.0	197.2	138.4	103.5	96.6	141.9	142.9	192.9
1980	101.4	93.8	85.3	111.3	151.0	151.4	98.2	99.1	90.7	98.1	100.0	596.3
1981	92.2	84.8	87.0	93.1	102.6	165.3	84.3	92.7	93.8	83.5	100.0	280.7
1982	104.6	107.8	98.1	105.7	125.8	105.7	104.9	105.4	105.3	104.9	130.0	103.8
1983	100.4	104.9	92.4	100.5	118.5	108.7	110.1	108.8	87.6	110.3	123.1	109.8
1984	100.0	108.6	92.6	98.4	133.8	105.3	98.8	112.2	84.7	97.9	162.5	101.9
1985	177.1	105.5	225.5	115.1	133.3	101.2	109.2	111.8	206.5	104.0	146.2	100.4
1986	110.8	142.3	114.5	89.9	100.0	109.3	104.4	127.1	81.4	105.2	118.4	113.5
1987	114.6	105.2	117.1	107.7	125.0	107.6	107.4	109.6	141.0	104.6	120.0	104.8
1988	107.0	100.2	100.6	142.2	120.0	98.5	111.4	106.3	120.5	110.9	124.1	99.8
1989	106.6	108.5	109.6	95.4	100.0	108.5	109.5	111.1	139.3	105.9	106.0	104.2
1990	100.9	98.3	100.7	102.4	133.3	100.5	107.4	106.6	115.0	106.3	126.8	99.4
1991	109.7	111.3	109.5	109.4	125.0	117.0	122.4	114.8	111.6	124.9	117.8	112.8
1992	120.2	113.9	120.6	120.5	120.0	116.8	111.9	116.1	150.9	105.7	133.0	116.4
1993	110.7	108.3	104.0	138.9	116.7	96.4	106.6	109.4	73.4	113.5	120.6	95.4
1994	95.7	105.7	92.9	101.7	142.9	96.3	113.9	107.0	103.6	116.0	140.6	92.4
1995	92.6	109.5	84.7	109.2	105.0	113.6	107.3	103.7	79.5	111.1	115.1	89.9
1996	86.1	106.6	87.3	78.0	114.3	102.2	81.0	101.1	93.0	78.4	118.9	98.2
1997	104.4	103.6	104.3	104.6	104.2	106.3	102.0	100.1	104.0	101.8	122.0	196.4
1998	102.2	98.3	104.7	95.5	112.0	132.7	90.0	98.7	108.8	86.3	122.8	285.4
1999	104.3	98.3	107.5	96.8	110.7	117.8	86.3	97.3	115.0	80.9	111.2	113.5
2000	106.0	106.0	106.7	103.4	100.0	110.6	102.8	104.7	110.7	101.1	118.3	99.1
2001	110.4	101.7	114.8	102.9	112.9	107.1	105.1	100.3	110.7	104.6	116.9	104.3
2002	104.1	95.8	107.1	99.4	120.0	101.2	100.2	93.6	110.2	98.8	131.8	96.4
2003	105.1	104.0	105.5	104.4	100.0	104.0	113.5	102.6	106.5	117.1	118.3	86.3
2004	108.4	126.8	105.1	108.6	116.7	117.9	113.1	119.7	107.1	113.7	112.4	124.8
2005	101.5	95.7	102.7	101.3	149.0	101.7	105.1	93.7	118.8	103.4	132.0	100.9
2006	108.9	86.7	114.8	104.1	108.1	117.8	106.3	104.2	114.9	102.7	107.2	226.8
2007	113.4	101.9	115.5	112.3	110.5	114.0	106.4	101.3	122.1	102.7	107.7	119.1
2008	109.9	102.3	111.9	104.6	97.1	112.3	100.7	102.3	117.4	94.6	91.3	117.3
2009	117.3	97.5	123.7	107.9	106.8	101.0	107.7	89.7	123.9	102.9	102.4	106.3
2010	114.1	108.1	113.5	117.7	128.1	114.9	120.1	106.4	115.5	124.0	175.1	111.2
2011	114.6	98.9	117.0	113.4	102.4	101.9	119.9	97.8	122.6	121.6	112.2	100.3
2012	111.5	99.7	113.5	109.1	107.9	100.7	116.0	95.0	113.3	119.5	114.6	100.3
2013	114.8	100.3	115.1	118.4	102.7	102.6	127.8	98.5	118.1	133.5	104.2	96.1
2014	107.8	92.5	107.4	112.2	110.0	105.7	123.0	91.1	116.7	126.3	115.5	102.0
2015	106.4	90.4	108.9	101.1	102.9	100.6	100.7	92.4	111.0	98.1	110.6	100.5
2016	108.0	100.6	106.6	113.4	107.6	109.3	150.2	100.2	108.8	164.0	109.5	99.7
2017	106.9	101.3	105.9	110.8	103.7	105.8	128.0	104.3	107.5	132.2	111.1	122.4
2018	106.1	105.0	105.5	107.9	106.5	106.9	101.6	99.7	107.0	100.7	107.3	107.4
2019	104.9	107.5	104.8	105.9	105.6	98.9	102.0	111.0	105.7	101.4	103.0	100.1
2020	95.0	95.8	96.4	91.7	99.8	97.9	99.8	93.6	98.4	99.9	103.6	109.1
2021	111.8	126.4	115.7	103.3	100.9	102.7	102.9	128.0	118.1	101.2	107.5	95.9
2022	91.4	95.5	90.6	91.1	91.8	106.9	100.2	100.1	90.9	101.3	96.5	100.5

15-8 各市货运量

Freight Traffic by City

单位：万吨 (10000 tons)

市　别	City	2005	2010	2015	2018	2019	2020	2021	2022
全　省	**Provincial Total**	**133992**	**205034**	**376434**	**424996**	**446018**	**356221**	**398420**	**364199**
广　州	Guangzhou	28026	51335	94303	124641	132922	89191	93968	85820
深　圳	Shenzhen	7837	25706	32331	32586	33982	41150	43657	40617
珠　海	Zhuhai	2225	7038	11626	12541	12883	7575	7947	7089
汕　头	Shantou	1703	3087	6469	6928	7533	7704	8651	7297
佛　山	Foshan	17354	19153	29428	32165	33311	23779	27128	26179
韶　关	Shaoguan	3251	6364	19024	20878	22570	10298	9358	8628
河　源	Heyuan	986	2244	6509	6861	6879	4372	6548	5769
梅　州	Meizhou	3751	4092	7820	8824	9070	9310	11211	10235
惠　州	Huizhou	4786	11104	23435	26080	27853	21387	24483	21844
汕　尾	Shanwei	1106	1232	2536	2879	3071	2260	3662	3221
东　莞	Dongguan	5127	9312	15923	17272	17653	17139	17449	15115
中　山	Zhongshan	5985	7820	17963	16640	11529	10666	10661	9668
江　门	Jiangmen	5626	7458	15407	15893	16901	17921	18568	17805
阳　江	Yangjiang	417	1752	11385	10231	10538	5499	7415	6623
湛　江	Zhanjiang	5016	6808	16528	19010	22177	18652	20726	17705
茂　名	Maoming	4388	4365	9895	11340	12486	10303	13236	12290
肇　庆	Zhaoqing	3689	2869	7303	7847	8509	8096	9705	8759
清　远	Qingyuan	3200	7155	15267	17318	19443	17594	25774	21697
潮　州	Chaozhou	1310	2339	4928	5976	6385	2795	2775	2541
揭　阳	Jieyang	2213	1945	3898	4448	4813	2422	2870	2876
云　浮	Yunfu	3286	2303	6099	6738	7141	6817	8903	8326
不分地区	Unclassified	22710	19553	18358	17901	18368	21291	23724	24097
按经济区域分	By Region								
珠 三 角	Pearl River Delta	103365	161348	266078	303566	313912	258195	277290	256992
东　翼	Eastern Region	6332	8603	17831	20230	21802	15181	17958	15934
西　翼	Western Region	9821	12925	37808	40582	45201	34454	41377	36618
山　区	Mountainous Region	14474	22158	54719	60618	65103	48391	61795	54655

注：分市数据仅含公路和水路运输，铁路、民航和管道运输在“不分地区”反映。下表同。

Note: Data by city only include the figures of highway and waterway transportation, whereas data of railway, civil aviation and pipeline transportation are reflected in the category “Unclassified by Region”. The same applies to the following table.

15-9 各市货物周转量

Freight Ton-kilometers by City

单位：亿吨公里 (100 million ton-km)

市 别	City	2005	2010	2015	2018	2019	2020	2021	2022
全 省	**Provincial Total**	**3917.43**	**5933.88**	**15130.59**	**28644.77**	**29230.88**	**27575.18**	**28388.06**	**28438.62**
广 州	Guangzhou	2431.16	2032.86	8225.53	21398.46	21737.17	21525.32	21760.26	22053.63
深 圳	Shenzhen	317.28	1627.56	2241.11	2156.25	2174.03	1987.07	2169.88	2212.30
珠 海	Zhuhai	84.89	168.12	167.01	206.48	237.64	442.37	459.28	335.21
汕 头	Shantou	38.41	101.79	170.80	162.25	175.31	78.41	83.43	78.30
佛 山	Foshan	182.11	152.08	266.40	323.76	336.53	238.96	295.92	306.27
韶 关	Shaoguan	26.97	118.91	359.42	391.58	430.09	187.06	161.56	149.26
河 源	Heyuan	8.48	34.02	87.46	94.65	97.83	36.39	56.01	52.71
梅 州	Meizhou	45.95	73.69	177.60	190.77	195.06	89.27	119.92	111.81
惠 州	Huizhou	40.29	152.97	476.75	481.45	505.40	375.63	409.37	410.35
汕 尾	Shanwei	8.60	13.44	29.30	34.26	36.06	20.58	31.23	27.24
东 莞	Dongguan	32.94	109.03	508.71	527.26	535.47	528.77	507.04	459.27
中 山	Zhongshan	43.03	64.81	167.46	138.98	98.83	74.55	82.26	76.01
江 门	Jiangmen	70.96	112.55	182.29	168.36	178.22	158.20	157.17	147.55
阳 江	Yangjiang	2.98	39.93	195.05	98.25	100.76	37.08	47.88	43.28
湛 江	Zhanjiang	57.47	177.54	469.13	591.61	595.97	398.17	461.70	445.82
茂 名	Maoming	23.78	92.42	211.71	267.16	283.52	227.90	279.39	256.84
肇 庆	Zhaoqing	24.87	38.56	76.11	81.21	84.95	67.78	80.94	81.10
清 远	Qingyuan	29.37	118.19	262.28	287.65	321.25	183.13	264.47	217.76
潮 州	Chaozhou	25.27	103.37	234.40	307.01	326.98	168.69	111.81	111.01
揭 阳	Jieyang	22.64	26.93	77.53	81.91	89.13	23.96	28.11	44.02
云 浮	Yunfu	17.26	36.83	59.85	78.42	81.69	79.77	101.38	95.63
不分地区	Unclassified	382.72	538.26	484.69	577.04	608.99	646.15	719.08	723.25
按经济区域分	By Region								
珠 三 角	Pearl River Delta	3610.25	4996.80	12796.07	26059.25	26497.23	26044.79	26641.18	26804.96
东 翼	Eastern Region	94.92	245.54	512.03	585.42	627.47	291.64	254.58	260.57
西 翼	Western Region	84.22	309.90	875.89	957.03	980.25	663.14	788.97	745.94
山 区	Mountainous Region	128.04	381.64	946.61	1043.07	1125.93	575.62	703.33	627.16

15-10 运输工具和线路拥有量

Number of Means of Transport and Length of Transport Routes

项　　目	Item	2000	2010	2015	2020	2021	2022
铁　路	**Railways**						
铁路机车　(台)	Number of Locomotives　(unit)	538	448	350	319	319	297
铁路营业里程　(公里)	Length of Railways in Operation　(km)	1942	2297	3859	4871	5101	5158
中央铁路	National Railways	694	629	629	629	633	633
地方铁路	Local Railways	1248	1668	3230	4302	4468	4525
公　路	**Highways**						
公路通车里程　(公里)	Length of Highways　(km)	102606	190144	216023	221873	222987	223081
民用汽车　(万辆)	Civil Motor Vehicles　(10000 units)	172.91	783.50	1472.33	2500.92	2702.55	2898.36
载客汽车　(万辆)	Passenger Vehicles　(10000 units)	85.34	629.30	1290.57	2231.96	2410.37	2602.63
(万客位)	Passenger Vehicle Seats　(10000 seats)	796.92	4148.85	7572.21	12502.03	13376.17	14301.67
私人轿车　(万辆)	Private Vehicles　(10000 units)	25.39	380.46	820.12	1359.83	1464.24	1576.00
载货汽车　(万辆)	Freight Vehicles　(10000 units)	84.38	147.53	174.90	259.49	281.77	285.08
(万吨位)	Tonnage of Freight Vehicles (10000 tonnages)	351.75	268.23	354.81	693.72	781.61	778.12
水　运	**Waterways**						
内河通航里程　(公里)	Length of Navigable Inland Waterways　(km)	13696	13596	12150	12252	12266	12266
机动船　(艘)	Number of Motor Vessels　(unit)	21733	8793	8716	6835	6646	6359
(万净载重吨)	Tonnage of Motor Vessels (1000 dead weight tonnage)	526.88	1140.71	2703.55	2251.25	2369.96	2305.98
(客位)	Number of Motor Vessel Seats　(seat)	149004	65960	80219	80815	80824	78925
(总功率万千瓦)	Total Power　(10000 kws)	307.42	420.54	688.33	587.97	619.56	609.66
民　航	**Civil Aviation**						
民用航空航线条数　(条)	Number of Civil Aviation Routes　(line)	329	815	963	1623	1629	1591
民用航空航线里程(万公里)	Length of Civil Aviation Routes(10000 kms)	50.03	180.74	237.29	369.21	339.56	273.44
民用运输飞机　(架)	Number of Civil Aircrafts　(unit)	106	441	625	886	901	909
管　道	**Pipelines**						
条　数　(条)	Number of Pipelines　(line)	45	105	116	156	154	156
输油(气)里程　(公里)	Length of Petroleum and Gas Pipelines　(km)	1535.57	6033.62	6500.90	10136.90	9664.23	11769.84

15-11 各市民用汽车拥有量（2022年）

Possession of Civil Vehicles by City (2022)

单位：辆 (unit)

市别	City	民用汽车总计 Total	载客汽车 Passenger Vehicles	#轿车 Sedan Cars	按车型分 By Vehicle Type 大型 Large	中型 Medium	小型 Small	微型 Minibuses
全省	**Provincial Total**	**28983604**	**26026292**	**16861574**	**146255**	**39503**	**25784087**	**56447**
广州	Guangzhou	3435035	2946483	1686190	31943	6720	2899892	7928
深圳	Shenzhen	3934683	3381247	1963981	29345	4765	3340064	7073
珠海	Zhuhai	894612	826165	545491	7869	1105	817175	16
汕头	Shantou	1039560	931770	625765	4354	1269	923322	2825
佛山	Foshan	3427854	3160769	2069202	11319	2605	3138926	7919
韶关	Shaoguan	540390	493985	327593	2066	1353	489354	1212
河源	Heyuan	546865	492516	346587	1909	1076	488511	1020
梅州	Meizhou	723609	640668	452465	3043	1188	634980	1457
惠州	Huizhou	1711003	1585474	1061938	6589	1393	1574691	2801
汕尾	Shanwei	377515	352961	240690	2217	602	349372	770
东莞	Dongguan	3908030	3651020	2311326	15633	2809	3628780	3798
中山	Zhongshan	1489604	1345263	897366	4891	863	1335605	3904
江门	Jiangmen	1120512	1008371	710180	3774	1087	1000661	2849
阳江	Yangjiang	566991	509187	380583	1226	391	506448	1122
湛江	Zhanjiang	928612	832723	593571	3464	1358	826600	1301
茂名	Maoming	993921	897030	657787	2941	2620	889118	2351
肇庆	Zhaoqing	733031	650868	436181	2675	1187	645867	1139
清远	Qingyuan	868560	773052	508898	3344	1615	766300	1793
潮州	Chaozhou	479332	422350	286256	967	384	418631	2368
揭阳	Jieyang	775370	693185	462621	3171	1041	687457	1516
云浮	Yunfu	453827	402806	289314	1273	996	399253	1284
不分地区	Unclassified	34688	28399	7589	2242	3076	23080	1
按经济区域分	By Region							
珠三角	Pearl River Delta	20689052	18584059	11689444	116280	25610	18404741	37428
东翼	Eastern Region	2671777	2400266	1615332	10709	3296	2378782	7479
西翼	Western Region	2489524	2238940	1631941	7631	4369	2222166	4774
山区	Mountainous Region	3133251	2803027	1924857	11635	6228	2778398	6766

15-11 续表 continued

单位：辆 (unit)

市 别	City	载货汽车 Freight Vehicles	按车型分 By Vehicle Type 重型 Heavy	中型 Medium	轻型 Light	微型 Mini Trucks	其他汽车 Others
全 省	**Provincial Total**	**2850830**	**553582**	**91236**	**2197316**	**8696**	**106482**
广 州	Guangzhou	468318	99021	18086	349854	1357	20234
深 圳	Shenzhen	534447	123805	10235	399506	901	18989
珠 海	Zhuhai	64998	13313	1374	50310	1	3449
汕 头	Shantou	105618	10120	1724	90802	2972	2172
佛 山	Foshan	258079	46061	10725	201167	126	9006
韶 关	Shaoguan	44405	8639	750	34977	39	2000
河 源	Heyuan	50614	10843	1612	38031	128	3735
梅 州	Meizhou	80374	14660	1471	63964	279	2567
惠 州	Huizhou	119252	27898	3353	87903	98	6277
汕 尾	Shanwei	23076	4557	1038	17433	48	1478
东 莞	Dongguan	248603	49034	12838	186590	141	8407
中 山	Zhongshan	141252	16807	4983	119411	51	3089
江 门	Jiangmen	108951	19747	3840	85283	81	3190
阳 江	Yangjiang	55563	12282	1967	41156	158	2241
湛 江	Zhanjiang	92467	15653	4210	72534	70	3422
茂 名	Maoming	93280	18318	2719	72155	88	3611
肇 庆	Zhaoqing	80177	16262	3454	60440	21	1986
清 远	Qingyuan	92194	24156	2646	65329	63	3314
潮 州	Chaozhou	54762	3216	957	49959	630	2220
揭 阳	Jieyang	80068	7393	1957	70418	300	2117
云 浮	Yunfu	49495	11779	1136	35436	1144	1526
不分地区	Unclassified	4837	18	161	4658		1452
按经济区域分	By Region						
珠 三 角	Pearl River Delta	2028914	411966	69049	1545122	2777	76079
东 翼	Eastern Region	263524	25286	5676	228612	3950	7987
西 翼	Western Region	241310	46253	8896	185845	316	9274
山 区	Mountainous Region	317082	70077	7615	237737	1653	13142

15-12 各市私人汽车拥有量（2022年）

Possession of Private Vehicles by City (2022)

单位：辆 (unit)

市别	City	汽车总计 Total	载客汽车 Passenger Vehicles	#轿车 Sedan Cars	载货汽车 Freight Vehicles	其它汽车 Others
全省	**Provincial Total**	**25461541**	**23950355**	**15659853**	**1476672**	**34514**
广州	Guangzhou	2741383	2547066	1365431	188646	5671
深圳	Shenzhen	3121731	3022285	1777592	96560	2886
珠海	Zhuhai	794407	754720	508749	38860	827
汕头	Shantou	977103	898932	611025	77395	776
佛山	Foshan	3083720	2935035	1947126	146307	2378
韶关	Shaoguan	498891	468290	315495	29820	781
河源	Heyuan	498702	460154	328568	36149	2399
梅州	Meizhou	661296	599314	429057	60681	1301
惠州	Huizhou	1510574	1449338	983643	59586	1650
汕尾	Shanwei	348951	331288	228933	16977	686
东莞	Dongguan	3446589	3318394	2129166	125995	2200
中山	Zhongshan	1359006	1270614	858847	87489	903
江门	Jiangmen	1022290	954336	685014	66980	974
阳江	Yangjiang	540342	495331	374193	43944	1067
湛江	Zhanjiang	882374	805287	581717	74999	2088
茂名	Maoming	938471	864622	640480	71481	2368
肇庆	Zhaoqing	666575	617247	420593	48500	828
清远	Qingyuan	767702	705777	471049	60514	1411
潮州	Chaozhou	457391	410260	280853	45882	1249
揭阳	Jieyang	731071	663297	446371	66428	1346
云浮	Yunfu	412972	378768	275951	33479	725
按经济区域分	By Region					
珠三角	Pearl River Delta	17746275	16869035	10676161	858923	18317
东翼	Eastern Region	2514516	2303777	1567182	206682	4057
西翼	Western Region	2361187	2165240	1596390	190424	5523
山区	Mountainous Region	2839563	2612303	1820120	220643	6617

15-13 各市公路基本情况（2022年）

Basic Conditions of Highways by City (2022)

单位：公里 (km)

市别	City	通车里程 Length of Highways	按等级分 By Class		按路面分 By Pavement			桥梁 Bridges	
			等级路 Expressways and Class I to IV Highways	等外路 Highways below Class IV	有铺装路面 Paved Highways	简易铺装路面 Simply-paved Highways	未铺装路面 Unpaved Highways	座 Number (unit)	米 Span (meter)
全省	**Provincial Total**	**223081**	**223013**	**67**	**222463**	**543**	**75**	**62112**	**6779767**
广州	Guangzhou	9075	9075		9074	0		4502	934928
深圳	Shenzhen	726	726		726			936	198630
珠海	Zhuhai	1505	1505		1505			516	173721
汕头	Shantou	4056	4054	2	4054		2	1578	244765
佛山	Foshan	5312	5312		5312			3554	763071
韶关	Shaoguan	17170	17170		17170			3293	354701
河源	Heyuan	17416	17402	14	17344	35	37	4695	343432
梅州	Meizhou	20841	20803	37	20567	273		4820	342293
惠州	Huizhou	13492	13490	1	13489	2	1	4310	395284
汕尾	Shanwei	5892	5892		5859	27	6	1628	106076
东莞	Dongguan	5266	5266		5266			1803	383348
中山	Zhongshan	2830	2830		2830			1397	278513
江门	Jiangmen	9877	9871	6	9877			3720	335158
阳江	Yangjiang	10830	10830		10766	62	2	3009	169110
湛江	Zhanjiang	22560	22560		22479	72	8	3078	189455
茂名	Maoming	19160	19160		19153	7		4925	260043
肇庆	Zhaoqing	14305	14305		14241	61	3	3636	338041
清远	Qingyuan	20662	20662		20651	1	10	4564	397653
潮州	Chaozhou	5538	5538		5535	0	3	1354	148857
揭阳	Jieyang	7634	7634		7632	0	2	2534	204813
云浮	Yunfu	8933	8927	7	8931	2		2260	217874
按经济区域分	By Region								
珠三角	Pearl River Delta	62387	62380	7	62320	63	5	24374	3800694
东翼	Eastern Region	23121	23118	2	23080	27	13	7094	704511
西翼	Western Region	52550	52550		52398	141	10	11012	618609
山区	Mountainous Region	85023	84965	58	84664	312	47	19632	1655953

15-14 公路通车里程和桥梁数

Length of Highways and Number of Bridges

项 目	Item	2000	2010	2015	2019	2020	2021	2022
通车里程 （公里）	**Length of Highways (km)**	**102606**	**190144**	**216023**	**220290**	**221873**	**222987**	**223081**
按等级分	By Class							
等级路	Expressways and Class Ⅰ to Ⅳ Highways	93695	170144	201456	214923	221651	222779	223013
高速公路	Expressways	1186	4839	7021	9495	10488	11042	11211
一 级	First Class	5391	10126	10936	11534	12021	12421	13337
二 级	Second Class	13397	19082	19213	19152	19636	19374	19122
三 级	Third Class	9156	16089	18662	19764	22403	23945	25299
四 级	Fourth Class	64565	120008	145624	154977	157103	155997	154045
等外公路	Highways below Class Ⅳ	8911	19999	14567	5368	222	208	67
按路面分	By Pavement							
有铺装路面	Paved Highways		123784	147976	186807	221024	222320	222463
简易铺装路面	Simply-paved Highways		5721	9418	4370	685	575	543
未铺装路面	Unpaved Highways		60638	58629	29113	164	92	75
桥 梁 （座）	**Number of Bridges (unit)**	**19668**	**42330**	**45589**	**49685**	**50036**	**51302**	**62112**
（米）	Span of Bridges (m)	819770	2340261	3205460	4397710	4693655	4924474	6779767
#永久式 （座）	Number of Permanent Bridges (unit)	19656	42233	45501	49584	49939	51243	62049
（米）	Span of Permanent Bridges (m)	819502	2337490	3202958	4394823	4691065	4923071	6778053
半永久式 （座）	Number of Semi-permanent Bridges (unit)	12	52	48	69	67	31	33
（米）	Span of Semi-permanent Bridges (m)	268	1391	1266	1753	1575	751	714
渡 口 （个）	**Number of Ferries (unit)**	**33**	**71**	**79**	**74**	**67**	**64**	**56**

15-15 输油(气)管道长度和运输量

Length and Traffic of Petroleum and Gas Pipelines

项 目	Item	2000	2010	2015	2019	2020	2021	2022
总 计	**Total**							
条 数 （条）	Number of Pipelines (line)	45	105	116	139	156	154	156
输送里程 （公里）	Length of Pipelines (km)	1535.57	6033.62	6500.90	9187.49	10136.90	9664.23	11769.84
输油(气)量 （万吨）	Pipeline Traffic (10000 tons)	2952	7267	8137	9944	13209	13564	14503
输油(气)周转量(万吨公里)	Ton-kilometers (10000 ton-km)	417432	1757891	1743309	2286693	2817764	2701993	2714244
原油管道	**Crude Oil Pipelines**							
条 数 （条）	Number of Pipelines (line)	7	17	25	43	44	45	45
输送里程 （公里）	Length of Pipelines (km)	352.67	634.18	595.38	729.70	741.80	745.80	841.61
输油量 （万吨）	Pipeline Traffic (10000 tons)	1912	3364	4474	5105	6347	5970	6322
输油周转量 （万吨公里）	Ton-kilometers (10000 ton-km)	189623	352764	382146	431203	450767	422756	428914
成品油管道	**Refined Oil Pipelines**							
条 数 （条）	Number of Pipelines (line)	27	62	53	44	44	48	45
输送里程 （公里）	Length of Pipelines (km)	211.00	3925.88	4283.67	6510.69	6300.69	7357.59	6628.99
输油量 （万吨）	Pipeline Traffic (10000 tons)	663	3015	3431	3953	3439	4306	3526
输油周转量 （万吨公里）	Ton-kilometers (10000 ton-km)	13250	1153210	1247144	1744326	1810463	1769311	1590619
其他管道	**Other Pipelines**							
条 数 （条）	Number of Pipelines (line)	11	26	38	52	68	61	66
输送里程 （公里）	Length of Pipelines (km)	971.90	1473.56	1621.85	1947.10	3094.41	1560.84	4299.24
输气量 （万吨）	Pipeline Traffic (10000 tons)	377	887	233	886	3423	3288	4655
输气周转量 （万吨公里）	Ton-kilometers(10000 ton-km)	214559	251917	114020	111164	556533	509926	694710

15-16 民航航站吞吐量

Throughput of Civil Aviation Airports

年 份 Year	合 计 Total			进 港 In-port			出 港 Out-port		
	架次（万次）Sorties (10000 sorties)	旅客（万人）Passenger Traffic (10000 persons)	货物（万吨）Freight Traffic (10000 tons)	架次（万次）Sorties (10000 sorties)	旅客（万人）Passenger Traffic (10000 persons)	货物（万吨）Freight Traffic (10000 tons)	架次（万次）Sorties (10000 sorties)	旅客（万人）Passenger Traffic (10000 persons)	货物（万吨）Freight Traffic (10000 tons)
1980	1.60	161	2.90	0.80	81	1.40	0.80	80	1.50
1985	4.00	318	6.20	2.00	160	3.00	2.00	158	3.20
1990	6.20	687	13.50	3.10	343	5.90	3.10	344	7.60
1995	17.70	1963	39.50	8.80	963	14.10	8.90	1000	25.40
1996	18.20	2025	45.60	9.10	993	15.90	9.10	1032	29.70
1997	19.00	1981	49.00	9.50	974	16.70	9.50	1007	32.30
1998	20.80	2010	55.80	10.40	986	20.80	10.40	1024	35.00
1999	22.20	1929	63.70	11.10	942	25.60	11.10	987	38.10
2000	23.60	2143	73.00	11.80	1044	30.90	11.80	1099	42.10
2001	25.10	2344	81.00	12.50	1136	33.90	12.60	1208	47.10
2002	28.00	2731	95.70	14.00	1340	40.40	14.00	1391	55.30
2003	28.10	2751	82.40	14.10	1351	34.90	14.00	1400	47.50
2004	34.70	3661	115.80	17.30	1801	50.80	17.40	1860	65.00
2005	38.40	4100	133.00	19.20	2023	58.60	19.20	2077	74.40
2006	42.36	4599	151.13	21.18	2262	64.40	21.18	2337	86.70
2007	46.61	5407	133.20	23.30	2614	53.00	23.31	2793	80.20
2008	49.33	5738	130.47	24.60	2756	52.70	24.60	2982	77.78
2009	54.20	6462	158.50	27.10	3150	65.30	27.10	3312	93.20
2010	58.56	7189	198.40	29.30	3533	83.00	29.30	3655	115.50
2011	61.18	7768	203.96	30.59	3837	84.56	30.59	3931	119.40
2012	65.60	8283	213.59	32.79	4090	86.81	32.81	4193	126.78
2013	70.83	9124	226.75	35.41	4502	91.96	35.42	4622	134.79
2014	76.90	9924	246.27	38.45	4877	99.93	38.45	5047	146.34
2015	79.90	10494	260.26	39.95	5170	108.06	39.96	5324	152.20
2016	85.65	11440	284.36	42.82	5642	118.26	42.83	5798	166.10
2017	94.30	12940	301.27	47.15	6408	125.95	47.15	6532	175.32
2018	100.29	14184	319.22	50.14	7019	133.28	50.15	7165	185.94
2019	105.69	15303	329.75	52.84	7560	133.22	52.85	7743	196.54
2020	84.16	9942	323.89	42.06	4990	126.96	42.10	4952	196.94
2021	85.01	9594	369.93	42.47	4764	138.70	42.53	4830	231.23
2022	60.41	5825	345.60	30.21	2873	126.43	30.21	2952	219.17

15-17 港口泊位及吞吐量

Berth and Throughput of Coastal Ports

项 目	Item	2000	2010	2015	2020	2021	2022
码头泊位合计 （个）	**Number of Berths (unit)**	**3191**	**3082**	**3093**	**2376**	**2295**	**2252**
沿海港口	**Coastal Ports**	**1373**	**1884**	**2005**	**1603**	**1488**	**1476**
#广州港	Guangzhou Port	141	633	584	621	497	493
湛江港	Zhanjiang Port	41	184	174	159	162	162
汕头港	Shantou Port	28	91	92	34	37	35
深圳港	Shenzhen Port	121	172	156	166	164	172
内河港口	**Ports of Inland Rivers**	**1818**	**1198**	**1088**	**773**	**807**	**776**
万吨级码头泊位合计 （个）	**Berths at 10000 Ton Class (unit)**	**126**	**245**	**291**	**342**	**349**	**368**
沿海港口	**Coastal Ports**	**126**	**245**	**291**	**342**	**349**	**368**
#广州港	Guangzhou Port	32	62	74	80	80	83
湛江港	Zhanjiang Port	24	31	33	42	44	44
汕头港	Shantou Port	6	18	19	11	14	14
深圳港	Shenzhen Port	34	69	67	75	74	76
内河港口	**Ports of Inland Rivers**						
码头泊位长度 （米）	**Length of Quay Line (m)**	**180238**	**252762**	**266828**	**248844**	**241392**	**244557**
沿海港口	**Coastal Ports**	**105193**	**176753**	**200025**	**193971**	**186842**	**191119**
#广州港	Guangzhou Port	13496	51673	51722	50011	40283	40265
湛江港	Zhanjiang Port	6635	17458	18419	22878	23577	23577
汕头港	Shantou Port	3152	9715	9898	5013	6029	5900
深圳港	Shenzhen Port	17150	31377	30627	34036	33736	34925
内河港口	**Ports of Inland Rivers**	**75045**	**76009**	**66803**	**54873**	**54550**	**53438**
货物吞吐量合计 （万吨）	**Total Volume of Freight Handled (10000 tons)**	**31649**	**122258**	**171109**	**202226**	**209600**	**204802**
沿海港口	**Coastal Ports**	**25495**	**105300**	**142059**	**175499**	**181604**	**175517**
#广州港	Guangzhou Port	11128	42526	50053	61239	62367	62906
湛江港	Zhanjiang Port	2038	13638	22036	23391	25555	25376
汕头港	Shantou Port	1284	3509	5181	3351	4138	4019
深圳港	Shenzhen Port	4224	22097	21706	26506	27838	27243
内河港口	**Ports of Inland Rivers**	**6154**	**16958**	**29050**	**26726**	**27996**	**29284**
集装箱吞吐量合计(万TEU)	**Total Volume of Containers Handled (10000 TEUS)**	**862.68**	**4360.14**	**5512.12**	**6728.95**	**7078.20**	**7064.83**
沿海港口	**Coastal Ports**	**655.15**	**3867.77**	**4914.73**	**6027.89**	**6428.94**	**6490.04**
#广州港	Guangzhou Port	142.98	1270.00	1739.66	2317.10	2417.96	2460.17
湛江港	Zhanjiang Port	7.48	32.01	60.12	122.54	140.47	153.54
汕头港	Shantou Port	11.44	93.50	117.86	159.38	179.99	176.50
深圳港	Shenzhen Port	395.84	2250.96	2420.45	2654.79	2876.76	3003.62
内河港口	**Ports of Inland Rivers**	**207.53**	**492.37**	**597.38**	**701.05**	**649.25**	**574.80**
旅客吞吐量合计 （万人）	**Total Volume of Passengers Handled(10000 persons)**	**1670.32**	**2483.21**	**3432.96**	**1699.27**	**1849.17**	**1464.19**
沿海港口	**Coastal Ports**	**1330.81**	**2109.39**	**2867.17**	**1696.87**	**1849.17**	**1464.19**
#广州港	Guangzhou Port	15.00	79.01	61.32	7.98	3.81	1.66
湛江港	Zhanjiang Port	29.60	1051.41	1299.79	1180.87	1252.53	1185.45
汕头港	Shantou Port	5.50					
深圳港	Shenzhen Port	203.36	333.88	586.52	222.03	259.92	113.31
内河港口	**Ports of Inland Rivers**	**339.51**	**373.82**	**565.79**	**2.40**		

注：从2019年起，港口统计数据采集方式改为企业一套表联网直报，统计范围是辖区内各港口。

Note: From 2019, the port statistical data collection method are changed to online reporting, and the statistical scope is all ports within the jurisdiction.

15-18 各市港口货物吞吐量

Freight Throughput of Ports by City

单位：万吨 (10000 tons)

市 别	City	2000	2005	2010	2015	2018	2019	2020	2021	2022
全 省	**Provincial Total**	**31649**	**70926**	**122258**	**171109**	**211037**	**191819**	**202226**	**209600**	**204802**
广 州	Guangzhou	12455	27283	42526	52096	61313	62687	63643	65130	65592
深 圳	Shenzhen	5697	15351	22098	21706	25127	25785	26506	27838	27243
珠 海	Zhuhai	1770	3557	6056	11209	13799	13838	13367	12826	10237
汕 头	Shantou	1284	1736	3509	5181	3963	3155	3351	4138	4019
佛 山	Foshan	2033	3951	5410	6147	8973	9636	9285	9341	8559
韶 关	Shaoguan	131	118	40	62	47	98	299	291	419
河 源	Heyuan	45	49							
梅 州	Meizhou	145	306	132	114					
惠 州	Huizhou	825	1515	4673	7013	8757	8956	9636	9644	9005
汕 尾	Shanwei	25	107	489	858	1245	1310	1274	1666	1751
东 莞	Dongguan	746	2280	5657	13149	16417	19808	19857	18896	17021
中 山	Zhongshan	635	2072	4798	7319	11965	1547	1312	1434	1539
江 门	Jiangmen	879	2438	4965	7525	9369	6832	10698	10510	9628
阳 江	Yangjiang	68	222	799	2139	2627	3235	3350	3403	3838
湛 江	Zhanjiang	2688	6620	13638	22036	30185	21570	23391	25555	25376
茂 名	Maoming	1104	1360	2284	2685	2540	2508	2683	2887	3162
肇 庆	Zhaoqing	189	520	1597	2945	3921	4057	4789	4657	4982
清 远	Qingyuan	193	461	639	2927	3894	1462	1864	2570	2478
潮 州	Chaozhou	60	80	635	1144	1458	824	1366	1737	1708
揭 阳	Jieyang	266	248	1290	2851	3080	1898	2370	2768	2990
云 浮	Yunfu	411	654	1023	2002	2357	2613	3186	4307	5257
按经济区域分	By Region									
珠 三 角	Pearl River Delta	25229	58966	97779	129108	159642	153147	159092	160276	153804
东 翼	Eastern Region	1635	2171	5924	10035	9746	7187	8361	10310	10468
西 翼	Western Region	3860	8202	16721	26860	35352	27312	29424	31845	32376
山 区	Mountainous Region	925	1588	1834	5106	6297	4173	5349	7169	8154

15-19 各市城市公共交通情况（2022年）

Basic Statistics on Public Transportation in Cities by City (2022)

市 别	City	公共汽电车 Public Bus and Trolly Bus				出租汽车 Taxi	
		运营车辆(辆) Number of Vehicles under Operation (unit)	运营线路条数(条) Number of operating lines	运营线路长度(公里) Length under Operation (Km)	客运量(万人) Passenger Traffic (10000 persons)	运营车辆(辆) Number of Vehicles in Operation (unit)	客运量(万人) Passengers Transported (10000 persons)
全　省	**Provincial Total**	**66145**	**6010**	**127333**	**307811**	**51668**	**75974**
广　州	Guangzhou	14907	1416	25745	100614	19602	36499
深　圳	Shenzhen	15961	958	20645	73947	19602	24592
珠　海	Zhuhai	2528	211	4403	24730	3219	5253
汕　头	Shantou	1989	147	4450	9911	606	503
佛　山	Foshan	6800	677	15143	26682	1467	1495
韶　关	Shaoguan	719	114	2015	3078	200	192
河　源	Heyuan	510	79	1420	1416	202	460
梅　州	Meizhou	1937	229	5593	6235	130	98
惠　州	Huizhou	2817	212	6448	8480	1234	1209
汕　尾	Shanwei	1105	107	2899	2744	196	223
东　莞	Dongguan	6330	444	8954	13704	1492	2453
中　山	Zhongshan	2640	229	4307	8908	778	508
江　门	Jiangmen	1775	372	6052	7418	176	299
阳　江	Yangjiang	406	74	1385	520	101	83
湛　江	Zhanjiang	1034	106	2188	3074	646	971
茂　名	Maoming	1047	111	2905	2176	817	247
肇　庆	Zhaoqing	1068	152	4134	5481	168	121
清　远	Qingyuan	1015	175	3760	3840	537	514
潮　州	Chaozhou	399	53	1295	1041	175	92
揭　阳	Jieyang	716	58	1774	2960	102	86
云　浮	Yunfu	442	86	1820	852	218	78
按经济区域分	By Region						
珠 三 角	Pearl River Delta	54826	4671	95829	269964	47738	72427
东　翼	Eastern Region	4209	365	10418	16656	1079	904
西　翼	Western Region	2487	291	6478	5770	1564	1301
山　区	Mountainous Region	4623	683	14608	15421	1287	1342

15-19 续表 continued

市 别	City	轨道交通 Subway, Light Rail and Streetcar				客运轮渡 Passenger Ferryboat	
		运营车数(辆) Number of Vehicles under Operation (unit)	运营线路条数(条) Number of operating lines	运营线路长度(公里) Length under Operation (km)	客运量(万人) Passengers Transported (10000 persons)	运营船舶(艘) Number of Vehicles under Operation (unit)	客运量(万人) Passengers Transported (10000 persons)
全 省	**Provincial Total**	**8495**	**41**	**1343**	**417585**	**52**	**1096**
广 州	Guangzhou	3680	18	643	236344	44	960
深 圳	Shenzhen	4284	17	560	175357		
珠 海	Zhuhai	30	1	9			
汕 头	Shantou					4	127
佛 山	Foshan	381	4	94	2644		
韶 关	Shaoguan						
河 源	Heyuan						
梅 州	Meizhou						
惠 州	Huizhou						
汕 尾	Shanwei						
东 莞	Dongguan	120	1	38	3240		
中 山	Zhongshan						
江 门	Jiangmen						
阳 江	Yangjiang						
湛 江	Zhanjiang					4	9
茂 名	Maoming						
肇 庆	Zhaoqing						
清 远	Qingyuan						
潮 州	Chaozhou						
揭 阳	Jieyang						
云 浮	Yunfu						
按经济区域分	By Region						
珠 三 角	Pearl River Delta	8495	41	1343	417585	44	960
东 翼	Eastern Region					4	127
西 翼	Western Region					4	9
山 区	Mountainous Region						

15-20 邮电业务总量和指数

Business Volume of Postal and Telecommunication Services and Their Indices

年份 Year	邮电业务总量(亿元) Business Volume of Postal and Telecommunication Services (100million yuan)			指数(上年=100) Indices (preceding year=100)		
	合计 Total	邮政 Postal Services	电信 Telecommunication Services	合计 Total	邮政 Postal Services	电信 Telecommunication Services
1978	0.90			103.4		
1979	0.96			106.7		
1980	1.05			109.4		
1981	1.15			109.5		
1982	1.17			101.7		
1983	1.31			112.0		
1984	1.56			119.1		
1985	2.05			131.4		
1986	2.54			123.9		
1987	3.49			137.4		
1988	5.11			146.4		
1989	10.33	0.75	9.58	135.9	90.4	141.5
1990	26.30	3.91	22.39	254.6	521.3	233.7
1991	38.89	4.60	34.29	147.9	117.6	153.1
1992	57.06	5.59	51.47	146.7	121.5	150.1
1993	94.25	7.10	87.15	165.2	127.0	169.3
1994	142.78	8.32	134.46	151.5	117.2	154.3
1995	204.93	9.63	202.60	143.5	115.7	150.7
1996	265.56	10.92	254.64	129.6	113.4	125.7
1997	330.38	11.44	318.94	124.4	104.8	125.3
1998	418.18	15.20	402.98	126.6	132.9	126.3
1999	542.65	19.72	522.93	129.8	129.8	129.8
2000	757.22	50.40	706.82	139.5	255.5	135.2
2001	782.67	42.13	740.54	129.9	105.1	131.7
2002	917.87	48.36	869.51	117.3	114.8	117.4
2003	1202.52	54.33	1148.19	131.0	112.3	132.1
2004	1781.78	55.12	1726.66	148.2	101.5	150.4
2005	2121.94	59.82	2062.12	119.1	108.5	119.4
2006	2540.54	69.48	2471.06	119.7	116.1	119.8
2007	3070.55	77.30	2993.25	120.9	111.3	121.1
2008	3564.85	87.97	3476.88	116.1	113.8	116.2
2009	3938.15	101.16	3837.00	110.5	115.0	110.4
2010	4832.94	118.57	4714.37	122.9	125.2	122.7
2011	1918.01	291.36	1626.65	116.4	129.9	114.3
2012	2174.67	395.18	1779.49	113.4	135.6	109.4
2013	2507.99	592.00	1915.99	115.3	149.8	107.7
2014	3394.39	859.81	2534.58	120.4	145.2	113.7
2015	4397.09	1228.75	3168.34	129.5	142.9	125.0
2016	6892.41	1886.25	5006.16	156.7	153.5	158.0
2017	6107.19	2526.29	3580.90	158.0	133.9	181.0
2018	11010.28	3215.75	7794.53	180.3	127.3	217.7
2019	16451.23	4403.44	12047.79	149.4	136.9	154.6
2020	20833.11	5807.81	15025.30	126.6	131.9	124.7
2021	4954.59	3021.10	1933.49	126.5	125.9	127.5
2022	5063.13	3112.87	1950.26	108.5	103.0	118.6

注：1.邮电业务总量1988年及以前按1980年不变价格计算，1989—2000年按1990年不变价格计算，2001—2010年按2000年不变价格计算，2011—2016年按2010年不变价格计算，2017年起，电信业务总量按2015年不变价格计算，邮政业务总量仍按2010年不变价格计算。2021年起，按2020年不变价计算。2022年，电信按照上年不变价就计算。指数按可比价格计算。

2.统计范围是辖区内全社会所有从事电信运营企业和国家邮政企业，以及获得快递业务经营许可的快递服务企业。

Notes:a) The business volume of postal and telecommunication services in and before 1998 was calculated at 1980 constant prices, that from 1998 to 2000 was calculated at 1990 constant prices, that from 2001 to 2010 was calculated at 2000 constant prices and that from 2011 to 2016 was calculated at 2010 constant prices. Since 2017, the total amount of telecommunications was calculated at 2015 constant prices, while the total amount of postal business was calculated at 2010 constant prices. From 2022,that was calculated at last year's constant prices. The index was calculated at comparable prices.

b) The statistical coverages of business volume of postal and Telecommunication services are all telecom enter prises, the national postal enterprises and express mail enterprises with express license.

15-21 各市邮电业务总量

Business Volume of Postal and Telecommunication Services by City

单位：亿元 (100 million yuan)

市 别	City	2000	2010	2015	2018	2019	2020	2021	2022
全 省	**Provincial Total**	**757.22**	**4832.94**	**4397.09**	**11010.28**	**16451.23**	**20833.11**	**4954.59**	**5063.13**
广 州	Guangzhou	168.26	1051.65	1092.94	2613.08	3814.51	4707.38	1298.94	1266.65
深 圳	Shenzhen	154.20	1031.26	1069.43	2769.27	3998.91	4917.38	1273.12	1281.50
珠 海	Zhuhai	22.31	137.61	91.22	198.58	315.81	403.91	71.55	66.57
汕 头	Shantou	36.61	173.81	134.46	357.95	537.54	735.30	210.94	232.51
佛 山	Foshan	66.29	428.72	282.87	686.93	1050.49	1336.25	288.80	311.75
韶 关	Shaoguan	11.11	69.58	45.17	103.44	170.58	219.63	35.74	36.80
河 源	Heyuan	6.26	46.33	41.85	103.58	170.72	217.26	35.02	35.63
梅 州	Meizhou	12.87	52.48	68.43	136.76	207.09	255.72	46.91	48.44
惠 州	Huizhou	27.19	201.02	146.50	381.31	606.36	786.86	137.20	143.04
汕 尾	Shanwei	11.10	48.01	38.05	87.89	140.18	184.88	33.69	35.79
东 莞	Dongguan	74.05	674.09	475.59	1282.22	1947.19	2562.96	521.90	532.09
中 山	Zhongshan	30.10	194.98	156.64	397.51	628.18	784.05	141.22	157.53
江 门	Jiangmen	32.02	135.08	102.06	258.22	382.65	462.90	80.23	83.59
阳 江	Yangjiang	8.60	50.67	45.30	104.34	165.89	216.27	43.43	48.62
湛 江	Zhanjiang	19.38	116.85	122.72	290.67	465.47	580.50	85.91	89.30
茂 名	Maoming	13.21	87.27	86.71	221.24	356.74	441.01	68.30	72.07
肇 庆	Zhaoqing	13.22	95.05	69.81	169.07	270.97	342.96	60.55	63.23
清 远	Qingyuan	9.96	56.06	61.24	150.30	235.91	301.45	47.94	50.75
潮 州	Chaozhou	12.78	54.52	46.13	122.21	197.87	272.79	70.47	78.98
揭 阳	Jieyang	20.81	94.01	96.30	373.97	575.54	830.84	305.00	325.62
云 浮	Yunfu	6.89	33.91	37.69	85.01	130.19	164.37	25.90	27.17
不分地区	Unclassified			85.99	116.72	82.42	108.45	71.83	75.50
按经济区域分	By Region								
珠 三 角	Pearl River Delta	587.64	3949.45	3573.05	8872.90	13097.48	16413.10	3945.34	3981.44
东 翼	Eastern Region	81.31	370.35	314.94	942.03	1451.14	2023.82	620.10	672.90
西 翼	Western Region	41.19	254.79	254.72	616.25	988.11	1237.77	197.63	209.99
山 区	Mountainous Region	47.09	258.35	254.38	579.10	914.50	1158.43	191.52	198.80

15-22 各市邮电业务情况（2022年）

Conditions of Postal and Telecommunication Services by City (2022)

市别	City	业务总量（亿元）Business Volume of Postal and Telecommunication Services (100million yuan)	#电信 Business Volume of Telecommunications	函件（万件）Number of Letters (10000 pcs)	报刊累计数（万份）Newspaper and Magazine Issue (10000 copies)	快递（万件）Pieces of Express Mail Services (10000 pcs)	移动电话用户（万户）Subscribers of Mobile Telephones (10000 subscribers)	固定互联网宽带接入用户(万户) Subscribers of Fixed Internet Broadband (10000 subscribers)	移动互联网用户（万户）Subscribers of Mobile Internet (10000 subscribers)
全　省	**Provincial Total**	**5063.13**	**1950.26**	**11036.58**	**71213.86**	**3013602.76**	**16650.76**	**4628.72**	**15097.28**
广　州	Guangzhou	1266.65	390.93	3614.95	19048.38	1013080.89	3210.09	765.30	2922.29
深　圳	Shenzhen	1281.50	381.05	1975.81	8553.90	579983.01	2817.52	674.28	2571.73
珠　海	Zhuhai	66.57	47.68	1324.86	1795.85	16985.21	385.22	122.71	352.57
汕　头	Shantou	232.51	55.58	97.87	3496.57	245711.62	652.77	173.91	598.15
佛　山	Foshan	311.75	146.73	998.67	4228.84	158426.18	1241.78	355.00	1144.29
韶　关	Shaoguan	36.80	27.20	69.28	1543.60	3464.02	298.43	98.82	265.34
河　源	Heyuan	35.63	27.64	16.80	3733.64	4155.81	276.22	89.95	248.49
梅　州	Meizhou	48.44	34.53	123.17	1972.98	7380.69	403.03	131.12	355.45
惠　州	Huizhou	143.04	89.36	163.16	3754.83	56061.66	744.41	278.48	684.43
汕　尾	Shanwei	35.79	21.53	9.58	665.91	13835.68	249.26	75.12	226.05
东　莞	Dongguan	532.09	201.39	1467.66	2862.05	288061.61	1644.68	434.52	1508.70
中　山	Zhongshan	157.53	78.83	111.25	1577.91	87148.87	691.94	215.77	634.81
江　门	Jiangmen	83.59	57.06	389.11	3862.41	18985.85	566.25	187.46	506.30
阳　江	Yangjiang	48.62	24.79	97.98	1145.04	24996.02	271.04	90.77	236.57
湛　江	Zhanjiang	89.30	68.39	104.22	2619.15	12061.81	732.73	207.70	642.44
茂　名	Maoming	72.07	51.97	166.48	2267.08	10299.99	601.43	156.80	527.90
肇　庆	Zhaoqing	63.23	39.49	104.66	1713.80	18832.19	417.80	130.09	372.23
清　远	Qingyuan	50.75	39.46	89.22	3008.83	5866.64	401.11	121.19	363.54
潮　州	Chaozhou	78.98	24.63	53.45	1457.00	73854.27	280.65	90.18	252.24
揭　阳	Jieyang	325.62	45.72	23.47	1053.66	372893.74	539.53	157.41	484.62
云　浮	Yunfu	27.17	20.80	34.93	852.43	1517.00	224.88	72.14	199.14
不分地区	Unclassified	75.50	75.50						
按经济区域分	By Region								
珠三角	Pearl River Delta	3981.44	1508.02	10150.13	47397.97	2237565.47	11719.68	3163.61	10697.35
东　翼	Eastern Region	672.90	147.45	184.37	6673.14	706295.31	1722.21	496.62	1561.06
西　翼	Western Region	209.99	145.16	368.68	6031.27	47357.82	1605.20	455.27	1406.91
山　区	Mountainous Region	198.80	149.63	333.40	11111.48	22384.16	1603.67	513.22	1431.96

15-23 邮政通信业基本情况

Basic Conditions of Postal and Telecommunication Services

项　目	Item	2000	2010	2015	2020	2021	2022
邮政业务量	**Business Volume of Postal Services**						
邮路长度 (万公里)	Length of Postal Routes (10000 km)	18.07	13.77	13.79	25.81	306.90	291.64
农村投递路线 (万公里)	Rural Delivery Routes (10000 km)	18.52	21.49	23.19	31.61	32.20	29.47
城市投递路线 (万公里)	Urban Delivery Routes (10000 km)		11.47	12.53	25.35	22.20	25.43
函件 (万件)	Number of Letters (10000 pcs)	106603	76204	64547	22840	13008	11037
包裹 (万件)	Package (10000 pcs)		332	182	206	225	271
快递 (亿件)	Pieces of Express Mail Services (10000 pcs)	0.13	5.91	50.13	220.82	294.57	301.36
报刊累计数 (万份)	Newspaper and Magazine Circulation (10000 copies)	107755	87895	91159	71120	69919	71214
全省平均每人每年发函件数 (件)	Annual Number of Per Capita Letter Mailed (pcs)	13.80	8.31	5.95	1.80	1.00	0.9
全省平均每百人每年订报刊数 (份)	Annual Average Number of Newspapers and Magazines Subscribed per 100 Persons(copies)	15.10	8.21	8.40	5.00	4.20	4.90
电信业务量	**Business Volume of Telecommunication Services**						
长途光缆线路长度 (公里)	Length of Long-distance Optical Cable Routes (km) (10000 lines)		46289	52662	57751	57870	62060
移动电话交换机容量(万户)	Capacity of Mobile Telephone Exchanges (10000 subscribers)	1825.40	14766.90	22025.80	23803.81	23803.81	24521.58
固定电话用户 (万户)	Number of Subscribers of Local Telephones (10000 subscribers)	1414.94	3169.14	2807.11	2131.88	2072.20	1944.08
移动电话用户 (万户)	Number of Mobile Telephones Subscribers (10000 subscribers)	1357.26	9710.09	15009.75	15536.92	16267.80	16650.76
固定互联网宽带接入用户 (万户)	Broadband Subscribers of Internet (10000 subscribers)	216.41	1523.22	2285.19	3889.99	4277.71	4628.72
移动互联网用户 (万户)	Number of Mobile Broadband Internet Subscribers (10000 subscribers)		6918.7	10950.25	14251.39	15070.27	15097.28
固定电话普及率 (户/百人)	Popularization Rate of Local Telephones (subscribers/100 persons)	18.40	30.38	25.87	16.89	16.34	15.36
移动电话普及率 (户/百人)	Popularization Rate of Mobile Telephones (subscribers/100 persons)	17.61	93.09	138.35	123.07	128.25	131.56

注：2020年前广东省邮路总长度(单程)指标由省邮政集团公司报送，不含单独机要，不含速递邮路长度，2021年该指标由省邮政管理局汇总后报送，包含邮政邮路(含单独机要邮路)、速递邮路。

Note: Before 2020，the total length (one-way) of postal routes in Guangdong Province submitted by the provincial postal group company，excluding Individual confidential information and the length of express postal routes，In 2021,the index submitted by the provincial postal administration after being summarized, including postal routes (including separate confidential postal routes) and express postal routes。

主要统计指标解释

铁路营业里程 又称营业长度(包括正式营业和临时营业里程)，指办理客货运输业务的铁路正线总长度。凡是全线或部分建成双线及以上的线路，以第一线的实际长度计算；复线、站线、段管线、岔线和特殊用途线以及不计算运费的联络线都不计算营业里程。该指标可以反映铁路运输业基础设施的发展水平，也是计算客货周转量、运输密度和机车车辆运用效率等指标的基础资料。

公路通车里程 指在一定时期内实际达到《公路工程技术标准 JTJ01-88》规定的等级公路，并经公路主管部门正式验收交付使用的公路里程数。包括大中城市的郊区公路以及通过小城镇街道部分的公路里程和桥梁、渡口的长度，不包括大中城市的街道、厂矿、林区生产用道和农业生产用道的里程。两条或多条公路共同经由同一路段，只计算一次，不得重复计算里程长度。该指标可以反映公路建设的发展规模，也是计算运输网密度等指标的基础资料。

内河航道里程 也称内河通航里程，指在一定时期内，能通航运输船舶及排筏的天然河流、湖泊水库、运河及通航渠道的长度。包括全年季节性通航累计三个月以上的航道，不包括仅供零散流放竹、木排的河道。该指标可以反映内河水运网的规模、水平和发展情况。

民用航空航线里程 指民航运输定期班机飞行的航线长度的总和。航线长度按机场之间的距离计算，通常有两种计算方法：一是将每条航线长度相加称为重复计算航线里程；一是将两线或两条以上航线经过同一区段里程，只计算一次航线长度称为不重复计算航线里程。一般常用的是后者，该指标可以确切反映民航运输网的规模，是表明民航事业为国民经济服务和方便人民生活程度的主要指标。

输油(气)管道里程 指油品(或天然气)的实际输送距离，一般按输油(气)管道的单线长度计算。若包括复线和备用线长度则称为输油(气)管道延展长度，是指管道铺设的实际长度。我们通常使用的是不包括复线的“输油(气)管道里程”，该指标可以反映管道运输的发展规模和水平。

货(客)运量 指在一定时期内，各种运输工具实际运送的货物(旅客)数量。该指标是反映运输业为国民经济和人民生活服务的数量指标，也是制定和检查运输生产计划、研究运输发展规模和速度的重要指标。货运按吨计算，客运按人计算。货物不论运输距离长短、货物类别，均按实际重量统计。旅客不论行程远近或票价多少，均按一人一次客运量统计；半价票、小孩票也按一人统计。

货物(旅客)周转量 指在一定时期内，由各种运输工具运送的货物(旅客)数量与其相应运输距离的乘积之总和。该指标可以反映运输业生产的总成果，也是编制和检查运输生产计划，计算运输效率、劳动生产率以及核算运输单位成本的主要基础资料。计算货物(旅客)周转量通常按发出站与到达站之间的最短距离，也就是计费距离计算。计算公式为：

货物（旅客）周转量=Σ（货物（旅客）运输量×运输距离）

港口货物吞吐量 指经水运进出港区范围，并经过装卸的货物数量，包括邮件及办理托运手续的行李、包裹以及补给运输船舶的燃料、物料和淡水。货物吞吐量按货物流向分为进口、出口吞吐量，按货物交流性质分为外贸货物吞吐量和国内贸易货物吞吐量。货物吞吐量的货类构成及其流向，是衡量港口生产能力大小的重要指标。

港口集装箱吞吐量 指用集装箱装载货物、按箱数表示的港口货物吞吐量。计量单位为国际标准箱（TEU）。将各种不同规格尺寸的集装箱自然箱数，按换算比例折合成 TUE（TWENTY FT EQUAL TO UNIT 的缩写）统计，即折合成 20 英尺标准箱统计，换算比例为：40 英尺箱为 1:2，35 英尺箱为 1:1.75，20 英尺箱为 1:1，10 英尺箱为 1:0.5。

民用汽车 指报告期末，在公安交通管理部门按照《机动车注册登记工作规范》，已注册登记领有民用车辆牌照的全部汽车数量。汽车统计的主要分类：根据汽车结构分为载客汽车、载货汽车及其他汽车；根据汽车所有者不同分为个人(私人)汽车、单位汽车；根据汽车的使用性质分为营运汽车、非营运汽车；根据汽车大小规格不同载客汽车分为大型、中型、小型和微型，载货汽车分为重型、中型、轻型和微型。

机动船 又称自航船，指装有各种发动机推进装置，以机械动力行驶的船舶。

驳船 指本身无动力装置，或只设简易动力装置，依靠拖船或推船带动的平底船。

船舶净载重量 指报告期末所拥有船舶的总载重量减去燃（物）料、淡水、粮食及供应品、人员及其行李等的重量及船舶常数后，能够装载货物的实际重量。

沿海港口 指位于海沿岸，具有一定设施和条件，供船舶停靠、旅客上下、货物装卸、生活物料供应等作业的港口。

内河港口 指位于江、河、湖沿岸，具有一定设施和条件，供船舶停靠、旅客上下、货物装卸、生活物料供应等作业的港口。

民用航空航线条数 民用航空航线指出于商业的目的，运输飞机从地球表面一点(起飞)飞到另一点(终点)的航行线路。应同时具备三个条件：一是有运输飞机定期飞行，二是有足以保证运输飞机飞行和起降所需要的机场及地面设施，三是经过批准并在一个航季中正常执行。计算条数时，来回程计为一条。分为国内航线、国际航线和地区航线。

民航运输飞机 从事公共航空运输的民用飞机。分为大中型飞机和小型飞机，大中型飞机指 100 座及以上的运输飞机，小型飞机指 100 座以下的运输飞机。

城市公共交通 指城市中供公众乘用的、经济方便的各种交通方式的总称。包括公共汽车、电车、轨道交通（地铁、轻轨、有轨电车、磁悬浮、索道、缆车等）、出租汽车、公共轮渡等客运交通设施。

运营线路网长度 指公共交通线路所通过的运营线路净长度。计算公式：运营线路网长度=运营线路总长度－Σ重复的线路长度

运营线路总长度 指全部运营线路长度之和。计算公式：运营线路长度=Σ各条运营线路长度=Σ〔1/2（上行起点至终点里程+下行起点至终点里程+上下行终点掉头里程〕。单向行驶的环行线路长度等于起点至终点里程与终点下客站至起点里程之和的一半，不包括折返、试车、联络线等非运营线路。

运营车辆数 指城市中用于公共交通运营业务的全部车辆数。地铁和轻轨在统计时一自然节为一辆。出租汽车指已经领取出租汽车专用牌照的运营车辆，包括技术完好的、在修的、长期行驶的以及拟报废尚未经上级机关批准的车辆。

轮渡运营船舶数 指用于城市客渡运营业务的全部船舶数。不含旅游客轮（长途旅游、市内供游人游览江、河、湖泊的船只）。

城市公共交通客运总量 指报告期内城市公共交通各种运输方式运送乘客的总人次。

邮电业务总量 指以价值量形式表现的邮电通信企业为社会提供各类邮电通信服务的总数量。邮电业务量按专业分类包括函件、包件、汇票、报刊发行、邮政快件、特快专递、邮政储蓄、集邮、公众电报、用户电报、传真、长途电话、出租电路、无线寻呼、移动电话、分组交换数据通信、出租代维等。计算方法为各类产品乘以相应的平均单价(不变价)之和，再加上出租电路和设备、代用户维护电话交换机和线路等的服务收入。该指标综合反映了一定时期邮电业务发展的总成果，是研究邮电业务量构成和发展趋势的重要指标。计算公式为：

邮电业务总量=Σ（各类邮电业务量×不变单价）+出租代维及其他业务收入
=邮政业务总量+通信业务总量

移动电话用户 指通过移动电话交换机进入移动电话网、占用移动电话号码的各类电话用户。包括签约用户和智能网预付费用户。一个移动电话号码统计为一户。

本地电话用户 指接入本地电信运营商固定电话网上的电话用户。包括：住宅用户、单位用户、公用电话用户等。

国际互联网用户 包括互联网窄带拨号用户和互联网宽带接入用户。互联网窄带拨号用户又分为互联网注册拨号用户、互联网主叫电话记费用户、互联网上网卡用户等几种。互联网注册拨号用户指由基础电信运营商用户提供的，使用固定帐号上网的一种方式，由用户到运营商的营业厅或业务代理商处申请办理，获得拨号上网帐号及密码，用户根据该帐号及密码拨叫上网特服号，通过认证获得动态 IP 地址接入宽带互联网。互联网主叫电话记费用户指用户不需要到运营商的营业厅或业务代理商处申请办理，只需要拨打某一运营商已经开通的主叫特服号码即可上网，上网费用随主叫电话收取。互联网上网卡用户指使用上网卡上的帐号和密码认证，通过 PSTN、N-ISDN 等方式接入宽带互联网的用户。互联网宽带接入用户指采用分组交换网、DDN 网、帧中继/ATM 网以及模拟专线、数字专线等方式，不经过基础电信运营商的宽带 IP 城域网，直接接入宽带互联网节点的用户，不含 XDSL、专线和 LAN 专线用户。

移动电话交换机容量 指移动电话交换机根据一定话务模型和交换机处理能力计算出来的最大同时服务用户的数量。

Explanatory Notes on Main Statistical Indicators

Length of Railways in Operation refers to the total length of the trunk line under passenger and freight transportation (including both regular operations and temporary operations). In the case of wholly or partially double or multiple track railways, calculation is based on the actual length of the first track, regardless of other tracks, station sidings, tracks under the charge of stations, branch lines, special-purpose lines and non-payable connecting lines. The length of railways in operation is an important indicator of the development of infrastructure for railway transport, as well as the foundation for the calculation of passenger-kilometers and freight ton-kilometers, traffic density and utilization efficiency of locomotives and carriages.

Length of Highways refers to the length of highways built in conformity with the grades specified by the Technical Standards JTJ01-88 for Highway Engineering, formally checked and accepted by highway authorities and put into use. The length of highways includes that of suburban highways at large and medium sized cities and highways passing through streets at small cities and towns, as well as the span of bridges and ferries. However, it does not include the length of streets in large and medium sized cities and highways built for production purposes at factories, mines, forest areas and agricultural areas. If two or more highways share the same segment, the length of the shared segment is only calculated for once and no duplication is allowed. The length of highways is an important indicator of the scale of development of highway construction, as well as the foundation for the calculation of transport network density and other indicators.

Length of Navigable Inland Waterways refers to the length of natural rivers, lakes, reservoirs, canals, and ditches open to navigation during a given period, which enables the transport by ships and rafts. This includes channels open to seasonal navigation for an accumulative period of over 3 months in a year, but excludes river courses used exclusively for wood or bamboo rafts on an irregular basis. This indicator reflects the scale, level and development situation of the inland waterway network.

Length of Civil Aviation Routes refers to the length of all routes for regular civil aviation flights. Calculation of route lengths is based on the distance between airports, usually in either of the following ways: duplicated calculation of route lengths, which directly sums up the length of every single air route, or singular calculation of route lengths, which calculates the same segments of aviation routes shared by two or more routes only once. In general practice, the latter is used, as it can precisely reflect the size of the civil aviation network and indicate the extent to which civil aviation serves the national economy and the needs of the people.

Length of Petroleum and Gas Pipelines refers to the actual transport distance of oil or gas products, generally calculated as the length of single pipelines. Inclusion of double pipelines and alternate pipeline in the calculation is termed the extension length of petroleum and gas pipelines, which indicates the actual length of the pipelines built. In general practice, the "Length of Petroleum and Gas Pipelines" exclusive of double pipelines is used, which reflects the scale and degree of development in pipeline transport.

Freight (Passenger) Traffic refers to the volume of freight (passengers) transported with various means. This indicator provides a quantitative measure of how the transport industry serves the national economy and the needs of the people, as well as an important reference for drafting and checking production plans in the transport industry and for studying the scale and speed of development in the transport industry. Freight transport is calculated in tons and passenger traffic is calculated in the number of persons. Freight transport is calculated in the actual weight of goods regardless of traveling distances and types of freight, while passenger traffic is calculated as the number of individuals traveling once, regardless of traveling distances, ticket prices, whether the passengers are traveling with half-price tickets or child tickets.

Freight Ton-kilometers (Passenger-kilometers) refer to the sum of the products of the volume of transported cargo (passengers) multiplied by the transport distance. These are important indicators of the total achievements of the transport industry, as well as the major foundation for drafting and checking production plans in the transport industry and for calculating the efficiency, labor productivity and the cost of transport enterprises. Normally, the shortest distance between the departure station and the destination station (i.e. the payable distance) is the basis to calculate the freight ton-kilometers and passenger-kilometers on. These indicators are calculated as follows:

Freight Ton-kilometers (Passenger-kilometers) = Σ (Freight (Passenger) Traffic × Transport Distance)

Volume of Freight Handled in Ports refers to the volume of cargo passing in and out of the harbor area that undergoes the loading and unloading processes, including mails, checked baggage and bales, as well as fuel, material and fresh water supplies to ships. The volume of freight handled may be classified by direction of flow as import volume and export volume, or by nature of cargo as volume of freight for domestic trade and volume of freight for foreign trade. The classification of volume of freight handled and its direction of flow are important indicators of the production capacity of ports.

Volume of Container Handled in Ports refers to the volume of freight handled in Ports that are loaded and unloaded in containers.The unit of measurement is TEU. The number of natural containers of various sizes of containers is converted into TEU (TWENTY FT EQUAL TO UNIT) according to the conversion ratio, that is to say, the conversion ratio is 1:2 for 40 foot container, 1:1.75 for 35 foot container, 1:1 for 20 foot container, and 1:0.5 for 10 foot container.

Possession of Civil Motor Vehicles refers to the total number of vehicles that are registered at transport management offices under the public security authorities and provided with civil vehicle licenses and tags according to the Work Standard for Motor Vehicles Registration at the end of the reference period. Major categories of vehicle are: passenger vehicles, freight vehicles and other vehicles in terms of structure; private vehicles and organization-owned vehicles in terms of ownership; commercial vehicles and non-commercial vehicles in terms of use; large, medium, small and mini passenger vehicles, and heavy, medium, light and mini trucks in terms of size.

Motor Vessels refer to vessels installed with power units and propelled by mechanical power. It is also known as self-propelled vessels.

Barges refer to flat-bottomed vessels driven by drawers or propellers. It has no power units or has only simple power units.

Dead Weight Tonnage of Vessels refers to the actual tonnage all the vessels within the reference period are capable of carrying. It equals the tonnage of all the vessels minus that of fuel, material and fresh water, foods, supplies, persons and luggage on vessels.

Coastal Seaports refer to seaports located alongside the coasts that have the right facilities and conditions for vessel mooning, passenger boarding and alighting, cargo loading and unloading, and supply of daily life materials.

Inland Ports refer to ports located along rivers and lakes that have the right facilities and conditions for vessel mooning, passenger boarding and alighting, cargo loading and unloading, and supply of daily life materials.

Number of Civil Aviation Routes refers to the number of all routes of commercial civil aviation flights from one point of the earth to another. Civil aviation routes shall meet three conditions. Firstly, there shall be regular flights. Secondly, there shall be adequate airport and ground facilities to ensure the flight, takeoff and landing. Thirdly, the flights are approved and carried out normally during the flight season. Singular calculation is used in calculating the number of routes. Civil aviation routes are divided into domestic routes, international routes and regional routes.

Civil Aviation Aircraft refer to aircraft used in public civil aero transport. They are divided into large and medium sized aircraft and small sized aircraft. The former refer to those with 100 seats and above, and the latter refer to those with less than 100 seats.

Urban Public Transportation refers to all the economical transport taken by the public in cities. It includes bus, trolley bus, rail transport (subway, light rail, streetcar, magnetically levitated trains, cableway, telpher, etc.), taxi, ferry boast, etc.

Length of Public Transportation Network refers to the net length covered by the public transportation routes. The following formula is used:

Length of Public Transportation Network=Length of Public Transportation under Operation - ΣLength of Repeated Routes

Length of Public Transportation under Operation refers to the sum of all public transportation routes under operation. The following formula is used:

Length of Public Transportation under Operation= -Σ(1/2 (length from starting station to terminal of forward trip+length from terminal to beginning station of backward trip+length of take-turning of both trips)

Number of Vehicles under Operation refers to the total number of vehicles under operation in public transportation in cities. For subway and light rail, each compartment is calculated as one unit. Taxi refers to all those with special operation license, including those in good condition, under maintenance, in long-term operation and with pending approval for writing-off.

Number of Ferry Boats refer to the total number of boats for ferry operation., excluding the long-distance or intra-city cruiser.

Total Passenger Traffic in Cities refers to the total number of persons transported by public transportation in cities.

Business Volume of Postal and Telecommunication Services refers to the total amount of postal and telecommunication services, expressed in value terms, provided by postal and telecommunication enterprises for the society. Postal and telecommunication services can be classified as letters, parcels, remittance, delivery of newspapers and magazines, fast mail service, express mail service, savings deposits, stamps for collection, public and individual telegraph service, facsimiles, long-distance telephone service, leasing of telephone lines, urban paging service, mobile telephone service, data communication through packet networks, network elements lease and maintenance, etc. To calculate the volume, the business volume of each product is multiplied by its average unit price (at constant prices), summed, and added to income from other services such as leasing of telephone lines and equipment, maintenance of telephone switchboards and lines on behalf of customers. This indicator reflects the overall achievements of postal and telecommunication services during a given period, and is an important reference for studying the composition of business volume and the development trend of postal and telecommunication services. This volume is calculated as follows:

Business Volume of Postal and Telecommunication Services = Σ(Business Volume of Each Product× Constant Unit Price) + Income from Leasing, Maintenance, and Other Services = Business Volume of Postal Services + Business Volume of Telecommunication Services

Mobile Telephone Subscribers refer to persons who own mobile telephone numbers and are connected with the mobile telephone communication network through mobile telephone switchboards, including contracted subscribers and pre-paid subscribers for intelligent network. One mobile telephone number is calculated as one subscriber.

Local Telephone Subscribers refer to subscribers that are connected to the local telecommunication service provider through fix line network, including household subscribers, institutional subscribers and public telephones.

Number of Internet Subscribers include both narrow-band dial-up users and broad-band access users of the internet. Narrow-band dial-up users are further classified into registered dial-up users, pay-per-calling users, and pre-pay card users. Registered dial-up service enables internet access through fixed accounts provided by basic telecommunication operators. Users of this service apply to the operators or their agents for accounts and passwords, with which they dial special numbers for internet connection and acquire dynamic IP addresses through authentification to gain access to the broad-band internet. Pre-pay calling service implies that instead of applying to the operators or their agents, users only need to dial a certain operator's special numbers to gain access to the internet and pay internet fees together with their calling fees. Pre-pay card users refer to those connected to the broad-band internet through PSTN and N-ISDN networks with accounts and passwords provided by the pre-pay cards. Broad-band access users (exclusive of XDSL and LAN users) refer to users directly connected to broad-band internet nodes through packet networks, DDN networks, frame relay/ATM networks, and special analog or digital lines, bypassing the broad-band IP MAN provided by basic telecommunication operators.

Capacity of Mobile Telephone Exchanges refers to the maximum number of subscribers that can be served simultaneously, calculated according to a certain calling model and the handling capacity of the mobile telephone exchanges.

十六、批发和零售业

WHOLESALE AND RETAIL TRADES

十六 批发零售业

简要说明

一、本篇资料反映包括批发零售业商品流通情况、社会消费品零售总额等。

二、本篇资料主要根据国家统计局《批发和零售业统计报表制度》进行搜集和加工整理。资料中限额以上批发和零售业采用全面调查的方法自下而上逐级综合汇总而得，限额以下企业及个体户资料采用抽样调查方法推算而得。

三、各表的调查范围：

限额以上批发和零售业统计限额标准：批发业年销售额2000万元及以上；零售业年销售额500万元及以上。

商品购、销、存总额表为各种经济类型的限额以上和限额以下批发零售业法人及产业活动单位和个体户。

社会消费品零售总额表为各种经济类型的法人及产业活动单位、个体户对城乡居民和社会集团的零售。

四、本篇资料由广东省统计局贸易外经统计处整理提供。

16 Wholesale and Retail Trades

Brief Introduction

Ⅰ. The date in this chapter show the development of Guangdong's domestic market，including mainly the circulation of commodities in the wholesale and retail trades and the total retail sales of consumer goods，etc.

Ⅱ. The data are collected and processed in accordance with the Statistical Reporting Scheme on Wholesale and Retail Trades stipulated by the National Bureau of Statistics. Data on basic conditions for all corporate enterprises of wholesale, retail above the designated size are collected through comprehensive reporting systems and data are reported level by level in a bottom-up manner. Data on small-size enterprises and individual enterprises below the designated size are collected through sample surveys.

Ⅲ. The statistical coverage in this chapter comes as follows:

Criteria for wholesale and retail sale trades above designated size is defined as follows：wholesale trade with annual sales of 20 million yuan or above, retail sale trade with annual sales of 5 million yuan or above.

The table of total purchases，sales and inventory include corporate units, establishments and individuals of various types of ownership both above and below designated size by category of commodities.

The table of total retail sales of consumer goods includes the retail sales of corporate units, establishments and individuals of various types of ownership to urban and rural residents and institutions.

Ⅳ. The data in this chapter are prepared and provided by the Division of Trade and External Economic Relations Statistics of Statistics Bureau of Guangdong Province.

16-1 批发零售业主要指标

Main Indicators on Domestic Trade

指　标	Item	2000	2010	2015	2020	2021	2022
社会消费品零售总额（亿元）	**Total Retail Sales of Consumer Goods (100 million yuan)**	**4320.73**	**16991.39**	**30326.76**	**40207.85**	**44187.71**	**44882.92**
按消费形态分	By pattern						
商品零售	Retail Sales			26574.66	36083.09	39427.05	40327.24
餐饮收入	Catering Income			3752.09	4124.76	4760.66	4555.68
按城乡分	By Urban and Rural Area						
城镇	Urban Areas	3292.69	14766.77	27089.25	35904.43	38923.93	39286.68
乡村	Rural Areas	1028.04	2224.62	3237.50	4303.42	5263.78	5596.24
批发零售业商品销售总额（亿元）	**Total Sales in Wholesale and Retail Trades (100 million yuan)**	**10316.88**	**47217.39**	**89778.91**	**136273.02**	**164806.14**	**170838.19**
按行业分	By Sector						
批发业销售额	Sales in Wholesale Trade	7053.14	30173.58	69695.48	108583.11	133290.44	138063.20
零售业销售额	Sales in Retail Trade	3263.74	17043.81	20083.43	27689.90	31515.70	32775.00
按规模分	By Size						
限额以上销售额	Sales above Designated Size	4922.10	30316.84	66166.10	105031.21	133208.82	143519.85
限额以下销售额	Sales below Designated Size	5394.78	16900.55	23612.81	31241.80	31597.32	27318.34
限额以上连锁总店数（个）	**Number of General Chain Stores above Designated Size (unit)**		**206**	**386**	**399**	**416**	**415**
限额以上连锁门店数（个）	**Number of Branch Chain Stores above Designated Size (unit)**		**23096**	**25903**	**34501**	**35112**	**36927**
限额以上连锁店销售总额（亿元）	**Total Sales of Chain Stores above Designated Size (100 million yuan)**		**3502.08**	**5241.15**	**3451.16**	**3827.81**	**4015.93**
#零售额	Retail Value		2980.36	4420.51	2883.53	3002.13	2967.19
亿元以上商品交易市场成交额（亿元）	**Transaction Value of Commodity Markets above 100 Million Yuan (100 million yuan)**		**4828.13**	**5576.63**	**5368.52**	**5534.20**	**5174.43**

注：本表社会消费品零售总额及批发零售业商品销售总额数据根据第四次全国经济普查资料进行了调整。

Note: The data of total retail sales of consumer goods and total sales of wholesale and retail goods in this table are adjusted according to the figure of fourth national economic census.

16-2 按城乡分社会消费品零售总额

Total Retail Sales of Consumer Goods by Urban and Rural Area

单位：亿元 (100 million yuan)

年份 Year	社会消费品零售总额 Total Retail Sales of Consumer Goods	按城乡分 By Urban and Rural Area	
		城镇 Urban Areas	乡村 Rural Areas
1978	79.86	38.42	41.44
1979	92.69	43.25	49.44
1980	117.67	66.72	50.95
1981	142.38	71.19	71.19
1982	164.23	82.77	81.46
1983	183.62	97.32	86.30
1984	226.13	131.61	94.52
1985	289.23	178.45	110.78
1986	327.02	172.67	154.35
1987	405.19	214.34	190.85
1988	568.07	306.19	261.88
1989	636.15	345.43	290.72
1990	667.36	457.34	210.02
1991	786.64	531.57	255.07
1992	1109.55	809.96	299.59
1993	1515.73	1137.96	377.78
1994	1984.58	1511.22	473.36
1995	2465.76	1865.49	600.27
1996	2754.06	2093.87	660.19
1997	3112.79	2363.79	749.00
1998	3530.86	2689.95	840.91
1999	3885.99	2962.03	923.96
2000	4320.73	3292.69	1028.04
2001	4783.01	3641.78	1141.23
2002	5301.86	4048.11	1253.76
2003	5918.30	4544.02	1374.28
2004	6741.88	5201.17	1540.71
2005	7777.23	5997.87	1779.36
2006	9019.22	6950.06	2069.16
2007	10509.88	8107.94	2401.94
2008	12699.80	9809.61	2890.20
2009	14531.85	11328.71	3203.14
2010	16991.39	14766.77	2224.62
2011	19693.70	17201.99	2491.71
2012	21954.29	19479.27	2475.02
2013	24589.96	21917.34	2672.62
2014	27436.68	24486.93	2949.75
2015	30326.76	27089.25	3237.50
2016	33303.21	29759.18	3544.02
2017	36598.59	32708.58	3890.01
2018	39767.12	35543.82	4223.30
2019	42951.75	38314.75	4637.00
2020	40207.85	35904.43	4303.42
2021	44187.71	38923.93	5263.78
2022	44882.92	39286.68	5596.24

注：本表1992—2018年数据根据第四次全国经济普查资料进行了调整。
Note: Data of 1992 to 2018 in this table have been adjusted in accordance with the figures from the forth national economic census.

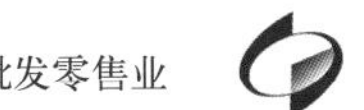

16-3 各市社会消费品零售总额（2022年）

Total Retail Sales of Consumer Goods by City (2022)

单位：亿元 (100 million yuan)

市 别	City	社会消费品零售总额 Total Retail Sales of Consumer Goods	按消费形态分 By Sector		按城乡分 By Urban and Rural Area	
			商品零售 Retail Sales	餐饮收入 Catering Income	城镇 Urban Area	乡村 Rural Area
广 州	Guangzhou	10298.15	9564.56	733.59	9960.69	337.46
深 圳	Shenzhen	9708.28	8744.59	963.69	9685.95	22.33
珠 海	Zhuhai	1044.67	960.03	84.65	1015.42	29.25
汕 头	Shantou	1485.03	1334.54	150.49	1073.51	411.52
佛 山	Foshan	3593.57	3345.13	248.44	3483.30	110.27
韶 关	Shaoguan	493.97	454.55	39.43	422.29	71.69
河 源	Heyuan	378.01	348.88	29.13	289.21	88.80
梅 州	Meizhou	656.82	597.42	59.40	493.50	163.32
惠 州	Huizhou	2040.52	1873.20	167.32	1634.46	406.06
汕 尾	Shanwei	475.53	415.71	59.82	344.24	131.29
东 莞	Dongguan	4254.87	3909.92	344.95	3840.49	414.38
中 山	Zhongshan	1593.42	1481.35	112.07	1454.16	139.26
江 门	Jiangmen	1309.05	1192.54	116.51	1017.13	291.92
阳 江	Yangjiang	495.63	442.97	52.67	382.86	112.77
湛 江	Zhanjiang	1826.63	1611.38	215.25	1477.28	349.35
茂 名	Maoming	1509.89	1324.21	185.68	1067.98	441.91
肇 庆	Zhaoqing	1117.07	1059.24	57.83	905.01	212.06
清 远	Qingyuan	581.16	553.44	27.72	480.39	100.76
潮 州	Chaozhou	487.08	449.55	37.53	401.44	85.64
揭 阳	Jieyang	1066.13	1022.81	43.32	763.34	302.80
云 浮	Yunfu	384.19	349.99	34.20	283.91	100.28
按经济区域分	By Region					
珠三角	Pearl River Delta	34959.60	32130.56	2829.05	32996.61	1963.00
东 翼	Eastern Region	3513.77	3222.61	291.16	2582.53	931.25
西 翼	Western Region	3832.16	3378.56	453.59	2928.12	904.04
山 区	Mountainous Region	2494.15	2304.27	189.88	1969.30	524.85

16-4 各市社会消费品零售总额

Total Retail Sales of Consumer Goods by City

单位：亿元 (100 million yuan)

市 别	City	2000	2005	2010	2015	2018	2019	2020	2021	2022
广 州	Guangzhou	1079.59	1765.01	3809.04	6994.42	8810.91	9551.57	9218.66	10122.56	10298.15
深 圳	Shenzhen	854.79	1757.85	3646.89	6419.78	8519.50	9144.46	8664.83	9498.12	9708.28
珠 海	Zhuhai	121.33	210.43	421.33	741.78	932.10	996.30	921.26	1048.24	1044.67
汕 头	Shantou	208.62	304.14	639.03	1101.82	1451.36	1562.73	1417.06	1503.84	1485.03
佛 山	Foshan	340.06	609.45	1470.02	2585.63	3425.44	3685.27	3289.09	3556.66	3593.57
韶 关	Shaoguan	75.98	111.72	219.10	359.20	439.64	477.55	445.25	488.16	493.97
河 源	Heyuan	38.91	74.41	153.54	271.31	356.93	386.83	360.74	387.62	378.01
梅 州	Meizhou	67.16	126.76	284.21	490.54	642.31	689.33	634.88	654.37	656.82
惠 州	Huizhou	143.35	291.29	652.02	1258.11	1769.13	1924.55	1746.08	1978.92	2040.52
汕 尾	Shanwei	60.56	98.42	219.60	339.09	407.21	442.26	435.65	477.30	475.53
东 莞	Dongguan	271.05	608.38	1456.27	2622.65	3637.37	4003.89	3740.14	4239.24	4254.87
中 山	Zhongshan	156.97	311.11	700.88	1206.61	1560.40	1617.09	1407.22	1530.11	1593.42
江 门	Jiangmen	191.38	301.36	542.35	854.97	1110.87	1206.96	1162.62	1278.10	1309.05
阳 江	Yangjiang	69.80	115.53	229.27	376.57	463.59	502.25	451.18	482.71	495.63
湛 江	Zhanjiang	174.57	289.73	657.45	1198.96	1575.26	1717.27	1638.76	1784.46	1826.63
茂 名	Maoming	134.85	241.37	554.67	1010.03	1324.07	1440.68	1356.48	1497.32	1509.89
肇 庆	Zhaoqing	86.31	162.25	362.34	727.62	1031.14	1107.52	1062.16	1160.82	1117.07
清 远	Qingyuan	67.35	105.37	265.04	420.67	529.78	573.94	520.09	579.62	581.16
潮 州	Chaozhou	58.70	93.58	201.06	345.92	450.89	490.84	444.88	480.70	487.08
揭 阳	Jieyang	80.38	131.34	365.23	751.47	994.32	1069.76	955.16	1055.76	1066.13
云 浮	Yunfu	39.05	67.75	142.08	249.62	334.87	360.69	337.24	375.50	384.19
按经济区域分	By Region									
珠 三 角	Pearl River Delta	3244.82	6017.12	13061.13	23411.58	30796.88	33237.60	31212.06	34412.76	34959.60
东 翼	Eastern Region	408.25	627.48	1424.92	2538.30	3303.78	3565.60	3252.74	3517.59	3513.77
西 翼	Western Region	379.22	646.63	1441.38	2585.55	3362.92	3660.20	3446.43	3764.49	3832.16
山 区	Mountainous Region	288.44	486.01	1063.96	1791.33	2303.53	2488.35	2298.21	2485.28	2494.15

注：本表数据根据第四次全国经济普查资料进行了调整。
Note: The data in this table have been adjusted in accordance with the figures from the forth national economic census.

16－5 批发零售业商品销售总额

Total Sales of Commodities in Wholesale and Retail Trades

单位：亿元 (100 million yuan)

项　目	Item	2010	2015	2020	2021	2022
合　计	**Total**	**47217.39**	**89778.91**	**136273.02**	**164806.14**	**170838.19**
按行业分组	By sector					
批发业	Wholesale Trade	30173.58	69695.48	108583.11	133290.44	138063.20
零售业	Retail Trade	17043.81	20083.43	27689.90	31515.70	32775.00
按规模分组	By Size of Enterprises					
限额以上企业和个体户	**Enterprises above Designated Size and Individuals**	**30316.84**	**66166.10**	**105031.21**	**133208.82**	**143519.85**
食品、饮料、烟酒类	Food, Beverages, Tobacco and Liquor	2635.17	7097.34	10080.56	11307.32	12541.48
粮油类	Grain and Edible Oil	366.51	1134.22	1700.26	1712.15	2031.89
肉禽蛋类	Meat, Poultry and Eggs	230.13	703.26	1207.09	1373.81	1787.91
饮料类	Beverages	192.76	1046.10	860.87	1079.32	1087.45
烟酒类	Tobacco and Liquor	1175.56	1939.10	2606.93	2847.79	2997.90
其它食品类	Other Food	670.21	2274.66	2706.72	3340.34	4636.34
服装鞋帽、针纺织品类	Garments,Footwear,Headgear,Knitwear and Textiles	1869.06	5244.01	2859.80	3600.19	3496.41
服装类	Garments	1133.19	3451.73	1695.49	2183.39	1918.92
鞋帽类	Footwear and Headgear	206.49	689.94	496.60	648.41	600.08
针、纺织品类	Knitwear and Textiles	529.38	1102.34	667.61	772.07	977.42
化妆品类	Cosmetics	138.83	401.67	860.15	796.74	790.04
金银珠宝类	Gold, Silver and Jewelry	221.13	1280.64	1006.14	1381.26	1401.30
日用品类	Daily-use Articles	762.55	2347.19	2595.20	2970.17	3142.29
#洗涤用品类	Detergents	232.11				
儿童玩具类	Toys for Children	32.61	96.89			
五金、电料类	Hardware and Electrical Appliances	266.24	761.81	1021.62	1250.84	1384.23
体育、娱乐用品类	Sports and Recreational Articles	153.92	168.46	317.44	451.05	409.42
书报杂志类	Newspapers and Magazines	77.67	161.28	198.35	191.57	205.74
电子出版物及音像制品类	E-journals and Video Products	23.12	29.96	13.76	17.32	10.20
家用电器和音像器材类	Household Appliances and Video Appliances	1221.85	2459.14	3223.93	3783.35	3673.59
中西药品类	Traditional Chinese and Western Medicines	1248.10	2957.35	4322.44	4958.16	5274.60
#西药	Western Medicines	848.37	1939.97	2941.52	3430.88	3762.64
中草药及中成药	Traditional Chinese Medicines	256.71	659.07	703.59	787.90	881.52
文化办公用品类	Articles for Cultural and Office Use	637.27	3586.88	2153.83	3192.55	3135.73
家具类	Furniture	189.07	542.19	624.02	765.24	726.42
通讯器材类	Communication Appliances	719.27	3176.14	4330.03	5599.90	5511.20
煤炭及制品类	Coal and Related Products	1144.17	1293.35	1707.50	2807.68	3015.13
木材及制品类	Timber and Related Products	60.20	163.68	493.07	743.07	818.39
石油及制品类	Petroleum and Related Products	7779.83	7792.01	10496.03	12347.91	14253.75
化工材料及制品类	Chemical Materials and Products	1566.66	3952.91	6582.43	8902.66	9663.72
金属材料类	Metal Materials	4380.16	8268.17	27657.15	37741.11	38508.14
建筑及装潢材料类	Construction and Decoration Materials	432.07	1171.45	3108.47	3811.46	3270.53
机电产品及设备类	Mechanical and Electrical Products and Equipment	1235.24	2888.60	5568.81	7584.80	8196.37
汽车类	Motor Vehicles	2773.14	6494.43	11260.63	12781.05	16680.58
种子饲料类	Seeds and Feedstuff	53.57	208.81	467.46	659.18	842.18
棉麻类	Cotton and Hemp	20.81	93.09	130.48	278.08	262.26
其它类	Others	707.74	3625.54	3951.91	5286.17	6306.15
限额以下企业和个体户	**Enterprises below Designated Size and Individuals**	**16900.55**	**23612.81**	**31241.80**	**31597.32**	**27318.34**

注：本表数据根据第四次全国经济普查资料进行了调整。

Note: The data in this table have been adjusted in accordance with the figures from the forth national economic census.

16-6 限额以上批发零售业商品批发额

Total Wholesale Value of Commodities in Wholesale and Retail Trades

单位：亿元 (100 million yuan)

项目	Item	2010	2015	2020	2021	2022
限额以上企业和个体户	**Enterprises above Designated Size and Individuals**	**24600.85**	**53553.50**	**91518.94**	**117680.13**	**126808.10**
食品、饮料、烟酒类	Food, Beverages, Tobacco and Liquor	2067.13	5863.76	8407.85	9444.53	10469.26
粮油类	Grain and Edible Oil	279.88	928.33	1451.73	1538.31	1836.05
肉禽蛋类	Meat, Poultry and Eggs	168.66	536.39	1029.53	1199.33	1562.08
饮料类	Beverages	134.29	907.60	669.50	820.44	806.60
烟酒类	Tobacco and Liquor	1065.75	1737.72	2338.65	2507.17	2639.84
其它食品类	Other Food	418.55	1753.72	2379.40	2534.95	3624.68
服装鞋帽、针纺织品类	Garments,Footwear,Headgear,Knitwear and Textiles	1385.88	3993.25	1934.23	2612.60	2641.46
服装类	Garments	786.06	2606.88	1039.20	1462.88	1301.90
鞋帽类	Footwear and Headgear	117.36	415.44	310.69	465.54	439.41
针、纺织品类	Knitwear and Textiles	482.46	970.93	584.25	687.87	900.15
化妆品类	Cosmetics	56.22	228.49	518.48	432.74	420.13
金银珠宝类	Gold, Silver and Jewelry	151.49	1045.36	762.07	1025.64	1039.81
日用品类	Daily-use Articles	569.53	1760.89	1840.31	2134.73	2274.36
#洗涤用品类	Detergents	166.98				
儿童玩具类	Toys for Children	19.52	61.29			
五金、电料类	Hardware and Electrical Appliances	241.86	635.55	983.95	1216.88	1349.27
体育、娱乐用品类	Sports and Recreational Articles	131.35	97.62	202.97	279.94	257.63
书报杂志类	Newspapers and Magazines	50.89	109.76	129.95	117.79	126.87
电子出版物及音像制品类	E-journals and Video Products	16.38	14.56	11.60	15.94	8.50
家用电器和音像器材类	Household Appliances and Video Appliances	790.44	1742.73	2349.56	2851.61	2703.46
中西药品类	Traditional Chinese and Western Medicines	957.64	2349.21	3715.33	4231.42	4432.71
#西药	Western Medicines	651.83	1524.78	2519.92	2922.80	3158.77
中草药及中成药	Traditional Chinese Medicines	216.34	571.22	623.97	694.51	772.54
文化办公用品类	Articles for Cultural and Office Use	570.14	3229.34	1751.45	2651.04	2592.18
家具类	Furniture	156.89	392.91	465.80	606.45	567.23
通讯器材类	Communication Appliances	639.96	2731.33	3604.56	4698.99	4487.87
煤炭及制品类	Coal and Related Products	1137.75	1264.48	1707.50	2807.67	3015.13
木材及制品类	Timber and Related Products	60.20	163.68	493.07	743.07	818.39
石油及制品类	Petroleum and Related Products	6488.12	5822.76	8881.90	10266.37	11867.42
化工材料及制品类	Chemical Materials and Products	1566.66	3952.91	6582.43	8902.66	9663.72
金属材料类	Metal Materials	4380.16	8268.17	27657.15	37741.11	38508.14
建筑及装潢材料类	Construction and Decoration Materials	392.48	1021.24	3059.01	3744.73	3200.17
机电产品及设备类	Mechanical and Electrical Products and Equipment	1200.20	2741.70	5532.01	7536.06	8134.55
汽车类	Motor Vehicles	920.60	2720.82	6509.55	7551.10	10986.64
种子饲料类	Seeds and Feedstuff	53.57	208.81	467.46	659.18	842.18
棉麻类	Cotton and Hemp	20.81	92.93	130.48	278.08	262.26
其它类	Others	594.50	3101.24	3820.27	5129.81	6138.75

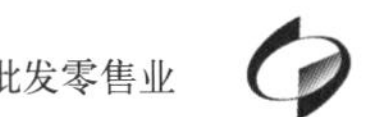

16-7 限额以上批发零售业商品零售额

Total Retail Value of Commodities in Wholesale and Retail Trades

单位：亿元 (100 million yuan)

项　目	Item	2010	2015	2020	2021	2022
限额以上企业和个体户	**Enterprises above Designated Size and Individuals**	**5715.99**	**12612.60**	**13512.27**	**15528.69**	**16711.75**
食品、饮料、烟酒类	Food, Beverages, Tobacco and Liquor	568.04	1233.58	1672.71	1862.79	2072.22
粮油类	Grain and Edible Oil	86.63	205.89	248.53	173.84	195.83
肉禽蛋类	Meat, Poultry and Eggs	61.47	166.87	177.56	174.48	225.82
饮料类	Beverages	58.47	138.50	191.37	258.88	280.85
烟酒类	Tobacco and Liquor	109.81	201.38	268.27	340.63	358.06
其它食品类	Other Food	251.66	520.94	327.32	805.39	1011.65
服装鞋帽、针纺织品类	Garments,Footwear,Headgear,Knitwear and Textiles	483.18	1250.76	925.57	987.59	854.95
服装类	Garments	347.13	844.85	656.29	720.51	617.02
鞋帽类	Footwear and Headgear	89.13	274.50	185.91	182.87	160.67
针、纺织品类	Knitwear and Textiles	46.92	131.41	83.37	84.20	77.27
化妆品类	Cosmetics	82.61	173.18	341.67	364.00	369.91
金银珠宝类	Gold, Silver and Jewelry	69.64	235.28	244.06	355.62	361.49
日用品类	Daily-use Articles	193.02	586.30	754.89	835.44	867.94
#洗涤用品类	Detergents	65.13				
儿童玩具类	Toys for Children	13.09	35.60			
五金、电料类	Hardware and Electrical Appliances	24.38	126.26	37.67	33.96	34.96
体育、娱乐用品类	Sports and Recreational Articles	22.57	70.84	114.47	171.11	151.79
书报杂志类	Newspapers and Magazines	26.78	51.52	68.39	73.77	78.87
电子出版物及音像制品类	E-journals and Video Products	6.74	15.40	2.16	1.39	1.69
家用电器和音像器材类	Household Appliances and Video Appliances	431.41	716.41	874.37	931.74	970.14
中西药品类	Traditional Chinese and Western Medicines	290.46	608.14	607.11	726.74	841.89
#西药	Western Medicines	196.54	415.19	421.60	508.08	603.87
中草药及中成药	Traditional Chinese Medicines	40.37	87.85	79.61	93.39	108.98
文化办公用品类	Articles for Cultural and Office Use	67.13	357.54	402.38	541.51	543.54
家具类	Furniture	32.18	149.28	158.22	158.79	159.19
通讯器材类	Communication Appliances	79.31	444.81	725.47	900.91	1023.34
煤炭及制品类	Coal and Related Products	6.42	28.87		0.01	
木材及制品类	Timber and Related Products					
石油及制品类	Petroleum and Related Products	1291.71	1969.25	1614.13	2081.54	2386.33
化工材料及制品类	Chemical Materials and Products					
金属材料类	Metal Materials					
建筑及装潢材料类	Construction and Decoration Materials	39.59	150.21	49.46	66.73	70.36
机电产品及设备类	Mechanical and Electrical Products and Equipment	35.04	146.90	36.80	48.74	61.82
汽车类	Motor Vehicles	1852.54	3773.61	4751.08	5229.94	5693.93
种子饲料类	Seeds and Feedstuff					
棉麻类	Cotton and Hemp		0.16	0.01		
其它类	Others	113.24	524.30	131.64	156.36	167.40

16-8 限额以上批发企业商品购、销、存总额（2022年）
Total Purchases, Sales and Inventory of Enterprises above Designated Size in Wholesale Trade (2022)

单位：亿元 (100 million yuan)

项　目	Item	企业单位数（个） Number of Enterprises (unit)	购进总额 Total Purchases	#进口 Imports	商品销售总额 Total Sales of Commodities
批发业合计	**Total Wholesale Trade**	**33171**	**117054.83**	**7182.43**	**121677.39**
#国有控股	State-owned and State-controlled Enterprises	967	31138.51	1323.01	31334.13
按登记注册类型分组	By Status of Registration				
内资企业	Domestic-funded Enterprises	31172	105337.23	5544.36	108777.83
国有企业	State-owned Enterprises	222	2938.64	95.35	3068.55
集体企业	Collective-owned Enterprises	27	22.99		24.00
股份合作企业	Share-holding Cooperative Enterprises	38	23.12	0.36	26.69
联营企业	Joint-operation Enterprises	7	38.15	0.08	38.42
国有联营企业	State-owned Joint-operation Enterprises	5	32.28	0.08	32.44
集体联营企业	Collective Joint-operation Enterprises	2	5.87		5.97
国有与集体联营企业	State-collective Joint-operation Enterprises				
其他联营企业	Other Joint-operation Enterprises				
有限责任公司	Limited Liability Corporations	4310	35574.72	1691.79	37137.21
国有独资企业	State Sole Investment Enterprises	150	3689.54	102.79	3888.71
其他有限责任公司	Other Limited Liability Companies	4160	31885.19	1589.00	33248.50
股份有限公司	Share-holding Corporations Ltd.	269	8087.43	85.31	7372.17
私营企业	Private Enterprises	26285	58635.86	3671.47	61091.86
私营独资企业	Private Sole Investment Enterprises	438	562.88	21.88	589.99
私营合伙企业	Private Partnership Enterprises	76	84.76	1.31	90.89
私营有限责任公司	Private Limited Liability Corporations	25547	57239.02	3569.56	59596.77
私营股份有限公司	Private Share-holding Corporations Ltd.	224	749.20	78.72	814.21
其他企业	Other Enterprises	14	16.31		18.94
港、澳、台商投资企业	Enterprises with Investment from Hong Kong, Macao and Taiwan	1259	6171.74	860.95	6971.36
合资经营企业	Joint Ventures	156	969.90	209.11	1021.93
合作经营企业	Cooperative Enterprises	8	93.00	0.01	94.02
独资经营企业	Sole Investment Enterprises	1034	4884.11	640.25	5587.02
投资股份有限公司	Share-holding Corporations Ltd.	27	86.68	1.85	123.21
其他港、澳、台商投资企业	Others	34	138.05	9.72	145.20
外商投资企业	Enterprises with Foreign Investment	740	5545.86	777.12	5928.20
中外合资经营企业	Sino-foreign Joint Ventures	121	2392.11	120.72	2582.20
中外合作经营企业	Sino-foreign Cooperative Enterprises	1	1.62		3.16
外资企业	Foreign-funded Enterprises	577	3033.79	652.90	3201.53
外商投资股份有限公司	Share-holding Corporations Ltd.	18	55.43	1.61	67.94
其他外商投资企业	Others	23	62.90	1.89	73.36
按国民经济行业分组	By Economic Sector				
农、林、牧、渔产品批发	Wholesale of Farm and Livestock Products	664	1808.82	174.10	1852.47
食品、饮料及烟草制品批发业	Wholesale of Food, Beverages and Tobacco Products	3411	8729.46	693.55	9695.13
#米、面制品及食用油批发业	Wholesale of Rice, Flour Products and Edible Oil	432	853.30	39.10	861.94
烟草制品批发业	Wholesale of Tobacco Products	42	1335.95	6.69	1821.96
纺织、服装及日用品批发业	Wholesale of Textiles, Garments and Daily-use Products	4241	6414.48	203.69	7171.29
#服装批发业	Wholesale of Garments	616	765.42	19.09	866.64
家用视听设备批发	Wholesale of Household Audio-visual Equipments	232	477.55	9.78	498.05
日用家电批发	Wholesale of Household Appliances	662	1673.00	28.35	1807.05
文化、体育用品及器材批发业	Wholesale of Cultural and Sports Articles and Appliances	1225	2944.95	60.65	3199.16
医药及医疗器材批发业	Wholesale of Medicines and Medical Appliances and Chemical Products	2095	4735.54	328.57	5259.76
矿产品、建材及化工产品批发	Wholesale of Mineral Products, Building Materials	12698	65150.31	2210.72	65602.48
#煤炭及制品批发业	Wholesale of Coal and Related Products	282	2819.89	218.11	2914.35
石油及制品批发业	Wholesale of Petroleum and Related Products	1015	11663.54	709.29	10817.63
金属及金属矿批发业	Wholesale of Metal and Related Products	4309	36889.01	704.62	37178.68
建材批发业	Wholesale of Building Materials	2427	4971.91	77.57	5415.30
化肥批发业	Wholesale of Chemical Fertilizers	96	205.76	8.79	216.57
机械设备、五金交电及电子产品批发业	Wholesale of Machinery, Hardware, Electric and Electronic Products	7725	22437.85	1980.11	23881.70
#汽车及零配件批发	Wholesale of Motor Vehicles and Parts	756	7319.98	75.33	7800.42
计算机、软件及辅助设备批发业	Wholesale of Computers, Software and Assistant Equipments	764	1909.57	162.10	1999.19
贸易经纪与代理	Trade Broker and Agency	309	2908.96	1365.35	2989.13
其他批发业	Other Wholesale Trades	803	1924.45	165.69	2026.26

16-8 续表 continued

单位：亿元 (100 million yuan)

项目	Item	批发额 Wholesale Trade	#出口 Exports	零售额 Retail Trade	年末库存总额 Inventory at the Year-end
批发业合计	**Total Wholesale Trade**	**120142.09**	**5312.67**	**1535.30**	**5569.74**
#国有控股	State-owned and State-controlled Enterprises	31010.22	708.72	323.91	1036.15
按登记注册类型分组	By Status of Registration				
内资企业	Domestic-funded Enterprises	107555.57	4726.64	1222.26	4864.99
国有企业	State-owned Enterprises	3040.66	62.48	27.89	197.56
集体企业	Collective-owned Enterprises	23.46	3.25	0.54	1.22
股份合作企业	Share-holding Cooperative Enterprises	24.84		1.86	3.24
联营企业	Joint-operation Enterprises	38.42	11.16	…	1.67
国有联营企业	State-owned Joint-operation Enterprises	32.44	11.16	…	1.66
集体联营企业	Collective Joint-operation Enterprises	5.97			0.01
国有与集体联营企业	State-collective Joint-operation Enterprises				
其他联营企业	Other Joint-operation Enterprises				
有限责任公司	Limited Liability Corporations	36809.16	1012.33	328.04	1220.08
国有独资企业	State Sole Investment Enterprises	3880.14	38.55	8.57	98.11
其他有限责任公司	Other Limited Liability Companies	32929.03	973.78	319.47	1121.97
股份有限公司	Share-holding Corporations Ltd.	7099.25	303.36	272.92	241.06
私营企业	Private Enterprises	60500.93	3334.06	590.93	3196.84
私营独资企业	Private Sole Investment Enterprises	584.56	26.77	5.43	37.80
私营合伙企业	Private Partnership Enterprises	87.19	1.71	3.70	6.69
私营有限责任公司	Private Limited Liability Corporations	59047.92	3272.41	548.85	3086.29
私营股份有限公司	Private Share-holding Corporations Ltd.	781.26	33.17	32.95	66.06
其他企业	Other Enterprises	18.85		0.08	3.32
港、澳、台商投资企业	Enterprises with Investment from Hong Kong, Macao and Taiwan	6837.80	162.57	133.56	462.79
合资经营企业	Joint Ventures	1010.81	44.71	11.12	76.86
合作经营企业	Cooperative Enterprises	93.13	1.22	0.89	0.84
独资经营企业	Sole Investment Enterprises	5473.90	104.19	113.11	363.85
投资股份有限公司	Share-holding Corporations Ltd.	121.81	1.17	1.40	12.44
其他港、澳、台商投资企业	Others	138.16	11.28	7.04	8.79
外商投资企业	Enterprises with Foreign Investment	5748.72	423.46	179.48	241.96
中外合资经营企业	Sino-foreign Joint Ventures	2426.37	59.82	155.83	37.42
中外合作经营企业	Sino-foreign Cooperative Enterprises	3.16			0.36
外资企业	Foreign-funded Enterprises	3180.29	361.57	21.24	192.62
外商投资股份有限公司	Share-holding Corporations Ltd.	65.75	1.10	2.18	8.45
其他外商投资企业	Others	73.14	0.97	0.22	3.12
按国民经济行业分组	By Economic Sector				
农、林、牧、渔产品批发	Wholesale of Farm and Livestock Products	1843.96	31.43	8.50	152.92
食品、饮料及烟草制品批发业	Wholesale of Food, Beverages and Tobacco Products	9579.43	246.60	115.69	719.72
#米、面制品及食用油批发业	Wholesale of Rice, Flour Products and Edible Oil	856.16	3.15	5.78	156.43
烟草制品批发业	Wholesale of Tobacco Products	1820.39	106.46	1.57	48.32
纺织、服装及日用品批发业	Wholesale of Textiles, Garments and Daily-use Products	6821.95	1578.62	349.34	528.00
#服装批发业	Wholesale of Garments	825.39	311.82	41.26	76.83
家用视听设备批发	Wholesale of Household Audio-visual Equipments	482.52	112.93	15.52	25.00
日用家电批发	Wholesale of Household Appliances	1706.13	291.22	100.92	119.95
文化、体育用品及器材批发业	Wholesale of Cultural and Sports Articles and Appliances	3035.37	120.77	163.79	389.27
医药及医疗器材批发业	Wholesale of Medicines and Medical Appliances and Chemical Products	5184.14	129.50	75.62	496.96
矿产品、建材及化工产品批发	Wholesale of Mineral Products, Building Materials	65084.15	609.39	518.33	1792.88
#煤炭及制品批发业	Wholesale of Coal and Related Products	2914.26	…	0.09	78.36
石油及制品批发业	Wholesale of Petroleum and Related Products	10391.72	130.31	425.91	367.13
金属及金属矿批发业	Wholesale of Metal and Related Products	37145.57	136.96	33.11	739.71
建材批发业	Wholesale of Building Materials	5377.76	187.31	37.55	260.04
化肥批发业	Wholesale of Chemical Fertilizers	215.73	2.75	0.84	19.66
机械设备、五金交电及电子产品批发业	Wholesale of Machinery, Hardware, Electric and Electronic Products	23600.79	2071.97	280.91	1354.28
#汽车及零配件批发	Wholesale of Motor Vehicles and Parts	7724.56	72.66	75.86	95.02
计算机、软件及辅助设备批发业	Wholesale of Computers, Software and Assistant Equipments	1951.26	230.44	47.93	137.93
贸易经纪与代理	Trade Broker and Agency	2984.43	348.60	4.70	55.62
其他批发业	Other Wholesale Trades	2007.85	175.79	18.41	80.09

16-9 限额以上零售企业商品购、销、存总额（2022年）
Total Purchases, Sales and Inventory of Enterprises above Designated Size in Retail Trade (2022)

单位：亿元 (100 million yuan)

项　目	Item	企业单位数(个) Number of Enterprises (unit)	购进总额 Total Purchases	#进口 Imports	商品销售总额 Total Sales of Commodities
零售业合计	**Total Retail Trade**	**8915**	**13594.84**	**375.68**	**16116.27**
#国有控股	State-owned and State-controlled Enterprises	543	1516.41	24.72	2584.78
按登记注册类型分组	By Status of Registration				
内资企业	Domestic-funded Enterprises	8408	10438.48	283.35	12357.58
国有企业	State-owned Enterprises	71	56.85	3.15	120.45
集体企业	Collective-owned Enterprises	87	42.81		50.29
股份合作企业	Share-holding Cooperative Enterprises	23	13.39		15.15
联营企业	Joint-operation Enterprises	26	16.92		19.98
国有联营企业	State-owned Joint-operation Enterprises	8	9.87		11.02
集体联营企业	Collective Joint-operation Enterprises	6	3.23		3.89
国有与集体联营企业	State-collective Joint-operation Enterprises	5	1.82		2.34
其他联营企业	Other Joint-operation Enterprises	7	2.00		2.73
有限责任公司	Limited Liability Corporations	1952	4334.52	131.64	4720.74
国有独资企业	State Sole Investment Enterprises	69	70.59	10.25	86.24
其他有限责任公司	Other Limited Liability Companies	1883	4263.94	121.39	4634.50
股份有限公司	Share-holding Corporations Ltd.	96	647.83	0.70	1465.33
私营企业	Private Enterprises	6150	5325.53	147.86	5964.99
私营独资企业	Private Sole Investment Enterprises	409	118.86	4.50	137.77
私营合伙企业	Private Partnership Enterprises	48	22.72		25.57
私营有限责任公司	Private Limited Liability Corporations	5632	5038.51	143.36	5617.32
私营股份有限公司	Private Share-holding Corporations Ltd.	61	145.44	…	184.33
其他企业	Other Enterprises	3	0.63		0.65
港、澳、台商投资企业	Enterprises with Investment from Hong Kong, Macao and Taiwan	290	1631.45	55.45	1907.05
合资经营企业	Joint Ventures	50	356.33	12.47	438.84
合作经营企业	Cooperative Enterprises	17	20.31		24.93
独资经营企业	Sole Investment Enterprises	211	1219.47	40.10	1402.87
投资股份有限公司	Share-holding Corporations Ltd.	7	18.97	2.88	23.59
其他港澳台投资企业	Others	5	16.37		16.84
外商投资企业	Enterprises with Foreign Investment	217	1524.92	36.88	1851.64
中外合资经营企业	Sino-foreign Joint Ventures	47	485.88	3.51	672.95
中外合作经营企业	Sino-foreign Cooperative Enterprises	2	3.69		4.38
外资企业	Foreign-funded Enterprises	150	961.96	28.23	1109.30
外商投资股份有限公司	Share-holding Corporations Ltd.	7	5.15		6.56
其他外商投资企业	Other Foreign Enterprises	11	68.25	5.15	58.45
按国民经济行业分组	By Economic Sector				
综合零售业	Comprehensive Retail Trade	689	1612.12	0.72	1825.86
#百货零售	Retail of General Merchandise	311	748.18	0.42	873.98
超级市场零售	Retail in Supermarkets	308	734.66	0.14	799.88
食品、饮料及烟草制品专门零售业	Retail of Food, Beverages and Tobacco Products	548	330.34	5.39	456.41
纺织、服装及日用品专门零售业	Retail of Textiles, Garments and Daily-use Products	549	460.00	11.93	701.43
#服装零售	Retail of Garments	263	187.68	5.38	301.06
文化、体育用品及器材专门零售业	Retail of Cultural and Sports Articles and Appliances	399	231.43	0.20	314.07
#体育用品及器材零售	Retail of Sports Articles and Appliances	21	7.62		11.36
图书、报刊零售	Retail of Books	163	54.64		65.14
医药及医疗器材专门零售业	Retail of Medicines and Medical Appliances	418	406.88	0.85	506.77
#西药零售	Retail of Western Medicines	334	380.54	0.64	471.19
中药零售	Retail of Traditional Chinese Medicines	52	19.38		24.16
汽车、摩托车、燃料及零配件零售业	Retail of Motor Vehicles, Motorcycles and Parts	3929	6440.95	322.65	7718.36
#汽车新车零售	Retail of Motor Vehicles	2662	5217.62	316.87	5455.40
机动车燃油零售	Retail of Motor Vehicle Fuels	993	1089.27	1.26	2118.12
家用电器及电子产品专门零售业	Retail of Household Appliances and Electronic Products	928	664.07	2.03	718.04
#家用视听设备零售	Retail of Household Audio-visual Equipments	33	26.79	1.78	26.60
日用家电零售	Retail of Household Appliances	402	320.31	0.01	349.43
计算机、软件及辅助设备零售业	Retail of Computers, Software and Assistant Equipments	237	81.06	0.09	87.71
通讯设备零售	Retail of Communication Equipments	175	208.64		223.33
五金、家具及室内装修材料专门零售业	Retail of Hardware, Furniture and Interior Decoration Materials	397	127.11	3.30	159.24
货摊、无店铺及其他零售业	Stall,Non-shop and Other Retails	1058	3321.94	28.61	3716.10

16-9 续表 continued

单位：亿元 (100 million yuan)

项　目	Item	批发额 Wholesale Trade	#出口 Exports	零售额 Retail Trade	年末库存总额 Inventory at the Year-end
零售业合计	**Total Retail Trade**	**1756.69**	**12.16**	**14359.58**	**1124.65**
#国有控股	State-owned and State-controlled Enterprises	673.20	0.07	1911.58	133.83
按登记注册类型分组	By Status of Registration				
内资企业	Domestic-funded Enterprises	1292.02	11.80	11065.56	887.57
国有企业	State-owned Enterprises	37.15	0.07	83.29	9.58
集体企业	Collective-owned Enterprises	2.37		47.92	2.09
股份合作企业	Share-holding Cooperative Enterprises	5.81		9.34	0.80
联营企业	Joint-operation Enterprises	0.99		19.00	1.13
国有联营企业	State-owned Joint-operation Enterprises	0.32		10.69	0.97
集体联营企业	Collective Joint-operation Enterprises	0.55		3.34	0.05
国有与集体联营企业	State-collective Joint-operation Enterprises			2.34	0.06
其他联营企业	Other Joint-operation Enterprises	0.11		2.62	0.05
有限责任公司	Limited Liability Corporations	327.05	0.55	4393.69	285.07
国有独资企业	State Sole Investment Enterprises	10.18		76.06	17.11
其他有限责任公司	Other Limited Liability Companies	316.88	0.55	4317.62	267.96
股份有限公司	Share-holding Corporations Ltd.	360.75		1104.58	39.19
私营企业	Private Enterprises	557.75	11.17	5407.24	549.67
私营独资企业	Private Sole Investment Enterprises	9.03		128.74	6.07
私营合伙企业	Private Partnership Enterprises	1.14		24.43	3.33
私营有限责任公司	Private Limited Liability Corporations	512.69	10.86	5104.63	526.97
私营股份有限公司	Private Share-holding Corporations Ltd.	34.90	0.32	149.44	13.31
其他企业	Other Enterprises	0.15		0.51	0.04
港、澳、台商投资企业	Enterprises with Investment from Hong Kong, Macao and Taiwan	167.89	0.29	1739.16	127.73
合资经营企业	Joint Ventures	50.14	0.09	388.70	28.37
合作经营企业	Cooperative Enterprises	0.11		24.82	0.92
独资经营企业	Sole Investment Enterprises	116.97	0.20	1285.90	96.57
投资股份有限公司	Share-holding Corporations Ltd.	0.28		23.30	1.04
其他港澳台投资企业	Others	0.39		16.44	0.82
外商投资企业	Enterprises with Foreign Investment	296.78	0.07	1554.87	109.35
中外合资经营企业	Sino-foreign Joint Ventures	226.06	0.06	446.89	36.13
中外合作经营企业	Sino-foreign Cooperative Enterprises			4.38	0.34
外资企业	Foreign-funded Enterprises	70.63	0.01	1038.67	70.11
外商投资股份有限公司	Share-holding Corporations Ltd.	0.02		6.54	0.55
其他外商投资企业	Other Foreign Enterprises	0.07		58.38	2.21
按国民经济行业分组	By Economic Sector				
综合零售业	Comprehensive Retail Trade	263.49	0.57	1562.37	133.61
#百货零售	Retail of General Merchandise	27.15	0.57	846.83	53.90
超级市场零售	Retail in Supermarkets	229.43		570.45	66.59
食品、饮料及烟草制品专门零售业	Retail of Food, Beverages and Tobacco Products	109.37	0.11	347.04	40.33
纺织、服装及日用品专门零售业	Retail of Textiles, Garments and Daily-use Products	120.39	1.83	581.04	133.39
#服装零售	Retail of Garments	44.45	1.19	256.61	67.82
文化、体育用品及器材专门零售业	Retail of Cultural and Sports Articles and Appliances	64.67	2.08	249.41	82.80
#体育用品及器材零售	Retail of Sports Articles and Appliances	0.38		10.98	1.38
图书零售	Retail of Books	12.29		52.84	13.37
医药及医疗器材专门零售业	Retail of Medicines and Medical Appliances	69.42		437.34	64.12
#西药零售	Retail of Western Medicines	62.78		408.41	57.21
中药零售	Retail of Traditional Chinese Medicines	2.04		22.12	5.54
汽车、摩托车、燃料及零配件零售业	Retail of Motor Vehicles, Motorcycles and Parts	714.45	0.01	7003.91	445.74
#汽车新车零售	Retail of Motor Vehicles	232.58	0.01	5222.82	389.19
机动车燃油零售	Retail of Motor Vehicle Fuels	468.83		1649.28	36.40
家用电器及电子产品专门零售业	Retail of Household Appliances and Electronic Products	118.34	0.27	599.69	67.63
#家用视听设备零售	Retail of Household Audio-visual Equipments	2.18		24.43	3.40
日用家电零售	Retail of Household Appliances	30.62	0.12	318.80	28.98
计算机、软件及辅助设备零售业	Retail of Computers, Software and Assistant Equipments	9.31		78.40	6.05
通讯设备零售	Retail of Communication Equipments	64.13		159.20	26.78
五金、家具及室内装修材料专门零售业	Retail of Hardware, Furniture and Interior Decoration Materials	30.13	0.70	129.11	20.29
货摊、无店铺及其他零售业	Stall,Non-shop and Other Retails	266.43	6.60	3449.67	136.74

16-10 各市限额以上批发零售企业商品购、销、存总额（2022年）

Total Purchases, Sales and Inventory of Enterprises above Designated Size in Wholesale and Retail Trades by City (2022)

单位：万元 (10000 yuan)

市别	City	商品购进总额 Total Purchases	#进口 Imports	商品销售总额 Total Sales	批发额 Wholesale Trade	#出口 Exports	零售额 Retail Trade	年末库存总额 Inventory at the Year-end
合计	**Total**	**1306496766**	**75581049**	**1377936642**	**1218987801**	**53248322**	**158948841**	**66943931**
批发业	**Wholesale Trade**	**1170548319**	**71824282**	**1216773897**	**1201420896**	**53126746**	**15353001**	**55697428**
广州	Guangzhou	476765986	17221754	486416566	480257417	9706185	6159149	19240247
深圳	Shenzhen	346657965	39006003	362881777	359020413	17737648	3861364	21095487
珠海	Zhuhai	48073577	5735407	50251011	49758080	4653713	492932	1601516
汕头	Shantou	16854647	878195	17709109	17534770	443483	174339	1093696
佛山	Foshan	134418695	2385083	139919482	138244576	5792050	1674906	4946850
韶关	Shaoguan	5259878	73340	6265556	5932047	5089	333509	210211
河源	Heyuan	751756	9245	935333	922887	69099	12445	64473
梅州	Meizhou	1792855	3111	2063717	2045213	6217	18504	98478
惠州	Huizhou	10344995	173038	11355772	10622961	269903	732812	420426
汕尾	Shanwei	788627		974431	969292	3244	5139	41957
东莞	Dongguan	57759864	2688520	61317364	60781618	5897829	535746	3266326
中山	Zhongshan	14728938	432494	15705671	15518667	3866197	187004	893031
江门	Jiangmen	11138223	617312	12053521	11852891	2724538	200630	588787
阳江	Yangjiang	1655799	10491	1946519	1930377	444322	16142	99328
湛江	Zhanjiang	8640560	510171	9146407	9011227	205267	135180	569284
茂名	Maoming	17028405	909065	17641096	17567169	13613	73927	460612
肇庆	Zhaoqing	5186612	491191	5483089	5476079	187531	7010	244269
清远	Qingyuan	4510069	387488	5417026	4864650	58113	552377	259981
潮州	Chaozhou	1176889	20193	1391532	1305126	34756	86406	65748
揭阳	Jieyang	5566664	121051	6267694	6185869	1007951	81825	383137
云浮	Yunfu	1447314	151132	1631225	1619566		11659	53585
零售业	**Retail Trade**	**135948446**	**3756767**	**161162745**	**17566905**	**121576**	**143595840**	**11246503**
广州	Guangzhou	44585774	914642	51993846	5281725	24164	46712121	2965159
深圳	Shenzhen	37378409	1231114	42260874	5951391	86310	36309484	4121933
珠海	Zhuhai	3518257	24508	4375761	271379	917	4104382	313746
汕头	Shantou	2622861	139657	2878400	263974	3936	2614426	199962
佛山	Foshan	8318024	253352	9150488	553845	3373	8596644	710067
韶关	Shaoguan	763920	16751	859718	30326		829392	90948
河源	Heyuan	1170699	32772	1211300	168767		1042533	72662
梅州	Meizhou	823252	20432	1243979	143521		1100458	78711
惠州	Huizhou	3973390	190968	5690868	656272		5034596	382684
汕尾	Shanwei	390277	6159	576153	65396		510758	36593
东莞	Dongguan	13035655	675463	15369349	609696	869	14759653	900778
中山	Zhongshan	4523590	118612	5979458	962150	1053	5017308	339694
江门	Jiangmen	3027599	3357	4051144	451772		3599372	253220
阳江	Yangjiang	767190	86	1212445	189562		1022883	67788
湛江	Zhanjiang	1549870	37840	2435993	412531		2023462	133696
茂名	Maoming	1490223	31041	2399221	633426		1765795	151619
肇庆	Zhaoqing	3812236	17924	4640484	556984		4083500	138505
清远	Qingyuan	924608	1577	1077077	71745		1005332	73454
潮州	Chaozhou	524103	18580	559411	43859		515552	46617
揭阳	Jieyang	1990055	3027	2350652	168610	953	2182042	81039
云浮	Yunfu	758455	18904	846123	79975		766148	87628

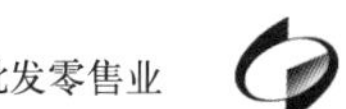

16-11 限额以上连锁批发零售业经营情况（2022年）

Business of Chain Stores above Designated Size in Wholesale and Retail Trade (2022)

项　目	Item	连锁总店数(个) Number of General Chain Stores (unit)	销售总额(万元) Total Sales Revenue (10000 yuan)	#零售额(万元) Retail Sales (10000 yuan)	营业面积(平方米) Operational Area (sq.m)
批发零售业合计	**Wholesale and Retail Trade**	**311**	**36281269**	**25924904**	**15933331**
按注册登记类型分	By Status of Registration				
内资企业	Domestic-funded Enterprises	262	24487916	18058735	7360777
国有企业	State-owned Enterprises	8	1715148	672549	348718
集体企业	Collective-owned Enterprises	1	37012	37012	4024
股份合作企业	Share-holding Cooperative Enterprises	1	19458	5723	7124
联营企业	Joint-operation Enterprises	1	82772	82772	16986
有限责任公司	Limited Liability Corporations	126	7986140	6616556	2838962
股份有限公司	Share-holding Corporations Ltd.	30	12741718	8953210	2838850
私营企业	Private Enterprises	95	1905670	1690915	1306113
其他企业	Other Enterprises				
港、澳、台商投资企业	Enterprises with Investment from Hong Kong, Macao and Taiwan	28	5813610	3649636	5757314
合资经营企业(港或澳、台资)	Joint Ventures	4	2223892	2073093	5178265
合作经营企业(港或澳、台资)	Cooperative Enterprises	2	41907	41907	6646
港、澳、台商独资经营企业	Sole Investment Enterprises	21	3516490	1513338	549540
港、澳、台商投资股份有限公司	Share-holding Corporations Ltd.	1	31321	21298	22863
外商投资企业	Enterprises with Foreign Investment	21	5979742	4216533	2815240
中外合资经营企业	Sino-foreign Joint Ventures	7	1416646	1252484	818873
中外合作经营企业	Sino-foreign Cooperative Enterprises	4	774325	492459	779467
外资企业	Foreign-funded Enterprises	9	3756672	2439491	1209750
其他外商投资	Others	1	32099	32099	7150
按零售业态分	By Type of Operation				
便利店	Convenience Store	7	748788	707926	154120
超市	Supermarket	42	3949913	2324391	2489884
百货商店	Department Store	17	5472239	4970783	7600519
专业店	Specialty Store	82	18048048	13029519	3596978
专卖店	Franchised Store	109	4391585	3131944	1573488
其他	Others	27	3371258	1570293	381259

16-11 续表 continued

项　　目	Item	从业人数(人) Number of Employed Persons (person)	连锁门店数(个) Number of Branch Chain Stores (unit)	直营店(个) Under Direct Management (unit)	加盟店(个) Through License Arrangement (unit)
批发零售业合计	**Retail Trade**	**181589**	**28943**	**22069**	**6874**
按注册登记类型分	By Status of Registration				
内资企业	Domestic-funded Enterprises	110819	22112	16316	5796
国有企业	State-owned Enterprises	2489	469	447	22
集体企业	Collective-owned Enterprises	250	6	6	
股份合作企业	Share-holding Cooperative Enterprises	154	29	29	
联营企业	Joint-operation Enterprises	660	214	149	65
有限责任公司	Limited Liability Corporations	55125	11551	9125	2426
股份有限公司	Share-holding Corporations Ltd.	23193	4033	3346	687
私营企业	Private Enterprises	28948	5810	3214	2596
其他企业	Other Enterprises				
港、澳、台商投资企业	Enterprises with Investment from Hong Kong, Macao and Taiwan	35457	4989	4337	652
合资经营企业(港或澳、台资)	Joint Ventures	17154	2273	1696	577
合作经营企业(港或澳、台资)	Cooperative Enterprises	155	6	6	
港、澳、台商独资经营企业	Sole Investment Enterprises	17532	2545	2536	9
港、澳、台商投资股份有限公司	Share-holding Corporations Ltd.	616	165	99	66
外商投资企业	Enterprises with Foreign Investment	35313	1842	1416	426
中外合资经营企业	Sino-foreign Joint Ventures	11246	782	613	169
中外合作经营企业	Sino-foreign Cooperative Enterprises	6563	468	422	46
外资企业	Foreign-funded Enterprises	17414	482	271	211
其他外商投资	Others	90	110	110	
按零售业态分	By Type of Operation				
便利店	Convenience Store	7466	2314	1232	1082
超市	Supermarket	28797	1576	1365	211
百货商店	Department Store	31662	896	844	52
专业店	Specialty Store	46623	7740	6889	851
专卖店	Franchised Store	42709	8094	7032	1062
其他	Others	20925	7299	3920	3379

16-12 亿元以上商品交易市场成交额

Turnover of Commodity Exchange Markets with Transaction Value over 100 Million Yuan

单位：亿元 (100 million yuan)

项　目	Item	2005	2010	2015	2019
合　计	**Total**	**1948.95**	**4828.13**	**5576.63**	**5495.80**
食品、饮料、烟酒类	Food, Beverages, Tobacco and Liquor	853.12	1591.87	1933.27	2199.17
#粮油类	Grain and Edible Oil	136.45	192.61	172.99	161.00
服装鞋帽、针、纺织品类	Garments,Footwear,Headgear,Knitwear and Textiles	457.60	1028.01	1294.61	1397.50
化妆品类	Cosmetics	8.18	15.69	18.67	16.49
金银珠宝类	Gold, Silver and Jewelry	1.14	47.17	21.98	66.97
日用品类	Daily-use Articles	42.93	209.48	197.15	151.52
五金、电料类	Hardware and Electrical Appliances	19.07	121.51	191.98	184.42
体育、娱乐用品类	Sports and Recreational Articles	5.09	7.44	10.09	10.97
书报杂志类	Newspapers and Magazines	2.37	4.75	2.64	1.91
电子出版物及音像制品类	E-journals and Video Products	2.22	5.84	11.52	0.78
家用电器和音像器材类	Household Appliances and Video Appliances	15.20	33.88	19.31	19.56
中西药品类	Traditional Chinese and Western Medicines	13.24	12.49	16.39	21.80
#中草药及中成药类	Chinese Herbal Medicines and Chinese Patent Medicines	12.52	11.76	13.49	17.91
文化办公用品类	Articles for Cultural and Office Use	62.63	66.35	57.66	20.83
家具类	Furniture	3.03	9.05	8.28	19.63
通讯器材类	Communication Appliances	2.24	52.00	38.80	12.45
煤炭及制品类	Coal and Related Products			0.17	
木材及制品类	Timber and Related Products	34.84	45.27	70.78	74.92
化工材料及制品类	Chemical Materials and Products	5.11	388.17	431.15	338.20
金属材料类	Metal Materials	82.11	485.52	418.28	164.79
建筑及装潢材料类	Construction and Decoration Materials	43.93	73.64	110.99	159.53
机电产品及设备类	Mechanical and Electrical Products and Equipments	17.68	28.11	47.40	51.01
汽车类	Motor Vehicles	175.68	531.59	555.89	491.76
种子饲料类	Seeds and Feedstuff		0.07	0.08	0.09
其他类	Others	101.54	70.23	119.54	91.49

16-12 续表 continued

单位：亿元 (100 million yuan)

项目	Item	2020	2021	2022
合 计	**Total**	**5368.52**	**5534.20**	**5174.19**
食品、饮料、烟酒类	Food, Beverages, Tobacco and Liquor	2151.80	2230.54	2327.72
#粮油类	Grain and Edible Oil	149.86	157.87	159.89
服装鞋帽、针、纺织品类	Garments,Footwear,Headgear, Knitwear and Textiles	1415.27	1439.38	1215.22
化妆品类	Cosmetics	11.95	13.90	11.48
金银珠宝类	Gold, Silver and Jewelry	57.19	35.25	29.23
日用品类	Daily-use Articles	139.52	163.63	160.34
五金、电料类	Hardware and Electrical Appliances	142.61	143.90	125.50
体育、娱乐用品类	Sports and Recreational Articles	7.11	6.43	3.69
书报杂志类	Newspapers and Magazines	1.21	1.32	1.81
电子出版物及音像制品类	E-journals and Video Products	0.42	0.42	0.49
家用电器和音像器材类	Household Appliances and Video Appliances	13.20	9.01	6.81
中西药品类	Traditional Chinese and Western Medicines	24.52	21.08	20.66
#中草药及中成药类	Chinese Herbal Medicines and Chinese Patent Medicines	20.77	20.42	19.94
文化办公用品类	Articles for Cultural and Office Use	17.32	13.38	13.98
家具类	Furniture	17.24	13.60	26.90
通讯器材类	Communication Appliances	9.96	9.66	9.60
煤炭及制品类	Coal and Related Products			
木材及制品类	Timber and Related Products	67.09	31.10	29.33
化工材料及制品类	Chemical Materials and Products	390.92	409.25	348.36
金属材料类	Metal Materials	163.96	159.23	82.00
建筑及装潢材料类	Construction and Decoration Materials	139.17	144.95	139.37
机电产品及设备类	Mechanical and Electrical Products and Equipments	45.15	48.28	50.99
汽车类	Motor Vehicles	463.52	489.38	416.33
种子饲料类	Seeds and Feedstuff	0.14	0.15	0.27
其他类	Others	89.25	150.36	154.13

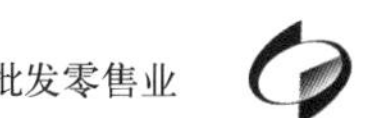

16-13 限额以上批发零售企业财务状况（2022年）

Financial Indicators of Enterprises above Designated Size in Wholesale and Retail Trades Services (2022)

单位：万元 (10000 yuan)

项　目	Item	批发零售业合计 Wholesale and Retail Trades	批发业 Wholesale Trade	零售业 Retail Trade
企业数 (个)	Number of Enterprises (unit)	42138	33214	8924
年初存货	Inventory at the Year-beginning	57202170	46789750	10412420
流动资产合计	Circulating Assets	465178203	407435226	57742976
#存货	Inventory	66290280	54827351	11462929
固定资产原价	Original Value of Fixed Assets	29632271	19625155	10007116
累计折旧	Accumulated Depreciation	13104922	8501433	4603489
#本年折旧	Depreciation Drawn in Current Year	1958757	1252709	706048
资产合计	Total Assets	590283781	511144870	79138911
负债合计	Total Liabilities	435587581	383119757	52467824
所有者权益合计	Total Creditors' Equity	154694642	127998553	26696088
实收资本	Paid-up Capital	77594595	63266526	14328069
#个人资本	Personal Capital	8731107	7108524	1622583
营业收入	Business Revenue	1249241522	1101355355	147886167
#主营业务收入	Main Business Revenue	1239224439	1095281818	143942620
营业成本	Business Costs	1171919618	1044439457	127480161
营业税金及附加	Tax and Extra Charges on Business	3713749	3169967	543782
其它业务利润	Profits from Other Businesses	2710455	1465988	1244467
销售费用	Marketing Expenses	38963284	24671262	14292022
管理费用	Management Expenses	18592959	13961679	4631280
财务费用	Financial Expenses	3282306	2643952	638354
#利息支出	Interests	3217236	2892731	324505
营业利润	Business Profits	18184986	17411921	773065
营业外收入	Non-operating Revenue	1259812	927353	332459
利润总额	Total Profits	18759119	17811427	947691
应交所得税	Income Taxes Payable	3644474	3024730	619744
本年应付职工薪酬	Total Wages Payable in Current Year	20579296	14291206	6288090
本年应交增值税	Value-added Tax Payable in Current Year	8167850	6352052	1815798

16-14 限额以上批发企业财务状况（2022年）

单位：万元

项 目	Item	企业数（个）Number of Enterprises	年初库存 Beginning Inventory	流动资产合计 Circulating Assets
批发业合计	**Total Wholesale Trade**	**33214**	**46789750**	**407435226**
#国有及国有控股	State-owned and State-controlled Enterprises	1196	11425305	83872110
按登记注册类型分	By Status of Registration			
内资企业	Domestic-funded Enterprises	31209	40115307	351838392
国有企业	State-owned Enterprises	225	1394393	9168245
集体企业	Collective-owned Enterprises	27	19347	90247
股份合作企业	Share-holding Cooperative Enterprises	38	30174	128622
联营企业	Joint-operation Enterprises	7	10798	162247
国有联营企业	State-owned Joint-operation Enterprises	5	8940	152967
集体联营企业	Collective Joint-operation Enterprises	2	1858	9280
国有与集体联营企业	State-collective Joint-operation Enterprises			
其他联营企业	Other Joint-operation Enterprises			
有限责任公司	Limited Liability Corporations	4316	11107930	120159812
国有独资企业	State Sole Investment Enterprises	150	933624	10239887
其他有限责任公司	Other Limited Liability Companies	4166	10174306	109919925
股份有限公司	Share-holding Corporations Ltd.	270	3331157	25268684
私营企业	Private Enterprises	26312	24197861	196765725
私营独资企业	Private Sole Investment Enterprises	438	328856	1851438
私营合伙企业	Private Partnership Enterprises	76	40016	282195
私营有限责任公司	Private Limited Liability Corporations	25573	23213362	188822754
私营股份有限公司	Private Share-holding Corporations Ltd.	225	615628	5809338
其他企业	Other Enterprises	14	23647	94811
港、澳、台商投资企业	Enterprises with Investment from Hong Kong, Macao and Taiwan	1263	4612902	33261717
合资经营企业	Joint Ventures	156	791839	4130884
合作经营企业	Cooperative Enterprises	8	11128	388860
独资经营企业	Sole Investment Enterprises	1038	3531913	26594823
投资股份有限公司	Share-holding Corporations Ltd.	27	134163	1495454
其它港澳台商投资企业	Others	34	143860	651697
外商投资企业	Enterprises with Foreign Investment	742	2061541	22335118
中外合资经营企业	Sino-foreign Joint Ventures	123	331924	7886051
中外合作经营企业	Sino-foreign Cooperative Enterprises	1	1768	6133
外资企业	Foreign-funded Enterprises	577	1543159	12619374
外商投资股份有限公司	Share-holding Corporations Ltd.	18	133349	1148309
其它外商投资企业	Others	23	51342	675251
按国民经济行业分	By Economic Sector			
农林牧产品批发业	Wholesale of Farm and Livestock Products	665	1445958	7451757
食品、饮料及烟草制品批发业	Wholesale of Food, Beverages and Tobacco Products	3413	6109145	39367209
#米、面制品及食用油批发业	Wholesale of Rice, Flour Products and Edible Oil	433	1323746	6299723
烟草制品批发业	Wholesale of Tobacco Products	42	394352	3896296
纺织、服装及日用品批发业	Wholesale of Textiles, Garments and Daily-use Products	4249	5213349	35693818
#服装批发业	Wholesale of Garments	618	741889	4425148
家用视听设备批发	Wholesale of Household Audio-visual Equipments	232	216579	2454793
日用家电批发	Wholesale of Household Appliances	665	1342648	8837503
文化、体育用品及器材批发业	Wholesale of Cultural and Sports Articles and Appliances	1227	3478793	14084444
医药及医疗器材批发业	Wholesale of Medicines and Medical Appliances	2096	4352918	27045652
矿产品、建材及化工产品批发	Wholesale of Mineral Products, Building Materials and Chemical Products	12715	15888904	166759871
#煤炭及制品批发业	Wholesale of Coal and Related Products	282	608442	6098190
石油及制品批发业	Wholesale of Petroleum and Related Products	1018	3567538	22631173
金属及金属矿批发业	Wholesale of Metal and Related Products	4316	6151269	75772698
建材批发业	Wholesale of Building Materials	2429	2469750	39238232
化肥批发业	Wholesale of Chemical Fertilizers	96	178509	939591
机械设备、五金交电及电子产品批发业	Wholesale of Machinery, Hardware, Electric and Electronic Products	7733	9084472	96532877
汽车零配件批发业	Wholesale of Motor Vehicles and Parts	756	2028243	29573665
计算机、软件及辅助设备批发业	Wholesale of Computers, Software and Assistant Equipments	765	1030880	6075960
贸易经纪与代理	Trade Broker and Agency	312	516597	12202559
其他批发业	Other Wholesale Trades	804	699615	8297039

Financial Indicators of Enterprises above Designated Size in Wholesale Trade (2022)

(10000 yuan)

固定资产原价 Original Value of Fixed Assets	累计折旧 Accumulated Depreciation	本年折旧 Depreciation Drawn in Current Year	资产合计 Total Assets	负债合计 Total Liabilities	所有者权益合计 Total Creditors' Equity	实收资本 Paid-up Capital	营业收入 Business Revenue	主营业务收入 Main Business Revenue
19625155	**8501433**	**1252709**	**511144870**	**383119757**	**127998553**	**63266526**	**1101355355**	**1095281818**
9208703	4016907	413829	116784364	74764369	42019995	16520654	318680100	317321293
16747571	7156599	1045734	439696156	336508536	103160050	52261596	985666119	981051173
1029345	409730	37857	12166851	6870892	5295958	1599081	27481992	27411813
32811	26346	342	136768	89493	47276	12919	257086	254935
10898	6648	486	140319	90591	49728	18943	241141	236619
41943	12136	1474	224879	116219	108660	24186	326070	324870
41274	11626	1464	215165	107321	107844	23478	273016	271817
669	510	11	9714	8898	816	709	53054	53054
4629192	1738735	252477	145094144	112450464	32643567	18784133	332852199	331605656
385404	147196	18267	13214310	8922228	4292082	1888798	34411864	34355414
4243788	1591539	234210	131879835	103528237	28351485	16895334	298440335	297250242
4621008	2239952	236127	42748185	24447286	18300899	6441587	76425236	75652089
6375804	2720733	516120	239084878	192407438	46649982	25376115	547910130	545393284
35514	12181	3621	1947046	1747116	199930	121491	5360075	5345460
3130	1473	526	287430	247094	40336	19103	819484	818117
5774616	2487630	472184	225519588	185595784	39896347	23972007	534283479	531914352
562544	219450	39789	11330814	4817444	6513370	1263513	7447093	7315355
6572	2319	850	100133	36153	63980	4633	172265	171908
1428168	592206	88395	43964570	27125639	16840066	7442423	62848116	62147602
246716	104383	12029	4923566	3916229	1007337	473399	9258604	9164518
11631	6529	716	493755	369543	124212	65670	794745	792160
1093947	449603	70993	35882821	21414352	14469604	6594950	50355784	49759257
60260	24074	3620	1990068	1018198	971869	199821	1103244	1097176
15614	7618	1037	674361	407318	267043	108583	1335739	1334491
1449415	752628	118580	27484144	19485582	7998438	3562506	52841120	52083044
851125	419479	68588	9787926	6724741	3063061	1450864	21597820	21371647
38	3	2	6168	4366	1802	144	28504	28504
572012	319924	48545	15178677	11297799	3880878	1674095	29942055	29422473
21865	11409	828	1721740	732373	989367	253284	613090	608746
4376	1813	616	789634	726304	63331	184120	659651	651674
653181	178270	29438	11094353	6870058	4224294	2462325	17508016	17395121
2931357	1187481	172501	47347835	33043789	14305263	4869827	89487175	88168103
676732	168021	21598	7680494	5736277	1944216	902286	8212566	8121872
541175	287500	30943	4582212	844528	3737685	56350	16193683	16180765
1592023	656113	107463	42494615	32733219	9761988	8328080	66250339	65625543
333626	130305	21170	5479955	4289271	1190878	1981600	8010808	7957625
44714	14700	2830	3916188	2922648	993540	2581359	4635408	4566105
278214	97905	18984	9347697	8131631	1216066	542044	16593519	16520125
552108	269438	41705	15816894	10695373	5121521	2210049	28900384	28639572
1264573	545753	101908	32159762	22524785	9632926	3528518	47137956	46474081
9414875	4266107	515151	221325168	169816863	51506613	27489934	596571778	594874421
314921	44763	10005	8244953	6254369	1990584	1186750	25445834	25352872
5239620	2551431	268480	33588821	22065738	11523083	5064675	108966641	108064908
1889213	820760	100063	93628261	74795097	18833153	11510757	330216366	329885057
894914	317792	61662	47206153	36586952	10617400	5095701	48870881	48703132
27350	12452	1714	1058727	848603	210123	121724	1996877	1993822
2593710	1145299	241121	113236164	88513925	24721708	10377382	214559258	213246666
332780	152081	45039	32618458	30060565	2557924	2293113	69147821	68867470
187244	78860	14976	6952039	5354593	1597446	906223	18194165	18043728
319335	108790	13415	14579960	11564050	3015909	1079905	22427456	22378398
303993	144182	30009	13090120	7357693	5708331	2920507	18512993	18479914

16-14 续表

单位:万元

项　目	Item	营业成本 Business Costs	营业税金及附加 Tax and Extra Charges on Business	其他业务利润 Profits from Other Businesses
批发业合计	**Total Wholesale Trade**	**1044439457**	**3169967**	**1465988**
#国有及国有控股	State-owned and State-controlled Enterprises	302870698	2674950	144721
按登记注册类型分	By Status of Registration			
内资企业	Domestic-funded Enterprises	939682108	2953960	792420
国有企业	State-owned Enterprises	26020980	443015	23704
集体企业	Collective-owned Enterprises	239537	451	652
股份合作企业	Share-holding Cooperative Enterprises	219832	687	-793
联营企业	Joint-operation Enterprises	304426	1110	216
国有联营企业	State-owned Joint-operation Enterprises	253548	1088	216
集体联营企业	Collective Joint-operation Enterprises	50879	22	
国有与集体联营企业	State-collective Joint-operation Enterprises			
其他联营企业	Other Joint-operation Enterprises			
有限责任公司	Limited Liability Corporations	317267277	1821525	260954
国有独资企业	State Sole Investment Enterprises	33049114	280297	18075
其他有限责任公司	Other Limited Liability Companies	284218162	1541228	242880
股份有限公司	Share-holding Corporations Ltd.	72563141	94915	49326
私营企业	Private Enterprises	522922387	592119	458360
私营独资企业	Private Sole Investment Enterprises	5092090	8618	505
私营合伙企业	Private Partnership Enterprises	776491	868	82
私营有限责任公司	Private Limited Liability Corporations	510303136	570327	417884
私营股份有限公司	Private Share-holding Corporations Ltd.	6750670	12306	39889
其他企业	Other Enterprises	144528	138	
港、澳、台商投资企业	Enterprises with Investment from Hong Kong, Macao and Taiwan	56558538	138154	275685
合资经营企业	Joint Ventures	8750189	17722	14049
合作经营企业	Cooperative Enterprises	782610	532	1846
独资经营企业	Sole Investment Enterprises	45080054	112825	258533
投资股份有限公司	Share-holding Corporations Ltd.	773812	5136	1182
其它港澳台商投资企业	Others	1171873	1941	75
外商投资企业	Enterprises with Foreign Investment	48198811	77853	397883
中外合资经营企业	Sino-foreign Joint Ventures	19742094	35972	61797
中外合作经营企业	Sino-foreign Cooperative Enterprises	13122	96	
外资企业	Foreign-funded Enterprises	27299144	38621	331173
外商投资股份有限公司	Share-holding Corporations Ltd.	559678	1376	2849
其它外商投资企业	Others	584773	1788	2065
按国民经济行业分	By Economic Sector			
农林牧产品批发业	Wholesale of Farm and Livestock Products	16966932	13306	24767
食品、饮料及烟草制品批发业	Wholesale of Food, Beverages and Tobacco Products	78662004	2022498	442705
#米、面制品及食用油批发业	Wholesale of Rice, Flour Products and Edible Oil	7769530	9171	29015
烟草制品批发业	Wholesale of Tobacco Products	11894693	1923236	1795
纺织、服装及日用品批发业	Wholesale of Textiles, Garments and Daily-use Products	58403720	194480	265040
#服装批发业	Wholesale of Garments	6961649	21391	29504
家用视听设备批发	Wholesale of Household Audio-visual Equipments	4289184	5639	9404
日用家电批发	Wholesale of Household Appliances	15354985	17106	40480
文化、体育用品及器材批发业	Wholesale of Cultural and Sports Articles and Appliances	26774519	65855	19646
医药及医疗器材批发业	Wholesale of Medicines and Medical Appliances	41368931	109845	152437
矿产品、建材及化工产品批发	Wholesale of Mineral Products, Building Materials and Chemical Products	581404920	477846	263957
#煤炭及制品批发业	Wholesale of Coal and Related Products	24646734	29031	8290
石油及制品批发业	Wholesale of Petroleum and Related Products	105184567	97961	56984
金属及金属矿批发业	Wholesale of Metal and Related Products	326837882	182890	57005
建材批发业	Wholesale of Building Materials	45628279	74885	35057
化肥批发业	Wholesale of Chemical Fertilizers	1883933	1913	2538
机械设备、五金交电及电子产品批发业	Wholesale of Machinery, Hardware, Electric and Electronic Products	201548008	254543	276087
汽车零配件批发业	Wholesale of Motor Vehicles and Parts	65281525	79422	12819
计算机、软件及辅助设备批发业	Wholesale of Computers, Software and Assistant Equipments	17200754	19980	7063
贸易经纪与代理	Trade Broker and Agency	21737723	11659	6022
其他批发业	Other Wholesale Trades	17572701	19937	15327

16-14 continued

(10000 yuan)

销售费用 Marketing Expenses	管理费用 Manag-ement Expenses	财务费用 Financial Expenses	营业利润 Business Profits	营业外收入 Non-operating revenue	利润总额 Total Profits	应交所得税 Income Taxes Payable	本年应付职工薪酬 Staff Salary Payable in Current Year	本年应交增值税 Value-added Tax Payable in Current Year
24671262	**13961679**	**2643952**	**17411921**	**927353**	**17811427**	**3024730**	**14291206**	**6352052**
5020615	1972110	433397	6717579	221532	6840275	1490167	3397312	2017382
19377833	11282242	2593868	12703391	574921	12850117	2246809	11286810	5302115
253926	273678	9482	718291	50963	763268	162843	359499	206356
5511	9024	767	2077	3518	4974	901	8395	2482
9807	9300	1174	3058	615	3070	584	10439	2543
8669	6732	-1689	6141	1428	5696	1337	9691	402
7578	6571	-1704	5255	1334	4716	1337	9444	282
1090	161	15	886	94	980	…	247	120
6059037	2582521	941307	4945987	109316	4956687	1106815	3210226	1848597
364873	205085	48784	571341	23339	581103	98714	279740	172552
5694164	2377437	892523	4374646	85976	4375584	1008101	2930486	1676045
2094067	605340	258823	1164022	65609	1161992	182813	1370248	430660
10919354	7790266	1383937	5868338	343270	5958768	791515	6300377	2810817
123126	85256	9870	41564	2464	41117	6144	87621	38008
12261	17914	1383	10476	157	10597	413	10939	7368
10467088	7467325	1310427	5450541	332549	5540811	754002	5995293	2691711
316879	219771	62258	365757	8100	366243	30956	206524	73731
27462	5382	67	-4523	202	-4338	2	17935	259
3214690	1514824	29329	3012529	235803	3173485	361133	1833970	632617
210088	120895	34407	134694	153060	277776	29664	118973	99869
6527	8309	4574	20	89	-587	-1160	6165	909
2676597	1315406	-8170	2717208	79541	2737868	326190	1612540	484562
201149	49591	-5853	159129	1766	158055	4579	69235	37217
120330	20623	4371	1477	1348	375	1860	27057	10060
2078739	1164614	20755	1696001	116629	1787826	416789	1170426	417320
831531	176770	-11891	1132256	47099	1171521	255352	349048	185462
12172	739	-3	2381	2	2380	572	2292	827
1120860	877703	27391	629091	64354	680945	154682	781744	210073
46949	94554	3350	-60321	1741	-62777	1107	10491	8997
67228	14848	1908	-7405	3433	-4244	5076	26852	11962
205279	225989	74381	95422	49135	139411	32315	171015	36600
3839352	2502715	18001	3014744	273643	3212877	718489	2620959	1097855
259870	156621	61184	95298	34429	93970	22363	183985	46715
257643	530239	-89888	1709476	891	1706304	432671	648798	554458
4699359	2107887	200360	696396	94484	702300	242694	2250767	786007
522776	397204	35031	1903	22433	5329	35356	360363	94858
239810	102899	45046	61089	3143	63058	6188	149686	32253
801255	252402	16122	147005	14763	155188	23235	333658	158441
1059586	680689	43198	642702	39784	657525	76595	885296	244235
3023320	1427633	161755	1543250	32276	1531482	247282	1482477	721352
6097287	3303000	1649085	6125111	279122	6230308	797570	3299837	1873110
255001	116115	98613	316536	20699	330221	52799	74942	128570
1843146	449164	291096	1244280	107707	1288292	244698	912828	449490
943957	797653	891594	2042653	64701	2075072	138650	711574	455410
1462242	836097	249695	1417930	39529	1413479	171358	775122	379115
47093	33941	4197	27903	1443	28890	4093	30543	4874
5185389	3231773	348888	4468230	135236	4502180	824351	3183727	1428127
2117663	291959	-32275	1499717	11949	1486745	431678	383518	365776
306165	297584	34189	210570	14821	219957	32808	318563	126656
160255	175702	98724	282173	14016	291257	46198	125000	63889
401436	306292	49560	543891	9657	544089	39235	272130	100877

16-15 限额以上零售企业财务状况（2022年）

单位：万元

项　目	Item	企业数（个）Number of Enterprises (unit)	年初库存 Beginning Inventory	流动资产合计 Circulating Assets
零售业合计	**Total Retail Trade**	**8924**	**10412420**	**57742976**
#国有及国有控股	State-owned and State-controlled Enterprises	615	1527702	9808654
按登记注册类型分	By Status of Registration			
内资企业	Domestic-funded Enterprises	8417	8353289	45774704
国有企业	State-owned Enterprises	71	68234	456187
集体企业	Collective-owned Enterprises	87	24045	132488
股份合作企业	Share-holding Cooperative Enterprises	23	7049	32125
联营企业	Joint-operation Enterprises	26	7330	51514
国有联营企业	State-owned Joint-operation Enterprises	8	5265	26770
集体联营企业	Collective Joint-operation Enterprises	6	126	6181
国有与集体联营企业	State-collective Joint-operation Enterprises	5	1077	6222
其他联营企业	Other Joint-operation Enterprises	7	863	12341
有限责任公司	Limited Liability Corporations	1954	2766154	15074768
国有独资企业	State Sole Investment Enterprises	70	203309	947811
其他有限责任公司	Other Limited Liability Companies	1884	2562845	14126957
股份有限公司	Share-holding Corporations Ltd.	97	504555	6249891
私营企业	Private Enterprises	6156	4975562	23774701
私营独资企业	Private Sole Investment Enterprises	410	66211	299439
私营合伙企业	Private Partnership Enterprises	48	21719	88824
私营有限责任公司	Private Limited Liability Corporations	5637	4726779	22644458
私营股份有限公司	Private Share-holding Corporations Ltd.	61	160852	741981
其他企业	Other Enterprises	3	360	3031
港、澳、台商投资企业	Enterprises with Investment from Hong Kong, Macao and Taiwan	290	1096248	6009678
合资经营企业	Joint Ventures	50	258883	1749994
合作经营企业	Cooperative Enterprises	17	9390	85854
独资经营企业	Sole Investment Enterprises	211	806065	3837250
投资股份有限公司	Share-holding Corporations Ltd.	7	13154	273628
其他港澳台商投资企业	Others	5	8755	62953
外商投资企业	Enterprises with Foreign Investment	217	962883	5958594
中外合资经营企业	Sino-foreign Joint Ventures	47	321375	1898858
中外合作经营企业	Sino-foreign Cooperative Enterprises	2	2241	22594
外资企业	Foreign-funded Enterprises	150	617791	3737360
外商投资股份有限公司	Share-holding Corporations Ltd.	7	5149	75728
其它外商投资企业	Others	11	16327	224054
按国民经济行业分	By Economic Sector			
综合零售业	Comprehensive Retail	690	1276956	8606301
#百货零售业	Retail of General Merchandise	312	522125	5545684
超级市场零售业	Retail in Supermarkets	308	667191	2561834
食品、饮料及烟草制品专门零售业	Retail of Food, Beverages and Tobacco Products	549	416181	3399283
纺织、服装及日用品专门零售业	Retail of Textiles, Garments and Daily-use Products	550	1290586	3788472
#服装零售业	Retail of Garments	263	647821	2032755
文化、体育用品及器材专门零售业	Retail of Cultural and Sports Articles and Appliances	399	397387	2538590
#体育用品及器材零售	Retail of Sports Articles and Appliances	21	17836	46355
图书零售业	Retail of Books	163	128923	590069
医药及医疗器材专门零售业	Retail of Medicines and Medical Appliances	418	636147	2280405
#西药零售	Retail of Western Medicines	334	575292	2097440
中药零售	Retail of Traditional Chinese Medicines	52	45210	119306
汽车、摩托车、燃料及零配件专门零售业	Retail of Motor Vehicles, Motorcycles and Parts	3934	4654907	23350374
#汽车新车零售	Retail of Motor Vehicles	2665	3914637	16013116
机动车燃料零售业	Retail of Motor Vehicle Fuels	994	544524	6499924
家用电器及电子产品专门零售业	Retail of Household Appliances and Electronic Products	928	582418	4637684
#家用视听设备零售	Retail of Household Audio-visual Equipments	33	27282	167921
日用家电零售	Retail of Household Appliances	402	280668	2795720
计算机、软件及辅助设备零售业	Retail of Computers, Software and Assistant Equipments	237	68678	588941
通讯设备零售业	Retail of Communication Equipments	175	181730	950738
五金、家具及室内装修材料专门零售业	Retail of Hardware, Furniture and Interior Decoration Materials	397	137576	688033
货摊、无店铺及其他零售业	Stall,Non-shop and Other Retails	1059	1020261	8453835

Financial Indicators of Enterprises above Designated Size in Retail Trade (2022)

(10000 yuan)

固定资产原价 Original Value of Fixed Assets	累计折旧 Accumulated Depreciation	本年折旧 Depreciation Drawn in Current Year	资产合计 Total Assets	负债合计 Total Liabilities	所有者权益合计 Total Creditors' Equity	实收资本 Paid-up Capital	营业收入 Business Revenue	主营业务收入 Main Business Revenue
10007116	**4603489**	**706048**	**79138911**	**52467824**	**26696088**	**14328069**	**147886167**	**143942620**
3257321	1559713	158672	17435968	4178501	13255369	2281809	23576560	23019905
7337675	3224319	508600	60352538	39818012	20559528	10439779	113752412	110791546
382709	190567	12171	1008948	160018	848930	195856	1083009	1053890
40735	19949	2868	171513	91237	80276	8924	456136	454111
10802	5121	1603	58018	25872	32146	14630	134563	133799
9568	6388	445	63499	32038	31462	6762	179875	175606
4487	2912	209	36103	24125	11977	4419	99436	98614
2010	1246	96	7087	3709	3377	267	35122	34997
1654	1114	96	7303	1059	6244	1637	21027	17991
1417	1117	45	13007	3144	9864	439	24291	24004
2733676	1148668	184721	20216771	14627101	5595478	4677244	43306845	41988458
162507	96674	9415	1590201	555274	1034927	409907	908933	866989
2571169	1051994	175306	18626570	14071827	4560551	4267338	42397911	41121469
1187929	558996	58415	9604249	1113738	8490511	487872	12859592	12605495
2972018	1294619	248368	29226315	23764866	5480642	5048440	55726026	54373823
98705	24440	5732	406601	250723	155877	52237	1270720	1263669
7534	4587	452	99401	83416	15984	22726	231643	229273
2727530	1196050	233157	27533696	22820845	4732044	4773662	52566433	51239794
138249	69542	9027	1186618	609882	576737	199816	1657230	1641086
238	12	9	3224	3143	82	50	6365	6365
1067417	575125	96518	8879185	5744667	3134518	2062687	17537314	16987129
311545	162068	27025	3194886	2079748	1115138	304293	3621868	3516046
21898	15760	1263	101382	54218	47164	43909	225472	221811
682986	374702	65484	4968679	3380857	1587822	1563985	13224348	12804726
45556	18219	2501	394476	126109	268367	53396	315360	295167
5431	4376	245	219762	103735	116027	97105	150265	149378
1602024	804045	100930	9907188	6905145	3002043	1825603	16596442	16163946
658487	308341	32872	3989147	2003374	1985773	754220	5633168	5492539
28844	21696	963	28876	17797	11079	8702	42674	39745
808802	439961	54960	5342654	4609230	733424	762253	10325756	10044713
57589	21879	7216	135683	70247	65437	54941	63064	57793
48303	12167	4919	410828	204498	206330	245489	531780	529155
2433346	1366111	163915	14764952	11428564	3336387	2512990	15894986	15101229
1237003	671501	69141	9642404	6568079	3074325	1264231	6919663	6595172
1068967	627310	77668	4355113	3883673	471441	1136968	7545270	7210583
446364	202280	28633	4659516	2385848	2273668	726123	3956269	3893023
291076	156517	24226	5081353	3820465	1275994	1208600	6046710	5952604
159610	79760	11179	2761573	1956977	819702	628666	2608447	2551628
375381	165127	25606	3324820	1983169	1341651	360697	2939050	2887798
28512	19534	3108	79772	62665	17108	16198	101347	100278
300730	117214	11627	1138865	698940	439924	162552	682976	651026
360367	90099	24036	2932456	2293811	638645	1318521	4644436	4568655
343224	82610	22495	2703415	2104660	598755	1276848	4315264	4247056
13904	5271	1042	158889	140204	18686	32274	222519	218898
4738072	2153326	372320	32315800	17367793	14958153	5705267	71260078	69495265
2533554	1127107	251556	20042375	15491915	4554783	4695062	50988471	49599816
1931528	887307	95846	11224229	1081458	10140672	725816	18895197	18599782
186760	88112	13171	5123907	4535674	588235	528999	6572324	6469076
10227	6173	765	180209	188057	-7848	11525	226128	222989
114527	50018	5684	3106187	2783644	322543	289886	3095365	3035806
21123	11698	2231	623356	469922	153434	94793	839999	827738
31193	14083	3355	1069312	994449	74865	101754	2111974	2084744
223713	67718	12585	966809	750188	216621	317737	1464234	1440487
952036	314200	41556	9969299	7902312	2066735	1649136	35108081	34134484

16-15 续表

单位:万元

项　　目	Item	营业成本 Business Costs	营业税金及附加 Tax and Extra Charges on Business	其它业务利润 Profits from Other Businesses
零售业合计	**Total Retail Trade**	**127480161**	**543782**	**1244467**
#国有及国有控股	State-owned and State-controlled Enterprises	21041366	70134	193587
按登记注册类型分	By Status of Registration			
内资企业	Domestic-funded Enterprises	99819032	406642	746013
国有企业	State-owned Enterprises	917448	3288	12104
集体企业	Collective-owned Enterprises	384608	1896	169
股份合作企业	Share-holding Cooperative Enterprises	120552	295	13
联营企业	Joint-operation Enterprises	149929	488	1819
国有联营企业	State-owned Joint-operation Enterprises	84618	210	
集体联营企业	Collective Joint-operation Enterprises	28833	113	
国有与集体联营企业	State-collective Joint-operation Enterprises	16838	86	10
其他联营企业	Other Joint-operation Enterprises	19640	79	1809
有限责任公司	Limited Liability Corporations	38541323	125485	233535
国有独资企业	State Sole Investment Enterprises	724155	5338	12338
其他有限责任公司	Other Limited Liability Companies	37817168	120147	221196
股份有限公司	Share-holding Corporations Ltd.	11707778	48544	33538
私营企业	Private Enterprises	47991495	226645	464836
私营独资企业	Private Sole Investment Enterprises	1065475	15408	1031
私营合伙企业	Private Partnership Enterprises	210286	414	127
私营有限责任公司	Private Limited Liability Corporations	45451990	206356	460987
私营股份有限公司	Private Share-holding Corporations Ltd.	1263743	4467	2691
其他企业	Other Enterprises	5899	2	
港、澳、台商投资企业	Enterprises with Investment from Hong Kong, Macao and Taiwan	14437377	82654	224059
合资经营企业	Joint Ventures	2749341	13933	92443
合作经营企业	Cooperative Enterprises	185637	636	3151
独资经营企业	Sole Investment Enterprises	11140687	66189	128128
投资股份有限公司	Share-holding Corporations Ltd.	231128	1299	328
其他港澳台商投资企业	Others	130583	597	10
外商投资企业	Enterprises with Foreign Investment	13223753	54486	274395
中外合资经营企业	Sino-foreign Joint Ventures	4333347	19577	102217
中外合作经营企业	Sino-foreign Cooperative Enterprises	32564	49	180
外资企业	Foreign-funded Enterprises	8343441	31794	169622
外商投资股份有限公司	Share-holding Corporations Ltd.	50113	136	936
其它外商投资企业	Others	464288	2931	1439
按国民经济行业分	By Economic Sector			
综合零售业	Comprehensive Retail	12726505	59597	528555
#百货零售业	Retail of General Merchandise	5297245	43248	208168
超级市场零售业	Retail in Supermarkets	6380284	13256	265269
食品、饮料及烟草制品专门零售业	Retail of Food, Beverages and Tobacco Products	2744186	20942	5233
纺织、服装及日用品专门零售业	Retail of Textiles, Garments and Daily-use Products	3907308	27097	32149
#服装零售业	Retail of Garments	1500110	11800	18398
文化、体育用品及器材专门零售业	Retail of Cultural and Sports Articles and Appliances	2082868	62498	23295
#体育用品及器材零售	Retail of Sports Articles and Appliances	66476	566	295
图书零售业	Retail of Books	494740	3057	15160
医药及医疗器材专门零售业	Retail of Medicines and Medical Appliances	3472884	11591	58379
#西药零售	Retail of Western Medicines	3231391	10445	57501
中药零售	Retail of Traditional Chinese Medicines	162466	730	819
汽车、摩托车、燃料及零配件专门零售业	Retail of Motor Vehicles, Motorcycles and Parts	65084527	222940	494101
#汽车新车零售	Retail of Motor Vehicles	46676015	169755	448830
机动车燃料零售业	Retail of Motor Vehicle Fuels	17160125	50610	42165
家用电器及电子产品专门零售业	Retail of Household Appliances and Electronic Products	5893499	34753	19891
#家用视听设备零售	Retail of Household Audio-visual Equipments	196615	672	2109
日用家电零售	Retail of Household Appliances	2839385	3971	7708
计算机、软件及辅助设备零售业	Retail of Computers, Software and Assistant Equipments	716065	26684	2007
通讯设备零售业	Retail of Communication Equipments	1882168	2923	7719
五金、家具及室内装修材料专门零售业	Retail of Hardware, Furniture and Interior Decoration Materials	1122296	12569	4061
货摊、无店铺及其他零售业	Stall,Non-shop and Other Retails	30446090	91795	78803

16-15 continued

(10000 yuan)

销售费用 Marketing Expenses	管理费用 Manag-ement Expenses	财务费用 Financial Expenses	营业利润 Business Profits	营业外收入 Non-operating revenue	利润总额 Total Profits	应交所得税 Income Taxes Payable	本年应付职工薪酬 Staff Salary Payable in Current Year	本年应交增值税 Value-added Tax Payable in Current Year
14292022	**4631280**	**638354**	**773065**	**332459**	**947691**	**619744**	**6288090**	**1815798**
1748408	496445	132701	164799	87406	224562	115840	1063356	255326
9456519	3294220	475837	661978	228657	791094	411626	4597960	1283569
99035	61792	6054	26557	10381	35262	4523	80383	11070
32524	14228	1429	21821	478	21929	4045	17535	7970
6304	1937	511	4890	49	4905	1271	3879	1622
10187	5685	422	13691	17	13689	3325	6993	2935
5153	3200	400	6366	1	6367	1582	4098	1152
2738	746	15	2678	1	2678	610	738	783
976	782	-16	2375	1	2368	600	1250	424
1320	957	24	2272	15	2277	534	907	577
3397923	886973	141075	292992	85158	357369	179269	1522087	460271
99477	45212	-8457	116582	5971	121037	14934	97091	11923
3298447	841761	149532	176411	79187	236333	164335	1424997	448348
823881	203642	56268	128604	32836	137302	41839	367340	133547
5086359	2119916	270053	173338	99738	220576	177354	2599595	666140
79611	53129	6046	51392	1318	51746	6857	42811	15624
10656	7276	407	1083	186	1042	227	6029	2257
4753419	1987396	255316	40020	98827	88636	162898	2422095	627103
242672	72115	8285	80843	-592	79152	7371	128660	21156
306	47	26	84		62	…	150	15
2323442	728479	49961	65655	43230	84835	101753	974576	252722
668353	183118	22634	59844	8678	62327	23743	323708	68377
22748	5443	51	12242	143	11946	3984	12228	4091
1564959	519860	25753	-23756	33366	-7644	72018	599084	170069
53580	18638	436	14523	268	14629	809	33797	7625
13802	1421	1089	2803	775	3577	1200	5759	2561
2512062	608581	112555	45433	60572	71762	106365	715554	279506
997084	190089	62530	-76657	36838	-45730	33949	308956	104882
9056	3458	408	-2015	542	-1452	225	5914	398
1400029	389594	49372	172034	23121	167157	81653	363575	164479
12651	2237	517	-1569	38	-1607	321	4850	769
93241	23202	-272	-46361	33	-46607	-9782	32259	8977
2403995	707649	149702	-207229	71183	-173765	76616	1152204	173270
1163329	317910	76835	118809	22162	119057	64129	528953	95967
970758	259843	64770	-304663	44796	-271041	8860	502388	53584
833002	234419	2780	198899	24805	214484	38765	317396	89500
1727680	453680	43313	-10566	23182	-3068	43315	693713	168289
809799	265133	19884	13076	10471	16882	22551	375825	78753
374958	286579	11903	191186	6087	193260	36785	258823	62387
23011	7765	1549	2579	253	2142	799	7706	3095
82642	97608	2651	25551	4152	28082	2692	91228	5458
962832	209066	18559	-34306	14831	-26303	16392	537898	75323
909283	179223	16526	-35403	13458	-28118	15311	493709	67649
41839	17872	1785	-1656	1121	-829	761	35063	4574
3367113	1585568	325670	961403	122927	1027068	304211	2179603	761619
2251576	1231670	205583	644129	75929	696991	214134	1630937	519628
1038486	295035	112564	332820	34550	334955	87066	480223	227922
476647	211743	34772	-80689	7609	-77867	1442	274762	54502
28158	7704	1471	-1369	519	-986	1207	10348	3925
211654	76632	16421	-57467	2641	-57209	-1031	85634	19852
64469	43636	3687	465	989	694	-507	60876	11026
156498	63365	12439	-20887	2686	-19471	1484	98830	16255
193475	108257	11868	16995	3031	19510	7521	96192	25915
3952320	834320	39787	-262627	58803	-225628	94699	777498	404993

16-16 各市限额以上批发零售企业财务状况（2022年）

单位：万元

市 别	City	企业数（个）Number of Enterprises (unit)	年初库存 Beginning Inventory	流动资产合计 Circulating Assets	固定资产原价 Original Value of Fixed Assets
批发零售业合计	**Total Wholesale and Retail Trades**	**42138**	**57202170**	**465178203**	**29632271**
批发业	**Wholesale Trade**	**33214**	**46789750**	**407435226**	**19625155**
广 州	Guangzhou	10482	17244186	125308414	7674868
深 圳	Shenzhen	9403	15243223	169197838	5591300
珠 海	Zhuhai	958	2130992	18180821	492495
汕 头	Shantou	789	896792	4359239	398347
佛 山	Foshan	3777	4276023	35488806	1191533
韶 关	Shaoguan	216	354462	1453319	161254
河 源	Heyuan	46	40693	462881	28270
梅 州	Meizhou	73	95899	749396	103744
惠 州	Huizhou	668	403529	3568706	432358
汕 尾	Shanwei	56	43474	270286	38694
东 莞	Dongguan	3190	2696855	20610501	1341845
中 山	Zhongshan	799	823539	5676075	421684
江 门	Jiangmen	698	625544	4304155	423777
阳 江	Yangjiang	165	107263	485729	166644
湛 江	Zhanjiang	493	479577	4866472	317165
茂 名	Maoming	564	436415	5045357	173385
肇 庆	Zhaoqing	175	184472	1660771	90486
清 远	Qingyuan	225	194531	2649856	178054
潮 州	Chaozhou	55	50406	362379	61986
揭 阳	Jieyang	322	366501	2046033	127358
云 浮	Yunfu	60	95375	688193	209911
零售业	**Retail Trade**	**8924**	**10412420**	**57742976**	**10007116**
广 州	Guangzhou	1895	2763728	15987218	2692972
深 圳	Shenzhen	1662	3463362	19920314	2613196
珠 海	Zhuhai	310	338089	2472786	286394
汕 头	Shantou	387	211822	758413	197731
佛 山	Foshan	695	711578	2957516	716215
韶 关	Shaoguan	189	92933	341994	79476
河 源	Heyuan	126	77144	1341892	117223
梅 州	Meizhou	128	92769	295281	157293
惠 州	Huizhou	523	332209	2014936	408637
汕 尾	Shanwei	105	49475	145172	62101
东 莞	Dongguan	715	852030	3701941	842797
中 山	Zhongshan	378	314853	1915253	375759
江 门	Jiangmen	396	243495	1758171	325313
阳 江	Yangjiang	105	73489	208688	106712
湛 江	Zhanjiang	224	182948	1325023	264319
茂 名	Maoming	225	155938	745587	175394
肇 庆	Zhaoqing	176	150871	834383	229489
清 远	Qingyuan	172	95835	302634	81906
潮 州	Chaozhou	82	41572	143073	45859
揭 阳	Jieyang	295	114443	402158	142273
云 浮	Yunfu	136	53839	170543	86056

Financial Indicators of Enterprises above Designated Size in Wholesale and Retail Trades by City (2022)

(10000 yuan)

累计折旧 Accumulated Depreciation	#本年折旧 Depreciation Drawn in Current Year	资产合计 Total Assets	负债合计 Total Liabilities	所有者权益合计 Total Creditors' Equity	实收资本 Paid-up Capital	营业收入 Business Revenue	主营业务收入 Main Business Revenue
13104922	**1958757**	**590283781**	**435587581**	**154694642**	**77594595**	**1249241522**	**1239224439**
8501433	**1252709**	**511144870**	**383119757**	**127998553**	**63266526**	**1101355355**	**1095281818**
3345692	468128	154328102	116154342	38175025	18952316	447560151	445074280
2525939	391018	217698607	167198505	50498370	27263292	321736286	319492181
194414	31941	21447311	15209046	6238265	2253397	45470718	45364614
170341	19783	5322598	3536755	1761093	800063	15864982	15839131
527417	79429	39688710	32396081	7291096	3817250	125154921	124989959
54498	8456	1783404	1141166	642238	354930	5597677	5555916
11663	2342	566551	204350	362201	36012	848224	845945
44591	5891	911366	675283	236083	60448	1881099	1876330
151340	27831	4445493	2978755	1466737	548832	10407650	10344367
12992	1898	297088	198175	98913	22207	879151	872134
553194	89641	28382517	19449839	8932869	4987687	56082366	55692529
200826	28564	7523999	5415107	2108892	710782	14428883	14285489
142558	26064	7441128	3613396	3827732	556067	11125301	11052195
75013	11732	651324	546527	104797	63228	1853459	1816587
109210	14749	6639907	4760414	1879493	1791595	8277722	8116976
76567	10742	5310844	3587957	1722887	300677	15791494	15718293
28730	3814	1797137	1602188	194949	86315	4903493	4901924
80738	8837	3242154	1985665	1256489	261152	5001503	4971634
32144	3078	472189	354056	118133	46724	1266990	1260021
51331	8480	2267465	1759988	507477	197445	5704373	5692904
112237	10292	926978	352162	574816	156109	1518914	1518410
4603489	**706048**	**79138911**	**52467824**	**26696088**	**14328069**	**147886167**	**143942620**
1213241	187793	23390282	17190498	6214890	3839118	47668952	46149524
1291182	214542	26370008	19134957	7234801	4811159	38790369	37886055
138145	20437	3066141	1743811	1322330	433664	4056767	3967598
81548	12499	1064372	553312	511060	174406	2620771	2562052
355267	50322	3945202	2929656	1015547	737174	8716365	8472104
42704	8744	451366	341831	109534	91319	804506	789636
48342	7905	1511397	1098039	413358	66300	1104881	1079980
69443	8569	493048	360216	132832	95589	1136974	1120428
163076	33631	2816322	1702864	1116216	299604	5185435	5068758
26323	2804	216512	96781	119732	22593	529816	513514
370497	54796	4995123	2631093	2371937	750042	14263666	13899102
171105	22045	2598574	985983	1612057	414606	5046290	4949405
165915	19488	2214243	1266946	947298	1289474	3703241	3599576
53439	8010	327260	-7951	335226	46280	1122482	1101282
97267	14479	1869837	833675	1036162	716997	2173389	2086595
75812	11113	1027224	227010	800214	94292	2190893	2091791
103834	8008	1241717	474243	767474	205987	4327103	4215578
36643	6313	412168	323678	88489	74044	982216	965394
24541	2878	212984	142569	70415	39010	528212	521344
39109	6067	604815	348056	256758	86081	2189208	2168969
36054	5606	310318	90559	219759	40331	744632	733935

16-16 续表

单位：万元

市 别	City	营业成本 Business Costs	营业税金及附加 Tax and Extra Charges on Business	其它业务利润 Profits from Other Businesses	销售费用 Marketing Expenses
批发零售业合计	**Total Wholesale and Retail Trades**	**1171919618**	**3713749**	**2710455**	**38963284**
批发业	**Wholesale Trade**	**1044439457**	**3169967**	**1465988**	**24671262**
广 州	Guangzhou	425438275	753481	479403	11080667
深 圳	Shenzhen	304048344	675454	728376	6550790
珠 海	Zhuhai	43367602	96683	19685	795989
汕 头	Shantou	14847307	138707	4610	336206
佛 山	Foshan	121111140	217742	120424	2108500
韶 关	Shaoguan	5183453	62284	3147	148261
河 源	Heyuan	692150	53683	517	21677
梅 州	Meizhou	1623705	73970	785	66430
惠 州	Huizhou	9596617	99491	7179	365416
汕 尾	Shanwei	731497	53916	126	20905
东 莞	Dongguan	52655558	209082	67297	1460735
中 山	Zhongshan	13264872	87953	9507	598289
江 门	Jiangmen	10407638	88986	3784	304605
阳 江	Yangjiang	1693924	38913	485	59000
湛 江	Zhanjiang	7758823	78684	6208	154122
茂 名	Maoming	15184186	69121	1663	163303
肇 庆	Zhaoqing	4658314	66250	1039	80656
清 远	Qingyuan	4624005	66166	7633	134971
潮 州	Chaozhou	1107892	51859	832	37790
揭 阳	Jieyang	5071615	148229	3034	157770
云 浮	Yunfu	1372541	39314	255	25183
零售业	**Retail Trade**	**127480161**	**543782**	**1244467**	**14292022**
广 州	Guangzhou	41165269	162704	453412	4978846
深 圳	Shenzhen	32336492	170663	306275	4695394
珠 海	Zhuhai	3459681	10380	40456	306172
汕 头	Shantou	2324796	17580	24573	168920
佛 山	Foshan	7616500	32077	69221	663505
韶 关	Shaoguan	687841	1623	6828	73450
河 源	Heyuan	979235	2505	4569	67859
梅 州	Meizhou	1018633	2669	3761	78525
惠 州	Huizhou	4544187	35398	18881	336965
汕 尾	Shanwei	487521	1088	8580	34805
东 莞	Dongguan	12936645	29198	140830	884958
中 山	Zhongshan	4085412	15399	36037	638705
江 门	Jiangmen	3209655	9125	32096	379850
阳 江	Yangjiang	1008398	1883	8385	70097
湛 江	Zhanjiang	1907752	3820	11742	158088
茂 名	Maoming	1988855	4663	17050	115198
肇 庆	Zhaoqing	3822956	8749	47715	374304
清 远	Qingyuan	854889	2116	5516	76975
潮 州	Chaozhou	485459	996	2839	28306
揭 阳	Jieyang	1891367	29714	3854	107230
云 浮	Yunfu	668619	1433	1850	53871

16-16 continued

(10000 yuan)

管理费用 Management Expenses	财务费用 Financial Expenses	营业利润 Business Profits	营业外收入 Non-operating revenue	利润总额 Total Profits	应交所得税 Income Taxes Payable	本年应付职工薪酬 Staff Salary Payable in Current Year	本年应交增值税 Value-added Tax Payable in Current Year
18592959	**3282306**	**18184986**	**1259812**	**18759119**	**3644474**	**20579296**	**8167850**
13961679	**2643952**	**17411921**	**927353**	**17811427**	**3024730**	**14291206**	**6352052**
4852165	726083	5595077	330409	5696719	1298603	5635722	2397658
5149944	1264831	6102259	386167	6301636	901671	4847884	1875720
407941	109466	813652	32763	832719	133913	394993	231893
202835	12813	323647	4897	322483	66140	143858	107934
919492	164508	1860437	71735	1904674	173256	976290	453576
91323	13689	101165	6972	105438	23689	97171	81347
30788	-77	83333	232	83037	12482	41277	18387
53908	4446	58675	1490	59233	15487	71210	32164
170778	10638	143565	5208	147146	33504	214533	93991
24857	-164	47638	252	47566	11851	26411	22785
944264	168565	927899	25143	923051	134730	823382	401834
232891	31237	252735	14063	261709	48208	299689	184045
172370	34909	333238	17491	343316	29796	164485	78316
57793	4952	-16273	1445	-16977	8894	67472	15925
160361	50366	91827	4207	92467	23620	100818	82637
89836	17187	279094	4305	278786	15951	88823	81065
56836	4375	37717	7052	44152	15915	68035	45310
157508	5942	69945	10769	78726	20270	81375	46506
25373	1126	41419	399	41024	11794	27864	23455
111277	18331	183949	1461	183675	38053	70073	63755
49141	730	80925	893	80849	6903	49843	13750
4631280	**638354**	**773065**	**332459**	**947691**	**619744**	**6288090**	**1815798**
1520331	203353	-175327	101096	-119579	167549	2035020	625682
1528208	174499	74328	135482	158145	204005	2066120	480713
127236	13783	165704	10161	166776	40066	173388	50740
70595	8528	19964	2460	18510	7967	74600	28753
282172	42210	117820	17820	130652	43606	351908	108095
32075	4623	6169	1320	6967	2612	52693	9121
27358	7070	22003	1127	20463	2311	41233	9826
28051	5793	3922	1159	3084	1577	45463	13466
125922	25936	102329	3559	100216	15031	200407	50824
19271	2140	-12021	358	-12763	246	24096	5384
279929	64025	86933	19864	99245	49304	426916	150028
151852	18830	149877	11208	154317	38012	192314	98536
95640	11927	13511	6259	15423	10355	153147	47330
17297	3893	19509	1479	20235	3600	38964	8722
56709	10198	38346	5685	41551	5469	111807	17023
40970	9155	34185	3852	37150	7106	72404	22613
94614	6676	24190	5162	25452	7935	71977	38489
34837	4914	10227	1812	11323	3968	52340	11879
10194	1472	1823	208	1783	996	19724	12618
67088	15732	73410	956	72181	6483	43215	17009
20932	3598	-3836	1432	-3438	1547	40354	8947

主要统计指标解释

社会消费品零售总额 指各种经济类型的批发零售业、住宿餐饮业和其他行业的企业（单位）或个体户，售予城乡居民用于生活消费和社会集团用于公共消费的商品金额的总和。

批发零售业商品购进总额 指从本企业以外的单位和个人购进（包括从国外直接进口）作为转卖或加工后转卖的商品金额。本指标由“从生产者购进额” “从批发零售业购进额” “进口额”和“其他购进”组成。 这个指标反映批发零售企业从国内、国外市场上购进商品的总量。

批发零售业商品销售总额 指售予本企业以外的单位和个人的商品金额（包括对国（境）外直接出口及售给本单位消费用的商品）。本指标由“对生产经营单位批发额” “对批发零售业批发额” “出口额”和“对居民和社会集团商品零售额”项目组成。这个指标反映批发零售业在国内市场上销售商品以及出口商品的总量。

批发 指除零售以外的一切商品销售活动。包括对生产经营单位批发、对批发零售业批发和出口。

对生产经营单位批发 指售给国民经济和社会各部门作为生产或经营使用的商品。

零售 指出售城乡居民用于生活消费商品和社会集团直接用于公用消费商品的活动。

批发零售业年末库存总额 指批发零售企业已取得所有权的全部商品。这个指标反映批发零售贸易企业的商品库存情况，对市场商品供应的保证程度。

批发零售业住宿餐饮业法人单位 指各种经济类型独立核算法人批发零售企业、住宿餐饮企业的单位个数。法人单位应同时具备以下条件：1. 依法成立，有自己的名称、组织机构和场所，能够独立承担民事责任；2. 独立拥有和使用资产，承担负债，有权与其他单位签订合同；3. 独立核算盈亏，并能够编制资产负债表。

批发业 是指从工农业生产者或从商品流通企业单位和个体户购进商品，转卖给工业、农业、建筑业、运输邮电业、住宿餐饮业、服务业等生产经营单位作为生产经营用，以及将商品转卖给其他批发企业或零售企业的商品流通企业(单位)和个体户。

零售业 是指从工农业生产者、批发业或居民购进商品，转卖给城乡居民作为生活消费和售给社会集团作为公共消费的商品流通企业(单位)和个体户。

Explanatory Notes on Main Statistical Indicators

Total Retail Sales of Consumer Goods refer to the sum of retail sales of consumer goods sold by enterprises (establishments) or individuals in wholesale，retail trade，accommodations, catering services and other industries of various types of ownership to urban and rural households for living consumption and to social institutions for public consumption.

Total Purchases of Commodities by Wholesale and Retail Trades refer to the purchases of commodities from other establishments or individuals (including direct import from abroad) for the purpose of reselling，either with or without further processing of the commodities purchased. This indicator includes the purchases from producers，the purchases from wholesale and retail trades，imports and other purchases. It is used to show the total value of purchases of commodities by wholesale and retail establishments from domestic and overseas markets.

Total Sales of Commodities by Wholesale and Retail Trades refer to the value of commodities sold to other establishments and individuals (including direct export and commodities sold to the sellers themselves for consumption). This indicator includes the value of wholesale to production and operation units，the value of wholesale to wholesale and retail trades，exports and retail sales to urban and rural households and social institutions. It is an indicator of the total value of sales of commodities at domestic markets and export.

Wholesale refers to all selling activities of commodities except retail trade, including wholesale to production and operation units, wholesale to wholesale and retail trades and export.

Wholesale to Production and Operation Units refers to commodities sold to departments of national economy and social departments for their production and operation.

Retail Sale refers to the selling of commodities to urban and rural households for living consumption and to social institutions for direct public consumption.

Total Inventory of Wholesale and Retail Trades at the Year-end refers to the total commodities possessed by wholesale and retail enterprises, which reflects the commodity stock level of various wholesale and retail enterprises and the potential for market supply.

Corporate Units in Wholesale and Retail Trades, Accommodations and Catering Services refer to the number of corporate enterprises of various types of ownership in the wholesale and retail trades, accommodations and catering services with independent accounting systems. An enterprise can be called a corporate enterprise only when it simultaneously meets the following requirements: (1)It is established according to law, with its own name, organization and location for business operation, as well as the capability to independently assume civil responsibility; (2)It owns and uses its assets independently, assumes liabilities and is entitled to sign contracts with other units; (3)It has an independent accounting system and is able to compile balance sheets.

Wholesale Trade refers to the commodity circulation enterprises (establishments) and individuals which purchase commodities from producers in industry and agriculture or from commodity circulation enterprises and individuals for the purpose of reselling them to establishments in industry, agriculture, construction, transportation, postal and telecommunications services, accommodations and catering services and other services for their production and operation as well as reselling them to other wholesale or retail enterprises.

Retail Trade refers to the commodity circulation enterprises (establishments) and individuals which purchase commodities from producers in industry and agriculture, wholesale trade or residents for the purpose of reselling them to urban and rural households for living consumption and to social institutions for public consumption.

十七、住宿餐饮业和旅游

HOTELS，CATERING SERVICES AND TOURISM

十七 住宿餐饮业和旅游

简要说明

一、本篇资料主要反映住宿和餐饮业的基本情况、经营情况和旅游产业的发展情况。主要内容包括：限额以上住宿和餐饮业基本情况、经营情况、财务情况；连锁餐饮业经营情况；经广东口岸入境游客人数（港澳台和外国人）、城市接待国内外旅游人数、旅行社组织接待人数以及旅游收入等基本情况。

二、本篇资料来源

本篇资料中住宿和餐饮业主要根据国家统计局《住宿和餐饮业统计报表制度》进行搜集和加工整理；旅游资料主要由广东省文化和旅游厅提供。

三、本篇资料的统计范围

限额以上住宿和餐饮业的企业、个体户；餐饮连锁集团；旅行社、星级饭店和旅游者。住宿业年营业额200万元及以上；餐饮业年营业额200万元及以上。

四、本篇的调查方法

限额以上住宿和餐饮业资料采用全面调查的方法自下而上逐级综合汇总而得，限额以下企业及个体户资料采用抽样调查方法推算而得。旅游部门基本情况、住宿设施接待人数、旅行社接待人数由各基层企业上报汇总，城市接待旅游人数、国内外旅游收入根据抽样调查资料测算。

五、本篇资料由广东省统计局贸易外经统计处整理、编辑。

17 Hotels,Catering Services and Tourism

Brief Introduction

Ⅰ. Data in this chapter reflect the development of hotel and catering services and tourism in China. They mainly include: the basic conditions, operating and financial status of hotel and catering services above the designated size; the operating status of chain catering services; number of international tourists entering China through ports in Guangdong (including foreigners, Chinese compatriots from Hong Kong, Macao and Taiwan), number of domestic and international tourists received by cities, number of tourists received by travel agencies, and earnings from tourism, etc.

Ⅱ. Data sources :

The data are collected and processed in accordance with the Statistical Reporting Scheme on Accommodations and Catering Services stipulated by the National Bureau of Statistics. The data in this chapter are provided by the Department of Culture and Tourism of Guangdong Province.

Ⅲ. The statistical coverage in this chapter comes as follows:

Data in this chapter cover the enterprises of hotel and catering services above the designated size, self-employed households of hotel and catering services; chain catering services, travel agencies, star-rated hotels and tourists; hotels with annual turnover of 2 million yuan or above, and catering services with annual turnover of 2 million yuan or above.

Ⅳ. The statistical coverage in this chapter comes as follows:

Data on basic conditions for all corporate enterprises of accommodations and catering services above the designated size are collected through comprehensive reporting systems and data are reported level by level in a bottom-up manner. Data on small-size enterprises and individual enterprises below the designated size are collected through sample surveys. Basic statistics on tourist agencies, the number of tourists received by lodging facilities, and the number of tourists received by travel agencies are summaries of reports from various enterprises, whereas the number of tourists received by cities and earnings from domestic and international tourism are estimates from sample surveys.

Ⅴ. The data in this chapter are prepared and edited by the Division of Trade and External Economic Relations Statistics of Statistics Bureau of Guangdong Province.

17-1 住宿、餐饮业、旅游主要指标

Main Indicators on Hotels, Catering Services and Tourism

指标	Item	2000	2010	2015	2019	2020	2021	2022
限额以上住宿餐饮业营业额（亿元）	**Business Revenue from Hotels and Catering Services above Designated Size (100 million yuan)**		**901.95**	**1600.72**	**1700.39**	**1424.61**	**1756.22**	**1765.90**
#客房收入	Revenue from Accommodations		189.48	326.56	354.09	254.85	315.85	325.74
餐费收入	Revenue from Restaurants		645.66	1153.00	1200.19	1031.14	1255.00	1260.98
商品销售收入	Revenue from Sales of Commodities		15.17	30.78	49.93	54.20	77.26	78.83
旅行社数（个）	**Number of Travel Agencies (unit)**	**504**	**1292**	**2150**	**3276**	**3425**	**3605**	**3764**
旅行社从业人员（人）	**Engaged Persons of Travel Agencies (person)**		**37841**	**62779**	**66507**	**52805**	**48418**	**39081**
星级宾馆(酒店)数(个)	**Number of Star-rated Hotels (unit)**	**750**	**1209**	**972**	**677**	**613**	**549**	**501**
接待过夜旅游者人数（万人次）	**Number of Tourists Staying Overnight Received (10000 person-times)**	**7662.95**	**21283.05**	**36225.18**	**53141.02**	**23059.46**	**25701.06**	**20307.15**
入境过夜游客	Inbound Tourists	1198.94	3141.09	3445.36	3731.40	468.85	320.44	190.16
外国人	Foreigners	212.85	732.25	781.83	856.96	80.46	64.48	44.46
港澳同胞	Chinese Compatriots from Hong Kong and Macao	813.84	2091.07	2382.48	2588.41	341.30	229.08	127.05
台湾同胞	Chinese Compatriots from Taiwan	172.25	316.74	281.05	286.03	47.09	26.87	18.65
国内旅游者	Domestic Tourists	6464.01	18141.96	32779.82	49409.62	22590.61	25380.63	20116.99
旅游收入（亿元）	**Earnings from Tourism (100 million yuan)**	**1149.95**	**3809.44**	**9080.76**	**15157.95**	**4690.59**	**5433.73**	**4213.51**
国际旅游收入	Foreign Exchange Earnings	340.08	844.85	1104.16	1417.93	162.28	144.51	116.84
国内旅游收入	Domestic Tourism Earnings	809.87	2964.59	7976.60	13740.02	4528.31	5289.21	4096.67

注：2020年起，接待过夜旅游者人数统计口径调整，由联网住宿企业根据公安系统网身份证登记信息统计过夜人数。接待过夜旅游者人数、旅游收入均与2019年以前年份不可比。

Note: From the year of 2020, the statistic caliber on the number of tourists staying overnight has been changed, networked hotels record the number according to ID card registration information in public security system, therefore the number of tourists staying overnight and earnings from tourism are incomparable with those in the year of 2019.

17-2 限额以上住宿业经营情况（2022年）

Business of Hotels above Designated Size (2022)

单位：万元 (10000 yuan)

项目	Item	企业(单位)数(个) Number of Enterprises (unit)	营业额合计 Business Revenue	#客房收入 Revenue from Hotels	#餐费收入 Revenue from Restaurants	#商品销售收入 Revenue from Sales of Commodities
住宿业合计	**Total Accommodations**	**3594**	**5129483**	**3117510**	**1179587**	**125559**
#国有及国有控股	State-owned and State-controlled Enterprises	224	8735701	3840512	2322371	412073
按登记注册类型分组	By Status of Registration					
内资企业	Domestic-funded Enterprises	3384	4415220	2780757	964533	98051
国有企业	State-owned Enterprises	76	291029	140226	67448	12356
集体企业	Collective-owned Enterprises	16	11908	4044	3895	2
股份合作企业	Share-holding Cooperative Enterprises	2	549	405	144	
联营企业	Joint-operation Enterprises	1	305	261		
国有联营企业	State-owned Joint-operation Enterprises					
集体联营企业	Collective Joint-operation Enterprises					
国有与集体联营企业	State-collective Joint-operation Enterprises	1	305	261		
其他联营企业	Other Joint-operation Enterprises					
有限责任公司	Limited Liability Corporations	735	1568701	864962	399438	52933
国有独资企业	State Sole Investment Enterprises	51	230581	102278	63047	12136
其他有限责任公司	Other Limited Liability Companies	684	1338120	762684	336391	40797
股份有限公司	Share-holding Corporations Ltd.	32	68011	36996	15971	4323
私营企业	Private Enterprises	2521	2473300	1732446	477637	28438
私营独资企业	Private Sole Investment Enterprises	188	157907	102295	27988	4260
私营合伙企业	Private Partnership Enterprises	36	21264	15547	3492	9
私营有限责任公司	Private Limited Liability Corporations	2268	2260685	1596191	435842	23577
私营股份有限公司	Private Share-holding Corporations Ltd.	29	33444	18413	10315	593
其他企业	Other Enterprises	1	1418	1418		
港、澳、台商投资企业	Enterprises with Investment from Hong Kong,Macao and Taiwan	151	440644	208437	142085	19811
与港澳台商合资经营企业	Joint Ventures	47	124945	61339	39627	3379
与港澳台商合作经营企业	Cooperative Enterprises	22	78672	30902	29293	8325
港澳台商独资经营企业	Sole Investment Enterprises	78	230356	114701	68427	7735
港澳台商投资股份有限公司	Share-holding Corporations Ltd.	1	751	729		
其他港澳台投资企业	Others	3	5920	767	4738	372
外商投资企业	Enterprises with Foreign Investment	59	273618	128316	72969	7697
中外合资经营企业	Sino-foreign Joint Ventures	19	90937	43930	31719	1459
中外合作经营企业	Sino-foreign Cooperative Enterprises	3	10766	5714	2980	
外资企业	Foreign-funded Enterprises	33	152534	64642	33876	5887
外商投资股份有限公司	Share-holding Corporations Ltd.	2	6141	3456	2439	
其他外商投资企业	Others	2	13240	10574	1955	351
个体工商户	Self-employed Individuals					
按国民经济行业分组	By Economic Sector					
旅游饭店	Tourist Hotels	1630	3412815	1794531	973141	103157
一般旅馆	General Hotels	1795	1471925	1147228	173368	20721
其它住宿服务	Others	169	244743	175752	33078	1682

17-3 限额以上餐饮业经营情况（2022年）

Business of Catering Services Enterprises above Designated Size (2022)

单位：万元 (10000 yuan)

项目	Item	企业(单位)数(个) Number of Enterprises (unit)	营业额 Business Revenue	#客房收入 Revenue from Hotels	#餐费收入 Revenue from Restaurants	#商品销售收入 Revenue from Sales of Commodities
餐饮业合计	**Total Catering Services**	**6639**	**12529471**	**139898**	**11430235**	**662731**
#国有及国有控股	State-owned and State-controlled Enterprises	70	460812	20346	336163	60404
按登记注册类型分	By Status of Registration					
内资企业	Domestic-funded Enterprises	6287	9263463	128846	8374836	550011
国有企业	State-owned Enterprises	15	21940	995	17729	1280
集体企业	Collective-owned Enterprises	16	21890	2287	13099	2439
股份合作企业	Share-holding Cooperative Enterprises	36	29659		29618	29
联营企业	Joint-operation Enterprises	2	10648		9294	1354
国有联营企业	State-owned Joint-operation Enterprises	1	10310		8957	1354
集体联营企业	Collective Joint-operation Enterprises					
国有与集体联营企业	State-collective Joint-operation Enterprises					
其他联营企业	Other Joint-operation Enterprises	1	338		338	
有限责任公司	Limited Liability Corporations	1002	2129779	44483	1936086	92872
国有独资企业	State Sole Investment Enterprises	19	74597	10891	47801	9114
其他有限责任公司	Other Limited Liability Companies	983	2055182	33592	1888285	83758
股份有限公司	Share-holding Corporations Ltd.	23	89670	2593	61983	15436
私营企业	Private Enterprises	5190	6958942	78488	6306118	436576
私营独资企业	Private Sole Investment Enterprises	569	382540	10292	357826	11279
私营合伙企业	Private Partnership Enterprises	78	73073	1136	70371	390
私营有限责任公司	Private Limited Liability Corporations	4505	6445431	64506	5838783	409784
私营股份有限公司	Private Share-holding Corporations Ltd.	38	57899	2554	39137	15123
其他企业	Other Enterprises	3	935		910	25
港、澳、台商投资企业	Enterprises with Investment from Hong Kong, Macao and Taiwan	268	1592706	5566	1463087	77315
与港澳台商合资经营企业	Joint Ventures	56	121884	3669	110049	3108
与港澳台商合作经营企业	Cooperative Enterprises	10	65560	381	55857	5294
港澳台商独资经营企业	Sole Investment Enterprises	187	1388784	1515	1280970	68805
港澳台商投资股份有限公司	Share-holding Corporations Ltd.	8	11634		11380	108
其他港澳台投资企业	Others	7	4845		4832	
外商投资企业	Enterprises with Foreign Investment	84	1673302	5487	1592312	35406
中外合资经营企业	Sino-foreign Joint Ventures	17	478099	2022	446085	13081
中外合作经营企业	Sino-foreign Cooperative Enterprises					
外资企业	Foreign-funded Enterprises	58	1167017	3465	1120667	20949
外商投资股份有限公司	Share-holding Corporations Ltd.	2	20112		18514	526
其他外商投资企业	Others	7	8073		7046	851
个体工商户	Self-employed Individuals					
按国民经济行业分	By Economic Sector					
正餐服务业	Restaurant Service	5455	6842236	137501	6378614	175245
快餐服务业	Fast Food Service	243	2556703	36	2447311	39212
饮料及冷饮服务业	Beverage and Cold Drink Service	168	1045689	63	952464	74486
其他餐饮服务业	Other Services	773	2084843	2299	1651846	373789

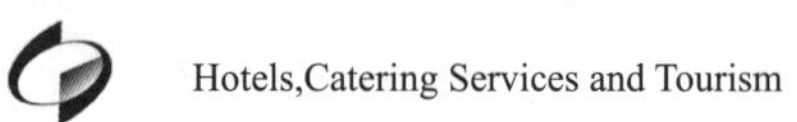

17-4 各市限额以上住宿餐饮业经营情况（2022年）
Business of Enterprises above Designated Size of Hotels and Catering Services by City (2022)

单位：万元 (10000 yuan)

市别	Item	企业(单位)数(个) Number of Enterprises (unit)	营业额 Business Revenue	#客房收入 Revenue from Hotels	#餐费收入 Revenue from Restaurants	#商品销售收入 Revenue from Sales of Commodities
合　计	**Total**	**10233**	**17658954**	**3257408**	**12609822**	**788290**
住宿业	**Accommodation**	**3594**	**5129483**	**3117510**	**1179587**	**125559**
广　州	Guangzhou	869	1516988	862343	326881	44544
深　圳	Shenzhen	707	1404433	977669	231401	11580
珠　海	Zhuhai	194	244936	149274	47725	9331
汕　头	Shantou	164	138593	95349	32648	2041
佛　山	Foshan	286	322465	168191	102710	17113
韶　关	Shaoguan	117	85680	50851	22360	2687
河　源	Heyuan	56	52505	32287	15048	2675
梅　州	Meizhou	48	42185	20821	14780	1398
惠　州	Huizhou	220	247323	165085	55591	4398
汕　尾	Shanwei	63	40613	31761	7102	103
东　莞	Dongguan	246	405591	208886	134612	8663
中　山	Zhongshan	128	120708	63034	39874	3285
江　门	Jiangmen	91	114559	54137	38008	7210
阳　江	Yangjiang	20	23451	17833	4019	158
湛　江	Zhanjiang	75	79582	44549	26380	3161
茂　名	Maoming	50	41227	24275	11375	802
肇　庆	Zhaoqing	59	44105	26003	14626	543
清　远	Qingyuan	75	96703	56285	28363	1386
潮　州	Chaozhou	38	21406	13879	5467	72
揭　阳	Jieyang	59	48368	33454	10175	2060
云　浮	Yunfu	29	38064	21545	10443	2348
餐饮业	**Catering Service**	**6639**	**12529471**	**139898**	**11430235**	**662731**
广　州	Guangzhou	1823	4448962	37250	4038101	274189
深　圳	Shenzhen	1649	4351523	26753	4061670	153593
珠　海	Zhuhai	262	341059	350	308592	27331
汕　头	Shantou	200	177421	108	170151	6826
佛　山	Foshan	658	651822	3393	592858	48523
韶　关	Shaoguan	127	61948	2565	55702	2773
河　源	Heyuan	33	26844	1968	24521	244
梅　州	Meizhou	19	14087	982	12753	107
惠　州	Huizhou	280	305837	18467	258800	13516
汕　尾	Shanwei	72	50053	2487	47026	80
东　莞	Dongguan	634	1124672	6308	999316	96259
中　山	Zhongshan	310	384304	294	352096	19415
江　门	Jiangmen	169	234790	1432	216719	6917
阳　江	Yangjiang	41	49614	4322	38140	3476
湛　江	Zhanjiang	118	117197	10793	101769	2244
茂　名	Maoming	72	40013	4005	35481	161
肇　庆	Zhaoqing	55	40827	3718	32728	3044
清　远	Qingyuan	31	34621	4316	28253	273
潮　州	Chaozhou	23	16003		15483	379
揭　阳	Jieyang	44	41787	8721	26258	3097
云　浮	Yunfu	19	16088	1668	13819	286

17-5 限额以上连锁住宿餐饮业经营情况（2022年）
Business of Chain Stores above Designated Size in Hotels and Catering Services (2022)

项　　目	Item	连锁总店数(个) Number of General Chain Stores (unit)	营业额(万元) Total Business Revenue (10000 yuan)	#零售额(万元) Retail Sales (10000 yuan)	营业面积(平方米) Operational Area (sq.m)
住宿餐饮业合计	**Catering Service**	**104**	**3878019**	**3747022**	**2067072**
按注册登记类型分	By Status of Registration				
内资企业	Domestic-funded Enterprises	66	1437223	1383129	677427
国有企业	State-owned Enterprises	2	32679	30959	3080
集体企业	Collective-owned Enterprises	1	7888	7123	12000
股份合作企业	Cooperative Enterprises	1	438	438	1440
有限责任公司	Limited Liability Corporations	27	755407	732136	324987
股份有限公司	Share-holding Enterprises	2	88185	80244	81403
私营企业	Private Enterprises	33	552626	532229	254517
其他企业	Other Enterprises				
港、澳、台商投资企业	Enterprises with Investment from Hong Kong, Macao and Taiwan	20	902548	867705	489362
与港澳台商合资经营企业	Joint Ventures	4	20420	19934	6007
与港澳台商合作经营企业	Cooperative Enterprises	1	20053	20053	22000
港澳台商独资经营企业	Sole Investment Enterprises	15	862076	827718	461355
港澳台商投资股份有限公司	Share-holding Corporations Ltd.				
外商投资企业	Enterprises with Foreign Investment	18	1538248	1496188	900283
中外合资经营企业	Sino-foreign Joint Ventures	3	467455	439955	268740
中外合作经营企业	Sino-foreign Cooperative Enterprises				
外资企业	Foreign-funded Enterprises	13	1049180	1034619	621863
外商投资股份有限公司	Share-holding Corporations Ltd.	1	17775	17775	8358
其他外商投资企业	Others	1	3839	3839	1322
按行业分	By Sector				
旅游饭店	Tour Hotel	4	26236	314	2001
一般旅馆	General Hotel	5	10722	451	100
正餐服务	Restaurant	38	918616	895680	497213
快餐服务	Fast Food	41	2113337	2050750	1188140
饮料及冷饮服务	Beverages and Cold Drinks Services	14	805270	795988	378296
其他餐饮业	Other Catering Industries	2	3839	3839	1322

17−5 续表 continued

项　　目	Item	就业人数(人) Number of Employed Persons (person)	连锁门店数(个) Number of Branch Chain Stores (unit)	直营店(个) Under Direct Management (unit)	加盟店(个) Through License Arran-gement (unit)
住宿餐饮业合计	**Catering Service**	**160054**	**7984**	**7846**	**138**
按注册登记类型分	By Status of Registration				
内资企业	Domestic-funded Enterprises	41799	2944	2868	76
国有企业	State-owned Enterprises	1009	60	60	
集体企业	Collective-owned Enterprises	441	2	2	
股份合作企业	Share-holding Cooperative Enterprises	13	2	2	
有限责任公司	Limited Liability Corporations	18234	1763	1704	59
股份有限公司	Share-holding Corporations Ltd.	2921	33	16	17
私营企业	Private Enterprises	19181	1084	1084	
其他企业	Other Enterprises				
港、澳、台商投资企业	Enterprises with Investment from Hong Kong, Macao and Taiwan	41185	1974	1912	62
与港澳台商合资经营企业	Joint Ventures	839	43	43	
与港澳台商合作经营企业	Cooperative Enterprises	602	6	6	
港澳台商独资经营企业	Sole Investment Enterprises	39744	1925	1863	62
港澳台商投资股份有限公司	Share-holding Corporations Ltd.				
外商投资企业	Enterprises with Foreign Investment	77070	3066	3066	
中外合资经营企业	Sino-foreign Joint Ventures	27316	685	685	
中外合作经营企业	Sino-foreign Cooperative Enterprises				
外资企业	Foreign-funded Enterprises	49042	2291	2291	
外商投资股份有限公司	Share-holding Corporations Ltd.	585	79	79	
其他外商投资企业	Others	127	11	11	
按行业分	By Sector				
旅游饭店	Tourist Hotel	730	21	21	
一般旅馆	General Hotel	471	34	34	
正餐服务	Restaurant	26756	1158	1141	17
快餐服务	Fast Food	110745	4264	4143	121
饮料及冷饮服务	Beverages and Cold Drinks Services	21225	2496	2496	
其他餐饮业	Other Catering Industries	127	11	11	

17-6 限额以上住宿餐饮企业财务状况（2022年）

Financial Indicators of Enterprises above Designated Size in Hotels and Catering Services (2022)

单位：万元 (10000 yuan)

项　目	Item	住宿和餐饮业合计 Total Hotels and Catering Services	住宿业 Hotels Services	餐饮业 Catering Services
企业数 (个)	Number of Enterprises (unit)	10233	3595	6638
年初存货	Inventory at the Year-beginning	994340	704370	289970
流动资产合计	Circulating Assets	17346714	11427378	5919336
#存货	Inventory	1027936	716055	311881
固定资产原价	Original Value of Fixed Assets	13214296	10430044	2784252
累计折旧	Accumulated Depreciation	6972101	5525181	1446920
#本年折旧	Depreciation Drawn in Current Year	536342	343372	192970
资产合计	Total Assets	31900935	21397921	10503014
负债合计	Total Liabilities	28746839	20175927	8570912
所有者权益合计	Total Creditors' Equity	3189899	1231545	1958354
实收资本	Paid-up Capital	10774979	8574906	2200072
#个人资本	Personal Capital	516134	286899	229235
营业收入	Business Revenue	16967127	4939047	12028081
#主营业务收入	Main Business Revenue	16643853	4786442	11857411
营业成本	Business Costs	9147126	2429990	6717136
营业税金及附加	Tax and Extra Charges on Business	85391	64843	20548
其它业务利润	Profits from Other Businesses	81020	44283	36737
销售费用	Marketing Expenses	5311053	1386762	3924292
管理费用	Management Expenses	3542586	1757774	1784813
财务费用	Financial Expenses	445477	337114	108364
#利息支出	Interests	257993	207637	50355
营业利润	Business Profits	-1387253	-941725	-445528
营业外收入	Non-operating Revenue	181666	90834	90831
利润总额	Total Profits	-1280457	-877221	-403236
所得税费用	Income Taxes Expenses	34211	6584	27627
本年应付职工薪酬	Total Wages Payable in Current Year	4647328	1616790	3030538

17-7 限额以上住宿企业财务状况（2022年）

单位:万元

项　目	Item	企业数(个) Number of Enterprises (unit)	年初库存 Beginning Inventory	流动资产合计 Circulating Assets
住宿业合计	**Total Hotels**	**3595**	**704370**	**11427378**
#国有及国有控股	State-owned and State-controlled Enterprises	224	34462	1436444
按登记注册类型分	By Status of Registration			
内资企业	Domestic-funded Enterprises	3385	599188	8690685
国有企业	State-owned Enterprises	76	12850	420777
集体企业	Collective-owned Enterprises	16	197	10774
股份合作企业	Share-holding Cooperative Enterprises	2	24	44
联营企业	Joint-operation Enterprises	1		709
国有联营企业	State-owned Joint-operation Enterprises			
集体联营企业	Collective Joint-operation Enterprises			
国有与集体联营企业	State-collective Joint-operation Enterprises	1		709
其他联营企业	Other Joint-operation Enterprises			
有限责任公司	Limited Liability Corporations	735	435412	4223686
国有独资企业	State Sole Investment Enterprises	51	4170	322875
其他有限责任公司	Other Limited Liability Companies	684	431241	3900810
股份有限公司	Share-holding Corporations Ltd.	32	1648	234743
私营企业	Private Enterprises	2522	149057	3799014
私营独资企业	Private Sole Investment Enterprises	188	28240	198724
私营合伙企业	Private Partnership Enterprises	36	505	9646
私营有限责任公司	Private Limited Liability Corporations	2269	119676	3555297
私营股份有限公司	Private Share-holding Corporations Ltd.	29	636	35348
其他企业	Other Enterprises	1		938
港、澳、台商投资企业	Enterprises with Investment from Hong Kong, Macao and Taiwan	151	83945	1035828
合资经营企业	Joint Ventures	47	70222	338388
合作经营企业	Cooperative Enterprises	22	3141	170722
独资经营企业	Sole Investment Enterprises	78	10281	523919
投资股份有限公司	Share-holding Corporations Ltd.	1		1794
其他港澳台商投资企业	Others	3	301	1005
外商投资企业	Enterprises with Foreign Investment	59	21238	1700865
中外合资经营企业	Sino-foreign Joint Ventures	19	4695	455720
中外合作经营企业	Sino-foreign Cooperative Enterprises	3	200	16273
外资企业	Foreign-funded Enterprises	33	16156	1021296
外商投资股份有限公司	Share-holding Corporations Ltd.	2	47	77328
其它外商投资企业	Others	2	140	130249
按国民经济行业分	By Economic Sector			
旅游饭店	Tourist Hotels	1631	578021	8559060
一般旅馆	General Hotels	1795	117792	2442123
其它住宿服务	Others	169	8557	426196
按控股情况分组	By Holdings			
国有控股	State Holdings	224	34462	1436444
集体控股	Collective Holdings	49	2250	190635
私人控股	Private Holdings	3131	370225	6906991
港澳台商控股	Hongkong,Macaw and Taiwan Holdings	137	280094	1444821
外商控股	Foreign Holdings	51	17269	1438144
其他	Others	3	70	10342
按星级分组	By Star Rating			
五星	Five Star	120	113872	3139915
四星	Four Star	262	151791	1154875
三星	Three Star	326	23108	515653
二星	Two Star	38	603	20838
一星	One Star	19	80	21790
其他	Others	2830	414916	6574306

Financial Indicators of Hotels above Designated Size (2022)

(10000 yuan)

固定资产原价 Original Value of Fixed Assets	累计折旧 Accumulated Depreciation		资产合计 Total Assets	负债合计 Total Liabilities	所有者权益合计 Total Creditors' Equity	实收资本 Paid-up Capital	营业收入 Business Revenue	主营业务收入 Main Business Revenue
		本年折旧 Depreciation Drawn in Current Year						
10430044	**5525181**	**343372**	**21397921**	**20175927**	**1231545**	**8574906**	**4939047**	**4786442**
2262369	1207401	35756	3820835	1974764	1813218	1245414	810286	788250
7452582	3808320	258504	16521002	15472258	1043802	7065694	4260655	4128824
607952	289257	-13513	1032761	718371	301879	176050	253690	240430
22351	16412	433	29265	46728	-17463	6660	11408	11190
3521	2785	34	2159	3752	-1593	490	558	558
1384	1334		888	161	727	1387	287	246
1384	1334		888	161	727	1387	287	246
3897754	1974669	143191	8139934	7135453	988845	4683101	1544970	1482522
590528	332040	17047	1057805	423201	631862	319906	219247	217670
3307226	1642629	126144	7082129	6712252	356984	4363196	1325723	1264852
184139	109511	5202	558723	218528	340196	89375	69968	63236
2735481	1414351	123158	6756335	7348441	-568900	2108614	2378398	2329267
148408	65119	5636	359745	283656	75461	65046	151809	148003
17978	12125	553	22142	18494	3365	7403	20543	19777
2556632	1328477	116409	6329294	7007700	-654290	2020991	2174284	2129882
12464	8631	561	45154	38590	6564	15174	31762	31607
			938	825	112	17	1375	1375
2182711	1249013	61137	2597780	2720521	-107632	1081895	416212	400886
663131	307029	16346	839869	960351	-120482	235961	118672	116291
459061	319709	7924	412219	392297	19823	277830	74091	73439
1060354	622241	36845	1340870	1359978	-3901	567934	217869	205576
135	17	11	3760	3897	-137		714	714
30	16	11	1062	3998	-2936	172	4867	4867
794751	467849	23730	2279138	1983148	295375	427317	262180	256732
280840	155217	8151	645429	568570	76244	89930	88115	87584
36947	29622	683	47601	26151	21449	31757	10161	10161
435758	248324	13792	1294660	1153870	140790	251091	145636	140796
4393	2899	185	79801	78688	1112	4269	5799	5799
36812	31787	920	211648	155868	55780	50270	12469	12393
8976801	4850627	269108	16874759	15820767	1069230	7417141	3306556	3198169
1270707	606562	64123	3837798	3617525	214648	1024104	1416972	1378473
182536	67992	10141	685364	737636	-52333	133662	215519	209800
2262369	1207401	35756	3820835	1974764	1813218	1245414	810286	788250
99799	72236	2776	288159	316426	-28267	28079	87638	78678
5233943	2669638	222738	12203663	13032841	-801882	5486466	3390449	3289610
2261732	1239938	64312	3181402	3123022	73489	1454991	423037	408618
572015	335873	17760	1889110	1722502	166608	357957	224553	218203
187	95	29	14752	6374	8378	2000	3084	3084
2972911	1839230	87141	5488190	4902218	585971	1377564	841838	811630
1148848	716870	9525	2224145	2080521	153038	597786	515672	496299
503670	324931	14100	927201	752837	168710	415621	286804	278773
22406	14292	642	52756	31846	21870	14244	25427	24757
43333	5168	737	69079	38436	30643	24531	35241	35241
5738876	2624691	231227	12636550	12370069	271314	6145160	3234066	3139743

17-7 续表

单位：万元

项　目	Item	营业成本 Business Costs	营业税金及附加 Tax and Extra Charges on Business	其它业务利润 Profits from Other Businesses
住宿业合计	**Total Hotels**	**2429990**	**64843**	**44283**
#国有及国有控股	State-owned and State-controlled Enterprises	488590	15559	6677
按登记注册类型分	By Status of Registration			
内资企业	Domestic-funded Enterprises	2115581	45691	39514
国有企业	State-owned Enterprises	145102	3325	4873
集体企业	Collective-owned Enterprises	5957	185	
股份合作企业	Share-holding Cooperative Enterprises	129	1	
联营企业	Joint-operation Enterprises	219	1	
国有联营企业	State-owned Joint-operation Enterprises			
集体联营企业	Collective Joint-operation Enterprises			
国有与集体联营企业	State-collective Joint-operation Enterprises	219	1	
其他联营企业	Other Joint-operation Enterprises			
有限责任公司	Limited Liability Corporations	763476	25517	15120
国有独资企业	State Sole Investment Enterprises	126386	4372	58
其他有限责任公司	Other Limited Liability Companies	637091	21145	15062
股份有限公司	Share-holding Corporations Ltd.	46945	1866	20
私营企业	Private Enterprises	1152597	14794	19501
私营独资企业	Private Sole Investment Enterprises	89548	1125	3362
私营合伙企业	Private Partnership Enterprises	9503	360	269
私营有限责任公司	Private Limited Liability Corporations	1042045	13252	15775
私营股份有限公司	Private Share-holding Corporations Ltd.	11501	57	95
其他企业	Other Enterprises	1156	2	
港、澳、台商投资企业	Enterprises with Investment from Hong Kong, Macao and Taiwan	175171	14379	2814
合资经营企业	Joint Ventures	41149	2147	774
合作经营企业	Cooperative Enterprises	34255	1364	17
独资经营企业	Sole Investment Enterprises	97428	10843	2023
投资股份有限公司	Share-holding Corporations Ltd.	122		
其他港澳台商投资企业	Others	2217	25	
外商投资企业	Enterprises with Foreign Investment	139237	4773	1955
中外合资经营企业	Sino-foreign Joint Ventures	53208	1680	118
中外合作经营企业	Sino-foreign Cooperative Enterprises	1699	200	1220
外资企业	Foreign-funded Enterprises	78037	2536	617
外商投资股份有限公司	Share-holding Corporations Ltd.	2586	55	
其它外商投资企业	Others	3707	302	
按国民经济行业分	By Economic Sector			
旅游饭店	Tourist Hotels	1581342	55388	33205
一般旅馆	Ordinary Hotels	716878	8205	10587
其它住宿服务	Others	131770	1251	491
按控股情况分组	By Holdings			
国有控股	State Holdings	488590	15559	6677
集体控股	Collective Holdings	39034	849	-546
私人控股	Private Holdings	1605396	26878	33561
港澳台商控股	Hongkong,Macaw and Taiwan Holdings	177354	18030	2704
外商控股	Foreign Holdings	116577	3525	1887
其他	Others	3039	1	
按星级分组	By Star Rating			
五星	Five Star	395663	21645	7321
四星	Four Star	237782	7896	7781
三星	Three Star	134908	2667	3140
二星	Two Star	13352	304	218
一星	One Star	27181	271	
其他	Others	1621104	32060	25822

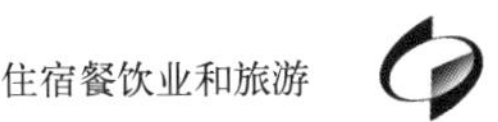

17-7 continued

(10000 yuan)

销售费用 Marketing Expenses	管理费用 Management Expenses	财务费用 Financial Expenses	营业利润 Business Profits	营业外收入 Non-operating revenue	利润总额 Total Profits	所得税费用 Income Taxes Expenses	本年应付职工薪酬 Staff Salary Payable in Current Year
1386762	**1757774**	**337114**	**-941725**	**90834**	**-877221**	**6584**	**1616790**
231607	335075	9919	-201041	24140	-178859	2445	419017
1189632	1492721	261197	-750184	73996	-698757	6185	1340387
91849	127594	3385	-92073	13010	-66787	363	152739
2950	3322	433	-1439	42	-1398	41	4770
280	190		-28		-29	1	298
	100	-1	-32	31	-1		229
	100	-1	-32	31	-1		229
465724	534245	151559	-333894	27310	-324484	1247	525180
53882	77872	2424	-34410	3880	-32004	1962	102948
411841	456373	149135	-299484	23430	-292480	-715	422232
8964	26202	2963	-14132	353	-16046	-63	29615
619865	801055	102857	-308790	33250	-290215	4594	627344
41011	28416	3067	-10448	551	-10586	1243	30325
3886	5857	84	920	215	777	102	5014
565160	752027	99502	-294602	32014	-276150	3233	583414
9809	14755	204	-4661	470	-4256	17	8591
	13		203	1	204	3	213
149883	175060	54005	-146192	7246	-140496	708	157139
45973	53081	11063	-33519	1083	-32559	-18	41794
22322	28472	1438	-13344	640	-12985	157	33145
78442	91978	41483	-97850	5474	-93517	570	80030
231	456	18	-113	4	-110		136
2915	1073	2	-1366	46	-1326		2035
47248	89993	21913	-45348	9592	-37968	-309	119264
10697	30477	14794	-22297	1433	-21564	5	25030
4696	3546	748	-666	57	-623	300	3477
30873	50107	6323	-22364	7932	-14722	-649	85244
416	3172	-15	-413	4	-409		2205
567	2692	63	392	165	-650	35	3309
998091	1170558	291590	-706897	63153	-656372	3294	1130635
326380	489600	39010	-155249	26629	-141799	1523	395067
62291	97616	6513	-79578	1053	-79051	1768	91088
231607	335075	9919	-201041	24140	-178859	2445	419017
22052	31268	7477	-12620	1287	-11503	179	25993
938206	1141948	210255	-507380	49344	-478416	4829	914461
149677	171389	94700	-182436	7333	-176775	-176	145731
45221	77444	14552	-37494	8731	-30913	-620	109900
	650	211	-754		-756	-73	1689
216241	315189	77489	-169243	11345	-163966	-1290	293991
166327	164761	26488	-84185	12435	-74123	1498	182822
84307	109675	7585	-39883	2884	-47554	2154	107680
7478	5849	106	-1020	146	-880	238	8466
1634	4215	899	1022	49	1071	322	2783
910776	1158086	224546	-648415	63975	-591769	3662	1021048

17-8 限额以上餐饮企业财务状况（2022年）

单位：万元

项　目	Item	企业数(个) Number of Enterprises (unit)	年初库存 Beginning Inventory	流动资产合计 Circulating Assets
餐饮业合计	**Total Catering Services**	**6638**	**289970**	**5919336**
#国有及国有控股	State-owned and State-controlled Enterprises	70	8425	394000
按登记注册类型分	By Status of Registration			
内资企业	Domestic-funded Enterprises	6286	236034	4750490
国有企业	State-owned Enterprises	15	448	12605
集体企业	Collective-owned Enterprises	16	523	13289
股份合作企业	Share-holding Cooperative Enterprises	36	747	9879
联营企业	Joint-operation Enterprises	2	134	4323
国有联营企业	State-owned Joint-operation Enterprises	1	134	3718
集体联营企业	Collective Joint-operation Enterprises			
国有与集体联营企业	State-collective Joint-operation Enterprises			
其他联营企业	Other Joint-operation Enterprises	1		605
有限责任公司	Limited Liability Corporations	1002	43285	945373
国有独资公司	State Sole Investment Enterprises	19	1312	36048
其他有限责任公司	Other Limited Liability Companies	983	41972	909325
股份有限公司	Share-holding Corporations Ltd.	23	3200	229632
私营企业	Private Enterprises	5189	187698	3535277
私营独资企业	Private Sole Investment Enterprises	569	12500	140668
私营合伙企业	Private Partnership Enterprises	78	4804	24055
私营有限责任公司	Private Limited Liability Corporations	4504	167667	3340743
私营股份有限公司	Private Share-holding Corporations Ltd.	38	2727	29812
其他企业	Other Enterprises	3		112
港、澳、台商投资企业	Enterprises with Investment from Hong Kong,Macao and Taiwan	268	31777	957308
合资经营企业	Joint Ventures	56	2391	120538
合作经营企业	Cooperative Enterprises	10	5232	31859
独资经营企业	Sole Investment Enterprises	187	23278	799825
投资股份有限公司	Share-holding Corporations Ltd.	8	811	4096
其他港澳台商投资企业	Others	7	66	990
外商投资企业	Enterprises with Foreign Investment	84	22159	211538
中外合资经营企业	Sino-foreign Joint Ventures	17	6119	47542
中外合作经营企业	Sino-foreign Cooperative Enterprises			
外资企业	Foreign-funded Enterprises	58	15872	155806
外商投资股份有限公司	Share-holding Corporations Ltd.	2	18	6960
其它外商投资企业	Others	7	151	1231
按国民经济行业分	By Economic Sector			
正餐服务	Dinner Service	5454	206342	3575745
快餐服务	Fast Food Service	243	29903	680857
饮料及冷饮服务	Beverage and Cold Drink Service	168	14305	803723
餐饮配送及外卖送餐服务	Food and Beverage Distribution and Takeout Service	483	29077	638710
其他餐饮业	Other Services	290	10343	220301
按控股情况分组	By Holdings			
国有控股	State Holdings	70	8425	394000
集体控股	Collective Holdings	26	658	61004
私人控股	Private Holdings	6212	229481	4353374
港澳台商控股	Hongkong,Macaw and Taiwan Holdings	252	33524	925619
外商控股	Foreign Holdings	74	17875	184920
其他	Others	4	7	420

Financial Indicators of Catering Services Enterprises above Designated Size (2022)

(10000 yuan)

固定资产原价 Original Value of Fixed Assets	累计折旧 Accumulated Depreciation	本年折旧 Depreciation Drawn in Current Year	资产合计 Total Assets	负债合计 Total Liabilities	所有者权益合计 Total Creditors' Equity	实收资本 Paid-up Capital	营业收入 Business Revenue	主营业务收入 Main Business Revenue
2784252	**1446920**	**192970**	**10503014**	**8570912**	**1958354**	**2200072**	**12028081**	**11857411**
337928	132903	14044	998381	608334	390047	261428	431695	422224
1783669	866859	125968	7399058	6602966	823224	1584446	8944757	8804427
13204	5682	396	44084	47349	-3265	8073	20853	19523
3276	2221	81	26563	10195	15580	4309	20481	19659
3671	2798	202	11673	10648	1752	985	27637	27560
817	633	99	6741	5200	1542	100	10629	10629
817	633	99	6137	4230	1907	100	10310	10310
			605	970	-365		319	319
637136	321058	38347	1788007	1787699	5876	453300	2074888	2042470
51529	35972	2177	80602	76986	3616	31777	70246	69431
585607	285086	36171	1707405	1710713	2261	421523	2004642	1973039
137733	28256	6121	600603	206659	393966	130528	83617	79761
987743	506200	80711	4921197	4535109	407690	987152	6705724	6603898
100974	40074	5934	245042	222692	21232	52222	368046	363925
22313	11553	2276	39908	35040	5392	12162	70535	69438
857751	453343	71953	4598622	4243513	376004	905645	6209078	6117841
6706	1230	547	37626	33865	5063	17124	58066	52694
90	12	12	190	107	83		927	927
572190	351982	42506	1963552	1250395	710908	439432	1504643	1492549
91404	55403	4392	190560	102656	89490	75441	117206	115694
35641	28812	812	50572	59739	-9167	21075	59575	57822
444133	267297	37092	1710592	1074174	633040	341492	1312138	1303981
858	406	192	10404	12760	-2591	492	11078	10412
155	64	18	1424	1066	136	933	4647	4640
428393	228079	24496	1140405	717551	424222	176194	1578681	1560435
178648	101330	6564	385404	130784	254836	32927	451649	451312
246035	125144	17291	738552	571795	167909	139942	1099862	1082502
2277	946	485	11549	10746	803	1000	19014	18998
1433	660	156	4900	4226	674	2325	8156	7623
1830649	942036	124160	6369241	5807686	578779	1690553	6610954	6487320
688563	372143	37789	2000326	1377408	622713	211688	2417541	2401509
130698	70959	14843	1071942	585514	497983	63750	991463	980481
101015	45611	12589	778457	573032	203513	171313	1457492	1444038
33326	16171	3588	283048	227272	55367	62768	550631	544063
337928	132903	14044	998381	608334	390047	261428	431695	422224
4942	3468	237	193818	169250	23780	6440	67126	66202
1443494	736784	108271	6237536	5775685	489771	1332733	8357968	8226973
743439	442828	52041	2290903	1408271	880383	442732	2014757	2003339
254370	130862	18370	781945	609389	173924	156730	1156063	1138213
79	75	8	431	-18	449	10	471	460

17-8 续表

单位：万元

项　目	Item	营业成本 Business Costs	营业税金及附加 Tax and Extra Charges on Business	其它业务利润 Profits from Other Businesses
餐饮业合计	**Total Catering Services**	**6717136**	**20548**	**36737**
#国有及国有控股	State-owned and State-controlled Enterprises	389180	1804	1557
按登记注册类型分	By Status of Registration			
内资企业	Domestic-funded Enterprises	5380631	17228	23944
国有企业	State-owned Enterprises	14937	50	337
集体企业	Collective-owned Enterprises	14986	313	20
股份合作企业	Share-holding Cooperative Enterprises	13434	37	20
联营企业	Joint-operation Enterprises	9550	30	
国有联营企业	State-owned Joint-operation Enterprises	9344	30	
集体联营企业	Collective Joint-operation Enterprises			
国有与集体联营企业	State-collective Joint-operation Enterprises			
其他联营企业	Other Joint-operation Enterprises	205		
有限责任公司	Limited Liability Corporations	1249874	3811	6075
国有独资公司	State Sole Investment Enterprises	54794	516	
其他有限责任公司	Other Limited Liability Companies	1195080	3295	6075
股份有限公司	Share-holding Corporations Ltd.	77276	603	12
私营企业	Private Enterprises	3999926	12384	17480
私营独资企业	Private Sole Investment Enterprises	228169	1730	1191
私营合伙企业	Private Partnership Enterprises	38336	229	857
私营有限责任公司	Private Limited Liability Corporations	3693682	10371	15433
私营股份有限公司	Private Share-holding Corporations Ltd.	39739	54	
其他企业	Other Enterprises	649		
港、澳、台商投资企业	Enterprises with Investment from Hong Kong,Macao and Taiwan	551724	2530	10701
合资经营企业	Joint Ventures	45896	572	1201
合作经营企业	Cooperative Enterprises	35629	215	3
独资经营企业	Sole Investment Enterprises	463484	1725	9497
投资股份有限公司	Share-holding Corporations Ltd.	4252	17	
其他港澳台商投资企业	Others	2463	2	
外商投资企业	Enterprises with Foreign Investment	784781	790	2093
中外合资经营企业	Sino-foreign Joint Ventures	157692	180	
中外合作经营企业	Sino-foreign Cooperative Enterprises			
外资企业	Foreign-funded Enterprises	616692	580	2077
外商投资股份有限公司	Share-holding Corporations Ltd.	6824	8	16
其它外商投资企业	Others	3574	22	
按国民经济行业分	By Economic Sector			
正餐服务	Dinner Service	3628945	15589	28716
快餐服务	Fast Food Service	1178294	1479	3405
饮料及冷饮服务	Beverage and Cold Drink Service	415579	683	1242
餐饮配送及外卖送餐服务	Food and Beverage Distribution and Takeout Service	1142687	2015	2478
其他餐饮业	Other Services	351632	782	897
按控股情况分组	By Holdings			
国有控股	State Holdings	389180	1804	1557
集体控股	Collective Holdings	50947	648	35
私人控股	Private Holdings	4914226	14957	23346
港澳台商控股	Hongkong,Macaw and Taiwan Holdings	727812	2495	9707
外商控股	Foreign Holdings	634827	643	2093
其他	Others	144	1	

17-8 continued

(10000 yuan)

销售费用 Marketing Expenses	管理费用 Management Expenses	财务费用 Financial Expenses	营业利润 Business Profits	营业外收入 Non-operating revenue	利润总额 Total Profits	所得税费用 Income Taxes Expenses	本年应付职工薪酬 Staff Salary Payable in Current Year
3924292	**1784813**	**108364**	**-445528**	**90831**	**-403236**	**27627**	**3030538**
59466	59970	2866	-13652	3175	-11299	732	156400
2419264	1495312	75523	-387376	65104	-354105	13454	2141144
7793	4390	706	-6959	471	-6551	-602	9980
1499	2912	-73	531	48	574	20	5007
11983	4205	234	-2569	283	-2400	26	8268
71	1018	89	-57	16	-62	99	2971
71	836	89	12	3	-6	99	2931
	182		-69	13	-56		40
593457	316759	25546	-84646	14389	-80236	6795	512966
19196	13406	1402	-18499	158	-18640	23	28082
574261	303353	24144	-66147	14231	-61596	6772	484883
8663	17931	-2914	17733	184	17705	456	34916
1795742	1147908	51934	-311438	49713	-283164	6659	1566730
87102	63002	3035	-16801	2575	-15708	580	91491
22470	11397	433	-2448	553	-2016	60	19858
1675698	1061068	48388	-286629	46101	-260239	5982	1442355
10472	12441	78	-5560	484	-5201	38	13027
57	191	1	29		29	1	306
867230	148706	11652	-64598	15823	-54831	7542	498519
57120	23748	705	-10310	1133	-9615	19	33842
26779	6847	166	-10690	185	-10625	-984	21373
775429	113991	10615	-40504	14394	-31028	8473	438024
6864	2641	165	-2768	73	-3273	34	4274
1039	1479	1	-326	38	-291		1005
637798	140794	21189	6446	9905	5700	6631	390875
257180	19856	4856	21684	1082	22238	5723	94697
364882	119684	16219	-14800	8716	-16020	875	290112
11798	223	20	3	39	29	32	3595
3938	1031	94	-441	69	-548	1	2470
2203426	1189967	69319	-415212	55247	-378132	14156	1761180
974928	245682	36826	1401	14418	1694	9394	645683
490530	95580	-4393	-17351	10047	-20554	2070	247781
139209	171661	4139	-5869	8217	1260	630	259125
116199	81923	2474	-8496	2903	-7504	1376	116768
59466	59970	2866	-13652	3175	-11299	732	156400
3728	5982	-250	5804	136	5738	1291	10527
2313333	1429384	69870	-405859	62574	-374285	7625	1969116
1147779	165366	19301	-14472	15546	-4855	17052	589180
399755	124106	16577	-17440	9396	-18630	925	305133
231	4		91	4	95	2	183

17-9 各市限额以上住宿和餐饮企业财务状况（2022年）

单位：万元

市别	City	企业数（个）Number of Enterprises (unit)	年初库存 Beginning Inventory	流动资产合计 Circulating Assets	固定资产原价 Original Value of Fixed Assets
住宿餐饮业合计	**Total Hotels and Catering Services**	**10233**	**994340**	**17346714**	**13214296**
住宿业	**Hotels**	**3595**	**704370**	**11427378**	**10430044**
广　州	Guangzhou	869	313473	3517102	2767859
深　圳	Shenzhen	707	25044	4211077	2285959
珠　海	Zhuhai	195	8838	413433	662585
汕　头	Shantou	164	3799	107829	301563
佛　山	Foshan	286	16759	584851	828233
韶　关	Shaoguan	117	7816	85418	157410
河　源	Heyuan	56	10886	108997	84007
梅　州	Meizhou	48	4556	109929	143455
惠　州	Huizhou	220	102072	550752	430953
汕　尾	Shanwei	63	1004	34130	70268
东　莞	Dongguan	246	103984	531842	1062943
中　山	Zhongshan	128	2561	119336	313650
江　门	Jiangmen	91	4069	188206	287784
阳　江	Yangjiang	20	253	15034	55725
湛　江	Zhanjiang	75	28131	294968	239709
茂　名	Maoming	50	2484	94633	53682
肇　庆	Zhaoqing	59	1619	96258	105146
清　远	Qingyuan	75	4234	156412	264776
潮　州	Chaozhou	38	33688	44081	185804
揭　阳	Jieyang	59	1396	55051	69413
云　浮	Yunfu	29	27703	108040	59122
餐饮业	**Catering Services**	**6638**	**289970**	**5919336**	**2784252**
广　州	Guangzhou	1822	78625	1687446	943910
深　圳	Shenzhen	1649	111222	2477334	727839
珠　海	Zhuhai	262	8607	165506	50843
汕　头	Shantou	200	3756	43213	13540
佛　山	Foshan	658	20266	265447	135962
韶　关	Shaoguan	127	2899	27363	29588
河　源	Heyuan	33	521	15046	9406
梅　州	Meizhou	19	1168	10253	8413
惠　州	Huizhou	280	7328	145025	150197
汕　尾	Shanwei	72	1015	21821	12662
东　莞	Dongguan	634	27120	495060	249447
中　山	Zhongshan	310	8808	136134	104091
江　门	Jiangmen	169	6600	98804	59664
阳　江	Yangjiang	41	1521	41653	30050
湛　江	Zhanjiang	118	3225	91136	126440
茂　名	Maoming	72	1428	40071	38948
肇　庆	Zhaoqing	55	1663	61243	24206
清　远	Qingyuan	31	1208	58125	23974
潮　州	Chaozhou	23	1150	3829	4322
揭　阳	Jieyang	44	929	28061	26472
云　浮	Yunfu	19	913	6769	14278

Financial Indicators of Enterprises above Designated Size of Hotels and Catering Services by City (2022)

(10000 yuan)

累计折旧 Accumulated Depreciation	#本年折旧 Depreciation Drawn in Current Year	资产合计 Total Assets	负债合计 Total Liabilities	所有者权益合计 Total Creditors' Equity	实收资本 Paid-up Capital	营业收入 Business Revenue	主营业务收入 Main Business Revenue
6972101	**536342**	**31900935**	**28746839**	**3189899**	**10774979**	**16967127**	**16643853**
5525181	**343372**	**21397921**	**20175927**	**1231545**	**8574906**	**4939047**	**4786442**
1522040	90253	6412944	5200961	1197260	1916343	1477526	1435895
1241986	52995	6640797	6134819	517818	1540784	1330476	1303472
390776	18410	1031950	1075162	-39229	582460	239434	229747
150925	7033	329564	345132	-15568	131997	131175	128203
490292	32895	1168842	1258694	-74756	424380	317385	292382
63667	8068	246918	219308	26525	67524	82088	80306
40014	3389	237362	197529	39832	1057040	51486	51105
77678	5908	204732	221455	-34323	1126724	39763	38753
202576	18048	897525	1020862	-122251	141761	244643	228285
32663	5977	109987	76614	33373	35783	39420	38927
584540	39775	1214800	1639103	-424304	298191	386350	378370
156934	10905	343182	335732	7450	663361	114942	113574
164460	11869	384560	366907	17653	218182	104843	101763
22857	2928	53727	49110	4617	15386	22294	21739
78090	7919	607212	664847	-57635	63936	74502	72139
23333	2409	206926	244972	-38062	12202	38619	37848
54065	4383	193446	220360	-24591	39462	41950	41348
131299	12141	496908	551800	-46938	104708	97769	89635
33075	2586	240502	92368	148135	24096	20904	20797
38121	2502	135145	111121	24724	44865	44255	43885
25791	2978	240894	149075	91814	65724	39223	38271
1446920	**192970**	**10503014**	**8570912**	**1958354**	**2200072**	**12028081**	**11857411**
529245	65989	3660715	2758193	912609	560904	4217092	4177842
396884	58797	3759154	3217666	565489	947806	4213131	4129920
30413	4361	230255	227641	3101	50025	331974	326416
6362	1402	61060	40654	20351	10989	170960	169171
70101	9611	436356	409376	27422	80505	635400	627175
13915	1724	51078	34939	15851	9701	60781	60035
4081	243	27517	20286	7231	4830	25652	23584
4224	475	15218	13227	1991	5021	13826	13816
78005	10042	276128	260579	15569	84246	302692	294662
7020	621	33600	20862	9316	2951	48151	46493
92251	15910	909763	541036	366675	197246	1080096	1072296
37414	4339	246605	220980	26985	137731	364995	364248
28628	3983	198767	174593	21983	31345	224971	221053
15616	1510	75864	64715	9579	5533	45466	42728
75175	6241	173041	195696	-22744	22056	111341	109225
10078	1972	80019	78592	25	10379	40627	40322
10944	1383	84746	99225	-13323	8787	38967	36977
11994	2105	114641	143658	-29017	11079	33129	32965
1043	167	7280	4102	3194	1556	15693	15513
15702	517	46092	21510	24332	16260	37462	37311
7827	1579	15116	23383	-8267	1123	15677	15660

17-9 续表

单位：万元

市别	City	营业成本 Business Costs	营业税金及附加 Tax and Extra Charges on Business	其它业务利润 Profits from Other Businesses	销售费用 Marketing Expenses
住宿餐饮业合计	**Total Hotels and Catering Services**	**9147126**	**85391**	**81020**	**5311053**
住宿业	**Hotels**	**2429990**	**64843**	**44283**	**1386762**
广州	Guangzhou	721052	22524	10116	395763
深圳	Shenzhen	693463	10826	10715	343911
珠海	Zhuhai	123381	3618	2259	74745
汕头	Shantou	62304	2126	417	37889
佛山	Foshan	159994	10120	2100	88936
韶关	Shaoguan	39639	869	702	22138
河源	Heyuan	20367	361	340	23545
梅州	Meizhou	21441	382	547	10167
惠州	Huizhou	112235	2980	708	70198
汕尾	Shanwei	23172	305	106	6149
东莞	Dongguan	153302	3166	9709	127079
中山	Zhongshan	58421	1045	355	37476
江门	Jiangmen	46720	1747	796	29046
阳江	Yangjiang	8479	395	106	7826
湛江	Zhanjiang	26872	1307	1979	32589
茂名	Maoming	22458	227	1013	8964
肇庆	Zhaoqing	25378	339	1253	13878
清远	Qingyuan	41385	1142	975	38358
潮州	Chaozhou	11948	331		5585
揭阳	Jieyang	30598	533		3687
云浮	Yunfu	27384	502	90	8834
餐饮业	**Catering Services**	**6717136**	**20548**	**36737**	**3924292**
广州	Guangzhou	2212427	4925	14312	1488381
深圳	Shenzhen	2188125	6279	12153	1654734
珠海	Zhuhai	205256	395	220	80855
汕头	Shantou	127500	610	175	23761
佛山	Foshan	402568	1883	2095	150083
韶关	Shaoguan	41429	138	20	9281
河源	Heyuan	17164	46	139	3963
梅州	Meizhou	10288	35		1323
惠州	Huizhou	184296	1247	647	65667
汕尾	Shanwei	32278	360		8373
东莞	Dongguan	747392	1633	3303	173238
中山	Zhongshan	223110	471	835	108228
江门	Jiangmen	131144	437	587	66618
阳江	Yangjiang	25991	269	7	11451
湛江	Zhanjiang	57228	279	1009	33189
茂名	Maoming	23038	402	647	9711
肇庆	Zhaoqing	22367	182	338	11453
清远	Qingyuan	18135	113	144	12498
潮州	Chaozhou	11759	68	107	1564
揭阳	Jieyang	25907	497		5875
云浮	Yunfu	9736	281		4045

17-9 continued

(10000 yuan)

管理费用 Management Expenses	财务费用 Financial Expenses	营业利润 Business Profits	营业外收入 Non-operating revenue	利润总额 Total Profits	所得税费用 Income Taxes Expenses	本年应付职工薪酬 Staff Salary Payable in Current Year
3542586	**445477**	**-1387253**	**181666**	**-1280457**	**34211**	**4647328**
1757774	**337114**	**-941725**	**90834**	**-877221**	**6584**	**1616790**
529886	94084	-237237	27599	-222785	4007	512055
495765	94021	-270589	25827	-257728	-1273	439834
92820	25023	-80010	4158	-77566	218	92287
34969	8527	-15228	2629	-13171	292	30720
119442	11441	-72279	11125	-67667	808	91948
32604	4124	-17824	2679	-15445	30	26159
14938	3169	-10709	533	-10439	-228	15317
16530	7267	-15618	999	-14725	14	14769
81477	12896	-33996	2327	-32593	699	71172
12406	238	-2637	132	-2534	51	12196
131899	31400	-59331	3484	-57077	893	121287
42304	2676	-26412	1131	-27907	638	38964
36813	5989	-14808	1898	-13125	80	33133
8333	1093	-3753	182	-3621	6	5248
23104	7292	-15213	874	-14507	158	25328
11498	6173	-9741	558	-9361	42	11634
13246	3621	-13725	1286	-12440	14	13540
34322	14063	-28775	2775	-26152	-84	30684
6590	465	-3679	57	11478	28	6051
9195	539	-282	125	-208	175	11583
9632	3014	-9882	458	-9650	17	12883
1784813	**108364**	**-445528**	**90831**	**-403236**	**27627**	**3030538**
628546	30871	-66866	27704	-55165	17986	1072221
601698	42695	-279455	38761	-266318	246	1138920
58509	3655	-16361	2323	-14559	406	76792
14260	812	3827	463	4316	274	25516
97974	4939	-24394	5602	-19127	1193	140070
9105	680	455	254	194	51	13087
4433	219	-164	127	-40	61	5389
2285	126	-400	68	-335	12	2866
54113	4001	-5413	1131	-5767	394	74309
7221	776	-909	138	-787	45	8960
160414	5532	-7331	6288	-3103	5403	232809
46644	1605	-15452	4346	-11834	664	91625
32436	2794	-7570	1082	-7396	421	61387
8674	1085	-2090	411	-1657	43	14231
25118	2727	-7992	523	-7213	103	29733
10652	960	-4327	461	-4210	75	10951
7907	1671	-4669	708	-4066	22	9436
8769	1961	-7728	320	-7572	19	9722
1527	71	672	45	733	53	3555
2392	1025	1394	34	1419	150	6059
2136	161	-755	43	-749	10	2901

17-10 各市住宿餐饮业营业额

Business of Enterprises above Designated Size of Hotels and Catering Services by City

单位：万元 (10000 yuan)

市 别	Item	2021		2022	
		住宿业 Hotels Service	餐饮业 Catering Service	住宿业 Hotels Service	餐饮业 Catering Service
广 州	Guangzhou	1696967	8608782	1613596	8366780
深 圳	Shenzhen	1657184	10973943	1524365	10263105
珠 海	Zhuhai	447571	931552	409869	912515
汕 头	Shantou	210764	1073201	188197	1064609
佛 山	Foshan	444643	2848668	415867	2832740
韶 关	Shaoguan	115101	362110	109013	359112
河 源	Heyuan	92945	375735	82696	361969
梅 州	Meizhou	88746	483537	79496	473913
惠 州	Huizhou	328072	1539417	302508	1516162
汕 尾	Shanwei	88374	630545	91782	620830
东 莞	Dongguan	517455	4904266	515083	4899398
中 山	Zhongshan	175042	1128499	159605	1114831
江 门	Jiangmen	190514	1267584	169946	1243733
阳 江	Yangjiang	49235	471734	50451	456411
湛 江	Zhanjiang	178366	2567394	168927	2505002
茂 名	Maoming	165125	1606415	156858	1560766
肇 庆	Zhaoqing	115811	952946	102720	921106
清 远	Qingyuan	150063	477300	123260	461967
潮 州	Chaozhou	40009	460087	37953	446653
揭 阳	Jieyang	139349	575392	113960	548208
云 浮	Yunfu	65413	329246	57371	324947
按经济区域分	By Region				
珠 三 角	Pearl River Delta	5573260	33155659	5213559	32070370
东 翼	Eastern Region	478497	2739225	431892	2680300
西 翼	Western Region	392727	4645543	376236	4522179
山 区	Mountainous Region	512269	2027928	451836	1981908

17-11 旅游部门基本情况

Basic Statistics on Tourism-related Agencies

指　标	Item	2000	2010	2015	2020	2021	2022
宾馆(酒店)　(家)	Number of Hotels　(unit)	2655	9179	16440	15696	17692	18314
按星级分：白金五星	By Star Rating:Platinum Five Star		1	1	1	1	1
五星	Five Star	19	93	116	101	94	90
四星	Four Star	61	194	178	135	136	127
三星	Three Star	283	661	566	338	292	263
二星	Two Star	339	246	107	36	25	20
一星	One Star	48	14	4	2	1	
未评星级	Unrated	1905	7970	15468	15083	17143	17813
宾馆(酒店)接待能力	Reception Capability of Hotels						
客房　(间)	Number of Guest Rooms　(unit)	202277	565582	982628	967022	1173307	1447484
床位　(张)	Number of Beds　(unit)	401718	938389	1535288	1451175	1742855	2125534
旅行社　(家)	Number of Travel Agencies　(unit)	504	1292	2150	3425	3605	3764

17-12 城市接待外国游客人数

Number of Foreign Visitors Received by Cities

单位：人次　(person-time)

国　别	Country	2000	2005	2010	2015	2020	2021	2022
总计	**Total**	**2128501**	**4639133**	**7322478**	**7818342**	**804613**	**584893**	**444588**
日本	Japan	413833	962727	1077329	892362	122929	124329	127194
韩国	Republic of Korea	71841	239213	418115	474549	35551	35948	24402
菲律宾	Philippines	20793	30847	47184	59613	6533	3005	3332
新加坡	Singapore	93762	179559	284832	285197	20860	20670	12833
泰国	Thailand	48341	150502	134313	147501	8542	7182	5699
印度尼西亚	Indonesia	63159	128428	158879	118720	7027	2706	2649
马来西亚	Malaysia	110384	220598	421556	351926	19545	12942	11008
美国	United States	196362	361224	645783	710768	79971	59688	44013
加拿大	Canada	35968	67844	133138	133020	16126	14451	11845
英国	United Kingdom	59123	105238	138353	146989	16312	13530	8130
法国	France	43578	99158	119850	148791	10059	10191	7836
德国	Germany	44707	87158	118332	142266	25600	18498	14063
意大利	Italy	19792	56071	86454	78488	5416	6973	7383
俄罗斯	Russia	10407	26692	58568	84489	17132	11856	9323
澳大利亚	Australia	34595	73346	149780	138169	14696	9844	10611
新西兰	New Zealand	5835	15702	24119	30740	4111	3313	3195
其他	Others	856021	1834826	3305893	3874754	394203	229767	141072

17−13 各市旅游宾馆(酒店)住宿设施（2022年）

Lodging Facilities of Tourist Hotels by City (2022)

市别	City	宾馆(酒店)(个) Number of Hotels (unit)	#白金五星级 Platinum Five Star	五星级 Five Star	四星级 Four Star	三星级 Three Star	二星级 Two Star	一星级 One Star	客房(间) Number of Rooms (unit)	床位(张) Number of Beds (unit)
全省	**Provincial Total**	**18314**	**1**	**90**	**127**	**263**	**20**		**1447484**	**2125534**
广州	Guangzhou	4439	1	23	29	61	11		302155	425524
深圳	Shenzhen	716		20	16	22	3		289085	374189
珠海	Zhuhai	542		6	7	21			53006	75664
汕头	Shantou	290		2	5	13			29876	41163
佛山	Foshan	1128		9	12	11			88427	122634
韶关	Shaoguan	675			2	29			34923	55216
河源	Heyuan	764		1	2	11	2		51926	109814
梅州	Meizhou	753		2	6	20			32117	49834
惠州	Huizhou	1077		4	5	7			77507	107559
汕尾	Shanwei	287		1	2	8			20340	30013
东莞	Dongguan	1542		9	7	1			132800	166600
中山	Zhongshan	553		2	1	8	1		41740	59935
江门	Jiangmen	1364		2	1	5			47000	71500
阳江	Yangjiang	833		3	2	6			46528	100290
湛江	Zhanjiang	690		2	6	7	1		48522	74977
茂名	Maoming	589		1	2	3			28690	67575
肇庆	Zhaoqing	538		1	7	19	1		32546	50532
清远	Qingyuan	629		1	4	3			37782	62152
潮州	Chaozhou	257			6	3	1		11948	16744
揭阳	Jieyang	343		1	4	2			22138	35619
云浮	Yunfu	305			1	3			18428	28000
按经济区域分	By Region									
珠三角	Pearl River Delta	11899	1	76	85	155	16		1064266	1454137
东翼	Eastern Region	1177		4	17	26	1		84302	123539
西翼	Western Region	2112		6	10	16	1		123740	242842
山区	Mountainous Region	3126		4	15	66	2		175176	305016

注：本表星级宾馆(酒店)指2022年底止已得到国家文化和旅游部或广东省文化和旅游厅批准的，不包已报未批部分。

Note: Star-rated hotels in this table refer to those approved by the National Culture And Tourism Ministry or Guangdong Provincial Culture and Tourism Department by the end of 2022, excluding hotels under examination.

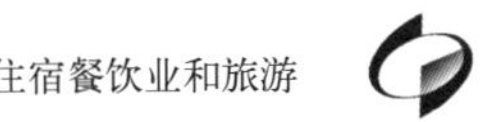

17-14 各市接待过夜旅游者人数

Number of Overnight Tourists by City

单位：万人次 (10000 person-times)

市 别	City	2021			2022		
		合计 Total	入境游客 Overseas Tourist Arrivals	国内游客 Domestic Tourists	合计 Total	入境游客 Overseas Tourist Arrivals	国内游客 Domestic Tourists
全 省	**Provincial Total**	**25701.06**	**320.44**	**25380.63**	**20307.15**	**190.16**	**20116.99**
广 州	Guangzhou	5795.30	67.95	5727.35	4956.94	71.08	4885.86
深 圳	Shenzhen	6364.32	131.49	6232.84	4896.03	55.13	4840.90
珠 海	Zhuhai	1004.72	42.44	962.27	608.08	18.35	589.73
汕 头	Shantou	493.15	1.75	491.40	383.62	1.56	382.06
佛 山	Foshan	1596.86	8.58	1588.28	1250.65	5.55	1245.11
韶 关	Shaoguan	464.91	0.75	464.16	362.81	0.60	362.21
河 源	Heyuan	317.87	0.50	317.37	267.45	0.33	267.13
梅 州	Meizhou	313.64	0.92	312.72	231.69	0.42	231.27
惠 州	Huizhou	1374.42	7.83	1366.58	1079.94	4.84	1075.10
汕 尾	Shanwei	430.13	4.20	425.93	331.40	2.20	329.20
东 莞	Dongguan	1961.56	22.88	1938.68	1588.44	7.43	1581.01
中 山	Zhongshan	782.61	6.92	775.68	512.94	7.87	505.07
江 门	Jiangmen	776.97	10.23	766.74	638.91	3.65	635.26
阳 江	Yangjiang	490.12	1.72	488.39	404.63	1.34	403.30
湛 江	Zhanjiang	807.23	1.61	805.62	657.80	0.74	657.06
茂 名	Maoming	557.27	0.68	556.59	464.23	0.44	463.78
肇 庆	Zhaoqing	618.19	1.32	616.87	455.46	1.98	453.48
清 远	Qingyuan	638.14	2.27	635.86	480.17	1.57	478.60
潮 州	Chaozhou	273.00	0.70	272.30	167.75	0.44	167.31
揭 阳	Jieyang	274.19	0.68	273.51	267.47	0.36	267.11
云 浮	Yunfu	366.47	5.01	361.46	300.72	4.29	296.44
按经济区域分	By Region						
珠 三 角	Pearl River Delta	20274.93	299.64	19975.29	15987.39	175.87	15811.52
东 翼	Eastern Region	1470.48	7.33	1463.15	1150.25	4.57	1145.68
西 翼	Western Region	1854.62	4.02	1850.60	1526.66	2.52	1524.15
山 区	Mountainous Region	2101.04	9.45	2091.58	1642.85	7.20	1635.64

17-15 各市旅游业收入

Tourism Earnings by City

单位：亿元 (100 million yuan)

市别	City	收入合计 Total Earnings		国际旅游收入 Foreign Exchange Earnings		国内旅游收入 Domestic Tourism Earnings	
		2021	2022	2021	2022	2021	2022
全　省	**Provincial Total**	**5433.73**	**4213.51**	**144.51**	**116.84**	**5289.21**	**4096.67**
广　州	Guangzhou	1424.21	1196.10	40.20	40.43	1384.01	1155.67
深　圳	Shenzhen	1598.98	1161.50	65.52	32.28	1533.46	1129.22
珠　海	Zhuhai	207.71	114.06	11.57	5.77	196.13	108.29
汕　头	Shantou	94.65	71.33	0.66	0.95	93.99	70.38
佛　山	Foshan	333.55	284.25	2.63	2.27	330.92	281.98
韶　关	Shaoguan	69.11	50.48	0.51	0.36	68.60	50.11
河　源	Heyuan	51.09	41.60	0.06	0.89	51.03	40.71
梅　州	Meizhou	54.72	40.64	0.34	0.25	54.38	40.39
惠　州	Huizhou	219.60	168.18	1.71	4.06	217.89	164.12
汕　尾	Shanwei	58.34	49.43	3.07	5.78	55.27	43.65
东　莞	Dongguan	379.58	307.41	8.59	6.46	370.99	300.94
中　山	Zhongshan	129.58	95.16	1.06	6.07	128.52	89.09
江　门	Jiangmen	124.83	94.88	2.11	1.38	122.72	93.51
阳　江	Yangjiang	85.47	68.93	0.45	0.37	85.03	68.56
湛　江	Zhanjiang	149.99	113.04	0.50	0.38	149.49	112.66
茂　名	Maoming	102.02	82.14	0.21	0.24	101.81	81.91
肇　庆	Zhaoqing	102.71	74.95	0.40	0.90	102.32	74.05
清　远	Qingyuan	111.40	91.49	1.17	6.26	110.22	85.22
潮　州	Chaozhou	30.62	17.89	0.51	0.18	30.10	17.71
揭　阳	Jieyang	41.59	40.33	0.20	0.03	41.39	40.30
云　浮	Yunfu	63.99	49.72	3.04	1.52	60.95	48.20
按经济区域分	By Region						
珠三角	Pearl River Delta	4520.75	3496.49	133.79	99.62	4386.96	3396.87
东　翼	Eastern Region	225.20	178.98	4.44	6.94	220.75	172.04
西　翼	Western Region	337.48	264.11	1.16	0.99	336.33	263.13
山　区	Mountainous Region	350.31	273.93	5.12	9.29	345.18	264.63

17-16 各市国际旅游外汇收入
Foreign Exchange Earnings from International Tourism by City

单位：万美元 (USD 10000)

市 别	City	2000	2005	2010	2015	2018	2019	2020	2021	2022
全 省	**Provincial Total**	**411221**	**639739**	**1243154**	**1788466**	**2051180**	**2052131**	**235267**	**224002**	**173705**
广 州	Guangzhou	150580	229400	468858	569601	648214	653027	80595	62311	60107
深 圳	Shenzhen	141669	200869	318058	496837	512094	500331	94272	101563	47990
珠 海	Zhuhai	39395	70148	122339	96263	146830	164980	15750	17934	8586
汕 头	Shantou	11705	5950	5016	8927	19874	21001	1430	1023	1418
佛 山	Foshan	15973	34485	72896	137548	161096	108054	5122	4084	3375
韶 关	Shaoguan	351	2782	10309	2848	2391	3108	949	788	539
河 源	Heyuan	798	850	1389	1420	2240	4098	172	93	1322
梅 州	Meizhou	1487	1975	2962	10321	17471	19542	1779	525	372
惠 州	Huizhou	5333	16549	50168	88494	104291	106940	3177	2651	6041
汕 尾	Shanwei	387	455	1175	2538	3390	3996	1522	4765	8595
东 莞	Dongguan	7618	28189	67592	157743	163012	159108	11696	13317	9610
中 山	Zhongshan	14692	21027	27591	29843	27227	30528	2518	1636	9026
江 门	Jiangmen	8295	10521	47657	96887	135315	176782	6802	3269	2049
阳 江	Yangjiang	230	852	1876	3729	4293	4841	491	692	549
湛 江	Zhanjiang	1004	1483	2716	7305	11724	12521	810	773	562
茂 名	Maoming	169	676	1198	1739	2815	3338	317	322	350
肇 庆	Zhaoqing	6264	4718	12440	32231	36152	21960	1693	620	1332
清 远	Qingyuan	834	2051	11062	15608	10168	11592	1199	1815	9313
潮 州	Chaozhou	3071	5264	13207	22296	34745	37193	973	794	265
揭 阳	Jieyang	701	587	2150	1820	2557	3361	318	316	43
云 浮	Yunfu	665	907	2499	4468	5280	5830	3682	4713	2263
按经济区域分	By Region									
珠 三 角	Pearl River Delta	389819	615907	1187597	1705447	1934231	1921710	221625	207384	148114
东 翼	Eastern Region	15864	12256	21547	35581	60566	65551	4243	6898	10321
西 翼	Western Region	1403	3012	5790	12773	18833	20700	1618	1787	1461
山 区	Mountainous Region	4135	8564	28220	34665	37550	44170	7781	7934	13809

注：本表数为广东省文化和旅游厅抽样调查测算数。

Note: Data in this table are obtained from the sample surveys of Guangdong Provincial Culture and Tourism Department.

主要统计指标解释

住宿业 是指为顾客提供临时住宿服务的企业(单位)和个体户。

餐饮业 是指从事食品的烹饪、调制并直接售给居民和社会集团的企业(单位)和个体户。

入境旅游人数 指来我国参观、访问、旅行、探亲、访友、休养 、考察、参加会议和从事经济、科技、文化、教育、体育、宗教等活动的外国人、华侨、港澳台同胞的人数。不包括外国在我国的常驻机构，如使领馆、通讯社、企业办事处的工作人员；来我国常驻的外国专家、留学生以及在岸逗留不过夜人员。

国际旅游外汇收入 指入境旅游的外国人、华侨、港澳台同胞在中国大陆旅游过程中发生的一切旅游支出，对于国家来说就是国际旅游外汇收入。

Explanatory Notes on Main Statistical Indicators

Hotel Services refers to the enterprises (establishments) and individuals engaged in providing temporary accommodation to customers.

Catering Services refer to the enterprises (establishments) and individuals engaged in food cooking, seasoning and selling food directly to households and social institutions.

Number of Overseas Visitor Arrivals refers to the number of foreigners, overseas Chinese, Chinese compatriots from Hong Kong, Macao and Taiwan coming to China for sight-seeing, visits, tours, family reunions, gatherings of friends, recuperation, inspection, conferences and other activities in the nature of business, science and technology, culture, education, sports, and religion. The statistics excludes representatives and employees of resident institutions of foreign countries in China such as embassies, consulates, news agencies and offices of foreign companies and organizations, as well as long-term foreign experts or students residing in China, and persons in transition without staying overnight in China.

Foreign Exchange Earnings from International Tourism refer to the total expenditures of foreigners, overseas Chinese, Chinese compatriots from Hong Kong, Macao and Taiwan during their stay in the mainland of China, or earnings of foreign exchange from international tourism in terms of national economy.

十八、房地产业

REAL ESTATE

十八　房地产业

简要说明

一、本篇资料反映广东省房地产开发企业经营活动情况，主要包括房地产开发企业土地开发和购置情况、投资规模及完成情况、房屋建筑情况及商品房销售情况等。

二、本篇资料由广东省统计局固定资产投资统计处整理提供。

三、本篇统计资料是根据《房地产开发统计报表制度》搜集和加工整理而得，全部数据采用全面调查的统计方法。

18 Real Estate

Brief Introduction

I. The information within this section reflects the operation and activities of real estate development enterprises within the Guangdong Province. The information focuses on the land development and purchasing activities of real estate development enterprises, the scope of investments and their completion, the construction of buildings, and the sale of commodity buildings

II. The information within this section was edited and provided by the Statistics Office on Investment in Fixed Assets from the Guangdong Statistics Bureau

III. The statistical information within this section was collected and further edited in accordance to the “Real Estate Development Statistics Reporting System,” all data has been compiled by full investigation.

18-1 房地产开发主要指标
Main Indicators on Real Estate Development

项　目	Item	2000	2010	2015	2020	2021	2022
土地开发及购置	**Land Development and Purchases**						
本年土地购置面积（万平方米）	Land Space Purchased in Current Year (10000 sq.m)	1942.30	1726.31	1478.80	1565.26	1637.98	738.18
本年完成投资额　（亿元）	**Investment Completed in Current Year (100 million yuan)**	**858.61**	**3659.69**	**8538.47**	**17312.74**	**17465.85**	**14962.97**
#住宅	Residential Buildings	593.74	2539.03	5890.51	11910.43	12438.31	10700.28
本年实际到位资金（亿元）	**Total Actual Funds in Place This Year (100 million yuan)**	**1064.51**	**7426.13**	**14164.30**	**26338.87**	**28156.22**	**18799.04**
#国内贷款	Domestic Loans	228.53	1256.11	2577.81	4799.69	4377.99	2781.86
利用外资	Foreign Investment	39.16	90.85	26.65	13.05	15.19	13.07
自筹资金	Self-raising Funds	287.71	1582.94	3933.40	8370.36	9183.75	7091.42
定金及预收款	Deposit and Advances Received	423.32	1537.64	4656.66	8485.31	9589.35	5799.01
个人按揭贷款	Personal Mortgage Loan		974.17	2322.61	3939.32	4231.62	2677.94
其他到位资金	Others	85.79	1984.42	647.17	731.14	758.32	435.73
房屋建筑面积（万平方米）	**Floor Space of Buildings(10000 sq.m)**						
施工面积	Floor Space under Construction	9922.12	29301.36	57941.86	91642.42	94247.53	88662.69
#住宅	Residential Buildings	7400.38	22253.76	40388.82	62695.09	63828.96	59483.86
竣工面积	Floor Space Completed	3161.39	5659.10	6044.43	7763.75	8043.47	8161.12
#住宅	Residential Buildings	2598.52	4589.22	4435.40	5573.29	5587.55	5641.97
竣工房屋价值　（亿元）	**Value of Buildings Completed (100 million yuan)**	**511.46**	**1587.46**	**2256.69**	**3760.73**	**4291.48**	**4779.71**
#住宅	Residential Buildings	415.94	1276.09	1639.45	2640.72	3094.66	3356.40
商品房销售面积（万平方米）	**Floor Space of Commercial Buildings Sold (10000 sq.m)**	**2259.95**	**7321.76**	**11681.01**	**14908.25**	**14011.26**	**10591.11**
#住宅	Residential Buildings	2009.34	6552.81	10497.62	12930.66	11826.26	8568.72
商品房销售额　（亿元）	**Total Sales of Commercial Buildings (100 million yuan)**	**729.50**	**5480.77**	**11442.80**	**22572.51**	**22320.27**	**15870.47**
#住宅	Residential Buildings	597.36	4589.82	9967.32	19829.63	19457.63	13428.51

注：2000年其他到位资金包括个人按揭贷款。
Note:Others funds in place in 2000 include personal mortgage loan.

18-2 按用途分房地产开发企业房屋建筑及销售情况

Situation of Real Estate Development, Corporate Building Construction and Sales by Purpose

指　标	Item	2005	2010	2015	2020	2021	2022
房屋施工面积　（万平方米）	**Floor Space under Construction (10000 sq.m)**	**15110.04**	**29301.36**	**57941.86**	**91642.42**	**94247.53**	**88662.69**
住宅	Residential Buildings	11399.99	22253.76	40388.82	62695.09	63828.96	59483.86
办公楼	Office Buildings	691.43	946.33	2607.81	5737.68	6103.22	5751.13
商业营业用房	Commercial Retail Buildings	1756.51	2621.92	6208.54	7937.75	7828.19	7185.81
其他	Other Buildings	1262.11	3479.35	8736.69	15271.90	16487.16	16241.89
房屋新开工面积（万平方米）	**Newly Started Constructing Floor Space (10000 sq.m)**	**4989.82**	**9904.38**	**12676.74**	**18407.77**	**16097.26**	**8535.40**
住宅	Residential Buildings	4010.39	7826.80	8681.76	12573.97	11392.51	5688.99
办公楼	Office Buildings	99.04	160.47	566.83	1133.75	584.57	465.10
商业营业用房	Commercial Retail Buildings	494.79	688.69	1573.31	1388.11	1009.17	601.35
其他	Other Buildings	385.61	1228.41	1854.85	3311.94	3111.00	1779.96
房屋竣工面积　（万平方米）	**Floor Space Completed(10000 sq.m)**	**4385.16**	**5659.10**	**6044.43**	**7763.75**	**8043.47**	**8161.12**
住宅	Residential Buildings	3476.73	4589.22	4435.40	5573.29	5587.55	5641.97
办公楼	Office Buildings	118.20	120.07	237.18	326.47	419.80	378.22
商业营业用房	Commercial Retail Buildings	427.16	474.79	504.54	593.35	627.82	668.40
其他	Other Buildings	363.08	475.01	867.30	1270.65	1408.30	1472.54
竣工房屋价值　（亿元）	**Value of Buildings Completed (100 million yuan)**	**829.35**	**1587.46**	**2256.69**	**3760.73**	**4291.48**	**4779.71**
住宅	Residential Buildings	632.53	1276.08	1639.45	2640.72	3094.66	3356.40
办公楼	Office Buildings	29.84	42.50	114.29	230.86	320.52	371.95
商业营业用房	Commercial Retail Buildings	98.59	154.56	234.71	418.36	371.91	484.53
其他	Other Buildings	68.40	114.32	268.24	470.79	504.38	566.83
商品房销售面积（万平方米）	**Floor Space of Commercial Buildings Sold (10000 sq.m)**	**5038.91**	**7321.76**	**11681.01**	**14908.25**	**14011.26**	**10591.11**
住宅	Residential Buildings	4546.32	6552.81	10497.62	12930.66	11826.26	8568.72
办公楼	Office Buildings	107.76	163.03	311.12	448.14	457.52	454.02
商业营业用房	Commercial Retail Buildings	277.08	371.91	479.21	610.92	725.69	656.75
其他	Other Buildings	107.75	234.01	393.05	918.54	1001.79	911.62
商品房销售额　（亿元）	**Total Sales of Commercial Buildings (100 million yuan)**	**2238.66**	**5480.77**	**11442.80**	**22572.51**	**22320.27**	**15870.47**
住宅	Residential Buildings	1886.39	4589.82	9967.32	19829.63	19457.63	13428.51
办公楼	Office Buildings	89.61	248.43	583.87	1189.86	1076.79	1077.22
商业营业用房	Commercial Retail Buildings	224.58	483.00	624.73	954.31	1143.97	848.19
其他	Other Buildings	38.09	159.52	266.87	598.71	641.87	516.55

18-3 按登记注册类型分组房地产开发投资情况

Investment in Real Estate Development

单位：亿元 (100 million yuan)

按登记注册类型分组	By Registration Status	2021 完成投资额 Investment Completed	2021 #住宅 Residential Buildings	2022 完成投资额 Investment Completed	2022 #住宅 Residential Buildings
全省	**Provincial Total**	**17465.85**	**12438.31**	**14962.97**	**10700.28**
内资	Domestic	15954.95	11420.62	13742.92	9901.05
国有	State-owned	666.53	473.78	734.03	549.70
集体	Collective-owned	48.48	36.12	52.26	28.85
股份合作	Cooperative	29.64	23.26	10.64	7.85
联营	Joint	6.30	5.27	7.05	5.08
有限责任公司	Limited Liability	8903.03	6459.78	7565.29	5496.92
股份有限公司	Share-holding	305.43	216.74	233.56	154.18
私营	Private	5975.48	4191.77	5072.39	3608.49
其他	Others	20.05	13.90	67.71	49.99
港、澳、台商投资	Funds from Hong Kong, Macao and Taiwan	822.38	491.32	690.07	454.09
外商投资	Foreign Funded	688.53	526.37	529.97	345.14

18-4 按登记注册类型分组房地产开发房屋建筑面积及价值（2022年）

Floor Space and Value of Buildings in Real Estate Development (2022)

按登记注册类型分组	By Registration Status	房屋建筑面积(万平方米) Floor Space of Buildings(10000 sq.m) 施工面积 Floor Space of Buildings under Construction	竣工面积 Floor Space of Buildings Completed	#住宅 Residential Buildings	竣工房屋价值（亿元）Value of Buildings Completed (100 million yuan)	#住宅 Residential Buildings
全省	**Provincial Total**	**88662.69**	**8161.12**	**5641.97**	**4779.71**	**3356.40**
内资	Domestic-funded Economy	80187.90	7368.44	5197.21	4297.92	3083.89
国有	State-owned	1481.61	22.25	13.66	22.87	14.10
集体	Collective-owned	411.12	15.80	13.29	5.54	4.71
股份合作	Cooperative	45.36				
联营	Joint	12.85				
有限责任公司	Limited Liability	43371.65	3965.53	2778.34	2297.48	1664.00
股份有限公司	Share-holding	1236.74	78.70	55.65	44.44	21.40
私营	Private	33554.08	3286.16	2336.28	1927.59	1379.69
其他	Others	74.48				
港、澳、台商投资	Funds from Hong Kong, Macao and Taiwan	5341.23	441.41	237.24	240.14	123.11
外商投资	Foreign Funded	3133.56	351.28	207.51	241.65	149.39

18−5 各市房地产开发企业投资总规模及完成情况（2022年）
The Total Investment Scale and Completion Status of Real Estate Development Enterprises By City (2022)

单位：亿元 (100 million yuan)

市别	City	计划总投资 Planned Total Investment	自开始建设至本年底累计完成投资 Accumulated Investment Completed From the Beginning of Construction to the End of this Year	本年完成投资 Completed Investment this Year	建筑安装工程 Construction and Installation	设备工器具购置 Purchase of Equipment and Instruments	其他费用 Others	土地购置费 Land Acquisition Fee
全省	**Provincial Total**	**133332.81**	**97402.38**	**14962.97**	**7840.67**	**106.63**	**7015.66**	**5884.83**
广州	Guangzhou	32232.16	24460.75	3431.90	1160.73	11.57	2259.59	1910.76
深圳	Shenzhen	25446.87	18495.83	3413.28	1491.04	8.23	1914.00	1574.36
珠海	Zhuhai	8309.01	5871.30	757.20	416.26	4.39	336.55	268.29
汕头	Shantou	2376.69	1935.24	377.76	264.74	6.30	106.71	98.55
佛山	Foshan	13522.88	10873.55	1956.52	973.96	10.41	972.15	899.09
韶关	Shaoguan	1753.18	1351.74	113.56	95.20	2.96	15.40	10.79
河源	Heyuan	1540.35	856.79	140.14	117.51	1.05	21.58	15.32
梅州	Meizhou	1931.58	1364.26	109.33	89.47	1.87	17.99	12.02
惠州	Huizhou	9633.32	6364.50	1086.98	765.15	21.03	300.80	254.44
汕尾	Shanwei	1342.07	842.17	122.54	100.38	3.10	19.07	9.97
东莞	Dongguan	7836.99	5709.56	895.90	397.20	3.06	495.64	445.50
中山	Zhongshan	4258.20	2975.38	398.56	236.29	1.47	160.79	125.30
江门	Jiangmen	4530.48	3600.06	538.30	407.27	3.29	127.74	103.18
阳江	Yangjiang	1380.92	881.11	76.97	70.50	1.49	4.97	1.39
湛江	Zhanjiang	3466.59	2161.78	333.43	256.35	1.74	75.34	36.27
茂名	Maoming	3071.98	1808.17	273.78	213.38	3.85	56.55	38.49
肇庆	Zhaoqing	3377.90	2455.92	315.08	280.21	5.99	28.88	18.66
清远	Qingyuan	3846.46	2929.65	274.87	208.28	6.16	60.43	35.88
潮州	Chaozhou	751.53	610.38	88.64	77.72	1.69	9.22	4.33
揭阳	Jieyang	1499.93	1120.03	161.90	129.43	5.76	26.71	18.37
云浮	Yunfu	1223.71	734.20	96.31	89.58	1.21	5.52	3.86
按经济区域分	By Region							
珠三角	Pearl River Delta	109147.80	80806.86	12793.73	6128.13	69.45	6596.16	5599.59
东翼	Eastern Region	5970.22	4507.82	750.85	572.27	16.86	161.72	131.22
西翼	Western Region	7919.50	4851.05	684.18	540.23	7.08	136.86	76.15
山区	Mountainous Region	10295.29	7236.65	734.21	600.04	13.24	120.93	77.87

18-6 各市房地产开发投资情况（2022年）
Investment in Real Estate Development by City (2022)

单位：亿元 (100 million yuan)

市别	City	完成投资额 Investment Completed	按用途分 By use #住宅 Residential Buildings	办公楼 Office Buildings	商业营业用房 Buildings for Business Use	其他 Others
全省	**Provincial Total**	**14962.97**	**10700.28**	**1073.22**	**1238.68**	**1950.78**
广州	Guangzhou	3431.90	2433.03	289.37	231.65	477.85
深圳	Shenzhen	3413.28	2029.79	528.74	421.88	432.88
珠海	Zhuhai	757.20	492.94	82.19	70.07	112.01
汕头	Shantou	377.76	265.46	9.92	19.02	83.36
佛山	Foshan	1956.52	1514.11	56.57	156.66	229.18
韶关	Shaoguan	113.56	89.69	0.61	12.68	10.58
河源	Heyuan	140.14	115.06	1.20	7.12	16.76
梅州	Meizhou	109.33	83.47	1.26	11.89	12.71
惠州	Huizhou	1086.98	878.38	16.44	69.88	122.28
汕尾	Shanwei	122.54	105.40	1.58	7.55	8.01
东莞	Dongguan	895.90	674.39	63.30	45.91	112.30
中山	Zhongshan	398.56	313.29	5.16	21.27	58.84
江门	Jiangmen	538.30	440.36	1.88	34.22	61.85
阳江	Yangjiang	76.97	67.64	0.38	5.12	3.83
湛江	Zhanjiang	333.43	268.15	2.74	21.37	41.16
茂名	Maoming	273.78	211.73	1.49	30.66	29.90
肇庆	Zhaoqing	315.08	255.45	2.81	27.76	29.05
清远	Qingyuan	274.87	207.68	2.27	18.40	46.52
潮州	Chaozhou	88.64	63.91	2.88	6.47	15.38
揭阳	Jieyang	161.90	117.53	2.29	10.54	31.55
云浮	Yunfu	96.31	72.81	0.16	8.57	14.77
按经济区域分	By Region					
珠三角	Pearl River Delta	12793.73	9031.74	1046.44	1079.30	1636.25
东翼	Eastern Region	750.85	552.30	16.67	43.58	138.30
西翼	Western Region	684.18	547.52	4.61	57.15	74.89
山区	Mountainous Region	734.21	568.72	5.50	58.66	101.34

18-7 各市房地产开发房屋建筑面积及价值（2022年）

Floor Space and Value of Buildings in Real Estate Development by City (2022)

市别	City	房屋建筑面积(万平方米) Floor Space of Buildings(10000 sq.m) 施工面积 Floor Space of Buildings under Construction	竣工面积 Floor Space of Buildings Completed	#住宅 Residential Buildings	竣工房屋价值(亿元) Value of Buildings Completed (100 million yuan)	#住宅 Residential Buildings
全　省	**Provincial Total**	**88662.69**	**8161.12**	**5641.97**	**4779.71**	**3356.40**
广　州	Guangzhou	12946.25	1351.74	851.84	854.57	584.79
深　圳	Shenzhen	10950.04	740.85	390.25	1097.30	622.79
珠　海	Zhuhai	3525.56	260.07	139.50	245.54	158.62
汕　头	Shantou	3285.34	198.88	136.00	85.53	60.36
佛　山	Foshan	8280.32	635.99	409.31	419.16	289.68
韶　关	Shaoguan	2053.56	227.34	180.46	60.15	49.16
河　源	Heyuan	1898.22	137.04	101.00	63.76	47.22
梅　州	Meizhou	2312.77	311.54	239.75	87.81	69.88
惠　州	Huizhou	8356.09	545.65	400.42	285.30	226.16
汕　尾	Shanwei	1504.35	184.10	113.41	86.97	65.18
东　莞	Dongguan	4261.89	287.80	206.63	234.28	187.79
中　山	Zhongshan	3971.91	502.65	358.36	218.49	167.33
江　门	Jiangmen	4228.73	614.50	457.85	247.09	200.45
阳　江	Yangjiang	1635.09	175.28	139.46	53.22	43.29
湛　江	Zhanjiang	3793.10	251.67	195.63	107.83	82.51
茂　名	Maoming	3764.05	430.58	353.96	165.72	133.93
肇　庆	Zhaoqing	3544.85	317.33	267.40	105.17	91.09
清　远	Qingyuan	4472.11	481.78	292.04	151.37	105.07
潮　州	Chaozhou	940.19	93.49	72.57	27.88	23.03
揭　阳	Jieyang	1422.40	188.23	141.82	89.48	64.37
云　浮	Yunfu	1515.88	224.60	194.32	93.11	83.70
按经济区域分	By Region					
珠三角	Pearl River Delta	60065.64	5256.59	3481.55	3706.90	2528.70
东　翼	Eastern Region	7152.28	664.70	463.80	289.86	212.94
西　翼	Western Region	9192.24	857.54	689.05	326.76	259.74
山　区	Mountainous Region	12252.54	1382.30	1007.57	456.19	355.02

18-8 按用途分商品房销售面积（2022年）

Floor Space of Commercial Buildings Sold by Use (2022)

单位：万平方米 (10000 sq.m)

按登记注册类型分组	By Registration Status	商品房销售面积合计 Floor Space of Commercial Buildings Sold	按用途分 By use 住宅 Residential Buildings	办公楼 Office Buildings	商业营业用房 Buildings for Business Use	其他 Others
全　省	**Provincial Total**	**10591.11**	**8568.72**	**454.02**	**656.75**	**911.62**
内资	Domestic-funded Economy	9835.70	7994.14	412.06	593.34	836.15
国有	State-owned	233.65	194.92	15.40	12.54	10.79
集体	Collective-owned	58.67	50.92	1.91	3.29	2.56
股份合作	Cooperative	17.62	17.45		0.12	0.04
联营	Joint	3.14	3.14			
有限责任公司	Limited Liability	5504.13	4434.74	256.58	322.01	490.80
股份有限公司	Share-holding	166.32	115.90	20.37	13.89	16.16
私营	Private	3839.26	3164.17	117.80	241.49	315.81
其他	Others	12.90	12.90			
港、澳、台商投资	Funds from Hong Kong, Macao and Taiwan	401.75	323.54	24.13	21.81	32.26
外商投资	Foreign Funded	353.67	251.03	17.83	41.60	43.21

18-9 按用途分商品房销售额（2022年）

Sales of Commercial Buildings by Use (2022)

单位：亿元 (100 million yuan)

按登记注册类型分组	By Registration Status	商品房销售额合计 Total sales of Commercial Buildings Sold	按用途分 By use 住宅 Residential Buildings	办公楼 Office Buildings	商业营业用房 Buildings for Business Use	其他 Others
全　省	**Provincial Total**	**15870.47**	**13428.51**	**1077.22**	**848.19**	**516.55**
内资	Domestic-funded Economy	14579.39	12373.77	973.78	767.39	464.46
国有	State-owned	687.94	594.39	79.59	8.94	5.02
集体	Collective-owned	62.68	54.62	2.23	4.42	1.42
股份合作	Cooperative	18.18	17.96		0.19	0.03
联营	Joint	3.66	3.66			
有限责任公司	Limited Liability	8288.17	7008.47	605.22	424.65	249.84
股份有限公司	Share-holding	313.32	226.22	51.88	30.05	5.17
私营	Private	5177.50	4440.51	234.86	299.14	202.99
其他	Others	27.94	27.94			
港、澳、台商投资	Funds from Hong Kong, Macao and Taiwan	757.82	632.62	65.86	32.13	27.21
外商投资	Foreign Funded	533.25	422.13	37.58	48.67	24.88

18-10 各市商品房屋销售情况（2022年）
Sales of Commercial Buildings by City (2022)

市别	City	商品房销售面积（万平方米）Floor Space of Commercial Buildings Sold (10000 sq.m)	#住宅 Residential Buildings	商品房销售额（亿元）Total Sales of Commercial Buildings (100 million yuan)	#住宅 Residential Buildings
全省	**Provincial Total**	**10591.11**	**8568.72**	**15870.47**	**13428.51**
广州	Guangzhou	1374.07	1026.53	3621.50	3023.64
深圳	Shenzhen	694.15	505.02	3520.01	2749.17
珠海	Zhuhai	339.63	266.21	675.98	576.36
汕头	Shantou	402.17	357.46	389.84	336.02
佛山	Foshan	1397.07	1017.08	2073.02	1769.86
韶关	Shaoguan	248.64	216.71	145.22	123.53
河源	Heyuan	256.86	212.21	144.37	128.64
梅州	Meizhou	248.63	229.54	137.91	126.58
惠州	Huizhou	1310.35	1136.56	1421.62	1292.17
汕尾	Shanwei	250.70	243.58	170.60	164.68
东莞	Dongguan	459.82	350.81	993.40	856.53
中山	Zhongshan	506.88	400.42	562.63	505.02
江门	Jiangmen	599.21	500.25	451.87	401.37
阳江	Yangjiang	241.19	214.53	131.63	116.67
湛江	Zhanjiang	364.90	335.51	324.24	294.72
茂名	Maoming	385.51	342.38	242.38	218.39
肇庆	Zhaoqing	457.79	367.48	246.05	208.58
清远	Qingyuan	505.05	361.21	296.27	243.27
潮州	Chaozhou	125.22	122.59	75.98	73.06
揭阳	Jieyang	196.99	190.31	141.69	134.02
云浮	Yunfu	226.28	172.33	104.24	86.23
按经济区域分	By Region				
珠三角	Pearl River Delta	7138.96	5570.36	13566.09	11382.71
东翼	Eastern Region	975.08	913.93	778.11	707.78
西翼	Western Region	991.60	892.42	698.25	629.78
山区	Mountainous Region	1485.46	1192.01	828.02	708.25

主要统计指标解释

本年土地购置面积 指房地产开发企业本年通过各种方式获得土地使用权的土地面积。

土地购置费 指房地产开发企业通过各种方式取得土地使用权而支付的费用。土地购置费按实际发生额填报，分期付款的应分期计入。项目分期开发的，只计入与本期项目有关的土地购置费。前期支付的土地购置费，项目纳入统计后计入。

房地产开发投资 指房地产开发企业本年完成的全部用于房屋建设工程、土地开发工程的投资额以及公益性建筑和土地购置费等的投资。

本年实际到位资金 指房地产开发企业本年实际到位的，可用于房地产开发的各种货币资金。包括国内贷款、利用外资、自筹资金、定金及预收款、个人按揭贷款和其他资金。

房屋施工面积 指房地产开发企业本年施工的全部房屋建筑面积。包括本年新开工的房屋建筑面积、上年跨入本年继续施工的房屋建筑面积、上年停缓建在本年恢复施工的房屋建筑面积、本年竣工的房屋建筑面积以及本年施工后又停缓建的房屋建筑面积。多层建筑应填各层建筑面积之和。

房屋新开工面积 指房地产开发企业本年新开工建设的房屋建筑面积，以单位工程为核算对象。不包括在上年开工跨入本年继续施工的房屋建筑面积和上年停缓建而在本年恢复施工的房屋建筑面积。房屋的开工应以房屋正式开始破土刨槽（地基处理或打永久桩）的日期为准。房屋新开工面积指整栋房屋的全部建筑面积，不能分割计算。

房屋竣工面积 指房地产开发企业本年按照设计要求已全部完工，达到住人和使用条件，经验收鉴定合格或达到竣工验收标准，可正式移交使用的各栋房屋建筑面积的总和。

商品房销售面积 指房地产开发企业本年出售商品房屋的合同总面积(即双方签署的正式买卖合同中所确定的建筑面积)。

商品房销售额 指房地产开发企业本年出售商品房屋的合同总价款(即双方签署的正式买卖合同中所确定的合同总价)。该指标与商品房销售面积同口径。

Explanatory Notes on Main Statistical Indicators

Land Area Purchased in Current Year refer to land area of land use right obtained by real estate development enterprises in various ways this year.

Land Purchase Fee refers to fees paid by real estate development enterprises for obtaining land use rights in various ways. The land purchase fee shall be filled in according to the actual amount, which paid by installments shall be counted by stages. If the project is developed by stages, only included the land purchase fees related to the current project. The land purchase fees paid in the previous period are included after the statistics.

Real Estate Development Investment refers to total investments completed by real estate development enterprises in this year for housing construction projects, land development projects, public welfare buildings and land acquisition costs.

Funds Actually Paid in this year refers to various monetary funds that actually in place by real estate development enterprises this year and available for real estate development. Including domestic loans, utilization of foreign capital, self raised funds, deposits and advances, personal mortgage loans and other funds.

Building Area under Construction refers to total area of houses constructed by real estate development enterprises in this year. Including the building area of newly started houses in this year, houses continued to be constructed from previous year to this year, houses suspended from construction in the previous year and resumed in this year, houses completed in this year and houses suspended from construction after construction in this year. For multi-storey buildings, the area of each floor shall be filled into total area.

New Construction Area refers to building area of the newly constructed houses of the real estate development enterprises in this year, which is accounted for by the unit project. It does not include the building area of houses that started in previous year and continued construction in current year and stopped construction in previous year and resumed construction in current year. The commencement of the house shall be subject to the date when the house officially starts the earth breaking and trenching (foundation treatment or permanent pile driving). The newly started area of the house refers to the total construction area of the whole house which cannot be calculated separately.

Building Area Completed refers to total area of each building that the real estate development enterprise has completed in accordance with the design requirements this year, has reached the occupancy and use conditions, passed the acceptance appraisal or reached the completion acceptance standard, and can be officially handed over for use.

Area of Commercial Building Sold refers to total contracted area of commercial buildings sold by real estate development enterprises in this year (i.e. the building area determined in the formal sales contract signed by both parties).

Sales of Commercial Building refers to total contract price of the commercial building sold by the real estate development enterprise this year (i.e. the total contract price determined in the formal sales contract signed by both parties). This indicator use the same caliber as area of commercial building sold.

十九、教育和科技

EDUCATION AND TECHNOLOGY

十九　教育和科技

简要说明

一、本篇资料主要反映广东教育、科学技术活动基本情况。

二、本篇资料主要包括：

1. 高、中、初等教育，幼儿教育和各种类型的各级成人教育，指标主要包括各级各类的学校数、在校生数、招生数、毕业生数、教职工数和专任教师数等。

2. 科技成果奖励和技术市场情况，专利申请受理量和批准量，研究与开发机构基本情况，高校研究与发展人员及经费，科协系统科技活动情况等数据。

三、本篇资料由广东省统计局社会和科技统计处负责整理、编辑。

四、统计资料来源：

教育统计资料根据广东省教育厅、广东省人力资源和社会保障厅提供的统计年报加工整理。科技统计资料根据广东省科技厅、广东省人力资源和社会保障厅、广东省教育厅、广东省科协等部门提供的统计年报加工整理。

19 Education and Technology

Brief Introduction

Ⅰ. The data in this chapter show the basic conditions on the development Guangdong's education, science and technology.

Ⅱ. The data in this chapter mainly include:

(1) The data on tertiary, secondary, primary, and kindergarten education and various types of adult education at all levels, including the number of schools, the number of students enrolled, the number of new enrollments, the number of graduates, the number of staff and workers, and the number of full-time teachers of various levels and categories.

(2) The data on scientific and technological achievements and prizes, conditions of technological markets, numbers of patent applications accepted and granted, basic conditions of R&D institutions, R&D personnel and funds in universities and colleges, and scientific and technological activities of associations of science and technology, etc.

Ⅲ. The data are prepared and edited by the Division of Social, Scientific and Technological Statistics of Statistics Bureau of Guangdong Province.

Ⅳ. Data sources:

Data on education are processed and prepared in accordance with the annual statistical reports provided by Guangdong Provincial Department of Education and Guangdong Provincial Department of Human Resources and Social Security. Data on science and technology are processed and prepared in accordance with the annual statistical reports provided by Guangdong Provincial Department of Science and Technology, Guangdong Provincial Department of Human Resources and Social Security，Guangdong Provincial Department of Education, Guangdong Provincial Department of Personnel and Guangdong Provincial Association of Science and Technology.

19-1 教育、科技主要指标
Main Indicators on Education, Science and Technology

指　标	Item	2000	2010	2015	2020	2021	2022
在校学生数 (万人)	Number of Total Enrollment (10000 persons)						
普通本专科	Regular Institutions of Higher Education	29.95	142.66	185.64	240.02	253.98	267.09
成人本专科	Institutions of Higher Education for Adults	20.14	46.40	66.45	110.31	97.51	110.27
中等学校	Secondary Schools	541.72	939.23	736.79	743.40	783.17	824.62
#普通中学	Regular Secondary Schools	460.69	709.05	560.72	595.82	629.98	665.38
高等教育毛入学率(%)	Gross Enrollment Rate of High Education (%)	11.35	28.00	33.00	53.41	57.65	60.07
高中毛入学率 (%)	Gross Enrollment Rate of Senior Secondary Schools (%)	38.70	86.20	95.70	97.29	97.71	97.58
学龄儿童入学率 (%)	Percentage of School-age Children Enrolled (%)	99.70	99.95	99.98	100.00	100.00	99.93
每万人口普通本专科在校学生数 (人)	Number of Students Enrolled in Regular Institutions of Higher Education per 10000 Population (person)	41.19	140.83	173.10	208.33	201.55	198.82
科技研究机构数 (个)	Number of R&D Institutions (unit)		4452	8164	31772	37172	
研究与实验发展(R&D)人员 (万人)	Number of R&D Personnel (10000 persons)		44.66	68.02	117.54	124.85	
R&D人员全时当量 (万人年)	Full-time Equivalent of (R&D Personnel (10 000 man-year)	7.11	36.47	50.17	87.23	88.52	
研究与实验发展(R&D)经费内部支出(亿元)	R&D Expenditure Internal Expenditure (100 million yuan)	107.12	808.75	1798.17	3479.88	4002.18	
#基础研究	Basic Research		16.72	54.21	204.10	274.27	
应用研究	Applied Research		37.32	165	319.89	356.72	
试验发展	Experimental Development		754.70	1478.96	2955.90	3371.19	
#政府资金	Government Funds	101.38	65.76	145.85	440.57	474.26	
企业资金	Enterprises Funds	86.44	708.93	1606.21	2988.29	3462.49	
R&D经费支出占地区生产总值比例 (%)	Percentage of Research and Development Expenditure in Provincial GDP (%)	0.99	1.74	2.43	3.14	3.21	
研究与实验发展(R&D)课题 (项目)数 (个)	Number of R&D Programs/Projects (item)		72747	112680	263694	284693	
省级及以上科技奖励成果 (项)	Number of Achievements in Science and Technology Awarded by Provincial-level and Higher Agencies(item)	289	296	269	212	176	211
专利授权量 (件)	Number of Patent Granted (piece)	15799	119346	241176	709725	872209	837276
#发明专利	Inventions	261	13691	33477	70695	102850	115080
技术合同成交额(亿元)	Transaction Value of Technological Contracts (100 million yuan)	48.21	242.5	663.53	3465.92	4292.73	4525.42

注：1.R&D经费支出占地区生产总值比例指标历史数据，已根据修订后的地区生产总值数据进行调整。
2.中等学校含中等职业学校、技工学校、普通高中、初中。

Note: a) Historical statistics on ratio of expenditure on R&D to GDP have been adjusted according to amended GDP statistics.
b) Secondary Schools include Secondary Technical Vocational Schools, Skilled Workers Schools, Ordinary High Schools and Junior High School.

19-2 各级各类学校在校学生数

Number of Total Enrollment by Level and Type of School

单位：万人 (10000 persons)

年份 Year	普通高等学校 General Colleges and Universities	中等学校 Secondary Schools 中等职业教育学校 Vocational Secondary Schools	技工学校 Technical Schools	普通中学 Regular Secondary Schools	小学 Primary Schools
1978	3.07	3.64		313.32	743.02
1979	3.79	4.51	0.71	268.73	743.81
1980	4.10	6.28	1.61	252.11	748.86
1981	4.47	6.12	1.39	218.71	734.78
1982	4.09	6.51	0.99	200.19	723.03
1983	4.56	9.96	0.92	199.59	705.34
1984	5.47	12.99	1.01	220.69	692.73
1985	6.99	18.01	1.45	236.45	671.25
1986	7.83	28.22	1.45	249.93	670.62
1987	8.63	34.26	2.63	252.60	677.37
1988	9.72	37.63	3.40	244.23	688.72
1989	10.04	42.09	3.93	235.73	715.15
1990	9.59	45.27	5.22	234.03	747.29
1991	9.27	44.74	5.63	238.28	788.93
1992	9.74	46.29	6.58	255.02	808.98
1993	11.70	50.24	7.68	277.19	832.14
1994	13.75	55.89	9.57	307.38	862.21
1995	15.18	66.67	11.10	339.46	883.19
1996	16.40	67.30	12.28	373.19	897.64
1997	17.47	72.70	13.29	400.85	911.34
1998	18.50	70.50	14.50	423.61	918.02
1999	22.08	69.50	23.00	443.91	920.96
2000	29.95	65.57	15.46	460.69	929.93
2001	38.19	62.00	16.67	489.70	952.98
2002	46.78	61.20	17.82	513.40	979.61
2003	58.78	63.08	23.90	545.91	1025.37
2004	72.69	65.54	28.11	580.86	1049.62
2005	87.47	71.02	32.81	611.69	1067.03
2006	100.86	80.84	38.16	639.29	1056.99
2007	111.97	90.76	45.81	655.38	1017.62
2008	121.64	100.08	53.54	679.65	956.47
2009	133.41	120.46	64.11	696.11	887.65
2010	142.66	154.78	75.56	709.05	848.55
2011	152.73	152.05	85.13	699.47	822.06
2012	161.68	149.57	88.52	668.40	808.24
2013	170.99	140.89	87.62	625.24	807.94
2014	179.42	128.22	62.26	590.77	831.91
2015	185.64	117.21	58.86	560.72	868.88
2016	189.29	106.57	53.26	545.22	905.22
2017	192.58	99.39	55.37	545.37	941.96
2018	196.32	86.73	54.27	556.18	988.37
2019	205.40	85.97	57.77	572.77	1033.43
2020	240.02	86.68	60.89	595.82	1057.11
2021	253.98	90.30	62.88	629.98	1079.01
2022	267.09	94.22	65.01	665.38	1084.05

注：1.普通高等学校包括大学，学院，独立学院，职业本科学校，高等专科院校，高等职业学校，其他普通高教机构，在校学生人数指普通本、专科人数，下同。

2.中等职业教育学校包括调整后中等职业学校，中等技术学校，中等师范学校，成人中等专业学校，职业高中学校，残疾人中等职业学校，技工学校，附设中职班，其他中职机构，下同；1986年前缺成人中专数据。

Notes: a) General colleges and universities include universities, colleges, independent colleges, vocational colleges, vocational colleges, higher vocational schools and other general institutions of higher education. The number of students in school refers to the number of students in regular universities with full undergraduate courses and colleges with specialized courses.The same applies to the following tables.

b) Secondary vocational education schools include adjusted secondary vocational schools, secondary technical schools, secondary normal schools, adult secondary specialized schools, vocational high schools, secondary vocational schools for the disabled, technical schools, secondary affiliated vocational classes, and other secondary vocational institutions, the same below; There are no adult secondary school data before 1986.

19-3 各级各类学校情况
Statistics on Various Levels and Types of Schools

项　目	Item	2000	2005	2010	2015	2020	2021	2022
普通高等学校	**Institutions of Higher Education**							
学校数　(所)	Number of Schools　(unit)	52	111	131	143	154	160	161
毕业生数　(万人)	Number of Graduates　(10000 persons)	5.00	15.71	33.42	47.69	55.01	57.44	63.38
本科	Universities with Full Undergraduate Courses	2.40	6.11	15.29	22.41	27.44	28.22	32.10
专科	Colleges with Specialized Courses	2.60	9.60	18.13	25.28	27.57	29.22	31.27
招生数　(万人)	Number of New Enrollments　(10000 persons)	12.08	30.70	44.02	56.15	91.72	75.19	79.56
本科	Universities with Full Undergraduate Courses	5.01	13.65	21.7	27.54	34.52	35.46	39.00
专科	Colleges with Specialized Courses	7.07	17.04	22.31	28.61	57.20	39.73	40.55
在校学生数(万人)	Number of Enrolled Students　(10000 persons)	29.95	87.47	142.66	185.64	240.02	253.98	267.09
本科	Universities with Full Undergraduate Courses	15.03	42.86	77.86	104.08	122.25	128.57	134.65
专科	Colleges with Specialized Courses	14.92	44.61	64.8	81.56	117.77	125.41	132.44
教职工数　(万人)	Number of Teachers and Staff (10000 persons)	4.68	9.08	11.4	14.54	17.79	19.03	19.81
#专任教师	Full-time Teachers	2.04	5.43	7.86	9.89	12.24	12.88	13.59
中等职业教育	**Vocational Secondary Schools**							
学校数　(所)	Number of Schools　(unit)	658	641	566	481	396	382	372
毕业生数　(万人)	Number of Graduates　(10000 persons)	21.54	18.91	33.17	41.73	26.61	26.05	27.19
招生数　(万人)	Number of New Enrollment　(10000 persons)	21.10	27.93	74.13	39.54	31.39	33.60	34.91
在校学生数(万人)	Number of Total Enrollment　(10000 persons)	65.57	71.02	154.78	117.21	86.68	90.30	94.22
教职工数　(万人)	Number of Teachers and Staff (10000 persons)	5.70	4.91	5.86	5.78	5.59	5.72	5.76
#专任教师	Full-time Teachers	3.70	3.37	4.35	4.50	4.38	4.49	4.59
技工学校	**Technical Schools**							
学校数　(所)	Number of Schools　(unit)	186	191	246	163	146	148	148
毕业生数　(万人)	Number of Graduates　(10000 persons)	4.28	9.60	12.80	14.46	15.39	15.45	17.33
招生数　(万人)	Number of New Enrollments　(10000 persons)	5.84	12.90	28.2	19.94	21.67	21.94	22.28
在校学生数(万人)	Number of Total Enrollment　(10000 persons)	15.46	32.81	75.56	58.86	60.89	62.88	65.01
教职工数　(万人)	Number of Teachers and Staff (10000 persons)	1.07	1.46	2.78	2.94	3.17	3.27	3.41
#专任教师	Full-time Teachers	0.68	1.03	1.98	2.10	2.40	2.49	2.63
普通中学	**Regular Secondary Schools**							
学校数　(所)	Number of Schools　(unit)	3964	4282	4334	4434	4783	4908	5024
毕业生数　(万人)	Number of Graduates　(10000 persons)	131.82	174.33	210.23	201.96	180.26	185.57	196.30
招生数　(万人)	Number of New Enrollments　(10000 persons)	171.16	219.64	241.96	182.89	209.14	225.14	236.55
在校学生数(万人)	Number of Total Enrollment　(10000 persons)	460.69	611.69	709.05	560.72	595.82	629.98	665.38
教职工数　(万人)	Number of Teachers and Staff (10000 persons)	27.57	36.03	44.53	47.54	66.13	70.93	73.72
#专任教师	Full-time Teachers	22.86	30.73	39.15	42.67	45.27	47.25	49.26

注：1.普通高等学校含大学，学院，独立学院，职业本科学校，高等专科院校，高等职业学校，其他普通高教机构。(下同)
2.根据教育部指标解释，对高等教育教职工取数口径从2012年开始调整为全口径教职工数，2011年及以前年份取校本部教职工数。(下同)
3.自2020年起，九年一贯制学校、十二年一贯制学校的教职工数计入普通中学教职工数；专任教师数则按教育层次进行归类。(下同)

Notes: a) General colleges and universities include universities, colleges, independent colleges, vocational colleges, vocational colleges, higher vocational schools and other general institutions of higher education. The same applies to the following tables.
b)According to the explanation of Ministry of Education indicators, the teachers and staff of higher education began to adjust to the whole caliber from 2012, fetched the number of main campus teachers and staff in 2011 and before. (The same below)
c) Since 2020,the number of teachers and staff in regular secondary schools include the number in nine-year and twelve-year education schools; The number of full-time teachers are grouped by education level. (The same below)

19−3 续表 continued

项 目	Item	2000	2005	2010	2015	2020	2021	2022
小学	**Primary Schools**							
学校数 (万所)	Number of Schools (10000 units)	2.42	2.12	1.68	1.01	1.06	1.06	1.06
毕业生数 (万人)	Number of Graduates (10000 persons)	148.48	167.43	174.19	121.49	146.95	159.08	166.09
招生数 (万人)	Number of New Enrollments (10000 persons)	155.73	164.16	135.92	165.80	177.07	183.80	175.91
在校学生数 (万人)	Number of Students Enrolled (10000 persons)	929.93	1067.03	848.55	868.88	1057.11	1079.01	1084.05
教职工数 (万人)	Number of Teachers and Staff (10000 persons)	42.08	46.37	48.78	51.44	49.10	51.15	51.70
#专任教师	Full-time Teachers	36.41	40.38	43.07	46.86	57.34	59.22	60.20
学龄儿童	**School-age Children**							
学龄儿童总数 (万人)	Total number (10000 persons)	905.39	1026.90	801.82	836.09	1007.79	1027.88	1041.06
已入学学龄儿童数 (万人)	Primary School Enrollment number (10000 persons)	902.65	1023.60	801.45	835.93	1007.79	1027.88	1040.28
学龄儿童入学率 (%)	Enrollment Rate (%)	99.70	99.68	99.95	99.98	100.00	100.00	99.93
小学毕业生	**Primary School Graduates**							
小学毕业生人数 (万人)	Number of Graduates (10000 persons)	148.48	167.43	174.19	121.49	146.95	159.08	166.09
已升学人数 (万人)	Number of Students Entering into Junior Secondary Schools (10000 persons)	142.77	162.66	166.37	116.45	141.96	154.62	161.63
幼儿园	**Kindergartens**							
幼儿园数 (所)	Number of Kindergartens (unit)	12027	10359	11161	16368	20747	21101	21566
在园幼儿数 (万人)	Number of Children in Kindergartens (10000 persons)	214.18	213.92	227.23	402.28	480.18	500.39	498.05
教职工数 (万人)	Number of Teachers and Staff (10000 persons)	12.91	15.90	23.68	43.62	61.13	65.28	66.78
#专任教师	Full-time Teachers	8.36	9.18	13.63	24.07	32.15	34.51	35.10
特殊教育学校	**Special Schools**							
特殊教育学校数 (所)	Number of Schools (unit)	61	67	75	116	143	150	152
招生数 (人)	Number of New Enrollments (persons)	2000	3363	3666	7303	12550	13198	13087
在校学生数 (人)	Number of Total Enrollment (persons)	27507	25752	26064	36048	63802	71170	74455

注：1.特殊教育学校是指盲人学校，聋人学校，弱智学校，其他特教学校，附设特教班
2.学龄儿童总数取6−11岁校内外学龄人口数，已入学学龄儿童数取6−11岁在校学龄人口数。
3.自2020年起，小学教职工数仅统计小学及小学教学点的教职工数；专任教师数则按教育层次进行归类。

Notes: a)Special schools refer to separate institutions providing regular or vocational primary and secondary education for blinded, dumb or mentally-retarded children, or other children and adolescents in need of special care in education.

b)The total number of School-age Children is the School-age population inside and outside the school aged 6-11,the Primary School Enrollment number is the School-age population aged 6-11.

c) Since 2020, the number of teachers and staff in primary school only counted the number in primary school and primary school place; The number of full-time teachers are grouped by education level.

19-4 研究生教育情况
Statistics on Postgraduate Education

项　目	Item	2000	2005	2010	2015	2020	2021	2022
培养单位数（个）	**Number of Institutions of Postgraduate Education (unit)**	**26**	**29**	**31**	**28**	**30**	**30**	**32**
高等学校	Institutions of Higher Education	18	21	23	25	27	27	29
科研单位	Research Institutions	8	8	8	3	3	3	3
招生数（人）	**Number of New Enrollments (person)**	**5672**	**17054**	**25798**	**30650**	**59918**	**64501**	**68644**
博士	Doctor	1053	2802	3307	3540	6394	7023	7687
高等学校	Institutions of Higher Education	1001	2599	3117	3532	6386	7015	7676
科研单位	Research Institutions	52	203	190	8	8	8	11
硕士	Master	4619	14252	22491	27110	53524	57478	60957
高等学校	Institutions of Higher Education	4510	13953	22135	27018	53399	57340	60767
科研单位	Research Institutions	109	299	356	92	125	138	190
在校学生数（人）	**Number of Enrolled Students (person)**	**13023**	**43942**	**72455**	**89404**	**151347**	**174309**	**195410**
博士	Doctor	2558	9049	12341	14474	22127	25020	27906
高等学校	Institutions of Higher Education	2445	8406	11706	14443	22100	24996	27877
科研单位	Research Institutions	113	643	635	31	27	24	29
硕士	Master	10405	34893	60114	74930	129220	149289	167504
高等学校	Institutions of Higher Education	10161	34066	59159	74682	128853	148888	167042
科研单位	Research Institutions	244	827	955	248	367	401	462
毕业生数（人）	**Number of Graduates (person)**	**2182**	**9489**	**17862**	**26174**	**36011**	**38911**	**45084**
博士	Doctor	417	1342	2436	2947	3393	3735	4506
高等学校	Institutions of Higher Education	387	1241	2288	2937	3386	3724	4500
科研单位	Research Institutions	30	101	148	10	7	11	6
硕士	Master	1765	8147	15426	23227	32618	35176	40578
高等学校	Institutions of Higher Education	1692	7941	15158	23151	32518	35071	40454
科研单位	Research Institutions	73	206	268	76	100	105	124

注：2014年起中国科学院大学下辖广州化学研究所、南海海洋研究所、华南植物研究所、广州能源研究所和广州地球化学研究所的教育事业报表统一归口中国科学院大学管理，并调整2013年起数据，从2013年起研究生数据均不含以上培养研究生单位数据。

Notes: Since 2014,Guangzhou Institute of Chemistry,South China Sea Institute of Oceanography,South China Institute of Botany,Guangzhou Institute of Energy and the Guangzhou Institute of Geochemistry's education statistics are under the centralized to the University of Chinese Academy of Sciences and since 2013 data has been adjusted and the number of students has excluded the number of students in these institutions.

19-5 各级各类继续教育在校学生数
Number of Total Enrollment by Level and Type of Continuing Education

单位：人　　(person)

项　目	Item	2000	2005	2010	2015	2020	2021	2022
成人高等教育	**Higher Education for Adults**	**201410**	**295618**	**463987**	**664495**	**1103093**	**975147**	**1102687**
成人高等学校	Institutions of Higher Education for Adults	84057	30081	22025	17556	276342	25174	25944
开放大学	The Open University	34242	10740	10980	10256	265802	12956	12378
职工高等学校	Schools of Higher Education for Staff and Workers	17147	6865	6344	5411	10540	12218	13566
管理干部学院	Colleges for Management Cadres	20142	2686	4398				
教育学院	Teachers' Colleges	12526	9790	303	1889			
普通、职业高等学校	Regular HEIs	117353	265537	441962	646939	826751	949973	1076743
函授	Correspondence	51028	100260	173761	281334	393209	538311	681925
业余	Spare time Schools	43063	141532	265713	365605	433542	411662	394818
脱产	Full-time Courses for Adults	23262	23745	2488				
网络教育本专科	**Online Education**		**43663**	**66875**	**93857**	**125820**	**398939**	**457604**
本科	Universities with Full Undergraduate Courses		34627	34263	42732	61575	87502	107329
专科	Colleges with Specialized Courses		9036	32612	51125	64245	311437	350275
成人中等教育	**Secondary Education for Adults**	**44006**		**29105**	**7341**	**4596**	**4943**	**5249**
成人中专学校	Specialized Secondary Schools for Adults			27327	7341	4596	4943	5249
成人中学	Secondary Schools for Adults	44006		5358				

注：2021年起，广东开放大学学生统计从成人教育学生调整为网络教育学生。

Notes: From 2021, the scope of student statistics in Guangdong Open University have been adjusted from adult education students to online education students.

19－6 高等学校情况（2022年）
Statistics on Institutions of Higher Education (2022)

项 目	Item	学校数(所) Number of Schools (unit)	毕业生数(人) Number of Graduates (person)	招生数(人) Number of New Enrollments (person)	在校学生数(人) Number of Total Enrollment (person)	教职工数(人) Number of Teachers and Staff (person)	#专任教师 Full-time Teachers
总 计	**Total**	**161**	**633760**	**795587**	**2670913**	**198115**	**135907**
#女性	Female		331716	407449	1336077	100705	68602
按隶属关系分	**Grouped by Relation of Leadership**						
中央属	Under Central Government	4	23328	26804	102511	21521	10703
地方属	Under Local Government	157	610432	768783	2568402	176594	125204
按学校类别分	**Grouped by Type of Institution**						
综合大学	University	72	280548	336412	1120389	91492	57883
理工院校	Science and Engineering College	36	176601	216220	723902	44792	33103
农业院校	Agriculture College	4	24797	28756	116727	8074	6096
医药院校	Medicine College	12	30153	40802	145267	14259	10432
师范院校	Teacher Education College	10	37499	47169	178684	14230	9760
语文院校	Language and Literature College	2	6939	7444	28768	3104	1997
财经院校	Economics and Finance College	14	63166	97702	296479	15907	12613
政法院校	Politics and Law College	2	3501	4034	12699	965	536
体育院校	Physical Culture College	3	3426	4084	15079	1667	1033
艺术院校	Art College	6	7130	12964	32919	3625	2454
其他	Others						
总计中：普通高等职业(专科)学校	General higher vocational (technical) schools	93	291247	399151	1267496	65608	51133

19－7 中等学校情况（2022年）
Statistics on Secondary Schools (2022)

项 目	Item	学校数(所) Number of Schools (unit)	毕业生数(人) Number of Graduates (person)	招生数(人) Number of New Enrollments (person)	在校学生数(人) Number of Total Enrollment (person)	教职工数(人) Number of Teachers and Staff (person)	#专任教师 Full-time Teachers
中等职业教育	**Vocational Secondary Education**	**372**	**271921**	**349075**	**942235**	**57553**	**45885**
调整后中等职业学校	Vocational Secondary Schools after Adjustment	229	162874	212407	568129	34933	27540
普通中专	General Secondary Schools	53	32622	43116	121007	6871	4734
成人中等专业学校	Specialized Secondary Schools for Adults	1	1472	1959	5249	246	207
职业高中学校	Vocational Senior Secondary Schools	89	63616	76165	205213	14638	12005
其他机构	Other Institutions	20	7098	8525	23604	865	702
附设中职班	Affiliated Vocational Class	42	4239	6903	19033		697
技工学校	**Technical Schools**	**148**	**173341**	**222783**	**650102**	**34099**	**26316**
普通中学	**Regular Secondary Schools**	**5024**	**1963029**	**2365455**	**6653826**	**737172**	**492630**
#高中	Senior Schools	1121	631295	749127	2117786	303581	164739

注：1．2011年起增加附设中职班。其他机构和附设中职班不计学校数。普通中专包括中等技术学校和中等师范学校。
2．自2020年起，九年一贯制学校教职工数计入普通初中教职工数、十二年一贯制学校及完全中学学校的教职工数计入普通高中教职工数；专任教师数则按教育层次进行归类。

Note: a) Since 2011, the item of Affiliated Vocational Class is added. The number of schools of other institutions and affiliated secondary vocational classes is not included in the total number schools of vocational secondary education. The general secondary schools include the secondary technical schools and secondary normal schools.
b)Since 2020, the number of teachers and staff in ordinary junior middle school include the number in nine-year education schools, the number of teachers and staff in ordinary high school include the number in twelve-year education school and complete secondary schools; the number of full-time teachers are grouped by education level.

19−8 各市普通中学情况（2022年）

Statistics on Regular Secondary Schools by City (2022)

市别	City	学校数（所）Number of Schools (unit)	毕业生数（人）Number of Graduates (person)	高中 Senior Secondary Schools	初中 Junior Secondary Schools	招生数（人）Number of New Enrollments (person)
广州	Guangzhou	555	176310	52616	123694	215716
深圳	Shenzhen	521	163312	48651	114661	226576
珠海	Zhuhai	90	35059	11046	24013	43446
汕头	Shantou	318	122989	46345	76644	142892
佛山	Foshan	235	123216	42684	80532	144638
韶关	Shaoguan	151	53083	17162	35921	62883
河源	Heyuan	201	73397	23539	49858	83298
梅州	Meizhou	241	83472	28583	54889	94464
惠州	Huizhou	309	114332	34354	79978	137031
汕尾	Shanwei	167	59130	18088	41042	66667
东莞	Dongguan	267	111667	29759	81908	147806
中山	Zhongshan	116	56717	17288	39429	71535
江门	Jiangmen	203	74647	27062	47585	84520
阳江	Yangjiang	122	50723	16144	34579	64161
湛江	Zhanjiang	300	136659	41751	94908	167195
茂名	Maoming	272	151872	53495	98377	169524
肇庆	Zhaoqing	208	80960	24285	56675	97112
清远	Qingyuan	193	72929	21495	51434	93668
潮州	Chaozhou	148	45829	16420	29409	51709
揭阳	Jieyang	301	126579	44802	81777	139518
云浮	Yunfu	106	50147	15726	34421	61096
按经济区域分	By Region					
珠三角	Pearl River Delta	2504	936220	287745	648475	1168380
东翼	Eastern Region	934	354527	125655	228872	400786
西翼	Western Region	694	339254	111390	227864	400880
山区	Mountainous Region	892	333028	106505	226523	395409

19-8 续表 continued

市 别	City	在校学生数（人）Number of Total Enrollment (person)	高中 Senior Secondary Schools	初中 Junior Secondary Schools	教职工数（人）Number of Teachers and Staff (person)	#专任教师 Full-time Teachers
广 州	Guangzhou	602372	170272	432100	76249	48728
深 圳	Shenzhen	616320	194735	421585	104037	50408
珠 海	Zhuhai	121634	38760	82874	12680	9186
汕 头	Shantou	403500	145159	258341	42541	29934
佛 山	Foshan	412660	137450	275210	46653	31154
韶 关	Shaoguan	175155	54644	120511	15789	12860
河 源	Heyuan	242572	80311	162261	25266	18736
梅 州	Meizhou	274283	88840	185443	25720	21097
惠 州	Huizhou	387240	120165	267075	42900	26832
汕 尾	Shanwei	189546	60358	129188	18774	13541
东 莞	Dongguan	404016	120953	283063	58252	28625
中 山	Zhongshan	198666	58586	140080	23640	13968
江 门	Jiangmen	243934	86087	157847	23393	17943
阳 江	Yangjiang	176456	54743	121713	17863	11810
湛 江	Zhanjiang	464487	136888	327599	41220	31678
茂 名	Maoming	485193	160672	324521	43796	36827
肇 庆	Zhaoqing	276097	84227	191870	26863	19168
清 远	Qingyuan	256878	76891	179987	24270	17714
潮 州	Chaozhou	148900	52640	96260	14861	11568
揭 阳	Jieyang	403385	145670	257715	38164	28861
云 浮	Yunfu	170532	49735	120797	14241	11992
按经济区域分	By Region					
珠 三 角	Pearl River Delta	3262939	1011235	2251704	414667	246012
东 翼	Eastern Region	1145331	403827	741504	114340	83904
西 翼	Western Region	1126136	352303	773833	102879	80315
山 区	Mountainous Region	1119420	350421	768999	105286	82399

注：自2020年起，九年一贯制学校、十二年一贯制学校的教职工数计入普通中学教职工数；专任教师数则按教育层次进行归类。

Note: Since 2020, the number of teachers and staff in regular secondary schools include the number in nine-year and twelve-year education schools; the number of full-time teachers are grouped by education level.

19-9 各市中等职业教育基本情况（2022年）

Basic Statistics on Vocational Secondary Education by City (2022)

市别	City	学校数（所）Number of Schools (unit)	毕业生数（人）Number of Graduates (person)	招生数（人）Number of New Enrollments (person)	在校学生数（人）Number of Total Enrollment (person)	教职工数（人）Number of Teachers and Staff (person)	#专任教师 Full-time Teachers
广州	Guangzhou	77	56396	55330	163313	8776	6606
深圳	Shenzhen	16	13448	15507	41829	4282	2962
珠海	Zhuhai	8	6889	6984	20358	1263	1035
汕头	Shantou	15	8704	12950	32577	2236	1812
佛山	Foshan	26	22138	25365	68499	5242	3981
韶关	Shaoguan	14	10484	11717	34386	2410	2060
河源	Heyuan	15	7187	14044	32593	1867	1412
梅州	Meizhou	16	7855	8712	24700	1248	984
惠州	Huizhou	25	13779	20277	55831	3048	2374
汕尾	Shanwei	10	4783	7690	19308	1088	938
东莞	Dongguan	20	17259	23879	62270	4519	3508
中山	Zhongshan	7	7799	9737	27755	1921	1589
江门	Jiangmen	16	9970	11932	33470	1934	1726
阳江	Yangjiang	6	4520	6891	18532	941	787
湛江	Zhanjiang	33	17801	29614	73320	3413	2890
茂名	Maoming	12	19469	26889	70453	3967	3441
肇庆	Zhaoqing	15	18689	23431	63776	3459	2878
清远	Qingyuan	14	9071	13264	36965	2247	1910
潮州	Chaozhou	8	2651	5163	12066	824	604
揭阳	Jieyang	11	7662	11563	29287	1761	1471
云浮	Yunfu	8	5367	8136	20947	1107	917
按经济区域分	By Region						
珠三角	Pearl River Delta	210	166367	192442	537101	34444	26659
东翼	Eastern Region	44	23800	37366	93238	5909	4825
西翼	Western Region	51	41790	63394	162305	8321	7118
山区	Mountainous Region	67	39964	55873	149591	8879	7283

19-10 各市小学情况（2022年）
Statistics on Primary Schools by City (2022)

市 别	City	学校数（所）Number of Schools (unit)	毕业生数（人）Number of Graduates (person)	招生数（人）Number of New Enrollments (person)	在校学生数（人）Number of Total Enrollment (person)	教职工数（人）Number of Teachers and Staff (person)	专任教师 Full-time Teachers
广　州	Guangzhou	992	164954	213837	1204223	59050	67290
深　圳	Shenzhen	353	161004	204997	1166852	34916	66513
珠　海	Zhuhai	149	28620	35372	203540	10137	10884
汕　头	Shantou	725	93381	89972	578465	24430	29868
佛　山	Foshan	423	97889	117674	686311	35495	37774
韶　关	Shaoguan	217	43988	39864	265341	14375	15284
河　源	Heyuan	359	53074	43229	294519	17908	20817
梅　州	Meizhou	448	63551	54574	365319	20902	21833
惠　州	Huizhou	590	98226	99814	630105	27309	34390
汕　尾	Shanwei	448	45293	44896	289512	16060	17075
东　莞	Dongguan	341	124538	133382	832701	35147	44603
中　山	Zhongshan	212	51758	60925	359892	14982	18507
江　门	Jiangmen	332	56209	57781	360358	16137	18356
阳　江	Yangjiang	166	44100	38617	255442	11651	15170
湛　江	Zhanjiang	914	118909	124364	776083	38554	41459
茂　名	Maoming	1400	114787	111128	709378	43219	41144
肇　庆	Zhaoqing	234	67081	61417	404118	18879	21595
清　远	Qingyuan	354	64521	65534	422369	21290	22898
潮　州	Chaozhou	567	35003	31868	208943	10656	11413
揭　阳	Jieyang	1207	90533	91531	567372	29663	30114
云　浮	Yunfu	183	43499	38292	259676	16226	15046
按经济区域分	By Region						
珠三角	Pearl River Delta	3626	850279	985199	5848100	252052	319912
东　翼	Eastern Region	2947	264210	258267	1644292	80809	88470
西　翼	Western Region	2480	277796	274109	1740903	93424	97773
山　区	Mountainous Region	1561	268633	241493	1607224	90701	95878

注：自2020年起，小学教职工数仅统计小学及小学教学点的教职工数；专任教师数则按教育层次进行归类。

Note: Since 2020, the number of teachers and staff in primary school only counted the number in primary school and primary school place; The number of full-time teachers are grouped by education level.

19-11 各市学龄儿童入学情况

Statistics on School-age Children Enrolled in Schools by City

市别	City	2021 学龄儿童人数（人）Number of School-age Children (person)	2021 已入学人数（人）Number of School-age Children Enrolled in Schools (person)	2021 入学率（%）Enrollment Rate (%)	2022 学龄儿童人数（人）Number of School-age Children (person)	2022 已入学人数（人）Number of School-age Children Enrolled in Schools (person)	2022 入学率（%）Enrollment Rate (%)
广　州	Guangzhou	1146179	1146179	100.0	1183978	1183978	100.0
深　圳	Shenzhen	1108367	1108367	100.0	1143995	1143995	100.0
珠　海	Zhuhai	189753	189753	100.0	197743	197743	100.0
汕　头	Shantou	561324	561324	100.0	557060	557060	100.0
佛　山	Foshan	649734	649734	100.0	671336	671336	100.0
韶　关	Shaoguan	262901	262901	100.0	257132	257132	100.0
河　源	Heyuan	288059	288059	100.0	282371	282371	100.0
梅　州	Meizhou	311597	311597	100.0	320967	317064	98.8
惠　州	Huizhou	626470	626470	100.0	623819	623819	100.0
汕　尾	Shanwei	282664	282664	100.0	286828	282214	98.4
东　莞	Dongguan	828959	828959	100.0	818057	818058	100.0
中　山	Zhongshan	345609	345608	100.0	355435	355435	100.0
江　门	Jiangmen	347264	347264	100.0	348233	348233	100.0
阳　江	Yangjiang	249033	249033	100.0	242902	242902	100.0
湛　江	Zhanjiang	739485	739485	100.0	746423	746423	100.0
茂　名	Maoming	638890	638888	100.0	682536	682533	100.0
肇　庆	Zhaoqing	346145	346145	100.0	343323	343323	100.0
清　远	Qingyuan	401745	401745	100.0	402645	402645	100.0
潮　州	Chaozhou	199315	199315	100.0	197274	197274	100.0
揭　阳	Jieyang	534416	534416	100.0	535307	535278	100.0
云　浮	Yunfu	220876	220876	100.0	213265	214024	100.4
按经济区域分	By Region						
珠三角	Pearl River Delta	5588480	5588479	100.0	5685919	5685920	100.0
东　翼	Eastern Region	1577719	1577719	100.0	1576469	1571826	99.7
西　翼	Western Region	1627408	1627406	100.0	1671861	1671858	100.0
山　区	Mountainous Region	1485178	1485178	100.0	1476380	1473236	99.8

注：学龄人口数取校内外学龄人口6-11岁人口数；已入学人数取在校学龄人口6-11岁人口数。

Note: The School-age population is the School-age population inside and outside school aged 6-11; the Primary School Enrollment number is the School-age population aged 6-11.

19-12 研究与试验发展(R&D)基本情况

Basic Statistics on Research and Development (R&D)

指　标	Item	2010	2015	2019	2020	2021
研究机构数　(个)	**Number of R&D Institutions (unit)**	**4452**	**8164**	**32347**	**31772**	**37172**
科学研究与技术开发机构	Scientific Research and Technological Development Institutions	186	189	187	193	201
全日制普通高等学校	Full-time Regular Institutions of Higher Education	450	850	1781	1873	2085
工业企业	Industrial Enterprises	3309	6553	25891	28262	32938
其他	Others	507	572	4488	1444	1948
研究与试验发展(R&D)活动人员　(人)	**Number of R&D Personnel (person)**	**446579**	**680237**	**1091544**	**1175441**	**1248474**
科学研究与技术开发机构	Scientific Research and Technological Development Institutions	9488	15739	24335	30356	34655
全日制普通高等学校	Full-time Regular Institutions of Higher Education	33865	57346	83351	85733	97638
工业企业	Industrial Enterprises	359476	534293	838891	911222	972954
其他	Others	43750	72859	144967	148130	143227
研究与试验发展(R&D)经费内部支出　(亿元)	**Internal Expenditure on R&D (100 million yuan)**	**808.75**	**1798.17**	**3098.49**	**3479.88**	**4002.18**
科学研究与技术开发机构	Scientific Research and Technological Development Institutions	21.35	63.98	112.16	180.04	194.35
全日制普通高等学校	Full-time Regular Institutions of Higher Education	28.58	62.97	185.78	202.94	222.62
工业企业	Industrial Enterprises	703.68	1520.55	2374.63	2996.70	2902.18
其他	Others	55.14	150.67	425.92	100.21	683.03
研究与试验发展(R&D)活动课题(项目)数　(个)	**Number of R&D Programs/Projects (item)**	**72747**	**112680**	**224904**	**263694**	**284693**
科学研究与技术开发机构	Scientific Research and Technological Development Institutions	3499	6712	7947	8851	9813
全日制普通高等学校	Full-time Regular Institutions of Higher Education	35749	61677	91361	100303	112442
工业企业	Industrial Enterprises	28423	37375	106340	132120	146858
其他	Others	5076	6916	19256	22420	15580

19-13 公有经济企业、事业单位专业技术人员年末人数

Number of Professional and Technical Personnel in State-owned Enterprises and Institutions at the Year-end

单位：人 (person)

年 份 Year	专业技术人员 Professional and Technical Personnel	#工程技术人员 Engineering	#农业技术人员 Agriculture	#科学技术人员 Scientific Research	#卫生技术人员 Health Care	#教学人员 Teaching
1978	211149	48836	16017	7852	53068	80287
1979	211117	48641	16975	7277	53155	79748
1980	291939	56144	18176	7356	61445	86192
1981	303892	60071	19017	6763	63536	97109
1982	328455	70699	19431	7822	69056	102178
1983	547038	85327	21636	5744	74183	109210
1984	579740	89348	22505	5573	79806	120016
1985	642542	102506	23030	6431	86174	133013
1986	656380	108210	23854	6368	89545	313009
1987	664085	118601	23553	6231	93553	333245
1988	674085	119167	19478	4904	85092	313419
1989	810130	137803	20644	5986	90751	364965
1990	838403	145535	21194	5731	92912	379894
1991	814651	140906	13050	4810	93141	398276
1992	883821	149916	13749	4566	104334	412681
1993	957725	163440	14246	4388	117959	434036
1994	1017804	174960	14670	4118	128079	460702
1995	1077848	180530	15219	4425	134586	511418
1996	1167583	186156	15449	4610	147155	573934
1997	1223897	191954	15779	4443	156889	613121
1998	1262343	190486	15703	4413	165721	649873
1999	1291078	184304	15660	4585	171461	677110
2000	1297804	180223	15083	4705	175521	696005
2001	1285708	168354	14151	4467	181703	710967
2002	1274140	160458	13386	4425	184192	721719
2003	1264983	135621	12575	4918	202548	734721
2004	1374679	149214	17321	5253	238886	774022
2005	1399042	146411	17407	5434	248547	791255
2006	1375416	137802	16999	5163	246679	805397
2007	1391934	140828	17311	5711	246480	824462
2008	1419852	144941	16701	5745	260940	837059
2009	1462861	153563	15805	5984	268796	856665
2010	1458044	149724	14084	4551	259131	885446
2011	1448011	151700	13475	5260	253992	879621
2012	1459018	151998	12256	5021	264976	861104
2013	1455605	139807	12538	3813	269147	888962
2014	1493095	155964	12772	5850	283499	888862
2015	1449255	139817	16076	6139	288384	928348
2016	1486082	151883	16681	7340	308402	893189
2017	1551010	169994	13161	10992	306208	897089
2018	1643815	178876	12111	12286	298778	883820
2019	1560074	195106	12001	7752	301505	901015
2020	1604988	214557	12214	8900	308073	913578
2021	1619331	215319	10926	6071	313637	924604
2022	1686386	246043	12223	4623	318987	942882

注：本表未包中央单位专业技术人员数。

Note: Data in this table do not include professional and technical personnel from the central units stationed in Guangdong.

19-14 高层次人才情况
Statistics on High-level Talents

单位：人 (person)

项 目	Item	2000	2005	2010	2015	2020	2021	2022
享受国家津贴新增人数	Number of Persons Granted State Allowances	164		137		168		
高级职称批准人数	Number of Persons with Senior Professional Titles	6111	19336	19031	16581	35649	36756	47467
博士后招收人数	Number of Persons in Working Stations for Post-doctoral Research	163	380	560	1297	4215	4427	4519
博士生情况	Status of Doctorate Students							
招生数	Number of New Enrollments	1053	2802	3307	3540	6394	7023	7687
在校生	Number of Enrolled Students	2558	9049	12341	14474	22127	25020	27906
毕业生	Number of Graduates	417	1342	2436	2947	3393	3735	4506

注：享受国家津贴的人数从2003年起逢双年评比一次。

Note: The number of persons granted state allowances has been appraised every double-digital year since 2003.

19-15 各类技术合同签订情况
Statistics on Technical Contracts Signed by Type

项 目	Item	2000	2005	2010	2015	2020	2021	2022
技术合同项目数（项）	**Number of Technical Contracts (item)**	**5464**	**14432**	**17558**	**17344**	**39845**	**49261**	**47892**
技术开发合同	Technical Development Contracts	921	5983	11629	13786	15990	19366	19054
技术咨询合同	Technical Consultation Contracts	572	1279	1649	430	3728	5699	3606
技术转让合同	Technical Transfer Contracts	297	639	868	1242	1486	2083	2446
技术服务合同	Technical Service Contracts	3674	6531	3412	1886	18641	22113	22786
技术合同金额（万元）	**Value of Technical Contracts (10000 yuan)**	**482104**	**1124740**	**2425045**	**6635253**	**34659205**	**42927258**	**45254248**
技术开发合同	Technical Development Contracts	142107	571458	1961788	2359626	9403438	14024662	15936000
技术咨询合同	Technical Consultation Contracts	12530	31696	48539	17050	1185716	417379	457788
技术转让合同	Technical Transfer Contracts	110279	288881	344264	2923722	5849315	7683299	5576242
技术服务合同	Technical Service Contracts	217188	232705	70454	1334855	18220736	20801917	23284218

19—16 科技成果项数

Number of Achievements for Scientific and Technological Research

单位：项 (item)

项　目	Item	2000	2005	2010	2015	2020	2021	2022
国家级科技奖励成果	**National Prizes for Scientific and Technological Research Achievements**	**24**	**15**	**36**	**32**	**36**		
国际合作奖	National Cooperation Prize							
国家发明奖	National Invention Prize		1	2	5	6		
国家自然科学奖	National Prize for Natural Sciences		1	1	5	2		
国家科技进步奖	National Prize for Progress in Science and Technology	24	13	33	22	28		
省级重大科技成果	**Major Provincial Scientific and Technological Achievements**				**2133**	**3302**	**2546**	**2601**
基础理论成果	Achievements in Fundamental Theory				126	854	602	605
应用技术成果	Achievements in Applied Technology				1990	2299	1779	1787
软科学成果	Achievements in Soft Sciences				17	149	165	209
省级科技奖励成果	**Provincial Prizes for Scientific and Technological Achievements**	**265**	**288**	**260**	**237**	**176**	**176**	**211**
省科技进步奖	Provincial Prize for Progress in Science and Technology	265	288	260	237	142	142	133
农业方面	Agriculture	46	51	31	31	13	11	10
工业方面	Industry	113	117	145	148	90	96	87
医药卫生方面	Medicine and Health Care	72	68	65	42	34	31	30
其他	Others	34	52	19	16	5	4	6

注：省级重大科技成果为全社会口径。

Note: Data of major provincial scientific and technological achievements are the whole society caliber.

19—17 县级政府部门属研究与开发机构基本情况

Basic Statistics on Research and Development Institutions under Government Departments at County Level

项　目	Item	2000	2005	2010	2015	2020	2021	2022
机构数 (个)	Number of Institutions (unit)	183	166	143	124	93	90	82
职工总数 (人)	Number of Staff and Workers(person)	4379	3433	2798	2054	1441	1517	1326
科技活动人员(人)	Scientists and Engineers (person)			1390	1119	1003	1120	984
经费收入 (万元)	Funds (10000 yuan)	13409	12229	16592	27162	26722	37671	31421
#来自政府的经费	Government Funds	5426	5187	9605	17467	20889	27776	25670

19-18 县级以上政府部门属研究与开发机构基本情况

Basic Statistics on Research and Development Institutions under Government Departments at and above County Level

项 目	Item	2000	2005	2010	2015	2020	2021	2022
总 计	**Total**							
机构数 (个)	Number of Institutions (unit)	296	192	181	184	189	196	192
职工总数 (人)	Number of Staff and Workers (person)	24926	14216	16922	22582	29376	33417	33387
科技活动人员 (人)	Scientists and Engineers			12819	17929	26107	30496	29912
经费收入 (万元)	Funds (10000 yuan)	358844	384866	665228	1450489	2717041	2934065	2474107
#政府拨款	Government Appropriations	98386	153946	332815	781376	2353141	2172171	1769817
经费支出 (万元)	Expenditures (10000 yuan)	330098	363973	674994	1363744	2458054	2712108	2542894
科技经费支出(万元)	Expenditures on Purchase of Assets(10000 yuan)			408216	962263	2231653	2475991	2334988
自然科学及技术领域	**Natural Sciences and Technology**							
机构数 (个)	Number of Institutions (unit)	263	163	156	158	167	176	171
职工总数 (人)	Number of Staff and Workers (person)	23623	13026	15601	21011	27637	31816	31750
科技活动人员 (人)	Scientists and Engineers			11738	16675	24601	29020	28381
经费收入 (万元)	Funds (10000 yuan)	345582	360334	626119	1375436	2622047	2834725	2370984
#政府拨款	Government Appropriations	89595	137906	306735	728278	2278854	2091386	1682902
经费支出 (万元)	Expenditures (10000 yuan)	317219	341823	634843	1297806	2362899	2610756	2437020
科技经费支出(万元)	Expenditures on Purchase of Assets(10000 yuan)			378555	919010	2153356	2394432	2254960
社会及人文科学领域	**Social Sciences and Humanities**							
机构数 (个)	Number of Institutions (unit)	16	13	10	10	10	11	12
职工总数 (人)	Number of Staff and Workers (person)	780	655	645	675	800	1045	1084
科技活动人员 (人)	Scientists and Engineers			567	616	723	928	980
经费收入 (万元)	Funds (10000 yuan)	6906	10914	18906	32129	53910	72870	78231
#政府拨款	Government Appropriations	5908	9370	14003	26643	50844	64383	70197
经费支出 (万元)	Expenditures (10000 yuan)	6897	10207	17585	30830	53609	74386	79306
科技经费支出(万元)	Expenditures on Purchase of Assets(10000 yuan)			14334	23636	45523	57684	56714
科技情报和文献机构	**Scientific-Technological Information and Literature Institutions**							
机构数 (个)	Number of Institutions (unit)	17	16	15	16	12	9	9
职工总数 (人)	Number of Staff and Workers (person)	523	535	676	896	939	556	553
科技活动人员 (人)	Scientists and Engineers			514	638	783	548	551
经费收入 (万元)	Funds (10000 yuan)	6356	13619	20203	42923	41085	26470	24893
#政府拨款	Government Appropriations	2883	6670	12078	26455	23443	16402	16718
经费支出 (万元)	Expenditures (10000 yuan)	5982	11944	22566	35108	41546	26966	26568
科技经费支出(万元)	Expenditures on Purchase of Assets(10000 yuan)			15327	19618	32774	23875	23313

19-19 各市县级及以上政府部门属研究与开发机构基本情况

Basic Statistics on Research and Development Institutions under Government Departments at and above County Level by City

市别	City	2021						
		机构数(个) Number of Institutions (unit)	就业人员(人) Number of Employed Persons (person)	#科技活动人员(人) R&D Personnel (person)	经费收入(万元) Funds (10000 yuan)	#政府拨款 Government Appropriations	经费支出(万元) Expenditures (10000 yuan)	科技经费支出(万元) R&D Expenditure (10000 yuan)
全 省	**Provincial Total**	**286**	**34934**	**31616**	**2971736**	**2199948**	**2750411**	**2502417**
广 州	Guangzhou	92	21165	19194	1694444	1065362	1620463	1446951
深 圳	Shenzhen	11	5913	5576	623536	529760	512644	500740
珠 海	Zhuhai	3	258	227	101878	101112	73923	70688
汕 头	Shantou	12	527	485	34949	33990	36694	34680
佛 山	Foshan	7	962	899	113619	116680	147055	141576
韶 关	Shaoguan	16	341	297	9488	7199	9196	7211
河 源	Heyuan	12	170	118	1947	1880	1947	1658
梅 州	Meizhou	22	322	277	8933	7909	10716	9241
惠 州	Huizhou	17	714	666	37041	35753	34011	31366
汕 尾	Shanwei	5	78	57	1518	6252	6025	5619
东 莞	Dongguan	12	2146	1842	192121	154168	147567	133734
中 山	Zhongshan	3	127	111	5166	4787	5340	4134
江 门	Jiangmen	9	212	172	9957	10927	10611	8535
阳 江	Yangjiang	4	132	111	16648	16377	7558	7127
湛 江	Zhanjiang	15	987	803	92777	80596	101548	77121
茂 名	Maoming	11	249	227	4920	4401	4948	4207
肇 庆	Zhaoqing	14	198	175	5912	5543	6439	5594
清 远	Qingyuan	6	66	49	1499	1333	1685	909
潮 州	Chaozhou	6	161	146	7135	6852	7859	7361
揭 阳	Jieyang	6	147	136	2527	2499	2498	2374
云 浮	Yunfu	3	59	48	5723	6569	1685	1592

19-19 续表 continued

市 别	City	2022 机构数(个) Number of Institutions (unit)	就业人员(人) Number of Employed Persons (person)	#科技活动人员(人) R&D Personnel (person)	经费收入(万元) Funds (10000 yuan)	#政府拨款 Government Appropriations	经费支出(万元) Expenditures (10000 yuan)	科技经费支出(万元) R&D Expenditure (10000 yuan)
全省合计	**Provincial Total**	**274**	**34713**	**30896**	**2505528**	**1795487**	**2575425**	**2360266**
广 州	Guangzhou	89	20487	18405	1494958	920068	1529699	1377904
深 圳	Shenzhen	14	6068	5383	408821	306802	394753	367012
珠 海	Zhuhai	3	323	291	22485	21211	49717	45145
汕 头	Shantou	12	548	494	66720	65657	71059	69038
佛 山	Foshan	7	1164	1117	104290	102143	149345	145498
韶 关	Shaoguan	15	327	281	8974	7135	9187	7156
河 源	Heyuan	10	130	101	1775	1691	1775	1524
梅 州	Meizhou	22	348	311	8970	8230	9113	7423
惠 州	Huizhou	15	666	639	74958	83054	58061	56434
汕 尾	Shanwei	5	81	67	3392	3384	2076	1887
东 莞	Dongguan	11	2222	1866	105992	79424	141858	132979
中 山	Zhongshan	2	143	117	5385	4698	5236	4341
江 门	Jiangmen	9	245	174	8723	7057	9089	6963
阳 江	Yangjiang	4	163	145	12982	12485	10892	10557
湛 江	Zhanjiang	14	955	772	153484	146492	105465	101986
茂 名	Maoming	10	232	188	7594	6951	7804	6234
肇 庆	Zhaoqing	11	166	143	4887	4754	5862	5118
清 远	Qingyuan	6	68	58	1538	1377	1511	1020
潮 州	Chaozhou	6	163	147	4924	4837	4661	4044
揭 阳	Jieyang	6	154	144	2496	2458	2631	2395
云 浮	Yunfu	3	60	53	2183	5581	5635	5612

19-20 三种专利申请量与授权量

Three Types of Patent Application and Granted

单位：件 (item)

年份 Year	申请量 Number of Patent Applications	发明 Inventions	实用新型 Utility Models	外观设计 Designs	授权量 Number of Patent Applic-ations Granted	发明 Inventions	实用新型 Utility Models	外观设计 Designs
1990	1948	231	1001	716	889	40	571	278
1995	7729	463	2367	4899	4611	57	1446	3108
2000	21123	1760	6033	13330	15799	261	4797	10741
2001	27596	2549	8144	16903	18259	301	5246	12712
2002	34339	3806	9972	20561	22760	351	6396	16013
2003	43186	6181	12985	24020	29235	953	7921	20361
2004	52201	8093	14682	29426	31446	1941	9307	20198
2005	72220	12887	18951	40382	36894	1876	11017	24001
2006	90886	21351	23886	45649	43516	2441	15644	25431
2007	102449	26692	25389	50368	56451	3714	21636	31101
2008	103883	28099	28883	46901	62031	7604	25072	29355
2009	125673	32247	39027	54399	83621	11355	27438	44828
2010	152907	40866	47706	64335	119346	13691	43901	61754
2011	196275	52012	67336	76927	128415	18242	51402	58771
2012	229514	60448	78731	90335	153598	22153	65946	65499
2013	264265	68990	93592	101683	170430	20084	77503	72843
2014	278351	75148	96136	107067	179953	22276	83202	74475
2015	355939	103941	135717	116281	241176	33477	105254	102445
2016	505667	155581	203609	146477	259032	38626	118157	102249
2017	627819	182639	283560	161620	332648	45740	169017	117891
2018	793819	216469	367938	209412	478082	53259	268508	156315
2019	807700	203311	369143	235246	527389	59742	282740	184907
2020	967204	215926	470055	281223	709725	70695	380882	258148
2021	980634	242551	456220	281863	872209	102850	484320	285039
2022	993480	236957	465463	291060	837276	115080	457716	264480

注：2017年起，专利申请量统计口径调整为国家知识产权局受理的按规定缴足申请费、符合进入初步审查阶段条件的专利申请数量，2017年前，该口径数据称为专利申请受理量。2020年起，国家知识产权局不再反馈各省专利申请量数据。

Note: Starting from 2017, the statistic for the number of patent applications accepted only includes patents that have passed initial review conditions and paid application fees as stipulated by the State Intellectual Property Office. Data before 2017 of this coverage were named as number of patent applications accepted. Since 2020, the State Intellectual Property Office will no longer feed back the data of patent applications in each province.

19-21 分市全社会研究与试验发展人员与经费（2021年）

Personnel and Intramural Expenditure on R&D by City (2021)

市 别	City	R&D活动人员（人）Number of R&D Personnel (person)	#企业 Enterprises	R&D经费内部支出（亿元）Internal Expenditure on R&D(100 million yuan)	#企业 Enterprises
全 省	**Provincial Total**	**1248474**	**1090330**	**4002.2**	**3536.0**
广 州	Guangzhou	235741	138895	881.7	563.8
深 圳	Shenzhen	443644	420383	1682.2	1613.1
珠 海	Zhuhai	37641	33891	113.7	110.3
汕 头	Shantou	14112	11203	31.2	24.4
佛 山	Foshan	104465	98455	342.4	321.8
韶 关	Shaoguan	7154	5836	19.1	21.7
河 源	Heyuan	5737	5541	8.9	8.8
梅 州	Meizhou	3741	2632	7.9	5.7
惠 州	Huizhou	74114	71722	169.0	162.7
汕 尾	Shanwei	1863	1647	8.1	7.7
东 莞	Dongguan	187637	182268	434.4	417.4
中 山	Zhongshan	36733	34895	81.1	79.5
江 门	Jiangmen	39989	38086	92.7	86.0
阳 江	Yangjiang	2863	2442	6.1	6.3
湛 江	Zhanjiang	8342	2918	18.7	11.5
茂 名	Maoming	8106	6193	17.2	12.9
肇 庆	Zhaoqing	13408	11296	29.5	27.0
清 远	Qingyuan	9120	8810	21.8	20.1
潮 州	Chaozhou	3746	3370	8.0	6.1
揭 阳	Jieyang	6421	6239	21.6	22.6
云 浮	Yunfu	3897	3608	7.0	6.8

19-22 规模以上工业企业的科技活动基本情况
Basic Statistics on Science and Technology Activities of Industrial Enterprises above Designated size

指标	Item	2020	2021	2022
企业基本情况	**Statistics on Industrial Enterprises**			
有R&D活动企业数 (个)	Number of Enterprises with R&D Activities (unit)	23081	26688	22742
有R&D活动企业所占比重 (%)	Percentage of Enterprises with R&D Activities (%)	39.5	40.3	33.1
R&D活动情况	**Statistics on R&D Activities**			
R&D人员全时当量 (万人年)	Full-time Equivalent of R&D Personnel (10 000 man-years)	70.00	70.91	77.26
R&D经费支出 (亿元)	Expenditure on R&D (100 million yuan)	2499.95	2902.18	3217.75
R&D经费支出与主营业务收入之比 (%)	Percentage of Expenditure on R&D to Sales Revenue (%)	1.67	1.67	1.79
R&D项目数 (项)	R&D Projects (item)	132120	146858	116888
R&D项目经费支出 (亿元)	Expenditure on R&D Projects (100 million yuan)	2566.01	3091.68	3554.68
企业办R&D机构情况	**Statistics on R&D Institutions**			
机构数 (个)	Number of R&D Institutions (units)	28262	32938	32434
机构人员数 (万人)	R&D Personnel (10 000 persons)	108.99	122.41	110.99
机构经费支出 (亿元)	Expenditure on R&D (100 million yuan)	4274.02	5046.84	4068.20
新产品开发及生产情况	Statistics on New Products Development and Production			
新产品开发项目数 (个)	Number of New Products (unit)	166140	201009	221782
新产品开发经费支出 (亿元)	Expenditure on New Products Development 100 million yuan)	4127.13	4636.98	5159.47
新产品销售收入 (亿元)	Sales Revenue of New Products (100 million yuan)	44313.05	49684.90	48075.11
#新产品出口	Export	13132.99	14296.30	13011.14
专利情况	**Statistics on Patents**			
专利申请数 (件)	Number of Patent Applications (piece)	305665	340935	354470
#发明专利	Inventions	127497	139727	149075
有效发明专利数 (件)	Number of Inventions in Force (piece)	435509	511717	572589
技术获取和技术改造情况	**Statistics on Technology Acquisition and Technology Reconstruction**			
引进国外技术经费支出 (亿元)	Expenditure for Acquisition of Foreign Technology (100 million yuan)	211.15	167.28	100.95
引进技术消化吸收经费支出(亿元)	Expenditure for Assimilation of Technology (100 million yuan)	2.99	2.70	2.25
购买国内技术经费支出 (亿元)	Expenditure for Purchase of Domestic Technology (100 million yuan)	233.89	152.77	153.85
技术改造经费支出 (亿元)	Expenditure for Technical Renovation (100 million yuan)	668.89	612.70	541.34

19-23 规模以上工业企业研究与发展经费内部支出

Internal Expenditures of Industrial Enterprises Above Designated Size

单位：亿元 (100 million yuan)

指　　标	Item	2020	2021	2022
总　计	**Totals**	**2499.95**	**2902.18**	**3217.75**
按登记注册类型分	**By Status of Registration**			
内资企业	Domestic Funded	1892.69	2179.69	2404.00
国有企业	State-owned Enterprises	7.25	12.39	5.20
集体企业	Collective-owned Enterprises	0.46	0.17	0.14
股份合作企业	Cooperative Enterprises	0.67	0.27	0.14
联营企业	Joint Ownership Enterprises	0.18	0.30	0.29
有限责任公司	Limited Liability Enterprises	780.31	897.35	1066.90
#国有独资	State Sole Funded Corporations	28.23	27.38	30.41
股份有限公司	Share-holding Corporations Limited	315.07	319.91	367.87
私营企业	Private Enterprises	788.74	949.17	963.02
其他企业	Other Enterprises	0.01	0.13	0.44
港、澳、台商投资企业	Enterprises with Funds from Hong Kong,Macao, and Taiwan	332.32	360.15	427.96
外商投资企业	Foreign Funded Enterprises	274.95	362.34	385.80
按企业规模分	**By Size of Enterprises**			
大型企业	Large Enterprises	1429.55	1684.46	1940.26
中型企业	Medium-sized Enterprises	487.25	549.18	599.92
小微型企业	Small Enterprises	583.15	668.55	677.57
按行业分	**By Industry**			
采矿业	**Mining**	**6.91**	**7.34**	**12.51**
煤炭开采和洗选业	Mining and Washing of Coal			
石油和天然气开采业	Extraction Petroleum and Natural Gas	5.29	4.87	8.67
黑色金属矿采选业	Mining and Processing of Ferrous Metal Ores	0.00	0.02	0.03
有色金属矿采选业	Mining and Processing of Non-ferrous Metal Ores	0.57	1.28	1.50
非金属矿采选业	Mining and Processing of Non-metal Ores	0.60	0.85	1.56
开采辅助活动	Support Activities for Mining	0.45	0.33	0.74
其他采矿业	Mining of Other Ores			
制造业	**Manufacturing**	**2461.82**	**2862.10**	**3163.55**
农副食品加工业	Processing of Food from Agricultural Products	23.70	22.69	24.54
食品制造业	Manufacture of Foods	20.40	21.44	20.90
酒、饮料和精制茶制造业	Manufacture of Liquor, Beverages and Refined Tea	4.47	4.75	6.70
烟草制品业	Manufacture of Tobacco	4.16	2.10	2.97
纺织业	Manufacture of Textile	10.86	12.54	10.75
纺织服装、服饰业	Manufacture of Textile, Wearing Apparel, and Accessories	13.59	15.14	17.39

19-23 续表 continued

单位：亿元 (100 million yuan)

指 标	Item	2020	2021	2022
皮革、毛皮、羽毛及其制品和制鞋业	Manufacture of Leather, Fur, Feather and Related Products and Footwear	11.69	12.68	14.30
木材加工和木、竹、藤、棕、草制品业	Processing of Timber, Manufacture of Wood,Bamboo, Rattan, Palm and Straw Products	3.72	6.53	3.83
家具制造业	Manufacture of Furniture	26.34	30.03	29.33
造纸和纸制品业	Manufacture of Paper and Paper Products	14.37	17.83	17.36
印刷和记录媒介复制业	Printing and Reproduction of Recording Media	18.48	13.56	19.19
文教、工美、体育和娱乐用品制造业	Manufacture of Articles for Culture, Education, Arts and Crafts, Sport and Entertainment Activities	12.89	14.62	13.30
石油加工、炼焦和核燃料加工业	Processing of Petroleum, Coking and Processing of Nuclear Fuel	4.72	5.54	4.56
化学原料和化学制品制造业	Manufacture of Raw Chemical Materials and Chemical Products	47.14	61.39	59.32
医药制造业	Manufacture of Medicines	58.73	80.35	96.06
化学纤维制造业	Manufacture of Chemical Fibers	2.10	3.10	1.71
橡胶和塑料制品业	Manufacture of Rubber and Plastics Products	83.57	97.23	97.72
非金属矿物制品业	Manufacture of Non-metallic Mineral Products	35.71	44.95	38.97
黑色金属冶炼和压延加工业	Smelting and Pressing of Ferrous Metals	9.36	11.09	19.41
有色金属冶炼和压延加工业	Smelting and Pressing of Non-ferrous Metals	11.68	18.81	16.62
金属制品业	Manufacture of Metal Products	78.04	98.64	101.54
通用设备制造业	Manufacture of General Purpose Machinery	105.36	121.34	124.23
专用设备制造业	Manufacture of Special Purpose Machinery	122.58	133.32	160.85
汽车制造业	Manufacture of Automobiles	129.57	169.51	226.79
铁路、船舶、航空航天和其他运输设备制造业	Manufacture of Railway, Ship, Aerospace and Other Transport Equipment	22.79	26.19	20.38
电气机械和器材制造业	Manufacture of Electrical Machinery and Apparatus	342.93	364.99	405.64
计算机、通信和其他电子设备制造业	Manufacture of Computers, Communication and Other Electronic Equipment	1182.61	1392.61	1539.58
仪器仪表制造业	Manufacture of Measuring Instruments and Machinery	45.71	43.32	51.63
其他制造业	Other Manufacture	7.26	8.17	8.09
废弃资源综合利用业	Utilization of Waste Resources	3.34	4.32	5.88
金属制品、机械和设备修理业	Repair Service of Metal Products, Machinery and Equipment	3.96	3.34	4.01
电力、热力、燃气及水生产和供应业	**Production and Supply of Electric Power, Heat Power, and Water**	**31.22**	**32.74**	**41.70**
电力、热力生产和供应业	Production and Supply of Electric Power and Heat Power	19.88	22.23	27.04
燃气生产和供应业	Production and Supply of Gas	7.22	7.19	10.91
水的生产和供应业	Production and Supply of Water	4.11	3.32	3.75

19-24 分市规模以上工业企业R&D活动人员和经费
R&D Personnel and Expenditure of Industrial Enterprises by City

市别	City	R&D活动人员(人) Number of R&D Personnel (person)			R&D经费内部支出(亿元) Internal Expenditure on R&D(100 million yuan)		
		2020	2021	2022	2020	2021	2022
全省	**Provincial Total**	**911222**	**957403**	**1026944**	**2499.95**	**2902.18**	**3217.75**
广州	Guangzhou	105364	96735	116321	315.11	377.92	401.00
深圳	Shenzhen	345344	351055	380604	1157.31	1259.73	1491.38
珠海	Zhuhai	34522	29707	36860	93.94	84.41	94.42
汕头	Shantou	11822	10549	11052	18.45	20.93	20.53
佛山	Foshan	98761	93184	91194	238.86	298.07	305.48
韶关	Shaoguan	5870	5587	5305	13.13	14.05	11.90
河源	Heyuan	2180	5182	4836	4.26	8.68	7.61
梅州	Meizhou	1574	2530	2257	2.77	5.61	3.88
惠州	Huizhou	57344	70360	81864	115.26	157.30	170.23
汕尾	Shanwei	1731	1603	2227	6.08	8.25	9.57
东莞	Dongguan	135841	175876	173176	308.42	405.61	411.00
中山	Zhongshan	32129	33794	39942	68.03	75.16	91.33
江门	Jiangmen	37269	37617	33327	70.13	82.33	73.21
阳江	Yangjiang	2045	2372	2938	5.23	4.46	7.29
湛江	Zhanjiang	2454	2763	4144	9.85	10.65	23.90
茂名	Maoming	6452	5868	5727	10.11	10.10	8.63
肇庆	Zhaoqing	10340	11159	13478	21.19	26.69	34.73
清远	Qingyuan	7831	8739	8875	14.01	19.71	19.11
潮州	Chaozhou	3692	3326	3194	4.57	5.84	4.68
揭阳	Jieyang	6606	5903	5818	20.82	20.22	22.74
云浮	Yunfu	2051	3494	3805	2.43	6.45	5.13
按经济区域分	By Region						
珠三角	Pearl River Delta	856914	899487	966766	2388.24	2767.22	3072.79
东翼	Eastern Region	23851	21381	22291	49.92	55.24	57.52
西翼	Western Region	10951	11003	12809	25.18	25.22	39.81
山区	Mountainous Region	19506	25532	25078	36.60	54.50	47.63

19-25 分市规模以上工业企业新产品开发与销售情况(2022年)

New Products Development and Sale by Industrial Enterprises by City(2022)

单位：亿元 (100 million yuan)

市别	City	新产品开发项目数(项) New Products (unit)	新产品开发经费支出 Expenditure on New Products Development	新产品销售收入 Sale Revenue of New Products	#出口 Exports
全省	**Provincial Total**	**221782**	**5159.47**	**48075.11**	**13011.14**
广州	Guangzhou	26824	567.02	6653.26	836.67
深圳	Shenzhen	64256	2399.24	15400.83	5750.80
珠海	Zhuhai	7382	171.90	1969.56	615.11
汕头	Shantou	3297	35.60	452.83	87.73
佛山	Foshan	28253	490.67	5448.51	1099.56
韶关	Shaoguan	1602	28.26	226.70	34.24
河源	Heyuan	1360	13.91	169.89	43.00
梅州	Meizhou	702	10.23	155.75	16.49
惠州	Huizhou	13467	245.50	3319.96	1210.46
汕尾	Shanwei	288	14.15	174.01	58.19
东莞	Dongguan	36897	663.02	8856.10	2010.01
中山	Zhongshan	13009	156.42	1592.67	534.38
江门	Jiangmen	10331	120.25	1397.64	419.68
阳江	Yangjiang	662	41.47	137.21	16.61
湛江	Zhanjiang	1303	34.06	245.62	11.67
茂名	Maoming	1022	15.45	116.77	10.24
肇庆	Zhaoqing	4517	57.05	659.60	59.65
清远	Qingyuan	2627	45.57	698.52	123.52
潮州	Chaozhou	1232	10.70	117.14	35.53
揭阳	Jieyang	1877	28.18	196.18	17.90
云浮	Yunfu	874	10.81	86.35	19.70
按经济区域分	By Region				
珠三角	Pearl River Delta	204936	4871.07	45298.13	12536.32
东翼	Eastern Region	6694	88.62	940.16	199.34
西翼	Western Region	2987	90.99	499.60	38.52
山区	Mountainous Region	7165	108.79	1337.22	236.96

19−26 科协机构及活动情况

Statistics on Associations for Science and Technology and Their Activities

项　目	Item	2000	2005	2010	2015	2021	2022
科协机构　（个）	**Number of Associations for Science and Technology (unit)**	**357**	**196**	**1026**	**142**	**141**	**141**
省科协	Provincial Associations	1	1	1	1	1	1
市科协	City Associations	21	21	21	21	21	21
县(市、区)科协	County (County-level City, District)Associations	123	120	121	120	119	119
厂矿科协	Factory and Mine Associations	212	54	883			
各级学会　（个）	**Number of Learned Societies (unit)**	**880**	**953**	**931**	**2417**	**1764**	**1783**
省级学会	Provincial Learned Societies	146	**151**	151	151	194	206
市级学会	City Learned Societies	734	802	780	838	1013	1042
县级学会	County Learned Societies				1428	557	535
农村专业技术协会　（个）	**Rural Specialized Technological Societies (unit)**	**2900**	**1948**	**1440**	**1360**	**400**	**332**
科协活动开展情况	**Activities of Associations for Science and Technology**						
举办各类学术交流会（次）	Number of Academic Meetings Held (time)	4769	1232	677	1466	1833	2000
举办科技科普展览　（次）	Number of Scientific and Technological Popularization Exhibitions Lectures (time)	2258	2319	3582	1561	893	1078
青少年科技竞赛　（次）	Number of Scientific and Technological Competitions for Adolescents (time)	1286	760	407	327	289	276
参加科协各类活动人次（万人次）	**Number of Participants in Activities Organized by Associations for Science and Technology (person-time)**	**836.76**	**871.69**	**1116.45**	**864.15**	**5012.74**	**13617.56**
参加各类学术交流会	Number of Participants in Academic Meetings	50.52	17.00	29.50	33.57	305.57	965.90
参加各类科技培训	Number of Participants in Training Programs	65.47	46.95	25.20	32.59	37.88	26.19
参加各类科普活动	Number of Participants in Scientific and Technological Popularization Activities	720.77	807.74	1061.75	797.99	4669.29	12625.47
主办科技期刊　（种）	**Publications of Academic Journals and Scientific and Technological Popularization Readings (kind)**	**582**	**216**	**611**	**110**	**42**	**42**
科技期刊总印数（万册、万份）	Number of Academic Journals and Scientific and Technological Popularization Readings Issued (10000 copies)	562	522	513	303	46	48

注：1.2013年，科协机构数不包括厂矿科协。
　　2.2013年起，主办科技期刊只统计在新闻出版机构注册登记，有正式刊号或内部准印证并由本单位直接主办、负责编辑的期刊。
　　3.各类科技培训统计口径变更为实用技术培训。

Note: a) In 2013, factory and mice associations are not included in number of associations for science and technology.
b)From 2013,publications of academic journals and scientific and technological popularization readings refer only to those with official numbers registered by press and publication or those with internal permit directly edited by the unit.
c)The scope of participants in training programs has been changed to operative technology training.

主要统计指标解释

普通高等学校 指按照国家规定的设置标准和审批程序批准举办，通过国家统一招生考试，收高中毕业生为主要培养对象，实施高等教育的全日制大学、独立设置的学院和高等专科学校，高等职业学校和其他机构。

成人高等学校 指按照国家有关规定审批、招收通过全国成人高教统一招生考试的具有高中毕业或同等学力的在职从业人员利用脱产、半脱产、业余或函授等多种形式对其实施高等学历教育，培养高等教育专科或本科毕业水平的专门人才，修业年限、课程设置和总学时的数按高等学历教育要求付诸实施的学校。包括广播电视大学、职工高等学校、农民高等学校、管理干部学院、教育学院、独立设置的函授学院等。

小学学龄儿童入学率 指调查范围内已入小学学习的学龄儿童占校内外学龄儿童总数（包括弱智儿童在内，但不包括盲聋哑儿童）的比重。

研究与试验发展(R&D) 指在科学技术领域，为增加知识总量，以及运用这些知识去创造新的应用进行的系统的创造性的活动，包括基础研究、应用研究、试验发展三类活动。国际上通常采用R&D活动的规模和强度指标反映一国的科技实力和核心竞争力。

基础研究 指为了获得关于现象和可观察事实的基本原理的新知识(揭示客观事物的本质、运动规律，获得新发现、新学说)而进行的实验性或理论性研究，它不以任何专门或特定的应用或使用为目的。其成果以科学论文和科学著作为主要形式。用来反映知识的原始创新能力。

应用研究 指为获得新知识而进行的创造性研究，主要针对某一特定的目的或目标。应用研究是为了确定基础研究成果可能的用途，或是为达到预定的目标探索应采取的新方法(原理性)或新途径。其成果形式以科学论文、专著、原理性模型或发明专利为主。用来反映对基础研究成果应用途径的探索。

试验发展 指利用从基础研究、应用研究和实际经验所获得的现有知识，为产生新的产品、材料和装置，建立新的工艺、系统和服务，以及对已产生和建立的上述各项作实质性的改进而进行的系统性工作。其成果形式主要是专利、专有技术、具有新产品基本特征的产品原型或具有新装置基本特征的原始样机等。在社会科学领域，试验发展是指把通过基础研究、应用研究获得的知识转变成可以实施的计划(包括为进行检验和评估实施示范项目)的过程。人文科学领域没有对应的试验发展活动。主要反映将科研成果转化为技术和产品的能力，是科技推动经济社会发展的物化成果。

R&D人员 指参与研究与试验发展项目研究、管理和辅助工作的人员，包括项目(课题)组人员，企业科技行政管理人员和直接为项目(课题)活动提供服务的辅助人员。反映投入从事拥有自主知识产权的研究开发活动的人力规模。

R&D人员全时当量 指全时人员数加非全时人员按工作量折算为全时人员数的总和。例如：有两个全时人员和三个非全时人员(工作时间分别为20%、30%和70%)，则全时当量为2+0.2+0.3+0.7=3.2人年。为国际上比较科技人力投入而制定的可比指标。

R&D经费支出合计 指调查单位用于内部开展R&D活动（基础研究、应用研究和试验发展）的实际支出。包括用于R&D项目（课题）活动的直接支出，以及间接用于R&D活动的管理费、服务费、与R&D有关的基本建设支出以及外协加工费等。不包括生产性活动支出、归还贷款支出以及与外单位合作或委托外单位进行R&D活动而转拨给对方的经费支出。

R&D经费支出中政府资金 指R&D经费内部支出中来自各级政府部门的各类资金，包括财政科学技术拨款、科学基金、教育等部门事业费以及政府部门预算外资金的实际支出。

R&D经费支出中企业资金 指R&D经费内部支出中来自本企业的自有资金和接受其他企业委托而获得的经费，以及科研院所、高校等事业单位从企业获得的资金的实际支出。

R&D项目（课题）数 指在当年立项并开展研究工作、以前年份立项仍继续进行研究的研发项目（课题）数，包括当年完成和年内研究工作已告失败的研发项目（课题），但不包括委托外单位进行的研发项目（课题）数。

新产品销售收入 指报告期企业销售新产品实现的销售收入。新产品是指采用新技术原理、新设计构思研制、生产的全新产品，或在结构、材质、工艺等某一方面比原有产品有明显改进，从而显著提高了产品性能或扩大了使用功能的产品。既包括经政府有关部门认定并在有效期内的新产品，也包括企业自行研制开发，未经政府有关部门认定，从投产之日起一年之内的新产品。

专利 是专利权的简称，是对发明人的发明创造经审查合格后，由专利局依据专利法授予发明人和设计人对该项发明创造享有的专有权。包括发明、实用新型和外观设计。反映拥有自主知识产权的科技和设计成果情况。

发明（专利） 指对产品、方法或者其改进所提出的新的技术方案。是国际通行的反映拥有自主知识产权技术的核心指标。

实用新型（专利） 指对产品的形状、构造或者其结合所提出的适于实用的新的技术方案。反映具有一定技术含量的技术成果情况。

外观设计（专利） 指对产品的形状、图案、色彩或者其结合所作出的富有美感并适于工业上应用的新设计。反映拥有自主知识产权的外观设计成果情况。

Explanatory Notes on Main Statistical Indicators

Regular Institutions of Higher Education refer to educational establishments set up according to government standards and evaluation and approval procedures, mainly enrolling graduates from senior secondary schools through uniform national matriculation examinations and providing higher education. Such institutions include full-time universities, independent colleges, technical colleges, professional colleges, and other institutions.

Institutions of Higher Learning for Adults refer to educational establishments approved according to relevant government rules, enrolling staff and workers with senior secondary or equivalent education through uniform national matriculation examinations, and providing them with regular higher education in various forms such as full-time, part-time, spare-time and correspondence courses in accordance with requirements of regular higher education in years of education, curricula, and total learning hours, so that they meet the standards for graduation of universities or junior colleges. Institutions of higher learning for adults include radio and TV universities, colleges for staff and workers, colleges for farmers, colleges for management cadres, teachers' colleges, and independent correspondence colleges.

Enrollment Rate of Primary School-age Children refers to the proportion of school-age children enrolled at primary schools in the total number of school-age children both in and outside schools (including retarded children, but excluding blind, deaf and dumb children).

Research and Development (R&D) refers to systematic and creative activities in the field of science and technology aiming at increasing the knowledge and using the knowledge for new application. R&D includes 3 categories of activities: basic research, applied research and experiments and development. The scale and intensity of R&D are widely used internationally to reflect the strength of S&T and the core competitiveness of a country in the world.

Basic Research refers to empirical or theoretical research aiming at obtaining new knowledge on the fundamental principles regarding phenomena or observable facts to reveal the intrinsic nature and underlying laws and to acquire new discoveries or new theories. Basic research takes no specific or designated application as the aim of the research. Results of basic research are mainly released or disseminated in the form of scientific papers or monographs. This indicator reflects the innovation capacity for original knowledge.

Applied Research refers to creative research aiming at obtaining new knowledge on a specific objective or target. Purpose of the applied research is to identify the possible uses of results from basic research, or to explore new (fundamental) methods or new approaches. Results of applied research are expressed in the form of scientific papers, monographs, fundamental models or invention patents. This indicator reflects the exploration of ways to apply the results of basic research.

Experiments and Development refer to systematic activities aiming at using the knowledge from basic and applied researches or from practical experience to develop new products, materials and equipment, to establish new production process, systems and services, or to make substantial improvement on the existing products, process or services. Results of experiment and development activities are embodied in patents, exclusive technology, and monotype of new products or equipment. In social sciences, experiment and development activities refer to the process of converting the knowledge from basic or applied researches into feasible programmes (including conduct of demonstration projects for assessment and evaluation). There are no experiment and development activities in the science of humanities. This indicator reflects the capability of transferring the results of S&T into technique and products, and measures the realization of S&T in spearheading the economic and social development.

R & D Personnel refer to persons engaged in research, management and supporting activities of R & D, including persons in the project teams, persons engaged in the management of S&T activities of enterprises and supporting staff providing direct service to the research projects. This indicator reflects the size of personnel engaged in R&D activities with independent intellectual property.

Full-time Equivalent of R&D Personnel refers to the sum of the full-time persons and the full-time equivalent of part-time persons converted by workload. For instance, if there are 2 full-time persons and 3 part-time workers (20%, 30% and 70% of working hours respectively on R&D activities), the full-time equivalent are 2+0.2+0.3+0.7=3.2 person-years. This is an internationally comparable indicator of S&T manpower input.

Total Expenditure of Funds on R&D refers to the real expenditure of surveyed units on their own R&D activities (basic research, applied research, experiments and development) including direct expenditure on R&D activities, indirect expenditure of management and services on R&D activities, expenditure on capital construction and material processing by others. Excluding the expenditure on production activities, return of loan, and fees transferred to cooperated or entrusted agencies on R&D activities.

Expenditure of Government Funds on R&D refers to the expenditure of funds on R&D activities from government agencies at different levels, including appropriate funds on science and technology from financial departments, scientific funds, operating expenses from education departments and the real expenditure of extra budgetary funds from government agencies.

Expenditure of Funds of Enterprises on R&D refers to the expenditure of funds on R&D activities from self-raised funds of enterprises and funds from other enterprises through entrustment, and the expenditure of funds of institutions, such as institution of scientific research and universities, from enterprises.

Number of R&D Projects (subjects) refers to the number of R&D projects (subjects) set up and implemented at the reference year, and the number of R&D projects (subjects) set up in former years and under implementation, including the projects (subjects) finished and failed at the reference year, excluding the projects (subjects) implemented by others through entrustment.

Sales Income of New Products refers to the sales income of new products of the enterprises at the reference period. New products refer to products developed and produced with new technologies and designs or improved in structure, material, process or other aspects so that their performance are improved or their functions expanded. New products include those affirmed by government authorities in their validity period and also those developed by enterprises without the affirmation of government authorities within one year after they are put into production.

Patent is an abbreviation for the patent right and refers to the exclusive right of ownership by the inventors or designers for the creation or inventions, given from the patent offices after due process of assessment and approval in accordance with the Patent Law. Patents are granted for inventions, utility models and designs. This indicator reflects the achievements of S&T and design with independent intellectual property.

Patented Inventions refer to new technical proposals to the products or methods or their modifications. This is universal core indicator reflecting the technologies with independent intellectual property.

Patented Utility Models refer to the practical and new technical proposals on the shape and structure of the product or the combination of both. This indicator reflects the condition of technological results with certain technical content.

Designs refer to the aesthetics and industrially applicable new designs for the shape, pattern and colour of the product, or their combinations. This indicator reflects the appearance design achievements with independent intellectual property.

二十、文化与体育

CULTURE AND SPORTS

二十　文化与体育

简要说明

一、本篇资料主要反映文化事业和体育的基本情况。

二、本篇资料主要包括：

1. 文化艺术、文物、图书馆、新闻出版、广播、电影、电视等文化事业的机构、人员及业务活动开展情况等。

2. 体育系统职工人数、群众体育活动开展情况及运动竞技成绩等。

三、本篇资料由广东省统计局社会和科技统计处负责整理、编辑。

四、统计资料来源：

文化、体育统计资料根据广东省文化和旅游厅、广东省广播电视局、广东省体育局及广东省档案局等有关部门提供的统计年报加工整理。

20 Culture and Sports

Brief Introduction

Ⅰ. The data in this chapter show the basic conditions on the development Guangdong's cultural undertakings. as well as sports.

Ⅱ. The data in this chapter mainly include:

(1) The data on institutions, personnel and business activities of culture and arts, cultural relics, libraries, news and publication, radio, film and television, etc.

(2) The number of staff and workers in sports departments， mass sports and athletics sports， etc.

Ⅲ. The data are prepared and edited by the Division of Social, Scientific and Technological Statistics of Statistics Bureau of Guangdong Province.

Ⅳ. Data sources:

The data on culture and sport are processed and prepared in accordance with the annual statistical reports provided by the Department of Culture and Tourism of Guangdong Province, Radio and Television Administration of Guangdong Province, Guangdong Provincial Bureau of Sports, Guangdong Provincial Bureau of Archives and the related departments.

20-1 文化、体育主要指标

Main Indicators on Culture and Education

指 标	Item	2000	2010	2015	2021	2022
电影放映单位 (个)	Number of Film Projection Units (unit)	1626	1392	1793	2839	3032
艺术表演团体 (个)	Number of Art Performance Troupes (unit)	138	133	72	76	76
文化馆 (个)	Number of Cultural Centers (unit)	118	129	146	144	144
公共图书馆 (个)	Number of Public Libraries (unit)	125	133	140	150	150
公共图书馆藏量 (万册、件)	Holdings of Public Libraries (10000 volumes)	2330	4615	7008	12687	14253
博物馆（含美术馆） (个)	Number of Museums (including arts museum) (unit)	131	169	193	385	393
博物馆藏品数(含美术馆) (万件)	Holdings of Museums (including arts museum) (10000 pieces)	49.09	84.46	101.83	268.17	277.42
全省每万人拥有公共文化设施面积 (平方米)	Area of Public Cultural Facilities per 10000 People (Sq m)		416.00	1189.24	1379.26	1477.57
档案馆 (个)	Number of Archives (unit)	161	205	217	189	190
利用档案 (万卷次)	Archives Utilized (10000 volume-times)	36.32	301.00	495.00	873.84	847.48
图书出版量 (万册)	Number of Books Published (10000 copies)	26978	23134	31287	50566	50591
杂志出版量 (万册)	Number of Magazines Published (10000 copies)	26299	21201	14458	9539	9113
报纸出版量 (亿份)	Number of Newspapers Published (100 million copies)	34.63	45.59	32.77	14.48	13.19
广播电台 (座)	Number of Radio Stations (unit)	106	22	22	2	2
电视台 (座)	Number of TV Stations (unit)	67	24	24	3	3
广播电视台 (座)	Number of Radio and Television Stations	83	79		95	95
广播综合人口覆盖率 (%)	Overall Population Coverage Rate of Radio (%)	96.0	98.0	99.9	99.98	99.98
电视综合人口覆盖率 (%)	Overall Population Coverage Rate of Television (%)	96.4	98.0	99.9	99.98	99.98
举办全民健身活动次数 (次)	Number of National Body-building Activities Held (time)		9477	5000	2000	2258
全省人均拥有体育场地面积 (平方米)	Per Capita Area of Sports Venues (Sqm)	1.91	2.01		2.54	2.68

注：1.由于文化部门改制，2012年起只统计事业单位和省直企业中的文化部门艺术表演团体。自2013年起，艺术表演团体口径进行调整，分为公有制艺术表演团体(事业)和公有制艺术表演团体(企业)。

2.2019年博物馆的统计范围增加了民办博物馆。

3.2019年起，广播电台、电视台数据只包含独立的广播电台和电视台，广播电台和电视台合并机构纳入广播电视台统计。

4.2020年全省人均体育场地面积数据依据最新人口统计数据统计。

Note: a)Due to institutional restructuring of cultural departments, the data of art performance troupes since 2012 only covers those of institutional organizations and directly under provincial jurisdiction.Since 2013,the coverage of art performance troupes has been adjusted to include public ownership art performance troupes(Institution) and public ownership art performance troupes(Enterprises).

b)The number of museums in 2019 includes private museums.

c)Since 2019, the number of radio stations and the number of television stations only include independent radio and television stations, and the combined institutions of radio and television stations are included in the radio and television stations.

d)Per capita area of sports venues in 2020 is based on the latest Census data.

20-2 文化艺术、文物事业机构数

Number of Institutions of Culture, Arts and Cultural Relics

单位：个 (unit)

年份 Year	电影放映单位 Film Projection Units	艺术表演团体 Arts Performance Troupes	文化馆 Cultural Centers	公共图书馆 Public Libraries	博物馆 Museums	档案馆 Archives
1978	6346	172	124	76	30	
1980	7375	195	113	97	26	
1985	6037	171	123	117	106	
1990	4024	130	113	103	106	138
1991	4041	122	110	104	107	147
1992	3917	125	113	108	108	150
1993	3974	126	115	110	108	148
1994	3750	132	116	111	111	156
1995	3668	134	115	114	113	155
1996	3670	136	115	115	114	157
1997	3463	138	117	119	117	157
1998	3621	139	117	120	122	157
1999	2938	140	117	121	128	162
2000	1626	138	118	125	131	161
2001	1794	139	118	129	140	175
2002	904	141	120	131	140	185
2003	840	144	117	129	144	185
2004	684	140	119	128	143	185
2005	720	139	117	129	146	185
2006	1542	138	120	129	147	186
2007	1844	128	122	130	153	186
2008	1450	130	121	132	152	188
2009	1265	127	128	133	160	197
2010	1392	133	129	133	169	205
2011	1357	100	134	134	161	209
2012	1419	61	137	137	168	209
2013	1506	75	147	137	191	214
2014	1673	72	147	138	192	218
2015	1793	72	146	140	193	217
2016	1974	72	146	142	192	192
2017	2323	74	146	143	197	192
2018	2490	74	145	143	199	188
2019	2666	72	145	146	259	189
2020	2845	71	144	148	324	186
2021	2839	76	144	150	385	189
2022	3032	76	144	150	393	190

注：由于全国文化文物统计制度统计口径的改变，2009年以后博物馆包含美术馆，其他年份博物馆不含美术馆。

Note: Due to the change in statistical coverage in national culture and cultural relics survey, the number of museums after 2009 includes arts museum and that of other years does not include arts museum.

20-3 文化部门艺术表演团体演出基本情况（2022年）

Basic Statistics on Performances of Art Troupes under(of) Cultural Departments (2022)

项　目	Item	剧团数(个) Number of Troupes (unit)	国内演出场次(万场) Number of Domestic Performances (10000 shows)	#到农村演出 Shows in Rural Areas	国内演出观众人次(万人次) Number of Domestic Spectators (10000 person-times)
合　计	**Total**	**76**	**0.52**	**0.24**	**326.73**
公有制艺术表演团体(事业)	Public Ownership Arts Performance Troupes (Institution)	29	0.17	0.06	134.64
国有	State-owned	29	0.17	0.06	134.64
集体	Collective-owned				
其他	Others				
公有制艺术表演团体(企业)	Public Ownership Arts Performance Troupes (Enterprises)	47	0.35	0.18	192.09
国有	State-owned	40	0.31	0.15	163.54
集体	Collective-owned				
其他	Others	7	0.04	0.03	28.55
按剧种分	**By Type of Art Performance Troupe**				
话剧、儿童剧、滑稽剧类	Modern Drama, Children Drama, Farce Drama	3	0.01		5.43
歌舞、音乐类	Dance, Music	22	0.14	0.04	67.49
京剧、昆曲类	Beijing Opera, Kunqu Opera				
地方戏曲类	Local Opera	41	0.31	0.20	216.65
杂技、魔术、马戏类	Magic, Acrobatics, Circus	3	0.01		13.00
曲艺类	Chinese Folk Art	5	0.02		8.17
乌兰牧骑	Nei Monggol Cultural Troupe Mounted on Horseback				
综合性艺术表演团体	Comprehensive Art Troupes	2	0.03		15.99

20–4 文化、文物机构及人员数（2022年）

Number of Institutions and Personnel in Culture and Cultural Relics (2022)

项　目	Item	合计 Total		文化部门 Cultural Departments		其他部门 Others	
		机构数（个） Number of Institutions (unit)	人数（人） Number of Personnel (person)	机构数（个） Number of Institutions (unit)	人数（人） Number of Personnel (person)	机构数（个） Number of Institutions (unit)	人数（人） Number of Personnel (person)
总　计	**Total**	**15520**	**248387**	**2535**	**43565**	**12985**	**204822**
文化合计	**Culture**	**15147**	**241148**	**2308**	**37716**	**12839**	**203432**
艺术事业	Arts	125	6305	118	6019	7	286
图书馆事业	Libraries	150	5444	150	5444		
群众文化事业	Mass Culture	1761	15352	1761	15352		
艺术教育业	Art Education	2	328	2	328		
文化市场经营机构(不含非公有制艺术表演团体)	Cultural Market Operating Units	12786	202102			12786	202102
文艺科研	Scientific Research on Arts	7	103	7	103		
艺术展览创作机构	Art Exhibition Creative Agency	60	825	42	649	18	176
文化行政主管部门	Administrative Department	152	8535	152	8535		
其他文化机构	Other Agencies	104	2154	76	1286	28	868
文物合计	**Cultural Relics**	**373**	**7239**	**227**	**5849**	**146**	**1390**
文物科研机构	Institutions for Cultural Relics	4	141	4	141		
文物保护管理机构	Agencies of Cultural Relics Preservation	26	316	24	316	2	
博物馆	Museums	340	6702	196	5312	144	1390
其他文物机构	Other Agencies	3	80	3	80		

20–5 公共图书馆、群众文化事业机构及人员数（2022年）

Number of Institutions and Personnel in Public Libraries and Mass Culture (2022)

项　目	Item	合计 Total		文化部门 Cultural Departments		其他部门 Others	
		机构数（个） Number of Institutions (unit)	人数（人） Number of Personnel (person)	机构数（个） Number of Institutions (unit)	人数（人） Number of Personnel (person)	机构数（个） Number of Institutions (unit)	人数（人） Number of Personnel (person)
图书馆事业	**Libraries**	**150**	**5444**	**150**	**5444**		
#少儿图书馆	Children's Libraries	5	243	5	243		
群众文化事业	**Mass Culture**	**1761**	**15352**	**1761**	**15352**		
群众艺术馆、文化馆	Mass Art Centers	144	2634	144	2634		
文化站	Cultural Stations	1617	12718	1617	12718		

20-6　各市文化、文物事业机构数（2022年）

Number of Institutions in Culture and Cultural Relics by City (2022)

单位：个　　　　(unit)

市　别	City	艺术表演团体 Art Troupes	文化馆 Cultural Centers	公共图书馆 Public Libraries	博物馆(含美术馆) Museums (including art museums)	档案馆 Archives
全　省	**Provincial Total**	**76**	**144**	**150**	**393**	**190**
广　州	Guangzhou	7	12	13	59	14
深　圳	Shenzhen	3	10	12	93	11
珠　海	Zhuhai	2	4	4	11	5
汕　头	Shantou	6	8	8	11	10
佛　山	Foshan	1	6	6	29	8
韶　关	Shaoguan	2	11	11	13	12
河　源	Heyuan	5	7	7	10	8
梅　州	Meizhou	6	9	10	28	13
惠　州	Huizhou	1	6	6	10	8
汕　尾	Shanwei	4	5	5	6	5
东　莞	Dongguan		1	1	20	2
中　山	Zhongshan		1	1	6	2
江　门	Jiangmen	1	8	8	15	13
阳　江	Yangjiang	1	5	5	9	6
湛　江	Zhanjiang	8	10	11	13	12
茂　名	Maoming	6	6	6	7	8
肇　庆	Zhaoqing	2	9	9	16	10
清　远	Qingyuan	4	9	10	9	10
潮　州	Chaozhou	2	4	4	12	5
揭　阳	Jieyang	5	6	6	7	6
云　浮	Yunfu	1	6	6	7	6
省直属单位	Units Directly under Provincial Government	9	1	1	2	16
按经济区域分	By Region					
珠三角	Pearl River Delta	17	57	60	259	73
东　翼	Eastern Region	17	23	23	36	26
西　翼	Western Region	15	21	22	29	26
山　区	Mountainous Region	18	42	44	67	49

注：1.自2013年起，艺术表演团体分为公有制艺术表演团体(事业)和公有制艺术表演团体(企业)。
　　2.各区域不包省直单位部分。

Note: a) The coverage of art performance troupes has been adjusted to include public ownership art performance troupes(Institution) and public ownership art performance troupes(Enterprises) since 2013.
b) By Region does not include agencies directly under provincial jurisdiction.

20-7 各市文化、文物事业机构的人员数（2022年）
Number of Personnel in Culture and Cultural Relics by City (2022)

单位：人 (person)

市别	City	艺术表演团体 Art Troupes	文化馆 Cultural Centers	公共图书馆 Public Libraries	博物馆(含美术馆) Museums (including art museums)	档案馆 Archives
全　省	**Provincial Total**	**4671**	**2634**	**5444**	**7409**	**2693**
广　州	Guangzhou	832	233	972	1453	420
深　圳	Shenzhen	378	361	1670	1422	149
珠　海	Zhuhai	248	74	129	204	64
汕　头	Shantou	207	113	116	230	136
佛　山	Foshan	54	154	335	740	164
韶　关	Shaoguan	75	185	110	234	127
河　源	Heyuan	139	126	117	135	78
梅　州	Meizhou	155	153	158	349	129
惠　州	Huizhou	87	114	138	203	116
汕　尾	Shanwei	231	70	80	98	56
东　莞	Dongguan		85	175	511	24
中　山	Zhongshan		30	52	122	112
江　门	Jiangmen	44	115	170	205	164
阳　江	Yangjiang	46	78	78	215	90
湛　江	Zhanjiang	343	124	135	204	121
茂　名	Maoming	168	67	140	78	90
肇　庆	Zhaoqing	69	123	180	246	122
清　远	Qingyuan	106	131	112	115	94
潮　州	Chaozhou	127	55	72	194	41
揭　阳	Jieyang	160	111	115	98	73
云　浮	Yunfu	39	86	95	92	72
省直属单位	Units Directly under Provincial Government	1163	46	295	261	251
按经济区域分	By Region					
珠三角	Pearl River Delta	1712	1289	3821	5106	1335
东　翼	Eastern Region	725	349	383	620	306
西　翼	Western Region	557	269	353	497	301
山　区	Mountainous Region	514	681	592	925	500

注：1.2012年起，分市数只统计事业单位的文化部门艺术表演团体。
　　2.各区域不包省直单位部分。

Note: a)Since 2012, the number of art troupes by city only covers data of art troupes of institutional organizations.
　　b)"By Region" does not include agencies directly under provincial jurisdiction.

20-8 图书、杂志、报纸出版数量

Number of Books, Magazines and Newspapers Published

项　　目	Item	2000	2005	2010	2015	2020	2021	2022
图书出版	**Books Published**							
种数　(种)	Number of Publications　(kind)	4374	5908	6354	10089	10970	11565	10557
总印数　(万册)	Total Printed Copies(10000 copies)	26978	22600	23134	31287	43448	50566	50591
总印张数(千印张)	Total Printed Sheets　(1000 sheets)	1482942	1514191	1597301	2434970	3394245	3982308	3967554
杂志出版	**Magazines Published**							
种数　(种)	Number of Publications　(kind)	337	366	380	382	380	380	380
总印数　(万册)	Total Printed Copies(10000 copies)	26299	20371	21201	14458	9887	9539	9113
总印张数(千印张)	Total Printed Sheets　(1000 sheets)	919514	116814	1251752	844427	492203	475097	452947
报纸出版	**Newspapers Published**							
种数　(种)	Number of Publications　(kind)	101	102	100	100	97	92	92
总印数　(万份)	Total Printed Copies(10000 copies)	346268	398152	455912	327660	153310	144834	131893
总印张数(千印张)	Total Printed Sheets　(1000 sheets)	17669099	28996964	43788152	20081573	5117384	4601690	3726676

注：1.本表图书种数、总印数和总印张不包含非“中国标准书号”部分。
　　2.2000年开始报纸出版统计不包校报、院报。

Note:a)Total Printed Copies and Total Printed Sheets does not include publications without “China International Standard Book Number”.
　　b)Since 2000, the number of newspaper published does not include that of college or institute newspaper.

20-9 图书出版情况（2022年）

Statistics on Books Published (2022)

门　　类	Category	图书出版种数(种) Number of Publications (kind)	#新出 New Public-ations	总印数(万册) Total Printed Copies (10000 copies)	总印张数(千印张) Total Printed Sheets (1000 sheets)
合　计	**Total**	**10557**	**4938**	**50591**	**3967554**
马克思主义、列宁主义、毛泽东思想	Marxism, Leninism and Mao Zedong Thought	19	7	4	315
哲学	Philosophy	132	82	91	11817
社会科学总论	General Social Sciences	80	44	33	4159
政治、法律	Politics and Law	245	176	1050	70797
军事	Military Affairs	30	12	22	2722
经济	Economy	489	339	239	35173
文化、科学、教育、体育	Culture, Science, Education and Sports	5902	1930	44376	3340642
语言、文字	Language, Philology	206	104	194	25738
文学	Literature	1371	848	3545	342251
艺术	Arts	448	330	325	44626
历史、地理	History and Geography	515	377	222	30192
自然科学总论	General Natural Sciences	22	18	11	1464
数理科学、化学	Mathematics, Physics and Chemistry	60	27	17	1944
天文学、地理科学	Astronomy and Geology	41	29	20	2095
生物科学	Biological Science	61	35	45	4142
医药、卫生	Medicine and Health Care	401	267	147	17713
农业科学	Agricultural Science	41	27	13	1460
工业技术	Industrial Technology	350	170	173	23516
交通运输	Transportation	23	12	25	716
航空、航天	Aeronautics and Aerospace	7	4	4	234
环境科学	Environmental Science	36	26	15	999
综合性图书	General Books	78	74	20	4839

注：本表图书种数、总印数和总印张不包含非“中国标准书号”部分。

Notes: Total Printed Copies and Total Printed Sheets does not include publications without “China International Standard Book Number”.

20-10 杂志出版情况（2022年）

Statistics on Magazines Published (2022)

项　目	Item	种数（种） Number of Publications (kind)	平均期印数（万册） Average Printed Copies per Issue (10000 copies)	总印数（万册） Total Printed Copies (10000 copies)	总印张数（千印张） Total Printed Sheets (1000 sheets)
合　计	**Total**	**380**	**412**	**9113**	**452947**
综　合	General	26	10	121	7078
哲学、社会科学	Philosophy, Social Sciences	97	199	4456	211042
自然科学、技术	Natural Sciences, Technology	180	144	3284	167816
文化、教育	Culture, Education	46	48	1147	58073
文学、艺术	Literature, Arts	31	10	105	8939

20-11 报纸出版情况（2022年）

Statistics on Newspapers Published (2022)

项　目	Item	种数(种) Number of Publications (kind)	平均期印数(万册) Average Printed Copies per Issue (10000 copies)	总印数(万册) Total Printed Copies (10000 copies)	总印张数(千印张) Total Printed Sheets (1000 sheets)
合　计	**Total**	**92**	**481**	**131893**	**3726676**
按类型分	**By Type**				
综合类	General Newspapers	46	387	119576	3385036
专业类	Specialized Newspapers	30	44	6918	243521
生活服务类	Life Service Newspapers	10	6	260	20503
读者对象类	Reader Oriented Newspapers	5	40	4735	69560
文摘类	Digest Newspapers	1	4	403	8056
按范围分	**By Region**				
省　级	Provincial-level Newspapers	31	214	53896	1816802
市　级	City-level Newspapers	61	266	77996	1909874

注：根据《全国报纸出版统计调查制度(2019)》，将报纸分为“综合类”“专业类”“生活服务类”“读者对象类”“文摘类”(以上为非高校校报)和“高校校报”六类。本表不包含高校校报。其中以前年度将“综合类”“生活服务类”“读者对象类”对应以前年度的“综合报”，将“文摘类”“专业类”对应以前年度的“专业报”。

Note: According to the 《National Newspaper Publishing Statistical Survey System (2019)》, newspapers are divided into six categories: "General", "Specialized", "Life Service", " Reader Oriented", "Digest"(the above are not college newspapers) and "college newspapers". This table does not include college newspapers. In the previous year, "General", "Life Service" and " Reader Oriented" correspond to "General Newspaper" , and "Digest" and "Specialized Newspaper" correspond to "Specialized Newspapers".

20-12　广播、电视事业发展情况

Statistics on Radio and Television Stations

项　目	Item	2000	2010	2015	2018	2019	2020	2021	2022
广播电台（座）	Number of Radio Stations (set)	106	22	22	22	2	2	2	2
中波广播发射台和转播台（座）	Number of Medium Wave Radio Transmission Stations and Relaying Stations (set)	10	21	27	27	26	22	22	28
电视台（座）	Number of Television Stations (set)	67	24	24	24	3	3	3	3
100瓦及以上电视发射台和转播台（座）	Number of Television Transmission and Relaying Stations at 1000 W and above (set)	49	83	83	83	103	95	95	98
广播电视台（座）	Number of Radio and Television Stations (set)	83	79	79	79	95	95	95	95
有线广播电视用户（万户）	Number of Subscribers to Cable Radio and Television (10000 subscribers)		1702	2089	1845	1767	1706	1710	1536
数字电视用户（万户）	Number of Subscribers to Digital Television (10000 subscribers)		950	1622	1761	1705	1639	1642	1477

注：1000瓦及以上电视发射台和转播台，从2006年起改为100瓦以上(含100瓦)电视发射台和转播台。

Note: Television transmission and relaying stations at 1000 W and above since 2006 have been replaced by television transmission and relaying stations at 100W and above.

20-13　广播电台宣传基本情况（2022年）

Basic Statistics on Radio Stations (2022)

项　目	Item	广播电视台（座）Number of Radio and TV Stations (set)	广播电台（座）Number of Radio Stations (set)	节目套数（套）Number of Programs (set)	平均每日播音时间（小时）Average Daily Broadcasting Hours (hour)				
						#自办节目时间 Self-produced Programs			
							#新闻节目 News Programs	#专题节目 Special Subject Programs	#文艺节目 Programs of Entertainment
合　计	**Total**	**95**	**2**	**140**	**2320**	**1783**	**426**	**395**	**313**
省　级	Provincial Level	1		9	215	206	29	74	35
市　级	City Level	19	2	60	1123	1012	154	199	138
县　级	County Level	75		71	982	565	243	122	140

20-14 电视台宣传基本情况（2022年）

Basic Statistics on Television Stations (2022)

项目	Item	广播电视台(座) Number of Radio and TV Stations (set)	电视台(座) Television Stations (set)	节目套数(套) Number of Programs (set)	平均每日播出音时间(小时) Average Daily Broadcasting Hours (hour)	#自办节目时间 Self-produced Programs	#新闻节目 News Programs	#专题节目 Special Subject Programs	#文艺节目 Entertainment Programs
合计	**Total**	**95**	**3**	**148**	**2293**	**732**	**379**	**315**	**77**
省级	Provincial Level	1		13	292	136	38	43	19
市级	City Level	19	3	64	1124	406	197	159	32
县级	County Level	75		71	877	190	144	113	26

20-15 各市广播、电视事业机构数（2022年）

Number of Institutions of Radio and Television by City (2022)

单位：座 (set)

市别	City	广播电台 Number of Radio Stations	中波广播发射台和转播台 Number of Medium Wave Radio Transmission Stations and Relaying Stations	电视台 Number of Television Stations	100瓦及以上电视发射台和转播台 Number of Television Transmission and Relaying Stations at 100 W and above	广播电视台 Number of Radio and Television Stations
广州	Guangzhou		4		5	5
深圳	Shenzhen	1	2	2	1	
珠海	Zhuhai				1	2
汕头	Shantou		1		2	4
佛山	Foshan	1		1	7	
韶关	Shaoguan				13	9
河源	Heyuan				5	6
梅州	Meizhou		2		4	8
惠州	Huizhou				5	5
汕尾	Shanwei				4	4
东莞	Dongguan				1	1
中山	Zhongshan				1	1
江门	Jiangmen				3	6
阳江	Yangjiang				2	4
湛江	Zhanjiang		1		10	6
茂名	Maoming				3	5
肇庆	Zhaoqing				7	7
清远	Qingyuan				8	8
潮州	Chaozhou				2	3
揭阳	Jieyang				4	5
云浮	Yunfu				4	5
省直属单位	Units Directly under Provincial Government		18		6	1

20-16 体育事业情况
Statistics on Sports

指　　标	Item	2010	2015	2020	2021	2022
体育系统年末职工人数（人）	**Number of Staff and Workers in Sports Departments at the Year-end (person)**	**9405**	**10620**	**12429**	**11987**	**10917**
正式运动员	Official Athletes	1036	1649	1679	2085	2208
体育教练员	Sports Coaches	1094	1485	1843	1942	1949
专职文化教师	Full-time Teachers for Literacy Classes	918	907	897	898	807
科技人员	Scientific and Technological Personnel	113	114	104	91	105
医务人员	Medical Personnel	97	60	100	110	112
管理人员	Administrative Personnel	3328	4401	5229	5076	4023
其他人员	Others	2819	2004	2577	1785	1713
体育比赛成绩	**Achievements in Sports Tournament**					
破世界纪录（项）	Number of World Records Chalked Up (item)	1	1	1	3	
获世界冠军（人次）	Number of World Championships Won (person-time)	27	27	1	10	14
破亚洲纪录（项）	Number of Asian Records Chalked Up (item)	2	4	2	6	
破全国纪录（项次）	Number of National Records Chalked Up (item-time)	5	5	5	8	1
获得全国冠军（项次）	Number of National Championships Won (item-time)	132	124	114	124	70
体育活动开展情况	**Sports Meets and Activities**					
举办全民健身活动次数（次）	Number of National Body-building Activities Held (time)	9477	5000	2959	2000	2258

主要统计指标解释

文化事业机构 指从事专业文化工作和为专业文化工作服务的独立建制的单独核算的单位。不包括这些单位另外举办独立核算的其他机构和各部门的业余文化组织。

艺术表演团体 指由文化部门主办或者实行行业管理（经文化行政部门审批并领取营业性演出许可证），专门从事表演艺术等活动的各类专业艺术表演团体，含民间职业剧团（不包括群众业余文艺表演团体）。

电影放映单位 指具有放映机器设备、固定或不固定的放映场所与专职或兼职的放映技术人员，经有关部门登记批准，经常为一定的观众对象放映电影的机构。包括经批准对外开放进行营业，并与电影发行放映管理机构分帐的专用放映单位和军委系统租片单位。

艺术表演观众人数（人次） 指售票、包场等有演出收入的场次和政府采纳的公益性演出场次及参加汇演等无演出收入的公开演出场次，不包括彩排审查和内部观摩演出的观看人次数。

Explanatory Notes on Main Statistical Indicators

Cultural Institutions refer to units which have their own organizational system and independent accounting system and specialize in or serve cultural development. They exclude other establishments with independent accounting system run by these cultural institutions and amateur cultural groups established by various departments.

Arts Performance Troupes refer to the various professional performing arts groups, which sponsored by the cultural sectors or guided by the cultural society (approved by the cultural administration authority, or registered and permitted with the relative certificate), including non-governmental troupes. The mass amateur arts performance troupes are not included.

Film Projection Units refer to units with film projection equipment, full or part-time projectionists, permanent or non-permanent cinemas, approved by and registered with related administrative departments to show films regularly for certain groups of audience, including film projection units which have been approved to give commercial shows and share profits with administrative agencies of film circulation and projection, as well as film renting units of the military system.

Number of Spectators at Art Performance (person-time) refers to the number of attendants at commercial shows, completely booked shows or free shows given in minority national areas, excluding the number of spectators at rehearsals for examination and internal shows for study.

二十一、卫生、社会福利、社会保障和其他

PUBLIC HEALTH, SOCIAL WELFARE, SOCIAL INSURANCE AND OTHERS

二十一　卫生、社会福利、社会保障和其他

简要说明

一、本篇资料主要反映广东卫生、社会福利、社会保险、安全生产及其他事业的发展情况。

二、本篇资料由广东省统计局社会和科技统计处负责整理、编辑。

三、卫生部分主要包括卫生事业机构、床位及人员数等，资料由广东省卫生健康委员会提供。

四、社会福利部分主要包括各种社会福利事业情况、城乡基层社会保障情况、婚姻登记状况等，资料由广东省民政厅提供。

五、社会保险部分主要包括城乡基本养老保险、失业保险、城乡基本医疗保险等基金征缴收入和参保人数，资料由广东省人力资源和社会保障厅提供。

六、亿元生产总值安全生产事故死亡率数据由广东省应急管理厅提供。

七、其他部分主要包括司法工作开展情况和交通、火灾事故发生情况等，资料由广东省司法厅 、广东省公安厅提供。

21 Public Health,Social Welfare,Social Insurance and Others

Brief Introduction

Ⅰ. The data in this chapter mainly show the development of Guangdong's public health，social welfare，social security, safe production and other undertakings.

Ⅱ. The data are prepared by the Division of Social，Scientific and Technological Statistics of Statistics Bureau of Guangdong Province.

Ⅲ. The data on public health mainly include the number of health institutions， hospital beds and personnel，etc. The data are provided by Health Department of Guangdong Province.

Ⅳ. The data on social welfare mainly include the social welfare services，grassroots social security in urban and rural areas and marriage registration status，etc. The data are provided by Guangdong Provincial Department of Civil Affairs.

Ⅴ.The data on social security mainly include the statistics on basic pension insurance for urban and rural residents, the unemployment insurance, the amount collected and percentage of collection and the number of persons participating in urban and rural basic medical care insurance.The data is provided by Guangdong Provincial Department of Human Resources and Social Security.

Ⅵ. The rate of death from work safety accidents per 100 million yuan of GDP is provided by the Department of Emergency Management of Guangdong Province.

Ⅶ. Other data mainly include judicial conditions and basic statistics on traffic and fire accidents，etc. The data are provided by Guangdong Provincial Department of Justice and Guangdong Provincial Department of Public Security.

21-1 卫生、社会福利和其他主要指标

Main Indicators of Sports, Public Health, Social Welfare, Environmental Protection and Others

指　标	Item	2000	2010	2020	2021	2022
医疗卫生机构数 (个)	Number of Health Care Institutions (unit)	8984	44880	55900	57955	59531
#医院、卫生院	Hospitals	2426	2444	2875	2935	2981
医疗卫生机构床位数 (万张)	Number of Beds in Health Care Institutions (10000 units)	16.81	30.01	56.47	58.90	60.83
#医院、卫生院床位	Hospital Beds	15.72	27.71	52.39	54.66	56.41
卫生技术人员数 (万人)	Number of Medical Technical Personnel (10000 persons)	26.50	45.55	83.21	87.58	91.84
#执业(助理)医师	Licensed Physicians & Physician Assistants	11.12	17.51	30.73	32.09	33.52
平均每千人口有卫生机构床位数 (张)	Number of Beds in health Institutions per 1000 Population (bed)	1.94	2.87	4.47	4.64	4.81
平均每千人口有卫生技术人员数 (人)	Number of Medical Technical Personnel per 1000 Population (person)	3.07	4.36	6.59	6.90	7.26
#执业(助理)医师	Licensed Physicians & Physician Assistants	1.29	1.68	2.43	2.53	2.65
社会救助总人数 (万人)	Total Number under Social Relief (10000 persons)	154.70	288.00	180.35	173.95	162.77
全省常住人口社保卡持卡率 (%)	Percentage of Permanent Provincial Residents with Social Security Card (%)		17.34	98.95	94.20	94.39
登记结婚件数 (对)	Registered Marriages (couple)	562118	857146	633341	591124	573050
离婚总数 (对)	Registered Divorces (couple)	47521	127048	245816	167209	184511
执业律师人数 (人)	Number of Full-time Lawyers (person)	7292	20230	54957	61946	70680
公证人员数 (人)	Number of Notarial Personnel (person)	1380	1694	2750	2928	3052
人民调解委员会调解人员数 (人)	Number of Mediators of People's Mediation Committees (person)	135192	194224	172816	182304	184727
亿元生产总值生产安全事故死亡率	Rate of Death from Work Safety Accidents per 100 Million Yuan of Gross Regional Product	1.080	0.153	0.023	0.019	0.016
交通事故发生数 (起)	Number of Traffic Accidents (unit)	66072	30480	26444	48206	38782
交通事故损失折款 (万元)	Losses from Traffic Accidents Converted into Cash (10000 yuan)	27526	8051	7673	10534	8649
火灾事故发生数 (起)	Number of Fire Accidents (unit)	8622	6065	54711	64134	55629
火灾事故损失折款 (万元)	Losses from Fire Accidents Converted into Cash (10000 yuan)	10065	17500	56007	79931	70995

注：2010年起医疗卫生机构、人员数总数含村卫生室数，千人口数据分母为常住人口。

Note: Since 2010,Data of village clinics was included in the total number of health care institutions and their personnel. The population of per 1000 persons used in this table are resident population.

21-2 医疗卫生机构、床位及人员数

Number of Health Care Institutions, Beds and Personnel

年份 Year	机构 (个) Health Institutions (unit)	#医院及卫生院 Hospitals	床位 (张) Beds (bed)	#医院及卫生院床位 Hospital Beds	卫生工作人员 (人) Medical Personnel (person)	#卫生技术人员 Medical Technical Personnel
1978	6949	1968	90645	84120	159583	126606
1979	7304	1974	91955	85144	171703	136568
1980	7649	1988	92506	84999	181480	144537
1981	8045	2002	94794	87010	191370	151971
1982	8331	2014	97441	88688	202162	160710
1983	8443	2037	100042	90851	208506	166543
1984	8525	2042	103231	93770	213193	170495
1985	8479	1853	107702	98231	220593	175337
1986	8713	1860	110022	99632	225526	180045
1987	8705	1880	114773	104932	230444	184126
1988	8820	1906	119328	109280	234807	187307
1989	8948	1886	122055	111816	240581	192147
1990	8989	1885	124015	114056	244039	194771
1991	9032	1906	129774	119079	249717	199051
1992	8989	1943	135527	124835	257043	205110
1993	8572	1968	139812	129317	267432	211874
1994	8720	2231	144865	134334	277398	220153
1995	8848	2267	148825	137756	288715	229894
1996	8921	2319	151553	141221	196108	237623
1997	8942	2348	155313	144496	305562	245862
1998	8805	2373	158351	147604	313737	252213
1999	8699	2415	162398	151367	320432	258591
2000	8984	2426	168143	157164	327065	264990
2001	8638	2444	172735	162197	330418	268347
2002	15500	2415	180791	165498	323294	262633
2003	15409	2410	188543	172981	336175	273620
2004	15744	2391	200056	183107	348203	283351
2005	16318	2428	209741	192551	364520	297334
2006	16953	2433	221886	204071	408972	332829
2007	16490	2435	234179	216951	452080	360674
2008	15821	2428	250497	231583	479462	383876
2009	16238	2442	271972	250364	513997	413444
2010	44880	2444	300083	277126	593503	455524
2011	45935	2411	325038	298070	627347	486356
2012	46556	2437	355274	324744	664825	520243
2013	47855	2447	378367	346478	710288	555498
2014	48087	2482	405707	372637	734345	584356
2015	48367	2539	435666	400745	771034	620004
2016	49124	2581	465228	428423	821880	667525
2017	49926	2666	492113	453022	866925	709894
2018	51527	2745	516973	477526	921703	757840
2019	53928	2817	545190	503893	964914	795132
2020	55900	2875	564701	523883	1009408	832061
2021	57955	2935	588953	546566	1062390	875803
2022	59531	2981	608258	564076	1111769	918430

注：从2002年开始，机构数中包含个体诊所机构数；从2010年开始机构、人员总计中含村卫生室数。

Note: Since 2002, the number of institutions has included the number of individual clinics;since 2010,number of village clinics was included in health care institutions.

21-3 医疗卫生机构、床位和人员数（2022年）

Number of Health Care Institutions, Beds and Personnel (2022)

机构类别	Type of Institution	机构（个） Number of Institutions (unit)	床位数（张） Beds (bed)	在岗职工（人） Employed Staff and Workers (person)	#卫生技术人员 Medical Technical Personnel	#执业(助理)医师 Licensed Physicians & Physician Assistants
医疗卫生机构数	**Health Care Institutions**	**59531**	**608258**	**1111769**	**918430**	**335181**
医　院	Hospitals	1812	497101	662717	549860	179691
卫生院	Health Centers	1169	66975	103114	88402	31629
康复医疗机构	Rehabilitation Medical Institution	13	634	882	537	189
社区卫生服务中心	Community Health Service Centers	1257	8933	62164	54083	22886
社区卫生服务站	Community Health Service Stations	1472	20	6386	5934	2671
门诊部、诊所、卫生所等	Outpatient Departments and Clinics	27434	188	141374	125966	61649
#诊所	Outpatient Departments	18340		58784	53785	28377
卫生所(医务室)	Clinics (Medical Stations)	2776		9847	9018	4768
急救中心(站)	Emergency Centers (Stations)	57		1102	629	148
采供血机构	Blood Taking and Supply Agencies	49		2990	2255	255
妇幼保健机构	Maternity and Child Care Centers	132	27642	60209	50763	16311
专科疾病防治院(所、站)	Specialized Prevention and Treatment Stations	124	6765	10197	7872	2910
疾病预防控制机构	Disease Prevention and Control Centers (Antiepidemic Stations)	145		11512	8629	4250
卫生监督所	Sanitation Supervision Stations	147		4394	2886	
卫生监督检验(监测、检测)所(站)	Sanitation Supervision Quarantine Stations	1		3		
医学科学研究机构	Research Institutions of Medical Science	10		168	35	19
医学在职培训机构	On-the-job Medical Training Institutions	4		620	128	18
健康教育所(站、中心)	Health Education Stations (Centers)	47		616	225	114
村卫生室	Rural Medical Stations	25304		31890	13528	11247
其他卫生机构	Other Health Agencies	354		11431	6698	1194

注：1.总数中含村卫生室数。
2.康复医疗机构包括疗养院和康复医疗中心。

Note: a) Number of village clinics was included in health care institutions.
b) Rehabilitation medical institutions include sanatoriums and rehabilitation medical centers.

21-4 各市医疗卫生机构、床位和人员数（2022年）

Number of Health Care Institutions, Beds and Personnel by City (2022)

市 别	City	机构（个）Number of Institutions (unit)	#医院 Hospitals	床位数（张）Beds (bed)	#医院床位 Hospital Beds	在岗职工（人）Employed Staff and Workers (person)	#卫生技术人员 Medical Technical Personnel	#执业(助理)医师 Licensed Physicians & Physician Assistants
全 省	**Provincial Total**	**59531**	**1812**	**608258**	**497101**	**1111769**	**918430**	**335181**
广 州	Guangzhou	6159	298	110505	100490	238147	195697	68687
深 圳	Shenzhen	5841	151	53984	50377	145248	118273	47234
珠 海	Zhuhai	1092	45	12431	10846	28458	23634	9072
汕 头	Shantou	2126	63	22326	19797	36847	31403	12292
佛 山	Foshan	2699	139	41027	37910	79986	68237	24685
韶 关	Shaoguan	2149	59	22126	16801	31127	25606	8355
河 源	Heyuan	2106	69	20555	13437	27651	22892	7567
梅 州	Meizhou	2936	59	23364	16453	34523	28620	10594
惠 州	Huizhou	3763	85	24979	19719	52082	43946	16911
汕 尾	Shanwei	1594	44	12261	8643	19330	15331	5464
东 莞	Dongguan	3696	121	35075	34145	77084	64626	24495
中 山	Zhongshan	1280	69	16994	16845	33393	29202	11163
江 门	Jiangmen	1767	57	26305	19556	42556	35999	12252
阳 江	Yangjiang	1832	65	16421	13235	22981	18350	6317
湛 江	Zhanjiang	3726	131	44914	34283	57280	46150	15497
茂 名	Maoming	3973	82	39039	23610	46232	38217	14214
肇 庆	Zhaoqing	3216	68	21012	15724	36992	29650	9835
清 远	Qingyuan	2657	64	19494	12934	32186	26761	9427
潮 州	Chaozhou	2233	32	8008	5917	15330	11541	4826
揭 阳	Jieyang	3243	79	25387	18873	34127	27789	10896
云 浮	Yunfu	1443	32	12051	7506	20209	16506	5398
按经济区域分	By Region							
珠 三 角	Pearl River Delta	29513	1033	342312	305612	733946	609264	224334
东 翼	Eastern Region	9196	218	67982	53230	105634	86064	33478
西 翼	Western Region	9531	278	100374	71128	126493	102717	36028
山 区	Mountainous Region	11291	283	97590	67131	145696	120385	41341

注：机构、人员数含村卫生室数。

Note: Number of village clinics was included in health care institutions.

21-5 各类医疗卫生机构、床位和人员数

Number of Health Institutions, Beds and Personnel by Type

指　　标	Item	2000	2005	2010	2015	2020	2021	2022
医疗卫生机构数（个）	**Number of Institutions (unit)**	**8984**	**40175**	**44880**	**48367**	**55900**	**57955**	**59531**
#医院	Hospitals	746	965	1088	1323	1700	1762	1812
卫生院	Health Centers	1680	1463	1356	1216	1175	1173	1169
门诊部、诊所、卫生所	Clinics, Health Stations and Community Health	5710	12224	11056	14068	23328	25782	27434
专科疾病防治院	Specialized Disease Prevention &Treatment Institution	158	157	147	131	130	128	124
疾病预防控制机构	Sanitation and Anti-epidemic Institutions	171	134	134	137	137	142	145
妇幼保健机构	Maternity and Child Care Centers	31	125	126	130	130	130	132
医学科学研究机构	Research Institutions of Medical Science	20	20	18	17	12	10	10
村卫生室	Rural Medical Stations	28913	23763	28339	27178	25887	25448	25304
床位数（张）	**Number of Beds (unit)**	**168143**	**209573**	**300083**	**435666**	**564701**	**588953**	**608258**
在岗职工（人）	**Employed Staff and Workers (person)**	**327065**	**364401**	**593503**	**771034**	**1009408**	**1062390**	**1111769**
卫生技术人员	Medical Technical Personnel	264990	271230	455524	620004	832061	875803	918430
#执业(助理)医师	Licensed Physicians & Physician Assistants	111172	120875	175100	229389	307289	320923	335181
注册护士	Nurses	83198	98681	168043	254430	374807	402047	420790
其他技术人员	Other Technical Personnel	8910	42559	54491	50033	55268	54729	55549
管理人员	Administrative Personnel	24320	21617	29541	30638	36995	38236	40223
工勤人员	Logistics Personnel	28845	28995	53947	70359	85084	93622	97567

注：从2002年开始，机构数中包含个体诊所机构数；门诊部(所)含门诊部、诊所、卫生所、医务室、护理站等；妇幼保健院归入妇幼保健机构统计；医生指执业(助理)医师。2008年起，门诊部(所)含护理站，不含社区卫生服务站(纳入其他卫生机构)。2010年起机构、人员数含村卫生室数。2021年起，管理人员为仅从事管理人员数。

Note: Since 2002, the number of institutions has included the number of individual clinics, covered in the category of outpatient departments (clinics); maternity and child care centers have been included in the number of maternity and child care institutions; doctors have referred to certified (assistant) doctors; and since 2008, clinics include nurse stations, but exclude community health stations, which is listed as Other Healthcare Institutions. Since 2010,Number of village clinics was included in health care institutions. Since 2021,the number of managers only includes the persons who are engaged in management.

21-6 各市社会保险基金征缴收入(2022年)

Amount Collected of Security Insurance (2022)

单位：万元 (10000 yuan)

市别	City	城镇职工基本养老保险基金征缴收入 Amount Collected of Urban Employee Basic Pension Insurance	城乡居民基本养老保险基金征缴收入 Amount Collected of Basic Pension Insurance for Urban and Rural Residents	城镇职工基本医疗保险基金征缴收入 Amount Collected of Urban Employee Basic Medical Insurance	城乡居民基本医疗保险基金征缴收入 Amount Collected of Basic Medical Care Insurance for Urban and Rural Residents	失业保险基金征缴收入 Amount Collected of Unemployment Insurance	工伤保险基金征缴收入 Amount Collected of Work Injury Insurance
全省	**Provincial Total**	**57971889**	**1125264**	**11839656**	**2665259**	**1137184**	**625071**
广州	Guangzhou	12158831	313794	3044084	221912	304786	113649
深圳	Shenzhen	15426524	1083	3136250	418250	347572	169432
珠海	Zhuhai	1951278	23698	388586	31403	36127	15313
汕头	Shantou	922437	97101	207589	138663	17481	6846
佛山	Foshan	4437009	25078	999630	141843	77682	51205
韶关	Shaoguan	658019	24103	198396	75747	10264	7667
河源	Heyuan	569595	39006	102128	83524	7198	5105
梅州	Meizhou	752363	44817	179062	114581	9356	5673
惠州	Huizhou	2317798	64151	384550	83466	34881	23598
汕尾	Shanwei	304313	19077	60191	84487	4035	3305
东莞	Dongguan	6152659	274	936562	49672	150074	95172
中山	Zhongshan	2312471	2371	435845	86776	44294	28662
江门	Jiangmen	1531013	19364	647319	93445	20918	15954
阳江	Yangjiang	450414	63643	95581	77945	4452	4965
湛江	Zhanjiang	943829	68614	238436	230842	14544	8886
茂名	Maoming	739153	52852	167144	216425	11975	6872
肇庆	Zhaoqing	806509	43458	162102	108218	12498	10122
清远	Qingyuan	835226	47247	183620	108266	13358	9493
潮州	Chaozhou	419114	41583	92144	74581	6040	3209
揭阳	Jieyang	568786	104438	77376	151769	4897	3533
云浮	Yunfu	363179	29511	103059	73443	4755	3757
省直	Directly under Provincial Government	3351370					32652
按经济区域分	By Region						
珠三角	Pearl River Delta	47094092	493271	10134929	1234987	1028832	523108
东翼	Eastern Region	2214650	262199	437300	449500	32453	16894
西翼	Western Region	2133396	185110	501162	525212	30971	20722
山区	Mountainous Region	3178381	184685	766265	455560	44929	31695

注：1.各区域数据不包含省直单位部分；本表生育保险收入不再单独填列，合并在职工医保收入中体现。

2.珠海、佛山、东莞、中山建立城乡一体化基本医疗保险制度，本表中4市居民基本医疗基金合并在职工基本医疗基金统计。

Note: a)The data of each region does not include the agencies directly under provincial jurisdiction. The Maternity Insurance income in this table are no longer filled in individually, consolidated in the Medical Care Insurance income of employees.

b)Zhuhai, Foshan, Dongguan and Zhongshan have established the urban-rural integrated basic medical insurance system.In this table, the urban employee medical care insurance in the four cities include the basic medical care insurance for urban and rural residents.

21-7 各市社会保险参保人数（2022年）

Number of Persons Participating in Social Insurance by City (2022)

单位：万人 (10000 persons)

市别	City	城镇职工基本养老保险参保人数 Urban Employee Basic Pension Insurance Contributors	城乡居民基本养老保险参保人数 Basic Pension Insurance for Urban and Rural Residents Contributors	城镇职工基本医疗保险 Urban Employees Basic Medical Care Insurance Contributors	城乡居民基本医疗保险参保人数 Basic Medical Care Insurance for Urban and Rural Residents Contributors	失业保险参保人数 Unemployment Insurance Contributors	工伤保险参保人数 Work Injury Insurance Contributors	生育保险参保人数 Maternity Insurance Contributors
全省	**Provincial Total**	**5229.21**	**2764.32**	**4856.02**	**6297.18**	**3751.12**	**4083.39**	**4061.98**
广州	Guangzhou	886.09	137.33	908.67	482.73	714.83	718.91	702.16
深圳	Shenzhen	1380.13	1.25	1337.62	333.62	1234.79	1276.20	1321.61
珠海	Zhuhai	154.02	13.60	175.87	74.37	122.02	129.14	132.15
汕头	Shantou	107.81	237.60	91.68	402.91	56.34	76.74	67.46
佛山	Foshan	455.61	72.38	449.07	232.58	326.01	359.35	363.53
韶关	Shaoguan	77.87	104.34	68.71	218.98	35.97	46.24	44.57
河源	Heyuan	55.94	131.99	52.55	252.16	29.50	39.67	47.65
梅州	Meizhou	106.72	166.36	58.22	370.47	39.18	49.39	42.19
惠州	Huizhou	215.31	115.82	241.82	246.10	166.83	171.18	220.58
汕尾	Shanwei	34.56	100.31	25.54	246.48	13.15	19.57	19.60
东莞	Dongguan	608.75	5.15	587.59	88.25	461.87	484.70	462.52
中山	Zhongshan	244.80	0.97	217.98	121.06	170.46	184.38	191.69
江门	Jiangmen	169.87	150.25	178.81	241.27	105.31	112.27	118.64
阳江	Yangjiang	45.02	126.45	37.02	222.71	20.95	35.75	28.27
湛江	Zhanjiang	110.58	286.84	96.69	589.93	48.91	55.35	60.66
茂名	Maoming	85.19	273.95	61.40	567.52	37.12	40.82	42.27
肇庆	Zhaoqing	90.95	164.86	90.06	326.69	54.13	68.46	64.34
清远	Qingyuan	92.48	187.06	85.95	316.57	51.19	63.12	62.86
潮州	Chaozhou	54.22	114.25	32.53	214.24	23.72	27.86	23.74
揭阳	Jieyang	64.53	253.18	27.01	529.87	19.34	31.68	20.04
云浮	Yunfu	38.04	120.38	31.23	218.67	19.50	24.33	25.45
省直	Directly under Provincial Government	150.70					68.31	
按经济区域分	By Region							
珠三角	Pearl River Delta	4206	662	4187.49	2146.67	3356	3505	3577.22
东翼	Eastern Region	261	705	176.76	1393.50	113	156	130.84
西翼	Western Region	241	687	195.11	1380.16	107	132	131.20
山区	Mountainous Region	371	710	296.66	1376.85	175	223	222.72

注：1.各区域不包省直单位部分。

2.2012年8月起，新型社会农村养老保险和城镇居民社会养老保险制度全覆盖工作全面启动，合并为城乡居民社会养老保险。

Note: a) “By Region” does not include agencies directly under provincial jurisdiction.

b) Since August 2012,system of new old-age insurance and urban basic pension insurance have started completely, and called basic pension insurance for urban and rural residents as total.

21-8 优抚、社会救济和福利事业情况

Statistics on Preferential Treatment and Resettlement, Social Relief and Welfare

项目	Item	2010	2015	2019	2020	2021	2022
优抚事业	**Preferential Treatment and Resettlement**						
优抚事业单位数 (个)	Number of Institutions for Preferential Treatment and Resettlement (unit)			33	39	42	42
优抚事业单位服务对象人数 (人次)	Number of Persons Adopted by Preferential Treatment and Resettlement Institutions (person-time)			2966	35347	42090	49679
优抚事业费用 (万元)	Expenses on Preferential Treatment and Resettlement (10000 yuan)			516766	542804	585915	631784
社会救助	**Social Relief**						
社会救助总人数 (万人)	Total Number under Social Relief (10000 persons)	288.00	227.25	176.64	180.35	173.95	162.77
城乡居民最低生活保障人数 (万人)	Number of Urban and Rural Residents Receiving Minimum Income Relief (10000 persons)	224.70	183.30	140.40	142.97	142.33	130.62
城镇	Urban Areas	40.70	29.69	15.66	15.21	15.00	14.78
农村	Rural Areas	184.00	153.60	124.74	127.76	127.33	115.84
城乡居民最低生活保障家庭户数 (万户)	Number of Urban and Rural Households Receiving Minimum Income Relief (10000 households)	91.80	86.39	58.65	59.52	58.63	54.29
城镇	Urban Areas	17.30	15.19	8.45	8.17	7.93	7.75
农村	Rural Areas	74.50	71.20	50.20	51.35	50.70	46.54
城乡居民最低生活保障金支出 (万元)	Expenditures on Minimum Income Relief for Urban and Rural Residents (10000 yuan)	244490	553022	646105	827367	794511	831586
城镇	Urban Areas	79665	159530	134570	151952	145289	150282
农村	Rural Areas	164825	393493	511535	675415	649222	681305
社会福利支出 (亿元)	Expenses on Social Welfare (100 million yuan)		40.89	109.50	117.74	131.47	143.42
社会救助支出 (亿元)	Expenses on Social Relief (100 million yuan)		94.79	103.26	124.34	118.65	125.51

21-8 续表 continued

项 目	Item	2010	2015	2019	2020	2021	2022
社会工作机构情况	**Social Welfare**						
提供住宿的社会工作机构(个)	Number of Social Welfare Institutions with Accommodations (unit)	2514	1588	1909	2039	2109	2058
编制登记	Registered with State Office for Scopes	256	1282	1419	1440	1455	1363
工商登记	Registered with Industry and Commerce Administration	27	48	148	215	272	304
民政登记	Registered with Civil Affairs Administration	1791	220	322	359	354	355
一个机构多块牌子	Unregistered	440	38	20	24	28	36
提供住宿的社会服务机构年末在院人数 (人)	Number of People Taken in by Social Welfare Institutions with Accommodations at the year-end (person)	92224	92043	98700	102212	101126	98395
编制登记	Registered with State Office for Scopes	26402	61360	51677	50335	47844	44786
工商登记	Registered with Industry and Commerce Administration	3188	8481	16617	19506	21160	23295
民政登记	Registered with Civil Affairs Administration	51516	20525	30037	32065	31555	29866
未登记	Unregistered	11118	1677	369	306	567	448
社区服务	**Community Service**						
社区综合服务机构和设施总数 (个)	Number of Community Nursing Service Facilities and Institution (unit)	15960	57108	71249	30978	31894	31950
社区服务指导中心	Community Service Guidance Centers		29	21	18	17	18
社区服务中心	Community Service Centers	1366	2893	1964	1863	2073	2108
社区服务站	Community Service Stations	1632	13284	25627	26605	27146	27116
社区专项服务机构和设施数	Number of Community Special Service Facilities and Institution	12962	40281	30890	2492	2658	2708
社区养老服务机构和设施数 (个)	Number of Community Nursing Service Facilities and Institution (unit)				22364	21450	21808
未登记和挂靠的特困人员救助供养机构	Unregistered and Affiliated Rescue and Feeding Institutions for the Poor People			45	16	11	11
全托服务社区养老服务机构和设施	Total Care Community Nursing Service Facilities and Institution				1442	1579	1587
日间照料社区养老服务机构和设施	Daily Care Community Nursing Service Facilities and Institution				14917	13698	13672
社区养老机构和设施	Community Nursing Facilities and Insitution		621	9469			
互助型养老设施	Community Mutual Aid Nursing Facilities			3233	3931	3936	3928
其他社区养老服务设施	Other Community Service Facilities				2058	2226	2610

注：1.2013年起，社会福利收养性事业单位数和社会福利收养性事业单位收养人数指标分别修改为提供住宿的社会服务机构数和提供住宿的社会服务机构年末在院人数。

2.2015年以前，一个机构多块牌子的机构为未登记注册机构。

3.2019年以前社区服务机构和设施总数包括(1)社区服务指导中心；(2)社区服务中心；(3)社区服务站；(4)未登记注册的特困人员供养机构；(5)社区养老照料机构和设施；(6)社区互助型养老设施；(7)其他社区服务机构和设施,数据填至2019年。从2020年起，根据《民政事业统计调查制度》，将社区综合服务机构和设施与社区养老服务机构和设施分开单独统计，2020年按新的口径进行填报。

Note: a) Since 2013, the indicator of number of social welfare institutions and number of people taken in by social welfare institutions are amended as the indicator of social welfare institutions with accommodations and number of people taken in by social welfare institutions with accommodations at year-end respectively.

b)Unregistered Institutions include one organization with a few brands.

c)The total number of community service facilities and institutions before 2019 includes(1)Community Service Guidance Centers;(2)Community Service Centers; (3)Community Service Stations; (4)Unregistered Feeding Institutions for the Poor People; (5)Community Nursing Facilities and Institution; (6)Community Mutual Aid Nursing Facilities;(7)Other Community Service Facilities, data to 2019. Since 2020, according to the Statistical Survey System of Civil Affairs, counted the Community Comprehensive Service Facilities and the Community Nursing Service Facilities and Institution separately and fill in new caliber in 2000.

21−9 婚姻登记情况
Statistics on Marriage Registration

项目	Item	2010	2015	2020	2021	2022
登记结婚件数 （对）	**Marriage Registration Number (couple)**	**857146**	**840411**	**633341**	**591124**	**573050**
内地居民登记结婚件数	Mainland Residents Marriage Registration Number	850448	832694	629197	586212	567609
涉外及华侨、港澳台居民登记结婚件数	Marriage Registration Number with Foreigners, Overseas Chinese and Citizens of HongKong, Macao and Taiwan	6698	7717	4144	4912	5441
登记结婚人数 （人）	**Nmber of Persons Registered (person)**	**1714292**	**1680822**	**1266682**	**1182248**	**1146100**
按居住地分类	By Place of Residence					
内地居民登记结婚人数	Number of mainland residents registered	1700896	1665442	1258394	1172424	1135218
涉外及华侨、港澳台居民登记结婚中	Number of Registered Marriages Involving Foreigners and Overseas Chinese, Hong Kong, Macao and Taiwan residents					
内地居民	Mainland Residents	6676	7676	4142	4901	5435
#女性	Female	5241	5324	1829	2570	2838
香港居民	Hongkong Residents	1552	2436	713	1575	1972
澳门居民	Macao Residents	765	827	579	616	594
台湾居民	Taiwan Residents	770	840	328	356	465
华侨	Overseas Chinese	1069	1526	98	106	202
外国人	Foreigners	2564	2129	2428	2270	2214
按婚前状况分类	By pre marital status					
初婚人数	Number of First Marriages	1583025	1501835	1065152	987392	968785
再婚人数	Number of Remarriages	131267	178987	201530	194856	177315
#女性	Female	57536	85208	105297	103362	95841
恢复结婚件数 （对）	Resumption of Marriages (couple)	12764	27356	27742	23364	23330
按年龄分类	By age					
#20～24	20～24	549611	490868	243187	184422	146421
25～29	25～29	703191	718631	550444	521992	520238
30～34	30～34	237064	230655	247435	258661	276867
35～39	35～39	105735	90905	93691	94449	96641
40以上	above 40	118691	149763	131925	122724	105933
离婚总数 （对）	**Total Number of Divorce (couple)**	**127048**	**193360**	**245816**	**167209**	**184511**
民政离婚登记 （对）	Registered Divorce (couple)	100759	167544	222287	144933	158096
内地居民登记离婚 （对）	Number of Mainland Residents Registered Divorces (couple)	99536	166142	220703	144402	157504
涉外及华侨、港澳台居民登记离婚 （对）	Divorce from Foreigners,Overseas Chinese and Citizens of Hong Kong, Macao and Taiwan (couple)	1223	1402	1584	531	592
#外国人 （人）	Foreigners (person)	397	290	202	138	194
法院调解离婚 （对）	Divorces through Law Court Mediation (couple)	17644	15268	13090	11821	15465
法院判决离婚 （对）	Divorces through Law Court Judgment (couple)	8645	10548	10439	10455	10950

21-10 律师、公证、基层司法基本情况

Basic Statistics on Lawyers, Notarization, Grassroots Judicial Work

项　　目	Item	2005	2010	2015	2020	2021	2022
律师工作	**Lawyers**						
律师事务所　(个)	Number of Law Offices (unit)	1110	1668	2290	3541	3857	4136
执业律师　(人)	Number of Full-time Lawyers (person)	15779	20230	28221	54957	61946	70680
担任常年法律顾问　(家)	Number of Units as Permanent Legal Advisors(unit)	20533	36484	59664	92416	100925	105979
民事案件诉讼代理　(件)	Agent of Civil Cases (case)	61800	150817	225385	610739	866545	903404
非诉讼代理　(件)	Agent of Non-litigious Legal Affairs (case)	157212	126726	174951	262059	390888	374785
刑事诉讼辩护及代理(件)	Defender of Criminal Cases (case)	18675	38116	30739	117566		103753
公证工作	**Notarization**						
公证处　(个)	Number of Notary Offices (unit)	114	139	146	156	154	154
工作人员（公证员、公证员助理）　(人)	Number of Notarial Personnel (person)	1374	1694	2190	2750	2928	3052
出证总数　(件)	Number of Notarized Documents (case)	1055486	1358974	1525912	1421210	1305061	1120370
国内公证	Domestic Notary	636337	912609	1044876	1235756	1066235	906707
涉外及涉台港澳公证	Foreign-related and Hong Kong, Macao and	419149	490745	481036	185454	238826	213663
基层司法行政工作	**Grassroots Judicial Work**						
基层司法所　(个)	Number of Law Service Offices (unit)	1647	1617	1616	1631	1628	1629
工作人员　(人)	Number of Personnel Working in Law Service Offices (person)	4938	4976	6036	8798	8896	8961
人民调解委员会　(个)	Number of People's Mediation Committees (unit)	28923	33789	32549	31494	31689	31827
调解人员　(人)	Number of Mediators (person)	163459	194224	181205	172816	182304	184727
调解纠纷总数　(件)	Number of Disputes Mediated (case)	169991	384531	326174	444984	489348	417242

注：自2021年起，司法部统计报表中将值班律师法律帮助案件以及法律援助受援人数不列入受理案件总数以及法律援助受援人数统计。

Note: Since 2021, the Ministry of Justice has excluded the legal assistance cases of duty lawyers and the number of legal aid recipients from the total number of cases accepted and the number of legal aid recipients in the statistical statements.

21-11　交通事故发生情况（2022年）

Statistics on Traffic Accidents (2022)

项　目	Item	合计 Total	按道路横断面位置分 By Cross-section Location of Roads				按事故发生道路类型分 By Type of Roads Where Accidents Occurs			
			机动车道 Roads for Motored Vehicles	非机动车道 Roads for Non-motored Vehicles	混合道 Mixed Roads	其他道 Others	高速公路 Express Highways	等级公路 Classified Highways	城市道路 Urban Roads	其他路 Others
发生　（起）	Number of Traffic Accidents (case)	38782	27472	1495	8676	1139	932	12161	22490	3199
死亡　（人）	Number of Deaths (person)	5318	4129	152	818	219	419	2144	2361	394
受伤　（人）	Number of Injuries (person)	37551	26193	1636	8756	966	1035	12837	21016	2663
损失折款（万元）	Losses Converted into Cash (10000 yuan)	8649	7046	208	1042	352	2193	2077	3942	437
平均每起事故损失（元）	Average Loss per Traffic Accident (yuan)	2230	2565	1391	1201	3090	23530	1708	1753	1366

注：1.等级公路分为一至四级公路和等外公路；
2.城市道路包括城市快速路和一般城市道路；
3.其他路包括单位小区自建路、公共停车场、公共广场、乡道、村道、田间地头、农垦区等区域。

Notes: a) Classified highways refer to highways of Class I to IV and Unclassified Highway.
b) Urban roads include express roads and normal roads in urban areas.
c) Other roads include roads within residential neighborhoods, public parking lots, squares, country roads, village roads, farm roads and reclaimed areas.

21-12　火灾事故发生情况（2022年）

Statistics on Fire Accidents (2022)

项　目	Item	合计 Total	特大 Extraordinarily Serious Accidents	重大 Serious Accidents	较大 Relatively Serious Accidents	一般 Ordinary Accidents
发生（起）	Number of Traffic Accidents (case)	55629	-	-	6	55623
死亡（人）	Number of Deaths (person)	123	-	-	24	99
受伤（人）	Number of Injuries (person)	233	-	-	10	223
损失折款（万元）	Losses Converted into Cash(10000 yuan)	70995	-	-	414	70581
平均每起事故损失(元)	Average Loss per Traffic Accident(yuan)	12762	-	-	690503	12689

注：2021年火灾事故发生起数、死亡人数、受伤人数、损失折款和平均每起事故损失为全口径统计数据。
Note: In 2021, the number of fire accidents,deaths,injuries,the loss of money and the average loss per accident were calculated by full caliber.

21-13 各市亿元生产总值生产安全事故死亡率

Rate of Death from Work Safety Accidents per 100 Million Yuan of Gross Domestic Product by City

单位：%　　(%)

市别	City	2010	2013	2014	2015	2016	2017	2018	2019	2020	2021	2022
全省	**Provincial Rate**	**0.153**	**0.100**	**0.092**	**0.085**	**0.050**	**0.041**	**0.034**	**0.029**	**0.023**	**0.019**	**0.016**
广州	Guangzhou	0.104	0.060	0.056	0.051	0.026	0.021	0.016	0.015	0.013	0.012	0.010
深圳	Shenzhen	0.071	0.040	0.033	0.032	0.020	0.014	0.012	0.011	0.010	0.008	0.007
珠海	Zhuhai	0.111	0.080	0.067	0.060	0.036	0.029	0.022	0.017	0.017	0.019	0.013
汕头	Shantou	0.181	0.130	0.110	0.107	0.035	0.044	0.035	0.027	0.027	0.014	0.012
佛山	Foshan	0.129	0.070	0.061	0.058	0.032	0.029	0.034	0.028	0.023	0.018	0.009
韶关	Shaoguan	0.356	0.220	0.196	0.170	0.116	0.113	0.104	0.091	0.062	0.057	0.045
河源	Heyuan	0.260	0.180	0.167	0.135	0.087	0.099	0.085	0.104	0.102	0.066	0.074
梅州	Meizhou	0.286	0.210	0.182	0.175	0.063	0.047	0.041	0.031	0.023	0.018	0.039
惠州	Huizhou	0.200	0.110	0.104	0.098	0.066	0.061	0.049	0.041	0.038	0.027	0.022
汕尾	Shanwei	0.302	0.230	0.198	0.188	0.139	0.167	0.102	0.089	0.062	0.048	0.034
东莞	Dongguan	0.135	0.100	0.089	0.084	0.052	0.043	0.039	0.028	0.021	0.016	0.012
中山	Zhongshan	0.185	0.120	0.114	0.108	0.065	0.047	0.049	0.057	0.056	0.045	0.028
江门	Jiangmen	0.261	0.200	0.174	0.162	0.080	0.061	0.036	0.029	0.024	0.016	0.037
阳江	Yangjiang	0.278	0.160	0.139	0.137	0.122	0.085	0.077	0.093	0.069	0.059	0.066
湛江	Zhanjiang	0.167	0.110	0.095	0.091	0.070	0.055	0.051	0.051	0.029	0.033	0.022
茂名	Maoming	0.190	0.120	0.109	0.104	0.043	0.032	0.028	0.025	0.020	0.013	0.014
肇庆	Zhaoqing	0.241	0.150	0.133	0.127	0.094	0.064	0.059	0.057	0.040	0.032	0.034
清远	Qingyuan	0.199	0.180	0.154	0.158	0.195	0.187	0.144	0.119	0.077	0.045	0.075
潮州	Chaozhou	0.172	0.110	0.155	0.156	0.070	0.052	0.049	0.051	0.036	0.035	0.025
揭阳	Jieyang	0.207	0.110	0.110	0.103	0.037	0.043	0.044	0.051	0.029	0.030	0.032
云浮	Yunfu	0.383	0.200	0.199	0.169	0.164	0.139	0.151	0.124	0.085	0.063	0.040

注：1.2005—2015年全省生产安全事故包括工矿商贸、道路交通、火灾、铁路路外、水上交通及渔业船舶死亡人数；各市生产安全事故包括工矿商贸、道路交通、火灾事故死亡人数。

2.2016年原国家安全监管总局开展生产安全事故统计改革，调整了生产安全事故统计范围。

Note:a) Work safety accidents from 2005 to 2015 of the Province include the number of deaths related to industry, mining,traffic,fire,railway,water traffic and fishing boats accidents, and work safety accidents of each city include the number of deaths related to mining, traffic and fire accidents.

b)Due to the statistics reform of production safety accident conducted by State Administration of Work Safety in 2016, the statistical coverage of production safety accident has been adjusted.

主要统计指标解释

卫生技术人员 指卫生事业机构支付工资的全部固定职工和合同制职工，现任职务为卫生技术工作的专业人员。包括中医师、西医师、中西医结合高级医师、护师、中药师、西药师、检验师、其他技师、中医士、西医士、护士、助产士、中药剂士、西药剂士、检验士、其他技士、其他中医、护理员、中药剂员、西药剂员、检验员，其他初级卫生技术人员。

医生 指经卫生部门审查合格，具有执业资格的医疗专业人员。

提供住宿的社会服务活动机构 根据《2014 年社会服务业统计制度》，提供住宿的社会服务活动机构包括：为老年人与残疾人提供收留抚养服务的机构、为智障与精神病人提供收留抚养服务的机构、为儿童提供收留抚养和救助服务机构以及其他提供住宿的服务机构。

律师 指受聘参加法律顾问处工作，提任法律顾问、刑（民）事代理人、刑事辩护人，办理非诉讼事件、解答法律询问，代写法律事务文书等主要从事律师事务的司法人员。

公证人员 指在国家公证机关依法办理公证事务的司法人员。包括公证员、助理公证员和在公证处工作的其他人员。

调解人员 在人民调解委员会担负调解民间一般民事纠纷和轻微违法行为所引起的纠纷的工作人员。包括调解委员会的委员和调解小组的调解员。

亿元生产总值生产安全事故死亡率 指一定时期内，每生产亿元生产总值，因各类生产安全事故造成的死亡人数。

Explanatory Notes on Main Statistical Indicators

Medical Technical Personnel refer to all permanent and contract medical staff and workers employed by medical institutions，including doctors of Chinese and Western medicine，senior doctors who integrate traditional Chinese therapeutics with Western therapeutics in practice，senior nurses，pharmacists of Chinese and Western medicine，laboratory specialists，other specialists，paramedics of Chinese and Western medicine，nurses，midwives，druggists in Chinese and Western medicine，laboratory technicians，other technicians，other practitioners of Chinese medicine，nursing attendants，pharmacological workers of Chinese and Western medicine，laboratory workers，and other primary medical personnel.

Doctors refer to qualified medical professionals approved to practice by public health departments.

Social Welfare Institutions with Accommodations In accordance with Statistical System of Social Service in 2014，Social Welfare Institutions with Accommodations includes: Institutions taking care of old people and handicapped people, institutions taking care of retarded people and mental patients, institutions adopting and salving children and other social welfare institutions with accommodations. That is, from 1995 to 2012 the caliber is Number of Social Welfare Institutions (unit); since 2013, due to the change of system in Ministry of Civil Affairs，the caliber changes to Social Welfare Institutions with Accommodations .

Lawyers refer to legal workers who are employed by legal counseling firms to act as legal advisers，agents in criminal or civil lawsuits，or defenders in criminal lawsuits，or to handle non litigious legal affairs，to advise on matters of law or to write legal papers for others.

Notary Personnel refer to judicial workers of the state notary offices handling notarization work according to law. They include notaries，assistant notaries，and other people working for notary offices.

Mediators refer to workers on people’s mediation committees responsible for mediating in civil disputes and cases of slight infraction of the law. They include members of the mediation committees and mediators of mediation groups.

Rate of Death from Work Safety Accidents per 100 Million Yuan of Gross Domestic Product refers to the number of deaths due to various work safety accidents in the production process of every 100 million yuan of gross domestic product within a certain period.

二十二、区域经济主要指标

MAJOR ECONOMIC REGIONS

二十二 区域主要经济指标

简要说明

一、本篇主要反映广东境内主要区域社会经济发展的基本情况，内容主要包括：珠三角、广州和深圳、东西两翼、山区县以及少数民族县等经济区域的主要统计指标数据。

二、本篇资料分别由广东省统计局各有关专业处整理提供，综合统计处负责编辑。

三、本篇资料根据国家统计局制定的各有关专业统计报表制度填报汇总而成。

四、本篇各项指标数据为各经济区域汇总数，由于部分年份各市生产总值等指标汇总数不等于全省数，因此仅适合反映该地区发展变化情况。

22 Major Economic Regions

Brief Introduction

Ⅰ. The data in this chapter mainly reflect the basic conditions of social and economic development of main economic regions in Guangdong, including the main indicators on the cities of the Pearl River Delta, Guangzhou and Shenzhen, the East and West Wings, counties in mountainous areas and minority counties.

Ⅱ. The data in this chapter are prepared and provided by the related specialized divisions and compiled by the Division of Comprehensive Statistics of Statistics Bureau of Guangdong Province.

Ⅲ. The data in this chapter are tabulated and reported in accordance with the various statistical reporting schemes stipulated by the National Bureau of Statistics.

Ⅳ. The indicators in this chapter are overall figures of various economic regions that only reflect the status of development of the corresponding regions, as the provincial total is not equal to the sum of indicators of various cities, such as gross domestic product.

22–1 区域主要经济指标

Main Indicators on Regional Economies

指标	Item	2021 珠三角 Pearl River Delta	2021 东翼 East Wing	2021 西翼 West Wing	2021 山区 Mountainous Areas
土地面积 (平方公里)	Land Area (sq.km.)	54767	15496	32682	76751
年末常住人口 (万人)	Permanent Population at the Year-end (10000 persons)	7860.60	1640.87	1587.13	1595.40
#城镇人口 (万人)	Urban Population (10000 persons)	6875.67	1002.08	750.87	837.90
地区生产总值 (亿元)	Gross Domestic Product (100 million yuan)	100914.59	7760.48	8772.55	7271.92
第一产业	Primary Industry	1705.36	617.17	1538.85	1123.32
第二产业	Secondary Industry	41360.66	3355.43	3250.70	2589.00
第三产业	Tertiary Industry	57848.57	3787.87	3983.01	3559.60
人均地区生产总值 (元)	Per Capita GDP (yuan)	128684	47425	55456	45630
地区生产总值指数 (上年=100)	Index of Gross Domestic Product (preceding year=100)	108.0	107.9	108.2	107.7
第一产业	Primary Industry	109.4	106.3	105.8	109.0
第二产业	Secondary Industry	109.5	106.9	109.3	106.8
第三产业	Tertiary Industry	107.0	109.0	108.4	108.0
人均地区生产总值指数 (上年=100)	Index of Per Capita Gross Domestic Product (preceding year=100)	106.8	107.8	107.6	107.7
规模以上工业增加值 (亿元)	Value-added of Industry above Designated Size (100 million yuan)	32036.61	1716.42	1752.31	1801.19
固定资产投资同比上年增长(%)	Growth Rate of Investment in Fixed Assets (%)	8.1	-10.5	16.7	2.9
#房地产开发投资 (亿元)	Investment in Real Estate Development (100 million yuan)	14202.86	1117.62	929.34	1216.04
社会消费品零售总额 (亿元)	Total Amount of Retail Sales of Consumer Goods (100 million yuan)	34412.76	3517.59	3764.49	2485.28
出口总额 (亿元)	Total Exports (100 million yuan)	48127.25	1069.80	570.38	758.04
进口总额 (亿元)	Total Imports (100 million yuan)	30806.57	316.90	472.05	560.58
实际外商直接投资 (亿元)	Foreign Direct Investment Actually Utilized (100 million yuan)	1747.69	16.94	40.25	31.40
地方一般公共预算收入 (亿元)	Local Public Budgetary Revenue (100 million yuan)	9366.17	330.21	386.49	501.05
地方一般公共预算支出 (亿元)	Local Public Budgetary Expenditure (100 million yuan)	12325.44	1268.25	1279.55	1822.80
金融机构本外币存款 (亿元)	Deposits in Renminbi and Foreign Currencies in All Financial Institutions (100 million yuan)	263012.21	10080.00	9368.24	10708.77
#本外币住户存款	Savings Deposits by Resident	76818.54	6965.80	6415.40	7398.83
金融机构本外币贷款 (亿元)	Loans in Renminbi and Foreign Currencies in All Financial Institutions (100 million yuan)	201530.79	5351.47	6802.13	8549.91
全体居民人均可支配收入 (元)	Per Capita Disposable Income of Households (yuan)	60729.7	27006.0	27538.1	27038.0
城镇居民人均可支配收入 (元)	Per Capita Disposable Income of Urban Households (yuan)	65118.6	32240.7	34861.6	34008.9
农村居民人均可支配收入 (元)	Per Capita Disposable Income of Rural Households (yuan)	30464.7	19211.4	21261.0	19599.6

22-1 续表 continued

指 标	Item	2022 珠三角 Pearl River Delta	2022 东 翼 East Wing	2022 西 翼 West Wing	2022 山 区 Mountainous Areas
土地面积 (平方公里)	Land Area (sq.km.)	54767	15496	32682	76751
年末常住人口 (万人)	Permanent Population at the Year-end (10000 persons)	7829.43	1643.42	1589.58	1594.37
#城镇人口 (万人)	Urban Population (10000 persons)	6848.95	1006.82	763.71	845.92
地区生产总值 (亿元)	Gross Domestic Product (100 million yuan)	104681.81	7913.42	9152.20	7371.15
第一产业	Primary Industry	1839.82	672.91	1633.23	1194.40
第二产业	Secondary Industry	43432.38	3356.46	3475.24	2579.43
第三产业	Tertiary Industry	59409.60	3884.06	4043.73	3597.31
人均地区生产总值 (元)	Per Capita GDP (yuan)	133437	48190	57621	46217
地区生产总值指数(上年=100)	Index of Gross Domestic Product (preceding year=100)	102.1	100.6	100.8	100.9
第一产业	Primary Industry	105.1	105.7	104.6	105.4
第二产业	Secondary Industry	103.1	98.1	99.0	99.1
第三产业	Tertiary Industry	101.3	102.0	100.6	100.7
人均地区生产总值指数 (上年=100)	Index of Per Capita Gross Domestic Product (preceding year=100)	102.0	100.3	100.4	100.8
规模以上工业增加值 (亿元)	Value-added of Industry above Designated Size (100 million yuan)	32444.89	1620.60	1594.31	1600.76
固定资产投资同比上年增长(%)	Growth Rate of Investment in Fixed Assets (%)	0.4	-13.4	-10.6	-14.4
#房地产开发投资 (亿元)	Investment in Real Estate Development (100 million yuan)	12793.73	750.85	684.18	734.21
社会消费品零售总额 (亿元)	Total Amount of Retail Sales of Consumer Goods (100 million yuan)	34959.60	3513.77	3832.16	2494.15
出口总额 (亿元)	Total Exports (100 million yuan)	50960.18	1065.73	571.22	722.33
进口总额 (亿元)	Total Imports (100 million yuan)	28389.16	290.98	578.24	520.27
实际外商直接投资 (亿元)	Foreign Direct Investment Actually Utilized (100 million yuan)	1720.08	16.12	48.78	34.03
地方一般公共预算收入 (亿元)	Local Public Budgetary Revenue (100 million yuan)	9049.47	309.90	353.99	481.78
地方一般公共预算支出 (亿元)	Local Public Budgetary Expenditure (100 million yuan)	12662.25	1266.24	1317.09	1839.23
金融机构本外币存款 (亿元)	Deposits in Renminbi and Foreign Currencies in All Financial Institutions (100 million yuan)	289656.10	11052.26	10036.79	11612.52
#本外币住户存款	Savings Deposits by Resident	90095.22	7938.99	7212.14	8308.40
金融机构本外币贷款 (亿元)	Loans in Renminbi and Foreign Currencies in All Financial Institutions (100 million yuan)	222640.84	5946.91	7795.89	9339.30
全体居民人均可支配收入 (元)	Per Capita Disposable Income of Households (yuan)	62700.0	28388.3	28713.6	28256.0
城镇居民人均可支配收入 (元)	Per Capita Disposable Income of Urban Households (yuan)	67092.6	33521.5	35906.0	35151.8
农村居民人均可支配收入 (元)	Per Capita Disposable Income of Rural Households (yuan)	31956.7	20335.4	22254.3	20627.7

注：1.珠三角包括：广州、深圳、珠海、佛山、惠州、东莞、中山、江门和肇庆。东翼指汕头、汕尾、潮州和揭阳。西翼指阳江、湛江和茂名。山区指韶关、河源、梅州、清远和云浮。

2.本表地区生产总值、工业增加值绝对数按当年价格计算，指数按可比价格计算，下表同。

Notes: a) The pearl river delta include Guangzhou, Shenzhen, Zhuhai, Foshan, Jiangmen, Dongguan, Zhongshan, Huizhou and Zhaoqing. The East Wing includes Shantou, Shanwei, Chaozhou and Jieyang. The West Wing includes Yangjiang，Zhanjiang and Maoming. The mountainous areas include Shaoguan, Heyuan, Meizhou, Qingyuan and Yunfu.

b) The figures in value terms on GDP and value-added of industry are calculated at current prices, whereas the index are calculated at comparable prices.The same applies to the following tables.

22-2 区域主要经济指标占全省比重

Percentage of Main Regional Economic Indicators to the Provincial Total

单位：% (%)

指　标	Item	2021 珠三角占全省比重 Percentage of Pearl River Delta to the Whole Province	东翼占全省比重 Percentage of East Wing to the Whole Province	西翼占全省比重 Percentage of West Wing to the Whole Province	山区占全省比重 Percentage of Mountainous Areas to the Whole Province
土地面积	Land Area	30.5	8.6	18.2	42.7
年末常住人口	Permanent Population at the Year-end	62.0	12.9	12.5	12.6
#城镇人口	Urban Population	72.6	10.6	7.9	8.9
地区生产总值	Gross Domestic Product	80.9	6.2	7.0	5.8
第一产业	Primary Industry	34.2	12.4	30.9	22.5
第二产业	Secondary Industry	81.8	6.6	6.4	5.1
第三产业	Tertiary Industry	83.6	5.5	5.8	5.1
规模以上工业增加值	Value-added of Industry above Designated Size	85.9	4.6	4.7	4.8
固定资产投资总额	Investment in Fixed Assets	76.1	9.3	6.5	8.1
#房地产开发投资	Investment in Real Estate Development	81.3	6.4	5.3	7.0
社会消费品零售总额	Total Retail Sales of Consumer Goods	77.9	8.0	8.5	5.6
出口总额	Total Exports	95.3	2.1	1.1	1.5
进口总额	Total Imports	95.8	1.0	1.5	1.7
实际外商直接投资	Foreign Direct Investment Actually Utilized	95.2	0.9	2.2	1.7
地方一般公共预算收入	Local Public Budgetary Revenue	88.5	3.1	3.7	4.7
地方一般公共预算支出	Local Public Budgetary Expenditure	73.8	7.6	7.7	10.9
金融机构本外币存款	Deposits in Renminbi and Foreign Currencies in All Financial Institutions	89.7	3.4	3.2	3.7
#本外币住户存款	Savings Deposits by Resident	78.7	7.1	6.6	7.6
金融机构本外币贷款	Loans in Renminbi and Foreign Currencies in All Financial Institutions	90.7	2.4	3.1	3.8

22-2 续表 continued

单位：% (%)

指 标	Item	2022 珠三角占全省比重 Percentage of Pearl River Delta to the Whole Province	东翼占全省比重 Percentage of East Wing to the Whole Province	西翼占全省比重 Percentage of West Wing to the Whole Province	山区占全省比重 Percentage of Mountainous Areas to the Whole Province
土地面积	Land Area	30.5	8.6	18.2	42.7
年末常住人口	Permanent Population at the Year-end	61.9	13.0	12.5	12.6
#城镇人口	Urban Population	72.4	10.6	8.1	8.9
地区生产总值	Gross Domestic Product	81.1	6.1	7.1	5.7
第一产业	Primary Industry	34.5	12.6	30.6	22.4
第二产业	Secondary Industry	82.2	6.4	6.6	4.9
第三产业	Tertiary Industry	83.8	5.5	5.7	5.1
规模以上工业增加值	Value-added of Industry above Designated Size	87.1	4.3	4.3	4.3
固定资产投资总额	Investment in Fixed Assets	78.6	8.3	6.0	7.1
#房地产开发投资	Investment in Real Estate Development	85.5	5.0	4.6	4.9
社会消费品零售总额	Total Retail Sales of Consumer Goods	78.0	7.8	8.6	5.6
出口总额	Total Exports	95.6	2.0	1.1	1.4
进口总额	Total Imports	95.3	1.0	1.9	1.7
实际外商直接投资	Foreign Direct Investment Actually Utilized	94.6	0.9	2.7	1.9
地方一般公共预算收入	Local Public Budgetary Revenue	88.8	3.0	3.5	4.7
地方一般公共预算支出	Local Public Budgetary Expenditure	74.1	7.4	7.7	10.8
金融机构本外币存款	Deposits in Renminbi and Foreign Currencies in All Financial Institutions	89.9	3.4	3.1	3.6
#本外币住户存款	Savings Deposits by Resident	79.3	7.0	6.4	7.3
金融机构本外币贷款	Loans in Renminbi and Foreign Currencies in All Financial Institutions	90.6	2.4	3.2	3.8

注：各指标在计算分区域占全省比重时，分母为21个市相加的合计数。

Notes: While calculating the percentage of each indicator of Pearl River Delta, East Wing, West Wing and Mountainous Areas to the whole province, the denominator is the sum of 21 cities.

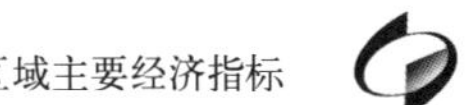

22-3 珠三角主要经济指标

Main Economic Indicators of the Pearl River Delta Economic Zone

年份 Year	年末常住人口 (万人) Permanent Population at the Year-end (10000 persons)	#城镇人口 Urban Population	年末户籍总人口 (万人) Total Population with Residence Registration at the Year-end (10000 persons)	城镇单位 就业人员 Employed Persons in Urban Areas
1990	2369.93	1696.63	2371.57	
1995	3292.03		2372.76	
2000	4289.78	2981.23	2563.60	495.46
2005	4547.14	3516.06	2763.32	636.10
2006	4735.47	3771.33	2821.27	675.38
2007	4930.68	3919.89	2872.47	718.88
2008	5138.48	4119.52	2920.82	724.38
2009	5361.72	4375.17	2967.02	767.05
2010	5622.95	4650.64	3024.57	823.67
2011	5937.94	4935.29	3073.87	927.40
2012	6216.60	5183.35	3105.01	969.59
2013	6446.86	5390.61	3156.02	1552.80
2014	6664.86	5590.56	3207.94	1555.45
2015	6868.51	5797.80	3265.69	1532.73
2016	7101.24	6018.53	3350.52	1547.13
2017	7338.07	6240.51	3475.10	1560.00
2018	7545.46	6463.52	3628.04	1603.20
2019	7683.95	6616.26	3767.72	1699.00
2020	7823.54	6825.60	3892.19	1719.68
2021	7860.60	6875.67	4015.66	1746.73
2022	7829.43	6848.95	4118.15	1717.30

注：2011—2019年年末常住人口根据2020年第七次全国人口普查初步汇总数进行平滑调整，城镇人口也作了相应的调整。

Note: The year-end populations from 2011 to 2019 have been adjusted in accordance with the preliminary sum figure obtained from the 7th National Population Census and the same applied to urban population.

22-3 续表 1 continued

年份 Year	地区生产总值 (亿元) Gross Domestic Product (100 million yuan)	第一产业 Primary Industry	第二产业 Secondary Industry	第三产业 Tertiary Industry	人均地区生产总值 (元) Per Capita Gross Domestic Product(yuan)
1990	1006.89	153.77	441.65	411.46	4612
1995	4077.74	346.94	1984.48	1746.32	13019
2000	8471.28	460.17	4044.38	3966.73	20369
2005	18426.64	559.23	9377.60	8489.80	40661
2006	21866.00	567.69	11266.58	10031.73	47112
2007	25971.88	631.40	13165.60	12174.88	53738
2008	30212.28	698.72	15107.89	14405.68	60010
2009	32478.00	694.61	15709.73	16073.65	61862
2010	38028.65	772.96	18655.55	18600.14	69281
2011	43890.08	876.91	21430.14	21583.03	76014
2012	47939.37	928.85	22670.54	24339.99	78967
2013	53472.83	984.03	24809.05	27679.75	84537
2014	57844.44	1030.07	26763.44	30050.94	88318
2015	62541.37	1073.87	28097.17	33370.33	92510
2016	68196.86	1153.92	29741.79	37301.15	97721
2017	74953.26	1181.53	32004.91	41766.82	103863
2018	80440.72	1265.53	34038.02	45137.18	108094
2019	87213.05	1430.38	35748.98	50033.69	114120
2020	89850.38	1576.19	35942.30	52331.89	115880
2021	100914.59	1705.36	41360.66	57848.57	128684
2022	104681.81	1839.82	43432.38	59409.60	133437

22-3 续表 2 continued

年份 Year	地区生产总值指数(上年=100) Index of Gross Domestic Product (preceding year=100)	第一产业 Primary Industry	第二产业 Secondary Industry	第三产业 Tertiary Industry	人均地区生产总值指数(上年=100) Index of Per Capita Gross Domestic Product(preceding year=100)
1990	117.3	107.4	119.9	118.6	116.1
1995	120.5	108.2	122.5	120.1	112.1
2000	113.9	104.4	114.6	114.1	106.5
2005	115.7	103.6	118.3	113.7	114.6
2006	116.8	98.5	118.7	115.8	113.9
2007	116.3	100.6	116.0	117.5	112.0
2008	112.8	101.7	111.9	114.5	107.9
2009	110.9	104.0	109.6	112.5	106.3
2010	113.1	104.1	115.5	110.9	108.2
2011	111.1	103.9	112.1	110.3	105.6
2012	109.5	103.3	108.8	110.4	104.1
2013	110.7	102.6	111.2	110.6	106.3
2014	108.6	102.9	108.7	108.7	104.9
2015	108.6	102.8	107.5	109.8	105.2
2016	108.0	102.2	107.2	108.9	104.6
2017	107.8	103.1	107.2	108.5	104.3
2018	106.8	104.8	107.2	106.4	103.6
2019	106.4	104.1	104.7	107.9	104.0
2020	102.4	105.3	101.7	102.9	100.5
2021	108.0	109.4	109.5	107.0	106.8
2022	102.1	105.1	103.1	101.3	102.0

22-3 续表 3 continued

年份 Year	公路通车里程(公里) Total Length of Highways in Operation (km)	货运量(万吨) Freight Traffic (10000 tons)	邮电业务总量(亿元) Total Business Volume of Postal and Telecommunication Services (100 million yuan)	本地电话年末用户(万户) Number of Subscribers of Local Telephones at the Year-end (10000 subscribers)	移动电话年末用户 (万户) Number of Subscribers of Mobile Telephones at the Year-end (10000 subscribers)	房地产开发投资(亿元) Investment in Real Estate Development (100 million yuan)	社会消费品零售总额(亿元) Total Retail Sales of Consumer Goods (100 million yuan)
1990							424.35
1995	20323		152.60				1793.50
2000	29029		587.64				3244.82
2005	32312	103365	1738.94	2355.10	5317.71		6017.12
2006	52139	113275	2068.19	2559.62	5497.75		6983.89
2007	53106	122408	2348.22	2651.33	6075.36		8136.58
2008	53418	120916	2754.77	2529.77	6463.22		9820.96
2009	54261	142733	2983.47	2400.25	6867.61	2583.17	11177.86
2010	55848	161348	3949.45	2269.84	7457.64	3118.66	13061.13
2011	56380	182281	1544.39	2284.31	8285.85	4022.87	15125.61
2012	58590	203570	1730.31	2295.29	9573.16	4483.67	16934.22
2013	59555	243500	2019.89	2288.94	11228.38	5362.75	19023.38
2014	61548	254491	2751.65	2195.47	11318.90	6293.55	21253.37
2015	63054	266078	3573.05	2086.68	11437.39	7075.57	23411.58
2016	63631	271565	5487.87	1954.24	10933.74	8601.16	25748.56
2017	64119	287210	4997.13	1801.51	10828.40	9827.78	28335.47
2018	62670	303566	8872.90	1659.62	12248.45	11490.33	30796.88
2019	61498	313912	13097.48	1706.89	11855.06	12849.54	33237.60
2020	62196	258195	16413.10	1579.55	10971.73	14106.37	31212.07
2021	62335	277290	3945.34	1540.60	11466.09	14202.86	34412.76
2022	62387	256992	3981.44	1447.76	11719.68	12793.73	34959.60

22-3 续表 4 continued

年份 Year	出口总额(亿美元) Total Exports (USD 100 million)	出口总额(亿元) Total Exports (100 million yuan)	进口总额(亿美元) Total Imports (USD 100 million)	进口总额(亿元) Total Imports (100 million yuan)	实际外商直接投资额(亿美元) Foreign Direct Investment Actually Utilized (USD 100 million)	实际外商直接投资额(亿元) Foreign Direct Investment Actually Utilized (RMB 100 million)	地方一般公共预算收入(亿元) Local Public General Budgetary Revenue (100 million yuan)
1990	222.21		196.77		12.36		97.98
1995	513.31		429.29		79.47		275.26
2000	847.77		743.15		103.87		599.06
2005	2273.18		1837.58		113.34		1218.48
2006	2887.45		2181.97		130.86		1460.77
2007	3540.85		2560.28		151.88		1882.01
2008	3872.08		2697.61		169.21		2248.16
2009	3417.77		2430.46		175.08		2522.29
2010	4318.02		3195.01		183.47		3139.58
2011	5064.89		3678.00		195.29		3674.70
2012	5477.09		3956.56		215.53		4129.09
2013	6070.93	37698.26	4403.38	27353.93	230.62		4669.16
2014	6137.68	37706.40	4153.86	25515.29	248.61		5375.37
2015	6087.57	37824.33	3664.49	22777.35	256.24		6391.70
2016	5650.87	37310.47	3450.88	22809.29	225.90		6923.98
2017	5902.41	39982.37	3709.89	25107.96	218.11		7455.96
2018	6152.58	40643.62	4239.27	27970.16		1350.73	7915.51
2019	5969.36	41173.44	3931.77	27108.47		1459.98	8277.81
2020	5972.95	41346.06	3805.68	26330.76		1551.42	8496.03
2021	7447.57	48127.25	4768.16	30806.57		1747.69	9366.17
2022	7644.09	50960.18	4261.73	28389.16		1720.08	9049.47

22-3 续表 5 continued

年份 Year	地方一般公共预算支出(亿元) Local Public Genera Budgetary Expenditure (100 million yuan)	金融机构本外币存款(亿元) Deposits in Renminbi and Foreign Currencies in All Financial Institutions (100 million yuan)	#本外币住户存款(亿元) Savings Deposits by Urban and Rural Residents (100 million yuan)	金融机构本外币贷款(亿元) Loans in Renminbi and Foreign Currencies in All Financial Institutions (100 million yuan)	全体居民人均可支配收入(元) Per Capita Disposable Income of Households (yuan)	城镇居民人均可支配收入(元) Per Capita Annual Disposable Income of Urban Households (yuan)	农村居民人均可支配收入(元) Per Capita Disposable Income of Rural Households (yuan)
1990	80.03						
1995	322.81						
2000	690.64	16211.75	7941.93	11227.42			
2005	1567.23	32962.25	16389.71	21073.93			
2006	1714.73	37367.68	18306.14	23613.32			
2007	2145.82	42555.31	18485.09	27982.87			
2008	2550.77	48512.14	22711.25	31044.80			
2009	2882.33	60618.78	25914.62	40608.44			
2010	3654.91	71294.51	29770.92	47159.74			
2011	4444.97	79575.13	33015.57	53133.57			
2012	4798.40	91585.24	37059.20	60568.45			
2013	5240.59	104255.28	40218.90	67988.65			
2014	5973.23	110800.56	41899.85	76017.12	33642.1	37063.7	15754.0
2015	8421.36	141609.04	42737.49	85741.78	36662.0	40284.5	17296.4
2016	9285.10	158966.41	46321.96	100149.59	40109.1	43967.4	19063.7
2017	10329.95	171937.41	48505.37	113683.01	43840.1	47926.9	20813.5
2018	10608.94	183537.91	54607.65	131084.22	47911.0	52129.1	22805.6
2019	11637.61	205988.39	61660.42	151816.93	52213.7	56638.7	25025.8
2020	11538.02	239220.69	70049.84	177090.87	54809.6	59225.1	26856.5
2021	12325.44	263012.21	76818.54	201530.79	60729.7	65118.6	30464.7
2022	12662.25	289656.10	90095.22	222640.84	62700.0	67092.6	31956.7

22-4 珠三角工业企业主要指标（2022年）

单位：亿元

项目	Item	企业单位数（个）Number of Enterprises (unit)
总　计	**Total**	**60305**
按经济类型分	Grouped by Ownership	
在总计中：国有控股经济	Of the Total: State-controlled Economy	1033
国有经济	State-owned Economy	111
集体经济	Collective-owned Economy	45
股份合作经济	Share-holding Cooperative Economy	30
股份制经济	Share-holding Economy	47840
外商投资经济	Economy with Foreign Investment	3539
港澳台投资经济	Economy with Investment from Hong Kong, Macao and Taiwan	7197
按轻重工业分	Grouped by Light and Heavy Industry	
轻工业	Light Industry	25901
重工业	Heavy Industry	34404
按企业规模分	Grouped by Size of Enterprise	
大型企业	Large	1288
中型企业	Medium	5603
小微型企业	Small and Micro	53414
按行业分	Grouped by Sector	
煤炭开采和洗选业	Mining and Washing of Coal	
石油和天然气开采业	Extraction of Petroleum and Natural Gas	2
黑色金属矿采选业	Mining and Dressing of Ferrous Metal Ores	2
有色金属矿采选业	Mining and Dressing of Nonferrous Metal Ores	2
非金属矿采选业	Mining and Dressing of Nonmetal Ores	91
开采专业及辅助性活动	Mining Specialized and Auxiliary Operations	7
其他采矿业	Mining and Dressing of Other Ores	
农副食品加工业	Processing of Farm and Sideline Food	687
食品制造业	Manufacture of Food	618
酒、饮料和精制茶制造业	Manufacture of Beverage	161
烟草制品业	Tobacco Products	38
纺织业	Textile Industry	1271
纺织服装、服饰业	Manufacture of Textile Garments, Footwear and Headgear	1814
皮革、毛皮、羽毛及其制品和制鞋业	Leather, Fur, Feather, Down and Related Products	1376
木材加工和木、竹、藤、棕、草制品业	Timber Processing, Bamboo, Cane, Palm Fiber & Straw Products	388
家具制造业	Manufacture of Furniture	1890
造纸和纸制品业	Papermaking and Paper Products	1392
印刷和记录媒介复制业	Printing and Record Medium Reproduction	990
文教、工美、体育和娱乐用品制造业	Manufacture of Cultural, Educational and Sports Articles	1626
石油、煤炭及其他燃料加工业	Petroleum, Coal and other Fuel Processing	83
化学原料和化学制品制造业	Manufacture of Raw Chemical Materials and Chemical Products	2747
医药制造业	Manufacture of Medicines	466
化学纤维制造业	Manufacture of Chemical Fibers	76
橡胶和塑料制品业	Plastic Products	5438
非金属矿物制品业	Nonmetal Mineral Products	2260
黑色金属冶炼和压延加工业	Smelting and Pressing of Ferrous Metals	402
有色金属冶炼和压延加工业	Smelting and Pressing of Nonferrous Metals	1020
金属制品业	Metal Products	6368
通用设备制造业	Manufacture of General-purpose Machinery	3867
专用设备制造业	Manufacture of Special-purpose Machinery	4000
汽车制造业	Manufacture of Automobile	1052
铁路、船舶、航空航天和其他运输设备制造业	Manufacture of Railway ,Ship,Aeronautics and Other Transport Equipment	512
电气机械和器材制造业	Manufacture of Electrical Machinery and Equipment	7761
计算机、通信和其他电子设备制造业	Manufacture of Communication Equipment, Computers and Other Electronic Equipment	9285
仪器仪表制造业	Manufacture of Instruments and Meters	1157
其他制造业	Other Manufactures	503
废弃资源综合利用业	Comprehensive Utilization of Waste	150
金属制品、机械和设备修理业	Manufacture of Metal Products,Machinery and Equipment Maintenance	78
电力、热力生产和供应业	Production and Supply of Electric Power and Heat Power	275
燃气生产和供应业	Production and Supply of Gas	176
水的生产和供应业	Production and Supply of Water	274

注：本表统计范围为年主营业务收入2000万元及以上的工业法人企业。

Main Indicators of Industrial Enterprises of the Pearl River Delta (2022)

(100 million yuan)

#亏损企业 Loss-making Enterprises	工业总产值(当年价) Gross Industrial Output Value (at current prices)	工业增加值(收入法) Value-added of Industry (by production approach)	年末资产总计 Total Assets at the Year-end	#产成品 Finished Products	流动资产合计 Total Current Asserts	年末负债合计 Total Liabilities at the Year-end
12977	**156731.60**	**32444.89**	**171047.63**	**7642.24**	**107112.04**	**99486.93**
208	24607.53	4786.35	33460.41	774.06	13017.94	19284.18
19	650.41	165.20	1204.85	20.40	440.34	626.46
16	30.98	10.32	52.14	0.57	27.83	39.20
8	53.14	10.50	16.85	1.84	12.19	7.87
10094	100017.86	20062.20	114834.66	4879.99	71070.31	68954.13
805	26545.27	5376.01	24538.24	1080.36	15186.84	13012.62
1801	28332.07	6623.32	29816.20	1626.55	19960.62	16443.44
5841	46475.04	10716.36	45753.02	2754.92	30667.04	25392.57
7136	110256.56	21728.53	125294.61	4887.32	76445.00	74094.37
156	73881.58	16936.04	91939.57	3543.12	55252.35	54055.25
1036	33815.85	7495.22	34551.93	1712.52	21068.73	18334.62
11785	49034.18	8013.63	44556.13	2386.59	30790.97	27097.06
	884.47	774.48	1014.11	2.43	279.55	702.41
	17.16	5.22	11.06	0.78	3.59	2.65
	19.67	1.68	3.60	0.06	0.56	0.63
33	142.02	23.60	222.23	6.06	73.39	171.19
	48.49	18.41	97.61	0.17	52.51	25.00
186	2861.88	272.52	1686.40	85.49	1133.78	1061.79
171	1761.55	565.57	1753.79	78.29	1036.94	818.29
38	1043.30	284.80	1050.78	41.98	665.91	513.56
8	403.15	299.64	323.81	5.62	250.51	62.08
329	1746.26	382.29	1331.35	88.02	810.42	679.61
468	1677.82	411.92	1376.01	155.98	991.35	706.20
228	1107.41	267.79	593.21	45.99	455.05	387.99
99	319.87	57.05	358.95	25.28	257.44	202.98
474	2106.03	474.43	1970.74	85.69	1372.75	1143.37
340	2319.61	368.75	2062.85	97.90	1224.63	1114.07
244	1183.00	304.22	1379.29	45.83	805.67	625.71
420	3496.23	518.28	2250.52	595.32	1862.68	1522.57
21	2376.34	425.68	912.94	41.43	448.72	606.55
496	6058.48	1014.98	5453.48	240.84	3281.76	2771.94
111	1899.05	687.76	3734.73	156.89	2149.47	1584.24
18	166.60	37.34	149.50	11.44	72.99	51.09
965	5403.22	1223.13	5124.35	263.47	3395.30	2847.27
527	5061.94	925.52	5164.08	236.64	3197.69	3296.74
101	1294.77	135.71	732.20	55.36	443.93	486.47
207	3811.29	317.54	1815.26	135.93	1370.70	1352.77
1219	7934.60	1638.63	5553.10	320.82	3891.12	3349.73
725	5464.83	1217.04	5869.38	403.22	4348.01	3325.35
833	5448.47	1505.50	7278.02	481.57	5338.78	3731.82
229	11384.83	2225.09	9800.76	310.88	6932.69	6296.60
113	1478.97	288.29	2009.34	60.63	1392.65	1325.92
1624	20245.22	4314.69	22542.66	1096.54	15849.01	13542.40
2215	45104.04	9047.98	54019.73	2246.49	36843.63	31503.58
207	1574.41	442.77	2151.48	141.47	1563.12	1046.65
89	606.72	168.25	651.77	30.33	502.28	311.62
41	470.51	44.51	362.16	30.77	243.07	244.12
11	230.51	66.75	294.87	4.21	207.92	177.38
67	6562.27	1229.11	15791.81	4.42	3115.93	9463.49
60	2269.85	165.14	1313.40	5.83	485.81	713.09
60	746.79	292.82	2836.31	2.14	760.72	1718.00

Notes: The statistical coverage of industry refers to the legal person industrial enterprises with annual main business revenue over 20 million yuan.

22-4 续表

单位：亿元

项　　目	Item	营业收入 Business Revenue
总　计	**Total**	**158741.80**
按经济类型分	Grouped by Ownership	
在总计中：国有控股经济	Of the Total: State-controlled Economy	24475.37
国有经济	State-owned Economy	657.98
集体经济	Collective-owned Economy	29.63
股份合作经济	Share-holding Cooperative Economy	54.00
股份制经济	Share-holding Economy	101113.91
外商投资经济	Economy with Foreign Investment	27429.15
港澳台投资经济	Economy with Investment from Hong Kong, Macao and Taiwan	28378.32
按轻重工业分	Grouped by Light and Heavy Industry	
轻工业	Light Industry	46940.20
重工业	Heavy Industry	111801.61
按企业规模分	Grouped by Size of Enterprise	
大型企业	Large	75096.94
中型企业	Medium	34289.75
小微型企业	Small and Micro	49355.11
按行业分	Grouped by Sector	
煤炭开采和洗选业	Mining and Washing of Coal	
石油和天然气开采业	Extraction of Petroleum and Natural Gas	785.15
黑色金属矿采选业	Mining and Dressing of Ferrous Metal Ores	19.75
有色金属矿采选业	Mining and Dressing of Nonferrous Metal Ores	19.40
非金属矿采选业	Mining and Dressing of Nonmetal Ores	128.51
开采专业及辅助性活动	Mining Specialized and Auxiliary Operations	48.01
其他采矿业	Mining and Dressing of Other Ores	
农副食品加工业	Processing of Farm and Sideline Food	3255.79
食品制造业	Manufacture of Food	1949.85
酒、饮料和精制茶制造业	Manufacture of Beverage	1114.29
烟草制品业	Tobacco Products	401.56
纺织业	Textile Industry	1723.74
纺织服装、服饰业	Manufacture of Textile Garments, Footwear and Headgear	1585.11
皮革、毛皮、羽毛及其制品和制鞋业	Leather, Fur, Feather, Down and Related Products	1098.33
木材加工和木、竹、藤、棕、草制品业	Timber Processing, Bamboo, Cane, Palm Fiber & Straw Products	306.17
家具制造业	Manufacture of Furniture	2045.03
造纸和纸制品业	Papermaking and Paper Products	2232.85
印刷和记录媒介复制业	Printing and Record Medium Reproduction	1182.33
文教、工美、体育和娱乐用品制造业	Manufacture of Cultural, Educational and Sports Articles	3448.36
石油、煤炭及其他燃料加工业	Petroleum, Coal and other Fuel Processing	2382.89
化学原料和化学制品制造业	Manufacture of Raw Chemical Materials and Chemical Products	6241.49
医药制造业	Manufacture of Medicines	1866.40
化学纤维制造业	Manufacture of Chemical Fibers	163.09
橡胶和塑料制品业	Plastic Products	5486.10
非金属矿物制品业	Nonmetal Mineral Products	4977.06
黑色金属冶炼和压延加工业	Smelting and Pressing of Ferrous Metals	1345.98
有色金属冶炼和压延加工业	Smelting and Pressing of Nonferrous Metals	4114.71
金属制品业	Metal Products	7833.64
通用设备制造业	Manufacture of General-purpose Machinery	5499.09
专用设备制造业	Manufacture of Special-purpose Machinery	5176.16
汽车制造业	Manufacture of Automobile	11931.16
铁路、船舶、航空航天和其他运输设备制造业	Manufacture of Railway ,Ship,Aeronautics and Other Transport equipment	1468.99
电气机械和器材制造业	Manufacture of Electrical Machinery and Equipment	20388.05
计算机、通信和其他电子设备制造业	Manufacture of Communication Equipment, Computers and Other Electronic Equipment	45908.83
仪器仪表制造业	Manufacture of Instruments and Meters	1599.21
其他制造业	Other Manufactures	607.95
废弃资源综合利用业	Comprehensive Utilization of Waste	485.05
金属制品、机械和设备修理业	Manufacture of Metal Products,Machinery and Equipment Maintenance	233.59
电力、热力生产和供应业	Production and Supply of Electric Power and Heat Power	6609.63
燃气生产和供应业	Production and Supply of Gas	2306.96
水的生产和供应业	Production and Supply of Water	771.54

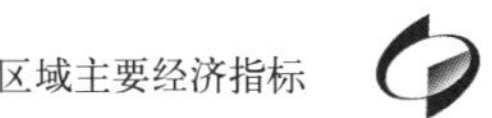

22-4 continued

(100 million yuan)

税金及附加 Tax and Extra Charges	利润总额 Total Profits	#亏损总额 Total Losses	利税总额 Total Pretax Profits	本年应交增值税 Value-added Tax Payable in Current Year	全部从业人员年平均人数（万人） Annual Average Number of Employed Persons (10000 persons)
1368.37	**9345.75**	**1465.08**	**13783.96**	**3069.84**	**1172.55**
779.94	1281.93	238.42	2485.73	423.86	62.58
2.89	54.17	5.06	71.59	14.53	2.85
0.15	-0.40	1.62	0.42	0.67	0.93
0.26	2.82	0.14	4.41	1.32	0.25
872.71	5681.91	872.40	8615.26	2060.65	706.26
307.90	1579.85	374.35	2355.75	468.00	164.20
179.80	1986.35	206.77	2666.62	500.47	287.89
404.31	3293.45	410.53	4887.13	1189.37	473.25
964.06	6052.30	1054.55	8896.83	1880.47	699.30
980.86	5484.16	337.10	7923.79	1458.76	407.87
215.60	2155.09	468.88	3059.02	688.33	309.91
171.91	1706.50	659.10	2801.15	922.74	454.77
43.29	450.04		561.09	67.76	0.32
0.09	3.18		3.83	0.56	0.05
0.06	0.93		1.06	0.08	0.06
3.81	0.83	14.29	9.11	4.47	0.46
0.09	8.12		8.78	0.58	0.14
5.31	106.50	11.97	140.27	28.46	7.67
12.60	209.86	17.93	303.68	81.22	14.84
20.33	90.32	4.41	148.05	37.41	6.44
190.34	34.94	0.31	258.63	33.35	1.51
7.56	103.46	13.18	151.44	40.41	18.10
7.51	52.90	22.07	101.77	41.37	34.08
4.73	37.19	8.67	60.17	18.26	23.59
1.77	7.93	4.27	18.43	8.73	3.74
9.67	134.88	15.23	193.41	48.86	29.47
9.51	32.67	26.44	105.54	63.36	16.94
4.84	79.04	8.50	109.61	25.73	17.56
9.46	112.01	15.58	152.25	30.78	40.83
304.35	13.53	7.96	340.89	23.01	1.18
29.26	319.28	101.54	483.07	134.53	27.94
13.11	334.26	79.23	427.91	80.54	13.70
0.80	16.65	3.31	20.78	3.34	1.02
21.90	337.95	33.89	471.09	111.23	70.85
22.18	202.37	57.33	347.81	123.26	34.09
3.51	30.17	13.41	48.81	15.13	3.37
8.58	86.56	12.39	136.34	41.20	12.59
30.59	408.38	43.04	608.63	169.67	82.28
21.33	355.08	46.42	490.84	114.44	55.92
25.83	500.46	78.53	653.79	127.51	63.41
272.51	691.47	80.89	1189.37	225.39	43.63
6.75	74.27	13.26	100.60	19.58	11.23
78.96	1496.67	123.01	2089.16	513.53	168.48
151.67	2336.93	444.29	3087.26	598.66	315.49
7.29	134.45	22.33	180.84	39.10	20.81
3.07	59.13	3.48	71.41	9.20	9.01
1.51	13.42	3.49	22.95	8.02	1.30
1.16	12.34	3.12	19.20	5.70	2.33
25.12	273.79	105.69	438.74	139.83	11.56
2.85	102.00	10.22	120.85	16.00	1.78
5.10	81.82	15.42	106.49	19.57	4.80

22–5 广州、深圳主要经济指标（2022年）

Main Economic Indicators of Guangzhou and Shenzhen (2022)

指　　标	Item	合计 Total	广州 Guangzhou	深圳 Shenzhen
土地面积（平方公里）	Land Area (sq.km)	9225.46	7238.46	1987.00
年末常住人口（万人）	Permanent Population at the Year-end (10000 persons)	3639.59	1873.41	1766.18
#城镇人口	Urban Population	3382.59	1620.12	1762.47
年末户籍总人口（万人）	Total Population with Residence Registration at the Year-end (10000 persons)	1689.65	1034.91	654.74
城镇单位就业人员	Employed Persons in Urban Areas	940.53	426.94	503.60
地区生产总值（亿元）	Gross Domestic Product (100 million yuan)	61226.68	28839.00	32387.68
第一产业	Primary Industry	343.94	318.31	25.64
第二产业	Secondary Industry	20315.18	7909.29	12405.88
第三产业	Tertiary Industry	40567.56	20611.40	19956.16
人均地区生产总值（元）	Per Capita Gross Domestic Product (yuan)	168002	153625	183274
地区生产总值指数（上年=100）	Index of Gross Domestic Product (preceding year=100)	102.2	101.0	103.3
第一产业	Primary Industry	103.0	103.2	100.8
第二产业	Secondary Industry	103.3	101.1	104.8
第三产业	Tertiary Industry	101.7	101.0	102.4
人均地区生产总值指数（上年=100）	Index of Per Capita Gross Domestic Product (preceding year=100)	102.2	101.0	103.2
公路通车里程（公里）	Total Length of Highways in Operation (km)	9800.3	9074.809	725.53
民用汽车拥有量（万辆）	Number of Civil Vehicles Owned (100 million unit)	737.0	343.5	393.5
私人汽车拥有量	Number of Private Vehicles Owned	586.3	274	312
邮电业务总量（亿元）	Total Business Volume of Postal and Telecommunication (100 million yuan)	2548.2	1266.65	1281.50
本地电话年末用户（万户）	Number of Subscribers of Local Telephones at the Year-end (10000 subscribers)	674.2	304	371
移动电话年末用户（万户）	Number of Subscribers of Mobile Telephones at the Year-end (10000 subscribers)	6027.6	3210	2818
房地产开发投资（亿元）	Investment in Real Estate Development (100 million yuan)	6845.18	3431.90	3413.28
社会消费品零售总额（亿元）	Total Retail Sales of Consumer Good (100 million yuan)	20006.43	10298.15	9708.28
出口总额（亿元）	Total Exports (RMB100 million)	28139.19	6195.42	21943.77
进口总额（亿元）	Total Imports (RMB 100 million)	19547.19	4752.76	14794.43
实际外商直接投资额（亿元）	Foreign Direct Investment Actually Utilized (RMB 100 million)	1288.46	574.13	714.33
地方一般公共预算收入（亿元）	Local Public Budgetary Revenue (100 million yuan)	5867.53	1855.10	4012.44
地方一般公共预算支出（亿元）	Local Public Budgetary Expenditure (100 million yuan)	8019.83	3022.45	4997.38
金融机构本外币存款（亿元）	Deposits in Renminbi and Foreign Currencies in All Financial Institutions (100 million yuan)	203895.59	80495.07	123400.52
#本外币住户存款	Savings Deposits by Residents	51806.85	26878.13	24928.72
金融机构本外币贷款（亿元）	Loans in Renminbi and Foreign Currencies in All Financial Institutions (100 million yuan)	152341.59	68918.60	83422.99
全体居民人均可支配收入（元）	Per Capita Disposable Income of Households (yuan)		71357.9	72718.2
城镇居民人均可支配收入（元）	Per Capita Disposable Income of Urban Households (yuan)		76849.4	72718.2
农村居民人均可支配 收入（元）	Per Capita Disposable Income of Rural Households (yuan)		36292.3	

22-6 粤东西北主要经济指标

Main Economic Indicators of the East and West and Mountainous Area

年份 Year	年末常住人口(万人) Permanent Population at the Year-end (10000 persons)	#城镇人口 Urban Population	年末户籍总人口(万人) Total Population with Residence Registration at the Year-end (10000 persons)	城镇单位就业人员 Employed Persons in Urban Areas
2000	4235.41	1787.22	4934.94	274.48
2001	4357.08		4970.09	262.55
2002	4427.40		5024.37	254.28
2003	4499.14		5062.96	255.45
2004	4594.16		5090.66	257.74
2005	4646.85	2098.62	5136.32	266.15
2006	4706.60	2191.04	5227.44	277.04
2007	4728.84	2202.07	5283.58	280.72
2008	4755.00	2216.23	5346.26	281.78
2009	4768.46	2256.19	5398.98	287.98
2010	4817.99	2259.21	5496.98	294.85
2011	4818.06	2268.59	5563.33	310.82
2012	4824.41	2275.05	5530.87	334.39
2013	4823.13	2283.13	5603.44	403.50
2014	4824.14	2293.19	5678.95	407.20
2015	4809.50	2319.58	5742.67	404.70
2016	4806.76	2334.93	5814.38	410.44
2017	4802.92	2348.03	5841.81	403.10
2018	4802.54	2403.58	5874.08	390.93
2019	4805.05	2457.00	5895.69	365.59
2020	4800.46	2538.38	5916.46	365.58
2021	4823.40	2590.85	5931.29	364.17
2022	4827.37	2616.45	5931.57	349.35

注：粤东西北地区包括汕头、汕尾、潮州、揭阳、阳江、湛江、茂名、韶关、河源、梅州、清远和云浮12市。

Note: East and West Wings and Mountainous areas in Guangdong include Shantou, Shanwei, Chaozhou, Jieyang, Yangjiang, Zhanjiang, Maoming, Shaoguan,Heyuan,Meizhou,Qingyuan and Yunfu.

22-6 续表 1 continued

年份 Year	地区生产总值(亿元) Gross Domestic Product (100 million yuan)	第一产业 Primary Industry	第二产业 Secondary Industry	第三产业 Tertiary Industry	人均地区生产总值(元) Per Capita Gross Domestic Product(yuan)
2000	2775.18	726.47	1054.10	994.61	6576
2001	2967.84	745.05	1141.98	1080.80	6908
2002	3181.57	778.07	1224.68	1178.82	7244
2003	3550.67	818.69	1426.03	1305.94	7955
2004	4083.32	897.96	1681.55	1503.81	8981
2005	4640.29	901.99	1989.52	1748.77	10043
2006	5464.89	957.22	2523.24	1984.43	11685
2007	6465.64	1062.06	3058.40	2345.19	13705
2008	7630.76	1208.84	3618.56	2803.36	16092
2009	8129.39	1256.17	3640.60	3232.62	17072
2010	9529.29	1433.71	4282.62	3812.96	19867
2011	11183.63	1667.60	4969.43	4546.59	23181
2012	12348.50	1808.63	5394.13	5145.74	25579
2013	13729.70	1916.89	6061.82	5750.99	28425
2014	14929.56	2018.70	6632.09	6278.78	30911
2015	15722.21	2145.60	6686.52	6890.10	32598
2016	16998.21	2345.85	6939.89	7712.48	35308
2017	18311.86	2428.58	7074.33	8808.96	38087
2018	19504.50	2570.99	7361.29	9572.22	40611
2019	20773.87	2920.23	7619.23	10234.41	43241
2020	21301.25	3156.55	7925.75	10218.95	44352
2021	23804.94	3279.34	9195.13	11330.47	49471
2022	24436.78	3500.54	9411.13	11525.10	50642

22-6 续表 2 continued

年份 Year	地区生产总值指数(上年=100) Index of Gross Domestic Product (preceding year=100)	第一产业 Primary Industry	第二产业 Secondary Industry	第三产业 Tertiary Industry	人均地区生产总值指数(上年=100) Index of Per Capita Gross Domestic Product (preceding year=100)
2000	108.2	105.3	108.1	110.4	107.5
2001	106.4	104.8	105.5	108.5	105.0
2002	108.5	105.4	109.3	109.9	106.5
2003	110.8	104.4	114.8	111.1	109.5
2004	112.3	104.5	115.8	113.5	110.4
2005	113.7	103.6	117.8	115.3	112.3
2006	115.3	104.7	121.3	114.0	114.6
2007	115.5	103.6	119.5	116.2	115.1
2008	111.5	103.1	111.6	115.0	111.0
2009	111.3	105.5	109.8	115.1	110.8
2010	114.1	105.0	116.3	114.7	113.3
2011	112.1	104.5	114.0	112.9	111.5
2012	110.3	104.8	112.9	109.1	110.2
2013	112.0	103.5	114.9	111.4	111.9
2014	109.3	103.6	111.7	108.0	109.3
2015	107.9	103.6	107.4	109.9	108.1
2016	107.4	103.0	105.9	110.3	107.6
2017	106.7	103.8	104.5	109.5	106.8
2018	105.2	104.5	104.7	105.9	105.3
2019	105.1	103.5	103.7	106.8	105.1
2020	102.2	103.3	103.1	101.2	102.2
2021	107.9	107.0	107.7	108.5	107.7
2022	100.8	105.1	98.7	101.1	100.5

22-6 续表 3 continued

年份 Year	公路通车里程(公里) Total Length of Highways in Operation (km)	货运量(万吨) Freight Traffic (10000 tons)	邮电业务总量(亿元) Total Business Volume of Postal and Telecommunication Services (100 million yuan)	本地电话年末用户(万户) Number of Subscribers of Local Telephones at the Year-end (10000 subscribers)	移动电话年末用户 (万户) Number of Subscribers of Mobile Telephones at the Year-end (10000 subscribers)	房地产开发投资(亿元) Investment in Real Estate Development (100 million yuan)	社会消费品零售总额(亿元) Total Retail Sales of Consumer Goods (100 million yuan)
2000	69133		169.58	549.37		73.33	1075.91
2001	70449	48307	168.33	641.30	543.26	80.39	1153.03
2002	73076	50111	189.63	730.86	706.06	95.52	1245.99
2003	74106	52616	236.67	848.28	888.71	99.40	1348.52
2004	74690	54202	333.87	1210.00	1317.44	112.74	1526.88
2005	77369	30627	383.01	1083.96	1448.30	142.70	1760.11
2006	124739	32636	472.35	1073.86	1620.17	179.68	2035.34
2007	128900	38046	722.32	1091.75	1766.69	281.61	2373.30
2008	129736	42258	810.08	1043.60	1932.03	370.54	2878.84
2009	130699	36989	954.68	966.38	2071.24	378.15	3353.98
2010	134296	43686	883.49	899.35	2252.45	541.04	3930.26
2011	134345	52697	373.62	862.85	2507.03	787.04	4568.09
2012	136354	62789	444.36	840.51	2894.83	869.12	5020.07
2013	143359	75952	488.10	810.96	3477.68	1126.85	5566.58
2014	150546	99242	642.75	753.98	3624.47	1344.90	6183.31
2015	152969	110358	824.04	720.43	3572.36	1462.90	6915.18
2016	154454	106080	1404.54	655.48	3415.21	1706.63	7554.65
2017	155461	113392	1110.06	604.59	3970.45	2247.92	8263.13
2018	155029	121430	2137.38	551.81	4574.81	2921.86	8970.24
2019	158793	132107	3353.75	596.40	4677.99	3002.62	9714.15
2020	159677	98026	4420.01	552.32	4565.20	3206.37	8997.37
2021	160652	121130	1009.25	531.60	4801.71	3262.99	9767.36
2022	160694	107207	1081.68	496.33	4931.08	2169.23	9840.08

22-6 续表 4 continued

年份 Year	出口总额(亿美元) Total Exports (USD 100 million)	出口总额(亿元) Total Exports (RMB 100 million)	进口总额(亿美元) Total Imports (USD 100 million)	进口总额(亿元) Total Imports (RMB 100 million)	实际外商直接投资额(亿美元) Foreign Direct Investment Actually Utilized (USD 100 million)	实际外商直接投资额(亿元) Foreign Direct Investment Actually Utilized (RMB 100 million)	地方一般公共预算收入(亿元) Local Public General Budgetary Revenue (100 million yuan)
2000	71.42		38.72		13.70		88.89
2001	45.92		34.34		14.14		101.53
2002	58.50		33.77		15.68		108.83
2003	77.92		44.27		19.14		121.96
2004	91.26		59.17		9.96		133.47
2005	108.53		60.74		10.30		176.54
2006	132.04		70.27		14.25		219.70
2007	151.53		87.68		19.38		278.37
2008	169.80		95.43		22.24		338.91
2009	171.79		91.17		20.27		400.35
2010	213.89		122.04		19.14		513.91
2011	253.04		137.41		22.70		619.29
2012	263.49		142.32		19.96		718.42
2013	292.71	1815.69	151.20	938.21	18.90		842.56
2014	323.19	1986.91	151.11	928.61	20.10		949.18
2015	347.12	2158.74	128.79	799.25	12.51		1011.79
2016	334.77	2210.07	116.33	769.86	7.59		990.73
2017	326.32	2210.50	128.17	868.03	10.95		1059.05
2018	317.88	2100.44	141.30	931.50		97.41	1058.94
2019	325.28	2242.60	139.37	959.88		60.59	1086.33
2020	310.04	2147.00	150.34	1038.82		68.87	1120.85
2021	371.02	2398.22	208.92	1349.53		88.59	1217.74
2022	354.93	2359.28	208.94	1389.49		98.94	1145.66

22-6 续表 5 continued

年份 Year	地方一般公共预算支出(亿元) Local Public Genera Budgetary Expenditure (100 million yuan)	金融机构本外币存款(亿元) Deposits in Renminbi and Foreign Currencies in All Financial Institutions (100 million yuan)	#本外币住户存款(亿元) Savings Deposits by Urban and Rural Residents (100 million yuan)	金融机构本外币贷款(亿元) Loans in Renminbi and Foreign Currencies in All Financial Institutions (100 million yuan)	全体居民人均可支配收入(元) Per Capita Disposable Income of Households (yuan)	城镇居民人均可支配 收入(元) Per Capita Disposable Income of Urban Households (yuan)	农村居民人均可支配收入(元) Per Capita Disposable Income of Rural Households (yuan)
2000	216.28	2871.90	2089.75	1984.98			
2001	239.76	3149.51	2321.72	2011.43			
2002	300.61	3511.40	2638.20	2134.33			
2003	348.73	4066.83	3037.48	2353.51			
2004	386.45	4547.77	3438.04	2312.68			
2005	438.76	5157.66	3878.05	2187.28			
2006	538.75	5894.51	4371.05	2321.86			
2007	673.46	6399.72	4528.21	2634.39			
2008	801.64	7607.15	5469.95	2791.07			
2009	965.51	9072.69	6221.71	3901.78			
2010	1184.81	10724.89	7194.83	4639.56			
2011	1464.85	12015.02	8045.99	5481.70			
2012	1726.82	13514.31	9206.38	6508.63			
2013	1983.95	15429.88	10419.74	7675.51			
2014	2323.42	17080.90	11316.03	8904.68	15397.9	20239.9	10935.7
2015	3230.36	18779.17	12271.21	9919.34	16843.9	22018.2	12019.1
2016	3263.41	20862.78	13446.79	10778.82	18364.5	23871.9	13147.1
2017	3473.17	22598.34	14436.89	12348.94	19948.4	25767.5	14297.8
2018	3882.98	24513.25	15685.83	14085.18	21578.1	27522.0	15570.2
2019	4245.80	26470.25	17298.73	16177.66	23383.7	29523.1	16992.8
2020	4434.79	28417.57	18926.81	18589.75	24716.7	30759.0	18176.9
2021	4370.61	30157.00	20780.03	20703.50	27191.4	33564.5	20112.8
2022	4422.56	32701.56	23459.54	23082.10	28451.6	34739.8	21153.3

22-7 东翼主要经济指标

Main Economic Indicators of the East Wing

指　　标	Item	2021	2022	2022年比2021年增长% Growth Rate in 2022 over 2021
土地面积 (平方公里)	Land Area (sq.km)	15495	15496	0.0
年末常住人口 (万人)	Permanent Population at the Year-end (10000 persons)	1640.87	1643.42	0.2
#城镇人口	Urban Population	1002.08	1006.82	0.5
年末户籍总人口 (万人)	Total Population with Residence Registration at the Year-end (10000 persons)	1930.05	1930.83	0.0
城镇单位就业人员	Employed Persons in Urban Areas	115.49	108.80	-5.8
地区生产总值 (亿元)	Gross Domestic Product (100 million yuan)	7760.48	7913.42	0.6
第一产业	Primary Industry	617.17	672.91	5.7
第二产业	Secondary Industry	3355.43	3356.46	-1.9
第三产业	Tertiary Industry	3787.87	3884.06	2.0
人均地区生产总值 (元)	Per Capita Gross Domestic Product (yuan)	47425	48190	0.3
地区生产总值指数 (上年=100)	Index of Gross Domestic Product (preceding year=100)	107.9	100.6	
第一产业	Primary Industry	106.3	105.7	
第二产业	Secondary Industry	106.9	98.1	
第三产业	Tertiary Industry	109.0	102.0	
人均地区生产总值指数(上年=100)	Index of Per Capita Gross Domestic Product(preceding year=100)	107.8	100.3	
公路通车里程 (公里)	Total Length of Highways in Operation (km)	23022	23121	0.4
邮电业务总量 (亿元)	Total Business Volume of Postal and Telecommunication (100 million yuan)	620.10	672.90	8.5
本地电话年末用户 (万户)	Number of Subscribers of Local Telephones at the Year-end (10000 subscribers)	212.40	197.36	-7.1
移动电话年末用户 (万户)	Number of Subscribers of Mobile Telephones at the Year-end (10000 subscribers)	1685.36	1722.21	2.2
房地产开发投资 (亿元)	Investment in Real Estate Development (100 million yuan)	1117.62	750.85	-32.8
社会消费品零售总额 (亿元)	Total Retail Sales of Consumer Goods (100 million yuan)	3517.59	3513.77	-0.1
出口总额 (亿元)	Total Exports (RMB 100 million)	1069.80	1065.73	-0.4
进口总额 (亿元)	Total Imports (RMB 100 million)	316.90	290.98	-8.2
实际外商直接投资额 (亿元)	Foreign Direct Investment Actually Utilized (RMB 100 million)	16.94	16.12	-4.8
地方一般公共预算收入 (亿元)	Local Public Budgetary Revenue (100 million yuan)	330.21	309.90	-6.2
地方一般公共预算支出 (亿元)	Local Public Budgetary Expenditure (100 million yuan)	1268.25	1266.24	-0.2
金融机构本外币存款 (亿元)	Deposits in Renminbi and Foreign Currencies in All Financial Institutions (100 million yuan)	10080.00	11052.26	9.6
#住户存款	Savings Deposits by Residents	6965.80	7938.99	14.0
金融机构本外币贷款 (亿元)	Loans in Renminbi and Foreign Currencies in All Financial Institutions (100 million yuan)	5351.47	5946.91	11.1
全体居民人均可支配收入 (元)	Per Capita Disposable Income of Households (yuan)	27006.0	28388.3	5.1
城镇居民人均可支配收入 (元)	Per Capita Disposable Income of Urban Households (yuan)	32240.7	33521.5	4.0
农村居民人均可支配收入 (元)	Per Capita Disposable Income of Rural Households (yuan)	19211.4	20335.4	5.9

22-8　西翼主要经济指标

Main Economic Indicators of the West Wing

指　　标		Item		2021	2022	2022年比2021年增长% Growth Rate in 2022 over 2021
土地面积	(平方公里)	Land Area	(sq.km)	32682	32682	0.0
年末常住人口	(万人)	Permanent Population at the Year-end	(10000 persons)	1587.13	1589.58	0.2
#城镇人口		Urban Population		750.87	763.71	1.7
年末户籍总人口	(万人)	Total Population with Residence Registration at the Year-end	(10000 persons)	1997.09	1998.48	0.1
城镇单位就业人员		Employed Persons in Urban Areas		110.50	107.70	-2.5
地区生产总值	(亿元)	Gross Domestic Product	(100 million yuan)	8772.55	9152.20	0.8
第一产业		Primary Industry		1538.85	1633.23	4.6
第二产业		Secondary Industry		3250.70	3475.24	-1.0
第三产业		Tertiary Industry		3983.01	4043.73	0.6
人均地区生产总值	(元)	Per Capita Gross Domestic Product	(yuan)	55456	57621	0.4
地区生产总值指数	(上年=100)	Index of Gross Domestic Product	(preceding year=100)	108.2	100.8	
第一产业		Primary Industry		105.8	104.6	
第二产业		Secondary Industry		109.3	99.0	
第三产业		Tertiary Industry		108.4	100.6	
人均地区生产总值指数	(上年=100)	Index of Per Capita Gross Domestic Product	(preceding year=100)	107.6	100.4	
公路通车里程	(公里)	Total Length of Highways in Operation	(km)	52518	52550	0.1
邮电业务总量	(亿元)	Total Business Volume of Postal and Telecommunication	(100 million yuan)	197.63	209.99	6.3
本地电话年末用户	(万户)	Number of Subscribers of Local Telephones at the Year-end	(10000 subscribers)	149.53	138.37	-7.5
移动电话年末用户	(万户)	Number of Subscribers of Mobile Telephones at the Year-end	(10000 subscribers)	1530.84	1605.20	4.9
房地产开发投资	(亿元)	Investment in Real Estate Development	(100 million yuan)	929.34	684.18	-26.4
社会消费品零售总额	(亿元)	Total Retail Sales of Consumer Goods	(100 million yuan)	3764.49	3832.16	1.8
出口总额	(亿元)	Total Exports	(RMB 100 million)	570.38	571.22	0.1
进口总额	(亿元)	Total Imports	(RMB 100 million)	472.05	578.24	22.5
实际外商直接投资额	(亿元)	Foreign Direct Investment Actually Utilized	(RMB 100 million)	40.25	48.78	21.2
地方一般公共预算收入	(亿元)	Local Public Budgetary Revenue	(100 million yuan)	386.49	353.99	-8.4
地方一般公共预算支出	(亿元)	Local Public Budgetary Expenditure	(100 million yuan)	1279.55	1317.09	2.9
金融机构本外币存款	(亿元)	Deposits in Renminbi and Foreign Currencies in All Financial Institutions	(100 million yuan)	9368.24	10036.79	7.1
#本外币住户存款		Savings Deposits by Residents		6415.40	7212.14	12.4
金融机构本外币贷款	(亿元)	Loans in Renminbi and Foreign Currencies in All Financial Institutions	(100 million yuan)	6802.13	7795.89	14.6
全体居民人均可支配收入	(元)	Per Capita Disposable Income of Households	(yuan)	27538.1	28713.6	4.3
城镇居民人均可支配收入	(元)	Per Capita Disposable Income of Urban Households	(yuan)	34861.6	35906.0	3.0
农村居民人均可支配收入	(元)	Per Capita Disposable Income of Rural Households	(yuan)	21261.0	22254.3	4.7

22-9 山区主要经济指标

Main Economic Indicators of Mountainous Areas

指　　标	Item	2021	2022	2022年比2021年增长% Growth Rate in 2022over 2021
土地面积 (平方公里)	Land Area (sq.km)	76751	76751	0.0
年末常住人口 (万人)	Permanent Population at the Year-end (10000 persons)	1595.40	1594.37	-0.1
#城镇人口	Urban Population	837.90	845.92	1.0
年末户籍总人口 (万人)	Total Population with Residence Registration at the Year-end (10000 persons)	2004.15	2002.26	-0.1
城镇单位就业人员	Employed Persons in Urban Areas	138.18	132.85	-3.9
地区生产总值 (亿元)	Gross Domestic Product (100 million yuan)	7271.92	7371.15	0.9
第一产业	Primary Industry	1123.32	1194.40	5.4
第二产业	Secondary Industry	2589.00	2579.43	-0.9
第三产业	Tertiary Industry	3559.60	3597.31	0.7
人均地区生产总值 (元)	Per Capita Gross Domestic Product (yuan)	45630	46217	0.8
地区生产总值指数 (上年=100)	Index of Gross Domestic Product (preceding year=100)	107.7	100.9	
第一产业	Primary Industry	109.0	105.4	
第二产业	Secondary Industry	106.8	99.1	
第三产业	Tertiary Industry	108.0	100.7	
人均地区生产总值指数 (上年=100)	Index of Per Capita Gross Domestic Product (preceding year=100)	107.7	100.8	
公路通车里程 (公里)	Total Length of Highways in Operation (km)	85112	85023	-0.1
邮电业务总量 (亿元)	Total Business Volume of Postal and Telecommunication (100 million yuan)	191.52	198.80	3.8
本地电话年末用户 (万户)	Number of Subscribers of Local Telephones at the Year-end (10000 subscribers)	169.67	160.60	-5.3
移动电话年末用户 (万户)	Number of Subscribers of Mobile Telephones at the Year-end (10000 subscribers)	1585.52	1603.67	1.1
房地产开发投资 (亿元)	Investment in Real Estate Development (100 million yuan)	1216.04	734.21	-39.6
社会消费品零售总额 (亿元)	Total Retail Sales of Consumer Goods (100 million yuan)	2485.28	2494.15	0.4
出口总额 (亿元)	Total Exports (RMB 100 million)	758.04	722.33	-4.7
进口总额 (亿元)	Total Imports (RMB 100 million)	560.58	520.27	-7.2
实际外商直接投资额 (亿元)	Foreign Direct Investment Actually Utilized (RMB 100 million)	31.40	34.03	8.4
地方一般公共预算收入 (亿元)	Local Public Budgetary Revenue (100 million yuan)	501.05	481.78	-3.8
地方一般公共预算支出 (亿元)	Local Public Budgetary Expenditure (100 million yuan)	1822.80	1839.23	0.9
金融机构本外币存款 (亿元)	Deposits in Renminbi and Foreign Currencies in All Financial Institutions (100 million yuan)	10708.77	11612.52	8.4
#本外币住户存款	Savings Deposits by Residents	7398.83	8308.40	12.3
金融机构本外币贷款 (亿元)	Loans in Renminbi and Foreign Currencies in All Financial Institution (100 million yuan)	8549.91	9339.30	9.2
全体居民人均可支配收入 (元)	Per Capita Disposable Income of Households (yuan)	27038.0	28256.0	4.5
城镇居民人均可支配收入 (元)	Per Capita Disposable Income of Urban Households (yuan)	34008.9	35151.8	3.4
农村居民人均可支配收入 (元)	Per Capita Disposable Income of Rural Households (yuan)	19599.6	20627.7	5.2

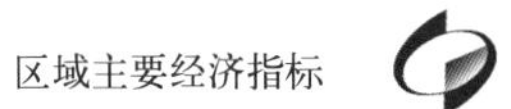

22-10 山区县(市、区)主要经济指标

Main Economic Indicators of Counties (County-level Cities and Districts) in Mountainous Areas

指　标	Item	2021	2022	2022年比2021年增长% Growth Rate in 2022 over 2021
年末户籍总人口　(万人)	Total Population with Residence Registration at the Year-end (10000 persons)	3497.00	3489.60	-0.2
地区生产总值　(亿元)	Gross Domestic Product (100 million yuan)	11808.73	12116.34	1.2
第一产业	Primary Industry	2216.29	2377.67	5.2
第二产业	Secondary Industry	4122.38	4186.28	-0.5
第三产业	Tertiary Industry	5470.06	5552.39	0.7
人均地区生产总值　(元)	Per Capita Gross Domestic Product (yuan)	44334	45425	1.1
地区生产总值指数　(上年=100)	Index of Gross Domestic Product (preceding year=100)	108.3	101.2	
第一产业	Primary Industry	108.9	105.2	
第二产业	Secondary Industry	107.5	99.5	
第三产业	Tertiary Industry	108.8	100.7	
人均地区生产总值指数(上年=100)	Index of Per Capita Gross Domestic Product(preceding year=100)	109.2	101.1	
房地产开发投资　(亿元)	Investment in Real Estate Development (100 million yuan)	1507.24	932.50	-38.0
社会消费品零售总额　(亿元)	Total Retail Sales of Consumer Goods (100 million yuan)	4283.54	4302.32	0.4
地方一般公共预算收入　(亿元)	Local Public Budgetary Revenue (100 million yuan)	543.43	570.18	4.9
地方一般公共预算支出　(亿元)	Local Public Budgetary Expenditure (100 million yuan)	2398.86	2490.97	3.8

注：50个山区县(市、区)包括:从化区、南澳县、曲江区、乐昌市、南雄市、仁化县、始兴县、翁源县、新丰县、乳源县、东源县、和平县、龙川县、紫金县、连平县、梅江区、兴宁市、梅县区、平远县、蕉岭县、大埔县、丰顺县、五华县、惠东县、龙门县、海丰县、陆河县、阳春市、信宜市、高州市、高要区、广宁县、德庆县、封开县、怀集县、英德市、连州市、佛冈县、清新区、连山县、连南县、阳山县、饶平县、潮安区、普宁市、揭西县、罗定市、新兴县、郁南县、云安区。

Notes: Counties(county-level cities and districts)in mountainous areas total 50, including Conghua District, Nan'ao County,Qujiang District,Nanxiong City, Lechang City,Renhua County, Shixing County, Wengyuan County, Xinfeng County, Ruyuan County, Dongyuan County, Heping County, Longchuan County, Zijin County, Lianping County, Meijiang District, Xingning City,Meixian County, Pingyuan County,Jiaoling County,Dabu County,Fengshun County,Wuhua County,Huidong County,Longmen County,Haifeng County,Luhe County,Yangchun City,Xinyi City,Gaozhou City, Gaoyao City, Guangning County,Deqing County, Fengkai County, Huaiji County,Yingde City, Lianzhou City, Fogang County, Qingxin County,Lianshan County, Liannan County,Yangshan County, Raoping County, Chao'an District, Puning City, Jiexi County, Luoding City, Xinxing County, Yunan County, and Yun'an District.

22-11 少数民族县主要经济指标（2022年）

Main Economic Indicators of Minority Counties (2022)

指标	Item	合计 Total	乳源县 Ruyuan County	连山县 Lianshan County	连南县 Liannan County
土地面积（平方公里）	Land Area (sq.km)	4758	2299	1218	1241
年末户籍总人口（万人）	Total Population with Residence Registration at the Year-end (10000 persons)	53.58	23.32	12.51	17.75
少数民族人口（万人）	Population of Minority Nationalities (10000 persons)	21.33	2.80	8.22	10.31
地区生产总值（亿元）	Gross Domestic Product (100 million yuan)	234.46	114.70	46.93	72.82
第一产业	Primary Industry	36.11	11.09	11.70	13.32
第二产业	Secondary Industry	90.23	58.82	10.63	20.78
第三产业	Tertiary Industry	108.12	44.79	24.60	38.72
人均地区生产总值（元）	Per Capita Gross Domestic Product (yuan)	55929	60914	49170	53761
地区生产总值指数（上年=100）	Index of Gross Domestic Product (preceding year=100)	103.3	103.2	102.3	104.3
第一产业	Primary Industry	107.7	115.8	102.6	105.7
第二产业	Secondary Industry	106.4	107.4	106.9	103.3
第三产业	Tertiary Industry	99.7	96.0	100.3	104.3
人均地区生产总值指数（上年=100）	Index of Per Capita Gross Domestic Product (preceding year=100)	103.1	102.8	102.1	104.1
公路通车里程（公里）	Total Length of Highways in Operation (km)	4194	2023	1015	1156
本地电话年末用户（户）	Number of Subscribers of Local Telephones at the Year-end (subscriber)	44539	26168	6418	11953
移动电话年末用户（户）	Number of Subscribers of Mobile Telephones at the Year-end (subscriber)	396923	173701	100337	122885
房地产开发投资（亿元）	Investment in Real Estate Development (100 million yuan)	6.96	3.74	1.39	1.84
社会消费品零售总额（亿元）	Total Retail Sales of Consumer Goods (100 million yuan)	38.97	22.51	5.44	11.02
地方一般公共预算收入（亿元）	Local Public Budgetary Revenue (100 million yuan)	10.07	5.24	2.44	2.40
地方一般公共预算支出（亿元）	Local Public Budgetary Expenditure (100 million yuan)	70.35	28.83	19.29	22.23
农村居民人均可支配收入（元）	Per Capita Annual Disposable Income of Rural Residents (yuan)		20149	17831	18198
普通中学（所）	Number of Regular Secondary Schools (unit)	27	8	10	9
在校学生数（人）	Number of Students Enrolled in Regular Secondary Schools (person)	26097	10807	6221	9069
小学（所）	Number of Primary Schools (unit)	50	12	8	30
在校学生数（人）	Number of Students Enrolled in Primary Schools (person)	43945	18354	10042	15549

二十三、县（市、区）主要经济指标

COUNTIES AND DISTRICTS UNDER CITY ADMINISTRATION

二十三　县（市、区）主要经济指标

简要说明

一、本篇资料反映广东县（市、区）经济发展基本情况，主要包括：各县（市、区）的地区生产总值、工农业总产值、主要农产品产量、固定资产投资、消费品零售总额、就业人员和工资水平、财政收支等内容。

二、本篇资料由广东省统计局各有关专业处整理提供，综合统计处负责编辑。

三、本篇资料依据国家统计局制定的各有关专业年度报表制度填报汇总而成。

四、本篇各县（市、区）生产总值、产值、财政类指标数据汇总数不等于全省数。

23 Counties and Districts Under City Administration

Brief Introduction

Ⅰ. The data in this chapter show the basic conditions of the economic development of counties and districts under city administration in Guangdong Province, mainly including gross domestic product, gross output value of industry and agriculture, output of major agriculture products, investment in fixed assets, total retail sales of consumer goods, number and wages of fully employed staff and workers, local government budgetary revenue and expenditure, etc.

Ⅱ. The data in this chapter are prepared and provided by the related specialized divisions and compiled by the Division of Comprehensive Statistics of Statistics Bureau of Guangdong Province.

Ⅲ. The data in this chapter are reported and compiled in accordance with related specialized annual report schemes formulated by the National Bureau of Statistics.

Ⅳ. The tabulated data on gross domestic product, output value and government finance of the counties and districts in this chapter do not sum up to the provincial total.

23-1 各县(市、区)地区生产总值

Gross Domestic Product by County (County-level City and District)

县(市、区)	County (County-level City and District)	地区生产总值(亿元) Gross Domestic Product (100 million yuan)		指数(上年=100) Index (preceding year=100)	
		2021	2022	2021	2022
广州市	Guangzhou				
越秀区	Yuexiu District	3606.39	3650.18	106.0	100.1
海珠区	Haizhu District	2405.20	2502.52	109.3	101.4
荔湾区	Liwan District	1203.11	1215.57	108.4	101.1
天河区	Tianhe District	6004.16	6215.72	108.2	102.4
白云区	Baiyun District	2532.84	2476.20	108.0	96.7
黄埔区	Huangpu District	4187.89	4313.76	108.2	101.5
花都区	Huadu District	1802.98	1770.81	106.6	98.9
番禺区	Panyu District	2657.70	2705.47	109.0	101.4
南沙区	Nansha District	2153.65	2252.58	109.6	104.2
从化区	Conghua District	415.92	410.92	103.6	98.1
增城区	Zengcheng District	1255.36	1325.27	110.7	104.0
深圳市	Shenzhen				
福田区	Futian District	5319.86	5514.49	108.6	103.0
罗湖区	Luohu District	2508.23	2630.19	106.1	103.4
盐田区	Yantian District	759.28	820.62	110.9	105.4
南山区	Nanshan District	7708.74	8035.88	109.6	103.3
宝安区	Baoan District	4419.06	4701.61	111.3	103.5
龙岗区	Longgang District	4968.61	5142.22	94.6	103.1
龙华区	Longhua District	2807.32	2951.67	109.8	103.1
坪山区	Pingshan District	910.09	1079.64	111.7	114.0
光明区	Guangming District	1348.43	1427.10	116.1	106.5
珠海市	Zhuhai				
香洲区	Xiangzhou District	2612.85	2682.23	106.6	101.6
金湾区	Jinwan District	814.85	861.96	111.3	103.5
斗门区	Doumen District	468.34	501.27	103.8	104.5
汕头市	Shantou				
金平区	Jinping District	594.30	611.33	106.3	101.6
龙湖区	Longhu District	605.58	614.37	106.7	100.2
澄海区	Chenghai District	489.66	513.28	106.1	103.5
濠江区	Haojiang District	185.45	184.92	106.8	98.4
潮阳区	Chaoyang District	533.02	534.77	106.1	99.1
潮南区	Chaonan District	506.55	522.84	106.7	102.0
南澳县	Nanao County	35.02	35.93	106.0	101.3
佛山市	Foshan				
禅城区	Chancheng District	2156.42	2283.81	108.4	103.1
南海区	Nanhai District	3565.66	3730.59	109.0	102.2
顺德区	Shunde District	4073.44	4166.39	108.4	100.8
高明区	Gaoming District	983.01	1045.18	107.3	103.5
三水区	Sanshui District	1407.20	1472.43	108.7	102.1
韶关市	Shaoguan				
浈江区	Zhengjiang District	228.78	226.81	106.1	99.2
武江区	Wujiang District	305.61	306.87	105.0	99.7
曲江区	Qujiang District	216.09	209.27	108.4	95.7
乐昌市	Lechang City	137.23	137.84	109.4	100.7
南雄市	Nanxiong City	131.05	132.25	106.7	100.7
仁化县	Renhua County	111.98	119.26	108.6	106.9
始兴县	Shixing County	98.64	101.89	114.0	102.1
翁源县	Wengyuan County	129.35	132.08	114.6	101.1
新丰县	Xinfeng County	81.89	82.97	109.1	99.3
乳源县	Ruyuan County	109.44	114.70	114.3	103.2

注：海丰县不包含深汕合作区地区生产总值数据。
Notes: GDP of Shenzhen-Shanwei Cooperation Zone not included Haifeng county.

23-1 续表 1 continued

县(市、区)	County (County-level City and District)	地区生产总值(亿元) Gross Domestic Product (100 million yuan) 2021	2022	指数(上年=100) Index(preceding year=100) 2021	2022
河源市	Heyuan				
源城区	Yuancheng District	522.71	532.23	110.3	101.3
东源县	Dongyuan County	167.18	172.31	112.6	102.7
和平县	Heping County	127.86	128.98	102.1	100.1
龙川县	Longchuan County	170.24	171.41	102.9	100.2
紫金县	Zijin County	188.10	189.39	108.7	100.2
连平县	Lianping County	97.82	100.26	105.5	100.9
梅州市	Meizhou				
梅江区	Meijiang District	287.34	287.73	104.3	100.2
梅县区	Meixian District	237.83	238.26	106.3	100.1
兴宁市	Xingning City	196.44	200.99	108.9	101.1
平远县	Pingyuan County	85.85	86.57	106.0	100.6
蕉岭县	Jiaoling County	106.56	105.68	105.1	99.6
大埔县	Dabu County	100.38	100.81	106.8	100.4
丰顺县	Fengshun County	118.92	119.29	102.4	100.2
五华县	Wuhua County	176.08	178.88	105.2	101.6
惠州市	Huizhou				
惠城区	Huicheng District	1809.06	1935.64	111.8	104.4
惠阳区	Huiyang District	1588.24	1719.23	107.9	105.0
惠东县	Huidong County	700.98	741.77	110.7	102.3
博罗县	Boluo County	745.58	801.39	112.8	103.7
龙门县	Longmen County	189.19	203.21	109.0	105.1
汕尾市	Shanwei				
市城区	Urban District	356.50	371.17	111.0	103.2
陆丰市	Lufeng City	423.03	418.02	113.9	97.3
海丰县	Haifeng County	405.31	426.81	113.5	103.8
陆河县	Luhe County	100.56	106.01	110.9	104.1
江门市	Jiangmen				
蓬江区	Pengjiang District	828.79	870.92	109.1	103.4
江海区	Jianghai District	289.77	302.10	109.9	102.4
新会区	Xinhui District	898.48	951.63	108.9	104.0
台山市	Taishan City	500.38	516.50	108.5	103.5
开平市	Kaiping City	435.90	456.07	108.3	102.8
鹤山市	Heshan City	436.82	458.51	109.7	102.8
恩平市	Enping City	207.91	217.68	107.1	102.6
阳江市	Yangjiang				
江城区	Jiangcheng District	567.28	579.92	110.4	101.2
阳东区	Yangdong District	342.01	341.44	107.9	100.2
阳春市	Yangchun City	366.26	357.62	105.7	99.0
阳西县	Yangxi County	235.63	256.02	108.5	103.8

23-1 续表 2 continued

县(市、区)	County (County-level City and District)	地区生产总值(亿元) Gross Domestic Product (100 million yuan) 2021	2022	指数(上年=100) Index(preceding year=100) 2021	2022
湛江市	Zhanjiang				
赤坎区	Chikan District	355.04	362.48	107.1	101.2
霞山区	Xiashan District	427.80	429.10	103.0	98.5
麻章区	Mazhang District	636.69	718.94	139.7	102.5
坡头区	Potou District	350.86	347.53	103.3	98.0
雷州市	Leizhou City	354.03	367.28	107.4	102.1
廉江市	Lianjiang County	513.18	533.14	107.0	102.0
吴川市	Wuchuan City	302.02	298.20	107.2	98.5
遂溪县	Suixi County	408.24	426.61	108.4	102.2
徐闻县	Xuwen County	217.60	229.27	108.1	103.0
茂名市	Maoming				
茂南区	Maonan District	1095.25	1160.99	106.0	96.9
电白区	Dianbai District	765.51	812.50	108.9	103.0
信宜市	Xinyi City	524.80	553.89	107.1	102.1
高州市	Gaozhou City	685.43	725.68	107.6	102.3
化州市	Huazhou City	624.91	651.57	108.4	101.6
肇庆市	Zhaoqing				
端州区	Duanzhou District	473.49	468.92	107.5	98.4
鼎湖区	Dinghu District	144.96	153.29	106.4	102.8
高要区	Gaoyao District	513.21	542.12	113.5	103.5
四会市	Sihui City	722.50	743.54	112.6	102.5
广宁县	Guangning County	176.22	180.58	108.0	102.3
德庆县	Deqing County	171.62	150.93	105.8	86.7
封开县	Fengkai County	163.87	170.98	110.0	102.4
怀集县	Huaiji County	279.94	294.68	112.2	103.6
清远市	Qingyuan				
清城区	Qingcheng District	709.19	717.85	105.4	101.1
清新区	Qingxin District	305.54	306.98	105.3	100.3
英德市	Yingde City	400.30	405.19	111.0	101.7
连州市	Lianzhou City	178.63	180.39	109.1	100.6
佛冈县	Fogang County	158.51	161.34	112.8	101.6
阳山县	Yangshan County	137.06	140.25	109.7	101.6
连山县	Lianshan County	45.32	46.93	107.6	102.3
连南县	Liannan County	66.14	72.82	109.8	104.3
潮州市	Chaozhou				
湘桥区	Xiangqiao District	305.48	318.73	109.8	102.5
潮安区	Chaoan District	618.97	651.67	108.2	101.4
饶平县	Raoping County	320.07	342.58	110.3	103.7
揭阳市	Jieyang				
榕城区	Rongcheng District	595.41	588.80	105.4	98.7
揭东区	Jiedong District	507.96	495.29	106.1	98.0
普宁市	Puning City	622.93	629.50	106.8	99.5
揭西县	Jiexi County	261.71	261.11	107.1	99.1
惠来县	Huilai County	292.96	286.28	107.6	98.3
云浮市	Yunfu				
云城区	Yuncheng District	248.91	256.80	108.1	102.5
云安区	Yunan District	130.23	134.29	109.2	102.5
罗定市	Luoding City	312.06	319.19	106.0	101.8
新兴县	Xinxing County	308.60	311.70	109.9	101.7
郁南县	Yunan County	138.06	140.45	108.1	102.9

23-2 各县(市、区)三次产业地区生产总值

Gross Domestic Product of the Three Strata of Industry by County (County-level City and District)

单位：亿元　　(100 million yuan)

县(市、区)	County (County-level City and District)	第一产业 Primary Industry 2021	2022	第二产业 Secondary Industry 2021	2022	第三产业 Tertiary Industry 2021	2022
广州市	Guangzhou						
越秀区	Yuexiu District			136.74	126.05	3469.65	3524.13
海珠区	Haizhu District	1.21	1.16	411.99	450.69	1992.00	2050.68
荔湾区	Liwan District	5.16	5.54	338.30	351.46	859.65	858.57
天河区	Tianhe District	2.36	2.58	439.86	447.33	5561.94	5765.81
白云区	Baiyun District	32.84	36.55	593.50	563.98	1906.49	1875.67
黄埔区	Huangpu District	4.44	5.19	2461.60	2529.15	1721.85	1779.42
花都区	Huadu District	50.27	52.06	793.82	762.20	958.88	956.54
番禺区	Panyu District	38.45	39.75	972.20	1016.19	1647.05	1649.53
南沙区	Nansha District	70.29	72.28	926.08	995.50	1157.28	1184.81
从化区	Conghua District	33.08	35.79	135.89	130.04	246.95	245.09
增城区	Zengcheng District	61.63	67.40	526.14	536.71	667.59	721.16
深圳市	Shenzhen						
福田区	Futian District	1.59	1.73	522.84	504.29	4795.43	5008.47
罗湖区	Luohu District	0.40	0.47	167.24	155.56	2340.59	2474.16
盐田区	Yantian District	0.14	0.32	127.25	151.43	631.89	668.87
南山区	Nanshan District	1.08	1.08	2215.27	2459.85	5492.39	5574.95
宝安区	Baoan District	0.85	0.90	2233.45	2371.83	2184.77	2328.88
龙岗区	Longgang District	2.08	2.61	3328.66	3460.03	1637.87	1679.57
龙华区	Longhua District	0.57	0.60	1404.34	1494.22	1402.41	1456.85
坪山区	Pingshan District	1.13	1.25	612.82	754.27	296.14	324.12
光明区	Guangming District	2.37	2.33	969.95	1016.97	376.10	407.81
珠海市	Zhuhai						
香洲区	Xiangzhou District	2.12	2.12	869.13	938.93	1741.60	1741.17
金湾区	Jinwan District	12.29	13.78	556.83	616.50	245.73	231.68
斗门区	Doumen District	39.78	44.62	225.15	252.65	203.41	204.00
汕头市	Shantou						
金平区	Jinping District	2.81	3.09	233.46	238.47	358.03	369.77
龙湖区	Longhu District	8.03	8.50	218.35	214.07	379.19	391.80
澄海区	Chenghai District	42.40	46.78	253.62	271.02	193.64	195.48
濠江区	Haojiang District	7.76	8.53	101.69	100.52	75.99	75.88
潮阳区	Chaoyang District	32.35	35.00	308.18	301.82	192.49	197.95
潮南区	Chaonan District	20.80	22.71	301.41	314.73	184.33	185.40
南澳县	Nanao County	12.26	12.36	5.31	5.81	17.45	17.77
佛山市	Foshan						
禅城区	Chancheng District	0.60	0.64	745.03	792.59	1410.79	1490.58
南海区	Nanhai District	59.47	66.24	1893.83	2006.09	1612.36	1658.26
顺德区	Shunde District	69.95	71.27	2398.24	2478.63	1605.25	1616.49
高明区	Gaoming District	29.82	37.32	734.58	783.85	218.61	224.01
三水区	Sanshui District	42.82	45.66	1009.26	1068.65	355.12	358.12
韶关市	Shaoguan						
浈江区	Zhengjiang District	8.36	8.17	65.47	61.38	154.95	157.25
武江区	Wujiang District	8.91	8.68	122.08	122.76	174.62	175.43
曲江区	Qujiang District	21.22	21.58	123.33	115.46	71.54	72.23
乐昌市	Lechang City	31.88	31.66	28.61	28.52	76.74	77.66
南雄市	Nanxiong City	36.89	37.49	29.59	29.23	64.58	65.53
仁化县	Renhua County	23.87	24.55	45.65	51.45	42.47	43.26
始兴县	Shixing County	25.85	28.37	30.99	31.01	41.81	42.50
翁源县	Wengyuan County	33.07	34.80	35.27	35.02	61.01	62.25
新丰县	Xinfeng County	15.64	18.16	24.89	23.04	41.36	41.77
乳源县	Ruyuan County	9.35	11.09	53.47	58.82	46.62	44.79

23-2 续表 1 continued

单位：亿元 (100 million yuan)

县(市、区)	County (County-level City and District)	第一产业 Primary Industry 2021	2022	第二产业 Secondary Industry 2021	2022	第三产业 Tertiary Industry 2021	2022
河源市	Heyuan						
源城区	Yuancheng District	3.57	3.94	245.31	250.55	273.83	277.74
东源县	Dongyuan County	28.59	30.74	62.98	65.27	75.62	76.29
和平县	Heping County	26.63	27.68	33.31	32.21	67.93	69.08
龙川县	Longchuan County	31.43	32.40	40.09	39.32	98.72	99.69
紫金县	Zijin County	42.27	44.61	56.05	54.73	89.78	90.04
连平县	Lianping County	20.72	23.03	26.70	27.06	50.39	50.16
梅州市	Meizhou						
梅江区	Meijiang District	8.35	9.37	124.85	123.58	154.14	154.79
梅县区	Meixian District	57.11	59.96	81.46	78.62	99.26	99.68
兴宁市	Xingning City	50.25	53.53	36.03	37.10	110.17	110.37
平远县	Pingyuan County	15.08	15.24	24.31	23.79	46.47	47.54
蕉岭县	Jiaoling County	17.12	18.70	48.35	45.54	41.09	41.43
大埔县	Dabu County	28.55	30.82	21.37	18.80	50.46	51.19
丰顺县	Fengshun County	23.98	26.99	45.79	42.37	49.15	49.93
五华县	Wuhua County	40.64	43.31	40.48	37.88	94.96	97.68
惠州市	Huizhou						
惠城区	Huicheng District	39.62	44.86	883.08	969.30	886.36	921.48
惠阳区	Huiyang District	24.28	25.37	1094.77	1242.13	469.20	451.73
惠东县	Huidong County	70.75	80.74	259.74	288.35	370.49	372.68
博罗县	Boluo County	80.42	88.50	397.78	436.48	267.38	276.41
龙门县	Longmen County	33.31	37.98	83.38	83.61	72.49	81.61
汕尾市	Shanwei						
市城区	Urban District	37.07	41.40	110.45	118.23	208.98	211.54
陆丰市	Lufeng City	73.55	84.32	168.90	146.72	180.58	186.98
海丰县	Haifeng County	40.27	44.81	184.25	196.04	180.79	185.97
陆河县	Luhe County	15.58	16.87	27.88	29.91	57.10	59.23
江门市	Jiangmen						
蓬江区	Pengjiang District	6.40	7.40	312.19	330.69	510.20	532.84
江海区	Jianghai District	6.25	7.91	176.87	184.29	106.65	109.90
新会区	Xinhui District	57.23	66.31	451.67	484.67	389.58	400.65
台山市	Taishan City	108.74	113.35	193.99	203.86	197.65	199.29
开平市	Kaiping City	52.26	56.50	208.23	217.57	175.40	181.99
鹤山市	Heshan City	31.90	36.46	222.32	240.53	182.60	181.52
恩平市	Enping City	32.11	36.68	57.99	62.03	117.80	118.97
阳江市	Yangjiang						
江城区	Jiangcheng District	52.96	57.24	222.77	225.07	291.55	297.61
阳东区	Yangdong District	59.30	58.91	180.70	178.78	102.01	103.75
阳春市	Yangchun City	68.23	66.55	113.74	107.30	184.28	183.77
阳西县	Yangxi County	65.09	68.73	72.90	85.19	97.64	102.11

23-2 续表 2 continued

单位：亿元 (100 million yuan)

县(市、区)	County (County-level City and District)	第一产业 Primary Industry 2021	2022	第二产业 Secondary Industry 2021	2022	第三产业 Tertiary Industry 2021	2022
湛江市	Zhanjiang						
赤坎区	Chikan District	1.40	1.47	77.15	79.09	276.50	281.91
霞山区	Xiashan District	3.11	2.90	188.31	181.53	236.37	244.67
麻章区	Mazhang District	49.46	53.13	463.91	539.42	123.32	126.39
坡头区	Potou District	23.56	24.18	226.00	219.78	101.30	103.57
雷州市	Leizhou City	146.58	153.64	40.18	44.31	167.28	169.33
廉江市	Lianjiang County	132.33	138.82	172.22	180.33	208.62	213.99
吴川市	Wuchuan City	37.40	37.87	103.50	96.57	161.11	163.75
遂溪县	Suixi County	142.24	154.73	89.78	92.49	176.22	179.39
徐闻县	Xuwen County	108.32	116.03	21.21	24.24	88.07	89.00
茂名市	Maoming						
茂南区	Maonan District	36.14	38.11	602.76	659.57	456.36	463.30
电白区	Dianbai District	156.84	165.40	267.91	302.58	340.77	344.52
信宜市	Xinyi City	142.54	158.04	86.72	99.58	295.53	296.26
高州市	Gaozhou City	165.87	185.17	166.53	184.44	353.03	356.08
化州市	Huazhou City	147.47	152.29	153.35	172.73	324.10	326.55
肇庆市	Zhaoqing						
端州区	Duanzhou District	0.23	0.26	144.33	135.83	328.93	332.83
鼎湖区	Dinghu District	11.34	11.92	63.59	70.43	70.03	70.94
高要区	Gaoyao District	108.51	114.51	269.34	289.21	135.36	138.40
四会市	Sihui City	70.41	72.71	386.14	406.22	265.94	264.62
广宁县	Guangning County	57.37	61.35	54.97	54.36	63.88	64.87
德庆县	Deqing County	41.20	44.30	68.15	43.68	62.28	62.96
封开县	Fengkai County	59.96	61.61	54.80	58.69	49.12	50.68
怀集县	Huaiji County	113.16	119.81	65.05	68.52	101.72	106.35
清远市	Qingyuan						
清城区	Qingcheng District	28.00	30.38	308.41	311.24	372.79	376.23
清新区	Qingxin District	55.93	60.09	128.72	124.46	120.90	122.42
英德市	Yingde City	79.97	87.61	159.66	157.16	160.66	160.43
连州市	Lianzhou City	46.76	51.38	49.83	46.14	82.03	82.87
佛冈县	Fogang County	22.71	25.85	75.50	74.23	60.31	61.26
阳山县	Yangshan County	47.18	50.26	24.35	22.94	65.53	67.05
连山县	Lianshan County	11.03	11.70	9.92	10.63	24.37	24.60
连南县	Liannan County	12.24	13.32	17.82	20.78	36.09	38.72
潮州市	Chaozhou						
湘桥区	Xiangqiao District	9.35	9.91	84.87	91.71	211.26	217.11
潮安区	Chaoan District	27.65	28.98	393.36	418.58	197.96	204.11
饶平县	Raoping County	78.98	85.99	103.72	115.23	137.37	141.37
揭阳市	Jieyang						
榕城区	Rongcheng District	13.71	14.22	246.92	230.76	334.78	343.82
揭东区	Jiedong District	43.40	45.77	234.99	216.04	229.56	233.48
普宁市	Puning City	44.21	47.91	206.01	198.96	372.71	382.63
揭西县	Jiexi County	48.46	52.84	75.74	67.10	137.52	141.17
惠来县	Huilai County	58.51	62.94	96.33	80.74	138.12	142.60
云浮市	Yunfu						
云城区	Yuncheng District	19.61	21.14	79.92	86.64	149.39	149.02
云安区	Yunan District	16.84	18.73	68.30	69.17	45.09	46.39
罗定市	Luoding City	64.24	68.11	83.16	83.80	164.67	167.29
新兴县	Xinxing County	76.01	77.49	106.73	107.51	125.86	126.70
郁南县	Yunan County	33.51	33.44	30.30	31.20	74.26	75.81

23-3　各县(市、区)三次产业地区生产总值指数

Gross Domestic Product of the Three Industries by County (County-level City and District)

上年=100　　(preceding year=100)

县(市、区)	County (County-level City and District)	第一产业 Primary Industry		第二产业 Secondary Industry		第三产业 Tertiary Industry	
		2021	2022	2021	2022	2021	2022
广州市	Guangzhou						
越秀区	Yuexiu District			100.8	92.4	106.2	100.4
海珠区	Haizhu District	75.9	91.8	112.2	105.5	108.8	100.6
荔湾区	Liwan District	108.5	102.2	107.0	103.8	108.9	100.1
天河区	Tianhe District	103.4	120.5	105.6	99.6	108.4	102.6
白云区	Baiyun District	94.8	105.2	111.2	96.0	107.3	96.7
黄埔区	Huangpu District	119.3	110.3	107.3	101.2	109.4	101.9
花都区	Huadu District	111.7	104.4	106.0	96.7	106.8	100.3
番禺区	Panyu District	107.2	97.6	114.6	105.6	106.1	99.2
南沙区	Nansha District	107.5	105.2	108.9	106.3	110.4	102.5
从化区	Conghua District	110.6	102.9	98.9	96.1	105.3	98.5
增城区	Zengcheng District	104.8	101.5	110.5	102.2	111.4	105.6
深圳市	Shenzhen						
福田区	Futian District	102.9	101.4	141.5	98.1	106.0	103.6
罗湖区	Luohu District	66.8	93.9	103.8	95.4	106.3	104.0
盐田区	Yantian District	120.3	1641.5	134.1	108.5	107.0	104.3
南山区	Nanshan District	137.7	99.4	111.9	105.9	108.7	102.2
宝安区	Baoan District	125.8	93.5	115.7	104.5	107.0	102.4
龙岗区	Longgang District	100.5	110.6	90.9	104.1	103.1	101.0
龙华区	Longhua District	114.3	88.7	108.1	104.4	111.7	101.7
坪山区	Pingshan District	115.6	105.3	117.5	118.8	101.3	104.2
光明区	Guangming District	101.8	85.2	124.1	106.2	99.8	107.1
珠海市	Zhuhai						
香洲区	Xiangzhou District	73.4	104.8	108.9	105.8	105.6	99.5
金湾区	Jinwan District	126.7	104.5	108.5	108.3	117.4	93.0
斗门区	Doumen District	104.1	108.2	107.0	109.4	100.5	98.6
汕头市	Shantou						
金平区	Jinping District	106.7	106.3	102.3	100.6	109.0	102.1
龙湖区	Longhu District	106.3	101.3	102.3	96.3	109.4	102.4
澄海区	Chenghai District	103.3	104.8	105.8	105.8	107.0	100.1
濠江区	Haojiang District	103.3	106.4	105.7	96.9	108.8	99.8
潮阳区	Chaoyang District	100.6	105.5	105.6	96.3	107.9	102.2
潮南区	Chaonan District	102.0	104.9	105.6	102.4	109.2	100.9
南澳县	Nanao County	101.9	99.5	106.9	107.7	108.8	100.8
佛山市	Foshan						
禅城区	Chancheng District	114.2	106.2	109.7	102.1	107.7	103.7
南海区	Nanhai District	107.9	107.0	108.8	103.1	109.2	101.1
顺德区	Shunde District	104.8	102.3	109.3	102.1	107.2	99.0
高明区	Gaoming District	110.1	116.3	106.3	103.9	110.1	100.3
三水区	Sanshui District	120.7	105.1	109.3	103.0	105.6	99.3
韶关市	Shaoguan						
浈江区	Zhengjiang District	109.5	100.1	102.8	92.6	107.2	101.7
武江区	Wujiang District	114.3	101.3	104.9	98.4	104.5	100.4
曲江区	Qujiang District	118.6	102.3	105.0	91.5	111.0	100.0
乐昌市	Lechang City	118.7	102.2	102.2	98.0	108.2	100.9
南雄市	Nanxiong City	107.1	102.3	94.9	97.3	112.3	101.1
仁化县	Renhua County	106.2	113.2	110.8	108.8	108.0	101.3
始兴县	Shixing County	109.6	106.9	118.4	98.3	114.0	101.6
翁源县	Wengyuan County	117.4	103.2	115.1	97.3	112.8	102.0
新丰县	Xinfeng County	115.4	106.7	97.7	90.9	113.7	100.9
乳源县	Ruyuan County	118.0	115.8	112.0	107.4	116.0	96.0

23-3 续表 1 continued

上年=100 (preceding year=100)

县(市、区)	County (County-level City and District)	第一产业 Primary Industry 2021	2022	第二产业 Secondary Industry 2021	2022	第三产业 Tertiary Industry 2021	2022
河源市	Heyuan						
源城区	Yuancheng District	108.1	104.8	116.0	101.5	105.8	101.0
东源县	Dongyuan County	119.1	108.0	117.3	103.2	107.0	100.2
和平县	Heping County	107.5	101.9	90.1	96.3	106.7	101.1
龙川县	Longchuan County	94.1	103.1	95.9	97.6	109.3	100.2
紫金县	Zijin County	114.5	105.3	109.8	97.3	105.9	99.8
连平县	Lianping County	107.2	105.0	105.6	101.4	104.8	98.8
梅州市	Meizhou						
梅江区	Meijiang District	105.5	106.9	103.2	99.0	105.2	100.7
梅县区	Meixian District	105.1	104.3	105.6	95.3	107.5	101.4
兴宁市	Xingning City	105.6	104.5	115.3	101.2	108.6	99.4
平远县	Pingyuan County	103.0	103.8	100.8	95.8	109.9	101.9
蕉岭县	Jiaoling County	107.8	107.3	100.6	93.7	109.5	102.9
大埔县	Dabu County	104.5	104.4	110.5	90.4	106.5	102.4
丰顺县	Fengshun County	101.1	104.5	96.3	93.9	109.0	103.2
五华县	Wuhua County	108.0	104.6	93.1	97.4	109.4	101.8
惠州市	Huizhou						
惠城区	Huicheng District	120.4	107.4	119.0	106.6	105.3	102.2
惠阳区	Huiyang District	110.8	102.2	116.9	109.1	91.4	95.7
惠东县	Huidong County	118.4	107.0	111.2	108.0	109.1	97.7
博罗县	Boluo County	119.5	106.7	118.0	105.4	104.3	100.4
龙门县	Longmen County	108.1	110.4	113.4	96.9	104.7	111.5
汕尾市	Shanwei						
市城区	Urban District	115.9	107.8	111.2	105.5	110.0	101.1
陆丰市	Lufeng City	106.8	107.4	118.9	87.4	112.9	101.7
海丰县	Haifeng County	108.0	107.1	114.6	104.9	113.8	101.8
陆河县	Luhe County	107.5	105.2	113.5	107.2	110.9	102.2
江门市	Jiangmen						
蓬江区	Pengjiang District	109.9	107.4	112.5	103.4	107.0	103.3
江海区	Jianghai District	110.6	107.7	113.7	102.3	104.4	102.1
新会区	Xinhui District	109.4	107.4	110.3	105.5	107.2	101.9
台山市	Taishan City	111.0	107.4	108.8	104.5	106.8	100.1
开平市	Kaiping City	110.3	106.8	112.2	102.6	103.6	101.7
鹤山市	Heshan City	106.3	106.5	114.1	105.4	105.4	98.9
恩平市	Enping City	110.8	105.0	103.1	104.5	107.9	100.9
阳江市	Yangjiang						
江城区	Jiangcheng District	99.0	101.0	121.6	99.5	105.9	102.4
阳东区	Yangdong District	102.8	102.2	110.8	99.2	106.1	100.7
阳春市	Yangchun City	104.7	103.4	102.4	95.3	108.0	99.1
阳西县	Yangxi County	97.5	100.4	119.5	107.7	110.4	103.7

23-3 续表 2 continued

上年=100 (preceding year =100)

县(市、区)	County (County-level City and District)	第一产业 Primary Industry 2021	第一产业 Primary Industry 2022	第二产业 Secondary Industry 2021	第二产业 Secondary Industry 2022	第三产业 Tertiary Industry 2021	第三产业 Tertiary Industry 2022
湛江市	Zhanjiang						
赤坎区	Chikan District	164.7	131.6	102.8	100.5	108.1	101.2
霞山区	Xiashan District	120.9	88.4	99.4	92.9	105.9	103.1
麻章区	Mazhang District	102.6	107.0	160.4	102.5	109.7	100.8
坡头区	Potou District	110.7	103.8	95.9	93.9	121.1	105.2
雷州市	Leizhou City	105.5	103.8	109.7	107.4	108.7	99.4
廉江市	Lianjiang County	106.7	102.9	110.1	102.5	104.7	100.8
吴川市	Wuchuan City	100.0	102.9	118.1	93.5	102.7	100.6
遂溪县	Suixi County	109.7	105.9	108.2	100.1	107.4	100.3
徐闻县	Xuwen County	104.9	104.3	112.7	109.3	111.2	99.9
茂名市	Maoming						
茂南区	Maonan District	100.7	103.8	100.5	92.7	113.8	101.3
电白区	Dianbai District	107.3	104.7	111.1	106.1	108.2	100.1
信宜市	Xinyi City	106.4	105.1	99.7	104.2	109.8	100.0
高州市	Gaozhou City	107.1	106.1	106.3	103.2	108.4	99.9
化州市	Huazhou City	110.4	105.8	110.0	100.8	106.8	99.9
肇庆市	Zhaoqing						
端州区	Duanzhou District	132.0	109.6	111.5	94.1	105.9	100.2
鼎湖区	Dinghu District	95.6	103.0	118.0	107.5	99.7	98.7
高要区	Gaoyao District	111.0	102.6	118.3	105.9	107.3	99.8
四会市	Sihui City	97.8	104.4	120.5	105.2	107.2	98.2
广宁县	Guangning County	111.3	109.0	105.8	98.2	106.9	99.6
德庆县	Deqing County	111.3	104.6	100.1	63.6	108.7	99.0
封开县	Fengkai County	110.4	100.8	111.0	105.4	108.4	101.2
怀集县	Huaiji County	107.9	103.6	125.7	104.8	110.0	102.7
清远市	Qingyuan						
清城区	Qingcheng District	103.1	106.8	108.4	99.5	103.3	101.9
清新区	Qingxin District	105.9	104.0	99.5	98.5	111.7	100.2
英德市	Yingde City	115.5	111.0	108.9	98.2	110.8	100.0
连州市	Lianzhou City	108.1	107.2	115.7	94.6	106.3	99.8
佛冈县	Fogang County	116.1	109.7	115.2	98.1	108.9	102.4
阳山县	Yangshan County	106.3	105.0	136.3	96.8	105.1	100.6
连山县	Lianshan County	108.5	102.6	145.2	106.9	97.7	100.3
连南县	Liannan County	106.2	105.7	112.4	103.3	110.0	104.3
潮州市	Chaozhou						
湘桥区	Xiangqiao District	104.9	111.5	105.5	103.2	111.9	101.8
潮安区	Chaoan District	106.4	103.5	106.3	101.2	112.2	101.7
饶平县	Raoping County	111.7	105.3	109.2	105.7	110.2	101.4
揭阳市	Jieyang						
榕城区	Rongcheng District	99.3	103.1	104.0	92.7	106.8	103.0
揭东区	Jiedong District	103.5	104.6	106.0	93.3	106.8	101.7
普宁市	Puning City	105.4	105.5	106.2	90.7	107.3	102.8
揭西县	Jiexi County	107.6	107.9	110.8	87.7	104.8	102.6
惠来县	Huilai County	103.7	104.8	110.2	86.8	107.6	103.5
云浮市	Yunfu						
云城区	Yuncheng District	111.6	102.9	107.7	108.5	107.9	99.5
云安区	Yunan District	109.4	105.4	108.2	100.9	110.9	103.8
罗定市	Luoding City	107.7	105.2	96.0	100.2	111.1	101.3
新兴县	Xinxing County	109.0	103.6	111.2	101.7	109.5	100.4
郁南县	Yunan County	114.3	105.3	98.6	101.8	109.6	102.3

23-4 各县(市、区)人均地区生产总值及指数

Per Capita Gross Domestic Product and Growth Rates by County (County-level City and District)

县(市、区)	County (County-level City and District)	绝对数（元） Absolute Figure (yuan) 2021	2022	指数(上年=100) Index(Preceding year=100) 2021	2022
广州市	Guangzhou				
越秀区	Yuexiu District	345837	351402	105.2	100.5
海珠区	Haizhu District	132096	138257	108.8	102.0
荔湾区	Liwan District	101477	107892	112.3	106.4
天河区	Tianhe District	267470	278713	107.0	103.1
白云区	Baiyun District	68012	67599	107.7	98.3
黄埔区	Huangpu District	339499	361029	110.0	104.8
花都区	Huadu District	107314	103692	102.9	97.3
番禺区	Panyu District	96804	96182	104.3	99.0
南沙区	Nansha District	246216	246211	105.3	99.6
从化区	Conghua District	57480	56018	102.2	96.8
增城区	Zengcheng District	83694	86068	107.6	101.3
深圳市	Shenzhen				
福田区	Futian District	341411	358433	107.6	104.4
罗湖区	Luohu District	218516	242839	104.6	109.6
盐田区	Yantian District	353402	384455	110.9	106.0
南山区	Nanshan District	426097	443469	107.2	103.1
宝安区	Baoan District	98486	104154	111.1	102.8
龙岗区	Longgang District	119286	122221	92.7	102.1
龙华区	Longhua District	110561	117477	107.5	104.1
坪山区	Pingshan District	162399	183737	107.8	108.7
光明区	Guangming District	121524	125924	110.7	104.2
珠海市	Zhuhai				
香洲区	Xiangzhou District	187295	191123	103.8	100.9
金湾区	Jinwan District	180997	190468	107.2	103.0
斗门区	Doumen District	76414	81374	101.4	104.0
汕头市	Shantou				
金平区	Jinping District	76536	78830	106.8	101.7
龙湖区	Longhu District	95067	95421	105.1	99.1
澄海区	Chenghai District	55885	58507	105.8	103.3
濠江区	Haojiang District	68748	68427	106.7	98.2
潮阳区	Chaoyang District	32145	32137	105.7	98.7
潮南区	Chaonan District	41021	42137	106.5	101.5
南澳县	Nanao County	54258	55797	105.6	101.5
佛山市	Foshan				
禅城区	Chancheng District	161276	170854	107.5	103.2
南海区	Nanhai District	96406	101178	107.7	102.6
顺德区	Shunde District	125240	128517	107.5	101.2
高明区	Gaoming District	208907	220921	106.7	103.0
三水区	Sanshui District	174386	174541	107.8	97.7
韶关市	Shaoguan				
浈江区	Zhengjiang District	62987	62579	106.6	99.4
武江区	Wujiang District	81083	80403	103.1	98.4
曲江区	Qujiang District	74410	72021	108.8	95.6
乐昌市	Lechang City	35821	36111	109.7	101.0
南雄市	Nanxiong City	36981	37438	106.3	101.0
仁化县	Renhua County	60261	64198	108.7	106.9
始兴县	Shixing County	49799	51358	114.0	102.0
翁源县	Wengyuan County	40099	40871	114.5	100.9
新丰县	Xinfeng County	41881	42389	109.3	99.2
乳源县	Ruyuan County	58306	60914	113.8	102.8

23-4 续表 1 continued

县(市、区)	County (County-level City and District)	绝对数（元） Absolute Figure (yuan) 2021	2022	指数(上年=100) Index(Preceding year=100) 2021	2022
河源市	Heyuan				
源城区	Yuancheng District	74059	75062	106.5	100.8
东源县	Dongyuan County	47834	48931	114.6	101.9
和平县	Heping County	36151	36517	102.2	100.2
龙川县	Longchuan County	28642	28891	104.6	100.3
紫金县	Zijin County	34207	34494	110.5	100.4
连平县	Lianping County	34322	35234	106.3	101.0
梅州市	Meizhou				
梅江区	Meijiang District	65782	65775	104.2	100.0
梅县区	Meixian District	42698	42840	106.0	100.2
兴宁市	Xingning City	25248	25965	110.4	101.6
平远县	Pingyuan County	45268	46037	107.2	101.4
蕉岭县	Jiaoling County	57976	58001	105.9	100.5
大埔县	Dabu County	30440	30909	107.6	101.5
丰顺县	Fengshun County	24798	24842	102.3	100.0
五华县	Wuhua County	19152	19377	105.9	101.2
惠州市	Huizhou				
惠城区	Huicheng District	86222	92299	111.5	104.5
惠阳区	Huiyang District	112335	121651	105.6	105.0
惠东县	Huidong County	68801	72848	110.2	102.3
博罗县	Boluo County	61544	66206	112.2	103.8
龙门县	Longmen County	59251	63701	108.9	105.2
汕尾市	Shanwei				
市城区	Urban District	78916	81873	111.1	102.8
陆丰市	Lufeng City	34179	33710	114.3	97.1
海丰县	Haifeng County	54794	57511	113.1	103.4
陆河县	Luhe County	40387	42542	110.9	104.0
江门市	Jiangmen				
蓬江区	Pengjiang District	96315	100453	107.1	102.6
江海区	Jianghai District	78178	80335	106.2	100.9
新会区	Xinhui District	98447	104220	108.1	104.0
台山市	Taishan City	55190	57259	108.9	104.0
开平市	Kaiping City	58108	60984	107.8	103.1
鹤山市	Heshan City	81671	84980	108.4	101.9
恩平市	Enping City	42943	45063	107.0	102.8
阳江市	Yangjiang				
江城区	Jiangcheng District	69266	70589	109.4	100.9
阳东区	Yangdong District	71230	70890	107.2	99.9
阳春市	Yangchun City	41677	40567	105.2	98.7
阳西县	Yangxi County	54125	58620	108.3	103.5

23-4 续表 2 continued

县(市、区)	County (County-level City and District)	绝对数（元） Absolute Figure (yuan) 2021	2022	指数(上年=100) Index(Preceding year=100) 2021	2022
湛江市	Zhanjiang				
赤坎区	Chikan District	84504	85120	104.4	99.8
霞山区	Xiashan District	64975	64673	101.1	97.7
麻章区	Mazhang District	119948	134181	138.2	101.5
坡头区	Potou District	103317	101736	102.7	97.4
雷州市	Leizhou City	26766	27725	107.5	102.0
廉江市	Lianjiang County	37598	39001	107.0	101.8
吴川市	Wuchuan City	33238	32746	107.2	98.2
遂溪县	Suixi County	49424	51511	108.7	102.0
徐闻县	Xuwen County	34308	36058	108.5	102.7
茂名市	Maoming				
茂南区	Maonan District	104834	109983	104.4	95.9
电白区	Dianbai District	50738	53623	108.5	102.6
信宜市	Xinyi City	51489	53975	105.9	101.4
高州市	Gaozhou City	51540	54632	107.2	102.4
化州市	Huazhou City	48174	49979	107.3	101.1
肇庆市	Zhaoqing				
端州区	Duanzhou District	77935	77113	105.6	98.3
鼎湖区	Dinghu District	68932	71747	104.2	101.2
高要区	Gaoyao District	69198	72969	113.6	103.3
四会市	Sihui City	112119	114904	111.4	102.1
广宁县	Guangning County	43201	44710	108.2	103.3
德庆县	Deqing County	51763	45088	105.9	85.9
封开县	Fengkai County	43751	45305	110.3	101.6
怀集县	Huaiji County	34755	36775	112.3	104.1
清远市	Qingyuan				
清城区	Qingcheng District	62944	63591	104.0	100.9
清新区	Qingxin District	49465	49640	106.1	100.1
英德市	Yingde City	42476	42925	110.9	101.5
连州市	Lianzhou City	47306	47748	109.1	100.5
佛冈县	Fogang County	50153	50978	112.7	101.4
阳山县	Yangshan County	37291	38127	109.7	101.5
连山县	Lianshan County	47553	49170	107.5	102.1
连南县	Liannan County	48959	53761	109.6	104.1
潮州市	Chaozhou				
湘桥区	Xiangqiao District	52993	55197	110.0	102.3
潮安区	Chaoan District	52607	55287	108.3	101.2
饶平县	Raoping County	39150	41832	110.7	103.6
揭阳市	Jieyang				
榕城区	Rongcheng District	63653	62639	105.4	98.2
揭东区	Jiedong District	54365	52845	106.2	97.7
普宁市	Puning City	31015	31148	106.8	98.9
揭西县	Jiexi County	38827	38694	108.3	99.0
惠来县	Huilai County	28021	27203	107.7	97.7
云浮市	Yunfu				
云城区	Yuncheng District	60822	62611	107.0	102.3
云安区	Yunan District	55183	56720	109.3	102.1
罗定市	Luoding City	33210	33857	105.8	101.5
新兴县	Xinxing County	71543	72127	109.8	101.5
郁南县	Yunan County	37088	37645	108.2	102.7

注：本表中，绝对数按当年价格计算，指数按可比价格计算。
Note: In this table, the absolute figures are calculated at current prices, and indices are calculated at comparable prices.

23−5 各县(市、区)规模以上工业、农林牧渔业总产值

Gross Output Value of Industry Enterprises above Designated Size and Agriculture by County (County-level City and District)

单位：万元 (10000 yuan)

县(市、区)	County(County-level City and District)	规模以上工业总产值 Gross Output Value of Industry Enterprises above Designated Size		农林牧渔业总产值 Gross Output Value of Agriculture	
		2021	2022	2021	2022
广州市	Guangzhou				
越秀区	Yuexiu District	747491	749349		
海珠区	Haizhu District	6827143	8092610	20824	20798
荔湾区	Liwan District	3731577	3656861	79303	82830
天河区	Tianhe District	9881616	10576627	96907	103492
白云区	Baiyun District	11888076	11349596	639388	682812
黄埔区	Huangpu District	89305478	89985962	84914	95125
花都区	Huadu District	28057691	25450966	869677	926465
番禺区	Panyu District	23456795	26712636	673501	650739
南沙区	Nansha District	35683830	40152040	1226562	1330324
从化区	Conghua District	5133642	5025300	592087	615819
增城区	Zengcheng District	16496685	17533878	1142341	1179282
深圳市	Shenzhen				
福田区	Futian District	24523414	18899969	41067	44157
罗湖区	Luohu District	11192393	12618400	7219	8459
盐田区	Yantian District	9680759	10768623	2715	5146
南山区	Nanshan District	68171843	75788627	29547	25784
宝安区	Baoan District	93590366	97234883	20522	21473
龙岗区	Longgang District	95520843	106392747	43961	49675
龙华区	Longhua District	58248768	64324368	9686	10123
坪山区	Pingshan District	22128121	34666107	20601	22437
光明区	Guangming District	35414965	40895195	44601	43080
珠海市	Zhuhai				
香洲区	Xiangzhou District	21691195	22762985	56070	65021
金湾区	Jinwan District	22461760	26611903	182337	231526
斗门区	Doumen District	8571441	9786012	750961	917599
汕头市	Shantou				
金平区	Jinping District	4852388	4816561	55059	60639
龙湖区	Longhu District	4776157	4954961	157755	169427
澄海区	Chenghai District	3007891	3425904	817101	902866
濠江区	Haojiang District	2715814	2776857	144396	157950
潮阳区	Chaoyang District	8677301	7684355	582284	623568
潮南区	Chaonan District	9711368	10324994	367520	398312
南澳县	Nanao County	41049	58120	236246	236775
佛山市	Foshan				
禅城区	Chancheng District	19727308	21902425	13485	14241
南海区	Nanhai District	70285149	74072719	1126573	1259584
顺德区	Shunde District	95691725	100583612	1312633	1340028
高明区	Gaoming District	36948612	40749915	594472	737042
三水区	Sanshui District	40472039	42345485	895253	943145
韶关市	Shaoguan				
浈江区	Zhengjiang District	1602409	1828285	146805	151187
武江区	Wujiang District	1870298	1707374	156494	143054
曲江区	Qujiang District	6426896	5772211	372245	359711
乐昌市	Lechang City	646850	619308	531556	525444
南雄市	Nanxiong City	773870	769904	615905	631070
仁化县	Renhua County	928857	1132471	384536	416771
始兴县	Shixing County	885000	811936	418564	443435
翁源县	Wengyuan County	924602	952079	566703	615996
新丰县	Xinfeng County	575825	543468	258819	289241
乳源县	Ruyuan County	1817673	2040999	152506	177942

23-5 续表 1 continued

单位：万元 (10000 yuan)

县(市、区)	County(County-level City and District)	规模以上工业总产值 Gross Output Value of Industry Enterprises above Designated Size		农林牧渔业总产值 Gross Output Value of Agriculture	
		2021	2022	2021	2022
河源市	Heyuan				
源城区	Yuancheng District	8192018	8552645	59881	65661
东源县	Dongyuan County	1987018	1667173	458052	491799
和平县	Heping County	746514	650984	417136	430776
龙川县	Longchuan County	1291114	1231206	493817	509657
紫金县	Zijin County	1542052	1637186	657637	689815
连平县	Lianping County	838089	859044	319052	349818
梅州市	Meizhou				
梅江区	Meijiang District	2847321	2796790	128891	142427
梅县区	Meixian District	1879818	1932497	901960	947985
兴宁市	Xingning City	733417	807489	828255	869357
平远县	Pingyuan County	512379	457285	239560	254743
蕉岭县	Jiaoling County	967399	795245	274927	297652
大埔县	Dabu County	497818	436729	431772	449403
丰顺县	Fengshun County	860062	947695	419418	439792
五华县	Wuhua County	356383	413046	661245	708005
惠州市	Huizhou				
惠城区	Huicheng District	36897458	38618029	595048	675434
惠阳区	Huiyang District	44684490	52713820	368987	384621
惠东县	Huidong County	3429540	3877087	1099682	1257747
博罗县	Boluo County	13128392	14573516	1284179	1421942
龙门县	Longmen County	1352894	1212106	526693	602754
汕尾市	Shanwei				
市城区	Urban District	4470376	4902706	588944	656257
陆丰市	Lufeng City	5133466	2980821	1239013	1377875
海丰县	Haifeng County	4139246	3567640	698976	764918
陆河县	Luhe County	882478	1059217	257466	293380
江门市	Jiangmen				
蓬江区	Pengjiang District	11776424	11999141	131981	161354
江海区	Jianghai District	6740638	6604854	107503	128165
新会区	Xinhui District	13662649	14406655	1070418	1128277
台山市	Taishan City	7034946	7244873	1912205	2252867
开平市	Kaiping City	5084601	5436623	1021613	1092619
鹤山市	Heshan City	8271721	8524771	607525	635771
恩平市	Enping City	1940939	2100117	571206	552904
阳江市	Yangjiang				
江城区	Jiangcheng District	13030177	14772611	860232	930471
阳东区	Yangdong District	3319092	3453682	992590	1000475
阳春市	Yangchun City	3286506	2914240	1202553	1188256
阳西县	Yangxi County	1610427	2066441	1015199	1084063

23−5 续表 2 continued

单位：万元 (10000 yuan)

县(市、区)	County (County-level City and District)	规模以上工业总产值 Gross Output Value of Industry Enterprises above Designated Size		农林牧渔业总产值 Gross Output Value of Agriculture	
		2021	2022	2021	2022
湛江市	Zhanjiang				
赤坎区	Chikan District	1106927	1149511	21685	23216
霞山区	Xiashan District	3135865	3558805	48352	46361
麻章区	Mazhang District	16520708	19777316	801828	868130
坡头区	Potou District	3013119	3426287	389842	395580
雷州市	Leizhou City	705913	808255	2316949	2425851
廉江市	Lianjiang County	1710111	1585156	2191400	2287562
吴川市	Wuchuan City	1029131	942889	675240	706942
遂溪县	Suixi County	2051376	2130004	2303768	2480945
徐闻县	Xuwen County	244849	333055	1683363	1806211
茂名市	Maoming				
茂南区	Maonan District	16804234	17975702	600199	602374
电白区	Dianbai District	2935501	3850105	2614285	2766526
信宜市	Xinyi City	229339	279485	2170644	2459654
高州市	Gaozhou City	1331747	1462595	2705029	3020354
化州市	Huazhou City	1009868	1207836	2337379	2451331
肇庆市	Zhaoqing				
端州区	Duanzhou District	3166128	3117007	3669	4019
鼎湖区	Dinghu District	2101140	2490869	232606	243253
高要区	Gaoyao District	11748061	11892079	1714702	1806470
四会市	Sihui City	19321887	21221504	1148001	1182059
广宁县	Guangning County	2123433	2163678	813805	867470
德庆县	Deqing County	2530707	1193625	655966	702527
封开县	Fengkai County	996094	987109	973351	997761
怀集县	Huaiji County	742107	788266	1675408	1790619
清远市	Qingyuan				
清城区	Qingcheng District	14509545	14862128	514627	566028
清新区	Qingxin District	4118938	3960635	900325	973175
英德市	Yingde City	5071296	4699560	1448948	1577607
连州市	Lianzhou City	1156470	1095698	769498	841342
佛冈县	Fogang County	3438661	3336084	353729	401171
阳山县	Yangshan County	226508	227511	747203	791633
连山县	Lianshan County	47940	65816	166366	175517
连南县	Liannan County	77932	85131	181999	197977
潮州市	Chaozhou				
湘桥区	Xiangqiao District	3715367	3302031	148598	155873
潮安区	Chaoan District	7956679	7584704	465916	484629
饶平县	Raoping County	2915964	2992551	1348226	1459396
揭阳市	Jieyang				
榕城区	Rongcheng District	8748105	8396148	211025	214398
揭东区	Jiedong District	9586915	8038356	673017	706573
普宁市	Puning City	6093939	4795518	655252	709331
揭西县	Jiexi County	2139343	1661004	826707	891755
惠来县	Huilai County	2438173	2137113	944394	1021712
云浮市	Yunfu				
云城区	Yuncheng District	1422214	1968932	310478	330863
云安区	Yunan District	1390035	1312356	261482	288350
罗定市	Luoding City	1458006	1421507	994289	1045061
新兴县	Xinxing County	1945357	1944601	1360763	1385381
郁南县	Yunan County	497056	521791	537668	532232

注：本表按当年价格计算。
Note: The data in this table are calculated at current prices.

23-6 各县(市、区)粮食产量
Output of Grain by County (County-level City and District)

单位：吨 (ton)

县(市、区)	County (County-level City and District)	粮食 Grain 2021	粮食 Grain 2022	#稻谷 Rice 2021	#稻谷 Rice 2022
广州市	Guangzhou				
越秀区	Yuexiu District				
海珠区	Haizhu District				
荔湾区	Liwan District				
天河区	Tianhe District				
白云区	Baiyun District	3120	3141	1114	2090
黄埔区	Huangpu District	2658	2706	1412	1772
花都区	Huadu District	11120	11206	3464	3668
番禺区	Panyu District	698	1304	315	553
南沙区	Nansha District	7032	7221	3933	5021
从化区	Conghua District	72686	73218	65622	64900
增城区	Zengcheng District	53455	55044	47049	47874
深圳市	Shenzhen				
福田区	Futian District				
罗湖区	Luohu District				
盐田区	Yantian District				
南山区	Nanshan District				
宝安区	Baoan District				
龙岗区	Longgang District	151	212	30	58
龙华区	Longhua District				
坪山区	Pingshan District				
光明区	Guangming District	146	940	135	110
珠海市	Zhuhai				
香洲区	Xiangzhou District	120	166	34	47
金湾区	Jinwan District	2087	2810	1322	1629
斗门区	Doumen District	26321	26972	24480	24726
汕头市	Shantou				
金平区	Jinping District	10759	10623	10536	10403
龙湖区	Longhu District	20477	20243	15495	15688
澄海区	Chenghai District	91333	91947	71880	72508
濠江区	Haojiang District	15068	15219	8474	8633
潮阳区	Chaoyang District	161414	163382	106659	107894
潮南区	Chaonan District	156544	156976	106879	106765
南澳县	Nanao County	3783	3855	1860	1758
佛山市	Foshan				
禅城区	Chancheng District				
南海区	Nanhai District	3787	5017	1946	3658
顺德区	Shunde District	168	213		
高明区	Gaoming District	35263	32238	30226	27147
三水区	Sanshui District	9396	12040	4923	8278
韶关市	Shaoguan				
浈江区	Zhengjiang District	19570	19913	18010	18413
武江区	Wujiang District	24559	24724	22990	22948
曲江区	Qujiang District	75931	76042	70483	69824
乐昌市	Lechang City	89940	90494	73007	72358
南雄市	Nanxiong City	207245	209679	189913	191783
仁化县	Renhua County	69343	69308	65520	58065
始兴县	Shixing County	74068	74831	69076	68971
翁源县	Wengyuan County	95260	95324	88235	88119
新丰县	Xinfeng County	54414	54690	48855	49456
乳源县	Ruyuan County	43892	44022	37240	36795

23-6 续表 1 continued

单位：吨 (ton)

县(市、区)	County (County-level City and District)	粮食 Grain 2021	粮食 Grain 2022	#稻谷 Rice 2021	#稻谷 Rice 2022
河源市	Heyuan				
源城区	Yuancheng District	11345	11370	10768	10198
东源县	Dongyuan County	153825	154443	146892	147276
和平县	Heping County	117956	118869	112392	113215
龙川县	Longchuan County	238790	239223	227484	227059
紫金县	Zijin County	199654	200643	190611	190966
连平县	Lianping County	89973	90895	85460	86077
梅州市	Meizhou				
梅江区	Meijiang District	22739	23034	17441	17914
梅县区	Meixian District	175410	161811	163600	150524
兴宁市	Xingning City	293526	293531	283956	282978
平远县	Pingyuan County	78016	80819	66192	70097
蕉岭县	Jiaoling County	66032	68008	61411	62643
大埔县	Dabu County	36556	45783	31154	40336
丰顺县	Fengshun County	119428	119304	102558	101877
五华县	Wuhua County	345191	345414	332275	330814
惠州市	Huizhou				
惠城区	Huicheng District	95331	81414	69037	65021
惠阳区	Huiyang District	44055	43003	25070	24476
惠东县	Huidong County	202061	205269	151259	149812
博罗县	Boluo County	155743	161227	124403	127216
龙门县	Longmen County	111879	112814	104906	106665
汕尾市	Shanwei				
市城区	Urban District	24509	25510	20396	22136
陆丰市	Lufeng City	181848	182120	155759	154707
海丰县	Haifeng County	169959	179950	151180	156632
陆河县	Luhe County	56954	57000	49860	50764
江门市	Jiangmen				
蓬江区	Pengjiang District	2301	2331	1360	1258
江海区	Jianghai District	422	639	371	586
新会区	Xinhui District	139659	136350	120442	117462
台山市	Taishan City	402672	404140	383356	384048
开平市	Kaiping City	232916	234877	217791	219289
鹤山市	Heshan City	63717	61280	56692	54191
恩平市	Enping City	144924	150706	139317	144757
阳江市	Yangjiang				
江城区	Jiangcheng District	81951	58256	78169	54876
阳东区	Yangdong District	136075	136966	122435	123753
阳春市	Yangchun City	274587	275747	246322	250912
阳西县	Yangxi County	129043	129595	117997	119710

23-6 续表 2 continued

单位：吨 (ton)

县(市、区)	County (County-level City and District)	粮食 Grain 2021	粮食 Grain 2022	#稻谷 Rice 2021	#稻谷 Rice 2022
湛江市	Zhanjiang				
赤坎区	Chikan District	1923	1913	1645	1661
霞山区	Xiashan District	4412	4626	4158	3673
麻章区	Mazhang District	84495	86511	73592	75239
坡头区	Potou District	65539	65711	56080	56364
雷州市	Leizhou City	376768	391372	336904	342570
廉江市	Lianjiang County	432309	435450	360371	362123
吴川市	Wuchuan City	170454	165619	156852	151602
遂溪县	Suixi County	246828	259217	198736	199753
徐闻县	Xuwen County	135280	136008	77854	77391
茂名市	Maoming				
茂南区	Maonan District	136017	136127	119902	119507
电白区	Dianbai District	298717	299186	265681	266266
信宜市	Xinyi City	344538	344800	261217	259893
高州市	Gaozhou City	405023	405147	387814	386350
化州市	Huazhou City	345845	346463	307108	305712
肇庆市	Zhaoqing				
端州区	Duanzhou District				
鼎湖区	Dinghu District	35536	35713	30063	29858
高要区	Gaoyao District	237818	240599	214495	217754
四会市	Sihui City	122210	122827	91334	92222
广宁县	Guangning County	180182	181273	153322	154143
德庆县	Deqing County	138480	139544	128591	128976
封开县	Fengkai County	216852	218907	194003	195728
怀集县	Huaiji County	293210	294747	268642	269154
清远市	Qingyuan				
清城区	Qingcheng District	69123	69232	66420	65985
清新区	Qingxin District	130403	131120	121458	121984
英德市	Yingde City	192018	192305	170705	169267
连州市	Lianzhou City	109172	109746	94645	94902
佛冈县	Fogang County	57405	57770	55179	55324
阳山县	Yangshan County	101267	101495	70797	69463
连山县	Lianshan County	40490	40745	37665	37889
连南县	Liannan County	33726	33878	21221	21714
潮州市	Chaozhou				
湘桥区	Xiangqiao District	24679	25457	19811	20427
潮安区	Chaoan District	96335	99976	75197	77765
饶平县	Raoping County	148656	152980	123713	128082
揭阳市	Jieyang				
榕城区	Rongcheng District	71036	71942	56557	57011
揭东区	Jiedong District	179852	182283	111414	110878
普宁市	Puning City	195992	197204	132154	133502
揭西县	Jiexi County	176498	177459	119522	120490
惠来县	Huilai County	178281	185287	100599	104155
云浮市	Yunfu				
云城区	Yuncheng District	49628	50776	45349	45990
云安区	Yunan District	70681	70765	56747	55950
罗定市	Luoding City	247899	247945	231388	231528
新兴县	Xinxing County	139847	139900	133372	133176
郁南县	Yunan County	133107	133100	120249	120879

23-7 各县(市、区)糖蔗、水果和蔬菜产量

Output of Sugarcane,Fruits and Vegetable by County (County-level City and District)

单位：吨 (ton)

县(市、区)	County (County-level City and District)	糖蔗 Sugarcane 2021	糖蔗 Sugarcane 2022	水果 Fruits 2021	水果 Fruits 2022	蔬菜 Vegetable 2021	蔬菜 Vegetable 2022
广州市	Guangzhou						
越秀区	Yuexiu District						
海珠区	Haizhu District			3993	3210	12359	13220
荔湾区	Liwan District					2945	2913
天河区	Tianhe District			367	228	6298	6424
白云区	Baiyun District			13151	10987	799689	846669
黄埔区	Huangpu District			16568	17519	63937	55332
花都区	Huadu District			28802	26293	539884	541002
番禺区	Panyu District			8251	7987	186433	181504
南沙区	Nansha District			261600	261774	710086	718948
从化区	Conghua District			147862	137530	318674	321094
增城区	Zengcheng District			338806	353030	1398105	1428580
深圳市	Shenzhen						
福田区	Futian District						
罗湖区	Luohu District			64	12	95	94
盐田区	Yantian District			2	1		2
南山区	Nanshan District			11812	4368	160	133
宝安区	Baoan District			1104	1234	22887	25095
龙岗区	Longgang District	57	361	547	512	22674	22830
龙华区	Longhua District				4	8975	8852
坪山区	Pingshan District			669	429	37436	39646
光明区	Guangming District			856	232	41332	40845
珠海市	Zhuhai						
香洲区	Xiangzhou District			5944	3397	4652	4580
金湾区	Jinwan District			76506	77156	45828	46359
斗门区	Doumen District			21165	19523	87920	89085
汕头市	Shantou						
金平区	Jinping District			1074	1084	46001	46738
龙湖区	Longhu District			204	330	211994	215102
澄海区	Chenghai District			112503	112690	712591	739918
濠江区	Haojiang District			769	905	62005	62310
潮阳区	Chaoyang District			148002	151686	349139	345478
潮南区	Chaonan District			34388	40675	372733	384427
南澳县	Nanao County			5140	5228	12278	12360
佛山市	Foshan						
禅城区	Chancheng District					3131	3344
南海区	Nanhai District			3538	3705	296959	308797
顺德区	Shunde District			8486	6698	86864	76689
高明区	Gaoming District			11302	11856	177006	180911
三水区	Sanshui District			23943	19019	288644	281886
韶关市	Shaoguan						
浈江区	Zhengjiang District			19957	20353	72720	67858
武江区	Wujiang District			12152	12918	87267	90197
曲江区	Qujiang District			38769	39690	112717	110415
乐昌市	Lechang City	204	20	175325	192216	257452	277689
南雄市	Nanxiong City			59131	63951	236472	253031
仁化县	Renhua County			141803	137006	103052	134714
始兴县	Shixing County	393	373	103359	132068	171465	184525
翁源县	Wengyuan County	27241	24744	71434	57561	137586	131093
新丰县	Xinfeng County	670	344	36878	35578	184699	187138
乳源县	Ruyuan County			13587	23021	59932	62902

23-7 续表 1 continued

单位：吨 (ton)

县(市、区)	County (County-level City and District)	糖蔗 Sugarcane 2021	糖蔗 Sugarcane 2022	水果 Fruits 2021	水果 Fruits 2022	蔬菜 Vegetable 2021	蔬菜 Vegetable 2022
河源市	Heyuan						
源城区	Yuancheng District	860		5092	5118	42314	45545
东源县	Dongyuan County	27058	25546	39906	42132	121623	127826
和平县	Heping County			42021	49037	140439	143702
龙川县	Longchuan County			83878	85648	156107	160809
紫金县	Zijin County			157568	160315	222244	235567
连平县	Lianping County			119955	130033	114919	117653
梅州市	Meizhou						
梅江区	Meijiang District			43898	41915	114513	122149
梅县区	Meixian District			800564	836594	500888	519971
兴宁市	Xingning City			178617	178861	814266	874518
平远县	Pingyuan County			93633	94121	70323	74697
蕉岭县	Jiaoling County	5472	2265	58149	61334	129990	144163
大埔县	Dabu County			223418	228195	206683	214423
丰顺县	Fengshun County			65473	68339	222547	232890
五华县	Wuhua County			91038	99622	395657	409452
惠州市	Huizhou						
惠城区	Huicheng District	2898	2735	47856	52269	588061	608786
惠阳区	Huiyang District	840		45515	47869	506069	550982
惠东县	Huidong County			124395	147386	900606	921842
博罗县	Boluo County	60611	45656	241662	259902	1064751	1100032
龙门县	Longmen County	5057	5111	501551	516711	339122	360401
汕尾市	Shanwei						
市城区	Urban District			14222	14519	76177	79644
陆丰市	Lufeng City			116675	148886	728197	749809
海丰县	Haifeng County	4964	5023	70152	77106	525000	553540
陆河县	Luhe County			122811	126776	110391	111865
江门市	Jiangmen						
蓬江区	Pengjiang District			2914	3160	80821	80766
江海区	Jianghai District			7786	7114	50274	54274
新会区	Xinhui District	2967	2587	171329	179514	190858	215338
台山市	Taishan City		153	82375	77611	561167	642101
开平市	Kaiping City			57061	57590	401326	441062
鹤山市	Heshan City			22346	22790	315079	324808
恩平市	Enping City	76808	73198	57464	55208	212214	216106
阳江市	Yangjiang						
江城区	Jiangcheng District			14278	17344	97676	99002
阳东区	Yangdong District	6170	3967	70747	70210	214213	222841
阳春市	Yangchun City	8744	8499	282494	284062	432713	447914
阳西县	Yangxi County			46389	47800	210038	213916

23−7 续表 2 continued

单位：吨 (ton)

县(市、区)	County (County-level City and District)	糖蔗 Sugarcane 2021	糖蔗 Sugarcane 2022	水果 Fruits 2021	水果 Fruits 2022	蔬菜 Vegetable 2021	蔬菜 Vegetable 2022
湛江市	Zhanjiang						
赤坎区	Chikan District	876		297	314	20781	18497
霞山区	Xiashan District			445	488	17665	12269
麻章区	Mazhang District	296228	310607	91554	89034	117268	134612
坡头区	Potou District	13665	16411	22030	20354	100653	107970
雷州市	Leizhou City	4237285	4249447	836567	864445	1008314	1040896
廉江市	Lianjiang County	325232	306156	486953	522964	1077001	1119521
吴川市	Wuchuan City	40058	81442	81614	77072	167395	189783
遂溪县	Suixi County	4275670	4228545	450055	484951	992890	1033314
徐闻县	Xuwen County	1000693	938816	1208876	1229940	895739	882476
茂名市	Maoming						
茂南区	Maonan District	16042	23817	51266	47927	396124	398074
电白区	Dianbai District	4680	5003	435268	442851	1009028	1050524
信宜市	Xinyi City			1202669	1255110	596206	631344
高州市	Gaozhou City	10167	10146	1954681	1981291	960452	1004753
化州市	Huazhou City	470833	491721	792616	848167	751642	786809
肇庆市	Zhaoqing						
端州区	Duanzhou District			864	764	5061	5102
鼎湖区	Dinghu District			25563	25929	122002	123795
高要区	Gaoyao District			210637	224586	1092704	1126697
四会市	Sihui City			183222	186363	323665	335055
广宁县	Guangning County			180856	181213	283512	284994
德庆县	Deqing County			494007	545199	291282	302325
封开县	Fengkai County	10985	11328	477216	477508	363459	371197
怀集县	Huaiji County	191	193	519190	535393	643981	669564
清远市	Qingyuan						
清城区	Qingcheng District	6123	3345	37559	41153	273880	288365
清新区	Qingxin District			279760	287403	698394	708760
英德市	Yingde City	241781	199815	63971	45806	861391	823625
连州市	Lianzhou City	115	13	144015	161291	833486	866682
佛冈县	Fogang County			125530	154259	241505	264396
阳山县	Yangshan County	255	158	90012	99211	701085	783424
连山县	Lianshan County			38605	42109	148435	155929
连南县	Liannan County			24513	26606	148121	156592
潮州市	Chaozhou						
湘桥区	Xiangqiao District			82905	85447	70845	72713
潮安区	Chaoan District			52671	47245	179225	177084
饶平县	Raoping County			163039	159529	303099	320160
揭阳市	Jieyang						
榕城区	Rongcheng District			40398	42460	204714	214991
揭东区	Jiedong District			40656	44449	669322	690756
普宁市	Puning City			266697	290778	471236	503286
揭西县	Jiexi County			175098	206355	381104	406562
惠来县	Huilai County			145112	150792	470561	478297
云浮市	Yunfu						
云城区	Yuncheng District			39279	42718	35603	36919
云安区	Yunan District			65897	65120	64851	74668
罗定市	Luoding City			77479	87244	120796	121689
新兴县	Xinxing County			130761	134579	376190	390177
郁南县	Yunan County			207060	198723	41253	39053

23-8　各县(市、区)猪肉产量、禽肉产量

Output of Pork and Output of Meat of Poultry by County (County-level City and District)

单位：万吨　　(10000 tons)

县(市、区)	County (County-level City and District)	猪肉产量 Output of Pork		禽肉产量 Output of Meat of Poultry	
		2021	2022	2021	2022
广州市	Guangzhou				
越秀区	Yuexiu District				
海珠区	Haizhu District				
荔湾区	Liwan District				
天河区	Tianhe District				
白云区	Baiyun District	0.31	0.39	0.80	0.83
黄埔区	Huangpu District				
花都区	Huadu District	1.16	1.23	0.70	0.60
番禺区	Panyu District			0.47	0.42
南沙区	Nansha District	0.73	0.83	0.31	0.31
从化区	Conghua District	1.73	1.85	0.71	0.79
增城区	Zengcheng District	0.76	0.76	2.10	1.45
深圳市	Shenzhen				
福田区	Futian District				
罗湖区	Luohu District				
盐田区	Yantian District				
南山区	Nanshan District				
宝安区	Baoan District				
龙岗区	Longgang District				
龙华区	Longhua District				
坪山区	Pingshan District				
光明区	Guangming District			0.02	0.02
珠海市	Zhuhai				
香洲区	Xiangzhou District				
金湾区	Jinwan District			0.07	0.09
斗门区	Doumen District	0.35	0.81	0.18	0.12
汕头市	Shantou				
金平区	Jinping District			…	…
龙湖区	Longhu District	0.06	0.02	0.76	0.79
澄海区	Chenghai District	1.13	1.26	2.90	3.55
濠江区	Haojiang District	0.22	0.19	0.08	0.07
潮阳区	Chaoyang District	1.27	1.32	0.30	0.10
潮南区	Chaonan District	1.58	1.69	0.03	0.03
南澳县	Nanao County	0.09	0.07	0.03	0.03
佛山市	Foshan				
禅城区	Chancheng District				
南海区	Nanhai District	1.15	1.26	0.60	0.32
顺德区	Shunde District	0.70	0.83	0.17	0.05
高明区	Gaoming District	1.61	2.12	2.02	2.70
三水区	Sanshui District	3.07	3.71	5.75	6.22
韶关市	Shaoguan				
浈江区	Zhengjiang District	1.07	1.14	0.09	0.07
武江区	Wujiang District	1.30	1.32	0.16	0.14
曲江区	Qujiang District	3.22	3.33	0.84	0.78
乐昌市	Lechang City	3.63	3.42	0.26	0.29
南雄市	Nanxiong City	3.48	3.48	1.31	1.40
仁化县	Renhua County	1.69	1.74	0.69	0.51
始兴县	Shixing County	1.53	1.41	0.48	0.40
翁源县	Wengyuan County	3.48	4.31	2.54	3.09
新丰县	Xinfeng County	1.07	1.33	1.12	1.44
乳源县	Ruyuan County	0.88	1.36	0.14	0.11

23−8 续表 1 continued

单位：万吨 (10000 tons)

县(市、区)	County (County-level City and District)	猪肉产量 Output of Pork		禽肉产量 Output of Meat of Poultry	
		2021	2022	2021	2022
河源市	Heyuan				
源城区	Yuancheng District	…	…	0.74	0.73
东源县	Dongyuan County	2.17	2.57	1.42	1.65
和平县	Heping County	1.89	1.85	1.51	1.62
龙川县	Longchuan County	2.62	2.61	0.94	1.04
紫金县	Zijin County	1.93	2.05	1.74	1.85
连平县	Lianping County	1.49	1.68	0.65	0.75
梅州市	Meizhou				
梅江区	Meijiang District	0.29	0.34	0.20	0.13
梅县区	Meixian District	2.43	2.49	1.36	1.21
兴宁市	Xingning City	3.68	3.73	2.12	2.25
平远县	Pingyuan County	0.87	1.03	0.31	0.32
蕉岭县	Jiaoling County	1.25	1.32	0.51	0.60
大埔县	Dabu County	1.24	1.49	0.83	0.82
丰顺县	Fengshun County	1.30	1.31	3.20	3.35
五华县	Wuhua County	4.06	4.19	1.64	1.75
惠州市	Huizhou				
惠城区	Huicheng District	1.30	1.67	0.79	0.70
惠阳区	Huiyang District	0.09	0.11	0.20	0.20
惠东县	Huidong County	4.36	4.37	1.18	1.40
博罗县	Boluo County	3.80	3.98	4.53	4.75
龙门县	Longmen County	1.01	1.22	0.78	0.88
汕尾市	Shanwei				
市城区	Urban District	0.49	0.44	0.26	0.25
陆丰市	Lufeng City	3.80	3.98	1.43	1.52
海丰县	Haifeng County	1.82	1.99	0.82	0.93
陆河县	Luhe County	1.01	1.05	0.38	0.43
江门市	Jiangmen				
蓬江区	Pengjiang District			0.27	0.10
江海区	Jianghai District			0.01	0.01
新会区	Xinhui District	1.83	2.14	3.14	2.73
台山市	Taishan City	4.23	4.19	1.55	2.92
开平市	Kaiping City	3.94	4.05	7.07	7.35
鹤山市	Heshan City	2.50	2.81	2.09	1.76
恩平市	Enping City	4.00	4.40	1.25	1.73
阳江市	Yangjiang				
江城区	Jiangcheng District	1.59	1.63	0.39	0.38
阳东区	Yangdong District	4.44	4.83	1.29	1.31
阳春市	Yangchun City	11.66	11.89	1.59	1.72
阳西县	Yangxi County	2.85	2.96	1.32	1.38

23-8 续表 2 continued

单位：万吨 (10000 tons)

县(市、区)	County (County-level City and District)	猪肉产量 Output of Pork 2021	猪肉产量 Output of Pork 2022	禽肉产量 Output of Meat of Poultry 2021	禽肉产量 Output of Meat of Poultry 2022
湛江市	Zhanjiang				
赤坎区	Chikan District			0.01	0.01
霞山区	Xiashan District			0.04	0.03
麻章区	Mazhang District	1.65	1.61	0.73	0.69
坡头区	Potou District	1.90	1.89	0.48	0.44
雷州市	Leizhou City	3.67	4.59	1.66	1.55
廉江市	Lianjiang County	10.66	11.12	2.93	2.91
吴川市	Wuchuan City	2.59	2.71	2.71	2.53
遂溪县	Suixi County	7.24	8.13	4.27	5.12
徐闻县	Xuwen County	1.40	2.10	0.73	0.59
茂名市	Maoming				
茂南区	Maonan District	4.44	4.96	3.55	4.10
电白区	Dianbai District	9.98	10.14	5.11	4.58
信宜市	Xinyi City	7.15	7.41	11.65	11.39
高州市	Gaozhou City	10.33	11.11	6.60	7.18
化州市	Huazhou City	13.07	13.60	3.25	3.13
肇庆市	Zhaoqing				
端州区	Duanzhou District				
鼎湖区	Dinghu District	0.19		0.35	0.35
高要区	Gaoyao District	6.18	6.03	5.71	6.18
四会市	Sihui City	3.05	3.79	5.36	5.41
广宁县	Guangning County	4.24	4.25	1.37	1.59
德庆县	Deqing County	0.87	0.59	0.99	0.94
封开县	Fengkai County	2.73	2.73	1.06	0.83
怀集县	Huaiji County	7.31	7.72	2.48	2.39
清远市	Qingyuan				
清城区	Qingcheng District	1.70	1.64	4.76	4.83
清新区	Qingxin District	2.82	2.87	4.39	4.32
英德市	Yingde City	7.69	8.99	2.92	3.93
连州市	Lianzhou City	3.27	3.44	0.77	0.88
佛冈县	Fogang County	1.31	1.38	0.41	0.43
阳山县	Yangshan County	4.31	4.02	1.97	2.19
连山县	Lianshan County	0.69	0.68	0.23	0.25
连南县	Liannan County	0.27	0.26	0.44	0.40
潮州市	Chaozhou				
湘桥区	Xiangqiao District	0.38	0.37	0.35	0.34
潮安区	Chaoan District	0.63	0.65	0.43	0.40
饶平县	Raoping County	2.26	2.38	2.13	2.29
揭阳市	Jieyang				
榕城区	Rongcheng District	0.35	0.37	0.04	0.05
揭东区	Jiedong District	1.60	1.65	0.71	0.84
普宁市	Puning City	2.09	2.21	0.37	0.41
揭西县	Jiexi County	3.07	3.20	1.69	1.85
惠来县	Huilai County	2.00	1.97	1.32	1.35
云浮市	Yunfu				
云城区	Yuncheng District	1.49	1.42	1.98	1.86
云安区	Yunan District	1.15	1.18	0.67	0.76
罗定市	Luoding City	2.94	3.32	2.11	2.31
新兴县	Xinxing County	4.67	4.82	16.23	16.03
郁南县	Yunan County	1.87	2.13	2.62	3.09

23-9 各县(市、区)规模以上工业企业单位数及利润总额

Number of Industrial Enterprises And Total Profits by County (County-level City and District)

县(市、区)	County (County-level City and District)	单位数（个） Number of Enterprises (unit)		利润总额（万元） Total Profit(10000 yuan)	
		2021	2022	2021	2022
广州市	Guangzhou				
越秀区	Yuexiu District	14	14	-23677	-70444
海珠区	Haizhu District	75	78	247093	166596
荔湾区	Liwan District	91	88	426534	452943
天河区	Tianhe District	150	136	239263	250445
白云区	Baiyun District	1058	1099	559498	473730
黄埔区	Huangpu District	1229	1263	7186701	6992730
花都区	Huadu District	1132	1154	1330589	1128040
番禺区	Panyu District	1209	1196	973664	1076620
南沙区	Nansha District	687	717	3206577	3928110
从化区	Conghua District	300	300	212771	289650
增城区	Zengcheng District	812	833	835886	593837
深圳市	Shenzhen				
福田区	Futian District	204	213	1777190	1037678
罗湖区	Luohu District	138	140	590554	648091
盐田区	Yantian District	75	89	337129	272780
南山区	Nanshan District	970	1012	7038301	9183491
宝安区	Baoan District	4937	5114	5695813	5745153
龙岗区	Longgang District	2290	2461	11467005	9961080
龙华区	Longhua District	1889	2022	2672731	3067248
坪山区	Pingshan District	703	794	781037	1556854
光明区	Guangming District	1718	1907	3222188	1642771
珠海市	Zhuhai				
香洲区	Xiangzhou District	710	760	3218074	3908546
金湾区	Jinwan District	637	697	1909491	1896642
斗门区	Doumen District	308	335	327378	160096
汕头市	Shantou				
金平区	Jinping District	305	321	306765	505486
龙湖区	Longhu District	289	305	224918	290937
澄海区	Chenghai District	354	375	-3465	49875
濠江区	Haojiang District	123	131	110152	52468
潮阳区	Chaoyang District	471	511	979613	595794
潮南区	Chaonan District	514	532	490083	489484
南澳县	Nanao County	5	6	5887	30268
佛山市	Foshan				
禅城区	Chancheng District	600	627	982670	950210
南海区	Nanhai District	4042	4344	4473933	4787720
顺德区	Shunde District	3053	3082	7373992	7944273
高明区	Gaoming District	605	662	3749818	4192833
三水区	Sanshui District	1070	1136	2230775	2180059
韶关市	Shaoguan				
浈江区	Zhengjiang District	57	57	29557	22857
武江区	Wujiang District	82	76	89403	76004
曲江区	Qujiang District	84	98	248997	-213338
乐昌市	Lechang City	66	78	1395	-42949
南雄市	Nanxiong City	71	80	-18383	-8381
仁化县	Renhua County	36	37	118702	155697
始兴县	Shixing County	41	45	53783	-3162
翁源县	Wengyuan County	64	65	60468	18043
新丰县	Xinfeng County	40	43	66376	-5741
乳源县	Ruyuan County	62	62	165126	210388

23-9 续表 1 continued

单位：万元 (10000 yuan)

县(市、区)	County (County-level City and District)	单位数（个） Number of Enterprises (unit) 2021	2022	利润总额（万元） Total Profit(10000 yuan) 2021	2022
河源市	Heyuan				
源城区	Yuancheng District	241	240	234127	127697
东源县	Dongyuan County	112	119	88368	33522
和平县	Heping County	45	41	113939	94117
龙川县	Longchuan County	72	70	52495	50106
紫金县	Zijin County	101	107	70961	149893
连平县	Lianping County	52	50	43354	70966
梅州市	Meizhou				
梅江区	Meijiang District	74	74	158408	145818
梅县区	Meixian District	101	110	205437	68718
兴宁市	Xingning City	83	88	-40	9037
平远县	Pingyuan County	54	54	30512	35755
蕉岭县	Jiaoling County	47	52	125227	-5467
大埔县	Dabu County	63	44	-53738	-25361
丰顺县	Fengshun County	64	71	14415	23323
五华县	Wuhua County	50	54	5068	20877
惠州市	Huizhou				
惠城区	Huicheng District	1293	1420	1335080	1410981
惠阳区	Huiyang District	1200	1374	2321891	858055
惠东县	Huidong County	329	383	169809	261307
博罗县	Boluo County	972	1104	485716	471951
龙门县	Longmen County	79	84	156178	41686
汕尾市	Shanwei				
市城区	Urban District	63	72	-11892	-13113
陆丰市	Lufeng City	83	97	55199	102517
海丰县	Haifeng County	117	119	64924	3999
陆河县	Luhe County	26	28	943	39686
江门市	Jiangmen				
蓬江区	Pengjiang District	549	612	374040	365974
江海区	Jianghai District	396	450	477927	337804
新会区	Xinhui District	649	707	813278	464737
台山市	Taishan City	281	311	165428	84054
开平市	Kaiping City	382	423	232911	250934
鹤山市	Heshan City	500	589	313006	406222
恩平市	Enping City	146	172	39959	26699
阳江市	Yangjiang				
江城区	Jiangcheng District	170	196	542282	274894
阳东区	Yangdong District	165	186	727264	820043
阳春市	Yangchun City	75	73	328111	216486
阳西县	Yangxi County	51	57	-11669	159155

23−9 续表 2 continued

单位：万元 (10000 yuan)

县(市、区)	County (County-level City and District)	单位数（个） Number of Enterprises (unit) 2021	2022	利润总额（万元） Total Profit(10000 yuan) 2021	2022
湛江市	Zhanjiang				
赤坎区	Chikan District	29	31	-34106	-56652
霞山区	Xiashan District	60	63	-2323	100530
麻章区	Mazhang District	108	104	1322810	434118
坡头区	Potou District	62	69	921734	1375687
雷州市	Leizhou City	59	64	-52121	-41295
廉江市	Lianjiang County	179	189	63980	23923
吴川市	Wuchuan City	132	129	8230	23087
遂溪县	Suixi County	115	120	74605	-29465
徐闻县	Xuwen County	44	46	54181	62655
茂名市	Maoming				
茂南区	Maonan District	114	117	1150383	-30786
电白区	Dianbai District	206	220	239014	-4975
信宜市	Xinyi City	50	51	13951	14418
高州市	Gaozhou City	154	163	73238	48620
化州市	Huazhou City	128	123	13341	20612
肇庆市	Zhaoqing				
端州区	Duanzhou District	138	137	204710	113111
鼎湖区	Dinghu District	95	107	37095	46996
高要区	Gaoyao District	391	430	804378	746843
四会市	Sihui City	560	610	663329	472921
广宁县	Guangning County	77	83	62037	177006
德庆县	Deqing County	90	88	54454	34417
封开县	Fengkai County	36	41	175657	134262
怀集县	Huaiji County	59	66	17280	14777
清远市	Qingyuan				
清城区	Qingcheng District	362	387	604397	597671
清新区	Qingxin District	167	175	259960	446461
英德市	Yingde City	204	228	503088	205222
连州市	Lianzhou City	63	71	155398	101088
佛冈县	Fogang County	109	122	255563	175766
阳山县	Yangshan County	24	28	27025	20210
连山县	Lianshan County	7	9	450	1215
连南县	Liannan County	13	14	1927	2109
潮州市	Chaozhou				
湘桥区	Xiangqiao District	161	183	99455	214088
潮安区	Chaoan District	730	754	536506	394702
饶平县	Raoping County	144	141	173620	216594
揭阳市	Jieyang				
榕城区	Rongcheng District	542	551	275624	248898
揭东区	Jiedong District	440	470	394515	439089
普宁市	Puning City	297	347	1016365	166823
揭西县	Jiexi County	93	112	284553	197489
惠来县	Huilai County	91	92	55834	-252288
云浮市	Yunfu				
云城区	Yuncheng District	101	99	9207	-55683
云安区	Yunan District	73	74	189430	31425
罗定市	Luoding City	89	81	111336	53439
新兴县	Xinxing County	111	111	50418	63219
郁南县	Yunan County	59	61	19265	573

23-10 各县(市、区)房地产开发投资

Investment in Fixed Assets by County (County-level City and District)

单位：万元 (10000 yuan)

县(市、区)	County (County-level City and District)	房地产开发投资 Investment in Real Estate Development 2021	2022
广州市	Guangzhou		
越秀区	Yuexiu District	224977	208391
海珠区	Haizhu District	2129236	2696311
荔湾区	Liwan District	2691586	2895261
天河区	Tianhe District	2541062	2455399
白云区	Baiyun District	4773908	3876970
黄埔区	Huangpu District	4663298	5147299
花都区	Huadu District	2280778	2222688
番禺区	Panyu District	3891642	4145750
南沙区	Nansha District	5358846	5863092
从化区	Conghua District	911808	364576
增城区	Zengcheng District	6797257	4443255
深圳市	Shenzhen		
福田区	Futian District	1842383	1798168
罗湖区	Luohu District	2619467	2041018
盐田区	Yantian District	771254	688039
南山区	Nanshan District	5156546	5738093
宝安区	Baoan District	5703132	7657201
龙岗区	Longgang District	5103233	5318208
龙华区	Longhua District	4578926	4623144
坪山区	Pingshan District	1141991	2205510
光明区	Guangming District	2873844	3846058
珠海市	Zhuhai		
香洲区	Xiangzhou District	6996628	4901609
金湾区	Jinwan District	3326278	1501234
斗门区	Doumen District	1298530	1169191
汕头市	Shantou		
金平区	Jinping District	875871	484290
龙湖区	Longhu District	1902935	1598003
澄海区	Chenghai District	712992	507628
濠江区	Haojiang District	630053	328460
潮阳区	Chaoyang District	494316	623262
潮南区	Chaonan District	185352	203951
南澳县	Nanao County	44226	32019
佛山市	Foshan		
禅城区	Chancheng District	4054423	4014813
南海区	Nanhai District	8155028	6011905
顺德区	Shunde District	7605724	7684628
高明区	Gaoming District	1410976	805304
三水区	Sanshui District	2202604	1048551
韶关市	Shaoguan		
浈江区	Zhengjiang District	143918	47446
武江区	Wujiang District	783458	366966
曲江区	Qujiang District	135308	106382
乐昌市	Lechang City	207110	96168
南雄市	Nanxiong City	229337	154184
仁化县	Renhua County	132252	66589
始兴县	Shixing County	104687	33680
翁源县	Wengyuan County	184929	118690
新丰县	Xinfeng County	180565	108086
乳源县	Ruyuan County	104497	37392

23-10 续表 1 continued

单位：万元 (10000 yuan)

县(市、区)	County (County-level City and District)	房地产开发投资 Investment in Real Estate Development	
		2021	2022
河源市	Heyuan		
源城区	Yuancheng District	1367593	750134
东源县	Dongyuan County	572027	269677
和平县	Heping County	171727	150464
龙川县	Longchuan County	274940	62024
紫金县	Zijin County	310889	132691
连平县	Lianping County	58277	36392
梅州市	Meizhou		
梅江区	Meijiang District	667923	257197
梅县区	Meixian District	332927	198618
兴宁市	Xingning City	355420	230659
平远县	Pingyuan County	81593	61125
蕉岭县	Jiaoling County	113452	56818
大埔县	Dabu County	97148	65324
丰顺县	Fengshun County	139542	66802
五华县	Wuhua County	390739	156734
惠州市	Huizhou		
惠城区	Huicheng District	5461622	4336360
惠阳区	Huiyang District	4288913	3756210
惠东县	Huidong County	1438345	1054858
博罗县	Boluo County	1770398	1554587
龙门县	Longmen County	273932	167808
汕尾市	Shanwei		
市城区	Urban District	997170	558180
陆丰市	Lufeng City	366020	248114
海丰县	Haifeng County	742128	292785
陆河县	Luhe County	314158	126344
江门市	Jiangmen		
蓬江区	Pengjiang District	1736300	1749085
江海区	Jianghai District	717126	397668
新会区	Xinhui District	1437777	1138055
台山市	Taishan City	1020131	824600
开平市	Kaiping City	734981	458964
鹤山市	Heshan City	874122	495340
恩平市	Enping City	504228	319335
阳江市	Yangjiang		
江城区	Jiangcheng District	408702	312649
阳东区	Yangdong District	193638	141795
阳春市	Yangchun City	217886	188145
阳西县	Yangxi County	222672	127077

23−10 续表 2 continued

单位：万元 (10000 yuan)

县(市、区)	County (County-level City and District)	房地产开发投资 Investment in Real Estate Development 2021	2022
湛江市	Zhanjiang		
赤坎区	Chikan District	920606	750830
霞山区	Xiashan District	744270	434922
麻章区	Mazhang District	411090	350319
坡头区	Potou District	381828	213682
雷州市	Leizhou City	133932	90423
廉江市	Lianjiang County	536557	191639
吴川市	Wuchuan City	692876	568262
遂溪县	Suixi County	307992	232378
徐闻县	Xuwen County	165379	100847
茂名市	Maoming		
茂南区	Maonan District	1026906	931663
电白区	Dianbai District	863632	656196
信宜市	Xinyi City	596442	424281
高州市	Gaozhou City	534248	463161
化州市	Huazhou City	388869	262493
肇庆市	Zhaoqing		
端州区	Duanzhou District	1031202	503602
鼎湖区	Dinghu District	1543739	653089
高要区	Gaoyao District	498091	334470
四会市	Sihui City	1534133	977208
广宁县	Guangning County	236033	119050
德庆县	Deqing County	60365	35068
封开县	Fengkai County	84238	86007
怀集县	Huaiji County	414372	442286
清远市	Qingyuan		
清城区	Qingcheng District	2198323	1749927
清新区	Qingxin District	269616	245658
英德市	Yingde City	481013	282711
连州市	Lianzhou City	148548	114683
佛冈县	Fogang County	395737	265297
阳山县	Yangshan County	81322	58222
连山县	Lianshan County	3683	13872
连南县	Liannan County	18838	18365
潮州市	Chaozhou		
湘桥区	Xiangqiao District	523012	413693
潮安区	Chaoan District	181392	211132
饶平县	Raoping County	298069	261582
揭阳市	Jieyang		
榕城区	Rongcheng District	1210583	480089
揭东区	Jiedong District	475260	350152
普宁市	Puning City	757999	435672
揭西县	Jiexi County	226634	113784
惠来县	Huilai County	238008	239327
云浮市	Yunfu		
云城区	Yuncheng District	448662	255692
云安区	Yunan District	56199	19761
罗定市	Luoding City	369387	341482
新兴县	Xinxing County	378858	228982
郁南县	Yunan County	170059	117212

注：湛江含市直数据，深圳含深汕合作区数据，分县区合计小于全市。
Note: Due to the projects that can't be classified by region and the development zone projects, the sum of the counties are less than the city.

23-11 各县(市、区)社会消费品零售总额

Total Retail Sales of Consumer Goods by County (County-level City and District)

单位：万元 (10000 yuan)

县(市、区)	County (County-level City and District)	社会消费品零售总额 Total Retail Sales of Consumer Goods		#商品零售 Retail Sales	
		2021	2022	2021	2022
广州市	Guangzhou				
越秀区	Yuexiu District	12533262	12232127	11478154	10868659
海珠区	Haizhu District	9742966	9589731	9027586	9017880
荔湾区	Liwan District	6440088	6470943	5541986	5598545
天河区	Tianhe District	20506402	20237930	18998888	18410521
白云区	Baiyun District	10763994	10696782	9625652	10031299
黄埔区	Huangpu District	12618338	14281849	12312536	14077754
花都区	Huadu District	7138354	7881521	6776845	7546519
番禺区	Panyu District	12710626	12639796	11613757	11738887
南沙区	Nansha District	2657093	2947894	2376911	2704372
从化区	Conghua District	1668257	1417064	1571283	1298242
增城区	Zengcheng District	4446224	4585896	4184584	4352970
深圳市	Shenzhen				
福田区	Futian District	22420358	22730642	19809287	20474294
罗湖区	Luohu District	13021525	12587077	11505040	11337626
盐田区	Yantian District	1452590	1526520	1283422	1374991
南山区	Nanshan District	13668141	13739930	12076352	12376041
宝安区	Baoan District	13895232	14320670	12276996	12899135
龙岗区	Longgang District	13607470	14876780	12022746	13400043
龙华区	Longhua District	12138222	12636705	10724607	11382327
坪山区	Pingshan District	1811549	1973406	1600576	1777516
光明区	Guangming District	2199031	2376487	1942932	2140586
珠海市	Zhuhai				
香洲区	Xiangzhou District	9198262	9069939	8296214	8335023
金湾区	Jinwan District	482208	575249	434919	528638
斗门区	Doumen District	801969	801552	723322	736604
汕头市	Shantou				
金平区	Jinping District	5331385	5232501	4758000	4662110
龙湖区	Longhu District	3113427	3055229	2843761	2786038
澄海区	Chenghai District	1805901	1794428	1667652	1654346
濠江区	Haojiang District	487731	481545	451895	445433
潮阳区	Chaoyang District	2175908	2169570	1940057	1931241
潮南区	Chaonan District	1933143	1928700	1716863	1710114
南澳县	Nanao County	190903	188299	158519	156101
佛山市	Foshan				
禅城区	Chancheng District	8144675	8195782	7746284	7785246
南海区	Nanhai District	12007378	12217473	10985132	11246137
顺德区	Shunde District	11830809	11954540	10960404	11137306
高明区	Gaoming District	1307195	1306369	1210703	1213306
三水区	Sanshui District	2276524	2261489	2080010	2069274
韶关市	Shaoguan				
浈江区	Zhengjiang District	1249645	1274553	1180032	1209949
武江区	Wujiang District	753258	780847	697059	725302
曲江区	Qujiang District	383748	384032	348127	347666
乐昌市	Lechang City	553532	559620	504645	510779
南雄市	Nanxiong City	467920	470196	422738	424923
仁化县	Renhua County	257408	257885	234005	233086
始兴县	Shixing County	288517	290018	261586	262030
翁源县	Wengyuan County	417855	427939	378436	387206
新丰县	Xinfeng County	268117	269496	242186	242762
乳源县	Ruyuan County	241601	225147	218090	201776

23-11 续表 1 continued

单位：万元 (10000 yuan)

县(市、区)	County (County-level City and District)	社会消费品零售总额 Total Retail Sales of Consumer Goods		#商品零售 Retail Sales	
		2021	2022	2021	2022
河源市	Heyuan				
源城区	Yuancheng District	1488020	1428202	1451201	1325782
东源县	Dongyuan County	436161	435164	392545	404702
和平县	Heping County	407963	395927	363339	356334
龙川县	Longchuan County	613853	608845	565543	560137
紫金县	Zijin County	570983	558152	468206	516271
连平县	Lianping County	359246	353851	330506	325542
梅州市	Meizhou				
梅江区	Meijiang District	1387662	1464667	1299668	1381612
梅县区	Meixian District	1493836	1450515	1361175	1321414
兴宁市	Xingning City	1040229	1031097	932995	925265
平远县	Pingyuan County	332966	332531	296780	297146
蕉岭县	Jiaoling County	393705	384177	353312	344633
大埔县	Dabu County	484120	479941	432141	429192
丰顺县	Fengshun County	557242	551457	497456	493422
五华县	Wuhua County	853950	873791	762585	781497
惠州市	Huizhou				
惠城区	Huicheng District	9072286	9238043	8438236	8480523
惠阳区	Huiyang District	2789766	3012835	2566586	2765783
惠东县	Huidong County	4118727	4230209	3749043	3883332
博罗县	Boluo County	3218352	3312361	2896886	3040747
龙门县	Longmen County	590068	611771	536961	561606
汕尾市	Shanwei				
市城区	Urban District	1148249	1153834	1002105	1007468
陆丰市	Lufeng City	1648877	1635820	1418433	1409026
海丰县	Haifeng County	1583735	1577811	1393975	1391724
陆河县	Luhe County	392107	387836	352288	348866
江门市	Jiangmen				
蓬江区	Pengjiang District	2607198	2672093	2450766	2434267
江海区	Jianghai District	633376	668772	507668	609249
新会区	Xinhui District	2943197	3017140	2501718	2748604
台山市	Taishan City	2252212	2301046	2072035	2096245
开平市	Kaiping City	1822157	1858056	1694606	1692682
鹤山市	Heshan City	1557892	1588613	1503366	1447221
恩平市	Enping City	964935	984735	887740	897090
阳江市	Yangjiang				
江城区	Jiangcheng District	2170371	2238545	1936475	2005586
阳东区	Yangdong District	691739	699358	617752	626743
阳春市	Yangchun City	1437273	1482408	1278381	1321928
阳西县	Yangxi County	527746	536011	467301	475400

23-11 续表 2 continued

单位：万元 (10000 yuan)

县(市、区)	County (County-level City and District)	社会消费品零售总额 Total Retail Sales of Consumer Goods 2021	2022	#商品零售 Retail Sales 2021	2022
湛江市	Zhanjiang				
赤坎区	Chikan District	4239723	4290108	3792605	3842785
霞山区	Xiashan District	3139495	3315785	2855838	3069903
麻章区	Mazhang District	1469349	1491433	1309052	1330015
坡头区	Potou District	428993	436410	364143	342956
雷州市	Leizhou City	1779510	1815745	1573641	1606559
廉江市	Lianjiang County	3052247	3113219	2634508	2689514
吴川市	Wuchuan City	1592352	1612093	1394837	1416979
遂溪县	Suixi County	1413148	1445302	1175493	1203167
徐闻县	Xuwen County	729747	746218	596600	611956
茂名市	Maoming				
茂南区	Maonan District	5124175	4830525	4748345	4485772
电白区	Dianbai District	2981567	3138454	2301769	2449139
信宜市	Xinyi City	2246025	2308912	2048940	2105806
高州市	Gaozhou City	2478247	2570851	2151428	2243479
化州市	Huazhou City	2143168	2250182	1847367	1957952
肇庆市	Zhaoqing				
端州区	Duanzhou District	2968937	2829910	2787040	2641551
鼎湖区	Dinghu District	1179401	1068265	1132397	1037230
高要区	Gaoyao District	910396	889465	818090	798142
四会市	Sihui City	4438309	4283078	4363895	4213356
广宁县	Guangning County	494785	495035	457609	458072
德庆县	Deqing County	527322	517484	485312	477448
封开县	Fengkai County	352011	350320	308167	307398
怀集县	Huaiji County	737005	737104	659082	659165
清远市	Qingyuan				
清城区	Qingcheng District	2801649	2824311	2646160	2706333
清新区	Qingxin District	715574	710081	675860	675717
英德市	Yingde City	988294	985116	933444	935590
连州市	Lianzhou City	402259	401183	379934	380083
佛冈县	Fogang County	391899	389157	370149	377189
阳山县	Yangshan County	332871	337181	314397	307945
连山县	Lianshan County	54437	54381	51416	50236
连南县	Liannan County	109255	110162	103191	101305
潮州市	Chaozhou				
湘桥区	Xiangqiao District	1391154	1411263	1275760	1297320
潮安区	Chaoan District	2368617	2397714	2192023	2222859
饶平县	Raoping County	1047183	1061818	961789	975414
揭阳市	Jieyang				
榕城区	Rongcheng District	3065439	3097962	2942821	2972089
揭东区	Jiedong District	2175092	2196697	2088088	2107435
普宁市	Puning City	3385400	3439416	3249387	3299650
揭西县	Jiexi County	902022	910576	865941	873575
惠来县	Huilai County	1029604	1037761	988420	995592
云浮市	Yunfu				
云城区	Yuncheng District	1154945	1184531	1061883	1081727
云安区	Yunan District	207724	212786	187203	192518
罗定市	Luoding City	1353496	1374853	1234006	1268725
新兴县	Xinxing County	588210	607073	518109	533557
郁南县	Yunan County	450672	462700	412674	423327

23-12 各县(市、区)财政收支

Local Government Budgetary Revenue and Expenditure by County (County-level City and District)

单位：万元 (10000yuan)

县(市、区)	County (County-level City and District)	地方一般公共预算收入 Local Government General Public Budget Revenue		地方一般公共预算支出 Local Government General Public Budget Expenditure	
		2021	2022	2021	2022
广州市	Guangzhou				
越秀区	Yuexiu District	540459	537001	1320258	1364528
海珠区	Haizhu District	557848	691968	1323801	1381284
荔湾区	Liwan District	531355	534341	1052182	1172425
天河区	Tianhe District	777556	813420	1605605	1377554
白云区	Baiyun District	694159	747474	1923530	1919114
黄埔区	Huangpu District	2068206	1820952	3579234	3357432
花都区	Huadu District	862669	757825	1709560	1488690
番禺区	Panyu District	1076711	1042625	1953780	1675581
南沙区	Nansha District	1082013	1170157	2713795	2949974
从化区	Conghua District	317736	272242	914845	889031
增城区	Zengcheng District	1138531	968549	1762934	1971038
深圳市	Shenzhen				
福田区	Futian District	2142921	1942706	2962862	3104741
罗湖区	Luohu District	1072857	893960	1832454	2051693
盐田区	Yantian District	364446	329097	678298	702781
南山区	Nanshan District	3610169	3616214	4024222	4342423
宝安区	Baoan District	2959961	2991877	4521591	4763327
龙岗区	Longgang District	3130525	2841726	4499416	5083488
龙华区	Longhua District	1522145	1514784	2923105	3312098
坪山区	Pingshan District	640284	547788	1578490	1752557
光明区	Guangming District	788157	808022	1823743	1788652
珠海市	Zhuhai				
香洲区	Xiangzhou District	414117	420835	975021	981973
金湾区	Jinwan District	481417	424882	930046	787729
斗门区	Doumen District	353948	230724	697185	734293
汕头市	Shantou				
金平区	Jinping District	95529	85968	338483	303832
龙湖区	Longhu District	189179	152398	372243	336539
澄海区	Chenghai District	163977	141765	418293	460046
濠江区	Haojiang District	63329	42947	213898	206593
潮阳区	Chaoyang District	184395	163077	749796	706067
潮南区	Chaonan District	98022	84137	571951	572874
南澳县	Nanao County	24117	12814	138437	126057
佛山市	Foshan				
禅城区	Chancheng District	1197372	1140247	1365771	1258454
南海区	Nanhai District	2665677	2584349	2894196	2688591
顺德区	Shunde District	2740080	2656521	2657726	2693925
高明区	Gaoming District	458124	441900	606298	603835
三水区	Sanshui District	715167	692536	816670	790466
韶关市	Shaoguan				
浈江区	Zhengjiang District	48975	39312	191854	175438
武江区	Wujiang District	61521	37339	196586	166993
曲江区	Qujiang District	72206	77573	262147	266800
乐昌市	Lechang City	82007	84924	410675	397948
南雄市	Nanxiong City	68899	75023	395196	416224
仁化县	Renhua County	47730	44303	257913	267146
始兴县	Shixing County	50545	41556	254274	253740
翁源县	Wengyuan County	79844	67295	346842	331794
新丰县	Xinfeng County	48139	48920	259726	254697
乳源县	Ruyuan County	61252	52416	290371	288312

23-12 续表 1 continued

单位：万元 (10000yuan)

县(市、区)	County (County-level City and District)	地方一般公共预算收入 Local Government General Public Budget Revenue		地方一般公共预算支出 Local Government General Public Budget Expenditure	
		2021	2022	2021	2022
河源市	Heyuan				
源城区	Yuancheng District	125927	107071	318867	284451
东源县	Dongyuan County	133904	126830	570408	555692
和平县	Heping County	61906	41316	387855	376462
龙川县	Longchuan County	83260	65668	676567	679183
紫金县	Zijin County	88981	83948	476523	511955
连平县	Lianping County	74860	46599	354800	347737
梅州市	Meizhou				
梅江区	Meijiang District	72767	59280	263063	274513
梅县区	Meixian District	163793	132291	561975	640055
兴宁市	Xingning City	106494	82562	692805	709259
平远县	Pingyuan County	52757	53478	290468	315987
蕉岭县	Jiaoling County	70242	60415	246220	291224
大埔县	Dabu County	65221	51505	453602	437546
丰顺县	Fengshun County	79205	65581	510013	489975
五华县	Wuhua County	121552	124300	840914	881547
惠州市	Huizhou				
惠城区	Huicheng District	440797	417359	810268	881518
惠阳区	Huiyang District	642828	684057	835883	871009
惠东县	Huidong County	314662	405813	877449	900820
博罗县	Boluo County	561168	662169	1044815	1104548
龙门县	Longmen County	194475	196465	433249	490692
汕尾市	Shanwei				
市城区	Urban District	77672	78483	284579	337969
陆丰市	Lufeng City	101735	114400	909064	945598
海丰县	Haifeng County	122776	135867	626794	695419
陆河县	Luhe County	42956	45746	329347	336836
江门市	Jiangmen				
蓬江区	Pengjiang District	314013	299551	426466	412092
江海区	Jianghai District	157493	142820	231011	241898
新会区	Xinhui District	585627	546809	977310	834111
台山市	Taishan City	356698	355166	771886	834627
开平市	Kaiping City	316450	307742	519363	566454
鹤山市	Heshan City	365090	357292	495123	489526
恩平市	Enping City	138899	134418	400959	410785
阳江市	Yangjiang				
江城区	Jiangcheng District	51031	49811	202367	243343
阳东区	Yangdong District	155386	161129	406708	440924
阳春市	Yangchun City	168309	168865	657162	737612
阳西县	Yangxi County	94930	136050	363550	392631

23-12 续表 2 continued

单位：万元 (10000yuan)

县(市、区)	County (County-level City and District)	地方一般公共预算收入 Local Government General Public Budget Revenue		地方一般公共预算支出 Local Government General Public Budget Expenditure	
		2021	2022	2021	2022
湛江市	Zhanjiang				
赤坎区	Chikan District	33829	29726	142385	140221
霞山区	Xiashan District	72039	65089	203024	175979
麻章区	Mazhang District	65827	66565	185295	158260
坡头区	Potou District	46087	45254	219381	200681
雷州市	Leizhou City	95504	88140	725211	721195
廉江市	Lianjiang County	175281	169956	830450	836460
吴川市	Wuchuan City	150060	88739	545034	527101
遂溪县	Suixi County	93058	57031	478724	530282
徐闻县	Xuwen County	140448	61403	486422	474107
茂名市	Maoming				
茂南区	Maonan District	106339	120630	462290	481962
电白区	Dianbai District	268787	277510	1032328	1134482
信宜市	Xinyi City	117249	124548	757169	808506
高州市	Gaozhou City	171842	173743	900466	915259
化州市	Huazhou City	136960	152410	827933	830672
肇庆市	Zhaoqing				
端州区	Duanzhou District	119698	111615	288419	287355
鼎湖区	Dinghu District	94045	81926	176942	155699
高要区	Gaoyao District	224353	281811	520668	539566
四会市	Sihui City	204427	184301	361177	426113
广宁县	Guangning County	71745	79421	345621	347827
德庆县	Deqing County	90031	47975	365504	341811
封开县	Fengkai County	118614	262218	373435	447896
怀集县	Huaiji County	72618	73857	540775	565965
清远市	Qingyuan				
清城区	Qingcheng District	170518	167666	543671	485909
清新区	Qingxin District	159618	170043	461878	527627
英德市	Yingde City	252618	291590	814403	839411
连州市	Lianzhou City	66244	62450	362796	375962
佛冈县	Fogang County	116073	127658	365780	381372
阳山县	Yangshan County	59128	63179	367142	387930
连山县	Lianshan County	22092	24380	176034	192898
连南县	Liannan County	21242	23959	207349	222277
潮州市	Chaozhou				
湘桥区	Xiangqiao District	48800	58181	245472	261034
潮安区	Chaoan District	126305	126791	597035	712828
饶平县	Raoping County	92638	89199	666341	632471
揭阳市	Jieyang				
榕城区	Rongcheng District	76151	55484	220737	317190
揭东区	Jiedong District	68271	64272	473931	515831
普宁市	Puning City	226636	217798	1015656	1056892
揭西县	Jiexi County	48191	37871	530136	603924
惠来县	Huilai County	89572	91725	609857	702791
云浮市	Yunfu				
云城区	Yuncheng District	58427	55638	272715	320717
云安区	Yunan District	57193	215113	264974	351233
罗定市	Luoding City	199687	135479	764543	699692
新兴县	Xinxing County	186244	142906	470642	414519
郁南县	Yunan County	63340	206254	340579	379568

23-13 各县(市、区)城镇居民人均可支配收入

Per Capita Disposable Income of Urban Households by County (County-level City and District)

县(市、区)	County (County-level City and District)	2021		2022	
		绝对值(元) Value (yuan)	增速(%) Ratio(%)	绝对值(元) Value (yuan)	增速(%) Ratio(%)
广州市	Guangzhou				
越秀区	Yuexiu District	82397	8.9	84621	2.7
海珠区	Haizhu District	76523	9.4	78130	2.1
荔湾区	Liwan District	74554	4.5	78133	4.8
天河区	Tianhe District	89206	12.3	93613	4.9
白云区	Baiyun District	75547	9.3	77511	2.6
黄埔区	Huangpu District	79474	12.7	83607	5.2
花都区	Huadu District	64352	8.8	66283	3.0
番禺区	Panyu District	70292	8.1	72541	3.2
南沙区	Nansha District	61559	6.3	64268	4.4
从化区	Conghua District	49339	9.1	51116	3.6
增城区	Zengcheng District	58419	9.2	61164	4.7
深圳市	Shenzhen				
福田区	Futian District	92608	9.6	95729	3.4
罗湖区	Luohu District	73911	9.3	76352	3.3
盐田区	Yantian District	73476	11.1	77604	5.6
南山区	Nanshan District	90378	9.5	95710	5.9
宝安区	Baoan District	66450	9.2	66587	0.2
龙岗区	Longgang District	60475	9.0	61284	1.3
龙华区	Longhua District	64341	12.5	66553	3.4
坪山区	Pingshan District	64154	12.3	66033	2.9
光明区	Guangming District	60002	9.0	63102	5.2
珠海市	Zhuhai				
香洲区	Xiangzhou District	73490	9.0	74353	1.2
金湾区	Jinwan District	45185	14.0	46584	3.1
斗门区	Doumen District	52892	11.3	54721	3.5
汕头市	Shantou				
金平区	Jinping District	42951	8.4	44767	4.2
龙湖区	Longhu District	44896	8.6	47250	5.2
澄海区	Chenghai District	33696	8.1	34436	2.2
濠江区	Haojiang District	31183	5.4	32732	5.0
潮阳区	Chaoyang District	30156	7.4	31365	4.0
潮南区	Chaonan District	28245	8.3	29462	4.3
南澳县	Nanao County	19292	9.4	20064	4.0
佛山市	Foshan				
禅城区	Chancheng District	60511	9.7	62965	4.1
南海区	Nanhai District	63840	10.0	66340	3.9
顺德区	Shunde District	67466	9.7	69981	3.7
高明区	Gaoming District	44231	9.5	46056	4.1
三水区	Sanshui District	48380	10.4	50270	3.9
韶关市	Shaoguan				
浈江区	Zhengjiang District	44886	8.4	45928	2.3
武江区	Wujiang District	45127	9.3	46454	2.9
曲江区	Qujiang District	36508	8.7	37473	2.6
乐昌市	Lechang City	31834	8.0	32860	3.2
南雄市	Nanxiong City	32418	8.8	33890	4.5
仁化县	Renhua County	33351	7.9	34295	2.8
始兴县	Shixing County	31896	10.1	32710	2.6
翁源县	Wengyuan County	32862	10.2	34022	3.5
新丰县	Xinfeng County	31758	7.9	32710	3.0
乳源县	Ruyuan County	32431	9.2	33827	4.3

23-13 续表 1 continued

县(市、区)	County (County-level City and District)	2021 绝对值(元) Value (yuan)	2021 增速(%) Ratio(%)	2022 绝对值(元) Value (yuan)	2022 增速(%) Ratio(%)
河源市	Heyuan				
源城区	Yuancheng District	35680	4.0	36366	1.9
东源县	Dongyuan County	27897	5.0	29052	4.1
和平县	Heping County	28819	8.6	29509	2.4
龙川县	Longchuan County	26468	6.9	27360	3.4
紫金县	Zijin County	25603	10.3	26630	4.0
连平县	Lianping County	27194	7.8	27874	2.5
梅州市	Meizhou				
梅江区	Meijiang District	40902	6.8	42620	4.2
梅县区	Meixian District	39822	8.1	41256	3.6
兴宁市	Xingning City	30434	8.9	31408	3.2
平远县	Pingyuan County	29628	9.8	30991	4.6
蕉岭县	Jiaoling County	31847	10.0	33026	3.7
大埔县	Dabu County	28146	8.2	29047	3.2
丰顺县	Fengshun County	29412	8.8	30383	3.3
五华县	Wuhua County	25090	9.7	26320	4.9
惠州市	Huizhou				
惠城区	Huicheng District	60987	6.9	61603	1.0
惠阳区	Huiyang District	50771	7.3	51297	1.0
惠东县	Huidong County	34306	6.2	35585	3.7
博罗县	Boluo County	40380	7.2	41938	3.9
龙门县	Longmen County	31107	8.4	32625	4.9
汕尾市	Shanwei				
市城区	Urban District	33623	10.2	35494	5.6
陆丰市	Lufeng City	30302	11.2	31922	5.3
海丰县	Haifeng County	37487	10.9	39238	4.7
陆河县	Luhe County	26382	9.2	27710	5.0
江门市	Jiangmen				
蓬江区	Pengjiang District	53591	7.3	55805	4.1
江海区	Jianghai District	49526	9.6	51460	3.9
新会区	Xinhui District	45962	10.8	48229	4.9
台山市	Taishan City	32782	8.1	33721	2.9
开平市	Kaiping City	34886	10.6	36220	3.8
鹤山市	Heshan City	37179	2.7	37959	2.1
恩平市	Enping City	29849	10.6	31250	4.7
阳江市	Yangjiang				
江城区	Jiangcheng District	37974	10.0	39519	4.1
阳东区	Yangdong District	36221	6.1	37489	3.5
阳春市	Yangchun City	32162	5.6	33079	2.9
阳西县	Yangxi County	29878	5.5	30715	2.8

23−13 续表 2 continued

县(市、区)	County (County-level and District)	2021 绝对值(元) Value (yuan)	2021 增速(%) Ratio(%)	2022 绝对值(元) Value (yuan)	2022 增速(%) Ratio(%)
湛江市	Zhanjiang				
赤坎区	Chikan District	42635	7.1	43923	3.0
霞山区	Xiashan District	51481	6.9	52010	1.0
麻章区	Mazhang District	33632	10.7	35220	4.7
坡头区	Potou District	36547	5.3	37109	1.5
雷州市	Leizhou City	26408	12.1	27401	3.8
廉江市	Lianjiang County	31293	9.6	32506	3.9
吴川市	Wuchuan City	29405	6.7	30809	4.8
遂溪县	Suixi County	28454	9.8	29517	3.7
徐闻县	Xuwen County	28996	7.7	29531	1.8
茂名市	Maoming				
茂南区	Maonan District	37205	10.2	38036	2.2
电白区	Dianbai District	31838	7.1	32722	2.8
信宜市	Xinyi City	30992	8.9	31842	2.7
高州市	Gaozhou City	31516	6.3	32263	2.4
化州市	Huazhou City	30918	7.0	31504	1.9
肇庆市	Zhaoqing				
端州区	Duanzhou District	43621	8.5	44128	1.2
鼎湖区	Dinghu District	33118	5.4	34384	3.8
高要区	Gaoyao District	33818	8.7	35017	3.5
四会市	Sihui City	41482	7.9	41934	1.1
广宁县	Guangning County	29232	7.9	30370	3.9
德庆县	Deqing County	30019	7.2	30783	2.5
封开县	Fengkai County	29692	9.4	30895	4.1
怀集县	Huaiji County	34152	6.8	35192	3.0
清远市	Qingyuan				
清城区	Qingcheng District	39749	7.3	40842	2.8
清新区	Qingxin District	35485	8.2	36502	2.9
英德市	Yingde City	32750	6.8	33686	2.9
连州市	Lianzhou City	34221	8.4	35574	4.0
佛冈县	Fogang County	34363	10.1	35475	3.2
阳山县	Yangshan County	32890	8.3	33700	2.5
连山县	Lianshan County	28853	9.8	30065	4.2
连南县	Liannan County	30130	9.1	31264	3.8
潮州市	Chaozhou				
湘桥区	Xiangqiao District	32551	7.3	34129	4.8
潮安区	Chaoan District	26454	8.9	27745	4.9
饶平县	Raoping County	25217	7.4	26492	5.1
揭阳市	Jieyang				
榕城区	Rongcheng District	30041	7.0	29881	-0.5
揭东区	Jiedong District	30879	8.9	31758	2.8
普宁市	Puning City	30774	8.9	31700	3.0
揭西县	Jiexi County	23867	5.3	24676	3.4
惠来县	Huilai County	25418	12.9	26364	3.7
云浮市	Yunfu				
云城区	Yuncheng District	31326	8.8	32662	4.3
云安区	Yunan District	30008	5.5	31653	5.5
罗定市	Luoding City	30465	10.4	32073	5.3
新兴县	Xinxing County	32255	7.6	33655	4.3
郁南县	Yunan County	30076	11.0	31264	4.0

23−14 各县(市、区)农村居民人均可支配收入
Per Capita Disposable Income of Rural Households by County (County-level City and District)

县(市、区)	County (County-level City and District)	2021		2022	
		绝对值(元) Value (yuan)	增速(%) Ratio (%)	绝对值(元) Value (yuan)	增速(%) Ratio (%)
广州市	Guangzhou				
越秀区	Yuexiu District				
海珠区	Haizhu District				
荔湾区	Liwan District				
天河区	Tianhe District				
白云区	Baiyun District	34791	10.5	36356	4.5
黄埔区	Huangpu District				
花都区	Huadu District	33141	10.3	34731	4.8
番禺区	Panyu District	46421	9.2	48696	4.9
南沙区	Nansha District	39818	7.8	42168	5.9
从化区	Conghua District	26381	10.6	27779	5.3
增城区	Zengcheng District	31740	10.9	33835	6.6
深圳市	Shenzhen				
福田区	Futian District				
罗湖区	Luohu District				
盐田区	Yantian District				
南山区	Nanshan District				
宝安区	Baoan District				
龙岗区	Longgang District				
龙华区	Longhua District				
坪山区	Pingshan District				
光明区	Guangming District				
珠海市	Zhuhai				
香洲区	Xiangzhou District				
金湾区	Jinwan District				
斗门区	Doumen District	34394	10.5	35829	4.2
汕头市	Shantou				
金平区	Jinping District				
龙湖区	Longhu District	25217	10.6	27038	7.2
澄海区	Chenghai District	23092	10.2	24162	4.6
濠江区	Haojiang District	20438	9.8	21698	6.2
潮阳区	Chaoyang District	19287	9.3	20482	6.2
潮南区	Chaonan District	20082	10.4	21355	6.3
南澳县	Nanao County	15811	11.7	16802	6.3
佛山市	Foshan				
禅城区	Chancheng District				
南海区	Nanhai District	43536	10.9	45651	4.9
顺德区	Shunde District				
高明区	Gaoming District	32291	11.9	33951	5.1
三水区	Sanshui District	35780	10.6	37635	5.2
韶关市	Shaoguan				
浈江区	Zhengjiang District	23009	9.5	23793	3.4
武江区	Wujiang District	24230	10.9	25175	3.9
曲江区	Qujiang District	22318	11.5	23207	4.0
乐昌市	Lechang City	19343	10.5	20175	4.3
南雄市	Nanxiong City	19522	10.0	20614	5.6
仁化县	Renhua County	21216	9.3	22369	5.4
始兴县	Shixing County	20276	10.8	21239	4.7
翁源县	Wengyuan County	19409	11.2	20330	4.7
新丰县	Xinfeng County	19005	10.3	20165	6.1
乳源县	Ruyuan County	18972	10.4	20149	6.2

注：深圳市因完成城市化，无农村居民相关数据。
Note: There is on data of Shenzhen city due to its total urbanization.

23-14 续表 1 continued

县(市、区)	County (County-level City and District)	2021 绝对值(元) Value (yuan)	2021 增速(%) Ratio(%)	2022 绝对值(元) Value (yuan)	2022 增速(%) Ratio(%)
河源市	Heyuan				
源城区	Yuancheng District	26455	12.1	27832	5.2
东源县	Dongyuan County	19520	8.3	20531	5.2
和平县	Heping County	18593	13.2	19845	6.7
龙川县	Longchuan County	19183	9.4	20137	5.0
紫金县	Zijin County	19573	12.1	20660	5.6
连平县	Lianping County	18932	13.9	20141	6.4
梅州市	Meizhou				
梅江区	Meijiang District	24170	7.8	25209	4.3
梅县区	Meixian District	24163	9.6	25468	5.4
兴宁市	Xingning City	21069	9.5	21996	4.4
平远县	Pingyuan County	21225	10.8	22456	5.8
蕉岭县	Jiaoling County	21017	11.2	22257	5.9
大埔县	Dabu County	17228	9.2	18038	4.7
丰顺县	Fengshun County	17251	10.4	18097	4.9
五华县	Wuhua County	15677	11.0	16617	6.0
惠州市	Huizhou				
惠城区	Huicheng District	28886	10.7	29785	3.1
惠阳区	Huiyang District	30470	10.4	31345	2.9
惠东县	Huidong County	26817	10.1	28067	4.7
博罗县	Boluo County	26717	10.2	27987	4.8
龙门县	Longmen County	25714	10.7	27107	5.4
汕尾市	Shanwei				
市城区	Urban District	20929	13.7	22286	6.5
陆丰市	Lufeng City	19643	11.8	21052	7.2
海丰县	Haifeng County	22072	14.6	23588	6.9
陆河县	Luhe County	15554	12.3	16478	5.9
江门市	Jiangmen				
蓬江区	Pengjiang District				
江海区	Jianghai District				
新会区	Xinhui District	27837	11.1	29754	6.9
台山市	Taishan City	21996	10.1	22937	4.3
开平市	Kaiping City	23001	10.9	24195	5.2
鹤山市	Heshan City	23424	14.7	24593	5.0
恩平市	Enping City	19249	12.0	20488	6.4
阳江市	Yangjiang				
江城区	Jiangcheng District	23624	8.7	24836	5.1
阳东区	Yangdong District	23633	12.5	24966	5.6
阳春市	Yangchun City	20799	11.0	21964	5.6
阳西县	Yangxi County	22517	11.9	23928	6.3

23-14 续表 2 continued

县(市、区)	County (County-level City and District)	2021 绝对值(元) Value (yuan)	2021 增速(%) Ratio(%)	2022 绝对值(元) Value (yuan)	2022 增速(%) Ratio(%)
湛江市	Zhanjiang				
赤坎区	Chikan District				
霞山区	Xiashan District	20544	5.3	21372	4.0
麻章区	Mazhang District	21981	11.5	23207	5.6
坡头区	Potou District	20468	9.4	21281	4.0
雷州市	Leizhou City	16798	11.7	17652	5.1
廉江市	Lianjiang County	22532	10.4	23708	5.2
吴川市	Wuchuan City	24081	6.8	25339	5.2
遂溪县	Suixi County	21596	10.8	22602	4.7
徐闻县	Xuwen County	21269	9.3	21818	2.6
茂名市	Maoming				
茂南区	Maonan District	22085	12.6	23051	4.4
电白区	Dianbai District	21682	8.7	22656	4.5
信宜市	Xinyi City	21521	9.9	22404	4.1
高州市	Gaozhou City	21666	10.0	22523	4.0
化州市	Huazhou City	21756	9.8	22529	3.6
肇庆市	Zhaoqing				
端州区	Duanzhou District				
鼎湖区	Dinghu District	29836	8.0	31061	4.1
高要区	Gaoyao District	26227	9.9	27381	4.4
四会市	Sihui City	29669	10.1	30488	2.8
广宁县	Guangning County	18847	10.0	19931	5.8
德庆县	Deqing County	24341	9.5	25154	3.3
封开县	Fengkai County	18668	10.8	19798	6.0
怀集县	Huaiji County	19890	10.2	20824	4.7
清远市	Qingyuan				
清城区	Qingcheng District	24851	9.3	26024	4.7
清新区	Qingxin District	19925	8.9	20867	4.7
英德市	Yingde City	20115	9.3	21230	5.5
连州市	Lianzhou City	17399	10.6	18428	5.9
佛冈县	Fogang County	19698	12.1	20684	5.0
阳山县	Yangshan County	18409	9.5	19131	3.9
连山县	Lianshan County	16788	11.8	17831	6.2
连南县	Liannan County	17210	11.3	18198	5.7
潮州市	Chaozhou				
湘桥区	Xiangqiao District	20893	10.9	22127	5.9
潮安区	Chaoan District	20856	10.6	22097	6.0
饶平县	Raoping County	18154	10.8	19272	6.2
揭阳市	Jieyang				
榕城区	Rongcheng District				
揭东区	Jiedong District	20750	9.1	21768	4.9
普宁市	Puning City	20271	10.1	21307	5.1
揭西县	Jiexi County	14427	8.4	15381	6.6
惠来县	Huilai County	15979	13.4	16931	6.0
云浮市	Yunfu				
云城区	Yuncheng District	20442	11.0	21583	5.6
云安区	Yunan District	19174	10.7	20376	6.3
罗定市	Luoding City	19061	10.6	20197	6.0
新兴县	Xinxing County	21983	10.8	23257	5.8
郁南县	Yunan County	18846	10.2	19656	4.3

附录

APPENDIX

附　录

简要说明

一、本篇资料包括部分省市社会经济主要指标、中国香港特别行政区、中国澳门特别行政区、中国台湾省主要统计指标及国际主要统计指标。

二、附录A、附录B、附录C资料来源于国家统计局编辑、中国统计出版社出版的《中国统计年鉴》和《中国统计摘要》。附录D资料来源于国家统计局编辑、中国统计出版社出版的《国际统计年鉴——2022》。

三、一些国际组织及其组成成员：

经济合作与发展组织（经合组织，OECD），成员国有38个：澳大利亚、奥地利、比利时、加拿大、智利、捷克、丹麦、爱沙尼亚、芬兰、法国、德国、希腊、匈牙利、冰岛、爱尔兰、以色列、意大利、日本、韩国、拉脱维亚、立陶宛、卢森堡、墨西哥、荷兰、新西兰、挪威、波兰、葡萄牙、斯洛伐克、斯洛文尼亚、西班牙、瑞典、瑞士、土耳其、英国、美国、哥伦比亚、哥斯达黎加。

欧洲联盟（欧盟，EU），成员国有27个：法国、德国、意大利、荷兰、比利时、卢森堡、丹麦、爱尔兰、希腊、西班牙、葡萄牙、奥地利、芬兰、瑞典、塞浦路斯、捷克、爱沙尼亚、匈牙利、拉脱维亚、立陶宛、马耳他、波兰、斯洛伐克、斯洛文尼亚、保加利亚、罗马尼亚和克罗地亚。

欧洲货币联盟（欧元区，Euro Area），成员国有19个：德国、比利时、奥地利、荷兰、法国、意大利、西班牙、葡萄牙、卢森堡、爱尔兰、芬兰、希腊、斯洛文尼亚、塞浦路斯、马耳他、斯洛伐克、爱沙尼亚、拉脱维亚和立陶宛。

东南亚国家联盟（东盟，ASEAN），成员国有10个：菲律宾、马来西亚、泰国、新加坡、印度尼西亚、文莱（1984年）、越南（1995年）、缅甸（1997年）、老挝（1997年）和柬埔寨（1999年）。

北美自由贸易区（NAFTA）：成立于1994年1月1日，成员国有3个，加拿大、墨西哥和美国。

西方七国（G7）：包括美国、日本、英国、德国、法国、意大利和加拿大。

四、一些国家(含地区)分类含义：

按收入分组国家：按照世界银行2021年分组标准，高收入国家指按图表集法计算的人均国民总收入13205美元及以上的国家，中等偏上收入国家指人均国民总收入4256美元至13205美元的国家，中等偏下收入国家指人均国民总收入1086美元至4255美元的国家，低收入国家指人均国民总收入1085美元及以下的国家。

发达国家或地区与发展中国家或地区：联合国统计司对“发达国家或地区”及“发展中国家或地区”没有一个明确的划分标准。通常是把亚洲的日本、塞浦路斯和以色列，北美的加拿大、美国、百慕大、格陵兰、圣皮埃尔和密克隆，大洋洲的澳大利亚、新西兰、赫德岛和麦克唐纳岛、诺福克岛、科科斯（基林）群岛、圣诞岛，欧洲，都列入发达国家或地区。国际货币基金组织指出“发达经济体”包括40个国家或地区，他们是：安道尔、澳大利亚、奥地利、比利时、加拿大、塞浦路斯、捷克、丹麦、爱沙尼亚、芬兰、法国、德国、希腊、中国香港、冰岛、爱尔兰、以色列、意大利、日本、韩国、拉脱维亚、立陶宛、卢森堡、中国澳门、马耳他、荷兰、新西兰、挪威、葡萄牙、波多黎各、圣马力诺、新加坡、斯洛伐克、斯洛文尼亚、西班牙、瑞典、瑞士、中国台湾、英国及美国。其他为新兴市场及发展中经济体。

五、2022年各省市资料均为快速年报数。

六、本篇资料由广东省统计局综合统计处负责整理、编辑。

Appendix

Brief Introduction

I. The data in this chapter include main social and economic indicators of some provinces and municipalities,main statistical indicators of Hong Kong and Macao Special Administrative Regions and Taiwan Province of the People’s Republic of China, as well as main international statistical indicators.

II. Data in Appendices A, B, C come from China Statistical Yearbook and China Statistical Abstract compiled by National Bureau of Statistics and published by China Statistics Press. Data in Appendix D come from International Statistical Yearbook compiled by National Bureau of Statistics and published by China Statistics Press.

III. International organizations and their members included are as follows:

Organization for Economic Co-operation and Development (OECD), has 38 members, i.e., Australia，Austria，Belgium， Canada, Chile，Czech Republic，Denmark，Estonia，Finland，France，Germany，Greece，Hungary，Iceland，Ireland，Israel， Italy，Japan，Korea，Latvia，Lithuania，Luxembourg，Mexico，Netherlands，New Zealand，Norway，Poland，Portugal，Slovak Republic，Slovenia，Spain，Sweden，Switzerland，Turkey，United Kingdom，United States，Columbia，Costa Rica.

European Union (EU), it expanded to 27 members, i.e., France, Germany, Italy, Netherlands, Belgium, Luxembourg, Denmark, Ireland, Greece, Spain, Portugal, Austria, Finland, Sweden, Cyprus, the Czech Republic, Estonia, Hungary, Latvia, Lithuania, Malta, Poland, Slovakia , Slovenia, Bulgaria, Romania and Croatia.

European Monetary Union (Euro Area), it has 19 members and member countries are Germany, Belgium, Austria, Netherlands, France, Italy, Spain, Portugal, Luxembourg, Ireland, Finland, Greece, Slovenia, Cyprus, Malta, Slovak, Estonia, Latvia and Lithuania.

Association of South East Asian Countries (ASEAN), it has 10 members, i.e., the Philippines, Malaysia, Thailand, Singapore, Indonesia, Brunei Darussalam (1984), Viet Nam (1995), Myanmar (1997), Lao People's Democratic Republic (1997) and Cambodia (1999).

North American Free Trade Area(NAFTA), was founded on January 1, 1994, with members unchanged hitherto, i.e., Canada, Mexico and the United States.

Group 7, includes the United States, Japan, the United Kingdom, Germany, France, Italy and Canada.

IV. Countries (territories) are classified as follows:

Countries by Income Group According to the criteria by the World Bank, countries and territories (referred to as economies) are classified into high income (higher than \$13205), higher middle income (between \$4256 and \$13205), lower middle income (between \$1086 and \$4255) and low income (\$1085 and below) groups by their per capita GNI (calculated by Atlas method)in the year 2021.

Developed and Developing Countries or Areas: There is no established convention for the designation of "developed" and "developing" countries or areas in the United Nations system. In common practice, Japan, Cyprus, Israelin Asia, Canada, the United States, Bermuda, Greenland, Saint Pierre and Miquelon in northern America, Australia, New Zealand, Heard Island and McDonald Islands, Norfolk Island, Cocos (Keeling) Islands, Christmas Island in Oceania, and Europe are considered "developed" regions or areas. Advanced economies in International Monetary Fund (IMF) are composed of 40 countries: Andorra,Australia, Austria, Belgium, Canada, Cyprus, Czech Republic, Denmark, Estonia, Finland, France, Germany, Greece, Hong Kong SAR, Iceland, Ireland, Israel, Italy, Japan, Korea, Latvia, Lithuania, Luxembourg, Macao SAR, Malta, Netherlands, New Zealand, Norway, Portugal, Puerto Rico, San Marino, Singapore, Slovak Republic, Slovenia, Spain, Sweden, Switzerland, Taiwan Province of China, United Kingdom, and United States. Others are emerging market and developing economies.

V. The data of various provinces and municipalities in 2022 all come from flash annual reports.

VI. The data in this chapter are prepared and compiled by the Division of Comprehensive Statistics of Guangdong Provincial Bureau of Statistics.

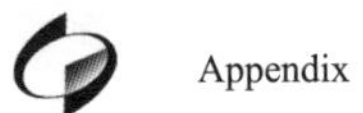

附录A-1 人口及地区生产总值（2022年）

Population and Gross Domestic Product (2022)

地 区	Province or Municipality	年末常住人口(万人) Year-end Permanent Population (10000 persons)	年末城镇人口比重 (%) Proportion of Urban Population (%)	地区生产总值(亿元) Gross Domestic Product (100 million yuan)	第一产业 Primary Industry	第二产业 Secondary Industry	第三产业 Tertiary Industry	地区生产总值比上年增长 (%) Increase by (%)	人均地区生产总值 (元) Per Capita GDP (yuan)	人均地区生产总值比上年增长 (%) Increase by(%)
全 国	**National Total**	**141175**	**65.22**	**1210207.2**	**88345.1**	**483164.5**	**638697.6**	**3.0**	**85698**	**3.0**
北 京	Beijing	2184	87.57	41610.9	111.5	6605.1	34894.3	0.7	190313	0.8
天 津	Tianjing	1363	85.11	16311.3	273.1	6038.9	9999.3	1.0	119235	1.8
河 北	Hebei	7420	61.65	42370.4	4410.3	17050.1	20910.0	3.8	56995	4.1
山 西	Shanxi	3481	63.96	25642.6	1340.4	13840.8	10461.3	4.4	73675	4.5
内蒙古	Nei Monggol	2401	68.60	23158.6	2653.7	11241.8	9263.1	4.2	96474	4.2
辽 宁	Liaoning	4197	73.00	28975.1	2597.6	11755.8	14621.7	2.1	68775	2.8
吉 林	Jilin	2348	63.72	13070.2	1689.1	4628.3	6752.8	-1.9	55347	-0.8
黑龙江	Heilongjiang	3099	66.21	15901.0	3609.8	4648.9	7642.2	2.7	51096	3.9
上 海	ShangHai	2475	89.33	44652.8	97.0	11458.4	33097.4	-0.2	179907	0.0
江 苏	Jiangsu	8515	74.42	122875.6	4959.4	55888.7	62027.5	2.8	144390	2.5
浙 江	Zhejiang	6577	73.38	77715.4	2324.8	33205.2	42185.4	3.1	118496	2.2
安 徽	Anhui	6127	60.15	45045.0	3513.7	18588.0	22943.3	3.5	73603	3.3
福 建	Fujian	4188	70.11	53109.9	3076.2	25078.2	24955.5	4.7	126829	4.3
江 西	Jiangxi	4528	62.07	32074.7	2451.5	14359.6	15263.7	4.7	70923	4.6
山 东	Shandong	10163	64.54	87435.1	6298.6	35014.2	46122.3	3.9	86003	3.9
河 南	Henan	9872	57.07	61345.1	5817.8	25465.0	30062.2	3.1	62106	3.5
湖 北	Hubei	5844	64.67	53734.9	4986.7	21240.6	27507.6	4.3	92059	3.4
湖 南	Hunan	6604	60.31	48670.4	4602.7	19182.6	24885.1	4.5	73598	4.8
广 东	Guangdong	12657	74.79	129118.6	5340.4	52843.5	70934.7	1.9	101905	1.7
广 西	Guangxi	5047	55.65	26300.9	4269.8	8938.6	13092.5	2.9	52164	2.6
海 南	Hainan	1027	61.49	6818.2	1417.8	1310.9	4089.5	0.2	66602	-0.5
重 庆	Chongqing	3213	70.96	29129.0	2012.1	11693.9	15423.1	2.6	90663	2.5
四 川	Sichuan	8374	58.35	56749.8	5964.3	21157.1	29628.4	2.9	67777	2.9
贵 州	Guizhou	3856	54.81	20164.6	2861.2	7113.0	10190.4	1.2	52321	1.2
云 南	Yunnan	4693	51.72	28954.2	4012.2	10471.2	14470.8	4.3	61716	4.7
西 藏	Tibet	364	37.39	2132.6	180.2	804.7	1147.8	1.1	58438	1.4
陕 西	Shaanxi	3956	64.02	32772.7	2575.3	15933.1	14264.2	4.3	82864	4.3
甘 肃	Gansu	2492	54.19	11201.6	1515.3	3945.0	5741.2	4.5	44968	4.7
青 海	Qinghai	595	61.43	3610.1	380.2	1585.7	1644.2	2.3	60724	2.1
宁 夏	Ningxia	728	66.34	5069.6	407.5	2449.1	2213.0	4.0	69781	3.5
新 疆	Xinjiang	2587	57.89	17741.3	2509.3	7271.1	7961.0	3.2	68552	3.3

注：地区生产总值为初步核算数。

Note: GDP is the preliminary calculated number.

附录A-2 固定资产投资完成情况（2022年）

Investment in Fixed Assets (2022年)

地 区	Province or Municipality	固定资产投资增速（不含农户）(%) Investment in Fixed Assets (excluding farmers) (%)	房地产开发投资额（亿元）Real Estate Development (100 million yuan)	商品房销售额（亿元）Total Sales of Commercial Housing (100 million yuan)	#住宅 Residential Buildings	房屋竣工面积（万平方米）Completion of Commercial Housing Area (10000 sq.m)	商品房销售面积（万平方米）Floor Space of Commercial Buildings Sold (10000 sq.m)
全 国	**National Total**	**5.1**	**132895.4**	**133307.8**	**116747.0**	**86222**	**135837**
北 京	Beijing	3.6	4178.5	3976.9	3545.3	1938	1040
天 津	Tianjing	-9.9	2127.9	1516.4	1421.6	1504	974
河 北	Hebei	7.9	4983.0	3702.1	3488.8	2523	4616
山 西	Shanxi	5.9	1764.2	1515.0	1418.4	2127	2257
内蒙古	Nei Monggol	17.6	978.3	868.0	808.7	1101	1381
辽 宁	Liaoning	3.6	2362.0	1814.7	1659.7	1946	2182
吉 林	Jilin	-2.4	1014.8	696.3	631.0	724	1001
黑龙江	Heilongjiang	0.6	628.6	569.4	506.7	732	926
上 海	ShangHai	-1.0	4979.5	7467.5	6937.8	1676	1853
江 苏	Jiangsu	3.8	12406.9	14811.6	13177.0	7892	12115
浙 江	Zhejiang	9.1	12939.5	12660.1	11061.4	6130	6815
安 徽	Anhui	9.0	6811.7	5487.9	4964.3	5945	7471
福 建	Fujian	7.5	5515.4	6502.4	5284.3	4063	6054
江 西	Jiangxi	8.6	2209.3	4905.2	4138.6	1463	6703
山 东	Shandong	6.1	9225.9	9807.7	8481.3	6686	11686
河 南	Henan	6.7	6793.4	6724.8	6152.3	6452	11141
湖 北	Hubei	15.0	6172.0	5413.3	4821.7	3281	6385
湖 南	Hunan	6.6	5180.3	4312.3	3800.1	3436	6793
广 东	Guangdong	-2.6	14963.0	15870.5	13428.5	8161	10591
广 西	Guangxi	0.1	2307.4	2390.1	1908.0	2345	4371
海 南	Hainan	-4.2	1158.4	1098.0	924.9	751	644
重 庆	Chongqing	0.7	3467.6	3101.6	2448.8	2796	4439
四 川	Sichuan	6.0	7500.0	8215.9	6966.7	4072	10340
贵 州	Guizhou	-5.1	2403.7	2193.6	1909.0	967	3847
云 南	Yunnan	7.5	3152.0	1999.4	1736.1	2565	2938
西 藏	Tibet	-18.0	60.7	50.7	43.7	36	60
陕 西	Shanxi	8.1	4254.8	3270.5	2958.8	1976	3309
甘 肃	Gansu	10.1	1481.7	835.5	780.5	918	1470
青 海	Qinghai	-7.6	296.1	145.0	127.7	248	204
宁 夏	Ningxia	10.2	419.9	502.1	451.0	627	716
新 疆	Xinjiang	7.6	1158.9	883.5	764.7	1141	1516

注：各地固定资产投资不含跨省投资。
Note: Trans-provincial investments are not included in the investment in fixed assets of various province.

附录A-3　居民人均收入与支出(2022年)

Per Capita Income and Expenditure (2022)

单位：元 (yuan)

地　区	Province or Municipality	全体居民 All residents		城镇居民 Urban resident		农村居民 Rural resident	
		人均可支配收入 Per Capita Disposable Income	人均消费支出 Per Capita Consumption Expenditure	人均可支配收入 Per Capita Disposable Income	人均消费支出 Per Capita Consumption Expenditure	人均可支配收入 Per Capita Disposable Income	人均消费支出 Per Capita Consumption Expenditure
全　国	**National Total**	**36883.3**	**24538.2**	**49282.9**	**30390.8**	**20132.8**	**16632.1**
北　京	Beijing	77414.5	42683.2	84023.1	45616.9	34753.8	23745.4
天　津	Tianjing	48976.1	31323.7	53003.2	33823.6	29017.8	18934.2
河　北	Hebei	30867.0	20890.3	41277.7	25071.3	19364.2	16270.6
山　西	Shanxi	29178.2	17536.7	39532.0	21922.6	16322.7	12090.9
内蒙古	Nei Monggol	35920.6	22298.4	46295.4	26666.8	19640.9	15443.6
辽　宁	Liaoning	36088.8	22603.7	44002.6	26652.2	19908.0	14326.1
吉　林	Jilin	27974.5	17897.5	35470.9	21834.9	18134.5	12729.2
黑龙江	Heilongjiang	28345.5	20411.9	35042.1	24011.0	18577.4	15161.8
上　海	ShangHai	79609.8	46045.4	84034.0	48110.5	39729.4	27430.3
江　苏	Jiangsu	49861.7	32848.1	60178.1	37795.7	28486.5	22596.9
浙　江	Zhejiang	60302.5	38971.1	71267.9	44511.2	37565.0	27483.4
安　徽	Anhui	32745.2	22541.9	45133.2	26832.4	19574.9	17980.4
福　建	Fujian	43117.7	30041.7	53817.1	35692.1	24986.6	20466.5
江　西	Jiangxi	32418.7	21707.9	43696.5	25975.5	19936.0	16984.4
山　东	Shandong	37560.1	22640.4	49049.7	28555.2	22109.9	14686.7
河　南	Henan	28222.4	19019.5	38483.7	23539.3	18697.3	14823.9
湖　北	Hubei	32913.6	24827.8	42625.8	29120.9	19709.5	18991.0
湖　南	Hunan	34036.0	24082.7	47301.2	29580.1	19546.3	18077.7
广　东	Guangdong	47064.6	32168.7	56905.3	36936.2	23597.8	20800.0
广　西	Guangxi	27980.7	18342.8	39703.0	22438.1	17432.7	14657.7
海　南	Hainan	30956.6	21500.4	40117.5	26417.6	19117.4	15145.5
重　庆	Chongqing	35665.9	25371.1	45508.9	30573.9	19312.7	16727.1
四　川	Sichuan	30679.2	22301.9	43233.3	27637.3	18672.4	17199.0
贵　州	Guizhou	25508.2	17938.7	41085.7	24229.9	13706.7	13172.5
云　南	Yunnan	26936.8	18950.8	42167.9	26239.7	15146.9	13308.6
西　藏	Tibet	26674.8	15885.6	48752.9	28265.4	18209.5	11138.9
陕　西	Shaanxi	30115.8	19848.4	42431.3	24765.8	15704.3	14094.2
甘　肃	Gansu	23273.1	17489.4	37572.4	25207.0	12165.2	11494.2
青　海	Qinghai	27000.0	17260.8	38735.8	21700.2	14456.2	12515.8
宁　夏	Ningxia	29599.3	19136.3	40193.7	24213.4	16430.3	12825.3
新　疆	Xinjiang	27062.7	17927.1	38410.2	24142.3	16549.9	12169.1

附录A-4 居民消费价格指数（2022年）

Consumer Price Indices (2022)

上年=100 (Preceding Year=100)

地 区	Province or Municipality	居民消费价格指数 Consumer Price Index	食品烟酒 Foods, Tobacco and Liquor	衣 着 Clothing	居 住 Residence	生活用品及服务 Daily Necessities and Services	交通和通信 Transportation and Communication	教育文化和娱乐 Education, Culture and Recreation	医疗保健 Health Care	其他用品和服务 Other Articles and Services
全 国	**National Total**	**102.0**	**102.4**	**100.5**	**100.7**	**101.2**	**105.2**	**101.8**	**100.6**	**101.6**
北 京	Beijing	101.8	103.1	100.6	100.6	101.6	105.0	100.6	100.7	101.6
天 津	Tianjing	101.9	102.2	101.4	100.3	101.6	105.9	101.8	100.2	100.3
河 北	Hebei	101.8	102.7	99.7	100.7	100.6	104.5	101.4	100.5	101.8
山 西	Shanxi	102.1	103.7	101.6	100.4	100.8	104.6	101.3	100.3	101.4
内蒙古	Nei Monggol	101.8	102.0	100.3	100.5	101.1	105.8	101.2	100.3	101.8
辽 宁	Liaoning	102.0	102.9	99.2	100.5	100.9	105.9	101.8	100.1	101.8
吉 林	Jilin	102.1	102.5	99.7	101.9	101.4	104.9	101.2	100.7	101.7
黑龙江	Heilongjiang	101.9	102.2	101.0	101.3	100.6	105.5	100.9	100.5	101.3
上 海	ShangHai	102.5	104.5	99.0	101.0	102.0	104.4	103.5	102.1	100.6
江 苏	Jiangsu	102.2	102.6	101.2	100.9	102.0	104.9	101.6	101.9	101.8
浙 江	Zhejiang	102.2	102.6	100.4	100.7	101.8	105.1	103.1	100.3	101.8
安 徽	Anhui	102.0	102.7	101.3	99.8	101.0	105.3	102.8	100.9	102.0
福 建	Fujian	101.9	102.4	100.0	100.9	101.3	104.9	101.4	100.3	101.5
江 西	Jiangxi	102.0	102.2	100.5	100.9	100.8	105.6	102.1	100.2	101.6
山 东	Shandong	101.7	102.3	100.3	100.5	101.1	104.8	100.4	100.4	101.8
河 南	Henan	101.5	102.1	100.4	100.1	101.1	104.4	101.3	100.7	101.4
湖 北	Hubei	102.1	102.2	101.0	101.4	101.4	104.7	102.3	100.3	102.4
湖 南	Hunan	101.8	101.4	101.3	100.7	101.2	106.3	100.9	101.0	101.6
广 东	Guangdong	102.2	102.9	100.6	100.6	101.2	105.8	102.2	100.4	101.6
广 西	Guangxi	101.9	101.9	100.7	100.4	100.5	104.5	104.0	100.9	101.0
海 南	Hainan	101.6	102.5	100.0	99.3	100.6	105.0	102.1	100.0	100.5
重 庆	Chongqing	102.1	103.9	100.0	99.9	101.4	105.5	101.6	99.7	100.6
四 川	Sichuan	102.0	101.9	101.4	101.0	101.3	105.4	102.0	100.6	101.7
贵 州	Guizhou	101.6	101.0	100.6	100.5	100.8	105.4	101.5	100.3	101.4
云 南	Yunnan	101.6	101.1	100.4	100.2	100.8	105.4	101.6	100.8	102.2
西 藏	Tibet	101.5	100.8	100.8	100.5	100.5	106.1	100.3	99.9	102.0
陕 西	Shaanxi	102.1	102.6	100.5	101.1	101.0	103.8	103.4	100.8	101.9
甘 肃	Gansu	101.9	102.8	100.4	100.8	100.9	105.0	100.9	100.5	101.2
青 海	Qinghai	102.4	102.8	101.5	101.1	101.2	104.7	103.6	100.4	100.9
宁 夏	Ningxia	102.3	102.2	99.2	100.9	101.4	106.8	101.5	102.3	101.1
新 疆	Xinjiang	101.8	101.4	99.8	101.4	101.0	106.1	100.7	100.0	102.3

附录A-5 农林牧渔业总产值和增速（2022年）
Gross Output Value of Farming,Forestry,Animal Husbandry and Fishery and Growth Rate (2022)

地 区	Province or Municipality	农林牧渔业总产值（亿元）Gross Output Value of Farming, Forestry, Animal Husbandry and Fishery (100 million yuan)	#农业 Farming	#林业 Forestry	#畜牧业 Animal Husbandry	#渔业 Fishery	农林牧渔业总产值比上年增长(%) Growth Rate in Gross Output Value of Farming, Forestry ,Animal Husbandry and Fishery (%)
全 国	**National Total**	**156065.9**	**84438.6**	**6820.8**	**40652.4**	**15468.0**	**4.4**
北 京	Beijing	268.2	129.8	86.5	42.3	3.9	-2.0
天 津	Tianjing	521.4	276.8	8.9	147.2	70.5	2.9
河 北	Hebei	7667.4	4035.7	266.6	2391.7	342.3	4.6
山 西	Shanxi	2211.6	1288.4	174.5	615.8	9.1	5.0
内蒙古	Nei Monggol	4316.8	2208.5	107.5	1876.3	31.3	4.9
辽 宁	Liaoning	5180.0	2258.3	161.7	1694.6	881.3	3.2
吉 林	Jilin	3217.9	1512.7	69.5	1482.6	61.6	4.1
黑龙江	Heilongjiang	6718.2	4320.5	212.3	1842.8	147.9	2.5
上 海	ShangHai	273.5	149.3	8.3	46.4	51.2	-1.1
江 苏	Jiangsu	8733.8	4685.7	185.6	1294.2	1856.9	3.9
浙 江	Zhejiang	3752.3	1769.8	183.0	405.7	1261.2	3.4
安 徽	Anhui	6278.0	2937.0	473.3	1812.5	660.3	4.5
福 建	Fujian	5502.6	2065.7	429.9	1066.3	1740.7	3.9
江 西	Jiangxi	4223.8	1916.7	416.9	1094.4	553.2	4.3
山 东	Shandong	12130.7	6206.5	227.3	3003.5	1729.7	4.8
河 南	Henan	10952.2	6948.3	149.5	2832.3	147.4	5.1
湖 北	Hubei	8939.3	4193.1	311.2	2128.2	1584.3	4.4
湖 南	Hunan	8160.1	3973.2	477.4	2466.9	617.8	3.8
广 东	Guangdong	8892.3	4308.2	549.2	1680.2	1898.2	4.8
广 西	Guangxi	6938.5	3977.7	548.5	1509.5	575.8	5.0
海 南	Hainan	2272.0	1236.8	118.7	340.5	466.6	3.5
重 庆	Chongqing	3068.4	1881.8	176.4	800.9	137.0	4.5
四 川	Sichuan	9859.8	5528.8	438.2	3281.7	343.1	4.5
贵 州	Guizhou	4908.7	3313.7	340.0	941.4	79.6	4.2
云 南	Yunnan	6635.8	3629.9	492.2	2192.3	119.9	5.5
西 藏	Tibet	278.6	121.0	7.0	143.4	0.2	4.8
陕 西	Shaanxi	4601.9	3310.4	86.1	925.4	36.2	4.6
甘 肃	Gansu	2680.7	1806.4	36.4	662.2	1.7	5.9
青 海	Qinghai	566.2	238.3	13.1	302.3	4.3	4.6
宁 夏	Ningxia	845.9	455.6	11.5	323.5	22.8	4.9
新 疆	Xinjiang	5469.0	3754.0	53.5	1305.3	32.1	5.8

注：本表绝对数按当年价格计算，增速按可比价格计算。
Note: the figures in this table are calculated at current prices, the growth rate is calculated at comparable prices.

附录A-6 主要农产品产量（2022年）
Output of Major Agricultural Products (2022)

单位：万吨 (10000 tons)

地 区	Province or Municipality	粮食 Grain	油料 Oil-bearing	糖料 Sugarcane	肉类 Meat	蔬菜 Vegetable	水果 Fruits
全 国	**National Total**	**68652.8**	**3654.2**	**11236.5**	**9328.4**	**79997.2**	**31296.2**
北 京	Beijing	45.4	0.9		4.3	198.9	38.3
天 津	Tianjing	256.2	0.4	…	29.5	256.4	57.8
河 北	Hebei	3865.1	115.4	70.2	478.8	5406.8	1533.9
山 西	Shanxi	1464.3	15.0	0.2	143.2	1010.3	1002.8
内蒙古	Nei Monggol	3900.6	170.0	387.1	284.1	1012.9	175.5
辽 宁	Liaoning	2484.5	113.4	1.3	446.2	2055.4	879.7
吉 林	Jilin	4080.8	81.6	1.4	291.0	514.8	166.0
黑龙江	Heilongjiang	7763.1	14.3	18.2	312.5	759.8	189.4
上 海	ShangHai	95.6	0.3	0.1	9.5	259.6	31.9
江 苏	Jiangsu	3769.1	96.3	5.9	318.1	5974.7	1002.1
浙 江	Zhejiang	621.0	33.0	39.2	108.5	1976.7	704.5
安 徽	Anhui	4100.1	173.4	9.3	475.3	2537.7	798.3
福 建	Fujian	508.7	23.6	28.8	296.3	1752.9	864.9
江 西	Jiangxi	2151.9	137.5	62.5	359.9	1786.9	749.4
山 东	Shandong	5543.8	274.0	…	844.5	9045.8	3095.5
河 南	Henan	6789.4	684.0	8.4	660.0	7845.3	2542.0
湖 北	Hubei	2741.1	374.2	26.6	441.2	4407.9	1143.2
湖 南	Hunan	3018.0	277.0	34.9	580.9	4356.7	1208.2
广 东	Guangdong	1291.5	117.4	1292.1	481.0	3999.1	1895.2
广 西	Guangxi	1393.1	76.5	7116.5	454.9	4236.5	3402.5
海 南	Hainan	146.6	7.5	76.7	69.2	605.4	563.6
重 庆	Chongqing	1072.8	70.8	8.3	205.3	2272.4	593.3
四 川	Sichuan	3510.5	433.8	38.5	685.7	5198.7	1380.5
贵 州	Guizhou	1114.6	105.6	41.3	241.0	3355.7	698.9
云 南	Yunnan	1958.0	63.5	1553.7	521.6	2857.9	1289.1
西 藏	Tibet	107.3	4.7	…	28.6	81.6	3.1
陕 西	Shaanxi	1297.9	56.3	0.3	132.1	2082.2	2240.8
甘 肃	Gansu	1265.0	61.3	15.8	142.6	1736.6	965.5
青 海	Qinghai	107.3	30.9		41.0	151.8	2.8
宁 夏	Ningxia	375.8	4.5	…	36.8	527.9	271.7
新 疆	Xinjiang	1813.5	37.2	399.1	204.7	1731.9	1672.6

注：水果产量含瓜果产量。
Note:The output of fruits includes melons in this table.

附录A－7　规模以上工业企业主要经济指标（2022年）

Main Economic Indicators of Industrial Enterprises above Designated Size (2022)

单位：亿元　　(100 million yuan)

地　区	Province or Municipality	营业收入 Business Revenue	营业成本 Business Cost	利润总额 Total Profit	应收账款 Accounts Receivable	产成品 Finished Goods	资产总计 Total Assets
全　国	**National Total**	**1379098.4**	**1168426.4**	**84038.5**	**216466.2**	**60363.2**	**1561196.7**
北　京	Beijing	26794.4	22310.9	1980.9	5765.8	1285.4	64237.4
天　津	Tianjing	23537.1	20080.7	1523.3	3397.7	926.6	24752.1
河　北	Hebei	52403.7	47132.4	1261.2	6958.5	2160.0	60192.4
山　西	Shanxi	37961.2	30397.5	3633.4	6673.2	1291.6	59676.4
内蒙古	Nei Monggol	28158.2	21559.7	4060.0	3268.5	948.1	42114.4
辽　宁	Liaoning	35854.2	30763.4	1540.9	5103.7	1703.4	43477.2
吉　林	Jilin	13835.9	11471.1	917.3	1926.3	586.5	19382.1
黑龙江	Heilongjiang	12418.8	10128.6	604.0	2110.8	565.3	19181.9
上　海	ShangHai	45264.8	37510.5	2793.6	9389.9	2089.1	54298.1
江　苏	Jiangsu	161506.0	138124.9	9061.9	34218.8	8864.0	169623.2
浙　江	Zhejiang	107956.6	92107.8	5863.6	21182.3	5980.0	125075.7
安　徽	Anhui	49051.1	42521.9	2449.7	9055.4	2153.9	55493.6
福　建	Fujian	70367.5	61346.1	4071.3	6639.6	2621.8	51807.6
江　西	Jiangxi	48295.5	41848.4	3456.1	5035.7	1467.6	33934.0
山　东	Shandong	108019.9	94572.5	4473.2	14912.2	5434.7	119195.8
河　南	Henan	60206.8	53255.8	2534.0	7005.0	2004.5	57668.8
湖　北	Hubei	53789.9	45878.5	3139.6	6292.6	2031.6	51829.6
湖　南	Hunan	47644.8	39668.6	2310.1	5508.8	1310.1	36454.6
广　东	Guangdong	183027.4	153237.9	10329.3	31814.7	8537.5	196419.2
广　西	Guangxi	23234.8	20861.2	702.3	3371.5	1197.3	25919.1
海　南	Hainan	2944.3	2399.3	135.2	440.6	102.0	4528.5
重　庆	Chongqing	28211.4	24190.3	1683.8	4179.9	957.6	26911.8
四　川	Sichuan	54932.4	45044.9	4836.3	7743.9	2103.4	64081.6
贵　州	Guizhou	10255.5	7785.7	1284.9	1820.2	460.0	18897.7
云　南	Yunnan	19682.8	15967.8	1330.5	2251.2	798.3	26815.1
西　藏	Tibet	498.5	360.8	61.5	98.6	18.8	2297.6
陕　西	Shaanxi	35208.7	27051.0	4570.3	4620.2	1275.3	44192.6
甘　肃	Gansu	10960.4	9337.8	594.6	1357.9	412.4	14787.9
青　海	Qinghai	4544.0	3421.6	828.9	686.8	157.8	7439.7
宁　夏	Ningxia	8107.3	6902.0	412.7	1093.6	315.7	13152.9
新　疆	Xinjiang	17573.8	13204.0	2462.3	2483.7	742.1	30237.0

注：本表除广东外均为快报数。
Note:The data in this table come from flash annual report except Guangdong's.

附录A-8 主要工业产品产量（2022年）

Output of Major Industrial Products (2022)

地 区	Province or Municipality	发电量（亿千瓦小时）Generating Capacity (billion kilowatt hours)	生 铁（万吨）Pig Iron (ten thousand tons)	钢 材（万吨）Steels (ten thousand tons)	水 泥（万吨）Cement (ten thousand tons)	农用化肥（万吨）Agricultural Chemical Fertilizer (ten thousand tons)	汽 车（万辆）Car (10000 vehicles)	家 用 电冰箱（万台）Household Refrigerators (10000 sets)	微型计算机设备（万台）Micro-computers Equipment (10000 units)
全 国	**National Total**	**88487.1**	**86382.8**	**134033.5**	**212951.3**	**5573.3**	**2718.0**	**8664.4**	**43418.2**
北 京	Beijing	467.1		184.3	203.4		87.1		858.6
天 津	Tianjing	764.9	1772.8	5543.7	529.5	47.8	60.3		0.1
河 北	Hebei	3792.9	19840.2	32169.2	10033.9	193.4	90.6		
山 西	Shanxi	4298.8	5833.5	6354.6	4844.6	364.9	16.5		3.6
内蒙古	Nei Monggol	6619.2	2188.8	3041.9	3597.0	400.9	5.4		
辽 宁	Liaoning	2256.8	7101.4	7727.5	3910.9	31.0	76.6	158.2	49.4
吉 林	Jilin	1056.9	1307.8	1532.0	1731.4	22.8	215.6		
黑龙江	Heilongjiang	1217.6	877.1	999.7	1881.1	80.5	8.3		
上 海	ShangHai	955.0	1390.0	1920.9	369.6	1.0	302.5		2760.7
江 苏	Jiangsu	6077.3	9637.9	14882.2	14235.7	161.8	94.4	1215.5	3330.5
浙 江	Zhejiang	4349.9	802.6	2934.8	12953.7	32.1	124.9	454.5	129.6
安 徽	Anhui	3298.8	2956.5	3963.0	14218.7	230.3	174.7	2633.5	2950.2
福 建	Fujian	3088.8	1382.5	3505.5	9692.9	48.2	33.9		1185.3
江 西	Jiangxi	1725.0	2384.7	3457.0	8997.2	111.7	41.4	70.8	4946.6
山 东	Shandong	6203.6	7371.3	10529.1	13522.5	430.3	101.9	832.1	0.7
河 南	Henan	3429.8	2743.0	4158.0	11488.4	396.4	55.3	173.9	97.2
湖 北	Hubei	3108.7	2832.3	3911.1	11056.2	591.4	189.6	518.5	1336.2
湖 南	Hunan	1768.1	2179.6	3038.3	9998.4	82.1	26.3		208.2
广 东	Guangdong	6093.8	2420.9	5627.4	15131.2	5.5	415.4	1773.3	6948.8
广 西	Guangxi	2115.9	3013.3	4995.6	10426.5	43.8	177.0	416.8	179.7
海 南	Hainan	405.7			1626.4	63.7	2.2		
重 庆	Chongqing	997.8	723.0	1690.6	5321.1	166.2	203.8	134.4	8631.9
四 川	Sichuan	4846.2	2036.4	3583.0	13070.1	381.8	72.5	115.2	9221.2
贵 州	Guizhou	2299.0	380.6	607.3	6428.1	247.5	4.6	156.6	0.1
云 南	Yunnan	4016.6	1583.3	2550.7	9693.7	245.1	2.2		571.0
西 藏	Tibet	128.2			792.7				
陕 西	Shaanxi	2852.1	1188.3	2010.5	6529.8	158.2	133.8	11.0	8.4
甘 肃	Gansu	1954.1	810.7	1091.6	4047.8	23.7			
青 海	Qinghai	998.1	99.4	120.6	978.5	555.4			
宁 夏	Ningxia	2235.1	497.7	578.5	1667.5	71.7			
新 疆	Xinjiang	4793.4	1027.1	1324.7	3877.5	383.6	1.4		

附录A-9　建筑业主要指标（2022年）

Indicators of Construction Industry (2022)

地　区	Province or Municipality	企业个数（个）Number of Enterprises (unit)	从事建筑业活动的从业人员平均人数（万人）Number of Employed Persons of Construction Enterprises (10000 persons)	建筑业总产值（亿元）Gross Output Value of Construction Enterprises (100 million yuan)	房屋建筑施工面积（万平方米）Construction Area of Housing Construction (10000 square meters)	房屋建筑竣工面积（万平方米）Completion Area of Housing Construction (10000 square meters)	按建筑业总产值计算的劳动生产率（元/人）Labor Productivity Calculated by Gross Output Value of Construction Industry (yuan/person)
全　国	**National Total**	**143621**	**6321.4**	**311979.8**	**1564518.2**	**405477.2**	**493526**
北　京	Beijing	2597	219.7	13866.1	89888.3	13815.4	631270
天　津	Tianjing	2547	81.5	4751.3	18808.4	2722.0	582963
河　北	Hebei	3579	112.1	6951.3	35918.4	7099.0	619862
山　西	Shanxi	3689	130.2	6145.5	22648.1	5634.9	472018
内蒙古	Nei Monggol	1040	24.1	1332.8	7045.5	1096.3	552567
辽　宁	Liaoning	5772	66.7	3936.9	13329.4	3633.2	590400
吉　林	Jilin	2936	37.3	2100.7	7047.1	1882.6	562465
黑龙江	Heilongjiang	2279	37.1	1414.5	3868.0	1056.8	381489
上　海	ShangHai	2351	128.0	9273.9	58203.1	8757.5	724666
江　苏	Jiangsu	13040	1045.1	40660.0	275135.4	76318.6	389048
浙　江	Zhejiang	9950	556.3	23861.1	171655.1	44915.4	428948
安　徽	Anhui	8362	230.7	11702.6	49670.7	14856.9	507177
福　建	Fujian	8699	511.6	17129.5	87432.9	20254.6	334833
江　西	Jiangxi	5782	199.8	10694.8	37048.4	14682.6	535204
山　东	Shandong	10643	309.3	17559.6	98827.9	22917.7	567710
河　南	Henan	9333	313.1	15086.9	66509.3	18282.6	481896
湖　北	Hubei	5927	264.7	21155.0	91309.9	33261.2	799201
湖　南	Hunan	3950	299.0	14481.0	76159.7	23988.5	484348
广　东	Guangdong	10960	398.3	22956.5	107372.7	24943.5	577358
广　西	Guangxi	2749	127.7	7275.8	27539.2	8561.0	569610
海　南	Hainan	325	8.9	467.2	1861.8	449.5	524564
重　庆	Chongqing	3762	232.7	10369.4	36185.8	12601.6	445629
四　川	Sichuan	8757	420.0	18675.2	77718.4	22398.7	444666
贵　州	Guizhou	2170	88.9	4820.2	16415.1	3375.3	541974
云　南	Yunnan	4254	168.1	8168.6	17690.2	5973.1	486080
西　藏	Tibet	410	4.2	203.8	262.6	117.5	484898
陕　西	Shaanxi	3987	168.6	10067.9	40252.7	6825.8	597007
甘　肃	Gansu	2466	51.4	2477.7	12228.8	2030.5	482127
青　海	Qinghai	417	8.5	566.5	971.5	174.8	665033
宁　夏	Ningxia	730	16.3	725.8	1802.3	559.3	445502
新　疆	Xinjiang	1861	62.2	3101.5	13718.3	2304.9	498730

注：本表为具有资质等级的施工总承包、专业承包建筑业企业(不含劳务分包建筑业企业)数据。

Note: Data in this table refer to construction enterprises with qualification grade of main contractor and professional contractors(not including labor subcontracting construction enterprises).

附录A-10　客运量和旅客周转量（2022年）

Passenger Traffic and Passenger-kilometers (2022)

地 区	Province or Municipality	客运量（万人）Passenger Traffic (10000 Persons)	铁路 Railways	公路 Highways	水运 Waterways	旅客周转量（亿人公里）Passenger-kilometers (100 million kilometers)	铁路 Railways	公路 Highways	水运 Waterways
全 国	**National Total**	**558738**	**167296**	**354643**	**11627**	**12921**	**6577.5**	**2407.5**	**22.6**
北 京	Beijing	25055	3950	21105		89	43.6	45.0	
天 津	Tianjing	8295	1311	6959	25	98	57.9	39.5	…
河 北	Hebei	8410	4114	4296		382	345.4	36.8	
山 西	Shanxi	6274	3716	2476	81	119	96.6	22.5	…
内蒙古	Nei Monggol	3557	1712	1844		89	68.5	20.4	
辽 宁	Liaoning	17579	4184	13151	244	269	201.1	66.3	1.7
吉 林	Jilin	7417	2052	5318	47	122	81.5	41.0	…
黑龙江	Heilongjiang	9203	3070	6016	118	126	91.7	34.4	0.1
上 海	ShangHai	7397	4313	2865	220	76	42.2	33.5	0.4
江 苏	Jiangsu	47077	12842	32652	1582	621	416.7	203.5	0.6
浙 江	Zhejiang	32659	12360	17938	2360	491	348.0	139.2	3.5
安 徽	Anhui	14672	7301	7284	87	484	407.8	75.6	0.1
福 建	Fujian	16567	6378	9651	538	260	191.7	68.1	0.5
江 西	Jiangxi	16217	6386	9734	97	456	394.2	61.3	0.1
山 东	Shandong	17536	8471	8247	818	415	313.8	98.3	3.2
河 南	Henan	26828	7512	19189	127	640	470.3	169.1	0.2
湖 北	Hubei	26050	8433	17412	205	475	377.6	96.2	0.8
湖 南	Hunan	38244	9779	27641	823	687	538.7	146.6	1.8
广 东	Guangdong	47623	17526	23730	884	1621	526.8	193.8	2.3
广 西	Guangxi	20654	5974	14479	201	378	245.2	131.8	0.8
海 南	Hainan	6688	1840	3447	1400	60	28.8	28.2	3.0
重 庆	Chongqing	19634	4824	14432	378	207	127.4	77.9	1.3
四 川	Sichuan	40221	9679	29816	726	393	223.1	168.6	0.9
贵 州	Guizhou	20323	4580	15537	205	320	207.2	112.2	0.4
云 南	Yunnan	16698	4724	11690	284	248	143.7	103.3	0.5
西 藏	Tibet	630	240	390		22	11.6	10.10	
陕 西	Shaanxi	13372	4825	8496	50	279	216.0	62.7	0.1
甘 肃	Gansu	8013	2444	5544	26	209	176.7	32.2	…
青 海	Qinghai	1118	366	721	31	43	33.1	10.2	…
宁 夏	Ningxia	2701	434	2195	71	37	17.5	19.0	…
新 疆	Xinjiang	12149	1766	10384		193	133.1	60.0	
不分地区	Not Classified by Region	25171				3914			

注：不分地区合计为民航完成数。

Notes: The total passenger-kilometers not classified by region refers to that completed by civil aviation.

附录A-11　货运量和货物周转量(2022年)
Freight Traffic and Freight Ton_Kilometers (2022)

地　区	Province or Municipality	货运量(万吨) Freight volume (10000 tons)	铁路 Railways	公路 Highways	水运 Waterways	货物周转量(亿吨公里) Turnover of goods (100 million tons)	铁路 Railways	公路 Highways	水运 Waterways
全　国	**National Total**	**5152571**	**498424**	**3711928**	**855352**	**231783**	**35946**	**68958**	**121003**
北　京	Beijing	18918	368	18549		1017	792	225	
天　津	Tianjing	52898	11754	30382	10761	2666	574	605	1487
河　北	Hebei	232136	30212	196727	5197	14234	5506	7890	838
山　西	Shanxi	211540	104514	107024	1	6473	3309	3164	…
内蒙古	Nei Monggol	211615	84906	126709		5221	3080	2141	
辽　宁	Liaoning	166281	22394	139403	4484	4611	1305	2778	529
吉　林	Jilin	46467	5654	40813		1874	597	1277	
黑龙江	Heilongjiang	52119	12955	38616	547	1852	969	846	36
上　海	ShangHai	141059	512	44846	95701	32370	21	844	31505
江　苏	Jiangsu	279143	10010	159936	109197	11829	382	3208	8240
浙　江	Zhejiang	321583	5453	205935	110195	13545	287	2650	10608
安　徽	Anhui	394061	7912	245982	140167	11282	849	3696	6737
福　建	Fujian	169091	4816	106939	57336	11340	206	1261	9873
江　西	Jiangxi	196926	5200	178366	13360	5120	619	4086	414
山　东	Shandong	334165	36174	276906	21085	14273	1897	7913	4464
河　南	Henan	259983	12156	230055	17772	11751	2748	7716	1287
湖　北	Hubei	209475	6279	144979	58217	7544	1224	2059	4261
湖　南	Hunan	213251	4827	186123	22301	2932	1016	1465	451
广　东	Guangdong	364199	9374	242474	97628	28439	363	2710	25005
广　西	Guangxi	213331	9805	163219	40307	5173	741	1886	2546
海　南	Hainan	30007	911	6844	22252	9964	13	40	9911
重　庆	Chongqing	135491	1899	111915	21678	3880	304	1063	2513
四　川	Sichuan	186423	8045	172329	6049	3202	1068	1858	276
贵　州	Guizhou	94999	6672	87870	456	1417	680	723	14
云　南	Yunnan	145857	6009	139217	630	2000	528	1463	8
西　藏	Tibet	4024	91	3934		130	28	103	
陕　西	Shaanxi	164723	43505	121188	30	4369	2498	1871	…
甘　肃	Gansu	72945	8861	64084		3681	1990	1690	
青　海	Qinghai	18467	3594	14874		703	527	175	
宁　夏	Ningxia	48623	10160	38463		874	276	598	
新　疆	Xinjiang	88293	21068	67225		2503	1550	954	
不分地区	Not Classified by Region	86868				5876			

注：不分地区合计中包括民航、管道等完成数。货运量和货物周转量的全国总计等于分省数与不分地区数据之和。

Notes: The Freight Traffic and freight ton-kilometers not classified by region refer to pipelines ,civil aviation and that completed by companies abroad under the China Ocean Shipping (Group) Company.The Freight Traffic and freight ton-kilometers is equal to the sum of the provinces and the not classified by region .

附录A-12 国内外贸易（2022年）

Retail Trades and Foreign Trades (2022)

地 区	Province or Municipality	社会消费品零售总额（亿元）Total Retail Sales of Social Consumer Goods (100 million yuan)	进出口总额（亿美元）Total Import and Export Volume (100 million dollars)	出口 Export	进口 Import	进出口总额（亿元）Total Import and Export Volume (100 million yuan)	出口 Export	进口 Import
全　国	**National Total**	**439732.5**	**63096.0**	**35936.0**	**27160.0**	**420678.2**	**239654.0**	**181024.2**
北　京	Beijing	13794.2	5465.0	881.7	4583.3	36445.5	5890.0	30555.5
天　津	Tianjing	3572.0	1267.6	571.8	695.7	8448.5	3803.6	4644.9
河　北	Hebei	13720.1	843.2	510.5	332.6	5629.0	3407.4	2221.6
山　西	Shanxi	7562.7	277.3	181.8	95.5	1845.6	1211.4	634.2
内蒙古	Nei Monggol	4971.4	227.7	94.3	133.4	1523.6	630.3	893.3
辽　宁	Liaoning	9526.2	1187.5	538.2	649.4	7907.3	3584.6	4322.8
吉　林	Jilin	3807.7	233.8	75.2	158.6	1558.5	502.3	1056.3
黑龙江	Heilongjiang	5210.0	396.9	81.3	315.6	2651.5	545.6	2106.0
上　海	ShangHai	16442.1	6272.4	2563.7	3708.7	41902.7	17134.2	24768.5
江　苏	Jiangsu	42752.1	8177.5	5225.9	2951.6	54454.9	34815.7	19639.2
浙　江	Zhejiang	30467.2	7034.4	5158.0	1876.5	46836.6	34325.4	12511.2
安　徽	Anhui	21518.4	1131.3	714.2	417.1	7530.6	4763.7	2766.9
福　建	Fujian	21050.1	2975.0	1820.4	1154.6	19828.5	12140.5	7688.0
江　西	Jiangxi	12853.5	1006.7	763.8	242.9	6713.0	5088.4	1624.6
山　东	Shandong	33236.2	4994.3	3047.7	1946.6	33324.9	20355.8	12969.1
河　南	Henan	24407.4	1279.0	787.6	491.4	8524.1	5247.0	3277.1
湖　北	Hubei	22164.8	927.3	632.2	295.1	6170.8	4209.3	1961.5
湖　南	Hunan	19050.7	1054.3	769.9	284.4	7058.2	5154.5	1903.6
广　东	Guangdong	44882.9	12469.7	7999.0	4470.7	83098.1	53319.5	29778.7
广　西	Guangxi	8539.1	980.5	546.8	433.7	6603.5	3705.4	2898.2
海　南	Hainan	2268.4	300.9	107.4	193.4	2009.5	722.6	1286.9
重　庆	Chongqing	13926.1	1228.3	790.9	437.4	8158.4	5245.3	2913.0
四　川	Sichuan	24104.6	1511.7	931.5	580.2	10076.7	6215.2	3861.6
贵　州	Guizhou	8507.1	119.1	77.8	41.2	801.2	523.6	277.6
云　南	Yunnan	10838.8	500.4	241.4	259.0	3342.3	1612.6	1729.8
西　藏	Tibet	726.5	6.9	6.5	0.4	46.0	43.1	2.9
陕　西	Shaanxi	10401.6	726.4	452.2	274.2	4835.3	3011.3	1824.0
甘　肃	Gansu	3922.2	88.3	19.1	69.2	584.2	127.3	456.9
青　海	Qinghai	842.1	6.5	4.0	2.5	43.0	26.5	16.5
宁　夏	Ningxia	1338.4	38.6	29.6	9.0	257.4	196.8	60.6
新　疆	Xinjiang	3240.5	366.8	311.1	55.7	2463.6	2091.2	372.4

附录B-1 中国香港特别行政区主要社会经济指标
Main Statistical Indicators of Hong Kong Special Administrative Region

指标	Item	1990	2000	2010	2020	2022
本地生产总值	**Gross Domestic Product (GDP)**					
按2020年环比物量计算①	At 2020Link Ratios①					
本地生产总值年增长率 (%)	Annual Growth Rate (%)	3.8	7.7	6.8	-6.5	-3.5@
本地生产总值 (亿港元)	GDP (HKD 100 million)	10513	15490	23087	26758	27484@
人均本地生产总值 (港元)	Per Capita GDP (HKD)	184290	232404	328675	357679	374135@
按当年价格计算	At Current Prices					
本地生产总值年增长率 (%)	Annual Growth Rate (%)	11.7	4.0	7.1	-5.9	-1.4@
本地生产总值 (亿港元)	GDP (HKD 100 million)	5993	13375	17763	26758	28270@
人均本地生产总值 (港元)	Per Capita GDP (HKD)	105050	200675	252887	357679	384831@
人口及生命统计	**Population and Vital Events**					
年中人口 (万人)	Mid-year Population (10000 persons)	570.4	666.5	702.4	748.1	734.6
粗出生率 (‰)	Crude Birth Rate (‰)	12.0	8.1	12.6	5.8	4.4
粗死亡率 (‰)	Crude Death Rate (‰)	5.2	5.1	6.0	6.8	8.4
劳动、就业	**Labor and Employment**					
劳动人口 (万人)	Labor Force (10000 persons)	274.8	337.4	363.1	391.8	377.6
劳动人口参与率 (%)	Labor Force Participation Rate (%)	63.2	61.4	59.6	59.7	58.2
失业率 (%)	Unemployment Rate (%)	1.3	4.9	4.3	5.8	4.3
政府收支、货币、金融（亿港元）	**Public Accounts, Money and Finance (HKD 100 million)**					
政府收入总额②	Total Government Revenue ②	895	2251	3765	5642	6222
政府支出总额②	Total Government Expenditure ②	856	2329	3014	8160	8105
货币供应量M3	Money Supply M3	12880	36928	71563	156440	165689
居民消费物价指数③	**Consumer Price Index③**					
(2019年10月至2020年9月=100)	(Oct. 2019 to Sep. 2020 = 100)					
综合消费物价指数	Composite Consumer Price Index	42.1	70.9	74.0	99.9	103.3
工业生产	**Industrial Production**					
工业生产指数④ (2015年=100)	Index of Industrial Production④ (2015=100)			101.9	95.8	101.2
工业电力消费量 (万亿焦耳)	Industrial Electricity Consumption (tera joules)	24934	17769	11080	10672	11087
工业煤气消费量 (万亿焦耳)	Industrial Gas Consumption (tera joules)	583	982	917	1653	1704
运输、旅游	**Transport and Tourism**					
进出香港的货物	Goods in and out of Hong Kong					
总卸下 (万吨)	Total disburden (10000 tons)	6076	13035	17282	18380	12904
总装上 (万吨)	Total laden (10000 tons)	2997	8692	12882	8900	7637
集装箱吞吐量⑤ (万标准集装箱单位)	Volume of Containers Handled⑤ (10000 TEUs)	510	1810	2370	1797	1669
访港旅客⑥ (万人次)	Visitor Arrivals⑥ (10000 person-times)	658	1306	3603	357	60
酒店入住率 (%)	Hotel Room Occupancy Rate (%)	79	83	87	46	66
对外商品贸易	**External Merchandise Trade**					
港产品出口 (亿港元)	Domestic Exports (HKD 100 million)	2259	1810	695	474	626
转口 (亿港元)	Re-exports (HKD 100 million)	4140	13917	29615	38801	44690
进口 (亿港元)	Imports (HKD 100 million)	6425	16580	33648	42698	49275
教育	**Education**					
小学学生人数⑦ (人)	Student Enrolment in Primary Schools⑦ (person)	531090	498175	334415	368255	337549
中学学生人数⑦⑧ (人)	Student Enrolment in Secondary Schools⑦⑧ (person)	481830	490039	486817	343478	334677

注：本表数据由香港特别行政区政府统计处提供，国家统计局整理编辑。

@数字将于日后进行修订。

①以环比物量计算的本地生产总值及其组成部分的参照年为2020年。

②财政年度数字。指当年4月1日至第二年3月31日。

③2019年10月起的消费物价指数是根据2019/20年住户开支统计调查所得的开支权数编制。较早的指数则是根据旧的开支权数而经过按比例换算与新基期的指数拼接。

④自2005年统计年度开始，所有工业生产指数均按《香港标准行业分类2.0版》编制。

⑤1998年起，采用一系列新的集装箱吞吐量数字，与1998年以前的数字不可比。

⑥1996年及以后的数字包括澳门访港的非澳门居民旅客人数。

⑦数字包括特殊学校的学生人数。

⑧数字亦包括夜校、技工级课程及毅进文凭课程的学生人数。

Notes: Data in this table are provided by the Census and Statistics Department of the Government of Hong Kong Special Administrative Region, and further prepared and edited by the National Bureau of Statistics.

@Figures are subject to revision as more data become available.

①The chain volume measures of GDP and its components have been re-referenced by 2020.

②Figures are as at end of the financial year. Financial year is from 1 April to 31 March of the next year,unless otherwise specified.

③The CPI from October 2019 is compiled based on the expenditure weights obtained from the 2019 / 20 household expenditure survey. The earlier indices are based on the old expenditure weights and split joint by converted in proportion to the indices of the new base period.

④Since 2005, all indices of industrial production are compiled based on the Hong Kong Standard Industrial Classification (HSIC) Version 2.0.

⑤Since 1998,new figures of container throughput are adopted,and therefore not comparable with the previous years.

⑥Figures of 1996 and after include arrival of non-Macao residents via Macao.

⑦Figures include students enrolled in special schools.

⑧Figures include students enrolled in night schools, technician level courses, and Yi Jin diploma courses.

附录B-2　中国澳门特别行政区主要社会经济指标

Main Statistical Indicators of Macao Special Administrative Region

指　　标	Item	1990	2000	2010	2020	2022
本地生产总值①	**Gross Domestic Product① (GDP)**					
以2020年环比物量计算	At 2020 Link Ratios					
本地生产总值实际增长率（支出法） (%)	Real Growth Rate of GDP by Expenditure	8.0	5.7	25.1	-54.2	-26.8
本地生产总值 (亿澳门元)	GDP (100 million MOP)	914.4	1190.2	3465.5	2034.0	1776.7
人均本地生产总值(万澳门元)	Per Capita GDP (10000 MOP)	27.3	27.6	64.5	29.9	26.2
按当年价格计算	At Current Prices					
本地生产总值名义增长率（支出法） (%)	Nominal Growth Rate of GDP by Expenditure	19.8	3.9	31.1	-54.3	-26.5
本地生产总值 (亿澳门元)	GDP (100 million MOP)	260.4	543.7	2260.0	2034.0	1772.7
人均本地生产总值(万澳门元)	Per Capita GDP (10000 MOP)	7.8	12.6	42.1	29.9	26.1
人口及生命统计	**Population and Vital Events**					
年中人口 (万人)	Mid-year Estimates of Population (10000 persons)	33.5	43.1	53.7	68.5	67.7
出生率 (‰)	Crude Birth Rate (‰)	20.5	8.9	9.5	8.1	6.4
死亡率 (‰)	Crude Death Rate (‰)	4.4	3.1	3.3	3.3	4.4
劳动、就业	**Labor**					
劳动人口 (万人)	Labor Force (10000 persons)	16.9	20.9	32.4	40.5	37.9
失业率 (%)	Unemployment Rate (%)	3.2	6.8	2.8	2.5	3.7
对外商品贸易	**External Trade**					
出口 (亿澳门元)	Exports (100 million MOP)	136.4	203.8	69.6	108.1	135.2
本地产品出口 (亿澳门元)	Domestic Exports (100 million MOP)		170.8	23.9	15.6	20.2
转口 (亿澳门元)	Re-exports (100 million MOP)		33.0	45.7	92.5	115.0
进口 (亿澳门元)	Imports (100 million MOP)	123.4	181.0	441.2	925.6	1398.1
工业生产	**Industrial Production**					
工业电力消耗量 (亿千瓦小时)	Industrial Electricity Consumption (100 million kwh)		1.5	1.5	1.4	1.5
运输、旅游	**Transport and Tourism**					
进出澳门货运车辆数目 (万辆)	Lorries Entering and Departing Macao (10000 times)	26.4	45.4	35.8	29.8	34.2
访澳旅客② (万人次)	Visitor Arrivals② (10000 person-times)		832.3	2496.5	589.7	570.0
酒店入住率 (%)	Hotel Room Occupancy Rate (%)	69	58	80	29	38
政府收支、货币、金融	**Government Accounts, Money and Finance**					
政府总收入① (亿澳门元)	Total Government Revenue① (100 million MOP)	60.2	153.4	884.9	1016.7	1044.9
政府总开支① (亿澳门元)	Total Government Expenditure① (100 million MOP)	55.1	150.2	383.9	961.3	995.9
货币供应（广义货币供应量M2） (亿澳门元)	Money Supply (M2) (100 million MOP)	307.5	849.2	2430.5	6923.6	7178.6
消费价格指数 (2018年4月至2019年3月=100)	**Consumer Price Index** (Apr.2018 to Mar.2019= 100)					
综合消费价格指数	Composite Consumer Price Index		56.90	70.66	102.60	103.70
教育③	**Education③**					
小学生 (人)	Students in Primary Education (person)	35514	46260	23785	35450	37854
中学生 (人)	Students in Secondary Education (person)	18283	39673	37224	27627	30274
高等教育学生 (人)	Students in Higher Education (person)	8864	9000	25539	39093	49594

注：本表数据由澳门特别行政区政府统计暨普查局提供，国家统计局整理编辑。
①数字在日后得到更多资料时会作出修订。
②自2008年开始，访澳旅客不包括外地雇员及学生等。
③不包括特殊教育学生。第n年的学生人数是指n/n+1学年年底学生人数。2007/2008学年起不包括回归教育学生人数；2010/2011学年起为注册学生人数。

Notes: Data in this table are provided by the Statistics and Census Services of the Government of Macao Special Administrative Region, and further prepared and edited by the National Bureau of Statistics.
①Figures are subject to revision as more data become available.
②Starting from 2008,foreign employees and students are not included in Macao Visitor arrivals.
③Special education students are not included.The number of students in year n refers to the number of students at the end of the n/n+1 academic year. The number of students returning to education will not be included from the 2007/2008 academic year.Starting from the 2010/2011 academic year, statistics only include registered students.

附录C　中国台湾省主要社会经济指标
Main Statistical Indicators of Taiwan Province

指　　标	Item	2000	2010	2020	2021	2022
国民经济核算	**National Accounts**					
本地居民生产总值(新台币亿元)	Gross National Product (NT$ 100 million)	104652	144761	204866	221975	232231
本地生产总值 (新台币亿元)	Gross Domestic Product (NT$ 100 million)	103285	140603	199148	217390	227065
经济增长率 (%)	Economic Growth Rate (%)	6.3	10.3	3.4	6.5	2.5
人均本地居民生产总值	Per Capita Gross Domestic Product					
新台币元	NT$	471734	625560	868732	945850	999125
美元	USD	15105	19765	29369	33756	33565
居民储蓄总额 (新台币亿元)	Gross Deposits (NT$ 100 million)	30597	47529	79409	95241	95991
储蓄率 (%)	Deposit Rate	29.2	32.8	38.8	42.9	41.3
人口	**Population**					
户籍登记人口数① (万人)	Year-end Population① (10000 persons)	2228	2316	2356	2338	2326
人口自然增加率 (‰)	Natural Population Growth Rate (‰)	8.08	0.91	-0.34	-1.27	-2.93
人口密度 (人/平方公里)	Population Density (persons/sq.km)	616	640	651	646	643
劳动、就业	**Labor and Employment**					
劳动力人口 (万人)	Labor Force (10000 persons)	978	1107	1196	1192	1185
失业率 (%)	Unemployment Rate (%)	3.0	5.2	3.9	4.0	3.7
工业	**Industry**					
工业生产指数 (2016年＝100)	Index of Industrial Production (2016=100)	54.4	87.7	116.1	131.7	132.9
制造业生产指数 (2016年=100)	Index of Industrial Production (2016=100)	52.6	87.0	117.2	133.9	135.1
对外贸易	**Foreign Trade**					
贸易额 (亿美元)	Total Value of Imports and Exports (USD 100 million)					
出口	Exports	1519	2774	3451	4464	4794
进口	Imports	1407	2557	2861	3820	4280
运输、旅游	**Transportation and Tourism**					
铁路客运人数 (亿人次)	Railways (100 million persons)	4.6	7.8	10.3	7.9	8.9
公路客运人数 (亿人次)	Highways (100 million persons)	11.5	11.1	10.8	7.9	8.4
航空客运人数 (亿人次)	Airway (100 million persons)	0.3	0.3	0.1		0.1
高速公路通行车辆数③(万辆次)	Vehicles for Motorway Transportation③ (10000 unit-times)	45381	55506	607532	579762	618001
每百人机动车辆数① (辆)	Vehicles per 100 Persons① (unit)	76.4	93.8	94.6	96.7	98.2
港埠货物装卸量 (万收费吨)	Inward and Outward Movements Cargo (10000 tons)	56695	65540	70299	75031	71827
观光 (万人次)	Tourism (10000 person-times)					
出岛旅客	Outbound Tourists	733	942	234	36	148
来台湾旅客	Inbound Tourists	262	557	138	14	90
财政、金融	**Public Accounts and Finance**					
赋税实征净额② (新台币亿元)	Revenue② (NT$ 100 million)	19298	16222	23987	28742	32479
货币供应量M2① (新台币亿元)	Money Supply M2① (NT$ 100 million)	188978	309544	501879	538752	575086
年增长率 (%)	Average Annual Growth Rate (%)	6.5	5.5	9.4	7.4	6.7
存款① (新台币亿元)	Deposits① (NT$ 100 million)	193087	310063	492197	527570	563301
物价年涨跌率 (%)	**Price Indices Annual Growth Rate (%)**					
批发	Wholesale Trade Price	1.81	5.46	-7.77	9.46	12.42
消费者	Consumer Price	1.26	0.97	-0.23	1.97	2.95

注：①年底数。
②为年度资料。
③从2013年12月30日起，国道高速公路由计次收费改为计程电子收费。

Notes: ① Year-end data.
② Annual data.
③Since 30th December 2013, toll for national highway has been charged for mileage instead of charged by the number of times.

附录D-1 部分国家和地区主要经济指标（2021年）

Main Economic Indicators of Some Countries and Territories (2021)

国家和地区	Country or Territory	国内生产总值（亿美元）Gross Domestic Product (USD 100 million)	人均国民总收入（美元）Per Capita Gross National Income (USD)	国内生产总值增长率(%) Growth Rate of GDP (%)	对GDP增长贡献率(%) Contribution Share in GDP Growth (%)		
					第一产业 Primary Industry	第二产业 Secondary Industry	第三产业 Tertiary Industry
世　界	World	961001	12070	5.8			
高收入国家	High Income	594454	47904	5.1			
中等收入国家	Middle Income	357859	5845	7.0			
中等偏下收入国家	Lower Middle Income	86833	2485	5.6			
中等偏上收入国家	Upper Middle Income	271043	10363	7.4			
中低收入国家	Low and Middle Income	363159	5298	6.9			
低收入国家	Low Income	5263	722	3.0			
最不发达地区	Least Developed	12729	1161	2.3			
中　国	China	177341	11890	8.1	6.5	40.0	53.5
巴　西	Brazil	16090	7720	4.6	-0.3	21.8	78.5
加拿大	Canada	19908	48310	4.6	-3.6	26.9	76.7
法　国	France	29375	43880	7.0	-0.1	23.5	76.6
德　国	Germany	42231	51040	2.9	-0.4	33.4	67.0
印　度	India	31734	2170	8.9	7.5	36.3	56.2
印度尼西亚	Indonesia	11861	4140	3.7	7.8	41.5	50.7
意大利	Italy	20999	35710	6.6	-0.3	49.3	51.0
日　本	Japan	49374	42620	1.6			
韩　国	Korea,Rep.	17985	34980	4.0			
马来西亚	Malaysia	3727	10930	3.1	-0.4	67.5	32.9
墨西哥	Mexico	12930	9380	4.8	2.3	39.9	57.8
俄罗斯	Russia	17758	11600	4.8	-1.2	34.9	66.4
新加坡	Singapore	3970	64010	7.6			
泰　国	Thailand	5060	7260	1.6			
英　国	United Kingdom	31869	45380	7.4	0.3	18.9	80.8
美　国	United States	229961	70430	5.7			

附录D-1 续表 continued

国家和地区	Country or Territory	GDP产业构成（%） Structure of GDP by Production Approach (%) 农业增加值占GDP比重 Agriculture	工业增加值占GDP比重 Industry	服务业增加值占GDP比重 Service Industry	能源生产量（2020年，万吨标准油） Energy Production (2020, 10000 tons of SOE)	能源最终消费量(2020年，万吨标准油） Total Energy Consumption (2020, 10000 tons of SOE)	货物进出口贸易总额（亿美元） Total Merchandise Imports and Exports (USD 100 million)	货物出口总额（亿美元） Merchandise Exports (USD 100 million)	货物进口总额（亿美元） Merchandise Imports (USD 100 million)
世　界	World	4.3	28.3	65.7①	1415461	957341	449147	223281	225866
高收入国家	High Income	1.3①	22.4①	71.8①					
中等收入国家	Middle Income	8.8	34.4	52.5					
中等偏下收入国家	Lower Middle Income	15.4	29.1	46.8					
中等偏上收入国家	Upper Middle Income	6.7	36.1	54.2					
中低收入国家	Low and Middle Income	9.1	34.3	52.2					
低收入国家	Low Income	25.6	24.9	35.5					
最不发达地区	Least Developed Countries	19.0	29.3	43.4					
中　国	China	7.3	39.4	53.3	279595	218191	60525	33638	26886
巴　西	Brazil	6.9	18.9	59.4	32178	22303	5155	2808	2347
加拿大	Canada	1.7②	24.6②	66.9②	51786	19004	10116	5076	5040
法　国	France	1.6	16.8	70.2	11988	13800	12989	5848	7141
德　国	Germany	0.8	26.6	63.0	9663	21389	30521	16319	14201
印　度	India	16.8	25.9	47.7	56799	59649	9683	3954	5729
印度尼西亚	Indonesia	13.3	39.9	42.8	44658	15154	4259	2299	1960
意大利	Italy	2.0	22.6	65.1	3519	10744	11678	6103	5575
日　本	Japan	1.0①	29.0①	69.5①	4337	26294	15250	7560	7690
韩　国	Korea,Rep.	1.8	32.5	57.3	5270	17466	12595	6444	6151
马来西亚	Malaysia	9.6	37.7	51.5	9177	6055	5370	2990	2380
墨西哥	Mexico	3.8	31.9	58.4	14806	9638	10172	4948	5225
俄罗斯	Russia	3.8	33.2	53.0	142992	50605	7978	4938	3040
新加坡	Singapore		24.9	69.4	60	1768	8636	4574	4062
泰　国	Thailand	8.5	34.8	56.7	6603	9667	5389	2720	2669
英　国	United Kingdom	0.6	17.7	71.6	11703	11405	11620	4682	6938
美　国	United States	1.1①	18.4①	80.1①	216005	146122	46896	17543	29353

注：①2020年数据。②2018年数据。
Note:①Data refer to 2020. ②Data refer to 2018.

附录D-2 部分国家和地区国内生产总值

Gross Domestic Product of Some Countries and Territories

单位：亿美元 (USD 100 million)

国家和地区	Country or Territory	2000	2005	2010	2015	2020	2021
世　界	**World**	**338309**	**477797**	**665961**	**751793**	**849068**	**961001**
高收入国家	High Income	277544	378255	457522	482584	536998	594454
中等收入国家	Middle Income	57670	94951	198509	261888	304338	357859
中等偏下收入国家	Lower Middle Income	15203	25644	52469	65260	75855	86833
中等偏上收入国家	Upper Middle Income	42466	69306	146040	196628	228483	271043
中、低收入国家	Low and Middle Income	59535	98026	204496	266613	309139	363159
低收入国家	Low Income	1914	3159	6132	4750	4810	5263
最不发达地区	Least Developed Countries	2174	3531	6861	9497	11620	12729
中　国	China	12113	22860	60872	110616	146877	177341
中国香港	HongKong SAR,China	1717	1816	2286	3094	3449	3681
中国澳门	Macao SAR,China	68	122	282	450	256	299
阿根廷	Argentina	2842	1987	4236	5947	3896	4915
澳大利亚	Australia	4156	6951	11476	13505	13278	15427
孟加拉国	Bangladesh	534	694	1153	1951	3739	4163
白俄罗斯	Belarus	127	302	572	565	615	682
巴　西	Brazil	6554	8916	22088	18022	14486	16090
保加利亚	Bulgaria	132	299	507	508	699	803
加拿大	Canada	7448	11731	16173	15565	16454	19908
捷　克	Czech Rep.	618	1371	2091	1880	2453	2823
埃　及	Egypt	998	896	2190	3294	3653	4041
法　国	France	13656	21969	26452	24392	26303	29375
德　国	Germany	19480	28469	33997	33576	38464	42231
印　度	India	4684	8204	16756	21036	26677	31734
印度尼西亚	Indonesia	1650	2859	7551	8609	10587	11861
伊　朗	Iran	1096	2265	4868	4082	2315	
以色列	Israel	1325	1427	2347	3001	4071	4816
意大利	Italy	11467	18582	21361	18366	18926	20999
日　本	Japan	49684	48315	57591	44449	50401	49374
哈萨克斯坦	Kazakhstan	183	571	1480	1844	1711	1908
韩　国	Korea,Rep.	5762	9349	11441	14658	16379	17985
马来西亚	Malaysia	938	1435	2550	3014	3370	3727
墨西哥	Mexico	7079	8775	10578	11719	10871	12930
蒙　古	Mongolia	11	25	72	116	133	151
缅　甸	Myanmar	68	106	378	630	789	651
荷　兰	Netherlands	4175	6853	8474	7656	9139	10180
新西兰	New Zealand	526	1147	1465	1781	2117	2500
尼日利亚	Nigeria	694	1761	3615	4868	4323	4408
巴基斯坦	Pakistan	820	1201	1772	2706	3003	3463
菲律宾	Philippines	837	1074	2084	3064	3618	3941
波　兰	Poland	1722	3061	4798	4778	5966	6740
罗马尼亚	Romania	373	985	1663	1777	2495	2841
俄罗斯	Russia	2597	7640	15249	13635	14883	17758
新加坡	Singapore	961	1278	2398	3080	3453	3970
南　非	South Africa	1518	2889	4174	3467	3354	4199
西班牙	Spain	5984	11537	14221	11956	12815	14253
斯里兰卡	Sri Lanka	163	244	567	806	810	845
泰　国	Thailand	1264	1893	3411	4013	4997	5060
土耳其	Turkey	2743	5063	7770	8643	7200	8153
乌克兰	Ukraine	324	892	1412	910	1566	2001
英　国	United Kingdom	16621	25448	24911	29566	27569	31869
美　国	United States	102509	130392	150490	182060	208937	229961
委内瑞拉	Venezuela	1171	1455	3932			
越　南	Viet Nam	312	576	1472	2393	3432	3626

附录D-3　部分国家和地区国内生产总值增长率

Growth Rates of GDP of Some Countries and Territories

单位：%　　(%)

国家和地区	Country or Territory	2000	2005	2010	2015	2020	2021
世　界	**World**	**4.5**	**4.0**	**4.5**	**3.1**	**-3.3**	**5.8**
高收入国家	High Income Countries	4.1	2.9	3.0	2.4	-4.5	5.1
中等收入国家	Middle Income Countries	5.9	7.3	8.0	4.5	-1.3	7.0
中等偏下收入国家	Lower Middle Income Countries	4.4	6.1	6.6	5.0	-3.3	5.6
中等偏上收入国家	Upper Middle Income Countries	6.4	7.7	8.4	4.3	-0.6	7.4
中低收入国家	Low and Middle Income Countries	5.8	7.3	7.9	4.4	-1.3	6.9
低收入国家	Low Income Countries	3.3	6.5	6.8	-0.2	0.1	3.0
最不发达地区	Most Underdeveloped Countries	4.3	7.4	6.2	2.5	0.6	2.3
中　国	China	8.5	11.4	10.6	7.0	2.2	8.1
中国香港	Hong Kong, China	7.7	7.4	6.8	2.4	-6.5	6.4
中国澳门	Macao, China	5.7	8.1	25.1	-21.5	-54.0	18.0
阿根廷	Argentina	-0.8	8.9	10.1	2.7	-9.9	10.3
澳大利亚	Australia	3.9	3.2	2.2	2.2		1.5
孟加拉国	Bangladesh	5.3	6.5	5.6	6.6	3.4	6.9
白俄罗斯	Belarus	5.8	9.4	7.8	-3.8	-0.9	2.5
巴　西	Brazil	4.4	3.2	7.5	-3.5	-3.9	4.6
保加利亚	Bulgaria	4.6	7.1	1.5	3.4	-4.4	4.2
加拿大	Canada	4.9	5.0	3.1	0.7	-5.2	4.6
捷　克	Czech Republi	4.0	6.6	2.4	5.4	-5.8	3.3
埃　及	Egypt	6.4	4.5	5.1	4.4	3.6	3.3
法　国	France	3.9	1.7	1.9	1.1	-7.9	7.0
德　国	Germany	2.9	0.7	4.2	1.5	-4.6	2.9
印　度	India	3.8	7.9	8.5	8.0	-6.6	8.9
印度尼西亚	Indonesia	4.9	5.7	6.2	4.9	-2.1	3.7
伊　朗	Iran	5.8	3.2	5.8	-1.4	1.8	
以色列	Israel	8.9	4.2	5.7	2.3	-2.2	8.2
意大利	Italy	3.8	0.8	1.7	0.8	-9.0	6.6
日　本	Japan	2.8	1.8	4.1	1.6	-4.5	1.6
哈萨克斯坦	Kazakhstan	9.8	9.7	7.3	1.2	-2.5	4.0
韩　国	Korea，Rep.	9.1	4.3	6.8	2.8	-0.9	4.0
马来西亚	Malaysia	8.9	5.3	7.4	5.1	-5.6	3.1
墨西哥	Mexico	4.9	2.3	5.1	3.3	-8.2	4.8
蒙　古	Mongolia	1.1	7.3	6.4	2.4	-4.6	1.4
缅　甸	Myanmar	12.4	13.6	10.1	3.3	3.2	-18.0
荷　兰	Netherlands	4.2	2.1	1.3	2.0	-3.8	5.0
新西兰	New Zealand	2.9	3.3	1.5	3.7	-1.3	4.6
尼日利亚	Nigeria	5.0	6.4	8.0	2.7	-1.8	3.6
巴基斯坦	Pakistan	4.3	6.5	1.6	4.7	-1.3	6.0
菲律宾	Philippines	4.4	4.9	7.3	6.3	-9.5	5.7
波　兰	Poland	4.6	3.5	3.7	4.2	-2.5	5.7
罗马尼亚	Romania	2.5	4.7	-3.9	3.0	-3.7	5.9
俄罗斯	Russia	10.0	6.4	4.5	-2.0	-2.7	4.8
新加坡	Singapore	9.0	7.4	14.5	3.0	-4.1	7.6
南　非	South Africa	4.2	5.3	3.0	1.3	-6.4	4.9
西班牙	Spain	5.2	3.7	0.2	3.8	-10.8	5.1
斯里兰卡	Sri Lanka	6.0	6.2	8.0	5.0	-3.6	3.7
泰　国	Thailand	4.5	4.2	7.5	3.1	-6.2	1.6
土耳其	Turkey	6.9	9.0	8.4	6.1	1.8	11.0
乌克兰	Ukraine	5.9	3.1	4.1	-9.8	-3.8	3.4
英　国	United Kingdom	3.7	2.6	2.1	2.6	-9.3	7.4
美　国	United States of America	4.1	3.5	2.7	2.7	-3.4	5.7
委内瑞拉	Venezuela	3.7	10.3	-1.5	-5.7		
越　南	Viet Nam	6.8	7.5	6.4	7.0	2.9	2.6

附录D-4　部分国家和地区人均国民总收入

Per Capita Gross National Income of Some Countries and Territories

单位：美元　　(USD)

国家和地区	Country or Territory	2000	2005	2010	2015	2020	2021
世　界	**World**	**5522**	**7394**	**9478**	**10664**	**11099**	**12070**
高收入国家	High Income	25415	34189	39344	41753	43855	47904
中等收入国家	Middle Income	1208	1821	3541	4915	5334	5845
中等偏下收入国家	Lower Middle Income	596	926	1669	2159	2281	2485
中等偏上收入国家	Upper Middle Income	1902	2882	5858	8449	9399	10363
中低收入国家	Low and Middle Income	1143	1716	3310	4507	4845	5298
低收入国家	Low Income	400	612	1073	760	689	722
最不发达地区	Least Developed Countries	299	445	777	1011	1103	1161
中　国	China	940	1760	4340	7890	10530	11890
中国香港	Hong Kong SAR,China	26930	28890	33620	41180	48560	54450
中国澳门	Macao SAR,China	14720	23950	45260	62090	46730	
阿根廷	Argentina	7470	4260	9270	12600	9080	10050
澳大利亚	Australia	21130	30390	46690	60490	53680	56760
孟加拉国	Bangladesh	440	550	800	1220	2340	2620
白俄罗斯	Belarus	10780	13240	15540	15760	15750	16720
巴　西	Brazil	3940	4000	9640	10170	7800	7720
保加利亚	Bulgaria	1660	3800	7010	7430	9630	10720
加拿大	Canada	22620	34810	44490	47590	43540	48310
捷　克	Czech Rep.	6340	12480	19400	18370	22130	24070
埃　及	Egypt	1420	1220	2370	3340	3000	3510
法　国	France	24990	35920	43970	41130	39500	43880
德　国	Germany	26180	35770	44680	45780	47520	51040
印　度	India	440	710	1220	1600	1910	2170
印度尼西亚	Indonesia	580	1220	2530	3430	3870	4140
伊　朗	Iran	1770	2960	6250	5710	3370	
以色列	Israel	19360	21500	29770	36200	42610	49560
意大利	Italy	21910	32480	37960	33000	32380	35710
日　本	Japan	36810	41280	43910	39380	40810	42620
哈萨克斯坦	Kazakhstan	1270	2930	7440	11380	8710	8720
韩　国	Korea,Rep.	11030	18520	22290	28720	32930	34980
马来西亚	Malaysia	3460	5270	8260	10680	10570	10930
墨西哥	Mexico	6210	8050	9040	10160	8530	9380
蒙　古	Mongolia	470	900	2000	3800	3740	3760
缅　甸	Myanmar	130	200	620	1170	1340	1140
荷　兰	Netherlands	28840	42110	54070	49850	51070	56370
新西兰	New Zealand	14080	25440	29680	40660	41480	45340
尼日利亚	Nigeria	470	1030	2150	2820	2000	2100
巴基斯坦	Pakistan	480	740	970	1260	1460	1500
菲律宾	Philippines	1180	1380	2370	3380	3430	3640
波　兰	Poland	4670	7340	12740	13310	15260	16670
罗马尼亚	Romania	1710	3880	8640	9600	12630	14170
俄罗斯	Russia	1710	4450	9980	11780	10740	11600
新加坡	Singapore	23680	28830	44930	53160	55010	64010
南　非	South Africa	3420	5610	6880	6610	6010	6440
西班牙	Spain	15790	25910	31970	28450	27360	29740
斯里兰卡	Sri Lanka	870	1210	2410	3760	3720	3820
泰　国	Thailand	1980	2790	4580	5710	7070	7260
土耳其	Turkey	4320	6820	10490	12030	9040	9830
乌克兰	Ukraine	680	1540	3030	2800	3570	4120
英　国	United Kingdom	29280	42810	41940	44730	39970	45380
美　国	United States	35960	46180	49150	56620	64140	70430
委内瑞拉	Venezuela	4120	4980	11810			
越　南	Viet Nam	380	630	1360	2460	3390	3560

附录D-5 部分国家和地区人均国内生产总值增长率

Growth Rates of Per Capita GDP of Some Countries and Territories

单位：%　　(%)

国家和地区	Country or Territory	2000	2005	2010	2015	2020	2021
世　界	**World**	**3.1**	**2.8**	**3.3**	**1.9**	**-4.3**	**4.8**
高收入国家	High Income	3.5	2.2	2.4	1.8	-4.9	5.1
中等收入国家	Middle Income	4.5	6.0	6.7	3.3	-2.2	6.0
中等偏下收入国家	Lower Middle Income	2.6	4.4	5.0	3.5	-4.6	4.2
中等偏上收入国家	Upper Middle Income	5.5	7.0	7.7	3.5	-1.1	7.0
中低收入国家	Low and Middle Income	4.3	5.8	6.5	3.0	-2.4	5.7
低收入国家	Low Income	0.5	3.5	3.9	-2.7	-2.5	0.3
最不发达地区	Least Developed Countries	1.7	4.8	3.8	0.1	-1.6	
中　国	China	7.6	10.7	10.1	6.4	2.0	8.0
中国香港	Hong Kong SAR,China	6.7	6.9	6.0	1.5	-6.2	7.4
中国澳门	Macao SAR,China	3.4	5.6	22.4	-23.1	-54.6	16.4
阿根廷	Argentina	-1.9	7.7	9.3	1.6	-10.8	9.2
澳大利亚	Australia	2.7	1.8	0.6	0.7	-1.3	1.3
孟加拉国	Bangladesh	3.3	5.0	4.4	5.4	2.4	5.9
白俄罗斯	Belarus	6.3	10.2	8.0	-4.0	-0.5	2.9
巴　西	Brazil	2.9	2.0	6.5	-4.4	-4.6	3.9
保加利亚	Bulgaria	5.1	7.9	2.2	4.1	-3.8	4.7
加拿大	Canada	3.9	4.0	2.0	-0.1	-6.3	4.0
捷　克	Czech Rep.	4.3	6.5	2.1	5.2	-6.0	3.3
埃　及	Egypt	4.3	2.6	3.1	2.1	1.6	1.4
法　国	France	3.2	0.9	1.4	0.8	-8.0	6.8
德　国	Germany	2.8	0.8	4.3	0.6	-4.6	2.9
印　度	India	2.0	6.2	7.0	6.8	-7.5	7.9
印度尼西亚	Indonesia	3.5	4.3	4.8	3.6	-3.1	2.6
伊　朗	Iran	4.5	2.0	4.6	-2.7	0.5	
以色列	Israel	6.1	2.3	3.8	0.3	-3.9	6.5
意大利	Italy	3.7	0.3	1.4	0.9	-8.6	7.3
日　本	Japan	2.6	1.8	4.1	1.7	-4.2	2.1
哈萨克斯坦	Kazakhstan	10.1	8.7	5.8	-0.3	-3.8	2.6
韩　国	Korea,Rep.	8.2	4.1	6.3	2.3	-1.0	4.2
马来西亚	Malaysia	6.4	3.3	5.6	3.7	-6.9	1.8
墨西哥	Mexico	3.4	0.9	3.6	2.0	-9.1	3.7
蒙　古	Mongolia	0.3	6.0	4.6	0.4	-6.1	-0.1
缅　甸	Myanmar	11.1	12.7	9.3	2.5	2.5	-18.6
荷　兰	Netherlands	3.5	1.8	0.8	1.5	-4.3	4.5
新西兰	New Zealand	2.3	2.2	0.4	1.7	-3.4	4.0
尼日利亚	Nigeria	2.4	3.7	5.2		-4.3	1.1
巴基斯坦	Pakistan	1.5	4.1	-0.6	2.6	-3.3	4.0
菲律宾	Philippines	2.2	3.0	5.6	4.7	-10.7	4.3
波　兰	Poland	5.7	3.6	4.0	4.3	-2.4	6.1
罗马尼亚	Romania	2.6	5.3	-3.3	3.4	-3.2	6.7
俄罗斯	Russia	10.5	6.8	4.5	-2.2	-2.5	5.2
新加坡	Singapore	7.2	4.9	12.5	1.8	-3.8	12.2
南　非	South Africa	2.7	4.0	1.6	-0.2	-7.6	3.6
西班牙	Spain	4.8	1.9	-0.3	3.9	-11.3	5.2
斯里兰卡	Sri Lanka	5.4	5.4	7.3	4.0	-4.1	2.5
泰　国	Thailand	3.4	3.5	7.0	2.7	-6.4	1.3
土耳其	Turkey	5.3	7.6	6.9	4.3	0.7	10.1
乌克兰	Ukraine	7.0	3.8	4.5	-9.4	-3.1	4.3
英　国	United Kingdom	3.3	1.9	1.3	1.8	-9.6	7.0
美　国	United States	2.9	2.5	1.9	2.0	-4.3	5.5
委内瑞拉	Venezuela	1.7	8.5	-2.9	-7.0		
越　南	Viet Nam	5.6	6.6	5.4	5.9	2.0	1.7

主要统计指标解释

国民总收入 国内生产总值减去生产税和进口税净额，减去支付给国外的雇员报酬和财产收入，加来自国外的雇员报酬和财产收入（即国内生产总值减去支付给非常住单位的初次收入，加上收到的非常住单位的初次收入）。按市场价格计算国民总收入的另一种方法是各部门所有初次收入的总和。国民总收入即国民生产总值，国民生产总值是以往国民核算中使用的概念。

按购买力平价计算的人均国民总收入 根据购买力平价计算的人均国民总收入。购买力平价国民总收入是用购买力平价比率、以国际元计算的国民总收入。国民总收入中一国际元的购买力等于美国一美元购买力。

香港居民消费价格指数 《香港统计年刊》中称为“消费物价指数”。香港特别行政区政府统计处编制不同的居民消费价格指数数列，以反映消费价格变动对不同开支范围的住户的影响。甲类、乙类及丙类消费价格指数分别根据较低、中等及较高开支范围的住户消费模式编制而成。而综合消费价格指数是根据上述住户的整体开支模式而编制，反映消费价格转变对全体住户的影响。

Explanatory Notes on Main Statistical Indicators

Gross National Income is gross domestic product (GDP) minus net taxes on production and imports, minus remuneration and property income for employees abroad, plus the corresponding items from employees abroad (in other words, GDP minus primary incomes payable to non-resident units plus primary incomes receivable from non-resident units). An alternative approach to measuring GNI at market prices is the sum of gross primary incomes from all sectors. Gross national income is identical to gross national product (GNP), as previously used in national accounts.

Per Capita GNI in PPP is per capita GNI based on purchasing power parity (PPP). PPP GNI is gross national income (GNI) converted to international dollars using purchasing power parity rates. An international dollar has the same purchasing power over GNI as a U.S. dollar has in the United States of America.

Consumer Price Index by Residents in Hong Kong refers to a series of consumer price indices reflected in Hong Kong Annual Digest of Statistics. The series of consumer price indices (CPIs) are compiled by the Census and Statistics Department of Hong Kong Special Administrative Region to reflect the impact of consumer price changes on households in different expenditure ranges. The CPI(A), CPI(B) and CPI(C) are compiled based on the expenditure patterns of households in the relatively low, medium and relatively high expenditure ranges. By aggregating the expenditure patterns of all households covered by the above three indices, a composite CPI is also compiled to reflect the impact of consumer price changes on the household sector as a whole.